# HARRY and WALLY's FAVORITE TV SHOWS

OTHER BOOKS BY HARRY CASTLEMAN AND WALTER J. PODRAZIK

*All Together Now:*
*The First Complete Beatles Discography*

*The Beatles Again?!*

*The End of the Beatles?*

*505 Radio Questions Your Friends Can't Answer*

*505 Television Questions Your Friends Can't Answer*

*TV & Movie Facts* (PODRAZIK ONLY)

*The TV Schedule Book: Four Decades of Network*
*Programming from Sign-on to Sign-off*

*Watching TV: Four Decades of American Television*

# HARRY and WALLY's FAVORITE

Harry Castleman and
Walter J. Podrazik

New York London Toronto Tokyo Sydney

Harry dedicates this book to Ida Gilberg Spitzer (1915–1989), who taught him how to enjoy life.

As always, Wally dedicates his work to the memory of Walter and Julia Podrazik.

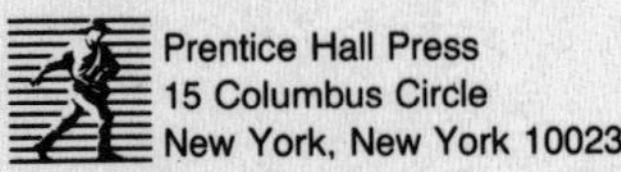

Prentice Hall Press
15 Columbus Circle
New York, New York 10023



**Library of Congress Cataloging-in-Publication Data**
Castleman, Harry
Harry and Wally's favorite TV shows
/ by Harry Castleman and Walter J. Podrazik.
p. cm.
Includes index.
ISBN 0-13-933250-2
1. Television serials—Reviews. I. Podrazik, Walter J.
II. Title.
PN1992.8.S4C35 1989
791.45'75'0973—dc20 89-3953
CIP

Designed by Richard Oriolo

Manufactured in the United States of America

10 9 8 7 6 5 4 3 2 1

First Edition

When was the Golden Age of Television?

Just check your calendar and circle today's date—you're in it!

Ironically, this is true even if you can't stand any new series currently being offered on television.

The reason?

Reruns.

Reruns on cable. Reruns on local independent stations. Reruns on network affiliates. Reruns on public television. Reruns on video cassettes and on videodiscs.

Increasingly, nearly everywhere you turn, you have your choice of the best moments in television's past. And, thanks to the time-shifting capabilities of home video tape recorders, you even have your choice of the best moments in television's present—available for viewing whenever you feel like watching.

*Harry and Wally's Favorite TV Shows* is a guide to some of the highs, lows, and obscure treats waiting for you out there, drawing from forty years of program offerings, right up to today.

Most important, this guide is presented from a contemporary vantage point. After all, in today's TV world, with all eras mixing together at the touch of the channel selector, it really doesn't matter how successful or critically popular a series was years ago. Today's TV viewers want to know: What's worth watching *now*?

From A to Z, this book provides the answers.

# CONTENTS

# INTRODUCTION

A decade ago we couldn't have done this book.

Back in the old days (the early 1980s, remember them?), talking about television series was usually limited to humming some half-forgotten theme songs and trying to remember a few character names. Sure, you could always find the latest batch of recent network hits in reruns (along with such perennials as *I Love Lucy*), but that was about it. Everything else was limited to a few summary anecdotes and statistics. How could you talk in detail about your favorite series with the individual episodes gathering dust on station and studio shelves?

Why were they there? Conventional wisdom at the time offered these explanations: Most series from the 1950s and 1960s were in black and white and no one would be interested in these today (beyond *I Love Lucy, Dick Van Dyke, Andy Griffith*, and *The Honeymooners*). Many series (especially from the 1970s) had too few episodes for a Monday-through-Friday rerun slot; you'd finish the entire cycle in less than a month. And, of course, a lot of series had not been big hits in the first place, so who would watch them in reruns? Mostly, though, the powers-that-be simply decided that most old series did not "fit in" with contemporary television programming. Whatever that was supposed to mean.

Guess what? They were wrong. Fortunately, the changing nature of television technology in the 1980s gave viewers plenty of chances to support their favorites. During that time, more than half the viewing households in the United States added VCRs and cable service to their lives. Videotape sales and rentals skyrocketed. Public broadcasting stations beefed up their schedules. And over-the-air independents began to court viewers more aggressively than ever. All of these changes seriously eroded the traditional hammerlock of ABC, CBS, and NBC on viewers. But, even more important, it also meant there were more television programmers than ever looking to fill more time than ever. On the one hand, the result was an unprecedented rush of brand-new first-run programming that completely bypassed ABC, CBS, and NBC. But countless hours were still left empty. Suddenly, some of those old series started looking better and better.

As a result, we now have a different television world. Naturally, new series are still the bread-and-butter flagship draw, but there is also a definite place in the equation for television's past, from the very recent to long-ago kinescopes. Maybe these won't outscore the latest number one programs in the weekly Nielsen ratings, but they have earned their niche. And, if programmed right, they can be quite profitable.

For dedicated viewers, then, these are really exciting times. You can watch the latest episodes of your favorite series, or you can reach back to another era for programs that first played when you were just a toddler. Whether on home video, as syndicated reruns, or through various cable services, you have the chance to judge so many of these offerings for yourself, perhaps discovering that the titles on your personal list of favorite series actually stretch from the 1980s back to the 1950s, and sometimes even beyond.

Of course, everything isn't out there yet. And sometimes you've vaguely heard of the series, but you want to know more about it before tuning in. Or, maybe there's a familiar title you feel like savoring one more time. That's what this book is for. We've combed through the files and selected more than 2,100 series and miniseries currently available for programming (even adding some that aren't, but should be), offering our observations—ranging from just a few lines to several pages.

Everyone loves to share thoughts on their favorites (and to chuckle over the turkeys), so we hope this guide makes your next flip through the pages of the TV schedule a bit more fun. With a little luck, you may even discover some previously hidden gems that become your new favorites. Or, perhaps you'll see a familiar title in a new light. Whatever the case, we know the feeling well. It's all part of the fun of watching TV.

# A GUIDE TO THE GUIDE

Each series write-up begins with basic background facts on that entry. The following is an item-by-item guide to our chosen style (and abbreviations).

## EXAMPLES

**A SERIES STILL IN PRODUCTION** **(**½) 30 min (33ep at Fall 1989 Color; 1987– Original Venue) Program Type** *with Key Performers as Key Characters*

**A STANDARD RERUN SERIES ENTRY** **(**½) 60 min (22ep & 90 min pilot Color; 1982–1983 Original Venue) Program Type** *with Key Performers as Key Characters*

**A TYPICAL MINISERIES ENTRY** **(**½) (8hr miniseries Color; 1982 Original Venue) Program Type** *with Key Performers as Key Characters*

**A TYPICAL OVERSEAS ENTRY** **(**½) 30 min (22ep Color; 1982–1983 Original Country and Venue) Program Type** *with Key Performers as Key Characters*

## EXPLANATION

### Entry Title

All entries are listed in alphabetical order, placed in what we feel are the most accessible and logical spots—even if that technically varies with exactly what appears on the screen.

For instance, the official title of a 1950s series featuring Charlie Chan is *The New Adventures of Charlie Chan*, but we have placed it under "C" (*Charlie Chan, The New Adventures of*) under the assumption that most people would think to look there first, rather than under "A" for "Adventures," "N" for "New," or "T" for "The." (Don't worry: There are cross-references at both "A" and "N" if you do happen to know the exact title wording.)

In searching for a title, remember the following:

- "A," "An," and "The" are not counted when alphabetizing titles, except for *T.H.E. Cat*, which can be found at the beginning of the *T*s.
- Abbreviations and call letters appear in front of whole words: Thus, series such as *M*A*S*H, F.D.R., S.W.A.T.*, and *SCTV* appear at the beginning of their respective letters.
- Titles beginning with "The Adventures of" can be found listed under the next hook word. (For instance, *The Adventures of Superman* is listed under "S" for *Superman, The Adventures of*.) The same is true of such prefixes as : "The Life and Legend of" (for *Wyatt Earp*), "The Life and Times of" (for *Grizzly Adams*), "The Saga of" (for *Andy Burnett*), and "The Days and Nights of" (for *Molly Dodd*).
- Titles with "The New" or "The Best of" can be found under the core name. For example, the write-up for *The New Odd Couple* is under "O" (*Odd Couple, The New*) following the discussion of the original *Odd Couple* series. However, titles appear under "N" or "B" if the words "New" or "Best of" clearly stand as a key part of the program identification (such as in *The New Land* or *Best of the West*).
- Names that precede the title (such as in *James Garner as Nichols* or *James Clavell's Noble House*) are not used for alphabetizing purposes. Both of these examples, therefore, would be found under "N."

### Star Rating

Entries are ranked on a zero to four-star (****) basis, within their own program types:

- Four-star series (****) represent what we feel are some of the best moments television has to offer.

These are highly impressive shows you can easily find yourself hooked on.

- Three- to three-and-one-half-star series (***, ***½) are all, to increasing degrees, highly recommended. We consider these worth the extra effort to find.
- Two-and-one-half-star series (**½) are also recommended, chiefly because they have some aspect that sets them apart from the pack—sometimes the presence of a particular personality or a slightly better than average treatment of a premise.
- Two-star series (**) are fifty/fifty propositions, acceptable but not outstanding. These are average shows.
- One-half- to one-and-one-half-star series (½, *, *½) are often likely to disappoint, though there may be personnel involved (writers, producers, performers) that make these worth catching once or twice.
- Zero-star series (zero) cannot be recommended. They are frequently embarrassingly bad. Oddly, though, these sometimes play as fascinating failures, so you may find yourself interested in them as historical curiosities. However, we doubt if you'll find them entertaining for more than one episode.

## Running Time

This refers to the length of the slot in which the program appears (generally 30, 60, 90 minutes or 2 hours). With few exceptions, the amount of actual program material is less than this time period, allowing room for a reasonable number of commercials.

When programs have had episode runs of different lengths (for example, *Gunsmoke* as a 30-minute and a 60-minute series), the details of that split are included under "Number of Episodes."

When a miniseries cannot be easily broken into such segments, the total running length of the entire miniseries is listed in hours in the "Number of Episodes" position.

## Number of Episodes

Each number is followed by a lowercase "ep" (for "episodes") except for miniseries, which are described by their total running time with a lower case "hr" (for "hours").

If a series is still in production at the time of this writing, the episode total to a particular point is given, designed by an "at" as follows:

"100ep at Fall 1989" means that there are 100 episodes up to but not including the season beginning in Fall 1989.

As for the number of episodes listed, ideally the total number currently available for rerun syndication should equal the number originally produced and aired. However, several factors affect that total: inclusion of the pilot or any sequels (possibly reedited into several episodes from a TV movie); dropping black-and-white episodes from a package in favor of just the color stories; and limited licensing of material produced overseas.

Generally, made-for-TV movie pilots and sequels are designated separately, unless the episode total clearly includes them. Theatrical movies based on (or inspired by) a TV series are not considered pilots or sequels.

It is assumed that double-length episodes (for instance a 60-minute version of a 30-minute series) are rerun as two standard-length epísodes.

This category is the trickiest one in the book, but the numbers cited reflect our best judgment (based on available industry information) of the total number of episodes produced. (The few exceptions to this are pointed out in the text of individual write-ups.)

## Color, Black and White (B&W), or Colorized

This indicates whether the episodes are in color, black and white, or colorized, with changeovers from one format to another noted.

## Original Era and Original Venue

The year(s) and venue(s) of each entry's first airing are given as a point of reference. The span of years indicates when the entry was first released or aired, which may be different from the years of production. Only the years when first-run product appeared are included, regardless of how long after that the series may have been slotted on a rerun basis.

The venues cited are only those over which the series offered first-run product.

Note that for most import series, the time frame and venue given are those of the original foreign airing. Thus, *Monty Python's Flying Circus* is not a 1974 PBS series but, rather, a 1969–1974 UK BBC series.

Among the venues cited in the United States are ABC, CBS, NBC, Fox, PBS, HBO, Showtime, Cinemax, A&E/The Entertainment Channel, CBN, Lifetime, and WTBS, along with Syndication (for first-run original material syndicated to individual stations); those cited in Britain include ABC, ATV/Central, BBC, C4 (Channel 4), Granada, ITV, LWT (London Weekend Television), Southern/TV South, Yorkshire, and Thames; the venues from Canada include CBC and CTV; and, for Australia, Nine Network and 0-10 Network.

## Program Type

This simply and arbitrarily draws distinctions between broad program types (situation comedy versus comedy-variety, for instance).

## Selected Cast List

The cast listing is italicized. It includes key cast members for the purposes of our discussion rather than every character who appears in the series.

## Video Index Entry Symbol

A small square ■ at the end of a write-up indicates that one or more episodes from the series are available on home video and are listed in "The Home Video Guide" chapter in the back of the book.

## A Note on the Titles Selected

This book contains write-ups on more than 2,100 television series and miniseries that originally aired (or currently play) in the evening viewing hours.

Only programs distributed nationally are dealt with. Local or regional series are not included.

The focus is primarily on comedy and drama series (including anthology titles), along with selected variety, music, and documentary packages. A key consideration throughout is whether or not this material is available for rerun packaging (or, in our opinion, that it should be).

One-time specials and TV movies are excluded, as are daytime soap operas, game shows, most talk shows, sports programs, and daily information packages (such as the nightly news or entertainment feature series).

A series can have as few as two episodes and still be included, though programs aired as reoccurring specials are not included (unless later packaged into a series).

A miniseries must run more than four hours to be listed; otherwise it is considered a long made-for-TV movie.

Of course, there are also a few titles included that violate the ground rules, because ultimately an entry is here because we felt like talking about it. After all, these are *our* favorite shows.

*Final Note:* For this book, the two of us turned out our respective write-ups with only minor collaboration, thus accounting for occasional conflicting opinions on the same series (especially in parenthetical cross-references). Naturally, whichever one of us you're talking to at the moment will gladly take credit for the parts you like, and blame the other for the sections you don't.

# HARRY AND WALLY'S FAVORITE TV SHOWS (from A to Z)

## ABC COMEDY HOUR (see *The Kopykats*)

## ABC MYSTERY MOVIE (1989– ABC)

An umbrella title Mystery Anthology series, beginning at Winter 1989 with *B. L. Stryker, Columbo,* and *Gideon Oliver.* See those titles for details.

## ABC STAGE '67 (***) 60 min (28ep Color; 1966–1967 ABC) Anthology

*ABC Stage '67* is perhaps as close to the "golden age" of 1950s TV as 1960s prime-time network TV ever got. Producer Hubbell Robinson is the overall boss for this fascinating potpourri of drama, documentary, musicals, and comedy. Each episode is very different from the others, and thus some are excellent, some only fair, but all are well produced.

Highlights include Truman Capote's *A Christmas Memory* (Capote narrates), with Geraldine Page as a kindly, slightly daffy older aunt to a young boy in Alabama (who represents Capote as a child); *The Human Voice,* David Susskind's production of a Jean Cocteau story about a middle-aged woman trying to end a love affair that consists entirely of the woman (Ingrid Bergman) talking to her unseen lover on the telephone; *The Legend of Marilyn Monroe,* a David Wolper documentary of the late film queen, with narration by John Huston; and *The Love Song of Barney Kempinski,* a comedy with Alan Arkin as a New York City bachelor on his last fling before his wedding.

The sad thing about *ABC Stage '67* is how rare and unique a show it is, and how it stands head and shoulders against the usual bland network TV fare of its era and the eras since.

## A. D. (ANNO DOMINI) (*) 12hr miniseries Color; 1985 NBC) Drama *with James Mason as Tiberius Caesar, Anthony Andrews as Nero, John McEnery as Caligula, Richard Kiley as Claudius, John Houseman as Gamaliel, Anthony Zerbe as Pilate, Neil Dickson as Valerius, Cecil Humphreys as Caleb, and Amanda Pays as Sarah the Slave Girl*

The decline and fall of trashy historical epics. Too long. Too dull. This one doesn't even work as a camp classic (not enough sleazy decadence). The actual tale of the decaying Roman empire is much better told in *I, Claudius.* But, while you're here you can watch future *Max Headroom* "control operator" Amanda Pays, whose character of Sarah has more screen time than most of the "big name" draws (typical miniseries move).

## A.E.S. HUDSON STREET (*½) 30 min (5ep Color; 1978 ABC) Situation Comedy *with Gregory Sierra as Dr. Antonio "Tony" Menzies, Rosana Soto as Nurse Rosa Santiago, and Stefan Gierasch as J. Powell Karbo*

Executive Producer Danny Arnold attempts, and mainly fails, to clone his success with *Barney Miller* by taking the same lighthearted, easygoing style and transplanting it from a New York City police station to a Gotham emergency medical ward (the "Adult Emergency Service" on Hudson Street). Gregory Sierra, who played a Hispanic detective on *Barney Miller,* is the island of stability amidst the chaos. In the 1977 pilot, Sierra's character is played by F. Murray Abraham, who later won an Oscar as envious composer Salieri in the 1984 film *Amadeus.*

## A. J. WENTWORTH (**) 30 min (6ep Color; 1982 UK Thames) Situation Comedy *with Arthur Lowe as A. J. Wentworth and Harry Andrews as the headmaster*

Final vehicle for Arthur Lowe (veteran of British hits *Coronation Street, My Dad's Army,* and *Bless Me, Father*), who plays an absentminded schoolmaster.

## A.K.A. PABLO (**) 30 min (13ep Color; 1984 ABC) Situation Comedy *with Paul Rodriguez as Pablo "Paul" Rivera, Joe Santos as Domingo Rivera, Katy Jurado as Rosa Maria Rivera, and Hector Elizondo as Jose Sanchez/Shapiro*

Norman Lear, whose *All in the Family* and *The Jeffersons* did so much to set the tone for the ethnic-based sitcoms of the 1970s, is about ten years too late in *a.k.a. Pablo.* Paul Rivera is an up-and-coming Hispanic stand-up comic who is still called Pablo, his real name, by the family. Paul/Pablo walks a tightrope in basing his humor on his ethnic background without hurting his family's pride.

Paul Rodriguez tries too hard as Paul/Pablo, though Hector Elizondo is funny as Paul's novice agent, who calls himself Jose Shapiro to fit into the heavily Jewish world of Hollywood moguls.

**THE A-TEAM (***) 60 min (96ep & 2 hr pilot Color; 1983–1987 NBC) Adventure** *with Mr. T as B. A. Baracus, George Peppard as Col. "Hannibal" Smith, Dwight Schultz as Capt. "Howling Mad" Murdock, Dirk Benedict as Lt. "Face" Peckman, Melinda Culea as Amy Allen, Eddie Velez as Frankie Sanchez, and Robert Vaughn as Gen. Hunt Stockwell*

A perfect vehicle for Mr. T. And one that he is so obviously pleased with that in real life he incorporates an allusion to his series character on the license plate of his flashy red Rolls-Royce convertible. It reads: "MR. TBA"—with the "BA" referring to his *A-Team* name, B. A. Baracus.

Mr. T has good reason to be pleased. This could have been just another routine action series, propped up by a familiar Hollywood veteran (George Peppard), some good character players (Benedict and Schultz), and Mr. T himself—fresh from his role as the fighting-mad challenger in the hit theatrical film *Rocky III.*

Instead, at its best, *The A-Team* offers something just a little bit different: a send-up of its own adventure genre, complete with a quirky mix of offbeat stories and personalities. This light approach is pretty well executed by Stephen J. Cannell's production company, whose roots reach back to other genre series done with such a touch, including *Black Sheep Squadron, The Rockford Files,* and *The Greatest American Hero.* In particular, *The A-Team* plays as a dead-on send-up of *Mission: Impossible.*

To veteran TV watchers, the always-in-control, planned-to-the-last-detail routine of the Impossible Missions force on *Mission: Impossible* has always been an especially ripe target for parody, and much of *The A-Team* seems structured with an almost deliberate disdain for their perfect execution. Both groups might triumphantly drive off in a mysterious van at the end of each story, but there are two completely different worlds at work.

For starters, the members of the A-Team are wanted by the government, not employed by it. They had been part of a crack commando squad in Vietnam in the 1970s that was falsely accused and convicted of treason in the last days of the war. But they promptly escaped from their maximum security prison and headed back to the States. There, in between bouts with pursuing army officers and MPs, they operate as modern-day soldiers of fortune.

As such, the A-Team charges for its services, rather than drawing from some blank-check government account. But, like all good fictional adventure heroes, the A-Team members waive their $100,000 fee often enough to make you wonder just how they ever balance their books.

Perhaps the most distinctive difference between the two teams is that the elaborate schemes of the A-Team more often than not carry a sense of backyard improvisation.

Team leader Hannibal Smith might begin an assignment with a plan, but usually has to adapt it to unexpected twists. In fact, his trademark line ("I love it when a plan comes together!") often carries more than a touch of irony. In some episodes the mission can't even begin until "Howling Mad" Murdock (a crack pilot who also happens to be clinically crazy) is sprung from the local psych ward; or until B. A. Baracus is tricked into taking a knockout drug so he can be loaded onto a waiting plane (he has a fear of flying); or until the smooth-talking Lt. Peck can con someone out of the cash or materials necessary for their transportation.

Even the hardware reflects this humorous spirit. While the Impossible Mission forces always seems to have the latest top-secret electronic hardware straight from the CIA's weapons warehouse, the A-Team usually has to make do with whatever is at hand (rolls of toilet paper, for instance).

And, in the ultimate caricature of TV adventure series conventions, despite all the guns and explosions in story after story, nobody really gets hurt. A car might careen, tumble, and crash, landing upside down . . . but the occupants will always be in one piece with just enough strength to pull themselves from the wreckage and run away before it explodes.

Unfortunately, after about two dozen really good episodes, *The A-Team* itself sometimes falls into the *Mission: Impossible* formula trap, grinding out generally interchangeable confrontations with generic bad guys. But, even then, its lighter tone manages to save the overall series, with such touches as unusual guest stars (including Mr. T's cohort from the wrestling circuit, Hulk Hogan, and pop singers Boy George and Rick James) and in-joke media allusions (for example, Dirk Benedict, who had previously played Starbuck in *Battlestar Galactica,* finds himself face-to-face with a man dressed in an alien Cylon costume).

For its final season, *The A-Team* swaps some of its *Fugitive* trappings (pursuit by the army) for formal entry into the espionage game. After facing a firing squad, they strike a deal to do some impossible missions for a rogue government agent, played by Robert Vaughn. This also provides the setup for a delightful tip-of-the-hat tribute to Vaughn's *The Man from U.N.C.L.E.* days, a story called "The Say UNCLE Affair" (with guest star David McCallum).

**AARON'S WAY** (**) **60 min (12ep & 2 hr pilot Color; 1988 NBC) Drama** *with Merlin Olsen as Aaron Miller, Belinda Montgomery as Sarah Miller, Kathleen York as Susannah Lo Verde, Samantha Mathis as Roseanne Miller, Jessica Walter as Connie Lo Verde, and Christopher Gartin as Mickey Lo Verde*

Traditional Amish values clash with the modern California lifestyle in *Aaron's Way.* Former NFL superstar Merlin Olsen (who previously appeared in such gentle series as *Little House on the Prairie* and *Father Murphy*) stars as Aaron Miller, a bearded Amish traditionalist with a large family in a secluded portion of the Pennsylvania Dutch region. In the pilot, Aaron must decide how to react when he learns that his oldest son Noah has died in California. Noah had left the Miller home and the Amish way of life, headed west, purchased a vineyard, and died in a surfing accident (how symbolic). At Noah's death, however, his girlfriend Susannah (a very modern young woman) was pregnant with Noah's child. Aaron decides to drag his clan to California, take over Noah's vineyard, and help raise Noah's child. The Miller's old-fashioned ways are at odds with those of Susannah, her brassy mother Connie, and California in general.

The conflict-of-cultures theme is a bit heavy-handed here, but *Aaron's Way* manages to keep its head above the mawkish most of the time. Even if the drama is often merely adequate, at least this is one California-based series devoid of killings and car chases.

**THE ABBOTT AND COSTELLO SHOW** (**) **30 min (52ep B&W; 1952–1954 Syndication) Situation Comedy** *with Bud Abbott, Lou Costello, Hillary Brooke, and Sid Fields as themselves*

Bud Abbott (the tall straight man) and Lou Costello (the short, fat, funny one) come from the old days of vaudeville and slapstick. This show, one of the first filmed comedies produced especially for syndication, is a "perfect" timepiece, capturing the old burlesque feel just as the format was disappearing.

The so-called setting is extremely loose. Abbott and Costello play themselves, or at least caricatures of themselves. They appear as struggling comedians living in a rooming house run by their henchman Sid Fields. Hillary Brooke is Lou's girlfriend, who lives down the hall. Other stock characters and stooges pop up over and over, Abbott and Costello drag out many of their famous routines from film and stage (including their most famous, the baseball-oriented "Who's on first?"), and the thin plots get lost in the shuffle.

This is not Abbott and Costello at their best (the production is frequently shoddy), but it does present a fair review of their best bits. The duo never were on the cutting edge of humor, but their broad-based slapstick always manages to bring a few smiles to even the most dour observer. ■

**THE ABSENT-MINDED PROFESSOR** (**½) **60 min (2ep at Summer 1989 Color; 1988– NBC)** *with Harry Anderson as Professor Henry Crawford, Mary Page Keller as Ellen Whitley, and James Noble as Dean Blount*

More than two decades after Fred MacMurray first played the eccentric Ned Brainard (in a pair of successful theatrical films), *Night Court*'s Harry Anderson takes up the mantle as the new absentminded professor. No relation, though. He's just the current physics prof at the local college, living in the same house that Brainard did. And that's where he comes across Brainard's old car, as well as his formula for flying rubber ("flubber"), leading to a new round of sky–high jinks with the flivver once again soaring overhead. Anderson's style is perfect for the character, which requires both a sense of silliness lurking beneath a veneer of homespun genius, and common sense behind spacey absentmindedness. The professor owns a computer named Albert that has the face of Albert Einstein (and was created by software designers Jay Johnson and Anderson himself). An excellent selection for a new continuing series launched in the fall of 1988 under the Walt Disney anthology series banner (then using the name *The Magic World of Disney*).

**ACAPULCO** (**½) **30 min (8ep B&W; 1961 NBC) Adventure** *with Ralph Taeger as Patrick Malone, James Coburn as Gregg Miles, Telly Savalas as Mr. Carver, Bobby Troup as himself, Jason Robards, Sr., as Max, and Allison Hayes as Chloe*

An intriguing attempt to salvage a failed Yukon goldrush series from 1960 (*Klondike*), *Acapulco* takes the two main actors of *Klondike* and turns them into totally new characters, set in another country and another era.

Ralph Taeger and James Coburn still portray roguish men of action, but they are set in twentieth-century Acapulco, Mexico, not turn-of-the-century Canada. Here, the duo play Korean War veterans who have dropped out long before that term became fashionable. The playboy pair earn the money needed for "booze and broads" by protecting Mr. Carver, a retired criminal lawyer always wary of attempts at revenge from mobsters he put away.

*Acapulco* is notable for the rare TV series appearance of James Coburn, the pre-*Kojak* role of Telly Savalas, and musician Bobby Troup (husband of Julie London and composer of "Route 66") playing himself as the owner of a small bar where the boys hang out.

**ACCIDENTAL FAMILY** (*) **30 min (16ep Color; 1967–1968 NBC) Situation Comedy** *with Jerry Van Dyke as Jerry Webster, Lois Nettleton as Sue Kramer, Teddy Quinn as Sandy Webster, and Ben Blue as Ben McGrath*

Undaunted by his failure in *My Mother the Car* from 1965, Jerry Van Dyke (younger brother of Dick) at last finds a role that somewhat fits his theatrical personality. Van Dyke plays Jerry Webster, a mediocre Las Vegas nightclub comic who is widowed and left with eight-year-old son Sandy. Jerry concludes Las Vegas is no place to raise his boy, so he buys a farm in California's San Fernando Valley, where Sandy is raised by pretty divorcée Sue Kramer, a tenant on the farm. Jerry spends weekdays in Vegas and weekends on the farm. What kind of Vegas comic has weekends off? No wonder Jerry never got very far.

Veteran stage and screen comic Ben Blue is Sue's uncle Ben. *Accidental Family* is produced by Sheldon Leonard (*Make Room For Daddy, The Andy Griffith Show,* and *The Dick Van Dyke Show*).

**ACE CRAWFORD, PRIVATE EYE (**) 30 min (5ep Color; 1983 CBS) Situation Comedy** *with Tim Conway as Ace Crawford, Joe Regalbuto as Toomey, Billy Barty as Inch, Shera Danese as Luana, and Bill Henderson as Mello*

This spoof of film noir private eyes *sounds* much funnier than it is. Tim Conway (in his *fifth* failure at headlining a sitcom) is Ace Crawford, the classic hard-as-nails gumshoe, who comes complete with trench coat and crumpled fedora. Ace actually is a complete klutz, yet he somehow solves the toughest cases and is surrounded by admiring women. Ace's assistant, Toomey, is a full-time accountant who idolizes the air Ace breathes. Ace hangs out at the Shanty, a sleazy bar with lots of atmosphere run by Inch, a midget. The Shanty features sexy chanteuse Luana, Ace's love interest, whose musical accompaniment is supplied by Mello, a blind pianist, played by real-life jazz star Bill Henderson.

**ADAM-12 (**½) 30 min (174ep Color; 1968–1975 NBC) Police Drama** *with Martin Milner as Officer Pete Malloy, Kent McCord as Officer Jim Reed, William Boyett as Sgt. MacDonald, and Gary Crosby as Officer Ed Wells*

Less preachy than Jack Webb's own 1967 *Dragnet* revival, this Webb-produced spinoff series follows a pair of likable patrol car cops (played by Martin Milner and Kent McCord) in their daily routine with the Los Angeles Police Department. "Adam-12" is their radio dispatch handle. Milner is the senior officer, probably because of clocking in so much road time on *Route 66.*

In 1989, production plans were announced for a new slate of *Adam-12* episodes with a completely new cast.

**ADAM'S RIB (**) 30 min (13ep Color; 1973 ABC) Situation Comedy** *with Ken Howard as Adam Bonner, Blythe Danner as Amanda Bonner, Dena Dietrich as Gracie Peterson, Edward Winter as Kip Kipple, and Ron Rifkin as Assistant D. A. Roy Mendelsohn*

An early 1970s "relevant" comedy, based on the 1949 Katharine Hepburn and Spencer Tracy theatrical film about a pair of married lawyers in court on opposite sides of a case. Repeated throughout the series, the setup allows for plenty of opportunities to "discuss issues," but there's no real sparkle among the characters. The performers are good, but they just don't click this time around slogging through "Today's Headlines," with Adam working at the D. A.'s office and Amanda at the law firm of Kipple, Kipple & Smith.

They all did much better TV work elsewhere: Howard on *The White Shadow,* Danner on *Tattinger's,* Rifkin on *When Things Were Rotten,* Winter on *M*A*S*H* (as Col. Flagg), and Dietrich in *The Ropers* and as an admonishing Mother Nature for Parkay margarine's campaign "It's not nice to fool Mother Nature."

**THE ADAMS CHRONICLES (***) 60 min (13ep Color; 1976 PBS) Drama** *with George Grizzard as John Adams, Kathryn Walker and Leora Dana as Abigail Adams, and David Birney and William Daniels as John Quincy Adams*

Long before the Kennedys, long before the Roosevelts, the premier first family of American politics was the Adams family of Massachusetts, not to be confused with the Addams family of Gomez and Morticia. The New England Adams family produced the only father-son presidential duo in American history (John and John Quincy), one of the nation's most intellectual and powerful first ladies (Abigail), a renowned diplomat (Charles Francis), and a noted historian (Henry).

*The Adams Chronicles* is a wonderful thirteen-part series following the family from prerevolutionary days to the dawn of the twentieth century. Both the personal and public lives of the various family members are featured, but, unlike many historical miniseries, the public part is not just window dressing for heated bedroom shenanigans. This tasteful touch reflects the PBS roots of the series, but, considering the usual PBS reliance on British programs, this historical family drama is special for having been made in America, about Americans and for Americans.

Various actors and actresses play the main characters as they grow older. Both David Birney and William Daniels take turns portraying John Quincy Adams. A few years later, the two actors appeared together again, in *St. Elsewhere,* playing very different roles. Birney played the libidinous Dr. Ben Samuels and Daniels was the straight-laced Dr. Mark Craig. Daniels also portrayed family patriarch John Adams in the Broadway and Hollywood versions of the musical *1776.*

**ADAMS OF EAGLE LAKE (*) 60 min (2ep & 2 hr pilot Color; 1975 ABC) Police Drama** *with Andy Griffith as Sheriff Sam Adams, Abby Dalton as Margaret Kelly, Nick Nolte as Jerry Troy, and Paul Winchell as Monty*

A failed effort at a series starring Andy Griffith as a sheriff in the resort town of Eagle Lake, California. The 1974 pilot is called *Winter Kill.* Executive producer Richard O. Linke had previously produced Griffith in *The New Andy Griffith Show* and *Headmaster.*

**THE ADDAMS FAMILY (***) 30 min (64ep B&W & 90 min Color sequel; 1964–1966 ABC) Situation Comedy** *with John Astin as Gomez Addams, Carolyn Jones as Morticia Addams, Jackie Coogan as Uncle Fester, Blossom Rock as Grandmama Addams, and Ted Cassidy as Lurch*

The Addams family members are some of the most Bohemian characters to be found in the annals of TV sitcoms. Based on the cartoon figures created by Charles Addams for *The New Yorker,* the Addams family members relish the joys of marching to the beat of a different drummer. The basic premise is that the family is a collection of ghouls, who live in a scary mansion surrounded by various manners of evil spirits. The humor is designed to come from the interaction of the Addams clan with "normal" society. There is humor in that vein, but the real beauties of *The Addams Family* are the finely crafted central characters and the accoutrements surrounding the family in their home.

Head of the clan is Gomez Addams, attorney-at-law, a pop-eyed bon vivant who lives the life of a man of great wealth. Gomez comes from old money, *very* old money, and does not need to work for a living. Nonetheless, when the fancy strikes him, Gomez is ready to pick up his dormant law practice and bring his own warped view of legal procedure to the aid of someone who has helped the family. Normally a man of leisure, Gomez is likely to be found in the basement with his great train collection, which he plays with merely to blow up. "Why else would a grown man play with trains?" he asks.

Wife Morticia is a sultry, sexy woman of class, who appreciates the finer things in life, such as a toxic concoction of food and drink, a poisonous plant, or a little relaxation on the torture rack. Gomez and Morticia rank as one of the sexiest couples on TV. It is hard to think of another marriage in TV history where both parties were so equal, so alive, and so totally in love with each other, even after years of marriage. And why not? Gomez keeps himself in good shape and radiates a form of dashing charm. Morticia slinks around in a form-fitting outfit that reveals her still-youthful figure and she has that quiet allure that women of undeniable beauty seem to exude. The mere mention of a word of French sends husband Gomez into waves of barely controllable passion. They still reminisce about their honeymoon, in a cave in Death Valley, "amid the soft flutter of bat wings."

Surrounding Gomez and Morticia are lesser lights who add great color to the household. Lurch, the seven-foot-tall zombie butler with the deepest voice on earth, is always good for a few laughs as the Addams clan tries to cheer him out of his eternal blue funk. The Addams's servant is Thing, a disembodied hand that pops up everywhere, from the mailbox (to collect the mail) to the card table (to play a hand of bridge).

The other characters are more mundane. Bald Uncle Fester is funny in a "crazy relative" sort of way. Grandmama Addams is cranky but is good at mixing magic potions. The two Addams children, pudgy Pugsley (Ken Weatherwax) and precocious Wednesday (Lisa Loring) are simply spoiled rich kids.

The plots in *The Addams Family* are, of course, totally meaningless. The beauty of the show is watching the actors go through their paces. In spite of the simple stories, the execution is exciting, funny, and lively. Viewers will come to share the Addams family pride in their eccentricity. Unlike the much more mundane Munster family (to whom the Addams clan will forever be compared), the Addamses have no illusion that they could fit into regular society. The Addamses care for people and always want to make friends, but they want friends who could appreciate the special quality of their type of life. If visitors come away from the Addams home scared, well, that's just too bad. *The Addams Family* celebrates eccentricity and is pure, unadulterated fun for viewers willing to take a walk on the wild side.

There is a ninety-minute 1977 reunion of the Addams family, *Halloween with the Addams Family,* with most of the original cast, that tries a bit too hard.

Beware of an animated version of *The Addams Family,* with none of the original cast's voices and none of the original show's excitement. The cartoon version is notable only because Jodie Foster (then eleven years old) supplies the voice of Pugsley.

**ADDERLY (***) 60 min (44ep Color; 1986–1988 Canada) Adventure** *with Winston Rekert as V. H. Adderly, Jonathan Welsh as Melville Greenspan, Dixie Seatle as Mona Ellerbee, and Ken Pogue as Major Clack*

For a former top agent in Covert Operations, it looks like quite a comedown: an office in the company basement, alongside the heating ducts and old file cabinets. But for V. H. Adderly, it represents the opportunity for a whole new career at ISI (International Security and Intelligence) after his left hand was virtually destroyed on a mission.

Sporting an artificial limb under a black leather glove, Adderly takes his reassignment to a Miscellaneous Affairs desk job in stride. He is good-humored, friendly, and conscientious. Adderly is also constantly following his instincts, returning to the field at a moment's notice to track miscellaneous cases that catch his eye. His good friend Mona, the department's administrative secretary, helps cover for him with their immediate superior, Melville Greenspan (a born paper pusher), and their boss upstairs, Major Clack.

However, unlike the faithful but forever desk-bound Miss Moneypenny in the James Bond novels, Mona occasionally gets into the action with Adderly. In fact, so does Greenspan, who obviously longs for the thrills of espionage operations, but only if they don't pose any real threat to him in the process. As a result, Greenspan and Adderly end up as perfect foils for each other: the nervous bureaucrat and his protective underling.

*Adderly* is one of those series that recognizes espionage as a game, sometimes very deadly, other times rather silly. It successfully balances a genuine sense of danger with a light touch of humor among the characters.

This series began as one of a handful of first-run offerings for the *CBS Late Night* slot. With a non-prime-time budget, it was produced, written, and filmed in Canada to hold down production costs. One happy by-product of a tighter budget was an emphasis in the scripts on clever plotting and dialogue rather than expensive car chases and elaborate shoot-outs.

**ADVENTURE THEATER (½) 30 min (10ep B&W; 1961 CBS) Drama Anthology**

A selection of unrelated thirty-minute dramas that were originally broadcast in 1959 and 1960 on *Schlitz Playhouse of Stars.*

**THE ADVENTURER (**) 30 min (26ep Color; 1972 UK ATV) Adventure** *with Gene Barry as Gene Bradley, Barry Morse as Parminter, and Catherine Schell as Diane Marsh*

Gene Barry is in his usual role as a suave sophisticate, this time playing an international film star doubling as a spy. Appropriate musical atmosphere is provided by veteran James Bond composer John Barry (who did the theme song) and *Man from U.N.C.L.E.* conductor Jerry Goldsmith (incidental music). Furtive glances and mysterious contact assignments courtesy of Morse and Schell.

**ADVENTURES AT SCOTT ISLAND (see *Harbourmaster*)**

**ADVENTURES IN PARADISE (*½) 60 min (91ep B&W; 1959–1962 ABC) Adventure** *with Gardner McKay as Capt. Adam Troy, Weaver Levy as Oliver Lee, James Holden as Clay Baker, and Guy Stockwell as Chris Parker*

*Adventures in Paradise* can be a lot of fun if you watch it as camp. If you look for *real* adventure, you'll be sorely disappointed. First, although allegedly set in the South Pacific, this show is really shot on the back lot of 20th Century Fox in Hollywood (only in the later seasons is some actual foreign footage added in). Second, the lead actor, Gardner McKay, shows little if any emotion as he cavorts through the southern seas as captain of the *Tiki,* an 85-foot schooner. McKay's only asset is his "hunk"-like chiseled features. There is no real reason for Capt. Troy to be in the South Pacific, the "adventures" Troy gets into are mild and predictable, and there is an unending supply of comely Polynesian lassies to spruce up the scenery.

Unfortunately, the comparative success of *Adventures in Paradise* during its original airing only taught TV executives that bland, undramatic series could capture an audience and be rerun for decades in syndication.

**ADVENTURES IN RAINBOW COUNTRY (*½) 30 min (26ep Color; 1972 Canada) Children's Adventure** *with Stephen Cottier as Billy Williams and Lois Maxwell as Nancy Williams*

Rainbow country? That's in Ontario near northern Lake Huron. Expect typical *Boy's Life* outdoor escapades with good location footage and (surprise) a mom played by James Bond's Miss Moneypenny (Lois Maxwell).

**THE ADVENTURES OF. . .**

To locate series titles that begin with "The Adventures of," go to the next word in the title. For example, *The Adventures of Superman* can be found under "S" for "Superman" (listed as *Superman, The Adventures of*).

**THE ADVENTURERS (*) 30 min (39ep B&W; 1966–1967 Syndication) Adventure** *with Edward Meeks and Yves Renier*

Edward Meeks and Yves Renier play two newspapermen who travel the world for stories and excitement. The stories they find and the excitement they have are far from memorable. In Europe, where this show was produced, it is called *The Globetrotters.*

**THE ADVOCATES (***) 60 min (B&W & Color; 1969–1974 & 1978–1979 PBS) Public Affairs**

A series of informative debates on public issues, presented in a courtroom trial setting, with proponents calling "witnesses" to bolster their case. Michael Dukakis, who became Governor of Massachusetts and ran unsuccessfully for President in 1988, moderated the show for a few years.

**AFRICAN PATROL (½) 30 min (39ep B&W; 1957–1958 UK) Crime Drama** *with John Bentley as African patrol chief Inspector Derek*

Potboiler jungle adventures filmed on location in East Africa. Derek's a part of the mobile African Police Patrol.

**THE AFRICANS (**½) 60 min (9ep Color; 1986 PBS) Documentary** *with Ali A. Mazrui as host*

Kenya-born professor Ali Mazrui presents a highly opinionated primer on Africa, its people, its history, and its current problems. The West is portrayed as villainous, but it is refreshing to have history presented from a different viewpoint. This documentary may spark debates as should any good documentary.

**AFTERMASH (*½) 30 min (31ep Color; 1983–1984 CBS) Situation Comedy** *with Harry Morgan as Dr. Sherman Potter, Jamie Farr as Max Klinger, William Christopher as Father Francis Mulcahy, Rosalind Chao* *as Soon-Lee Klinger, Brandis Kemp as Alma Cox, John Chappell as Mike D'Angelo, Jay O. Sanders as Dr. Gene Pfeiffer, and David Ackroyd as Dr. Boyer*

You know something's wrong halfway through the first episode of this spin-off series from *M*A*S*H* when Klinger's speech on veterans' rights and dreams brings everything to a screeching halt. The problem is obvious. They're trying to do *M*A*S*H* as it was toward the end of its successful run—funny, if at times smug and preachy. But, despite the title and the inclusion of three former *M*A*S*H* performers in the cast (Morgan, Farr, and Christopher), this is really a new show that has to earn its own stripes, in particular the right to be "relevant." To do that, the series has to be funny. And, for the most part, it isn't.

Besides the writing, another part of the problem is the "seniority" system in the casting, pushing Potter, Klinger, and Mulcahy as the three main characters. Of that trio, only Potter really belongs up front (and Harry Morgan does a good job as an administrator who can't believe the amount of red tape he faces on the home front). But, there should have been some fresh and eager comic faces to dispense Hawkeye- and Trapper-type lines, rather than Klinger's old ethnic jokes or Mulcahy's sensitive consoling. At the beginning, Dr. Pfeiffer attempts to fill that role, but he is generally ineffectual. Toward the end, David Ackroyd's Dr. Boyer character also tries to break through the morass, but the series never catches fire.

Definitely for *M*A*S*H* completists only, with a guest shot episode featuring Gary Burghoff as Radar (on his wedding day). Of course, fanatic fans would also like to see a video release of Burghoff's *Walter* pilot (Radar as a cop) as well as a complete collection of the ultimate *M*A*S*H* cast reunion: the series of late 1980s IBM computer commercials showcasing all the main cast members, even Alan Alda.

In the closing credits, *AfterMASH* is officially identified as "a continuation of *M*A*S*H*." There aren't too many stations these days taking that cue and mixing these episodes into their *M*A*S*H* rotation.

**AGAINST THE WIND (***) 60 min (13ep Color; 1978 Australia) Drama** *with Mary Larkin as Mary Mulvane, Bryan Brown as Michael Connor, Peter Gwynne as Francis Mulvane, and Kerry McGuire as Polly McNamara*

Sort of an Australian version of *Roots, Against the Wind* follows Mary Mulvane from the poverty of Ireland through conviction for some petty crime and sentencing to a penal colony in New South Wales, Australia. In her new home, she and her family and the other new immigrants to Australia (many of whom are also convicts) struggle to establish a just society in the newly colonized continent.

Bryan Brown, a standout in other Australian-based miniseries (*The Thorn Birds* and *A Town Like Alice*) is watchable as always in this exciting series.

**THE AGATHA CHRISTIE HOUR (**½) 60 min (9ep Color; 1982 UK Thames) Mystery Anthology**

A leisurely set of Agatha Christie mysteries without any of her personal superstars like Miss Marple or Hercule Poirot grabbing the spotlight. Instead, these are generally staged as 1920s and 1930s period pieces, often involving ordinary people unexpectedly thrust into dangerous, even murderous, situations. But sometimes (as in "The Manhood of Edward Robinson") there isn't any murder or mayhem at all, just a whimsical adventure in an otherwise ordinary life. Through them all, you can also see some of the preliminary models for investigative character traits and story structures later used in Christie's more famous works. Overall, though, this is a low-expectation series, with some simple, unassuming tales and a nice range of guest stars (Jeremy Clyde in "Magnolia Blossom," for instance). These episodes first aired in the United States on *Mystery!*, beginning in 1983.

**AGATHA CHRISTIE'S . . .** **(see *Miss Marple; Partners in Crime*)**

**AGONY (***) 30 min (20ep Color; 1979–1981 UK London Weekend Television) Situation Comedy** *with Maureen Lipman and Simon Williams*

Well-staged comedy about a newspaper advice columnist (played by Maureen Lipman) who fearlessly doles out solutions to her readers' problems but finds her own personal circles an intricate, complicated mess. To start, she and her husband (played by Simon Williams, James Bellamy on *Upstairs, Downstairs*) are frequently at odds (they even separate for a while) and often find themselves in the most awkward situations (such as when he falls in love with a shrink). Then there's her gay friends who quarrel more than an old married couple. Not to mention the apparent revolving door to her office that seems to bring everyone in for a few "personal words." After all this, the problems in the letters from her readers must seem like a cakewalk. Though the setup may seem like an all-too-obvious comic contrast (advisor badly in need of advice), it happens to work superbly.

The series concept was hatched by a real-life practitioner in the advice game, Anna Raeburn, and was later adapted for Stateside viewing as *The Lucie Arnaz Show*.

**AIR POWER (**½) 30 min (26ep B&W; 1956–1957 CBS) Documentary** *with Walter Cronkite as narrator*

Another rehash of World War II, by CBS News. Ostensibly tracing the history of the airplane from Kitty Hawk to jet planes, *Air Power* focuses mostly on the dogfights of the second World War. German and Japanese footage get almost equal billing with allied sources. *Air Power* was produced by CBS with the "cooperation" of the U.S. Air Force, so don't look for any critical comments from Uncle Walter.

**AIRWOLF (**) 60 min (79ep & 2 hr pilot Color; 1984–1987 CBS & USA) Adventure** *with Jan-Michael Vincent as Stringfellow Hawke, Ernest Borgnine as Dominic Santini, Alex Cord as Michael Archangel, Jean Bruce Scott as Caitlin O'Shannessy, Barry Van Dyke as St. John Hawke, Anthony Sherwood as Jason Lock, Michele Scarabelli as Jo Santini, and Geraint Wyn Davies as Maj. Mike Rivers*

*Airwolf* stars a super-secret U.S. government helicopter that can add, subtract, multiply, and divide all on its own (not to mention fly all over the world and bomb the bejesus out of bad guys). The problem is, this modern flying marvel (called "Airwolf") has been stolen and taken to . . . Libya! (boo! hiss!) and only our hero, Stringfellow Hawke (is that his *real* name?), can get it back. Hawke retakes Airwolf for Uncle Sam, but then will *not* give it back unless the feds agree to look for his long-lost brother (St. John), who is missing in action in Vietnam (are you following all this?). So, while the government looks for Hawke's big bro, Hawke hides in the hills, plays the cello, acts cool, and occasionally lowers himself to crank up Airwolf and go bomb somebody the government wants eliminated.

The best that can be said about *Airwolf* is that Jan-Michael Vincent is awfully good-looking and the air action scenes are exciting. However, Ernest Borgnine, who was so good in *McHale's Navy*, seems miscast playing Hawke's buddy and copilot Dominic Santini.

For the final season, the entire cast changes. Stringfellow is knocked out of commission when another helicopter he is riding is blown up by those nasty foreign terrorists. Ernest Borgnine's character is killed off, and his pretty young niece (Jo) replaces him. Wonder of wonders, Stringfellow's long-lost brother St. John is rescued and returns to the states, where he picks up where his little brother left off. Without Vincent and Borgnine, *Airwolf* is just a bland, routine action filler.

**ALAS SMITH AND JONES (**) 30 min (24ep Color; 1984–1987 UK BBC) Comedy-Variety** *with Mel Smith and Griff Rhys Jones*

Two members of the *Not the Nine O'Clock News* comedy team reunite for this series, emphasizing sketches and their comedy dialogues a bit more than the latest topical jibes. Thus, it's a good, relatively timeless mix—and deserving of a permanent spot on the rerun schedule by virtue of its punning title alone, which is guaranteed to add an element of surprise to some viewers searching for the western adventure *Alias Smith and Jones*.

**THE ALASKANS (*½) 60 min (36ep B&W; 1959–1960 ABC) Adventure** *with Roger Moore as Silky Harris, Jeff York as Reno McKee, Dorothy Provine as Rocky Shaw, and Ray Danton as Nifty Cronin*

A laughable effort by Warner Bros. to take their *77 Sunset Strip* concept of two hunks, a shapely lass, and an exotic clime and set it in the Yukon gold rush of 1898. Moore is appropriately named "Silky" and Dorothy Provine is the same squeaky clean singer that she played in *The Roaring Twenties*. The gold rush was a dirty, nasty business, but Silky and his buddy Reno avoid anything that would get them dirty.

**ALCOA PREMIERE (***) 30 min (14ep B&W; 1961–1963 ABC) Drama Anthology** *with Fred Astaire as host*

From the early 1960s, the later era of TV drama anthologies, *Alcoa Premiere* is a collection of *filmed*, not live dramas, with an excellent roster of acting talent. Charlton Heston, Cliff Robertson, Telly Savalas, Lee Marvin, Elizabeth Montgomery, and Robert Redford (earning his only Emmy award nomination to date) appear in various episodes. There are also 39 hour-long dramas from this series, but they are currently packaged separately as *Fred Astaire Presents*.

**ALCOA THEATER** (see ***Turn of Fate and The Golden Age of Television***)

**THE ALDRICH FAMILY (**) 30 min (B&W; 1949–1953 NBC) Situation Comedy** *with Robert Casey, Richard Tyler, Henry Girard, Kenneth Nelson, and Bobby Ellis as Henry Aldrich, House Jameson as Sam Aldrich, Lois Wilson, Nancy Carroll, and Barbara Robbins as Alice Aldrich, Charita Bauer, Mary Malone, and June Dayton as Mary Aldrich, and Jackie Kelk, Robert Barry, and Jackie Grimes as Homer Brown*

*The TV version of The Aldrich Family* is even more cloying and artificial than the long-running radio series it was based on. The Aldriches are a "typical" upper middle-class suburban family (they live on Elm Street in Centerville, which is as middle of the road an address as you can get).

The focus is on teenage son Henry and his parents and sister. Henry is always involved in escapades with partner-in-high-jinks Homer Brown. The memorable opening line of Mrs. Aldrich calling and calling son Henry, followed by Henry's whiny reply "Coming, mother!" was effectively mocked in a ribald version on Firesign Theatre's "Georgy Tirebiter" skits.

The constant cast changes indicate that the TV version never really jelled. The early episodes were performed live. Jean Muir was to have succeeded Nancy Carroll as Alice Aldrich in 1951, but Muir was "blacklisted" by the sponsor, due to alleged leftist ties, setting off the first public debate over the McCarthy-era casting practice. ■

**ALF (***) 30 min (77ep at Fall 1989 Color; 1986– NBC) Situation Comedy** *with Max Wright as Willie Tanner, Anne Schedeen as Kate Tanner, Andrea Elson as Lynn Tanner, Benji Gregory as Brian Tanner, and Paul Fusco as the voice of Alf*

If your family dog could talk, it would probably sound a lot like Alf. Blunt. Wisecracking. Constantly quoting television shows it spends far too much time watching. It might also attempt some alibis when caught poking around where it shouldn't. Or for casting an evil eye on the family cat. Ultimately, though, being able to talk would make that soft furry creature an even more treasured member of the family. Which is what Alf is to Willie Tanner and his clan.

Alf won the Tanners over almost from the moment he crash-landed his spaceship into their garage roof. For one thing, Alf (their acronym name for him as an *A*lien *L*ife *F*orm) was a stranger in a strange land, the sole survivor of his home planet (Melmac), and obviously in need of the Tanners' help to deal with Earth customs. Or at least to avoid being put in a dog pound or under some scientist's dissecting blade and microscope. Besides, he got on fabulously with the kids and promised to keep under control his love of cats as a fine dining treat. (Though that goes against the customs of his home planet where they say, "The only good cat is a stir-fried cat.")

Alf is a clever combination of character threads: warm and loving like E. T. or one of the muppets, full of one-liners and mischief like a typical sitcom kid, and a storehouse of arcane media bits and voices like Robin Williams. He also borrows a page from Mister Ed's script, using the telephone at all hours of the night to do everything from calling "ratings households" urging them to watch his favorite polka show (it finishes number one for the week) to using Willie's name to order from a home shopping program. Like Mork from Ork, Alf is conveniently naive in enough Earth practices to be constantly learning some lesson of life. Yet he is also equipped with sufficient scientific know-how to run his own low-powered television signal and to set off small explosions that wreck various rooms in the house.

Above all, *Alf* is a showcase for Alf as a pop personality—just the type of program a visiting alien might line up to make a splash here. There's a veteran producer (Tom Patchett, from *The Bob Newhart Show*) and a strong Earthling cast, led by Max Wright (the put-upon boss of *Buffalo Bill*). Willie Tanner and the rest of the humans do an excellent job reacting to the scene-stealing alien, whether he greets them from the bathtub (having just consumed a bar of soap), at the dinner table with a bad case of super hiccups, or belching in the living room after overeating. Food is his constant fixation and, ironically, the Tanners end up encouraging extra snacks by sending Alf to the kitchen every time there's someone at the door. Fortunately, though, everyone is the household does know about Alf, so at least Willie isn't alone like Wilbur Post was with Mister Ed.

*Alf* became one of NBC's top characters of the late 1980s, even spawning a Saturday morning cartoon show looking at life on Melmac before he left and placing him in historical settings (*Alf Adventures*). Like Kermit and Miss Piggy, he also turned up everywhere, from awards shows to *The Tonight Show* set, appealing to adults as well as to children. He's an "articulated puppet," meaning that his ears, eyes, and mouth all move, so such real-life appearances are surprisingly effective and believable. Perhaps a lot of thirtysomethings were initially lured to the show and its furry star by their little ones, but once there they were won over by Alf's personality.

**ALFRED HITCHCOCK PRESENTS (***) 30 min (266ep B&W; 1955–1962 CBS & NBC), then as THE ALFRED HITCHCOCK HOUR 60 min (93ep B&W; 1962–1965 CBS & NBC); Revived as ALFRED HITCHCOCK PRESENTS 30 min (73ep at Fall 1989 plus 2 hr pilot Color; 1985– NBC & USA) Suspense Anthology** *with Alfred Hitchcock as host*

Though already a popular and respected film director for more than two decades, Alfred Hitchcock did not become a household name until he stepped into television as the producer, occasional director, and (most important) on-camera host to his own anthology series.

There he won legions of fans with his droll opening comments that showcased his talents as a superb tongue-in-cheek performer willing to don any costume or pose in any setting for the sake of absurd, macabre humor.

As a scarecrow, Hitchcock complained of a bothersome little girl and a tin woodsman that wanted him to go dancing up the road with them. Standing in a wine vat, he described the fate of another person who had been with him stomping grapes—he sank without a trace, but with a drunken smile on his face. And so it went, with Hitchcock as a farmer, a bagpipe player, a clerk at the "Dead Letter Office," a mop-top drummer for a rock band. No matter what the guise, though, Hitchcock remained Hitchcock, never breaking from his deadpan delivery and never failing to set the mood for what followed.

Each opening bit ended with a lead-in to a commercial message, identified by Hitchcock in such glowing terms as "tedious," "calculated but confusing," and "a one-minute anesthetic." But viewers and sponsors loved it, accepting the ribbing as part of the total package.

Which, by the way, also included some dramatic suspense tales that filled the time until Hitchcock's closing remarks. They also happened to be very good productions involving top-notch talent, including performers Burt Reynolds, Robert Redford, Steve McQueen, and Robert Duvall, directors Robert Altman, William Friedkin, Sydney Pollack, and Hitchcock himself, writers Ray Bradbury, Roald Dahl, Ellery Queen, and the team of Richard Levinson and William Link.

The stories themselves usually involved murder, blackmail, revenge, lust, deceit, and other "popular sports" of the Hitchcock world. the key element in all of them was a surprise turn of events at the end. These "tales with a twist" soon became known as Hitchcock's storytelling trademark, even though only a handful of his feature films—such as *Psycho,* made halfway into the run of the TV series—contained such surprise twists.

For most of its original run, the Alfred Hitchcock anthology series used a half-hour format. This was perfect for a quick hit on the audience: Set up a premise, work in the complications, and then pull some switch. Such classics as "Lamb to the Slaughter" (a woman murders her husband with a frozen leg of lamb) and "Man from the South" (a gambler bets his little finger that a lighter will ignite ten times in a row) appeared in this format.

There were also nearly 100 episodes in the *Alfred Hitchcock Hour* version of the series. Though the additional time certainly allowed the performers a greater opportunity to develop their characters, too often the stories themselves seemed padded and were less effective. One problem was that viewers had more time to anticipate the twists. Still there are some excellent episodes, usually containing more involved plotting and strong individual scenes leading to the finale. Among the ones worth watching are: "I Saw the Whole Thing" (Hitchcock's final directorial effort for television), "Dear Uncle George" (written by *Columbo* creators Richard Levinson and William Link), and "The Life Work of Juan Diaz" (written by Ray Bradbury).

Two decades after Hitchcock's series ended its run (and nearly five years after his death), the program was revived—with him once again as host, thanks to a newly developed method of colorizing black and white film. This process allowed Hitchcock to continue his role as Master of Suspense on recycled old intros, first in a made-for-TV movie pilot, then in a series. The stories themselves were freshly filmed, mixing new scripts with generally effective restagings of selected episodes from the original run. ■

**ALIAS SMITH AND JONES** (**½) **60 min (43ep Color; 1971–1973 ABC) Western** *with Peter Deuel (a. k. a. Duel) and Roger Davis as Hannibal Heyes/Joshua Smith and narrator, Ben Murphy as Jed "Kid" Curry/Thaddeus Jones, and J. D. Cannon as Harry Briscoe*

Here is a light and breezy western that combines some action with some nice humorous byplay. Kid Curry and Hannibal Heyes are two members of the outlaw Devil Hole Gang who decide to go straight. They are promised a pardon if they can last a year without breaking the law, so the duo go underground, adopt new identities (Smith and Jones), and try to stay out of trouble. Staying clean is not easy when most lawmen think the pair are still wanted men and the duo's former outlaw associates have several old scores they want to settle.

Keep a sharp eye out for a post–*Flying Nun* Sally Field, who appears a few times as Clementine Hale, a pal of Kid Curry. Peter Deuel (who also spelled his name Duel) died of an apparent suicide after sixteen episodes. Narrator Roger Davis stepped in to fill the Heyes/Smith role. Much of the jaunty air of this series can be credited to the deft hand of executive producer Roy Huggins, of *Maverick* fame. Glen A. Larson, the producer of *Alias Smith and Jones,* later went on to produce other lightweight action shows such as *B. J. and the Bear, The Fall Guy, Manimal,* and *Sheriff Lobo.*

**ALICE** (***) **30 min (185ep Color; 1976–1985 CBS) Situation Comedy** *with Linda Lavin as Alice Hyatt, Vic Tayback as Mel Sharples, Polly Holliday as Flo Castleberry, Beth Howland as Vera Gorman, and Philip McKeon as Tommy Hyatt*

*Alice* is blessed with a wonderful supporting cast that allows the show to remain interesting through a very long run. Linda Lavin, the headliner, is a marvelous actress, but she could never have sustained a hit comedy for nine years without generous helpings of Mel, Flo, and Vera. Combine the top-notch backup with a wonderfully flexible setting and you have a hit show that turned out 185 episodes.

Alice is someone who has not quite adjusted to life, but is trying to. An aspiring singer recovering from the trauma of the death of her husband, Alice packs her belongings and leaves New Jersey, along with twelve-year-old son Tommy, looking for a new life out west. Before she is able to launch her singing career, Alice begins to run out of money and, reluctantly, takes a job as a waitress in Mel's Diner, a roadside eatery near Phoenix, Arizona.

Alice does not really think of herself as better than the gang at Mel's (as literary hopeful–turned-barmaid Diane Chambers does in *Cheers*), but being a waitress is definitely not what Alice wants to do for the rest of her life. She never quite gives up hope of becoming a singer and so she is always struggling to deal with the toughness of her life as single mom/waitress in a dusty Arizona truck stop.

Alice's fellow waitress Flo is a TV sitcom gem. She is the embodiment of hundreds of waitresses across the land who have been serving the same old slop to the same old slobs for longer than they care to remember. Flo's charm is that she is hardly ever dragged down by her lot in life, but rather rises to the challenge. Having seen quite a parade of humanity pass through the truck stop, Flo is not impressed by much and will not put up with any lip from anybody (Mel included). Her classic retort "Kiss my grits!" was a popular exclamation during the show's run.

Mel is more than the stereotypical tyrannical TV boss. He will rant and rave at everyone, but Mel really does care about his waitresses, even though he is convinced they are all nuts. He will defend them when they are under attack from outsiders, but, being a good father figure, Mel will chew them out when they falter or try to slip one past him.

Alice's son Tommy is somewhat of a cipher, not providing much more than the simple fact of being Alice's son. Tommy merely serves as the basis of several plot complications for Alice as she tries to raise the boy on her own. Tommy grows up during the series, but never develops much character. Vera, the third waitress at Mel's, also does not add much at first, except as foil to Mel, Flo, and Alice. Later episodes focus more and more on Vera, as she finally comes out of her shell (she even gets married near the end), but her ultrasensitive nature gets tiring after a while.

The setting of *Alice,* a roadside diner, is the perfect locale to have all sorts of interesting characters, both regular and irregular, drop in to add color and launch the plot of an episode. This workable setting was based on Martin Scorcese's 1975 theatrical film *Alice Doesn't Live Here Anymore*.

Naturally, nine seasons is a long time for any sitcom, and the final years of *Alice* are not the best. For one thing, the cast starts changing. Polly Holliday takes Flo on her own to star in a spin-off (*Flo*). Diane Ladd, who had played the original Flo in the "Alice" movie, replaces Flo in the TV series, but as a different character, Belle Dupree. Belle leaves after one year, to be replaced by Jolene Hunnicutt (Celia Weston). They are both OK, but they are *not* Flo.

It is always nice to see a long-running program produce a good last episode that brings the curtain down on a successful run. *Alice* winds up with a nice tear-jerker as Mel sells his diner and the gang all go their separate ways. Alice finally makes it to Nashville to start her singing career and Vera has recently married. The closeness the cast must have felt comes through in the real emotion of the last episode.

**ALL CREATURES GREAT AND SMALL (***) 60 min (70ep & two 2 hr specials at Fall 1989 Color; 1977–1980 & 1987– UK BBC) Drama** *with Christopher Timothy as James Herriot, Peter Davison as Tristan Farnon, Robert Hardy as Siegfried Farnon, and Carol Drinkwater and Lynda Bellingham as Helen Herriot*

Based on the autobiographical books of country veterinarian James Herriot, this series offers a warm slice of small-town life in northeast England (Yorkshire) from the 1930s to the 1950s. The focus is on three vets who serve the farmers in the area: James (the dedicated idealist), Siegfried (his mentor), and Tristan (Siegfried's lighthearted younger brother). As the series opens, the three share residence at Skeldale House (with housekeeper, Mrs. Hall), exchanging stories and medical advice between meals, cases, and socializing.

The stories themselves are low-key but marvelously personal, ranging from simple misunderstandings (often involving Tristan) to vigils over sick, pregnant, or injured animals. Yet despite the tone of the title, this isn't a cuddly animal series, or a blissful ode to small-town living. In fact, as the vets consistently make clear to starry-eyed visitors from the city, this is a good life, but a hard one. To start, the patients (cows, pigs, sheep) are big, sometimes ornery, and inevitably resting in spots that leave the vets up to their knees in muck and mud. Their owners are even worse, often crotchety and suspicious, and certainly slow to pay their bills. And, of course, conveniences and services a city dweller might be accustomed to are often nowhere to be found. But the rewards are also considerable (if less tangible): a beautiful countryside, small-town camaraderie, and satisfaction with a job well done.

The first batch of *All Creatures Great and Small* stories was produced in the late 1970s. In the mid-1980s, most of the original cast returned to continue the program, bringing the timeline into the early 1950s. ■

**ALL FOR LOVE (**½) 60 min (12ep Color; 1982–1983 UK Granada) Drama Anthology**

Short stories with a common element: love. Not exactly the British version of *Love, American Style* (no laugh track), but rather a mix of light and serious fare. In "A Dedicated Man," for instance, a waiter and a waitress pretend to be married to land a job at a respectable resort, even inventing a son who's "away at school." On the other hand, "Mona" concerns a teenager taking care of a reclusive former soldier still suffering the effects of being gassed in World War I. The material is taken from a variety of writers, including Francis King, William Trevor, and Elizabeth Taylor (no, not *that* one). Five of these tales appeared on *Masterpiece Theatre* in the mid-1980s.

**ALL IN THE FAMILY (***½) 30 min (207ep Color; 1971–1979) Situation Comedy** *with Carroll O'Connor as Archie Bunker, Jean Stapleton as Edith Bunker, Sally Struthers as Gloria Bunker Stivic, Rob Reiner as Michael Stivic, Isabel Sanford as Louise Jefferson, Mel Stewart as Henry Jefferson, Sherman Hemsley as George Jefferson, Mike Evens as Lionel Jefferson, and Danielle Brisebois as Stephanie Mills* **ARCHIE BUNKER'S PLACE (**½) 30 min (97ep Color; 1979–1983) Situation Comedy** *with Carroll O'Connor as Archie Bunker, Jean Stapleton as Edith Bunker, Danielle Brisebois as Stephanie Mills, Martin Balsam as Murray Klein, Allan Melvin as Barney Hefner, Anne Meara as Veronica Rooney, Barry Gordon as Gary Rabinowitz, and Denise Miller as Billie Bunker*

By all rights, *All in the Family* should be a prime candidate for obsolescence, doomed to gather dust at the Smithsonian Institution (right next to Archie Bunker's favorite easy chair). After all, the scripts are filled with references to real-life events of the 1970s, ranging from comments on the "latest" inflation and unemployment rates to the Watergate hearings and Richard Nixon's career. The characters bandy about the names of such public political figures as Henry Kissinger, George McGovern, and Gerald Ford. (Didn't one them almost get elected president of the United States?) How could anyone even remotely care about all that today?

The answer is, most people don't. But, surprise, those points are almost irrelevant to the continued success of the stories. Despite its almost mythical status as a topical ground breaker, from a contemporary perspective *All in the Family* is not really about the "latest" headline news—it's about family life. And these days the series works on two levels.

The first (and most obvious) is as a broad comedy. With his loud mouth, propensity for malapropism, and pig-headed stubbornness, Archie Bunker is a blustery paper tiger in the fine tradition of Ralph Kramden on *The Honeymooners.* He is constantly frustrated by his wife (Edith), son-in-law (Mike), and daughter (Gloria), who are always doing the wrong things. For starters, Gloria married Mike (whom Archie refers to as "Meathead"), a card-carrying liberal who doesn't have a job (he's a student, so the couple is living with Archie and Edith), doesn't respect his elders (especially Archie), and disdains religion, the flag, and sexual restraint. The two clash constantly on virtually every subject.

Archie's problems don't end with Mike, though. Sometimes it seems the whole family is operating on a completely different plane. For example, when Edith accidentally dents a parked car with a can of cling peaches she is foolish enough to leave a note with her name and phone number! Or when an artist friend of Mike's asks if Gloria would pose in the nude, she agrees to. And, worst of all, the whole family seems to get on with their black next-door neighbors, the Jeffersons. In the course of dealing with such issues (and many others) there's plenty of back-and-forth shouting, especially between Archie and Mike. But their comments are usually funny and, in most of these, Archie is the loser, getting his comeuppance from all corners (even Sammy Davis, Jr., in an early guest spot).

On that level, *All in the Family* is a reasonably funny vehicle, with quips just a few notches below the scripts on such series as *Mary Tyler Moore* or *Bob Newhart.* (A few of the really "heavy" topical stories are uncomfortably dated, but you'll be able to spot them almost immediately and quickly seek refuge elsewhere.) However, what makes the series something special today is watching it as a character study. For example, when Archie and Mike argue about the latest issues, consider that as a mask for something else: Archie is saying, "How *dare* you marry my little girl and not be able to provide for her!" When Mike finally does get a teaching job (and eventually moves into the house next door to Archie and Edith), Archie's tone is noticeably softer. He still may not be thrilled with his daughter's choice, but at least they're starting to look like a young family should: a house, a job, and (best of all) a child (Joey). Mike, too, begins to appreciate Archie more, especially as he begins to feel the stings of reality in the outside world (for instance, despite his professed beliefs, feeling resentful at losing a new job to an equally qualified, but black, competitor).

But the growth doesn't stop there. Archie's view of the world at large changes considerably over the course of the series, especially when you look at what he does rather than merely listen to what he says. Archie may engage in argument after argument, but when the shouting has died down, he's the one who inevitably changes. Inch by inch, issue by issue, when the crunch comes, he learns to see things from a different point of view, especially when things move from vague generalities to specific people. For instance, he may subscribe to the general rhetoric of some neighborhood Ku Klux Klan members, but when they earmark Michael and Gloria's house for a burning cross, Archie is a thundering bull proudly citing the black blood in his veins (from a transfusion during a gall bladder operation) and threatening to call on his "black blood brothers" to help stomp on any "honkies" who want to mess with him. In addition, when Archie changes jobs from the warehouse docks to owning his neighborhood tavern, he simply has to become a much more reasonable figure—he's a small businessman now.

Perhaps the most fascinating aspect of the series is watching it as a contrast in marriages between Archie and Edith's generation and Mike and Gloria's. This is something that can only be appreciated in reruns, because we can see the actions of earlier episodes with the knowledge of how everything eventually does turn out. On that level, the older generation definitely "wins."

Michael and Gloria are from the speak-your-mind, be-open-and-honest generation. They profess all the "ideologically correct" positions on all the issues (the war in Vietnam, affirmative action, equal rights, and sexual freedom). They talk constantly about commitment, and are proud of their son. Yet (as later revealed in episodes of *Archie Bunker's Place* and on the *Gloria* spin-off series) the two will go through some rocky times, separate, and eventually divorce. Knowing that outcome brings a strange intensity to their rough times throughout the *All in the Family* run, especially at those moments when you look at them and say, "I could see it coming." The happy moments are still happy, but the uncertain ones become especially touching.

Archie and Edith, on the other hand, are anything but "liberated." Yet just as Archie grows, so does Edith, evolving from an all-too-naive "dingbat" into a quietly understanding and deeply principled person. Over the course of the series, keep a close eye on them. They don't parade their sexuality (Edith doesn't "burn her bra"), but after all the shouting is over, they clearly enjoy their intimate moments. Even when Archie has a "dalliance" with another woman, their love survives. In fact, he seems to appreciate Edith even more. It's really no surprise that, for them, marriage indeed means "till death do us part."

*All in the Family* slides into *Archie Bunker's Place,* with the main storyline shifting to the neighborhood tavern. Edith, Mike, and Gloria all turn up in the first season of the "new" series, though, so it's hard to think of it as a separate entity. The real cutoff comes at the beginning of the second season, with the death of Edith. This is a stunning and effective episode, set a month *after* her death, with Archie still refusing to deal with his pent-up grief. It's worth keeping an eye on the *Archie Bunker's Place* rerun rotation just to catch this story.

Otherwise, *Archie Bunker's Place* is a good showcase for the Archie character on his own, but nothing extraordinary. He takes on a variety of associates and partners (starting with Martin Balsam as Murray Klein). During its final season, there is also a spin-off solo *Gloria* series, but except for the pilot episode, there is no major interaction between Archie and his little girl.

*All in the Family* was based on the hit British comedy *Till Death Us Do Part,* and brought to the States by Norman Lear and Bud Yorkin. Lear used its success to launch a host of other series, with *The Jeffersons* and *Maude* direct *All in the Family* spin-offs.

**ALL IS FORGIVEN** **(**) 30 min (11ep Color; 1986 NBC) Situation Comedy** *with Bess Armstrong as Paula Russell, Terence Knox as Matt Russell, Carol Kane as Nicolette Bingham, Shawnee Smith as Sonia Russell, Judith-Marie Bergan as Cecile Porter-Lindsey, David Allen Grier as Oliver Royce, and Bill Wiley as Wendell Branch*

This series probably seems absolutely hilarious (and all too familiar and lifelike) to the writers and production people behind it. For viewers safe at home, the verdict is decidedly mixed. Much of the humor is hooked to the cynical, insecure, and slapdash world of television production, in this case for the fictional daytime soap opera *All Is Forgiven.* Paula Russell lands her job as program producer there by sheer luck, standing in the production office as the only available body at the moment her predecessor departs. She doesn't even see her employer because the whole transaction takes place over the company's intercom system. Yet within moments, Paula is running the show and instantly finds herself overwrought, overbudget, behind schedule, and chain-smoking. But she does gain a fast "friend for life" in one of the soap opera's writers, spacy but literate Nicolette Bingham, who is overjoyed that Paula picks up an allusion to Tennessee Williams, exclaiming in amazement, "You *read*!" Nicolette then arranges for Paula to end her first day (unexpected new job notwithstanding) with her planned marriage ceremony by transforming the studio set into a perfect wedding backdrop at the end of the shooting schedule. As this falls into place over a thirty-second whir of activity, you get a hint as to why these people stick around, because sometimes their television work can be absolute magic.

Unfortunately, there aren't many more such moments. For the most part, the series carries a cynical chip on its shoulder, with Paula's home and office life filled with petty problems and personal antagonism. Her new husband's teenage daughter can't stand her (and vice versa) and she's constantly caught in clashes of personality at the office (usually between the self-centered star, Cecile, and everybody else, especially the writing staff). As a result, Paula is always working far too long at the office on a program she doesn't really respect, and when she gets home to her husband (who she really loves), there's always jealous Sonia to contend with.

Now maybe this reads like the typical personal diary for some television writers, but turning it into entertaining comedy is a tricky proposition. It can be done (*Buffalo Bill* and *The Dick Van Dyke Show* prove that, succeeding with totally opposite tones), but in this case the whole package doesn't quite work. Even with an appropriately exaggerated performance by Carol Kane as Nicolette (complete with a cutting southern accent), and a solid "loving couple" portrayal by Armstrong and Knox, what you really want is to catch these people in another setting. Look for Kane in *Taxi,* Knox in *St. Elsewhere,* and Armstrong in *Lace.*

**ALL PASSION SPENT** **(**½) 60 min (3ep Color; 1988 BBC) Drama** *with Wendy Hiller as Lady Slane, Harry Andrews as Fitzgeorge, Hilary Mason as Edith, Phyllis Calvert as Carrie, Graham Crowden as Herbert, John Franklyn-Robbins as Kay, and Maurice Denham as Bucktrout*

This leisurely adaptation of a 1931 novel by Vita Sackville-West features Wendy Hiller as an independent eighty-five-year-old woman, newly widowed after sixty-eight years of marriage to a British prime minister. Much to the astonishment of her children, she decides to strike off and live by herself, setting up housekeeping in the Hampstead area—which is where she finds herself courted by a long-time admirer. This warm character showcase for Hiller first aired in the States on *Masterpiece Theatre.*

**ALL THAT GLITTERS** **(**½) 30 min (65ep Color; 1977 Syndication) Serial Comedy** *with Lois Nettleton as Christina Stockwood, Chuck McCann as Bert Stockwood, Anita Gillette as Nancy Langston, Barbara Baxley as L. W. Carruthers, Vanessa Brown as Peggy Horner, Jessica Walter as Joan Hamlyn, Linda Gray as Linda Murkland, and Gary Sandy as Dan Kincaid*

A true male/female role reversal series, running under the assumption that it's been a "woman's world" since the dawn of time. Or, as Kenny Rankin's opening theme song ("Genesis Revisited") explains, that's the way God meant it since the time She created us all. Of course, there are the obvious switches, such as the leering comments directed toward company secretary Dan Kincaid (Gary Sandy, later Andy Travis on *WKRP*) by the corporate bigwigs ("nice behind!"). But, once the setup is in place, the series moves along nicely within its own world, with the women easily slipping into the typically male hard-knocking corporate characterizations, and the men taking their turn in the secretarial and domestic roles.

Chuck McCann (then most familiar to viewers as the face behind the medicine cabinet mirror in Right Guard deodorant commercials) is particularly effective in his portrayal of executive Christina Stockwood's housekeeping husband, bringing a puppy dog vulnerability to his character. In fact, though this was touted as another comic soap opera serial developed by Norman Lear (like *Mary Hartman, Mary Hartman*), the prevailing mood is actually more a touching sense of sadness. That didn't play very well in the time periods in which *Mary Hartman* had done so well (right before or after prime time), and since there also was no overnight star like Louise Lasser to boost interest in the series, it did very poorly in the ratings. As a result, even though *All That Glitters* has a sufficient number of otherwise familiar cast members (Gary Sandy, Chuck McCann, Linda Gray, Jessica Walter, Lois Nettleton), it is rarely rerun.

**ALL THE RIVERS RUN (**½) (8hr miniseries Color; 1983 Australia) Drama** *with Sigrid Thornton as Philadelphia ("Dilly") Gordon/Edwards, John Waters as Brenton ("Teddy") Edwards, Adrian Wright as Alastair Raeburn, Darius Perkins as Ben Mitchell, Don Barker as Geroge Blakeney, Celia De Burgh as Imogen, and John Alansu as Ah Lee*

An entertainingly soapy tale following the aspirations of Philadelphia Gordon, a sensitive but strong-willed young woman in turn-of-the-century Australia. She excels at anything she sets her mind to, so ultimately her most daunting task is deciding between a passion for the earthy river life (where she is co-owner and operator of a riverboat bearing her name) and the lure of hobnobbing in the big city art circles as a successful painter.

There's a devoted man for her in either port (the rugged and passionate skipper Brenton Edwards or wealthy art critic and patron Alastair Raeburn), so the real issue here seems to be which path will let her excel best as a strong, independent woman.

Based on a hit novel (by Nancy Cato), the series is somewhat reminiscent of the 1979 Australian theatrical film, *My Brilliant Career.* Sigrid Thornton also appears as the heroine in the Australian-produced *Man from Snowy River* theatrical feature films. ■

**ALL YOU NEED IS LOVE (**½) 60 min (16ep Color; 1977 UK London Weekend Television) Documentary**

Though this well-researched history of popular music covers a wide range of styles and performers, programmers often air just one episode from the series, treating it as a one-time Beatles special. Not surprisingly, it's the hour containing the group's performance of the title song as part of a worldwide television hookup back in 1967. However, that isn't the only time the Beatles appear in *All You Need Is Love,* nor is this episode devoted entirely to them (about half focuses on other performers from the "summer of love" era). In any case, the entire package is worth watching as a basic overview of twentieth-century pop music, as seen through British eyes. Perhaps the most dated aspect of the series is the selection of rare footage—far more has surfaced since 1977, even turning up regularly as "special videos" on MTV.

**ALL'S FAIR (**½) 30 min (24ep Color; 1976–1977 CBS) Situation Comedy** *with Richard Crenna as Richard C. Barrington, Bernadette Peters as Charlotte "Charley" Drake, Judy Kahan as Ginger Livingston, and Michael Keaton as Lanny Wolf*

This is executive producer Norman Lear's most overtly political series, other than the never-aired black congressman sitcom *Mr. Dugan. All's Fair* is set in Washington, D. C., and features the love/hate battle between arch-conservative political columnist Richard Barrington and his youngish liberal girlfriend/photographer Charley Drake. The conflicts are political, sexual, and generational, all guaranteeing lots of witty, topical banter back and forth, a staple of Norman Lear series.

Late in the series, Barrington is appointed an assistant to President Carter, where he encounters presidential joke writer Lanny Wolf, played by a very young Michael Keaton in his first TV series role.

**'ALLO, 'ALLO (**½) 30 min (54ep at Spring 1989 Color; 1984– UK BBC) Situation Comedy** *with Gordon Kaye as Rene, Carmen Silvera as Edith, Vicki Michelle as Yvette, Sam Kelly as Geering, and Richard Marner as Von Strohm*

Sometimes the missions taken on by the men from *Hogan's Heroes* would involve leaving their German prisoner-of-war camp and teaming up with some contacts in a nearby town, often at a cafe or bar. This BBC-produced series uses such a cafe setting as its main focus, offering a new round of World War II resistance humor done as broad farce under the self-serving manipulations of Rene, owner and operator of the cafe.

Actually, he is not quite as selfless and dedicated a fighter as Col. Hogan. Though he loves good food, fine wine, and beautiful women, Rene is also quite happy and willing to sell sausage and other rationed foodstuffs to the German officers, led by Von Strohm. Not that he likes them—it's just good business. They, in turn, conveniently look the other way when he's receiving his shipments and stocking his shelves. Not that they'd notice anything really suspicious if they tried; they're from the sitcom academy of Nazi soldiering, no doubt taught by its chief practitioner, Col. Klink. Instead, Rene's problems come from members of the resistance, who are always eager to use his facilities, and him, as a key point in their ongoing sabotage missions. He reluctantly agrees, probably most inspired by some of the beautiful women he sees working for the cause.

Though this is not a cliffhanger-style series, there is a more or less continuing set of subplots, most notably tracing the disposal of seized art objects by the Nazis. Naturally, local officers like Van Strohm scheme to line their own pockets at the expense of the home office, even as the resistance works to outwit both ends. Of course, some people find the very idea of humorous Nazis offensive but, as with *Hogan's Heroes,* if you accept the initial premise, all the rest flows easily, if predictably.

In 1988, there was a successful live theatrical version of *'Allo, 'Allo* staged at London's West End, using members from the series cast.

**ALMOST GROWN (**) 60 min (9ep & 2 hr pilot Color; 1988–1989 CBS) Drama** *with Timothy Daly as Norman Foley, Eve Gordon as Suzie Long Foley, Albert Macklin as Joey Long, Nathaniel Moreau and Raffi DiBlasio as Jackson Foley, Ocean Hellman as Anya Foley, Malcolm Stewart as Dr. Bob Keyes, Rita Taggart as Joan Foley, Richard Schaal as Dick Long, and Anita Gillette as Vi Long*

The ups and downs of the relationship of Norman and Suzie are traced over three decades in *Almost Grown,* with plenty of background period music, in case you needed more help to set the scene. In the early 1960s, the couple met in high school and dated. In the swinging 1970s, they married. Now it's the 1980s, they have two kids (Anya and Jackson), are divorced, and, as the series opens, Suzie is planning to get married again, this time to Dr. Bob Keyes. She can't seem to get down the aisle, however, without reliving a few more moments of her life with Norman. *Almost Grown* manages to toss in nearly every clichéd expression of the three decades it covers.

**ALOHA PARADISE (½) 60 min (13ep Color; 1981 ABC) Situation Comedy** *with Debbie Reynolds as Sydney Chase, Bill Daily as Curtis Shea, Pat Klous as Fran Linhart, and Mokihana as Evelyn Pahinui*

This sappy effort by Aaron Spelling and Douglas Cramer to clone their hit *The Love Boat* transplants the same frothy multiple-story vignette format of that successful series to another exotic setting. This time, instead of the cruise ship, the locale is Paradise Village, a resort on the Kona coast in Hawaii. Debbie Reynolds is annoyingly chipper as manager of the resort. Like *The Love Boat, Aloha Paradise* has a schmaltzy theme song, sung by Steve Lawrence. Without the swank allure of the seagoing setting of *The Love Boat, Aloha Paradise* resembles a second class resort that makes for a very trying holiday. Stick to the original, instead.

**THE ALVIN SHOW (**½) 30 min (26ep Color; 1961–1962 ABC) Cartoon** *with voice of Ross Bagdasarian as Dave Seville, Simon, Theodore, and Alvin*

After scoring several hit records during the late 1950s (including the novelty Christmas chart-topper, "The Chipmunk Song"), the Chipmunks broke into television in 1961 as part of the animation invasion of network prime time. Under the strict supervision of creator Ross Bagdasarian (who created and voiced the chipmunk characters of Simon, Theodore, and Alvin, along with his own alter ego, Dave Seville), they performed in a variety-show-style setting (like *The Bugs Bunny Show*), rather than the half-hour adventure structure of *The Flintstones, The Jetsons,* and *Top Cat.* This allowed "the boys" plenty of time for short skits and adventures, as well as musical performances. They introduced young viewers to such old-fashioned pop songs as "On Top of Old Smokey" and "A Bicycle Built for Two," as well as more contemporary Chipmunk favorites including "Alvin's Harmonica" and "The Alvin Twist." They even dug out one of Dave's (er, Ross's) pre-Chipmunk hits, "The Witch Doctor."

These half-hour programs are rounded out with the adventures of Clyde Crashcup (voiced by Shepard Menken) and Leonardo (who speaks only in an inaudible whisper to Crashcup). Clyde Crashcup immodestly claims to be the inventor of everything, from the bathtub to music to Egypt.

Though the Chipmunks lasted only one season in prime time, the series immediately hit the kiddie cartoon rerun cycle. In 1983, more than a decade after the death of Ross Bagdasarian, his son (Ross Jr.) took up the tradition, supervising (and voicing) a new series of half-hour cartoon packages (78 at the Fall of 1988), *Alvin and the Chipmunks.* These played first on NBC's Saturday morning lineup, then hit the syndication trails. Though the animation is fairly basic, all of the programs (especially the originals) capture the entertaining sense of youthful mischief that have kept the Chipmunks performing favorites for all these years.

**AMANDA'S (**½) 30 min (8ep Color; 1983 ABC) Situation Comedy** *with Beatrice Arthur as Amanda Cartwright, Tony Rosato as Aldo, Simone Griffeth as Arlene Cartwright, Fred McCarren as Marty Cartwright, Rick Hurst as Earl Nash, and Keene Curtis as Clifford Mundy*

Here's how American producers handle the *Fawlty Towers* premise of a guest house by the sea.

Unlike its British cousin, *Amanda's* leaves no doubt who is in charge here. So while Amanda may possess Basil Fawlty's love of insults, sarcasm, and browbeating, she has none of his shackles, i.e., a domineering mate. (He's deceased, so Amanda's son Marty is the day-to-day hotel manager.) Of course, that plot accommodation also reflects the fact that there probably isn't anyone at Central Casting who could convincingly dominate a Beatrice Arthur character. She would pulverize him with just a glare.

Among the supporting characters, Marty's wife, Arlene, comes closest to actually taking on Amanda, who can't stand the fact that she married her son. The two frequently exchange barbs as Amanda prays for the day that their marriage falls apart. At the other extreme, Aldo, the foreign bellman who can barely utter a coherent sentence in English, is totally terrified of his boss.

So the overall tone of this series is far different from *Fawlty Towers* in handling some good old-fashioned drawing room comedy misunderstandings, preferably with a sexual tone. For instance, in one story Amanda sees several people in seemingly romantic embraces, so naturally assumes they are all sexually involved. They, in turn, see her in a similar situation and think she is having affairs with several men at once. Which leads to everyone accusing everyone else in the hotel lobby. But could anyone really believe that Amanda would *think* of having an affair with Aldo?

As such a short-run series, *Amanda's* is probably best viewed as an amusing seaside stopover for Beatrice Arthur between *Maude* and *The Golden Girls.*

## THE AMAZING SPIDER-MAN (see *Spider-Man*)

## AMAZING STORIES

**(**) 30 min (45 ep: forty-three 30 min & two 60 min; 44 Color & 1 B&W; 1985–1987 NBC) Fantasy Anthology** *produced by Steven Spielberg*

The opening sequence celebrates storytellers.

They bask in the warm glow of the campfire, all eyes fixed on them spinning their tales. Then, sweeping through the ages and technologies, there is a montage of images from their stories, all leading us back to another warm glowing campfire. This time, it's coming from a living room television screen, with a typical American family gathered to watch and listen.

This nifty intro is a classic. Unfortunately, the same cannot be said for many of the entries in this series.

Part of the problem with *Amazing Stories* was unrealistically high expectations. Steven Spielberg attracted a great deal of attention when he agreed to produce a television anthology series in 1985. After all, he had begun his career as a television director (handling an episode of *Columbo,* a segment on the *Night Gallery* pilot, and the made-for-TV movie *Duel*), but graduated quickly to theatrical feature films, where he turned out some of the biggest box office successes in movie history. If Spielberg was coming back to his TV roots, then the product was expected to be . . . pretty amazing.

Some of it was. But, as with any television anthology series, some of it wasn't. It just depended on how each episode's script, direction, and characters fell into place. Unfortunately, given the expectations raised by the success associated with such Spielberg blockbusters as *Jaws, E. T.,* and *Raiders of the Lost Ark,* the week-in week-out grind of series television could not help but be a letdown. And, ironically (given the series title), the most consistent flaw was in the stories themselves, which often seemed in need of just one more good rewrite.

Still, there were moments, especially humorous ones such as a horror movie actor rushing to the birth of his child without removing his "mummy" costume ("Mummy, Daddy" with Bronson Pinchot); an ancient ring that transformed a frumpy wife into a femme fatale, determined to murder her husband ("The Wedding Ring" starring real-life husband and wife Danny DeVito and Rhea Perlman); a dog's-eye view of the annoying world of humans (the animated "Family Dog"—later released as a theatrical film short); and every student's nightmare, a demanding but crazed teacher ("Go to the Head of the Class," a one-hour special reuniting *Back to the Future* director Robert Zemeckis with one of that film's stars, Christopher Lloyd).

Perhaps the best development to come from *Amazing Stories* was that it helped remove some of the "stigma" associated with "doing television" after success in theatrical features. Spielberg attracted other cinema veterans to his series, resulting in episodes directed by Martin Scorsese ("Mirror, Mirror"), Clint Eastwood ("Vanessa in the Garden"), Burt Reynolds ("Guilt Trip"), and Joe Dante ("Boo"). Paul Bartel ("Eating Raoul," "Lust in the Dust") went one step further and used his *Amazing Stories* guest segment to remake his own 1966 short film about a woman who suspected that her life was being secretly filmed and then run in theaters as a slapstick serial ("Secret Cinema").

Unfortunately, sometimes even these big names couldn't overcome some pretty weak scripts. Perhaps Spielberg should have presented the entire series as a director's or actor's showcase, emphasizing experiments in style rather than plot. He might have even acted as host, setting the tone for each one with a few pithy introductory remarks. As *Steven Spielberg Presents* or *The Spielberg Zone* it just might have worked.

## AMEN

**(**½) 30 min (64ep at Fall 1989 Color; 1986– NBC) Situation Comedy** *with Sherman Hemsley as Deacon Ernest Frye, Clifton Davis as Rev. Reuben Gregory, Barbara Montgomery as Casietta Hetebrink, Roz Ryan as Amelia Hetebrink, and Anna Maria Horsford as Thelma Frye*

Sherman Hemsley burrowed his way into the American psyche through his twelve-year run as George Jefferson, first on *All in the Family* and then on *The Jeffersons.* In *Amen,* he gets to play a very similar character: the energetic, egocentric Deacon Frye, who oversees operations at the First Community Church in Philadelphia (founded by his father). Not surprisingly, Frye assumes he can browbeat anybody to his side of an issue—until his new minister, Rev. Reuben Gregory, turns up. Gregory has a smooth, strong personality of his own that proves to be quite effective in their battle of wills.

Clifton Davis, who plays Rev. Gregory, certainly had the right resumé for the job, since he is a Seventh Day Adventist pastor in real life and the son of an evangelist. This lends an authentic tone to his portrayal. In addition, the church setting provides a believable backdrop for getting involved in the community's everyday problems (large and small), while the choice serves as a creditable excuse for some soulful music performances (with stand-out work by Roz Ryan's Amelia Hetebrink).

But perhaps the best aspect of the First Community Church setting is that it helps to keep Hemsley's abrasive and manipulative character somewhat in check. After all, in spite of his self-centered flaws, Deacon Frye is still a sincerely dedicated man of the cloth. As a result, he seems to take his inevitable comeuppance a lot better than George Jefferson ever could.

**AMERICA (****) 60 min or 30 min (13ep at 60 min or 26ep at 30 min Color; 1972 UK BBC) Documentary** *with Alistair Cooke as writer and narrator*

*America* was written and produced just as *Masterpiece Theatre* was getting off the ground on PBS and establishing Alistair Cooke as the man to introduce Stateside audiences to classy British television. Appropriately, this series (subtitled "A Personal History of the United States") allowed him to take the next step and bring U.S. viewers a mini-tour of their own country's history. It's a lovingly detailed documentary actually done for both British and U.S. consumption, first broadcast in 1972 by the BBC and NBC.

Cooke became a U.S. citizen in 1941 (just past thirty years old), and so brings the perspective both of a man raised outside the States and that of a well-informed citizen proud of his adopted country. He draws on his knowledge of both countries and clearly explains how events were perceived on both sides of the Atlantic. Cooke is especially good with the on-point anecdote, whether it's describing the hellish journeys taken by settlers heading across the mountains and deserts of California, or the political courage and statesmanship of the men pounding out their great experiment in democracy, the American Constitution. One constant theme throughout is that what people expected of the new country was far different from the immediate and present-day reality.

*America* originally aired in the one-hour format, anticipating the U.S. bicentennial celebrations of 1976. Cooke subsequently recorded new wraparound material for the half-hour versions. ■

**AMERICA 2NIGHT** **(see *Fernwood 2-Night*)**

**THE AMERICAN DREAM (*) 60 min (6ep Color; 1981 ABC) Drama** *with Stephen Macht as Danny Novak, Karen Carlson as Donna Novak, Tim Waldrip as Casey Novak, Michael Hershewe as Todd Novak, Andrea Smith as Jennifer Novak, Hans Conried as Abe Berlowitz, and John McIntire as Sam Whittier*

*The American Dream* is a heavy-handed effort to present meaningful drama to prime-time viewers. The upper middle-class Novak family takes the unprecedented step (for TV) of voluntarily moving from swank suburban Arlington Heights, Illinois, to the gritty reality of a racially mixed decaying neighborhood in Chicago. The change is supposed to be good for the Novaks' souls, but it does take some getting used to.

Amidst the plasticity of the Novak clan, the best character is old hand Hans Conried (Uncle Tonoose in *Make Room for Daddy* and the voice of Snidley Whiplash on *Bullwinkle*). Conried plays the neighborhood curmudgeon who sells the Novaks their inner-city home and becomes a friend of the family. Barry Rosenzweig produced both this series and *Cagney & Lacey*.

**AN AMERICAN FAMILY (**) 60 min (12ep B&W & 60 min sequel; 1973 PBS) Documentary**

On the surface, this series has the simplest of goals: documenting the lives of a middle-class American family. Producer Craig Gilbert and his crew filmed more than 300 hours over seven months in and about the household of the Loud family in Santa Barbara, California. The 300 hours were edited into a twelve-hour series that presents the Louds to America.

As one can imagine, a lot of the family's activities appear as ordinary, run-of-the-mill suburban banality. Most people's lives would seem deathly dull to even themselves if memorialized in a TV documentary. What makes the Louds' lives memorable is that, as the series progresses, the family begins unraveling in front of the camera. First, son Lance reveals he is a homosexual. Then, the parents' marriage crumbles, wife Pat opts for divorce, and husband Bill moves out of the house. All of this is preserved for the nation's entertainment.

The fact that so much drama happened to occur while the film crew was present raises very difficult questions. Assuming the kernel of all the Louds' problems existed before filming started, did the presence of the cameras exacerbate problems that might have been resolved otherwise? Did the cameras cause family divisions that did not exist before? Were the Louds crazy for allowing outsiders to take over their lives and expose fissures in their family unity that all families work to overcome? Were the Louds cynically manipulated by the film crew, in order to make the documentary more "sexy"?

It is impossible, even after watching the series, to answer many, if any of these questions. Even if the filmmakers are given every benefit of the doubt, a viewer is left with a disturbing feeling that the television camera does more than just blindly record the history going on around it. *An American Family* is a valuable lesson that the camera must be thought of as a participant in the events it records.

A one-hour postscript to the series was produced in 1983 for HBO by Gilbert's two assistants, Alan and Susan Raymond. *An American Family Revisited: The Louds 10 Years Later* presents filmed interviews with family members, discussing how being the focus of a national documentary changed their lives.

For an effective putdown of the entire *An American Family* issue, catch the witty 1979 Albert Brooks film, *Real Life,* in which Brooks plays a shifty producer who films a "typical" American family.

**THE AMERICAN GIRLS (zero) 60 min (11ep Color; 1978 CBS) Adventure** *with Priscilla Barnes as Rebecca Tomkins, Debra Clinger as Amy Waddell, David Spielberg as Francis X. Casey, and William Prince as Jason Cook*

In this botched mix of *Charlie's Angles* and *60 Minutes,* Rebecca and Amy are field researchers for the fictional TV news magazine "The American Report." The two lassies roam the countryside, attempting to turn up hard-hitting stories while still looking beautiful. Francis Casey is the TV producer who, "Charlie"-like, gives the girls their assignments.

Priscilla Barnes later was one of Suzanne Somers' replacements in *Three's Company.*

**AMERICAN PLAYHOUSE (***½) (Color; 1982– PBS) Drama Anthology**

This umbrella title has been used by PBS for a variety of dramatic presentations of varying lengths (from 60 minutes to 2 hours), ranging from multi-part filmed docudramas such as *Oppenheimer* to adaptations of theatrical plays such as Sam Shepard's *True West* (starring John Malkovich and Gary Sinise). Most are one-shot offerings, though, making this a bit like PBS's version of an ABC/CBS/NBC made-for-TV movie slot. ■

**AMERICAN SHORT STORY (***) 60 min (13ep Color; 1977–1980 PBS) Drama Anthology** *with Colleen Dewhurst and Henry Fonda as hosts*

These well-staged adaptations of short stories by American authors include such works as "Bernice Bobs Her Hair" by F. Scott Fitzgerald (with Shelley Duval), "I'm a Fool" by Sherwood Anderson (with Ron Howard and Amy Irving), "Barn Burning" by William Faulkner (with Tommy Lee Jones), and "Almos' a Man" by Richard Wright (with LeVar Burton). This originally aired as an occasional series for PBS, with the running time for a particular story anywhere from thirty minutes to the full hour (with some packaged as "double features"). In reruns and home video, the individual stories sometimes stand alone, even if they run an odd time such as thirty-nine minutes. ■

**THE AMERICANS (**) 60 min (17ep B&W; 1961 NBC) War Drama** *with Darryl Hickman as Ben Canfield and Dick Davalos as Jeff Canfield*

Produced during the one-hundredth anniversary of the Civil War, *The Americans* presents the war between the states from the perspective of one border state family, the Canfields. Elder brother Ben joins the Union blue, while younger brother Jeff sides with the Confederate gray.

Darryl Hickman, who plays Ben, had a much more pacific relationship with his real-life brother Dwayne, the star of *Dobie Gillis* (where Darryl made several guest appearances as Dobie's brother Davey).

**AMERIKA (***) (14-½hr miniseries Color; 1987 ABC) Drama** *with Kris Kristofferson as Devin Milford, Robert Urich as Peter Bradford, Sam Neill as Col. Andrei Denisov, Mariel Hemingway as Kimberly Ballard, Christine Lahti as Alethea Milford, Cindy Pickett as Amanda Bradford, Armin Mueller-Stahl as Gen. Petya Samanov, Ford Rainey as Will Milford, and Don Reilly as Justin Milford*

It may be overly long, but *Amerika* is one of the most innovative miniseries of the 1980s. Set in 1997, *Amerika* supposes a world where, somehow or other, the Russians peaceably took over the United States about a decade before. Exactly how they did it is never made very clear, and the idea is very improbable. If, however, you simply assume that original premise, the rest of the series makes a great deal of sense. The point is that people, any race of people, will react in different ways to sudden, seismic change. Some will knuckle under and accept the change meekly. Some will be "pragmatic" and play along, trying to do their best in a bad situation. Some will relish the change as an opportunity to personally benefit from a new status quo. Others will never give in and will fight to the death. This scenario was played out in the 1930s and 1940s as the Nazis took over Germany, first, then most of the rest of Europe. It happened again after World War II, as the Russians occupied eastern Europe. What *Amerika* asks is, how would Americans, who have not known foreign domination for more than two centuries, react to sudden occupation?

The differing reactions of Americans are personified in the two main characters, Peter Bradford and Devin Milford. Bradford is the pragmatist, who becomes the chief American administrator of the Midwest, under Soviet supervision. Bradford dislikes the Russians, but feels he is doing the best for his people by trying to win the little battles that can be won through bureaucratic wrangling with the overlords. Devin Milford is the rebel, the losing presidential candidate in 1988, who has been a political prisoner of the Russians for a decade and is now released. Returning to his home in Milford, Nebraska (named for his family), he encounteres boyhood friend Bradford and the two soon part company. Milford refuses to accept the Soviet yoke, and he begins to lead a guerrilla resistance band.

Kris Kristofferson, a Rhodes scholar turned country singer turned movie actor, is messianic as Milford. He is given some heavy speeches to make, and he just stares a lot, but his acting is quite powerful. Robert Urich as Peter Bradford is the perfect local politician, trying to make do with what he has. His small tinges of ego help him play along with the Russians for a while. Sam Neil, an Australian actor who starred in *Reilly, Ace of Spies,* is the "good" villain as the top Russian KGB official in the United States. As with most big miniseries, the secondary cast is made up of large numbers of well-known actors and actresses.

*Amerika* created a firestorm of protest when it first aired, but it will be difficult to remember what all the hubbub was about when watching the series. *Amerika* is a little heavy-handed, and the ending is overly dramatic, but it deals with issues of personal political conscience that few, if any, other TV series have touched.

**AMOS AND ANDY (***) 30 min (78ep B&W; 1951–1953 CBS) Situation Comedy** *with Tim Moore as George "The Kingfish" Stevens, Spencer Williams as Andy Brown, Alvin Chidress as Amos Jones, and Ernestine Wade as Sapphire Stevens*

It's not true! All those awful things you have heard about *Amos and Andy* just are not true. The show is not a dangerous insult to black Americans, filled with harmful stereotypes that demean an entire race. Unfortunately, because the program is rarely seen these days, it is very difficult to convince many people that *Amos and Andy* is no more a threat to the nation than old reruns of *Sanford and Son* or *Good Times.*

*Amos and Andy* is the televised version of the most popular sitcom of the radio era (which ran from 1929 all the way to 1960). The show, set in Harlem, was created by Freeman Gosden and Charles Correll, two Southern whites who supplied most of the voices for the black characters in the radio version. At first, the focus was on Amos, a calm, laconic cab driver, and Andy, a dim-witted bachelor. As the radio show grew in popularity, the character of George Stevens, the "Kingfish" of the local black men's club (the Mystic Knights of the Sea Lodge), came to the forefront and the character of Amos faded into the background. The Kingfish was a loud, bombastic blowhard, always out for a quick buck at someone else's expense (usually Andy's).

When *Amos and Andy* came to TV, Gosden and Correll served as producers, but relinquished the acting roles to TV's first all-black cast. Various black organizations protested the show, alleging that it demeaned blacks and reinforced negative stereotypes. *Amos and Andy* lasted only two years on TV before going into reruns and, in 1966, at the height of the civil rights movement, it was withdrawn from syndication. Due to its bad reputation, *Amos and Andy* is now being held hostage. The distributor will not distribute the show and it is virtually impossible to see the program on television.

What a viewer will find most surprising today upon viewing *Amos and Andy* is how *un*impressive it is. If you come to the program expecting outrageously offensive characterizations of blacks, you will be sorely disappointed. Perhaps in the early 1950s, when the very concept of blacks on TV was highly unusual, *Amos and Andy* appeared controversial. Nowadays, after more than thirty years of watching an endless stream of screwball characters of every race and religion on TV sitcoms, the folks in *Amos and Andy* look just like everybody else.

Sure, there are many unflattering characters in *Amos and Andy,* but Fred Sanford, George Jefferson, and Jimmie Walker's J. J. in *Good Times* are not very morally uplifting either. Unlike most all of the black sitcoms of the 1970s, *Amos and Andy* never harps on racial issues, never features black-on-white antagonisms. Instead, *Amos and Andy* keeps to the all-black world of Harlem, where blacks are seen in all walks of life. In the series, a black might run his own business (a taxi company, for example), be a lawyer (such as Algonquin J. Calhoun, Esquire) or push a broom (as does Lightnin', the lodge's janitor).

The writing in *Amos and Andy* is spotty, the acting is overly broad, but, in spite of everything, the show is funny. Not all of the time, but enough. Perhaps the emphasis on dialect seems unsettling now, but in the era when *Amos and Andy* was born, an era when America was filled with many people who spoke with an accent, obvious ethnicity was not something to shy away from. In *The Goldbergs* or *Life with Luigi,* sitcoms that were contemporaries of *Amos and Andy,* there were plenty of Yiddish and Italian dialects mangling the King's English.

What mortally wounded *Amos and Andy* was that it was the first all-black sitcom. It appeared at a time when the image of blacks in the mass media was, at best, typified by servile maids and butlers. Blacks were highly sensitive to *any* portrayal of blacks that seemed at all negative or less than commendable. Coming from that background, it may not be surprising that the screwball nature of *Amos and Andy* rubbed some raw nerves in the early 1950s. But, almost forty years have gone by. TV has proved its lowest-common-denominator equality by portraying most every racial and social group as silly, juvenile sitcom characters. *Amos and Andy* has served its sentence. It is time for the show to be released from purgatory and be rerun to death on UHF stations and cable outlets like all other hit sitcoms of the past. It is time to see *Amos and Andy* for what it truly is: just another silly sitcom. No more. No less.

The only glimpse TV viewers have had of *Amos and Andy* in almost two decades comes through a sixty-minute syndicated special from 1983, "Amos and Andy: Anatomy of a Controversy," hosted by talented black comic George Kirby. With appearances by figures such as Jesse Jackson and Redd Foxx, the special emphasizes the breakthrough the *Amos and Andy* series was in the 1950s to black actors who then had few roles on national TV. The "Kingfish Sells a Lot" episode is shown and Kirby has nice things to say about the program.

Except through that special (and a visit to a broadcast museum), the best way (currently) to see *Amos and Andy* is to track down the twenty-two-volume video cassette collection of forty-four episodes. ■

**AMOS BURKE, SECRET AGENT (see *Burke's Law*)**

**AMY PRENTISS (*½) 2 hr & 90 min (3ep: two 2 hr & one 90 min Color; 1974–1975 NBC) Police Drama** *with Jessica Walter as Amy Prentiss, Helen Hunt as Jill Prentiss, Steve Sandor as Sgt. Tony Russell, and Arthur Metrano as Det. Rod Pena*

Beautiful thirty-five-year-old widowed Amy Prentiss is the new chief of detectives of the San Francisco Police Department. Jessica Walter is unconvincing as Prentiss in this lame stab at feminist police drama. The *Amy Prentiss* pilot aired as an episode of *Ironside,* another, far better, show about a chief of detectives in San Francisco.

**AND MOTHER MAKES THREE (**) 30 min (26ep Color; 1971–1974 UK Thames) Situation Comedy** *with Wendy Craig*

A young widow struggles to bring up two young sons while upholding the traditional sitcom portrait of a scatter-brained housewife. This routine British program evolved from *Not in Front of the Children* and later became *And Mother Makes Five,* neither of which is currently syndicated in the United States.

**THE ANDROS TARGETS (*) 60 min (13ep Color; 1977 CBS) Crime Drama** *with James Sutorious as Mike Andros, Pamela Reed as Sandi Farrell, Roy Poole as Chet Reynolds, and Alan Mixon as Norman Kale*

Mike Andros is a crusading do-gooder, writing for the mythical *New York Forum,* in this forgettable effort at capturing the mid-1970s post-Watergate hero worship of investigative reporters. Where's Geraldo Rivera when you need him?

**ANDY BURNETT, THE SAGA OF (**) 60 min (6ep B&W; 1957–1958 ABC) Adventure** *with Jerome Courtland as Andy Burnett, Jeff York as Joe Crane, Andrew Duggan as Jack Kelly, and Slim Pickens as Bill Williams*

Originally broadcast as part of *Walt Disney Presents,* this short series follows young farmer Andy Burnett as he heads west in the 1820s to the Missouri frontier.

**THE ANDY GRIFFITH SHOW (****) 30 min (249ep: 159 B&W & 90 Color & 2 hr sequel; 1960–1968 CBS) Situation Comedy** *with Andy Griffith as Andy Taylor, Don Knotts as Barney Fife, Ron Howard as Opie Taylor, Frances Bavier as Bee Taylor, Jim Nabors as Gomer Pyle, George Lindsey as Goober Pyle, Howard McNear as Floyd Lawson, Hal Smith as Otis Campbell, Aneta Corsaut as Helen Crump, Betty Lynn as Thelma Lou, and Jack Burns as Warren Ferguson* **MAYBERRY, R.F.D. (**½) 30 min (78ep Color; 1968–1971 CBS) Situation Comedy** *with Ken Berry as Sam Jones, Buddy Foster as Mike Jones, Frances Bavier as Bee Taylor, George Lindsey as Goober Pyle, Arlene Golonka as Millie Swanson, and Alice Ghostley as Aunt Alice*

You will not find the town of Mayberry on any map of North Carolina, because Mayberry does not exist, in a strictly literal sense. On the other hand, Mayberry exists in the minds of millions of viewers who are intimately familiar with the town, thanks to regular visits with its residents through the medium of television.

Mayberry is the archetypal small rural locale that supposedly used to fill America. Everybody knows everybody else—there is no crime to speak of, no racial tensions, no youth rebellion, no rush hours, no suburban sprawl, no action, no thrills, no precocious TV kids, no car chases, no . . . nothing. Just the local inhabitants going through life at an easygoing pace, with troubles of their own that they think are huge.

At the center of Mayberry is Andy Taylor, local sheriff, who never carries a gun and rarely has to deal with any crime wave more virulent than the weekly drunken binge of town sot Otis Campbell. Sheriff Taylor is a widower who lives with his young son Opie and his spinster Aunt Bee. He dates various local women off and on (such as schoolteacher Helen Crump), but romance is not a big concern for Andy. He'd probably prefer to chew the fat with Floyd the barber. The chief problem in the sheriff's life is his hypertense deputy, Barney Fife, who treats every traffic case and every jaywalking ticket as if it were an outbreak of wanton lawlessness.

From this simple setting, with these simple people, comes *The Andy Griffith Show,* one of the great sitcoms of the 1960s, a show that is both a trendsetter and a unique program almost impossible to copy. When the gang from Mayberry first popped up on TV, rural settings were exceedingly rare. Previously, only *The Real McCoys* had blazed a trail away from the cities, and the prognosis was shaky for Mayberry at first. The steady, stable popularity of *The Andy Griffith Show* helped pave the way for the hordes of rural-based shows (*The Beverly Hillbillies, Green Acres,* et. al) to come.

While a harbinger of trends to come, *The Andy Griffith Show* accomplished something few, if any, of the resulting rural-based TV shows could. It managed to be funny while still presenting the locals as mostly normal human beings, not as people one step away from inbreeding-based lunacy.

Chief credit for keeping the show on an even keel must go to Andy Griffith himself and to executive producer Sheldon Leonard. Griffith had played the country bumpkin before (in the TV and film version of *No Time for Sergeants*), but in Sheriff Taylor he found a more sympathetic character. The sheriff is a perfect combination of easygoing relaxation and fatherly even-handedness, and is the logical choice to be the de facto leader of the town. His relationship with Opie rings of true human warmth, without leaking into the artificial buddiness that many TV dads exude. Andy Taylor will try hard to guide and discipline his son, but the sheriff feels somewhat awkward and ill at ease around the boy at times accentuating the lack of a mother's guidance to balance his occasional fatherly preoccupation with other matters. Aunt Bee helps around the house and provides some motherly fussing over the boy, but in the end, Andy and Opie are two guys more at ease in the world of men than the strangely different world of females.

Barney Fife is perhaps the funniest TV character of his decade. Barney's megalomania, paranoia, persecution complex, and psychological inadequacies combine to produce one certifiable basketcase who should never be given a gun and a badge. Fortunately, Barney is under Andy's watchful eye and the slow pace of life in Mayberry does not provide many chances for Barney to really hurt himself or others. If Andy is soothing to watch, Barney is an electric shock, always shooting off on some tangent that can fill an otherwise slow episode. Barney's boastful motto, that there are only two types of cops, "the quick and the dead," simply does not apply to Mayberry, since both Andy and Barney are neither of those two. Don Knotts, a veteran at playing high-strung types, helped develop the Andy-Barney relationship before the series was created, while playing an army psychiatrist to Andy Griffith's country GI in the 1958 film version of *No Time for Sergeants.*

The other regulars in *The Andy Griffith Show* fill in the background ably. Floyd the barber is the epitome of every hick know-it-all who has never been to the big city. Otis the town drunk provides comic relief. The Pyles, on the other hand, are a bit much. Gomer and cousin Goober, gas station attendants at the local filling station, provide the country bumpkin figures city folk are familiar with. Their goofy stupidity is an acquired taste and conflicts with the general tone of the show.

Still, it is Gomer who is first "spun-off" to his own hit series, *Gomer Pyle, U.S.M.C.,* where Gomer joins the Marines and his geeky country ways become more grating. One season later, after 159 episodes, the central fulcrum of *The Andy Griffith Show* breaks as Barney Fife leaves Mayberry to hit the big time as a detective in Raleigh, the state capital. From that point on, *The Andy Griffith Show* begins a slow, stately but steady decline. Jack Burns, late of stand-up comedy pair Burns and Schreiber, arrives as new deputy Warren Ferguson. Ferguson has some of the same jumpy tendencies as Barney, but he overplays his hand and loses the deft relation to reality that made Knotts's Fife so special.

After seven full seasons, Andy Taylor himself shuffles off. He and long-time flame Helen Crump are married, the couple (and Opie) move out of town, and the program mutates into *Mayberry, R.F.D.*. While technically a different show, *Mayberry, R.F.D.* is really *The Andy Griffith Show* without Andy Griffith, at least not in front of the camera. Griffith serves as executive producer of the "new" show, which is still set in Mayberry and features many of the same cast. Goober is still pumping gas and Aunt Bee is still caring for a motherless boy and a widower, but this time it is Sam Jones and his young son Mike. Jones, a local farmer who becomes a member of the town council and a big cheese in Mayberry, is supposed to have the same gentle, calm, lovable way about him as Andy Taylor did. Unfortunately, Ken Berry is no Andy Griffith. Instead of a kindly modern father figure, Jones is the same simple, bumbling wimp that Berry played in *F Troop* (as Capt. Parmenter). Jones cannot hold the aging series together, although the residual popularity of the Andy Taylor years kept *Mayberry, R.F.D.* popular through its original run.

After two years on *Mayberry, R.F.D.,* Aunt Bee is eased out of the show, to be replaced by the more brash Alice Ghostley, thus breaking the last major link to the Andy Griffith years. After another two seasons, the town of Mayberry drifts into the mists, not to be seen again for another fifteen years.

In 1986, in *Return to Mayberry,* most of the original Andy Griffith-era regulars return for a wonderful two-hour TV movie reunion. Andy and wife Helen are back in Mayberry just in time to disrupt the plans of perennial number two Barney Fife, who is running for sheriff, the job he always lusted over. It turns out Andy wants his job back also, and the mix of welcome returns and jealous feelings combine to create one of the better of the plethora of TV "reunion" shows of the 1980s.

The pilot for *The Andy Griffith Show* originally aired on the old *Danny Thomas Show* (a.k.a. *Make Room for Daddy*) in 1960, with Andy Griffith, Ron Howard, and Frances Bavier. Andy Taylor was also Mayberry's justice of the peace and newspaper publisher in the pilot, while Bavier's character is named Henrietta Perkins. The difference between the slow, down-home feel of Andy Taylor's Mayberry and the rush-rush world of Danny Williams (the Danny Thomas character) make it all the more amazing to realize that Danny Thomas helped create the show, and that Thomas's producer, Sheldon Leonard, produced both shows.

*The Andy Griffith Show* was originally rerun under the title *Andy of Mayberry.* ■

**ANDY GRIFFITH SHOW, THE NEW** **(**) 30 min (10ep Color; 1971 CBS) Situation Comedy** *with Andy Griffith as Andy Sawyer, Lee Meriwether as Lee Sawyer, Ann Morgan Guilbert as Nora, Lori Rutherford as Lori Sawyer, and Marty McCall as T. J. Sawyer*

You couldn't get much closer to the old *Andy Griffith*

Show than *The New Andy Griffith Show.* Andy Griffith plays Andy Sawyer, not Andy Taylor. Sawyer is the mayor (as opposed to the sheriff) of a small North Carolina town (Greenwood, not Mayberry). There are some differences, though. Unlike Andy Taylor, Andy Sawyer's wife is still alive, and they have a son *and* a daughter, not just a son.

Unfortunately, there is no Don Knotts to liven things up, so *The New Andy Griffith Show* is mostly just bucolic passages of life and family in Greenwood.

**THE ANDY WILLIAMS SHOW (**) 60 min (52ep Color; 1969–1971 NBC) Musical-Variety** *with Andy Williams, Charlie Callas, and Irwin Corey*

The low-key crooner sails through these amiable hours of song and banter, in what was already his third prime-time series. As befits the late 1960s, an effort is made to be "hip," with psychedelic sets and guest rock acts. The musical director for this show is the then-young Mike Post, who later went on to fame as the writer of the theme songs to *The Rockford Files* and *Hill Street Blues,* among others.

**THE ANDY WILLIAMS SHOW (*) 30 min (26ep Color; 1976–1977 Syndication) Musicial-Variety** *with Andy Williams and Wayland Flowers*

A poor music-variety entry in the waning days of that genre. The easy-going "Moon River" man is poorly matched with brassy comic Wayland Flowers (and his naughty puppet Madam).

**ANGEL (*) 30 min (39ep B&W; 1960–1961 CBS) Situation Comedy** *with Annie Farge as Angel Smith, Marshall Thompson as John Smith, Doris Singleton as Susie, and Don Keefer as George*

The excuse used here for screwball misunderstandings at least makes sense: Newlywed Angel is from France and so has trouble with both the language and the customs in her new country. *I Love Lucy's* Jesse Oppenheimer is one of the producers behind this effort, but it still falls short as unexceptional and derivative.

**ANGIE (**) 30 min (36ep Color; 1979–1980 ABC) Situation Comedy** *with Donna Pescow as Angie Falco Benson, Robert Hays as Brad Benson, Debralee Scott as Marie Falco, Sharon Spelman as Joyce Benson, John Randolph as Randall Benson, and Doris Roberts as Theresa Falco*

What they never tell you in stories like "Cinderella" is what happens after the poor young peasant girl is swept away by her Prince Charming. What does she do? How does she get along with her royal in-laws? And, just how *do* they live "happily ever after"? If *Angie* is any indication, they do just fine, thank-you.

As a modern-day Cinderella, Angie is taken from her job as a coffee shop waitress and brought into the rich household of young pediatrician Brad Benson. He's every mom's secret dream: not only a doctor, but one from an "old-money" Philadelphia family. What's more, he's so understanding that when she misses all her friends at work, he helps her arrange to buy the coffee shop. Later, she trades it in for a beauty parlor. Angie even hires her mom (Theresa) and younger sister (Marie) to work with her—a fair reward for all the years Theresa sold papers at a newsstand to support the family. No wonder she loves her new son-in-law.

Of course, his side of the family is not very happy about the arrangement, but despite their carping there's not much they can do. Angie and Brad love each other and, even when they have an argument, they always make up. Sniping at the Falco family doesn't help much either because Theresa is well-equipped to return their best shots. So, Angie and Brad live happily ever after. Which is a wonderful fairy tale, but not very engrossing as a comedy. In fact, this series is best described as a premise in search of a conflict. About the best they can do is have the Falco and Benson families face off on *Family Feud* (with a guest appearance by Richard Dawson). Guess who wins?

This is not a bad series, just a very nice, very bland visit with some generally nice people. The ones you really want to see are familiar from other sources: Donna Pescow (the theatrical film *Saturday Night Fever* and the *Out of This World* series), Robert Hays (the theatrical film *Airplane!* and the *Starman* series), and Doris Roberts (Mildred Krebbs on *Remington Steele*). With *Angie,* they're in the sort of harmless comedy fluff you might see at a suburban dinner-theater. Minor conflicts. Happy endings. Pass the dessert.

**ANIMAL WORLD (**½) 30 min (147ep Color; 1968–1976 NBC & CBS & ABC & Syndication) Documentary** *with Bill Burrud as host and narrator*

Well done wildlife footage shot on location throughout the world, under the supervision of producer Bill Burrud (who had previously done some theatrical nature films). During the late 1960s and early 1970s, this series turned up as a safe network sub in the spring and summer schedules, thereafter spinning off into rerun syndication with a sprinkling of new episodes.

**THE ANN SOTHERN SHOW (**½) 30 min (93ep B&W; 1958–1961 CBS) Situation Comedy** *with Ann Sothern as Katy O'Connor, Ernest Truex as Jason Macauley, Ann Tyrrell as Olive Smith, Don Porter as James Devery, Louis Nye as Dr. Delbert Gray, Ken Berry as Woody, and Jesse White as Oscar Pudney*

Ann Sothern was one of the pioneer independent women of American TV, along with Eve Arden (*Our Miss Brooks*). While most women on TV were slaving in the kitchen, Ann Sothern, first in *Private Secretary* (a.k.a. *Susie*), and then in *The Ann Sothern Show,* portrayed a working woman with guts, spunk, and responsibility.

Here she plays Katy O'Connor, the assistant manager of a fancy Manhattan hotel, who must deal with the trying guests and the often frustrating staff. After only 13 episodes, Ernest Truex is canned as Katy's boss, to be replaced by Don Porter, who played Sothern's boss in *Private Secretary*. Ann Tyrrell, who plays Katy's roommate Olive, is another carryover from *Private Secretary,* where she also played Sothern's chum. Look for a young Ken Berry (*Mayberry, R.F.D., F Troop*) as Woody, the bellhop, and Louis Nye, in his usual ingratiating manner, as a dentist who courts and eventually marries Olive. In the program's final episode, 1950s sensibilities win out, as Porter's character proposes to Katy.

Ann Sothern has a special place in TV lore as the voice of "mother" in *My Mother the Car.*

**THE ANN SOTHERN SHOW (see also *Private Secretary*)**

**ANNA AND THE KING (**½) 30 min (13ep Color; 1972 CBS) Situation Comedy** *with Yul Brynner as the King of Siam, Samantha Eggar as Anna Owens, Keye Luke as Prince Kralahome, Lisa Lu as Lady Thiang, and Rosalind Chao as Princess Serena*

There really *was* an Anna. She was Anna Leonowens, who really did tutor the children of the King of Siam in the late 1800s. Margaret Landon turned Anna's story into a novel called *Anna and the King of Siam,* which was the name of the first (1946) movie of this tale. In 1951, the story became *The King and I*, a hit Rodgers and Hammerstein Broadway play starring then-unknown Yul Brynner, who first shaved his head for the role. In 1956, the hit play became a hit movie, again starring Brynner, who thereafter never could shake the character of the King.

Brynner dons the fancy pants of the Oriental despot again in this flopped sitcom. Compared to the hit movie, this TV version is pretty lame. Look for Rosalind Chao as the King's eldest daughter, Serena. She later gained a measure of fame as Soon-Lee, the wife of Corporal Klinger in the waning days of *M*A*S*H* (and in *After MASH*). Gene Reynolds, the producer of *Anna and the King,* also produced *M*A*S*H.*

**ANNA KARENINA (**) 60 min (10ep Color; 1978 UK BBC) Drama** *with Nicola Pagett as Anna Karenina, Stuart Wilson as Count Alexei Vronsky, Mary Morris as Countess Bronsky, Nicholas Jones as Nikolai Levin, Robert Swann as Konstantin Levin, Eric Porter as Alexei Karenin, and Margot van der Burgh as Countess Lydia Ivanovna*

Detailed portrait of nineteenth-century upper-class Russia produced by Donald Wilson (*The Forsyte Saga, The First Churchills*) from his adaptation of the Leo Tolstoy novel. Like the literary original, the story is good but goes on far too long, filling the time by lingering over the "decadent" society author Tolstoy may have come from but was in the midst of rejecting himself. The main victim of this society is the beautiful and romantic young Anna, wife of respected businessman Karenin. Though a married woman, she finds herself in love with a visiting soldier, Count Vronsky, and eventually runs off with him. But that means they both have to face the full judgmental forces of "proper society," which is the only world in which they really feel comfortable. Russian upper-class circles may be stifling, even disintegrating from within, but the alternative is boredom—along with their own doubts and guilt. And it all comes to a head as Anna contemplates (and contemplates and contemplates) suicide as a possible solution to everything, eventually standing ready to throw herself in front of a speeding train.

Nicola Pagett is quite good in the title role, with strong support from Stuart Wilson as Vronsky. Nonetheless, the best strategy on this novelization is to watch the beginning and the ending sections, then search out the much shorter (only four episodes) *Madame Bovary,* a similarly plotted tale set in France. Or you can try any of the theatrical film versions of *Anna Karenina,* up through the 1985 U.S. made-for-TV movie presentation (with Jacqueline Bisset, Christopher Reeve, Paul Scofield, and Ian Ogilvy) though that latest one is a bit stiff, even at three hours.

**ANNETTE (***) 12 min (20ep B&W; 1958 ABC) Situation Comedy** *with Annette Funicello as Annette McCleod, Richard Deacon as Dr. Archie McCleod, Sylvia Fields as Lila McCleod, Tim Considine as Stephen Abernathy, David Stollery as Mike Martin, and Shelley Fabares as Corey*

This largely-forgotten production is due for reemergence in the videotape era. Not, under a strict definition, a TV series, these twenty episodes orignally aired as part of *The Mickey Mouse Club* in the 1950s. Annette, the first among equals in the Mouseketeer clan, plays an innocent country girl who is transplanted to the big city and moves in with her aunt and uncle.

There isn't much to the story, but watching Annette at her peak of popularity is fun, and the other stars are familiar. Richard Deacon is better known as Fred Rutherford (*Leave It to Beaver*) and Mel Cooley (*The Dick Van Dyke Show*). Tim Considine is another Disney alumnus (*Spin and Marty*) who was the eldest son, Mike, on *My Three Sons.* David Stollery was the Marty of *Spin and Marty.* Shelley Fabares later turned up as daughter Mary on *The Donna Reed Show.*

**ANNIE MCGUIRE (**½) 30 min (8ep Color; 1988 CBS) Situation Comedy** *with Mary Tyler Moore as Annie Block McGuire, Denis Arndt as Nick McGuire, Bradley Warden as Lewis Block, Adrien Brody as Lenny McGuire, Cynthia Marie King as Debbie Mc-*

*Guire, Eileen Heckart as Emma Block, and John Randolph as Red McGuire*

After twelve years as the co-star or star of hit sitcoms (*The Dick Van Dyke Show, The Mary Tyler Moore Show*), Mary Tyler Moore littered the networks with a long string of failed variety shows and sitcoms (many of which were better than their brief track record indicates). *Annie McGuire* is another try by Moore to catch on with the viewing public. Mary plays Annie Block, a liberal Manhattan divorcée with a twelve-year-old son. At the start of the series, Annie meets and marries Nick McGuire, a conservative Bayonne, New Jersey, widower with a fourteen-year-old son and a nine-year-old daughter. Along with Nick comes his cantankerous and reactionary father, Red, who is a perfect sparring partner for Annie's mother Emma, an ultra-leftist of the old school.

All is not political posturing on *Annie McGuire*, however. There are elements of drama in the series, as when Annie befriends a crippled Vietnam veteran who tries to rob her. The mix of humor and poignancy is sometimes clunky and the series seems confused as to what it is doing, but at least Moore has calmed her character down from the fluttering miss we've seen so often before. She had already proved, in films such as *Ordinary People*, that she could effectively play dramatic roles, and the addition of a little serious material in *Annie McGuire* is a nice try at staking out new ground on television.

The original pilot for this series cast Edward J. Moore (no relation) as Mary's new husband. At the last moment, the pilot was reshot and Denis Arndt took over the role.

**ANNIE OAKLEY (**½) 30 min (80ep B&W; 1954–1957 Syndication) Western** *with Gail Davis as Annie Oakley, Brad Johnson as Dep. Sheriff Lofty Craig, and Jimmy Hawkins as Tagg Oakley*

Cute but deadly Annie is the sure shot of Diablo County, Arizona, in this popular kiddie Western from the 1950s. Annie and her brother Tagg are orphaned and live with their uncle, the sheriff, who is hardly ever around. This leaves Annie free to be courted by tall, silent deputy Craig. ■

**ANOTHER DAY (½) 30 min (4ep Color; 1978 CBS) Situation Comedy** *with David Groh as Don Gardner, Joan Hackett as Ginny Gardner, and Hope Summers as Olive Gardner*

*Another Day* is an early attempt at a Yuppie sitcom. Don and Ginny Gardner are two working parents with three bratty kids. Don's mother, Olive, lives with her son and daughter-in-law, takes care of the young ones, and is free with her child-rearing advice to Don and Ginny.

David Groh had more success as the sometimes-husband in *Rhoda*. James Komack (*The Courtship of Eddie's Father, Welcome Back, Kotter*) serves as producer of *Another Day*, and Paul Williams supplies the theme song.

**ANYTHING BUT LOVE (**½) 30 min (6ep at Summer 1989 Color; 1989– ABC) Situation Comedy** *with Jamie Lee Curtis as Hannah Miller, Richard Lewis as Marty Gold, Louis Giambalvo as Norman Keil, Richard Frank as Jules Kramer, Sandy Faison as Pamela Peyton-Finch, and Bruce Kirby as Leo Miller*

Best known as a movie actress (*Trading Places, A Fish Called Wanda*), Jamie Lee (daughter of Tony) Curtis is appealing as Hannah Miller, an ex-teacher whose life perks up through a chance airplane meeting with writer Marty Gold. Hannah and Marty hit it off right away, and he helps her secure a job as a researcher for the *Chicago Monthly*, the magazine he writes for. The office setting is filled with familiar character types (such as the gruff-but-lovable boss and the catty gossip columnist), but *Anything But Love* works because of the chemistry between Curtis and Richard Lewis, who plays Marty. A popular stand-up comic (who previously appeared in the short-lived sitcom, *Harry*), Lewis is an appealing bundle of neuroses, whose dead-pan style meshes well with Curtis's lively enthusiasm.

**APPLE PIE (***) 30 min (7ep Color; 1978 ABC) Situation Comedy** *with Rue McClanahan as Ginger-Nell Hollyhock, Dabney Coleman as "Fast" Eddie Murtaugh, Jack Gilford as Grandpa Hollyhock, Caitlin O'Heaney as Anna Marie Hollyhock, and Derrel Maury as Junior Hollyhock*

This wonderfully wacky sitcom deserves more attention than it originally received (only two episodes aired before the show was yanked). The premise is novel and nutty. In 1933 Kansas City, lonely hairdresser Ginger-Nell wants a family, so she gets one, by placing classified ads in local papers. Her new husband, Fast Eddie, is a slick con man. Crotchety grandpa is blind, the daughter tap dances, and the son wants to fly like a bird.

The cast is superb (Rue McClanahan starred in *Maude* and *Golden Girls*, while Dabney Coleman is a veteran of *Mary Hartman, Buffalo Bill*, and *"Slap" Maxwell*) and the broad touch of executive producer Norman Lear (*All in the Family*) is evident. A hidden gem.

**APPLE'S WAY (**) 60 min (28ep Color; 1974–1975 CBS) Drama** *with Ronny Cox as George Apple, Lee McCain as Barbara Apple, Vincent Van Patten as Paul Apple, Eric Olson as Steven Apple, Patti Cohoon as Cathy Apple, and Franny Michel and Kristy McNichol as Patricia Apple*

Homespun moralizing about the simple things in life, created by *Waltons* guru Earl Hamner, Jr. For this one, successful architect George Apple decides to leave the big city rat race and bring his wife and children back to his hometown of Appleton, Iowa. Frankly, the kids aren't thrilled with the move and some of the townspeople think George is pretty silly, too, especially when he gets in a lather about some symbolic cause (usually ecological). Still, that's not really enough conflict to keep this one from coming off as far too unbelievably super-sweet. If you like sentimental family drama, stick with the activities at Waltons' mountain, instead.

**THE AQUANAUTS/MALIBU RUN** (*½) **60 min (32ep B&W; 1960–1961 CBS) Adventure** *with Keith Larsen as Drake Andrews, Jeremy Slate as Larry Lahr, and Ron Ely as Mike Madison*

*The Aquanauts* is a tepid clone of *Sea Hunt* by Ivan Tors, the man responsible for that Lloyd Bridges classic. In the first 13 episodes, the focus of *The Aquanauts* is on Drake Andrews and Larry Lahr, two salvage divers in the Pacific who get involved in lots of nautical scrapes. In episode 14, Andrews returns to the Navy and is replaced by Mike Madison (played by *Tarzan*-to-be Ron Ely). After episode 19, the format changes and the name does too. As *Malibu Run,* the show puts Larry and Mike in trendy Malibu Beach, California, where the duo wile away the time as diving instructors and part-time private eyes.

**ARCHER** (*) **60 min (6ep & 2 hr pilot Color; 1975 NBC) Detective Drama** *with Brian Keith as Lew Archer, and John P. Ryan as Lt. Barney Brighton*

Lew Archer is yet another ex-cop who becomes a private eye after leaving the force in this bland series based on some successful Ross McDonald novels. Brian Keith could use the help of old *Family Affair* co-star Sebastian Cabot, who put in his detective hours in *Checkmate.*

The 1974 pilot is called *The Underground Man.*

**ARCHIE BUNKER'S PLACE** (see *All in the Family*)

**ARE YOU BEING SERVED** (**) **30 min (60 ep Color; 1974–1977 UK BBC) Situation Comedy** *with Mollie Sugden as Mrs. Slocombe, John Inman as Mr. Humphries, Frank Thornton as Capt. Peacock, Arthur Brough as Mr. Grainger, Trevor Bannister as Mr. Lucas, Wendy Richard as Miss Brahms, and Nicholas Smith as Mr. Rumbold*

What this mid-1970s British series serves is enough sexual innuendo to make Benny Hill blush, snickering insinuation far beyond *Three's Company,* and outright farce subbing for plots to an extent we'd never dream of here. It all takes place at the Grace Brothers department store, with the staff winking, nudging, and rolling their eyes through each episode. Nonetheless, if you can tolerate the leering stereotypes, you'll find this is a pretty funny package filled to the brim with simple-minded silliness and caricatures (including a swishy portrayal of the gay Mr. Humphries).

Sure, you'll probably feel guilty about it in the morning, but you'll also come away with a whole new appreciation for (or dissatisfaction with) the comparatively restrained approach of U.S. sitcoms. For instance, the 1979 pilot for a Stateside version of this series included in the cast the laid-back Tom Poston, along with John Hillerman, Charlotte Rae, and Alan Sues (as Mr. Humphries).

**ARMCHAIR THEATER** (**) **60 min (61ep: 60 Color & 1 B&W; 1969–1974 UK Thames) Drama Anthology**

Actually, this long-running British series began in 1956, as a prestige production of that country's independent ABC company. Its golden days were in the late 1950s and early 1960s under producer Sydney Newman, who emphasized contemporary plays on contemporary themes, an approach that continued after Newman went over to the BBC in 1963 (where he was one of the initial guiding lights behind *Doctor Who*). In 1968, Thames (corporate successor to ABC) revived the title, which is where the material in this syndicated package comes from. The stories still reflect a commitment to then-contemporary (early 1970s) issues, but otherwise there's nothing particularly outstanding about this version of the series.

**ARNIE** (**½) **30 min (48ep Color; 1970–1972 CBS) Situation Comedy** *with Herschel Bernardi as Arnie Nuvo, Sue Ane Langdon as Lillian Nuvo, Roger Bowen as Hamilton Majors, Jr., Herb Voland as Neil Ogilvie, and Charles Nelson Reilly as Randy Robinson*

The intriguing premise of *Arnie* is lost amidst the bland scripts of this average sitcom. Arnie Nuvo is a blue-collar foreman who is promoted to management as head of the company's product improvement division. Arnie feels somewhat guilty about leaving his old pals behind on the loading dock, but is excited about his new status.

Charles Nelson Reilly is funny as Arnie's neighbor, the star of a TV cooking show "The Giddyap Gourmet," but what is the brassy Reilly doing in this generally low-key sitcom?

**AROUND THE WORLD IN 80 DAYS** (**) **(6hr miniseries Color; 1989 NBC) Adventure** *with Pierce Brosnan as Phileas Fogg, Eric Idle as Passepartout, Peter Ustinov as Detective Fix, and Julia Nickson as Princess Auoda*

Jules Verne's 1873 novel (made by Michael Todd into a lavish 1956 film starring David Niven) becomes an airy TV miniseries, with suave Pierce Brosnan (from *Remington Steele*) as nineteenth-century globetrotter Phileas Fogg. In order to prove a point (and win a bet) with his upper class society cronies, Fogg sets out to circle the planet in a mere eighty days—a feat they declare impossible. Accompanied by his French valet Passepartout, Fogg leaves London armed with one carpet bag and 30,000 pounds in cash, ready to hire, beg, or borrow a wide assortment of nineteenth-century transport (including high-speed trains, a hot air balloon, and an Indian elephant). What Fogg doesn't realize is that, soon after departing, he is identified as the man who just robbed the Bank of England, and for most of the journey is pursued by the blustery Detective Fix.

Brosnan carries himself well enough as the aloof and passionately punctual Fogg, but Monty Phython's Eric Idle (as Passepartout) and Peter Ustinov (as Fix) never seem to catch fire in their bits of business. Part of the problem is that both the script and the direction of the series lack a comic edge, aspiring to a light and breezy touch but coming off as just routine and mechanical. Even the attempts to embellish Verne's original story (which, for a full-length novel, is surprisingly simple) merely stretch out scenes rather than add any substance to the plot. As a result, *Around the World in 80 Days* ends up less an epic adventure than a mildly amusing romantic travelogue with some celebrity cameos and plenty of fancy location scenery.

**ARREST AND TRIAL (*½) 90 min (30ep B&W; 1963–1964 ABC) Crime Drama** *with Ben Gazzara as Det. Sgt. Nick Anderson and Chuck Connors as John Egan*

It's tempting to consider this an innovative approach to relative guilt and innocence. During the first half (forty-five minutes) of each episode in this series, Los Angeles police detective Nick Anderson investigates a crime, tracking and arresting his suspect, then handing them over for trial. In the second half, though, attorney John Egan, attempts to get them *acquitted.* So, the two heroes of this series are constantly working in opposition to each other, with guilt and innocence truly a relative term.

Unfortunately, the stories don't hang together well, with very little effective interplay between the two setups. Instead, it's more like a cop show followed by a lawyer show saving money by using some of the same guest stars on both, then treating them almost like different characters with the same names. In truth, the real innovation of this series was probably just the idea of splitting a longer time period between two segments, using an umbrella title, and hoping viewers would stick around for both. They didn't back then and there's no reason to expect them to now, except for a chance to see Ben Gazzara and Chuck Connors.

**THE ASCENT OF MAN (***) 60 min (13 ep Color; 1974 UK BBC) Documentary** *with Dr. Jacob Bronowski as host*

Following in the footsteps of such BBC productions as Sir Kenneth Clark's *Civilisation,* this series traces the scientific and philosophical history of Western civilization. Polish-born California scientist Dr. Jacob Bronowski conceived and hosted the package (shortly before his death), taking viewers through such essential developments as the use of basic tools, the beginnings of architecture, and the roots of mathematics and chemistry. He also examines less starry moments such as the trial of Galileo, the effects of the Industrial Revolution, and scientific responsibility in a world that created the Nazi death camps. Sharply conceived, well paced, and ultimately upbeat and inspirational. ■

**ASPEN (***) (5hr miniseries Color; 1977 NBC) Drama** *with Sam Elliott as Tom Keating, Perry King as Lee Bishop, Gene Barry as Carl Osborne, Michelle Phillips as Gloria Osborne, and Debi Richter as Angela Morelli*

*Aspen* was one of the first TV miniseries to really wallow in the sleaze, a habit that quickly caught on with other shows. As the title implies, the setting is the glitzy Colorado ski resort, where lots of apres ski romance takes place. Veteran miniseries preppy hunk Perry King (*Captains and the Kings, The Last Convertible*) plays Lee Bishop, a man unjustly convicted of the rape and murder of fifteen-year-old sexpot Angela Morelli. Sam Elliott plays the good-guy lawyer trying to get Bishop released. Meanwhile, real estate mogul Carl Osborne (played by the slick Gene Barry) wants to turn the entire area into condos. If you like racy trash, this is for you.

*Aspen* also has run as *The Innocent and the Damned,* which sounds much too biblical for something of this ilk.

**THE ASPHALT JUNGLE (**½) 60 min (13ep B&W; 1961 ABC) Police Drama** *with Jack Warden as Matthew Gower, Arch Johnson as Capt. Gus Honochek, and Bill Smith as Sgt. Danny Keller*

A better-than-average cop show about a squad of New York City plain-clothes detectives battling the mob. The theme music is by Duke Ellington.

**THE ASSASSINATION RUN (**½) 60 min (3ep Color; 1982 UK) Drama** *with Malcolm Stoddard as Mark Fraser, Mary Tamm as Jill Fraser, Sandor Eles as Vladimir Ilyich Grigor, and Leon Sinden as Bartlett*

This modern spy saga from England concerns a British intelligence hit man, Mark Fraser, who resigns after his job finally becomes too odious to bear. Retirement is not so quiet for Fraser, as his wife Jill is kidnapped by German left-wing terrorists, who use her to blackmail Fraser into assassinating a right-wing publisher. Fraser must try to string the captors along until he can free Jill.

**ASSIGNMENT FOREIGN LEGION (*) 30 min (26ep B&W; 1956–1957 UK BBC) Adventure Anthology** *with Merle Oberon as host and The Correspondent*

An early British production that turned up in the States, this program dramatizes the French Foreign Legion in North Africa during World War II. Former Hollywood beauty Merle Oberon narrates and occasionally stars as a foreign correspondent.

**ASSIGNMENT-UNDERWATER (½) 30 min (39ep B&W; 1960–1961 Syndication) Adventure** *with Bill Williams as Bill Greer and Diane Mountford as Patty Greer*

*Flipper,* without the dolphin. Bill Greer and daughter Patty run the charter boat "The Lucky Lady" in Florida and become involved in mild, forgettable adventures.

**ASSIGNMENT: VIENNA (**) 60 min (8ep & 2 hr pilot Color; 1972–1973 ABC) Adventure** *with Robert Conrad as Jake Webster, Charles Cioffi as Maj. Bernard Caldwell, and Anton Diffring as Inspector Hoffman*

Well-known tough guy Robert Conrad is an American spy who doesn't like playing by the book. His cover is operator of Jake's Bar & Grill, a Vienna version of Rick's Cafe American in the film *Casablanca.* The TV series was actually shot in Vienna. The pilot is called *Assignment: Munich.*

Conrad is believable enough as a spy, but the stories are routine. Executive producer Eric Bercovici went on to produce the *Shogun* miniseries.

**THE ASSOCIATES (***) 30 min (13ep Color; 1979–1980 & 1982 ABC The Entertainment Channel) Situation Comedy** *with Martin Short as Tucker Kerwin, Wilfred Hyde-White as Emerson Marshall, Joe Regalbuto as Eliot Streeter, Alley Mills as Leslie Dunn, and Tim Thomerson as Johnny Danko*

*The Associates* presents a lighthearted view of lawyers, in a setting that the majority of lawyers might actually recognize: the restrictive confines of a big-city law firm. Television usually portrays lawyers in an overly serious light, just one step down from those noble angels-in-white of the medical profession. At least doctors have been shown in some fairly realistic settings, toiling away in hectic hospitals, with patients to tend to all the time. Lawyers, on the other hand, invariably are shown in wildly stereotypical confrontational settings, such as the theatrical courtroom climaxes of *Perry Mason* or *The Defenders'* moralistic philosophizing. In *The Associates,* the producers of *Taxi* bring together a great cast to break this legal mold.

Martin Short, in his pre-*SCTV,* pre–*Saturday Night Live,* era, is Tucker Kerwin, a moderately idealistic recent graduate from a prestigious law school. Kerwin, along with a few other apprentice lawyers (called associates) in the powerful firm of Bass & Marshall, find out quickly that succeeding in the real world and succeeding in school require fairly different skills. Kerwin's idealism is nicely set off by the personalities of Eliot Streeter, an amoral young partner who will stop at nothing to advance his own interests, and Emerson Marshall, the somewhat fatherly, somewhat intimidating, senior partner.

The best episode of *The Associates* is a real insider's chuckle, with John Ritter (then the star of the smarmy *Three's Company*) guest starring as the headliner of a popular risqué TV sitcom that gets into a script censorship battle with its network. The network calls in its lawyers, the firm of Bass & Marshall. Tucker Kerwin is sent to Los Angeles and learns firsthand how TV comedies can be ruined by layers of lawyers and network censors. The episode ends with a worn-out Kerwin musing that it is probably impossible to write a funny script about lawyers. *The Associates* proves otherwise.

As an extra treat, catch B. B. King's appropriate theme song, the pre-Yuppie angst of "Wall Street Blues."

Only nine episodes aired in this series' original run. A few years later, the final four episodes debuted on the Entertainment Channel, a cable service that later became the Arts and Entertainment Channel (A&E).

**AT EASE (**) 30 min (14ep Color; 1983 ABC) Situation Comedy** *with Jimmie Walker as Sgt. Tyrone Valentine, David Naughton as Pvt. Tony Baker, Roger Bowen as Col. Clarence Clapp, Richard Jaeckel as Maj. Hawkins, Jourdon Fremin as Cpl. Lola Grey, and George Wyner as Cpl. Wessel*

An honest attempt to take the *Sgt. Bilko* military shenanigans formula and place it in the 1980s, *At Ease* is set in the peacetime somnambulance of Camp Tar Creek, Texas. Sgt. Valentine is the Bilko character who outwits the brass (Col. Clapp and Maj. Hawkins) with the help of his aide de camp (Pvt. Baker). In a nod to changed times, Sgt. Valentine is black.

The actors here are much better than the material. Jimmie Walker finally gets a role to use the smart-mouth persona he developed as "J. J." on *Good Times.* David Naughton is better known for his starring roles in musical Dr. Pepper ads of the era. Part of the reason *At Ease* fails is that the show's executive producers, Aaron Spelling and Douglas Cramer, are better at sudsy fluff (*The Love Boat, Aloha Paradise*) than trenchant humor.

**AUSTIN CITY LIMITS (**½) 60 min (Color; 1976— PBS) Musical-Variety**

In the 1970s, Austin, Texas, became the focal point of a vibrant branch of country music, the so-called outlaw sound, championed by Willie Nelson and Waylon Jennings. The Austin sound was a reaction to the stylized world of Nashville, the acknowledged capital of country music. Where Nashville symbolized heavily produced, mainstream music, Austin became the haven for a looser, more imaginative, more "down-home" sound.

*Austin City Limits* was created to capture the feel of the Austin branch of country music and spread its gospel around the country. In essence, it is a very simple show. For one hour, one or two performers run through their songs in front of a live audience and some TV cameras. Most of the older shows feature such Texas "outlaw" favorites as the aforementioned Willie and Waylon, plus Jerry Jeff Walker, Asleep at the Wheel, and Townes Van Zandt. Many of these artists had labored for years as regional or cult favorites, and *Austin City Limits* was their first major chance for national exposure. After featuring most of the country stars that had blossomed in the Austin area, the show broadens its scope and begins covering acts ranging from rock to blues to Cajun to country swing to folk to downright undefinable.

This eclectic choice of artists and dedication to the pure art of performing music is the real joy of *Austin City Limits*. In an age marked by trends toward separating and insulating various types of popular music, *Austin City Limits* demonstrates that apparently diverse strains of music can be blended together in harmony.

During the earlier, more "Texas" years, the *Austin City Limits* theme song was the rabidly pro–Lone Star State anthem "London Homesick Blues," more popularly known as "Home with the Armadillos," performed by Gary P. Nunn and the Lost Gonzo Band, the former backups for Jerry Jeff Walker. This song was eventually dropped in favor of a more "modern," jazzier theme without the lyrics.

In syndication, *Austin City Limits* also appears as an edited thirty-minute series.

**AUTOMAN (**½) 60 min (12ep & 90 min pilot Color; 1983–1984 ABC) Adventure** *with Desi Arnaz, Jr., as Walter Nebicher, Chuck Wagner as Automan, Robert Lansing as Lt. Jack Curtis, Gerald S. O'Loughlin as Capt. E. G. Boyd, and Heather McNair as Roxanne Caldwell*

This contrived but innovative crime saga is one of the first TV series to focus on computers. Walter Nebicher, a drone in the police computer department, creates Automan, a computer-generated holographic superhero who cracks all the tough cases, with the help of "Cursor," an electronic dot that can create objects out of thin air. It all seems pretty silly, but you must give the show credit for trying something different. Executive producers Glen A. Larson and Larry Brody had more luck with *The Fall Guy*.

**THE AVENGERS (****) 60 min (161ep: 104 B&W & 57 Color; 1961–1969 UK ABC) Adventure** *with Patrick Macnee as John Steed, Diana Rigg as Emma Peel, Linda Thorson as Tara King, Patrick Newell as Mother, Ian Hendry as Dr. David Keel, and Honor Blackman as Cathy Gale* **THE NEW AVENGERS (***) 60 min (26ep Color; 1976–1977 UK ITV) Adventure** *with Patrick Macnee as John Steed, Joanna Lumley as Purdey, and Garret Hunt as Mike Gambit*

Reminiscing about this classic series on *The Tonight Show*, Patrick Macnee noted that one of its key groundbreaking innovations (a male and female pair of adventurers as fighting co-equals) came about partially by accident. In Britain, where the series began in 1961, *The Avengers* started as the adventures of two male heroes, Dr. David Keel (played by Ian Hendry) and his mysterious friend from the cloak-and-dagger world, John Steed. Keel was a civilian doctor whose fiancée, an innocent bystander to a drug pickup, had been killed by the dealers (they feared she could identify them). Heartbroken and outraged, he agreed to team up with Steed to pursue her killers (hence, the "avengers" title hook), and soon found himself co-opted into a new sideline career, that of a freelance crime fighter.

What really set this potentially derivative crime series apart was its off-beat approach, especially to the characters. Generally, Steed, the government operative, would come to Keel for help on his latest case, setting up a relationship of two strong, independent figures tackling an assignment. Neither was the other's second banana. They were serious, sophisticated, yet they also displayed a confident almost tongue-in-cheek touch that took some of the grim edge off the tales. Because these stories were still staged as live drama presentations, the limits on movement, sets, and scene shifting made the attitude of the characters stand out even more.

Then came the accident. In the midst of this first season of *The Avengers*, an actor's strike shut down production after twenty-six episodes. During that time, Hendry decided not to continue in his role, leaving the producers with a stack of unused scripts. They decided to continue the series, but with a new partner for Steed—another "civilian," but this time a woman, Mrs. Cathy Gale (played by Honor Blackman), a professional anthropologist. However, they were not about to go back and change Steed's partner into a typical damsel-in-distress. Instead, they simply adapted the existing scripts for the new character, retaining the strong sense of shoulder-to-shoulder individual independence. And that attitude carried into the new stories as well, with the resulting chemistry between Steed and Gale being a smashing success.

The fifty-two episodes featuring the Macnee/Blackman team originally played in Britain between 1962 and 1964 (in two seasons of twenty-six, done live on videotape), firmly establishing the distinctive slick and sophisticated style of *The Avengers:* Steed's expertly tailored Edwardian wardrobe, Cathy Gale's rugged leather outfits (nothing kinky, just practical for fight scenes), their respective classy apartments, lush original music, and stories that pepper first-rate adventure plots with a sense of the bizarre (involving everything from pet cemeteries to a murder that takes place on a live television interview show). Above all, there is the energy between Steed and Mrs. Gale. She is cool, in control, a widow, and very attractive. He is a perfect gentleman, handsome, the epitome of sophistication, yet also a thorough professional in the business of espionage. If ever sexual sparks could fly, it's between them. And they do, because the two obviously enjoy each other's company, but never in any bed-thrashing cliché sort of way. Instead, the exact nature of their personal relationship is kept deliciously unstated, with the air of mystery allowing it to go any way a viewer cares to imagine. The only certainty: They're a great team.

In fact, they made such a perfect pair that when Honor Blackman decided to leave the series in 1965 for feature film work (most notably as Pussy Galore in the

James Bond thriller, *Goldfinger,*) there was serious concern about a successor. But when Diana Rigg stepped into the role of Mrs. Emma Peel, all doubts vanished.

And that's where the story of *The Avengers* actually begins for U.S. viewers. None of the previous versions of the series ever turned up on this side of the Atlantic, even the final Blackman season (which was sold internationally). This was no doubt due in part to the slightly "stagy" look of the videotaped series. By then, U.S. viewers subsisted almost entirely on a diet of film, especially for their action programs. So, beginning with the first Diana Rigg season, *The Avengers* went to film, bringing aboard some new production people, including Albert Fennell and Brian Clemens (who would continue to champion *The Avengers* even into the 1970s *The New Avengers* revival). Ironically, in the 1980s, the Cathy Gale episodes also turned up on film (transferred from videotape), but they have not played in the States.

There are only two seasons of Diana Rigg episodes (twenty-six in black and white, twenty-four in color, plus a transition episode to her successor). Nonetheless, these are the ones that turned *The Avengers* into a truly international hit, even landing a spot on the U.S. ABC network schedule beginning in 1966. For British viewers, of course, there was the necessary transition to a new female foil to Steed (the early black-and-white stories even have a pre-credits sequence describing Emma Peel as his "new partner"), but they were pleased to see the spirit of the Steed/Gale relationship preserved. And for American fans, it was love at first sight.

This was a program hitting its stride just as it reached our shores, so the package packed a powerful character and storytelling punch. The relationship between Emma Peel and John Steed came off as ground-breaking and amazing, instantly clicking with viewers of both sexes who admired their easy banter, sophisticated lifestyle, mutual respect, and keen reflexes in the field of battle. Like her predecessors, Emma Peel is independent, a wealthy widow (her husband, Peter Peel, had been lost in a plane crash) who enjoys "coming out to play" with Steed. For his part, he delights in thinking of new ways to make his simple request: "Mrs. Peel, We're Needed." Separately and together, they're ready to solve another case.

By this time, the writers had thrown open Pandora's box and pulled out anything they could get away with, setting Steed and Mrs. Peel against alien invading plants, cybermen, a mind-switching device, and time travel. But, they pulled it off, thanks to the credibility of their leads and the insistence that while individual moments might be absurd, the thriller itself was to be taken seriously (within its own universe). There might be raised eyebrows, but no obvious "mugging to the camera." They also made certain to include standard espionage and blackmail tales in the mix, along with a few apparently incredible stunts that turned out to be hoaxes, to keep viewers guessing as to which direction a particular story would take.

The Emma Peel and John Steed run of *Avengers* episodes set a standard that performers and viewers continue to use even today. Viewers enjoy finding a stylish show reminiscent of *The Avengers,* while performers relish the thought of capturing the flavor of that classic. (And that's not limited just to the world of TV series—the music video to the 1985 hit by the Pretenders, "Don't Get Me Wrong," is filmed just like an *Avengers* episode, complete with footage of Patrick Macnee.)

In 1967, Diana Rigg left the series, meaning that at the height of its popularity, *The Avengers* itself faced the challenge of measuring up to its own standards. Unfortunately, the thirty-two episodes with the character of Tara King (Linda Thorson) often fall short. Part of the problem was the decision to change the nature of the relationship between Steed and his new female cohort. Unlike her predecessors, Tara was from government espionage service, just like Steed. She was also much younger, so instead of a pair of mature co-equals, there was more of a mentor/student attitude. But Tara learned quickly and could soon hold her own with Steed. Unfortunately, they both lost their vital independence to plot lines that constantly put them at the beck-and-call of a wheelchaired ministry superior, Mother. Even worse, the writers finally went off the deep end and filled far too many episodes (especially those with Mother) with campy set pieces and sadly outdated spy antics. Instead of innovating, *The Avengers* often seemed to be copying not just itself but its imitators. The fact that Tara and Steed come through this in one piece with some good episodes is amazing. Still, after one season with Tara King, *The Avengers* closed shop.

But that wasn't quite the end. In the mid-1970s, following a Linda Thorson/Patrick Macnee reunion for a French television champagne commercial, Albert Fennell and Brian Clemens decided to take on *The Avengers* legend with *The New Avengers.* Amazingly, they succeed. This series has a distinctive look, a wry (occasionally cynical) sense of humor, a strong cast, and clever stories. This time Steed has two partners, Mike Gambit and Purdey, with all three agents from some conveniently vague arm of British intelligence. Gambit and Purdey are young but seasoned, with tremendous respect for Steed, whom they look on as the man who wrote the book on espionage. Purdey also finds Steed very sexy, but (in the best *Avengers* tradition), we never see if that leads to a liaison.

At his end, Steed plays the part of senior operative, spending his off-hours on a country estate, but still ready to send his steel-rimmed bowler into action when necessary. He's a key part of every story, even if Purdey and Gambit end up doing most of the legwork, because he's especially adept at thinking his way out of the most complex traps, drawing on his years of experience and training. In an odd way, we probably learn more about Steed's career here than in any other version of the series, with several episodes involving characters from his past, forcing him to look at his college days, World War II, and his years as a Cold War operative. One of the best is "To Catch a Rat," which brings back Patrick Macnee's original *Avengers* co-star, Ian Hendry, cleverly cast as one of Steed's old espionage partners missing for more than a dozen years. It's a well-paced story giving Hendry center stage as he attempts to complete a mission begun in the Kennedy administration. If you enjoy dotting the *i's* of television series continuity, be sure to catch that episode.

Appropriately, *The New Avengers* wraps up the memory scrapbook with a brief cameo appearance by Diana Rigg as Emma Peel (in the two-hour episode "K Is for Kill"). Be forewarned—it's a brief sequence, zipping by in the first ten minutes of the story.

In the late 1980s, work began on a proposed movie, but with a new cast. ■

**THE AWAKENING LAND (**½) (7hr miniseries Color; 1978 NBC) Drama** *with Elizabeth Montgomery as Sayward Luckett, Jane Seymour as Genny Luckett, and Hal Holbrook as Portius Wheeler*

An epic drama of a woman's triumph over hard times on the edge of the frontier, *The Awakening Land* is set in the Ohio wilderness around the start of the nineteenth century. The miniseries is based on the novel by Conrad Richter.

**B.A.D. CATS (zero) 60 min (5ep & 90 min pilot Color; 1980 ABC) Police Drama** *with Asher Brauner as Nick Donovan, Steve Hanks as Ocee James, Michelle Pfeiffer as Samantha Jensen, and Vic Morrow as Eugene Nathan*

Here we have a rancid example of the worst of the anti-establishment car-chase school of cop shows from the late 1970s (though it originally aired in the first months of the 1980s). Nick and Ocee are two ex-stock-car racers who join some unit of the L.A.P.D. called *B*urglary *A*uto *D*etail, *C*ommercial *A*uto *T*hefts (B.A.D. C.A.T.s) and commence to race all over the City of Angels at ridiculous speeds and crash numerous cars. For some reason, Nick and Ocee can't understand why their superior, bad old Capt. Nathan, is tough on them.

It's quite hard to tell the bad guys from the cops on *B.A.D. Cats.* Aaron Spelling and Douglas Cramer, the producers of *B.A.D. Cats,* also produced *The Love Boat,* which seems like serious television drama compared to this series. ■

**B. J. AND THE BEAR (**) 60 min (47ep & 2 hr pilot Color; 1979–1981 NBC) Adventure** *with Greg Evigan as Billie Joe "B. J." McCoy, Claude Akins as Sheriff Elroy P. Lobo, Mills Watson as Deputy Sheriff Perkins, Slim Pickens as Sheriff Beauregard Wiley, Richard Deacon as Sheriff Masters, Conchata Ferrell as Wilhelmina "The Fox" Johnson, Murray Hamilton as Rutherford T. Grant, and Sam as Bear*

*B. J. and the Bear* is an innocuous and lively show about a good-looking independent trucker named B. J., who always seems to run into a slew of corrupt cops, especially Sheriff Lobo (who was so corrupt, he got his own series). B. J.'s constant companion is Bear, his pet chimpanzee.

After about thirty episodes, the format alters, as B. J. (and Bear) settle down in Los Angeles (where else?) to run their own trucking business, called Bear Enterprises. With the big trucking firms against B. J., he is forced to hire only curvaceous female drivers, with names like "Stacks." It's a rough life out there in Los Angeles.

This amiable time filler is produced by Glen A. Larson.

**B. L. STRYKER (**½) 2 hr (5ep at Fall 1989 Color; 1989– ABC) Detective Drama** *with Burt Reynolds as B. L. Stryker*

Before heading to superstardom in the world of theatrical feature films (during the mid 1970s), Burt Reynolds turned in distinctive "loner cop" performances in two TV series, *Hawk* (1966) and *Dan August* (1970). Appropriately, for his return to television in 1989, Reynolds is once again a policeman, B. L. Stryker, though this time he's retired (from the New Orleans force). But he's still on the job, only in Florida (Palm Beach) as a private investigator. This is a fast-moving Reynolds tough cop vehicle, with plenty of shot-on-location through-the-palm-trees car chases and tense confrontations with the bad guys. Reynolds gives his title role plenty of zest, and also shares executive producer chores with *Magnum, P.I.* veteran Tom Selleck.

This series first aired as one of three elements playing under the umbrella title *The ABC Mystery Movie,* rotating the slot with *Gideon Oliver* and a revival of *Columbo.*

**BAA BAA BLACK SHEEP** **(see *Black Sheep Squadron*)**

**BABY BOOM (**½) 30 min (7ep at Summer 1989 Color; 1988– NBC) Situation Comedy** *with Kate Jackson as J. C. Wiatt, Kristina and Michelle Kennedy as Elizabeth Wiatt, Joy Behar as Helga, Daniel Bardol as Ken Aronburg, Robyn Peterson as Arlene Kincaid, Susie Essman as Charlotte Elsman, and Sam Wanamaker as Fritz Curtis*

Writers Nancy Meyers and Charles Shyer take another pass at their tale of Yuppie motherhood, turning their hit 1987 threatrical film (directed by Shyer and starring Diane Keaton) into a series. By dealing with the story on the installment plan, they have the chance to shift the emphasis, linger on particular moments, and restage some scenes virtually intact from the film (such as a class for turning toddlers into "superbabies"). They can also dispense with some of the film's plot twists that really don't hold up to close scrutiny (such as J. C.'s illogical purchase of a dilapidated house in the country). They never get to redo the entire film but, because of some important changes they make from the beginning, they don't have to.

The series begins five months after super-executive J. C. Wiatt finds herself the instant parent of two-year-old Elizabeth—her inheritance from a distant cousin in England. This eliminates the film's awkward initial scenes of J. C. trying to decide whether to keep the child (foolishly hurting her own career by dragging the child around to the office and key business encounters). Instead, for the series, J. C. starts in control, having followed the sensible strategy of any wealthy executive—hire somebody else to do the day-to-day dirty work, then deal with the follow-up. That's an important move because it eliminates the sense of J. C.'s situation being merely unjustified whining from an immature Yuppie. She's rich, she uses her money to help deal with this new twist in her life, and then moves on to the really important ramifications. So, while she continues on the office fast track at Sloane Curtis & Co. (albeit at a more leisurely pace), Helga, Elizabeth's nanny, takes care of the child during the day. This may be a tricky balancing act, but J. C. has decided she likes being a mom and she likes her job. And she seems to have figured out a way to do both.

That's miles ahead of the feature film version of J. C., who doesn't reach that point of control until the wrap-up final confrontation with her boss (played in both the film and series by Sam Wanamaker). So with the front end and back end already covered, the series version of *Baby Boom* focuses on the middle: the day-to-day life of mom and daughter. Here the series seems to borrow a page from the stylistic approach of *The Days and Nights of Molly Dodd* or such Woody Allen films as *Annie Hall,* breaking the episodes into much shorter segments (often set off by title graphics), complete with voiceover narration by J. C. The result is a fragmented story line of major and minor crises (at home and at the office), peppered with moments of frustration, triumph, and warm hugs—a rhythm real-life moms can certainly recognize.

As in the film version, *Baby Boom* scores most of its outright comedy points mocking the exaggerated concerns of the yuppie world of big business advancement and professional motherhood. For her encounters with practicing "supermoms," for instance, Kate Jackson brings just the right touch of polite amazement to her character as she attempts to understand the rationale behind training children for the New York art and social scene while they're still toddlers. Readings from Feodor Dostoyevski's *The Idiot* (in Russian), lectures on Van Gogh, violin lessons, and full immersion swimming lessons are fine, but how about a walk in the park for her two-year-old?

Ultimately, *Baby Boom* is an unabashed pep talk on parenting. One of the best of these moments comes in a dream visit from Jane Wyatt (Margaret Anderson on *Father Knows Best*) and Barbara Billingsley (June Cleaver on *Leave It to Beaver*), who turn up to counsel her, complete with milk and cookies and a vacuum cleaner.

Like *Molly Dodd,* this is a low-key but imaginative series. The two might play well together in rerun tandem, perhaps with PBS's *Trying Times* rounding out the package.

**BABY, I'M BACK (*½) 30 min (12ep Color; 1978 CBS) Situation Comedy** *with Demond Wilson as Raymond Ellis, Denise Nicholas as Olivia Ellis, Kim Fields as Angie Ellis, Tony Holmes as Jordon Ellis, Helen Martin as Luzelle Carter, and Ed Hall as Col. Wallace Dickey*

A tricky premise for a sitcom: A man who one day just abandoned his wife and two children because he couldn't take the pressures of married life suddenly reappears after seven years. The reason? She's had him declared legally dead and he disagrees with that diagnosis. Once he returns, though, he finds his affections for the family stirred. Now he wants to be reconciled and have a chance to be the father and the husband he never was. Only trouble is, she's engaged to a stable, responsible Pentagon man.

Back in the old days, plots like this were set up by a more involuntary separation such as having the spouse lost at sea or suffering from amnesia. But, once you get over an initial dislike for the estranged husband's past actions, this plays well enough as a broad triangle comedy carried chiefly by its two appealing leads: Demond Wilson, the former son on *Sanford and Son,* and Denise Nicholas, the former Liz McIntyre on *Room 222.* As with similar conflicts in such theatrical features as *My Favorite Wife* or *Move Over, Darling,* it's hard not to root for a reunion.

Future *Facts of Life* star Kim Fields plays their young daughter.

**BABY MAKES FIVE (*) 30 min (5ep Color; 1983 ABC) Situation Comedy** *with Peter Scolari as Eddie Riddle, Louise Williams as Jennie Riddle, Janis Page as Blanche Riddle, and Priscilla Morrill as Edna Kearney*

Ignore this sitcom. It concerns the Riddles, a young couple with three small kids, along with a newly born set of twins. Peter Scolari (who plays Papa Riddle) is much better in *Bosom Buddies* and *Newhart.*

**BACHELOR FATHER (**½) 30 min (157ep B&W; 1957–1962 CBS & NBC & ABC) Situation Comedy** *with John Forsythe as Bently Gregg, Noreen Corcoran as Kelly Gregg, and Sammee Tong as Peter Tong*

John Forsythe, later famous as Charlie in *Charlie's Angels* and the ultra-rich Blake Carrington on *Dynasty,* lands his first TV starring assignment in *Bachelor Father.*

Forsythe is already into the role of rich dilettante here as he plays Bently Gregg, a well-heeled Hollywood attorney who is a bachelor and womanizer. Gregg's social whirl is disrupted when he becomes guardian of his thirteen-year-old niece Kelly after her parents died in a car crash.

Although the single-parent gambit became wildly popular later on (*Family Affair, Alice, Kate & Allie*), it was still fairly new in the 1950s. *My Little Margie* tried it at the start of that decade and *The Rifleman* and *My Three Sons* would pick up the idea after *Bachelor Father* caught on, but Bently Gregg is the real beginning of the trend.

This single-parent concept violated the prime directive of 1950s sitcoms: glorifying normal, wholesome families living in suburbia. Nuclear suburban families are all well and good, but too much of anything is no fun and the bachelor father/single-parent angle is rich in script possibilities. For one thing, the parent can have various romantic interests, and so can the child, thus doubling the chance for touches of passion. In *Bachelor Father,* the setup is perfect: Kelly can't really object to Bently's romancing, since he is not her father and no "disloyalty" to Kelly's departed mother is involved.

Forsythe and Corcoran are acceptable as Bently and Kelly. All the expected plot twists about interruptions of his ritzy life-style and her budding teen crushes occur. The best character is house "boy" Peter Tong, a somewhat smart-mouthed old coot who manages to say things to the head of the household that no friend or relative could, just like most domestics in TV sitcoms.

One special event to watch for is a 1960 appearance of Linda Evanstad as one of Kelly's girlfriends. More than twenty years later, Evanstad, then known as Linda Evans, played wife to John Forsythe in *Dynasty*.

## THE BACHELORS (see *It's a Great Life*)

## BACKSTAIRS AT THE WHITE HOUSE (***) (9hr miniseries Color; 1979 NBC) Drama *with Olivia Cole as Maggie Rogers, Tania Johnson and Leslie Uggams as Lillian Rogers, Louis Gossett, Jr., as Levi Mercer, and Leslie Nielsen as Ike Hoover and narrator*

Sort of an American version of *Upstairs, Downstairs,* this miniseries follows American history from the Taft to the Eisenhower administrations from the vantage point of the largely black White House staff. Chief Maid Maggie Rogers, her daughter, and successor Lillian are the focus.

Numerous guest celebrities pop up as bigwig politicos, such as Victor Buono as Pres. Taft, Robert Vaughn as Pres. Wilson, Harry Morgan as Pres. Truman, and Andrew Duggan as Pres. Eisenhower.

## THE BAD NEWS BEARS (*) 30 min (23ep Color; 1979–1980 CBS) Situation Comedy *with Jack Warden as Morris Buttermaker, Catherine Hicks as Emily Rappant, Phillip R. Allen as Roy Turner, Meeno Peluce as Tanner Boyle, Tricia Cast as Amanda Whirlitzer, Sparky Marcus as Leslie Ogilvie, and Corey Feldman as Regi Tower*

The "Bad News Bears" concept had already been sequeled to death in the movies before this disappointing TV version arrived. *The Bad News Bears* was a good movie in 1976, with Walter Matthau and Tatum O'Neal. Then came the inferior *The Bad News Bears in Breaking Training* and the pointless *The Bad News Bears Go to Japan.* Who needs yet another version?

The TV story is the same as the original film, with Jack Warden as the cantankerous swimming pool cleaner who is sentenced to coach a Junior High baseball team, instead of going to jail for driving a nasty client's car into a pool. Warden looks like he's only in this for the money. The acting by the kids is spotty. Among the youngsters, Meeno Peluce did better in *Best of the West* and *Voyagers,* Corey Feldman later turned up in the film *Goonies,* and Sparky Marcus is best known as child evangelist Jimmy Joe Jeeter in *Mary Hartman, Mary Hartman.*

## THE BAILEYS OF BALBOA (*) 30 min (36ep B&W; 1964–1965 CBS) Situation Comedy *with Paul Ford as Sam Bailey, Les Brown, Jr. as Jim Bailey, Sterling Holloway as Buck Singleton, John Dehner as Cecil Wyntoon, and Judy Carne as Barbara Wyntoon*

There is precious little to recommend in this very unfunny show from the mid-1960s. Paul Ford (Col. Hall from *Sgt. Bilko*) plays a grouchy old coot who runs a slapdash charter fishing business amidst the polished splendor of Balboa, a resort yachting community. This is one of Judy Carne's earliest sitcom roles, a few years before she hit it big on *Laugh-In.*

## BAKER'S DOZEN (**) 30 min (6ep Color; 1982 CBS) Situation Comedy *with Ron Silver as Mike Locasale, Cindy Weintraub as Terry Munson, Doris Belack as Capt. Florence Baker, and John Del Regno as Jeff Diggins*

Mike Locasale and Terry Munson are male and female New York City undercover cops who must keep their affair a secret from their female boss, Capt. Baker, who frowns on interoffice romances. The series is shot on location in New York City. The scenery is nice, but the predictable plots and cumbersome basic premise result in only mild entertainment.

## BALL FOUR (**) 30 min (13ep Color; 1976 CBS) Situation Comedy *with Jim Bouton as Jim Barton, Jack Somack as John "Cap" Capogrosso, Ben Davidson as Ben "Rhino" Rhinelander, Bill McCutcheon as Harold "Pinky" Pinkney, and Lenny Schultz as Lenny "Birdman" Siegel*

This sports-based sitcom grew out of former major league pitcher Jim Bouton's "kiss and tell" book *Ball*

*Four.* Unlike the book, the TV show centers on fictional players on a fictional baseball team (probably to avoid lawsuits). Bouton stars as one of the players on the Washington Americans and also serves as writer for some of the scripts. The idea here is good, but spotty scripts and poor direction result in *Ball Four* never living up to its potential. The theme song is composed and sung by Harry Chapin.

**BANACEK (**) 90 min (16ep & 2 hr pilot Color; 1972–1974 NBC) Mystery** *with George Peppard as Thomas Banacek, Ralph Manza as Jay Drury, Murray Matheson as Felix Mulholland, and Christine Belford as Carlie Kirkland*

The gimmick here is theft rather than murder. But these are no ordinary thefts. Instead they involve seemingly impossible situations, such as a star quarterback's disappearance from under a pile of players—during a game, in plain view of a packed stadium and the TV cameras. Or a prize race horse that disappears some time between the beginning and end of a race. Or an armored car filled with gold bullion that vanishes in the middle of a deserted Texas highway.

Enter Thomas Banacek, an independent investigator who, for a hefty 10 percent finder's fee, promises to save the insurance company a small fortune in payouts on the missing object (or person). Though the local police sometimes resent this well-heeled bounty hunter entering the case, they have to admit Banacek's good. And he knows it.

Unfortunately, the investigations themselves are fairly routine, so in a ninety-minute slot the program often comes off as padded. And, it doesn't take too long to figure out what kind of illusion was used to pull off each caper.

Still, on the positive side, Banacek's confidants Jay Drury (his chauffeur) and Felix Mulholland (owner of a rare book shop in Boston) provide some good sidebar bits. And, for about half the stories, Christine Belford spices things up as another independent insurance investigator in competition with Banacek.

Peppard makes his character come across as a likable, confident person—and one proud of his ethnic roots (Banacek is Polish and constantly drops references to Polish proverbs). Not surprisingly, these traits won the series popularity points among Polish ethnics, who enjoyed seeing a handsome, successful, and worldly wise Polish character take home those fat contingency fees.

**BANYON (**) 60 min (13ep & 2 hr pilot Color; 1972–1973 NBC) Detective Drama** *with Robert Forster as Miles C. Banyon, Joan Blondell as Peggy Revere, Richard Jaeckel as Lt. Pete McNeil, Julie Gregg as Abby Graham, and Teri Garr as Mabel*

Banyon is a hard-on-the-outside/warm-on-the-inside shamus in the film noir world of 1930s Los Angeles in this run-of-the-mill retread of the Sam Spade/Philip Marlowe school of private eyes. Joan Blondell, an actress who survived a stint as a blonde bombshell in the *real* Hollywood of the 1930s, is fun as Peggy Revere, the proprietress of a secretarial school in Banyon's building who supplies him with free secretaries (including a young Teri Garr).

**BARBARA MANDRELL AND THE MANDRELL SISTERS (***) 60 min (32ep Color; 1980–1982 NBC) Musical-Variety** *with Barbara Mandrell, Louise Mandrell, Irene Mandrell, and the Krofft Puppets*

One of the few successful variety shows to emerge out of the 1980s, this series has a decidedly country & western slant, as befits the hostesses, country star Barbara Mandrell and her two younger sisters. As with most musical-oriented variety shows, there are lots of singing guests, some small talk, and a lot of numbers performed by the hosts.

**BARBARA STANWYCK THEATER (**½) 30 min (36ep B&W; 1960–1961 NBC) Drama Anthology** *with Barbara Stanwyck as host*

In contrast to the usual practice with such anthologies, Barbara Stanwyck performed in nearly all the episodes, even though this meant playing more than two dozen different characters. For this, she drew on a long and successful theatrical film career, firmly established in the 1930s and 1940s with such movies as *Meet John Doe* and *Double Indemnity.* As with other stars whose box office appeal softened in the fifties, she decided to join the competing medium.

One character she did repeat three times in her anthology was that of Josephine Little, owner of a successful import–export business in Hong Kong. This was pitched as an extended pilot for a proposed series, but never got picked up. A few years later, though, she landed the lead role in *The Big Valley.*

**BARBARY COAST (**) 60 min (13ep & 2 hr pilot Color; 1975–1976 ABC) Western** *with William Shatner as Jeff Cable, Doug McClure as Cash Conover, Richard Kiel as Moose Moran, and Dave Turner as Thumbs, the piano player*

Undercover government agent Jeff Cable is a man of a thousand disguises, operating in San Francisco's wild "Barbary Coast" during the 1870s. His unlikely ally is Cash Conover, owner of the Golden Gate Casino. Together, the two score a few points for truth and justice in this otherwise wild and reckless boomtown. The series attempts to play it tough yet slightly humorous, a mix reminiscent of *The Wild, Wild West.* It's close, but not quite there, though Shatner seems particularly geared to adding the appropriate comic touches. In the pilot film, Dennis Cole had the role of Conover, but for the series they turned to McClure, a western veteran (nearly a decade as cowhand Trampas on *The Virginian*).

Right after the series ended, 7′2″ Richard Kiel went from casino bouncer in the old West to the deadly Jaws, the super-chomping foe of James Bond in *The Spy Who Loved Me.*

**THE BARCHESTER CHRONICLES (**½) 60 min (7ep Color; 1982 UK BBC) Drama** *with Donald Pleasance as Rev. Septimus Harding, Nigel Hawthorne as Dr. Grantly, Janet Maw as Eleanor Harding, Geraldine McEwan as Mrs. Proudie, Alan Rickman as Slope, and Susan Hampshire as Madeline*

Life in Barchester, the fictitious Victorian cathedral city that serves as the setting for six satirical novels by Anthony Trollope (author of *The Pallisers*). *The Warden* and *Barchester Towers* are the two adapted for this series, which begins with accusations of corruption raised against the simple and honest Rev. Harding by—of all people—his daughter's suitor, John Bold (David Gwillim). But this is just the first of many public and private manipulations for power in town, as ambitious men and women set their sights on such influential positions as dean, warden, and bishop.

A nicely staged series of double-dealing intrigue.

**BARE ESSENCE (*) (4-½hr miniseries & 11ep 60 min Color; 1982–1983 CBS & NBC) Drama** *with Genie Francis as Patricia "Tyger" Hayes, Linda Evans (then Jennifer O'Neill) as Lady Bobbi Rowan, Bruce Boxleitner (then Al Corley) as Chase Marshall, Lee Grant (then Jessica Walter) as Ava Marshall, and Ian McShane as Niko Theophilus*

*Bare Essence* is a sudsy, racy tome on the loves and intrigues of the perfume business, and is one of the few miniseries that graduated to the world of weekly series. Genie Francis, relocated from a daytime soap opera (*General Hospital*) is Tyger Hayes, the typical headstrong young and beautiful woman who makes a miraculous rise in the world, only to encounter evil nasty people along the way (along with gorgeous hunks). Tyger develops a smash new perfume and marries the boss's son in the miniseries. In the weekly show, Tyger's husband is conveniently disposed of in the first episode (he dies in a racing accident), and she vies to become head honcho at the office.

**BAREFOOT IN THE PARK (**) 30 min (12ep Color; 1970–1971 ABC) Situation Comedy** *with Scoey Mitchlll as Paul Bratter, Tracy Reed as Corie Bratter, Thelma Carpenter as Mabel Bates, and Nipsey Russell as Honey Robinson*

Neil Simon's play *Barefoot in the Park* had already been turned into a hit 1967 film (starring Robert Redford and Jane Fonda) before this TV version came along. For video, the Simon story of a young married couple trying to make it in New York City is transposed onto an all-black setting. Scoey Mitchlll (that's no typo, that's how he spells his name) plays Paul Bratter, a new lawyer at a big downtown firm. Paul and his wife Corie live in a small top-story Manhattan apartment. Corie's mother Mabel and her friend Honey frequently stick their noses into Paul and Corie's life and apartment. It's a nice try to do something different with a familiar concept, but, for a quality late 1960s sitcom on a sensible young couple, *Love on a Rooftop* is funnier.

In syndication, *Barefoot in the Park* has been grafted into the *Love, American Style* series and appears as a continuing segment of that program.

**BARETTA (**) 60 min (82ep Color; 1975–1978 ABC) Police Drama** *with Robert Blake as Tony Baretta, Dana Elcar as Inspector Shiller, Edward Grover as Hal Brubaker, Michael D. Roberts as Rooster, Chino Williams as Fats, and Lala as Fred*

Antiestablishment cops from the 1970s are a dime a dozen. Each one has some unique personality quirk or trademark, but the concept is always the same. The rogue cop is the only one in the department who *really* knows how to capture the bad guys, since the old-fashioned bureaucrat police honchos are too by-the-book to know what's going on. The renegade star always hangs out on the street, wearing unconventional garb, talking unconventional lingo, and feeling empathy for the poor slobs who make up the oppressed underbelly of that show's nameless urban megalopolis.

*Baretta* is a pure "formula" antiestablishment cop show. Tony Baretta is an undercover police detective in some big city. He lives in some squalid little hotel room with his roommate Fred, a pet cockatoo. The cockatoo gimmick is not half bad. It's better than sucking lollipops and saying "Who loves ya', baby?" a lot, as Theo Kojak did. At least Tony Baretta can talk to Fred, thereby allowing some light to be shed on Baretta's usually tight-lipped personality.

Every antiestablishment cop has to have some frustrated police superior, in order to demonstrate how independent the hero is. Tony Baretta is so independent that he goes through two bosses during the series. Inspector Shiller lasts only the first few months, with Lt. Brubaker picking up the thankless task of supervising Baretta for the rest of the run.

Robert Blake puts a lot of soul into his performance as the undercover cop Tony Baretta, but he takes himself much too seriously and the few light touches in the show seem misplaced. Viewers will come to appreciate the hard work Baretta performs in his many undercover disguises, but he really can be a giant pain in the rear with his insistence on doing everything his own way. When you begin feeling sympathy for the by-the-book police superior, you know that this antiestablishment cop show has pushed its premise too far.

*Baretta* has a catchy theme song, "Keep Your Eye on the Sparrow," sung by Sammy Davis, Jr.

**BARNABY JONES** **(**½) 60 min (177ep Color; 1973–1980 CBS) Detective Drama** *with Buddy Ebsen as Barnaby Jones, Lee Meriwether as Betty Jones, Mark Shera as Jedediah Romano "J. R." Jones, and John Carter is Lt. John Biddle*

The always classy Quinn Martin produces this highly competent private-eye series. Like Frank Cannon, the central character in another Quinn Martin private-eye show of the 1970s, Barnaby Jones is neither young, handsome, a wisecracker, nor a fast mover, and those are all pluses. Jones works carefully to crack his cases. Jones' simple manner often lures villains into assuming he is a bit thick, but, somewhat akin to Lt. Columbo, Jones is only letting the guilty incriminate themselves in an off-guarded moment.

In the final four seasons, Barnaby is teamed up with his young cousin, J. R., who does some of the legwork that the aging Barnaby can't. This is one of the first of the insidious instances of TV producers feeling they must provide a young hunk to offset the assumed unattractiveness of an elderly leading man private eye.

**BARNEY MILLER** **(****) 30 min (170ep and pilot Color; 1975–1982 ABC) Situation Comedy** *with Hal Linden as Capt. Barney Miller, Max Gail as Det. Stan Wojciehowicz, Abe Vigoda as Det. Sgt. Phil Fish, Jack Soo as Det. Sgt. Nick Yemana, Ron Glass as Det. Sgt. Ron Harris, Gregory Sierra as Det. Sgt. Chano Amenguale, Steve Landesberg as Det. Sgt. Arthur Dietrich, Linda Lavin as Det. Janice Wentworth, Barbara Barrie as Elizabeth Miller, Ron Carey as Officer Carl Levitt, and James Gregory as Inspector Frank Luger*

At first, this comedy about police life at New York's Twelfth Precinct (Greenwich Village area) is structured along fairly standard lines of the time. There is a cast of diverse ethnic types, including Barney Miller (Jewish), Ron Harris (Black), Chano Amenguale (Hispanic), Nick Yemana (Asian), Stan Wojciehowicz (Polish), and Phil Fish (old and Jewish). The action takes place at a variety of settings: the station house, Barney's apartment (where he has a loving wife and two teenage kids), and in the field (on a stakeout, for instance). It seems a fairly typical home and office comedy, though with particularly good dialogue.

Very quickly, however, the visual look of the show changes, with the scenes increasingly limited to just two main sets: the detectives' "bullpen" booking room (complete with a small holding cell) and Barney's office. And as that happens, the series begins to take on the aura of a close-knit theater piece, with most of the main action off stage. What we see are the characters, up close and personal, as they enter the precinct office for processing—as suspects, witnesses, or victims. When they tell their stories (or as the particular detectives describe what happened when they arrived on the scene), the picture created in our mind's eye captures the action more effectively than any that could ever be shot.

It's old-fashioned storytelling at its finest, leading us to the real high point of the action: resolving the situation causing the trouble in the first place. That's when *Barney Miller* truly shines, because the detectives see their task as one of creative compromise and diffusing tensions, especially in "disturbing the peace" disagreements. So they all use the processing time at the station as an opportunity to have people let off steam and cool down. In many cases, that's all those involved need: the chance to have someone listen to their tale. Or the opportunity to confront long-time antagonists in a situation where they can't avoid dealing with a particular problem. In fact, often the detectives intentionally leave the two sides to themselves for a while (usually with one "in the cage"), hoping that they'll work things out. When the time comes to sign the complaint and make it official, many end up declining to do so. And that's considered a good day's work. It's better in the long run for them, and it sure eliminates a lot of permanent paperwork.

Given that premise, there's never any shortage of characters and offbeat situations coming through the precinct doors (ranging from a kidnapped antique doll to a man who thinks he's the Messiah to a bomb hidden in a suitcase). However, it's the detectives themselves who provide the solid foundation for all this activity. Over the course of the series, each of them emerges as a well-rounded and distinctive personality. In their banter and interrogations, they don't just crack jokes (though they deliver plenty of funny lines); they deal with situations precisely and perfectly as themselves. As a result, *Barney Miller* emerges as one of the finest character comedy showpieces ever, celebrating tone, expression, and dialogue every bit as much as plot.

Though the individual stories are all self-contained, there are continuing threads that run over the course of the series. One of the more elaborate ones follows cocky and self-centered Harris as he develops from a casual writer to a published novelist, turning out *Blood on the Badge,* inspired by events and characters at the Twelfth Precinct. Over several seasons, we see him go from scribbling notes during particularly odd events at the station, to churning out his manuscript, landing a publisher, and basking in its success (to the occasional annoyance of everybody else). When the book results in a libel suit by Arnold Ripner (Alex Henteloff), an ambulance-chasing attorney who hangs around the precinct, we also see the flip side, including an expensive trial and Harris's attempts to recover with a new book.

Harris's venture is the most eleaborate, but all the characters have their moments in the spotlight. The continuing subtext for Barney is his frustration at being unable to advance beyond the rank of captain, along with some rocky times in his marriage (again, mostly off-screen). He also serves as the father figure (OK, uncle figure) to the other men, even going so far as to help his superior, Inspector Luger, court a mail-order bride by composing a few love letters. Barney sets the overall tone at the precinct and consistently supports his men and his principles.

Wojo is soft-hearted, well-meaning, but sometimes fairly irresponsible, especially when he lets his libido do his thinking for him. (It's no surprise, for instance, when he gets involved with one of the female detectives temporarily assigned to the precinct, Janice Wentworth, played by future *Alice* star Linda Lavin.) Yemana taps the secret gambler in all of us, symbolized by his love of horse racing. (You know he picks up lottery tickets every day.) And Fish is the grizzled veteran who seems to regard work as a vacation from growing old at home, though eventually he does retire and devotes full attention to the far more demanding schedule of domestic life (in a *Fish* spin-off).

Gregory Sierra's Chano departs after only two seasons, with his replacement, Arthur Dietrich, symbolic of the clear direction of the series by then. Dietrich is not another ethnic type. Instead, he is the epitome of a brilliantly sardonic intellectual, a verbal wit who is often used by the other characters as a walking encyclopedia. Also joining the cast at about the same time is a uniform officer "from downstairs," Carl Levitt, who dreams of becoming a detective.

Real-life police departments have praised *Barney Miller* as being one of the most realistic cop shows around. The detectives rarely draw their guns, and they spend more time in conversation, paperwork, and resolving minor neighborhood squabbles than in blowing away some Mr. Big drug king. Of course, they're also some of the most articulate and witty people you'll ever meet (and who wouldn't mind coming off like that?). In any case, this series is well worth repeated visits.

The original pilot for *Barney Miller* (under the title "The Life and Times of Barney Miller," with Abby Dalton as his wife) aired just once (summer 1974) on *Just for Laughs,* one of those anthology series of rejected pilots. Fortunately, this one got new life.

## THE BARON (*) 60 min (26ep Color; 1965–1966 UK ATV) Spy Drama *with Steve Forrest as John "The Baron" Mannering, Sue Lloyd as Cordelia Winfield, Colin Gordon as John Alexander Templeton-Green, and Paul Ferris as David Marlowe*

The Baron is a wealthy Yank in London, who uses a cover as an art dealer to mask his undercover spy work for British intelligence. This undistinguished British series is based on short stories by John Creasey. Leading man Steve Forrest also starred as "Hondo" Harrelson in the very American *S.W.A.T.*

## BAT MASTERSON (**½) 30 min (108ep B&W; 1958–1961 NBC) Western *with Gene Barry as Bat Masterson*

Gene Barry's first hit series, and already he's quite adept at the role of debonair sophisticate, even in the crude and dusty old West of the 1880s. Bat Masterson wears impeccably tailored clothes (including a derby hat), carries a gold-topped cane, and wields a custom-made gun. Though a lawman, he's assigned to no particular town, so he wanders throughout the territory from Kansas to California. He also prefers his wits and his cane to a fistfight or shoot-out, but he's capable of both if necessary.

The stories are pretty good, with Masterson riding into each new town just in time to protect the innocent and win the hearts of the ladies. As you follow the series, though, consider this: How does Masterson manage to literally trip up 200-pound fleeing villains merely by tossing his cane? What does it do, wrap itself around their legs? And, by the way, how does someone swinging a stick beat a fast draw? Watch the close-ups and see if you can figure it out.

## BATMAN (***½) 30 min (120ep Color; 1966–1968 ABC) Adventure *with Adam West as Bruce Wayne/Batman, Burt Ward as Dick Grayson/Robin, Alan Napier as Alfred Pennyworth, Madge Blake as Harriet Cooper, Yvonne Craig as Barbara Gordon/Batgirl, Neil Hamilton as Police Commissioner James Gordon, and William Dozier as narrator*

*Batman* is 1960s pop culture in a nutshell. This one program combines the rise of the young baby-boom generation weaned on comic books and TV, and the campy, sarcastic, offbeat view that came to permeate most of popular culture in that troubled decade.

The original Batman, created by Bob Kane in *Detective Comics* in 1939, was a very sober, square-jawed type of guy, without much fun in his life. Bruce Wayne, Batman's alter ego, was a rich orphan raised by his family's butler, Alfred. Becoming the so-called "world's greatest detective," Wayne created the Batman figure to strike fear into the hearts of criminals. Operating out of the Batcave below the Wayne mansion and aided by Wayne's ward (young orphan Dick Grayson a.k.a. Robin, the Boy Wonder), the Caped Crusader battles crime in sprawling Gotham City. Only old, loyal Alfred knows the true identities of the Dynamic Duo. The crime fighters are on twenty-four-hour call from the Gotham City police, whose commissioner summons them via the Batphone or the Batsignal searchlight.

This is all standard comic book superhero stuff, similar to the Superman legend that produced a classic TV series in the 1950s. The TV *Batman,* however, is a different bird altogether. In the hands of executive producer William Dozier, Batman is camped up for the 1960s. Poking fun at the seriousness overflowing in most superhero comic books of the times, Dozier exaggerates the "square" good-citizen nature of Batman and Robin, in order to set them against a menagerie of colorful, rebellious, antiestablishment villains. The mix works perfectly. The Dynamic Duo are so morally upright (Batman refuses to start the Batmobile unless Robin buckles his seat belt) that they are hilarious.

Surrounded by the enticing allurements of the crime world, such as beautiful women, money, and power, Batman and Robin do not feel envy but rather revulsion at how these villains have strayed so far from the Calvinistic American work ethic. In opposition to Batman and Robin, the paragons of virtue, the villains seem almost appealing in their free-spirited drive to stay independent and individualistic.

This symbiosis of superheroes and villains is just right for the 1960s, when the clichéd homilies of the established culture were in the process of being rejected by many young Americans, *Batman*'s target age group. In *Batman,* viewers can laugh at the system through laughing at Batman and Robin and their cornball ways. Yet the show ostensibly champions the crime fighters and so is immune from charges of subversiveness.

Even without this sociological interpretation, *Batman* is great fun. All the various "Bat" items (mobile, cave, phone, copter, pole, etc.) are gaudily marked and humorously gauche (why does Batman bother with such silly names?). Robin's propensity for atrocious puns ("Holy ice cubes, Batman!" as the pair are being frozen) and the outright stupidity of the Gotham police, who can't solve a pickpocket case without Batman, make entertaining fare. On top of that comes the imaginative and proto-psychedelic production. Rich in splashy colors, the program accentuates the obligatory fisticuffs with large cartoonish captions ("Biff!" "Bamm!" "Ouch!") and tilted camera work. The very structure of the show lampoons the style of the 1930s and 1940s movie adventure serials, which always ended in a cliff-hanger to entice viewers to return. In *Batman,* one adventure is hardly closed before another crisis has beset the Caped Crusader and the Boy Wonder. Producer Dozier steps in and plays the unctuous narrator who drags out every ounce of drama by postulating, in virtually every episode, that *this,* surely, *must* be the end of the line for Batman and Robin, but tune in next time, just in case they get out of the jam somehow.

Without a doubt, the choicest morsels in *Batman* are the weekly villains. Once the program caught on with viewers (almost immediately), every big name and hasbeen in Hollywood clamored to have a stint as Batman's foil. Some became virtual regulars, such as Burgess Meredith (The Penguin), Frank Gorshin (The Riddler), and Cesar Romero (The Joker). Others only popped up once or twice, such as Ethel Merman (Lola Lasagne), Julie Newmar (Catwoman), Rudy Vallee (Lord Marmaduke Ffogg), Victor Buono (King Tut), Joan Collins (The Siren), Liberace (Chandel), and Milton Berle (Louie the Lilac). The opportunity to overact on national TV was too enticing to pass up, and the relish the actors who play the villains put into their work is uplifting.

*Batman* is so stylized and unique that it becomes a cliché almost as fast as it catches an audience. By the later episodes, the fun of camping up a superhero begins to wear off. Batman and Robin start smirking at their own uptightness, and an unnecessary addition is made to the cast. Commissioner Gordon's daughter joins the cast as Batgirl, and it gets somewhat confusing as she does not know Batman and Robin's true identity and they do not know hers.

During the height of the series' popularity, a theatrical movie, also called *Batman,* was produced, with all the TV regulars, many of the best villains, and Lee Meriweather as Catwoman. After *Batman* left the air, Adam West and Burt Ward briefly returned to their roles as the voices of the Dynamic Duo in two animated Saturday morning cartoon series, *The New Adventures of Batman* and *Batman and the Super Seven.*

In 1989, the Batman saga was revived in a new big-budget theatrical film starring Michael Keaton as the Caped Crusader (and Jack Nicholson as the Joker). ■

## BATTLESTAR GALACTICA/GALACTICA 1980 (*½)

**60 min (29ep plus 3 hr pilot Color) (1978–1980 ABC) Science Fiction Adventure** *with Lorne Greene as Commander Adams, Dirk Benedict as Lt. Starbuck, Richard Hatch as Capt. Apollo, Herbert Jefferson, Jr., as Lt. Boomer, Terry Carter as Col. Tigh, John Colicos as Count Baltar, Maren Jensen as Athena, Jonathan Harris as the voice of Lucifer, Patrick Macnee as the voice of the Imperious Cylon Leader, Noah Hathaway as Boxey, Kent McCord as Capt. Troy (Boxey grown up), Barry Van Dyke as Lt. Dillon, and Robyn Douglass as Jamie Hamilton*

In the beginning, *Battlestar Galactica* looks promising, if ponderous.

There is all the stuff of legends in the making. Characters carry the names of Greek gods or star constellations such as Apollo, Athena, and Cassiopeia. White-haired leaders in flowing robes talk of war and peace and great galactic civilizations.

But evil aliens known as the Cylons hover over all, their warriors clad in shining jet-black armor, ready to strike. And they do, launching a deadly attack on the Twelve Colony Planets of the humans even as the leaders of both sides are in the midst of ratifying a peace treaty meant to end a thousand years of conflict.

When the smoke clears, all that remains of the human forces are a few full-size battleships out in space, led by the battlestar *Galactica.* She is soon joined by about two hundred other vessels to form a "rag tag fugitive fleet," determined to fight the Cylons the best they could, but also driven by another dream. Like the biblical tribes of Israel, the survivors of the Twelve Colony Planets take off into deep space to find their Promised Land, a legendary thirteenth human colony called Earth.

All this was first set in a three-hour prime-time première in 1978 (and also as a theatrical film release later that year), meant to mark the beginning of an epic television legend that would be on a par with *Star Wars, Flash Gordon,* and *Star Trek,* appealing to fans of all ages.

It didn't quite turn out that way.

Despite all the mythic trappings, *Battlestar Galactica* ended up as a very, very expensive space adventure series popular chiefly with children. The stories quickly lost the sense of danger and true horror that had accompanied the première setup (and first few episodes), settling instead into a mechanical formula of gun battles, cute kids, and mechanical pets. There was nothing wrong with that, but it hardly justified state-of-the-art special effects and a record-breaking budget for that time of $1 million per episode. With increasingly soft ratings, the series soon shut down production.

But before the end, there are moments. In one ("The Man with Nine Lives"), guest Fred Astaire borrows a page from *It Takes a Thief* (where he played dad to international jewel thief Alexander Mundy) and appears as an interplanetary con man claiming to be the long-lost father of Galactica fighter pilot Lt. Starbuck (Dirk Benedict). In another ("War of the Gods"), Patrick Macnee plays a mysterious space wreck survivor who turns out to be the devil incarnate, enticing members of the fleet with his ability to make their dreams come true.

In all the episodes, Lorne Green plays *Galactica* Commander Adama, the leader of the spaceship fleet and concerned father figure to them all. Green is the lone holdover regular to continue in the follow-up/revival title, *Galactica 1980,* an eight-episode package set on present-day Earth at the end of a long interstellar journey. For its final episode, Starbuck turns up as well. ■

**THE BAXTERS (*) 30 min (24ep Color; 1979–1981 Syndication) Situation Comedy/Drama/Discussion** *with Larry Keith as Fred Baxter, Anita Gillette as Nancy Baxter, Sean McCann as Jim Baxter, and Terry Tweed as Susan Baxter*

An intriguing failure, *The Baxters* is an eleven-minute comedy/drama about a middle-class family in the suburbs facing all the big problems of modern life. After the actors set up the problem, the scene shifts to the TV audience and a moderator, who fill out the half hour by debating what the resolution of the problem should be. This innovative concept was brought to national syndication by sitcom experimenter Norman Lear.

Even a pioneer such as Lear had to admit that *The Baxters* flopped, and Lear pulled out after one season. The second season, with Jim and Susan Baxter replacing Fred and Nancy Baxter, came from Toronto, and is even more turgid than the first.

**BAY CITY BLUES (***) 60 min (8ep Color; 1983 NBC) Drama** *with Michael Nouri as Joe Rohner, Kelly Harmon as Sunny Hayward, Pat Corley as Ray Holtz, Bernie Casey as Ozzie Peoples, Dennis Franz as Angelo Carbone, Peter Jurasik as Mitch Klein, Ken Olin as Rocky Padillo, Michele Greene as Judy Nuckles, and Perry Lang as John "Frenchy" Nuckles*

Minor league baseball has become a mostly ignored subculture of the sports world where has-beens bump against wanna-bes and where major league success seems just a pitch away. *Bay City Blues* is a valiant attempt to capture that world, by focusing on both the on- and off-the-field lives of the Bay City (California) Bluebirds.

Once you know that this show was created by Steven Bochco, the co-creator of *Hill Street Blues,* you know everything you need to know about *Bay City Blues.* It's the same idea, transplanted from the ghetto precinct house to the AA League diamond. There is the same plethora of characters, the same interweaving of story lines, and the same deft combination of drama, character study, and humor. Unfortunately, it is a lot easier to create gripping story lines when writing about a ghetto police station than when writing about twenty-year-old pitching phenoms and forty-year-old wash-outs.

The best reason to seek out *Bay City Blues* is the same reason you would go to a minor league baseball game, to watch the stars of tomorrow before they hit it big. *Bay City Blues* is a literal training ground for actors who were later called up to *Hill Street Blues* (or who were sent down from the hit series for more "seasoning"). Dennis Franz, whose corrupt cop character (Sal Benedetto) had been killed off in *Hill Street,* softens that characterization a bit in *Bay City* as Angelo Carbone, a seedy, slightly shady coach, and he then took virtually the same role back to *Hill Street* as Norman Buntz. Peter Jurasik, who would be Sid, the snitch in the Buntz-era *Hill Street,* is a similar fast-talking con artist in *Bay City,* where he plays Mitch Klein, the team radio announcer. Pat Corley, who had been the hypertensive coroner in *Hill Street,* is the equally tense owner in *Bay City.* Ken Olin, the womanizing Rocky Padillo in *Bay City,* became Harry Garibaldi, a sensitive cop with a roving eye, on *Hill Street* (and went on to greater fame as Michael Steadman in *thirtysomething*). Michele Greene, who plays the wife of pitcher Frenchy Nuckles, later starred as idealistic young lawyer Abby Perkins in Bochco's post–*Hill Street Blues* series, *L.A. Law.*

Maybe *Bay City Blues* is not a great show and maybe the script writers try too hard to be dramatic. Maybe nobody cares about minor league baseball anymore and maybe the series deserved to be canceled after a while. Nonetheless, *Bay City Blues* was pulled from the lineup much too fast. This show could have been a contender.

**THE BEACHCOMBER (*) 30 min (39ep B&W; 1961–1962 Syndication) Adventure** *with Cameron Mitchell as John Lackland, Don Megowan as Capt. Huckabee, and Sebastian Cabot as Andrew Crippen*

This obscure saga of a dropout from society comes from the pre-hippie days of the early 1960s. John Lackland, a San Francisco merchandising executive, leaves the rat race behind and becomes a beach bum in the South Pacific who helps people in distress. Too bad he never was able to rescue Gilligan and his pals, who must have been nearby.

**BEACON HILL** (**) **60 min (12ep & 2 hr pilot Color; 1975 CBS) Drama** *with Stephen Elliott as Benjamin Lassiter, Nancy Marchand as Mary Lassiter, David Dukes as Robert Lassiter, Kathryn Walker as Fawn Lassiter, Meave McGuire as Maude (Lassiter) Palmer, Edward Herrmann as Richard Palmer, Linda Purl as Betsy Bullock, George Rose as Mr. Hacker, Paul Rudd as Brian Mallory, Kitty Winn as Rosamond Lassiter, Susan Blanchard as Marueen Mahaffey, and Beatrice Straight as Emmaline Hacker*

Eyeing the success of *Upstairs, Downstairs* imports on public television, CBS slotted a similar period drama in 1975, but one with a Stateside setting. Like the British original, there were plenty of soapy complications focusing on both the wealthy upstairs family and the members of their downstairs household staff. Only instead of pre–World War I London, it was all set in 1920s Boston in the fashionable Beacon Hill area at the home of the Lassiter family.

Though the pilot scored well, ratings quickly sagged as the network discovered that it takes more than a few surface trappings to win a dedicated audience. In fact, though, it's hard to imagine how CBS thought this would possibly be an immediate commercial network success. Even *All in the Family* (an Americanized version of a British comedy) took a while to build its following. To expect instant loyalty to a large-cast soap opera (even one similar to a top-ranked PBS series) was quite presumptuous, especially with the respected British original still fresh in viewers' minds for one-on-one comparisons.

Ultimately, though, the series could have overcome such problems. What really hurt *Beacon Hill* was that far too much attention was paid to the lavish sets and elaborate costumes at the expense of character development and plot. In short, the program was all dressed up with no idea of where to go. There were too many characters dumped into the setup at the beginning, so most were reduced to a few quick caricature traits (an embittered son, a hard-nosed husband, a bohemian daughter, a faithful butler). Plots quickly settled into a series of promotional "grabbers"—the son gets drunk, the daughter throws a scandalous party, the father faces political embarrassment.

Toward the end of the thirteen-episode run, production people from *Upstairs, Downstairs* were brought in to help, but *Beacon Hill* had already lost its chance to lure an audience to upper-class Boston. Hope the cast got to keep their outfits.

**BEANS BAXTER, THE NEW ADVENTURES OF** (**) **30 min (16ep & 1 hr pilot Color; 1987–1988 Fox) Adventure** *with Jonathan Ward as Benjamin "Beans" Baxter, Jr., Jerry Wasserman as Number Two, Elinor Donahue as Susan Baxter, Scott Bremner as Scooter Baxter, Rick Lenz as Benjamin Baxter, Sr., Kurtwood Smith as Mr. Sue, Karen Mistal as Cake Lase, and Stuart Fratkin as Woodshop*

Beans is a high school student in suburban Washington, D.C. whose father, Benjamin Baxter, is a courier for the Network, a secret spy organization. Baxter, Sr., disguises his actions by posing as a mailman, until he is whisked away by agents of UGLI, a terrorist outfit. Beans picks up where his dad left off and begins serving as a courier for the Network, by hiding messages in vending machines. While all this is going on, Beans is trying to lead a seminormal life in high school, without breaking his cover.

What makes *Beans Baxter* so cute are its humorous touches of placing the bureaucratic world of spies into the mundane high school setting that Beans inhabits. Beans' mother, Susan, is played by *Father Knows Best* alumnus Elinor Donahue.

Oh, by the way, despite this show's title, there never were any *old* adventures of Beans Baxter.

**BEARCATS!** (*) **60 min (13ep & 2 hr pilot Color: 1971 CBS) Adventure** *with Rod Taylor as Hank Brackett and Dennis Cole as Johnny Reach*

Two adventurers roam the American Southwest, circa 1914, in a Stutz Bearcat automobile instead of a horse. This contrived program is eminently ignorable. The pilot is called *Powderkeg*.

**BEAUTY AND THE BEAST** (***) **60 min (42ep at Summer 1989 Color; 1987– CBS) Drama** *with Linda Hamilton as Catherine Chandler, Ron Perlman as Vincent, Roy Dotrice as Father, and Jay Acavone as Joe Maxwell*

The beauty of *Beauty and the Beast* is not really Linda Hamilton (although she qualifies for that title), but rather the tone of selfless compassion that runs through this program. While most other shows of its era championed the "What's in it for me?" philosophy rampant in the U.S., *Beauty and the Beast* supposes an idealism and integrity far beyond anything viewers are likely to come across in real life. While this approach may be cause for claiming *Beauty and the Beast* is an unrealistic fairy tale, credit should go to the producers for daring to even pretend that people can be so noble in our time.

At the start of the series, Linda Hamilton's beautiful lady lawyer (Catherine) is mugged in the jungle of downtown Manhattan. She is found and cared for by the mysterious Vincent, who lives, with his father, in a subterranean labyrinth beneath the New York City streets. The catch here is that Vincent looks like a beast, and is not all human. His father looks normal, but Vincent looks like the cowardly lion of *Wizard of Oz* fame, and his visage is enough to cause men to shudder and women (such as Catherine) to scream. Ah, but once Catherine gets over her initial shock, she learns that

Vincent is a kind, gentle giant who likes to read poetry and shies away from any physical relationships. He certainly is not the average guy she'd meet in the meat market singles bars of Manhattan.

As the series develops, Catherine, still dealing with the shock of her attack and Vincent's help in her convalescence, leaves her fancy corporate law job. She takes a more "meaningful" job, as an Assistant D. A. Thus she is more likely to get involved in dangerous cases, and to need the help of the mysterious Vincent, who seems to be able to know just when and where she could use the help of a tall, superhumanly strong guy with a scary face.

Vincent and his father are always on the verge of having their peaceful underground sanctuary violated by the hordes of nasty Manhattan vermin who lurk on the surface. Catherine is always struggling to figure out how to deal with her strong feelings for the man/beast who dotes on her so and yet shies away from her touch. The plots themselves may be weak at times, but *Beauty and the Beast* is just so different from standard TV fare, you can overlook the occasional story lapse.

Vincent is clearly a figure from fairy tales, and he sets a staggeringly pristine model that mortal men will never match. Still, when 99 percent of TV drums home the message that surface appeal is the basis for quality, that relationships between men and women revolve around physical lust or economic dependency, and that the noble nature of figures from mythology is just something to smirk at, *Beauty and the Beast* does its part to provide a little equal time for opposing views.

One major surprise about this show is that it comes from Paul Junger Witt and Tony Thomas, two producers who previously gave us well-made but more broadly played shows such as *Soap, Benson,* and *It's a Living/ Making A Living.* ■

**BEGGERMAN, THIEF (see *Rich Man, Poor Man*)**

**BEHIND CLOSED DOORS (*) 30 min (26ep B&W; 1958–1959 NBC) Spy Drama** *with Bruce Gordon as Commander Matson*

Bruce Gordon, who played Frank Nitti on *The Untouchables,* is the only continuing character in this anthology of stories of U.S. Naval Intelligence, based on the files of real-life Admiral Ellis M. Zacharias.

**THE BEIDERBECKE AFFAIR (**½) 60 min (6ep Color; 1985 UK YTV) Mystery Adventure** *with Barbara Flynn, James Bolam, Dudley Sutton, Terence Rigby, Colin Blakely, and Dominic Jephcot*

A jazz fan's/record collector's heroic fantasy, with the key to a mystery tied in to some old Bix Beiderbecke records. Good mix of music and action.

**BEN CASEY (**½) 60 min (153ep & 2 hr sequel Color; 1961–1966 ABC) Medical Drama** *with Vince Edwards as Dr. Ben Casey, Sam Jaffe as Dr. David Zorba, Betty Ackerman as Dr. Maggie Graham, Franchot Tone as Dr. Daniel Freeland, Jeanne Bates as Nurse Wills, and Harry Landers as Dr. Ted Hoffman*

Man. Woman. Birth. Death. Infinity.

Those words (spoken off-camera) and those symbols, (usually written on a chalk board) open the show. They offer an instant summary of the dramatic extremes of hospital work: Life begins, life ends, the universe goes on.

Doctors Ben Casey and David Zorba are the two key figures at County General Hospital and they provide a perfect dramatic center for the series. Casey is the brilliant, handsome, and headstrong neurosurgeon. Zorba is his experienced mentor, guiding him through procedures in both the operating room and the bureaucratic front office. Working together, they usually succeed, but not every time. Casey's darkly brooding manner clearly shows that he doesn't enjoy losing, even if the case was a hopeless one to begin with. At times his total lack of humor is hard to take, but that's when Zorba steps in to break the grim mood.

This is a well-written series, fairly realistic for its time, and supported by a strong lineup of guest stars. These include a good number of otherwise famous performers from theatrical films and other TV series, including George C. Scott, Colleen Dewhurst, Rod Steiger, Bruce Dern, Jerry Lewis, Robert Blake, Jack Klugman, and Robert Culp.

The first few seasons of *Ben Casey* are probably the best, while the final two dozen stories suffer from the absence of Sam Jaffe's Dr. Zorba (replaced by Franchot Tone as Dr. Freeland) and an increased emphasis on blatantly soapy cliff-hangers and love affairs. One of these final shows includes a rather strained multipart tale of a young woman (Jane Hancock, played by Stella Stevens) who had just wakened from a thirteen-year coma.

*Ben Casey* was created by James Moser, who was also responsible for a respected medical series of the 1950s, *Medic.* A two-hour 1988 TV-movie, *The Return of Ben Casey,* brought Edwards back to the title role in a thinly disguised pilot for a new series, but the package comes across as stuffy, stiff, and dated.

**BENJAMIN FRANKLIN (***) 90 min (4ep Color; 1974 CBS) Drama Documentary** *with Beau Bridges, Richard Widmark, Eddie Albert, Lloyd Bridges, and Melvyn Douglas all as Benjamin Franklin*

An excellent production tracing the life and career of one of the key founding fathers of the United States, from before the Revolutionary War to his final years.

**THE BENNY HILL SHOW (**½) 30 min (125ep Color; 1969–1982 UK Thames) Comedy-Variety** *with Benny Hill, Henry McGee, Bob Todd, Jackie Wright, and Nicholas Parsons*

It's nice to know that British television isn't all *Masterpiece Theatre*–type drama and BBC documentaries. *The Benny Hill Show* demonstrates that low-brow humor is universal, and that the British have a special flare for it.

Pudgy, smirking Benny Hill plays the perpetual lecher, forever surrounded by and chasing after an unending stream of scantily clad beauties (who are far *less* clad in the British originals, before American censors snipped out several scenes for U.S. syndication). Like the Red Skelton and Jackie Gleason show of old, *The Benny Hill Show* is a collection of skits, blackouts, and continuing characters. Hill is naughty but never nasty, silly but never stupid. At times, the show seems like nothing more than an R-rated adult version of the "Road Runner" cartoons (constant chases with no climax), but vaudeville (*real,* sexy vaudeville) has rarely been done so sprightly on TV.

Since the regular production of *The Benny Hill Show* ceased, several new specials and "best of" compilations have aired. ■

**BENSON (***) 30 min (158ep Color; 1979–1986 ABC) Situation Comedy** *with Robert Guillaume as Benson DuBois, James Noble as Governor Gene Gatling, Inga Swenson as Gretchen Kraus, Missy Gold as Katie Gatling, Lewis J. Stadlen as John Taylor, Caroline McWilliams as Marcie Hill, Ethan Phillips as Pete Downey, Didi Conn as Denise Stevens Downey, and Rene Auberjonois as Clayton Endicott III*

Benson was one of the best characters on the Susan Harris-produced comedy *Soap.* There, he functioned as far more than just family butler to the Tates—he was the sharp-tongued voice of sanity who (barely) kept the silly household from collapsing into a muddled mess. And he had some of the program's funniest lines, directed especially against Jessica Tate's philandering husband, Chester.

The character was the obvious choice for a spin-off series, so about halfway through *Soap* Benson left to work for Jessica's cousin, Governor James Gatling. In doing so, he exchanged one out-of-joint family for an executive household sorely in need of his management skills.

Governor Gatling is well-meaning, principled, but often quite naive in both his personal and professional life. Though Benson starts out with the vaguely defined role of Gatling's household manager, the governor quickly comes to rely on him for help in just about everything, especially raising his young daughter, Katie (Gatling is a widower). The rest of the executive staff also comes to welcome Benson as a reassuring force at the mansion—except for Kraus and Taylor, who resent his encroachment on their respective territories: food and legislative fodder. That's fine, because they provide Benson with two perfect targets for his biting putdowns. Kraus (Inga Swenson) is the combative housekeeper (a character similar to Swenson's manipulative Inga Svenson on *Soap*) while Taylor is the governor's officious, self-serving personal aide who glories in his position (but does manage to get the job done). Taylor is replaced after one season by the similarly styled Clayton Endicott III, the governor's chief-of-staff.

Unlike *Soap*'s serial structure, *Benson* plays as a regular sitcom with self-contained episodes. This allows for a great latitude of plots, ranging from domestic conflicts to legislative budget battles to special offbeat settings (such as a murder mystery aboard a cruise ship).

Over the long haul, there is also slow but steady plot and character development. The most obvious is Benson's rising star in government. On his first day, in fact, he steps in to save a staff report presentation, quickly demonstrating his ability to handle ticklish situations, to charm the bureaucrats and legislators, and to make tough, effective decisions. Despite those obvious talents, he's promoted anyway, becoming budget director for the state, then lieutenant governor. In the program's final season, he even takes a stab at the governor's office.

Governor Gatling, too, evolves from a truly dumb, gaffe-prone bumbler (who confuses Benson with the Rev. Jesse Jackson the first time they meet) to a more firm and disciplined leader. The other characters also grow, even Gretchen Kraus, who gets promoted from the kitchen to appointment secretary.

*Benson* is one of those solid workhorse comedies that may not have a reputation as a "ground breaker" (like *All in the Family* or *Soap*), but it does consistently deliver top-notch humor. Fortunately, it even outlasted its parent series, allowing *Soap* the opportunity to resolve (sort of) the final season's cliff-hanger, with a mysterious (rather ghostly) visit from Jessica Tate, who stops by Benson's office on her way to the afterlife.

**BERGERAC (*½) 60 min (13ep Color; 1981 UK BBC) Police Drama** *with John Nettles as Det. Jim Bergerac and Cecile Paoli as Francine*

Jim Bergerac is a British police detective who only works on the cases the *regular* police detectives can't solve (can't you name eight or ten other shows that have that same premise?). Nothing unusual occurs here.

**BERLIN ALEXANDERPLATZ (***) 60 min (14ep Color; 1979 West Germany & Italy) Drama** *with Gunter Lamprecht as Franz Biberkopf, Gottfried John as Reinhold, Barbara Sukowa as Mieze, and Hanna Schygulla, Ivan Desny, Karin Baal, and Brigitte Mira*

Rainer Werner Fassbinder's epic adaptation of Alfred Doblin's novel looking at German life on the eve of Nazism. Lamprecht plays a reformed criminal who attempts to reestablish himself in the outside world following a five-year prison sentence for killing a prostitute. Despite the hedonistic forces buffeting him on all sides (this is freewheeling Berlin in the late 1920s), he valiantly fights to maintain his dignity and commitment to live a good life.

At times grim, depressing, and downright confusing. In 1980, this was edited into a monumental-length theatrical release (more than fifteen hours, with previously unused footage), providing ample empirical evidence that there are some films best digested via television.

**BERNSTEIN/BEETHOVEN (***) (11ep Color; 1982 PBS) Music** *with Leonard Bernstein as conductor and Maximilian Schell as commentator*

Leonard Bernstein conducts the Vienna Philharmonic Orchestra through Beethoven's nine symphonies and assorted other works of the famed composer.

**BERRENGER'S (½) 60 min (11ep & 90 min pilot Color; 1985 NBC) Drama** *with Sam Wanamaker as Simon Berrenger, Ben Murphy as Paul Berrenger, Yvette Mimieux as Shane Bradley, Andrea Marcovicci as Gloria Berrenger, Robin Strand as Billy Berrenger, Anita Morris as Babs Berrenger, Jack Scalia as Danny Krucek, Laura Ashton as Laurel Hayes, and Leslie Hope as Cammie Springer*

A major department store is a world unto itself, with big-money international contracts, cut-throat competition, and a surprisingly large bureaucracy and staff hidden behind those flashy sales counters. It's perfectly fair game for drama, but in this series it doesn't work, especially as a prime-time soap. Young Cammie Springer is far too innocent—at one point she stands in the lobby, eyes glistening with wonder while whispering the store name, "Berrenger's." Wow! She takes this far too seriously to be believed. Of course, so do the members of the Berrenger family, with their complicated marital and corporate intrigues. But much as it tries, *Berrenger's* just doesn't sizzle, especially in comparison to the larger-than-life characters and plots on *Dallas* or even *Dynasty*. It's like hoping for Bloomingdale's and ending up at K-mart.

**BERT D'ANGELO/SUPERSTAR (*½) 60 min (12ep Color; 1976 ABC) Police Drama** *with Paul Sorvino as Bert D'Angelo, Robert Pine as Inspector Larry Johnson, and Dennis Patrick as Capt. Jack Breen*

One of Quinn Martin's more forgettable crime series, *Bert D'Angelo/Superstar* deserves its anonymity. D'Angelo is a veteran of the New York City police force who now operates as a police detective on the San Francisco force. His impressive success at rounding up criminals earns him the nickname "Superstar."

**THE BEST OF . . .**

Even if a series has "The Best of" in its current rerun title (*The Best of Saturday Night Live,* for instance), it is still listed under the original program title. In addition, *The Best of Groucho* is listed under *You Bet Your Life.*

**BEST OF THE WEST (***) 30 min (22ep Color; 1981–1982 ABC) Situation Comedy** *with Joel Higgins as Marshal Sam Best, Leonard Frey as Parker Tillman, Carlene Watkins as Elvira Best, Meeno Peluce as Daniel Best, Tracey Walter as Frog Rothchild, Jr., Valri Bromfield as Laney Gibbs, and Tom Ewell as Doc Jerome Kullens*

An old-fashioned genre spoof, with Joel Higgins as the upright but inadvertent western hero, Sam Best (thus, the series title). Sam is a Civil War vet from Philadelphia who moves to the town of Copper Creek to run a general store—with his Southern belle wife, Elvira, and ten-year-old son, Daniel, unhappily in tow. In short order, Sam comes face-to-face with Parker Tillman, the sharpie who sold him the store, and who also happens to run the lawless town's protection racket. Sam refuses to pay, then accidentally scares off a gunfighter terrorizing the town, and before you can say "series premise," he's appointed marshal.

It's a good setup and the entire cast does an excellent job with their comic caricatures. Tillman is conniving and duplicitous. Sam is pure-of-heart but appropriately bumbling. His wife and son are perfectly miserable in their new home. And the rest of the standard western types are all there, just slightly out of sync: the inebriated town doctor (Doc Kullens), the dim-witted henchman (Frog), and the fearsome gunfighter (the incompetent Calico Kid—an occasional role for Christopher Lloyd, moonlighting from *Taxi*).

There's a good mix of slapstick (attempting to prove his competence in the marshal's job, Sam shoots himself in the leg), silly scenes (a frustrated Elvira attempts to sweep all the dirt from the floor of their new home, only to discover it's a dirt floor), and appropriately absurd plots (the Calico Kid signs on as a saloon cook, swearing never again to kill anything that can't be breaded and sautéed).

*Best of the West* lasted only one season, but it was a good stopover for Higgins between *Salvage 1* with Andy Griffith (who turns up for an episode as Elvira's dad, Lamont Devereaux) and *Silver Spoons* with Ricky Schroder.

**BEST SELLERS (1976–1977 NBC) Drama**

Four miniseries, *Captains and the Kings, Once an Eagle, Seventh Avenue,* and *The Rhineman Exchange,* originally aired under this umbrella title. See each title for details.

**THE BEST TIMES (*½) 60 min (6ep & 30 min pilot Color; 1985 NBC) Drama** *with Janet Eilber as Joanne Braithwaite, Beth Ehlers as Mia Braithwaite, David Packer as Neil "Trout" Troutman, Jim Metzler as Dan Bragen, and Jay Baker as Tony Younger*

Youth is pictured as the "best times" in this sudsy drama set in a southern California beach town. The focus is on John F. Kennedy High School, where divorcée

Joanne Braithwaite has just joined the faculty as an English teacher, while daughter Mia tries to fit in as a student. There is a whole menagerie of characters tossed in, both on the teacher and the student level, but the ponderous pontificating by many drags *The Best Times* down.

The thirty-minute pilot from 1984 is titled *Things Are Looking Up* and features Gretchen Corbett in the lead role of Joanne Braithwaite.

**BETTER DAYS** (*) **30 min (4ep Color; 1986 CBS) Situation Comedy** *with Raphael Sbarge as Brian McGuire, Dick O'Neill as Harry Clooney, Chip McAllister as Luther Cain, Guy Killum as Anthony "Snake" Johnson, and Randee Heller as Harriet Winters*

Brian McGuire is a blond Beverly Hills boy who, much to his initial chagrin, reverses thirty years of TV history and moves from California to Brooklyn when his parents suffer financial ruin. Brian moves in with his grandfather, Harry Clooney, in an apartment above the old man's vegetable stand, but the young man finds it difficult to relate with the inner city kids he meets, and they feel the same way about him. All that the boys share is an interest in basketball. The basic premise is novel, but it's hard to get to know the characters over such a small number of episodes.

**THE BETTY HUTTON SHOW** (**) **30 min (26ep B&W; 1959–1960 CBS) Situation Comedy** *with Betty Hutton as Goldie Appleby, Gigi Perreau as Pat Strickland, Richard Miles as Nicky Strickland, and Dennis Joel as Roy Strickland*

The 1940s film star Betty Hutton plays Goldie, a showgirl turned manicurist, who lucks upon a rich old man who dies and leaves her as executrix of his vast financial estate and guardian of his three bratty kids. This show is also known as *Goldie*.

**THE BETTY WHITE SHOW** (**½) **30 min (14ep Color; 1977–1978 CBS) Situation Comedy** *with Betty White as Joyce Whitman, John Hillerman as John Elliot, Georgia Engel as Mitzi Maloney, Caren Kaye as Tracy Garrett, Barney Phillips as Fletcher Huff, and Alex Henteloff as Doug Porterfield*

Betty White's first series following her stint on *The Mary Tyler Moore Show* broke from the approach used in the MTM-produced vehicles for other alums from the program. Instead of taking the same character to another setting (as was done with Rhoda, Phyllis, and Lou Grant), MTM put aside White's Sue Anne Nivens persona in favor of a new (but similar) sharp-tongued show business type, television actress Joyce Whitman. She's a just-past-her-peak film performer who has finally consented to "do television." Unfortunately, her chosen vehicle is a sleazy crime adventure show, *Undercover Woman.* Although we never see a finished episode of this series-within-the-series, it's pretty clear that *Undercover Woman* embraces and (only slightly) exaggerates all the worst empty-headed aspects of such programs. If you're keeping score, in real life at that time *Police Woman* was a prime-time hit, and, for a while, slotted against MTM's *Lou Grant.*

In the home scenes of *The Betty White Show,* Georgia Engel (Ted's girlfriend Georgette on *Mary Tyler Moore*) plays Joyce's apartment mate and best friend, Mitzi. At the studio, in the long breaks between filming, Joyce spars with Tracy Garrett, a sexy young actress who plays her partner in the *Undercover Woman* series. Tracy will do anything to advance her career, so Joyce never misses an opportunity to put her down (though she seems beyond embarrassment). Joyce (and the rest of the crew) also direct plenty of antagonism toward Doug Porterfield, the bumbling CBS network liaison to *Undercover Woman.*

But Joyce's main comic foil on the set is the acerbic director of the series, John Elliot (played by John Hillerman), who was also Joyce's former husband. That past history between them tempers the antagonism with genuine affection and concern, making both of them more believable characters. In fact, watching those two in action is probably the chief reason to catch this series. MTM obviously recognized that potential spark and had both performers (and Engel) signed on to work together even before the particular premise had been set up (at one time there was even talk of making the women nuns teaching at a Catholic school run by Hillerman, playing a priest).

Perhaps some other setting would have worked better for them because, overall, *The Betty White Show* doesn't quite hang together. At the very least, most of the action should have been staged at Joyce and Mitzi's apartment, bringing all the characters to that world and never bothering with the studio—where it too often feels dull, cramped, and listless (just like in real life, no doubt). Or how about an estate in Hawaii? Or a retirement community in Florida?

**BETWEEN THE WARS** (**½) **30 min (16ep Color; 1978–1979 Syndication) Documentary** *with Eric Sevareid and Richard Basehart as narrators*

The years between World War I and World War II in America are the focus of this nicely done documentary, produced by Alan Landsburg (*In Search Of . . . ; That's Incredible*). ■

**BEULAH** (*) **30 min (B&W; 1950–1953 ABC) Situation Comedy** *with Ethel Waters and Louise Beavers as Beulah, William Post, Jr. and David Bruce as Harry Henderson, Ginger Jones and June Frazee as Alice Henderson, Butterfly McQueen as Oriole, and Percy "Bud" Harris and Dooley Wilson as Bill Jackson*

It's hard to say who is demeaned more in this show, the black domestics or the white employers. On the one hand, *Beulah* is the first nonmusical TV network show with a black in a leading role. Or course, the leading role is that of a maid, Beulah, who caters to the white Henderson family. Beulah is the "Queen of the Kitchen" and she is always solving crises here and there, but her character is sort of embarrassing, especially in the ridiculous regular opening, when the big black maid cries "Somebody bawl fo' Beulah?"

The other blacks are not much help. Beulah's boyfriend, Bill Jackson, defines the word *shiftless,* but Beulah's pal Oriole, another maid, is lively and fun.

Still, when talking about demeaning portrayals in *Beulah,* lets not overlook the abysmal Hendersons, the whites. They are one of the most idiotic, klutziest families in TV history. They can't seem to do anything right, unless Beulah helps, of course.

*Beulah* is a show best left forgotten. ■

**BEULAH LAND (*½) (6hr miniseries Color; 1980 NBC) Drama** *with Lesley Ann Warren as Sarah Pennington Kendrick, Meredith Baxter Birney as Lauretta Pennington, Paul Rudd as Leon Kendrick, Hope Lange as Deborah Kendrick, Eddie Albert as Felix Kendrick, and Don Johnson as Bonard Davis*

This listless miniseries, based on novels by Lonnie Coleman, centers on two rival clans in the pre- and post-Civil War South. The only spice comes from lots of forceful women and heaving breasts. Check out the pre–*Miami Vice* Don Johnson as heir to the Oaks plantation.

**THE BEVERLY HILLBILLIES (***) 30 min (274ep: 106 B&W & 168 Color & 2 hr sequel; 1962–1971 CBS) Situation Comedy** *with Buddy Ebsen as Jed Clampett, Irene Ryan as Daisy "Granny" Moses, Donna Douglas as Elly May Clampett, Max Baer, Jr., as Jethro Bodine, Raymond Bailey as Milburn Drysdale, and Nancy Kulp as Jane Hathaway*

Time has been kind to *The Beverly Hillbillies.* When the show first burst upon the national scene, it was lambasted for its low-brow humor and its silly characters. In spite of the critical brickbats, *The Beverly Hillbillies* shot to the top of the ratings and stayed a very popular show throughout the 1960s, spawning an entire genre of rural-based sitcoms.

Now that a generation has passed, it is time for TV critics to swallow hard and admit what most Americans have known all along, *The Beverly Hillbillies* is a wonderfully funny show that wears the badge "popular TV sitcom" proudly. The show has aged well, still can elicit a generous helping of laughs, and even evidences some aspects of biting social sarcasm that few cultural observers noted when the show first appeared.

As most TV viewers are aware, *The Beverly Hillbillies* is the saga of Jed Clampett, an Ozark mountain widower, his mother-in-law Granny, his daughter Elly May, and his nephew Jethro. One day, while hunting for food, Jed comes across some "bubbling crude" on his land. It's "black gold," Texas tea," or, in more mundane parlance, *oil.* Lots of oil. Jed becomes a millionaire almost overnight, as he sells the drilling rights on his land to the OK Oil Company. As long as the oil keeps flowing from Jed's land, the money keeps rolling into Jed's pocket.

As a man of wealth, Jed is advised to move up in the world. He loads his family and belongings on the Clampett jalopy, hillbilly-style, and they drive to the fabled realms of Beverly Hills, California, land of "swimmin' pools and movie stars." The Clampett fortune, originally $25 million, is deposited in the Commerce Bank run by Milburn Drysdale, an erudite social climber with a snobby wife. As the largest depositor in the Commerce Bank, Jed Clampett becomes Mr. Drysdale's main concern in life, for if the Clampett fortune is shifted elsewhere, Drysdale's career will be ruined. To keep an eye on his treasured clients, Mr. Drysdale arranges for Jed to purchase an enormous mansion right next door to the Drysdale's own spread.

The most obvious laughs in *The Beverly Hillbillies* come at the expense of the Clampetts, who are mostly befuddled when exposed for the first time to things city folk take for granted, such as indoor plumbing and door bells. The better laughs come from the other direction, as the so-called urbane, cultured Beverly Hills set stops at nothing to cater to the whims of the Clampetts, due solely to the hillbillies' newfound fortune. The shallowness of the alleged sophisticates is laid bare, as all their assumed high standards give way in the face of the Clampetts' money.

All but one of the characters in *The Beverly Hillbillies* is a caricature, and the broad painting of these roles allows the show to run away on light flights of fancy that would be impossible with more realistic portrayals. Granny is an inveterate cynic, an unreconstructed Confederate who sees nothing in the city that can beat the old mountain ways she grew up with. Her answer to most problems is to concoct a witchlike brew that will cast a spell, break a spell, or just taste awful. If it fails, Granny is the first to get out the rifle and prepare for combat against anyone threatening the family's peace.

Elly May is the ultimate innocent. Blessed with a starlet's figure (shown off well in her tight-fitting jeans), Elly is never able to figure out that most every man she meets has designs upon her. She also can't understand why her passion for wild animals and wrestling seems to cool off her army of suitors.

Jethro is the country rube personified. Struggling to complete his grade school education as he enters his twenties, Jethro's head is turned around by all the pretty girls and fancy cars available to him. The only occupation that appeals to Jethro is that of professional playboy, but he never seems to get the hang of it as his hulking, country ways show through every time.

Milburn Drysdale is marvelously shameless as he panders to every desire of his Ozark neighbors. Drysdale will wear stupid clothes, say silly things, turn his life upside down just to avoid angering the Clampetts. Drysdale's aide-de-camp, Jane Hathaway, is peerless in her female martinet role. She personifies the bloodless yet efficient corporate type who sees life only as business and sees business as all of life. The Clampetts always try to get Jane to loosen up a bit, to no avail.

The only sensible person in the lot is Jed. Amidst all the wild hubbub that always develops, Jed can be counted on to keep his cool and come up with a solution. Jed is the only character who successfully blends the two cultures in the show. He relies on his Ozark common sense, but he also learns what is valuable from urban society and tries to marry the best of both worlds.

Numerous colorful secondary characters come and go throughout the show's run. Bea Benadaret plays Pearl Bodine, Jed's sister and Jethro's mother, who stayed home in the hills when the family hit it rich. Benadaret turns up frequently in the first season but disappears to star in the first *Beverly Hillbillies*-inspired spin-off, *Petticoat Junction.* Louis Nye, who made a living overacting, appears early as the Drysdales' good-for-nothing overage playboy son Sonny. Elly May's beau during the show's middle years is Dash Riprock, a bubble-headed pretty boy movie star, whose real name had been Homer Noodleman before coming to Hollywood. Bluegrass music legends Lester Flatt and Earl Scruggs, who wrote the delightful theme song "The Ballad of Jed Clampett," turn up about once a year as old-time pals of Jed's. Keep an eye out, in the early episodes, for the character of Janet Trego, one of Drysdale's secretaries, who was portrayed by Sharon Tate, a young actress who would meet a grizzly fate in real life at the hands of Charles Manson and his group before *The Beverly Hillbillies* left the air.

Nine years is a long time for any sitcom, and *The Beverly Hillbillies* probably could have done better by calling it quits after five or six. Still, the free-for-all looseness and lightness of the show and the deftly daft characters keep the program watchable for a long time. *The Beverly Hillbillies* does not aim to do much more than make you laugh, but it succeeds in its aim more often than not.

Producer Paul Henning, never known for high-brow TV series, milked the rural humor vein he tapped in *The Beverly Hillbillies* in later spin-offs such as *Green Acres* and *Petticoat Junction.*

In a 1981 two-hour made for TV movie, *The Return of the Beverly Hillbillies,* most of the original cast update the family's exploits since they left weekly TV. Jed has moved back to the simpler life of the Ozarks now that Granny has died. Elly May runs her own zoo, Jane Hathaway works for the U.S. Department of Energy, and Jethro (portrayed in the sequel by Ray Young) has found his perfect niche as head of Mammoth Film Studios in Hollywood, where he is never far from an unending stream of starlets. ■

**BEVERLY HILLS BUNTZ (**) 30 min (9ep Color; 1987–1988 NBC) Situation Comedy** *with Dennis Franz as Norman Buntz, Peter Jurasik as Sidney "Sid the Snitch" Thurston, and Dana Wheeler-Nicholson as Rebecca Giswold*

Producers never really learn that second bananas rarely can make it on their own show. *Beverly Hills Buntz* is a classic example of the problems inherent in taking an interesting secondary character from a hit show and trying to send him on his own.

In *Hill Street Blues,* Norm Buntz was one of the highlights of the later seasons, combining his repulsively banal tastes and habits with an utterly noble and courageous personality that cut through a lot of the surface trappings many people take for significant attributes. In the *Hill Street* finale, Buntz punches out pompous Police Chief Daniels and quits the force. In *Beverly Hills Buntz,* we see Norm resettled from the cold and dreary streets of *Hill Street* to the sunny beaches of Los Angeles. Accompanied by his unshakable informer ("snitch") Sidney Thurston, Buntz sets up shop in Beverly Hills as a private eye, and tries to adapt his brutally honest personality to the laid-back lifestyle of the West Coast.

It all sounds like a rather workable format, but it never goes anywhere. *Beverly Hills Buntz* never knows if it is a sardonic black comedy or a topical drama. With Buntz being the leading character now, the producers feel obligated to tone down the more abrasive (but fascinating) aspects of Buntz's personality. Norm's erstwhile buddy Sidney is more and more irrelevant, being used only as the source of geeky humor. When Norm winds up having an affair with a policeman's widow from "back home," it is evident that Norm Buntz has become just another wisecracking private eye in sunny California. Buntz should have stayed on Hill Street.

**BEWITCHED (***) 30 min (252ep: 72 B&W & 180 Color; 1964–1972 ABC) Situation Comedy** *with Elizabeth Montgomery as Samantha Stephens, Dick York and Dick Sargent as Darrin Stephens, Agnes Moorehead as Endora, David White as Larry Tate, Alice Pearce and Sandra Gould as Gladys Kravitz, Paul Lynde as Uncle Arthur, Marion Lorne as Aunt Clara, and Alice Ghostley as Esmerelda*

The concept of *Bewitched* is appealing. Samantha is a comely lass engaged to marry upwardly mobile adman Darrin Stephens. Just before the nuptials, Samantha reveals her deep, dark secret to Darrin. She's a witch. A real witch, with supernatural powers, who's been around hundreds, if not thousands, of years. Tired of all the magical folderol that goes along with being a working witch, Samantha decides to chuck it all and marry the mortal she is in love with. Darrin, taken aback as anybody would be by this revelation, decides to go ahead with the marriage, but on the condition that "Sam" curtail her use of witchly powers to the absolute minimum.

Darrin is always desperate to hide his wife's background from the rest of the world. Samantha is constantly trying to please her husband by sticking to the mortal straight and narrow, but cannot help backsliding into a little witchcraft now and then (especially when doing housework). Samantha's resolve is sorely tested by her relatives (particularly her mother Endora) who oppose this "mixed" marriage and urge her to return to the supernatural fold.

A lot of fun comes from Samantha's magic tricks, which are caused by her twitching her pretty little nose. Samantha can move objects through the air, make things disappear, and call up characters out of history.

Headliner Elizabeth Montgomery (daughter of veteran thespian Robert Montgomery) brings a sensual, yet dignified, quality to Samantha, as she demonstrates that witches have problems just like everybody else. Agnes Moorehead is regal as the never forgiving mother-in-law who is mortified that a mortal has made off with her daughter. Alice Ghostley is fun to watch as Esmeralda, the timid maid/witch, who will disappear when spoken to harshly. Paul Lynde is his usual overacting self as Samantha's noisy Uncle Arthur, who plays well off the icy Endora. Rounding out the primary cast are nosy neighbor Gladys Kravitz and Samantha's addle-brained Aunt Clara.

The concept of the mixed witch/mortal marriage is great, but the placement of the characters in an extremely bland suburban setting detracts from the fun. Husband Darrin is a real bore, always trying to stifle any signs of life and excitement in Samantha. Darrin is the typical 1950s male white-collar slave, always bowing and scraping before his all-powerful boss (in this case, Larry Tate). You begin to wonder why on earth Samantha gave up the exciting world of witchcraft to do housework drudgery for a boring guy like Darrin Stephens. Since it is mostly the witches and warlocks who are the most interesting characters in *Bewitched,* viewers may come to agree with Endora. Maybe Sam *did* make a big mistake.

In the middle of the second season, the Stephens' first child, Tabitha, is born, resulting in lots of syrupy sweet cute baby witch shticks. At the start of the sixth season, a son, Adam, is born, but he does not make much of a splash in the show. Adam appears just after Dick Sargent replaces Dick York as Darrin. The change is minimal. Sargent's Darrin is slightly more appealing, but not by much. On the whole, the last few seasons are forgettable, and can be avoided without losing much.

Since *Bewitched* is a good, but not great, show, it is not surprising to know that its executive producer, Harry Ackerman, produced several other good, but not great, sitcoms, such as *Bachelor Father, Dennis the Menace, The Farmer's Daughter, Gidget, Love on a Rooftop, Occasional Wife,* and *The Second Hundred Years.* A brief and forgettable spin-off from *Bewitched* appeared in 1977 and 1978, called *Tabitha,* which focused on the now-grown daughter of Samantha and Darrin. Tabitha's brother Adam appears in the show also, but the only carryover from the cast of *Bewitched* is Bernard Fox, as the very minor character of Dr. Bombay (Samantha's physician in the original series).

**BEYOND WESTWORLD (*) 60 min (5ep Color; 1980 CBS) Science Fiction** *with Jim McMullan as John Moore, James Wainwright as Simon Quaid, William Jordan as Joseph Oppenheimer, and Connie Sellecca as Pamela Williams*

A lame follow-up to two fairly successful (and entertaining) movies (*Westworld* and *Futureworld*), *Beyond Westworld* presents a variation of the familiar tale of a mad scientist (in this case, Simon Quaid) who wants to take over the world. Quaid's convoluted evil plot uses his lifelike robots, who populate Westworld, an amusement park where visitors can live out their fantasies.

Avoid this series and look for the two original films instead.

**BIFF BAKER, U. S. A. (**½) 30 min (26ep B&W; 1952–1953 CBS) Adventure** *with Alan Hale, Jr., as Biff Baker and Randy Stuart as Louise Baker*

One of the earliest examples of the globe-hopping spy to turn up on TV, Biff Baker is a secret U.S. operative whose cover is the importing business. While Biff is always running into trouble in his travels, at least he has the thoughtfulness to bring his wife along. Hence, there are not many romantic encounters with beautiful Soviet agents for Biff.

The chief interest in *Biff Baker* is the leading man, Alan Hale, Jr., who is better known to TV fans as The Skipper in *Gilligan's Island.* Biff Baker is a much better spy than The Skipper is a boat captain. Baker, at least, never gets lost.

**BIG EDDIE (**) 30 min (13ep Color; 1975 CBS) Situation Comedy** *with Sheldon Leonard as "Big" Eddie Smith, Sheree North as Honey Smith, Quinn Cummings as Ginger Smith, Billy Sands as Monte "Big Bang" Valentine, and Alan Oppenheimer as Jessie Smith*

Sheldon Leonard is known as a behind-the-scenes man, for his role as producer of *Make Room for Daddy, The Andy Griffith Show,* and *The Dick Van Dyke Show,* among others. He turned up as an actor infrequently in all those sitcoms, but only in *Big Eddie* did he finally land a starring role. Unfortunately, *Big Eddie* comes nowhere near the quality of Leonard's previous hit productions. Leonard plays Big Eddie, a reformed gangster who milks his Brooklyn mobster "dem, dese, dose" dialect to the maximum, and then some. Big Eddie's reformation is caused by the presence of Ginger, his granddaughter, who moves in with Eddie and his wife Honey.

Credit must be given to the broad, loose humor of *Big Eddie.* After all, Honey must be the only lead female character in a sitcom who used to be a stripper, and Leonard is fun as the lumbering ex-mob man. *Big Eddie* is produced by Bill Persky and Sam Denoff, the producers of *That Girl* and colleagues of Leonard in the *Dick Van Dyke* production team.

**THE BIG EVENT Various (Color; 1976–1981 NBC) Variety**

For four seasons, NBC aired a grab bag of special programming under the umbrella title *The Big Event.* Contents of the series tended to big-scale movies (*Gone with the Wind, 2001: A Space Odyssey, The Godfather Saga*), made-for-TV films (*Sybil, The Father Knows Best Reunion*), and miniseries (*Holocaust, Centennial*).

**BIG HAWAII (*½) 60 min (12ep & 2 hr pilot Color: 1977 NBC) Drama** *with Cliff Potts as Mitch Fears, John Dehner as Barrett Fears, Lucia Stralser as Karen "Keke" Fears, and Bill Lucking as Oscar Kalahani*

Sort of a Hawaiian permutation of *Dallas,* this sprawling soaper is set on the huge Paradise ranch on the island of Hawaii. The central focus is on the conflict between boss man Barrett Fears and his prodigal, rebellious son Mitch.

The pilot is called *Danger in Paradise.*

**THE BIG PICTURE (*) 30 min (B&W; 1951–1964 Syndication & ABC) Documentary** *with Capt. Carl Zimmerman as narrator*

If you want to see what TV of the 1950s *really* looked like, watch *The Big Picture.* Sure you could spend your time checking out Lucy and Desi or the fabled dramatic offerings of *Playhouse 90,* but those were just the few big ticket items that garnered all the attention. If you really lived in the 1950s and just happened to flip on your big screen Philco or Zenith, you could not watch for long without bumping into *The Big Picture.*

This was a series produced and directed by the U.S. Army. They recycled a lot of Signal Corps film footage, added a narrator and, *voila,* had a "documentary" series that served as a great public relations gimmick to present the Army's view of the world and itself. One week you might see the test firing of a new nuclear missile, while the next week's show might present a view of American tanks rumbling into some far-off land, seeking to pacify the unruly natives. ABC, which had more than its share of dead air space in the 1950s, ran the show throughout the decade. Local stations, with oodles of time to fill, snapped up the show and ran it well into the 1960s, in time slots all over the schedule.

The series may seem archaic now, but in an era of mostly live in-studio shows, *The Big Picture* was one of the few sources of rock-'em sock-'em action in the great outdoors. Consequently it did have a certain undeniable appeal to those local programmers seeking something more lively than *Winky Dink and You.*

**BIG SHAMUS, LITTLE SHAMUS (*½) 60 min (13ep Color; 1979 CBS)** *with Brian Dennehy as Arnie Sutter, Doug McKeon as Max Sutter, George Wyner as George Korman, Kathryn Leigh Scott as Stephanie Marsh, and Cynthia Sikes as Jingles Lodestar*

You've seen Brian Dennehy in guest shots, supporting roles, and occasional leads in dozens of theatrical feature films, made-for-TV movies, and television series. He's a big man with an expressive face, so he often gets cast as a tough cop or detective, usually a maverick type. After one such role on *Cagney and Lacy,* he was even offered a spin-off series with that character. Based on what happened with *Big Shamus, Little Shamus,* it's easy to understand why he turned that down. In its original network run, only two episodes of the series ever aired, though more were produced.

The setting is Atlantic City, following the legalization of gambling. Dennehy plays Arnie Sutter, a long-time house detective for the once-dying Ansonia Hotel that suddenly finds business booming with new hustling clientele. Arnie is divorced but lives with his thirteen-year-old son, Max (the "little shamus" of the title), and that pushes the series tone more in the direction of a warm family drama—even while dealing with hookers and thieves. Rounding out the cast are faces familiar from other series, including George Wyner (*Hill Street Blues*) as Arnie's boss, Cynthia Sikes (*St. Elsewhere*) as an undercover security agent, and Kathryn Leigh Scott (the daytime soaper *Dark Shadows*) as the assistant manager.

**THE BIG SHOW (*) 90 min (13ep Color; 1980 NBC) Variety Anthology** *with various guest hosts*

A last-gasp revival of the lavish, big-budget prime-time network variety series, launched by NBC when it was mired in the ratings cellar. The program certainly stood out from the competition, but not enough to justify the huge network investment. Instead, it only seemed to confirm that the era for such a truly mixed-bag approach to variety had passed. Audiences might enjoy grandiose fountains, ice skating, water ballet, and comedy sketches (with performers ranging from Dean Martin to Monty Python's Graham Chapman)—just not all on the same TV show. Available for rerun syndication, but don't expect to see it very often.

**THE BIG STORY (*) 30 min (39ep B&W; 1957–1958 Syndication) Drama Anthology** *with Burgess Meredith as host*

Dramatic recreations of then-famous newspaper stories (both human interest and crime related), usually including the reporters in the wraparound narration. The series originally ran on NBC from 1949 to 1957, then continued for one season in snydication. Those are the episodes still available. Throughout the run, the writers received a $500 cash award for use of their story. Obviously, these decades-old stories are rather dated now.

**BIG TOWN** (see *By-Line: Steve Wilson*)

**THE BIG VALLEY** (***) **60 min (112ep Color; 1965–1969 ABC) Western** *with Barbara Stanwyck as Victoria Barkley, Richard Long as Jarrod Barkley, Peter Breck as Nick Barkley, Lee Majors as Heath Barkley, and Linda Evans as Audra Barkley*

Take the sprawling western nature of *Bonanza,* mix in a heaping dose of intrafamily squabbling from *Falcon Crest,* and, voila, you have *The Big Valley.* Like *Bonanza,* there is an aging single parent running a huge ranch in the old West, with a brood of grown and frisky offspring to contend with. Like *Falcon Crest,* a powerful female matriarch rules the clan.

Barbara Stanwyck is intense and tough as the chief Barkley, and she is helped out by top-flight acting talent in her TV offspring. Refined son Jarrod, the lawyer, is played by Richard Long, (of *Bourbon Street Beat* and *77 Sunset Strip* fame). Hot-tempered ranch foreman Nick is played by Peter Breck, whose dark handsome looks were largely ignored by viewers in *Black Saddle* in the late 1950s. *Dynasty* glitter queen-to-be Linda Evans has her first TV starring role as Audra, the beautiful headstrong daughter. The perfect match for Evans' good looks is superhunk Lee Majors (*The Six Million Dollar Man, The Fall Guy*), also in his first starring role, as the half-breed Barkley, the product of an illicit liaison by the deceased Mr. Barkley with an Indian squaw.

*The Big Valley*'s three producers, Jules Levy, Arthur Gardner, and Arnold Laven, also produced *The Rifleman* and *Honey West.* ■

**THE BILL DANA SHOW** (**½) **30 min (42ep B&W; 1963–1965 NBC) Situation Comedy** *with Bill Dana as Jose Jimenez, Jonathan Harris as Jerome Phillips, Gary Crosby as Eddie Martin, and Don Adams as Byron Glick*

Bill Dana's Jose Jimenez character was a national favorite in the late 1950s and early 1960s, first on the old Steve Allen TV show and then on several hit comedy albums. Jose was a simple, nervous Latin American who spoke with a heavy accent. He was forever getting into sticky situations due to his uncertain understanding of habits north of the border and his naive trust in human kindness. Part of Jose's appeal was the easy laughs obtained by his dialect-filled mangling of English. Audiences did not, however, just laugh *at* Jose's malapropisms. They also laughed *with* him as Jose lampooned the super-serious world of American culture through some simple-minded but astute comments on our culture.

In *The Bill Dana Show,* Jose turns up as a bellhop in a swank New York City hotel. Being a bellhop is just about the sum total of Jose's life, because not only does he work long shifts at the hotel but he also lives there in a small apartment supplied by hotel management (in lieu of salary, no doubt). Some of Jose's relatives drop by now and then, but the series is mostly Jose, the hotel, and the people found there.

The hotel staff and guests add a lot of flavor to *The Bill Dana Show.* Jonathan Harris, later the loathsome Dr. Scott in *Lost in Space,* plays the equally odious hotel manager, Mr. Phillips, who has little patience for Jose's predicaments. Don Adams (in his first major TV role) appears as klutzy house detective Byron Glick, in a virtual dry run of Adams's Maxwell Smart character from *Get Smart.* Gary (son of Bing) Crosby is Eddie Martin, another hotel bellhop, one not so trusting of human nature as Jose.

Aside from the great cast, *The Bill Dana Show* has two pros behind the cameras, executive producers Danny Thomas and Sheldon Leonard. Leonard was Danny's producer in *Make Room for Daddy,* and went on to produce *The Dick Van Dyke Show.* Yet in spite of all this talent, The Bill Dana Show does not age very well. The writing is not that good and the very character of Jose Jimenez is a quaint relic of an older era before ethnic-oriented humor became a politically charged topic. The great cast and a chance to see Bill Dana at his height of popularity make *The Bill Dana Show* worthwhile watching for an episode or two, but not much more.

**BILL MOYERS' JOURNAL** (***) **60 min (1972–1976 & 1979–1981 PBS) Documentary** *with Bill Moyers*

An eclectic and wonderful series of public affairs programs from Lyndon Johnson's former press secretary, produced between Moyers' stints at CBS. This series combines documentaries, essays, and discussions into a mix that represents some of the best TV journalism of the 1970s. ■

**BILLY** (½) **30 min (13ep Color; 1979 CBS) Situation Comedy** *with Steve Guttenberg as Billy Fisher, James Gallery as George Fisher, Peggy Pope as Alice Fisher, Paula Trueman as Grandma, and Michael Alaimo as Norval Shadrack*

Billy daydreams. A perfectly normal trait for a nineteen-year-old boy. Understandable considering his job (an assistant mortician's clerk at Shadrack and Shadrack funeral home). But unlike everybody else, his dreams come to life, at least for a little while—thanks to the magic of Hollywood special effects (and celebrity promotion). So the real action stops and Billy's daydreams take hold, often involving famous personalities or TV characters such as the Incredible Hulk or Suzanne Somers, who actually appear on camera. Oddly, having the real performers there hurts the effect because, instead of coming off like a dream come true, it's more like switching channels between a couple of different TV programs. The sequences focusing just on his personal aspirations and fantasies are more effectively dreamlike, but the whole program is pretty much an unfocused mess.

Based on the British series *Billy Liar.* Steve Guttenberg has had much greater success with such theatrical features as the *Police Academy* films and *Three Men and a Baby.*

**BING CROSBY SHOW (*½) 30 min (28ep B&W; 1964–1965 ABC) Situation Comedy** *with Bing Crosby as Bing Collins, Beverly Garland as Ellie Collins, Carol Faylen as Janice Collins, and Diane Sherry as Joyce Collins*

Bing Crosby's one and only regular TV series is a pure formula TV sitcom. The show is modeled after Danny Thomas's *Make Room for Daddy,* in that Crosby plays a *thinly* disguised version of himself. The difference is that Bing Collins (as opposed to Bing Crosby) is retired from the hectic world of professional crooning to enjoy the pleasures of family living in Nameless Suburb, U.S.A. Bing's TV wife Ellie is not content with staying at home. She craves to enter the glamorous world of show business herself, and bugs Bing to get her a break (shades of *I Love Lucy*). Bing is saddled with two typical sitcom daughters, Janice, a fifteen-year-old battling her way through puberty, and Joyce, a ten-year-old who is a child genius. Even though Bing is supposed to be retired, he still manages to sing a song or two per episode.

Bing was one of the last of the radio superstars to take the plunge into weekly television production. If Bing could resist the allurement of TV for so long, it's too bad he had to wind up on such a boring sitcom. If you are a fan of the "Old Groaner," wait for a rerun of one of his numerous classy variety specials. There was not much reason to watch *The Bing Crosby Show* when it was made and there is precious little reason to watch it now. ■

**BIOGRAPHY (**½) 30 min (91ep: 65 B&W & 26 Color; 1961–1964 & 1979–1980 Syndication) Documentary** *with Mike Wallace (B&W) and David Janssen (Color) as narrator*

*Biography* is a video scrapbook of the lives of a wide range of celebrities from the twentieth century. Politicians are heavily represented, both the famous (Winston Churchill) and the infamous (Adolf Hitler), but so are scientists, artists, athletes, and entertainers.

The series is produced by David Wolper (*Making of the President, Roots*) and the original black-and-white run is narrated by Mike Wallace (*60 Minutes*). The later, inferior, color version uses David Janssen (*The Fugitive*) as narrator.

Don't look to *Biography* for any thoughtful analysis of historical trends, but it does provide a virtually timeless scrapbook overview of numerous characters you may want to know more about.

**THE BIONIC WOMAN (**½) 60 min (58ep Color; 1976–1978 ABC & NBC) Science Fiction** *with Lindsay Wagner as Jaime Sommers, Richard Anderson as Oscar Goldman, and Martin E. Brooks as Dr. Rudy Wells*

In the world of comic-book-style fiction, nothing as insignificant as death ever gets in the way of a good plot. Or a good spin-off series.

The character of Jaime Sommers first appeared in several episodes of *The Six Million Dollar Man* as a love interest for Steve Austin. They had once been engaged, but Austin's career as an astronaut got in the way and they split. Then Steve Austin had the flight accident, which led to the operation that turned him into a bionic superman.

A skydiving accident put Jaime in the same situation, with the same result: an operation replacing some of her crushed limbs with bionic parts. Sporting new legs, a new right arm, and a new right ear, Jaime Sommers became the Bionic Women. She and Austin might have become the perfect "super" couple, but then complications set in and she ended up close to death.

But not *that* close. She recovered completely, except for parts of her memory, including her feelings for Austin. So for the duration of the series, they were destined to be "just good friends," especially once the Bionic Woman went off to her own program.

This calculated spin-off even brought along Oscar Goldman, Steve Austin's boss at the Office of Scientific Information (OSI), to supply dangerous missions for Jaime. Still, Lindsay Wagner managed to bring a slightly different feel to her series, if only because she was a female hero battling those aliens, robots, spies, and other evil forces. She even got her own pet Bionic Dog, a German Shepherd named Max.

And at least she didn't have to wear some silly outfit like Lynda Carter's in *Wonder Woman.* ■

**BIZARRE (**) 30 min (125ep Color; 1980–1984 Showtime) Comedy-Variety** *with John Byner as host*

Producers Allan Blye and Bob Einstein, two behind-the-scenes veterans of the *Smothers Brothers Comedy Hour* (Einstein also appeared onstage as Officer Judy), created this vanguard cable TV comedy series. With the extra freedom that cable provides, *Bizarre* sometimes veers toward the intentionally outrageous, but the bluer segments have been deleted for the over-the-air syndication version of the show. Popular comic impressionist John Byner does well as host. A tame pilot of the series ran on ABC in 1979, with Richard Dawson as host.

**THE BLACK ADDER (***) (18ep at Summer 1989 Color; 1983 & 1985 & 1987 UK BBC) Comedy** *with Rowan Atkinson as Edmund (the Black Adder), Tony Robinson as Baldrick, Brian Blessed as Henry VII, Miranda Richardson as Queen Elizabeth I, Stephen Fry as Lord Welchett, Patsy Byrne as Nursie, Hugh Laurie as George, Tim McInnerny as Lord Percy, and Helen Atkinson-Wood as Mrs. Miggins*

A crude but very funny "alternative" history of Britain, ostensibly setting the record straight on wars, royalty, and personal heroics, beginning with the battle of Bosworth Field in 1485 and continuing through Elizabethan times. Actually, considering most Americans don't know much about what really happened in England back then, for us it might be more accurate to call *The Black Adder* the perfect antidote for one-too-many super-serious British historical dramas. It's a period piece black comedy, complete with anachronisms, insults, and plenty of lusty violence (including an inadvertent beheading in the very first story).

*Not the Nine O'Clock News* veteran Rowan Atkinson (who co-created the series) plays the title character (also known as Edmund), a lazy, weaselly liar who slithers his way into increasing power and influence, though still feeling deprived of what he knows he *really* deserves. In the first six episodes, Brian Blessed (Augustus on *I. Claudius*) is his father, Richard IV, who comes to power after the luckless Richard III (Peter Cook) fails to make it home after a triumphant victory on the battlefield. (Edmund knows why, but he's not telling anyone how the king, er, lost his head.)

For the next round of episodes (*Black Adder II*), the setting changes to the court of Queen Elizabeth I, with Edmund considerably more confident and aggressively insulting. Those traits reach their caustic heights in *Black Adder the Third,* with Edmund as the personal aide to Percy, the Prince of Wales—a terribly stupid member of the royal family with nothing to do. He deserves everything Edmund dishes out. In each setting, the loyal manservant Baldrick is there at Edmund's side.

The series is extremely well written, with elaborate verbal insults and twists on historical and literary allusions worthy of *Monty Python.* Most viewers agree that *Black Adder II* and *Black Adder the Third* are less violent and more polished than the first group of episodes, but all have a sharp, caustic edge. In 1989, A&E and the BBC began work on an additional round of episodes, *Black Adder IV.*

**BLACK BEAUTY (**½) 60 min (5ep Color; 1978 NBC) Drama** *with Kristoffer Tabori as Luke Gray, Martin Milner as Tom Gray, Eileen Brennan as Annie Gray, William Devane as John Manly, Edward Albert as Lewis Barry, Mel Ferrer as Nicholas Skinner, Ike Eisenmann as Luke Gray (as a child), and Warren Oates as Jerry Baker*

The often heartbreaking journeys of the horse Black Beauty, separated from its loving owner (young Luke Gray) as a colt. For the next thirteen years, the horse moves through a succession of owners (some kind, some cruel), while Luke dreams of being reunited with his special childhood companion. Appropriately sentimental rendition of the Anna Sewell novel.

**BLACK BEAUTY, THE ADVENTURES OF (**) 30 min (52ep Color; 1972–1973 UK London Weekend TV) Adventure** *with William Lucas as Dr. James Gordon, Judi Bowker as Victoria Gordon, Roderick Shaw as Kevin Gordon, Stacy Dorning as Jenny Gordon, and Charlotte Mitchell as Amy Winthrop*

Set in Victorian England (1877) on a comfortable country estate, the adventures of young Judi Gordon and her beautiful stallion, Black Beauty. Despite the title, this is not the setting and story by Anna Sewell, but something closer to Walter Farley's *The Black Stallion.* Judi's dad, brother, sister, and housekeeper also occasionally get involved. ■

**BLACK SADDLE (***) 30 min (38ep B&W; 1959–1960 NBC & ABC) Western** *with Peter Breck as Clay Culhane, Russell Johnson as Marshal Gib Scott, and Anna Lisa as Nora Travers*

*Black Saddle* is a compelling and intriguing western that, unfortunately, originally got lost in the shuffle in the waning days of the TV western craze. Clay Culhane is a gunfighter who chose to go straight after losing his brothers in gunfights. Clay goes *all* the way straight, all the way to law school. After earning his degree, he winds up in the New Mexico territory, providing assistance to those needing legal help. Who said all those TV westerns are too violent?

Peter Breck later played one of the Barkley boys in *The Big Valley* and Russell Johnson, as "The Professor," later found himself shipwrecked on *Gilligan's Island.*

*Black Saddle* is syndicated, along with episodes of *Johnny Ringo, Law of the Plainsman, The Westerner,* and other 1950s westerns, as part of a series titled *The Westerners.*

**BLACK SHEEP SQUADRON (***½) 60 min (52ep & 2 hr pilot Color; 1976–1978 NBC) War Drama** *with Robert Conrad as Maj. Gregory "Pappy" Boyington, Dana Elcar as Col. Lard, Simon Oakland as Gen. Moore, John Larroquette as Lt. Bob Anderson, Dirk Blocker as Lt. Jerry Bragg, Larry Manetti as Lt. Bob Boyle, Robert Ginty as Lt. T. J. Wiley, W. K. Stratton as Lt. Lawrence Casey, James Whitmore, Jr., as Capt. Gutterman, Jeb Adams as Lt. Jeb Pruitt, Jeff McKay as Lt. Donald French, Katherine Cannon as Capt. Dottie Dixon, and Nancy Conrad as Nurse Nancy*

The exploits of a crack squad of World War II fighter pilots in the Pacific, saddled for its first season with one of television's sillier titles for an action series, *Baa Baa Blacksheep.* This misleading moniker was changed to *Black Sheep Squadron,* which is how the entire series currently plays in rerun syndication.

This is one of producer Stephen J. Cannell's best efforts, perfect for his patented mix of action, humor, and heroics. He makes excellent use of World War II newsreel-style footage to frame scenes, and also works wonders editing a relatively limited amount of airborne "dog-fight" material to maximum effect. Best of all, he has an ideal lead to carry the stories, with Robert Conrad turning in one of his best series performances ever as World War II flying ace Gregory "Pappy" Boyington. And the real Boyington, in fact, acted as a consultant to the series.

Pappy is leader to a squad of military misfits, dubbed the Black Sheep Squadron. What they lack in discipline, though, they more than make up for in their missions which is what allows Pappy to buck the by-the-books brass and (usually) get away with it. Just like the members of the 4077th on *M*A*S*H,* they win many bureaucratic battles simply by getting the job done on the front lines, with victory forgiving their many sins. Eventually their nominal superior officers in the region, Col. Lard and Gen. Moore, become their biggest unofficial boosters.

Though Conrad's Pappy clearly remains the central focus throughout the series (even narrating each episode), the strong supporting cast is used quite well. Over time, this cast even includes Conrad's own daughter, Nancy, as one of the young nurses assigned to their island base (part of a team christened "Pappy's Lambs"). Among the pilots, there are also three next-generation performers, Jeb Adams (son of Nick), Dirk Blocker (son of Dan), and James Whitmore, Jr.

Many of the Black Sheep also went on to success in subsequent series, including John Larroquette (on *Night Court*), Larry Manetti (on *Magnum, P. I.*), Robert Ginty (on *The Paper Chase*), Jeff McKay (on *Tales of the Gold Monkey*), Katherine Cannon (on *Father Murphy*) and Dana Elcar (on *MacGyver*).

**BLACKE'S MAGIC (**) 60 min (12ep & 2 hr pilot Color; NBC 1986) Mystery** *with Hal Linden as Alexander Blacke and Harry Morgan as Leonard Blacke*

A murder mystery series from one of the creators of *Murder, She Wrote* (Peter Fischer). Hal Linden plays Alexander Blacke, a retired magician who finds himself solving murder mysteries in his spare time, beginning with the death of a close friend. He's aided by his con-man dad, Leonard, who finds such tasks far more interesting than life in any retirement home.

The setup has potential, alternating between an emphasis on magic tricks, con games, and murder, but never quite finds its rhythm. However, it's a fine short-run vehicle for Morgan and Linden, who play the father and son team quite nicely.

**BLAKE'S 7 (**½) 60 min (52ep Color; 1978–1981 UK BBC) Science Fiction** *with Gareth Thomas as Roj Blake, Paul Darrow as Kerr Avon, Jacqueline Pearce as Servalan, Michael Keating as Vila, Peter Tuddenham as the voice of computers Orac, Slave, and Zen, Stephen Greif and Brian Croucher as Commander Travis, Josette Simon as Dayna, Steven Pacey as Tarrant, Jan Chappell as Cally, Sally Knyvette as Jenna, Glynis Barber as Soolin, and David Jackson as Gan*

Sometime beyond the twenty-sixth century, Earth is headquarters for the Federation, a ruthless empire that has extended its grip throughout the galaxy. Fighting against it is a small band of rebels, spearheaded by a savvy, principled leader named Roj Blake. His goal: Smash the Federation.

At first glance, this British science fiction series looks to be pretty standard space opera stuff, albeit well done. There's plenty of action, most of the episodes are self-contained, and the main characters are well equipped for a sustained romp through the galaxy.

Blake is the consummate heroic rebel, a born leader whose exploits have assumed legendary proportions. He and his crew specialize in sabotage, determined to disrupt Federation computers, communication, trade, and colony control every chance they get. They are pursued by two key agents, Commander Travis (a rogue officer and a hated foe of Blake's from Earth) and Supreme Commander Servalan (an ambitious woman driven by the desire for ultimate power).

All this is in the best tradition of the running battles in such classics as *Flash Gordon, Buck Rogers,* and *Star Wars,* with dedicated heroes set against the leaders of an evil empire (Flash versus Ming, Buck versus Killer Kane, Luke Skywalker versus Darth Vader). But stay with *Blake's 7* a while and you'll notice more than a few unusual twists.

The most obvious one is that Blake and his crew don't get along very well—individual members don't just argue among themselves, sometimes they don't even trust each other. It's clear that they're in the business of revolution for ego, self-protection, or because there's no other option open to them.

Most of them are convicted criminals. Vila is a professional safecracker and break-in artist. Avon was behind a multimillion-dollar computer credit fraud scheme. Blake himself was (falsely) charged with corrupting young children. Even allowing for extenuating circumstances (Gan, for instance, murdered a Federation guard that he saw rape his girlfriend) the fact is that Blake's Seven probably have more in common with the criminal misfits of the Dirty Dozen than Luke Skywalker and Flash Gordon.

Computer genius Kerr Avon is the ultimate in heroic opposites—cold, cynical, manipulative, distrustful, and perfectly willing to shoot someone in the back. He would not hesitate to trade another's life to save his own. Yet Avon stands just a hair behind Blake, respecting his natural leadership abilities but ready to assume control of the ship and crew for his own ends the moment Blake falters or disappears. For about half the series run, Avon gets his wish and does end up as leader.

To what end? That's the most striking aspect of *Blake's 7:* an unmistakable sense of futility. Though Blake's crew manages to destroy some key bases, upset several grand schemes, and even depose a few leaders, the system generally remains intact. They are far better at meting out punishment to deserving evildoers than dismantling the Federation or helping other revolutionaries survive. So the real subtext of the series turns out to be a question of their own survival: How long will

Blake and his various followers hold out against an entrenched empire? How many of them will make it to the final credit roll?

Series creator Terry Nation was certainly no stranger to bleak visions of the future when he put together *Blake's 7.* Not only did he create the ruthless Daleks for *Doctor Who* but he also showcased them in some of the most brutal stories and settings ever to appear on that series. *Blake's 7* simply takes this vision to its frightening conclusion, with ordinary people rather than a Time Lord leading the battle against apparently overwhelming forces.

*Blake's 7* originally ran in Britain for four seasons, with a cliff-hanger dilemma placed at the end of each thirteenth episode. So to keep track of cast and crew changes, be sure to catch the last and first few episodes of each cycle. Above all, don't miss "Blake," the final episode of the entire series—it's a stunner.

And, no, you haven't lost the ability to count—there are *never* seven people in the *Blake's 7* crew at any one time. To reach that magic number, you have to count one or more of the three computer characters: Zen, Orac, and Slave.

**BLANSKY'S BEAUTIES (*½) 30 min (13ep Color; 1977 ABC) Situation Comedy** *with Nancy Walker as Nancy Blansky, Scott Baio as Anthony DeLuca, Eddie Mekka as Joey Luca, Pat Morita as Arnold, Caren Kaye as Bambi Benton, and Lynda Goodfriend as Ethel "Sunshine" Akalino*

Nancy Walker as wisecracking den mother and producer to ten beautiful Las Vegas showgirls. Loud and leering. And just a stopover for Scott Baio and Lynda Goodfriend (moonlighting while working on *Happy Days*), Pat Morita (between stints on *Happy Days* and *Mr. T and Tina*), Caren Kaye (*The Betty White Show* was next), and, of course, Nancy Walker. After years of success as a strong second banana on two series simultaneously (*MacMillan and Wife* and *Rhoda*), this marked Walker's second unsuccessful solo series within one season (*The Nancy Walker Show* being the other). Her next attempt came a decade later (*Mama's Boy*), though in all that time she never gave up her most famous role: Rosie, the diner waitress with the quickest (most absorbent) paper towels in town.

**BLEAK HOUSE (***) 60 min (8ep Color; 1985 UK BBC) Drama** *with Diana Rigg as Lady Dedlock, Denholm Elliott as John Jarndyce, Philip Franks as Richard Carstone, Lucy Hornak as Ada Clare, Donald Sumpter as Capt. Nemo, Bernard Hepton as Krook, Suzanne Burden as Esther Summerson, Robin Bailey as Sir Leicester Dedlock, and T. P. McKenna as Skimpole*

Excellent adaptation of the satirical Charles Dickens novel, painting a typically gloomy picture of the Victorian legal system in action (or rather, nonaction). In this case, it's the Chancery court, originally set up to settle disputed estates, but in fact guaranteed to drag any case well past the lifespans (and financial resources) of everyone involved. So while the would-be heirs (cousins Richard and Ada) await developments, they're shipped off as wards of the court to their bachelor cousin, John Jarndyce. Their companion Esther Summerson joins them there as well. And that's when the narrative really starts rolling, unfolding in layers as a genuine mystery. There's an aristocratic lady with a mysterious past (Lady Dedlock), mysterious deaths (including a case of "spontaneous combustion"), double identities, a surprising romance, and a deadly obsession with the legal system.

**BLESS ME FATHER (**½) 30 min (21ep Color; 1979–1982 UK London Weekend TV) Situation Comedy** *with Arthur Lowe as Father Duddleswell, Peter de Anda, and Gabrielle Daye*

Based on a series of humorous novels (by Peter de Rosa) set in the 1950s, this series looks at the lighter side of Catholic parish life in Britain—not laughing at the faith but at the funny things that happen to the faithful. In this case, they're all at St. Jude's (patron saint of hopeless causes), under the watchful eye of Father Duddleswell, a feisty pastor who stands somewhere between *Going My Way*'s sainted Father Charles O'Malley and *Hell Town*'s street-smart Father Noah "Hardstep" Rivers. He and his newly ordained young cleric (played by Peter de Anda) are there to keep the parishioners on track through preaching, example, and an understanding involvement in their lives. Which means, as in any good comedy, they sometimes find themselves in downright silly situations—whether it's challenging a neighborhood superstition about an unlucky bar stool (Father Duddleswell sits on it) or trying to arrange new bells for the church building. There are also some uniquely Catholic moments, such as a miswired new loudspeaker system that crosses into the private confessional box and broadcasts a confession to the congregation at the church (every Catholic's nightmare).

But it's all done with wry good humor, with the priests emerging as loving, very human members of the community trying to cope with the occasional silliness of the world—just like everyone else.

**BLIND AMBITION (***) (8hr miniseries Color; 1979 CBS) Drama** *with Martin Sheen as John Dean, Theresa Russell as Maureen "Mo" Dean, Rip Torn as Pres. Richard Nixon, Lawrence Pressman as H. R. "Bob" Halderman, Graham Jarvis as John Ehrlichman, and John Randolph as John Mitchell*

After *Washington: Behind Closed Doors,* this is the best Watergate TV miniseries. Based on two books (*Blind Ambition* and *Mo*) by John and Maureen Dean (respectively), *Blind Ambition* views the Nixon era and the Watergate crisis through the eyes of the Dean family.

Dean, White House counsel during the early 1970s, and his wife are an otherwise boring Yuppie couple caught in the growing political furor. Rip Torn is a riot as Nixon, with all the ticks and quirks of the original intact. Martin Sheen (who played Bobby Kennedy in *The Missiles of October,* another great political miniseries) gives a very human portrayal of John Dean, making him seem a lot nicer than he seemed in real life. David Susskind serves as executive producer. An unnecessary gimmick of the miniseries is using some of the transcripts of the Nixon-era White House tapes as the script for key scenes in the Oval Office. The gambit backfires, since the *real* dialogue comes across as highly *un*real and stilted. ■

**BLONDIE (**) 30 min (26ep B&W; 1957 NBC) Situation Comedy** *with Arthur Lake as Dagwood Bumstead, Pamela Britton as Blondie Bumstead, Florenz Ames as Julius C. Dithers, and Hal Peary as Herb Woodley*

In this series, the first attempt to bring Chic Young's popular comic strip to TV, Blondie is the one always trying to keep bumbling husband Dagwood in line. Arthur Lake had already played Dagwood in several Hollywood movies in the 1940s (to Penny Singletons' Blondie) and his plaintive cry of "Blondie!" opens each episode. Pamela Britton, this version of Blondie, later played Lorelei Brown, the nosy landlady on *My Favorite Martian.*

**BLONDIE (**) 30 min (26ep Color; 1968–1969 CBS) Situation Comedy** *with Will Hutchins as Dagwood Bumstead, Patricia Harty as Blondie Bumstead, Jim Backus as Julius C. Dithers, Henny Backus as Cora Dithers, Peter Robbins as Alexander Bumstead, Pamelyn Ferdin as Cookie Bumstead, and Bryan O'Bryne as Mr. Beasley*

The second television version of the Bumstead family came a decade after the first, with Will Hutchins (the soft-spoken cowboy of *Sugarfoot*) and Patricia Harty (the part-time spouse of *Occasional Wife*) a perfectly acceptable (if unexceptional) Blondie and Dagwood. However, Jim Backus is perfectly cast as Mr. Dithers, Dagwood's sputtering boss (and, bringing a touch of real life to the setting, Henny Backus—Jim's wife—is there beside him as Cora Dithers, the boss's wife).

All of the characters are played, appropriately, as fairly straightforward comic strip caricatures, though the chief criticism of this version is that, at times, it's a bit too restrained. The series needs more scenes like Dagwood's smashing into Mr. Beasley, the mailman, on his mad dash to work. Silly, sure, but that's *Blondie.*

**THE BLUE AND THE GREY (**½) (8hr miniseries Color; 1982 CBS) Drama** *with John Hammond as John Geyser, Stacy Keach as Jonas Steele, Colleen Dewhurst as Maggie Geyser, and Lloyd Bridges as Ben Geyser*

Sugar-coated Civil War history is presented through the eyes of *Harper's Weekly* correspondent John Geyser, who conveniently happens to be on the scene for all the major events of the War Between the States. Gregory Peck is august in a bit role as Pres. Lincoln. ■

**THE BLUE ANGELS (*) 30 min (39ep B&W; 1960–1961 Syndication) Adventure** *with Dennis Cross as Cmdr. Arthur Richards, Warner Jones as Capt. Wilbur Scott, Michael Galloway as Lt. Russ MacDonald, and Don Gordon as Lt. Hank Bertelli*

The Blue Angels are a four-man team of precision Navy pilots, who show up at promotional air shows. This TV series, based on their exploits, goes to extremes to drag in some international intrigue and crime-fighting action. The best part is the stock footage of the real Blue Angels in action.

**THE BLUE KNIGHT (***) (8hr miniseries & 23ep 60 min & 90 min pilot Color; 1973 & 1975–1976 NBC & CBS) Police Drama** *with William Holden and George Kennedy as William "Bumper" Morgan and Lee Remick and Barbara Rhoades as Carrie Williamson*

One of the earliest of the "gritty" school of TV cop shows that later bloomed with *Hill Street Blues, Blue Knight* begins as a miniseries starring William Holden as Bumper Morgan, the classic cop on the beat, four days away from retirement. Bumper prefers walking to riding around in some fancy patrol car, and the folks in the neighborhood respond by helping him out when they can.

In the series, with George Kennedy as Bumper, retirement is not mentioned. The producers of the series, Lee Rich and Philip Capice, later tended for more mainstream drama, with *Dallas* and *Knots Landing.* ■

**BLUE LIGHT (**½) 30 min (17ep Color; 1966 ABC) Spy Drama** *with Robert Goulet as David March*

*Blue Light* came and went in a flash, but is worth seeking out, if you can find it. The show appears at first to be a run-of-the-mill adventure yarn, focusing on an American spy posing as a turncoat Nazi sympathizer in World War II Germany. A more careful examination reveals that *Blue Light* has several attributes that distinguish it from similar series.

The show's producer, Buck Houghton, was the original producer of the original *Twilight Zone,* and *Blue Light* has some of the same class and attention to detail as Rod Serling's masterpiece. *Blue Light* stars Robert Goulet, who became famous as a smooth pop singer with a devastatingly handsome physique. Goulet's character (David March) is a pretty-boy correspondent supposedly taken in by the master race philosophy of the Nazis. March is actually working deep undercover as an American agent in the super-secret spy organization code-named Blue Light. Goulet effectively plays slightly against type, since his solid performance as tough-guy spy is a surprising change from the more effete, playboyish character he usually projected as a singer (and continues to present in *Blue Light* in his cover as a supposed Nazi convert).

To make his cover effective, March renounces his American citizenship and spouts Nazi ideology. As a result, he must endure the fervent hatred of his own countrymen who believe that he is a traitor. March must keep one step ahead of both the SS, who are trying to uncover the identity of the Blue Light agents, and other branches of Allied intelligence, who want to kill the American they think has turned against his own.

It is a great concept, somewhat reminiscent of *The Fugitive*, but more limited. David March's extreme precariousness in *Blue Light* does not lend itself to a long series. After all, how many suicide missions could March survive, and how long would it take the SS to find him out? Perhaps it is best that *Blue Light* only lasts a short while. It works better as a miniseries anyway.

**BLUE SKIES (**) 60 min (8ep Color; 1988 CBS) Drama** *with Tom Wopat as Frank Cobb, Season Hubley as Annie Cobb, Kim Hauser as Zoe Cobb, Alyson Croft as Sarah Cobb, Danny Gerard as Charley Cobb, and Pat Hingle as Henry Cobb*

A warm family drama set under the blue skies of the Pacific Northwest with former *Dukes of Hazzard* star Tom Wopat playing a widowed but now remarried advertising man leaving New York for a new life in his old Oregon home town. Even though he and his wife were both previously married (Annie is divorced), the two feel almost like newlyweds exploring new territory, except there are three children between them: He has a sensitive twelve-year-old daughter, Sarah, and a ten-year-old son, Charley, while she has a glib twelve-year-old daughter, Zoe. All of them have to get used to their new mom or dad, which provides an underlying source of conflict throughout the series. So, for instance, when Annie gets pregnant, Sarah is not particularly thrilled. Zoe, on the other hand, is sorely tempted by the reappearance of her natural father, who offers her an invitation to return with him to New York.

Frank and Annie also have adjustments to make, as they begin to settle into a lifestyle quite different from New York City. Overall, a low-key but effective limited-run series.

**BLUE THUNDER (*) 60 min (6ep Color; 1984 ABC) Police Drama** *with James Farentino as Frank Chaney, Dana Carvey as Clinton "Jafo" Wonderlove, Bubba Smith as Lyman "Budda" Kelsey, and Dick Butkus as Richard "Ski" Butowski*

A bad series based on a nasty film, *Blue Thunder* features a maniacal helicopter operated by (who else?) the Los Angeles Police Department. The helicopter does all sorts of mean, nasty things to mean, nasty, bad guys (who do not have their own helicopter to fight back). Ex–pro football jocks Bubba Smith and Dick Butkus are unintentionally hilarious as the ground-based support staff for the flying behemoth. "Jafo" Wonderlove is one of the first of the classic characters of 1980s high-tech shows: the computer whiz/nerd who plays off of the good-looking hunks.

**THE BOAT (Das Boot) (**½) 60 min (6ep: 5 60 min & 1 90 min Color; 1982 West Germany) Drama** *with Juergen Prochonow, Herbert Gronemeyer, Hubertus Bengsch, Klaus Wennemann, Bernd Tauer, Martin Semmelrogge, and Erwin Leder*

A six-episode version of the 1980 theatrical feature film, expanding on the original footage. It's the story of a German U-boat on a World War II mission in the Atlantic, with Juergen Prochonow as the commander directing the strategy. Realistic and surprisingly engrossing—remember, these are supposed to be the bad guys—with an appropriately claustrophobic feel. ■

**BOB & CAROL & TED & ALICE (*) 30 min (7ep Color; 1973 ABC) Situation Comedy** *with Robert Urich as Bob Sanders, Anne Archer as Carol Sanders, David Spielberg as Ted Henderson, Anita Gillette as Alice Henderson, and Jodie Foster as Elizabeth Henderson*

In 1969, Paul Mazursky directed a hit sex film comedy, *Bob & Carol & Ted & Alice,* starring Robert Culp and Natalie Wood as a swinging young couple trying to loosen up their friends, Elliott Gould and Dyan Cannon. The two couples wind up swapping mates, learning a lot about each other, and having fun. In 1973, a TV series based on the film appeared, starring virtually unknown actors at that time, and the show stinks. It is a perfect example of how TV tends to turn funny, sexy ideas into smarmy Pablum.

Needless to say, no wife swapping goes on in the TV version. The hip young couple are the Sanders (he is a filmmaker) and the stodgy couple are the Hendersons (he is a boring lawyer). Lots of lip service is paid to the sexual revolution and there are a lot of allusions to sex, but nothing ever *happens* on this show. It's all talk and no action, just like *Love, American Style,* another titillating sex comedy of the era.

Robert Urich makes his first TV starring role as Bob Sanders, playing the type of sensitive hunk he later became famous for (in shows such as *Vega$* and *Spenser: For Hire*). Anne Archer, who plays Urich's wife, came to fame much later in the movies as the wronged wife in *Fatal Attraction.* Keep an eye peeled for Jodie Foster as the Henderson's little girl. Three years after the TV series was filmed, Foster became a movie superstar as an underage prostitute in Martin Scorsese's violent *Taxi Driver.*

**THE BOB CRANE SHOW (*½) 30 min (14ep Color; 1975 NBC) Situation Comedy** *with Bob Crane as Bob Wilcox, Trisha Hart as Ellie Wilcox, Todd Susman as Marvin Susman, and Jack Fletcher as Dean Lyle Ingersoll*

The star of *Hogan's Heroes* strikes out as a forty-two-year-old insurance executive who leaves the business world to fulfill his lifelong dream of becoming a doctor, by entering medical school. The laughs are few and far between as Crane plays the oldest student in his class. He is an acting trouper, but the concept never seems to click. This is one of the early failures of the MTM production company.

**THE BOB CUMMINGS SHOW (see also *Love That Bob*)**

**THE BOB CUMMINGS SHOW (**) 30 min (22ep B&W; 1961–1962 CBS) Situation Comedy** *with Bob Cummings as Bob Carson, Murvyn Vye as Lionel, and Roberta Shore as Henrietta "Hank" Gogerty*

Not to be confused with Cummings's hit series *Love That Bob* (which was officially known as *The Bob Cummings Show*), this series places Cummings's familiar character of a leering playboy in the role of a charter pilot who is always becoming involved in adventures and romantic escapades. One angle of the show that was meant at the time to be trendy but now seems dated is Bob's use of an "aerocar," a small plane that could easily be converted to an automobile. This series is also known as *The New Bob Cummings Show.*

**BOB HOPE PRESENTS THE CHRYSLER THEATER (**½) 60 min (114ep Color; 1963–1967 NBC) Drama Anthology** *with Bob Hope as host*

After the so-called golden age of TV drama in the middle and late 1950s, this series was the last weekly drama anthology on network TV, and it demonstrates what TV drama had turned into by the mid-1960s. Many of the episodes are really just failed pilots for projected series or early versions of the TV movie, which did not develop a life of their own until the late 1960s. Bob Hope serves as host, tossing in some *bons mots* at the start and end, much like Alfred Hitchcock did in his series.

There are a few standouts here, however, such as a 1963 production of "One Day in the Life of Ivan Denisovich" (with Jason Robards) and a 1964 musical production of "The Seven Little Foys" with Mickey Rooney and the Osmond Brothers.

**THE BOB HOPE SHOW (**) 60 min (B&W & Color; 1950– NBC) Comedy-Variety** *with Bob Hope and various guest stars*

Bob Hope has been the exception to an otherwise iron-clad rule: You can't keep scoring big TV ratings with a straightforward combination of monologue, guests, skits, and music. That's right out of vaudeville or the old network radio comedy-variety shows. It just doesn't fly today.

Except, for Bob Hope, it has worked—whether in the 1950s, 1960s, 1970s, or 1980s. Though taking full advantage of TV technology (especially editing), he's never made a fundamental change to *how* he approaches his television appearances. Unlike friends Jack Benny or George Burns, for instance, Hope has never set up some show-within-a-show sitcom structure. More basic, he's never done a *weekly* TV comedy program. Even when his name was on a weekly series slot in the 1960s (*Bob Hope Presents the Chrysler Theater*), on most episodes he merely introduced a drama anthology presentation. His comedy-variety hours in the slot were presented as *specials.* In short, when Bob Hope does a Bob Hope comedy show, he wants it regarded as something special. And that's how he has continued to work, staging several comedy specials each year even after that regular slot was gone.

There's one unfortunate by-product of that approach. Bob Hope does not have a neat, timeless television vehicle (like a sitcom) that can carry his particular style of humor long after he's gone. The closest he comes are the many comedy-variety hours he handled in the 1950s (under a variety of umbrella titles) and the *Chrysler Presents a Bob Hope Special* programs that ran regularly in his *Chrysler Theater* slot from 1963 to 1967. But these rarely turn up, except in collectors' circles.

Of course, even those programs suffer from (ironically) one of the elements that made them so entertaining in the first place: Hope's references to contemporary events, whether in his choice of skits, guest stars, or zingers in his opening monologues. Some do hold up decades later. Many don't, as the chuckle from immediate recognition at the time turns into a sense of mild puzzlement years later. Still, at least these contain basic Bob Hope in pretty good form. If some of the material is dated, other skits still work.

Sad to say, with only a few exceptions, Hope's many specials since the late 1960s often come off as very shopworn, no matter how glitzy and packed with stars. Whether it's a salute to the Superbowl, America's Bicentennial, another of his birthdays or personal showbiz anniversaries, they inevitably threaten to bury their host in a sea of guest stars, drop-ins, edited effects, and cue-card references. And it's pretty unlikely there will ever be much call for a syndicated package with such titles as "Bob Hope's All Star Comedy Look at the Fall [1981 TV] Season: It's Still Free and Worth It!" Even his monologues in these shows are chopped to pieces, obviously edited from a considerably longer performance.

Thus, there is not much of a clue here as to why people such as Woody Allen and Dick Cavett have long admired Hope's style. Ironically, Hope's most accessible video work may turn out to be such pre-television movies as *Ghost Breakers* (1940) and, of course, the many "Road" pictures, where he perfected his patented cowardly braggadocio mixed with a genuine sense of heroism.

Or, perhaps, we could hope that a full-length Bob Hope live concert surfaces, preferably one not originally intended for TV. He's done thousands—surely there must be film or videotape of at least one from each decade of his career. On stage, alone, just like back in vaudeville, laying joke upon joke upon joke to an appreciative audience. That might be the best video Hope we can hope for. ■

**THE BOB NEWHART SHOW** **(****) 30 min (142ep Color; 1972–1978 CBS) Situation Comedy** *with Bob Newhart as Bob Hartley, Suzanne Pleshette as Emily Hartley, Bill Daily as Howard Borden, Peter Bonerz as Jerry Robinson, Marcia Wallace as Carol Kester Bondurant, Jack Riley as Elliott Carlin, Florida Friebus as Mrs. Bakerman, John Fiedler as Emil Peterson, and Oliver Clark as Mr. Herd*

Bob Newhart is one of television's great reactors. Like Jack Benny, he can get tremendous mileage out of a hurt look, a sustained glare, or an outraged double take. Also like Benny, Newhart knows when not to react, delivering humorous asides with a devastating deadpan.

Best of all, Newhart can play an "Everyman" type character with ease, bringing to everyday situations the type of nervous energy most of us can easily recognize in ourselves.

Bob Newhart has also been blessed with two superb situation comedy setups that allow him to showcase his performing personality perfectly. *Newhart* is his 1980s vehicle, but this series is his classic 1970s setup playing Chicago psychologist Bob Hartley.

Casting Newhart as a shrink was inspired because, for that job, he was supposed to sit, listen, and react. Which he does, without ever getting close to a cure for the likes of neurotic Elliott Carlin, henpecked Emil Peterson, the obsessively inferior Mr. Herd, or any of his other regular patients. And when they are finished, Bob's co-workers such as secretary Carol Kester or orthodontist Jerry Robinson step in, also looking for a sympathetic ear and advice they will probably ignore. Or take, and then blame Bob for the consequences.

As with any other well-rounded career comedy, the scenes at home are just as effective. There, Bob and his wife Emily have the ultimate in intrusive, imposing, but also sweetly helpless neighbors, Howard Borden—an airline navigator who sometimes needs directions to his own apartment across the hall. Or Howard might come in to borrow a cup of milk for his cereal, then remember he also needs sugar, fruit, a spoon, a bowl, *and* the cereal.

Then there's Emily. As played by Suzanne Pleshette, she is one of the most confidently sexy sitcom wives ever to come along. For most of the series, she pursues a career of her own as a grammar school teacher and administrator while Bob is at the office. Some of Bob and Emily's best moments are at the end of the day in bed together, exchanging humorous comments before turning out the lights.

One reason *The Bob Newhart Show* wears so well is that the excellent scripts are filled with a wide variety of humor: simple wordplay, running gags, clever setups, and even occasional slapstick. In addition, Newhart wisely steps back at times and lets all of the characters have a chance to be funny. This is truly an ensemble comedy.

*The Bob Newhart Show* was only the second series produced by Mary Tyler Moore's MTM company, but it certainly won a special place in the hearts of its cast and crew. Long after the final season ended, *Bob Newhart* alumni continued to drop allusions to it. One of the cabbies on *Taxi* chose Carol from *The Bob Newhart Show* as his dream date. On *Alf,* Bill Dailey reversed roles and played a psychiatrist, with Jack Riley there as one of his patients. Riley also appeared as a patient on *St. Elsewhere* along with Oliver Clark, with both playing characters strikingly similar to their *Bob Newhart* roles from ten years before. In a perfect "full circle," Riley also turned up on *Newhart* as a patient for a different psychologist, one who blamed "some quack in Chicago" for the sorry state of Riley's character.

For a while in daily syndication, *The Bob Newhart Show* became the jumping off point for a college student drinking game called "Hiya Bob." The rules were simple: Every time a character greeted Bob either at home or at the office, you had to down some beer. Try it yourself sometime, with your own favorite indulgence. You'll see Bob is quite a popular guy!

**BOBBIE GENTRY'S HAPPINESS HOUR** **(*) 60 min (4ep Color; 1974 CBS) Musical-Variety** *with Bobbie Gentry as hostess*

Bobbie Gentry, the singer renowned for "Ode to Billie Joe," hosts a brief variety series that features an early appearance of Valri Bromfield, a Canadian comedienne who graduated from the Second City comedy troupe and also appeared in two brief but interesting series, *The New Show* and *Best of the West.*

**THE BODY HUMAN** **(***) 30 & 60 min (15ep: eleven 60 min & four 30 min Color; 1977–1983 CBS) Documentary**

Various facets of the human body (genes, senses, gestation, reproduction, heart, brain, etc.) are handled with skill, respect, and entertainment in this acclaimed series of specials. Various celebrities (Marlo Thomas, Cicely Tyson, Ken Howard, Mike Farrell) serve as hosts.

**THE BOLD ONES** **60 min (86ep Color; 1969–1973 NBC) Drama**

This is the umbrella title for *The Doctors, The Lawyers, The Protectors,* and *The Senator.* See each of those titles for more details.

In syndication, episodes of the brief early 1970s series *Sarge* (with George Kennedy) have been added to the original four segments of *The Bold Ones,* in order to boost the series close to the 100-episode mark.

**BOLD VENTURE** (*) **30 min (39ep B&W; 1959 Syndication) Adventure** *with Dane Clark as Slate Shannon, Joan Marshall as Sailor Duval, and Bernie Gozier as narrator King Moses*

Loosely based on a 1951 radio adventure series starring Humphrey Bogart and Lauren Bacall and set in the West Indies. For this typical 1950s exotic location action series, Dane Clark plays expatriate Slate Shannon and Joan Marshall plays his young ward, Sailor Duval. Together they operate a hotel (called Shannon's Place) and a sixty-foot sloop (called *The Bold Venture*) in Trinidad, rounding up the usual assortment of people in need of help, usually against smugglers, thieves, and thugs. It's an extremely well-worn path. In the early 1970s, Clark played Lt. Tragg in that short-run revival of *Perry Mason.*

**BONANZA** (****) **60 min (430ep & 2hr sequel Color; 1959–1973 NBC) Western** *with Lorne Greene as Ben Cartwright, Michael Landon as Joseph "Little Joe" Cartwright, Dan Blocker as Eric "Hoss" Cartwright, Pernell Roberts as Adam Cartwright, David Canary as Candy, Lou Frizzel as Dusty Rhoades, Mitch Vogel as Jamie Hunter, Tim Matheson as Griff King, Ray Teal as Sheriff Roy Coffee, and Victor Sen Yung as Hop Sing*

Throughout the 1960s and into the 1970s, *Gunsmoke* and *Bonanza* were two of the most popular series on television. They essentially kept the western alive in prime time long after most of the other "oaters" had faded. *Gunsmoke*'s well-deserved reputation was as TV's first and best adult western. *Bonanza* earned its following as the definitive family western, a tag that serves it well even today.

This is the story of the Cartwrights—Ben and his sons Adam, Hoss, and Little Joe—a stable, respected family that owns, works, and lives on the thousand-acre Ponderosa ranch near Virginia City, Nevada. They're leaders in the community, champions of fair play, and the solid center for literally hundreds of stories.

One reason *Bonanza* works so well is that each of the central characters has such a distinctive personality: Ben is the firm but loving father, oldest brother Adam is the most serious and introspective, Hoss is the occasionally naive huge bear of a man with a heart of gold, and Little Joe is the impetuous romantic. As a result, the series can shift among the characters, sometimes focusing on the entire family, in other cases showcasing just one or two members. So it's like having a half-dozen different series leads under one title, offering a wide range of characters interacting not only among themselves but with the weekly guest stars as well.

That same variety applies to the stories, too. Though *Bonanza* includes plenty of horseplay (and Hoss play), gunfights, and other typical western hooks, it isn't tied down to one formula. Some episodes are straightforward, serious drama. Others are soapy and sentimental. And sometimes (especially when Hoss and Little Joe team up), the tales are intentionally, undeniably hilarious. (One *unintentionally* humorous moment, though, comes at the end of the first story, when Ben, Adam, Hoss, and Little Joe ride off into the sunset *singing* the words of the *Bonanza* theme. It remained an instrumental thereafter.)

Over the nearly fourteen-year run of the series, there were remarkably few cast changes. Pernell Roberts left after six seasons, and, while a variety of ranch hands (Candy, Jamie, Dusty) stepped in as "practically family," this change really made the bond between the remaining Cartwrights tighter than ever. Just before the end of the series, Dan Blocker died unexpectedly, virtually guaranteeing that the following season would be the last. It was.

By the end there were more than 400 episodes, quite a respectable run. Oddly, even though all of them are in color (unusual for a series begun in the late 1950s), for years about a hundred of these were not included in the syndication package. Then, in the late 1980s, with the success of such closet-cleaning ventures as the "lost episodes" of *The Honeymooners,* the *Bonanza* episodes were returned to syndication under a similar "lost episodes" banner.

At the same time, *Bonanza* also took a cue from another revival hook: continuing the basic premise with a new cast (the strategy used for *Star Trek: The Next Generation*). Lorne Greene was even committed to be part of the 1987 filming for *Bonanza: The Next Generation* (a two-hour pilot), but passed away before his work could be done. Instead, only his portrait (as Ben Cartwright) appears, with the role of father figure going to Ben's brother, Aaron (John Ireland). Rounding out the new Cartwright clan are Barbara Anderson as Anabelle (Little Joe's wife), Michael Landon, Jr., as Ben (their son), Brian A. Smith as Josh (long-lost son of Hoss), Robert Fuller as Ponderosa foreman Charley Poke, and John Amos as family cook and ranch hand Mr. Mack. They all take part in a typical Ponderosa conflict, even edging into modern times with the appearance of those "new-fangled" horseless carriages.

In a way, though, the real continuation of *Bonanza* was *Little House on the Prairie,* as Michael Landon became head of his own western family. It may have been a different character, decade, and setting, but in the cross-pollinating world of series television, it was really "Little Joe" all grown up and on his own. ■

**BONKERS!** (*) **30 min (24ep Color; 1978–1979 Syndication) Musical-Variety** *with Bill Hudson, Brett Hudson, Mark Hudson, and Bob Monkhouse*

This silly variety series (produced by Jack Burns, of the comedy duo Burns & Schreiber) features The Hudson Brothers, a mediocre singing group that TV executives kept trying to pass off as stars throughout the 1970s.

**BOONE** (**½) **60 min (13ep Color; 1983–1984 NBC) Drama** *with Tom Byrd as Boone Sawyer, Greg Webb as Rome Hawley, Barry Corbin as Merit Sawyer, Elizabeth Huddle as Faye Sawyer, and Kitty Moffat as Susannah Sawyer*

The words "Elvis Presley" are never spoken in this series, but they haunt every scene and every aspect of the show. After all, if you were told this series was about a young boy from near Nashville, who leaves high school in 1953, hoping to become a star by playing guitar and singing funked-up country songs, what name would come to your mind? If you then are told that the boy's loving mother dotes all over him and his father wants him to forget singing and get a real job at the filling station, but that the boy perseveres, only to be tossed off the Grand Ol' Opry for being too wild, would any name *but* Elvis Presley be on your mind?

Well, *Boone* is *not* about the late Mr. Pelvis, but rather about Boone Sawyer. Sawyer does not have the sultry sneer of Elvis and looks far too clean-cut to be a rebel (he doesn't even have an outrageous ducktail hairdo, which was de rigueur among proto-rockers in the South). Chalk up the cleanliness to the influence of executive producer Earl Hamner (creator of the equally clean *The Waltons*). A little more gritty reality in *Boone* would have helped.

**BOOTS AND SADDLES—THE STORY OF THE FIFTH CAVALRY** (**) **30 min (39ep B&W; 1957–1958 Syndication) Western** *with Jack Pickard as Capt. Shank Adams, Patrick McVey as Lt. Col. Hayes, and Gardner McKay as Lt. Kelly*

*Boots and Saddles* is yet another run-through of the Old West in the amorphous 1870s, focusing on the good guys (the Cavalry) versus the bad guys (the Injuns). This is the first major role for superhunk Gardner McKay, who practices going through wild adventures without mussing up his hair, in preparation for his appearance in *Adventures in Paradise.*

**BORDER PATROL** **(see *U.S. Border Patrol*)**

**BORDERTOWN** (**) **30 min (24ep at Summer 1989 Color; 1988– CBN) Western** *with John Brennan as Cpl. Clive Bennett, Richard Comar as Marshal Jack Craddock, and Sophie Barjac as Dr. Marie Dumont*

Canadian corporal Clive Bennett (from the Royal Canadian Mounted Police) and U.S. marshal Jack Craddock (a former Texas Ranger) are rival lawmen sharing an office on the border between their two countries. Bennett is a by-the-books RCMP man while Craddock is free-wheeling and headstrong. Naturally, when necessary, they work together, though the competitive spirit between the two extends long past office hours, especially in their respective romantic designs on the town's only doctor, Marie Dumont.

Well, at least by setting this western at the forty-ninth parallel between Canada and the U.S., all that cheaper-to-film-up-there-than-here footage from "up North" makes sense. This is a co-production of CBN and Canada's Global TV.

**BORIS KARLOFF PRESENTS THRILLER** **(see *Thriller*)**

**BORN FREE** (**½) **60 min (13ep Color; 1974 NBC) Adventure** *with Gary Collins as George Adamson, Diana Muldaur as Joy Adamson, Hal Frederick as Makedde, and Peter Lukoye as Nuru*

Well-meaning but ultimately boring, this series is set in a game reserve in East Africa. Gary Collins is the bwana who teaches conservation to the natives. Co-star billing should go to Elsa, the lioness, who is raised by the Adamsons through the series. *Born Free* is based on a novel of the same name by the real Joy Adamson and two hit movies, *Born Free* (1966) and its sequel *Living Free* (1972).

**BOSOM BUDDIES** (***) **30 min (37ep Color; 1980–1982 ABC) Situation Comedy** *with Tom Hanks as Kip and Buffy Wilson, Peter Scolari as Henry and Hildegarde Desmond, Wendie Jo Sperber as Amy Cassidy, Donna Dixon as Sonny Lumet, Telma Hopkins as Isabelle Hammond, Lucille Benson as Lilly Sinclair, and Holland Taylor as Ruth Dunbar*

Two guys in drag. Hence the term "bosom" buddies. A perfect setup for cheap sight gags straight out of 1940s burlesque-style television.

But, surprise, this is one of the true gems of early 1980s comedy, closer in spirit to Billy Wilder's classic two-guys-in-drag film *Some Like It Hot* than Uncle Miltie's muggings.

The reason given for Kip Wilson and Henry Desmond to dress as women is convoluted but convincing: Newly arrived in New York City, Kip and Henry are desperate for a reasonably priced apartment when a wrecking ball levels their first choice (with them in it). Their friend Amy tells them about a vacancy where she lives, only there is one catch. The Susan B. Anthony Residential Hotel is open only to women. So, with Amy's help, they don costumes and manage to convince anybody who asks that they are Buffy and Hildegarde, sisters of Kip and Henry.

And, sure enough, there are some predictable (but still highly entertaining) plots, including other men falling in love with them, being recognized by their parents, and just barely sidestepping an unmasking.

However, the series really excels in emphasizing the *buddies* over the *bosoms.* Tom Hanks and Peter Scolari play their characters perfectly (all four of them), conveying a comfortable sense of comic give-and-take. For instance, when they introduce themselves in their female costumes for the first time, they end up sticking each other with the most off-the-wall monikers they could both think of. First, Kip introduces Henry as "Hildegarde," so Henry strikes back immediately by identifying Kip as "Buffy." They both hate their new names!

Just as important to the buddy relationship, Kip and Henry come off as real friends who would support and encourage each other. They both work at an ad agency (along with Amy), but also dream of more creative projects. Henry, a copywriter, wants to do a novel (probably about their lives as women), while Kip, an illustrator, wants to be a serious painter. In more immediate dreams, Amy lusts after Henry while Kip has his heart set on Amy's roommate, a beautiful blond dancer named Sonny.

With their dual identities, Kip and Henry soon find themselves buddies with the women at the hotel as well, offering words of encouragement in both guises. Besides Amy and Sonny, they also become friends with a model named Isabelle (played by Telma Hopkins, a former member of Tony Orlando's backing group, Dawn).

About halfway through the series, Kip and Henry decide that their friends should know what is really going on. Soon afterward the scripts virtually eliminate any appearances by Buffy and Hildegarde, with the previous plot hook acknowledged only by an occasional verbal reference or high-pitched "Who is it?" when someone knocks at their apartment door.

The scene also shifts primarily to a new job setting for Kip and Henry, 60 Seconds Street, an independent production company they form with Amy and their former ad agency boss, Ruth. In that setting, all the characters have a chance to pursue their individual dreams in some excellent ensemble episodes.

In the real world, Tom Hanks made the jump to theatrical films (beginning with *Splash*) soon after this series while Peter Scolari had a long and successful run on *Newhart.*

**BOSS LADY (***) 30 min (22ep B&W; 1952 NBC) Situation Comedy** *with Lynn Bari as Gwen F. Allen, Nicholas Joy as Mr. Allen, Glenn Langan as Jeff Standish, and Lee Patrick as Aggie*

Here is an intriguing oddity from the paleozoic era of women on TV. Gwen F. Allen is that extreme rarity of 1950s sitcoms, a working woman. Odder still, Gwen is not just a worker drone but she is the *boss*! The only caveat is that she assumed the role only because her bumbling father is Chairman of the Board of the company, a home construction firm. Nonetheless, *Boss Lady* is fascinating for observing how the producers coped with the perverse notion of a woman executive in the fifties. Gwen's main problem is that, due to her beauty, her male underlings are constantly falling in love with her.

Lynn Bari is perfect for the role, as she spent most of the 1930s and 1940s playing forceful, independent women (mostly the philandering "other woman") in numerous "B"-grade films. *Boss Lady* is a marked change of pace for Jack Wrather, the producer of both this series and the ultratraditional *Lassie.*

**BOSTON BLACKIE (***) 30 min (58ep B&W & Color; 1951–1953 Syndication) Detective Drama** *with Kent Taylor as Boston Blackie, Lois Collier as Mary Wesley, and Frank Orth as Inspector Faraday*

The primary force in nonnetwork independent TV series in the 1950s was the Ziv company. *Boston Blackie* is one of the earlier and one of the better Ziv productions. As with most syndicated series from the 1950s, the production budget is evidently small, but the sprightly tone and the colorful characters make up for the lack of opulence present in the big-budget network shows.

Boston Blackie, a private eye, has no evident connection to the Massachusetts capital, other than perhaps an air of debonair sophistication the city used to exude. Blackie is a dapper ex-con now living the straight and narrow as a detective. As with most private-eye stories, the police consider Blackie to be a criminal who only *acts* reformed, and so Blackie must battle both the cops and the criminals. Blackie's romantic interest and girl Friday, Mary Wesley, tags along with Blackie frequently, and their repartee is entertaining.

The Boston Blackie character has a long history, beginning at the start of this century in magazine stories, moving up through several novels by George Randolph Chester and then numerous movies and a network radio show.

**BOURBON STREET BEAT (**) 60 min (39ep B&W; 1959–1960 ABC) Detective Drama** *with Andrew Duggan as Cal Calhoun, Richard Long as Rex Randolph, Arlene Howell as Melody Lee Mercer, and Van Williams as Kenny Madison*

One of the minor icons of the Warner Bros.–produced detective series from the late 1950s, *Bourbon Street Beat,* like the others of its ilk (*77 Sunset Strip, Hawaiian Eye, Surfside Six*), sticks to rigid formula: a small detective agency in an exotic locale (the French Quarter in New Orleans), with a young hunk (Van Williams) and a pretty face (Arlene Howell, Miss America 1958). In *Bourbon Street Beat,* the producers went a bit overboard on alliterative names, with three of the four lead characters qualifying.

Another tradition of the family of Warner Bros. series from this era was the swapping of stars between shows. After *Bourbon Street Beat* folded, Richard Long and Van Williams not only moved to *77 Sunset Strip* and *Surfside Six,* respectively, but they continued playing the same characters in their new series as well.

**BOYD Q.C. (*½) 30 min (77ep B&W; 1963–1964 UK Associated Rediffusion) Courtroom Drama** *with Michael Denison and Charles Leno*

Michael Denison plays British barrister Boyd, with Charles Leno as his clerk. As in *Perry Mason* Boyd always gets the guilty party.

**BOYS WILL BE BOYS (½) 30 min (11ep Color; 1988 Fox) Situation Comedy** *with Matthew L. Perry as Charles "Chazz" Russell, William Gallo as Francis*

*"Booch" Lottabucci, Demian Slade as Eugene Bloober-man, and Terri Ivens as Debbie Miller*

The short-lived comedy series *Second Chance,* with Kiel Martin as a dead man named Charles Russell who returns to his past to guide the young teenage version of himself, was bad enough. What's worse is that when the original premise didn't work the producers dumped the Kiel Martin dead man character, retitled the show *Boys Will Be Boys,* and simply focused on the juvenile exploits of young Charles (called "Chazz"), his Fonzie-esque pal Booch, and nerdy pal Eugene. These three guys are stupid enough that they could use some adult guidance (not that they would listen to any). Ignore this at all costs.

**BRACKEN'S WORLD (**½) 60 min (41ep Color; 1969–1970 NBC) Drama** *with Warren Stevens and Leslie Nielsen as John Bracken, Eleanor Parker as Sylvia Caldwell, Peter Haskell as Kevin Grant, Dennis Cole as Davey Evans, and Elizabeth Allen as Laura Deane*

An early example of the corporate melodrama school of TV series championed by *Dallas, Bracken's World* revolves around Century Studios in evil, nasty, sexy Hollywood. At first, studio honcho John Bracken is never seen, just heard (through the voice of Warren Stevens) in speaker phone conversations with his executive secretary Sylvia Caldwell (a gambit later used in *Charlie's Angels*). After the first sixteen episodes, Century Studios goes through a major shake-up, Caldwell is out, and Mr. Bracken himself, now in the person of Leslie Nielsen, appears to run things firsthand.

**THE BRADY BRIDES (½) 30 min (7ep & 90 min pilot Color; 1981 NBC) Situation Comedy** *with Maureen McCormick as Marcia Brady Logan, Eve Plumb as Jan Brady Covington, Jerry Houser as Wally Logan, Ron Kuhlman as Philip Covington III, Ann B. Davis as Alice Nelson Franklin, and Florence Henderson as Carol Brady*

As if the world really needed more adventures of the Brady gang once *The Brady Bunch* died, the whole clan reunites for a TV movie, *The Brady Girls Get Married,* in which Marcia and Jan Brady marry a laid-back toy designer and a preppy college chemistry teacher, respectively. The TV movie serves as a pilot for *The Brady Brides* series, where Marcia and Jan set up house, in the *same* home (to save money). Mama Brady and ex-maid Alice pop over now and again to butt into the young couples' lives. As with the original *The Brady Bunch, The Brady Brides* is produced by Sherwood Schwartz.

**THE BRADY BUNCH (*½) 30 min (117ep & 2 hr sequel Color; 1969–1974 ABC) Situation Comedy** *with Robert Reed as Mike Brady, Florence Henderson as Carol Brady, Ann B. Davis as Alice Nelson, Maureen McCormick as Marcia Brady, Eve Plumb as Jan Brady, Susan Olsen as Cindy Brady, Barry Williams as Greg Brady, Christopher Knight as Peter Brady, and Mike Lookinland as Bobby Brady*

At one time, the wholesome family sitcom ruled the air waves. The tumult and social revolt of the 1960s changed all that, and for a long time, topical, relevant sitcoms were the rage. *The Brady Bunch* is the last remnant of the 1950s wholesome brand of sitcom, and the series dragged on until the mid 1970s.

*The Brady Bunch* is nothing if not loud and boisterous. Mike Brady, a widower with three sons, and Carol Martin, a widow with three daughters (remember, this is before divorce was recognized as conceivable by network programmers), marry and move their combined broods into one four-bedroom house in the typical Los Angeles suburb where all the other traditional TV sitcoms are set. The focus is on the tumultuous interaction of the two clans, along with veteran housekeeper Ann B. Davis (who had apprenticed under Bob Cummings in *Love That Bob*), a pet cat, and Tiger, a shaggy dog.

*The Brady Bunch* is amiable fluff that becomes sickeningly sweet after extended viewing. The series and its progeny, *The Brady Bunch Hour* and *The Brady Brides,* are all produced by Sherwood Schwartz (of *Gilligan's Island* fame).

Aside from two follow-up Brady series (*The Brady Bunch Hour* and *The Brady Brides*), the Brady family reunite once more in a two-hour 1988 TV movie, *A Very Brady Christmas,* where most of the offspring are flown home by mom and dad to spend yuletide with the folks.

**THE BRADY BUNCH HOUR (zero) 60 min (9ep Color; 1977 ABC) Comedy-Variety** *with Robert Reed as Mike Brady, Florence Henderson as Carol Brady, Ann B. Davis as Alice Nelson, Maureen McCormick as Marcia Brady, Geri Reischl as Jan Brady, Susan Olsen as Cindy Brady, Barry Williams as Greg Brady, Christopher Knight as Peter Brady, and Mike Lookinland as Bobby Brady*

Why would anyone want to revive *The Brady Bunch* in a variety format? The characters here are the same as in the series (with a new actress playing daughter Jan), but the Bradys have left the suburbs for a southern California beach house, where they practice becoming TV stars (the only logical career for a Californian). Along with the squeaky clean Brady family antics, there are singers, dancers, and comedy sketches. Even fans of the original series will be hard-pressed to stay tuned to this one.

**THE BRAIN (***) 60 min (8ep Color; 1984 PBS) Documentary** *with George Page as host*

The mysteries of the workings of the human brain are examined in this well-produced documentary series. ■

**BRANDED (**) 30 min (48ep: 13 B&W & 35 Color; 1965–1966 NBC) Western** *with Chuck Connors as Jason McCord*

One of the unfinished series of the 1960s. The premise of this western is simple, concisely described in the title song that opens each episode. Only one man survived an Indian attack at Bitter Creek, Wyoming—U.S. Army Captain Jason McCord. But the army brass doesn't believe he was inadvertently spared after being knocked unconscious during the fight. They think he ran and hid. Maybe worse, but they can't prove it. So they strip him of his rank and drum him from the service, branded a coward.

Frankly, even McCord's not totally sure of the events. But he sets out on the well-worn paths of the 1870s television West, out to prove to the world (and maybe to himself) that he really isn't a coward. And maybe to find someone else—an Indian, a civilian, anyone—who might have seen what happened that fateful day.

The stories along the way are slightly above average western fodder, with the first dozen or so the best of the lot. Realistically, someone in that situation probably never would find out the absolute truth. But that doesn't change the feeling of frustration at the end of the run. Though a few people (including an Indian survivor) seem to confirm his innocence, there really should have been a wrap-up episode clearly showing the audience, if not McCord, just what happened. As it is, we can only guess, looking at Connors's subsequent series for a clue: Could those mysterious *Werewolf*-type tracks at the site have anything to do with McCord's disappearance during the battle?

**BRAVE EAGLE** (***) **30 min (39ep B&W; 1955–1956 CBS) Western** *with Keith Larsen as Brave Eagle, Keena Nomkeena as Keena, Kim Winona as Morning Star, and Bert Wheeler as Smokey Joe*

*Brave Eagle* is a hidden treasure worth seeking. Amidst the endless stream of cookie-cutter TV westerns that disgorged from the tube during the 1950s, *Brave Eagle* is virtually the *only* TV western that tells the story of the Old West from the *Indian's* point of view. In what is even a more staggering development, most of the Indian roles (other than the lead) are played by real Indians, or at least actors with a fair amount of Indian blood. For these reasons, *Brave Eagle* is unique.

The character of Brave Eagle is the chief of a peaceful tribe of Cheyenne, who raises his foster son Keena while romancing comely Morning Star. The series focuses both on the interaction among other tribes of Indians and the problems caused by the ever-encroaching white man, whose presence is changing the tribe's way of life. ■

**BREAKING AWAY** (**½) **60 min (8ep Color; 1980–1981 ABC) Comedy Drama** *with Shaun Cassidy as Dave Stohler, Vincent Gardenia as Ray Stohler, Barbara Barrie as Evelyn Stohler, Jackie Earle Haley as Moocher, Thom Bray as Cyril, Tom Wiggin as Mike, and John Ashton as Roy*

Even with some cast changes for television, this series version of the theatrical feature film *Breaking Away* (a "sleeper" hit in 1979) is very faithful to the tone and spirit of the original. It's a college town (Bloomington, Indiana) where the university fraternity guys look down on the local kids, mere high school graduates. As in the film, locals Dave, Moocher, Cyril, and Mike are wondering what to do with their lives. But, in the meantime, Dave enjoys riding his bike, and all of them take delight in tweaking the noses of the college crowd every chance they get. Script writers for the series include Steve Tesich (who won an Oscar for the film screenplay) and Glen Gordon Caron (creator of *Moonlighting*). Thom Bray went from here to *Riptide*.

**BREAKING POINT** (*) **60 min (30ep B&W; 1963–1964 ABC) Medical Drama** *with Paul Richards as Dr. McKinley "Mac" Thompson and Eduard Franz as Dr. Edward Raymer*

The success of *Ben Casey* and *Dr. Kildare* in the early 1960s caused a brief flurry of medical shows, including this heavy-headed series about two psychiatrists who deal with the hordes of mentally unbalanced patients who walk in off the streets of Los Angeles.

**BRENNER** (***) **30 min (25ep & 90 min pilot B&W; 1959 & 1964 CBS) Police Drama** *with Edward Binns as Det. Lt. Roy Brenner and James Broderick as Off. Ernie Brenner*

Herb Brodkin, a much-acclaimed TV producer of drama (*Alcoa Hour, Studio One,* and *The Defenders*), produces this quality half-hour cop show. *Brenner* deals with two generations of policemen from the same family. The elder Brenner (Roy) is the classic hard-nosed veteran cop with more than twenty years under his belt. Young, idealistic son Ernie is walking the beat, dealing with the harsh realities of life that are not explained in police academy. Father and son, as you might guess, disagree about most things, but the family bond forces them to work out their problems. James Broderick, who plays Ernie, is better known as the amiable father on *Family* and as the father of film star Matthew Broderick (*Ferris Bueller's Day Off*).

The ninety-minute pilot for *Brenner* is called "The Blue Men," and aired on *Playhouse 90* in 1959 with Richard LePore as young Ernie. In a rarity for TV in the early days, the cast and crew of *Brenner* were reassembled in 1964, five years after production of the original fifteen episodes, to create an additional ten episodes.

**BRET MAVERICK** (***) **60 min (16ep & 2hr pilot Color; 1981– 1982 NBC) Western** *with James Garner as Bret Maverick, Ed Bruce as Tom Guthrie, Darleen Carr as Mary Lou Springer, Richard Hamilton as Cy Whittaker, John Shearin as Sheriff Mitchell Dowd, Ramon Bieri as Elijah Crow, David Knell as Rodney Catlow, Priscilla*

*Morrill as Estelle Springer, and Stuart Margolin as Philo Sandine*

It is the Super Bowl of poker games. That's why Bret Maverick rides into the small town of Sweetwater, Arizona: He is out to win one of the biggest gambling pots ever. Only before it is over he finds himself in the most unexpected situation of his life—settled down. As owner of a ranch (the Lazy Ace) and half owner of a saloon (the Red Ox), Bret Maverick is suddenly in a new, more leisurely, phase of his life.

That's the setup for the revival of one of television's legendary characters. And, for the most part, it works very well. James Garner is relaxed and comfortable as ever in the role, and he has a good supporting cast and some excellent writing to see him through. There's even a great title song, sung by country & western star Ed Bruce (Garner sings along in the pilot, but lets Bruce handle the tune solo for the regular series), who also does a surprisingly strong job as Maverick's partner in the saloon, former sheriff Tom Guthrie. Even more unexpected, Tom (not Bret) is the subject of the major continuing love interest of the series, Mary Lou Springer, the emancipated and independent publisher of the town's newspaper. However, "ML" does eye Bret . . . as a subject ripe for coverage. He's an outsider, a gambler, and also a genuine western legend. That fact occasionally turns up to haunt Bret (as in the story "The Ballad of Bret Maverick"), though it also helps explain his continued willingness to help other people (even Billy the Kid)—he knows things are not always what they seem.

Perhaps the only major flaw with the series is that the writers deal Bret Maverick too good a hand. He always seems to be working on some con game (in contrast to the original series, when he pulled such stunts only when necessary). The man obviously has too much time on his hands and no one to keep him in line. Tom is the only one who really understands what makes Maverick tick, and he's Bret's partner. Though the manipulative banker, Elijah Crow, and his hand-picked sheriff, Mitchell Down, talk a good game, they're no match for the master. In the wrap-up episode of the first season, though, there are a few new wrinkles introduced to the setup, giving Maverick more of a challenge at the saloon and at the sheriff's office. Unfortunately, just as these fell into place, *Bret Maverick* was canceled—one of those borderline cases that would have probably made the renewal sheet a decade later or just slid to some cable network. (Ironically, that same bad timing occurred in the 1970s with Garner's other western series, *Nichols,* which was canceled shortly after reworking its premise for an anticipated second season.)

That's too bad because, even though Bret's brother Bart (Jack Kelly) turns up in the final episode, there was never a chance for the ultimate *Maverick* reunion: Bret, Bart (we'll ignore Brent), nephew Ben (from the series *Young Maverick*), and cousin Beau (played by Roger Moore). Would Moore (then the highly paid theatrical James Bond) have done it? If anyone could have talked him into it, James "cousin Bret" Garner would have been the one.

**THE BRETTS (**) 60 min (19ep: eighteen 60 min & one 90 min Color; 1987 UK) Drama** *with Norman Rodway as Charles Brett, Barbara Murray as Lydia Brett, David Yelland as Edwin, Belinda Lang as Martha, George Winter as Thomas, Lysette Anthony as Daphne, Tim Wylton as Sutton, Bert Parnaby as Brewster, and Janet Maw as Jean Lacy*

British theater in the 1920s, as lived and performed by a renowned family of thespians, the Bretts, led by Charles and Lydia. They have five grown children, a dedicated staff, and plenty of melodramatic off-stage conflicts to keep themselves in practice for their latest curtain raiser. For instance, when Charles hires a new secretary (beautiful and young and covered with furs), Lydia storms out threatening divorce—but one suspects as much for the chance to do a dramatic exit as out of anger over his choice. The children have similar streaks in them, raising family conflicts and arguments to the level of "high art."

Though the series has pretty good writing and a fairly consistent cast, at times it really is hard to take their showbiz concerns too seriously. (The fate of the empire is not exactly resting on such questions as, "Shall we do a brand-new script for our next production or go with a revival of an old favorite?") These choices may be no more mundane than, say, the day-to-day meal menu decisions on *Upstairs, Downstairs,* but at least you believe the kitchen staff there actually cares about the answer. With *The Bretts,* you suspect they're just posturing again. It's not just "the show must go on"—for them it never stops.

**THE BRIAN KEITH SHOW (**) 30 min (46ep Color; 1972–1974 NBC) Situation Comedy** *with Brian Keith as Dr. Sean Jamison, Shelley Fabares as Dr. Anne Jamison, Victoria Young as Nurse Puni, and Roger Bowen as Dr. Austin Chaffee*

Brian Keith, the star of *Family Affair,* plays Dr. Sean Jamison, an affable pediatrician in practice with his daughter Anne in Hawaii. Their love for the "little people" (their young patients, not leprechauns) causes the Jamisons to dispense free service to many. Titled *The Little People* during its first season, the show becomes *The Brian Keith Show* for the second and final season. Anne is played by *Donna Reed Show* graduate Shelly Fabares.

**BRIDESHEAD REVISITED (****) 60 min (13ep Color; 1981 UK Granada) Drama** *with Jeremy Irons as Charles Ryder, Anthony Andrews as Sebastian Flyte, Laurence Olivier as Lord Marchmain, John Gielgud as Edward Ryder, Diana Quick as Lady Julia Flyte, Claire Bloom* *as Lady Marchmain, Phoebe Nicholls as Lady Cordelia Flyte, Simon Jones as Brideshead, Nickolas Grace as Anthony Blanche, John Grillo as Mr. Samgrass, Charles Keating as Rex Mottram, Jane Asher as Celia Mulcaster*

A meticulously faithful adaptation of the Evelyn Waugh novel about aristocratic Anglo-Catholics during the 1920s, written in a passionate frenzy over just four months in 1944. That, in fact, is the setting that frames the main story—the closing days of World War II, with British Army Captain Charles Ryder discovering that his unit's new temporary bivouac is at Brideshead Castle, on the grounds of the Marchmain estate. He's been there before, and that's where this story really begins, twenty years earlier, in the 1920s.

As with the book, this television version is about both the passing of an era and coming of age. Charles first encounters the estate's family (beginning with Sebastian) while at Oxford College. It's the heady days of pre-Depression extravagance, one World War behind them, another hidden beyond the horizon. People, especially headstrong college students, have plenty of time to be whoever and whatever they want, if they can ever figure out just what that might be in the first place. When Charles meets Sebastian (who stumbles drunkenly into his room one night), such considerations take on aspects he never before dreamed of. He's fascinated by this magically beautiful man who soon draws him into a brand new world.

This includes the expansive and luxurious Marchmain estate, which Charles visits as Sebastian's house guest. These are particularly effective scenes because, despite the fact that the two are grown men, there is a childlike sense of fun and personal discovery between them. Charles is almost like a kid "sleeping over" at a friend's house, fascinated by every aspect of someone else's life: personal objects, family members, and conversations. Their sense of play is most evident at one visit when Sebastian is confined to a wheelchair due to an injury to his ankle. Charles pushes his self-indulgent friend around the grounds, almost like a child playing with a wagon or a bicycle. And Sebastian loves every minute of it.

Yet there is also a feeling of awe at the staggering size of the castle and estate—there's a beautiful garden, fountain, dozens of guest rooms, and even a private Catholic chapel. Which leads to one of the most unusual aspects of Charles' encounter with Sebastian and his family: the influence of the Catholic religion on their lives. Whether active or nonpracticing, the family members cannot seem to escape the personal effects of their religion—it permeates their lives and relationships, especially between the estranged Lord and Lady Marchmain. That's a situation Charles finds puzzling because he had come to regard such beliefs as essentially irrelevant or, at best, an intellectual hobby.

But at times in the story they seem positively alluring, like part of a magic, secret society. No doubt Waugh's own conversion to Catholicism at age twenty-seven served as inspiration for this tone, and for the many questions raised in conversations about the meaning of it all. This ongoing theme is so strong that it adds an extra sense of importance to scenes and decisions that might be regarded as trivial in another context, for instance, should a priest be brought to someone's deathbed, even against their wishes? In this way, *Brideshead Revisited* is quite unusual, even compared to other British novel adaptations. There is a conscious effort to deal with the personal whys and hows of belief, a very tricky area.

And it works. When *Brideshead Revisited* first aired in 1981 and 1982, it attracted great followings in both the United States and Britain. Viewers seemed as mesmerized as Charles at the peculiar splendor of this self-involved (at times decadently self-indulgent) world. The performances and character conflicts are uniformly excellent, with Laurence Olivier, John Gielgud, and Claire Bloom particularly effective as the standard bearers of their fading era. ■

**BRIDGES TO CROSS** **(**) 60 min (6ep & 2 hr pilot Color; 1986 CBS) Drama** *with Suzanne Pleshette as Tracy Bridges, Nicholas Surovy as Peter Cross, Roddy McDowall as Norman Parks, Jose Ferrer as Morris Kane, and Eva Gabor as Maria Talbot*

Suzanne Pleshette, best known to TV viewers as Bob Newhart's wife Emily in *The Bob Newhart Show*, gets a brief moment to shine on her own as Tracy Bridges, a reporter for Washington-based *World Week* magazine, who spends her time interviewing the rich and famous. Bridges is constantly locking horns with her ex-husband, Peter Cross, who is also a reporter for *World Week*. The result is one of the corniest title puns in some time, *Bridges to Cross.* Sounds more like two-thirds of a baseball double-play combination.

The backup characters are a plus in this series. Roddy McDowall (finally off of the planet of the apes) is Tracy's secretary. Deep-voiced actor Jose Ferrer is the nononsense editor of *World Week*, while Eva Gabor, last seen in *Green Acres*, is back where she belongs, the big city, as a socialite who provides valuable gossip to Tracy.

**BRIDGET LOVES BERNIE** **(**½) 30 min (24ep Color; 1972–1973 CBS) Situation Comedy** *with Meredith Baxter as Bridget Fitzgerald, David Birney as Bernie Steinberg, Harold J. Stone as Sam Steinberg, and David Doyle as Walt Fitzgerald*

Back in the 1920s, there was a hit Broadway play, *Abie's Irish Rose,* about a rich Irish girl who marries a poor Jewish boy. The families, of course, do not get along, but love conquers all in the end. *Bridget Loves Bernie* is a modern update of this concept. Meredith Baxter plays the rich Irish girl who weds David Birney's nice Jewish boy character. Birney plays the proverbial struggling writer who earns a living driving a cab. David Doyle (Charlie's male flunkie in *Charlie's Angels*) is the exasperated Irish father of the bride. Audra Lindley (Mrs. Roper from *Three's Company*) is Doyle's wife. The Semitic in-laws are veteran character actor Harold J. Stone (one of the actors who portrayed Papa Jake in *The Goldbergs*) and Bibi Osterwald. Executive producer is Douglas S. Cramer, who went on to produce *The Love Boat.*

*Bridget Loves Bernie* is a fun show. The plot concept is old hat (it was already old back in the 1920s), but the cast does their best to wring some laughs out of it. In a real-life ending you would think could only happen in the movies, Baxter and Birney fell in love while filming this series and were married in 1973. No wonder their chemistry is so good in *Bridget Loves Bernie.* (The couple did, however, split up in 1989.)

Meredith Baxter-Birney went on to play Michael J. Fox's TV mother in one of the top sitcoms of the 1980s, *Family Ties.*

**BRING 'EM BACK ALIVE (**) 60 min (17ep Color; 1982–1983 CBS) Adventure** *with Bruce Boxleitner as Frank Buck, Cindy Morgan as Gloria Marlowe, Clyde Kusatsu as Ali, Ron O'Neal as the Sultan of Johore, John Zee as G. B. Von Turgo, Harvey Jason as Bhundi, and Sean McClory as Myles Delany*

A period-piece exotic action series, dusting off an adventure character from radio, the movies, and comic strips (there had even been a TV pilot kicking around in the late 1950s) to cash in on the success of the first Indiana Jones film, *Raiders of the Lost Ark,* in 1981. Boxleitner plays famed explorer Frank Buck as a rough-and-tumble adventurer living and operating out of Singapore in 1939, just before World War II. He battles Nazis, smugglers, and other assorted baddies, with his best buddy, Ali, at his side, and the affections of Gloria Marlowe (the new American vice-consul in Singapore) just a heart-tug away. His Highness, the Sultan of Johore, also backs Frank in his quests, especially against the area's top underworld figures, G. B. Von Turgo and his associate, Bhundi.

This is far too tame for its pulp-magazine premise, and the straight-faced Boxleitner looks downright silly in his jungle hat. *Tales of the Gold Monkey,* released at the same time as this series, does a much better job on the Indiana Jones trail. Boxleitner, meanwhile, is more appropriately cast as a contemporary agent in his next series, *Scarecrow and Mrs. King.*

The real-life Frank Buck's exploits (in truth, limited to animal trapping) can be seen in the 1932 feature film also called *Bring 'em Back Alive,* which was his motto, and how he did his job.

**BRINGING UP BUDDY (*) 30 min (34ep B&W; 1960–1961 CBS) Situation Comedy** *with Enid Markey as Violet Flower, Doro Merande as Iris Flower, and Frank Aletter as Buddy Flower*

Frank Aletter has the dubious distinction of starring in some of the worst sitcoms of the early 1960s. Aside from his lead in the truly awful *It's About Time* and the little known *Cara Williams Show,* Aletter stars as the very unlikable Buddy Flower in this unlikable show. Buddy is an eligible young investment broker who decides to live with his two elderly maiden aunts, Violet and Iris (get it yet? the family name is Flower). The aunts spend their time trying to marry Buddy off. *Bringing Up Buddy* is produced by Joe Connelly and Bob Mosher, the team that produced the classic *Leave It to Beaver.*

**BROADSIDE (*) 30 min (32ep B&W; 1964–1965 ABC) Situation Comedy** *with Kathy Nolan as Lt. Anne Morgan, Edward Andrews as Cmdr. Rogers Adrian, Dick Sargent as Lt. Maxwell Trotter, Lois Roberts as Molly McGuire, Sheila James as Selma Kowalski, and Jimmy Boyd as Marion Botnik*

Essentially a female version of *McHale's Navy, Broadside* is a rather unfunny show that has four comely WAVES assigned to an otherwise all-male U.S. Navy outpost in the South Pacific during peacetime. The presence of the women, of course, throws everyone into turmoil, especially the commander, Rogers Adrian, who had it pretty cushy before the ladies arrived. The similarity to *McHale's Navy* is intentional, since Edward J. Montagne produced both shows.

The only value in watching *Broadside* is to see the typical 1950s old-fashioned view of women in the military, and to see some familiar faces. Dick Sargent was the second Darrin Stephens in *Bewitched,* Kathy Nolan played Richard Crenna's wife in *The Real McCoys* (and was the first woman elected as president of the Screen Actors Guild), and Sheila James was Zelda Gilroy in *Dobie Gillis.*

**BROADWAY OPEN HOUSE (**) 60 min (52ep B&W; 1950–1951 NBC) Variety** *with Jerry Lester and Dagmar*

*Broadway Open House* is the first late-night network TV talk show, the predecessor to the venerable *Tonight* show. Unlike the slightly cerebral *Tonight* hosts, such as Steve Allen and Jack Paar and the boyish charmer Johnny Carson who hosted *Tonight* for more than a quarter century, the host of *Broadway Open House,* Jerry Lester, is pure vaudeville. There is lots of raucous humor from Jerry, lots of pointless jokes about "beanbags" (were these funny in 1950?) and some celebrity guests. The most intriguing star is Dagmar (a.k.a. Virginia Ruth Egnor), a tall Nordic goddess with an alluring figure who played the dumb blonde role. Dagmar is clearly no dummy, however, and she frequently steals the show. Her role and Lester's leering remarks are quite out of style these days.

Morey Amsterdam, later Buddy Sorrell in *The Dick Van Dyke Show,* alternated with Lester as host of *Broadway Open House,* but it is only highlights of Lester's shows that are available today (under the title *Jerry Lester and Dagmar*).

**BROKEN ARROW** (**) **30 min (72ep & 60 min pilot B&W; 1956–1958 ABC) Western** *with John Lupton as Tom Jeffords, Michael Ansara as Cochise, Tom Fadden as Duffield, and Russ Bender as Marshal Stuart Randall*

A 1950s TV western, which at least concedes that the Indians might not be all that bad, *Broken Arrow* follows the tale of Tom Jeffords, U.S. government Indian agent to the Apaches. Jeffords tries peacefully negotiating with the Indians (and Apache Chief Cochise) instead of shooting them. The pilot episode, broadcast as a segment of *The Twentieth Century Fox Hour,* casts Ricardo Montalban (later the star of *Fantasy Island*) as Cochise. The *Broken Arrow* series is sometimes syndicated under the title *Cochise.*

**BRONCO** (**½) **60 min (69ep B&W; 1958–1962 ABC) Western** *with Ty Hardin as Bronco Layne*

One of the second-string Warner Bros. westerns, following the adventures of a former Confederate Army officer, Bronco Layne, wandering the West after the war. There he meets the usual band of Warners supporting cast performers, along with appearances by others such as Jack Nicholson, Joel Grey, and Robert Vaughn.

Originally, *Bronco* was conceived as a fill-in for the Cheyenne character during a contract dispute with the star of that series, Clint Walker. Later, when Walker was back in the fold, there were crossover appearances on *Cheyenne* and another Warner Bros. western, *Sugarfoot,* when all three programs alternated in the same slot.

**BRONK** (**) **60 min (24ep Color; 1975–1976 CBS) Police Drama** *with Jack Palance as Lt. Alex "Bronk" Bronkov, Joseph Mascolo as Mayor Pete Santori, Dina Ousley as Ellen Bronkov, and Tony King as Sgt. John Webber*

Jack Palance does not often play cool, sympathetic guys, but Lt. Alex Bronkov is one such case. Produced in the mid-1970s, when all TV cops had some offbeat personality quirk, Bronk is a pipe-smoking policeman with a crippled daughter. Bronk works with his old buddy, the mayor of Ocean City, California, to clean up the town from the vermin of the sort Palance usually plays in movies and TV.

Carroll O'Connor (*All in the Family's* Archie Bunker) and Bruce Geller (producer of *Mission Impossible*) teamed up to produce this bland show.

**THE BRONX ZOO** (**½) **60 min (21ep Color; 1987–1988 NBC) Drama** *with Ed Asner as Joe Danzig, Kathryn Harrold as Sara Newhouse, David Wilson as Harry Barnes, Kathleen Beller as Mary Caitlin Callahan, Nicholas Pryor as Jack Felspar, Janet Carroll as Carol Danzig, Jerry Levine as Matthew Littman, Mykel T. Williamson as Gus Butterfield, Gail Boggs as Roz Hemphill, Adam Carl as Warren Snyder, Randee Heller as Jeannie Barnes, and Betty Karlen as Virginia Biederman*

Anyone tuning in expecting to see *Lou Grant II* is in for a surprise. This series takes Ed Asner's principled, outspoken character type (embodied for more than a decade in Lou Grant) and places it in a much tougher setting—far from the safe haven of the WJM management office (on *Mary Tyler Moore*) or the city editor's desk of the *Los Angeles Tribune* (on *Lou Grant.*) In *The Bronx Zoo,* Asner's Joe Danzig is on the front lines, with a put-up or shut-up challenge: Within a year, he must hammer into shape the facilities, faculty, and students of Benjamin Harrison High School (nicknamed "The Bronx Zoo"), or the city school board will close its doors for good. That's not quite as glamorous as getting the news out by deadline time. And, ironically, it means that if Danzig succeeds his reward will be even more time at that trouble-ridden site.

To kick off the series, the workaholic Danzig accepts the challenge, much to the bitter disappointment of his wife. (And the two are having marriage problems to begin with.) What follows is a generally well-done drama focusing primarily on the lives of Danzig and his teaching staff as they attempt to make a grossly inadequate system work. Surprisingly, Asner's character steps aside quite often in the initial episodes in favor of the teachers, most of whom fall into the truly dedicated mold of *Mr. Novak* and *Room 222:* Sara (English), Harry (history), Mary Caitlin (art), Matthew (math substitute), and Gus (science and gym). Trading barbs with them and Danzig is Vice-Principal Jack Felspar, a decent but dedicated bureaucrat disappointed at not getting the principal's job (no doubt to use as a stepping stone to a better assignment—nobody except Danzig could possible *want* this job). There's plenty of humor, sex (Sara and Harry are an item), and good character interaction, though at times it's hard to shake off a disheartening sense of helplessness at the situation they all face.

Over time, there's an attempt to be a bit more upbeat as the series focuses more on Danzig as a father figure, both symbolically for the students, and then literally at home when his wife gives birth late in life to a baby girl. Some of these later episodes are probably the best in the run.

One unusual aspect of this Gary David Goldberg-produced series is its linkage back to previous projects. In 1981, he had pitched two ideas to CBS: a one-hour drama on changing attitudes between the 1960s and 1980s generations (*Family Ties*), and a thirty-minute sitcom about a city high school (*Making the Grade*). CBS bought the sitcom and gave it a six-episode tryout in 1982, while Goldberg reworked the drama into a half-hour comedy for NBC. In 1986, with *Family Ties* a huge hit, Goldberg dusted off the idea of a school setting but flipped it from the comedy world of urban St. Louis to the dramatic world of New York's inner city.

But, he carried over a few character names (Jack Felspar, Harry Barnes, and probably Sara), perhaps as an affectionate allusion to the original venture.

**BROTHERS** (**½) **30 min (115ep Color; 1984–1989 Showtime) Situation Comedy** *with Paul Regina as Cliff Waters, Robert Walden as Joe Waters, Brandon Maggart as Lou Waters, Philip Charles MacKenzie as Donald, Hallie Todd as Penny Waters, Robin Riker as Kelly, and Mary Ann Pascal as Samantha "Sam" Waters*

One of the earliest continuing series produced especially for cable TV, *Brothers* is a somewhat heavy-handed look at the three Waters brothers. Big brother Lou is the father figure of the trio. Middle brother Joe owns a restaurant and is divorced with a young daughter (Penny). Youngest brother Cliff walks out of his own wedding at the last moment because he is gay.

Cliff's sudden coming out of the closet is the original main theme in *Brothers*, as Lou and Joe must deal with Cliff's sexual preference. Cliff has none of the stereotypical mannerisms traditionally deemed homosexual, but his platonic pal Donald has every one, which may strike some viewers the wrong way. Robert Walden, who plays Joe, is best known as brash reporter Joe Rossi from *Lou Grant*.

**THE BROTHERS** (**) **30 min (26ep B&W; 1956–1957 CBS) Situation Comedy** *with Gale Gordon as Harvey Box, Bob Sweeney as Gilmore Box, Ann Morriss as Dr. Margaret Kleeb, Nancy Hadley as Marilee Dorf, and Barbara Billingsley as Barbara*

What a surprise! Gale Gordon, for once, does not play Lucille Ball's boss or at least somebody's boss. Gordon plays Harvey Box, who runs a photography studio in San Francisco with his brother Gilmore. The two brothers, both single, are enmeshed in various romantic adventures with local ladies. Not much really goes on here. Look for Barbara Billingsley (June Cleaver in *Leave It to Beaver*) as Harvey's girlfriend.

**BROTHERS AND SISTERS** (*) **30 min (11ep Color; 1979 NBC) Situation Comedy** *with Chris Lemmon as Milos "Checko" Sabolcik, Randy Brooks as Ronald Holmes III, William Windom as Dean Larry Krandall, Mary Crosby as Suzi Cooper, Amy Johnston as Mary Lee, Jon Cutler as Stanley Zipper, and LaWanda Page as Hattie*

This is one of the many failed attempts by the TV networks to translate the popular, bawdy film *Animal House* to TV. This attempt is memorable, if at all, for its use of celebrity offsprings Chris Lemmon (son of Jack) and Mary Crosby (daughter of Bing). Mary Crosby is better known for playing Kristin Shepard, the revengeful mistress who shot J. R. Ewing on *Dallas*.

**THE BROTHERS BRANNAGAN** (*) **60 min (39ep B&W; 1960–1961 Syndication) Detective Drama** *with Steve Dunne as Mike Brannagan and Mark Roberts as Bob Brannagan*

From the early 1960s, long before wisecracking private eyes became the rage, the brothers Brannagan swap smart remarks and operate a private-eye operation in Phoenix, Arizona (then a very unlikely setting for a TV series).

**THE BUCCANEERS** (*) **30 min (39ep B&W; 1956–1957 CBS) Adventure** *with Robert Shaw as Capt. Dan Tempest, Peter Hammond as Lt. Beamish, Brian Rawlinson as Gaff, and Paul Hansard as Taffy*

If cowboys and Indians can succeed on TV, why not sailors and pirates, eh, matey? *The Buccaneers* is set in the early 1700s, on an island in the Caribbean Sea, where Lt. Beamish is the newly appointed royal governor. Beamish enlists reformed pirate Dan Tempest (what a name for a sailor!) to battle the likes of Blackbeard. Robert Shaw, who plays Capt. Tempest, is only practicing for his most important naval encounter, his 1975 movie battle (he was the veteran shark hunter) with that popular "eating machine," the title character of *Jaws*.

**BUCK JAMES** (**) **60 min (19ep Color; 1987–1988 ABC) Medical Drama** *with Dennis Weaver as Buck James, Shannon Wilcox as Jenny James, Alberta Watson as Rebecca Meyer, Kirk Sisco as Kyle Grant, Jon Maynard Pennell as Clint James, and Elena Stiteler as Dinah James*

Dennis Weaver as crack surgeon Buck James, who heads the trauma unit at a Texas university hospital. The usual life-and-death crises are set against domestic problems that Buck finds a lot tougher to handle, especially when it comes to his ex-wife, Jenny, and their two children. At times this show seems to be striving for a *St. Elsewhere* feel, but the writing is nowhere as skillful and, as a result, some salty language and sexual innuendo come off more as crude than clever. It's not McCloud becomes a doctor, but it's not terribly engrossing, either.

**BUCK ROGERS** (**) **30 min (39ep B&W; 1950–1951 ABC) Science Fiction** *with Kem Dibbs and Robert Pastene as Buck Rogers, Lou Prentis as Lt. Wilma Deering, Harry Sothern as Dr. Huer, and Harry Kingston as Black Barney Wade*

This is the first attempt to bring Buck Rogers, hero of comics, radio, and movie serials, to television. Buck is a red-blooded American from the twentieth century who, through various mumbo jumbo, winds up in the twenty-fifth century, where he does remarkably well in adapting to the newfangled devices. Before you know it, he's saving the universe operating from his headquarters, Niagra.

This version of Buck's adventures is on the cheap side, but is fun to watch. This series is not to be confused with the big-budget *Buck Rogers* series from the 1980s, with Gil Gerard.

**BUCK ROGERS IN THE 25TH CENTURY (**) 60 min (36ep & 2 hr pilot Color; 1979–1981 NBC) Science Fiction** *with Gil Gerard as Captain William "Buck" Rogers, Erin Gray as Colonel Wilma Deering, Tim O'Connor as Dr. Huer, Henry Silva and Michael Ansara as Kane, Pamela Hensley as Princess Ardala, Thom Christopher as Hawk, and Wilfrid Hyde-White as Dr. Goodfellow*

This space adventure followed right on the unsuccessful heels of *Battlestar Galactica,* so Universal Studios had a pretty good idea of what would not work. To the company's credit, it applied these lessons quite well to the production and packaging of *Buck Rogers.* For starters, the pilot film played as a theatrical release several months before the fall season, not after it (which *Battlestar Galactica* had done). Thus, *Buck Rogers* earned not only up-front revenue but also some surprisingly positive reviews.

The film (and subsequent series) also used a number of leftover models, spaceships, and other hardware from *Battlestar Galactica.* However, *Buck Rogers* did not adopt the same somber approach to storytelling. Instead, from the beginning, the new series managed to treat these larger-than-life tales with just the right tone of irreverence, especially on the part of star Gil Gerard. As the twentieth-century man thrown 500 years off track, he just shrugs his shoulders, fights for the forces of good, smiles knowingly as Wilma Deering (his rarely pursued love interest), and enjoys all the neat hardware he has at his disposal—down to his small robot aide, Twiki (with a voice usually done by Mel Blanc).

Even when the series shifts from an Earth base to a space patrol setup (aboard the *Searcher*), Buck and his companions do not lose their sense of humor. Some characters and gimmicks even add to it, including an obnoxious new robot, Crichton (no doubt an allusion to Michael Crichton, who wrote the science fiction novel *Andromeda Strain*), Admiral Asimov, commander of the spaceship (ostensibly descended from science fiction writer Isaac Asimov), and Dr. Goodfellow, the definitive "funny old scientist." ■

**BUCKSKIN (*) 30 min (39ep B&W; 1958–1959 NBC) Western** *with Tommy Nolan as Jody O'Connell, Sallie Brophy as Annie O'Connell, Michael Road as Marshal Tom Sellers, and Michael Lipton as Ben Newcomb*

*Buckskin* is a bland western focusing on ten-year-old Jody O'Connell and his widowed mother, who eke out a living running a boardinghouse in Buckskin, Montana, in the ever-popular 1880s. Jody narrates each episode and plays elementary harmonica to set the tone for the show.

**BUDGIE (*½) 60 min (13ep: 4 B&W & 9 Color; 1971–1973 UK Thames) Crime Drama** *with Adam Faith, Georgina Hale, and Iain Cuthbertson*

Crime drama with a touch of humor, following the (mostly unsuccessful) schemes of a small-time crook (played by Adam Faith) operating out of London's Soho area. The show is of interest mainly to see Faith, an extremely successful pop singer in Britain from the early to mid-1960s. The thirteen episodes in the U.S. syndication package are only about a third of the episodes produced.

**BUFFALO BILL (***) 30 min (26ep Color; 1983–1984 NBC) Situation Comedy** *with Dabney Coleman as Bill Bittinger, Joanna Cassidy as Jo Jo White, John Fiedler as Woody, Max Wright as Karl Shub, Geena Davis as Wendy Killian, and Charles Robinson as Newdell Spriggs*

Dabney Coleman has made a career out of playing intriguing boors. From Merle Jeeter, the slimy mayor of Fernwood in *Mary Hartman,* to the piggish boss in the movie *9 to 5,* to "Slap" Maxwell, an abrasive minor-league-caliber sports writer, Coleman's characters always come across as a man everyone would love to punch in the mouth. Yet, somehow, they are fun to watch and viewers actually wind up feeling somewhat sorry for him, in spite of his bad qualities. This may be because, for all their faults, these characters are blatantly honest in their self-centeredness. After all, each of us has some amount of that Dabney Coleman personality lurking in us, yearning to break free of the restraints of kindness and consideration instilled in us since childhood.

*Buffalo Bill* is Coleman's first opportunity to shine as the headliner, and it is wonderfully refreshing to find a leading man who is not a nice guy. Coleman plays "Buffalo" Bill Bittinger, an insensitive host of a local TV talk show in Buffalo, New York. By setting Bittinger up as a heel, the writers have many avenues of plot lines open to them that would be closed off by focusing on the average nice guy. Bittinger constantly gets into trouble by asking outrageous and insulting questions of his guests on his TV show, makes amazingly intrusive demands on Jo Jo, his director and on-again off-again girlfriend, and treats most of his staff as peons.

Aside from the pleasure of watching an acting pro like Coleman go through his nasty paces, *Buffalo Bill* provides wonderful inside satire on the world of television. Coleman effectively skewers the all-too-real self-centered egomaniacal broadcasting types, who will stop at nothing and will step over anybody in order to get ahead. In one telling episode, Bittinger appears to be in line for an important TV job in New York City and he can't wait to leave behind the small-town atmosphere of Buffalo. When, however, Bittinger fails to get the job, he launches into a maudlin on-the-air speech about how he could have had the job, but just couldn't bear to leave the warm, friendly people of Buffalo.

Because Coleman's character is so aggressively grating, *Buffalo Bill* takes some getting used to by viewers weaned on lovable guys like Dick Van Dyke. Those who enjoyed Jackie Gleason in *The Honeymooners,* however, will take to Bill Bittinger right way.

*Buffalo Bill* is produced by the talented team of Tom Patchett and Jay Tarses, the men behind the old Bob Newhart psychiatrist series. The *Buffalo Bill* opening is a great montage featuring Coleman and several celebrity look-alikes, making it appear as if Bill Bittinger really had interviewed Henry Kissinger, Burt Reynolds, and Liza Minnelli.

*Buffalo Bill* is the first TV series for Max Wright (here, jittery station manager Karl Shub, but later Willie Tanner, the lead human on *Alf*), Geena Davis (here, Bill's alluring research assistant Wendy Killian, but later the star of her own TV series, *Sara,* and lead actress in movies such as *The Accidental Tourist*), and Charles Robinson (here, gruff black make-up man Newdell Spriggs, but later clerk Mac Robinson on *Night Court*).

**THE BULLWINKLE SHOW/ROCKY AND HIS FRIENDS (***½) 30 min (147ep Color; ABC & NBC 1959–1963) Animated Cartoon** *with the voices of Bill Scott as Bullwinkle J. Moose and Mr. Peabody, June Foray as Rocket J. Squirrel, Natasha Fatale, and Nell Fenwick, Paul Frees as Boris Badenov and Inspector Fenwick, Walter Tetley as Sherman, Charles Ruggles as Aesop, Daws Butler as Aesop, Jr., Hans Conried as Snidley Whiplash, and William Conrad as narrator*

In 1983, film snobs and cultural elitists at the Chicago International Film Festival were rather distressed to discover that the hottest ticket at their event was for a retrospective honoring the television work of Jay Ward, culminating with his most popular cartoon series: *The Bullwinkle Show.*

It was a well-deserved honor. Even with animation that is often rather crude, there is simply no denying that Rocky, Bullwinkle, Boris, and Natasha (and their friends) are some of the best defined, best written, and most entertaining characters ever to appear on television. Their stories are in the best tradition of the theatrical cartoons of the 1930s and 1940s (which were designed to appeal to adults as well as to children), with multiple layers of gags and satirical references. This includes supporting characters with such silly names as Mr. Big, Fearless Leader, Capt. "Wrongway" Peachfuzz, and King Bushwhack the 33rd, and such unusual plot hooks as a scheme to manufacture counterfeit cereal box-tops, giant metal-munching robot mice who devour television antennas, Bullwinkle as the star quarterback of Watsamatta U., the search for Mt. Flatten, repository of the antigravity metal "upsidasium", and—most famous of all—the legendary Kirwood Derby, which turned the world's dumbest people into the most brilliant. (That hat also had an unexpected side effect: Garry Moore's variety show sidekick, Durward Kirby, was so annoyed that the story was pulled from the *Bullwinkle Show* rerun packages.)

The adventures of Rocky and Bullwinkle first played weekday afternoons (as *Rocky and His Friends* on ABC) in 1959, but within two years it had won a prime-time slot as *The Bullwinkle Show.* After one year in prime time, the series shifted to the world of Saturday and Sunday morning cartoons, where it began its cycle of endless reruns that continues today. Originally, the backup features to the Rocky and Bullwinkle segments on each show included "Peabody's Improbable History" (time travel with a genius dog, Peabody, and his boy, Sherman), "Bullwinkle's Corner" (humorous poetry readings), and "Fractured Fairy Tales" (narrated by Edward Everett Horton). These were later joined by "Aesop and Son" (fables with a pun-filled twist), "Mr. Know-It-All" (Bullwinkle offering wrongheaded advice), and "Dudley Do-right of the Mounties" (a frantic send-up of turn-of-the-century blue-eyed heroics). Currently all the material that originally appeared on *Rocky and His Friends* and *The Bullwinkle Show* is arbitrarily split in half to fill two half-hour syndication packages: one under the Bullwinkle banner, the other using Rocky as the title hook.

Appropriately, some of the characters from the series even crossed over from the animated world. Bullwinkle himself appeared briefly as a hand puppet to introduce segments of the *Bullwinkle* cartoon series when it first moved to NBC. Even better, in 1989, Boris and Natasha headed toward the silver screen in a live-action adventure with Dave Thomas and Sally Kellerman in the title roles. ■

**BULMAN (**½) 60 min (20ep Color; 1985 & 1987 UK Granada) Adventure** *with Don Henderson as George Bulman and Siobhan Redmond as Lucy McGinty*

Retired from the police force, former Chief Inspector Bulman sets up an antique and clock-mending shop, but soon finds himself taking on private investigation cases as well. (Old habits die hard.) You can't miss Bulman—he's the one with the woolly gloves and carrier bag, assisted by Lucy McGinty, the daughter of a former colleague.

Don Henderson and his Bulman character originated in another British series, *Strangers* (which ran from 1978 to 1982). The twenty-episode *Bulman* series followed, though the U.S. syndication package sometimes trims both the number of episodes and the running time of each.

**BURKE'S LAW (**½) 60 min (64ep B&W; 1963–1965 ABC) then AMOS BURKE, SECRET AGENT (*½) (17ep B&W; 1965–1966 ABC) Mystery-Adventure** *with Gene Barry as Capt. Amos Burke, Gary Conway as Det. Tim Tilson, Regis Toomey as Det. Sgt. Les Hart, Leon Lontoc as Henry, Eileen O'Neill as Sgt. Ames, and Carl Benton Reid as "The Man"*

Police Captain Amos Burke is an honest cop who happens to be filthy rich. So even as he puts in a hard day's work—he's head of homicide investigations for the Los Angeles Police Department—Captain Burke doesn't forget the little comforts of life, such as his personal limousine, fully stocked bar, and romantic encounters with beautiful women. As the one in charge, he also assigns himself to only the interesting cases, usually involving the rich and famous.

This series is probably one of the best for Gene Barry, with his suave sophisticated character type in an unlikely but quite likable setting. The supporting cast is adequate (Detective Tilson and Sergeant Hart do the heavy legwork, and chauffeur Henry takes care of the limo), while the large cast of guest stars gives Burke plenty of suspects to question. Though the killer's identity is always held to the end, there is not a standard moment of revelation formula, as in *Murder, She Wrote.* Except, of course, that it's always Captain Burke who unmasks the killer.

*Burke's Law* producer Aaron Spelling went on to use the extensive guest cast gimmick in his many subsequent anthology series such as *The Love Boat* and *Fantasy Island. Columbo* creators William Link and Richard Levinson wrote several episodes of *Burke's Law* as did science fiction author Harlan Ellison. One episode ("Who Killed the Jackpot?") introduced Anne Francis and John Ericson as characters for the series *Honey West.*

*Burke's Law* changed formats in its final season to cash in on the spy craze of the mid-1960s, so Captain Burke became *Amos Burke, Secret Agent.* Unfortunately, the character was turned from a unique millionaire sleuth to just another pretty-boy agent. The only other regulars in that phase of the series are Burke's mysterious boss, "The Man," and his limousine—only *without* the chauffeur!

**THE BURNS AND ALLEN SHOW** **(see *The George Burns and Gracie Allen Show*)**

**BUS STOP (**½) 60 min (25ep B&W; 1961–1962 ABC) Drama** *with Marilyn Maxwell as Grace Sherwood, Rhodes Reason as Will Mayberry, Joan Freeman as Elma Gahringer, and Richard Anderson as Glen Wagner*

Extremely loosely based on William Inge's play and the 1956 hit film of the same name, *Bus Stop* fits into the *Route 66/The Fugitive* school of TV drama. Like those other two series, *Bus Stop* is really a slice-of-life show, with continuing characters used mainly as the foundation for what is really a drama anthology. Set in the Sherwood Bus Depot and Diner in sleepy Sunrise, Colorado, *Bus Stop* has only a few regulars. Grace Sherwood is the owner and operator of the diner, while Elma Gahringer is the diner's one and only waitress. Sheriff Will Mayberry and D. A. Glenn Wagner deal with the outbreaks of crime that seem to follow the arrival of newcomers each week.

Keep an eye out for the episode "A Lion Walks Among Us" (directed by Robert Altman). Teen singer Fabian Forte guest stars as a wacked-out youth who goes on a murder binge. This episode caused one of the earliest public outcries against TV violence. Rhode Island Senator John Pastore said, after viewing the episode, "I looked at it and I haven't felt clean since. I still have the stench in my nose." With almost thirty years of more explicit TV and film violence since then, the modern viewer will wonder what all the hubbub was about.

**BUSTIN' LOOSE (*) 30 min (26ep Color; 1987–1988 Syndication) Situation Comedy** *with Jimmie Walker as Sonny Barnes, Vonetta McGee as Mimi Shaw, Larry Williams as Rudey Butler, Aaron Lohr as Nickky Robison, Tyren Perry as Trish Reagan, and Marie Lynnwise as Sue Ann Tyler*

Based on the 1981 Richard Pryor film about an ex-con escorting a busload of handicapped kids (under the care of their teacher, played by Cicily Tyson) to a new home. In that setting, there's lots of "earthy" language, as Pryor's character takes on all comers, even the Ku Klux Klan. Needless to say, the premise is cleaned up and simplified for the television series run. Jimmie Walker plays Sonny, a carefree smart-talkin' bachelor who gets assigned to five years of community service after a run-in with the law. His task: keeping house for Mimi, a beautiful social worker trying to raise four foster kids. Needless to say, Sonny wins the kids over immediately. They think of him as a combination Eddie Murphy, Bill Cosby, and Alf. Mimi, on the other hand, requires a little more time, which Sonny has plenty of. A more restrained character for Walker than his J. J. on *Good Times* (but that would probably be true of virtually any role), though the series goes for put-downs by rote a bit too often.

**BUSTING LOOSE (*) 30 min (26ep Color; 1977 CBS) Situation Comedy** *with Adam Arkin as Lenny Markowitz, Jack Kruschen as Sam Markowitz, Pat Carroll as Pearl Markowitz, Barbara Rhoades as Melody Feebeck, and Paul B. Price as Ralph Cabell*

Lenny Markowitz, a twenty-four-year-old engineering grad student, leaves the overprotective wing of his typical Jewish parents and takes up the swinging singles life, moving into an apartment with a hot babe next door. You've seen all this before somewhere.

**BUTTERFLIES (**) 30 min (20ep Color; 1980–1981 UK BBC) Situation Comedy** *with Wendy Craig as Ria Parkinson, Geoffrey Palmer as Ben Parkinson, Andre Hall as Russell Parkinson, Nicholas Lyndhurst as Adam Parkinson, Joyce Windsor as Ruby, and Bruce Montague as Leonard Dunn*

Ria Parkinson has hit her forties, her two sons have grown, and her husband is only interested in his work (dentistry) and his hobby (collecting butterflies). Like any self-respecting "modern" woman, Ria considers having an affair, in this case with recently divorced Leonard

Dunn. This British sitcom handles the situation with the naturalistic humor that American TV producers of sex comedies find hard to duplicate.

**BY THE SWORD DIVIDED (**) 60 min (16ep Color; 1983–1985 UK) Drama** *with Sharon Mughan as Anne Fletcher, Timothy Bentinck as Sir Thomas Lacey, Rob Edwards as John Fletcher, Lucy Aston as Lady Lucinda Ferrar, Julian Glover as Sir Martin Lacey, Gareth Thomas as Major General Horton, Judy Buxton as Susan, Malcolm Stoddard as Captain Marsh, and Jeremy Clyde as King Charles I*

Adequate tale of the English Civil War of 1640 (the Roundheads versus the Royalists), with the principal focus on one family (led by Sir Martin Lacey) fiercely divided over the war. Plenty of personal and political intrigues at their stronghold castle Arnescote, including a prolonged siege and a secret mission to deliver silver to the king. Created by period drama veteran John Hawkesworth.

**BY-LINE: STEVE WILSON (*) 30 min (39ep B&W; 1955–1956 NBC) Crime Drama** *with Mark Stevens as Steve Wilson, Doe Avedon as Diane Walker, and Barry Kelley as Charlie Anderson*

Crime in Big Town, U. S. A., as reported and exposed by the crusading Steve Wilson and his newspaper, *The Illustrated Press.* The series began as a radio show in the late 1930s and came to television in 1950—first as a live show, then on film from 1952. During the 1950s and early 1960s, the filmed adventures played in rerun syndication under such titles as *Heart of the City* (ninety-one episodes), *Headline* (the next forty-two episodes), and *By-Line: Steve Wilson* (the final thirty-nine episodes). The last title is the only one currently available, with Wilson the managing editor of the paper, Diane his girlfriend, and Charlie his best friend.

Occasionally, there are some interesting guest stars (such as Robert Vaughn, Dennis Weaver, and Sal Mineo), but for the most part this is either a terribly *chic* example of television *film noir* or just a laughable grade-B adventure series with reporter rejects even the *Daily Planet* wouldn't hire.

**CBS REPORTS (***) 60 min (B&W & Color; 1959– CBS) Documentary**

After the death of CBS's acclaimed *See It Now* documentary series, *CBS Reports* became the umbrella title for most of the network's documentaries. Over the years, numerous hosts and producers have come and gone on the irregularly scheduled series, and the title has sometimes changed to *CBS News Hour* and *CBS News Special.*

The very first *CBS Reports* broadcast, *Biography of a Missile* (the development of the Juno 2 rocket), is narrated by Edward R. Murrow and produced by Fred W. Friendly, the duo responsible for *See It Now.* Other memorable broadcasts include *KKK—The Invisible Empire* (the power of the Ku Klux Klan in the South) from 1966, *Hunger in America* (the continuing problem of hunger among America's poor) from 1969, *The Selling of the Pentagon* (the Pentagon's expensive public relations program) from 1971, and *The Guns of Autumn* (an attack on animal hunting in America) from 1975.

**C.P.O. SHARKEY (**) 30 min (25ep Color; 1976–1978 NBC) Situation Comedy** *with Don Rickles as C. P. O. Otto Sharkey, Harrison Page as C. P. O. Robinson, Elizabeth Allen as Capt. Quinlan, Peter Isacksen as Seaman Pruitt, Richard X. Slattery as Capt. "Buck" Buckner, and Jonathan Daly as Lt. Whipple*

Don Rickles is perfect for guest spots on television variety shows, but he seems unable to succeed as the star of his own show. He's tried hosting a variety show and several sitcoms, and none lasted very long. The reason? Rickles is probably too intense, too liable to go for the jugular to please the ever-somnambulant regular TV watcher.

*C.P.O. Sharkey* is about as good a sitcom format as Don Rickles could ask for. He plays an abrasive Chief Petty Officer at the San Diego Naval Training Center, whose job is to browbeat green recruits into tough fighting men. Thus, he can yell and scream and insult his men, slide into humorous ethnic material usually considered taboo in these ultrasensitive days, and it all fits into the plot. Unfortunately, the producers decided (probably correctly) that thirty minutes of unrelieved Rickles zings would be tiring on a viewer. So they tried to leaven Rickles' character by showing his "soft" side, his caring side. Don Rickles looks silly being a soft, caring guy and the whole show sinks under the weight of balancing the "good" Rickles and the funny "bad" Rickles.

**CADE'S COUNTY (***) 60 min (24ep Color; 1971–1972 CBS) Western** *with Glenn Ford as Sam Cade, Edgar Buchanan as J. J. Jackson, Taylor Lacher as Arlo Pritchard, Victor Campos as Rudy Davillo, and Peter Ford as Pete*

Glenn Ford is Sheriff Sam Cade, based in the town of Madrid, but responsible for law enforcement in the entire county. He's assisted by deputies J. J. Jackson (the old pro) and Arlo, Victor, and Pete (the next generation, including Glenn Ford's real-life son as Pete). Together they tackle a wide range of cases (much like executive producer David Gerber's showpiece series, *Police Story*), though often focusing on the sensitive relationships between Native Indian Americans and the white man. There are strong guest star performances (including Chief Dan George in "The Witness," Bobby Darin in "A Gun for Billy," and Martin Sheen in "Safe Deposit") supported by consistently effective and authentic scripts. This one-season venture has recycled a few of its stories into feature-length episodes (*The Marshal of Madrid* and *Slay Ride*) for the TV movie slots.

**CAESAR'S HOUR (***½) 60 min (B&W; 1954–1957 NBC) Comedy-Variety** *with Sid Caesar, Carl Reiner, Howard Morris, Nanette Fabray, Pat Carroll, and Janet Blair*

It is not quite as good as Caesar's classic, *Your Show of Shows,* but *Caesar's Hour* is one of the better, more imaginative, comedy hours from the 1950s. Most of the *Your Show of Shows* crew is here (except co-star Imogene Coca and producer Max Liebman) and the flavor is much the same. The absence of Coca is felt as a parade of competent but unspectacular leading ladies come and go. Like "The Honeymooners" in the somewhat similar *Jackie Gleason Show, Caesar's Hour* has a recurring featured skit, "The Commuters," featuring Caesar, Carl Reiner, and Howard Morris as suburban men taking the train in and out of the city each day, which sometimes expands to almost fill the hour.

Some of the skits from *Caesar's Hour* turn up in the *Best of Your Show of Shows* package. ■

**CAGNEY AND LACEY (***) 60 Min (125ep & 2 hr pilot Color; 1982–1988 CBS) Police Drama** *with Sharon Gless and Meg Foster as Detective Chris Cagney, Tyne Daly as Detective Mary Beth Lacey, Al Waxman as Lieutenant Bert Samuels, Martin Kove as Detective Victor Isbecki, Carl Lumbly as Detective Mark Petrie, Sidney Clute as Detective Paul La Guardia, Harvey Atkin as Sergeant Ronald Coleman, Barry Primus as Sergeant Dory McKenna, Robert Hegyes as Detective Manny Esposito, Dick O'Neill as Charlie Cagney, and John Karlen as Harvey Lacey*

New York police detectives Chris Cagney and Mary Beth Lacey are a "buddy cop" team that does more than just round up the usual suspects. They are also fully developed characters outside the squad room, with two completely different approaches to life. Mary Beth is very happily married, with a hard-working husband (Harvey) in the construction business and two young sons (later in the series they add a daughter). They're salt-of-the-earth types, living in a tight but comfortable New York apartment, with dreams of owning a proper house someday (eventually they save enough and make the big move). Chris is single, lives in a Manhattan loft, dresses very well, and has an active sex life. She's very close to her dad, Charlie, a former policeman (and a problem drinker), and has two major relationships over the course of the series (one with another cop, Dory McKenna, and the other with a lawyer, David Keeler).

Even though Mary Beth may leave work in a bowling shirt, while Chris wears a stylish fur, they complement each other perfectly. They are both good detectives, with Chris usually (but not always) the more impulsive of the two. Both aspire to the rank of sergeant, but they are smart enough not to let any competition run their relationship because a good partner is irreplaceable. When there's a crunch of any sort, they make certain to talk it out, usually using the women's room for their personal one-on-one discussions (covering everything from the particulars of a case to deeply personal issues). That's a particularly effective set piece, turning the rest room into a safe haven that no male character dares to invade.

During its original run, *Cagney and Lacey* acquired a reputation for turning out strong topical dramas. (*Ms. Magazine* founder Gloria Steinem went so far as to call it the best show on TV for a *TV Guide* article, citing episodes dealing with date rape and alcoholism). Don't let that scare you off. Yes, there are a few ringers (an episode about bombing abortion clinics seems particularly pedantic and even brings back that favorite strawman villain from the 1970s, the manipulative and misguided protester) but, for the most part, the series keeps the heavy-handed preachiness in check. Besides, *Cagney and Lacey* is enough of a traditional cop show to include a large proportion of familiar plot hooks in the episode mix, deftly avoiding the trap of repeated (and dated) relevancy.

In fact, because Chris and Mary Beth are such well-developed characters, their regular cases come off as exceptionally effective. Two of the best feature Chris in pursuit of a classy international jewel thief, Albert Grand. She dreams of being the first detective in the world to snare him, avidly reading through his book (*Grand Hotels*) looking for clues to the way his mind works. Mary Beth perceptively notes exactly what's going on: "He's world class—so if you capture him do you think that makes *you* world class?" Chris may protest, but that's exactly what's on her mind. One of Mary Beth's best showcases has her grabbed by a gunman in a railroad yard. It sounds like a typical hostage story setup, except that she is her own best hope, deftly playing her captor's emotions while the rescue forces wait for the right moment to move in.

*Cagney and Lacey* remains remarkably consistent over its run, so this is a reliably entertaining package. The original 1981 TV movie pilot features Loretta Swit (from *M*A*S*H*) as Chris Cagney, and is not included in the syndication package. Meg Foster won the Cagney role for the series, but Sharon Gless replaced her after the first half dozen episodes. However, stations rarely begin their rotation of *Cagney and Lacey* with the Meg Foster episodes, preferring to sneak them in later in the run. Tyne Daly plays Mary Beth throughout.

**CAIN'S HUNDRED (*) 60 min (30ep Color; 1961–1962 NBC) Crime Drama** *with Mark Richman as Nicholas "Nick" Cain*

*Cain's Hundred* is an overly serious attempt to spruce up an otherwise run-of-the-mill crime show with flourishes of "docudrama." Nick Cain is a former mob lawyer who switches sides and now travels the country, trying to lock up the criminals he formerly protected (his aim is to get the top 100 mobsters in the land). The episodes, we are told, are based on true stories, just like *Dragnet.*

Paul Monash, the producer of *Cain's Hundred,* had more luck with a legal setting in *Judd, For the Defense,* and struck paydirt with the seminal TV prime-time soaper, *Peyton Place.*

**CAKES AND ALE** (**½) **(3ep Color; 1976 UK BBC) Drama** *with Michael Hordern as Willie, Paul Aston as Willie (as a young man), Judy Cornwell as Rosie, Mike Pratt as Driffield, Peter Jeffrey as Alroy Kear, Lynn Farleigh as Amy, James Grout as Lord George Kemp, and Kevin Stoney as the Vicar*

Adaptation of Somerset Maugham's 1930 novel about life in a small country town, told in the context of an eager biographer coming to document his literary hero's life, a grand old man of English literature. Actually, it's a satirically cruel tale aimed by Maugham at the highbrow literary establishment at the time, with the two main characters representative of contemporary writers: The biographical subject is generally seen as Thomas Hardy, while the smarmy researcher (and hero worshiper) is novelist Hugh Walpole. The researcher comes to town determined to present a "cakes and ale" version of his subject (an expression meaning "hunky dory" or "just fine"). He will show his hero as wise and stately, especially for choosing a sophisticated woman of the world as his second wife (replacing a "trollop barmaid" he married in his youth). But the truth is far different and the first wife, Rosie, is the most affectionately warm and generous human being in the tale. Worse yet, the literary hero is actually a raunchy braggart and his new wife is a pretentious nag. Unless you're a very serious literature fan (digesting *Masterpiece Theatre* weekly for nearly two decades), the particulars of such after-the-fact celebrity gossip probably won't entertain you as much as the frankly nasty tone applied to most of the characters. It's an occasionally flawed but mostly fun presentation.

**CALIFORNIA FEVER** (½) **60 min (10ep Color; 1979 CBS) Adventure** *with Jimmy McNichol as Vince Butler, Marc McClure as Ross Whitman, Michele Tobin as Laurie Newman, and Lorenzo Lamas as Rick*

This mindless hour is merely a vehicle to push the overhyped career of Jimmy McNichol, brother of actress Kristy McNichol. The young McNichol plays Vince, who lives the life of the cool L.A. dude crusing through high school with his buddy Ross. The duo are into music, cars, and girls. Ross drives a souped-up auto, dubbed "The Grossmobile." The show's only redeeming feature is that *California Fever* is the first series role for one of the star hunks of the 1980s, Lorenzo Lamas (son of Fernando) who came to fame as Lance Cumson on *Falcon Crest.*

Paul R. Picard, producer of *California Fever,* also turned out *The Dukes of Hazzard, Enos,* and *Scruples.*

**THE CALIFORNIANS** (**) **30 min (69ep B&W; 1957–1959 NBC) Western** *with Adam Kennedy as Dion Patrick, Sean McClory as Jack McGivern, Herbert Rudley as Sam Brennan, Richard Coogan as Matthew Wayne, Carole Mathews as Wilma Fansler, and Arthur Fleming as Jeremy Pitt*

*The Californians* starts off trying to do something different in the cookie-cutter world of 1950s westerns, but winds up just like all the others. Set in the young town of San Francisco in the 1850s (in the wake of the gold rush of 1849), *The Californians* first focuses on the ad hoc law enforcement efforts of two men, Dion Patrick, ex-gold prospector and now crusading newspaperman, and Jack McGivern, owner of the big local general store. With few, if any, real lawmen around, and with gold fever cascading through the hordes of new arrivals in the city by the bay, the locals must try to keep the peace as they see fit, and Patrick and McGivern head up an unofficial peacekeeping force. It's a novel idea, but, it does tend to smack of vigilantism. After the first twenty episodes or so, Patrick and McGivern are phased out and much more traditional western hero, Matthew Wayne, is phased in. Wayne is the new sheriff (later marshal), and his crime-fighting efforts are rather familiar to veteran watchers of TV oaters.

The primary reason to seek out *The Californians* is to watch for young lawyer Jeremy Pitt, who blows into town around the same time lawman Wayne does. Pitt is played by Arthur Fleming, best known to couch potatoes as Art Fleming, the original (and best) host of TV's quiz show classic, *Jeopardy.*

**CALL MR. D.** (see ***Richard Diamond, Private Detective***)

**CALL TO GLORY** (**½) **60 min (19ep Color; 1984–1985 ABC) Drama** *with Craig T. Nelson as Col. Raynor Sarnac, Cindy Pickett as Vanessa Sarnac, Elisabeth Shue as Jackie Sarnac, Gabriel Damon as R. H. Sarnac, David Hollander as Wesley Sarnac, and Keenan Wynn as Carl Sarnac*

*Call to Glory* is more interesting as a historical and social artifact than as a regular TV show. It represents one of the first efforts on network TV to dramatize the turbulent 1960s from a retrospective point of view, and it is one of the first (of many) series about the 1960s that relies on snippets of music from that era to set the mood. It also is one of the first TV drama series to deal with the U.S. involvement in Vietnam.

Col. Raynor Sarnac (who thought up that name?) is a seriously patriotic Air Force jet pilot who, in best miniseries style, winds up being involved in, or dealing with, most of the important news events of his day (the Cuban missile crisis, the Vietnam war, the assassination of John F. Kennedy). The primary focus of the show, however, is Col. Sarnac's family life, rather than his military exploits.

At times, *Call to Glory* is on the verge of being a very good show. Craig Nelson, of the *Poltergeist* films, is riveting as Col. Sarnac. However, muddy plots and a desire to drag in too many real-life news events ultimately drag *Call to Glory* down to earth. ■

**CALLAN (***) 60 min (52ep: 30 B&W & 22 Color; 1967–1973 UK Thames) Spy Drama** *with Edward Woodward as David Callan*

Essential viewing for fans of *The Equalizer,* presenting Edward Woodward as cold-blooded British secret service agent David Callan. Though not directly connected to the 1980s series, it might as well be, going a long way to explain just why an agent like Robert McCall might one day retire from the service and go into action as an avenging angel for the otherwise helpless common citizens. One day he probably looked in the mirror and decided, after a lifetime of double-dealing and dispensing death, the time had come for a change.

In *Callan* we see Woodward playing a relatively young professional, the epitome of a gritty, sometimes shabby, and ultimately very alone agent of the government, whose nasty business is murder. As such, he is an important cog in the game of international intrigue, but not one proudly paraded by his own people. He's an outsider among them, and often appears glum and disappointed with his own life (much like Richard Burton's character in the 1965 feature film *The Spy Who Came in from the Cold*). In a way, he's much closer to Ian Fleming's original portrayal of James Bond in the early novels as a sometimes frightening killer.

The series ran successfully in Britain for about half a decade, with most of the episodes also available for Stateside syndication. In 1974, Woodward starred in a theatrical film based on the character (*Callan*) and, in 1981, a few years before taking the role of McCall for *The Equalizer,* he played Callan one more time in a one-episode special, "Wet Job," with the aging agent facing his grim past, present, and future.

**CALLUCCI'S DEPARTMENT (**½) 30 min (13ep Color; 1973 CBS) Situation Comedy** *with James Coco as Joe Calucci, Candy Azzara as Shirley Balukis, Jose Perez as Ramon Gonzales, and Jack Fletcher as Oscar Cosgrove*

James Coco was a success on Broadway and in Hollywood, but his two sitcoms (*Calucci's Department* and *The Dumplings*) both flopped. *Calucci's Department* has all the makings of a fairly funny show, but, unfortunately, it was canceled long before it had a chance to develop. Coco plays the harassed supervisor of a branch office of the New York State Unemployment Office (not exactly your typical sitcom setting). Coco's chief problem at work is his nitpicking, incompetent staff of ethnically mixed goldbricks. It's a great chance for Coco to use his somewhat overrefined personality to great comic effect.

**CALVIN AND THE COLONEL (**½) 30 min (26ep Color; 1961–1962 ABC) Animated Cartoon** *with the voices of Freeman Gosden as Col. Montgomery J. Klaxon, Charles Correll as Calvin Burnside, and Paul Frees as Oliver Wendell Clutch*

*Calvin and the Colonel* is *Amos and Andy* without any of the controversy. The result demonstrates once and for all that Freeman Gosden and Charles Correll created a wonderful universal comic concept with *Amos and Andy,* one that transcends its original racial setting.

Gosden and Correll created *Amos and Andy* in the late 1920s, and the comedy about blacks in Harlem quickly became the first big comedy sensation of network radio. Gosden and Correll, two Southern whites, provided most of the voices for the radio show, which lasted over three decades. An effort was made in the 1950s to transform *Amos and Andy* into a television show, with an all-black cast, but the program was not as popular as the radio version, and charges of racial stereotyping dogged the TV *Amos and Andy,* eventually forcing the reruns off the air.

After the radio version of *Amos and Andy* finally closed shop in 1960, Gosden and Correll took the concept and presented it in the more noncontroversial form of a cartoon, called *Calvin and the Colonel.* To make certain that no racial group could take offense, all the characters are animals. Col. Klaxon, the equivalent of George "Kingfish" Stevens of *Amos and Andy* fame, is a cunning schemer, always ready to fleece an unwary mark. Calvin Burnside, the revamped Andy Brown, is the dim-witted but kindly confederate of the Colonel. Andy Brown of the TV version of *Amos and Andy* resembled a gentle bear and, appropriately, Calvin Burnside *is* a big bear. Col. Klaxon, fittingly enough, is a fox.

Calvin and the Colonel follows the adventures of Col. Klaxon and Calvin Burnside, two Southerners who are struggling with adapting to life in the North. Also around to provide color is the Colonel's nagging wife Maggie Belle (voice of Virginia Gregg) and shyster lawyer Oliver Wendell Clutch (with voice by Paul Frees, who also provided the voice for Boris Badenov in *Bullwinkle*). The stories are funny, if somewhat simple. The Colonel, like the Kingfish, always is good for some laughs as he tries to hoodwink the world, while avoiding his wife's vengeful temper. Calvin is always around to somehow disrupt the Colonel's latest scheme.

The producers of *Calvin and the Colonel* are Joe Connelly and Bob Mosher, the duo who created *Leave It to Beaver.*

**CAMEO THEATER** (**) **60 min (26ep Color; 1955–1958 NBC) Drama Anthology**

Umbrella title used for selected episodes from a daily afternoon drama anthology (*NBC Matinee Theater*) that originally ran on NBC from 1955 to 1958. *Matinee Theater* was one of the first programs to be regularly broadcast in color, and, in its initial season, the performances usually went out as live broadcasts from Los Angeles. After a while, the network turned to presentations on film instead, which still meant several hundred episodes over the course of three seasons. This anthology package includes stories with such performers as June Lockhart, Dean Stockwell, and Sarah Churchill. Oddly, there was another prime-time anthology fill-in series called *Cameo Theater,* which played on NBC earlier in the 1950s, but that series has nothing to do with this one.

**CAMERA THREE** (**½) **30 min (26ep Color; 1979–1980 PBS) General Interest**

For twenty-six years, *Camera Three* was a Sunday morning staple on CBS, presenting a potpourri of education, the arts, and public affairs, all on a shoestring budget. These twenty-six episodes come from the series' brief prime-time coda on PBS. Unfortunately, the best episodes are the old, live, black and white ones on CBS, which are mostly lost.

**CAMP RUNAMUCK** (*) **30 min (26ep Color; 1965–1966 NBC) Situation Comedy** *with Dave Ketchum as Counselor Spiffy, Arch Johnson as Commander Wivenhoe, David Madden as Counselor Pruett, Alice Nunn as Mahalia May Gruenecker, and Frank DeVol and Leonard Stone as Doc Joslyn*

As sitcoms go, *Camp Runamuck* is as mediocre as they come. Still, the show does have its share of laughs. Camp Runamuck, you see, is a summer camp for young boys, just across the lake from Camp Divine for young girls. That setup alone is a fertile setting for yucks. Unfortunately, anyone who went to summer camp will have a number of stories that are as funny, if not funnier, than those in *Camp Runamuck.* You could probably guess what sort of characters are in this show without much effort. There is the nasty camp director who hates kids. There are some overage smart-alecky kids. There are screwball counselors who let the kids run all over them. There are curvaceous female counselors in tight T-shirts. Lots of people fall into the lake. People get lost in the woods. Get the picture? You can tell that this show is from a more innocent era because there are no dirty words and nobody (not even the counselors) comes even close to having a sexual encounter.

**THE CAMPBELLS** (**½) **30 min (100ep for Fall 1989 Color; 1985– Canada CTV) Adventure** *with Malcolm Stoddard as Dr. James Campbell, Amber-Lea Weston as Emma Campbell, Eric Richards as John Campbell, and Cedric Smith as Capt. Thomas Simms*

Set in the 1830s, *The Campbells* concerns a Scottish doctor who moves to the Canadian wilderness with his two children. Presto! The Campbells are pioneers.

The production budget here is not great, but the stories are well-produced and amiable. Dr. Campbell's children are a bit wooden, but Malcolm Stoddard is good as the independent-minded physician making a new life out in the wilds.

**CANDID CAMERA, THE NEW** (**) **30 min (130ep Color; 1974–1978 Syndication) Comedy** *with Allen Funt, John Bartholomew Tucker, Phyllis George, Jo Ann Pflug, and Betsy Palmer*

Allen Funt came up with the idea of recording people's candid reactions to highly unusual situations while he was in the Army during World War II. In 1947, Funt brought the idea to network radio as *Candid Microphone,* the title he used when his show first appeared on television in 1949. Not much of a hit, the show bounced around the networks until 1953, quickly retitled *Candid Camera.* It returned, for a more popular run, from 1960 to 1967 on CBS, with Durward Kirby as co-host most of the time. These old black and white episodes are no longer available in reruns.

The 1970s episodes, titled *The New Candid Camera* to set them apart from the old series, are the first to be produced in color. The format is the same as before. Funt, looking like the world's greatest smart aleck, introduces most of the segments with lip-smacking expectations. The man never seems to tire of seeing how people so easily make fools of themselves when out-of-the-ordinary situations disrupt their normal routine. In these syndicated episodes, Funt goes through a lengthy list of co-hosts, from the pretty-boy naughtiness of John Bartholomew Tucker, to the vapidity of Phyllis George, to the more sedate sensibility of Betsy Palmer.

Tricking people is only one aspect of *Candid Camera.* The show also frequently presents little nontrick features, such as simply watching as normal people go about their life, albeit in unusual ways. These snippets include popular clips of traffic cops who act as conductor to the flow of traffic or the oft-used candid interviews with children, who, as Art Linkletter always knew, "say the darndest things." ■

**CANNON** (**½) **60 min (122ep & 2 hr pilot & 2 hr sequel Color; 1971–1976 CBS) Detective Drama** *with William Conrad as Frank Cannon*

One of the more entertaining and least pompous of the antiestablishment cop/private-eye shows of the 1970s, *Cannon* broke the standard mold of crime shows by the casting of its lead actor. William Conrad, formerly the radio voice of Marshall Dillon on the original *Gunsmoke* and the narrator of both *The Fugitive* and the Rocky and Bullwinkle segments of *Bullwinkle,* is fatter and surlier than nine-tenths of the other cops and private eyes on TV. As private-eye Frank Cannon,

Conrad finally finds a good vehicle for his quirky personality.

Cannon only takes cases when he feels like it, or needs the cash to finance his grandiose epicurean habits. He is as likely to snarl at his clients as he is to snarl at his suspects. As might be expected with a private-eye show starring an overweight middle-aged actor, there is little running and fighting in *Cannon.* Instead, there are plenty of car chases and lots of verbal attacks by the always alert Cannon. Another plus for this show is that it comes from the era before it was felt that every nonhandsome leading man had to have a young hunk as a sidekick to keep the attention of female viewers (as was the case in Conrad's later and far grumpier series, *Jake and the Fat Man*).

The suspense and plotting are good, but not exceptional. The show is just good-quality middle-of-the-road TV by two masters of good taste, William Conrad and producer Quinn Martin (who produced *The Fugitive,* among other hits). The two-hour sequel from 1980, *The Return of Frank Cannon,* is actually a failed pilot that tried to revive the series. The sequel is lackluster (Quinn Martin was not involved) and Conrad is merely going through the paces. The only cute touch is that in this version Cannon has given up private-eye work in order to run a restaurant, a task closer to his heart.

**CANNONBALL (**½) 30 min (39ep B&W; 1958–1959 Syndication) Adventure** *with Paul Birch as Mike Malone and William Campbell as Jerry Austin*

Long before overproduced country & western ballads about truck drivers became musical clichés, there was *Cannonball,* the original TV trucker saga. This no-nonsense show is neither flashy nor hyped up. It is simply thirty minutes of competent video adventure, with a workable, flexible format, the sort of show independent TV producers were churning out without much fanfare in the 1950s.

Mike Malone and Jerry Austin are two truckers, always on the road and always winding up in the midst of some human or mechanical crises. Neither is a pretty boy (the type favored in silly 1970s trucking shows such as *B. J. and the Bear*), but both are hard-working Joes who gallantly represent the trucking fraternity. Their quiet poise and bravery make trucking seem awfully attractive to a youngster with wanderlust. The theme song of *Cannonball* is real catchy.

**THE CAPTAIN & TENNILLE (*) 60 min (19ep Color; 1976–1977 ABC) Musical-Variety** *with Daryl "The Captain" Dragon and Toni Tennille*

It was a sure sign the TV musical-variety was moribund in the 1970s when *The Captain & Tennille* was the best of that genre on the air. The program still seems turgid today. The married headliners sing amiable tunes ("Love Will Keep Us Together"), but they have little to no stage presence. The Captain barely talks, while Tennille stands around, looking pretty.

**CAPTAIN DAVID GRIEF (*½) 30 min (39ep B&W; 1956–1957 Syndication) Adventure** *with Maxwell Reed as Captain David Grief and Maureen Hingert as Anura*

Captain David Grief roams the South Seas around Melanesia (near Australia) in search of adventure, with Anura along as his permanent passenger and companion. Together they battle typhoons, headhunters, pirates, and stock footage. Actually, the stark and simple feel of the series is rather appropriate to the original Jack London material this series is loosely based on, though this result is probably more a reflection of budget restraints than artistic integrity.

**CAPTAIN GALLANT OF THE FOREIGN LEGION (*½) 30 min (65ep B&W; 1955–1957 Syndication) Adventure** *with Larry "Buster" Crabbe as Captain Michael Gallant, Cullen Crabbe as Cuffy Sanders, Al "Fuzzy" Knight as Private Fuzzy Knight, Gilles Queant as Sgt. Du Val, and Norma Eberhardt as Carla*

Kiddie adventure series showcasing Buster Crabbe, one of the kings of the 1930s theatrical cliff-hanger serials (he starred in *Flash Gordon* and *Buck Rogers*). For this venture, Crabbe and his real-life son, Cullen, take on the shifting sands of North Africa (or Northern Italy, in later location shooting), stationed at a remote outpost of the French Foreign Legion. Crabbe plays a pure-of-heart (one might say gallant) soldier, while Cullen is his young ward, the son of a slain officer. Unfortunately, the tales are strictly kids' stuff—if you ever thought some of those old theatrical serials seemed hokey, this will make them look positively profound in comparison, with the landscape better plotted than the adventures. Definitely worth seeing, though, to catch Crabbe between his legendary serial characters and his farewell cameo shots in such programs as the 1980s version of *Buck Rogers in the 25th Century* series.

For a while, this series played in the syndicated rerun circuit as *Foreign Legionnaire.* ■

**CAPTAIN MIDNIGHT (**½) 30 min (39ep B&W; 1954–1956 CBS) Adventure** *with Richard Webb as Captain Midnight/Jet Jackson, Sid Melton as Ichabod "Icky" Mudd, and Olan Soule as Aristotle "Tut" Jones*

The two and one-half stars listed for this show do not signify dramatic quality, but rather camp cuteness, since *Captain Midnight* might well be the lamest kiddie adventure series of the 1950s. It certainly looks like one of the cheapest.

Captain Midnight, a war ace, is the top gun of some ridiculous organization known as the Secret Squadron, which battles evil. His top aide, impossibly enough, is played by borscht belt graduate Sid Melton (best known as Danny Thomas's manager in *Make Room for Daddy*). For a while after this show's network run, the original sponsor (Ovaltine) made the producers delete all references to "Captain Midnight" when the show went into syndicated reruns. Thus, the program was temporarily retitled *Jet Jackson, Flying Commando* and a poor job of vocal overdubbing attempted to alter all uses of the old name during each episode. The original *Captain Midnight* prints are now the version more likely to appear. ■

**CAPTAIN NICE (**) 30 min (15ep Color; 1966–1967 NBC) Situation Comedy** *with William Daniels as Carter Nash/Captain Nice and Alice Ghostley as Mrs. Nash*

In the mid-1960s, all the networks were stumped by the success of *Batman,* with its campy style and tongue-in-cheek humor. Numerous efforts were made to produce similar shows. None caught on. The two closest clones of *Batman* were *Captain Nice* and *Mr. Terrific.* They both flopped. Both deserved to die quick deaths, but *Captain Nice* is the only one remotely worth hunting for now.

*Captain Nice* is the brainchild of Buck Henry, the same man who succeeded with *Get Smart* in lampooning the spy trend with a comedy takeoff. So, with *Captain Nice,* why not a successful takeoff on superheroes? William Daniels, later renowned as the uptight Dr. Mark Craig of *St. Elsewhere,* stars as meek, mild-mannered Carter Nash, a police chemist who accidentally develops a potion that, when drunk, bestows super powers, such as tremendous strength and the ability to fly. Unfortunately, the potion does nothing to alter Nash's meek personality, and he is forever trying to muster courage as he uses his superpowers to combat the villains in his town.

Daniels is quite funny as the mouse-turned-superman. Alice Ghostley is the standard bossy Jewish mother who tries to run her superhero son's life. There are some good superhero shticks, such as having Captain Nice wear an ill-fitting outfit and having him *not* want to fight crime (it was all his mother's idea). The concept should work, but something is missing. Perhaps the problem is that the original of the mold, *Batman,* was so much a parody itself that *Captain Nice* is a parody of a parody and that may be one level too far. The great cast and crew and the great concept make *Captain Nice* a flop to look for.

**CAPTAIN VIDEO AND HIS VIDEO RANGERS (**) 30 min (B&W; 1949–1956 DuMont & Syndication) Science Fiction** *with Richard Coogan and Al Hodge as Captain Video, Don Hastings as The Ranger, and Hal Conklin as Dr. Pauli*

From TV's dark ages, this is the premier TV sci-fi show, produced by the perennially broke DuMont network, and the lack of money shows. In the distant future, Captain Video, "Guardian of the Safety of the World," battles the evil Dr. Pauli, and assorted other fiends, with the help of The Ranger, his young sidekick. Few episodes remain intact.

**CAPTAINS AND THE KINGS (**) (9hr miniseries Color; 1976 NBC) Drama** *with Richard Jordan as Joseph Armagh, Joanna Pettet as Katherine Hennessey, Charles Durning as "Big" Ed Healey, Patty Duke Astin as Bernadette Hennessey Armagh, Robert Vaughn as Charles Desmond, Jane Seymour as Marjorie Chisholm Armagh, and Perry King as Rory Armagh*

Adapted from Taylor Caldwell's novel of the same name, *Captains and the Kings* is about Joseph Armagh, a Joseph P. Kennedy–type character who comes, impoverished, to America from Ireland in the 1850s and struggles until he becomes one of the nation's most powerful men. His ultimate goal, to have his son Rory become the first Irish Catholic elected as president, comes to naught as Rory is assassinated while campaigning. Sound vaguely familiar?

**CAPTURED** **(see *Gangbusters*)**

**CAR 54, WHERE ARE YOU? (**½) 30 min (60ep B&W; 1961–1963 NBC) Situation Comedy** *with Joe E. Ross as Gunther Toody, Fred Gwynne as Francis Muldoon, Bea Pons as Lucille Toody, and Paul Reed as Capt. Martin Block*

*Car 54, Where Are You?* is second-banana heaven. All the people involved in his show have great track records as supporting characters (or second bananas) in other shows, but there is something missing from the final recipe and *Car 54* ultimately falls short. It almost makes it to the category of a lost classic, but instead is relegated to the more populated collection of shows that are interesting for mostly historical, not entertainment, reasons.

The most noteworthy aspect of *Car 54* is the impressive resumes of its cast and crew. The man behind the show, Nat Hiken, produced Phil Silvers' Sgt. Bilko series *You'll Never Get Rich,* and the Hiken/Bilko stamp is all over *Car 54.* Like the Bilko show, *Car 54* is a comedy about men in uniform who fall far short of the usual public image associated with their position. With Bilko the setting was the U.S. Army and with *Car 54* the setting is a police precinct house in the Bronx section of New York City. The policemen are as unlikely a bunch of crime fighters as the Bilko brigade was an unbelievable assortment of fighting men. As with the Bilko show, it is the incongruity of watching out-of-shape borscht-belt comedians play roles that, in real life, would be filled by well-conditioned younger men that provides a lot of the humor in *Car 54.*

The primary cast crossover from the Bilko show is Joe E. Ross, who played the short, dumpy Rupert Ritzik with Phil Silvers. In *Car 54,* Ross plays short, dumpy Gunther Toody. Toody and Ritzik are exactly the same character, with only the name changed. In the Bilko show, Ritzik was another of the amusing troupe of goldbricks that surrounded master manipulator Ernie Bilko. Ritzik was memorable for his trademark expression of "oooh-oooh-oooh," which is not much of a trademark expression when you think about it. Toody still has Ritzik's "oooh-oooh-oooh" expression, Ritzik's bumbling good-natured personality, and even Ritzik's wife. Beatrice Pons, who played Mrs. Ritzik, turns up in *Car 54* as Mrs. Toody and is just as nagging as she was in the Bilko show.

The other lead in *Car 54* is best known for what he did after *Car 54.* A young, gangly Fred Gwynne is Toody's partner, Francis Muldoon, a low-key earlobe-pulling Irishman who provides a good balance to Toody's short, bubbly Jewishness. Gwynne went on to greater fame as Herman Munster in *The Munsters,* and observing how Gwynne towers over the other in *Car 54,* it's easy to see how he got the role of the hulking Frankenstein-ish Munster.

Toody and Muldoon are a good pair, but they are too lightweight to carry a show on their shoulders. Toody's childlike exuberance wears thin real fast and his "oooh-oooh-ooohing" looses whatever humor it has after an episode or two. Toody and Muldoon are simply not distinctive enough. If they were true charlatans, like Bilko, the show would be more fun. If the pair were more normal, then the other crazies in the precinct would fill in the dead spots and *Car 54* would be *Barney Miller* in black and white. Sadly, *Car 54* stagnates somewhere in between.

As with the Bilko show, Nat Hiken fills *Car 54* with a top-notch crew of supporting performers. Veteran character actor Paul Reed plays Toody and Muldoon's boss, Capt. Martin Block, with just the right touch of authority and exasperation. Another officer, Leo Schnauser, is played by Al Lewis, whose huge grin and bad teeth accompanied Fred Gwynne to *The Munsters,* where Lewis played the vampirish Grandpa Munster. Officer Schnauser's wife, Sylvia, is portrayed by Charlotte Rae, later a star in *The Facts of Life.* Nipsey Russell, later a popular stand-up comedian, is Officer Anderson, one of the few nondomestic black characters on TV before the mid-1960s.

One thing that stands out in *Car 54* is its authentic New York feel. Shot entirely on location in New York, *Car 54* reeks of the hustle and bustle of Gotham and the vibrant nature of overlapping ethnic groups that gives the nation's largest city a lot of its charm. Even the show's theme song, which Hiken co-wrote, is a homage to New York. It tosses in references to various boroughs and lists numerous incidents that would be calamities in a smaller town, but are just everyday occurrences in the Big Apple.

**THE CARA WILLIAMS SHOW (**) 30 min (28ep B&W; 1964–1965 CBS) Situation Comedy** *with Cara Williams as Cara Bridges/Wilton, Frank Aletter as Frank Bridges, Paul Reed as Damon Burkhardt, Reta Shaw as Mrs. Burkhardt, and Jack Sheldon as Fletcher Kincaid*

Mildly amusing setup, more timeless than it might appear at first glance (just check with your company's personnel department). Cara and Frank are in love and married. Unfortunately, their employer (Fenwick Diversified) specificially forbids people who are married to each other from both working at the company. So they choose a time-honored American solution: they lie. Cara continues to use her own name (Wilton) as secretary to Damon Burkhardt, keeping her association with Frank (a company efficiency expert) during their after-hours secret. When the truth comes out, though, it's Frank who faces the punishment of pounding the pavement (Cara's complex filing system has made her irreplaceable), until his wife convinces the company to change its policy. Almost lost in all the silly subterfuge is the rather innovative concept (for the times) of a childless, two-career couple. Of course, to keep things consistent with sitcom clichés of the era, Cara is the semiobligatory scatterbrained secretary and housewife. Still, it is a pleasantly executed production.

Previously, Cara Williams played Gladys in the 1960 *December Bride* spin-off, *Pete and Gladys.*

**CARIBE (**) 60 min (13ep Color; 1975 ABC) Police Drama** *with Stacy Keach as Lt. Ben Logan, Carl Franklin as Sgt. Mark Walters, and Robert Mandan as Comm. Ed Rawlings*

One of the lesser-known crime series from prolific producer Quinn Martin, *Caribe* predates *Miami Vice* by almost a decade, but contains many of the same elements. The show is set in Miami, features a white cop (Ben Logan) and his black partner (Mark Walters), and contains lots of Latin flavoring. Logan and Walters work a special police unit, the Caribbean Force, that roams the Caribbean, fighting for truth, justice, and the (North) American way.

**CAROL BURNETT SHOW (****) 60 min (244ep Color; 1967–1978 CBS) also packaged as CAROL BURNETT & FRIENDS 30 min (175ep) Comedy-Variety** *with Carol Burnett, Vicki Lawrence, Harvey Korman, Tim Conway, Lyle Waggoner, and Dick Van Dyke*

Carol Burnett's program was the last of the weekly hour-long comedy-variety series, running from the late 1960s to the late 1970s. One reason Burnett's series lasted so long is that she emphasized the *comedy* in comedy-variety. Each program had at least two major comedy sketches, with a nice mix of subjects. There were popular film and television series parodies, humorous commercials, and recurring characters such as Mr. Tudball and Mrs. Wiggins, Ed and Eunice and her Mama, and the cleaning lady who usually closed down the set at the end of the season.

Naturally, Burnett herself played in nearly every sketch, but she was also wise enough to step aside occasionally and let her extremely able supporting players run with a routine. Vicki Lawrence, Harvey Korman, and Tim Conway put in some of their best work ever as part of this team. Korman and Conway are particularly amusing as they consistently try to top each other on stage.

Most of the episodes of the hour-long version of the

series (complete with opening routines and musical guests) are available for syndication, but rarely turn up. Instead, programmers usually slot the more compact comedy-only half-hour cutdowns. These are some of the best and most effective comedy-variety showcases ever packaged, assuring Carol Burnett of exposure to new generations of viewers long after her variety series itself ended. The frequent repetition of these sketches also paved the way for the success of a 1980s spin-off series featuring company member Vicki Lawrence, *Mama's Family.* ■

**CARSON COMEDY CLASSICS (**) 30 min (130ep Color; 1983–1985 Syndication) Comedy-Variety** *with Johnny Carson and Ed McMahon*

The *Tonight* program, which debuted on NBC in 1954, popularized the form of late-night talk shows. First hosted by Steve Allen and then by Jack Parr, *Tonight* developed into a loose combination of comedy and celebrity chitchat. In 1962, after Parr moved to prime time, daytime quiz show host Johnny Carson took over the show and stayed for more than twenty-five years. Carson, orginally a stage magician and stand-up comic, never completely gave up performing on his own on *Tonight,* and frequently followed his opening monologue with comedy skits starring himself. He portrayed a popular collection of familiar characters, such as super-hick Floyd R. Turbo, pompous magician Carnac the magnificent, and old Aunt Blabby.

In the mid-1980s, with large amounts of Carson's comedy bits (and those featuring Carson's numerous guests) in the can, a thirty-minute collection of comedy highlights from Carson's years on *Tonight* was assembled as *Carson Comedy Classics,* with Ed McMahon, ever the second banana, serving as host. Outside of Carson's annual anniversary retrospectives on *Tonight, Carson Comedy Classics* provides the best way to relive the highlights of Carson's long reign as late-night comedy king.

**CARTER COUNTRY (**) 30 min (44ep Color; 1977–1979 ABC) Situation Comedy** *with Victor French as Chief Roy Mobey, Kene Holliday as Sgt. Curtis Baker, Richard Paul as Mayor Teddy Burnside, Harvey Vernon as Deputy Jasper DeWitt, Jr., and Guich Koock as Deputy Harley Puckett*

When Jimmy Carter became president in early 1977, the nation thought it was quaint that he came from a small rural town such as Plains, Georgia. For a brief moment, there was a spell of "redneck chic" in the land, which was reflected on television by shows such as *The Dukes of Hazzard* and *Carter Country.*

Set in Clinton Corners, Georgia, just down the road from Plains (hence the title), *Carter Country* is a harmless effort to take the central concept of the 1967 hit film *In the Heat of the Night* and turn it into a sitcom. Roy Mobey is a died-in-the-wool Confederate white police chief with a kind heart. Chief Mobey now must contend with his first black deputy, Curtis Baker, who is full of big (northern) city learning and attitudes. The two distrust each other, but yet get along well out of common respect. Many of the jokes are racially edged, which wears thin after a few viewings.

**CASABLANCA (*) 60 min (10ep B&W; 1955–1956 ABC) Spy Drama** *with Charles McGraw as Rick Jason, Marcel Dalio as Capt. Louis Renaud, Dan Seymour as Ferrari, and Clarence Muse as Sam*

This is the first attempt to translate the 1942 Bogart–Bergman film classic *Casablanca* to television. The attempt fails miserably, with Charles McGraw quite wooden as the American expatriate in North Africa (whose name is inexplicably altered here from Bogart's Rick Blaine to Rick Jason). Marcel Dalio, star of two Jean Renoir film masterpieces (*The Grand Illusion* and *Rules of the Game*) provides whatever class exists in this series in the Claude Rains role of local French police chief.

**CASABLANCA (*½) 60 min (5ep Color; 1983 NBC) Spy Drama** *with David Soul as Rick Blaine, Hector Elizondo as Capt. Louis Renault, Reuven Bar-Yotam as Ferrari, Scatman Crothers as Sam, and Patrick Horgan as Maj. Heinrik Strasser*

This 1980s version of the 1942 Humphrey Bogart-Ingrid Bergman film is slightly more palatable than the bland 1950s adaptation, but not by much. Primarily, the fault lies with insisting on casting a he-man type as Rick (the Bogart role). Where Humphrey Bogar deftly combined strength, irascibility, and vulnerability in his character, this TV version only emphasizes the strength, thus resulting in a more run-of-the-mill spy saga. David Soul tries hard, but his California stud image, quite useful in his portrayal of "Hutch" in *Starsky and Hutch,* does not belong in Casablanca, sparring with Nazis and pining away for lost loves.

The splashy, flashy production of this *Casablanca* is typical of popular producer David L. Wolper (*Roots, The Thorn Birds*).

**CASANOVA (**½) 60 min (6ep Color; 1971 UK BBC) Drama** *with Frank Finlay as Giovanni Casanova, Zienia Merton as Christina, Norman Rossington as Lorenzo, Christine Noonan as Barbarina, Patrick Newell as Carlo, Geoffrey Wincott as Senator Bragadin, and Ronald Adam as the Senior Inquisitor*

Eighteenth-century Italian poet, writer, and lover, Giovanni Casanova, sits in his cell, reflecting on the many accusations that he has led a wicked life. You'll have plenty of opportunities to judge for yourself as this series traces his fabled career, complete with some fairly explicit language, nudity, and detailed sexual writings. (You may have to rewind and watch several times, just to render a fair verdict.) The series was written by Dennis Potter, creator of *Pennies from Heaven,* and played in first-run syndication in the United States.

**THE CASE OF THE DANGEROUS ROBIN (*) 30 min (18ep B&W; 1960–1961 Syndication) Crime Drama** *with Rick Jason as Robin Scott and Jean Blake as Phyllis Collier*

Future *Combat* lead Rick Jason toils away as a contemporary insurance investigator with fast karate moves and a nose for customer fraud. A formula crime adventure series with a theme song by Red Skelton's orchestra leader (David Rose) and a title more intriguing than any of the cases.

**THE CASES OF EDDIE DRAKE (½) 30 min (13ep B&W; 1951 DuMont) Crime Drama** *with Don Haggerty as Eddie Drake and Patricia Morrison as Karen Gayle*

Private detective Eddie Drake works the seamier side of New York City, with a female psychologist at his side. A formula crime adventure series originally shot on a shoestring budget in the late 1940s/early 1950s, and left sitting on the shelf for quite a while. There's a good reason.

**CASEY JONES (**½) 30 min (32ep B&W; 1957–1958 Syndication) Adventure** *with Alan Hale, Jr., as Casey Jones, Bobby Clark as Casey Jones, Jr., Mary Lawrence as Alice Jones, Dub Taylor as Willie Simms, Eddy Waller as Red Rock, and Pat Hogan as Sam Peachpit*

A great opportunity to see Alan Hale, Jr., steer something other than the ill-fated *Minnow* of *Gilligan's Island.* He's the engineer behind the legendary *Cannonball Express,* riding the Midwest rails in the 1890s for the Illinois Central Railroad, with his wife and young son at his side. This is a simple, kid-oriented adventure series with Saturday matinee-style plots and an always triumphant crew of good guys. Though inspired by a famous ballad that ends in the crash of the *Cannonball* and the death of Casey, no such grisly fate awaits him here.

**CASSIE & COMPANY (**) 60 min (13ep Color; 1982 NBC) Detective Drama** *with Angie Dickinson as Cassidy "Cassie" Holland, John Ireland as Lyman "Shack" Shackelford, Dori Brenner as Meryl Fox, and Alex Cord as Mike Holland*

Angie Dickinson has always been known for her good looks, from a leading role as a leggy dance hall girl in the 1959 film *Rio Bravo* (when she was twenty-eight), to the starring role as Pepper Anderson in *Police Woman* (in her forties). *Cassie & Company,* filmed after Dickinson had kissed age fifty good-bye, could well be her last role as a sexpot. Cassie Holland is mostly an update of Pepper, now off the force and running a detective business she bought from Shack Shackelford. Cassie does her share of flirting to crack a case, and the help of Mike Holland, her ex, now city District Attorney, is a big plus to her as well. Grover Washington, Jr. wrote and performs the theme song.

**THE CAVANAUGHS (***) 30 min (26ep Color; 1986–1989 CBS) Situation Comedy** *with Barnard Hughes as Francis Cavanaugh, Christine Ebersole as Kit Cavanaugh, Peter Michael Goetz as Chuck Cavanaugh, Mary Tanner as Mary Margaret Cavanaugh, Danny Cooksey as Kevin Cavanaugh, Parker Jacobs as John Cavanaugh, and John Short as Fr. Chuck Cavanaugh, Jr.*

You can practically smell the corned beef and cabbage in this light family sitcom about three generations of the very Irish–American Boston Cavanuaghs living under one roof. The role of the crotchety old head of the clan was practically tailor-made for Barnard Hughes, and he gives it his all. He's demanding, judgmental, and interfering with his children (Kit and Chuck) and grandchildren (Mary Margaret, Kevin, John, and Fr. Chuck), merely expecting them to conform to all his expectations and values in work, play, religion, and sex. Naturally, as he reminds them time and again, he's only acting out of love. True enough, but he's also a stubborn Irishman determined to get his own way, no matter what!

The two special prizes in Pop's eyes are Mary Margaret and Kit, his one-time estranged daughter who had left the family household years ago for the world of show business. She's returned home after nearly two decades to help raise her brother Chuck's kids (after the death of his wife) and to take a break from showbiz. Pop is naturally delighted to see her, though occasionally annoyed when she becomes the center of attention (especially to Mary Margaret), spinning tales of celebrity circles and limousine luxury—balanced with memories of her association with an ill-fated talk show venture hosted by Alan Thicke (an odd in-joke reference to Thicke's real-life 1983 *Thicke of the Night* show). Christine Ebersole does a good job as Kit, giving the program a strong central core: Kit and Pop. The familiar father–daughter patter begins practically from the moment she first comes through the door, only now as an adult Kit is equipped with far more ammunition for battle than ever before. And with for more appreciation for just how special her dad really is.

This is a well-paced comedy with plenty of wisecracks and minor family conflicts. Occasionally, Art Carney also turns up as Pop's brother, James Cavanaugh, giving Hughes a chance for some scenes of sibling rivalry as well. This is perfect accompaniment to a mug of green beer on St. Patrick's day, but can be viewed straight the rest of the time.

**CELANESE THEATER (**½) 60 min (20ep B&W; 1951–1952 ABC) Drama Anthology**

One of ABC's first prestigious production vehicles, a live drama series presenting one-hour adaptations of top-quality plays by writers such as Eugene O'Neill, Maxwell Anderson, Philip Barry, and Elmer Rice. Though the kinescope film recordings of the series are not available for syndication, a handful of episodes have turned up on home video, including "Winterset" (by Maxwell Anderson with Eduardo Ciannelli, Ralph Morgan, and Richard Carlyle), "Yellowjacket" (by Sidney Howard and Paul de Kruif with Richard Kiley, MacDonald Carey, and Jack Klugman), and "On Borrowed Time" (by Paul Osborn and Lawrence Edward Watkin with Ralph Morgan, Mildred Dunnock, and Billy Chapin). ■

**CELEBRITY** **(**) (6-½hr miniseries Color; 1984 NBC) Drama** *with Michael Beck as T. J. Luther, Joseph Bottoms as Mack Crawford, Ben Masters as Kleber Cantrell, James Whitmore as Clifford Casey, Hal Holbrook as Calvin Sledge, Karen Austin as Ceil Shannon, and Debbie Allen as Regina Brown*

In Texas, 1950, three high school senior boys, T. J., Mack, and Kleber, are involved in a rape/murder of a young girl. They all agree to cover up the evidence. Twenty-five years later, T. J. is a televangelist, Mack is a movie star, and Kleber is a writer. They reunite, trouble develops, and the old rape/murder charge resurfaces. This overly glitzy series is based on the Thomas Thompson novel.

**CENTENNIAL** **(***) (26hr miniseries Color; 1978–1979 NBC) Drama** *with David Janssen as the Narrator/Paul Garrett, Robert Conrad as Pasquinel, Richard Chamberlain as Alexander McKeag, Michael Ansara as Lame Beaver, Gregory Harrison as Levi Zandt, Alex Karras as Hans Brumbaugh, Timothy Dalton as Oliver Seccombe, Lynn Redgrave as Charlotte Buckland, Brian Keith as Axel Dumire, William Atherton as Jim Lloyd, Doug McKeon as Philip Wendell, Barbara Carrera as Clay Basket, Stephen McHattie as Jacques Pasquinel, Chad Everett as Capt. Maxwell Mercy, Cliff DeYoung as John Skimmerhorn, and Robert Vaughn as Morgan Wendell*

An appropriately epic television adaptation of James A. Michener's massive novel, following the growth of America in microcosm by focusing on the developments taking place in one particular slice of territory (a piece of land in the Colorado Rocky Mountains). The story begins in the late 1700s with the arrival of the first white men to lay claim to the area, French–Canadian trader Pasquinel and his partner, trader Alexander McKeag, a Scottish fugitive. They find the spot breathtakingly beautiful. Years later, so does Mennonite Levi Zandt, who establishes the town of Centennial there, with farmers, ranchers, and miners following in his wake. And so the town grows over the years into the twentieth century, with struggles for power, control, and influence over the area continuing from generation to generation. By the end, we've reached contemporary times, with Paul Garrett (descendant of Pasquinel) facing off against businessman Morgan Wendell.

*Centennial* is truly a star-studded, big-budget, sharp-looking package. Even the cast highlights in the list above leave out dozens of familiar names, who all turn in strong performances. In an odd way, though, the real star just might be the setting itself. It stands tall, confident, and proud at the beginning, boldly challenging the awestruck newcomers. By the end, the area is still majestic, but considerably scuffed, nicked, battered, and beaten by the encroachment of civilization. Though not quite an ecological *Roots, Centennial* does offer a hint of the tremendous impact personal aspirations and visions have had on the development (for better or worse) of our country's topography and, by extension, its spirit.

This lengthy package plays in many forms, originally running as a miniseries of two- and three-hour films but later broken into one-hour segments as well.

**CESAR'S WORLD** **(**) 30 min (39ep Color; 1968–1969 Syndication) Documentary** *with Cesar Romero as host*

Cesar Romero, the suave Latin lover of Hollywood days gone by, is an odd choice to host this series that focuses on the nitty-gritty of various cultures around the world. Romero would probably feel more at home at a local posh nightclub, with a dry martini in his hand.

**CHAMPION, THE ADVENTURES OF** **(*) 30 min (26ep B&W; 1955–1956 CBS) Adventure** *with Barry Curtis as Ricky North and Jim Bannon as Sandy North*

Gene Autry's horse Champion prances out in his own series (produced by Autry's company). Set in the ever-popular 1880s, the series focuses on the stallion and twelve-year-old Ricky, the only human Champion will tolerate on his back.

**THE CHAMPIONS** **(**) 60 min (30ep Color; 1967 UK ATV) Adventure** *with Stuart Damon as Craig Stirling, Alexandra Bastedo as Sharon Macready, William Gaunt as Richard Barrett, and Anthony Nicholls as W. L. Tremayne*

Stirling, Macready, and Barrett are three spies for Nemesis, a mysterious crime-fighting group based in Geneva, Switzerland, who are given superhuman powers by some hermits in Tibet. The trio then return to work with a marked improvement in their job performance, as you might expect.

**CHANNING** **(**½) 60 min (26ep B&W; 1963–1964 ABC) Drama** *with Henry Jones as Dean Fred Baker and Jason Evers as Prof. Joseph Howe*

Something of a *Dr. Kildare* on campus, *Channing* concerns craggy old Dean Baker and bright young Prof. Howe, who interact with the other faculty and the students of midwestern Channing University.

Don't bother with the two forgotten stars here—look for the background cast of semi-regulars. You'll find such familiars as Marion Ross (Mrs. Cunningham in *Happy Days*), Suzanne Pleshette (Bob's wife, Emily, in the 1970s *Bob Newhart Show*), Barbara Harris (from Broadway's *The Apple Tree* and Hollywood's *Nashville*), Forrest Tucker (Sgt. O'Rourke in *F Troop*), Dawn Wells (Mary Ann in *Gilligan's Island*), Keir Dullea (astronaut Bowman in *2001: A Space Odyssey*), Joey Heatherton (the singer/dancer), Yvonne Craig (Batgirl on *Batman*), Leslie Nielsen (Disney's *Swamp Fox,* star of *Police Squad!* and the film *Airplane!*), Bob Crane (star of *Hogan's Heroes*), and Leo G. Carroll (star of *Topper* and Mr. Waverly in *The Man from U.N.C.L.E.*).

**CHARLES IN CHARGE (**) 30 min (94ep at Fall 1989; 1984–1985 & 1987–1989 CBS & Syndication) Situation Comedy** *with Scott Baio as Charles, Julie Cobb as Jill Pembroke, James Widdoes as Stan Pembroke, Willie Aames as Buddy Lembeck, Jennifer Runyon as Gwendolyn Pierce, James Callahan as Walter Powell, Sandra Kerns as Ellen Powell, and Ellen Travolta as Lillian*

Scott Baio, a teen hunk in the early 1980s, went from second banana in *Happy Days* (as the Fonz's younger cousin Chachi), to star of his own short-lived series (*Joanie Loves Chachi*) only to find happiness in this mild domestic sitcom about a young male stud college student who becomes live-in houseboy to a well-off suburban family, the Pembrokes. The point here is to set off Baio's macho cool image against the cuddly nature of his role of keeping an eye on the wild Pembroke brood. "Can a man's man raise kids?" is what *Charles in Charge* is really asking, though the setting is played up for laughs.

After one season, the format alters as the Pembrokes are out and the Powells are in. It is explained that the Pembrokes had moved out of town and sold their home to the Powells. Naturally, Charles comes along with the house. The basic concept, however, stays the same, since the Powells have three young teens for Charles to supervise. Soon thereafter, Charles's mother, Lillian, moves into town and buys Charles's favorite pickup joint, Sid's Pizza Parlor. Veteran Baio watchers will note that Ellen Travolta (sister of John), who plays Lillian, also played Baio's mother in *Joanie Loves Chachi.*

**CHARLIE & COMPANY (*) 30 min (18ep Color; 1985–1986 CBS) Situation Comedy** *with Flip Wilson as Charlie Richmond, Gladys Knight as Diana Richmond, Ray Girardin as Walter Simpson, and Della Reese as Aunt Rachel*

Flip Wilson and Gladys Knight (without her old backup group, the Pips) move from variety to sitcoms in this tepid copy of *The Cosby Show.* Flip and Gladys play Charlie and Diana Richmond, a successful middle-class black couple with three cute but exasperating kids. The already frantic pace of zingy one-liners picks up even further when Diana's smart-mouthed Aunt Rachel moves in.

**CHARLIE CHAN, THE NEW ADVENTURES OF (*) 30 min (39ep B&W; 1957 UK ITC)** *With J. Carrol Naish as Charlie Chan and James Hong as Barry Chan*

The original theatrical Charlie Chan films from the 1930s and 1940s have often been played by local stations like a series, with their general running time of between sixty-five and seventy-five minutes being cut or stretched to fill holes as short as an hour or as long as ninety minutes. Actually, though, with a few exceptions most of these stories are totally disposable: the real attraction is watching the Charlie Chan character calmly and quietly face off against his suspects, the guilty party, and, of course, his number one and/or number two sons. He disarms them with his homey aphorisms, his even tones, and, when necessary, a touch of sarcasm.

Of the three main theatrical leads, Warner Oland (who took the role from 1931 to 1937) is the best, Sidney Toler (1937 to 1946) is a good successor, especially at the beginning of his stint, and Roland Winters (to the end in 1949) is the weakest. Unfortunately, the Charlie Chan films have not been at the top of the preservation and restoration lists, so broadcast copies are often in horrid condition, especially those of the fifty-year-old Oland offerings. Among the titles to look for are *Charlie Chan at the Opera, Charlie Chan on Broadway,* and *Charlie Chan at Treasure Island.*

No doubt observing the success of the Charlie Chan films as television fodder, Britain's ITC production company turned out one season's worth of episodes (syndicated in the United States), with Chan operating out of London. They are no substitute for the originals. Neither is *The Amazing Chan and the Chan Clan,* an absurd 1972 cartoon series (sixteen episodes for CBS Saturday mornings) that follows the adventures of ten children of Charlie Chan throughout the world.

**THE CHARLIE FARRELL SHOW (**½) 30 min (13ep B&W; 1956 CBS) Situation Comedy** *with Charlie Farrell as himself, Charles Winninger as Dad Farrell, Richard Deacon as Sherman Hull, and Leon Askin as Pierre*

The real Charlie Farrell was one of Hollywood's leading men in the 1920s and 1930s (especially with co-star Janet Gaynor). In the 1940s, he left show biz and made a fortune founding the Palm Springs Racquet Club. In the 1950s, the dapper graying ex-star was elected mayor of Palm Springs and returned to the screen, albeit the small glowing one and not the silver version. First, Farrell played the exasperated dad in *My Little Margie,* the ultimate 1950s male urban business type. In this series, he sticks to a role model closer to home: himself. The fictional Farrell, like the real one, runs a Palm Springs health resort and must deal with all the daily hassles of keeping the staff in line and pleasing his pampered patrons. Keep an eye open for the resort manager, played by Richard Deacon (*Leave It to Beaver, The Dick Van Dyke Show*), and the chef, played by Leon Askin (Gen. Burkhalter in *Hogan's Heroes*).

**CHARLIE'S ANGELS** (*½) **60 min (115ep Color; 1976–1981 ABC) Detective Drama** *with Kate Jackson as Sabrina Duncan, Farrah Fawcett as Jill Munroe, Jaclyn Smith as Kelly Garrett, Cheryl Ladd as Kris Munroe, Shelley Hack as Tiffany Welles, Tanya Roberts as Julie Rogers, David Doyle as John Bosley, and John Forsythe as Charlie Townsend*

This is a series roundly panned for the wrong reason. Almost from the beginning in the mid-1970s, the chief accusation against *Charlie's Angels* was that it exploited its beautiful female stars by parading them in swimsuits, exercise tights, and other revealing garb at every opportunity. Of course that happened. But there was a lot more going on, too.

For instance, there's the very premise of the series: that these beautiful women were stuck in humdrum law enforcement jobs that ignored their considerable talents, just because they were women. Charlie Townsend knew better and hired them to be the chief field operatives for his detective agency.

In that setting, there were a number of twists on what was until then the usual television detective setup. To start, these women really did do the legwork, fighting, and final collar of each episode's villain. In doing so, they developed the type of buddy relationship previously reserved for male heroes. So even when one of the angels did end up in a damsel in distress role, it was another damsel (er, angel) that did the rescuing, not some dashing leading man type.

Best of all, John Bosley, the only male regular seen on the series, was not a hulking superstud but rather an average looking, slightly chunky nice guy. He played administrative flunky to Charlie, who never showed his face on camera, preferring to give his instructions and assignments over a speaker phone. Though Bosley helped out in the field, he was also the one who ended up doing all the paperwork at the end of each case—tasks previously reserved for such gal Fridays as Maggie (Sharon Gless) on *Switch* or Peggy (Susan Saint James) on *The Name of the Game. Charlie's Angels* may not be a feminist diatribe, but it is an effective switch on some tried and true TV clichés.

So what's the problem with the series? A familiar one: weak scripts. No wonder everybody ends up focusing on the angels themselves. Our favorite lineup: Sabrina, Kelly, and Kris (with visits from Jill). Worst lineup: Kelly, Kris, and Tiffany (too many blondes).

Since the series ended production in 1981, all of the former angels (especially Farrah Fawcett and Kate Jackson) have had success in other projects, sometimes deliberately playing against their familiar image (Fawcett in *The Burning Bed,* for instance). Still, there's always a market for fresh pin-up fantasy, so in 1988, producer Aaron Spelling held auditions for some new angels, with an eye toward producing a TV movie revival (and perhaps a limited series) for the Fox network. The winners: Clayre Yarlette, Karen Kopins, Sandra Canning, and Tea Leoni.

**THE CHARMER** (**½) **60 min (6ep 1988; Color UK London Weekend) Drama** *with Nigel Havers as Ralph Gorse, Bernard Hepton as Donald Stimpson, Rosemary Leach as Joan Plumleigh-Bruce, Fiona Fullerton as Clarice Mannors, Judy Parfitt as Alison Warren, and Abigail McKern as Pamela Bennett*

Set in the roadhouses and seaside resorts of England during the late 1930s Depression era, this series follows the amorous amoral aspirations of social climber Ralph Gorse. Smartly played by Nigel Havers, he's a good-looking "charmer" who knows just what buttons to push and what tales to spin in his seductive courting of women. After getting what he wants through them (money or power, preferably both), Gorse callously tosses them aside and moves on to his next conquest. However, when he swindles a thousand pounds from Joan Plumleigh-Bruce, a wealthy middle-aged widow, Gorse makes an enemy for life: Donald Stimpson, the woman's close friend and suitor, who is determined to bring him to justice.

Clearly Gorse is meant to be seen as the worst kind of social interloper, but what gives this series a slightly schizophrenic edge is that his glib tongue and smooth techniques are just so seductive. For a while, you can't help but admire his audacious style (especially against truly snooty upper-class types), even though you know retribution awaits him at the wrap-up.

This series is based on characters created by Patrick Hamilton in an unfinished 1950s trilogy (*The West Pier, Mr. Stimpson and Mr. Gorse* and *The Unknown Assailant*) that chronicles the life and times of Ralph Gorse. Hamilton also wrote *Gaslight* and *Rope,* two character classics turned into movies also dealing with greed, power, and stylish manipulators.

**THE CHARMINGS** (**½) **30 min (22ep Color; 1987–1988 ABC) Situation Comedy** *with Caitlin O'Heaney and Carol Huston as Snow White Charming, Christopher Rich as Prince Eric Charming, Judy Parfitt as Queen Lillian White, Cork Hubbert as Luther, and Paul Winfield as the voice of the mirror*

*The Charmings* deserves a lot of credit for taking a familiar concept and standing it on its head and then turning it inside out. The result is often silly, but the program is innovative enough and cute enough to be worth a watch.

The idea is to first take two characters from a popular fairy tale (Snow White and Prince Charming) and then to place them, for no good reason, smack dab in the 1980s, living in suburbia, with two kids, a live-in troll or two, a wicked witch mother-in-law, and a magic mirror. In a manner somewhat akin to *Bewitched,* the figures from mythical times must learn to adapt to modern life.

Snow White (called "Snow") and her prince (just "Eric" now) are so ultrastraight looking that they easily fit in to the white-bread L.A. tract development they live in. Lillian, Snow's nasty stepmother, is a blast as the cranky old witch who relies on her magical powers to cope with a society that treasures youth and beauty (neither of which she has). Lillian's confidant is her magic mirror, which talks back to her in the best streetwise honesty of our times. Paul Winfield, who has played a long string of noble and honorable black figures, almost steals the show with his wry put-downs as the voice of the mirror.

**CHARTERS AND CALDICOTT (**½) (6ep Color; 1985 UK BBC) Mystery** *with Robin Bailey as Charters and Michael Aldridge as Caldicott*

A short-run British mystery series showcasing a pair of comic sleuths introduced more than forty years before in two theatrical films, Alfred Hitchcock's *The Lady Vanishes* (1938) and *Night Train to Munich* (1940). In those shows, Charters and Caldicott (played by Basil Radford and Naunton Wayne) were two minor characters used by script writer Sidney Gilliat as humorous relief against a backdrop of tense espionage adventure. They were perfect, well-meaning twits, more comfortable discussing cricket than Nazi spies. For this series, though, the two have to carry the investigative ball because, much to their dismay, a dead body inexplicably turns up in Caldicott's home. Robin Bailey and Michael Aldridge do a fine job in the title roles, though it might have been a better idea to have two multiepisode tales rather than stretching this single case into six parts. At least they would have had more time at the cricket field, which (no surprise) is where they end up in the concluding chapter of this tale.

**CHASE (*½) 60 min (24ep & 90 min pilot Color; 1973–1974 NBC) Police Drama** *with Mitchell Ryan as Captain Chase Reddick, Wayne Maunder as Sgt. Sam MacCray, Reid Smith as Officer Norm Hamilton, Michael Richardson as Officer Steve Baker, Brian Fong as Officer Fred Sing, Albert Reed as Inspector Frank Dawson, Craig Gardner as Officer Tom Wilson, and Gary Crosby as Officer Ed Rice*

A Jack Webb production created by Stephen J. Cannell and following the exploits of yet another elite police squad in Los Angeles. This time, it's a four-person unit under the watchful eye of Captain Chase Reddick, who dispatches his expert with trained dogs (MacCray), an ace copter pilot (Hamilton), a hot-rod jockey (Baker), and a motorcycle demon (Sing). Even with Cannell's eye for mayhem and occasional humor, this one can't rise above its predictable format.

**THE CHEATERS (*) 30 min (26ep B&W; 1960–1961 UK) Crime Drama** *with John Ireland as John Hunter and Robert Ayres as Walter Allen*

Future *Rawhide* team member John Ireland toils away as a contemporary insurance investigator in London with a hard-working assistant and a nose for customer fraud. Last seen scanning the scripts of *The Case of the Dangerous Robin* (featuring another insurance man) for possible leads and referrals.

**CHECK IT OUT! (**) 30 min (66ep at Summer 1989 Color; 1985– Canada CTV) Situation Comedy** *with Don Adams as Howard Bannister, Henry Beckman as Alf Scully, Tonya Williams as Jennifer Woods, Dinah Christie as Edna Moseley, and Jeff Pustil as Jack Christian*

Don Adams, best known as Agent 86 on *Get Smart,* gets to use one of his trademark schticks, appearing exasperated, as supermarket manager Howard Bannister. Surrounded by a menagerie of incompetent help, Bannister is forever fuming in this simple but sometimes satisfying sitcom.

**CHECKING IN (*) 30 min (4ep Color; 1981 CBS) Situation Comedy** *with Marla Gibbs as Florence Johnston, Larry Linville as Lyle Block, Liz Torres as Elena Beltran, and Patrick Collins as Earl Bellamy*

A collection of second bananas, *Checking In* transplants Marla Gibbs and her character of cheeky maid Florence from *The Jeffersons* and Larry Linville's spineless and stuffy wimp character (similar to his Maj. Frank Burns on *M*A*S*H*) to a swank Manhattan hotel. Florence is executive housekeeper (translation: chief maid) and Linville's Lyle Block is the hotel manager.

Following the brief run of *Checking In,* Marla Gibbs checked back into *The Jeffersons,* and later found more solo success in *227.*

**CHECKMATE (***) 60 min (70ep B&W; 1960–1962 CBS) Detective Drama** *with Anthony George as Don Corey, Doug McClure as Jed Sills, Sebastian Cabot as Carl Hyatt, and Jack Betts as Chris Devlin*

An intelligent detective series from the late 1950s/early 1960s era, *Checkmate* is one of the few of that genre not produced by Warner Bros. (home of *77 Sunset Strip*). Checkmate, Inc. is a posh San Francisco detective agency, run by the requisite hunks, Don Corey and Jed Sills. What sets *Checkmate* apart from its Warner Bros. competition is that the Warners detective series always added some offbeat male for laughs and some pretty young thing for looks. *Checkmate* totally eschewed the "bubble-headed babe" and its offbeat male (Carl Hyatt) is presented as the mental superior of the two pretty boys. Hyatt (played by rotund and British Sebastian Cabot) is a trained criminologist, who is frequently frustrated by the thickness of his sleeker associates.

Cabot's superior acting was later largely wasted in his most famous series, *Family Affair,* where he played a prissy nanny named French.

**CHEERS (****) 30 min (168ep at Fall 1989 Color; 1982– NBC) Situation Comedy** *with Ted Danson as Sam Malone, Shelley Long as Diane Chambers, Rhea Perlman as Carla Tortelli, Kirstie Alley as Rebecca Howe, Nicholas Colasanto as Ernie "Coach" Pantusso, Woody Harrelson as Woody Boyd, Kelsey Grammer as*

*Dr. Frasier Crane, Bebe Neuwirth as Dr. Lilith Sternin, John Ratzenberger as Cliff Clavin, and George Wendt as Norm Peterson*

It's lust at first sight. Or at least by the end of the first episode. That's when down-to-earth Boston bartender Sam Malone and self-conscious grad student turned barmaid Diane Chambers start walking that thin line between love and hate. On the surface, they have absolutely nothing in common: He's a former baseball pitcher with plebeian tastes and an outgoing personality, while she's an overeducated English major with perfect breeding and a preference for the classics. The only reason she even enters the Cheers bar in the first place is to have a drink with her literature professor/paramour, Sumner Sloan, before the two of them rush off to the islands. But then Sumner decides to go back to his wife, leaving a distressed Diane looking for employment, so Sam offers her a job as a cocktail waitress (pointing out that with her degrees and lack of real-world experience, she wasn't qualified for much else). Rationalizing this as an opportunity to help her writing by getting to know the "common people," Diane accepts the job. In reality, of course, they agree to this arrangement because, no matter how illogical it may seem, they find themselves attracted to each other.

At first, Sam and Diane hide their emotions with quips and put-downs. (She makes fun of his uneducated ways and he mocks her pretentious mannerisms.) By the end of the first season, though, they at last admit their true feelings in one of the funniest, sexiest reverse seductive scenes ever. Following a passionately angry argument in Sam's office (with the entire bar listening at the door), they stand face to face, fire in their eyes, as Sam suddenly asks: "Are you as turned on as I am?" "More!" Diane comes back in response.

The two then carry on an intense affair for one season, but it's a stormy situation so their barroom comments are still peppered with quips and put-downs. That sharp edge continues through every subsequent phase of their relationship as they split, continue to work together, flirt with other people (Diane nearly marries her psychiatrist, Frasier Crane), and, eventually, agree to marriage.

The ceremony takes place at Cheers (with the bar patrons exchanging bets as to whether or not they'll really go through with it), at the end of Shelley Long's fifth and final season as a regular with the program. It's a very clever episode that manages to write the character of Diane Chambers out of the storyline yet still bring the Sam and Diane relationship to a satisfying and upbeat conclusion.

There are two parallel plots; a fantasy flash-forward and the actual story. In the latter, the two split by the end of the episode, but it's an amicable arrangement. Diane goes off to complete her half-finished (but just sold) novel, promising to return for a wedding in six months. Somehow Sam knows that will never happen, and he watches quietly as she disappears out the door and out of his life. However, in the fantasy track, it's all quite different. In that, the two are content in their golden years, looking back over a happy life together. This part of the story is very effective and demonstrates why, frankly, the two of them *should be* married. They complement each other perfectly, with Diane helping Sam to be more genuinely affectionate, considerate, and responsible, while he makes her feel more comfortable with people and self-confident about herself. In the final fantasy scene, they dance lovingly together in the romantic light of their living room.

Of course, the best aspect of the Sam and Diane relationship is that it provides a continuing sexually charged lure to the series. But what sets *Cheers* apart from an average comedy offering is that the story doesn't stop with them. Instead, while Sam and Diane are carrying on, so is everyone else, turning this into one of the best written and executed situation comedies ever (courtesy of the MTM-groomed creative team behind *Taxi*). There are two wonderful Gracie Allen-type illogical innocents (the Coach and his successor, Woody), a sharp-tongued waitress who hates Diane (Carla), a know-it-all yakker (postman Cliff Clavin), a deadpan intellectual (Frasier, Diane's old psychiatrist), and a beer-drinking schlub (the rotund Norm Peterson, whose entrance into the bar is greeted with a chorus of "Norm!" from the patrons). All of these characters are clearly defined and remain true to type (even if it means coming off as slovenly or obnoxious), with every one given showpiece episodes and excellent lines. As a result, this is a series with throwaway background comments that are as funny as the main punchlines (for example, while Sam and Diane once again ponder the state of their relationship, the bar patrons engage in a passionate discussion on the fine points of the *Road Runner* cartoons).

A highly recommended series, even after the departure of Diane. Wisely, the producers opted not to do the same type of relationship over again with the new female foil (Kirstie Alley's Rebecca Howe), letting Rebecca and Sam simply spar while he tries to score, more for ego than love. (She takes over as manager of Cheers while Sam works as the chief bartender.) With all the other cast members firmly established by then, *Cheers* plays out even more as a pure ensemble comedy in those seasons. And, though Sam and Diane failed to tie the knot, the series still adds some husband and wife plots to the story repertoire with two other weddings: Carla and hockey player Eddie Lebec (Jay Thomas), and Frasier and fellow psychiatrist Lilith Sternin (Bebe Neuwirth).

The outside facade of a Cheers-type bar really does exist in Boston, though the place is called the Bull & Finch Pub. The *Cheers* continuity also intersects with that of another Boston-based series (from another production company), *St. Elsewhere.* On *Cheers,* Carla mentions going to St. Eligius hospital to give birth, while on one episode of *St. Elsewhere* several of the characters stop by the bar for a few drinks (and interact with Carla, Cliff, and Norm).

**CHER (**) 60 min (26ep Color; 1975–1976 CBS) Musical-Variety with Cher and Gailard Sartain**

Produced after Cher's divorce from Sonny Bono and in between her two stints with Sonny as co-host of *The Sonny and Cher Comedy Hours, Cher* is not hurt by the absence of Mr. Bono. Numerous top rock acts of the day appear as guests, portly Gailard Sartain (of *Hee-Haw*) supplies laughs on a regular basis, and George Schlatter (*Laugh-in*) produces.

**CHEYENNE (**½) 60 min (107ep B&W; 1955–1963 ABC) Western** *with Clint Walker as Cheyenne Bodie*

One of the granddaddys of TV hour-long adult westerns, *Cheyenne* is also one of the first forays into TV production by the Warner Bros. film studio. There is not much to the plot here, as tall, laconic, rugged Cheyenne Bodie, an ex-frontier scout, roams the West in the days after the Civil War. Bodie is always hooking up with people who need help or who are looking for trouble. It's not a meaty concept, but it's done well enough to keep you occupied for an hour.

**THE CHICAGO STORY (**½) 90 min (13ep & 2hr pilot Color; 1982) Drama** *with Maud Adams as Dr. Judith Bergstrom, Vincent Baggetta as Lou Pellegrino, Molly Cheek as Megan Powers, Dennis Franz as Officer Joe Gilland, Daniel Hugh-Kelly as Det. Frank Wajorski, Richard Lawson as Det. O. Z. Tate, Kristoffer Tabori as Dr. Max Carson, and John Mahoney as Lieutenant Roselli*

A chunky ninety-minute package that takes the concept of a rotating umbrella series and squeezes all the segments together. The result is *The Bold Ones,* sardine style, with separate titles such as *The Doctors, The Lawyers, and The Senator* replaced by a narrative focusing on different circles in the same episodes. There are dedicated doctors (Judith Bergstorm, Max Carson), lawyers (public defender Lou Pellegrino, district attorney Megan Powers, state's attorney Kenneth A. Dutton), and police officers (street cop Joe Gilland, plainclothes partners Frank Wajorski and O. Z. Tate), all forced to face the effects of contemporary crime in Chicago. And it's not like the old days of *The Untouchables* when there was the illusion that if only you could knock off "Mr. Big" and his main lieutenants (or if Prohibition were repealed) everything would be fine. Here crime has been completely interwoven into the fabric of city life, with no easy way to isolate and remove it. So the doctors, lawyers, and police officers have to do their best to live with it.

Though some of the stories meander, the overall series is quite effective, with an especially solid lineup of up-and-coming performers, writers, and directors. Because much of the series was filmed on location, this is a great opportunity for spotting Chicago-trained talent (such as Dennis Franz before his success on *Hill Street Blues,* or Bruce Young before *E/R*). In fact, any Chicago-based performers that don't turn up in even a walk-on role in *The Chicago Story* were probably out of town. Or still nursing the bandages from *The Blues Brothers* movie.

**THE CHICAGO TEDDY BEARS (*) 30 min (13ep Color; 1971 CBS) Situation Comedy** *with Dean Jones as Linc McCray, John Banner as Uncle Latzi, Art Metrano as Nick Marr, Jamie Farr as Lefty, Marvin Kaplan as Marvin, and Huntz Hall as Dutch*

This extremely lightweight sitcom is set in a Chicago speakeasy during the Prohibition era of the 1920s. Linc McCray and his Uncle Latzi run the joint, while Linc struggles to keep his mobster honcho cousin, Big Nick Marr, from muscling in on the profitable business.

Watch this show only to see the actors. Dean Jones starred in Disney's *The Love Bug,* John Banner was Sgt. Schultz in *Hogan's Heroes,* and Marvin Kaplan was the voice of Choo Choo in *Top Cat* and played Henry, one of the regulars in *Alice.* This is the first regular series role for Jamie Farr, before he played Cpl. Klinger on *M*A*S*H.* Finally, Huntz Hall, one of the charter members of the Dead End Kids/Bowery Boys from the 1930s and 1940s movie serials, makes his one and only appearance as a regular in a TV series in this show.

**CHICO AND THE MAN (**½) 30 min (88ep Color; 1974–1978 NBC) Situation Comedy** *with Jack Albertson as Ed "The Man" Brown, Freddie Prinze as Chico Rodriguez, Scatman Crothers as Louie Wilson, and Gabriel Melgar as Raul Garcia*

As with many hit sitcoms of the 1970s, *Chico and the Man* revolves around racial tension. Here the races are Anglo and Latino. Representing the Yankees is Ed Brown, the cantankerous old owner/operator of a garage in a neighborhood in East Los Angeles that is now all Hispanic (other than Brown, it seems). Representing the Chicanos is Chico Rodriguez, a lively, energetic young Mexican-American with an urge to improve his lot in life. Chico ingratiates himself with "The Man," becomes Brown's assistant, and winds up improving the garage's business. The stories revolve around the cultural differences between the two principals and their growing, if mostly unspoken, admiration and trust of each other.

Much of the pleasure of this series comes from the charm of Freddie Prinze, a young stand-up comedian who gained instant national notoriety from this show. Apparently unable to handle the sudden changes in his life, Prinze committed suicide at the end of the show's third season. The fourth and final season is a questionable effort to keep the hit show going without its central focus. Chico is said to have left to go into business with his father, and Mr. Brown finds himself with a new

Hispanic ward, Raul, a twelve-year-old Mexican who smuggled himself across the border in Brown's car trunk when the old codger was in Mexico for a quick fishing trip. This final season is in the *Webster/Diff'rent Strokes* mold, with a kind benevolent white folk caring for a deprived, cute, but mischievous minority kid.

James Komack, of *The Courtship of Eddie's Father* and *Welcome Back, Kotter* fame, produces *Chico and the Man,* while Jose Feliciano provides the theme song.

**CHIEFS (**½) (6hr miniseries Color; 1983 CBS) Drama** *with Charlton Heston as Hugh Holmes, Keith Carradine as Foxy Funderburke, Stephen Collins as Billy Lee, Wayne Rogers as Will Henry Lee, Brad Davis as Sonny Butts, and Billy Dee Williams as Tyler Watts*

Martin Manulis, a *Playhouse 90* producer in the 1950s, brings some class to the usually trashy world of TV miniseries in this tale of forty years in the small southern town of Delano. The story is about a murder in Delano that takes three generations and three police chiefs to solve. ■

**CHINA BEACH (***) 60 min (24ep at Fall 1989 & 2 hr pilot Color; 1988– ABC) War Drama** *with Dana Delany as Coleen McMurphy, Chloe Webb as Laurette Barber, Nan Woods as Cherry White, Michael Boatman as Pvt. Sam Beckett, Robert Picardo as Dr. Dick Richards, Concetta Tomei as Lila Garreau, Marg Helgenberger as Karen Charlene "K. C." Koloski, Brian Wimmer as Pvt. Boonewell "Boonie" Lanier, Megan Gallagher as Wayloo Marie Holmes, and Nancy Giles as Frankie*

There are innumerable TV series about war from the man's point of view, but *China Beach* could well be the first TV series telling a war story from a largely female perspective. The war is the Vietnam war, the time is around 1967, and the place is a medical unit in Vietnam near the ocean (an area nicknamed China Beach). Colleen McMurphy is the war-weary head nurse. Laurette Barber is a perky USO entertainer in the war zone to boost morale. Cherry White is a naive Red Cross volunteer disconcerted by the bloodshed. K. C. is the local whore. Along with some of the male medical help at the unit, the women deal with the nastiness of being near combat as best they can. There are touches of *M*A*S*H*-like black humor, along with soapy-style drama. As in any good war series, *China Beach* undergoes several cast changes over time. Laurette Barber leaves after the first six episodes to join a USO tour. Soon after the start of the show's second season, Cherry White is killed by mortar fire during the Tet offensive.

*China Beach,* and its more male-oriented contemporary, *Tour of Duty,* manage to pull off the tough task of making the Vietnam War worth watching.

**CHINA SMITH, THE AFFAIRS OF (½) 30 min (52ep B&W; 1952 & 1954–1955 Syndication) Adventure** *with Dan Duryea as China Smith*

These "overseas" adventures (set in the Orient but certainly not filmed anywhere near there) make even grade-B movies look good, with cheesy scenery, wooden plots, and plodding performances. The hook for all this is independent private eye China Smith, a rough-and-tumble kind of guy who operates out of Singapore and who doesn't hesitate to use his gun or his fists. In its original run, the series came in two nonconsecutive seasons of 26 episodes, with the second batch dubbed *The New Adventures of China Smith.* These days, however, the program turns up most often as one entry in *The Golden Years of TV* anthology of 1950s series. ■

**CHIPS (*½) 60 min (138ep Color; 1977–1983 NBC) Police Drama** *with Erik Estrada as Officer Frank "Ponch" Poncherello, Larry Wilcox as Officer Jon Baker, Robert Pine as Sgt. Joe Getraer, Lou Wagner as Harlan, Tom Reilly as Officer Bobby Nelson, and Lew Saunders as Officer Gene Fritz*

Two young hunks patrol the Los Angeles freeway system as members of the California Highway Patrol. They help average citizens, fight crime, and try to keep traffic flowing on the busiest highway system in the world. Most important, though, they look super cool in uniform aboard their motorcycles and, after hours, in their civilian togs as two very eligible bachelors. Jon is a serious one, while Ponch is the more relaxed free spirit. The series uses their likable personalities to carry rather routine tales of everyday police work, with each episode consisting of a mix of light and semiserious incidents. It's not a Jack Webb production, but it might as well have been. Unfortunately, stretching these meandering episodes into one-hour shows really strains the formula. The program would have worked much better in the half-hour *Adam-12* format, though during the original airing of the series the popularity of the two stars (especially Estrada) among teens kept the series going strong for several seasons (and the fan magazines filled with Ponch pinups).

**THE CHISHOLMS (**) (12hr miniseries & 9ep 60 min Color; 1979–1980 CBS) Western** *with Robert Preston as Hadley Chisholm, Rosemary Harris as Minerva Chisholm, Ben Murphy as Will Chisholm, Stacey Nelkin and Delta Burke as Bonnie Sue Chisholm, James Van Patten as Bo Chisholm, and Brian Kerwin and Brett Cullen as Gideon Chisholm*

One of the few miniseries to be brought back as a weekly series, *The Chisholms* follows a clan of Virginians who lose their family farm in a legal dispute. In the miniseries, the clan packs up and heads west, making it as far as Wyoming. In the series, the Chisholms push on to the promised land, California. Set in the pre–Civil War 1840s (quite unusual for TV westerns, which usually prefer the more amorphous 1880s), the series was created by David Dotort, who cut his teeth in western family sagas by producing *Bonanza.* ■

**CHOPPER ONE** (*) 30 min (13ep Color; 1974 ABC) **Adventure** *with Dirk Benedict as Officer Gil Foley, Jim McMullan as Officer Dan Burdick, Ted Hartley as Capt. McKeegan, and Lou Frizzel as Mitch*

Formula police action series, with future *Battlestar: Galactica* space pilot Dirk Benedict cruising an even more unusual corridor of the universe, the skies above California. As a member of the California Police Department's Chopper One squad, Gil Foley and his partner Dan Burdick are part of an airborne highway patrol, scanning the ground below for signs of crime and/or evil—anything from muggers to snipers. Totally disposable. Keep under cover and wait for Benedict's signature role on *The A-Team* instead.

**CHRISTABEL** (***) (4ep Color; 1988 UK BBC) **Drama** *with Elizabeth Hurley as Christabel Burton/Bielenberg, Stephen Dillon as Peter Bielenberg, Geoffrey Palmer as Mr. Burton, Ann Bell as Mrs. Burton, and Nigel Le Valliant as Adam Von Trott*

Dennis Potter (*Pennies from Heaven, The Singing Detective*) turns in an excellent adaptation of the bestselling British autobiography, *The Past Is Myself,* by Christabel Bielenberg. It's the story of a beautiful young English woman (the niece of British Lord Northcliffe) in 1934 who defies her father's wishes and marries a German lawyer, Peter Bielenberg. She and her husband then move to Berlin just as Hitler's brownshirts are taking to the streets. Peter in particular is torn and horrified by the situation—he wants his country to be a viable, strong nation, but he desperately wishes for an end to Hitler's particular vision of success. So they stay in Germany, even when war is declared, but at the same time also find themselves drawn into the anti-Hitler movement. (Eventually, there's even an assassination plot.)

Through all this, Peter and Christabel have to negotiate day-to-day living, reconciling the big picture of outrage with their own personal safety and that of their children. Christabel ends up spending the entire war in Germany, surviving both the rise and fall of Nazi power—all the while doing her best to participate in attempts at change, no matter how futile they might appear.

At the time of this production, the real-life Christabel Bielenberg was still alive and living in Ireland, able to see the success of both her book and this series. This drama first aired in the United States on *Masterpiece Theatre.*

**CHRISTOPHER COLUMBUS** (**½) (6hr miniseries Color; 1985 CBS) **Drama** *with Gabriel Byrne as Christopher Columbus, Rossano Brazzi as Diego Ortiz DeVilhegas, Virna Lisi as Dona Moniz Perestrello, Faye Dunaway as Queen Isabella, Oliver Reed as Martin Pinzon, Raf Vallone as Jose Vizinho, Max Von Sydow as King John, Eli Wallach as Hernando DeTalavera, and Nicol Williamson as King Ferdinand*

Lorimar Productions (the studio that gave us *Dallas* and *The Waltons*) teams up with RAI, an Italian TV outfit, to create a rich version of the life of Christopher Columbus. The story begins in his early days in Genoa, focuses on his bumping into North America while looking for Asia, and concludes with the explorer as an old man making one more trip to the New World. Unlike most historical miniseries, the history here gets predominance over the romance.

**CHRYSLER THEATER, BOB HOPE PRESENTS THE** (see *Bob Hope Presents The Chrysler Theater*)

**THE CHUCK BARRIS RAH-RAH SHOW** (zero) 60 min (6ep Color; 1978 NBC) **Comedy-Variety** *with Chuck Barris as host*

In this nadir for TV variety, game show maven Chuck Barris brings his deliberately gross *Gong Show* format of laughing at *really* bad acts and presents it in a variety hour setting. The few professional acts that are tossed in are interesting, but they suffer by the company they must keep. Jaye P. Morgan is around to leer at the men, just as she does on *The Gong Show.*

**CIMARRON CITY** (*) 60 min (16ep B&W; 1958–1959 NBC) **Western** *with George Montgomery as Matthew Rockford and narrator, Audrey Totter as Beth Purcell, John Smith as Lane Temple, and Dan Blocker as Tiny Budinger*

*Cimarron City* is a run-of-the-mill western set in Cimarron City, Oklahoma, during the oil and gold booms of the late 1800s. The only note of interest is the presence of pre-*Bonanza* Dan Blocker ("Hoss") as a local citizen who aids Sheriff Temple.

**CIMARRON STRIP** (*½) 90 min (23ep Color; 1967–1968 CBS) **Western** *with Stuart Whitman as Jim Crown, Percy Herbert as Mac Gregor, Randy Boone as Francis Wilde, and Jill Townsend as Dulcey Coopersmith*

A wandering, often tedious western that no doubt won its original network slot due to the success of another ninety-minute oater, *The Virginian.* Unfortunately, this one doesn't come up with the scripts to fill those wide-open spaces, stretching the material to the breaking point in a typically loose western premise: Marshal Jim Crown, based in Cimarron City, is assigned the task of patrolling a thousand miles of wild borderland between Kansas and the Indian territory (the "Cimarron strip"), which is where he usually encounters the weekly guest stars. A grade-B western with a grade-A length. ■

**CIRCLE OF FEAR** (see *Ghost Story*)

**CIRCUS BOY** (**½) 30 min (49ep B&W; 1956–1958 NBC & ABC) **Adventure** *with Mickey Braddock as Corky, Noah Beery, Jr., as Joey the Clown, Robert Lowery as Big Tim Champion, Andy Clyde as Circus*

*Jack, Guinn Williams as Pete, and Leo Gordon as Hank Miller*

A breezy children's series following the turn-of-the-century life of Corky, a young circus orphan boy, and his adventures under the big top. He's the adopted ward of Big Tim Champion, owner and operator of the traveling Champion Circus, who took the boy in when he bought the one-ring show and discovered Corky's circus-folk parents had been killed in a high-wire accident. Corky's job with the show is far safer: He's water boy to Bimbo, his pet baby elephant.

Of course, for baby-boomer rock fans, the best part of *Circus Boy* is the chance to see twelve-year-old Mickey Braddock in the title role, a decade before he played under his own name (Micky Dolenz) on the teen-oriented hit series, *The Monkees.*

**THE CISCO KID** **(***) 30 min (156ep Color; 1950–1956 Syndication) Western** *with Duncan Renaldo as The Cisco Kid and Leo Carrillo as Pancho*

Only *The Lone Ranger* predates *The Cisco Kid* in the annals of successful TV westerns, and only the masked man and Tonto can challenge the Cisco Kid and Pancho for pure kiddie western quality. Much like his Anglo compadre, the Lone Ranger, the Mexican-bred Cisco Kid is always polite, ever chivalrous, never gets dirty even after battling bad guys on the plains, and hardly, if ever, kills anyone. He and portly Pancho roam the Mexican-American border regions in the late 1800s, righting wrongs, subduing evildoers, and charming the ladies. Much like the Lone Ranger, Cisco is viewed by local law enforcement officials as an outlaw of some type, so he must keep a low profile and vamoose pronto after doing his good deed for the day, in order not to be detained by any nosy federales. Or course, Cisco is no outlaw at all, but the added threat of capture by lawmen as well as banditos adds some spice to the plots. Pancho, in the best kiddie western sidekick tradition (a la Andy Devine's Jingles for Wild Bill Hickok) is mostly around for laughs, but he can be counted on in a pinch to help Cisco subdue the enemy at hand.

The character of the Cisco Kid originated in an O. Henry short story and developed through a comic strip, a radio series, and several silent and talking pictures (some later ones starring the same Duncan Renaldo who starred in the TV series). Produced by the Ziv company, the masters of quality low-cost 1950s syndication, *The Cisco Kid* was filmed in color, a rarity in the early 1950s, since color TV was still a few years away. The gamble paid off and the fact that all of the episodes are in color (unlike *The Lone Ranger* or *The Adventures of Superman,* which both have a fair number of black-and-white episodes) ensured *The Cisco Kid* a long run in syndication when many of its contemporary black-and-white series were passed over as looking too old-fashioned. ■

**THE CITADEL** **(**½) 60 min (10ep Color; 1983 UK BBC) Drama** *with Ben Cross as Dr. Andrew Manson, Clare Higgins as Christine Barlow, Gareth Thomas as Dr. Philip Denny, Jack Walters as Thomas, Cynthia Grenville as Blodwen Page, Beryl Nesbitt as Annie Hughes, Tenniel Evans as Dr. Page, John Garvin as Dr. Bramwell, Olwen Griffiths as Mrs. Bramwell, Richard Davies as Mr. Watkins, and Janet Davis as Mrs. Watkins*

A crusading young doctor, Andrew Manson (well played by Ben Cross) takes on the seemingly impregnable citadel of the medical bureaucracy, beginning with his practice in a Welsh mining town of the 1920s. Based on a novel by A. J. Cronin (also made into a successful feature film in 1938), this series traces Dr. Manson's frustration with corrupt officials, his sagging idealism, and his fateful career decisions—especially when he relocates to London. There he must face the question of just what he is prepared to do to become a finanacial success. Though there are definitely some stacked odds along the way, this all eventually leads to a dramatic final episode confrontation when Dr. Manson is brought up on charges before a medical board. This is no *St. Elsewhere,* but it plays with more passion than an average episode of *Ben Casey.*

**CITY DETECTIVE** **(*) 30 min (65ep B&W; 1953–1955 Syndication) Police Drama** *with Rod Cameron as Lt. Bart Grant*

New York City police detective Bart Grant dukes it out with hoodlums nationwide in this nondescript cop show. *City Detective* is the first TV series produced by Blake Edwards, before he became famous with *Peter Gunn* and the Pink Panther movies.

**CITY OF ANGELS** **(**) 60 min (13ep Color; 1976 NBC) Detective Drama** *with Wayne Rogers as Jake Axminster, Elaine Joyce as Marsha, Clifton James as Lt. Murray Quint, Timmie Rogers as Lester, and Philip Sterling as Michael Brimm*

A period-piece detective series, set in the 1930s and clearly inspired by the success of Jack Nicholson's 1974 theatrical hit, *Chinatown.* As with the movie, the backdrop is Los Angeles (the "city of angels") and the hero, Jake Axminster, is a marginally successful straight-talking detective cut from the pulpy world of Raymond Chandler tales. Wayne Rogers (in his first post-*M*A*S*H* series) does a good job with the role—a mix of seriousness with a sly sense of humor—and looks quite authentic in costume behind the wheels of the vintage automobiles.

Unfortunately, while *Chinatown* and Chandler can easily get away with some convoluted (at times, inexplicable) plot twists, that same indulgence is much harder to pull off in a series, especially at the beginning. So, even with veteran *Maverick* producer Roy Huggins supervising, *City of Angels* never really places a strong storyline into the meticulously designed stage. The best way to sample this series is with the movie-length packaging of the first story, "The November Plan," a three-hour, three-part tale.

**CIVILISATION** **(****) 60 min (13ep Color; 1969 UK BBC) Documentary** *with Kenneth Clark as host*

Sir Kenneth Clark presents this sweeping journey through the history of Western Europe driven by a simple premise: to seek out what makes human beings truly human. Truly civilized.

For Clark, this means noting necessary technological developments but focusing his emphasis on art, music, architecture, and philosophy. This is a history of ideas, not just of dates, conquests, and gadgets. And Clark pays particular attention to those who could rightly be labeled "genius" in this pursuit, from David to Rembrandt to Van Gogh.

But Clark never forgets that he is doing a television series, either. He takes full advantage of the documentary form to make his points, traveling throughout Europe to show firsthand just what he is talking about. Frequently the camera lingers at some painting, sculpture, or great hall, while music from the period plays in the background and Clark's gentle voice offers helpful hints on just what to look for. Often in these sequences, though, he remains silent for a bit, allowing the works to speak for themselves.

*Civilisation* is the definitive television crash course on Western European culture, admittedly selective in its scope but remarkably consistent in its vision. Clark summarizes this vision aptly in the final segment, confessing a preference for order over chaos, creation over destruction, gentleness to violence, and forgiveness to vendetta. Above all, he believes that it is essential that we learn about ourselves from our own history.

With *Civilisation,* he certainly shows us how. ■

**CLIFFHANGERS** **60 min (10ep Color; 1979 NBC) Adventure**

Three twenty-minute serial dramas, *Stop Susan Williams, The Secret Empire,* and *The Curse of Dracula,* aired under this umbrella title. See each title for details.

**CLIMAX** **(***) 60 min (165ep B&W; 1954–1958 CBS) Drama Anthology** *with William Lundigan and Mary Costa as hosts*

One of the better (and more popular) anthology programs of the era, with an emphasis on tales of suspense and adventure. Though the series itself is not currently available for syndication, individual episodes often turn up on home video releases, especially when they offer the chance to tout a familiar title or performer, or both. Among these are two 1954 productions, "A Christmas Carol" (with Basil Rathbone and Frederic March) and the video debut of James Bond in "Casino Royale." This adaptation of Ian Fleming's first 007 novel has Barry Nelson as Bond (and Peter Lorre as his foe, Le Chiffre) and is of particular interest to fans because it bears some resemblance to Fleming's original text even though it presents the character as an American agent who is less than suave. The adaptation is in contrast to the 1967 theatrical film, which merely used the title and concept as a jumping-off point for a general spy parody.

Of course, every episode of *Climax* was not a key moment in pop culture history, but if you see the title listed as the source of some video production you can usually assume an offering that is better than average. ■

**CO-ED FEVER** **(½) 30 min (1ep Color; 1979 CBS) Situation Comedy** *with Heather Thomas as Sandi, Jillian Kesner as Melba, David Keith as Tucker Davis, Alexa Kenin as Maria "Mousie," Christopher S. Nelson as Doug, and Jane Rose as Mrs. Selby*

Somewhat more than a pilot, somewhat less than a series, *Co-Ed Fever* is one of the contestants in the "shortest-lasting TV series in history" contest. Planned as CBS's entry in the three networks' scramble to clone the film hit *National Lampoon's Animal House* (ABC had the "official" spin-off, *Delta House,* while NBC had *Brothers and Sisters*), *Co-Ed Fever* aired but once (in a special "preview" airing) and has yet to be seen again. Probably more than one episode was produced, but the series has never been syndicated, so it is not clear how many exist.

The show, for the record, is set at Baxter College, an eastern girls school that just went co-ed, with most of the main characters living in Brewster House, where Mrs. Selby served as housemother. The humor is, appropriately, very sophomoric.

**COACH** **(**½) 30 min (13ep at Fall 1989 Color; 1989– ABC) Situation Comedy** *with Craig T. Nelson as Hayden Fox, Jerry Van Dyke as Luther, Clare Carey as Kelly, Shelley Fabares as Christine Armstrong, and Bill Fagerbakke as Dauber*

Best known as a dramatic actor (the TV series *Call To Glory* and the first two theatrical *Poltergeist* films), Craig T. Nelson nimbly tackles comedy here, as he plays beefy-but-caring Hayden Fox, head football coach at Minnesota State University. Divorced for years, Coach Fox has had few contacts with his young daughter Kelly, until she enrolls as a freshman at Minnesota State. Suddenly, the coach has to exercise his rusty fathering skills. The results are somewhat formulaic (such as when he wants to punch out a faculty member he suspects is dating Kelly), but Nelson's well-rounded portrayal of Coach Fox as a "man's man" makes up for a lot of plot thinness. Shelley Fabares (daughter Mary Stone long ago in *The Donna Reed Show*) plays the coach's romantic interest, a sportscaster at the local TV station. Jerry (brother of Dick) Van Dyke plays Assistant Coach Luther in a manner reminiscent of the thick-headed Ernie ("Coach") Pantusso from the first three years of *Cheers.*

**CODE NAME: FOXFIRE** (**) **60 min (7ep & 2 hr pilot Color; 1985 NBC) Spy Drama** *with Joanna Cassidy as Elizabeth "Foxfire" Towne, Sheryl Lee Ralph as Maggie Bryan, Robin Johnson as Danny O'Toole, John McCook as Larry Hutchins, and Henry Jones as Phillips*

A somewhat more palatable version of the *Charlie's Angels* concept, *Code Name: Foxfire* presents the story of Elizabeth Towne, a female ex-CIA agent unjustly convicted and jailed. Now out of the slammer, she is recruited by Larry Hutchins, brother of the president, to spy again for Uncle Sam, this time as the den mother to two beautiful lassies. Maggie Bryan is a cat burglar from Detroit, while Danny O'Toole is a comely Manhattan cab driver. You just never know when Elizabeth might need a good cab driver to get out of a tight jam in some foreign capital.

**CODE R** (*) **60 min (13ep Color; 1977 CBS) Crime Drama** *with James Houghton as Rick Wilson, Martin Kove as George Baker, Tom Simcox as Walt Robinson, and Susanne Reed as Suzy*

Frantic trauma series such as *S.W.A.T.* and *Emergency!* are at least mildly believable due to their setting in Los Angeles, where violent crime is never more than a moment away, as all good couch potatoes know. *Code R* does not even have this slim shred of veracity, as it is set on tiny Channel Island off the southern California coast. Viewers are asked to believe that in such a sparse setting, constant crises are possible in order to occupy fire chief Wilson, beach chief Baker, and police chief Robinson.

**CODE RED** (*) **60 min (13ep & 90 min pilot Color; 1981–1982 ABC) Adventure** *with Lorne Greene as Joe Rorchek, Julie Adams as Ann Rorchek, Andrew Stevens as Ted Rorchek, Sam J. Jones as Chris Rorchek, and Martina Deignan as Haley Green*

The Rorcheks are no Cartwrights, and *Code Red* is no *Bonanza.* Lorne Greene, the paterfamilias in both the popular western and this lame 1970s action series, only walks through his paces as Joe Rorchek, head of a family of firefighters and arson investigators. Irwin Allen, producer of other high-tech series such as *Lost in Space, Voyage to the Bottom of the Sea* and *Land of the Giants* (not to mention such cinema classics as *The Towering Inferno* and *The Poseidon Adventure*), is behind the scenes in *Code Red,* and tries to toss in a few crumbs of educational fire-prevention lore for children in order to give the series a gloss of redeeming virtue.

**CODE 3** (*) **30 min 39ep B&W; 1956–1957 Syndication) Police Drama** *with Richard Travis as Sheriff Barnett, Denver Pyle as Sgt. Murchison, and Sheriff Eugene W. Biscailuz as himself*

A low-rent version of *Dragnet, Code 3* is based on real-life police case histories. Real-life Los Angeles County Sheriff Biscailuz appears at the end of many episodes. "Code 3" is police lingo for an emergency requiring immediate response.

**THE COLBYS** (*½) **60 min (49ep Color; 1985–1987 ABC) Drama** *with Charlton Heston as Jason Colby, John James as Jeff Colby, Stephanie Beacham as Sable Scott Colby, Barbara Stanwyck as Constance Colby, Katharine Ross as Francesca Scott Colby, Ken Howard as Garrett Boydston, Tracy Scoggins as Monica Colby, Ricardo Montalban as Zachary Powers, Maxwell Caulfield as Miles Colby, and Emma Samms as Fallon Carrington Colby*

At the front end, this series almost has to be run in conjunction with the appropriate *Dynasty* episodes because of some intertwining plot setups. To get things rolling, John James comes from *Dynasty* as Jeff Colby to live in Los Angeles, to search for his missing bride (Fallon, who has amnesia), and to claim his stake in the Colby family empire. Charlton Heston, Stephanie Beacham, and Katharine Ross take the surrogate Blake, Krystle, and Alexis roles, growl a bit in *Dynasty*'s direction (especially at rival Blake), and then settle down to their own machinations. In its original airing, the series even changed its name from *Dynasty II: The Colbys* to just *The Colbys* shortly after it premiered, though this change was probably as much a reflection of the spin-off's disappointing ratings as a desire for a separate identity. In any case, most of the connections to the parent series disappear midway into the first batch of episodes as *The Colbys* begins to stand on its own.

Considering how weak *Dynasty* itself is in the fine art of plots, it seems almost unfair to expect much better from the spin-off. Still, even by those standards of lowered expectations, many of the first season's conflicts are dull formula affairs, setting up the semiobligatory rich versus rich concerns that might have looked good on paper but just don't generate sparks on screen. Everything looks expensive and serious and important, but nothing sticks.

*The Colbys* lasted only two seasons, so the forty-nine episodes cycle through rather quickly in reruns. Keep an eye out for the last dozen or so, because they're the most fun. By then, everyone seems to have adopted a go-for-broke attitude, so the stories and performances carry an extra zing. This reaches a peak at the main cliff-hanger of the final episode in which the always-in-demand Fallon is carried off in an alien spaceship—a plot twist more appropriate to *Soap* or *Mary Hartman, Mary Hartman* than to the *Dynasty* families. Perhaps the writers just wanted to give the supermarket tabloids a dream headline ("Soap Star Abducted by Aliens!") for their program send-off. Whatever the reason, Fallon later turns up again (no explanations, please) on *Dynasty* (as does Stephanie Beacham's Sable), while the remaining Colbys disappear into the ether.

**COLDITZ** (**½) **60 min (28ep Color; 1972–1973 UK BBC) War Drama** *with Robert Wagner, David McCallum, Bernard Hepton, Anthony Valentine, and Jack Hedley*

At the beginning of World War II, the Nazis set up a POW camp for high-level prisoners at Colditz Castle. An imposing, nearly impregnable site, this location was touted as escape-proof, but some dedicated Allied soldiers thought otherwise. This series follows the schemes and adventures both inside and outside the walls with a first-rate cast and some well-written stories. Perhaps the most unusual aspect of this production, though, is that it never had a first-run network airing in the United States despite its success in Britain and the inclusion of the very familiar faces of Robert Wagner and David McCallum. Even today, only fifteen of the available episodes are offered in the Stateside syndication package. So, if you spot this one, be sure to catch it, especially if you're a Wagner fan. You won't be disappointed.

**COLONEL FLACK** (**½) **30 min (39ep B&W; 1957–1959 Syndication) Situation Comedy** *with Alan Mowbray as Col. Humphrey Flack and Frank Jenks as Uthas P. Garvey*

Col. Flack used to be a colonel, but now he is retired, and he spends his time traveling the globe, living the good life, and beating various con artists at their own game. His partner in high-jinks is Uthas P. (for Patsy) Garvey. Alan Mowbray, ubiquitous character actor in numerous movies from the 1930s to the 1950s, is the charming "veddy" British colonel. An earlier live version of this series aired on the doomed DuMont network in 1953 and 1954. The Col. Flack character first appeared in stories by Everett Rhodes Castle in *The Saturday Evening Post.*

**COLONEL MARCH OF SCOTLAND YARD** (**) **(26ep B&W; 1953–1954 UK) Crime Drama** *with Boris Karloff as Colonel Perceval March, Ewan Roberts as Inspector Ames, and Eric Pohlmann as Inspector Gordon*

Boris Karloff, complete with a black eye patch (over his left eye), gets the chance to step away from horror films and suspense anthologies for this standard crime drama. He plays the head of a special investigative division of Scotland Yard (D-3), an expert criminologist given the puzzling cases typically handed over to television sleuths. The stories are routine and the sets occasionally cheesy, but it is fun to see Karloff in this type of role.

**COLT .45** (**) **30 min (67ep B&W; 1957–1960 ABC) Western** *with Wayde Preston as Christopher Colt and Donald May as Sam Colt, Jr.*

In this Warner Bros. western from the late 1950s, Christopher Colt, handsome young son of the inventor of the Colt .45 revolver, travels the West undercover as a gun salesman, while actually spying for Uncle Sam. During the middle episodes, star Wayde Preston was eased out of the series due to contract disputes (a frequent occurrence among Warner Bros. shows of the era). Preston was temporarily replaced by Donald May, who played Sam Colt, Jr., Chris's cousin, who performs the same tasks Chris handled. May was rewarded by Warners for his stepping in at the last minute by being shifted to another of the studio's series (*The Roaring Twenties*) when Preston returned to the fold.

**COLUMBO** (****) **90 min & 2 hrs (43ep: thirty-eight 90 min & nine 2-hr & two 2-hr pilots Color; 1971–1978 NBC & 1989– ABC) Mystery** *with Peter Falk as Lt. Columbo*

The best part of any murder mystery is the ending—when you find out who done it, and how. Then the killer's elaborate scheme is spelled out in detail, with all the twists and turns and red herrings and fatal errors knowingly explained, usually by a brilliant attorney, a hard-working gumshoe, or a disarming amateur detective.

*Columbo* takes just the opposite tack. For about the first twenty minutes of each episode, the audience is shown the killer (the main guest star) at work, cleverly executing what seems to be a near-perfect crime. Then Lieutenant Columbo (Peter Falk) enters the scene. So now you know who did it, how it was done, and who's going to figure it all out. What possible reason could there be to stick around for the rest of a ninety-minute episode? To watch the battle of wits.

There is no regular supporting cast in *Columbo.* The series is carried entirely by the interaction between Falk and the guest stars, who form one of the best lineups of villains since *Batman.* They include Patrick McGoohan as an iron-fisted commandant of a boys' military academy, Donald Pleasance as a dedicated wine connoisseur, Dick Van Dyke as an ambitious professional photographer, Johnny Cash as a top-selling religious singer–songwriter, John Cassavettes as a philandering maestro, Louis Jourdan as an extortionist food critic, and William Shatner as an impeccably dressed television detective. (Some performers even returned for another go-around, though playing completely different murderers.)

In each case, the rumpled, persistent, but always ever-so-polite lieutenant almost immediately spots the guilty party. (Perhaps he had been watching the opening segment of the show before arriving.) For the rest of the story, he picks at alibis, uncovers clues, and builds his case. Mostly, though, he spends time jousting with his number one suspects, admiring their accomplishments, learning about their professions, and asking for their "advice" and observations at every step of the investigation. All the while, the once apparently perfect crime slowly unravels, as viewers race with Columbo to put their finger on the fatal flaw in the scheme.

Columbo ultimately trips up his foes by getting inside their heads and learning how they think. He doesn't just learn *how* they did it—he understands *why.* For those engaged in a cold-hearted grab for money or power, he takes great professional pride in confronting them with the damning evidence—usually self-incrimination as the result of their own carelessness, overconfidence, arrogance, or fear of capture. (Watch the stunned look of realization on the face of Dick Van Dyke in "Negative Reaction.")

Occasionally, there are otherwise good people who resorted to murder as the only solution they could see to a desperate situation. Before turning them in, the lieutenant sometimes offers a moment of sympathetic friendship, such as sharing a farewell bottle of wine with Donald Pleasance in "Any Old Port."

Before watching an episode of *Columbo,* make certain that the time slot is at least ninety minutes (preferably two hours). The series suffers considerably when heavily edited (as it was for a while on *CBS Late Night*), losing the rhythm of the interaction between Columbo and his foes.

Often, the two made-for-TV movie pilots that introduced the character of Columbo ("Prescription: Murder" and "Ransom for a Dead Man") are not shown as part of the series itself. Instead they usually air in a station's movie slots.

Columbo creators Richard Levinson and William Link, who obviously loved mystery series, were also responsible for *Ellery Queen* and *Murder, She Wrote.* In 1989, shortly after the death of Levinson, Link revived *Columbo,* with Peter Falk as one segment in a new series of made-for-TV mystery movies on ABC. Same raincoat (really), plus a new set of puzzling "perfect crimes," beginning with a murder-in-a-locked-room scheme by guest villain Anthony Andrews. ■

**COMBAT (***) 60 min (152ep: 127 B&W & 25 Color; 1962–1967 ABC) War Drama** *with Rick Jason as Lt. Gil Hanley, Vic Morrow as Sgt. Chip Saunders, Pierre Jalbert as Paul "Caje" Lemay, Jack Hogan as Pvt. William G. "Wildman" Kirby, Dick Peabody as Littlejohn, Steven Rogers as Doc Walton, and Conlan Carter as Doc*

*Combat* lasted five seasons, longer than any of the other World War II sagas that turned up in the 1960s, when that war had receded enough into the past to be safe and nostalgic. The focus is on the men of K Company, Second Platoon, U.S. Army Infantry, as they slog their way through Europe from D-Day through V-E Day a short year later. To any real Army dogface engaged in the fight, that year must have seemed like five, but in the case of *Combat,* it really *was* five years long, which is longer than the entire U.S. involvement in World War II. Oh well, TV's *M*A*S*H* lasted far longer than the real Korean War.

The best thing about *Combat* is that the presentation of the GI's life is fairly realistic for series TV. Soldiers come and go, the miseries are numerous, and the so-called honor of warfare is scarce. War is mostly a game of tactics, guts, and luck. The two leads, Lt. Hanley and Sgt. Saunders, are two manly men without any of the self-doubts and personality flaws that pop up in more antiestablishment films and series of the late 1960s and 1970s. After all, this is World War II, our last war where everyone was gung ho.

Aside from the usual grab bag of recruits that make up K Company, keep an eye out for Pvt. Braddock, the company comic in the first season's shows, played by borscht-belt stand-up comic Shecky Greene. *Combat* comes from a time when ethnicity was such a thing to be avoided on TV that someone as obviously Jewish as Shecky plays a character with as bland a name as Braddock.

The grittiness of *Combat* is helped by the series being filmed in black and white and the insertion of some real combat footage. When the show goes to color for its last year, it loses part of its charm. Robert Altman, who went on to direct the original movie version of *M*A*S*H,* served as occasional producer, director, and writer on the first season's episodes of *Combat.*

**THE COMEDY SHOP (*) 30 min (75ep Color; 1978–1979 Syndication) Comedy-Variety** *with Norm Crosby as host*

Boston-born stand-up comic Norm Crosby serves as host to a collection of aspiring comedians, who get three minutes each of national TV time to show their talent. Veteran comics such as Red Buttons and Larry Storch also appear.

**THE COMEDY ZONE (**) 60 min (5ep Color; 1984 CBS) Comedy-Variety** *with Ann Lange, Mark Linn-Baker, Joe Mantegna, Audrie J. Neenan, Bob Gunton, and Bill Randolph*

Here is an extreme rarity: a comedy variety series from the 1980s. Something akin to an updated version of *Love, American Style, Comedy Zone* features varying-length comedy bits and musical numbers. The setting is New York, and the writing tries hard to be hip but succeeds only occasionally. One of the regulars, Mark Linn-Baker, is better known as the American cousin in *Perfect Strangers.*

**COMING OF AGE (**½) 30 min (15ep Color; 1988–1989 CBS) Situation Comedy** *with Alan Young as Ed Pepper, Glynis Johns as Trudie Pepper, Paul Dooley as Dick Hale, Phyllis Newman as Ginny Hale, and Kevin Pollak as Brian Binker*

Dick Hale is unhappy, forced to retire from his job as an airline pilot at age sixty due to his company's official policy on cockpit personnel. To compound his distress, he and his wife, Ginny, have moved into a retirement community in Arizona, the Dunes, where he faces the prospect of just fading away under the blazing sun. Or, even worse, of becoming like their chipper, bouncy, happy neighbors, the Peppers. Ed and Trudie Pepper are glad to be there, glad to chat with their new best friends, glad to jog and play, and glad-glad-glad to share their latest cooking creations. (Ed has even learned to bake bread.) About the only time they get rankled is over some of the rules imposed by the retirement community's young director, Brian Biker, a condescending bureaucrat—and even then they know all they have to do is work with the systern and things will change.

This is a harmless fluff piece, with the upbeat Peppers a surprisingly pleasant shot of energy for the series and an effective contrast to Dick's dour attitude. What gives the series added credibility is the fact that the four leads have been around in television for quite a while (most notably Alan Young with *Mister Ed* and Phyllis Newman on *That Was the Week That Was*), so—like *The Golden Girls*—it's fun to see them in a vehicle that has them all going strong even after "retirement." In that spirit, one of the most enjoyable segments of the program is the photo montage in the opening credits, taking each one's picture scrapbook from their wonder years through their thirtysomethings until they're almost grown.

**COMMANDO CODY (*½) 30 min (12ep B&W; 1955 NBC) Science Fiction** *with Judd Holdren as Jeff King/ Commando Cody, William Schallert as Ted Richards, Aline Towne as Joan Albright, and Greg Gay as Retik*

As television took hold in the 1950s, movie studies found the airwaves the perfect place to give some of their old product new life. The Saturday matinee cliffhanger series from the 1930s and 1940s were perfect programming filler, with a few of the really good ones (most notably, *Flash Gordon*) even winning local prime-time slots. In 1955, Republic Pictures went one better, developing a serial that played like a regular television adventure series (each half-hour episode was self-contained), eventually ending in a final confrontation with the ultimate bad guy (just like a traditional serial). After some very limited theatrical play, they released *Commando Cody* to television, first as Saturday morning summer filler for NBC, then in endless local reruns throughout the schedule.

True to the genre form, many of the special effects and disaster shots are simply stock footage, sometimes lifted from previous serials (such as Republic's 1949 *King of the Rocket Men*). In addition, some of the scientific mumbo jumbo is plainly preposterous (for starters, try to figure out how Commando Cody keeps his legs from being burned by his rocket exhaust, how he stays alive wearing just his insulated leather jacket in space, and how the moon can be knocked from its orbit with a few well-placed surface explosions). But, skipping from episode one to twelve, it's always fun to see the evil genius get his due, even if he does look like someone in a badly designed Pharaoh costume on Halloween.

This is truly silly stuff, but fun in limited doses. And, if you look closely in the first few episodes, you'll see veteran William Schallert (later, Patty's dad on *The Patty Duke Show*) as one of Commando Cody's assistants.

**CONCEALED ENEMIES (***) 60 min (4ep Color; 1984 PBS) Drama** *with Edward Herrmann as Alger Hiss, John Harkins as Whittaker Chambers, Peter Riegert as Richard Nixon, Raymond Serra as J. Edgar Hoover, and Maria Tucci as Priscilla Hiss*

A dramatized version of the bitter real-life conflict between Alger Hiss and *Time* magazine editor Whittaker Chambers, set in the anti-Communist "witch-hunt" period of the late 1940s and early 1950s. The central conflict eventually boils down to charges by Chambers that Hiss was a Soviet spy, and Hiss's attempt to clear his name through a libel suit. Perhaps the most effective aspect of the drama is its demonstration of how devastating the accusation process itself becomes, with the actual facts or truth of the case increasingly irrelevant in the flurry of charges, counter-charges, and political posturing. Herrmann and Harkins are excellent as the fuming rivals, with Peter Reigart's portrayal of young congressman Richard Nixon (eager to exploit the case) quite telling as well.

This was a co-production between Thames Television in Britain and PBS's WGBH in Boston, where much of the filming took place. It first aired Stateside on the drama anthology series *American Playhouse*.

**CONCRETE COWBOYS (**) 60 min (6ep & 2 hr pilot Color; 1981 CBS) Adventure** *with Jerry Reed as Jimmy Lee "J. D." Reed and Geoffrey Scott as Will Ewbanks*

"When You're Hot, You're Hot," was the title of Jerry Reed's hit tune from the 1970s, and *Concrete Cowboys* proves, again, the truth of that axiom. Reed, a popular country and western singer, tries to cash in on the wave of "country chic" that percolated in the United States during the late 1970s (the Carter years). Reed's character, also named Reed, and his buddy Will Ewbanks, are two Montana drifters in the modern West, bumping into trouble and adventure each week. Unfortunately for Reed, he wasn't quite as hot as he thought, for *Concrete Cowboys* contains little that is memorable, and only lasted a short time.

The pilot episode, from 1979, presents a more promising match, with Reed paired with pre–*Magnum, P. I.* Tom Selleck in the Will Ewbanks role.

**CONDO (*) 30 min (11ep Color; 1983 ABC) Situation Comedy** *with McLean Stevenson as James Kirkridge, Brooke Alderson as Margaret "Kiki" Kirkridge, Mark Schubb as Scott Kirkridge, Luis Avalos as Jesus "Jesse" Rodriguez, Yvonne Wilder as Maria Rodriguez, and Julie Carmen as Linda Rodriguez*

Another entry in the "failed sitcoms with McLean Stevenson" category, Condo is a slapdash effort to graft the classic Romeo and Juliet idea with allegedly topical racial humor (which really means thirty minutes of ethnic put-down). Snooty Southern California WASP James Kirkridge and clan are in a bit of an economic pickle and have to move from a vast house in sunny suburbia to a condominium (think of the shame!). There, the Kirkridges rub shoulders with the Hispanic Rodriguezes, on the way up the social ladder from the barrio. Much sputtering ensues between the two camps, and love triumphs when Anglo son Scott and Latino lass Linda start a family and marry each other (in that order).

**CONFLICT (**) 60 min (19ep B&W; 1956–1957 ABC) Drama Anthology** *with Gig Young as host*

"People in conflict" is the theme of these unconnected dramas originally aired as part of the *Warner Bros. Presents* series.

**CONNECTIONS (***) 60 min (10ep Color; 1978 UK BBC) Documentary** *with James Burke as host*

The history of technology is brought alive in this sprightly British series that follows the apparently unrelated connections between numerous small advances in science and changes in politics and social structures throughout history. Host James Burke is a pint-size dynamo who is not at all the usual stuffy, boring, English talking head type that usually host "serious" English TV documentaries. Burke drags the viewer along a breathtaking and tiring road of human knowledge, while speaking in plain, simple language. Pay attention, though—Burke fits a lot of information into his quick phrases. ■

**CONRAD NAGEL THEATER (*½) 30 min (26ep B&W; 1955 Syndication) Drama Anthology** *with Conrad Nagel as host*

Obscure drama series hosted by Conrad Nagel, a Hollywood romantic lead in dozens of films in the 1920s and 1930s, then a strong character actor in the 1940s. Offstage he was a co-founder (and one-time president) of the Academy of Motion Picture Arts and Sciences and helped the organization set up its Academy Awards system. Shortly before beginning work on his last set of films in 1956, he attached his name to this series, also coming aboard to introduce the stories. Though the offerings are generally routine, a few performers such as Sebastian Cabot turn up, almost repertory style, in several episodes of the program's one and only season.

**THE CONSTITUTION: THAT DELICATE BALANCE (***) 60 min (13ep Color; 1984 PBS) Discussion** *with Fred Friendly as host*

Suppose you're the president of the United States, facing a tense, top-secret situation. Or, suppose you're a reporter who has just been given a lead to a story that might seriously embarrass the president and undermine the nation's confidence in him. Now imagine both events taking place at the same time, racing on a collision course with each other. What rights can the president or the reporter invoke, citing the U.S. Constitution for support?

That's the type of hypthetical setup (only far more detailed and complicated) you'll find in this series of seminars staged at Congress Hall in Philadelphia. What sets this apart from just an ordinary academic discussion show is the caliber of the participants, ranging from former U.S. President Gerald Ford to CBS news anchor Dan Rather—all of whom have had to face analogous situations in real life. In fact, it's fun to see all of them forced to explain their positions with more than a few public relations phrases, especially when the hypothetical situations veer awfully close to the real thing.

Former CBS News President Fred Friendly offers background comments to open and close each episode. ■

**THE CONTENDER (½) 60 min (5ep & 90 min pilot Color; 1980 CBS) Drama** *with Marc Singer as Johnny Captor, Katherine Cannon as Jill Sindon, Moses Gunn as George Beifus, and Tina Andrews as Missy Dinwittie*

In this sentimental and starchy saga, Johnny Captor, a bright white boy, inexplicably leaves the good life of college in Oregon to become a championship fighter. Jill, his teacher girlfriend, can't understand why he did it. Fight trainer and ex-champ George Beifus thinks Johnny is the next great white hope. This show could *never* be a contender.

**CONVOY (*½) 30 min (13ep B&W; 1965 NBC) War Drama** *with John Gavin as Commander Dan Talbot, John Larch as Merchant Captain Ben Foster, Linden Chiles as Chief Officer Steve Kirkland, and James Callahan as Lieutenant Dick O'Connell*

A grim, almost documentary-like World War II series (shot in black and white) following the journey of some two hundred American ships across the Atlantic. Will the ships make it to Europe intact? Unfortunately this isn't one of those widely known true-life journeys, so there's no automatic curiosity in seeing familiar history played out. Instead we need to get involved with the stories and characters, but they're generally formula-flat and predictable. So all that's left is a lot of fleet footage. With that as the only enticement, you might as well just switch to a real-life documentary series such as *Victory at Sea*.

One odd continuity note: Someone was obviously paying attention to performer resumes when they made James Callahan's character on the 1980s *Charles in Charge* an ex–World War II Navy officer.

**COOL MILLION (*) 90 min (4ep Color; 1972–1973 NBC) Detective Drama** *with James Farentino as Jefferson Keyes, Adele Mara as Elena, and Ed Bernard as Tony Baylor*

The concept here is offbeat enough to be interesting, but the show just does not jell into anything memorable. Jefferson Keyes is an independently wealthy ex-government spy now out on his own as a private detective. Keyes is so exclusive that he charges a "cool" million dollars for each assignment, though he guarantees money back if not satisfied. Clients contact him through Elena, a woman in Lincoln, Nebraska, with enough time on her hands to act as messenger for Keyes.

*Cool Million* comes from producer Roy Huggins, who also produced such tangy sleuth sagas as *77 Sunset Strip, Alias Smith and Jones,* and *Maverick.*

**THE COP AND THE KID (½) 30 min (13ep Color; 1975–1976 NBC) Situation Comedy** *with Charles Durning as Frank Murphy, Tierre Turner as Lucas Adams, Patsy Kelly as Brigid Murphy, and Sharon Spelman as Mary Goodhew*

During the 1970s, the TV networks seemed convinced that the viewing public couldn't get enough of stories about white people raising adorable black kids. *The Cop and the Kid* is yet another of these shows, each one of which seems overly forced and overly cute in retrospect. The only redeeming feature here is that Lucas, the resident black orphan, is not really adorable. He is more of a pain in the rear who takes advantage of his unlikely guardian, middle-aged bachelor cop Frank Murphy.

**THE CORAL JUNGLE (**½) 60 min (12ep Color; 1975–1976 Syndication) Documentary** *with Leonard Nimoy as host/narrator, and Ben Cropp and Eva Cropp as themselves*

The wonders of the Australian Great Barrier Reef are shown through the diving exploits of Ben and Eva Cropp, while well-known Vulcan Leonard Nimoy adds very logical narration.

**CORKY AND THE WHITE SHADOW (**½) 12 min (15ep B&W; 1956 ABC) Adventure** *with Darlene Gillespie as Corky Brady, Buddy Ebsen as Matt Brady, Lloyd Corrigan as Uncle Dan, and Chinook as White Shadow*

Originally a serial seen as part of *The Mickey Mouse Club* in the 1950s, *Corky and the White Shadow* stars Mouseketeer Darlene Gillespie. With the help of her faithful dog, White Shadow, she tracks down a criminal sought by her father, the local sheriff (played by Buddy Ebsen, who is more famous for playing Ozark millionaire Jed Clampett and Davy Crockett's pal Georgie Russel).

**THE CORNER BAR (**) 30 min (16ep Color; 1972–1973 ABC) Situation Comedy** *with Gabriel Dell as Harry Grant, Langhorn Scruggs as Mary Ann, Vincent Schiavelli as Peter Panama, Anne Meara as Mae, Eugene Roche as Frank Flynn, and Ron Carey as Donald Hooten*

Virtually two series under one title, *The Corner Bar*'s first ten episodes concern Grant's Tomb, a Manhattan bar owned and operated by Harry Grant (played by Gabriel Dell, one of the original Dead End Kids, a.k.a. the Bowery Boys). In the last six episodes, the place is renamed The Corner Bar (which is the name of the show all along) and comes with two new owners, Frank and Mae. Some of the regulars turn up in both permutations, some just in one or the other.

Considering that *The Corner Bar* is produced by stand-up comedy master Alan King and *Your Show of Shows* graduate Howard Morris, it's a surprise and a pity that this show isn't funnier. For a more satisfying, tall, cool laugh, move up the east coast to Boston's *Cheers.*

**CORONADO 9 (*) 30 min (39ep B&W; 1959–1960 Syndication) Detective Drama** *with Rod Cameron as Dan Adams*

Tall, good-looking Dan Adams is one of the horde of TV private eyes operating in California, this time on the Coronado peninsula near San Diego. "Coronado 9" is his telephone exchange, in the pre–"all numbers" era when people still *had* such things.

**CORONATION STREET (**) 30 min (B&W & Color; 1960– UK Granada) Drama** *with Violet Carson as Ena Sharples, William Roache as Ken Barlow, Pat Phoenix as Elsie Tanner, Margot Bryant as Minnie Caldwell, Doris Speed as Annie Walker, Arthur Lowe as Mr. Swindley, Jean Alexander as Hilda Ogden, Bernard Young as Stan Ogden, and Jack Howarth as Albert Tatlock*

And the cast list could go on and on, just as in any U.S. soaper. *Coronation Street* is Britain's champion sudser, set in the northern England working class world of old terraced houses in industrial Lancashire. More than 2,500 episodes have gone out (twice weekly, in the early evening) since its première in December 1960, though the program has never been successfully exported Stateside. Like our daytime soap offerings, it may be that such leisurely paced drama doesn't cross cultures as easily as the high glitz of a *Dallas* or a *Dynasty.* Nonetheless, a curiosity to sample while on a visit to Britain, or browsing through a broadcast museum's card file, just for a taste of another world that viewers take as seriously as soap fans take soap operas in the United States. Which may be why even the real-life Queen of England and Prince Philip turned up for a visit with the fictional characters there. *Monty Python* may have to use cardboard cutouts of royalty in its comedy sketches, but the residents of *Coronation Street* get the real thing.

**CORONET BLUE (***) 60 min (11ep Color; 1967 CBS) Adventure** *with Frank Converse as Michael Alden*

The history of *Coronet Blue* is almost as exciting as the offbeat show itself. In early 1965, CBS agreed to run this one-hour mystery series from Herbert Brodkin, a star producer from TV drama's golden age in the 1950s who also produced the critically acclaimed hit series *The Defenders* in the early 1960s. CBS had a change of heart and canceled its order for *Coronet Blue* shortly before Brodkin began shooting the series. Brodkin, believing in the show, went ahead and filmed eleven episodes, in the hopes that the series would find a prime-time slot soon enough.

The 1965 season came and went and none of the networks took a chance on the program. The 1966 season came and again *Coronet Blue* was passed over. Admitting defeat, Brodkin agreed to let the series run during the summer of 1967, in order to make some money out of the doomed effort. With little fanfare, CBS stuck *Coronet Blue* into its summer schedule and was as shocked as anyone when it became the top-rated summer series of 1967. The network then wanted to keep the show going, but that was not to be. By the fall of 1967, Brodkin was involved in other projects and star Frank Converse was hard at work filming *N.Y.P.D.*, a new cop series set to première on ABC. Thus, *Coronet Blue* faded away at the end of the summer.

It is not that hard to guess why CBS originally passed on *Coronet Blue,* since the premise is so out of the ordinary, especially by 1965 standards. Frank Converse plays a man fished out of New York's East River with nonlethal gunshot wounds and a severe case of amnesia. Converse's character cannot recall anything of his past, not even his name, but he knows somebody tried to kill him and he is told that he was mumbling the words "Coronet Blue" when he was rescued. Converse's character, who is given the name Michael Alden during his recuperation, spends his time trying to rediscover his past and unlock the mystery of the phrase "Coronet Blue," which, he believes, will help unravel the details of his attempted murder.

Alden's quest leads in the direction of spies, secret organizations, and powerful interests that might have tried to kill him for what he knew. Alden is followed by confederates of his would-be killers, who stand ready to try to kill him again, if he regains his memory or begins to get too close to the truth about his background.

*Coronet Blue* has a lot of spy mystery elements to it, which CBS must have liked, but the amnesia angle is very odd, and Alden is a lonely man on a lonely quest, with few friends and few clues to his past. There is little of the surface trappings of fancy gadgets or beautiful women found in popular spy sagas featuring James Bond or Napoleon Solo that would make *Coronet Blue* easy home viewing.

It is, however, just these touches of quirkiness that turn *Coronet Blue* into such a gem. Like the viewer, Alden has no idea if he was an honorable man about to uncover some nefarious doings or just a common hood slated for execution in yet another gangland war. This dilemma adds an intriguing touch to Alder's search—he is afraid at times to find the answer to his questions, since his real past may not be what he hopes.

The format of searching for Alden's past is a limited one. *Coronet Blue* could never have become a long-running series, which was what all prime-time series were supposed to aim for in 1965. Coronet Blue could only have been what it became, a successful limited-run series. The major fault, of course, is that producer Brodkin never filmed a concluding episode, since he hoped the series would be picked up to run for another season. After all eleven episodes, both Michael Alden and the viewer still are not much closer to resolving who Alden really is or what "Coronet Blue" means. Perhaps, someday, Frank Converse will star in a TV movie sequel to wrap up the loose ends. Some people have been waiting more than two decades for an answer.

**COS (**½) 60 min (7ep Color; 1976 ABC) Comedy-Variety** *with Bill Cosby*

Though Bill Cosby first scored monster television ratings in the 1960s with his series of comedy-variety specials, this follow-up venture turned out to be a short-run ratings fizzle in its original ABC airing, lasting less than two months. Nonetheless, it is a well-produced *Sesame Street*–like program aimed directly at young children with flashy effects, puppets, music, and comedy narratives along with guest celebrities and a company of regulars (including Jeff Altman, Willie Bobo, and Buzzy Linhart). Obviously, Cosby would do better with his next prime-time venture.

**THE COSBY SHOW (****) 30 min (123ep at Fall 1989; 1984– NBC) Situation Comedy** *with Bill Cosby as Cliff Huxtable, Phylicia Rashad (née Ayers-Allen) as Clair Huxtable, Lisa Bonet as Denise Huxtable, Malcolm Jamal Warner as Theo Huxtable, Sabrina LeBeauf as Sondra Huxtable Tibideaux, Tempestt Bledsoe as Vanessa Huxtable, Keshia Knight Pulliam as Rudy Huxtable, and Geoffrey Owens as Elvin Tibideaux*

Situation comedy in the 1980s is neatly divided into two eras, B. C. (*B*efore *C*osby) and A. C. (*A*fter *C*osby).

When *The Cosby Show* came along in 1984, sexy prime-time soap operas were the hot television format. Everyone wanted another *Dynasty* or *Dallas.* Right behind that format were adventure and detective series modeled after such favorites as *Magnum P. I.* or *The A-Team.*

Sure, there were popular sitcoms such as *Kate and Allie* or *Newhart,* but they didn't hold the same tantalizing prospect of chart-topping ratings. In fact, in some circles the sitcom format was being written off as "played out."

Bill Cosby's series changed all that. *The Cosby Show* was not just a hit—it was a big hit. In an era of declining network audience shares (fragmented by dozens of other offerings on cable), Cosby's show sometimes attracted more than half the television households in America. During just its second season, there were thirteen episodes of the series among the fifteen most-watched shows of the entire year (only "Superbowl XX" and its postgame show prevented a clean sweep by Cosby).

Thanks to Bill Cosby, NBC was assured a solid run as the number one television network of the 1980s. Led by Bill Cosby's show, situation comedy staged a remarkable comeback throughout the prime-time schedule. At individual local stations, when episodes of *The Cosby Show* were offered for rerun syndication in 1987, they fetched record prices.

But that's all commerce, a necessary by-product of any series that changes the face and direction of television. *The Cosby Show* is really all about family life, as warmly recounted by Bill Cosby. For viewers (and probably Cosby himself) the series represents the culmination of a lifetime of performing, with Bill Cosby playing his best role ever: himself.

Almost from the beginning of his career in the 1960s, Bill Cosby had been winning over audiences as a storyteller, showing an uncanny sense for tapping memories of growing up in America (no matter what neighborhood or ethnic group). At first, his monologues focused on family life and his childhood in Philadelphia during the 1940s. This setting eventually found its perfect television embodiment in the ten-year run of the *Fat Albert and the Cosby Kids* cartoon show.

By the 1980s, Cosby's emphasis in his stage routines shifted more and more to his own family life, as the Philadelphia child became a father. Now thoroughly familiar with both points of view, Cosby often replaced the tales of his own youthful mischief with knowing descriptions of the more recent joys (and tribulations) of family life. As the baby-boom generation began its own new baby boom in the 1980s, it was the perfect time in Cosby's career to bring his family-oriented style of storytelling to a regular sitcom slot.

Cosby himself described *The Cosby Show* as "an extension of my real life, and also of my stand-up comedy." If you want to see that for yourself, compare the 1982 concert film *Bill Cosby—"Himself"* to the first (pilot) episode of *The Cosby Show*. Some of the same lines and situations turn up in both.

As co-creator, co-producer, and executive consultant for *The Cosby Show,* Cosby fashioned the program into a perfectly tailored "alternate reality" to his own happy home life. Bill Cosby, the successful entertainer and educator with a savvy professional wife (Camille) and five children (daughters Erika, Erinn, Ensa, and Evin, and son Ennis), became Cliff Huxtable, a successful obstetrician with a savvy lawyer wife (Clair) and five children (daughters Rudy, Vanessa, Denise, and Sondra, and son Theo). The Huxtables live in a comfortable Brooklyn townhouse with a living room that closely resembles the one in Cosby's own Massachusetts home. Best of all, in contrast to typical sitcom families, the Huxtable parents are clearly in charge. The kids may be cute, but mom and dad have the last word.

Humor in *The Cosby Show* revolves around the everyday complications of family life. Should the family have another baby? What do you tell a son or daughter who wants to quit school? How do you teach responsibility to your daughter when she asks her parents to buy her a new car? Where do you put the pumpkin dad carved for the children's Halloween party? And where did dad leave that power drill he borrowed from the next-door neighbors?

Some of these situations don't even have a kicker punchline, and many would barely sustain any other comedy series. For a while, it was even fashionable to put down *The Cosby Show* for its low-key formula and squeaky clean image of upper middle-class success. Yet that simply ignores the growth among all the family members, especially the children, as they begin to go off into the real world (with Sondra as a married mom of twins, Denise as a world traveler after a year in college, and so on). Besides there is no denying that Cosby's very gentle approach works, especially when he is on camera. No matter how thin the plot, Cosby is able to keep the scenes moving just like a tale from one of his own stage routines. In doing so, he finds an audience greater than any he could dream of reaching even in a lifetime of stand-up comedy performances.

Whether in its first-run days or in syndication, *The Cosby Show* is a Cosby comedy album come to life, offering viewers the opportunity to visit and grow with the types of characters they had come to know and love in Bill Cosby's family tales.

## COSMOS (***½) 60 min (13ep Color; PBS 1980–1981) Documentary *with Carl Sagan as host/narrator*

Cornell astronomer Carl Sagan became a media celebrity through this sumptuously produced TV primer on the universe at large. Sagan insists he *never* babbled the phrase "billions and billions of stars" during the show, but that has become the trademark phrase by which comedians turn out a quick, cheap impersonation of the lively scientist.

Topics on *Cosmos* range wide and far, from deep space "black holes," to the "canals" on Mars, to Egyptian hieroglyphics and communication between whales. ■

## THE COUNT OF MONTE CRISTO (*) 30 min (39ep B&W; 1955–1956 Syndication) Adventure *with George Dolenz as Edmond Dantes/Count of Monte Cristo, Faith Domergue as Princess Anne, and Nick Cravat as Jacopo*

This is a tepid version of the classic Alexander Dumas story of Edmond Dantes, an eighteenth-century Frenchman falsely imprisoned for treason. Dantes escapes, finds a fortune, and sets himself up as a nobleman on the island of Monte Cristo, where he fights crime and injustice.

The only noteworthy highlight here is that leading man George Dolenz is the father of Micky Dolenz, star of *The Monkees.*

**COUNTER POINT (**) 30 min (26ep B&W; 1952 ABC) Drama Anthology**

This undistinguished series of suspense-based dramas originally aired under the title *Rebound.*

**COUNTERSPY (*) 30 min (39ep B&W; 1958 Syndication) Spy Drama** *with Don Megowan as David Harding*

After fifteen years as a network radio series (from the creator of *Gang Busters*), *Counterspy* turned up for one season as a syndicated television adventure program. Unfortunately, it didn't have the budget to make the jump properly, playing as a typical stock-set crime drama with little chance of contemporary rerun syndication.

**COUNTERTHRUST (½) 30 min (13ep B&W; 1959–1960 Syndication) Spy Drama** *with Tod Andrews, Diane Jergens, and Victor Diaz*

Tired Cold War espionage adventures filmed on location in the Far East, with three American agents battling to keep the Red Menace from tipping the first of the dominoes eventually leading to the front doors of Everytown, U. S. A.

**COUNTRY MATTERS (***) 60 min (13ep Color; 1972 UK Granada) Drama Anthology**

These short stories set in the English countryside are taken from the writings of Herbert E. Bates and Alfred E. Coppard. Though nearly three decades apart, both writers specialized in rural-based tales generally focusing on stoicism in adversity, first loves, and betrayal, with the elder Coppard somewhat more cynical (declaring as one of his themes: "Do unto others what ought to have been done unto them long ago.") This anthology series is generally very well done, with consistently good performances from the ever-changing cast. And, of course, you'll probably spot faces familiar from other British-produced series and miniseries, such as Pauline Collins (from *No, Honestly*) in the story "Crippled Bloom," Rachel Kempson (from *Elizabeth R.* and *The Jewel in the Crown*) in "Breeze Anstey," and Jeremy Brett (from *Sherlock Holmes*) in "An Aspidistra in Babylon." Most of the episodes were slotted on *Masterpiece Theatre* during the late 1970s.

**COURT MARTIAL (**) 60 min (26ep & 2 hr pilot B&W; 1966 ABC) Law Drama** *with Bradford Dillman as Capt. David Young, Peter Graves as Maj. Frank Whittaker, and Kenneth J. Warren as Sgt. John MacCaskey*

Perhaps the only dramatic TV series set during World War II that is almost devoid of battlefield scenes, *Court Martial* focuses instead on lawyers of the U.S. Army Judge Advocate General's office (that is, the Army's law firm). Capt. Young and Maj. Whittaker travel across Europe to track down evidence before the inevitable courtroom denouement.

The 1963 pilot, titled *The Case Against Paul Ryker,* guest stars Lee Marvin as Sgt. Ryker, a U.S. soldier accused of treason.

**THE COURTSHIP OF EDDIE'S FATHER (**½) 30 min (73ep Color; 1969–1972 ABC) Situation Comedy** *with Bill Bixby as Tom Corbett, Brandon Cruz as Eddie Corbett, Miyoshi Umeki as Mrs. Livingston, Kristina Holland as Tina Rickles, and James Komack as Norman Tinker*

A low-key series featuring Bill Bixby as magazine publisher and writer Tom Corbett raising his loving young son, Eddie. As Harry Nilsson's opening theme to the program reminds us, the two are "Best Friends," with Eddie especially dedicated to finding his widower dad a new romantic interest. Though none of these women lead to a new mom, Eddie should seriously consider a dating service as a sideline—most singles would love to meet even half the prospects he comes up with.

The stories are well done, if sometimes overly cute and sentimental, with good support work from Miyoshi Umeki as the family housekeeper, and executive producer James Komack, who gave himself the role of a photographer at Tom's magazine. Komack went on to produce series such as *Welcome Back, Kotter,* while Bixby still had *The Magician, The Incredible Hulk,* and *Goodnight Beantown* (among others) to look forward to.

**COUSIN BETTE (**½) 60 min (5ep Color; 1972 UK BBC) Drama** *with Margaret Tyzack as Bette Fischer, Colin Blakely as Steinbock, Thorley Walters as Baron Hulot, Harriet Harper as Hortense, Helen Mirren as Valerie, Edmond Knight as General Hulot, and Ursula Howells as Adeline*

Adaptation of the 1847 novel by Honore de Balzac about a vain womanizer (Baron Hulot), his influential family, and their poor relation, Cousin Bette Fischer. She's fortyish, a spinster, and, to begin the story, generous to a poor sculptor (Steinbock), taking him into her modest apartment. He becomes her protégé, but also soon falls for the Baron's daughter, crushing Bette and stirring in her a thirst for revenge—against him and, more importantly, against the Hulots, especially the Baron. Fortunately for her, the Baron's egotistic eagerness to take up with a particular mistress allows her to put into motion schemes targeted to leave the Hulot family impoverished and in disgrace. Spitefully amusing.

**COVER UP (**) 60 min (22ep & 2 hr pilot Color; 1984–1985 CBS) Adventure** *with Jennifer O'Neill as Danielle Reynolds, Antony Hamilton as Jack Striker, Jon-Erik Hexum as Mac Harper, Dana Sparks as Ashley, Irena Ferris as Billie, and Richard Anderson as Henry Towler*

A flashy formula adventure series using fashion photography as the cover-up for globe-trotting espionage. Jennifer O'Neill plays a top-flight photographer who jumps into the spy game after the death of her diplomat husband, Mark, from a car bomb. She soon discovers that he was really an intelligence agent known as an "outrider," a person put in a critical situation without any official outside help. So Jennifer decides to bring his killers to justice herself and enlists an "outrider" of her own, a combat-savvy agent from special services who once posed as a gun-toting beefcake poster boy. The two make a perfect hunk-and-honey pair: He poses, she shoots, they both spy. Warily, Mark's old boss, Henry Towler (played by Richard Anderson, in a role similar to his Oscar Goldman character on *The Six Million Dollar Man*), decides to help them on their first case, then quickly agrees that they would be a fine team on a permanent basis.

Originally Jon-Erik Hexum was appropriately cast as the hunk (he already had the made-for-TV movie *The Making of a Male Model* under his belt). However, shortly after the series premiered, he died after a freak accident on the set (holding and discharging a stage gun at his own head).

The series continued, sidestepping the tricky problem of potentially exploiting the tragic situation by quietly bringing in a new performer (Australian Antony Hamilton) to play a different character, Jack Striker—though exactly the same character type. (That's why they call it "formula" television.) There was no elaborate new origin, just the continuation of the initial premise, with Danielle told (at first) that Mac was on another assignment and she should work with Jack this time around. But at the end of their first case together, she learns the truth from Henry ("He's not coming back, is he?"), quietly crying while Jack comforts her. (In a nod to reality, Richard Anderson even steps out of character with a voice-over explanation of Hexum's death, read over the episode's final freeze frame.)

But, after that moment, the series rolls on virtually unchanged, with slightly better-than-average espionage adventures against an assortment of occasionally intriguing foes (such as Matine Beswicke as a vengeful black-widow type).

Perhaps the most annoying aspect of *Cover-Up* is its enthusiastic use of knock-off cover versions of top-forty tunes as background music, beginning with a barely adequate version of Bonnie Tyler's "Holding Out for a Hero" over the opening and closing credits. However, since these tunes are usually played during totally extraneous photo sessions featuring pinup-style poses by both male and female models, that sin is usually forgiven.

**COWBOY G-MEN (*) 30 min (39ep B&W & Color; 1952–1953 Syndication) Western** *with Russell Hayden as Pat Gallagher and Jackie Coogan as Stoney Crockett*

*Cowboy G-Men* deserves some sort of award for the ultimate 1950s kiddie TV series title. Amidst the popularity of *The Lone Ranger* and *Hopalong Cassidy,* the first word in the show's title is that all-important word, *cowboy.* Wait! There's more! These guys aren't just cowboys—they are also *G-men,* a term from the 1930s and 1940s indicating government law enforcement types, such as FBI men (or, in this case, undercover government agents). So the two mother lodes of male-oriented kiddie fiction in mid-century, cowboys and Indians and cops and robbers, are united in *one* show. Which isn't any good.

The stars of *Cowboy G-Men* are two movie has-beens. Russell Hayden was Lucky Jenkins in several hit Hollywood westerns in the 1930s. Jackie Coogan was a child film star in the 1920s, beginning with *The Kid* (co-starring Charlie Chaplin), who later went through numerous lawsuits, to reach his childhood earnings, and numerous divorces. Post–World War II viewers know him best as the absurd Uncle Fester in *The Addams Family.*

**COWBOY IN AFRICA (*) 60 min (26ep Color; 1967–1968 ABC) Adventure** *with Chuck Connors as Jim Sinclair, Tom Nardini as John Henry, Ronald Howard as Howard Hayes, and Gerald Edwards as Samson*

The title says it all. Chuck Connors, star of *The Rifleman,* plays an American rodeo star who is hired by a wealthy landed Englishman in Kenya, in order to help protect wildlife in a big game preserve. Ronald Howard, son of film star Leslie Howard, plays the British land baron.

*Cowboy in Africa* grew out of a 1967 film, *Africa—Texas Style!* starring Hugh O'Brian and John Mills.

**THE COWBOYS (*) 30 min (13ep Color; 1974 ABC) Western** *with Moses Gunn as Jebediah Nightlinger, Diana Douglas as Annie Andersen, Jim Davis as Bill Winter, Robert Carradine as Slim, Adolf "A" Martinez as Cimarron, and Clint Howard as Steve*

Picking up where the 1972 movie of the same name (that starred John Wayne) left off, *The Cowboys* features seven teenage boys incongruously set on a New Mexico ranch in the 1870s, helping out the widow of the man who brought them together on his cattle drive.

**CRAIG KENNEDY, CRIMINOLOGIST (*) 30 min (26ep B&W; 1952 Syndication) Crime Drama** *with Donald Woods as Craig Kennedy*

Gangsters, cops, and Craig Kennedy, a scientific detective who works with the New York City police in cracking crimes. Yet another low-budget pulp adventure package best left interred.

**CRANE (*½) 60 min (26ep B&W; 1965–1966 UK Rediffusion) Adventure** *with Patrick Allen as Crane*

Typical early sixties adventure series following the well-worn style of such U.S. productions as *Hawaiian*

*Eye* and *Surfside Six.* Patrick Allen is the good-looking owner of a boat and a local cafe in Morocco, where he inevitably finds himself dealing with beautiful women, heavy-handed thugs, and secret smuggling plots.

**CRAZY LIKE A FOX (**½) 60 min (35ep & 2 hr sequel Color; 1984–1986 CBS) Detective Adventure** *with Jack Warden as Harry Fox, John Rubinstein as Harrison K. Fox, Penny Peyser as Cindy Fox, and Robby Kiger as Josh Fox*

Lovable middle-aged private eye Harry Fox can con his lawyer son Harrison into anything, especially helping out dad on a case. Before long, the two are locked in yet another car chase, bouncing through the streets of San Francisco with Harrison aghast and Harry only a shade less concerned. But they're also having the time of their lives, which is why this lighthearted detective series comes off. The cases are about average (part mystery, part adventure), but by the time they finish their father and son routine, almost irrelevant. After a while, Harrison's wife Penny and even his son Josh really start to enjoy his second career, helping out whenever they can.

Jack Warden came to this role as a very familiar face, with appearances in dozens of series and films (including such theatrical releases as *Shampoo* and *Heaven Can Wait* with Warren Beatty and such television series as *The Bad News Bears* and *The Wackiest Ship in the Army*). John Rubinstein also carried some impressive credentials, chiefly as a Broadway musical performer and composer (the son of classical pianist Artur Rubinstein).

The series ran about two years on CBS, went on hiatus, and returned in 1987 with a successful two-hour movie (*Still Crazy Like A Fox,* set in London with a guest shot from *Monty Python's* Graham Chapman), but the network did not order any additional first-run episodes.

**CREATIVITY WITH BILL MOYERS (***) 30 min (17ep Color; 1982 PBS) Interview** *with Bill Moyers*

This Emmy award-winning series examines the process of creativity by discussing the topic with successful, innovative people in the arts, sciences, agriculture, and industry. ■

**CRIME AND PUNISHMENT (**½) 60 min (4ep Color; 1980 UK BBC) Drama** *with John Hurt as Raskolnikov, Timothy West as Inspector Porfiry, Anthony Bate as Svidrigailov, Yolanda Palfrey as Sonia, Frank Middlemass as Marmeladov, Sian Phillips as Katerina Ivanova, Carinthia West as Lizaveta, and David Troughman as Razumihin*

Philosophy leads to murder. In this adaptation of the nineteenth-century Russian novel by Feodor Dostoyevsky, John Hurt (fresh from his work as Caligula on *I. Claudius*) plays one of literature's classic wrong-headed thinkers, Raskolnikov, who feels nothing but contempt for the rest of society. To satisfy his sense of moral superiority, he commits a meaningless murder to demonstrate that he can do anything he wants, without any sense of guilt or remorse (and without any normal motive to tie him into the crime). But Raskolnikov soon discovers that he is neither God nor Superman, as he is forced to confront the consequences of his actions. First he must deal with the inner voice of his own conscience (which is not as irrelevant as he first assumed), and then with the real world—in the form of Inspector Porfiry, a cunning police investigator (played with great subtlety by Timothy West). Over the course of the story, Porfiry gets inside Raskolnikov's head, helping to steer him toward the final punishment that avaits him.

If all that sounds vaguely familiar, try following this show with an episode of *Columbo,* such as the original made-for-TV movie/pilot, *Prescription: Murder* available as a rental video tape). It's nice to see that the good lieutenant has such strong roots in the classics. Actually, this four-part series would have probably played better as a long movie like *Columbo,* allowing the cumulative effects of Porfiry's investigation and Raskolnikov's internal guilt to build in one self-contained sweep.

Finally, if you're in a really silly mood, take this opportunity to fully appreciate yet another clever allusion from *The Bullwinkle Show* and say Raskolnikov's name in your best Boris Badenov voice. Recognize Boris's high-class curse ("Roz-kol'-ne-kuf!")?

**CRIME INC. (**½) 60 min (7ep Color; 1984 UK Thames) Documentary**

A solid, British-produced basic primer on the history of organized crime in the United States. Or one more reason that U.S. tourists to Europe can usually expect to hear the sound of a mock tommy-gun ("eh-eh-eh-eh-eh") after they introduce themselves, especially if they're from Chicago or New Jersey. But it's hard to argue with this production. Series writer (and director) Martin Short (no, not the one from *SCTV* and *Saturday Night Live*) and staff have done a superb job combining material from Stateside news, film, and photo archives with brand new interviews. These include on-camera discussions with FBI informants, law enforcement agents, and family friends, who share some disquieting comments about the whys and hows of the business of murder. The discussions are tied together by off-screen narration, so the correspondent does not supplant the story (unlike the opening of Al Capone's secret vault by Geraldo Rivera).

**CRIME REPORTER** **(see *Official Detective*)**

**CRIME STORY (***) 60 min (48ep & 2 hr pilot Color; 1986–1988 NBC) Police Drama** *with Dennis Farina as Lt. Mike Torello, Anthony Denison as Ray Luca, John Santucci as Pauli Taglia, Stephen Lang as David*

*Abrams, Bill Smitrovich as Sgt./Det. Danny Krychek, Joseph Wiseman as Manny Weisbord, Jon Polito as Phil Bartoli, and Darlanne Fluegel as Julie Torello*

*Crime Story* contains most of the allure of the Florida-based hit series *Miami Vice,* with hardly any of its weaknesses. Producer Michael Mann takes the attention to period detail, liberal use of background music, and colorful characters that worked for him in *Miami Vice* and transplants them back two decades to an era before Miranda warnings and court rulings forced police to "go easy" on criminals.

The first thirteen episodes of *Crime Story* are set in Chicago, in the early 1960s. The wonderful period film clips (in appropriately washed-out colors) of the Windy City and the re-recorded strains of Del Shannon's 1961 hit "Runaway" used over the opening credits immediately inform you of the era and the locale. The program follows the crime-fighting efforts of the Major Crime Unit (MCU), a special task force set up to battle the mob. As viewers familiar with the old *Untouchables* series will know, mob influence in Chicago is a time-honored tradition, dating back at least to the 1920s and Al Capone. So discovering that gangsters still have a big say in Chicago in the 1960s is not a shock.

Leader of the MCU is a no-nonsense cop, Mike Torello (played by former real-life Chicago cop Dennis Farina). The rest of the unit consists of a few nameless lugs of varying ethnic persuasions who surround Torello and do his bidding, but for all practical purposes, Torello is the MCU.

Right from the start, Torello locks in on a rising young star of the underworld, Ray Luca. While the MCU is aware of Luca's growing power, Torello and his boys never can seem to get enough evidence on the young punk to put him away. By the end of the original thirteen episodes, Luca has knocked off virtually the entire top echelon of the Chicago mob and become a powerful local figure on his own. He sides with national mob lord Manny Weisbord in a seismic effort to relocate the mob's efforts to Las Vegas. Out West, the front offered by legalized gambling offers unlimited possibilities to the gangsters to increase their power base and expand their operations. The days of neighborhood shakedowns are gone. The era of the national and international crime cartels is just beginning.

Not content to stay in the Midwest and chase Luca's subordinates, Torello manages to have his MCU absorbed by the federal authorities and so he, too, moves his headquarters to Las Vegas for the second half of the first season. Out west, with new, flashier graphics over the opening credits, *Crime Story* begins to look more and more like *Miami Vice.* Swank gambling parlors serve as backdrops as Luca muscles out all the honest casino owners.

Torello learns the ways of Vegas fast enough, but his MCU has no better luck putting Luca behind bars. By the end of the first season, it appears as if Luca is trapped when his thick-headed flunky, Pauli Taglia, squeals to the MCU, out of pique at Luca's indifference. Luca is then almost killed in a violent shoot-out in the streets of Vegas. Luca survives, Pauli escapes the MCU, and has a rapprochement with his boss. Pauli takes Luca to the desert to recuperate, but, dense as always, Pauli holes up at an Army A-bomb test site. The first season comes to a radioactive end as Luca and Pauli try to race out of the test range as a nuclear bomb is detonated.

The second, and final, season of *Crime Story* opens without Luca (for the moment), but with some more imaginative story lines. Thinly disguised caricatures of Marilyn Monroe and Sen. Jack Kennedy turn up and Torello has to save the senator from being blackmailed by the mob. The not always arm's-length relationship between the mob and the government becomes a major theme in the final season. Luca (showing few effects of his radiation bath) returns and begins to look beyond the limited scope of the United States. Soon Luca has virtually taken control of a Latin American country, in order to further expand his power and to advance his new, lucrative drug-pushing business. Torello and the MCU, ever on Luca's heels, follow him south of the border, where another climactic battle ensues. When the local puppet president turns against Luca, the mobster means to escape by air. Torello jumps on board as the plane taxis down the runway, and the two-year-long battle between Luca and Torello finally comes down to an old-fashioned one-on-one, mano a mano fistfight. We never learn who is stronger. In one of the weirdest endings in TV series history, Luca's Achilles heel, Pauli, shoots the pilot for insulting his intelligence and the plane nosedives to a certain-death crash with Pauli, Luca, and Torello on board. Somehow it was always clear that the only way Torello could stop Luca was to give up his own life as well.

The early Chicago-based episodes of *Crime Story* are the best. The unique setting, the gritty reality, and the blue-collar ambience are virtually unrivaled in TV cop show history. These early installments almost revel in allowing the MCU cops to beat up on suspects. This may strike some viewers as disturbing, but it does add a lot of electricity to the goings-on.

The move to Las Vegas may have been unavoidable in order to appeal to more viewers, but *Crime Story* loses a lot of its charm when it heads for the bright lights. Still the Vegas episodes are quite entertaining. The second season's emphasis on how government corruption and criminal activities go hand in hand is one of the strongest statements of that topic in an entertainment series. The decision to turn Luca into Torello's sole nemesis is both a plus and a minus. It is good to have a well-recognized villain for Torello to rail at, but after a while you begin to wonder if Luca could really be so invincible and so powerful after such a relatively brief career in crime. Unlike *Miami Vice,* it is always clear what the *Crime Story* plots are about, and the gorgeous dollops of style never overpower the story. While two seasons is a short run for such an exciting series, *Crime Story* decided on maintaining a limited story line, so perhaps it is best that the program kept to a limited run. Consider it an extended miniseries when it turns up in reruns. ■

**CRIMES OF PASSION** (**½) **60 min (30ep Color; 1974 UK ATV) Crime Drama** *with Anthony Newlands as the Judge, Daniel Moynihan as Maitre Saval, and John Phillis as Maitre Lacan*

Set in France, this European import begins each episode with a crime of the heart, works through the courtroom trial, with Maitre Saval for the defense and Maitre Lacan for the prosecution, and concludes with a verdict from the Judge.

**CROSSBOW** (**½) **30 min (72ep at Fall 1989 Color; 1986– CBN) Adventure** *with Will Lyman as William Tell, David Barry Gray as Matthew Tell, and Jeremy Clyde as Gov. Gessler*

Set in medieval England, *Crossbow* takes the famous historical figure of William Tell (the one who shot an apple on his son's head), and uses him as the center of a sprightly adventure series. All the standard accouterments of medieval stories (castles, knights, sorcerers, duels) are mixed together nicely, will Tell as the focus, along with his wife and son. Tell's nemesis is Gov. Gessler, played by Jeremy Clyde, once one-half of the English rock duo Chad and Jeremy. Clyde's former partner, Chad Stuart, puts in a guest appearance in the opening episode.

In England, this series is known as *William Tell.*

**CRUNCH AND DES** (*½) **30 min (39ep B&W; 1955–1956 Syndication) Adventure** *with Forrest Tucker as Crunch Adams, Sandy Kenyon as Des Smith, and Joanne Bayes as Sari Adams*

Light adventure series following the exploits of the Bahamas charter boat *Poseidon* and its owners and operators, Crunch Adams and Des Smith. Naturally in each episode they follow their program formula map and steer themselves (and Crunch's sister, Sari) straight into some dangerous new situation. Though cheap and predictable, this is worth a glance for Forrest Tucker, a decade away from his TV signature role as Sgt. O'Rourke on *F Troop.*

**CRUSADE IN EUROPE** (***) **30 min (26ep B&W; 1949 ABC) Documentary** *with Westbrook Van Voorhis as narrator*

Arguably the *first* documentary series produced especially for television, *Crusade in Europe* is based on Gen. Dwight D. Eisenhower's book on the Allied effort in Europe during World War II. Produced by the team responsible for radio's *March of Time,* the series uses the overly dramatic Westbrook Van Voorhis as deep-voiced narrator.

**CRUSADER** (**) **30 min (52ep B&W; 1955–1956 CBS) Adventure** *with Brian Keith as Matt Anders*

The first starring role for the ever-irascible Brian Keith (famous for *Family Affair*), *Crusader* is a Cold War melodrama of a freelance American writer who spends his time trying to free enslaved victims of the Red Menace held behind the Iron Curtain.

**THE CURSE OF DRACULA** (**½) **20 min (10ep Color; 1979 NBC) Serial Drama** *with Michael Nouri as Count Dracula, Stephen Johnson as Kurt von Helsing, and Carol Baxter as Mary Gibbons*

Where else would a 500-year-old vampire superstar turn up in modern-day America besides sunny California? The Transylvanian Count is on the loose once more, this time posing as a professor of European history in a small college, where nubile young lovelies with luscious necks hang on his every word. The suave Count is tracked by the grandson of his 19th century nemesis, Prof. von Helsing.

This cute effort to update the Dracula classic is helped by the dark sexiness of Michael Nouri in the ageless leading role.

The series originally aired under the title *Dracula '79,* as part of the umbrella series *Cliffhangers.*

**CUSTER** (**) **60 min (17ep Color; 1967 ABC) Western** *with Wayne Maunder as Lt. Col. George A. Custer, Slim Pickens as Joe Milner, Peter Palmer as Sgt. James Bustard, and Michael Dante as Crazy Horse*

Produced in the midst of the Swinging Sixties, *Custer* tries to present infamous George Armstrong Custer as just some misunderstood rebel with a cause. The proto-hippie Custer has long blond hair, riles the establishment with unconventional behavior, and acts cool.

It's a bit hard to swallow this portrayal of Custer, but at least the series focuses on his lesser-known early military career, before his debacle at Little Big Horn. At this point, Custer has just been busted from Major General to Lt. Colonel, and the boy wonder of the Army is given a rag-tag bunch of ex-Confederates and crooks to shape up. Needless to say, he succeeds, and his troop becomes known as the "Fighting Seventh" Cavalry.

**CUTTER TO HOUSTON** (½) **60 min (7ep & 90 min pilot Color; 1983 CBS) Medical Drama** *with Jim Metzler as Andy Fenton, Shelley Hack as Beth Gilbert, and Alec Baldwin as Hal Wexler*

An early Yuppie drama series focusing on the personal and professional crises of three young MDs who, for various reasons, are transferred from a high-tech hospital conglomerate in Houston to a rinky-dink backwater facility in crummy Cutter, Texas. Andy Fenton likes it, since he grew up in Cutter. Hal Wexler doesn't mind it too much since he's serving out a probation for a prescription-forging scandal. Beth Gilbert is pissed, since there aren't any good shopping malls in Cutter.

**THE D. A.** **(*) 30 min (13ep & two 2 hr pilots Color; 1971–1972 NBC) Police/Courtroom Drama** *with Robert Conrad as Paul Ryan, Harry Morgan as H. M. "Staff" Stafford, and Julie Cobb as Katherine Benson*

From the Jack Webb crime factory comes *The D. A.*, which is slightly different from the usual Jack Webb police series. For one thing, *The D. A.* is not about grunt police work, at least not exclusively. The first segment of the show does follow D. A. Paul Ryan in his detective phase, solving the crime. The second segment moves to the courtroom (not a popular spot in most Jack Webb shows), where Ryan serves as prosecutor, usually against Public Defender Katherine Benson.

Harry Morgan, Webb's partner in the 1960s version of *Dragnet,* is second banana in *The D. A.*, while *Wild, Wild West* graduate Robert Conrad receives top billing. The first pilot for this program, from 1969 (*The D. A.: Murder One*), has Howard Duff in the secondary role, while the second pilot, from 1971 (*The D. A.: Conspiracy to Kill*), has Conrad working solo.

**THE D. A.'s MAN** **(*½) 30 min (26ep B&W; 1959 NBC) Police Drama** *with John Compton as Shannon, Ralph Manza as Al Bonacorsi, and Herb Ellis as Frank LaValle*

Now here's a switch—a TV series about a private eye who quits and becomes a cop, and not vice versa. Shannon trades in his gumshoe license to be an undercover investigator for the New York City District Attorney.

**D. C. FOLLIES** **(**½) 30 min (36ep at Fall 1988 Color; 1987– Syndication) Comedy** *with Fred Willard and the Krofft puppets*

Fred Willard plays owner and operator of a Washington watering hole, D. C. Follies, where familiar faces from the world of politics, sports, and showbiz all seem to turn up. There's even an ex-presidents table, with Richard Nixon, Jimmy Carter, Gerald Ford, and Ronald Reagan constantly swapping stories and personal observations. Of course, the trick is that except for Willard and any special guest stars, all the characters are puppets made in the spitting image of the real-life figures (courtesy of program creators Sid and Marty Krofft).

Doing topical celebrity lampoons in a syndicated series is a tough balancing act calling for a careful mix of timeless traits (the shifty-eyed Nixon, the easily distracted Reagan, the preppy George Bush) and the latest character developments (Oprah Winfrey's almost magical weight loss). For the most part, *D. C. Follies* manages to keep the elements reasonably fresh without being dated (easily adding new faces to the puppet wall in just a few days), though obviously long-term rerun packaging will focus on highlight compilations. Still the bar setting provides the perfect excuse for such unlikely drinking buddies as Ted Koppel, Sylvester Stallone, and Jack Nicholson, talking the way you might imagine they would with the cameras off and no one near to overhear them. Good for a healthy chuckle and certainly easier to take than the more vitriolic puppet lampoons of the British-made *Spitting Image* series.

**DADS** **(*) 30 min (9ep Color 1986–1987 ABC) Situation Comedy** *with Barry Bostwick as Rick Armstrong, Carl Weintraub as Louie Mangiotti, Skye Bassett as Kelly Armstrong, Eddie Castrodad as Allan Mangiotti, and Jason Naylor as Kenny Mangiotti*

Rick Armstrong and Louie Mangiotti were best buddies in high school. Since graduation, they went their separate ways, got married, had children, and got divorced. Now single again, the two old friends reunite and decide to share a home in Philadelphia. Rick brings along his thirteen-year-old daughter Kelly, while Louie brings his two sons, sixteen-year-old Allan and twelve-year-old Kenny. The problem is that Rick has turned into a fussy Yuppie reporter, while Louie is a Joe six-pack blue-collar stonemason. The two dads use every opportunity to disagree with each other, leaving *Dads* a noisy, grating series.

Barry Bostwick, who plays Rick, is a fine actor who appeared in several sumptuous miniseries such as *Scruples* and *George Washington.*

**THE DAIN CURSE** **(***) (6hr miniseries Color; 1978 CBS) Mystery** *with James Coburn as Hamilton Nash, Nancy Addison as Gabrielle Leggett, Martin Cassidy as Eric Collinson, Jean Simmons as Aaronia Haldorn, Jason Miller as Owen Fitzstephan, Hector Elizondo as Ben Feeney, Beatrice Straight as Alice Dain Leggett, Roland Winters as Hubert Collinson, and Paul Stewart as The Old Man*

A well-written adaptation of a 1929 Dashiell Hammett mystery, complete with authentic period-piece costumes and sets, gritty action, and a witty script. Most important, the cast is excellent, led by James Coburn as the appropriately skeptical Hamilton Nash, a private eye hired by the insurance company to look into what should be a two-bit claim. Eight cheap, imperfect diamonds were taken from the Leggett household, but Nash is puzzled by the elaborate measures apparently used by the thieves to acquire the stones. Why go to all that trouble? Before long, he finds himself in an increasingly complex affair filled with murder, drugs, a deadly family curse, and a mysterious religious cult. Though at times this story seems excessively complicated that's just a reflection of the original material (Hammett's trademark is the multi-layered tale). Stick around till the end—it's worth it.

Though sounding like a perfect entry for the PBS's *Mystery!,* this big-budget series had its première on CBS in 1978. ■

**THE DAKOTAS** (**) **60 min (19ep & 60 min pilot B&W; 1963 ABC) Western** *with Larry Ward as Marshal Frank Ragan, Jack Elam as Deputy J. D. Smith, Chad Everett as Deputy Del Stark, and Mike Greene as Deputy Vance Porter*

Mostly a routine western from the Warner Bros. TV factory, *The Dakotas* is memorable only for two of its stars: the deputies helping out Marshal Ragan in the post–Civil War Dakota Territory. One, J. D. Smith, is played by Jack Elam, usually typecast as a hulking bad guy in Hollywood westerns (such as *The Sundowners*). The other is Del Stark, played by Chad Everett, usually typecast as a hunk (*Medical Center*). Everett makes his first TV starring role here.

The pilot episode, from 1962, called *A Man Called Ragan,* does not have the Vance Porter character.

**DAKTARI** (***) **(89ep Color; 1966–1969 CBS) Adventure** *with Marshall Thompson as Dr. Marsh Tracy, Cheryl Miller as Paula Tracy, Yale Summers as Jack Dane, Hari Rhodes as Mike, Hedley Mattingly as Hedley, Ross Hagen as Bart Jason, and Erin Moran as Jenny Jones*

If you're going to have scene-stealing animals, it might as well be a whole jungle's worth. This kid's-stuff series follows the adventures of an American animal doctor, Marsh Tracy, at an animal preserve and research center in Africa. There he and his daughter work with the natives (who call him Daktari, their word for *doctor*) and other transplanted types (including American Jack Dane and British game warden Hedley) in protecting the wildlife, especially from poachers. In between, they enjoy the opportunity to travel through the area (usually with someone sitting on the hood of the jeep) and to spend time with their personal camp pets, a cross-eyed lion named Clarence and a chipmanzee named Judy. Mike is their best friend among the natives. For the last season's worth of episodes, they are joined by Bart Jason, a hunter turned safari guide (cameras only, though), and Jenny Jones, a seven-year-old orphan (played by future *Happy Days* daughter Erin Moran).

*Daktari* was filmed in Africa, U.S.A., a wild-animal park near Los Angeles. The series was created by *Sea Hunt* mentor Ivan Tors as a spin-off from his successful 1965 theatrical feature film, *Clarence the Cross-Eyed Lion.* Though the image of a great white medicine man among the natives is sometimes an awkward image for contemporary audiences, the animal characters keep most of this series rather timeless.

**DALGLIESH** (***) **60 min (24ep at Fall 1988 Color; 1983– UK Anglia) Mystery** *with Roy Marsden as Chief Inspector Adam Dalgliesh and John Vine as Massingham*

Adam Dalgliesh is a scholarly policeman, a successful poet, and an intense (occasionally brooding) thinker. When there's a murder to be solved, he's also a no-nonsense investigator, one of London's top talents. Formal but not snobbish, Dalgliesh enters each case with an air of clear confidence and authority, expecting answers to his pointed queries, even as he examines the many possible twists and turns in the scenario for murder. Roy Marsden's portrayal of the inspector is very effective and so true to the original books that their author, English magistrate P. D. James, confessed to being unable to envision anyone but him while working on her new Dalgliesh novels.

Fortunately, unlike the typical cops and robbers setup, the television rendition also retains the author's affection for multilayered plots and characters, so this series demands your attention. It also manages the very difficult task of sustaining each mystery tale over about a half dozen episodes, with Dalgliesh piecing together a solution step-by-step, with occasional help from his young foil, Massingham. Sometimes even the inspector doesn't like what he discovers (as in *Shroud for a Nightingale*), but as the consummate professional he feels duty-bound to bring the guilty party to justice.

The *Dalgliesh* stories first aired in the United States on *Mystery!,* beginning in 1985, with adaptations of four different novels playing in that slot: *The Black Tower* (6ep) and *Cover Her Face* (6ep), both produced in Britain in 1985, and *Death of an Expert Witness* (6ep) and *Shroud for a Nightingale* (5ep), produced in Britain in 1983.

**DALLAS** (***½) **60 min (305ep at Fall 1989 & 3 hr prequel Color; 1978– CBS) Drama** *with Larry Hagman as J. R. Ewing, Patrick Duffy as Bobby Ewing, Barbara Bel Geddes and Donna Reed as Miss Ellie Ewing, Victoria Principal as Pamela Barnes Ewing, Linda Gray as Sue Ellen Ewing, Jim Davis as Jock Ewing, Steve Kanaly as Ray Krebbs, Charlene Tilton as Lucy Ewing, Priscilla Presley as Jenna Wade, and Ken Kercheval as Cliff Barnes*

Suppose Romeo and Juliet had lived. Instead of a double suicide that shamed their two feuding families into patching up their differences, imagine the pair of young lovers alive to confront their kin with this: "We're in love. We've been secretly married. And we intend to live together on the family homestead."

The inevitable conflicts from such a defiant declaration would have given William Shakespeare enough plotting fodder to carry a full-blown sequel to one of his most famous plays. Or, in modern dress, maybe a weekly television series, set in Texas oil country. Only instead of Montague versus Capulet, it's Barnes versus Ewing.

Okay, so maybe *Dallas* isn't quite the work of the Bard, but it does use basic, durable, and classic conflicts to sustain more than a decade's worth of plots. Almost all of these boil down to one thing: family (challenges from outside and conflicts within). Knowing that things like family pride and honor really matter to these characters gives the stories their extra edge, transforming potentially petty squabbles among some rich folks into matters of great personal importance that are easy to identify with. Of course, it also helps to have the sheen of power, money, influence, and sex as part of the package, too, for the proper dose of fantasy living from your easy chair.

Still, when Bobby Ewing rides onto the Southfork Ranch with his new bride in scene one, episode one of *Dallas,* it's the affront to his family that makes this a truly tense moment. The reaction is instant outrage. How dare he! How dare she! How dare they! Pam is the daughter of Digger Barnes, hated enemy of the Ewings! In particular, Bobby's brother, J. R., vows to do all in his power to end that union and, true to his word, he never misses a chance to do so over the next ten years. Bobby, for his part, remains firm in his resolve: He loves Pam, and that's that. And, except for J. R., everyone else eventually comes to accept Pam as part of the family, especially J. R.'s wife, Sue Ellen, who sees in her a potential ally in the conflicts with her husband.

Besides, just because he married Pam doesn't mean Bobby has abandoned his family in everything else. Far from it. Though he prefers a more principled life (certainly in comparison to his brother, J. R.), Bobby remains true to the Ewings, especially when any outside force comes to challenge them. Over time, it also becomes clear that he's one of the few who can stand up to J. R. when his brother's latest schemes threaten to endanger the family's stability more than any stranger possibly could.

And so it goes. *Dallas* successfully pumps more than ten years' worth of excellent stories from these key avenues of conflict: the Ewings versus Barnes, the Ewings versus outsiders, the Ewings versus each other, and J. R. Ewing versus the world. Along the way, the series touched off a gusher of prime-time network soap operas (including its own spin-off series, *Knots Landing*). But, even though challengers like *Dynasty* briefly outscored it in the ratings, *Dallas* remains one of the few with plots that are fun to follow in reruns.

Besides Bobby and Pam versus the family, of course, there are the numerous schemes of J. R. Ewing. As played by Larry Hagman, J. R. is one of the most delightfully fun bad guys ever on television. He's always there with an extra twist or a complicated scheme destined to leave everyone it touches fuming. Early on, in fact, that's what helped put *Dallas* on the international viewing map as people around the world speculated on the identity of the mysterious assailant who gunned down J. R. late one night at his office. "Who shot J.R.?" they wondered. Those episodes are worth taping in the rerun circuit just to see if the eventual explanation holds up to what plays in the preceding episodes. Keep a close eye on the gun Sue Ellen waves when visiting her sister Kristin's apartment, especially in the flashback sequence. (Kristin—played by Mary Crosby—did the deed.)

The other famous *Dallas* cliff-hanger is the "Bobby's in the shower/it was all a dream" revelation. In this, Pam Ewing wakes up at the end of one *Dallas* season to find Bobby taking a shower, even though he supposedly died in a car accident the year before. How did he get there? Simple. Apparently Pam dreamed it all: not only Bobby's death, but also one entire season's worth of episodes. Actually, what's fun here it to watch the reruns from the season that's supposed to disappear as a bad dream and see if there were plot points that they didn't deal with properly when Pam "woke up." One instance is a crossover visit by Pam to *Knots Landing* (with Gary Ewing's reaction to Bobby's death and Val's decision to name one of her new twins Bobby in his honor), which obviously never happened if Bobby didn't die.

*Dallas* received a lot of criticism for that gimmick, though any fan of the series who suffered through the eventually negated season would have to agree it deserved its fate. Besides that was the only way to get Patrick Duffy back in the cast as Bobby Ewing. That was essential because, after Bobby's death, the writers soon discovered that removing him from the story was one step shy of removing J. R.—it totally upset the balance of conflicts. Pam had absolutely no reason to stick around and J. R. had no one who could keep him in line. They tried bringing in an ersatz Bobby in the form of cousin Jack Ewing (Dack Rambo), but he was just another outsider posing no threat to the well-established J. R. So after some personal lobbying by Larry Hagman, Duffy as Bobby was back. J. R. would have been proud of the behind-the-scenes negotiations.

There is also an excellent prequel to the series, *Dallas: The Early Years,* a three-hour TV movie released in 1986. Larry Hagman's J. R. serves as the opening narrator to the tale, which follows the Ewing and Barnes clans from the Depression to the early 1950s, revealing just why the conflict between the two families is so deep and bitter. Even if you never watch the regular *Dallas* episodes, try to catch this one.

**DALTON'S CODE OF VENGEANCE (**) 60 min (2ep & two 2 hr pilots Color; 1986 NBC) Adventure** *with Charles Taylor as David Dalton*

A cross between Chuck Norris, Charles Bronson, and Shane, with Charles Taylor playing David Dalton, a tight-lipped Vietnam vet wandering the country as a self-styled friend to the helpless. Based on two successful made-for-TV movies (*Code of Vengeance* in 1985 and *Dalton: Code of Vengeance II* in 1986), the series features plenty of drug dealers, crazed killers, military misfits, and—above all—opportunities for shin-kicking revenge. If you like that type of thing and there isn't a Bronson or Norris film readily available, this is an acceptable, somewhat less violent, substitute. The original TV movies turn up most often.

**DAMON RUNYON THEATER (**) 30 min (39ep B&W; 1955–1956 CBS) Drama Anthology** *with Donald Woods as host*

Dramas based on the short stories and character concepts of author-journalist Damon Runyon, who specialized in portraits of lower-class life in New York City. As a laureate of the illiterate, he focused on hard-boiled (but sentimental) sorts: safecrackers, horseplayers, beer barons, crapshooters, and the like. (These were all key players in his best-known work, the musical *Guys and Dolls,* adapted from his writings several years after his death in 1946.) For this series, the low-life characters are there in abundance, done rather well by the likes of Broderick Crawford, Sheldon Leonard, James Whitmore, and William Frawley (among many others). Though at times the affection for the New Yorkese underworld seems woefully misplaced and naive, the stories are reasonably faithful to the author.

**DAN AUGUST (**½) 60 min (26ep Color; 1970–1971 ABC) Police Drama** *with Burt Reynolds as Det. Lt. Dan August, Norman Fell as Sgt. Charles Wilentz, Richard Anderson as Chief George Untermeyer, Ned Romero as Sgt. Joe Rivera, and Ena Hartmann as Katy Grant*

A gritty Quinn Martin production giving Burt Reynolds one of his better detective character roles. Dan August is a tough, experienced cop working in the southern California community he grew up in. As a result, he gets personally involved in helping people get the justice they're looking for. Though the program suffers from a few uncomfortable bouts of early 1970s relevancy (in one story, an evil killer turns out to be—surprise—a rabble-rousing student dissident), it delivers some acceptable police action. Not long after this series, Reynolds hit a hot streak at the box office propelled largely by lighter vehicles such as *Smokey and the Bandit,* but also peppered with detective dramas such as *Fuzz, Shamus,* and *Hustle.* That's probably the reason episodes of this series often turn up in TV movie slots disguised as a Burt Reynolds detective film. Actually they're just several different cases edited together into an "instant" movie. Ironically they often come off better than the more heavy theatrical films such as *Hustle.*

**DAN RAVEN (*½) 60 min (13ep B&W; 1960–1961 NBC) Police Drama** *with Skip Homeier as Lt. Dan Raven, Dan Barton as Det. Sgt. Burke, and Quinn Redeker as Perry Levitt*

His beat: Hollywood's famed Sunset Strip. His assignment: Keep the nightclubs, jazz houses, coffee shops, and parking lots safe. The result: a police series with plenty of opportunities for cameos and guest star shots by performers such as Bobby Darin, Buddy Hackett, Mel Torme, and Paul Anka, but not much in the way of interesting stories. Stick with the "other" Sunset Strip detectives (at *77 Sunset Strip*)—who have a catchier theme song and a really good-looking parking lot attendant.

**DANGER (**½) 30 min (239ep B&W; 1950–1955 CBS) Drama Anthology** *with Richard Stark as host/narrator*

Murder most foul is the ever-present theme of this series from the days of live New York TV drama. Numerous celebrities-to-be (such as Steve Allen, Jack Lemmon, Paul Newman, Grace Kelly, and James Dean) turn up. Yul Brynner directs several episodes.

**DANGER BAY (**½) 30 min (98ep at Summer 1989 Color; 1985– Disney Channel) Adventure** *with Donnelly Rhodes as Grant "Doc" Roberts, Cristopher Crabb as Jonah Roberts, Ocean Hellman as Nicole Roberts, Deborah Wakeham as Joyce Carter, Susan Walden as J. L. Duval, and Hagan Beggs as Dr. George Dunbar*

Donnelly Rhodes, best known to TV viewers as Dutch, the convicted murderer who escaped from prison with Chester Tate in *Soap,* stars as Doc Roberts, a marine biologist raising two rambunctious teenagers in the Canadian northwest. Roberts is frequently called upon to rescue either animals or people (or both) who get into trouble in his neck of the woods. This is a quality low-key series (maybe a little *too* low-key) that pushes the concepts of conservation and animal protection.

**DANGER MAN** **(see *Secret Agent/Danger Man*)**

**DANGER UXB (**½) 60 min (13ep Color; 1978–1979 UK Thames) Drama** *with Anthony Andrews as Lieutenant Brian Ash, Maurice Roëves as Sergeant James, Judy Geeson as Susan Gillespie, Norman Chappell as Captain Mould, George Innes as Wilkins, Deborah Watling as Norma Baker, Ken Kitson as Corporal Horrocks, Jeremey Sinden as Ivor Rogers*

A British war series following an unusual band of specialists in World War II: the bomb disposal squad, also known as "sappers." Their assignment is to disarm the unexploded bombs (UXBs) that litter the London area and the surrounding countryside in the wake of the Nazi air strikes. It's a daunting assignment because the hastily assembled unit starts out with only a rudimentary knowledge of German detonators and booby traps, and has to learn on the job. Which is precisely what newly arrived Lieutenant Brian Ash finds himself doing to open the series, dealing with a bomb in a position to destroy an important part of London's electrical powerline system. Of course, mistakes in this type of work can be fatal.

Taken from the wartime memoirs of British Major A. P. Hartley, this series offers an authentic glimpse of a truly frightening day-to-day by-product of the ongoing war. The defusing team in particular is always on edge, fully aware that hours (even days) after an air raid there is still potential danger everywhere (from a shopping area to a school yard), ready to explode without a moment's notice. Thus, the sequences showing their painstaking defusing efforts are riveting—and oddly reminiscent of those moments in *Mission: Impossible* when Barney Collier does his surreptitious technical work (usually squeezed into some dangerous space like an elevator shaft with the car hovering above).

Apart from the unusual specialty of the sappers and the focus on their technical skills, this series offers fairly good wartime character types, settings, and stories—all under the supervision of creator John Hawkesworth (producer of *Upstairs, Downstairs* and *The Duchess of Duke Street*). Anthony Andrews went on to *Brideshead Revisited.*

**DANGEROUS ASSIGNMENT (*) 30 min (39ep B&W; 1952 Syndication) Spy Adventure** *with Brian Donlevy as Steve Mitchell*

Steve Mitchell is one more loyal American spy battling for freedom against Communist subversion, all on behalf of Uncle Sam, in this Cold War saga.

**DANIEL BOONE (**) 60 min (4ep B&W; 1960–1961 ABC) Western** *with Dewey Martin as Daniel Boone, Mala Powers as Rebecca Boone, and Richard Banke as Squire Boone*

This version of the Daniel Boone legend originally aired as part of *Walt Disney Presents,* and provides a more traditional view of the frontiersman than the more familiar Fess Parker mid-1960s Boone series. In this Disney version, Boone is mostly concerned with leading his pioneer clan to the promised land of Kentucky.

**DANIEL BOONE (***) 60 min (165ep: 45 B&W & 120 Color; 1964–1970 NBC) Western** *with Fess Parker as Daniel Boone, Patricia Blair as Rebecca Boone, Ed Ames as Mingo, Albert Salmi as Yadkin, Roosevelt Grier as Gabe Cooper, and Jimmy Dean as Josh Clements*

Fess Parker is best known for his TV work as Davy Crocket in the early Disney TV efforts of the 1950s, but Parker also put in a few years in the mid-1960s playing Daniel Boone, another American folklore figure from the Revolutionary War era. Parker's Daniel Boone is a calm, cool, peaceful man, with a wife and children. Boone is always chumming around with Indians (such as the Oxford-educated Mingo) or runaway black slaves (such as Gabe Cooper, played by Roosevelt Grier, in one of his first acting roles after leaving the NFL). There is very little messy violence here, and lots of bucolic warmth somewhat akin to *The Waltons* or *Little House on the Prairie.*

*Daniel Boone* is one of the first series from Aaron Spelling, who went on to produce *The Love Boat, Fantasy Island,* and *Charlie's Angels.*

**THE DANNY KAYE SHOW (***) 60 min (96ep: 48 B&W & 48 Color; 1963–1967 CBS) Comedy-Variety** *with Danny Kaye, Harvey Korman, and Joyce Van Patten*

Kaye was one of the most gifted performers of the post–World War II era. He could tell jokes, sing, dance, perform in mime, and act, and he did it all with tremendous class. This variety series, produced by Perry Lafferty, is constantly top-quality, and Harvey Korman, as frequent second banana to Kaye, serves an able apprenticeship for his starring role in *The Carol Burnett Show,* which began just as the Kaye show ceased production.

**THE DANNY THOMAS SHOW** **(see *Make Room for Daddy*)**

**DANTE'S INFERNO (**) 30 min (26ep B&W; 1960–1961 NBC) Adventure** *with Howard Duff as Willie Dante, Alan Mowbray as Stewart Styles, Tom D'Andrea as Biff, and James Nolan as Inspector Loper*

A delayed spin-off of sorts from *Four Star Playhouse,* where Dick Powell first played the role of smooth-talking gambler Willie Dante. For this series, Howard Duff (radio's original Sam Spade in the late 1940s) takes over the character, a reformed con man determined to operate a legitimate nightclub in San Francisco. Unfortunately his reputation has preceded him, and the local police are always certain he's up to something. As a result, he can't help but get involved in some of their cases, if only to keep his own newly scrubbed image relatively clean.

This is a typical early-1960s TV version of sophisticated adventure with Dante often deadpanning comments to Stewart, his British maitre d', and Biff, his bartender and old-time conning sidekick. Overall, though, the series manages to pull off its premise successfully only about half the time.

**DARKROOM (*) 60 min (7ep Color; 1981–1982 ABC) Suspense Anthology** *with James Coburn as host*

This stilted suspense hour pales before the masters of TV suspense such as Rod Serling and Alfred Hitchcock, but it is one of the few attempts at the format in the 1980s. The *Darkroom* tales are strictly ordinary, and James Coburn seems miscast in the role of the super-serious host who is trying to act spooky.

**A DATE WITH JUDY (*) 30 min (39ep B&W; 1951–1953 ABC) Situation Comedy** *with Patricia Crowley and Mary Linn Beller as Judy Foster, Judson Rees and John Gibson as Melvyn Foster, Anna Lee and Flora Campbell as Dora Foster, and Jimmy Sommers as Ogden "Oogie" Pringle*

Set in sunny southern California, this fluffy family sitcom is an outgrowth of a popular radio series of the 1940s. Judy is a precocious high school bobby-soxer who exasperates her sedate parents. Most of the entire cast changes after the first season (when, originally, the program moved from Saturday mornings to prime time).

**A DATE WITH THE ANGELS** (**) **30 min (24ep B&W; 1957–1958 ABC) Situation Comedy** *with Betty White as Vicki Angel, Bill Williams as Gus Angel, Richard Reeves as Hal "Murph" Murphy, Burt Mustin as Mr. Finley, and Richard Deacon as Roger Finley*

In *A Date with the Angels,* the angels are Gus and Vicki Angel, two peppy, young, recently married suburbanites. He is an insurance salesman, she is . . . the wife of an insurance salesman.

The only aspect of this series worth noting is the cast. This is not Betty White's first TV series (*Life with Elizabeth was),* but it is from her first years of stardom. Handsome hubby Bill Williams is best known to veteran viewers as Kit Carson. Burt Mustin played crotchety quasi-senile old coots through three decades of TV shows (up through *Phyllis,* when he was in his nineties). Richard Deacon is in the TV second banana hall of fame for his portrayal of Fred Rutherford in *Leave It to Beaver* and Mel Cooley in *The Dick Van Dyke Show. Date with the Angels* is produced by Don Fedderson, who had better luck with *My Three Sons* and *Family Affair.* ■

**DAVE ALLEN AT LARGE** (***) **30 min (51ep Color; 1975 UK BBC) Comedy-Variety** *with Dave Allen as host*

Then there's the one about this Irish fella who convinces the BBC to give him a television comedy series.

Of course, the show has a small group of regular players who back him in about a dozen short sketches each outing. But the heart of the program is devoted to a pub-loving Irishman's dream job: sitting onstage in front of a live audience and telling stories, always with a cigarette and drink at hand. (His glass is supposed to be filled with water, though odds are it was drawn from the same tap used to make Jackie Gleason's onstage cup of "coffee.")

The humor is timeless. Which is to say, it's cut from cloth very familiar to pub crawlers—drinking, sex, religion, death, God, and a touch of politics—but without any names or topical references to date it. Just say "The Pope," "The Queen," or "The Prime Minister," and get on with the story.

But here's the punchline. Irishman Dave Allen pulls it off. His *Dave Allen at Large* wears well more than a decade after it first aired in Britain. His delivery is comfortably ingratiating, his dialects quite effective, and he knows how to milk a bad pun or mild double entendre for the camera as well as for the studio audience.

For maximum enjoyment, the program should be accompanied by a pint of Guinness—because it really is like a visit with a neighborhood saloon storyteller. And for a special treat, try to see it with someone who's Catholic or Irish (preferably both). They bring an amusing fear of divine retribution for some of Allen's semi-sacrilegious material.

**DAVID CASSIDY—MAN UNDERCOVER** (*½) **60 min (13ep Color; 1978–1979 NBC) Police Drama** *with David Cassidy as Dan Shay, Wendy Rastatter as Joanne Shay, and Simon Oakland as Sgt. Walt Abrams*

In his early twenties, David Cassidy became a teen heartthrob through *The Partridge Family* and numerous hit records associated with that show (such as "I Think I Love You"). *David Cassidy—Man Undercover* is Cassidy's heartfelt, yet doomed, attempt to be taken seriously as an actor, as he portrays a youthful undercover cop named Dan Shay. The focus on Shay's nervous yet brave wife Joanne and their young daughter Cindy is sappy. Simon Oakland is perfect, as always, as the harassed, ornery police superior, a role he duplicated in *Toma* and *Kolchak: The Night Stalker.*

Produced by David Gerber (*Medical Story, Joe Forrester,* and *Police Story*), *David Cassidy—Man Undercover* originated as an episode of *Police Story.*

**DAVID COPPERFIELD** (**½) **Drama in two major series versions:**

**60 min (6ep Color; UK BBC 1975)** *with Jonathan Kahn and David Yelland as David Copperfield, Arthur Lowe as Mr. Micawber, Patricia Routledge as Mrs. Micawber, Patience Collier as Aunt Betsey Trotwood, Martin Jarvis as Uriah Heep, Ian Hogg as Mr. Peggotty, and Pat Keen as Nurse Peggotty*

**60 min (5ep Color; UK 1988)** *with Colin Hurly, Nolan Hemmings, and David Dexter as David Copperfield (older/teen/young), Oliver Cotton as Mr. Murdstone, Sarah Crowden as Jane Murdstone, Paul Brightwell as Uriah Heep, Simon Callow as Mr. Micawber, Sandra Payne as Mrs. Micawber, Jenny McCracken as Nurse Peggotty, Brenda Bruce as Aunt Betsey Trotwood, John Savident as Mr. Creakle, Francesca Hall as Dora, Artro Morris as Mr. Wickfield, Sophie Green as Agnes Wickfield, and Jeremy Brundenell as Steerforth*

Charles Dickens admitted that this was his favorite of all his works. It contains many autobiographical references, most notably young David's exploited labors at a Blackfriars warehouse, which recalls a similar incident in Dickens' own boyhood. The novel also has several classic villains, including the humorless Mr. Murdstone, the whip-cracking Mr. Creakle, and the insidiously humble Uriah Heep. There's also the more ambiguously complex Steerforth, a man admired by young David but seen in a new light later in his life. And there are exploited children and adults on all sides, including the far too trusting Mr. and Mrs. Micawber, Mr. Wickfield, and Little Em'ly. But, despite the many instances of gloom and doom, the story is ultimately one of survival, of getting through childhood and reaching adulthood with the belief that things can be different.

Of the two serialized versions, the 1975 presentation wins by a nose. There's also a less effective made-for-TV movie version (done in 1970) that is saved by its star-studded cast (including Ralph Richardson, Ron Moody, Richard Attenborough, and Laurence Olivier).

**THE DAVID FROST REVUE (**½) 30 min (52ep Color; 1971–1973 Syndication) Comedy-Variety** *with David Frost, Marcia Rodd, and Jack Guilford*

David Frost is best known to Americans as a somewhat overly glib talk show host, but he began in England performing topical satire (on the original *That Was the Week That Was,* for example). Here Frost leads a troupe of comics in collections of trenchant comments on life and politics. This was all fairly tame even in the early 1970s, and has lost much of its luster.

**DAVID L. WOLPER SPECIALS OF THE SEVENTIES (**½) 60 min (30ep Color; 1971–1973 ABC & CBS & NBC) Documentary** *with various narrators including Cliff Robertson, Hal Holbrook, Alexander Scourby, Lorne Greene, and Rod Serling*

Though best known as one of the guiding lights behind *Roots* in 1976, previously David Wolper was also responsible for a number of imaginatively conceived documentary specials. About a dozen of these consist of historical reconstructions treated as being shot at the time of such events as "The Crucifixion of Jesus," "Showdown at the O.K. Corral," "The Plot to Murder Hitler," and "Surrender at Appomattox." Others are flashy pop documentaries (such as Rod Serling narrating "Monsters! Mysteries or Myths?"). And, for better or worse, there are about a half dozen episodes that helped turn George Plimpton into a true pop culture figure, a self-styled modern renaissance man demonstrating his instinctive skills in such areas as football ("Plimpton! The Great Quarterback Sneak"), road racing ("Plimpton! At the Wheel"), elephant hunting ("Plimpton! Adventures in Africa"), and westerns ("Plimpton! Shoot-out at Rio Lobo," with John Wayne). Plimpton! later went on to the ultimate in prestige jobs, hosting *Mousterpiece Theatre* on the Disney Channel.

**THE DAVID NIVEN SHOW (**½) 30 min (13ep B&W; 1959 NBC) Drama Anthology** *with David Niven as host*

Popular film actor David Niven hosts a series of entertaining drama vignettes, a few of which he appears in. The other episodes feature guests such as Barry Nelson, Fay Wray, Dan Duryea, and Keefe Brasselle. This show is also titled *The David Niven Theater.*

**DAVY CROCKETT (***) 60 min (5ep Color; 1954–1955 ABC) Western** *with Fess Parker as Davy Crockett, Buddy Ebsen as Georgie Russel, Helen Stanley as Polly Crockett, Hans Conried as Thimbelrig, Kenneth Tobey as Jim Bowie, and Jeff York as Mike Fink* **DAVY CROCKETT (**½) 60 min (4ep & 2 hr pilot at Fall 1989 Color; 1988– NBC) Western** *with Tim Dunigan and Johnny Cash as Davy Crockett and Gary Grubbs as Georgie Russel*

When it first aired beginning in late 1954 on Walt Disney's *Disneyland* anthology, the original three-part tale of Davy Crockett touched off a national fad. Genuine imitation Davy Crockett coonskin caps were everywhere, the "Ballad of Davy Crockett" topped the charts, and every boy wanted a toy rifle just like Davy's "ol' Betsy." Even more than three decades later, it's easy to see why the *Davy Crockett* series was such a success: This is a simple story of frontier courage, very well told. Fess Parker is completely believable as the title character, combining a canny hunter's instinct with a *Mr. Smith Goes to Washington* dedication to truth, honesty, and peace. Even in his role as Indian fighter, Crockett seems more interested in negotiating a fair peace than in winning a battle, and he brings that attitude to the halls of Congress as well. But there's never any doubt about his bravery, especially as he stands with his lifelong friend Georgie Russel alongside the men at the Alamo, fighting General Santa Anna's forces to the bitter end.

However, that dramatic and irrevocable conclusion left Walt Disney little choice for a much-demanded sequel. It had to be a *pre*quel, looking at Crockett's life anytime before the Alamo. Those two stories (also featuring the character of Mike Fink) take place in Crockett's more carefree days exploring the river areas in Illinois and Ohio. All five episodes regularly turn up in reruns on the Disney channel. The original three-part story was also edited into a feature film for quick theatrical release in 1955.

*Davy Crockett* effectively typecast Fess Parker as a brave western hero (not a bad image to be stuck with), which he later translated into a successful six-season run as *Daniel Boone.* Buddy Ebsen, of course, went on to play a savvy mountain man of a different sort as Jed Clampett on *The Beverly Hillbillies.*

In 1988, the character of Davy Crockett was revived as part of a general revamping of the Walt Disney anthology series (then called *The Magic World of Disney*). To launch this version, Johnny Cash plays Davy as an elder statesman reminiscing about his younger days. And then it's forward, into the past, for all new adventures of Davy Crockett and Georgie Russel. Naturally these stories don't have quite the same impact or innocence as the originals, but the link to one of Disney's original television hits represented a nice touch. ■

**DAY BY DAY (**½) 30 min (33ep at Summer 1989 Color; 1988– NBC) Situation Comedy** *with Linda Kelsey as Kate Harper, Doug Sheehan as Brian Harper, Christopher Barnes as Ross Harper, Courtney Thorne-Smith as Kristin Carlson, and Julia Louis-Dreyfus as Eileen Swift*

With the birth of their second child, a fast-track Yuppie career couple (lawyer Kate and stockbroker Brian) suddenly realizes they missed seeing their son, Ross, grow up. He's now fifteen years old and a happy teen with girls on his mind. In order to spend more time with him and with their new baby, Kate and Brian decide to change jobs so they can work out of their home. They open a preschool day-care center. It's a typical Yuppie solution to a perceived problem, turning the desire for family time into a new career, but the result fills a community need and produces a warm, entertaining comedy.

Linda Kelsey (from *Lou Grant*) and Doug Sheehan (from *Knots Landing*) play Kate and Brian, an affectionate couple that seems genuinely sincere about their new lifestyle, taking great delight in leading hordes of kids in games, snacks, naps, and sing-alongs. Their chief assistant is Kristin Carlson, an attractive college student majoring in child psychology—and she is probably the main reason son Ross has decided to give his folks' new venture a chance. Just to keep things from getting too snug, warm, and sugary, one of the Harpers' old business associates, stockbroker Eileen Swift (played by former *Saturday Night Live* cast member Julia Louis-Dreyfus), is always dropping by. She's a wonderful contrast to the touchy-feely world of day-care, dismissing the kids as "a bunch of yammering little shrimps" and shamelessly embracing all the trappings of a lucrative, competitive business lifestyle. Eileen is sure Kate and Brian will come to their senses someday, but in the meantime she still enjoys inviting them out. Besides, when they're with her, some of their old competitive tendencies definitely come out. Kate and Brian may have changed careers, but they're still themselves.

This series was co-created by *Family Ties* producer Gary David Goldberg, who even has the characters of Steve and Andrew Keaton (Michael Gross and Brian Bonsall) stop by in a crossover visit.

## THE DAY OF THE TRIFFIDS (**½) 60 min (6ep Color; 1981 UK BBC) Science Fiction *with John Duttine as Bill Masen, Emma Relph as Jo, Emily Dean as Susan, and Maurice Colbourne as Jack Coker*

Based on the paranoiac 1963 British film about flaming meteors that blind most of the world's population and bring spores of flesh-eating plants (called "triffids") that menace civilization as we know it, this British-made series keeps the basic plot of the film, but adds a very 1980s touch. In the TV series, the big, bad oil conglomerates are tied in with the triffids. The extraterrestrial plants have some sort of oil the companies want, and before the oil companies realize the danger inherent in the plants, the nasty things have escaped and threaten all of Mankind.

## THE DAY THE UNIVERSE CHANGED (***) 60 min (10ep Color; 1985 UK BBC) Documentary *with James Burke as host*

As in his previous historical documentary series, *Connections*, in *The Day the Universe Changed* British writer James Burke attempts to explain the significance of events in scientific history. In doing so, he continues to preach a gospel that he has championed since the 1960s: Make science accessible (even understandable) to nonscientists. His reason seems abundantly clear: Science profoundly affects our lives.

How well this series works for you may depend on how much of Burke and his message you've seen and heard before. He's not really covering too much new ground, so if you are already familiar with the general thrust of the material and many of the particulars, you may find yourself focusing more on his editing techniques than on the text.

That's an education in itself, though, because *The Day the Universe Changed* seems designed first and foremost for a TV world with a very short attention span. There's always movement on screen, either by cutting from scene to scene or just following Burke as he walks while he talks. At times it looks a bit silly, beginning sentences at the bottom of a staircase and completing them at the top. But it certainly keeps the program from coming off as a long history lecture delivered from a teacher's podium, which in fact is just what it is (albeit an excellent one).

And, on closer examination, there seems to be some method to Burke's having the pictures do so much walking, especially in contrast to the overall structure of his previous series, *Connections.* In that program, Burke followed some simple (sometimes fairly obscure) scientific development from about as far back as it could go, tracing its ramifications to the present. Sometimes the jumps he made along the way seemed rather arbitrary, almost as if he were stacking the deck leading to his conclusion.

For *The Day the Universe Changed,* Burke limits his meandering through all of history and instead more effectively sets the stage for each important scientific development in its own time frame. Here's what life was like then; now here comes the discovery; now here's what life became. It's all much cleaner and easier to digest, eventually leading to a surprisingly philosophical final episode.

This series is the type that easily inspires a desire for follow-up discussion. For U.S. distribution of the program in 1985, South Carolina public television produced a brief postscript to each episode. Benjamin Dunlop does a mini-interview with Burke, taking a second look at the points he has just raised (on film) as well as the techniques used in the show itself.

## THE DAYS AND NIGHTS OF MOLLY DODD (see *Molly Dodd, The Days and Nights of*)

## DEADLINE (*) 30 min (39ep B&W; 1959–1960 Syndication) Drama Anthology *with Paul Stewart as host/narrator*

Paul Stewart, veteran of Orson Welles's Mercury Theater's famous "War of the Worlds" broadcast and feature player in Welles' film gem *Citizen Kane,* is the no-nonsense host of this minor series dramatizing stories about American newspaper reporters.

**THE DEAN MARTIN SHOW (**½) (52ep Color; 1965–1974 NBC) Comedy-Variety** *with Dean Martin*

During the original decade-long run of his comedy-variety series, "Dino" worked hard at being relaxed and informal. He wouldn't even turn up on the set until each week's taping day (that was in his contract). Then he'd slide down the fireman's pole (or just come through the ground-level door) into his cozy soundstage living room, complete with a couch, drinks, and a grand piano (played by accompanist Ken Lane). He'd welcome guest stars, sing some songs, present comedy skits, tell a few jokes, and ogle the pretty women. It was essentially a timeless Las Vegas show (sans blatantly off-color jokes), and it kept Martin a network fixture through the 1960s and early 1970s.

Over the course of the series, he makes plenty of references to his "rat-pack" friends and they, in turn, pop up every once in a while. (For example, Frank Sinatra appears to put an end to a running-gag mock contest in which his recording of "Strangers in the Night" is played, followed by Martin's request for viewers to write in and tell him the name of that mysterious singer—insisting week after week that no one had guessed his identity.) Though he never kept a company of repertory players, Martin did showcase such regulars as The Golddiggers (slotting them several times as his summer replacement series), The Ding-a-Ling Sisters (A Golddiggers spin-off), and Les Brown and His Band. Eventually he even developed one routine, a celebrity roast, into a spin-off series of specials.

Despite the successful track record, though, Martin's show faces the same problem that haunts virtually every old variety program. The world of syndicated reruns demands something different. Though not hurt by outdated topicality (this was not a headline-oriented satire show), over the long rerun haul the program comes off as terribly repetitious—like watching every performance in a six-week Vegas nightclub stint. Wisely, the syndicators have gone with a selection of episodes (two packages of twenty-six) rather than trying to sell everything. Some nice highlights packages are left to be culled, perhaps for some future, laid-back video release. ■

**DEAN MARTIN'S CELEBRITY ROASTS (**½) 60 min (26ep Color; 1968–1985 NBC) Comedy** *with Dean Martin*

Never a regular series of its own, *Dean Martin's Celebrity Roasts* collects various episodes from Dean's weekly variety series from the late 1960s and early 1970s that were devoted to mock tributes to famous celebrities. The "roast" format proved so successful that they continued as specials into the mid-1980s after Martin left the grind of weekly TV behind, and these later episodes turn up in this collection as well. Martin's drinking buddies, Foster Brooks, Nipsey Russell, Don Rickles, et al., are usually around to get in their digs at the "lucky" celeb featured each week. The "roastees" include Bob Hope, Danny Thomas, Frank Sinatra, Jackie Gleason, Lucille Ball, Telly Savalas, and Dino himself. In spite of the men's club ambience, the shows do present famous personages in a somewhat unguarded moment.

**DEAR DETECTIVE (**) 60 min (3ep & 2 hr pilot Color; 1979 CBS) Police Drama** *with Brenda Vaccaro as Det. Sgt. Kate Hudson, Arlen Dean Snyder as Prof. Richard Weyland, Ron Silver as Det. Schwartz, Michael MacRae as Det. Brock, Lesley Woods as Mrs. Hudson, and Jet Yardum as Lisa*

Based on the 1977 French film *Tendre Poulet,* this series begins with a full-fledged remake of the original as a new TV movie, then continues with the same characters for three more episodes. Brenda Vaccaro is good as the independently minded Los Angeles police sergeant whose off-hours activities include raising a young daughter (Lisa) from a previous marriage and pursuing a romantic affair with a local college professor. Under the guidance of veteran *Columbo* writer Dean Hargrove, this mix might have turned into a long-running vehicle for Vaccaro, but instead just played out as a short-run miniseries (though the movie remake is all you need to catch). For the fun of it, though, try to find the original subtitled film and compare the American and French approaches to essentially the same story. (*Tendre Poulet* is available on videotape either under its original French title or *Dear Detective* or *Dear Inspector.*)

**DEAR JOHN (**) 30 min (22ep at Fall 1989 Color; 1988– NBC) Situation Comedy** *with Judd Hirsch as John Lacey, Jane Carr as Louise, Harry Groener as Ralph, Isabella Hofmann as Kate, Jere Burns as Kirk, Christine Rose as Gloria, Carlene Watkins as Wendy Lacey, and Billie Bird as Mrs. Philbert*

With two graduates from *Taxi* (star Judd Hirsch and producer Ed. Weinberger), *Dear John* should be funnier than it is. Hirsch plays John Lacey, a New York City high school teacher who literally received a "Dear John" letter when his wife took up with his best friend. Now divorced and living alone, John joins a neighborhood singles group for adults, the One-to-One Club. Run by Louise, who sees sexual meaning in everything, the One-to-One gang resembles the group of loonies who used to turn up on the old *Bob Newhart Show.* Ralph is a nerd-type whose Bulgarian wife left him at their wedding reception. Kirk is a refuge from the disco years, a macho poser who can't figure out why women shun him. Kate looks normal enough, but won't say why her husband left her. Mrs. Philbert is a widow whose late husband was a crackpot.

There are some laughs in the One-to-One bantering back and forth, but everybody tries much too hard, leaving the characters more cardboard than human.

**DEAR PHOEBE** **(**½) 30 min (39ep B&W; 1954–1955 NBC) Situation Comedy** *with Peter Lawford as Bill Hastings (a.k.a. Phoebe Goodheart), Marcia Henderson as Mickey Riley, and Charles Lane as Mr. Fosdick*

*Dear Phoebe* is an intriguing little show that dabbled in sexual role reversals long before the concept became trendy. Bill Hastings is a college professor of psychology who leaves the ivy-covered walls behind to break into journalism as a reporter. He lands a job with the Los Angeles *Daily Blade,* but not as a reporter. Instead he is given a lovelorn advice column, where he writes under the pen name Phoebe Goodheart. Not really happy with the assignment, Hastings still is angling for a reporter's job, as is Mickey Riley, the *Blade's* brash female sports reporter, who is, of course, Hastings's girlfriend. The fact that Miss Riley has a traditionally male name is not coincidental, since she is holding down a job that was decidedly off-limits for the fairer sex in the 1950s. Thus, she is an interesting match for Hastings, who is saddled with a job considered the private domain of women.

The concept of *Dear Phoebe* is usually better than the exposition, but Peter Lawford's eternal cool is enough to cover up some bland spots in the scripts.

**DEATH VALLEY DAYS** **(**½) 30 min (532ep B&W & Color; 1952–1972 Syndication) Western Anthology** *with Stanley Andrews, Ronald Reagan, Robert Taylor, and Dale Robertson as hosts*

One of the truly venerable series in TV history, *Death Valley Days* dug up good, simple stories about the pioneer West for twenty years, with very few lapses in quality.

*Death Valley Days* had already enjoyed a healthy fifteen-year run (1930–1945) on network radio before it was resurrected in the early 1950s as one of the first TV shows produced especially for syndication. The concept of the series is simplicity itself: a western anthology. The characters come and go with dizzying speed, opening up tremendous vistas for the writers, since people can be killed off at will and stories can range far and wide in search of a central concept.

The only continuing character in the show, aside from the narrator, is Death Valley itself, a huge track of largely inhospitable desert in southern California that somehow attracted numerous pioneers, prospectors, and bandits over the years. Not coincidentally, Death Valley is where borax is mined, and the long-time sponsor of *Death Valley Days* was 20 Mule Team Borax. This explains the show's traditional opening that features the twenty-mule team hauling borax out of the hot, nasty desert.

The stories are simple tales of the Old West. Many were filmed in and around Death Valley and most lack production polish, but they have a lot of heart. After more than a decade with Stanley Andrews (the "Old Ranger") as host/narrator, former B-movie star Ronald Reagan steps in to shill the borax until he is called away to run for governor of California (thus not straying far from Death Valley). Former film and TV stars Robert Taylor and Dale Robertson split the remaining six years as host/narrator.

Various episodes of *Death Valley Days* have been repackaged over the years and syndicated under other names, with new hosts in many cases. *The Pioneers* is a group of 104 black-and-white episodes from 1956 to 1958, with Will Rogers, Jr. as narrator. *Trails West* presents 130 black-and-white episodes from 1958 to 1960, with Ray Milland. *Western Star Theater* consists of 104 episodes from 1963 to 1965 in black and white, with Rory Calhoun as host. *Call of the West* is 52 color episodes from 1966 to 1967, with John Payne as host. *Frontier Adventures* is 52 episodes from 1970 to 1972, and keeps the original early 1970s narrator, Dale Robertson. ■

**THE DEBBIE REYNOLDS SHOW** **(**) 30 min (26ep Color; 1969–1970 NBC) Situation Comedy** *with Debbie Reynolds as Debbie Thompson, Don Chastain as Jim Thompson, Patricia Smith as Charlotte Landers, and Tom Bosley as Bob Landers*

Jess Oppenheimer, producer of *I Love Lucy,* unsuccessfully takes the "daffy wife wants to break into her husband's career" setting and applies it to popular film star Debbie Reynolds. In this case, the career is newspaper reporting, not show business, but Debbie is just as airy and silly as Lucy Ricardo. Furthermore, hubby Don Chastain lacks the befuddled humor of Desi Arnaz. In the 1970s, when women really were entering the world of careers in force, the idea of a wife wanting a job like her husband's no longer seemed as humorous as it did in the 1950s.

Look for a young Tom Bosley (Mr. Cunningham in *Happy Days*) as next-door neighbor Bob Landers.

**DECEMBER BRIDE** **(**) 30 min (154ep B&W; 1954–1959 CBS) Situation Comedy** *with Spring Byington as Lily Ruskin, Frances Rafferty as Ruth Henshaw, Dean Miller as Matt Henshaw, Verna Felton as Hilda Crocker, and Harry Morgan as Pete Porter*

*December Bride* could qualify in one sense as the perfect 1950s sitcom, not because of its quality but because of its inherent blandness, the most distinctive trait of the decade. *December Bride* is fun, lively, and full of nice people who are somewhat interesting, but rather bland. There is nothing in the series even remotely controversial, and it was a rerun staple for years after it ended its original run.

Lily Ruskin is an aging widow with plenty of spunk. She lives with her daughter Ruth and son-in-law Matt

Henshaw, who are constantly trying to "marry the old lady off" (hence, to make her a December bride). Lily's cohort Hilda also keeps an eye out for eligible old smoothies (too bad they never run into Vern Albright of *My Little Margie,* who'd be a perfect match).

The best side angle of *December Bride* is next-door neighbor Pete Porter (Harry Morgan, in his first series role). Porter is forever taking refuge in the Henshaw household to avoid the continual bickering of his occasionally heard but never seen wife, Gladys. When *December Bride* ceased production (with Lily still single, by the way), Morgan's Pete Porter character become one of the first in TV history to be spun-off into his own series (*Pete and Gladys*), where Gladys finally appears on screen.

## DECISION: THE CONFLICTS OF HARRY S TRUMAN

**(***) 30 min (26ep B&W; 1964–1965 Syndication) Documentary**

The major events of the Truman presidency (1945–1953) are examined in this thoughtful and well-produced series. The aging but still feisty former president himself appears in many episodes, to give a firsthand account of how certain decisions were made. Other ex-presidents could well model their video memoirs after this.

## DECOY

**(**) 30 min (39ep B&W; 1957–1958 Syndication) Police Drama** *with Beverly Garland as Patricia "Casey" Jones and Frank Campanella as Lt. Torry (a.k.a. Harris)*

Something of a female version of *Dragnet, Decoy* presents dramatizations from the real-life files of New York City's Policewomen's Bureau. Beverly Garland, who plays Casey Jones, the beautiful decoy, gained a bit more TV notoriety in 1969 on *My Three Sons,* when she played Barbara Harper, who marries Steve Douglas (Fred MacMurray), one of the tube's perennial single men. *Decoy* is also known as *Policewoman Decoy.* ■

## THE DEFENDERS

**(***½) 60 min (132ep B&W; 1961–1965 CBS) Law Drama** *with E. G. Marshall as Lawrence Preston and Robert Reed as Kenneth Preston*

*The Defenders* provides a nearly perfect synthesis of the glories of TV's so-called golden age of drama and the demands of regular weekly series production. From the 1950s era of drama anthologies come the high-class writing and concern for issues of public controversy. From the more modern era of weekly series with familiar and continuing characters comes an easily approachable series concept with two appealing lead actors. That the result works is best evidenced by *The Defenders* winning a major Emmy award each of the four seasons the show originally aired.

The core of the program is the father and son duo of Lawrence and Kenneth Preston, partners in the law firm of Preston & Preston. Lawrence, the father, is a sagacious veteran of courtroom intrigue, legal maneuvering, and protection of defendant's rights. Son Kenneth is just out of law school, filled with great ideals and legal theories, but unschooled in the realities of legal practice.

What puts *The Defenders* far above average TV crime fare are the well-crafted scripts and the expert production. While most TV series of the era avoided any hint of controversy, *The Defenders* courted issues of public debate. The very first episode deals with mercy killing. Later shows focus on the long-taboo topic of blacklisting in the entertainment field, abortion (a topic scarcely alluded to on TV at the time), and the government's right to prohibit travel of U.S. citizens.

*The Defenders* takes such hot issues and presents them in an approachable, dramatic, entertaining way that is still challenging to the intellect. With the Prestons arguing over the merits of a case and the ensuing drama of a courtroom trial, *The Defenders* sugarcoats the debate over issues and allows a wider audience to be drawn in. The 1950s drama anthologies also loved to feature big issues, but they tended to be preachy, and the lack of continuing, familiar characters to anchor the dramas seemed to scare off viewers.

*The Defenders*'s executive producer, Herbert Brodkin, came directly from *Alcoa Hour* and *Studio One,* the best of the 1950s drama anthologies, and star E. G. Marshall appeared in numerous dramas from the golden age. Filmed in New York, *The Defenders* is blessed with a "Who's Who" of great acting talent for guest stars, such as Jack Klugman, Gene Hackman, Martin Sheen, Jon Voight, James Earl Jones, Robert Redford, Dustin Hoffman, and Ossie Davis. Robert Reed, a fine actor making his TV series debut in *The Defenders,* found greater fame starring in *The Brady Bunch* in the late 1960s.

*The Defenders* is *literally* an outgrowth of the 1950s drama series, as its pilot was a two-part 1957 episode of *Studio One,* called "The Defender," written by Reginald Rose and starring Ralph Bellamy and William Shatner.

## THE DELPHI BUREAU

**(**) 60 min (8ep & 2 hr pilot Color; 1972–1973 ABC) Spy Drama** *with Laurence Luckinbill as Glenn Garth Gregory and Anne Jeffreys as Sybil Van Loween*

Produced at a time when the existence of President Nixon's "plumbers" unit of covert operations was coming to light in the Watergate scandal, *The Delphi Bureau* concerns a somewhat similar unit, a secret national security outfit called the Delphi Bureau that is responsible only to the president. Glenn Garth Gregory is one of the Delphi Bureau's chief agents, a man with total recall who keeps his contact with his bosses to a minimum out of security concerns. Gregory's only direct communication with the shadowy agency is through Sybil Van Loween, a woman whose cover is a Washington society hostess.

In the original pilot, Celeste Holm plays Sybil, but Anne Jeffreys (the whimsical ghost of Marion Kirby in *Topper*) takes over the role in the series.

**DELTA HOUSE** (*½) **30 min (13ep Color; 1979 ABC) Situation Comedy** *with Josh Mostel as Jim "Blotto" Blutarsky, Stephen Furst as Kent "Flounder" Dorfman, John Vernon as Dean Vernon Wormer, Bruce McGill as Daniel "D-Day" Day, James Widdoes as Robert Hoover, and Peter Fox as Eric "Otter" Stratton*

*Delta House* is low-cal, no sugar, caffeine-free *Animal House,* and it leaves the expected bad taste in your mouth. Following the huge success of the 1978 film *National Lampoon's Animal House,* the networks craved a TV version. Naturally the outrageous language and humor and the flagrant sex of the movie had to go, so what does that leave? Well, lots of juveniles running around behaving in an obnoxious manner. In *Animal House,* that worked, because the acting was good, the writing was funny, and there *was* outrageous language and humor and flagrant sex. In *Delta House,* without those elements, not much works at all.

The setting is literally the same as in *Animal House,* the Delta House fraternity at Faber College. The Delts are the black sheep of the fraternity system at Faber, and they are always engaging in wild parties, playing raucous rock music, and getting into trouble with the administration. Blotto is the younger brother of Bluto, the John Belushi character from the movie. Dean Wormer and three of the Delta brothers (Flounder, D-Day, and Hoover) are played by the same actors as in the movie. There is the same ongoing battle with the goody-goody Omega frat house, the same intense interest in females, and the same fixation on alcohol consumption. Still, without the liberty allowed in films, and without the film's actors such as Belushi, Tim Matheson, Thomas Hulce, Peter Riegert, and Donald Sutherland, *Delta House* is a course not even worth auditing.

**DELVECCHIO** (**½) **60 min (22ep Color; 1976–1977 CBS) Police Drama** *with Judd Hirsch as Sgt. Dominick Delvecchio, Charles Haid as Sgt. Paul Shonski, Michael Conrad as Lt. Macavan, George Wyner as Asst. D. A. Dorfman, and Mario Gallo as Tomaso Delvecchio*

On the surface level, *Delvecchio* is only a mildly interesting antiestablishment cop series from the 1970s. Dominick Delvecchio is a law school graduate who turns to police detective work rather than to legal practice. The result is that he is somewhat of a more cerebral cop than usually found on the tube.

The more interesting aspect of *Delvecchio* is its cast and crew. Star Judd Hirsch makes his first regular TV series appearance in this show, before going on to greater fame in *Taxi.* Aside from Hirsch, three regulars who would later be teamed up in *Hill Street Blues* appear in *Delvecchio.* Delvecchio's partner is played by Charles Haid (*Hill Street's* Andy Renko). Michael Conrad (Phil "Let's be careful out there" Esterhaus in *Hill Street*) plays Delvecchio's superior, and George Wyner, who plays Assistant D. A. Bernstein in *Hill Street,* plays the same type of role here. With all these casting coincidences, it is not surprising to discover that two of the chief writers of *Delvecchio,* Steven Bochco and Michael Kozoll, went on to produce *Hill Street Blues.*

**DEMPSEY AND MAKEPEACE** (*½) **60 min (26ep & 2 hr pilot Color; 1985–1986 UK London Weekend Television) Police Drama** *with Glynis Barber as Det. Sgt. Harriet (Harry) Makepeace, Michael Brandon as Lt. James Dempsey, and Ray Smith as Superintendent Gordon Spikings*

A hands-across-the-water coupling, with New York City cop James Dempsey teaming up overseas with high-born English policewoman Harriet Makepeace as part of an elite Scotland Yard undercover unit. Naturally they don't like each other at first (he feels she's too snooty; she finds his preference for gunplay quite improper), but soon they discover they're perfect complements to each other. He has the streetwise skills; she has connections in high places. There are also hints that this male/female coupling might result in some romantic sparks, but it never develops very far. That's not too surprising because we really don't learn much about the characters to help move such things along. Overall, this is an average contemporary shoot-em-up (noticeably more violent than most), with pure formula stories featuring interchangeable terrorists, kidnappers, and thieves, along with plenty of explosions, car crashes, and gunplay. In short, Britain's idea of an ideal 1980s export to the U.S. market.

**THE DENNIS O'KEEFE SHOW** (*) **30 min (39ep B&W; 1959–1960 CBS) Situation Comedy** *with Dennis O'Keefe as Hal Towne, Hope Emerson as Amelia "Sarge" Sargent, Rickey Kelman as Randy Towne, and Eloise Hardt as Karen Hadley*

Tall, rugged Dennis O'Keefe, a leading man in numerous Hollywood films in the 1940s, plays Hal Towne, a Los Angeles newspaperman who writes a column called "All Around Towne." Towne is the typical TV widower with a cute kid and an eye for the ladies. The formidable Hope Emerson plays the tough Sarge, Towne's housekeeper.

**DENNIS THE MENACE** (**) **30 min (146ep B&W & Colorized & 2 hr Color sequel; 1959–1963 CBS) Situation Comedy** *with Jay North as Dennis Mitchell, Herbert Anderson as Henry Mitchell, Gloria Henry as Alice Mitchell, Joseph Kearns as George Wilson, Gale Gordon as John Wilson, and Billy Booth as Tommy Anderson*

Dennis Mitchell *is* a menace, and that is the big problem with *Dennis the Menace.* At the start of the series, Dennis is six years old, and full of the good-hearted mischief that young boys are prone to. The series, based on the long-running comic strip by Hank Ketcham, is designed to focus on Dennis's escapades, and how the surrounding adults never seem to be able to handle the young dynamo in their midst. Dennis is supposed to be wild, but cute, so as to still be appealing to viewers.

Dennis, unfortunately, is one of those kids who only exists on television. He is always saying profound yet supposedly cute statements that cut through all the adult's gobbledygook. Dennis gets in trouble, sure, but (we are led to believe) it's only because the adults don't understand the simple kindness he has in his heart. In reality, Dennis comes across more as a somewhat spoiled and pampered child. He causes the adults around him far more headaches than he ought to, and he usually escapes any punishment by turning on his humble act and displaying the cloying cuteness with which the producers have endowed him. Dennis would be a whole lot easier to take if he just did something out of spite for once, the way real kids do. His artificial goodness of character is annoying and clashes with his always-turbulent antics.

The best reason to watch *Dennis the Menace* is to see the early episodes with Joseph Kearns as long-suffering neighbor Mr. Wilson. Dennis is always underfoot at the Wilsons', since Mrs. Wilson can always be counted on to load the kid up with piles of freshly baked cookies. Mr. Wilson, who is a bit of a snit, is forever trying to shoo the brat away. Invariably, in the end, Dennis's wildness turns out to have saved Mr. Wilson's life or something, and the elderly neighbor must swallow his shame and apologize to the brash urchin. After a few episodes, sympathy tends to go to Mr. Wilson in his never-ending battles to avoid Dennis.

Joseph Kearns died during the third season, and he was replaced by Gale Gordon, playing Mr. Wilson's brother. Gordon, who made a career out of playing Lucille Ball's boss, is much more annoying than Kearns. As he used to do with Lucy, Gordon is forever becoming exasperated and overplaying his aggression. Kearns was a far more believable neighbor.

*Dennis the Menace* is produced by Harry Ackerman, producers of other hit sitcoms such as *Bachelor Father, Bewitched, Gidget,* and *The Flying Nun.*

Based on a long-running comic strip by Hank Ketcham, *Dennis the Menace* was turned into an animated cartoon series in 1986. A 1987 two-hour made-for-TV movie (also called *Dennis the Menace*) serves as a 1980s sequel to the 1960s TV series. Victor DiMattia steps into the title role (playing Dennis as a six-year-old) while William Windom (Congressman Glen Morley in *The Farmer's Daughter* and Dr. Seth Hazlitt in *Murder, She Wrote*) plays the ever put-upon Mr. Wilson.

**DEPARTMENT S (*½) 60 min (28ep Color; 1970–1971 UK ATV) Adventure** *with Peter Wyngarde as Jason King, Joel Fabiani as Stewart Sullivan, Rosemary Nicols as Annabell Hurst, and Dennis Alaba Peters as Sir Curtis Seretse*

More routine international adventure, created by genre veterans Dennis Spooner (*The Avengers, Bergerac, The Baron*) and Monty Berman (*The Adventurer, The Champions, The Baron*). King, Sullivan, and Hurst are the team of special operatives working for Interpol's Department S. It continued for a second year as *Jason King,* focusing on the solo exploits of the title character.

**THE DEPUTY (**½) 30 min (76ep B&W; 1959–1961 NBC) Western** *with Henry Fonda as Chief Marshal Simon Fry, Allen Case as Deputy Clay McCord, Wallace Ford as Marshal Herk Lamson, and Read Morgan as Sgt. Hapgood Tasker*

When a series title refers to a supporting character rather than a big-name draw (the deputy instead of Henry Fonda's marshal), you know you won't be seeing much of the more-famous face. In this case, Fonda turns up for just a handful of stories (though he does narrate all of them), with the weekly action shifting instead to the character of Deputy Clay McCord. That disappointment aside, this is still a pretty good western series, focusing on McCord's reluctance to take on a role that virtually demands his willingness to use his guns in life or death situations. He's a level-headed young storekeeper who would prefer to keep firearms in their holsters or gun racks, and he often tries to figure out less violent resolutions to traditional western conflicts. This oater is out of the ordinary and well worth seeing. And even without Fonda on screen in every episode, the themes and texture are perfectly suited to his personal approach to the Old West.

**DESIGNING WOMEN (***) 30 min (66ep at Fall 1989 Color; 1986– CBS) Situation Comedy** *with Delta Burke as Suzanne Sugarbaker, Dixie Carter as Julia Sugarbaker, Annie Potts as Mary Jo Shively, and Jean Smart as Charlene Frazier*

"Buddy" shows about men are a dime a dozen, but "buddy" shows about women are rare. Set in Atlanta, this series features four women who run their own decorating business (hence the title). They're confident, sexy, and also happen to be the best of friends. Julia Sugarbaker is the savvy founder of the company. Suzanne is her younger sister, a former beauty contest winner who knows just how to use her good looks and winning smile (as her string of ex-husbands attests). Mary Jo is divorced and raising two teenagers, while business manager Charlene starts out as the only one never married (a situation rectified by the end of the third season). Though they're all given some familiar sitcom traits (for instance, beauty queen Suzanne is quite self-centered), the characters ultimately emerge as authentic people—due to excellent performances by the ensemble and an exceptionally clear vision of the entire setting by series creator Linda Bloodworth-Thomason (a veteran writer from the likes of *M*A*S*H* and *Rhoda,* who turns out most of the scripts). When the characters exchange quips, even the catty comments come off as perfectly natural dialogue among long-time friends.

Of course, the *Designing Women* moniker is also a double entendre, reflecting the fact that the four are sharp, calculating business people. They have to be because, even in the self-proclaimed "capital of the New South," the myth of the southern belle dies hard. But that's part of the charm of the series, as the women successfully deal with the outside world—whether it's facing an antediluvian male client or just visiting Graceland. They are there for each other when it really counts, which is what a "buddy" premise is all about.

**DESILU PLAYHOUSE (**½) 60 min (47ep B&W; 1958–1960 CBS) Drama Anthology** *with Desi Arnaz as host*

A production of the Desilu studio set up by Lucille Ball and Desi Arnaz to produce *I Love Lucy, Desilu Playhouse* is a fine collection of filmed hour-long dramas. Most of the *Lucy* cast (including series host Desi Arnaz) turn up in various dramas. The two-part pilot for *The Untouchables* and what is, in effect, the pilot for *The Twilight Zone* (called *The Time Element*) originally aired as part of *Desilu Playhouse.*

**DESTRY (**½) 60 min (13ep B&W; 1964 ABC) Western** *with John Gavin as Harrison Destry*

If you take *The Fugitive,* put it in the Old West, and add a little humor, you have *Destry*. Harrison Destry is the gun-shy son of fabled lawman and gunman Tom Destry. Like most sons of famous heroes, Harrison was never able to live up to the reputation of the "old man." The son did manage to secure a job as sheriff somewhere, but he was jailed on trumped-up embezzlement charges. The *Destry* series follows the reluctant Destry, now out of jail, as he searches for the men who framed him, in order to clear his name.

Handsome Hollywood leading man John Gavin has fun with the Destry character, one that was created in several novels in the early part of the twentieth century and memorialized in a collection of fine films by the likes of Tom Mix, James Stewart, and Audie Murphy.

**DETECTIVE IN THE HOUSE (**) 60 min (6ep Color; 1985 CBS) Drama** *with Judd Hirsch as Press Wyman, Cassie Yates as Diane Wyman, and Jack Elam as Nick Turner*

*Detective in the House* is a very 1980s-ish tale about a husband who decides to stay at home and take care of the kiddies while mom works. The catch is that dad, an engineer (played by Judd Hirsch of *Taxi*), is starting his own detective business and operating it out of the home. The ever-craggy Jack Elam plays Nick Turner, an eccentric retired detective who gives tips to novice gumshoe Hirsch.

**DETECTIVE SCHOOL (*) 30 min (13ep Color; 1979 ABC) Situation Comedy** *with James Gregory as Nick Hannigan, Randolph Mantooth as Eddie Dawkins, and LaWanda Page as Charlene Jenkins*

With the wide assortment of private eyes popping up on TV, you wonder how they all got training for the job. *Detective School* provides a mostly unfunny answer. Nick Hannigan, aging gumshoe, opens up a fleabag night school for aspiring detectives and winds up with an ethnically mixed bag of students: a shoe salesman, a housewife, a model, etc. The idea is funnier than the series. The three main stars all were better in the shows they became famous for: *Barney Miller* (James Gregory), *Emergency!* (Randolph Mantooth), and *Sanford and Son* (LaWanda Page).

**THE DETECTIVES, ROBERT TAYLOR'S (**½) 30 min & 60 min (97ep: sixty-seven 30 min & thirty 60 min B&W; 1959–1962 ABC & NBC) Police Drama** *with Robert Taylor as Capt. Matt Holbrook, Tige Andrews as Lt. John Russo, Lee Farr as Lt. James Conway, Russell Thorson as Lt. Otto Lindstrom, Mark Goddard as Sgt. Chris Ballard, Ursula Thiess as Lisa Bonay, and Adam West as Sgt. Steve Nelson*

Gritty, generally effective cop show with Robert Taylor as Matt Holbrook, the head of a group of plain-clothes detectives tackling the usual gang of TV bad guys. The half-hour *Detectives* programs move at a rapid clip, with Holbrook or his men efficiently chasing down the episode's drug dealer, thief, or murderer. Each one gets some time in the team spotlight, with the final collar alternating between Lieutenant Lindstrom (the veteran of the squad), Lieutenant Conway (the swinging bachelor), and Lieutenant Russo (a tough-talking cop played by Tige Andrews, later better known as Captain Greer on *The Mod Squad*). This half-hour package also offers Captain Holbrook a chance for romance, which comes in the form of Robert Taylor's then real-life wife, Ursula Thiess, as police reporter Lisa Bonay.

In the hour version of the series (which went under the title *Robert Taylor's Detectives* in its original network airing), future *Batman* star Adam West comes aboard as Sergeant Nelson, and the stories take the extra time to meander the back-lot streets of New York. Perhaps with half an eye toward *Naked City,* the scripts occasionally include somewhat topical plot threads, though the overall strength of this series still remains the swift, almost dispassionate, dispatching of justice.

**THE DEVLIN CONNECTION (*) 60 min (13ep Color; 1982 NBC) Detective Drama** *with Rock Hudson as Brian Devlin, Jack Scalia as Nick Corsello, Leigh Taylor-Young as Lauren Dane, and Louis Giambalvo as Lt. Earl Baorden*

The extremely forced concept of *The Devlin Connection* tries to squeeze in as many sexy concepts as possible, with the result being a mixed-up jumble. Rock Hudson (in his last TV series lead role) is a former private eye/military hero who now runs the Los Angeles Cultural Arts Center. Rock runs into Jack Scalia, who plays an aspiring detective who also works as a racquetball pro at a health club and just happens to be the son Rock never knew he had as a result of a wartime fling with a French filly. Father gets to know son and the two work together to solve crimes on the side. Rock wears lots of fancy clothes and drives expensive cars. Jack sweats a lot and shows off his muscles. ■

**DIAGNOSIS: UNKNOWN** **(*½) 60 min (39ep B&W; 1960 CBS) Crime Drama** *with Patrick O'Neal as Dr. Daniel Coffee, Phyllis Newman as Doris Hudson, Cal Bellini as Dr. Motilal Mookerji, Martin Huston as Link, and Chester Morris as Capt. Max Ritter*

An early 1960s version of *Quincy, M. E., Diagnosis: Unknown* features Dr. Daniel Coffee, the chief pathologist at a big New York City hospital, who helps the police solve murder through forensic science.

**DIAL 999** **(*½) 30 min (39ep B&W; 1958 UK) Police Drama** *with Robert Beatty as Inspector Michael Maguire*

Covering programming bases on both sides of the Atlantic, this routine crime series places a member of the Royal Canadian Mounted Police in England to study modern British crime detection methods at Scotland Yard. That's where he learns how to reach emergency help in London: dial 9-9-9 (their version of 9-1-1). An adequately done bread-and-butter cop show.

**DIAMONDS** **(**½) 60 min (44ep at Fall 1989 Color; 1987– CBS & USA) Adventure** *with Nicholas Campbell as Mike Devitt, Peggy Smithhart as Christina Towne, Alan Feiman as Darryl, and Tony Rosato as Lt. Lou Gianetti*

Mike and Christina once played a pair of married private eyes for a television series, *Diamonds*. Following the cancellation of that series, and their own divorce, they decided to stick together as a professional team and try detective work for real with their own "Two of Diamonds" agency. That's where we find them for this series, which also happens to be called *Diamonds*. (At last report, real-life series stars Nicholas Campbell and Peggy Smithhart have not gotten married to each other, or divorced, or gone into the detective business.) Oddly, one reason they seem to be qualified for their new profession is that their sleuthing often resembles a TV detective's scenario, requiring costumes, props (usually supplied by Darryl, the special-effects expert from their former studio), and the outright staging of situations.

*Diamonds* began in the wake of *Remington Steele* and *Moonlighting's* success, obviously intent on setting up yet another pair of hesitant, teasing detective lovers. Surprisingly, it works, with Mike and Christina coming across as a very natural and funny pair who are obviously attracted to each other (after all, they were married), yet also very careful about jumping back into an intimate relationship (after all, they were divorced). In between, they take on reasonably entertaining cases, with Mike's cousin at the police force, Lou (played by former *SCTV* and *Saturday Night Live* member Tony Rosato), inevitably drawn into their latest caper to provide the badly needed firepower and street savvy.

This series was filmed in Canada. Campbell previously appeared on a short-lived newspaper drama from 1986, *The Insiders,* where his resemblance to either Sting or David Bowie (or both) was dutifully noted.

**DIANA** **(**) 30 min (13ep Color; 1973 NBC) Situation Comedy** *with Diana Rigg as Diana Smythe, David Sheiner as Norman Brodnik, Barbara Barrie as Norma Brodnik, Richard B. Shull as Howard Tolbrook, Robert Moore as Marshall Tyler, Carol Androsky as Holly Green, and Richard Mulligan as Jeff Harmon*

Diana is a British divorcée in her thirties, just arrived in Manhattan and ready to begin a new Stateside career as a fashion coordinator to a major department store. She lives in her brother's apartment (available because he's an anthropologist exploring somewhere in South America), though she instantly discovers that over the years he's given out keys to many casual and intimate friends. As a result, at any inappropriate time (this is a comedy, after all), some stranger is likely to walk through the door.

At her office world she attempts to explain her view of the fine art of fashion as it applies to Brodnik's department store, running into conflicts with the copywriter (Howard), the head of merchandising (Norma, the boss's wife), and, of course, the store's owner (Norman Brodnik). Through it all, star Diana Rigg looks sharp, does the appropriate deadpans, curls her lip, and probably wonders why she came all the way to the States just for this.

And that was the chief problem with this series in its original airing: baggage from the past. It happens with any popular performer attempting to strike gold with a different vehicle—expectations are unrealistically high, so that the new program had better be great within the first five minutes, or else. In this case, the rather ordinary setting was judged as a colossal letdown and not worthy of Mrs. Emma Peel (Rigg's cult figure character on *The Avengers*). Today, though, *Diana* has its own legitimate attraction as an opportunity to see Rigg in a light comedy half a decade after *The Avengers*. On that level, it works fine, with a pair of bonuses thrown in: regular Richard Mulligan (later on *Soap* and *Empty Nest*) plays Diana's mystery-writing friend, Jeff, and (of course) there's a one-time guest star appearance by Patrick Macnee, her old *Avengers* cohort.

**DICK AND THE DUCHESS** **(*) 30 min (B&W; 1957–1958 CBS) Situation Comedy** *with Patrick O'Neal as Dick Starrett, Hazel Court as Jane Starrett, Richard*

*Wattis as Peter Jamison, and Michael Shepley as Inspector Stark*

Dick is a common American insurance investigator. He is married to Jane, a real life English duchess. They live in London. Her family does not like him. She is somewhat daffy. Sometimes she gets in the way of his work. Still, they are happy. Say, don't they have a dog named Spot?

**DICK CLARK'S LIVE WEDNESDAY (*½) 60 min (13ep Color; 1978 NBC) Variety** *with Dick Clark as host*

In this failed attempt from the 1970s to bring the Ed Sullivan–type variety format back to prime time, *American Bandstand* honcho Dick Clark plays host to a wide variety of performers. The guests include rock'n'roll pioneers, pop stars, Hollywood celebrities, and (to emphasize the pointless feature that the show was aired live) some magician or stuntman performing some amazing trick or stunt. Considering that the show is, of course, no longer live and that it may or may not run on a Wednesday, anybody running this show would be advised to use a different title (*Dick Clark's Show That Used to Be Live and Originally Ran on Wednesday*?). In the fall of 1988, Clark revived this very same limited concept for a few episodes, titled *Live! Dick Clark Presents.*

**DICK POWELL THEATER (**) 60 min (59ep B&W; 1961–1963 NBC) Drama Anthology** *with Dick Powell as host*

Dick Powell, popular as a young crooner in Hollywood musicals of the 1930s, hosts this drama anthology from the 1960s. The series is typical for its era because it is really just a spot to run pilots for projected series (such as *Burke's Law* and *Saints and Sinners,* which got their start here). A few straightforward dramas, more typical of the 1950s drama anthologies, do turn up, including the Emmy-winning "The Price of Tomatoes" starring Peter Falk and Inger Stevens. Powell died before production of this series ended and various guests serve as guest host in the last few episodes. While Powell was alive, the series was titled *The Dick Powell Show.*

**DICK POWELL'S ZANE GREY THEATER** **(see *Zane Grey Theater*)**

**DICK TRACY (*) 30 min (B&W; 1950–1951 ABC) Police Drama** *with Ralph Byrd as Dick Tracy and Joe Devlin as Sam Catchem*

Chester Gould's popular comic-strip police detective Dick Tracy turns up on TV in this violent, poorly produced effort from the early 1950s. Ralph Byrd also played Tracy in several B-grade Hollywood films of the 1940s.

**THE DICK VAN DYKE SHOW (****) 30 min (158ep & pilot B&W; 1961–1966 CBS) Situation Comedy** *with Dick Van Dyke as Rob Petrie, Mary Tyler Moore as Laura Petrie, Rose Marie as Sally Rogers, Morey Amsterdam as Buddy Sorrell, Richard Deacon as Mel Cooley, Jerry Paris as Jerry Helper, Ann Morgan Guilbert as Millie Helper, Larry Mathews as Ritchie Petrie, and Carl Reiner as Alan Brady*

Originally, Carl Reiner thought he'd be perfect for the role of Rob Petrie. After all, he created the concept, drawing on his own real-life experiences as a writer for such 1950s comedy-variety vehicles as *Your Show of Shows* and *Caesar's Hour.* If his own personal home and office life back then seemed to border on situation comedy, how could he miss with cleaverly crafted scripts about some fictional characters he had total control over? So, in 1959, he put together a cast (with himself as Rob) and turned out a pilot for a proposed series called *Head of the Family.*

Good idea, wrong time and personnel. (It aired in 1960 on one of those summer series for failed pilots.) A short time later, Reiner found himself working with veteran producer Sheldon Leonard, assembling another version of the premise. For this one, Reiner willingly surrendered the lead to Dick Van Dyke, taking instead the less prominent character of Alan Brady, the star of the series Rob Petrie writes for. This time, everything worked, and *The Dick Van Dyke Show* was on its way. Today it still plays as a nearly flawless combination of superb writing and performing. In addition, the series also carries an extra nostalgic tinge, providing photo album impressions of middle-class life in the early 1960s. (Everyone's pretty clean cut, with Mary Tyler Moore's hair style vaguely reminiscent of the one worn at the time by First Lady Jacqueline Kennedy.) About the only problem ever caused by the show was the image left on impressionable young kids, who had to wonder why their mom and dad were forced to sleep in the same bed while Rob and Laura each had their own. (Are we poor? Can't the folks afford two beds?)

Even if sales of twin beds did not skyrocket as a result of the show, in nearly every other way *The Dick Van Dyke Show* set a style for comedy that still works today. (In fact, *The Mary Tyler Moore Show* and the entire MTM school of production are the spiritual descendants of *Dick Van Dyke.*) That's probably why the original continues to play so well: It's the basic formula done to perfection.

There are two main settings, the home world of New Rochelle and the office world of New York City. Rob, Laura, their son Ritchie, and neighbors Jerry and Millie Helper are the main characters in the suburb setting. At the office, it's Rob and fellow writers Buddy and Sally. Since they're being paid to write jokes, they have a very good reason to be constantly exchanging wisecracks with each other. As a result, these sequences often come off as an instant vaudeville routine, with Buddy in particular always ready with one more quip. (In real life, Morey Amsterdam proudly boasted that he could turn out a joke about any subject, instantly.) The main target of his witticisms: bald producer Mel Cooley, brother-in-law to star Alan Brady.

The series carefully mixes the home and office worlds, sometimes adding a third hook: flashbacks to the past following Rob and Laura in their early days of courtship, marriage, and job hunting. These flashbacks give the series a touch of *This Is Your Life* and, more important, also allow an episode to begin with a particularly intriguing hook that leads to the flashback story. (For instance, Rob explains that soon after bringing Ritchie home he thought he had the wrong baby. Why? Well . . .) Sometimes even present-day stories are told in flashback form, beginning the episode near the end of the action in order to get viewers wondering: "How did *that* happen?" For instance, one story opens with Laura coming to bail Rob out of jail. The charge: gambling and assault.

But no matter how they're framed, the main reason these stories endure is that they present believable characters in unusual but ultimately explainable situations. And they're executed by an incredibly gifted cast. Dick Van Dyke is at his slapstick best, making perfect use of his tall, skinny form and his rubbery face. Mary Tyler Moore also has great moves, along with a demeanor that comes across as natural and real, not sitcom forced. Her sob of "Oh, Rob" is a world away from Lucille Ball's whine of "But, Ricky." Both are funny, but Laura Petrie is part of a different, more believable world. Rose Marie and Morey Amsterdam are lifelong showbiz hoofers, perfectly suited to the playing of just such characters. And Carl Reiner, of course, spent more than a few moments performing on comedy-variety shows.

Because the producers and cast deliberately ended production after just five seasons, the quality of this series remains consistently high throughout. As a result, it's definitely worth following *The Dick Van Dyke Show* from beginning to end. That way, you can really focus on Rob and Laura's past history, in everything from a disastrous wedding ceremony to Laura's spaced-out first meeting with Rob's parents (the result of taking someone else's prescription drugs). You can also savor such classic setups as "Coast-to-Coast Big Mouth" (Laura reveals on television that Alan Brady wears a wig), "Obnoxious, Offensive, Egomaniac, Etc." (the writers attempt to retrieve "their" copy of Alan's script, containing all the insults they direct his way), and "The Curious Thing About Women" (Laura can't control her curiosity over a mysterious package that has arrived for Rob).

The series ends as it began (at least, behind the scenes). This time, it's the character of Rob Petrie who has been doing some writing (we see him working on his manuscript throughout the series). The result is a book, based on his life, focusing in particular on his career as a writer for a comedy-variety show. Appropriately, Carl Reiner's Alan Brady decides that the book would be the perfect basis for a new television sitcom, which he plans to produce and star in. (Wonder if that includes tripping on an ottoman to open the show?)

*The Dick Van Dyke Show* was a tough act to follow. After all, most performers have only one change-the-face-of-television production in them. Amazingly, though, Moore landed in another, *The Mary Tyler Moore Show,* in the early 1970s. Carl Reiner and Dick Van Dyke reunited for the well-done (but not quite ground-breaking) *The New Dick Van Dyke Show* in the 1970s. Otherwise, Reiner has concentrated most of his energies on theatrical feature films (ranging from *Oh, God* with George Burns to *Dead Men Don't Wear Plaid* with Steve Martin).

**DICK VAN DYKE SHOW, THE NEW (**½) 30 min (72ep Color; 1971–1974 CBS) Situation Comedy** *with Dick Van Dyke as Dick Preston, Hope Lange as Jenny Preston, Angela Powell as Annie Preston, Fannie Flagg as Mike Preston, Marty Brill as Bernie Davis, Nancy Dussault as Carol Davis, David Doyle as Ted Atwater, Dick Van Patten as Max Mathias, Barry Gordon as Dennis Whitehead, Henry Darrow as Alex Montenez, Barbara Rush as Margot Brighton, Chita Rivera as Connie Richardson, and Richard Dawson as Richard Richardson*

There are two different premises here, as Dick Van Dyke and writer-producer Carl Reiner take another run at sitcom history. Though they don't come up with another Rob and Laura and Buddy and Sally package, they do manage several seasons worth of well-written and executed comedy once again split between home life and the world of showbiz.

For the first forty-eight episodes, Dick Preston works as the host of a local talk show in Phoenix, Arizona (the series was filmed on location in Carefree, Arizona). This version comes complete with the semiobligatory collection of odd-ball guests, production meetings reminiscent of the original *Dick Van Dyke Show,* advice from his manager (which he occasionally heeds), and helpful interference from his sister-secretary-counselor (which he simply can't avoid). At home, Dick and his wife have a happy, healthy relationship, a loving young daughter, and a college-age son (who's generally away at school). And, no surprise, as a local television celebrity Dick gets a few chances to perform his patented physical schtick.

In the last twenty-four episodes, the scene shifts to Hollywood as Dick accepts a major role in a daytime soap opera, *Those Who Care,* and moves his family to California. This setup seems a more deliberate attempt to duplicate the original *Dick Van Dyke* show, with a faster pace and more emphasis on behind-the-scenes banter among the performers, writers, and the producer. Dick Van Patten shines here as the program's producer, with Barry Gordon taking the old Rob Petrie role of head writer. On the home front, Richard Dawson is particularly strong as one of Dick's next-door neighbors.

Overall, *The New Dick Van Dyke Show* (which dropped the "New" for its final season in its original airing) is solid, if not exactly groundbreaking, with an old pro working well in a slightly different sitcom universe. Remember, this show originally aired in the early 1970s. So, for instance, unlike Rob and Laura Petrie (who hopped into separate beds when they went to sleep), Dick and Jenny had to face reality, as in one episode (controversial at the time) in which Annie comes upon her parents in bed together, having just made love. (Actually, they did too good a job there; CBS did not air the episode, though it does turn up in syndication.) Yet even with such contemporary demands, the old Van Dyke and Reiner comedy sparkle still gets through, reminding us of just why they hold such a special place in viewers' hearts.

**DICKENS OF LONDON** (**) **60 min (10ep Color; 1977 UK Yorkshire TV) Drama** *with Simon Bell as Charles Dickens (as a boy), Roy Dotrice as Charles Dickens (as an old man) and as John Dickens, Gene Foad as Charles Dickens (as a young man), Diana Coupland as Catherine Dickens, Adrienne Burgess as Kate Macready Dickens, Christine McKenna as Georgiana Hogarth, and Henrietta Baynes as Fanny Dickens*

Apparently, more has been written about Charles Dickens than just about any other author, except William Shakespeare. Such is the legacy of generations of literature classes around the world. So to help cram for that first-semester final, here's a dramatized biography following the life of Dickens, based on his memoirs and anecdotes from his final lecture tour of the States. Appropriately, Dickens as an old man is used in a framing device to each episode, looking back at his own past. (Keeping family resemblance intact, that role is taken by Roy Dotrice, the same actor playing John Dickens, Charles' father—though fans of *Beauty and the Beast* will recognize him as a father figure of a different sort from that 1980s series.) The story goes from childhood to about age thirty-two, by which time Dickens had already written *The Pickwick Papers, Oliver Twist, Nicholas Nickleby, The Old Curiosity Shop,* and *A Christmas Carol.*

Unless you're a dedicated Dickens fan, though, this series really isn't strong enough to keep you for the duration. Your best bet is probably the front end, with stories of Charles as a young boy and the powerful effect those years had on his own work. Thus, it's easy to understand why the exploitation of helpless children was one of the most prevalent themes in his writing. Oddly, these harrowing years are also the best part if you are a Dickens connoisseur, because it's always a challenge trying to spot any real-life models for characters that turned up later in his books. So pay particular attention to his mother and father.

**DIFF'RENT STROKES** (**) **30 min (189ep Color; 1978–1986 NBC & ABC) Situation Comedy** *with Conrad Bain as Philip Drummond, Gary Coleman as Arnold Jackson, Todd Bridges as Willis Jackson, Dana Plato as Kimberly Drummond, Charlotte Rae as Mrs. Edna Garrett, Nedra Volz as Adelaide Brubaker, Mary Jo Catlett as Pearl Gallagher, Shaver Ross as Dudley Ramsey, Janet Jackson as Charlene DuPrey, Danny Cooksey as Sam McKinney, and Dixie Carter and Mary Ann Mobley as Maggie McKinney*

In the days immediately before *The Cosby Show,* cynical viewers may well have wondered if the only way a young black kid could grow up in a comfortable home was to be adopted by some kind-hearted white folks. Now maybe that was making a lot out of just two programs (*Diff'rent Strokes* and *Webster,* which followed five years later), but in the early 1980s they stood out.

Of the two lead characters, Emmanuel Lewis's Webster would probably win the cutie-pie contest, but Gary Coleman's Arnold Jackson scores plenty of points on his own. He's a blunt, manipulative imp, thoroughly enjoying the opportunity fate has dealt him and his brother, Willis: the chance to grow up on the right side of the tracks. It all comes about when widower Philip Drummond, wealthy head of a huge conglomerate, agrees to honor the dying wish of his black housekeeper and look after her boys. Drummond takes the task to heart and brings them into his own home to live with him and his daughter, Kimberly. He calls them his sons, they call him their dad, and after a while he even legally adopts them.

With all the characters in place, *Diff'rent Strokes* gets down to business, playing with two main approaches to comedy. The first harkens back to the *All in the Family* relevancy days (no accident, this is from Norman Lear's Embassy company), with topical and controversial issues frequently used as the jumping-off point for plots. These include such setups as Drummond's mother being prejudiced against blacks, his old prep school refusing to accept Arnold and Willis because they're black, Arnold pretending to be a bedwetter in order to gain attention, and (in one of the program's more famous episodes) Nancy Reagan's appearance to plug her "Just Say No!" campaign against drug abuse.

Though these message hooks are the ones that win commendations, they also tend to be somewhat heavy-handed and tiresome. Frankly, the series owes its longevity to a simultaneous emphasis on old-fashioned family sitcom basics: the joys and pains of growing up, simple misunderstandings, family deceptions, and plenty of chances for sharp-tongued mugging to the camera, especially by Gary Coleman's Arnold. He's a con man, a sweet-talker, a dancing fool, a warm and cuddly son, and, increasingly over the course of the series, a really annoying smart aleck. Fortunately, the rest of the cast (especially Conrad Bain's Philip Drummond) play off Coleman pretty well and manage to keep the show from completely degenerating into a one-character schtick. During the eight-years of the program, everyone gets the chance to grow a little, even Philip, who remarries and brings new bride Maggie McKinney and her young son, Sam, into the household for the final two seasons of the series.

During the course of its original run, *Diff'rent Strokes* included appearances with two other Embassy-produced series: *The Facts of Life* (a legitimate spin-off for Charlotte Rae's character of Mrs. Garrett) and *Hello, Larry* (an ultimately unsuccessful production that tried to ride on the *Diff'rent Strokes* coattails by making its lead an old Army buddy of Drummond, who also owned the radio station Larry worked for).

**A DIFFERENT WORLD (**½) 30 min (46ep at Fall 1989; 1987– NBC) Situation Comedy** *with Lisa Bonet as Denise Huxtable, Jasmine Guy as Whitley Gilbert, Dawnn Lewis as Jaleesa Vinson, Kadeem Hardison as Dwayne Wayne, Mary Alice as Lettie Bostic, Charnele Brown as Kim Reese, Darryl Bell as Ron Johnson, Cree Summer as Freddie Brooks, Sinbad as Walter Oakes, and Glynn Turman as Colonel Clayton Taylor*

With *The Cosby Show* turning in some of the best program ratings of the mid-1980s (almost single-handedly making NBC the most successful network of the era), it was almost inevitable that the golden slot immediately following Cosby would be requested for a spin-off show from the same company. What they filled it with was a big surprise. Rather than go with a very obvious hook (perhaps the family adventures of Huxtable daughter Sondra and her husband Elvin running a safari goods store), they took daughter Denise (Lisa Bonet) and put her in *A Different World.*

Set at Hillman College, alma mater of Cliff Huxtable, this is one series that truly lives up to its name, capturing the insulated feel of campus life. Denise and her fellow students are kids on their own for the first time, trying to establish themselves in a world that magnifies relatively simple things like dorm meetings, roommate scraps, decisions about courses, dating, and even homework into major concerns. All this can seem pretty trivial and puzzling to an outsider. Unfortunately, for its first season *A Different World* seems uncertain of its own identity as well (going through several producers).

Former *Fame* star Debbie Allen (sister of Phylicia Rashad of *The Cosby Show*) takes over behind-the-scenes reins for the second season, instituting flashier opening graphics and a new version of the title song (sung by Aretha Franklin), helping the program settle into what it seemed to be headed toward anyway: a light ensemble comedy about campus life.

As such, it does a fairly good job with some low-key complications peppered with occasional flashes of *Fame*-style techniques (fantasy dream sequences, for instance). Ironically, as *A Different World* finds its focus, the series also loses its original main star, Lisa Bonet, who went on maternity leave before production for the second season began. As a result, though, the series emerges with a more truly balanced ensemble just as likely to showcase the humorous homelife concerns of a tough professor like Colonel Taylor as the dorm life conflicts of the style-conscious Whitley Gilbert.

All of that is straight out of Debbie Allen's *Fame* yearbook, which is just fine. After all, that was a pretty "different world" of its own.

**DIRTY DANCING (**½) 30 min (12ep Color; 1988–1989 CBS) Drama** *with Patrick Cassidy as Johnny Castle, Melora Hardin as Francis "Baby" Kellerman, McLean Stevenson as Max Kellerman, Constance Marie as Penny, John Wesley as Sweets, Paul Feig as Norman, Charlie Stratton as Neil, and Mandy Ingber as Robin*

A surprisingly faithful adaptation to the 1987 hit nostalgic film (set in 1963), even with a number of superficial changes. In the theatrical original, young Francis (nicknamed "Baby") is the daughter of a successful WASP doctor vacationing at a cheesy Catskills resort, who ventures from her family's watchful eye into the bump-and-grind world of the hired staff. There she loses her heart to street-smart dance instructor Johnny Castle, learns some sweaty, sexy dance moves, and begins to assert herself in an aching transition from daddy's little girl to a young woman. With the 1963 backdrop, there are plenty of opportunities for "we were right in hindsight" generational confrontations over such issues as an illegal abortion, a career at any cost, and—most of all—that suggestive "dirty" dancing done to that "sinful" rock beat.

For the series, it's still 1963 in the Catskills but Baby has become the daughter of the resort owner (Max Kellerman), there to spend the summer getting reacquainted with her divorced dad before heading off to Mt. Holyoke College. Eager to please, Max makes Baby the official talent coordinator (overseeing Johnny) over her objections, tries to set her up with a premed life guard (Neil), and rooms her with boy-crazy cousin, Robin. Those are sensible plot changes, though, and make Baby's continued involvement with the hired help more believable, especially their tolerance for her. Baby comes through for them, taking advantage of her "apple of daddy's eye" influence to make sure Johnny's dance routines get performed. But, much to her dad's (and Robin's) disappointment, she had no interest in the self-centered Neil (even if he is a hunk). Instead, Baby has fallen instantly for Johnny, and he can't help but notice her—if only as the boss's daughter—to the annoyance of his regular partner (in more ways than one), Penny.

Like the film, there are extended dance sequences (probably the most such numbers in a nonvariety format since *Fame*), bare-chested males, and lots of period-piece oldies, all toned down only slightly for television.

They go over with little resistance from either Max or the Catskills audience, reflecting more contemporary attitudes than those of the time. (This isn't really the early 1960s; it's more the way we might see the period through 1980s eyes.) Above all, there are Baby's internal rumblings as she steps into young adulthood, epitomized by the undercurrent of sexual tension between her and Johnny. They come from different social backgrounds and may only have this summer together—will this turn out to be "the time of their lives"? Not a bad rendition of soft-core teen fantasies, though ardent fans of the original film probably prefer simply rerunning their favorite scenes from that.

**THE DIRTY DOZEN: THE SERIES** (*½) **60 min (7ep & 2 hr pilot Color; 1988 Fox) War Drama** *with Ben Murphy as Lt. Danko, John Bradley as Jonathan Farrell, John Di Aquino as Jean Lebeq, John Slattery as Dylan Leeds, Jon Tenney as Janosz Feke, Mike Jolly as Vern, and Glenn Withrow as Roy*

First there was the exciting 1967 film *The Dirty Dozen* (with Lee Marvin, Ernest Borgnine, and Jim Brown) about twelve convicts released from Allied jails in 1943 to engage in a suicide mission against the Nazis. A full eighteen years later, a mediocre TV movie (*The Dirty Dozen: The Next Mission*) brought back Marvin and Borgnine in their old roles (along with some youngsters) in order to sneak into the Aryan fatherland one more time.

The TV series version of the dirty dozen saga pales before even the TV movie in its effort to update the same concept. In this gangster twelvesome there is a demolition expert, forger, intelligence man, and a male model. This crew would have trouble infiltrating a Hollywood cast party—never mind the Axis empire.

**DIRTY SALLY** (**) **30 min (13ep Color; 1974 CBS) Western** *with Jeanette Nolan as Sally Fergus and Dack Rambo as Cyrus Pike*

A western comedy with Jeanette Nolan as a hard-drinking, tobacco spitting, ornery old junk dealer wandering the Old West of the 1880s with a young ex-gunfighter, Cyrus Pike, the son she never had. He wants to get over to California and pan for gold, which is also her plan except she insists on following in that grand tradition of TV sagebrush stars: She gets involved in other people's problems along the way. So Cyrus has to wait, since it is her worthless mule pulling the wagon. (Whoops, make that: It's her mule, Worthless, pulling the wagon.)

*Dirty Sally* is amusing, but not as effective as such classics as *F Troop* or even *Best of the West.* Previously, Nolan appeared in the westerns *Hotel De Paree, The Virginian* (with her husband, John McIntire), and *Gunsmoke,* where she introduced the character of Sally Fergus (on the episode "Pike"). Dack Rambo's other western credits include *The Guns of Will Sonnett* and (in a more contemporary setting) *Dallas.*

**DISNEY/THE DISNEY SUNDAY MOVIE/DISNEY'S WONDERFUL WORLD/DISNEYLAND** **(see *Walt Disney*)**

**DISNEY'S DUCKTALES** **(see *DuckTales*)**

**DISRAELI: PORTRAIT OF A ROMANTIC** (***) **60 min (4ep Color; 1979 UK ATV) Drama** *with Ian McShane as Benjamin Disraeli, Mary Peach as Mary Anne Wyndham Lewis, Rosemary Leach as Queen Victoria, John Carlisle as Dr. William Ewart Gladstone, Mark Dignam as Lord Lyndhurst, Leigh Lawson as Count Alfred D'Orsay, Madelena Nedeva as Henrietta Sykes, William Russell as Wyndham Lewis, and Margaret Whiting as Lady Marguerite Blessington*

Good biographical drama that shows the growth of nineteenth-century British statesman Benjamin Disraeli from a dandy writing romantic novels to an articulate and respected prime minister under Queen Victoria. Actually the segments showing his early days are a lot of fun—he's a good-looking guy, well-off, popular with women, incredibly vain, and dressed to the teeth in brightly colored outfits (green velvet suit, blue dressing gown) complete with fashionable hats and gold pinky rings. He looks for all the world like an irresponsible overindulgent twit—and, in fact, he loses one of his first bids for public office because of that perception. But, clearly, there's far more to the man behind that facade, a self-confident independence that sees him through tough public and private decisions (including a change in religious beliefs and his choice of Mary Anne Lewis as his wife). And in his politicial life, "Dizzy" (his popular nickname) ends up surprising a lot of people, beginning with his maiden address in Parliament, and continuing through his face-offs with partisan opponent William Gladstone and his service as prime minister of England.

**DOBIE GILLIS, THE MANY LOVES OF** (***½) **30 min (145ep B&W & 30 min Color sequel & 2 hr Color sequel; 1959–1963 CBS) Situation Comedy** *with Dwayne Hickman as Dobie Gillis, Bob Denver as Maynard G. Krebs, Frank Faylen as Herbert T. Gillis, Florida Friebus as Winnie Gillis, Sheila James as Zelda Gilroy, Tuesday Weld as Thalia Menninger, Warren Beatty as Milton Armitage, William Schallert as Leander Pomfritt, Doris Packer as Clarice Armitage/Clarissa Osborne, and Stephen Franken as Chatsworth Osborne, Jr.*

Teenagers didn't amount to much on TV in the 1950s. When they appeared at all, it was as secondary characters designed merely to garner a few easy laughs. With *Dobie Gillis,* that all changed and TV was dragged, kicking and screaming, into the 1960s.

*Dobie Gillis* is mostly about teenagers, their lives and loves and hopes and dreams. This focus makes *Dobie Gillis* much more modern in its outlook than its traditional sitcom contemporaries, such as *My Three Sons.*

As a result, *Dobie Gillis* is eminently watchable three full decades after its production. Fashion styles may have changed since the late 1950s, but teenagers are just as self-absorbed and lively as in Dobie's day.

At the center of *Dobie Gillis* is, of course, Dobie Gillis, the slightly offbeat son of Herbert T. Gillis, owner and proprietor of the Gillis Grocery Store. Gillis the elder is from the old school, where working hard to provide for your family was just about all there was in life. His hopes for his son extend merely to having the boy buckle down, work hard, and take over the grocery store when it's time to retire. Dobie, on the other hand, sees life somewhat differently. To him, the primary drive in life is love, hence the full title of the show. Dobie is struggling through the later high school years, and his goals are simply to win the heart of the most beautiful girl around and to (somehow) suddenly become independently wealthy without having to work very hard. At the start of each episode he is usually found in the city park, unconsciously mocking the pose of the local replica of Rodin's statue "The Thinker," caught up in some reverie concerning a deep mystery of life. In a style somewhat reminiscent of George Burns' asides to the TV viewers, Dobie will break from his thoughts to talk directly to the TV audience, to let them know what's on his mind.

While Dobie's tendency to ponder big questions sets him somewhat apart from the usual TV teen, his best friend and good buddy, Maynard G. Krebs, is clearly a complete break from all that had come before. Maynard is TV's first regular beatnik, the bongo-playing predecessors to the hippies. While Dobie may think differently from other teens, he dresses and talks "normally." Maynard, on the other hand, is *well* off the beaten track. Garbed in sweatshirts and sneakers, goateed, and full of hipster lingo such as "cool," "daddy-o," and "man," Maynard wants no part of the American dream of wealth, fame, and beauty that Dobie strives for so diligently (the very mention of the word *work* makes Maynard jump). Yet the two are buddies. The reason is that, deep down, Dobie is not sure whether he really wants all those typical goals either. Dobie might just chuck it all and become a beatnik too . . . maybe.

*Dobie Gillis* goes through quite a few major format changes during its four-year run. At first, Dobie has very whitish blond hair, to make him look more swank. He spends his time lusting after cool, icy, money-hungry Thalia Menninger, who only has eyes for darkly handsome Milton Armitage (Warren Beatty, in one of his few TV series roles). Armitage's mother Clarice is a royal pain, with her snooty, overbearing manner. Dobie, meanwhile, is fending off the ardent amorous efforts of Zelda Gilroy, a short, smart, but very plain girl who can make Dobie twitch by just twitching her nose.

Halfway through the first season, Thalia and Milton disappear, and the chief bane of Dobie's existence becomes fabulously wealthy Chatsworth Osborne, Jr. (who is Milton's cousin). Chatsworth gets a charge out of disrupting Dobie's romantic efforts by utilizing his vast bankroll to distract the attention of Dobie's latest flame. Chatsworth's mother, Clarissa, is played by the *same* actress who played Milton Armitage's mother Clarice just a few episodes previously! The two mothers are virtually the same (well, they *are* supposed to be sisters), but Mrs. Osborne's snootiness seems much more in place with the Osborne fortune behind it.

In the middle of the second season, Dobie (whose hair has slowly been returning to Dwayne Hickman's natural brown) and Maynard graduate from high school and enlist in the Army (Maynard in the *Army*!?). The Army episodes of *Dobie Gillis* only last a few months, and they do not work at *all*.

At the start of the third season, Dobie and Maynard finish their Army stints and enter junior college back in their home town. Once again reunited with most of the old regulars, Dobie and Maynard complete the program's final two seasons doing what comes naturally, that is, avoiding work, searching for love, and trying to "find" themselves.

The wonderful pairing of Dobie and Maynard is the engine that drives *Dobie Gillis.* Still, the supporting cast is top-notch as well. Credit for the high quality of the production goes to executive producer Martin Manulis, a respected producer from such hoary classics as *Playhouse 90,* who usually did not "stoop" to producing sitcoms.

There are two sequels to the Dobie saga. In 1977, most of the central cast reunited in *Whatever Happened to Dobie Gillis?,* a thirty-minute pilot aimed at reviving the show. Thalia was long gone, so Dobie had married Zelda and they had a son named Georgie (played by Stephen Paul) who was now entering the troubled teen years himself. Dobie had, in fact, gone to work with the "old man" and now both ran Gillis Grocery Store. Maynard, ever offbeat, still is marching to his own tune, but is now an entrepreneur. The 1977 pilot episode went nowhere and no series revival took place.

In 1988, a more formal reunion, *Bring Me the Head of Dobie Gillis,* succeeded more than the 1977 effort. With Frank Faylen (who played Dobie's father) deceased, Dobie now runs the grocery himself. He and Zelda still have a son named Georgie, who is *still* a teen (but is now played by Scott Grimes). Thalia (played by Connie Stevens) returns to town as a rich widow trying to find true love with Dobie, the boy she had rejected in her claw to the top. Dobie, after thinking about it, turns Thalia down and escapes her wrath when she offers the whole town "oodles of money" if Dobie is killed. Maynard, Zelda, Chatsworth, and even high school teacher Mr. Pomfritt appear, all looking a lot older, but essentially the same. Middle-aged Dobie, never having really grown up, still thinks aloud by the statue of "The Thinker" and still struggles to figure out life.

The character of Dobie Gillis first appeared in a book by Max Shulman. In 1953, Bobby Van (later star of the 1970s Broadway revival of *No, No Nanette*) played Dobie as a silly and flighty collegian in the forgettable film *The Affairs of Dobie Gillis.*

**DOC** (**½) **30 min (31ep Color; 1975–1976 CBS) Situation Comedy** *with Barnard Hughes as "Doc" Joe Bogert, Elizabeth Wilson as Annie Bogert, Mary Wickes as Miss Tully, Irwin Corey as "Happy" Miller, Judith Kahan as Laurie Fenner, John Harkins as Fred Fenner, Linda Kelsey as Gwen Bogert, Audra Lindley as Janet Scott, David Ogden Stiers as Stanley Moss, Lisa Mordente as Teresa Ortega, and Ray Vitte as Woody Henderson*

This series offers two different performing arenas for the character of crusty old Doc Bogert: The first places him in a cozy New York brownstone surrounded by family and friends (for twenty-five episodes), while the second locates him in a private west-side clinic flying solo with only his office associates for company. In both cases, Barnard Hughes simply steps on stage with his patented irascible old codger persona (scowling on the outside, soft on the inside) that served him so well as Bob Hartley's dad on *The Bob Newhart Show,* a Polish priest on *All in the Family,* and, appropriately, a crusty old doctor in Paddy Chayefsky's 1971 theatrical film *The Hospital.*

Of the two settings for *Doc,* the first is more satisfying, if occasionally confusing—Doc's large Catholic family has a lineup of grandchildren even he can't remember. But the family also inspires some of the program's best lines, especially those caustic comments he directs at his son-in-law, Fred (who he can't stand), and those leveled at his patients by his wife (who is harder on them than he is). This series (both versions) was created and developed specifically for Hughes by MTM veterans Ed. Weinberger and Stan Daniels (who also did *Phyllis*), but it still wasn't the best showcase for his special character type—that wouldn't come until the 1980s with his role as the interfering head of the family in *The Cavanaughs.*

**DOC CORKLE** (*) **30 min (3ep B&W; 1952 NBC) Situation Comedy** *with Eddie Mayehoff as Doc Corkle, Billie Burke as Melinda, Arnold Stang as Winfield Dill, and Hope Emerson as Nellie Corkle*

For a long time, *Doc Corkle* held the record for the TV series with the shortest run. In an era when even the worst shows usually limped through an entire season, *Doc Corkle* was axed after only three episodes.

Doc Corkle is a dentist with money problems and family problems. His stepsister Melinda is the usual source of high jinks. Arnold Stang (the voice of Top Cat) plays slightly against type as a young millionaire engaged to marry Doc's daughter Laurie.

**DOC ELLIOT** (**½) **60 min (15ep & 90 min pilot Color; 1974 ABC) Medical Drama** *with James Franciscus as Dr. Benjamin Elliot, Noah Beery, Jr., as Barney Weeks, Neva Patterson as Mags Brimble, and Bo Hopkins as Eldred McCoy*

James Franciscus plays a New York doctor in search of fulfillment and more personal involvement with his patients, so he packs his bags and heads west, stopping in Colorado. There he sets up a small clinic and makes many of his house calls in a four-wheel-drive camper equipped with a two-way radio. For more inaccessible spots, he relies on pilot Eldred McCoy. This series is modest but quietly effective, with Franciscus bringing a touch of warm humor to his role. Produced by Lee Rich and Lorimar while *Dallas* was still a few years away. These days, the ninety-minute movie pilot is the way you'll most likely sneak a peak at this series.

**THE DOCTOR** (**) **30 min (44ep B&W; 1952–1953 NBC) Medical Anthology** *with Warner Anderson as The Doctor and host/narrator*

A pioneer among medical series on television, *The Doctor* is light-years away from *Dr. Kildare* and *Marcus Welby, M. D.,* in that this series is an anthology, dealing with different medical crises and different medical heroes each week. Host Warner Anderson occasionally stars in a few episodes as an unnamed general practitioner. This series has also been syndicated as *The Visitor.*

**DOCTOR CHRISTIAN** (*½) **30 min (39ep B&W; 1956 Syndication) Drama** *with Macdonald Carey as Dr. Mark Christian and Jean Hersholt as Dr. Paul Christian*

A television wrap-up to the long-running career of Jean Hersholt as Dr. Christian, which began in a radio series in 1937 and spawned a series of theatrical films beginning in 1939. Through these permutations the setup remained the same: the low-key adventures of a simple country doctor. For the television series, Hersholt let his character edge into retirement as the good doctor's nephew became the *new* Dr. Christian. But his assignment remained unchanged: caring for the patients in his small town. Unfortunately, after the long run of the original, "Dr. Christian—The Next Generation" seems a rather tired concept, not helped much by the typically limited production values of 1950s syndication. The idea still works most effectively as a pleasant, nostalgic period piece, best appreciated in its original radio broadcasts or feature film formats.

**DOCTOR FU MANCHU, THE ADVENTURES OF** (*) **(13ep B&W; 1956 Syndication) Adventure** *with Glen Gordon as Dr. Fu Manchu, Lester Stevens as Sir Dennis Nayland Smith, Laurette Luez as Lia Elthram, Clark Howat as Dr. Jack Petrie, and Lester Matthews as Malik*

Republic Studios essentially remade one of its old

cliff-hanger serials for television syndication in the 1950s, dusting off the adventures of writer Sax Rohmer's pulp classic, though with limited success. In fact, the initial pilot (in 1950, with John Carradine as Dr. Fu Manchu) was rejected, so the project stayed on the shelf until 1955. Then using a pair of directors (William Witney, who had directed the 1940 version of the tale, and Franklin Adreon), a thirteen-episode package was created. It's reasonably faithful to the old films (for what that's worth), complete with the required face-off between the two sides: the revenge-driven title character and his similarly bent daughter (Lia) versus their brave British nemesis (Nayland Smith) and his scientific ally (Dr. Petrie). Nonetheless, this is still a pretty hokey slice of pulp fiction with barely adequate sets, scripts, and performances. It's best consigned to an obscure camp classics slot on some overnight cable program.

**DR. HUDSON'S SECRET JOURNAL (*) 30 min (78ep B&W; 1955–1957 Syndication) Medical Drama** *with John Howard as Dr. Wayne Hudson, Cheryl Callaway as Kathy Hudson, and Olive Blakeney as Mrs. Grady*

Based on a character in Lloyd C. Douglas's book *Magnificent Obsession* (which became a 1935 movie starring Robert Taylor), this run-of-the-mill medical show centers on widower Dr. Wayne Hudson, a famed neurosurgeon at Center Hospital, his niece Kathy, and his housekeeper, Mrs. Grady.

**DOCTOR IN THE HOUSE (**½) 30 min (90ep Color; 1970–1973 UK London Weekend Television) and continued as DOCTOR AT SEA (13ep Color; 1974), DOCTOR AT LARGE (29ep Color; 1974), DOCTOR ON THE GO (26ep Color; 1975) Situation Comedy** *with Barry Evans as Dr. Michael Upton, Robin Nedwell as Dr. Duncan Waring, Geoffrey Davies as Dr. Dick Stuart-Clark, Ernest Clark as Prof. Geoffrey Loftus, Ralph Michael as The Dean, George Layton as Paul Collier, and Richard O'Sullivan as Dr. Bingham*

For sheer quantity, there are few other British comedies that can match the number of episodes turned out for the various *Doctor in the House* series. Surprisingly, the cast and writers also manage to make this offering very consistent in the process, with pranks, schemes, slapstick, and the pursuit of beautiful women the constant creed of these medical students. They begin their saga of irreverence in the hallowed halls of Saint Swithin's Teaching Hospital in London and never look back, not even after beginning private practice. And, in the time-honored tradition of the madcap surgeons of *M*A*S*H,* they get away with a lot, because the medicos actually can do the job when it counts.

This resilient setting was first conceived in the 1950s as a series of books by a recent medical graduate, Dr. Richard Gordon. These books quickly turned into a series of theatrical films, most starring Dirk Bogarde, and eventually evolved into a 1970s series for British television. In this television version, the action focuses primarily on Michael Upton, who is there for the first batches under the title *Doctor in the House,* then shifts more to Duncan Waring, Dick Stuart-Clark (the most upright of the bunch), and Paul Collier—with Professor Loftus as their unsmiling nemesis most often. The setting also changes over the successive series as they all move from the med school to the outside world and, eventually, to the staff of a British hospital. On signing up there, the young doctors are even sternly warned that they must keep their noses clean. *(Right.)*

Of the doctors, Richard O'Sullivan's face is most familiar from his other hit comedies, *A Man About the House* and *Robin's Nest.* Also, during the *Doctor at Large* run, look for scripts written by Monty Python's John Cleese and Graham Chapman.

**DR. KILDARE (***) 60 & 30 min (200ep: one hundred-forty-two 60 min B&W & fifty-eight 30 min Color; 1961–1965 NBC) Medical Drama** *with Richard Chamberlain as Dr. James Kildare and Raymond Massey as Dr. Leonard Gillespie*

*Dr. Kildare* combines the best of soap operas and prime-time dramas to create a high-quality, high-gloss series. Young, handsome Richard Chamberlain (in his first major TV role) plays young, handsome James Kildare, a new intern at mammoth Blair General Hospital specializing in internal medicine. Kildare is always under the watchful eye of craggy old Dr. Gillespie, senior staff physician at Blair General. Week after week, Kildare struggles through the traumas of dealing with patients with mysterious maladies and trying to please Gillespie, who always is ready with criticisms.

This medical format is now quite familiar (though it was somewhat novel when *Dr. Kildare* first aired), but what still sets this show apart is the character of Kildare and the workings of the Kildare/Gillespie relationship.

Kildare is truly an angel in white. Other medical shows (*Ben Casey, Trapper John. M. D., St. Elsewhere*) at least suggest the possibility of nuances of character in the leads, but in *Dr. Kildare* there is only one character question: Can Kildare cut it as a physician? No other aspects of his personality are developed to any extent. Kildare is just a healing animal, untrained perhaps, but voracious in his desire to cure. Yes, he is devastatingly handsome, but it is almost as if he does not quite realize it. Women seem to flutter around Kildare, and he notes that with some interest. Still he never allows that interest to distract him from his twenty-four-hour job of healing the sick. This constant theme of hard work gives *Dr. Kildare* a harsh, Calvinistic tinge that is somewhat oppressive. What is missing in *Dr. Kildare* are a few more human faults or touches of reality in Kildare's character.

Dr. Gillespie is obviously a father figure. Kildare is forever trying to impress the senior physician the way a young boy might try to impress his dad while playing little league baseball. Gillespie acts as the younger man's conscience, reminding him to be more careful, to try harder, to be a better doctor, to never let up in his concentration.

The soap opera aspects of *Dr. Kildare* develop as the series progresses. Kildare becomes a resident, is more sure of himself, eases up a bit, and starts noticing the ladies. The number of beautiful young women suffering from temporary amnesia rises dramatically in the neighborhood of Blair General and Kildare treats them all. The Kildare/Gillespie relationship is downplayed and more attention is devoted to each week's guest patients. In the show's last season, the producers flaunt the soap opera aspects of *Dr. Kildare* by turning the sixty-minute show into a thirty-minute program (which originally aired twice in one week) and by stretching story lines over several episodes.

The Dr. Kildare character has a long history. He was created by author Max Brand (the pen name for Frederick Schiller Faust) in a series of short stories. Several popular movies were made between 1938 and 1947, starring Lew Ayres as Kildare and Lionel Barrymore as the forever crusty Dr. Gillespie. A network radio series aired in the early 1940s. After this popular 1960s TV series, a revival of sorts occurred in 1972, with *Young Dr. Kildare,* a syndicated series starring Mark Jenkins and Gary Merrill.

**DOCTOR SIMON LOCKE (*) 30 min (39ep Color; 1971–1972 Syndication) Medical Drama** *with Sam Groom as Dr. Simon Locke, Jack Albertson as Dr. Andrew Sellers, Nuala Fitzgerald as Nurse Louise Wynn, and Len Birman as Chief Dan Palmer*

Set in the small Canadian town of Dixon Mills, these are the low-budget syndicated adventures of Dr. Simon Locke, a dedicated young surgeon (played by Sam Groom, a graduate from the daytime soap *Another World*) and his crusty but compassionate medical mentor, Dr. Andrew Sellers (played by Jack Albertson, a few years before *Chico and the Man*). They find the usual assortment of criminals, diseases, and heart-tugging situations, often working with the local police chief, Dan Palmer, in making life in the community better for all. In the wake of scathing reviews at the nickel and dime production values of this series, Albertson left the program after a single season. It carried on, though, under a new title, *Police Surgeon.*

**DOCTOR WHO (***½) 30 min & 60 min & 90 min (672ep comprising 158 stories at Fall 1989; B&W for first 50 stories, B&W or Color next 24, Color only thereafter; 1963– UK BBC) Science Fiction** *with William Hartnell as the First Doctor (134ep comprising 29 stories), Patrick Troughton as the Second Doctor (119ep comprising 21 stories), Jon Pertwee as the Third Doctor (128ep comprising 24 stories), Tom Baker as the Fourth Doctor (160ep comprising 41 stories), Peter Davison as the Fifth Doctor (71ep comprising 19 stories & one 90 min special), Colin Baker as the Sixth Doctor (32ep comprising 11 stories), and Sylvester McCoy as the Seventh Doctor (28ep comprising 12 stories at Fall 1989)*

One great fantasy shared by both children and adults is the ability to travel through space and time, going backward and forward anywhere in the universe to see what was and what will be. Britain's *Doctor Who* has been taking that journey more or less continuously since 1963.

The initial premise was really quite simple. Two British school teachers decided to visit the home of one of their exceptional students (named Susan) who seemed to know a lot of details about historical events, almost as if she had been there. It turned out that her "home" was a blue police call box (telephone booth). Once inside, the teachers were astonished to discover plenty of room because, in reality, the box was a combination time machine and space ship, in disguise.

The vehicle was called the TARDIS (an acronym for Time and Relative Dimensions in Space) and its canny operator (known as the Doctor—never "Doctor Who") was a man from another planet who looked to all the world like a kindly old grandfather. Within a few minutes, the Doctor and his traveling companions (Susan and the two teachers) were off. And so it would continue for more than twenty years, with new companions (and new Doctors) carrying on the adventures.

*Doctor Who* premiered in Britain on November 23, 1963, as the BBC began to resume regularly scheduled programming after extensive coverage of the assassination of President John F. Kennedy. Slotted in an early Saturday evening time period, the program took dead aim at fantasy-oriented adults and children, even structuring each story as a multiepisode cliff-hanger reminiscent of the old Saturday afternoon movie serials. Within two months, the series was one of the most talked about subjects in Britain. The reason? In just the second serial, the Doctor and his companions were locked in deadly combat with an evil race of robotlike creatures called the Daleks.

As the seven-week battle with the Daleks unfolded, their cold metallic voices and strangely shaped bodies (which looked a bit like overgrown pepper mills) became the subject of a national fad. In the process, *Doctor Who* turned into a bona-fide all-ages hit.

Except for two theatrical film adaptations (*Doctor Who and the Daleks* and *The Daleks: Invasion Earth 2150 A.D.*), none of these shows reached the United States until about ten years later.

By then, *Doctor Who* was in color and much more salable in syndication. There was also a completely different cast, including a new performer (Jon Pertwee) in the role of the Doctor. Actually, Pertwee was the third one to take the part, with each succeeding performer bringing a decidedly different look to the character. (These changes were all explained in the series as part of a "regeneration" process the Doctor experienced every once in a while.)

By the end of the 1970s, *Doctor Who* was playing throughout the United States (primarily on public broadcasting stations), with yet another performer (Tom Baker) in the lead role. This version really caught on, turning the series into a year-round staple that attracted a fiercely loyal (and vocal) audience.

Unlike the BBC, which by then produced and aired only about twenty-six weeks worth of *Doctor Who* episodes per year, most U.S. stations ran the series either in strip form (half-hour episodes five days a week) or edited together into complete weekly stories (about ninety minutes each). As a result, they went through about eight seasons worth of episodes in just one year, easily catching up with the British cycle by the early 1980s.

The BBC continued to turn out new episodes throughout the decade (going through three more Doctors), but at a much slower rate than before. To help meet the now seemingly insatiable appetite of U.S. viewers, the BBC dug into its archives and released every complete *Doctor Who* serial on its shelves, starting with the very first adventure from 1963. Most of these shows were in black and white, but that didn't seem to matter. Viewers who had come to enjoy the continuity of the series welcomed the opportunity to see the adventures from beginning to end. Programmers were also happy because they now had about 120 stories to use in a weekly cycle that could run about two and one-half years without a repeat.

Perhaps the biggest surprise to U.S. viewers from this retrospective viewing was the discovery that *Doctor Who* did not just "get good" with Tom Baker or Jon Pertwee. The series had obviously settled quite quickly into an effective mix of clever plots, scary alien monsters, and genuine heroics, including a willingness to let the heroes lose every once in a while (especially against the Daleks), wiping out entire civilizations in the process. On the lighter side, the tightly cut garb on some of the female characters (obviously designed with adult males in mind) was also there practically from the beginning.

There are a few technical distractions in the black-and-white episodes. State-of-the-art costumes and television special effects look particularly primitive twenty years later. Also, at the time they probably were not shooting with endless reruns in mind, so there were no retakes on mildly muffed lines. Consequently, first-time viewers should probably watch the black-and-white episodes only after getting familiar with the parameters of the series in any of the subsequent color adventures.

Over the years, each new performer brought his own distinct flavor to the Doctor, in effect creating a self-contained series within the overall series. A brief scorecard on each follows.

William Hartnell's Doctor is a kind but stubborn eccentric old professor type. His best companions: Carole Ann Ford as Susan Foreman, William Russell as Ian Chesterton, and Jacqueline Hill as Barbara Wright, the initial trio of fellow travelers with the series. Among the best stories: "The Daleks," "The Dalek Invasion of Earth," "The Planet of Giants," "The Aztecs," "The Space Museum," and "The Romans" (cleverly played like an ancient Roman comedy). About thirteen of the Hartnell stories are lost or incomplete.

Patrick Troughton's Doctor is a more playful, almost Chaplinesque figure, sometimes referred to as the "cosmic hobo." His best companions: Frazier Hines as Jamie McCrimmon and Wendy Padbury as Zoe. Also introduced in this era: Nicholas Courtney as Brigadier Lethbridge-Stewart. Unfortunately, more than half the stories from this period are lost or incomplete. The best among those remaining: "The Seeds of Death," "The Krotons," and "War Games" (a ten-part epic easily ranking as one of the best stories in the entire series).

Jon Pertwee's Doctor is a man of action, supremely confident, articulate, yet also warmly reassuring. Best companions: Katy Manning as Jo Grant and Elisabeth Sladen as Sarah Jane Smith. Also introduced in this era: Roger Delgado as The Master, a brilliant rogue time traveler and a continuing foe for the Doctor. Among the best stories: "Carnival of Monsters," "The Three Doctors" (a team-up of the first three performers), "Colony in Space," "The Monster of Peladon," and "Inferno" (a terrific parallel-Earth story with dual roles for most of the cast). The color prints for four of the Pertwee stories are currently lost, though black and white copies are around.

Tom Baker's Doctor is the man with the long scarf, floppy hat, curly hair, and dedicated determination that exploring the universe should be fun! His best companions: Louise Jameson as Leela, Elisabeth Sladen continuing as Sarah, and Mary Tamm as Romana. Also introduced in this era: K-9, the mechanical computer dog, and Anthony Ainley taking over the role of The Master. Among the best stories: "The Talons of Weng-Chiang," "The Pirate Planet," "Genesis of the Daleks," and "The Invisible Enemy" (a *Fantastic Voyage*–style journey through the Doctor's own body). Tom Baker's run as the Doctor was the longest and most successful in the program's history.

Peter Davison's Doctor is young, good-humored, gentle, and at times almost boyishly naive. He had the unenviable task of succeeding Baker, and wisely played the character quite differently from his predecessor. His best companions: Janet Fielding as Tegan Jovanka and Mark Strickson as Turlough. Among the best stories: "Enlightenment," "Arc of Infinity," "Earthshock," and "The Five Doctors" (a twentieth anniversary special teaming the first five performers).

Colin Baker's Doctor is a conscious return to some of the blatantly eccentric trappings of the previous Baker (no relation), but with a more abrasive, irrational, even arrogant tone at times reminiscent of the original William Hartnell portrayal. Although there are touches of humor, the stories in general are particularly weak, especially in the scripting for the Doctor's main companion, Nicola Bryant as Peri Brown (who is all too often presented as just a whiney, self-centered American). The pacing of the series is also hurt with a one-season (six stories) changeover in the length of individual episodes from thirty minutes to fifty minutes (just when you think there should be a cliff-hanger pause, there isn't). This run is probably one of the least successful ones in the series, though it does end with a clever set of four stories under one umbrella title, "The Trial of a Time Lord." (Look for a guest shot by Brian Blessed in that one.) Other noteworthy tales in the Colin Baker run: "Twin Dilemma" and "The Two Doctors" (with guest Patrick Troughton).

Sylvester McCoy's interpretation of the Doctor is the most deliberately comic one since Patrick Troughton's, and marks a return to a more relaxed approach to the series. Less physically dominating than his predecessors, he takes particular delight in silly wordplay and light banter. And he actually seems to like his companions (Bonnie Langford as Melanie and Sophie Aldred as Ace). Among the best stories (so far): "Paradise Towers," "Delta and the Bannerman" (a magical mystery trip to 1959 Wales), and "Remembrance of the Daleks." ■

**THE DOCTORS (**½) (44ep Color; 1969–1973 NBC) Medical Drama** *with E. G. Marshall as Dr. Benjamin Craig, David Hartman as Dr. Paul Hunter, John Saxon as Dr. Ted Stuart, Robert Walden as Dr. Martin Cohen, and Sally Kemp as Nurse Robbins*

This is the only segment airing under *The Bold Ones* umbrella title to last the entire four-year run of the series. It's a reliable, if not groundbreaking, setup, with E. G. Marshall as the head (and founder) of The Benjamin Craig Institute, a medical research center based in Los Angeles. He and his protégés tackle a wide range of patient ailments, and even manage to keep the emphasis more on issues and characters rather than on sudsy soap-opera-style complications. Though at times the series suffers bouts of early 1970s relevancy, at least it's appropriate for Marshall, who tackled his share of hot issues as a lawyer in *The Defenders* back in the early 1960s. Some of the episodes run under the title *The New Doctors,* though all of them are part of the same basic setup. David Hartman went directly from this series to the lead in *Lucas Tanner,* while Robert Walden eventually landed at another issue-oriented program, *Lou Grant.*

**THE DOCTORS AND THE NURSES** **(see *The Nurses/The Doctors and the Nurses*)**

**DOCTORS' HOSPITAL (**) 60 min (13ep & 2 hr pilot Color; 1975–1976 NBC) Medical Drama** *with George Peppard as Dr. Jake Goodwin, Zohra Lampert as Dr. Norah Purcell, Victor Campos as Dr. Felipe Ortega, Albert Paulsen as Janos Varga, and John Larroquette as Dr. Paul Herman*

From Bing Crosby Productions and executive producer Matthew Rapf, the folks who brought you the classy angst of *Ben Casey,* comes *Doctors' Hospital,* a capable show focusing on a half-dozen medicos, rather than just one. George Peppard, more familiar to most viewers as the cigar-chomping Hannibal Smith from *The A-Team,* is the lead doctor, a neurosurgeon at gargantuan Lowell Memorial Hospital in Los Angeles. John Larroquette, the lascivious Dan Fielding in *Night Court,* makes his first series appearance here.

The 1975 pilot is titled *One of Our Own.*

**DOCTORS' PRIVATE LIVES (*½) 60 min (4ep & 2 hr pilot Color; 1979 ABC) Medical Drama** *with Ed Nelson as Dr. Michael Wise, John Gavin as Dr. Jeffrey Latimer, Randolph Powell as Dr. Rick Calder, Phil Levien as Kenny Wise, William Smithers as Dr. Trilling, and Elinor Donahue as Mona Wise*

The title says it all—these are soapy personal conflicts at a large hospital, focusing in particular on two heart surgeons: Dr. Wise, the hospital's chief of surgery, and Dr. Latimer, chief of the cardiovascular unit. They are in never-ending angst about ethics, relationships, love, and passion, occasionally paying attention to the concerns of the other characters (family, friends, patients). Donna Mills (later Abby on *Knots Landing*) appears in the 1978 made-for-TV movie pilot as Dr. Beth Demery.

**DOG AND CAT (**) 30 min (7ep & 90 min pilot Color; 1977 ABC) Situation Comedy** *with Lou Antonio as Sgt. Jack Ramsey, Kim Basinger as J. Z. Kane, and Matt Clark as Lt. Arthur Kipling*

In police lingo, a "dog and cat" team is a squad car unit made up of one male and one female officer. That, in a nutshell, is all there is to the plot of *Dog and Cat.* He is a veteran of the LAPD. She is a beautiful (naturally), highly skilled (naturally) policewoman. He doubts she can take the heat. She wants to prove she can. As a comedy, there is much light and breezy banter. One reason to search for this show is to see Kim Basinger before she became a sexy film queen (*9½ Weeks, Never Say Never Again, The Natural*).

**DOLLY (***) 30 min (26ep Color; 1976–1977 Syndication) Musical-Variety** *with Dolly Parton*

As opposed to Dolly Parton's big-budget network variety flop of the 1980s, this simple, plain series from the 1970s is a wonderful stage for the real Dolly Parton, as she jokes and sings with some of her best friends in the entertainment world. Set in and around Nashville, the show is an easygoing half hour with a lot of music, a little laughing, and some talented guests. Look for the episode featuring the team of Parton, Emmy Lou Harris, and Linda Ronstadt, a full decade before the three singers released their joint album *Trio.*

**DOLLY (*½) 60 min (22ep Color; 1987–1988 ABC) Musical-Variety** *with Dolly Parton*

Country and western singing superstar Dolly Parton joins the ranks of those who tried, and failed, to revive the lost art of the big-budget network prime-time variety series in the 1980s. Dolly tries awfully hard to make this work, but it just doesn't. At first, Dolly is packaged just like any pop star, but one who happens to have a country twang. This packaging writes off Dolly's natural basis for popularity—her country charm and ways. Midway through the series, the producers change and the tone becomes more down home, more natural. It's too late, though, since the show sinks by its own production weight. Parton should have stuck with the simple format that worked in her 1970s syndicated series of the same name.

**DOLPHIN COVE (**) 60 min (8ep Color; 1989 CBS) Adventure** *with Frank Converse as Michael Larson, Trey Ames as David Larson, Karron Graves as Katie Larson, Virginia Hey as Alison Mitchell, Ernie Dingo as James "Didge" Desmond, and Nick Tate as Mr. Trent*

*Dolphin Cove* is what passes for late 1980s wholesome family drama on TV. Frank Converse (the amnesiac of *Coronet Blue* and the idealistic cop in *N.Y.P.D.*) plays Michael Larson, a Yuppie dolphin researcher whose wife just died in a nasty car crash. Larson relocates his career and his two kids to Australia, where he can start a new life (and where this economy series was filmed, in order to avoid higher American production costs).

Things are not all hunky-dory down under. Larson has problems dealing with the Aussie dolphins. Teenage son David is homesick for the United States. Young daughter Katie, who was in the car during the accident that killed her mother, has not spoken since the crash. Alison Mitchell, the beautiful therapist, is frustrated in her efforts to coax Katie back to normal speech. But wait! Katie somehow starts communicating with the all-knowing dolphins. The cerebral aquatic mammals keep turning up at opportune times to assist the young girl, who has the habit of frequently finding herself in trouble. Chances are, the dolphins know the Larsons are from the United States and they are angling for a major role in a remake of *Flipper.*

**THE DOM DELUISE SHOW (*) 30 min (26ep Color; 1987–1988 Syndication) Situation Comedy** *with Dom DeLuise as Dom DeLuca, George Wallace as George Henry Wallace, Maureen Murphy as Maureen, Angela Aames as Penny, Michael Chambers as Michael Chambers, and Lauren Woodland as Rosa*

Dom DeLuise, the rotund comic who appears in several Burt Reynolds films (such as *The End*), wastes his time here as a widower raising his ten-year-old daughter Rosa. Dom plays a barber with his shop across the street from a big Hollywood studio. Consequently, famous Hollywood stars (Burt Reynolds, Dean Martin, Zsa Zsa Gabor) are always dropping by. Dom makes frequent asides to the home audience, and many members of the backup cast are proficient stand-up comics on their own. Unfortunately all this talent goes mostly to waste as the plots never go beyond some cute one-liners.

**DOMESTIC LIFE (**) 30 min (10ep Color; 1984 CBS) Situation Comedy** *with Martin Mull as Martin Crane, Christian Brackett-Zika as Harold Crane, Judith-Marie Bergan as Candy Crane, Megan Follows as Didi Crane, Mie Hunt as Jane Funakubo, Robert Ridgely as Cliff Hamilton, and Hoyt Axton as Rip Steele*

Martin Mull's style of smug comic mockery works best when he is slightly removed from the action and aligned more with his audience. That way, he can wink at them, knowingly arch his eyebrows, and say (or imply) the question, "Can you believe *those people* are so out of it?" That style serves him well in the put-on talk show format of *Fernwood/America 2Nite* and the pseudodocumentary *The History of White People in America.* The problem with *Domestic Life* is that, for a parody, it's remarkably similar to lots of real sitcoms, leaving Mull just a half step away from the type of production he normally would skewer mercilessly.

What rescues the series from comedy hell is its willingness to embrace some tradtional sitcom elements with a vengeance. If comedies of the 1950s and 1960s too often cast their dad characters as lovable but dumb (especially when compared with the kids), *Domestic Life* does them one better. Son Harold is by far the most intelligent and articulate member of the family, especially in matters of business. He patiently lectures dad on management of the family household, investments with the highest potential yield, and the best tax strategies. Unfortunately this advice usually comes too late—after a while you wish Martin would just give Harold the job of family investment counselor and be done with it. (Of course, Harold will get it all anyway just on interest charges on the money he lends his folks!) Usually the way sitcoms balance off the genius child is with parental expertise in less technical fields, such as love, courtship, and dating. Harold had best stick with the newspaper advice columns—dad and mom are not much help here, either. (On that front, his number one female friend is Sally Dwyer, played by Tina Yothers, moonlighting from *Family Ties.*)

The kicker joke in the premise is that Martin is a commentator for a Seattle television station, hosting a news show segment called "Domestic Life," in which he talks about the funny side of family living. There, Mull's wit at last finds juicier targets—they're only defenseless adults—such as fellow news team members Cliff Hamilton and Jane Funakubo, as well as maverick station owner Rip Steele (played by country singer Hoyt Axton), a former cowboy movie star.

Steve Martin served as executive producer for this series and, not surprisingly, Mull sings the title song.

**DON KIRSHNER'S ROCK CONCERT** (**½) **90 min (144ep Color; 1973–1981 Syndication) Musical-Variety** *with Don Kirshner as host*

If you can ignore the introductions by Mr. Kirshner, this series is a pretty good collection of mid-1970s rock music in action (Fleetwood Mac, Black Sabbath, Paul McCartney and Wings, the Rolling Stones, Blondie, the Ramones). Unfortunately, it is a bit hard to ignore Mr. Kirshner, who has about as much stage presence as Ed Sullivan on quaaludes. Kirshner, a famous music producer and promoter who can take credit for the success of Bobby Darin, the Monkees, and the Archies, loves to drop names of his well-known friends and tries real hard, to no avail, to act cool and relaxed. Like most of the rock music series of the 1970s, Kirshner's series is a collection of edited live concert appearances.

For a lovely set of parodies of Kirshner's bland hosting style, look for Paul Shaffer's unerring impressions in several late 1970s episodes of *Saturday Night Live.* ■

**THE DON RICKLES SHOW** (*½) **30 min (13ep Color; 1972 CBS) Situation Comedy** *with Don Rickles as Don Robinson, Louise Sorel as Barbara Robinson, Erin Moran as Janie Robinson, and Robert Hogan as Tyler Benedict*

The formula appears to be great: Take master stand-up comedian Don Rickles, put him in a sitcom as a frazzled advertising executive who is always popping off at the craziness around him, then let TV comedy genius Sheldon Leonard (*Make Room for Daddy, The Andy Griffith Show, The Dick Van Dyke Show*) be executive producer and let Hy Averback, a man with a track record of dealing with broad humor on TV (*F Troop, The Dukes of Hazzard*), be the producer. The result? A flop.

Rickles is simply too volatile, too wild to be hog-tied into a "normal" role as a suburban corporate executive. Rickles as loving husband? Doting father? No way. His style of torrential put-downs is best suited for the open stage, or at least the loose atmosphere of a late-night talk show.

Check out Erin Moran, in her pre–Joanie Cunningham (*Happy Days*) phase, as Rickles's daughter. Moran was only eleven when *The Don Rickles Show* was produced, but this series is already her second (she appeared in *Daktari* at age seven).

**THE DONNA FARGO SHOW** (**) **30 min (13ep Color; 1978–1979 Syndication) Musical-Variety** *with Donna Fargo as hostess*

The Osmond Brothers produced this mild variety series starring Donna Fargo, a popular country and western singer.

**THE DONNA REED SHOW** (**½) **30 min (175ep B&W; 1958–1966 ABC) Situation Comedy** *with Donna Reed as Donna Stone, Carl Betz as Dr. Alex Stone, Shelley Fabares as Mary Stone, Paul Peterson as Jeff Stone, Patty Petersen as Trisha Stone, Bob Crane as Dr. Dave Kelsey, and Ann McCrea as Midge Kelsey*

There are many challengers for the "Most Wholesome Sitcom Family of the 1950s" award, since wholesomeness was a prized commodity in those days. The Cleavers of *Leave It to Beaver* spring to mind, of course. Serious consideration must also go to the Andersons of *Father Knows Best* and the Nelsons of *Ozzie and Harriet,* but a dark horse candidate is the Stones of *The Donna Reed Show.* What gives the Stones an edge is that there really is not one member of the Stone family who has any sort of peculiar personality trait to set them apart from average suburbanites. All of the Stones are, well, wholesome.

Considering that *The Donna Reed Show* is named after the actress playing the mother, it is not too surprising that the father in the Stone household is somewhat of a cipher. Dr. Alex Stone, a small-town pediatrician, is a nice enough chap, who shows the wry bemusement with his family's antics that is required of sitcom dads of the 1950s. Having Dr. Stone be a pediatrician is a convenient plot device to get him out of the home at all hours of the day and night (for wholesome reasons), leaving the star, Donna Reed, as the primary focus. Dr. Stone is no wimp like Ozzie Nelson; rather, he is much more in the Ward Cleaver mold. Like Ward, Alex means well but has little time to do much more than provide a few sage words of advice and make bumbling attempts to be pals with his offspring.

*The Donna Reed Show* is one of a handful of 1950s family sitcoms featuring the wife as the lead. The others of this ilk (*I Love Lucy, The Goldbergs*) were popular enough, but they featured more comical, offbeat female leads. Reed plays Donna Stone straight down the middle. She displays her share of typical housewife fluster when trying to deal with problems on her own, but this is normal for the times. Reed earned the star billing based on her successful film career, where she portrayed everything from a prostitute (*From Here to Eternity*) to the more traditional faithful wife character (*It's a Wonderful Life.*) Reed's real-life husband, Tony Owen, served as producer of *The Donna Reed Show* and obviously took care to be certain his wife came across in a favorable light.

If the parents in *The Donna Reed Show* are such straight arrows, what about the kids? Well, they are pretty wholesome too. Mary, the Stones' oldest, is cute, but not gorgeous. She spends most of the series in the high school dating years, where puppy love complications abound. The Stones' son Jeff is rambunctious and interested in cars and is making his own first fumbling efforts to woo the fairer sex. Once again, though, this is all pretty standard for the times, and there is nothing about Mary or Jeff to make them memorable.

So we've written off the entire Stone family as nice but bland. The final area to look for some color in a wholesome family sitcom is the neighbors, and here *The Donna Reed Show* finally shows a glimmer of distinctiveness. For two seasons in the middle years of the series, Bob Crane livens up the program as the madcap Dr. Dave Kelsey, yet another pediatrician, who displays a great deal more zaniness than Dr. Stone. This must be chalked up to the fact that Dr. Kelsey and his wife Midge do not seem to have any children. Therefore, they can be allowed the occasional flight of fancy. Crane's success in his role as Dr. Kelsey led directly to the starring role in his own sitcom (*Hogan's Heroes*).

The omnipresent wholesomeness of *The Donna Reed Show* is both its strength and its weakness. Wholesomeness does not necessarily mean boredom, and this show must be recognized as a well-crafted series that has many enjoyable, humorous episodes. The humor is realistic and the characters are friendly. The unremitting wholesomeness does become a drag after a while, though. One longs for a slimy character like Eddie Haskell of *Beaver* fame, or some screwball like Lucy Ricardo, to inject some unusual flavor. *Leave It to Beaver* and *Father Knows Best* proved that quality humor can come out of a normal family setting, but both those shows added enough flair to make at least some of the characters memorable. None of the major characters in *The Donna Reed Show* are any more interesting than anybody you might meet in the average suburban development. *The Donna Reed Show* tries very hard to be sober, reasonable, family entertainment. The problem is that it succeeds too well.

Shelley Fabares and Paul Peterson both followed Ricky Nelson's lead and used their starring roles in a family sitcom to launch singing careers. Both Fabares ("Johnny Angel") and Petersen ("She Can't Find Her Keys" and "My Dad") scored with hits (that were performed in various episodes of this series), but their singing fame faded as soon as they lost their prime-time showcase. Soon after her character was sent off to college, Fabares left the series to pursue a career in the movies (she appeared in several Elvis Presley flicks, such as *Girl Happy*, *Clambake*, and *Spinout*). Shortly after Fabares left, Petersen's real-life younger sister, Patty, joined the cast as a wayward orphan taken in by the kindly Stone family. Could we expect anything but such generosity from such a wholesome family?

**DON'T CALL ME CHARLIE** **(*½) 30 min (26ep B&W; 1962–1963 NBC) Situation Comedy** *with Josh Peine as Pvt. Judson McKay, Linda Lawson as Pat Perry, John Hubbard as Col. U. Charles Barker, Alan Napier as Gen. Steele, and Arte Johnson as Cpl. Lefkowitz*

Set in Paris, *Don't Call Me Charlie* does not really focus on Col. U. Charles Barker, who hates it when his men call him Charlie, but rather on country bumpkin Judson McKay, who came to Paris directly from the farms of Iowa. It is McKay's persistence in keeping to his rural roots amidst the allures of the city of lights that provides most of the comedy fodder for this show. By the way, Col. Barker commands a unit of Army veterinarians, not fighting men.

Alan Napier is best known for his role as Alfred, the butler, in *Batman* while Arte Johnson's claim to fame is as a cast member of *Rowan & Martin's Laugh-In.*

**THE DORIS DAY SHOW** **(**½) 30 min (128ep Color; 1968–1973 CBS) Situation Comedy** *with Doris Day as Doris Martin, Denver Pyle as Buck Webb, Fran Ryan as Aggie Thompson, Rose Marie as Myrna Gibbons, McLean Stevenson as Michael Nicholson, Kaye Ballard as Angie Palucci, Bernie Kopell as Louie Palucci, John Dehner as Cy Bennett, and Peter Lawford as Dr. Peter Lawrence*

It would take a half hour to explain all the format changes in this thirty-minute sitcom. Suffice it to say that you can watch the role of the modern TV woman evolve during the course of this series. At first, Doris Day, the star of numerous fluffy romantic films of the 1950s (starring Rock Hudson and Cary Grant), is the typical 1950s TV mom, with two kids and a dog but no husband (he's dead). She and her brood move from the city back to the country to live on her father's farm. In year two, Day begins to change. She gets a job, back in the city, but just as a secretary to pre-*M*A*S*H* McLean Stevenson (in his first series role), who plays the editor of a weekly news magazine. Thus, Day has become a commuting mom, alternating from country to city, worker to mother, each day. Her pal here is veteran TV working woman Rose Marie (of *The Dick Van Dyke Show*).

In year three, the bucolic country atmosphere vanishes, as Day moves her kids and dog back to the city, into an apartment above the Paluccis, who run an Italian restaurant. In this stage, Doris Day moves up from the "pink collar" world of the secretary pool to the exalted position of part-time reporter. Finally, in year four, Day truly becomes the TV woman of the 1970s, as her kids and her dog magically disappear and she is now a swinging single-woman reporter, dating a handsome doctor (played by Peter Lawford).

Day gets to sing her big movie hit, "Que Sera Sera," each week, which is a bit more often than might be desired.

**DOROTHY** **(*) 30 min (4ep Color; 1979 CBS) Situation Comedy** *with Dorothy Loudon as Dorothy Banks, Russell Nype as Burton Foley, Kenneth Gilman as Jack Landis, and Priscilla Morrill as Lorna Cathcart*

Dorothy Loudon, an actress and singer hot (in the late 1970s) from a starring role in the Broadway musical *Annie,* headlines a nondescript sitcom set in a private girl's school in Connecticut. Amidst the prim and proper locale, Dorothy Banks is an odd bird, a divorced ex-showgirl who teaches the girls music and drama and something about real life.

**DOUBLE DARE** (**) 60 min (6ep Color; 1985 CBS) **Police Drama** *with Billy Dee Williams as Billy Diamond, Jennifer Warren and Janet Carroll as Lt. Samantha Warner, and Ken Wahl as Ken Sisko*

*Double Dare* is a sprightly adventure yarn with sleek Billy Dee Williams in his first leading role in a TV series. Williams plays Billy Diamond, a cat burglar who avoids jail after his arrest by agreeing to work undercover as a police agent. Ken Sisko is Billy's partner who is sprung from prison in order to team up again with Billy, this time on the side of law and order. Ken Wahl, who plays Sisko, makes his first TV series appearance here. He went on to a juicier role as Vinnie Terranova, the lead character is *Wiseguy.*

**THE DOUBLE LIFE OF HENRY PHYFE** (*½) 30 min (17ep Color; 1966 ABC) **Situation Comedy** *with Red Buttons as Henry Wadsworth Phyfe, Fred Clark as Gerald B. Hannahan, Zeme North as Judy Kimball, and Marge Redmond as Florence Kimball*

From the era of tongue-in-cheek spies and super heroes (*Get Smart, Mr. Terrific, Captain Nice*) comes Henry W. Phyfe, the archetypal mild-mannered accountant. Henry, however, has the misfortune to be an exact double of U-31, a secret U.S. government spy who has just been killed in a mundane hit-and-run accident. The government, in the person of loud, obnoxious Gerald Hannahan, recruits Phyfe to impersonate the spy, who was suave, brave, and intelligent, everything Henry is not. Only Hannahan knows what Henry's up to, so Henry's girlfriend Judy and her mother Florence are always befuddled by the changes in Henry's lifestyle.

This just can't compare with *Get Smart.* Red Buttons, a star of Broadway revues in the 1940s, tries too hard in a show too loud and stilted for its own good.

**DOUBLE TROUBLE** (*) 30 min (23ep Color; 1984–1985 NBC) **Situation Comedy** *with Jean Sagal as Kate Foster, Liz Sagal as Allison Foster, Barbara Barrie as Margo Foster, Jonathan Schmock as Billy Batalato, James Vallely as Charles Kincade, and Donnelly Rhodes as Art Foster*

The setting of this frothy sitcom shifts halfway through its run. The focus throughout is the Foster twins (played by the real-life Sagal twins, who appeared as cheerleaders in the film *Grease II*), two pretty sixteen-year-olds from Iowa. Kate Foster is the spunky, rambunctious one, while Allison is the sober, studious one. People are always mixing up the two, which is where a lot of the yucks are supposed to come from. At first, the twins are at home with Art, their widowed dad. After eight episodes, the scene shifts to New York City, where the pretty duo have gone to make it in the big time, Kate as an actress, Allison as a fashion designer.

**DOUGLAS FAIRBANKS, JR. PRESENTS** (**½) 30 min (117ep B&W; 1953–1957 Syndication) **Drama Anthology** *with Douglas Fairbanks, Jr., as host*

Douglas Fairbanks, Jr., one of Hollywood's top leading men from the 1930s and 1940s, serves as host, executive producer, and occasional star in this series of entertaining dramas. Originally the show's title included the sponsor's name; for example, *Douglas Fairbanks, Jr., Presents the Rheingold Theater.*

**DOWN AND OUT IN BEVERLY HILLS** (*½) 30 min (8ep Color; 1987 Fox) **Situation Comedy** *with Hector Elizondo as Dave Whiteman, Anita Morris as Barbara Whiteman, Tim Thomerson as Jerry Baskin, Evan Richards as Max Whiteman, Eileen Seeley as Jenny Whiteman, April Ortiz as Carmen, and Mike as Matisse*

The original 1986 Paul Mazursky movie *Down and Out in Beverly Hills* was a riot with Richard Dreyfuss, Bette Midler, and Nick Nolte starring in a rollicking saga of how a homeless bum stumbles into the lives of a nouveau riche Beverly Hills family, changing them all forever. The lame TV version loses a great deal in the translation to video. As is often the case with remakes from films, the TV version is toned down and cleaned up, lacking the zing and punch of the original. Furthermore, the characters are tidied up for TV, making them less interesting and more like all the other TV families we see.

The pity is that the TV cast is quite talented. Hector Elizondo, taking over Richard Dreyfuss's role as the neurotic clothes-hanger tycoon, is a fine actor usually wasted in clichéd Latino roles (*Freebie and the Bean* and *a.k.a. Pablo*). Tim Thomerson, in for Nick Nolte as the hippie-turned-bum, has played intriguing crackpots in *Quark* and *The Associates.* The only cast carryovers from the movie are Evan Richards as the closet psychotic son and Mike the dog, who stole the film as Matisse, the crafty and aggressive family canine.

**DOWN TO EARTH** (*½) 30 min (104ep Color; 1985–1987 Syndication) **Situation Comedy** *with Dick Sargent as Richard Preston and Carol Mansell as Ethel*

Dick Sargent already has experience dealing with roommates with unusual powers. He had a three-year stint as Dick York's replacement in the husband role of Darrin Stephens in *Bewitched.* Now, as widower Richard Preston, Sargent must cope with Ethel, a housekeeper sent from heaven, who keeps tabs on the three boisterous Preston children.

**DOWNTOWN** **(*½) 60 min (13ep Color; 1986–1987 CBS) Crime Drama** *with Michael Nouri as John Forney, Robert Englund as Dennis Shothoffer, Millicent Martin as Harriet Conover, Blair Underwood as Terry Corsaro, Mariska Hargitay as Jesse Smith, Virginia Capers as Delia Bonner, and David Paymer as Capt. David Kiner*

The excuse for this band of independent investigators to be working together is that they're all parolees, serving out-time at an ad-hoc halfway house. Actually it's the home of Harriet Conover (played by former *That Was the Week That Was* ensemble performer Millicent Martin), a genteel older woman whose involvement in fraud helped land her in this setup. She and her fellow inmates are not judged dangerous enough to be a physical threat to society, but they do have to serve some punishment. So the younger kids (Terry, Jesse, and Dennis) are supposed to help fix Harriet's home, while all of them look for respectable jobs and cooperate with their social worker (Delia Bonner) and their parole officer (John Forney). While the social worker is eager to see this plan succeed, Detective Forney can't believe he's stuck on babysitting detail, his punishment for stepping out of line with his bosses one too many times. His charges compound the sentence by constantly getting involved in his latest cases, drawing on their personal enthusiasm and streetwise skills: Harriet is a creditable con artist, Terry is a former pickpocket, Jesse is a whiz at karate, and Dennis is a master of impersonation (an appropriate skill for the future Freddy Krueger character of *Nightmare on Elm Street*). An adequate adventure series with by-the-numbers group escapades.

**DRACULA '79** **(see *The Curse of Dracula*)**

**DRAGNET** **(***) 30 min (361ep: 263 B&W & 98 Color & 2 hr Color pilot; 1951–1959 & 1967–1970 NBC) Police Drama** *with Jack Webb as Joe Friday, Barton Yarborough as Sgt. Ben Romero, Barney Phillips as Sgt. Ed Jacobs, Herb Ellis and Ben Alexander as Frank Smith, and Harry Morgan as Bill Gannon*

*Dragnet* has made the complete circle in popular culture, from a breakthrough in style to an instantly recognizable standard (and, at times, a virtual self-caricature). Thus, to understand *Dragnet,* a viewer must see where the show came from and what it became.

When Jack Webb first developed the series on radio in 1949, and two years later on TV, *Dragnet* was a breath of fresh air in the world of pop culture cops. Before *Dragnet,* crime fighting was usually portrayed on radio and TV in an overly romantic light. Policemen or private eyes would effortlessly deduce the criminal's identity and then outtrick the felon, while engaging in witty repartee and romancing some young lovely at the same time.

While this image is fine for light entertainment now and then, it paints a wildly distorted image of what real policemen go through. *Dragnet* changed all that. In *Dragnet,* thanks to Jack Webb's unwavering dedication to realism, you see the boredom, the red tape, the hard work, the long hours, and the frustration of real police work.

In semidocumentary style, *Dragnet* follows Sgt. Joe Friday of the Los Angeles Police Department and his partner (there are five, serving at various times) as they investigate and solve each week's crime. The cases were said to be based on actual case histories of the L.A.P.D. Friday serves as narrator as well, and a short summary by an offscreen announcer at the end of each episode provides information as to what happened to that week's villain after Sgt. Friday turns him over to other parts of the criminal justice system.

*Dragnet* fulfills its original goals admirably. It does present a much more realistic view of policemen, and viewers come away with a better understanding of what makes the average cop tick. *Dragnet,* however, has become a prisoner of its success and its own view of policemen is now a new stereotype.

*Dragnet* was an instant hit when it came to TV and all of its quirks and idiosyncrasies have since become standard elements of pop culture. The foreboding four-note musical opening, the deadpan narration, the overabundance of police jargon, the "just the facts, ma'am" style of Sgt. Friday, the somber epilogue at the end, even the sweaty hand chiseling the name of Webb's production company (Mark VII) in stone after the closing credits, all have been indelibly etched into the national conscience. They have been parodied by generations of comedians, from Stan Freberg ("St. George and the Dragonet" in 1953) to Dan Aykroyd (the 1987 film *Dragnet*).

The TV *Dragnet* is so easy to mimic because the program is extremely predictable. Friday is a police automaton. He has no wife, hardly any girlfriends, little family, and no outside interests other than apprehending lawbreakers. His partner is designed merely to provide a little comic relief and appear stumped by situations ultimately solved by Sgt. Friday, serving as Dr. Watson to Friday's Sherlock Holmes.

One aspect of Friday's personality that is always lurking beneath the surface is his basic distrust, almost dislike, for anyone who is not a working-stiff cop. He has true disdain for confessed and suspected criminals alike, but he also exudes a barely sublimated condescension for victims and eyewitnesses as well. It is as if he is disgusted with the noncop, noncriminal characters for their lack of precision and attention to detail and for not being as tuned in to the nuances of police procedure as he is. Sure, he is always calling everyone "sir" and "ma'am," but not very convincingly. Friday even evidences a little revulsion for his police superiors. Maybe not in the case of his immediate bosses, who he deals with on a daily basis, but definitely in the case of the upper echelon, those too far removed from the day-today grunt work that Friday revels in and knows to be the heart and soul of police work.

This holier-than-thou attitude is somewhat understandable. Those who are forced to confront daily the worst that life has to offer have a lot of trouble dealing with civilians who can avoid or ignore the harsh realities of life. If somewhat understandable, this trait is not very admirable. After watching several episodes of *Dragnet,* you want to tell Joe Friday to cool out, relax a bit, and cut the whole world just a little bit of slack. Friday, though, never changes, and at times the viewer may almost prefer to root for the criminals.

The original 1951–1959 black and white episodes of *Dragnet* (formerly syndicated under the title *Badge 714*—Friday's badge number) are not seen as often as the color episodes from the 1960s. The 1950s version is more low-key (if that is possible) and even features a fiancée for Friday (Dorothy Abbott as Ann Baker), although that romance is short-lived. Friday's partner in the 1950s episodes is usually the easygoing Frank Smith, but in the earliest episodes Friday is teamed with Ben Romero (played by Barton Yarborough, a carryover from the original radio series) and then Ed Jacobs. There is also a 1954 theatrical movie of *Dragnet,* with Ben Alexander in the Frank Smith role.

In the color 1960s episodes, Bill Gannon carries on the style of Frank Smith. Gannon has a wife and kids and provides a valuable symbol of normality that Friday never emulates. These later episodes also stray into the topical realm of student protesters and drug abuse. Here, Friday's bad tendencies are exacerbated. Friday never could deal with people who were just a little out of the ordinary, and he lets his inner venom spill out over and over when dealing with the new counterculture. After all, they oppose all the things Friday holds dear . . . blind obedience to form and unswerving insensitivity to those who stray from the straight and narrow. Times may have changed since the 1950s, but Friday never changed. If anything, he just became grumpier and less sympathetic.

When all is said and done, *Dragnet* serves a purpose. The shows are almost uniformly well written and produced, due, no doubt, to Webb's devotion to all aspects of the show's production. While freeing policemen from one set of TV stereotypes, however, Joe Friday only saddled them with another, one that took years (and shows such as *Barney Miller* and *Hill Street Blues*) to wear off.

In 1989, MCA announced plans to revive *Dragnet* with an entirely new cast, as a first-run syndicated series. ■

**DREAM STREET (*½) 60 min (5ep & 90 min pilot Color; 1989– NBC) Drama** *with Dale Midkiff as Denis Debeau, Peter Frechette as Harry Debeau, Thomas Calabro as Joey Coltrera, Cecil Hoffmann as Joni Goldstein, Jo Anderson as Marianne McKinney, Victor Argo as Anthony Coltrera, Debra Mooney as Lillian Debeau, Tom Signorelli as Peter Debeau, Christine Moore as Kara, and David Barry Gray as Eric Debeau*

From the creators of *thirtysomething, Dream Street* maintains that earlier show's focus on the day-to-day intricacies of human relationships, but shifts the setting to the blue-collar world of Hoboken, New Jersey. In the pilot, Peter Debeau, owner of a refrigeration business, is laid low by a stroke, and he turns over control of the family enterprise to his middle son, Denis. This causes friction between Denis and his older, but more lackadaisical, brother Harry. Youngest son Eric is still preoccupied with getting drunk and chasing girls all night.

Meanwhile, Denis's best friend, Joey, also is moving up in a family business, but in Joey's case that means the local Mafia outfit. The two boyhood chums now must deal with each other on the more unforgiving level of inner city business, and sparks fly.

Joey is engaged to the blond, beautiful and Jewish Joni, who chooses to overlook Joey's seamy family enterprise while focusing on the riches she hopes Joey will amass. Denis takes up with a brainy but tough school teacher, Marianne McKinney, whose middle-class sensibilities clash with her blue-collar surroundings.

*Dream Street* tries very hard to be insightful and noncondescending to its characters, but it still comes over as too forced. The bluesy soundtrack and hazy setting of the local bar (a popular locale for the Debeau boys) sometimes make *Dream Street* look more like a beer commercial than a drama.

**DREAMS (*) 30 min (5ep Color; 1984 CBS) Situation Comedy** *with John Stamos as Gino Minnelli, Jami Gertz as Martha Spino, Cain Devore as Phil Taylor, Albert Macklin as Morris Weiner, Valerie Stevenson as Lisa Copley, and Ron Karabatsos as Frank Franconi*

Music videos, a new fad in the early 1980s, are used in *Dreams* to breathe some life into this comedy about a struggling rock group from Philadelphia. Most of the group members, including lead hunk Gino, are from blue-collar backgrounds, but new singer Lisa, daughter of a U.S. senator, has a more pampered past.

The music is bland, the comedy is mediocre. *Dreams* deserved its quick cancellation.

**THE DUCHESS OF DUKE STREET (***) 60 min (31ep Color; 1976–1977 UK BBC) Drama** *with Gemma Jones as Louisa Trotter, Christopher Cazenove as Charles Tyrrell, Victoria Plucknett as Mary, John Welsh as Merriman, John Cater as Starr, Richard Vernon as Major Smith-Barton, Ian Francis as Irene Baker, Donald Burton as Augustus Trotter, June Brown as Mrs. Leyton, John Rapley as Mr. Leyton, Mary Healey as Mrs. Cochran, and Holly De Jong as Violet*

Louisa Trotter is the duchess, a Cockney-born working-class cook who becomes the no-nonsense proprietress of the Bentinck Hotel in London. The setup is based on the real-life character of Rosa Lewis, who allegedly landed management of the fashionable Cavendish Hotel in London as one result of her rumored affair with Prince Edward of Wales (later Edward VII). In any case, this background is the jumping-off point for a careful mix of historical events, business and political intrigues, domestic concerns, and romantic entanglements. Any similarity to 165 Eaton Place (*Upstairs, Downstairs*) should be no surprise because this series is also produced by John Hawkesworth. It comes complete with his meticulous eye for detailed atmosphere and characters, including (appropriately) such hotel "downstairs" types as the doorman (Mr. Starr), the cook (Mrs. Cochran), and the maid (Violet). There's even an eccentric retired military man, Major Smith-Barton, who never has any money to pay for his room, but who earns his keep by helping Louisa in other ways.

But she definitely remains the main force in the series, whether it's juggling the affections of royalty, visiting the battlefields of France during World War I, or considering a bad marriage just to expedite an affair with someone else. It's her hotel and her complicated life. Overall, not quite as stable and satisfying as *Upstairs, Downstairs,* but certainly a worthy neighbor.

This was a joint production between the BBC and Time-Life Television.

**THE DUCK FACTORY (**½) (13ep Color; 1984 NBC) Situation Comedy** *with Jim Carrey as Skip Tarkenton, Teresa Ganzel as Mrs. Sheree Winkler, Jack Gilford as Brooks Carmichael, Julie Payne as Aggie Aylesworth, Nancy Lane as Andrea Lewin, Don Messick as Wally Wooster, Clarence Gilyard, Jr. as Roland Culp, and Jay Tarses as Marty Fenneman*

Young Skip Tarkenton is on the verge of fulfilling the ultimate childhood dream, turning thousands of hours of youthful fascination with classic cartoons into a job alongside some of the veterans of the animation business. He's left his Midwest home and arrived in Los Angeles on the doorstep of Buddy Winkler Productions, ready to begin work. The only problem is that Buddy just recently died and the animation house is floundering, desperate to keep its one network product on the air, *Dippy Duck.* Before you can say "youthful energy and enthusiasm," Skip is an accepted member of the animation crew, appearing to be the fresh talent who just might be able to pump some new life into the cartoon star.

He tries his best, delivering naively upbeat pep talks to the veterans no longer quite sure of their own skills, such as animation director Brooks, gag writer Marty, and voice-over narrator Wally. Luckily, he's fully supported by the new owner of the studio, sexy young Sheree, the late Buddy's bride of three weeks. But she and the crew often find themselves facing off against Aggie, the company's financial manager, who feels driven to maintain Buddy's old skinflint standards, especially when it comes to any compensation to the staff.

This show has a potentially clever premise that never quite sorts out all the details. For instance, one look at Buddy's estate (where Sheree now lives) reveals that he certainly had money. Was that all from *Dippy Duck*? Or just from cutting corners at the studio? Maybe Aggie really is the only one who can keep the operation afloat, despite the good intentions of Sheree and Skip. Yet if they're all working on the same side, where's the conflict of the series?

In any case, even if *The Duck Factory* never quite finds its overall comic rhythm, it does hang around long enough to take a few welcome digressions down animation row. For instance, clips of *Dippy Duck* are frequently intercut with the action—demonstrating one strange Saturday morning offering. Other times the bullpen takes an enthusiastic break to reminisce, with Skip prompting the old-timers to do sketches and voices just like the good old days. The most welcome bit, though, is probably the visit by the faces behind two of television's most familiar cartoon voices: June Foray and Bill Scott (best known for, respectively, Rocky the Flying Squirrel and Bullwinkle J. Moose). In one delightful episode, they even do their renditions of several cartoon theme songs including the tunes to *Superchicken, The Road Runner,* and *George of the Jungle.*

**DUCKTALES, DISNEY'S (***) 30 min (65ep at Fall 1989 Color; 1987– Syndication) Cartoon Adventure** *with the voices of Alan Young as Scrooge McDuck, Russi Taylor as Huey, Dewey, Louie, and Webigail, Hal Smith as Gyro Gearloose and Flintheart Glomgold, and Terence McGovern as Launchpad McQuack*

Dedicated fans of Disney's ducks have been aware of one ironic secret for decades: Over the past forty years, the best stories featuring Donald Duck and his clan did not appear on the silver screen. Instead they turned up in authorized, Disney-licensed comic books. Many of these classics came from the pen of artist and writer Carl Barks, who turned out hundreds of Duck stories for a quarter of a century (1942 to 1967).

In his tales, Barks created a spectacular world of comic adventure that included a rich selection of major and minor characters. The most famous of these was Donald Duck's uncle, Scrooge McDuck—the world's richest duck.

How rich is he? McDuck's ready cash fills a concrete money bin measuring three cubic acres and comes to well over one multiplujillion nine obsquatumatillion dollars. Scrooge is always traveling the world to keep an eye on his investments or (more likely) going in search of yet another long-lost treasure. To help him out, he brings along Donald and his nephews, Huey, Dewey, and Louie.

Until *DuckTales,* cartoon viewers rarely saw the ducks in this light. In fact, they barely saw Scrooge at all. With a handful of exceptions, they saw Donald and his nephews presented chiefly as charismatic but silly (sometimes even slapstick) stars.

Like the comic book stories, the *DuckTales* adventures are funny, but they also allow the ducks to display intelligence, courage, and responsibility. They can be heroic as well as funny. No doubt to keep the spotlight on Scrooge, Donald Duck is written out of most of the stories, with a new character (Launchpad McQuack) taking his place.

Carl Barks retired in the 1970s, so he's obviously not the one doing the animation for these new cartoons. But the art is very good, and his spirit is there, along with frequent story and writing credits. Best of all, many concepts and characters first introduced in print by Barks at last get their long overdue animation showcase, including inventor–genius Gyro Gearloose, evil sorceress Magica De Spell, the thieving Beagle Boys, and that font of all human knowledge, Huey, Dewey, and Louie's *Junior Woodchuck Guidebook.*

In a bit of ironic casting, the voice of Scrooge McDuck is done by Alan Young, who (as Wilbur Post on *Mr. Ed*) used to spend his TV time listening to a talking horse. ■

**DUET (**½) 30 min (55ep Color; 1987–1989 Fox) Situation Comedy** *with Matthew Laurance as Ben Coleman, Mary Page Keller as Laura Kelly, Alison LaPlaca as Linda Phillips, Chris Lemmon as Richard Phillips, Jodi Thelen as Jane Kelly, and Arleen Sorkina as Geneva*

A comfortable romantic comedy with two couples trying to make their respective relationships work. Ben and Laura start out the series as the fresh-faced courting pair. He's an aspiring writer, she runs a catering business, and they both soon find themselves sizing each other up. They date, fight, break up, reunite (at an Alcholics Anonymous meeting, no less), and then move in together. Even with their occasional rough spots, you know they'll make it because they're so sweet. A perfect couple.

Richard and Linda, on the other hand, have plenty of rough spots to work out. Linda starts out in the Hollywood fast track pulling deals and bossing everyone she can (especially Richard), graduates to motherhood, and eventually joins Laura in her business (after getting canned from the studio). She's one of those characters you can't imagine ever really having as a friend, but who adds that extra zing to a sitcom setup.

When Duet ended its run, Linda became the focus of a Fall 1989 spinoff series, *Open House*, set in a real estate office.

**THE DUKE (*) 60 min (3ep & 2 hr pilot Color; 1979 NBC) Detective Drama** *with Robert Conrad as Oscar "Duke" Ramsey, Larry Manetti as Joe Cadillac, Red West as Sgt. Mick O'Brien, and Patricia Conwell as Dedra Smith*

Popular TV tough guy Robert Conrad, a one-time professional boxer in his youth, plays a retired pugilist who turns to private detective work when his partner in a restaurant venture is murdered. *The Duke* is produced by Stephen J. Cannell, who had better luck with Conrad in *Black Sheep Squadron.*

**THE DUKES OF HAZZARD (**) 60 min (147ep Color; 1979–1985 CBS) Comedy Adventure** *with Tom Wopat as Luke Duke, John Schneider as Bo Duke, Catherine Bach as Daisy Duke, Denver Pyle as Uncle Jesse Duke, James Best as Sheriff Roscoe P. Coltrane, Sonny Shroyer as Deputy Enos Strate, Rick Hurst as Deputy Cletus, and Sorrell Booke as Jefferson Davis "Boss" Hogg*

This series gets extraordinary mileage out of the good-lookin' Duke cousins (Luke, Bo, and Daisy), their supercharged flashy red Dodge Charger (the General Lee), the stupidity of the local law enforcement officers (Sheriff Roscoe and Deputy Enos), and the unmitigated greed of the local political heavyweight (the white-suited "Boss" Hogg). The episodes are all virtually interchangeable, though well done in their particular genre, with everyone playing their cartoon caricature roles faithfully and with good humor. It all comes off like stories around the campfire, with the best banjo picker and singer in town sharing the latest tall tales about a local legend. In this case, country and western outlaw–singer Waylon Jennings sets the tone from the very first episode, playing the role of program narrator, as well as author (and performer) of the hit title song—dedicated to those good old boys in Hazzard County. They lead a simple but entertaining life. Cars crash, tumble, and spin. Boss Hogg fumes. Daisy looks great. Enos gawks. And moonshine justice prevails again.

Despite the formula setup, this series does provide several opportunities to test your TV-watching alertness: Be on the lookout for Deputy Cletus during the time Enos is on his own series (*Enos*), and see if you notice when Luke and Bo Duke are briefly replaced by long-lost cousins Coy (Byron Cherry) and Vance (Christopher Mayer) Duke (a change that took place when Tom Wopat and John Schneider were involved in a contract dispute).

Appropriately, there is also a Saturday morning cartoon adventure spin-off (sixteen episodes first aired in 1983) following the Dukes and Boss Hogg on an around-the-world auto race. All the voices are done by members of the original cast (including cousins Coy and Vance along with Bo and Luke), though the narrator's role is taken over by Uncle Jesse (Denver Pyle).

**THE DUMPLINGS (**) 30 min (13ep Color; 1976 NBC) Situation Comedy** *with James Coco as Joe Dumpling, Geraldine Brooks as Angela Dumpling, George S. Irving as Charles Sweetzer, and George Furth as Frederic Steele*

Famed 1970s TV sitcom creator Norman Lear deserves some credit for daring to flat out do a show about fat people. The Dumplings (cute name, huh?) are not chubby, not a little portly, not trying to go on some new fad diet. No, the Dumplings are FAT, and proud of it. Good for them.

Appropriately, the fat Dumplings run a luncheonette in a big Manhattan office building, where they can deal with their first love—food—every day, and make a living out of it to boot. The best thing about *The Dumplings* is that the Dumplings are not made fun of because they are fat. Instead, *The Dumplings* is a sitcom that happens to be about fat people, with most of the humor coming from the antics of the assorted patrons who frequent the luncheonette. James Coco got mileage out of his girth for years, and he plays the role with relish, as it were. The scripts are a bit weak, but this is worth a watch or two.

*The Dumplings* is based on a comic strip of the same name by Fred Lucky.

**DUNDEE AND THE CULHANE** (*) **60 min (13ep Color; 1967 CBS) Western** *with John Mills as Dundee and Sean Garrison as The Culhane*

The lead character here, simply called Dundee (no first name), is a British barrister inexplicably roaming the open vistas of the American Old West in the always popular 1870s. Dundee abhors violence, is very sophisticated, and tries his best to bring a touch of civilization to the backward outposts of one of Britain's former colonies. Dundee's aide, The Culhane (no, there never is an explanation of what this name means or where it came from) is a young hunk/apprentice lawyer who just happens to be a crack gun shot, a trait that comes in handy out there on the old prairie. This odd couple turn up here and there, helping some of those in need on the frontier.

This offbeat show is produced by Sam H. Rolfe (*The Man from U.N.C.L.E.*) and David Victor (*Marcus Welby, M. D.*).

**DUPONT SHOW OF THE MONTH/WEEK** (***½) **90 & 60 min (132ep: forty-two 90 min & ninety 60 min; 1957–1964 CBS & NBC) Anthology**

Everything from serious drama to musicals to home movies of Hollywood stars is likely to show up in this collection of some of the best of American television from the late 1950s and early 1960s. Stars such as George C. Scott, Harpo Marx, Mike Nichols, Elaine May, Richard Burton, Lee J. Cobb, and Sir John Gielgud pepper the lineup. ■

**DUSTY'S TRAIL (zero) 30 min (26ep Color; 1973–1974 Syndication) Situation Comedy** *with Bob Denver as Dusty, Forrest Tucker as Mr. Callahan, Ivor Francis as Carter Brookhaven, Lynn Wood as Daphne Brookhaven, Bill Cort as Andy, Jeannine Riley as Lulu McQueen, and Lori Saunders as Betsy*

You would think that Sherwood Schwartz would have been satisfied with inflicting *Gilligan's Island* on us. Well, *Gilligan* rides again in *Dusty's Trail*, but with a slightly altered format.

Instead of a pleasure cruise in the South Pacific, we now have a wagon train heading for California in the 1880s. Instead of "The Skipper," we now have wagon master Mr. Callahan (Forrest Tucker from *F Troop*). Bob Denver plays Dusty, the inept trail scout who is a clone of his earlier Gilligan character. Instead of the stuffy Howells, we have the stuffy Brookhavens. Instead of slinky Ginger, we have sultry Lulu (Jeannine Riley from *Petticoat Junction*). The correlation goes on and on. The wagon train, of course, gets hopelessly lost and Gilligan er . . . Dusty and Mr. Callahan impotently try to lead the group to California.

Avoid this show at all costs. If you insist on torturing yourself, watch one of the several interminable sequels of *Gilligan's Island*.

**DYNASTY** (**½) **60 min (217ep Color; 1981–1989 ABC) Drama** *with John Forsythe as Blake Carrington, Linda Evans as Krystle Jennings Carrington, Joan Collins as Alexis Carrington Colby, Pamela Sue Martin and Emma Samms as Fallon Carrington Colby, John James as Jeff Colby, Al Corley and Jack Coleman as Steven Carrington, Gordon Thomson as Adam Carrington (a.k.a. Michael Torrance), Heather Locklear as Sammy Jo Dean, Lloyd Bochner as Cecil Colby, Diahann Carroll as Dominque Deveraux, Billy Dee Williams as Brady Lloyd, Rock Hudson as Daniel Reece, and Catherine Oxenberg as Amanda*

Legend has it that money is the root of all evil. That may help to explain why so many people keep doing so many nasty things in this show, since money flows through *Dynasty* like blood flows through *M*A*S*H*. One of the two consummate prime-time soap operas of the 1980s (along with the older *Dallas*), *Dynasty* flaunts its characters' wealth with a vividness and a conviction unrivaled in TV lore. The homes, the jewels, the clothes, the cars, the *skin* of all these characters is so flawless, so luxurious that mere mortal viewers must stand back and watch, agape, at the rarefied lives led by these gods and goddesses (who have, of course, feet of clay).

To properly document all the doings of the Carrington/Colby pantheon of figures would require a novella, at least, but the core setup is somewhat straightforward. Blake Carrington is a Denver-based zillionaire, whose financial empire is tied to oil. Blake was married to Alexis and had three children, Adam, Steve, and Fallon. Blake later split from Alexis and, as the series starts, he marries Krystle, his youngish ex-secretary. After a while, Alexis returns to the scene and becomes the chief villain of the piece. First she tries to get rid of Krystle so she can reclaim Blake; then she tries to destroy the entire Carrington empire. Son Steven first is a homosexual, then isn't, then is blown up, then has plastic surgery (to explain a new actor playing the role). Daughter Fallon sleeps around, then marries Jeff, son of Alexis' new husband (who, naturally, is Blake's rival). Long-lost son Adam turns up with another name. Other secondary characters come and go, many played by top-name actors and actresses (such as Rock Hudson, in his last major TV role, as Daniel Reece, who courts Krystle).

*Dynasty* triumphs with style over content, even when compared to the other style-conscious prime-time soap operas. At first, this strategy pays off. The regal style in *Dynasty* is breathtaking, and the dramatic wave after wave of crises and climaxes cover up a lot of wooden performances and slapdash scripting. Alexis is a character for the ages. Her vile and venomous nature knows no bounds and is devilishly alluring. She is evil matched against Krystle's simple, pure goodness. Their royal cat fights are the best female combat on TV since the days of Roller Derby.

What finally drags *Dynasty* down is its unending reliance on opulence and convoluted plotting. After milking dry its basic Alexis versus Krystle and Alexis versus Blake themes, there is not enough left to hold the gaudy show together. When *Dynasty* is at its peak (the first three or four seasons), however, it is truly a jewel to behold. Like the Taj Mahal, *Dynasty* is impressive to look at, but it is not a workable home on a day-to-day basis.

**E/R (EMERGENCY ROOM) (**½) 30 min (22ep Color; 1984–1985 CBS) Situation Comedy** *with Elliott Gould as Dr. Howard Sheinfeld, Marcia Strassman and Mary McDonnell as Dr. Eve Sheridan, Lynne Moody as Nurse Julie Williams, Luis Avalos as Dr. Esquivel, William Schilling as Richard the orderly, Conchata Ferrell as Nurse Joan Thor, Shuko Akune as Maria Amardo, and Bruce A. Young as Officer Fred Burdock*

Disguised as a spin-off from *The Jeffersons* (George Jefferson appears in the first story visiting his niece Julie in her new job), *E/R* is actually an adaptation of a long-running Chicago theatrical production set in a hospital Emergency Room. The concept was developed by the Organic Theater Company, whose ensemble members researched the topic by visiting real-life emergency rooms for a sense of the truth is stranger than fiction routine there. The play *E/R* was a huge success and proved particularly popular with medical people, who nodded knowingly at such incidents as Dr. Sheinfeld's removal of a bloody light bulb, intact, from the rectum of a patient.

Though the series version attempts to carry on some of that cutting room absurdity (as an urban version of *M*A*S*H*), the execution is toned down for network television sensibilities. The result is a Band-Aid *Barney Miller,* attempting to mix story lines that showcase both the crazy world of urban medicine and the personal lives of the ensemble, led by Elliott Gould as the irreverent Dr. Sheinfeld. Gould turns in some of his best television work ever and it almost works. The problem is that, although Sheinfeld is always living on the edge of bankruptcy (with two ex-wives and several Chicago sports teams to support), he still breezes through situations much too easily. The logical foil to keep him in check, Dr. Eve Sheridan, starts out as his equal in the pilot, but for the rest of the series she is softened and recast, with Mary McDonnell replacing Marcia Strassman (Gabe Kotter's no-nonsense wife on *Welcome Back Kotter*). It's a good potential romance, but not strong enough on the hard-nosed administrative side.

Still, even with its limitations, it is frankly refreshing to have a non-Los Angeles/New York setting, conceived and nurtured by writers and performers who have some idea of the local (Chicago) flavor. Two members of the original *E/R* theatrical cast even continue their stage roles for the series, Bruce Young and Shuko Akune. Other faces familiar to Chicago theater audiences also turn up in guest shots, including original *E/R* theatrical company members Carolyn Purdy-Gordon (as Mrs. Dobbs), Richard Fire (as Dr. Klimaszewski), and Gary Houston (as Dr. Krell), along with Dennis Franz (better known as Norman Buntz on *Hill Street Blues*).

**EAST OF EDEN (***) (8hr miniseries Color; 1981 ABC) Drama** *with Timothy Bottoms as Adam Trask, Bruce Boxleitner as Charles Trask, Jane Seymour as Cathy Ames, Sam Bottoms as Cal Trask, Hart Bochner as Aron Trask, Soon-Teck Oh as Lee, Karen Allen as Abra, and Warren Oates as Cyrus Trask*

Good adaptation of the 1952 John Steinbeck novel, following internal family conflicts across three generations. It all begins in Connecticut shortly after the Civil War, with two teenage brothers, Adam (sensitive, dependable) and Charles (unruly, volatile), vying for the affections of their dad, Union veteran Cyrus Trask. Complicating all their lives is the arrival of the beguiling young Cathy Ames, who teases and toys with the brothers' affections. Jane Seymour does a marvelously effective portrayal of Cathy, sometimes as an innocent looking for help, more often maliciously malevolent, even venomous. Eventually she marries one of them and the trials continue in California with the next generation of brothers, Cal and Aron.

*Dynasty* co-creator Richard Shapiro did the script adaptation for this miniseries. The 1955 theatrical film version featured James Dean as Cal. ■

**EAST SIDE, WEST SIDE (**½) 60 min (24ep B&W; 1963–1964 CBS) Drama** *with George C. Scott as Neil Brock and Cicely Tyson as Jane Foster*

This show certainly can't be faulted for not having its

heart in the right place. George C. Scott, in one of his rare TV series roles, plays Neil Brock, a young social worker in New York, trying to deal with the oppressive problems of poverty and injustice. Cicely Tyson plays Brock's secretary. Each week the program focuses on some new facet of the sordid side of life. One week it is poverty, then racism, then welfare, followed by drug addiction, crime, aging, etc. Clearly, this is not *The Love Boat.*

While *East Side, West Side* is an admirable effort to dramatize serious issues, it is a bit heavy-handed, especially when viewing the show in retrospect. When the program first aired, many of the problems dealt with were hardly mentioned on TV, and certainly never in prime time. Thus, *East Side, West Side* is fascinating for its historical role, being such a groundbreaker in dealing with current social issues and featuring blacks in major dramatic roles. Nowadays, however, all of these issues, and more, are featured fairly regularly on everything from news documentaries to celebrity talk shows. The earnest intensity, the almost religious fervor of *East Side, West Side,* seems too strident now. This is not to say that these problems are not serious or real today, but we know about them and it is not shocking to see them portrayed.

As pure theater, the show is well worth watching. Executive producer David Susskind, one of the giants of TV drama's golden age, deftly mixes political education and intriguing stories. With Scott and Tyson as the leads, it is no surprise that the acting is good. The guest stars, such as James Earl Jones, are no slouches either.

*East Side, West Side* is great drama, but it is tough to imagine keeping up with it every week. The bleakness, the air of despondency is intended, but a bit hard to take after a while. As one social worker in a big city, there is only so much Neil Brock can do. Halfway through the series, things brighten up a bit as Brock gets a new job, working for a New York congressman (Linden Chiles) who can, presumably, do something to improve the situation of the downtrodden. It takes more than sixty minutes of drama to change any of the issues dealt with in *East Side, West Side,* and that is why the series is so unique and why it was too far ahead of its time and had such a short run.

**EASTENDERS (**) 30 min (195ep Color; 1985– UK BBC) Drama**

It seems only fair that Britain send back its own hit soaps in return for the likes of our *Dallas* or *Dynasty,* and this show is one of their biggest. Only the decades-old *Coronation Street* is more popular, though that has never managed to achieve even a toe-hold Stateside. In contrast, *EastEnders,* the relative newcomer (begun on the BBC in 1985), has built a cult following here over a surprisingly short time (since about 1987).

As with any soap, the characters and plot twists are long and complicated, though the distinctive difference with this one is that most of the action takes place in the Cockney world of London's East End (at Albert Square in the borough of Walford, though don't bother checking a map because the address is pure fiction). As in most British neighborhoods, the main gathering point is the local pub—in this case, the Queen Vic, run by Angie and Den. There the Cockney accents fly by fast and unadulterated, with these salt-of-the-earth types making the best of tough times and their prerequisite affairs, personal double dealings, births, deaths, and, of course, clashes of culture. (Unlike the States, money alone doesn't buy respectability—it's all a matter of breeding, background, and education.)

A must for soap opera fans, just to catch the contrasts with our efforts. It's also worth a look by more casual viewers, if only for a slice of British pop culture that definitely won't turn up on *Masterpiece Theatre.*

**EASY STREET (**½) 30 min (22ep Color; 1986–1987 NBC) Situation Comedy** *with Loni Anderson as L. K. McGuire, Jack Elam as Alvin "Bully" Stevenson, Lee Weaver as Ricardo Williams, Dana Ivey as Eleanor Standard, and James Cromwell as Quentin Standard*

One of the running gags on *WKRP in Cincinnati* was that Loni Anderson's character of receptionist Jennifer Marlowe had more money than everyone else at the station, combined. For *Easy Street, WKRP* creator Hugh Wilson once again puts wealth in some unlikely hands, with Anderson as L. K. McGuire, a former Las Vegas showgirl who married the owner of the casino. The sitcom begins shortly after his death, with L. K. the heiress to a multimillion dollar fortune. The only people contesting the will: her husband's sister, Eleanor, and Eleanor's husband, James—who both also happen to live on the estate.

Ironically, L. K. would much rather have had her husband, Ned, back in place of the fortune. So she goes looking for her own family and drops in on an uncle she hasn't seen in some twenty years, Bully Stevenson. Lucky for him. When she visits his cheap retirement home, Bully is on the verge of trying to commit suicide by drowning himself in the bathtub, fully dressed. Instead, still dripping wet, he and his perfectly dry apartment mate, Ricardo, end up accepting L. K.'s invitation to spend a weekend at her estate, which quickly turns into a request that they stay for good—first, because L. K. is genuinely appalled at their dreary apartment setting and can't imagine them returning there; and second, because she really enjoys the way they get under Eleanor and Quentin's skins. Much to her in-laws' horror, Bully and Ricardo agree to stay.

Much like the theatrical hit film *Down and Out in Beverly Hills,* the series chugs along on basic snobs-versus-slobs humor, carried almost exclusively by the appeal of the lead performers. Anderson is quite comfortable as the nouveau riche showgirl who once wore a model of the Chrysler Building on her head (and not much below that), while Elam and Weaver play the self-described "old coots" with glee. The stories are predictably dumb (in the first episode, Bully gets everyone to stick spoons to their noses) but funny, with your tolerance for tales of the idle rich pretty much determining your tolerance for the premise. In its original run, it stuck around 3.66 times as long as the television version of *Down and Out in Beverly Hills.*

**THE ED SULLIVAN SHOW (***) 60 min (250ep B&W & Color; 1948–1971 CBS) Variety** *with Ed Sullivan as host*

The world of *The Ed Sullivan Show* has disappeared. The show is from a time when filling an hour with Broadway dancers, foreign ballerinas, borscht-belt comedians, nervous pop stars, dancing bears, and a talking mouse guaranteed a huge audience. It is from a time when a host with stooped shoulders, homely features, awkward mannerisms, and a nasal voice seemed warm and familiar. It is from a time when the entire family, and most of the country, watched the same show at the same time on a Sunday night.

For twenty-three years, Ed Sullivan used his keen sense of talent to present the cream of the entertainment world to the folks at home, which was miracle enough for the time. Television was new, and it did not take much to capture an audience. The very notion that the country's best entertainers (not to mention stars of other lands) would perform for you, in your house, every week, at no charge, was revolutionary. There was no need for frills.

You could say that *The Ed Sullivan Show* is not really television so much as it is vaudeville, with a TV camera added. The truth is that early television was just vaudeville, with a camera added, and Ed Sullivan was early television. Today *The Ed Sullivan Show* serves mostly as an invaluable treasure trove of artistic history. The highlights of the hours and hours of Sullivan kinescopes and videotapes capture performances of a literal "Who's Who" of mid-century entertainment.

What is particularly fascinating about watching the old *Sullivan* tapes now is to see early performances of artists who later became superstars. Jerry Lewis and Dean Martin made their TV debut on Sullivan's show (on the very first episode, which is not currently available in syndication). Elvis Presley made three memorable appearances just as he was changing from rock'n'roll star to social phenomenom. The Beatles made their heralded American debut on the *Sullivan* show, and instantly became teen music icons.

In the pre–Johnny Carson *Tonight* era, the *Sullivan* show was the main proving ground for stand-up comics. Alan King, Henny Youngman, Jack E. Leonard, Jackie Mason, and Myron Cohen represent classical vaudeville comedy. Allan Sherman, Shelly Berman, Bob Newhart, and Bill Cosby represent stand-up comedy with the topical relevance of the 1960s. George Carlin and Richard Pryor represent the harbingers of the post-*Sullivan* counterculture comedians that thrived in the 1970s. They all put in their time on Sullivan's Sunday night show.

Because *The Ed Sullivan Show* only really works as history now, much of its content seems archaic and clunky. For every appearance of world-class talent such as Russia's Moiseyev Dancers, there seem to be three appearances of run-of-the-mill jugglers or acts that spin plates in the air at one time. Sullivan's habit of pointing out celebrities in the audience may have been thrilling in TV's early days, but seems pointless and self-serving now. His kissy-kissy relationship with the cute Italian-accented mouse puppet Topo Gigio now appears strained, perhaps an effort in the show's later years to soften up the image of a man dubbed "old stone face."

Sullivan himself must be seen to be believed. He truly has no stage presence. He constantly stumbles over words and frequently looks as if he doesn't really care about some of the acts he introduces. These attributes are prime examples of everything a TV variety host is not supposed to be, and that is why watching Sullivan is worth the effort. He was good because he was a good packager of entertainment. He could spot talent, knew how to balance an hour program, and didn't waste time calling attention to himself. We could use more hosts like him now.

There were far more than 250 episodes of *The Ed Sullivan Show,* but only 250 are currently syndicated, most all of which come from the 1955–1971 period. From 1948 to 1955, the show was called *Toast of the Town.* In 1980, a series of 13 half-hour compilations of material from the *Sullivan* years was syndicated as *The Best of Sullivan,* with comedian John Byner as host. ■

**THE ED WYNN SHOW (*½) 30 min (15ep B&W; 1958–1959 NBC) Situation Comedy** *with Ed Wynn as John Beamer, Jacklyn O'Donnell as Laurie Beamer, Sherry Alberoni as Madge Beamer, and Herb Vigran as Ernest Henshaw*

Ed Wynn made a name for himself as a giggling vaudeville clown in the early decades of this century. He was one of the first of the big-name comedians to try TV in the late 1940s, and he created some wonderful moments of live comedy in his 1949 variety series called *The Ed Wynn Show* and as one of the regular hosts of *Four Star Revue* (a.k.a. *All Star Revue*) in the early 1950s. Unfortunately, this series (also called *The Ed Wynn Show*) is best left ignored, even though it is his one stab at a filmed weekly sitcom. Wynn plays an old widower raising his two orphaned granddaughters, eighteen-year-old Laurie and nine-year-old Midge. Wynn tries hard, but he cannot fit into the limitations of the weekly sitcom format.

**THE EDDIE CAPRA MYSTERIES (**) 60 min (13ep Color; 1978–1979 NBC) Law Drama** *with Vincent Baggetta as Eddie Capra, Wendy Phillips as Lacey*

*Brown, Ken Swofford as J. J. Devlin, and Michael Horton as Harvey Winchell*

On the surface, Capra looks and acts like a private eye. He is dark, handsome, a man of the earth, who spends his time cracking tough murder cases that seem to befuddle everybody else. The twist? Capra is *not* a detective—he's a lawyer. He's not just any lawyer—he's an unorthodox lawyer who angers the stuffed shirts running the prestigious firm he works at. Yet Capra's success in handling murders allows him the freedom to act as he pleases. The action here is exciting, but the series has a bit too much of the 1970s, "anti-establishment" trendiness for its own good.

**THE EDGAR WALLACE MYSTERY THEATER (**) 60 min (39ep B&W; 1960–1963 UK BBC) Mystery Anthology** *with Edgar Wallace as host*

Popular British writer Edgar Wallace acts as an English Rod Serling, introducing acceptable hour-long stories of suspense.

**EDGE OF DARKNESS (**½) 60 min (6ep Color; 1985 UK BBC) Espionage Adventure** *with Joe Don Baker as Darius Jedburgh, Bob Peck as Ronald Craven, Jack Watson as James Godbolt, Joanne Whalley as Emma Craven, John Woodvine as Ross, Tim McInnerny as Terry Shields, and Charles Kay as Pendleton*

A British north country murder mystery that turns into an international thriller with ominous topical overtones. It starts with a Yorkshire police officer, Ronald Craven, refusing to accept the official department explanation of the shotgun death of his own daughter. They say she was the victim of a criminal seeking revenge for Craven's own arresting activities, but his independent digging uncovers a far more complicated web, involving British intelligence, a flamboyant CIA agent (played by American Joe Don Baker from *Eischied*), nuclear waste, illegal stockpiles, and a plot to break into a nuclear facility. A message miniseries that still manages to work as murderous intrigue under the guidance of two behind-the-scenes veterans from the *Reilly—Ace of Spies* adventures (director Martin Campbell and writer Troy Kennedy Martin). Eric Clapton does an appropriately bluesy score.

**THE EDISON TWINS (**½) 30 min (78ep Color; 1984–1987 Disney) Adventure** *with Andrew Sabiston as Tom Edison, Marnie McPhail as Ann Edison, and Sunny Thraser as Paul Edison*

With an affectionate eye towards such classic teen adventures as the Hardy Boys (preferably the old *Mickey Mouse Club* version), this Disney-produced series (done with Canada's CBC network) offers a brother-and-sister pair of teenage sleuths, Tom and Ann Edison, along with their younger brother, Paul. Naturally, they bring teen expertise at basic science and history to their cases, along with a creditable affection for pop music, sweet desserts, and sharp-looking transportation. Overall, this is a good contemporary package with just the right sense of nostalgic familiarity. ■

**EDWARD AND MRS. SIMPSON (***) 60 min (7ep Color; 1978 UK Thames) Drama** *with Edward Fox as Prince Edward, Cynthia Harris as Wallis Warfield Simpson, Peggy Ashcroft as Queen Mary, David Waller as Stanley Baldwin, Andrew Ray as the Duke of York, and Marius Goring as King George V*

A stylish period piece of twentieth-century royal love, following the real-life, sometimes scandalous, exploits of young Edward, Prince of Wales. It all takes a turn for the romantic when he falls for a decidedly nonroyal, twice-divorced American, Wallis Simpson. As the story unfolds, Edward finds himself forced to choose between his expected path to the throne and the woman he loves. It reaches a touching climax with his pointed, personal message over the airwaves to the British public in 1936.

With excellent performances throughout, *Edward and Mrs. Simpson* is an effective reminder that concerns about royal behavior and the intricacies behind succession to the crown did not end in Victorian times. One fascinating contrast for contemporary royalty watchers, though, takes place about halfway through the series. When faced with the potentially juicy tale of a possible shipboard liaison between Edward and Wallis, Britain's "Fleet Street" shows incredible restraint with its coverage. While the rest of the world touts banner headlines, the British press is discreet. When was the last time you heard that description used for the British tabloids? ■

**EDWARD ARNOLD THEATER (*½) 30 min (26ep B&W; 1954 Syndicated) Drama Anthology** *with Edward Arnold as host*

Bland drama anthology hosted by portly character actor Edward Arnold, whose film credits stretched back to 1915, including lead roles in *Diamond Jim*, *Meet Nero Wolfe,* and *You Can't Take It with You.* He died just two years after the original run of this series.

**EDWARD THE SEVENTH/EDWARD THE KING (**½) 60 min (13ep Color; 1975 UK ATV) Drama** *with Timothy West as Edward (as an adult), Charles Sturridge as Edward (as a teen), Annette Crosbie as Queen Victoria, Robert Hardy as Prince Albert, Deborah Grant and Helen Ryan as Alexandra of Denmark, and John Gielgud as Benjamin Disraeli*

Scrupulously detailed account of the life and times of Britain's turn-of-the-century monarch. He had a particularly long wait for the crown because his mother, Queen Victoria, reigned for sixty-eight years! That left him decades to fill with all sorts of royal distractions, though eventually he did marry Alexandra of Denmark. By the time it was his turn as king, however, he was almost old enough for retirement from a normal job. Packaged for U.S. syndication as *Edward the King,* with wraparound background narration by Robert MacNeil.

**THE EDWARDIANS (**½) 60 min (8ep Color; 1972 UK BBC) Drama Anthology**

A series of four historical dramas set in the turn-of-the-century Edwardian age, looking at such figures as fiery British Cabinet minister Lloyd George, automobile innovators Charles Rolls and Frederick Royce, and Sherlock Holmes creator Arthur Conan Doyle. Solid biographical presentations that first aired in the United States during the mid-1970s on *Masterpiece Theatre.*

**EIGHT IS ENOUGH (***) 60 min (112ep & 2 hr sequel Color; 1977–1981 ABC) Comedy Drama** *with Dick Van Patten as Tom Bradford, Diana Hyland as Joan Bradford, Betty Buckley as Sandra Sue Abbott ("Abby") Bradford, Mark Hamill and Grant Goodeve as David Bradford, Lani O'Grady as Mary Bradford, Laurie Walters as Joannie Bradford, Susan Richardson as Susan Bradford, Kimberly Beck and Dianne Kay as Nancy Bradford, Connie Needham (Newton) as Elizabeth Bradford, Willie Aames as Tommy Bradford, and Adam Rich as Nicholas Bradford*

A family comedy drama of the late 1970s led by Dick Van Patten, one of the few television children to later preside over his own video brood. His own eight-year stint as a sibling began in 1949 when (at twenty) he landed the role of sixteen-year-old brother Nels Hansen on the long-running family comedy series, *Mama.* Two decades after *Mama* ended, Van Patten was a proud TV papa in a big way, with eight kids.

Though *Eight Is Enough* has a laugh track, its sixty-minute length and overall approach push it away from group sitcoms like *The Brady Bunch* and closer to family dramas such as *The Waltons* (no coincidence, since it was from the same producers). It is structured to deal with family situations from the very young (eight-year-old Nicholas) through the teen years and into young adulthood (twenty-three-year-old David), with a middle-aged dad (Van Patten) trying to make sense of it all. Perhaps the most striking thing about *Eight Is Enough* is that it honestly tries to reconcile the generations, using all the right buzz words of its era about communication, freedom, and honesty to handle everything from premarital cohabitation to losing a school football game. Though occasionally a few of the plot situations are forced to make an ideologically correct point (usually in the area of sex or sexism), it is still refreshing to see the old-fashioned family approach of *Ozzie and Harriet, My Three Sons,* and *Mama* applied to 1970s and 1980s sensibilities.

The series was based on the autobiography of Tom Braden, a Washington columnist, but almost immediately departed from the original's scenario when Diana Hyland (who played Joan Bradford, mom of the clan) passed away after appearing in only five shows. Rather than recast, they let Tom become a widower, though he soon married again (he and Abby, a tutor from the kids' high school, fell in love). In another cast change, Mark Hamill played David in the first two episodes, which originally aired just as the first *Star Wars* films premiered. Soon thereafter Grant Goodeve took over the character.

The series played out probably just long enough, with most of the kids getting the chance to face a mix of adolescent and young adult situations (including marriage) without getting too repetitious. Then again, when the series staged "Eight Is Enough: A Family Reunion" in 1987, it was to celebrate Tom's fiftieth birthday . . . something he had already done on the regular series. Luckily, Mary Frann (taking the role of Abby for Betty Buckley) didn't let on.

**87TH PRECINCT (**½) 30 min (30ep B&W; 1961–1962 NBC) Police Drama** *with Robert Lansing as Det. Steve Carella, Norman Fell as Det. Meyer Meyer, Ron Harper as Det. Bert Kling, Gregory Walcott as Det. Roger Havilland, and Gena Rowlands as Teddy Carella*

Not quite *Hill Street Blues,* but a pretty good cop showcase for its time—grim, gritty, and violent—mixing in both the home and station house concerns of its characters, especially Robert Lansing's Steve Carella. In an unusual twist, Carella's wife (played by Gena Rowlands) is a deaf mute. Based on a long-running series of mystery books by Evan Hunter (writing under the pseudonym of Ed McBain).

**EISCHIED (***) 60 min (13ep & 3 hr pilot Color; 1979–1980 NBC) Police Drama** *with Joe Don Baker as Chief Earl Eischied, Alan Fudge as Deputy Commissioner Jim Kimbrough, Alan Oppenheimer as Capt. John Finnerty, Eddie Egan as Ed Parks, and Suzanne Lederer as Carol Wright*

With hefty portions of the gritty style of police series popularized by *Hill Street Blues, Eischied* usually succeeds in presenting tight, taut, police drama. The program's problem is that it is full of the anti-establishment cop conventions that clogged the airways in the 1970s.

Earl Eischied (TV columns were forever misspelling the name) is a mean, tough southerner who is chief of the New York City Police Detective bureau. Eischied's sole goal in life, like that of *Dragnet*'s equally grim Joe Friday, is to rid the city of the hordes of criminal vermin infesting its streets. Unlike Friday, however, Eischied will use whatever methods are needed, fair or foul. Eischied's tenacity is always getting him in hot water with the wishy-washy, politically ambitious Deputy Commissioner Jim Kimbrough. This is to be expected, since 1970s TV cops are obligated to spend half their time battling officious bureaucratic bosses who want only to go by the book. Eischied has no family and no home life, other than his pet cat. Who else would put up with his growling, snarly personality?

Joe Don Baker, the original Sheriff Buford Pusser in the original film *Walking Tall*, is riveting as the Dixie cop in Yankeeland. The 1978 pilot for *Eischied* is titled *To Kill a Cop. Eischied* is produced by David Gerber, the man who almost single-handedly began the modern era of realistic police shows with *Police Story*.

**EISENHOWER & LUTZ (*) 30 min (13ep Color; 1988 CBS) Situation Comedy** *with Scott Bakula as Barnett "Bud" Lutz, Jr., DeLane Matthews as Megan O'Malley, Patricia Richardson as Kay Dunne, Rose Portillo as Millie Zamora, Leo Geter as Dwayne Spitler, and Henderson Forsythe as Barnett "Big Bud" Lutz, Sr.*

Bud Lutz, a cheesy lawyer who squeaked his way through law school, sets up practice at a former hot-tub showroom area in a suburban minimall in Palm Springs, California. It's near an intersection known to have a high number of auto accidents, so there's even the chance for a lot of walk-up (crawl-over?) business. Bud's dad, a professional sign painter, points out the value of a catchy name and gives his son's firm the title Eisenhower & Lutz (even though there is no Mr. Eisenhower anywhere near). The junior Lutz agrees and, in short order, is attempting to lure clients in, with his girlfriend Megan, his secretary Millie, and his intern Dwayne all taking their turns out front pretending Bud Lutz is really a busy, well-qualified guy.

Frankly he doesn't deserve their loyalty. Even as the paint dries on his dad's sign, Bud is trying to figure out the best ways to exploit a former girlfriend's affections for him—chiefly because Kay is a partner in a very successful local firm. And if it means possibly pushing Megan to the sidelines, he's more than willing to consider that option. Fortunately, Lutz regularly gets his comeuppance, and Megan seems destined to hang on to her man (why she'd want to is another question entirely). This series had a short run in its original airing, though without a major revamping in the overall plotting, it's hard to imagine what direction it might have taken in a longer stint.

**EISENHOWER: THE WAR YEARS (***) (6hr miniseries Color; 1979 ABC) War Drama** *with Robert Duvall as Gen. Dwight D. Eisenhower, Lee Remick as Kay Summersby, Darren McGavin as Gen. George S. Patton, Dana Andrews as Gen. George C. Marshall, J. D. Cannon as Gen. Walter B. Smith, Laurence Luckinbill as Maj. Richard Arnold, Wensley Pithey as Winston Churchill, Bonnie Bartlett as Mamie Eisenhower, and Lowell Thomas as himself*

Robert Duvall shines as Dwight Eisenhower in this miniseries focusing on the general's wartime exploits. And that includes some discreet time with his personal driver, Kay Summersby (whose book, *Past Forgetting*, is the adaptation source for this production), well played by Lee Remick. Naturally there's also plenty of epic battle footage, strategy sessions among the generals, and an undeniably exciting wrap-up with the D-Day invasion and the Battle of the Bulge. Veteran CBS newsman Lowell Thomas provides the narration. Of course, you might walk away thinking Eisenhower was the only real genius at work here, but then again, it's his series. For other versions of the heroics, consult films and miniseries focusing on such figures as General Patton or Winston Churchill. (Were these men all at the same war?)

This show originally aired as a six-hour miniseries called *Ike*, but currently carries the title *Eisenhower: The War Years*. It plays in syndication at its original length or as cut-downs running either three or four hours.

**THE ELEVENTH HOUR (*) 60 min (62ep B&W; 1962–1964 NBC) Medical Drama** *with Wendell Corey as Dr. Theodore Bassett, Jack Ging as Dr. Paul Graham, and Ralph Bellamy as Dr. L. Richard Starke*

This heavy-handed, very serious medical show is populated with quality actors, but the leaden tone and the dreary atmosphere drag the series down into a morass. In the beginning, *The Eleventh Hour* focuses on Drs. Bassett and Graham, two psychiatrists who share an office as well as a passion for solving the perplexing psychiatric problems of people with mental disorders (those who seek help in the "eleventh hour," just before a mental collapse). Dr. Bassett works with the state police, so many psychopathic criminals come his way.

In the series' second season, Dr. Bassett is out and Dr. Starke is in. Dr. Starke has no ties to the police, so the show spends more time on run-of-the-mill psychos, those who have not chopped up their family or blown up their office . . . yet.

Veteran Hollywood greats Wendell Corey and Ralph Bellamy try hard, but it would be nice if the doctors could lighten up a bit and crack some jokes. *The Eleventh Hour* is produced by Norman Felton, a graduate of the successful *Dr. Kildare* series, who went on to produce the much lighter *Man from U.N.C.L.E.*

**ELFEGO BACA, THE NINE LIVES OF (**½) 60 min (10ep B&W; 1958–1960 ABC) Western** *with Robert Loggia as Elfego Baca, Robert F. Simon as Sheriff Morgan, Leonard Strong as Zangano, and Valerie Allen as Lucita*

Originally broadcast as part of *Walt Disney Presents*, this is an attempt to take the successful *Zorro* format and give it a bit more believability. Set in New Mexico in the 1880s, *Elfego Baca* follows the exploits of sheriff/lawyer Elfego Baca as he tries his best to clean up his town (without resorting to wearing a mask like Zorro). As with many series of the 1950s that deal with Mexicans, *Elfego Baca* uses actors of mainly Italian descent (such as Robert Loggia) to play the Mexican roles. ■

**ELIZABETH R** (***½) **90 min (6ep Color; 1971 UK BBC) Historical Drama** *with Glenda Jackson as Queen Elizabeth I, Ronald Hines as Secretary of State Cecil, Peter Jeffrey as King Philip, John Woodvine as Sir Francis Drake, Bernard Hepton as Archbishop Cranmer, Robin Ellis as the Earl of Essex, Stephen Murray as Walsingham, Ronald Hines as William Cecil, Robert Hardy as Robert Dudley, Rosalie Crutchley as Catherine Parr, John Ronane as Thomas Seymour, and Rachel Kempson as Kat Ashley*

That's how she signed her name on royal documents: *Elizabeth R*—short for Elizabeth Regina or Elizabeth the Queen. She was the last of the Tudor rulers, reigning through five decades (1558–1603) during one of the most dramatic periods of British history, the English Renaissance. It was the age of Shakespeare, Sir Francis Drake, and the Spanish Aramada. This era was also one of relative peace, due in no small part to Elizabeth's astute political senses. And that's what this series is all about: Elizabeth the Queen in control.

Glenda Jackson is outstanding in the title role, projecting a sense of imperial presence and confidence. She seems well suited to power, and the story line illustrates this point time and again as it follows her life from age fifteen to sixty-nine. Whether it's negotiating a treaty, protecting herself from assassination plots, or even teasing potential suitors with the prospect of marriage, Elizabeth carefully and successfully manages events, lives, and emotions. Especially her own.

**THE ELLEN BURSTYN SHOW** (**½) **30 min (12ep Color; 1986–1987 ABC) Situation Comedy** *with Ellen Burstyn as Ellen Brewer, Elaine Stritch as Sydney Brewer, Megan Mullally as Molly Brewer Ross, and Jesse Tendler as Nick Ross*

An intelligent sitcom that never gathered much attention during its original airing, *The Ellen Burstyn Show* features the actress who originated the role of Alice Hyatt, in the film *Alice Doesn't Live Here Anymore.* In this show, Burstyn plays a writer and college professor who lives with her feisty mother (played by Elaine Stritch, a great character actress from stage and screen), her twenty-five-year-old divorced daughter, and five-year-old grandson. There is too much witty bantering going on here, but the characters are good enough to merit catching a few episodes.

**ELLERY QUEEN, THE FURTHER ADVENTURES OF (A.K.A. MYSTERY IS MY BUSINESS)** (*½) **30 min (32ep B&W; 1954 Syndicated) Mystery** *with Hugh Marlowe as Ellery Queen, Florenz Ames as Inspector Richard Queen, and Charlotte Keane as Nikki Porter*

**ELLERY QUEEN** (***) **60 min (24ep & 2 hr pilot Color; 1975–1976 NBC) Mystery** *with Jim Hutton as Ellery Queen, David Wayne as Inspector Richard Queen, Tom Reese as Sgt. Velie, Ken Swofford as Frank Flannigan, and John Hillerman as Simon Brimmer*

A half dozen different performers have played Ellery Queen in four or five different television series (depending how you count revamping and recasting) showcasing the character. Only two series are currently in circulation. The 1954 version stars Hugh Marlowe (one of four who had the role on radio) and runs under the title *Mystery Is My Business.* It's a straightforward reading of the character setup: Mystery writer Ellery Queen helps his police inspector dad piece together solutions to mysteries. Despite the invitation to solve the mystery before Ellery does, the series is not much different from most other routine crime shows of the time.

The 1975 program takes a lighter, more nostalgic approach to the premise, setting the action as a 1940s period piece. Hutton is excellent as the soft-spoken Ellery, while Wayne is sufficiently crusty and wise as his dad. The real treat is the competition between Queen and criminologist Simon Brimmer, a radio detective played by the acerbic John Hillerman. Sometimes they thrash out their conflicting theories right in the radio studio, with Inspector Queen and newspaper columnist Frank Flannigan ready to act as soon as the guilty party is identified. That's a clear, impossible-to-miss moment because, in the final segment, Ellery turns to the camera and asks if the audience has figured the mystery out yet. He has and he's about to reveal his solution. And stay alert—some of these solutions get quite convoluted. The production team for this version of *Ellery Queen* included Peter S. Fischer, Richard Levinson, and William Link, ardent mystery lovers who did it again a decade later with *Murder, She Wrote.*

**ELLIS ISLAND** (**½) **(7hr miniseries Color; 1984 CBS) Drama** *with Faye Dunaway as Maud Charteris, Richard Burton as Phipps Ogden, Claire Bloom as Rebecca Weiler, Ann Jillian as Nellie Byfield, Ben Vereen as Roscoe Haines, and Melba Moore as Flora Mitchum*

There are no surprises in this miniseries set on the island in New York harbor that served as the entry port for thousands of immigrants to the United States. The time is 1907 and all major religious and ethnic groups among the era's wave of immigrants are represented. The series is based on the novel by Fred Mustard Stewart. ■

**EMERALD POINT N.A.S.** (**½) **60 min (21ep Color; 1983–1984 CBS) Drama** *with Dennis Weaver as Adm. Thomas Mallory, Maud Adams as Maggie Farrell, Jill St. John as Deanna Kincaid, Andrew Stevens as Lt. Glenn Matthews, Susan Dey as Celia Mallory Warren, Patrick O'Neal and Robert Vaughn as Harlan Adams, Stephanie Dunnam as Kay Mallory Matthews, Charles Frank as Lt. Cmdr. Jack Warren, and Doran Clark as Ensign Leslie Mallory*

Most of the prime-time soaps from the 1980s are all set in the world of private finance. *Emerald Point N.A.S.* deserves some credit for moving the setting to a U.S.

Navy air station (in California), where the focus is on the personal and professional intrigue among the top brass. The series revolves around Adm. Mallory, widowed commander of the base, and his three young and beautiful daughters: Celia, the antimilitary one married to a Navy lawyer; Kay, the flirt who marries an ex-Navy man convicted of manslaughter; and Leslie, a recent graduate from Annapolis who makes the old man proud.

As with most prime-time soaps, the villain is the most interesting character. First Patrick O'Neal and then Robert Vaughn are wonderfully venal as the corrupt town business magnate Harlan Adams. Look for Susan Dey as renegade daughter Celia, as Dey begins to move away from her bubblegum role as Laurie Partridge and toward the icy cool lawyer Grace Van Owen in *L. A. Law*. The producers of *Emerald Point N.A.S.*, Richard and Esther Shapiro, created the megahit *Dynasty.*

**EMERGENCY! (*½) 60 min (132ep & 2 hr pilot & four 2 hr sequels Color; 1972–1977 NBC) Crime Drama** *with Robert Fuller as Dr. Kelly Brackett, Julie London as Dixie McCall, Bobby Troup as Dr. Joe Early, Kevin Tighe as Roy DeSoto, and Randolph Mantooth as John Gage*

*Emergency!* takes the mentality of local TV news, which loves to air carnage simply for its shock value, and transposes it to weekly TV drama. The focus is on the members of Squad 51 of the Los Angeles County Fire Department's Paramedic Rescue Service, who round up each week's bloody victims and transport them to Rampart Hospital, where the emergency staff is always on call. This format allows for a great deal of pointless, unconnected violence and gore. Nothing gut-wrenching, mind you, but still just mindlessly riveting enough to capture viewers.

Considering the amount of work the *Emergency!* paramedics are involved in, you would think that Los Angeles County was one gigantic trauma center, with mayhem and tragedies around every corner. There is no time for minor details such as character development, just a few free moments for witty repartee among the hunks on the paramedic squad and some flirting with the nurses at the hospital.

This toning down of personality is a trademark of the executive producer of *Emergency!*, Jack Webb, creator and star of *Dragnet* and creator of other soulless shows such as *Project UFO.* The only interesting personality aspect about *Emergency!* is that female lead Julie London was Webb's ex-wife, and she was married to one of the male leads, Bobby Troup, when the show was filmed.

Aside from the original two-hour pilot from 1971, there are four two-hour episodes of *Emergency!* that aired sporadically for a year after the show left the weekly prime-time schedule in 1977.

**EMERGENCY ROOM** **(see *E/R [Emergency Room]*)**

**EMPIRE (**½) 60 min (32ep B&W; 1962–1963 NBC) Drama** *with Richard Egan as Jim Redigo, Terry Moore as Constance Garret, Anne Seymour as Lucia Garret, Ryan O'Neal as Tal Garret, and Charles Bronson as Paul Moreno*

In *Empire,* an early 1960s attempt at the big-business quasi-soap-opera format that would not catch on until the late 1970s, Jim Redigo is the foreman of a huge ranch in modern-day New Mexico owned by the wealthy Constance Garret. The romantic aspects of *Empire* are positively Victorian compared with the *Dallas*-era soaps. Mucho macho film star Charles Bronson (*Death Wish*) makes a rare TV appearance as ranch hand Paul Moreno.

The character of Jim Redigo later moved up to lead status in a spin-off of *Empire* called *Redigo.*

**EMPIRE (**½) 30 min (6ep Color; 1984 CBS) Situation Comedy** *with Dennis Dugan as Ben Christian, Patrick Macnee as Calvin Cromwell, Richard Masur as Jack Willow, Caren Kaye as Meredith Blake, Christine Belford as Jackie Willow, and Howard Platt as Roger Martinson*

Corporate intrigue is skewered nicely in this charming little sitcom. Calvin Cromwell is the chairman of the board of Empire Industries, an international conglomerate headquartered in New York City. Cromwell is a positive tyrant who believes that anxiety breeds excellence, and so he terrorizes the other executives until they will endure any humiliation in order to win Cromwell's praise. Into this den of psychos comes Ben Christian, the new vice-president for research and development, who lacks the nasty, sycophantic traits of the other executives, and so is disliked by everyone.

While *Empire* sometimes gets silly, it is filled with such wild abandon that it is catchy. The cast is superior, with Patrick Macnee (*The Avengers*) deliciously evil as Cromwell, and Dennis Dugan (*Richie Brockelman, Private Eye*) appropriately wide-eyed as the aptly named Christian.

**EMPTY NEST (***) 30 min (22ep at Fall 1989 Color; 1988– NBC) Situation Comedy** *with Richard Mulligan as Dr. Harry Weston, Kristy McNichol as Barbara, Dinah Manoff as Carol, Park Overall as Nurse Laverne, David Leisure as Charley, and Bear as Dreyfuss*

A solid and reliable Richard Mulligan vehicle created and produced by Susan Harris (and company), operating just down the Florida retirement road from *The Golden Girls* (yet another slice of the Harris universe). Mulligan (best known as nutty Burt Campbell on Harris's *Soap*) brings his patented physical schtick and put-upon persona (with that touch of nervous uncertainty in his voice) to the role of widower pediatrician Harry Weston, who divides his comic time between dealing with the kids at his office and fretting about his two grown daughters also living in town. Barbara's job is bad enough (she's a Florida cop), but Carol is still a relatively recent divorcée and Harry doesn't want her hurt again. (Barbara represents yet another *Soap* connection, having played Burt Campbell's ill-fated daughter-in-law, Elaine.)

The best aspect of the relationship between Harry and his daughters is that there is obviously mutual love and affection at work here, with the family members in that rare situation of dealing with each other as adults (rather than grown kids sharing the same roof). However, Harry does save some of his innermost thoughts for someone else, the sweet, sad-eyed old dog, Dreyfuss. This gives Mulligan a chance for some very effective monologues, sharing jokes, doubts, and heartfelt observations alone in the apartment with his special confidant and companion. Overall, this is a nicely balanced package.

**THE ENGLISH GARDEN** (**½) **30 min (7ep Color; 1980 UK Thames) Documentary** *with Sir John Gielgud as host*

A history of gardens, including guided tours through some of England's most spectacular displays. With plenty of pretty pictures, this show is a magazine-come-to-life program, accompanied by impeccable narration from Sir John Gielgud. A perfect substitute for actually *doing* any gardening.

**ENOS** (½) **60 min (16ep Color; 1980–1981 CBS) Comedy/Adventure** *with Sonny Shroyer as Enos Strate, Samuel E. Wright as Turk Adams, John Dehner as Lt. Jacob Broggi, and John Milford as Capt. Dempsey*

A spin-off from the simple-minded *Dukes of Hazzard, Enos* has none of the amiable fun of its progenitor and all of its faults. Ultra-hick Enos, a deputy sheriff in Hazzard County, is miraculously hired by the Los Angeles Police Department after making a bumbling capture of the two most wanted men in the land. In the City of Angels, Enos is teamed up with black streetwise partner Turk Adams.

Much like the favorite rube of the 1960s, Gomer Pyle, Enos is always flashing a stupid grin, giving everyone the impression that he is dense. Yet somehow the country bumpkin usually manages to get his man by the end of the episode. The inanity of the characters and the script make *Enos* almost unwatchable, even for fans of the Duke clan.

**ENSIGN O'TOOLE** (**) **30 min (32ep B&W; 1962–1963 NBC) Situation Comedy** *with Dean Jones as Ensign O'Toole, Jay C. Flippen as CPO Homer Nelson, Jack Mullaney as Lt. Rex St. John, Harvey Lembeck as Gabby Di Julio, Jack Albertson as Lt. Cmdr. Virgil Stoner, and Beau Bridges as Howard Spicer*

Based on two novels by Bill Lederer, *Ensign O'Toole* is a harmless half hour of military shenanigans somewhat more refined than *McHale's Navy*, but not as sharp as Phil Silvers' Sgt. Bilko series. Set aboard the U.S. Navy destroyer *Appleby* in the peacetime South Pacific, *Ensign O'Toole*'s main character is a charming know-it-all who makes himself scarce when there is work to do.

The cast is the chief drawing card for this series. Dean Jones entertained millions in the Disney *Love Bug* series of movies. Jack Mullaney, who plays the ship's vain supply officer, had the bad fortune to co-star in *It's About Time.* Harvey Lembeck is a graduate of the Bilko series (where he played Rocco Barbella). Jack Albertson starred in *Chico and the Man* a decade after *Ensign O'Toole.* Beau Bridges, son of Lloyd, and later a movie star on his own (*Norma Rae*), has his first role as a TV series regular here.

**THE EQUALIZER** (***) **60 min (86ep at Summer 1989 Color; 1985–1989 CBS) Adventure** *with Edward Woodward as Robert McCall, Robert Lansing as Control, William Zabka as Scott McCall, and Ron O'Neal as Lt. Isadore Smalls*

In the urban jungle it's *us versus them,* and *them* definitely seems to have the upper hand at every turn. That's the message of the shadowy opening montage to this series, with people alone late at night on the streets, in dark alleys, or waiting for a nearly empty train to take them home, all apparently just half a step away from some personal assault. But, there's also hope: Emerging from the dark urban landscape is the formidable figure of one Robert McCall, a self-styled "equalizer" in the game of threats, counterthreats, and psychological terror.

That's a powerful image and, in the hands of Edward Woodward in the title role, this series manages to stake out its distinctive niche in the one-man-versus-the-system genre. Woodward plays a former U.S. government agent, the best in the field, who quit the business after a few too many years of frequently amoral double-dealing. Instead he has chosen to dedicate his considerable skills to attacking problems closer to home, advertising his services in the local New York papers: "Got a problem? Odds against you? Call The Equalizer." Though this ad turns up a good number of kooks, McCall screens the calls on his answering machine carefully and chooses the ones that seem truly in need—usually those with that frightened, nervous catch in their voices. Soon the game is once again afoot.

What makes McCall so creditable is that he harbors no Pollyanna illusions. Even if he was eventually unwilling to continue officially as a government agent, he knows the need for such an approach in dealing with the cold-blooded ruthless characters of the world. Sometimes, in fact, he takes on freelance missions for his old boss (Robert Lansing plays his agency contact), or calls on old associates to help him tackle his latest urban bully. They respond because they respect McCall as one of their own, an articulate, tasteful gentleman living in a comfortable Manhattan apartment, but with the battle scars from a lifetime of service in the intelligence community. One excellent example of his expertise in action comes in an episode that finds McCall part of a group of hostages held by terrorists in a New York hotel. He knows enough to bide his time, waiting for the right moment to strike, even if it means gritting his teeth during the torture of some fellow hostages.

Actually, despite the mugger on the streets image of the opening, McCall's clients are not just threatened by street violence—often they are victims of corporate injustice, with some arrogant business types exploiting employees or customers. In taking on such nebulous tasks (for instance, getting a corporation to provide compensation for a product one of its administrators stole from an inventor), McCall might use some of the more elaborate mind-game illusions familiar to fans of *Mission: Impossible* or *The A-Team*. Even in these the emphasis is not on the clever mechanical gimmicks (pulling some plastic mask from the face of an undercover double), but rather on the characters, with McCall there to peel back the illusions of self-serving justification. He knows their game—he's played it himself—and he won't stand for it any longer.

And this is an underlying theme to the whole series—characters forced to face the consequences of their actions. McCall, in fact, does so on a very personal level, with one of his personal continuing threads being his relationship with his once estranged son, Scott. On this level, McCall is not so much The Equalizer as The Conscience, or even The Avenging Angel. Fortunately, Woodward usually manages to keep his character just this side of the line between morality and the blatant vigilante style of a typical Chuck Norris or Charles Bronson film. Though at times McCall does get a bit preachy, he emerges from it all as someone you'd not only be glad to have on your side but that you'd like to have as a trusted friend.

For a taste of what McCall's life as an agent might have been like, search for the late 1960s–early 1970s British series *Callan,* in which Woodward plays a British operative with a license to kill. Even the distinctive signature theme to *The Equalizer* has an obtuse espionage connection, composed and conducted by Stewart Copeland, son of a CIA agent, though better known as one of the members of the hit group The Police. ■

## ERNIE KOVACS, THE BEST OF (***) 30 min (10ep B&W; 1977 Syndication) Comedy *with Ernie Kovacs and Jack Lemmon as narrator*

The word *genius* is bandied about quite freely in discussing some of the big stars of early TV, but even under a strict definition of the word, Ernie Kovacs must be included in any list of TV geniuses. Not because he was the funniest man ever to appear on TV, which he wasn't, but because he, before almost everyone else, intuitively understood what makes television different from radio or movies or the stage, and he developed the first truly television form of humor.

Kovacs was an oddball, as are most geniuses. He was not the easiest person to get along with, nor was he the type who instantly appealed to great masses of viewers. He bounced around several short-lived TV series throughout the early 1950s, garnering a modicum of fame and honing his comedy talent.

The advent of videotape in the late 1950s allowed Kovacs to perfect his craft. Freed from the restraints of live TV, he could string together short, unconnected bits, called "blackouts" (due to the quick cuts to black in between them) in order to develop a comedy theme. The first real test of this system was an NBC special from January 1957, which contained not a single word of dialogue, just video images set to music. By orchestrating the movements of people, scenery, and supposedly inanimate objects to the tempo of the music, Kovacs created a video opera of sorts that was light-years ahead of the standard vaudeville-based comedy then all over TV.

While serving as host of a few silly game shows on the low-rated ABC network in the early 1960s, Kovacs was allowed to produce a series of monthly specials. It is these specials that provide us with the purest examples of Kovacs' TV comedy. The highlights of these shows were re-edited in 1977 and rerun as *The Best of Ernie Kovacs.*

The specials were produced on an extraordinarily small budget, and the lack of funds shows in the cheap sets and poor lighting. Still, the magic of Kovacs' mind shines through. He portrays his large cast of characters that he invented and performed over the years, such as lisping, soused poet Percy Dovetonsils, horror movie host Auntie Gruesome (who scared "her"self with descriptions of films), and German disk jockey Wolfgang Sauerbraten. Appearing along with Kovacs' alter egos are the Nairobi Trio, three people in ape masks, baggy suits, and hats, who try to keep time with a simple record over and over again, with something *slightly* different going wrong each time.

Aside from trotting out Kovacs' cast of familiars, his ABC specials allow him to experiment further with video tricks. Again there are no-dialogue music segments, with simple props apparently moving on their own to the beat. Kovacs uses sight gags such as superimposing himself in old silent movies, in order to "direct" the actors. The out-of-the-ordinary is always occurring, such as twenty people climbing out of a soapy tub Ernie is lying in, or written credits on a sink suddenly washing down the drain, to be replaced by new credits.

When watching these old specials, just recall that there was little money available to spend, and that these truly are experimental in nature. Sometimes a bit will work; sometimes five in a row will not. The point is that nobody else was doing anything anywhere near what Kovacs was doing at the time. Kovacs' work in these specials is the direct ancestor of the style made popular by *Rowan and Martin's Laugh-In* years later. Kovacs' death in an early 1962 car accident put an end to his innovations, but he blazed the trail that many others would follow thereafter. ■

**THE ERROL FLYNN THEATER (**) 30 min (16ep B&W; 1957 Syndication) Drama Anthology** *with Errol Flynn as host*

Errol Flynn, the premier dashing romantic hero of Hollywood in the 1940s, acts as host to a series of thirty-minute dramas, some of which star Mr. Flynn. ■

**ESCAPE (*) 30 min (4ep Color; 1973 NBC) Suspense Anthology** *with Jack Webb as narrator*

*Dragnet* major-domo Jack Webb produces and narrates this series that dramatizes the exploits of people caught in dangerous situations.

**ESPIONAGE (**½) 60 min (24ep B&W; 1963–1964 UK ATV) Drama Anthology**

A British-produced anthology of fact-based espionage stories, filmed on location throughout Europe. This show came out just a half-step ahead of the mid-1960s wave of tongue-in-cheek spy adventures and, as a result, treats double-dealing intrigues with a much more somber and downbeat tone. There's a good lineup of British and American guest performers throughout the series, including Dennis Hopper, Jim Backus, Fritz Weaver, Bernard Lee (M in the James Bond films), and Patrick Troughton (the second Doctor Who).

**THE ETHEL BARRYMORE THEATER (**) 30 min (13ep B&W; 1956 Syndication) Drama Anthology** *with Ethel Barrymore as hostess*

Like many fading stars of stage and screen during the 1950s, Ethel Barrymore, member of the fabled Barrymore family of actors and actresses, serves as hostess and occasional star of a series of passable dramas.

**EUREKA STOCKADE (**) 2 hr (2ep Color; 1983 Australia) Drama** *with Bryan Brown as Peter Lalor, Amy Madigan, Carol Burns, Bill Hunter, Penelope Stewart, and Brett Cullen as Charles Ross*

More than a century before Paul Hogan and Crocodile Dundee helped turn Australia into one of the top ten tourist spots of the world, the country had a minor cash flow problem: It went bankrupt. No doubt the time was terribly traumatic for everyone there (it led to armed rebellion among the country's gold miners and other "free men"), but today it's just an obscure footnote to history. Still, this workmanlike if dull and sprawling production covering the events does offer Australian Bryan Brown (from *The Thorn Birds* and such films as *Cocktail*) as Peter Lalor, the rebel leader, and Canadian-American Brett Cullen as Charles Ross, the designer and defender of the Australian rebel flag. (Well, maybe you had to be there.) Also look for Amy Madigan (from such films as *Field of Dreams* and *Roe versus Wade*) in the cast.

**THE EVE ARDEN SHOW (*½) 30 min (26ep B&W; 1957–1958 CBS) Situation Comedy** *with Eve Arden as Liza Hammond, Allyn Joslyn as George Howell, Karen Greene as Mary Hammond, Gail Stone as Jenny Hammond, and Frances Bavier as Nora*

What do writers do between royalty checks? For starters, they find jobs that pay a bit more frequently and lucratively. In the case of author Liza Hammond, she hits the lecture circuit, leaving her two children (and housekeeping chores) with Nora (played by Frances Bavier, just two years away from her role as Aunt Bee on *The Andy Griffith Show*). The series is based on an autobiography by novelist Emily Kimbrough. A short-run disappointment for Eve Arden after four seasons of success with *Our Miss Brooks.*

**EVENING AT THE BOSTON POPS (***) 60 min (26ep Color; 1979–1982 PBS) Music**

Recorded live in Boston Symphony Hall, the Boston Pops Orchestra performs the best of popular and classical music, conducted by John Williams. Similar concerts, with legendary maestro Arthur Fiedler, aired on PBS from 1970 to 1979, but are no longer syndicated.

**EVERGLADES (**) 30 min (38ep Color; 1961–1962 Syndication) Adventure** *with Ron Hayes as Lincoln Vail and Gordon Cosell as Chief Anderson*

Lincoln Vail is a policeman for the Everglades County police in Florida, battling lawbreaking gators and other swamp creatures.

**EVERGREEN (**) (6hr miniseries Color; 1985 NBC) Drama** *with Lesley Ann Warren as Anna Friedman, Armand Assante as Joseph Friedman, Ian McShane as Paul Lerner, Brian Dennehy as Matthew Malone, Betty Buckley as Mrs. Bradford, Robert Vaughn as John Bradford, Patricia Barry as Mrs. Lerner, and Kate Burton as Agatha Bradford*

Anna Friedman is a poor Polish-Jewish immigrant to the United States at the turn of the century. She begins life in America as a seamstress in a sweaty shop, moves up to household maid to a rich WASP family on Fifth Avenue, and reaches the top as wife to a successful suburban contractor. In spite of her success, she still carries a torch for the son of the WASP family on Fifth Avenue.

Based on the Belva Plain best-selling novel, *Evergreen* is directed by TV drama veteran Fielder Cook (*Kraft Television Theater, The Defenders*).

**THE EVERLY BROTHERS SHOW (**½) 60 min (13ep Color; 1970 ABC) Musical-Variety** *with Don Everly, Phil Everly, Joe Higgins, and Ruth McDevitt*

The singing rock'n'roll brothers host a sprightly variety hour that originally served as a substitute for Johnny Cash's program, hence its original title: *Johnny Cash Presents The Everly Brothers Show.*

**EVERYTHING'S RELATIVE (½) 30 min (7ep Color; 1987 CBS) Situation Comedy** *with Anne Jackson as Rae Matthews, Jason Alexander as Julian Beeby, John Bolger as Scott Beeby, and Gina Hecht as Emily Cabot*

Anne Jackson is a real, honest-to-God *act*ress, who appears in *serious* plays and films (*The Bell Jar, Lovers and Other Strangers*). So it is a bit disappointing to see her in this absolutely dreadful sitcom. Hopefully, she used the money to finance an Ibsen festival or something equally worthwhile.

For the record, in *Everything's Relative* Jackson plays the domineering mother of two grown sons who room together in swinging Manhattan. Older son Julian runs a product-testing company, while younger son Scott works in construction.

**EXECUTIVE SUITE (**) 60 min (19ep Color; 1976–1977 CBS) Drama** *with Mitchell Ryan as Don Walling, Stephen Elliott as Howell Rutledge, Sharon Acker as Helen Walling, Leigh McCloskey as Brian Walling, and Wendy Phillips as Stacey Walling*

*Executive Suite* is another lifeless attempt at a soapy drama set in the world of big business that predates *Dallas.* It was not until J. R. Ewing that the networks realized the key to corporate drama was nasty villains, and none of the bad guys in this series merit inclusion in the same class as J. R. In *Executive Suite,* Don Walling is president of the huge, amorphous Cardway Corporation, located in California.

**THE EXPERT (**½) 60 min (54ep Color; 1970–1975 UK BBC) Crime Drama** *with Marius Goring as Dr. John Hardy, Ann Morrish as Dr. Jo Harding, Virginia Stride as Susan Bartlett, and Victor Winding as Inspector Fleming*

Doctor John Hardy helps the local police in Warwickshire, England, crack their latest mystery with his unique expertise in forensic medicine. As with *Quincy, M. E.,* this show is chiefly a character showcase, though unlike his Stateside colleague, Hardy has a controlled, self-effacing demeanor.

**EYE TO EYE (**½) 60 min (6ep Color; 1985 ABC) Detective Drama** *with Charles Durning as Oscar Poole and Stephanie Faracy as Tracey Doyle*

Apparently there's this code among pulp fiction private eyes that you have to avenge your partner's murder, even if the two of you haven't worked together in years. Then there's this creed among writers and producers that when the right crime-fighting duo clicks, they're usually opposites—and they lead to ratings gold. This combination is one that doesn't quite make it, though it comes close with plenty of snappy patter and fast-moving action all in place. Durning plays a set-in-his-ways, over-the-hill gumshoe who finds his routine upset when the daughter of his ex-partner turns up, determined to work with him on solving her dad's murder. So (to quote the program touts), they "dance a tango, hijack a plane, get in a gunfight, and nab a killer"—and, of course, then team up on a permanent basis. Of the two leads, Durning is probably more familiar (with dozens of roles in television and theatrical films, including *The Best Little Whorehouse in Texas*), while Faracy has a strong base in comedy (she was the inept baker on *The Last Resort* and the sexy feature reporter on *Goodnight, Beantown*).

**THE F.B.I. (**½) 60 min (234ep Color; 1965–1974 ABC) Police Drama** *with Efrem Zimbalist, Jr. as Lewis Erskine, Philip Abbott as Arthur Ward, Stephen Brooks as Jim Rhodes, William Reynolds as Tom Colby, and Lynn Loring as Barbara Erskine*

The two greatest producers of TV crime dramas from the 1950s through the 1970s were Jack Webb and Quinn Martin, and the two of them had very different styles. Webb, best known for *Dragnet, Adam-12,* and *Emergency!,* emphasized the grim, no-nonsense hard work of the police, with a minimum of human warmth evident in his lead characters. Martin, on the other hand, through shows such as *The Untouchables, The Fugitive, Cannon,* and *Streets of San Francisco,* almost always focused on the human aspect of drama, with colorful, interesting characters in the forefront.

*The F.B.I.* is Quinn Martin trying to copy Jack Webb. If not for Quinn Martin signatures such as a deep-voiced offscreen announcer and screen titles breaking each hour into four acts (plus an epilogue), *The F.B.I.* could easily pass for a Jack Webb production. Like *Dragnet, The F.B.I.* is based on cases from the files of the authorities, in this case, J. Edgar Hoover's Federal Bureau of Investigation. Like *Dragnet, The F.B.I.* has a male lead who is laconic, almost emotionless, and humorless, and the stories just stick to the facts, ma'am, with little time for off-duty vignettes.

Even so, Inspector Lewis Erskine, a pure company man, displays some kindness at times, even to suspects and apprehended felons. Though he is working for the F.B.I., the organization in the forefront of combating the antiestablishment elements of the 1960s, Inspector Erskine lacks the burning hatred that typified Joe Friday's run-ins with the California counterculture on *Dragnet.*

Nevertheless, Lewis Erskine is still mostly a colorless cop, tracking down his suspect without much style. He is a far cry from Efrem Zimbalist's other great role, that of swank, sophisticated private-eye Stuart Bailey of *77 Sunset Strip* (a show, interestingly enough, that Jack Webb radically altered as producer in its final season). Erskine has a cool but correct relationship with his immediate superior, Assistant F.B.I. Director Arthur Ward, and acts kind and paternal to his underlings, first Jim Rhodes and then Tom Colby. In the first season, a romance develops between Jim Rhodes and Erskine's daughter Barbara, one that Erskine does not condone. Both the romance and the daughter disappear by the second season, so *The F.B.I.* can concentrate full-time on the gritty work of tracking down criminals. Private lives are out, work is in.

It is a shock to realize that this show lasts for nine full seasons. The quality stays fairly constant, and the F.B.I. is always a fertile source for new stories, but after a few seasons, the lack of diversions from Erskine's quest for justice builds viewer indifference. In the end, Quinn Martin's effort to emulate Jack Webb is self-defeating.

In the early 1980s, ABC tried to revive this same concept in *Today's F.B.I.,* starring Mike Connors as FBI man Ben Slater. This later series is even closer to the Jack Webb school of crime fighting, and bears no direct character connection to the Efrem Zimabalist/Quinn Martin series.

**F.D.R. (**½) 30 min (26ep B&W; 1965 ABC) Documentary** *with Arthur Kennedy as narrator*

Drawing on extensive newsreel and archives film footage, this series presents an excellent, detailed portrait of the public life of President Franklin Delano Roosevelt. The series is generally chronological, with emphasis on appropriate themes such as FDR's attempts to "pack" the Supreme Court or the role of Eleanor Roosevelt as a politically astute activist. Charlton Heston reads excerpts from Roosevelt's writings to convey the president's more private thoughts. Eleanor Roosevelt herself also appears in a few segments filmed shortly before her death.

**F TROOP (***) 30 min (65ep: 34 B&W & 31 Color; 1965–1967 ABC) Situation Comedy** *with Forrest Tucker as Sgt. Morgan O'Rourke, Larry Storch as Cpl. Randolph Agarn, Ken Berry as Capt. Wilton Parmenter, Melody Patterson as Wrangler Jane, and Frank DeKova as Chief Wild Eagle*

The contrived setting of *F Troop* is a bit unusual, even by TV sitcom standards. In the last days of the Civil War, a bumbling easygoing private (Wilton Parmenter) lucks into a promotion to captain. With the war over, Parmenter is assigned to command F Troop at Fort Courage, a sleepy backwater Kansas outpost on the frontier. Parmenter may reign, but Sgt. O'Rourke rules, through his subrosa business dealings with the neighboring Hekawi Indians (who claim to be lovers, not fighters). Parmenter is usually preoccupied in fending off the amorous advances of comely cowgirl Wrangler Jane, whose object is matrimony. Most of the humor in the show comes from Parmenter's bumbling attempts to exert his authority as Captain, while O'Rourke and company try to keep their business dealings hidden and the men of F Troop try to avoid any strenuous physical activity.

*F Troop* shows how the old style of vaudeville and the new medium of television can amicably live side by side. As in vaudeville, the acting in *F Troop* is very broad, edging towards farce. Forrest Tucker, as O'Rourke, and Larry Storch, as his aide-de-camp Cpl. Agarn, are both vaudeville-style troopers from the old days and they bring a wonderful joy to their characters. O'Rourke is the traditional sharp operator, smart enough to never overplay his hand and adept at maintaining Parmenter's purely nominal position as commander. Agarn is the classic second banana, always wishing to supplant O'Rourke but never bright enough to outfox the master. The other members of F Troop include a bugler who can't play a good note, a legally blind lookout, and a private who only speaks German. The only other military outfit on TV comparable in ineptitude to Capt. Parmenter's F Troop in Fort Courage is Sgt. Bilko's Company B at Fort Baxter.

The Hekawis are carbon copies of the men of F Troop, only with feathers. Chief Wild Eagle is as canny a businessman as O'Rourke. Whenever a visiting Army busybody threatens to disrupt the tribe's profitable relationship with the paleface soldiers, the chief knows enough to stage a mock attack that O'Rourke can easily fend off, in order to impress the visiting brass. Crazy Cat (Don Diamond), Wild Eagle's Agarn, is just as anxious as the Corporal to inherit the top spot, and just as inept at running his own operation.

In the later episodes, the vaudeville aspects of *F Troop* loom larger. The abilities of Tucker and Storch to overact with style shine as they take turns playing double (or triple) roles, as long-lost relatives who turn up at Fort Courage. Thus, Tucker plays Angus O'Rourke, the Sergeant's father from the old sod. Agarn plays a crazy quilt variety of Agarn cousins, one Mexican, one French, and one Russian, but all equally as crackpot as the original American.

The guest stars on *F Troop* sometimes steal the show from the regulars. Edward Everett Horton, narrator of "Fractured Fairy Tales" on *Bullwinkle,* plays the aged Hekawi medicine man Roaring Chicken. Other veteran pros such as Phil Harris (Flaming Arrow), Don Rickles (Bald Eagle), and Milton Berle (Wise Owl) don Hekawi garb for a show or two. On the Army side, Paul Lynde appears as a singing Canadian Mountie (shades of Dudley Do-right), George Gobel eases in as a cousin to Wrangler Jane, and Henry Gibson (pre-*Laugh-In*) is Private "Wrongo" Starr (to cash in on the Beatles' fame, no doubt).

*F Troop* is pure entertainment, with no claim to relevancy, just like old vaudeville. Maybe the pies in the face and baggy pants of burlesque are missing, but the easy laughs are plentiful.

**THE FACTS OF LIFE** (**½) **30 min (181ep Color; 1979–1988 NBC) Situation Comedy** *with Charlotte Rae as Edna Garrett, Lisa Whelchel as Blair Warner, Kim Fields as Tootie Ramsey, Mindy Cohn as Natalie Green, Nancy McKeon as Jo Polniaczek, MacKenzie Astin as Andy Moffet, and Cloris Leachman as Beverly Ann Stickle*

Originally presented as a spin-off from *Diff'rent Strokes*, featuring Mrs. Garrett (the former housekeeper to the Drummonds), this series quickly took on a distinct identity of its own. The setting is the Eastland boarding school where Mrs. Garrett acts as a housemother, surrogate parent, and confidante to the young women in her charge. The lineup changes over the years (including Molly Ringwald as Molly Parker for one year), but the four we see through essentially the entire run are Blair, Tootie, Natalie, and Jo. During that nearly decade-long run, they mature from high school teens to young college women to young adults ready to take on the world. Along the way, they also work after-hours at Mrs. Garrett's gourmet food store (about four seasons into the series), later transformed into a 1950s malt shop. And when Mrs. Garrett leaves to get married, they welcome her sister, Beverly Ann, as their new housemom.

This series is steady and reliable with a nicely balanced cast, reasonaly funny scripts, and remarkably restrained plots. There's no scene-stealing Gary Coleman type to hog most of the good lines, and the morals of the stories are simple, but generally not heavy-handed. Best of all, there is a genuine sense of mutual friendship among the young women. It is easy to understand why they consider the years they've spent together as some of the most important in their lives.

The current syndicated package also includes a pair of two-hour TV movies sliced into half-hour episodes: *The Facts of Life Goes to Paris* (1982) and *The Facts of Life Down Under* (1988). Both are on film rather than videotape.

**FAERIE TALE THEATER** (***½) **60 min (27ep Color; 1982–1987 Showtime) Anthology** *with Shelley Duvall as hostess*

This collection of modern, frequently tongue-in-cheek, adaptations of classic children's fairy tales is blessed with a superstar array of stars and producers. The writing is splendid, the sets are not expensive but still resourceful, and the stories are told with a lovely mix of respect for tradition and the tone of modern sensibilities. These fables are definitely for the older set of children, who already think of themselves as grown up. Children over the age of twenty will enjoy these tales most of all.

Some examples of the series include Robin Williams (*Mork & Mindy*) and Teri Garr (*Young Frankenstein*) in "The Tale of the Frog Prince," Herve Villechaize (*Fantasy Island*) and hostess Shelley Duvall in "Rumpelstiltskin," Alan Arkin (*The In-Laws, The Russians Are Coming*) and Art Carney (*The Honeymooners*) in "The Emperor's New Clothes," Pee-wee Herman (*Pee-wee's Playhouse*) in "Pinocchio," and Ricky Schroder (*Silver Spoons*) and Joan Collins (*Dynasty*) in "Hansel and Gretel."

Tall, gangly actress Shelley Duvall (*Nashville* and *Three Women*), who is both executive producer and hostess here, deserves the major credit for the quality of the series. She set the high-quality level yet fun tone and attracted the big stars on what must have been a shoestring budget. ■

**FAIR EXCHANGE** (**) **60 min and 30 min (28ep: fifteen 60 min & thirteen 30 min B&W; 1962–1963 ABC) Situation Comedy** *with Judy Carne as Heather Finch, Lynn Loring as Patty Walker, Eddie Foy, Jr., as Eddie Walker, and Victor Maddern as Tommy Finch*

The first regular series role for Judy Carne on her way to overnight stardom on *Laugh-In* (a half decade later). She plays Heather Finch, a British teen longing to visit the United States. Meanwhile, in New York, Patty Walker, the daughter of her dad's old army buddy, dreams of studying in London. So the two families agree to a one-year fair exchange: Heather comes to live with the Walker clan in New York, while Patty moves in with the Finch family in London. The stories focus on the adjustments both girls have to make in their respective new countries. It would be fun to slot *Fair Exchange* reruns back-to-back with *The Patty Duke Show*—after all, both series use a trans-Atlantic teen connection as an initial hook.

This comedy began with a one-hour format for half its episodes, then switched to a half-hour structure for the remainder of its run.

**FALCON CREST** (**) **60 min (206ep at Fall 1989 Color; 1981– CBS) Drama** *with Jane Wyman as Angela Channing, Robert Foxworth as Chase Gioberti, Susan Sullivan as Maggie Gioberti, Lorenzo Lamas as Lance Cumson, William R. Moses as Cole Gioberti, David Selby as Richard Channing, and Abby Dalton as Julia Cumson*

The third of the big three prime-time soap operas of the early 1980s (behind *Dallas* and *Dynasty*), *Falcon Crest* is co-produced by the disparate duo of Earl Hamner (*The Waltons*) and Michael Filerman (*Flamingo Road*). *Falcon Crest* contains all the necessary elements for a successful soap: incalculable wealth, an evil villain, good-looking young people, and sexual intrigue. Unlike the other giants of the genre, the money in this series does not ooze from oil, but rather drips from wineries (located somewhere in California's Napa Valley).

The Falcon Crest wineries are huge and successful, and control of them is the engine that turns most of the plot complications. Evil matriarch Angela Channing rules Falcon Crest and seeks to rule everybody in her family, as well as the entire county, if possible. Her noble nephew Chase is the main roadblock in her path, as he uses his own nearby wine holdings to block Angela's ever-increasing efforts to obtain more "lebensraum" for her grapes. Chase actually briefly wrestles control of Falcon Crest away from Angela at one point, but that only spurs her on to more dastardly plots.

Angela's chief henchman is her playboy grandson Lance, who she manipulates and uses to accomplish some of her complex maneuvers. Her other main adversary, the competing evil genius, is unprincipled newspaper publisher Richard Channing, Angela's stepson. He, too, is forever trying to obtain control of Falcon Crest, or at least destroy it if he can't have it.

*Falcon Crest* does not have the opulence of *Dynasty,* nor the playful nastiness of *Dallas,* which all combine to give the program a tone that is a bit too serious for this kind of show. Instead of the jewel-bedecked bitchiness of an Alexis–Krystle cat fight, or the sweet seductiveness of J. R.'s cobralike smile as he destroys another competitor, *Falcon Crest* viewers must make do with Angela's shriveled grimaces, Chase's goody-two-shoes altruism, and Lance's airhead hunkiness. It's still enough to capture those who like a good, complicated, romance-tinged melodrama, but *Falcon Crest,* believe it or not, ultimately fails to achieve cult status because it is *too* realistic (at least when compared to its contemporary competitors). What prime-time soap fans crave is outrageous opulence and exaggerated characters. Instead, in *Falcon Crest,* we get mere extreme wealth and ultradetermined personalities, who seem to be only mild dramatizations of real small-time big wheels.

The role of Angela provides a welcome change in attitude for Jane Wyman. The former wife of Ronald Reagan spent years in Hollywood first playing bimbos and then sensitive victims. For several years in the mid-1950s, she was resplendent as the gowned hostess of *Fireside Theatre,* a drama anthology. Angela is her first major role as a villainess, and Wyman really sinks her teeth into the part, wonderfully playing against type. The other chief attraction on *Falcon Crest* is Lorenzo Lamas (son of Fernando), who covers up his limited acting experience with a thick layer of Latin good looks that goes a long way in sudsy shows like this.

**THE FALL AND RISE OF REGINALD PERRIN** **(see *Reginald Perrin, The Fall and Rise of*)**

**THE FALL GUY (**½) 60 min (150ep Color; 1981–1986 ABC) Adventure** *with Lee Majors as Colt Seavers, Douglas Barr as Howie Munson, Heather Thomas as Jody Banks, Jo Ann Pflug as "Big Jack," and Markie Post as Terri Michaels/Shannon*

If Burt Reynolds had been available for TV series work in the early 1980s, this would have been the perfect vehicle for him, cut from the same cloth as such light theatrical features as *Smokey and the Bandit* and *The Cannonball Run.* As it turned out, Lee Majors did just fine moving from the super-straight adventures of *The Six Million Dollar Man* to those of a tongue-in-cheek modern-day bounty hunter.

*The Fall Guy* cleverly mixes two of Hollywood's favorite fantasy worlds, law enforcement and filmmaking, with Majors playing a top-line stuntman who also doubles as a bail bond agent. (He brings back people who jumped bail and skipped town.) Why does he bother? For extra money—much of it no doubt used to repair his poor abused pick-up truck after chasing another fugitive down some bumpy back road.

This series is pure cartoon fun with simple plots, plenty of grimaces, and double takes by Majors, and comic sidekick relief from Douglas Barr. Majors sets the tone in the opening credits, singing (in his best country and western drawl) "The Ballad of the Unknown Stuntman," complete with sly references to being "seen with Farrah" (Fawcett, his former wife) and to being underappreciated for making stars like Clint Eastwood and Robert Redford look "so fine" by doing their stunts.

Film buffs should enjoy the opening credits in the first few seasons, which incorporate clips involving famous stunts from real theatrical features (including *The Silver Streak, Butch Cassidy and the Sundance Kid, Mother, Jugs & Speed,* and, appropriately, *The Stuntman*). The series also constantly drops the names of real-life stars that Colt Seavers is supposedly doing stunts for, ranging from Robert Wagner (presumably for *Hart to Hart*) to Roger Moore (playing some famous British secret agent).

For those uninterested in such arcane matters, Heather Thomas also parades through the series in plenty of tight, revealing outfits.

**THE FALL OF EAGLES (**) 60 min (13ep Color; UK BBC 1974) Drama** *with Curt Jurgens as Otto von Bismarck, Gemma Jones as Princess Victoria, Patrick Stewart as Vladimir Lenin, Barry Foster as Kaiser Wilhelm II, and Marius Goring as Paul von Hindenburg*

The road to and through World War I, as taken by the ruling dynasties of Austria–Hungary, Germany, and Russia. An intensely detailed saga following the story from Austrian Emperor Franz-Joseph's era to the departure of Germany's Kaiser Bill into exile. Overall, a grim tale, though the performances are for the most part pretty good. This was a co-production with Time-Life television, with Patricia Neal serving as host to the series in its U.S. packaging.

**FALLEN HERO (**) 60 min (12ep Color; 1978–1979 UK Granada) Drama** *with Del Henney, Wanda Ventham, Marged Esli, and John Wheatley*

The hook is a good one: a professional sports figure's career is sidetracked (perhaps permanently) after he's injured in a game. There are marital difficulties, problems with self-esteem, and the very practical reality of not having a job. The chief problem with this series for U.S. viewers is that it's all about a rugby star, not exactly part of our national pastime. Only half the twelve episodes produced in England are currently available here.

**FAME** **(***½) 60 min (136ep at 60 min or 90ep at 30 min Color; 1982–1986 NBC & Syndication) Drama** *with Debbie Allen as Lydia Grant, Gene Anthony Ray as Leroy Johnson, Albert Hague as Benjamin Shorofsky, Michael Thoma as Gregory Crandall, Lee Curreri as Bruno Martelli, Carlo Imperato as Danny Amatullo, Carol Mayo Jenkins as Elizabeth Sherwood, Ken Swofford as Quentin Morlock, Ann Nelson as Gertrude Berg, and Janet Jackson as Cleo Hewitt*

If ever a theatrical feature should have been a television series, the 1980 film version of *Fame* was it. There just wasn't enough time available to present what director Alan Parker tried to do: follow no less than a half-dozen characters at a special New York high school for the performing arts, from registration/audition, through crises in freshman, sophomore, junior, and senior years, to graduation. With little more than two hours to work with, the result was a highly charged collection of unfinished character sketches. Still, with its eye-catching dance numbers and incessant beat, it was a hit film, with the title song an international top-ten smash by Irene Cara.

As a one-hour series, *Fame* has the chance to do the job right from start to finish. And it does. Several performers and most of the characters from the film come over to the television version (including Debbie Allen, Gene Anthony Ray, Lee Curreri, and Albert Hague). Over the course of the series, they go through school the old-fashioned way: week by week, course by course, crisis by crisis, year by year. So, for instance, we get to see characters such as dancer Leroy Johnson (one of the standouts in the film) not only grow and mature but also handle the cold reality of the toughest decision of all: What do I do next? It's something all the students (and the teachers) have to face, which makes their time in the protective cocoon of the school very precious. They know they have to make the most of it.

Thus, as in the film, at any time along the way any of the characters are liable (and likely) to break into song or dance or a musical rap or even some lines from a play. But it comes off as believable because they're in this school to perform. And sometimes these bits evolve into full-fledged fantasy sequences that occasionally fill an entire episode (two of the best involve tributes to *The Wizard of Oz* and Sherlock Holmes). Yet through all this, the series hangs together because the connecting characterizations and story lines are very well done. And there's always that underlying theme: the quest to excel and celebrate the performing arts, and by extension, the human spirit.

Such heady stuff was trumpeted by NBC in its original presentation of the series, but the untypical setup barely lasted a season and a half on the network (even as part of "the best night of television on television"). Nonetheless, the producers and studio continued the series in first-run syndication, where it thrived for several more years. What really kept the venture profitable, though, was the international market. In England, for instance, not only was the program a hit but so were concert appearances by "The Kids from *Fame*" (who had two top-selling albums in 1982). They met similar success in other countries such as Japan and Israel, and several episodes of the series incorporate these overseas concert performances.

After a healthy run, the series held its final graduation and everyone had to face the inevitability of life after classes (albeit fictional ones). This reality included the producers, who had to make adjustments to the series itself for the rerun syndication market, packaging the episodes in both one-hour and half-hour formats. (Go with the full-length versions.) Among the graduates, the two most successful at this point are Debbie Allen (who came aboard in the second season of *A Different World* to help rework the series) and international pop star Janet Jackson.

**FAMILY** **(**½) 60 min (86ep Color; 1976–1980 ABC) Drama** *with James Broderick as Doug Lawrence, Sada Thompson as Kate Lawrence, Elayne Heilveil and Meredith Baxter-Birney as Nancy Lawrence Maitland, Gary Frank as Willie Lawrence, Kristy McNichol as Letitia "Buddy" Lawrence, and John Rubinstein as Jeff Maitland*

An intriguing mixture of quality drama and typical soapy fare, *Family*'s dichotomy is best indicated by the identity of its three executive producers. Two of the producers, Aaron Spelling and Leonard Goldberg, teamed up to produce some of the gaudiest glitter of the 1970s, such as *Charlie's Angels, Fantasy Island,* and *S.W.A.T.* The third producer, Mike Nichols, made his name as a director of intelligent and successful plays, such as *Barefoot in the Park* and *The Odd Couple.*

The family members in *Family* are the Lawrences, an upper-middle-class clan living in the sunniness of Pasadena, California, who have a slew of personal problems that complicate their lives. Daughter Nancy discovers her husband Jeff cheating on her, so she gets a divorce and later enters law school. Son Willie quits school and hopes to become a famous writer; meanwhile he marries a woman with a terminal illness. Teenage daughter Buddy goes through puberty and briefly runs away from home. Matriarch Kate develops breast cancer and patriarch Doug, a lawyer, is temporarily blinded in a car crash.

In spite of the constant churning of crises, *Family*

does a fairly good job of setting compelling drama in a home environment. The series served as Kristy McNichol's entrance to stardom, and like most young TV stars, she went on to star in several hit movies (such as *The Night the Lights Went Out in Georgia*). She later returned to TV in *Empty Nest.*

*Family* has a tendency toward oppressive seriousness but, like any good sudsy drama, it's easy to get caught up in the tribulations of the characters. The lack of *Dynasty*-like opulence is refreshing, even if the plots are equally convoluted.

**FAMILY AFFAIR (**½) 30 min (138ep Color; 1966–1971 CBS) Situation Comedy** *with Brian Keith as Bill Davis, Sebastian Cabot as Giles French, Anissa Jones as Buffy Davis, Johnnie Whitaker as Jody Davis, and Kathy Garver as Catherine "Cissy" Davis*

Nice. *Family Affair* is nice. Very nice. The grown-ups are nice; the kids are nice. If you like nice, this is the show for you. If you get filled up with nice pretty quickly and yearn for flashes of realism, or even just some pointed barbs, then avoid *Family Affair.*

You simply can't fault *Family Affair* on many grounds other than unrelenting niceness. Bill Davis is a swinging New York bachelor/engineer whose life of ease in his Manhattan apartment, with his English manservant Mr. French, comes to a crashing halt when Davis's brother and sister-in-law die in a car accident. Davis's two nieces, fifteen-year-old Cissy and six-year-old Buffy, and his nephew Jody (Buffy's twin), are suddenly orphans in need of a home and Davis reluctantly agrees to raise them. The entire series revolves around the dichotomy of the single, very un-fatherlike Davis coping with the responsibilities of fatherhood, while the ultra-British Mr. French at first abhors having to deal with the three urchins, though the large fellow comes to really love the brood.

As Bill Davis, Brian Keith is wonderful. Keith is almost unmatched at projecting slow, burning frustration, a trait Bill Davis exudes frequently when the kids get into some mischief. Sebastian Cabot takes a step back from his exciting role as criminologist Carl Hyatt in *Checkmate,* since Cabot must overact as the stuffy, snooty Brit. Cissy, Jody, and Buffy (and viewers) see through the front pretty quickly.

With two such qualified actors, *Family Affair* has a solid base, but that base is constantly nibbled away by the unrelenting sugary characters of the children, especially Jody and Buffy. These kids are too good to be true and the plot lines get bogged down over and over with sappy stories of the cute tykes and their innocent escapades. Teenager Cissy doesn't attract much attention, since she is getting to the dating age and that sensitive topic is too risque for a show as nice as *Family Affair.*

Produced by Don Fedderson, *Family Affair* always strikes home with a sizable number of viewers who like their characters pure and their plots simple. Unfortunately, life is rarely like that, as the story of the later adventures of Anissa Jones (who plays Buffy) proves. Only thirteen when *Family Affair* ceased production, she died of a drug overdose at eighteen.

There are a handful of episodes in *Family Affair*'s first season without Sebastian Cabot, who was ill during production. John Williams (the elderly British actor, not the American composer of the *Star Wars* theme) fills in for Cabot in these shows as Mr. French's brother, Nigel.

**THE FAMILY HOLVAK (*½) 60 min (13ep & 2 hr pilot Color; 1975 NBC) Drama** *with Glenn Ford as Rev. Tom Holvak, Julie Harris as Elizabeth Holvak, Lance Kerwin as Ramey Holvak, and Elizabeth Cheshire as Julie Mae Holvak*

A minor-league *Waltons, The Family Holvak* brings us yet another very sensitive Appalachian family of poor whites during the depression of the 1930s. The cast is good, making up for many faults in the slow plots. Hollywood star Glenn Ford makes a rare turn in a TV series as a preacher. Julie Harris, who plays the preacher's wife, also is better known for her roles in movies (*Requiem for a Heavyweight*) and in plays (*The Member of the Wedding*). Lance Kerwin, as their son, gained a smidgen of notoriety as the lead in *James at 15.*

The 1974 pilot is titled *The Greatest Gift.*

**FAMILY MAN (**) 30 min (7ep Color; 1988 ABC) Situation Comedy** *with Richard Libertini as Shelly Tobin, Mimi Kennedy as Andrea Tobin, Alison Sweeney as Rosie Tobin, Whitby Hertford as Josh Tobin, and Keeley Mari Gallagher as Sara Tobin*

When a series focuses on the home life of a comedy writer, it's pretty hard not to regard it as somewhat autobiographical. Or, more cynically, as not much of a creative stretch. But in the case of *Family Man,* at least it doesn't look like your typical wisecracking sitcom. Instead, like its contemporary, *Molly Dodd,* it is low-key and has no laugh track.

Mimi Kennedy (Nan on *The Two of Us*) and Richard Libertini (the Godfather on *Soap*) play Shelly and Andrea, married a few years with three children (two from her previous marriage and one of their own). Shelly is the terribly anxious one, worried about his writing (especially since Andrea doesn't always share his sense of humor), the state of their marriage, and how well they're bringing up the kids. (Does he favor their youngest over hers? Or vice versa?) Breaking through the exaggerated anxiety are some cute kid scenes and a few more typical comedy hooks (mom and dad go on a diet, mom's battle against a persistent mosquito).

With only a half-dozen episodes, this show never really has a chance to go anywhere, though it is hard to see exactly where it is supposed to go. A B+ for effort, a C for script execution.

**FAMILY TIES** (***) **30 min (176ep & 2 hr special Color; 1982–1989 NBC) Situation Comedy** *with Michael J. Fox as Alex Keaton, Meredith Baxter-Birney as Elyse Keaton, Michael Gross as Steven Keaton, Justine Bateman as Mallory Keaton, Tina Yothers as Jennifer Keaton, Brian Bonsall as Andy Keaton, Marc Price as Skippy Handelman, Scott Valentine as Nick Moore, Tracy Pollan as Ellen Reed, and Courteney Cox as Lauren Miller*

What happens when an idealistic couple from the 1960s finds that, despite their best efforts, their son has grown into his teen years as a very intelligent political conservative, a success-oriented pragmatist perfect for the Ronald Reagan/George Bush era? If it's a typical sitcom execution, not much—maybe a few obvious digs at role reversal (conservative kid rebelling against liberal parents) and a few cheap shots at 1960s hypocrisy (always an easy target). Or you could get *Family Ties.*

This series takes that potentially heavy-handed premise and turns it into a genuinely affectionate comedy, with gentle revelations between generations rather than savage put-downs. And the key to maintaining that tone is Michael J. Fox as Alex P. Keaton, a genuine conservative who also happens to be a loving son.

Fox has one of the most naturally likable screen personas around. With his ingratiating smile, nervous self-confidence, and puppy dog charm, he's almost impossible to dislike, even when delivering a sarcastic line to another character (such as his younger sister, Mallory), or working with a weak script (in such theatrical feature films as *Teen Wolf* or *The Secret of My Success*). Fortunately, with *Family Ties* he generally has very strong material perfectly suited to his character.

Over the course of the series, Alex remains true to his conservative leanings (which apparently took hold practically at birth), but also learns to explore his emotions with far greater depth than he ever expected. One pivotal moment takes place when he falls in love for the first time, losing his heart to Ellen Reed, an art student at his college. At first, Alex can't even figure out how to tell her about his feelings because he doesn't understand them himself. When she boards a train to visit her current boyfriend at another college (and probably agree to marry him), the opportunity seems gone forever. But on the way to a prestigious college party, Alex impulsively turns the car away and drives several hundred miles to meet Ellen at the station (about 3:00 A.M.). His shy nervousness when uttering the words "I love you" for the first time is delightfully innocent, and before long they seem the perfect couple.

And they are, though not for long on screen—Tracy Pollan leaves the series after about a season. However, in real life, she and Fox fell in love and eventually got married.

Another showpiece moment comes in a one-hour story dealing with the death of one of Alex's friends in a car accident. The event leaves Alex deeply troubled chiefly because he was supposed to have been in that car too, only he skipped the ride because he didn't want to help his friend move. In short, Alex was saved because he was selfish and lazy. The second half of the story is an *Our Town*–style monologue by Alex, who desperately tries to avoid really talking to an off-screen psychiatrist by talking instead about everything else in his life.

With Fox as the dependable foundation, the rest of the characters have plenty of time to grow as well. Alex's parents come off surprisingly well, softening their 1960s rhetoric just as Alex takes the hard edge from some of his conservative values. Mallory and Jennifer are acceptable younger sister types, though in later episodes Alex saves most of his energy for indoctrinating his younger brother Andy on the glories of capitalism.

Ironically, when *Family Ties* was first in development (initially pitched as an hour-long drama set-up before evolving into a thirty-minute comedy), creator Gary David Goldberg encountered resistance from NBC's Brandon Tartikoff to his choice of Fox as Alex. According to program legend, Tartikoff didn't think Fox's chemistry was quite right, dismissing the performer as someone whose face would "never end up on a lunch box." Goldberg held firm, and when *Family Ties* became a big hit for NBC, Tartikoff received a custom-made lunch box sporting Fox's likeness.

There is also a 1985 TV movie, *Family Ties Vacation*, set in London.

**THE FAMILY TREE** (**) **60 min (6ep Color; 1983 NBC) Drama** *with Frank Converse as Kevin Nichols, Anne Archer as Annie Benjamin-Nichols, Martin Hewitt as Sam Benjamin, Melora Hardin as Tess Benjamin, Jonathan Hall Kovacs as Toby Benjamin, James Spader as Jake Nichols, and Joanna Cassidy as Elizabeth Nichols*

So this is what happened to Michael Alden (Frank Converse), the man who couldn't remember his identity on *Coronet Blue.* As Kevin Nichols, he faces a challenge even tougher than the spy game: making a marriage work. Actually, making a second marriage work, as he and another divorced parent, Annie, tie the knot and combine their families. She has three children (Sam, Tess, and her youngest, Toby—a deaf character played by a real-life deaf actor), while he has one (Jake). Now the six of them have to begin to work out new relationships with memories of a previous mother and father figure still fresh in everyone's mind. Created by *Family* producer Carol Evan McKeand, this short-run series never had a chance to really go anywhere.

**FANTASTIC JOURNEY** (*) **60 min (10ep Color; 1977 NBC) Science Fiction** *with Jared Martin as Varian, Roddy McDowall as Dr. Johnathan Willaway, Carl Franklin as Dr. Fred Walters, Ike Eisenmann as Scott Jordan, and Katie Saylor as Liana*

TV just doesn't tend to do science fiction very well, and *Fantastic Journey* does nothing to rectify this situation. The plot somehow ties in the Bermuda Triangle, aliens, and a time/space warp. Through some mumbo-jumbo, five beings from various times and places team up to try and find their way home, or at least an explanation of how they came to be brought together. Varian is from the twenty-third century, Dr. Walters is from our present, Dr. Willaway is a refuge from the swinging sixties who dabbles in robotics, Scott is a young telepath, and Liana is a mysterious lady from Atlantis or the Crab Nebulae or Toledo, or neither, or all of the above. Nothing is ever resolved during the series.

**FANTASY ISLAND (*) 60 min (152ep & two 2 hr pilots Color, also available as 260ep at 30 min; 1978–1984 ABC) Drama Anthology** *with Ricardo Montalban as Mr. Roarke and Herve Villechaize as Tattoo*

Everyone has a personal fantasy and for a mere $10,000 Mr. Roarke can make it come true. Sort of, as long as you fly to his private island resort and don't wish for anything too tough (like leading a Chicago or Boston baseball team to a World Series championship). Of course, you may discover unexpected consequences, but isn't that why you wondered in the first place? "What would happen if . . ."

Actually one obvious question is: How does Roarke stage all those elaborate fantasy scenarios, maintain the island, and keep his white suits and Cordoba clean for such a small fee? The answer is: It's magic. In fact, toward the end of the series, that aspect is played up more and more with Roarke even taking on the devil. It's too bad they never went all the way and turned this entire setup into an adventure series focusing on Ricardo Montalban's Roarke and Herve Villechaize's Tattoo. By far, they are the most intriguing performers and characters in the series. Even their brief conversations sizing up the people disembarking from the plane are far more interesting than the stories that follow.

The problem with the guest star fantasies is that ultimately they're a cheat. While the people involved may learn some lesson about themselves, it's all part of a staged, self-contained island universe. These stories might as well be just hypnotic dreams induced by Roarke on arrival. Come to think of it, maybe that's exactly what they are. Maybe Roarke is just a benign Freddy Krueger, tapping the inner psyche of each visitor . . . and of each viewer. Just to be safe, it might be wise to use Tattoo's cry of "The Plane! The Plane!" as warning to seek refuge in some safer programming, like a heavy-metal music video or a rerun of *Poltergeist III*. ■

**THE FAR PAVILIONS (**½) (6hr miniseries Color; 1984 HBO) Drama** *with Ben Cross as Ashton Pelham-Martyn, Amy Irving as Princess Anjuli, Christopher Lee as Kaka-Ji Rao, Omar Sharif as Koda Dad, and John Gielgud as Cavagnari*

The sun hasn't even begun to think about setting on the British Empire during the era covered by this star-studded miniseries. Set in British-ruled India in the late 1800s, *The Far Pavilions* has lots of battles, political intrigue and, more than anything, a forbidden love story between Indian-born-and-bred British officer Ashton Pelham-Martyn and his former childhood playmate Hindu Princess Anjuli. Amy Irving (*The Competition, Yentl, Crossing Delancey*) plays the Hindu Princess as a slightly tanned Jewish–American princess. ■

**FARADAY AND COMPANY (**) 90 min (6ep Color; 1973–1974 NBC) Detective Drama** *with Dan Dailey as Frank Faraday, James Naughton as Steve Faraday, Sharon Gless as Holly Barrett, and Geraldine Brooks as Louise "Lou" Carson*

*Faraday and Company* is a pleasant jaunt of a show, one that doesn't aim high, and it manages to fulfill most of its modest goals. Frank Faraday is a private eye who was framed twenty-five years ago for the death of his partner and spent the next quarter century twiddling his thumbs in some stinking South American jail. Now released and returned to his home, Los Angeles, Faraday finds out his old secretary/girlfriend Lou gave birth to his son, Steve, soon after Frank went incommunicado. Steve, it conveniently turns out, now is also a gumshoe, so the old man and the recently found chip-off-the-block team up. Pops is all Philip Marlowe-ish, with tough talk and fast fists. Sonny boy is seventies cute and more of a high-tech whiz than a bruiser.

Dan Dailey, a charmer from the old Hollywood days of movie musicals, is still an old smoothie. Sharon Gless, the actress who came to fame playing Chris Cagney in *Cagney & Lacey*, makes her TV series debut as the Faraday's current secretary. Leonard Stern, of *Get Smart* and *McMillan and Wife* fame, provides the amiable production.

**THE FARMER'S DAUGHTER (**½) 30 min (102ep: 74 B&W & 28 Color; 1963–1966 ABC) Situation Comedy** *with Inger Stevens as Katrin "Katy" Holstrum, William Windom as Congressman Glen Morley, Cathleen Nesbitt as Agatha Morley, Mickey Sholdar as Steve Morley, and Rory O'Brien as Danny Morley*

Katy Holstrum is a pretty, young, naive, blond woman from the farms of Minnesota, but of recent Swedish extraction. She comes to Washington, D.C. in hopes of obtaining her congressman's assistance in securing a government job teaching underprivileged children in the Congo (this woman is *truly* wholesome). Instead, the widowed congressman winds up talking Katy into living in his home as governess to his two boys, Danny (age eight) and Steve (age fourteen). Before the series ends, the congressman and Katy are married. Apparently the underprivileged children of the Congo will have to get along on their own.

Looking at *The Farmer's Daughter* with modern eyes, you have to wonder whether Congressman Morley could have found Katy a position of somewhat more responsibility than as live-in nanny to his two kids. We all know about the types of jokes that the title "The Farmer's Daughter" came from, and Katy's beauty and unmarried status are not lost on the congressman when he invites her to live in his house.

Nonetheless, this show is from the early 1960s, not the looser, libidinous 1970s or 1980s, so the underlying theme of sex and sexual roles is buried deep, deep inside *The Farmer's Daughter.* There are no scandals about an aging widowed congressman living with a gorgeous naive country bumpkin, the kids do not make smart-aleck remarks about fixing up old Dad and Katy, and, for goodness sake, the Congressman *does* marry her near the end, so everybody comes out OK. Things must have been much simpler back then.

*The Farmer's Daughter* is based on a 1947 film of the same title, starring Joseph Cotten and Loretta Young (who won as Oscar for Best Actress for the role). A one-hour pilot for the TV series aired in early 1962, with a completely different cast and crew. Lee Remick played Katy and Peter Lawford played the congressman, while TV drama veterans Fred Coe and Fielder Cook served as producer and director, respectively.

**FAST TIMES (**) 30 min (7ep Color; 1986 CBS) Situation Comedy** *with Claudia Wells as Linda Barrett, Courtney Thorne-Smith as Stacy Hamilton, Dean Cameron as Jeff Spicoli, James Nardini as Brad Hamilton, Patrick Dempsey as Mike Damone, Vincent Schiavelli as Hector Vargas, and Ray Walston as Arnold Hand*

*Fast Times at Ridgemont High* was a fun-filled 1982 film about high schoolers in the early 1980s (which gave Sean Penn his first big role). *Fast Times* is a bland TV copy of the film. The concept is the same (a gang of semiwild, sex-obsessed kids going through all the usual traumas of puberty), but without any of the blunt honesty and frank sexuality of the film, what's the point? The only cast carryovers are Vincent Schiavelli as Mr. Vargas, the spaced-out science teacher, and the always sprightly Ray Waltson (*My Favorite Martian*) as the beleaguered history teacher, Mr. Hand.

**FATHER BROWN (**½) 60 min (26ep Color; 1974 UK ATV) Mystery** *with Kenneth More as Father Brown*

He has an unimposing look about him: the round face, clear eyes, and quiet demeanor of an innocent cleric. But behind surface appearances this is a parish priest with a difference. Father Brown is an expert sleuth who brings his finely honed abilities at judging human behavior to the task of doling out justice here on earth, searching out the truth behind rash assumptions, conjecture, and murder. Kenneth More is quite good in this adaptation of the popular G. K. Chesterton hero of the 1930s, tackling such cases as finding the killer of a teetotaling philanthropist, helping a young woman ward off a blackmailer, and helping a French chief of police deal with a decapitated corpse that turns up at his own garden party.

This series first aired in the United States on *Mystery!* in 1982, though the program used only four of the available twenty-six episodes. There has also been an American made-for-TV movie version of the character, transplanting him Stateside for a 1980 offering starring Bernard Hughes.

**FATHER DEAR FATHER (**½) 30 min (39ep Color; 1968–1973 UK Thames) Situation Comedy** *with Patrick Cargill as Patrick Clover, Natasha Pyne as Anna Glover, Ann Holloway as Karen Glover, Ursula Howells as Barbara Mossman, and Noel Dyson as Matilda Harris*

Well-staged screwball farce with Patrick Cargill (the Scotland Yard inspector in the Beatles' film *Help!*) at his no-nonsense straight-laced best. He plays a divorced mystery writer who seems to be living a comfortable, carefree life (driving a classic car and living in a spacious house), stepping out on his own . . . except for the task of trying to keep his two beautiful, very available, daughters in line. And dealing with his ex-wife, Barbara, who turns up at the most awkward times. Or managing his well-meaning but interfering housekeeper, "Nanny" Harris. Then there's his mother, brother, publisher . . .

More than a dozen of the thirty-nine episodes from the series are not included in the current U.S. syndication package.

**FATHER DOWLING MYSTERIES (**½) 60 min (8ep & 2 hr pilot at Summer 1989 Color; 1989– NBC) Mystery** *with Tom Bosley as Father Frank Dowling, Tracy Nelson as Sister "Steve" Stephanie, and Mary Wickes as Marie*

After years of playing straightman cop Amos Tupper to Jessica Fletcher on *Murder, She Wrote,* Tom Bosley at last gets the chance to be the one to explain the solution to the latest mystery. It's a well-deserved promotion, and a breezy character showcase from veteran producer Dean Hargrove (also responsible for the *Return of Perry Mason* and *Matlock* series), who gives Bosley the fun role of a soft-spoken but stubborn Catholic priest, Father Frank Dowling. (The character is originally from a series of books by Ralph McInerny.)

Dowling is in charge of one of those traditional Chicago Catholic parishes (St. Michaels) that seems plucked from the set of *Going My Way.* The church building is filled with dozens of statues, polished wooden benches, a high vaulted ceiling, and a huge organ that fills the space with music, while the rectory has a comfortable old dining room, wide wooden doors and staircases, and a faithful housekeeper (Marie) to keep things in order. It's a wonderfully nostalgic, yet surprisingly authentic, physical setting for this series, even reflecting more contemporary times with just a skeleton staff of priests and nuns. Essentially Father Dowling and his chief assistant, Sister Stephanie, are in charge of everything. And, in this case, that includes solving mysteries. When they do their parish work (including the most demanding daily mass schedule ever posted) is probably the only mystery they'll never adequately explain.

Even though the stories spend a tad too much time focusing on victims of murder, drugs, and prostitution, what makes the series work are the light pieces more concerned with cute moments for Dowling and Sister Stephanie than grim complications. And the pair responds, properly garbed (collar and habit), dutifully dashing into darkened warehouses, dodging bullets, and offering the local district police the same type of hunches and observations that used to drive Amos Tupper bananas. Tracy Nelson (daughter of *Ozzie and Harriet*'s Rick Nelson) is particularly amusing as Sister Stephanie, mixing proper deference to her superiors with natural curiosity and the ability to bend the rules to her investigating advantage. She's a street-kid-turned-nun, and knows every angle.

Though not quite up to the caliber of such British-produced cleric series as *Father Brown* (more emphasis on plot in those), *Father Dowling Mysteries* does offer a return to the days when Bing Crosby's Father O'Malley could walk from his parish into the secular world and do just about anything he tried.

**FATHER KNOWS BEST (***) 30 min (203ep B&W & two 90 min sequels; 1954–1960 CBS & NBC) Situation Comedy** *with Robert Young as Jim Anderson, Jane Wyatt as Margaret Anderson, Elinor Donahue as Betty "Princess" Anderson, Billy Gray as James "Bud" Anderson, Jr., and Lauren Chapin as Kathy "Kitten" Anderson*

The Andersons of *Father Knows Best* are middle-of-the-road middle Americans, right out of a civics lesson filmstrip. They live on South Maple Street in Springfield, somewhere in the Midwest. Jim is an insurance agent for the General Insurance Company (could any name be more bland?) and Margaret is a housewife, pure and simple. At the start of the show, Betty is seventeen, Bud is fourteen, and Kathy is nine. As the show moves on, Betty and Bud graduate from high school and enter State College, right there in Springfield, so they can continue living with their family.

The Andersons live in a lovely home, in a lovely neighborhood, and nothing really awful ever happens to them, and these are all reasons the famiily seems so odd today. We have come to expect the unexpected from sitcoms. Great issues, from racism to child molesting, must be played out in every sitcom worth its salt.

Usually the real problem with 1950s suburban sitcoms is not the relatively bland setting but the silly type of people who tend to show up and the blandness of many scripts. When a suburban family show is put together with care, like *Father Knows Best,* the result can be timeless.

What sets *Father Knows Best* above many of its contemporaries is the finely crafted characters. Neither parent is a raving lunatic (a real breakthrough) and, in spite of the embarrasingly chauvinistic title, Mother is just as perceptive and level-headed as Father. The children are fairly normal for 1950s suburbia. The kids got through all the trials and trip-ups of adolescence and their parents learn the hard lesson that much of life must be learned firsthand, since there is only so much a parent can do for a child.

The Andersons may be idealized, since they all *care* so much about each other and try so hard to be good. That behavior now seems odd just because caring and goodness are currently out of style, or at best, embarrassing to acknowledge. In the 1950s, viewers were overdosed on nice families. Since then, crackpot familes have been the norm. It is somewhat soothing to watch an old-fashioned family these days. This urge to get away from oddity, no doubt, was a big factor in the rise in popularity of *The Cosby Show* in the late 1980s, when warm family sitcoms made a reappearance.

Among the strong points of *Father Knows Best* are the three children. In spite of their surface trappings of frilly formality (a remnant of the pre-rock'n'roll image of teens), all three have moments when they each turn angry and self-centered. This refreshing wave of reality helps spice up the overly starched mood of their parents. Jim and Margaret Anderson are *very* kind and thoughtful parents: they rarely get more than slightly peeved. The emotions of their offspring keep *Father Knows Best* believable, even in this age of cynicism.

Two sequels serve as acceptable follow-ups to the Anderson family story, with both coming from 1977. *The Father Knows Best Reunion* is just that, a get-together for Jim and Margaret's thirty-fifth anniversary, while *Father Knows Best: Home for Christmas* is a traditionally syrupy holiday special, ending with a battle to keep the Anderson home in the family (Jim and Margaret wind up selling the family homestead to Bud and his wife, while the old folks take off in a Winnebago to see the U.S.A.).

*Father Knows Best* began on radio in 1949, and lasted for five years there, running right up until its TV debut. Robert Young was the only cast member to make the leap from audio to video.

**FATHER MURPHY (**) 60 min (55ep & 2 hr pilot Color; 1981–1982 NBC) Drama** *with Merlin Olsen as John Michael Murphy, Moses Gunn as Moses Gage, Katherine Cannon as Mae Woodward Murphy, and Timothy Gibbs as Will Adams*

From Michael Landon, master of *Little House on the*

*Prairie,* comes this equally wholesome tale of goodness on the frontier. Hulking ex-NFL star Merlin Olsen, a refuge from *Little House,* plays John Murphy, a large miner who disguises himself as a preacher in order to shelter an entire army of kids who were orphaned in a battle between the mine boss and his peons. "Father" Murphy is eventually unmasked and then marries sweet schoolmarm Mae. The newlyweds, of course, legally adopt all the wee ones.

Never fear when watching *Father Murphy*—the good guys always win and the bad guys can be spotted in fifteen seconds.

**FATHER OF THE BRIDE (*) 30 min (34ep B&W; 1961–1962 CBS) Situation Comedy** *with Leon Ames as Stanley Banks, Ruth Warrick as Ellie Banks, Myrna Fahey as Kay Banks Dunston, Rickie Sorensen as Tommy Banks, and Burt Metcalfe as Buckley Dunston*

Based on a great 1950 film starring Spencer Tracy and Elizabeth Taylor, *Father of the Bride* loses most of its pizazz in the transition to the small screen. Daddy Banks is still uneasy about his princess's plans to get married to Buckley Dunston. Mother Ellie is behind daughter Kay's wedding plans, and in mid-series the young couple do get hitched. The focus then shifts to postnuptials as Buckley and Kay set up house and the Bankses, now almost empty nesters (except for son Tommy), adjust to the change.

The lack of big name stars (compared to the movie version) and the simple, merely adequate scripts hurt this show badly. Actor Burt Metcalfe, the groom, later served as one of the producers of *M*A*S*H.*

**FATHER'S DAY (**½) 30 min (14ep Color; 1983 UK C4) Situation Comedy** *with John Alderton*

Based on a *Punch* column by British writer Hunter Davies detailing the trials and tribulations of raising a teenage daughter, this series casts John Alderton as the harried dad. Alderton raised his share of kids in the school comedy *Please, Sir,* while Davies made his international mark as author of the official biography of the Beatles in 1968.

**FATHERS AND SONS (**) 30 min (5ep Color; 1988 NBC) Situation Comedy** *with Merlin Olsen as Buddy Landau, Jason Late as Lanny Landau, Kelly Sanders as Ellen Landau, Andre Gower as Sean Flynn, and Ian Fried as Matt Bolen*

Former *Father Murphy* lead (and L.A. Rams football player) Merlin Olsen tries his hand at a sitcom, once again playing an understanding father figure (this time, Buddy Landau). He's a role model and advisor not only to his own son, Lanny, but to the other kids as well. This is all mildly amusing, but nothing more.

**FAVORITE SON (**½) (6hr miniseries Color; 1988 NBC) Drama** *with Harry Hamlin as Sen. Terrence "Terry" Fallon, Linda Kozlowski as Sally Crain, Robert Loggia as Nick Mancuso, James Whitmore as Pres. Sam Baker, Lance Guest as Ross, Mitchell Ryan as Vice-Pres. Dan Eastman, and Ronny Cox as William Rieker*

Political intrigue and steamy sex make an interesting combination in this miniseries set in Washington. Terry Fallon, a freshman Texas senator, is wounded in the assassination of a Nicaraguan contra leader. Fallon's impassioned remarks on live TV coverage of the shooting's aftermath create a groundswell to have him replace the sitting vice-president at the political conventions set to begin in nine days. Fallon's comely press aide (and secret lover), Sally Crain, angles to put her man in line for the nod from incumbent president Sam Baker. FBI agent Nick Mancuso, investigating the shooting, begins to turn up very suspicious clues that lead him to uncover a major conspiracy.

Harry Hamlin, Michael Kuzak from *L. A. Law,* really gets into his role as an ambitious hot-headed senator. Linda Kozlowski, from the *Crocodile Dundee* films, is alluring as his love interest. Robert Loggia, almost steals the show as the crude and cynical aging FBI man (his character even lands a Fall 1989 spin-off series, *Mancuso FBI*). Steve Sohmer wrote the original novel and served as executive producer of the series.

**FAWLTY TOWERS (****) 30 min (12ep Color; 1975, 1979 UK BBC) Situation Comedy** *with John Cleese as Basil Fawlty, Prunella Scales as Sybil Fawlty, Andrew Sachs as Manuel, Connie Booth as Polly Sherman, and Ballard Berkeley as Major Gowen*

As part of the *Monty Python* troupe, John Cleese developed a sketch comedy persona that excelled in biting sarcasm, explosions of anger, and broad physical schtick (most notably, a funny walk). He found a perfect home for these traits in the guise of innkeeper Basil Fawlty.

In *Fawlty Towers,* Cleese and writing partner (and wife at the time) Connie Booth (who plays housekeeper Polly) fashioned a very funny bedroom farce filled with character misunderstandings, closely timed entrances and exits, and some broad physical routines. They also set the stage for some marvelous verbal exchanges, usually between Basil Fawlty and just about anyone, especially the guests and staff at the inn.

Often the sources of Basil's frustrations are easy to spot. Though he and his wife Sybil are joint owners and operators of their guest house by the sea in Torquay, she seems to spend most of her time sitting and gossiping, either on the phone or with the guests. Their bellman, Manuel, barely speaks English (he's from Barcelona) and so constantly misunderstands orders. Even some of the guests are every innkeeper's nightmare: pushy, demanding, and obnoxious.

So Basil strikes back with his tongue, usually in a voice dripping with sarcasm. In confronting a demanding guest named Mrs. Richards (a woman too cheap to turn on her hearing aid because it would run down the batteries), he picks a speck from the floor and asks, "Excuse me, is this a piece of your brain?" And in an exasperated conversation with Manuel, he says condescendingly, "Please try to understand before one of us dies."

Sometimes, though, Basil's problems are his own fault, resulting from his deep conviction that he is a perfect judge of people and situations. In fact, he's prone to rash assumptions about both, compounded by a pigheaded determination to put on a good face and press on, no matter what. For instance, he easily mistakes conversations among people gathered for a family reunion as plans for illicit sex back in their rooms. Or when he hears that some hotel inspectors are in the area, he quickly attempts to curry favor with any guest he suspects might be one of them—inevitably guessing wrong on each attempt.

All of these situations are made even funnier by a running incongruity in the whole series. Despite all his posturing and bellowing at the guests and hired help, Basil is easily cowed by figures of authority such as health or hotel inspectors. Even more important, Basil is absolutely terrified of his wife. He may be taller and stronger and louder, but she clearly rules the roost. His only recourse is an insult or two (usually muttered under his breath) or seizing an everyday situation to prove that he's better at running the inn than she is.

This gives an added edge to the silliness, especially with situations in which all of Basil's posturing, misjudgments, and misdirected fawning converge. Not only does he have to deal with the consequences of his actions but he also has to face Sybil. They may not be the most unhappy couple in situation comedy history, but they give new meaning to the concept of marriage as a mutual "life sentence."

*Fawlty Towers* was originally presented in Britain in two short-run seasons four years apart. As a result, nearly every episode is a gem, with many standout moments such as Basil's agonized shriek in "The Hotel Inspectors," his crazed Nazi impression in "The Germans," and his nonchalant final encounter with Manuel's pet rodent (named Basil) in "Basil the Rat." ■

**FAY (**) 30 min (8ep Color; 1975 NBC) Situation Comedy** *with Lee Grant as Fay Stewart, Joe Silver as Jack Stewart, Audra Lindley as Lillian, Bill Gerber as Danny Cassidy, and Norman Alden as Al Messina*

One of writer Susan Harris's early comedy productions (before such hits as *Soap* and *The Golden Girls*), this series got caught in one of network television's bouts with moral posturing in its original run in 1975. Unfortunately, that made it pretty hard to carry through *Fay*'s premise of a good-looking divorcée in her forties pursuing the life of a swinging single. Still, the cast and writers do their best, with veterans Lee Grant and Joe Silver turning in strong performances as the sparring divorced couple. (He wants them to get back together; she can't take his philandering ways any longer.) Overall the series is rough compared to later Harris productions, but worth catching for some prototype conflicts. Ironically, one character type even turned up in a completely different kind of series: Andra Lindley's Lillian, an unhappily married friend of Fay's—within a few years, Lindley had a similar part, Helen Roper, in a prime-time series dripping with sexual innuendo, *Three's Company*.

**THE FEATHER AND FATHER GANG (**) 60 min (13ep & 90 min pilot Color; 1976–1977 ABC) Adventure** *with Stefanie Powers as Toni "Feather" Danton, Harold Gould as Harry Danton, Frank Delfino as Enzo, Monte Landis as Michael, Lewis Charles as Lou, Joan Shawlee as Margo, Edward Winter as J. C. Hadley, and Allen Williams as Binkwell*

Barely adequate television rendition of the con-game hook used so successfully at the time in the 1973 theatrical film hit, *The Sting*. Appropriately, Harold Gould, one of the chief operators in that movie, takes a similar role for the series. He plays a somewhat reformed con man dedicated to helping his attorney daughter, Toni, on her cases with a few well-staged *Sting*-like operations. Old mates Enzo, Michael, Lou, and Margo help father out, while Toni (Feather) has to deal with her partners and J. C. Hadley from the D. A.'s office. Stefanie Powers went from here to considerably greater success with *Hart to Hart*. Oddly, her future *Hart* mate, Robert Wagner, also had a run in a con-game series, *Switch*, but that series was far more effective than hers.

**FELONY SQUAD (**½) 30 min (73ep Color; 1966–1969 ABC) Police Drama** *with Howard Duff as Sgt. Sam Stone, Dennis Cole as Det. Jim Briggs, Ben Alexander as Sgt. Dan Briggs, Barney Phillips as Capt. Ed Franks, and Frank Maxwell as Capt. Nye*

A wonderful time piece, *Felony Squad* is one of the last of the old-fashioned cop shows, before the era of reactionary goons (*S.W.A.T., Emergency!*), selfcentered antiestablishment loners (*Kojak, Baretta*), and smart-talking pretty boys (*Starsky and Hutch*). The cops in *Felony Squad* get their man the old-fashioned way: They go at it, man to man, in a knock-down, drag-out battle of wits, fists, and ammo. The only foreshadowing of times to come is young and handsome Jim Briggs, who looks a lot nicer than the other mugs in the station house.

Ben Alexander is perfect to play Jim Briggs' dad, desk sergeant Dan Briggs, the cops' "den mother," since Alexander put in his time as Joe Friday's main partner, Frank Smith, in the 1950s version of *Dragnet*.

One thing *Felony Squad* lacks is any trace of humor. Its deadpan serious tone is an obvious target for satire on the entire police show format. For laughs try watching an episode of *Felony Squad* and then immediately watch an episode of the very effective police parody *Police Squad!* It will be difficult to tell them apart at times.

**FERNWOOD 2-NIGHT/AMERICA 2NIGHT (***½) 30 min (130ep Color: 65 Fernwood and 65 America; 1977–1978 Syndication) Talk Show Satire** *with Martin Mull as Barth Gimble, Fred Willard as Jerry Hubbard, and Frank DeVol as Happy Kyne*

*Fernwood 2-Night* constitutes the first serious attempt to poke fun at the TV talk show. Created by Norman Lear as a summer replacement for *Mary Hartman, Fernwood 2-Night* brings the same delightful sense of wicked satire to talk shows that *Mary Hartman* brings to soap operas. Set in the same small Ohio town of Fernwood as *Mary Hartman, Fernwood 2-Night* is hosted by Barth Gimble, twin brother of Garth Gimble, a character from *Mary Hartman* who died from impaling himself on an aluminum Christmas tree. Gimble considers himself the epitome of sophistication, but his true nature is given away by his used-car-salesman wardrobe. Sidekick Jerry Hubbard is the classic midwestern good ol' boy, who knows little of the world beyond the county line and shows off his ignorance every time he tries to ask a serious question.

Much of the fun of this show comes from the outrageous guests that turn up every night. Fernwood's high school principal appears once to demonstrate the proper method of spanking a troublesome student. The student used for the demonstration, however, turns out to be a nicely developed sixteen-year-old coed. A set of local parents complains one night that their son has been taken in by some crazed religious cult that insists on its adherents wearing dark robes and speaking in foreign tongues. The strange cult is the Roman Catholic church, which is foreign enough in all-WASP Fernwood. On the opening show, a Jew from Toledo whose car broke down in Fernwood is brought on for the education of local residents who probably never had seen a Jew before. Occasionally, an out-of-town celebrity or two shows up, such as gravelly voiced singer Tom Waits, who declares "I would rather have a bottle in front of me than a frontal lobotomy."

After their summer stint, Barth and Jerry reappear as hosts of *America 2Night,* on the "United Broadcasting System" (which boasts of putting the "U" before the "BS"), from Alta Coma, California, the unfinished furniture capital of the world. The move to the west coast helps liven up the show, as more famous celebrities from nearby Hollywood can drop in. Charlton Heston, Robin Williams, Elke Sommer, and others come by to put up with uncouth questioning from Barth and Jerry.

Two of the secondary figures on this show deserve credit. Frank DeVol, as Happy Kyne, the mirthless bandleader of the off-key Mirth Makers, had dabbled in sitcoms before, in *Camp Runamuck* and *I'm Dickens . . . He's Fenster* in the 1960s. DeVol's real claim to fame was as a writer of theme songs for TV shows, such as *Family Affair* and *My Three Sons.* Alan Thicke, a very talented Canadian who produced both the Fernwood and California versions of the series, later tried to bring some of the zaniness of *Fernwood 2-Night* to mainstream America as host of his own "real" late-night talk show, *Thicke of the Night,* which bombed. Thicke wound up starring in an amusing sitcom, *Growing Pains.* Meanwhile, stars Martin Mull and Fred Willard went on to team up for an appropriately offbeat group of comedy specials, Mull's cable production of *The History of White People in America.*

*Fernwood 2-Night* is probably too weird for many viewers. Its relentlessly satirical tone, however, helped pave the way for more middle-of-the-road comedians such as David Letterman, who succeeded in hosting a late-night talk show that mostly spoofs the established trends of the talk show format.

**FIBBER MCGEE AND MOLLY (**) 30 min (26ep B&W; 1959–1960 NBC) Situation Comedy** *with Bob Sweeney as Fibber McGee, Cathy Lewis as Molly McGee, and Harold Peary as Mayor Charles La Trivia*

*Fibber McGee and Molly*? Isn't that a radio show? Yes, it is, but it's a television show, as well. For the old-timers who actually remember listening to the long-running (1935–1957) radio show, this TV version will be a big disappointment.

The original radio version starred Jim Jordan and his real-life wife Marian as the McGees, a homey couple who lived at 79 Wistful Vista. Fibber was, by nature, a spinner of tall tales, hence his name. Molly was the level-headed one who always took care of the practical problems caused by Fibber's absentmindedness. The chief running gag of the show was Fibber's perpetually overstuffed hall closet, which Molly always vainly admonished him never to open. Fibber never listened and the elongated clunks, crashes, and crunches heard when the closet was opened always brought a laugh from the radio audience.

Well, that was radio. The television version of *Fibber McGee and Molly* has little to offer. The lead actors (Bob Sweeney and Cathy Lewis) are different and they show little sparkle as a couple. The sprightly repartee of the radio version betwen the real-life spouses is sorely lacking on TV. Sweeney and Lewis do not seem at all like man and wife, but rather just two actors, putting in a day's work.

Then there is the fabled hall closet. Seeing a real stuffed closet takes away all the fun. No real closet on TV could ever match the mythical closet of radio, for the radio one could keep disgorging junk far longer, and at odder intervals.

The only real plus of the TV version is the appearance of Hal Peary, who originated the bombastic character of Throckmorton P. Gildersleeve on the radio version of the show. After starring in his own radio series (*The Great Gildersleeve*), Peary returned to his roots in the TV *Fibber McGee and Molly,* in the thinly disguised Gildersleeve-ish character of Mayor La Trivia.

**THE FILES OF JEFFREY JONES** (*½) **30 min (39ep B&W; 1954–1955 Syndicated) Crime Drama** *with Don Haggerty as Jeffrey Jones and Gloria Henry as Michele "Mike" Malone*

Low-budget detective adventures set in New York City, with Don Haggerty as a G. I. turned P. I. and Gloria Henry as his newspaper reporter girlfriend. Just a few years after this show, Henry turned up in much more pleasant surroundings as Mrs. Mitchell on *Dennis the Menace.*

**FILTHY RICH** (*) **30 min (15ep Color; 1982–1983 CBS) Situation Comedy** *with Slim Pickens and Forrest Tucker as "Big Guy" Beck, Delta Burke as Kathleen Beck, Dixie Carter as Carlotta Beck, Charles Frank as Stanley Beck, Jerry Hardin as "Wild" Bill Weschester, Michael Lombard as Marshall Beck, and Ann Wedgeworth as Bootsie Weschester.*

There is something inherently funny about the rich falling all over themselves while grabbing for more dough, but *Filthy Rich* overdoes that concept. The setup is great, with Tennessee land baron Big Guy Beck dropping dead, yet still running his family's lives by means of his video-taped "living" will. The will (more of which keeps popping up in various episodes) requires snobby son Marshall and wife Carlotta to share the Beck mansion (Toad Hall) with the unsophisticated Bill (Big Guy's illegitimate son) and Bill's bimbo wife Bootsie. Meanwhile, young and sexy Kathleen, Big Guy's final wife, is on the prowl for a new sugar daddy.

*Filthy Rich,* however, squanders all the humor inherent in its concept. The characters are caricatures with few shreds of reality and the scripts are silly. Producer Linda Bloodworth-Thomason and co-stars Delta Burke (who plays young Kathleen) and Dixie Carter (who plays wife Carlotta) all graduated to *Designing Women,* a far funnier series.

**FINDER OF LOST LOVES** (**) **60 min (23ep Color; 1984–1985 ABC) Detective Drama** *with Tony Franciosa as Cary Maxwell, Deborah Adair as Daisy Lloyd, Anne Jeffreys as Rita Hargrove, and Richard Kantor as Brian Fletcher*

*Finder of Lost Loves* is a detective series in name only. Aging lothario Tony Franciosa plays Cary Maxwell, a wealthy widower who still bemoans the death of his wife. In order to spare others the pain he suffered, Cary hires himself out as a detective for those poor souls who are searching for former loves whose whereabouts are unknown. From this bare-bones plot, the real structure of the show emerges, that is, a *Love Boat*-ish collection of two or three vignettes of love, with Cary as Cupid. The *Love Boat* analogy is apt, since *Finder of Lost Loves* is another schmaltzy series from Aaron Spelling and Douglas Cramer, the duo responsible for that aquatic-based program. One point of note here is that Anne Jeffreys, the lovely Marion Kirby in *Topper,* play Cary's office manager with her usual aplomb.

**A FINE ROMANCE** (**½) **60 min (8ep Color; 1989 ABC) Comedy/Drama** *with Christopher Cazenove as Michael Trent, Margaret Whitton as Louisa Phillips, Ernie Sabella as George Shipman, Kevin Moore as Miles, and Dinah Lenney as Friday*

American Louisa Phillips and Briton Michael Trent used to be married. They also used to be the co-hosts of a TV travel show called *Ticket to Ride* (do The Beatles know about this?). Now they are divorced, and he has left the series, with plans to remarry. Louisa can't stand his replacement as co-host, and isn't wild about the idea of Michael's upcoming nuptials, either. Through some of Louisa's brash shenanigans, the new wedding ceremony never occurs and she and Michael are reunited, as co-hosts but not as a couple. Together (somewhat) the bickering pair bounce around Europe, accompanied by their production unit, always in search of some picturesque scenery for their show. One way or another, they also always find a murder or a mystery that needs solving. The dialogue is brisk and witty, and meant to remind you of *The Thin Man* and *Remington Steele.* The adventures the couple become involved in are somewhat far-fetched. The European scenery is nice, though.

Christopher Cazenove, who plays Michael, previously appeared in *Dynasty* as Ben Carrington. In the original (never-aired) pilot episode, the role of Michael was played by Anthony Andrews.

**FIREHOUSE** (*) **30 min (13ep Color; 1974 ABC) Adventure** *with James Drury as Capt. Spike Ryerson, Richard Jaeckel as Hank Myers, Michael Delano as Sonny Caputo, and Bill Overton as Cal Dakin*

*Firehouse* is one of the more forgettable crime-fighting series of the 1970s, and a rare example of a program produced by Aaron Spelling and Leonard Goldberg that was neither a popular favorite nor an outrageous effort at hyping a flashy concept. *Firehouse* is much more in the Jack Webb (*Emergency!*) vein of laconic heroes battling evil with quiet grace. The firehouse crew of Engine Company 23 of the Los Angeles Fire Department, led by grizzled veteran Spike Ryerson, dash around, putting out fires and saving simple citizens.

**FIRESIDE THEATRE** (*½) **30 min (100ep B&W; 1950–1954 NBC) Drama Anthology**

One of television's first filmed drama series, this originally ran for nearly the entire decade of the 1950s, eventually (in 1955) adopting the name of its most popular program host, Jane Wyman (see *The Jane*

*Wyman Show*). This was not one of the front-line prestige programs of the time. The stories are workmanlike but nothing special, with casts including a good number of later-famous television performers (ranging from Gene Barry to Ernest Borgnine to Amanda Blake), but few superstars. Though this series played in endless syndicated reruns during the 1950s and into the early 1960s, its lack of fondly remembered continuing characters means that it rarely turns up today.

The current syndication package offers only about 100 of the more than 300 episodes produced. Sometimes episodes turn up under the syndicated rerun title *Return Engagement.* ■

**1ST & TEN (**½) 30 min (49ep at Summer 1989 Color; 1985– HBO) Situation Comedy** *with Delta Burke as Diane Barrow, Leah Ayres Hendrix as Jill Schrader, Reid Shelton as Ernie Denardo, Stan Kamber as Coach Grier, Prince Hughes as Bubba Kincaid, Cliff Frazier as Jethro Snell, and O. J. Simpson as T. D. Parker*

The trials and tribulations of owning (and playing on) a professional football team form the basis for this moderately effective sports comedy. It all starts when Diane Barrow (played by pre-*Designing Women* Delta Burke) gets control of the California Bulls (of the NAFL league) as part of her divorce settlement and decides to put her own stamp on running the organization. Initially, the players are less than thrilled, but they decide to cooperate on the chance that new blood might just lead to a championship. No surprise—eventually it does.

Along the way, there's also plenty of locker room highjinks, romantic intrigues, and turnover among the players (linemen Bubba and Jethro manage to hang on the longest). There's also quite a bit of turbulence in the front office, with the team president constantly fighting Diane for control. Eventually, she is tricked out of her position, though her replacement is also a woman, Jill Schrader. Later, the players unsuccessfully attempt to run the team themselves before a corporation buys the franchise and installs another woman (played by Shanna Reed) as front office director. In all but a few episodes, Coach Ernie Denardo (Reid Shelton) handles the team on the field. Former real-life NFL star O. J. Simpson also appears as a regular for several batches of episodes, playing front office general manager T. D. Parker.

After the first dozen episodes, the series has usually carried a subtitle after the *1st & Ten* title: *Training Camp: The Bulls Are Back* (6 episodes), *The Championship* (4 episodes), *Going for Broke* (14 episodes), and *The Bulls Mean Business* (13 episodes).

**THE FIRST CHURCHILLS (**) 60 min (12ep Color; 1969 UK BBC) Drama** *with Susan Hampshire as Sarah Churchill, John Neville as John Churchill, John Standing as Sidney Godolphin, James Billiers as Charles II, John Westbrook as York, Lisa Daniely as Princess Mary, Frederick Peisley as Shaftsbury, and Margaret Tyzack as Princess Anne*

The life and times of John and Sara Churchill, ancestors to Sir Winston in the 1600s. Husband John is a successful British general equally adept at battlefield strategy and political intrigue, while his wife, Sara, is lady-in-waiting to Princess (later Queen) Anne—and his most valuable ally. Together they weave their way through the arcane politics of the royal court, with John parlaying his successful military career under four monarchs (Charles II, James II, William of Orange, and Queen Anne) into being named the first Duke of Marlborough.

This was the premier offering on *Masterpiece Theatre* in 1971. It may well have been selected because of its connection to the popular *Forsyte Saga,* which enjoyed a very successful run on public television the previous year. Written, produced, and directed by *Forsyte* producer Donald Wilson, and featuring one the most popular cast members of that series, Susan Hampshire, *The First Churchills* is, nonetheless, only a limited success. The manipulations among similarly costumed characters from all over Europe are very hard to follow and the entire series could have been improved considerably with half as many episodes.

**FIRST IMPRESSIONS (**) 30 min (8ep Color; 1988 CBS) Situation Comedy** *with Brad Garrett as Frank Dutton, Sarah Abrell as Donna Patterson, Thom Sharp as Dave Poole, Brandy Gold as Lindsay Dutton, Ruth Kobart as Mrs. Madison, and James Noble as Raymond Voss*

As a welcome change of pace, this comedy is set in Omaha, Nebraska. Unfortunately, it must still be impossible for the Hollywood set to conceive of life in any environment outside the usual California or New York settings, so one of the running gags is, of course, that anybody with any sense wants to leave town. In fact, that's part of the basic premise: Advertising writer Frank Dutton faces life as a single parent after the departure of his wife Barbara, who left town for the coast "to find herself." (Sigh.) Will they ever learn?

In any case, Frank takes care of their young daughter, Lindsay (played by Brandy Gold, younger sister to Missy Gold from *Benson* and Tracey Gold from *Growing Pains*), with some nanny-ish help from Mrs. Madison, his next-door neighbor. At the office ("Media of Omaha"), he trades lines with the rest of the small agency's crew: Dave, an old school chum; Donna, the overprotected daughter of a local evangelist; and the sincere but laid-back Raymond (a character similar to James Noble's role as the governor on *Benson*). Frank also does his share of odd impressions (thus the series title), including interpretations of such stars as Jack Nicholson and Christopher Lloyd (no surprise there because that's just the type of thing Brad Garrett does in real life as part of his stand-up comedy act). Unfortunately, in its short run, there's very little chemistry among the characters, so none of this show leaves much of an impression. Well, you might notice Harry Nilsson's vocals on the opening song.

**FISH** (*½) **30 min (35ep Color; 1977–1978 ABC) Situation Comedy** *with Abe Vigoda as Phil Fish, Florence Stanley as Bernice Fish, Lenny Bari as Mike, Denise Miller as Jilly, Todd Bridges as Loomis, and Barry Gordon as Charlie Harrison*

Mix *Barney Miller* and *Welcome Back, Kotter* and what do you have? Whatever it is, it's not *Fish,* which, in its efforts to steal concepts from both these hit shows, winds up neither fish nor fowl, but just something smelly.

Detective Phil Fish, the aging towering behemoth from *Barney Miller,* is spun off here into his own show where he and long-suffering wife Bernice suffer a lapse of sanity and decide to become foster parents for five wild and unruly street kids. Oh, it's quite noble of the Fishes, but the wild urchins quickly grate on the nerves (of viewers and Fishes alike) and one can only wonder whether Phil and Bernice deserved a more peaceful life in their autumn years.

**FITZ & BONES** (**) **60 min (4ep & 2 hr pilot Color; 1981 NBC) Crime Drama** *with Tom Smothers as Bones Howard, Dick Smothers as Ryan Fitzpatrick, Diana Muldaur as Terri Seymour, Mike Kelin as Robert Whitmore, and Roger C. Carmel as Lawrence Brody*

This is the only TV series in which the two Smothers brothers, Dick, the dark-haired straight man, and Tom, the seemingly silly funny one, do *not* play brothers. They do, however, play partners, in that Dick is Ryan Fitzpatrick, a crusading telejournalist in San Francisco and Tom is his somewhat klutzy cameraman. Together they roam the city by the bay, ferreting out scoops and engaging in light banter, while fending off the competition (Lawrence Brody, played by rotund Roger C. Carmel).

It took guts to cast the Smothers Brothers in a basically straight dramtic role, but the world does not need another crusading TV reporter, and this show goes essentially nowhere.

The pilot is known as *Terror at Alcatraz.*

**THE FITZPATRICKS** (**) **60 min (13ep Color; 1977–1978 CBS) Drama** *with Bert Kramer as Mike Fitzpatrick, Mariclare Costello as Maggie Fitzpatrick, Clark Brandon as Sean Fitzpatrick, James Vincent McNichol as Jack Fitzpatrick, Michele Tobin as Maureen "Mo" Fitzpatrick, and Sean Marshall as Max Fitzpatrick*

An Irish *Waltons, The Fitzpatricks* is set in Flint, Michigan, near the steel mills. The good and gracious Fitzpatrick family struggles through some fearsome bad times, but comes out okay, while learning some valuable lessons about life. All in all, not a bad way to spend an hour, once you get to know the players.

**FIVE FINGERS** (***) **60 min (16ep B&W; 1959–1960 NBC) Spy Drama** *with David Hedison as Victor Sebastian, Luciana Paluzzi as Simone Genet, and Paul Burke as Robertson*

Until the success of the James Bond movies in the early 1960s, most TV spy series were heavy-handed morality plays, with tough stolid leads. *Five Fingers* predates the James Bond films, but it has a lot of the same cool yet witty flavor that Bond brought to the screen and Napoleon Solo brought to TV (in *The Man from U.N.C.L.E.*). This show is definitely worth searching for.

Victor Sebastian is a double agent, who leads three lives. He spies for the United States in Cold War Europe by fronting as a Communist operative, in order to dig up info on the Reds. His third "life" is his cover, as a theatrical agent who books musicians throughout Europe. This job allows Sebastian to travel to all the hot spots of the 1950s and get involved in exciting action. Sebastian's only contact with home is Robertson, a more traditional American agent.

Sebastian usually travels Europe with his love interest, Simone Genet, a fashion model who yearns to be a singer. She figures Sebastian's show biz connections can be of help, but, here's the catch, she doesn't know Sebastian is a spy. Keeping Simone in the dark takes a lot of fancy footwork by the ever-alert Sebastian.

Aside from the snappy plots, *Five Fingers* has other pluses, such as production from Martin Manulis (a great talent in both serious drama, *Playhouse 90,* and popular comedy, *Dobie Gillis*), and lead acting from David Hedison, who later had more success as Lee Crane in *Voyage to the Bottom of the Sea.* Also, don't overlook Paul Burke (*Naked City, 12 O'Clock High*) and the sexy Luciana Paluzzi, a leading lady in European films best known in the United States for her role as Fiona in the James Bond film *Thunderball* (but more often seen in the States in dogs such as *The Green Slime*).

*Five Fingers* is loosely based on a nice 1952 film starring James Mason that is set during World War II.

**FLAMBARDS** (***) **60 min (12ep Color; 1979 UK Yorkshire) Drama** *with Christine McKenna as Christina Parsons, Edward Judd as Uncle Russell, Steven Grives as Mark Russell, Alan Parnaby as William Russell, and Sebastian Abineri as Dick*

A trilogy of books by K. M. Pyton is the basis for this tale of an oppressed young woman in World War I-era England. Christina, a teenaged orphan girl, is farmed out to her despotic uncle in the countryside. Amidst the decaying splendor of the estate (called Flambards), Christina grows up under her uncle's extremely harsh rule. Heir to the Flambards fortune is the equally sadistic Mark, who aims to make Christina his wife. Mark's sensitive younger brother William is more in tune with Christina's personality, but his interest in the new science of airplanes takes him away. The war changes everything, and Christina has many travails to go through before the show ends.

The best thing about *Flambards* is that, unlike many of the English society dramas that British TV churned out in the 1970s (many of which wound up on *Masterpiece Theater*), the people in *Flambards* seem real and the concerns are more modern in scope. The theme song is cute, too.

**THE FLAME TREES OF THIKA (***) 60 min (7ep Color; 1981 UK Thames) Drama** *with Hayley Mills as Tillie Grant, Holly Aird as Elspeth Grant (Huxley), David Robb as Robin Grant, John Nettleton as Major Breeches, Morgan Sheppard as Mr. Roos, Carol Macready as Mrs. Nimmo, and Ben Cross as Ian Crawfurd.*

Based on Elspeth Huxley's memoirs (*The Flame Trees of Thika* and *The Mottled Lizard,* with the author also consulting on the production), this series describes her childhood growing up on a coffee plantation in a desolate section of Kenya, Africa. The program follows Elspeth and her family beginning a new life in 1913 as they relocate into yet another piece of Britain's far-flung pre–World War I empire. As such, it offers a glimpse of how the British acted while ruling portions of Africa (analogous to the picture of British Indian rule in *The Jewel in the Crown*). The main difference, though, is that this picture is a reflection of a child's-eye view of the world, which brings an innocent, homey, personal feel to the stories. So besides inevitable major historical events in the background, there are also such vivid memories as the trees (from the title) along the plantation driveway, a traumatic first experience with some cruel school kids in Nairobi, and—most of all—a sense of the vast space surrounding the Grant family home. Elspeth truly grew up in isolation. The story ends at the outbreak of World War I, with the family and their friends leaving Kenya and scattering.

A very popular family series, with particularly strong performances by Holly Aird as young Elspeth Grant (Huxley) and Hayley Mills as her mom. (Appropriately, Mills and series co-producer John Hawkesworth had first worked together when she was a budding child performer and he gave her a starring role in the 1958 film *Tiger Bay.*) There is a sequel to *The Flame Trees of Thika,* but only in book form, *Out in the Midday Sun: My Kenya,* published in 1987.

**FLAMINGO ROAD (**½) 60 min (37ep Color; 1981–1982 Color) Drama** *with Howard Duff as Sheriff Titus Semple, Cristina Raines as Lane Ballou, John Beck as Sam Curtis, Kevin McCarthy as Claude Weldon, Morgan Fairchild as Constance Weldon, Stella Stevens as Lute Mae, Mark Harmon as Fielding Carlyle, Woody Brown as Skip Semple, Barbara Rush as Eudora Weldon, Peter Donat as Elmo Tyson, and David Selby as Michael Tyron*

Turned out by the same company responsible for *Dallas,* this series draws its initial soapy setup from a 1949 theatrical film (starring Joan Crawford and Sidney Greenstreet) and a steamy 1942 novel (by Robert and Sally Wilder). Though there are plenty of trappings of wealth (as on *Dallas* or *Dynasty*), this series is not just another round of internecine battles among self-indulgent rich folks; it's a deliciously sleazy series of conflicts between the haves and have-nots of a small Florida town (Truro). The ultimate "have" is Sheriff Titus Semple (Sidney Greenstreet's role in the 1949 film), who may not be the wealthiest or classiest person in town but is the most influential. He keeps a treasure trove of dirt on everybody, and doesn't hesitate to use it for any political, social, or personal scheme.

For cold hard cash, there's the Weldon family, living on a luxurious Flamingo Road estate. Thanks to the sheriff, the two are intimately intertwined, with Semple's political protégé, Fielding Carlyle, married to Constance, the adopted daughter of Claude and Eudora Weldon. But Fielding is still in love with local singer Lane Ballou (Joan Crawford's role in the 1949 film), who works at the nightspot/bordello of Lute Mae Sanders. Besides, Constance is spoiled and self-centered, and maybe it's about time someone stood up to Semple. So . . .

This is a relatively short-run series (barely lasting two seasons in its original airing), with the performers playing their characters like the penny-ante kingmakers and small-time hustlers that they really are. As a result, *Flamingo Road* comes off as entertaining pulp trash, even sliding into good old-fashioned deep South voodoo in its last batch of episodes. Those are the ones featuring the ruthless Michael Tyrone, who comes to town bent on avenging the death of his father, a man wrongly convicted and executed for murder. His schemes push things into borderline camp, with a final episode twist best left dangling without any attempt at an explanation.

Most of the *Flamingo Road* lead cast members have a long history with other series and feature films. Some of their subsequent ventures include David Selby as Richard Channing on *Falcon Crest,* Morgan Fairchild on *Paper Dolls* (as Racine) and *Falcon Crest* (as Jordan Roberts), and Mark Harmon as Dr. Robert Caldwell on *St. Elsewhere.*

**FLASH GORDON (*½) 30 min (39ep B&W; 1953 Syndication) Science Fiction** *with Steve Holland as Flash Gordon, Irene Champlin as Dale Arden, and Joseph Nash as Dr. Alexis Zarkov*

When *Star Wars* first hit the theaters in 1977, it seemed instantly, thrillingly familiar and accessible to several generations of baby boomers. If you want to see why, just catch the three original Flash Gordon theatrical serials: *Flash Gordon* (1936), *Flash Gordon's Trip to Mars* (1938), and *Flash Gordon Conquers the Universe* (1940).

In the days before television, the adventures of Flash

Gordon played as a newspaper adventure strip, which was then adapted into the three multiepisode cliffhanger "shorts," though in many cases movie house patrons were there first and foremost to see the *Flash Gordon* adventure, not the "main" feature.

Millions more thrilled to those epics on television, slotted as weekly half-hour adventures, especially in the 1950s. They usually turned up on Saturday or Sunday mornings, but occasionally landed a prime-time berth as well. The serials left a lasting impression whenever they played, establishing Larry "Buster" Crabbe's Flash Gordon, Charles Middleton's Ming the Merciless, and Jean Rogers's Dale Arden as (respectively) the definitive heroic figure, hissable villain, and maiden in distress.

Of the three tales, *Flash Gordon's Trip to Mars* probably wears the best, with special effects (such as a bridge of light) advanced just enough to be acceptable and a plot that centers around two villains, Ming the Merciless and Azura, Queen of Magic (Beatrice Roberts).

However, the original *Flash Gordon* series is still essential viewing, with a mysterious, at times even erotic, aura all its own. Though the plot is ostensibly about saving Earth, in fact that's just an excuse for Flash, Zarkov, and Dale to visit the different civilizations of Mongo (shark men, lion men, hawk men) in search of allies. Naturally, every male rules on Mongo lusts after Dale (she's a sultry blond in this one) while Ming's daughter Aura (Priscilla Lawson) pursues Flash. Of course, Flash loves only Dale. She, in turn, ardently declares, "I'd do *anything* for Flash."

It's all wonderful viewing and a reminder that the television adventure series has roots stretching back into the golden days of Hollywood. No doubt George Lucas and Steven Spielberg soaked up quite a bit of this in their own living rooms as kids.

Naturally, such a rich history was also ripe for further exploitation with all-new tales made specifically for television. Unfortunately, the 1953 German-produced *Flash Gordon* series (with Steve Holland in the title role) looks tacky and cheap—and doesn't even have Ming. To the production company's credit, though, the action is updated to the future, just like the setting adopted by the *Flash Gordon* newspaper strip at the time.

Much better is the 1979 animated series for NBC's Saturday morning cartoon line-up. This plays much closer in style to the original cliffhanger serials.

Also in 1979, Buster Crabbe made one more appearance in a television space epic, doing a cameo in the two-hour premiere episode ("Planet of the Slave Girls") of a new television series version of *Buck Rogers in the 25th Century.* Appropriately, back in the 1930s, Crabbe had played Buck Rogers as well as Flash. ■

**FLATBUSH** **(½) 30 min (5ep Color; 1979 CBS) Situation Comedy** *with Joseph Cali as Presto Prestopopolos, Adrian Zmed as Socks Palermo, Vincent Bufano as Turtle Romero, Randy Stumpf as Joey Dee, and Sandy Helberg as Figgy Figueroa*

You can't fault this series for not being ethnic enough (just check out the names of the characters), but you can't credit it with being funny either.

*Flatbush* is about five guys from an Italian neighborhood in the Flatbush section of Brooklyn who recently graduated from high school and are now working at various jobs. The fellows also belong to a loosely knit social club, the Flatbush Fungos. They become involved in numerous lighthearted escapades, but it is doubtful that many viewers will watch this show long enough to care what happens.

**FLICKERS** **(**½) 60 min (6ep Color; 1981 UK ITC) Comedy** *with Bob Hoskins as Arnie Cole, Frances de la Tour as Maude, Fraser Cains as Llewellyn, Sherrie Hewson as Letty, Dickie Arnold as Corky Brown, Sheri Shepstone as Violet, and Wilfred Grove as Sad Galloway*

A roguish but lovable cockney con man, Arnie Cole, is out to make a killing in the fledgling British film industry of the early twentieth century by producing scores of ten-minute flicks. Only one thing stands between him and his dreams of being a mini-mogul: lack of operating cash. But then he meets the razor-tongued Maude, a wealthy woman with ready cash . . . and a problem. She's pregnant and needs a husband and a father, both to save her reputation and to help raise her child. Arnie can't resist her plea and purse, so they're soon off on a marriage of convenience that lends itself perfectly to comedy. For example, on their first day of married life, he's off making movie deals while she awaits his return, steaming. So when he returns . . .

A good vehicle for the versatile Bob Hoskins (lead in such theatrical features as *Mona Lisa, The Long Good Friday,* and *Who Framed Roger Rabbit?*), though with the one-hour running time it's more a period-piece drama done with a light touch rather than an intense comedy (like *Fawlty Towers*). Series writer Roy Clarke subsequently revisited England's early motion picture industry in another series, *Pictures.*

**THE FLINTSTONES** **(**) 30 min (166ep Color; 1960–1966 ABC) Animated Cartoon** *with the voices of Alan Reed as Fred Flintstone, Jean Vander Pyl as Wilma Flintstone, Mel Blanc as Barney Rubble, and Bea Benaderet and Jerry Johnson as Betty Rubble*

Now mostly thought of as just another TV cartoon show, *The Flintstones* began life as one of the pioneering prime-time efforts in TV animation by William Hanna and Joseph Barbera, the famed producers of *Tom and Jerry, Quick Draw McGraw, Huckleberry Hound,* and *Scooby-Doo.* The long-lasting popularity of *The Flintstones* demonstrates the show's appeal to young viewers. Older viewers may, however, find their attention wandering after they get over the nostalgia of revisiting an old friend.

The premise is, of course, to transform suburban American concepts to a Stone Age setting, focusing on the neighboring Flintstone and Rubble families. Some of the humor comes from transposing modern electronic concepts to prehistoric counterparts, such as having a car that is operated by foot power, or a garbage disposal that is really a hungry bird hiding under the sink. These sight gags are always good for a few laughs, but after a while, they begin to wear thin.

The primary failure of *The Flintstones* (as viewed through adult eyes) is the characters. Loosely based on the Kramdens and the Nortons from Jackie Gleason's *The Honeymooners,* the Flintstones and the Rubbles lack all the qualities that made Gleason's characters so memorable. Both Fred Flintstone and Ralph Kramden are loud, bossy blowhards, but Kramden has the touch of the tragic to him. Kramden is basically a loser, struggling in every way he know to be a somebody. Flintstone, on the other hand, has no real problems, just a nasty boss (George Slate) and an overactive pet dinosaur, Dino. Thus, Fred's noisy nature has no counterpoint (other than Wilma's sarcasm). He is just a loudmouth who yells "Yabba Dabba Doo" a lot.

Likewise, Barney Rubble is no Ed Norton. Rubble has none of the exciting flights of fancy or the expressive vocal mannerisms that made Norton great. The wives are more in line with the *Honeymooner* model, in that Wilma Flintstone has some of Alice Kramden's sly smarts that enable her to get her way without wounding the enormous male ego of her husband. Betty Rubble, like Trixie Norton, is a virtual nonentity.

Even when not measured up against such august competition as *The Honeymooners, The Flintstones* must be considered only a qualified success. The stories are too simple, the tenor is too brassy, and the humor is too mundane. Young viewers, always excited by loud action and catch-phrases, can enjoy *The Flintstones* for what it is—competent middle-of-the-road animated fun. Older viewers, who need a little more substance to their diet, will come away feeling like they just ate too much cotton candy (it's too sugary and mostly just air).

The weakness of *The Flintstones* is certainly not due to the cast, since the voices of the major characters belong to respected and talented performers. Alan Reed, the voice of Fred, had contributed his hefty gait and distinctive deep voice to *Duffy's Tavern* and *Life with Luigi.* Bea Benaderet was an alumni of the Burns and Allen show and left *The Flintstones* (where she was the voice of Betty) to devote full time to her starring role in *Petticoat Junction.* Mel Blanc (Barney Rubble) was a legend in cartoon circles, having created some of the most memorable voices of the era, such as Bugs Bunny, Daffy Duck, and Porky Pig.

Producers Hanna and Barbera created a long string of popular cartoon series, of which *The Flintstones* is but one well-known example. While the duo *did* turn out a few programs with some bite to them (*Jonny Quest, Top Cat*), as a rule, Hanna-Barbera seemed satisfied with attracting just children. Many cartoon shows from other producers that were aimed mostly at youngsters, such as *Bullwinkle, George of the Jungle,* and *Underdog,* contained a high level of writing that could capture an adult's imagination.

Aside from the basic package of *The Flintstones,* the characters of Fred, Wilma, Barney, Betty, and their progeny, turn up in a plethora of other TV formats. Over the years, *The Flintstones Comedy Hour, The New Fred and Barney Show, Flintstones Funnies, Fred and Barney Meet the Thing, Fred and Barney Meet the Schmoo* (?!), and *Fred Flintstone and Friends* (among others) have kept the Bedrock folk in front of a constant parade of new generations of kiddies. ■

**THE FLIP WILSON SHOW (**½) 60 min (52ep Color; 1970–1974 NBC) Comedy-Variety** *with Flip Wilson*

Most variety shows do not age well, and *The Flip Wilson Show* is no exception. The feeling of the early 1970s permeates this show, with lots of hip references to drugs and hippies. The very premise of Wilson's persona ("Hey, I may be black, but I'm not threatening, I'm still funny") is old hat now. Still, Wilson is a very funny guy, who is not seen much anymore. This series captures him in full bloom and is still good for some laughs.

Wilson's two funniest characters are Rev. LeRoy of the Church of What's Happening Now, a man of God who is not above an easy con or an amorous advance, and Geraldine Jones, a sassy and spunky lady who likes to flirt and then warn pursuers of her steady boyfriend, "Killer."

*The Flip Wilson Show* lives and dies with Flip. He is the whole show. There are lots of celebrity guest stars (such as Johnny Carson, Raymond Burr, Andy Williams, Redd Foxx, Red Skelton, and the Muppets), but the only reason to watch is to see Flip flip out.

There were more than fifty-two episodes of *The Flip Wilson Show,* but these are the only ones currently available in syndication.

**FLIPPER (**½) 30 min (88ep Color; 1964–1968 NBC) Adventure** *with Brian Kelly as Porter Ricks, Luke Halpin as Sandy Ricks, Tommy Norden as Bud Ricks, and Susie as Flipper*

It is well known that dolphins are intelligent animals. Okay, they are *very* intelligent animals, but *Flipper* pushes this concept just a bit too far. After watching a few episodes, you will be convinced that Flipper can probably talk like Mr. Ed, but unlike Mr. Ed, Flipper probably is so frustrated trying to get humans to pay attention to him that he chooses *not* to speak, out of spite.

The supposed masters of this show are the Ricks family members, headed by widower/hunk Porter Ricks. He is the chief ranger at Coral Key Park, Florida, home of flora, fauna, and foolish divers. Porter must protect them all, along with his two motherless sons, fifteen-year-old Sandy and ten-year-old Bud. The kids (and their father) lead a pretty idyllic life by the tropical sea, but trouble is always close at hand, be it bad guys on the run or pretty young scuba-divers with the bends.

The Ricks clan would be stumped by most problems if it were not for their pet male dolphin Flipper (played by trained female dolphin Susie), who is really Lassie in a wet suit. Like Lassie, Flipper is always the first to figure out something is wrong, and the thick humans never seem to understand the warnings he tries to give. Only Sandy and Bud know that Flipper is reliable, but even they can rarely figure out the problem without Flipper's guidance.

Beyond the amazing perceptiveness of the porpoise, *Flipper* can be enjoyed as a picturesque half hour of good fun and excitement, but you keep wishing the humans would wise up. *Mad* magazine's spoof of *Flipper* captured this tendency perfectly by having a desperate Flipper, after trying all his usual tricks to alert the humans, write out the problem in perfect English in the sand, using a stick held in one of his flippers. The humans still didn't get the message.

*Flipper* is another of the animal and nature-rich series produced by Ivan Tors, the man responsible for *The Aquanauts, Daktari, Gentle Ben,* and *Sea Hunt.* Coming from the early 1960s, the era before movie-length TV pilots, *Flipper* had its two pilots released as regular theatrical films. *Flipper,* from 1963, features Luke Halpin as Sandy, but stars Chuck Connors (*The Rifleman*) as the father. The second pilot, *Flipper's New Adventure,* from 1964, keeps Halpin and introduces Brian Kelly as Porter Ricks. ■

**FLO (**) 30 min (29ep Color; 1980–1981 CBS) Situation Comedy** *with Polly Holliday as Flo Castleberry, Geoffrey Lewis as Earl Tucker, Joyce Bulifant as Miriam Willoughby, Sudie Bond as Velma Castleberry, Lucy Lee Flippin as Fran Castleberry, Stephen Keep as Les Kincaid, and Jim B. Baker as Farley Waters*

What better way to do a spin-off from *Alice* than to do *Alice* all over again? Or something pretty close. After four seasons as the feisty "Kiss My Grits" waitress at Mel's Diner, Flo takes off for a posh new job in Houston. But along the way she makes the mistake of stopping at her hometown (Cowtown, Texas), and—on a dare—buys a rundown roadhouse there. So Flo ends up staying, determined to make "Flo's Yellow Rose" (as it's rechristened) a viable business, if only to prove that she can indeed make it on her own. If you liked Flo's pushy personality on *Alice,* you'll love this series. It's all built completely around her, with put-down foils at every turn: Velma, her spirited mother; Earl, the bartender who hates the idea of working for a woman; Fran, her sober-sided sister; Miriam, her chief waitress; Les, the piano player; and Farley, the obnoxious banker holding the mortgage on Flo's place. If none of that appeals to you, Hoyt Axton's theme song for the series is pretty good.

**THE FLYING DOCTOR (*½) 30 min (39ep B&W; 1959 Australia) Adventure** *with Richard Denning as Dr. Greg Graham, Jill Adams as Mary, Peter Madden as Dr. Harrison, and Alan White as Charley*

In these Australian-produced medical heroics, American physician Dr. Greg Graham fearlessly attends to needs in the outback country down under. He and his nurse and assistant reach those out-of-the-way places in a small plane (piloted by Charley), often bringing in lifesaving medicine just in time. Cleanly done though obviously dated today (they should have set it in the automatically nostalgic 1930s rather than in 1959). Actually the only reason for watching is for lead Richard Denning, more familiar from his stints on *Hawaii Five-O* (as Governor Philip Grey) and *Mr. and Mrs. North* (he was Mr.).

**FLYING HIGH (½) 60 min (18ep & 2 hr pilot Color; 1978–1979 CBS) Comedy-Drama** *with Pat Klous as Marcy Bowers, Connie Sellecca as Lisa Benton, Kathryn Witt as Pam Bellagio, and Howard Platt as Capt. Doug March*

Pointless, banal, cheap, sexploitive, boring. These are all words that can be used to dismiss this brainless effort to outjiggle *Charlie's Angels.* Other than that, suffice it to say that *Flying High* is about three perky, sexy white girls who are stewardesses for Sunwest Airlines, based in (need you ask?) Los Angeles. The *only* reason to catch *Flying High* is to see Connie Selleca in her first series. In *The Greatest American Hero* and *Hotel,* she proved that she could really act. You'd hardly guess it from *Flying High.*

**THE FLYING NUN (*) 30 min (82ep Color; 1967–1970 ABC) Situation Comedy** *with Sally Field as Elsie Ethington/Sister Bertrille, Marge Redmond as Sister Jacqueline and narrator, Madeleine Sherwood as the Mother Superior, Shelley Morrison as Sister Sixto, and Alejandro Ray as Carlos Ramirez*

*The Flying Nun* is really just mindless fluff. It's not that the show is unwatchable, far from it. In fact, it does tend to grow on you, though like mold on a pile of wet clothes. Still, if you seek anything other than silly situations and sugary-sweet resolutions, just hit the remote control button quickly whenever *The Flying Nun* buzzes into your home.

The basic plot here is that young Elsie Ethington follows in the path of her missionary aunt, and gets herself to a nunnery. Ah, but not just any nunnery. No, tiny, lightweight (90 lbs.) Elsie (who is ordained as Sister Bertrille) is assigned to the Convent San Tanco on a hill near San Juan, Puerto Rico, where the Caribbean trade winds blow most all the time. Now if you think like a TV programmer, you could imagine that nuns situated in such a windy place would wear outlandish headdresses (called coronets), with bent-down sides that resemble a bird's wings. So tiny Sister Bertrille, with the funny headdress, on the windy hill, can . . . well, fly, sort of. The wind blows her up and about, she learns to maneuver a bit, and she "flies." Big deal. If you take out the entire "flying" angle, this show would still be just a time-filler with no real humor or focus. *With* the flying, *The Flying Nun* seems to have gone over the edge in its effort to find some memorable hook to drag in an audience.

It is always nice to see Sally Field on screen, but *The Flying Nun* is a real step backward from her previous show *Gidget.* At least in *Gidget,* Field played an interesting young teen, struggling through puberty. In *The Flying Nun,* Field looks silly being buffeted by the winds and she does not really come across as much of a nun, either. As for the rest of the cast, the straight-laced Mother Superior is around just to be made fun of and Sister Jacqueline is there to provide some sage advice to the struggling airborne novice. The local Puerto Ricans are portrayed as "noble savages," ever thankful for the wisdom and beneficence of the female North Americanos with the silly hats.

One local worth watching is millionaire/playboy Carlos Ramirez, who skims the top off his worldly winnings and regularly donates cash to the convent. Carlos struggles with his undeniable attraction to the perky Sister Bertrille, and is about the only one in the show who seems to find the fact that Sister Bertrille can "fly" to be odd. For that alone, he deserves credit.

**FOLEY SQUARE (**½) 30 min (14ep Color; 1985–1986 CBS) Situation Comedy** *with Margaret Colin as Alex Harrigan, Hector Elizondo as Jesse Steinberg, Cathy Silvers as Molly Dobbs, Sanford Jensen as Carter DeVries, Michael Lembeck as Peter Newman, Vernee Watson-Johnson as Denise Willums, Israel Jurabe as Angel Gomez, and Jon Lovitz as Mole*

A good mix of home and office comedy, with Margaret Colin playing a dedicated young assistant D. A. with five years front-line experience on the job and even longer in the trenches of the dating scene. The series neatly balances both worlds, with complications occasionally crossing back and forth between the two (as when Alex's attempts at an uninterrupted date on the eve of her thirtieth birthday are consistently thwarted by an assignment to protect a witness in a murder trial). D. A. Jesse Steinberg directs activities on the office front, where Alex shares assignments with two other assistants (innocent newcomer Molly and the pushy and ambitious Carter) and exchanges quips with the ex-con office messenger (Angel) and the department's secretary (Denise). Back in her apartment building, Alex's best friend is Peter Newman, a local school teacher.

For a short-run series, this show hits its comic stride surprisingly fast—making the decision to drop the program in its original airing all the more disappointing. Afterward, Margaret Colin went on to play a former assistant D. A. in *Leg Work.* One of the other cast members moved even faster, with Jon Lovitz appearing as a new cast member of *Saturday Night Live* just as the first few episodes of *Foley Square* (with his Mole character) were broadcast.

**FOLLOW THAT MAN** **(see *Man Against Crime*)**

**FOLLOW THE SUN (*) 60 min (30 ep B&W; 1961–1962 ABC) Adventure** *with Barry Coe as Ben Gregory, Brett Halsey as Paul Templin, Gary Lockwood as Eric Jason, and Gigi Perreau as Katherine Ann Richards*

*Hawaiian Eye* is not that great a show to begin with, so saying that *Follow the Sun* is almost as good as *Hawaiian Eye* is truly damning with faint praise. Ben Gregory and Paul Templin are freelance magazine writers (rather than detectives, as in *Hawaiian Eye*) based in sunny Honolulu, who are always getting involved in drama while tracking down a story. Kathy Richards is the perky female that always seems to be required in this sort of show and Eric Jason is the "go-fer" for Ben and Paul.

**FOOT IN THE DOOR (½) 30 min (6ep Color; 1983 CBS) Situation Comedy** *with Harold Gould as Jonah Foot, Kenneth Gilman as Jim Foot, Diana Canova as Harriet Foot, and Marian Mercer as Mrs. Griffin*

Aside from the barely funny play on words in the show's title (relating to the name of the main character), *Foot in the Door* has little to offer. Aging widower Jonah Foot, after the death of his domineering, boring wife of forty years, decides to leave his rural New Hampshire home and barge in on his young son Jim and Jim's new bride. So, Foot, the elder, muscles his way into the small New York City apartment of Foot, the younger, therefore providing the thin basis for the show's title. In the big city, Pops hopes to take part in the swinging single night life he craved all those years. This highly artificial plot quickly collapses from its own weight, leaving a very poor show that wastes the time of Harold Gould, an otherwise quality actor who played the father on *Rhoda. Foot in the Door* is based on a British series, *Tom, Dick & Harriet.*

**FOR LOVE AND HONOR (**) 60 min (12ep Color; 1983 NBC) Drama** *with Cliff Potts as First Sgt. Eugene Allard, Yaphet Kotto as Platoon Sgt. James "China" Bell, Shelley Smith as Capt. Carolyn Engel, Gary Grubbs as Cap. Stephen Wiecek, Rachel Ticotin as Cpl. Grace Pavlik, Amy Steel as Sharon (Dolan), and Kelly Preston as Mary Lee*

This version of "Today's Army" has to give Cpl. Grace Pavlik serious second thoughts about her career choice.

She's a young recruit in an airborne outfit of paratroopers led by an ambitious commanding officer, Captain Wiecek, who doesn't particularly care for females breaking into this previously all-male barracks. Luckily, recruit supervisor First Sgt. Allard has more of a tolerance for women—well, at least for medical Capt. Carolyn Engel, with whom he's quite smitten. That leaves the workout sessions in the capable hands of Platoon Sgt. Bell, a Vietnam vet and one-time boxing champ with an unmistakable voice of authority. Of course, for the men, there are always workouts of a different sort with the flirtatious Mary Lee, the base commander's oversexed, adopted young daughter.

In short, this is a familiar young-recruits-in-training series, structured as a continuing serial drama, much like *Dallas* or *Knots Landing* or even the soapy but popular theatrical film *An Officer and a Gentleman.*

**FOR THE PEOPLE (***) (13ep B&W; 1965 CBS) Law Drama** *with William Shatner as David Koster, Howard DaSilva as Anthony Celese, Lonny Chapman as Frank Malloy, and Jessica Walter as Phyllis Koster*

The chief claim to fame of *For the People* is that it is the reason William Shatner did *not* star in the original pilot of *Star Trek.* While Gene Roddenberry used Jeffrey Hunter as the original Captain of the *USS Enterprise,* Shatner was busy starring in this heartfelt crime series. The quick cancellation of *For the People* left Shatner out of work and available when Roddenberry decided to revamp *Star Trek* before production of the series began.

The *Star Trek* connection aside, *For the People* stands on its own as a nice piece of quality TV. Shatner plays David Koster, a forceful assistant district attorney in New York, battling crime in a place where crime abounds. Koster is something of a workaholic (how can he rest when criminals walk free?) and he is full of the "we can change the world" vigor of the Kennedy years, but he is vulnerable as well. His wife, Phyllis, is a classical musician whose profession sometimes conflicts with the demands of David's job, resulting in one of the first two-career couple clashes in TV history.

Shatner's skill is, of course, a major plus for *The the People,* but do not overlook the contribution of executive producer Herbert Brodkin, who was a giant of the 1950s drama era (*Studio One*) and had succeeded with the rather similiar-toned *The Defenders.*

**FOR THE TERM OF HIS NATURAL LIFE (*½) (6hr miniseries Color; 1983 Australia) Drama** *with Anthony Perkins, Patrick Macnee, Colin Friels, and Samantha Eggar*

Australian melodrama set in the 1860s, with a young Englishman framed for murder and banished to the Botany Bay penal colony for life. There's plenty of heartache and physical torture, though it does play as rather perfunctory. Patrick Macnee probably comes off best as a humane governor with an attractive daughter.

**FOREIGN INTRIGUE (*½) 30 min (156ep B&W; 1951–1955 Syndicated) Espionage Adventure** *with James Daly as Michael Powers, Jerome Thor as Robert Cannon, Synda Scott as Helen Davis, Robert Arden as Steve Powers, Anne Preville as Patricia Bennett, and Gerald Mohr as Christopher Storm*

This early 1950s formula adventure series, shot in Europe, actually has three distinct setups playing under the same umbrella title. The first focuses on foreign correspondents Robert Cannon, Helen Davis, and Steve Powers, who carry the first seventy-eight episodes (subsequently syndicated as *Dateline Europe*). Paris-based correspondents Michael Powers and Patricia Bennett take over for the next thirty-nine stories (subsequently snydicated as *Overseas Adventures*). The hook and setting change for the final thirty-nine episodes (syndicated as *Cross Current*), following the adventures of Christopher Storm, owner of a Vienna hotel, who helps people caught in the grip of the international underworld.

The only lead of any real interest (decades later) is James Daly (who plays Michael Powers), because he subsequently appeared in many other programs, most notably as the experienced older doctor, Paul Lochner, in the 1970s *Medical Center.*

**FOREVER FERNWOOD** **(see *Mary Hartman, Mary Hartman*)**

**FORREST RANGERS (**) 30 min (104ep Color; 1965–1966 Syndication) Adventure** *with Graydon Gould as Ranger George Keeley, Michael Zenon as Joe Two Rivers, Gordon Pinsent as Sgt. Scott, and Rolland Bedard as Uncle Raoul*

Set in the Canadian north woods, *Forrest Rangers* is a workmanlike kiddie-oriented adventure yarn where a group of six children—four boys and two girls—all members of the Junior Ranger Club, help out the real rangers in the great white north.

**THE FORSYTE SAGA (***½) 60 min (26ep B&W; 1967 UK BBC) Drama** *with Kenneth More as Jolyon "Jo" Forsyte, Eric Porter as Soames Forsyte, Joseph O'Connor as Jolyon Forsyte, Sr., Nyree Dawn Porter as Irene Forsyte, Margaret Tyzack as Winifred Forsyte, Susan Hampshire as Fleur Forsyte, and Nicholas Pennell as Michael Mont*

The series that set the mold for numerous generational sagas of monied English families, *The Forsyte Saga* is a sumptuous adaptation of John Galsworthy's novels of the well-to-do Forsyte clan. Set in England from 1879 to 1926, during the wane of the Victorian era and the start of the social upheaval brought on by World War I, *The Forsyte Saga* focuses on old Jolyon Forsyte and his number one son, Jo. There is much posturing, much romantic intrigue, and much lust for lucre. It is instructional to watch this program now and compare it to *Dallas,* to see how well this high-brow series was translated into the more mass-popular American setting.

**FORTUNE DANE (**½) 60 min (6ep Color; 1986 ABC) Detective Drama** *with Carl Weathers as Fortune Dane, Daphne Ashbrook as Kathy "Speed" Davenport, Penny Fuller as Mayor Amanda Harding, and Joe Dallesandro as Perfect Tommy*

More an adventure series than a cop show, with Carl Weathers (Rocky Balboa's number one opponent, Apollo Creed, in the *Rocky* films) in the title role. He plays a tough, honest police detective who quits the force when some department mob corruption hits close to home. In a new town (Bay City), Dane becomes the chief troubleshooter for an equally independent and honest mayor, Amanda Harding. Fast-moving formula, especially fun to watch when Weathers is in action.

**FORTUNES OF WAR (**) 60 min (7ep Color; 1987 UK BBC) Drama** *with Emma Thompson as Harriet Pringle, Kenneth Branagh as Guy Pringle, Ronald Pickup as Prince Yakimov, Charles Kay as Dobson, James Villiers as Inchcape, Robert Graves as Simon, and Diana Hardcastle as Edwina*

A World War II love story based on two trilogies by Olivia Manning ("The Balkan Trilogy" and "The Levant Trilogy"), though the basic plot simply comes down to young marrieds attempting to survive in truly trying times. At first, the world seems dismissible as Guy and Harriet Pringle arrive in Bucharest, Romania. He's an English teacher and an outgoing, supportive person. Harriet is more reserved and, in particular, thinks that Guy gets taken advantage of by his university associates. But as the war begins to roll into their lives, they find themselves seriously inconvenienced at home (one of Guy's friends, Prince Yakimov, moves into their apartment), pushed into travel abroad, and then separated several times.

A competent but generic wartime saga.

**48 HOURS (**) 60 min (Color; 1988– CBS) Documentary** *with Dan Rather as host*

Not so much of a documentary (in the traditional sense) as more of a slice of life, *48 Hours* takes a few CBS News correspondents and plunks them down into one story (drug use, Hollywood, infertility, a hurricane, etc.) for two days. Host Dan Rather pieces all the segments together, sort of, so that the viewer gets a feel for the topic. While there may be few deep insights provided into the topic of the week, at least a surface familiarity is conveyed. Despite all the bold talk about how this series is an example of the new wave of TV documentaries, *48 Hours* really looks like an attempt to churn out a "prestige" program in just two days, with the major concern being the considerable cost savings from the old-style, in-depth documentary.

**FOUL PLAY (*) 60 min (10ep Color; 1981 ABC) Comedy-Adventure** *with Barry Bostwick as Det. Tucker Pendleton, Deborah Raffin as Gloria Munday, Richard Romanus as Capt. Vito Lombardi, Greg Rice as Ben Bernard, and John Rice as Beau Bernard*

One more failure at adapting a hit film comedy to TV, *Foul Play* has none of the zip of the Chevy Chase–Goldie Hawn movie original. Barry Bostwick is worthy of something more than the silly role of Tucker Pendleton, a clumsy San Francisco police detective. Pendleton solves crimes, or at least tries to, with the help of his girlfriend Gloria, who starts out as a librarian but soon becomes a TV star.

**FOUR-IN-ONE 60 min (24ep Color; 1970–1971 NBC) Drama**

This is the original overall title for four separate series: *McCloud, San Francisco International Airport, Night Gallery,* and *The Psychiatrist.* See those titles for details.

**FOUR JUST MEN (**½) 30 min (39ep B&W; 1959 Syndication) Adventure** *with Dan Dailey as Tim Collier, Jack Hawkins as Ben Manfred, Richard Conte as Jeff Ryder, and Vittorio DeSica as Rico Poccari*

There is lots of European action in *Four Just Men,* a watchable crime series that is blessed with four talented leading men. The quartet of the show's title were comrades in fighting Nazism during World War II, but went their separate ways after 1945. Brought back together more than a decade later by their old commander to help battle more mundane enemies, each of the four battles crime in his own way. American Tim Collier is a newspaper reporter, Briton Ben Manfred is a detective, Jeff Ryder is (believe it or not from his name) a French attorney, and Rico Poccari is an Italian hotel operator.

The primary allure of *Four Just Men* is its quality cast, recruited from the world of film. Dan Dailey starred in Hollywood musicals in the 1940s and played Dizzy Dean in *The Pride of St. Louis* in the 1950s. Raspy-voiced Jack Hawkins starred in *The Bridge on the River Kwai* and *Ben-Hur.* Richard Conte was a popular leading man for the Fox studios (*New York Confidential*). Vittorio DeSica won awards not only as an actor but also as a director (*The Bicycle Thief* and *The Garden of the Finzi-Continis*).

**THE FOUR SEASONS (**½) 30 min (11ep & 60 min pilot Color; 1984 CBS) Situation Comedy** *with Jack Weston as Danny Zimmer, Marcia Rodd as Claudia Zimmer, Allan Arbus as Boris Elliott, Barbara Babcock as Lorraine Elliott, Tony Roberts as Ted Callan, Joanna Kerns as Pat Devon, Elizabeth Alda as Beth Burroughs, Beatrice Alda as Lisa Callan, and Alan Alda as Jack Burroughs*

In this continuation of Alan Alda's 1981 hit film about the friendships between three pairs of middle-aged couples, only Jack Weston and Alda's two real-life daughters return with their characters for the television version. Alda himself also turns up in his Jack Burroughs role to help launch the series (which he produced), bidding farewell to friends Danny and Claudia Zimmer as they pick up stakes and head from New York to Los Angeles. The result is a puzzle, though, that didn't quite connect at the time. Maybe it was a few years too early for such *thirtysomething* Yuppie plots as Danny fretting over lending money to Ted for a "risky agricultural investment," or everyone flying out to Las Vegas to help Danny identify and claim his stolen Mercedes. (Not exactly *Honeymooners* or *Happy Days* territory there.)

More likely, though, the series simply suffered from a second banana ailment—too many performers who previously made thier marks as strong supporting characters (in everything from *M*A*S*H* and *Hill Street Blues* to various Woody Allen films). While uniformly good, the cast needs scripts that are less democratic, allowing someone (okay, someone *other than* Weston's whining hypochondriac character) to stand apart and really attempt to drive the series. Maybe even another character for additional seasoning. Too bad Alan Alda had decided to concentrate his own career at the time on films rather than television. This series could have been a nice post-*M*A*S*H* civilian showcase for him. Instead it's merely a good mixture of familiar faces in search of a hit between their usual assignments. Within a few years, Joanna Kerns (Pat Devon) found her hit teamed with Alan Thicke in *Growing Pains.*

## FOUR STAR PLAYHOUSE (see *Star Performance*)

## FRACTURED FLICKERS (***) 30 min (26ep B&W; 1961 Syndication) Comedy *with Hans Conried as host*

Surely one of the more bizarre series in TV history, *Fractured Flickers* took scenes from hoary old silent film classics, such as *The Hunchback of Notre Dame* (1923), *Dr. Jekyll and Mr. Hyde* (1920), and *The Mark of Zorro* (1920), and added humorous synchronized dialogue that turned the old adventure films into camp humor. This concept had been tried by TV comedy genius Ernie Kovacs in the 1950s and may have been the inspiration for Woody Allen's second film *What's Up Tiger Lily?,* which pulled the same trick with a Japanese film.

Host of this irreverent riot is Hans Conried, the loud Uncle Tonoose from *Make Room for Daddy* and the voice of Snidley Whiplash in *The Bullwinkle Show.* The Bullwinkle connection is the key, as *Fractured Flickers,* like *The Bullwinkle Show,* came from the fertile minds of Jay Ward and Bill Scott.

## FRANK'S PLACE (***½) 30 min (22ep Color; 1987–1988 CBS) Situation Comedy *with Tim Reid as Frank Parrish, Daphne Maxwell Reid as Hanna Griffin, Francesca P. Roberts as Anna-May, Frances E. Williams as Miss Marie, Tony Burton as Big Arthur, Charles Lampkin as Tiger Shepin, Robert Harper as Sy "Bubba" Weisberger, William Thomas, Jr., as "Cool" Charles, Don Yesso as "Shorty" La Roux, Virginia Capers as Bertha Griffin-Lamour, and Lincoln Kilpatrick as Rev. Deal*

*Frank's Place* deserves honorable mention in the TV Hall of Fame for being one of the first black-oriented TV series (along with *The Cosby Show*) to portray blacks as normal human beings, rather than as loud, silly buffoons or as noble, ever-suffering martyrs. Unfortunately *Frank's Place* did not last long enough to fulfill its promise of being one of the comic TV highlights of the late 1980s.

Tim Reid (Venus Flytrap on *WKRP* and Downtown Brown on *Simon & Simon*) plays Frank Parrish, an erudite college professor of Renaissance history from Boston. As the series starts, Frank is quite surprised to learn that he has inherited a small creole restaurant ("Chez Louisiane") in the black section of New Orleans from his late father, who Frank barely knew. Frank intends to sell the place, but he is taken in by the simple charm of the eatery and the close-knit atmosphere of the staff. As a result, Prof. Parrish moves to the Crescent City and takes over management of the restaurant (popularly known as the "Chez").

Among the crew at Frank's place are Big Arthur (the no-nonsense ex-boxer chief cook), Anna-May (the sassy chief waitress), Miss Marie (the waitress emeritus who only waits on her old customers), and Tiger (the grizzled bartender who has seen it all). Usually hanging out in the bar are the Rev. Deal (a cleric with no current pulpit but with an eye for get-rich-quick schemes) and Bubba Weisberger (a low-key southern Jewish lawyer and one of the few resident whites). Frank's love interest is Hanna Griffin, the gorgeous daughter of Bertha Griffin-Lamour (the local undertaker who is the matriarch of the black community). Hanna is played by Reid's real-life wife Daphne.

The series does an excellent job of character development. Over the few episodes produced, each of the characters is fleshed out and made even more believable than at the start, while the program still maintains a fine air of laughter. Nothing is taken very seriously here, which is appropriate for a show set in New Orleans, a city with a lot of tolerance for eccentrics.

Credit for the finely crafted work on *Frank's Place* goes to the star and co-executive producer, Tim Reid. Equal credit goes to Hugh Wilson, the other executive producer, who performed the same task in Reid's first series (*WKRP,* which is very similar in feel). Keep an eye out for the fascinating episode about a homeless bum who takes up residence in the alley behind the Chez. It is directed by Frank Bonner, another *WKRP* alumnus (he played salesman Herb Tarlek).

The fact that only one season's worth of episodes of *Frank's Place* were produced is a shame. The general consensus at the time it was canceled, among TV critics and network executives alike, was that the viewing public truly did not know what they were missing.

**FRED ASTAIRE PRESENTS** (**) **60 min (39ep B&W; 1961–1963 ABC) Drama Anthology** *with Fred Astaire as host*

These unrelated dramas originally aired under the title *Alcoa Premiere,* which is still the title used for thirty-minute dramas that Astaire also hosted from 1961 to 1963.

**FREDDY'S NIGHTMARES** (*½) **60 min (22ep at Fall 1989 Color; 1988– Syndicated) Horror Anthology** *with Robert Englund as Freddy Krueger*

A television spin-off from the tremendously successful *Nightmare on Elm Street* theatrical films, with Robert Englund continuing his ghoulish role as dream master Freddy Krueger. The kick-off episode is directed by Tobe Hooper (*Texas Chainsaw Massacre, Poltergeist*) and sets up the conflict between the outraged citizens of Springwood and Freddy, who they see released from police custody through a technical loophole in the law. Then it's a citizens' vigilante group versus the man with the talon-tipped glove. Guess who wins?

The rest of the series focuses chiefly on Freddy as narrator/host, with occasional forays into particular narratives. There is also more emphasis on the stories themselves rather than on the roller-coaster ride of special effects that carry most of the theatrical *Elm Street* films. Obviously this emphasis reflects budget limitations as much as deliberate script structure, though (ironically) it doesn't dilute the messy horror much at all. For one thing, there's plenty of graphic gore, with severed body parts (fingers, a pulsating heart) and splattered blood turning up everywhere. For off-camera action it's even worse. As Alfred Hitchcock demonstrated decades before, implication is usually the most frightening special effect possible, as the audience members fill in the details with their own deepest nightmares (a most appropriate prospect for Freddy). So, for instance, when Freddy attacks someone sitting helplessly in a dentist's chair, you don't need to see *exactly* what he's doing to know the victim's teeth will never be the same again.

The main problem with the series (as with the films) is the arbitrary unfairness of it all. There's virtually no justification for Freddy's behavior, and the same holds true for many of the pawns in the non-Freddy stories. Perhaps, ironically, this unfairness makes the series the most lifelike one on television, with evil too often rewarded and admired while the good simply suffer as helpless victims. It's a sadly cynical approach, but it definitely stands out from the even-handed justice that often neatly wraps up stories in so many other series. Definitely not for the squeamish or fair-minded, but, then again, neither are the theatrical films.

**FREE COUNTRY** (**½) **30 min (5ep Color; 1978 ABC) Comedy-Drama** *with Rob Reiner as Joseph Bresner, Judy Kahan as Anna Bresner, Larry Gelman as Leo Gewurtzman, and Renee Lippin as Ida Gewurtzman*

A neat Rob Reiner comedy project sandwiched in between the end of his stint as the "Meathead" on *All in the Family* and his sucess in the 1980s as a feature film director. For this series, he stays with an ethnic hook, trading his Polish Mike Stivic role for that of Lithuanian immigrant Joseph Bresner. The twist is that he plays the character both as an eighty-nine-year-old looking back, and as a hopeful young man, beginning in 1906. It's an admittedly sentimental tale, but it effectively covers some very familiar ground for twentieth-century ethnics, touching on such basic problems as getting used to a big city like New York, homesickness for the old country, and fear of possible deportation. In addition to Reiner, the rest of the central cast has solid comedy roots on such series as *The Bob Newhart Show* (Gelman as Bernie Tupperman, Lippin as the insecure Michele) and *Mary Hartman, Mary Hartman* (Kahan as Penny Major). Reiner created this series with Phil Mishkin, his partner on a 1972 project, *The Super.*

**FREE TO CHOOSE** (***) **60 min (10ep Color) (1980 PBS) Documentary** *with Milton Friedman*

The beauty of the free enterprise system is the focus for this series, hosted by famed economist Milton Friedman. ■

**FREEBIE AND THE BEAN** (*) **60 min (9ep Color; 1980–1981 CBS) Comedy-Drama** *with Tom Mason as Sgt. Tim "Freebie" Walker, Hector Elizondo as Sgt. Dan "The Bean" Delgado, and William Daniels as Walter W. Cuikshank*

The 1974 film of *Freebie and the Bean* was mildly funny, presenting the lighthearted exploits of solid, by-the-book Hispanic cop Dan Delgado (Alan Arkin), embarrassingly called "The Bean," and his odd-couple partner Tim Walker (James Caan), a freewheeling moocher. The TV version of the film lacks whatever loud charm the film had. There is a depressingly high number of unnecessary car chases and crashes and lots of pointless wise-guy banter. William Daniels is, as always, appealing as a snooty boss, a role similar to his role as Dr. Mark Craig in *St. Elsewhere.*

**THE FRENCH ATLANTIC AFFAIR** (**½) **(6hr miniseries Color; 1979 ABC) Drama** *with Chad Everett as Harold Columbine, Telly Savalas as Craig Dunleavy, Michelle Phillips as Jennie, Louis Jourdan as Charles Girodt, and Shelley Winters as Helen Wabash*

Aaron Spelling and Douglas Cramer, producers of *The Love Boat,* take the same concept of a floating luxury liner full of celebrities and warp it slightly by adding some terror that wouldn't work on the Pacific

Princess. Here the ship is hijacked by a religious cult leader and his fanatical followers. This entertaining miniseries is based on a novel by Ernest Lehman.

**FRESH FIELDS** (***) **30 min (26ep Color; 1984 UK Thames) Situation Comedy** *with Julia McKenzie as Hester Fields, Anton Rodgers as William Fields, Ann Beach as Sonia, Philip Bird as Peter Richardson, Debbie Cumming as Emma Richardson, and Fanny Rowe as Nancy Pemrose*

William and Hester Fields rise to the challenge of starting fresh after the kids have moved out, in between their everyday essential tasks (he as a CPA, she as a homemaker and part-time caterer).

As such, they're an untypical television sitcom couple. They look comfortable together. They're playful and sexy and display a sense of humor. It's reminiscent of the relationship between Bob and Emily Hartley on *The Bob Newhart Show:* an adult couple having a laugh at life together rather than always trying to pull some screwball fast one on each other.

For instance, when Hester asks William to serve as bartender for one of her first private catering jobs, he has some initial misgivings but agrees. Since this is a sitcom, William promptly runs into a business associate at the party, so he has to pretend to be both a guest and a bartender. But both he and his wife are in on the deception—they're trying to fool everyone else.

Another time, when William needs help at the office, Hester jumps in. While there, she deftly manages to convince a waiting client that her husband's services are in demand by the likes of *Vogue,* nailing down that account.

Overall, there's slightly more emphasis on the domestic rather than the office humor, but it's a nice mix. Hester's mom (Nancy) lives next door and—like the Stateside Hartleys—the Fields have a mooching next-door neighbor (Sonia) who shares Howard Borden's uncanny knack for turning up at meal time.

**FRESNO** (**½) **(6hr miniseries Color; 1986 CBS) Serial Comedy** *with Carol Burnett as Charlotte Kensington, Dabney Coleman as Tyler Cane, Teri Garr as Talon Kensington, Gregory Harrison as Torch, Charles Grodin as Cane Kensington, Valerie Mahaffey as Tiffany Kensington*

Could you take one of those *Carol Burnett Show* movie or television parodies, expand it, and switch it for the real thing? And if you did, would anybody notice the difference? *Fresno* is a game attempt, a soap opera/miniseries send-up running without a laugh track (one was added in reruns) or sly mugging to the camera. Instead everyone puts their all into the story's fierce battles over control of the raisin capital of the world, Fresno, California—"a turbulent town tossed in a tempest of unchained passion . . . unspeakable greed . . . and unlimited parking." The result is very dry, understated humor, unlike the gag and pratfall approach taken in other genre parodies such as *Police Squad* or *When Things Were Rotten.* (No surprise there, it was hatched by *Newhart* producer Barry Kemp.) Yes, the action is funny, but just how funny depends on how silly you find most soap opera-type intrigues to begin with—after the style over substance glitz of *Dynasty* or the traumas of the wine country on *Falcon Crest,* cornering the market on raisins in high-gloss *Fresno* isn't that much of an exaggeration.

Instead it's best to approach the series as an opportunity to see some excellent comic performers (Carol Burnett, Dabney Coleman, Teri Garr, Charles Grodin) add their extra zip to an otherwise straightforward set of soapy complications. Who will triumph in the raisin game? The widowed matriarch (Burnett) of the Kensington clan? Her bitter competitor, Tyler Cane (Coleman)? Or perhaps her power-mad son, Cane (Grodin)? And what about Talon (Garr), Cane's voluptuous wife, who has fallen for a bare-chested drifter straight out of *The Long, Hot Summer* (the aptly named Torch played by Gregory Harrison—nicely poking fun at his own bare-chested hunk image from the made-for-TV movie *For Ladies Only*)? It's worth sticking around to find out the answers to these and many other questions.

**FRIDAY THE 13TH: THE SERIES** (**½) **60 min (52ep at Fall 1989 Color; 1987– Syndication) Suspense Drama** *with John Lemay as Ryan Dallion, Robey as Micki Foster, and Chris Wiggins as Jack Marshak*

Beginning with *Friday the 13th* in 1980, a lengthy, disgusting, gory series of theatrical films revolving around the character of Jason (an unstoppable killing machine who terrorizes a teen summer camp) somehow captured a large audience. This TV series tries to cash in on the popular film title, while actually bearing few, if any, connections to the rancid celluloid originals.

The TV version revolves around the haunted trinkets distributed by Lewis Vendredi, an antiques dealer who sold his soul to the devil. Now that Satan has collected on his bargain, Vendredi's store has passed to his pretty niece Micki. Seeking to undo the harm her late uncle caused, Micki, her cousin Ryan, and a kindly retired magician (Jack Marshak, former friend of Vendredi), try to save unsuspecting people from tragedy caused by the hexed objects. The trio's efforts to find and recover the dangerous items lead them to encounter some very nasty individuals. Some are corrupted by the spooked antiques, while some are just bad to begin with. The stories are delightfully creepy, the special effects are nice and the violence is gaudy. The writing and acting may be a bit overblown, but that can easily be ignored while focusing on the style. It's a pity the series felt the need to associate itself with the movies that are of far lower quality.

**FRIDAYS** (**) **60 min (100ep Color; 1980–1982 ABC) Comedy-Variety** *with Mark Blankfield, Maryedith Burrell, Melanie Chartoff, Larry David, Darrow Igus, Brandis Kemp, Bruce Mahler, Michael Richards, and John Roarke*

This series was launched by ABC just as *Saturday Night Live's* original cast was winding up its final season. Recognizing that comparisons were inevitable, *Fridays* mocked that fact from the very first episode, lining up the cast and identifying particular *Saturday Night Live* knock-off concepts they did and didn't want to use. Not surprisingly, the initial episode was not very good. But very quickly the show improved, with a hungry young cast eager to make its mark. They specialized in raunchy, loud, almost swaggering humor, starting as strong individuals and trying to learn how to do ensemble work. By the fall of 1980, as NBC unveiled the disastrous new *Saturday Night Live '80, Fridays* was hitting its stride and looking better and better in comparison.

With the dawn of the Ronald Reagan presidency at hand, *Fridays* jumped wholeheartedly into the business of political satire. This satire was not limited merely to caustic comments on the humorous newscasts (anchored by Melanie Chartoff), but began up front, with elaborate parody productions (often including original musical numbers) operning the show. In send-ups of such films as *Popeye, The Rocky Horror Picture Show, Close Encounters of the Third Kind,* and a typical Bob Hope and Bing Crosby "Road" picture (with the two turning up in Central America) the cast left no doubt of what they thought of the "Gipper" (Reagan) and his vision of the world.

Though the program began without using any guest hosts, that feature was quickly added. George Carlin, the first guest host for *Saturday Night Live,* was also the first to fill that slot for *Fridays.* The running time of the show also changed over its original run, ranging from just over an hour to nearly two hours. As a result, the program benefits considerably from editing for rerun repackaging, which trims the episodes to a one-hour length.

None of the *Fridays* cast members ever reached the Eddie Murphy-Bill Murray-Chevy Chase level of subsequent success, so the reruns don't offer the opportunity to see such future superstars in the making. (However, they do constantly turn up in other TV series and in movies, so you'll recognize their faces.) Unfortunately, political humor (even very well done) dates rather quickly. In addition, because the cast never really jelled as a truly comfortable ensemble, the program comes off more like a series of solo comedy spots—individually very good, but still yesterday's news, especially when some cable channel is probably offering a marathon of new talent right now.

A prime candidate for a single-volume highlights video, quickly, before people forget who this Reagan character was in the first place.

**FRIENDS** (*½) **60 min (5ep Color; 1979 ABC) Comedy-Drama** *with Charles Aiken as Pete Richards, Jill Whelan as Nancy Wilks, and Jarrod Johnson as Randy Summerfield.*

In a bit of a change of pace for Aaron Spelling and Douglas Cramer, producers of glitzy shows such as *The Love Boat* and *Vega$,* their series *Friends* is supposed to be a warm, cuddly show about life, seen from the point of view of three eleven-year-olds living in suburban Westerby, California. The goal is admirable, but the scripting is weak and does not ring true. Catch *The Wonder Years* instead.

**FRIENDS AND LOVERS** **(see *The Paul Sand Show*)**

**FRIENDS OF MAN** (**½) **30 min (52ep Color; 1973–1974 Syndication) Documentary** *with Glenn Ford as narrator*

The relationship between animals and humans is the focus of this program that adults will think is more interesting for children than children will.

**FROM A BIRD'S EYE VIEW** (**) **30 min (18ep Color; 1970 UK ITC) Situation Comedy** *with Millicent Martin as Millie Grover, Pat Finley as Maggie Ralston, Peter Jones as Clyde Beauchamp, Robert Cawdron as Bert Grover, and Noel Hood as Miss Fosdyke*

Screwball comedy of two stewardesses assigned to the international London route: Millie, the scatterbrained British native, and Maggie, her level-headed American friend. Appropriately, the program title is a pun on the British slang for a woman ("bird"). It's a tried-and-true setup that works, filmed in England by veteran producer Ralph Levy (*Jack Benny, George Burns and Gracie Allen*). Previously, Millicent Martin had been one of the key performers in the British version of *That Was the Week That Was,* while Pat Finley went on to *The Bob Newhart Show* (playing Bob's sister). Their boss, played by Peter Jones, soared even farther, playing the voice of the book in the science fiction comedy *The Hitchhiker's Guide to the Galaxy.*

**FROM HERE TO ETERNITY** (**) **(6hr miniseries & thirteen 60 min ep Color; 1979–1980 NBC) Drama** *with William Devane as Sgt. Milt Warden, Natalie Wood and Barbara Hershey as Karen Holmes, Steve Railsback as Pvt. Robert E. Lee Prewitt, Roy Thinnes as Capt./Maj. Dana Holmes, Joe Pantoliano as Pvt. Angelo Maggio, Kim Basinger as Lorene Rogers, Peter Boyle as Sgt. James "Fatso" Judson, and Don Johnson as Jefferson Davis Prewitt*

First came the James Jones book; next came the Oscar-winning 1953 movie, starring Burt Lancaster, Donna Reed, and Frank Sinatra. In 1979 came the six-hour TV miniseries, followed by the 1980 hourly TV series. The setting is Pearl Harbor, December 1941.

It is always risky for a TV miniseries to try to remake

a film with which most viewers are very familiar. The movie memories will always jar against the new video version. Still, the six-hour TV miniseries of *From Here to Eternity* is a fine attempt to remake a classic. While missing the award-wining acting of the film, the miniseries (with Natalie Wood as Karen Holmes) holds its own. It makes up for its shortcomings by accentuating the sexual angles in Jones's book that the 1953 film downplayed.

Like the movie, the miniseries focuses on the time just before and after the Japanese attack on Hawaii. Tough-as-nails Sgt. Milt Warden is having an affair with Karen Holmes, wife of his commanding officer, Dana Holmes. Meanwhile, Warden is also trying to get his men in fighting shape. Warden's biggest challenge is unaggressive Pvt. Robert E. Lee Prewitt, whose many names indicate he has a long family tradition of military glory to uphold. Instead of short-order drills, Prewitt would prefer to spend time with Lorene Rogers, the local prostitute. The miniseries, like the film, comes to a climax when the "day of infamy" arrives.

The 1980 TV series picks up where the book, the movie, and the miniseries left off, which is its central problem. No longer in the familiar ground set by James Jones, the story is set in Honolulu in 1942 and is a bit loose. Sgt. Warden and Karen Holmes (now played by Barbara Hershey) are still fooling around behind Dana's back, but then Sgt. Warden has a heart attack and Karen leaves them both, to spend the duration of the war Stateside.

Meanwhile, Robert Prewitt is dead, shot while AWOL, and his younger brother, Jefferson Davis Prewitt (do you think the Prewitts are from the South?) turns up, looking to avenge his brother's death. He takes up with Robert's old tart/girlfriend, Lorene Rogers, and then marries her.

Hey, what about the war? The attack on Pearl Harbor has come and gone, but all these military types are still sitting on their duffs in Hawaii. What gives? Well, the answer is that the TV series downplays the battle of arms for the battle of the heart. After all, if the boys go off to war, what will the girls do?

Look for a pre-*Miami Vice* Don Johnson as the younger Prewitt. Unlike his dead older brother, Jeff Prewitt has no problem with being aggressive and macho. Kim Basinger, who went on to star in movies such as *Batman* and *9½ Weeks,* plays the prostitute in both the miniseries and series.

**FRONTIER (**½) 30 min (30ep B&W; 1955–1956 NBC) Western Anthology** *with Walter Coy as narrator*

*Studio One*'s Worthington "Tony" Miner produced these tales of the Old West, based on newspaper stories from the 1800s.

**FRONTIER CIRCUS (*½) 60 min (26ep B&W; 1961–1962 CBS) Western** *with Chill Wills as Col. Casey Thompson, John Derek as Ben Travis, and Richard Jaeckel as Tony Gentry*

You know the networks were scraping the bottom of the barrel of the western format in the early 1960s when they came up with a show like *Frontier Circus.* Almost every other conceivable permutation of format dealing with the Old West had been tried, so why not a series about a *circus* traveling through the Southwest in the 1880s? Thus, you can show circus acts *and* have shootouts with Indians and other assorted bad guys!

Casey Thompson and Ben Travis run the T&T Circus, while Tony Gentry is the advance man. The cast provides some marginal interest to seasoned couch potatoes. Chill Wills was a staple of Hollywood westerns (such as *The Alamo*), and provided the off-screen voice for Francis, the Talking Mule (Hollywood's precursor to Mr. Ed). Richard Jaeckel, here making his first series appearance, is a veteran of numerous shows, but always as a supporting actor (he was police Lt. Quirk in *Spencer: For Hire*). Last but not least, *Frontier Circus* is the one and only TV series starring John Derek, the movie director (*Tarzan: The Ape Man*) best known for marrying some of the world's most beautiful women, such as Ursula Andress, Linda Evans, and Bo Derek.

**FRONTIER DOCTOR (*½) 30 min (39ep B&W; 1956–1957 Syndication) Western** *with Rex Allen as Dr. Bill Baxter*

*Frontier Doctor* is about the trials and tribulations of a doctor on the edge of civilization, in this case the Arizona Territory at the turn of the century. Star Rex Allen had a lengthy show biz career before *Frontier Doctor,* as a country and western singer and star of numerous B movies about the Old West for Republic.

This show has also been known as *The Man of the West* and *Unarmed.*

**THE FUGITIVE (****) 60 min (120ep: 90 B&W & 30 Color; 1963–1967 ABC) Drama** *with David Janssen as Dr. Richard Kimble, Barry Morse as Lt. Philip Gerard, Bill Raisch as Fred Johnson, and Diane Brewster as Helen Kimble*

Not many people think of *The Fugitive* when lists of "best ever" TV shows are assembled, but it definitely belongs in that select group. In a simple, unassuming way, it excels in all the basic categories by which TV dramas are judged.

First of all, the premise is perfect. Loosely based on a mixture of the later part of Victor Hugo's classic *Les Miserables* and the long-running legal saga of Dr. Sam Sheppard, *The Fugitive* concerns Dr. Richard Kimble, a middle-class, middle-of-the-road guy whose wife Helen cannot conceive children. The tension that problem creates has eroded their marriage until they do not get along. One night an argument erupts over whether the Kimbles should try adopting a baby. He says yes, she says no, and he storms out of the house and drives off, causing quite a scene that their suburban neighbors cannot help but notice.

After driving around for a while, Dr. Kimble cools off and returns home. Upon pulling into his driveway, Dr. Kimble almost runs over a ratty-looking one-armed man who is fleeing from the Kimble home. In a flash, the one-armed man is gone and Dr. Kimble goes into his house and discovers his wife's body. He assumes she had been killed by the one-armed man who had broken into the house in a burglary attempt.

Nobody else saw the one-armed man. Kimble himself only got a fleeting look at the fellow. Everybody knew the Kimbles had not been getting along. Nobody else believes there ever was a one-armed man. Based on circumstantial evidence, Dr. Kimble is convicted of the murder of his wife and sentenced to death. While Kimble is being transported by train to the state penitentiary with Indiana State Police Lt. Philip Gerard, the train accidentally derails. In the confusion, Kimble escapes and becomes a fugitive from the law, always fearing recapture by local police or the relentless Lt. Gerard who is obsessed with the idea of tracking Kimble down. On the other hand, Kimble tries to clear his name and avoid execution by somehow tracking down the mysterious one-armed man (whose name turns out to be Fred Johnson).

This premise, which is succinctly recalled at the start of each episode of *The Fugitive,* has several good points. It is completely elastic. Kimble can go anywhere, do anything, and it all makes sense. After all, the man is on the run from the law—he cannot stay in one place too long. Kimble must keep moving and must keep changing jobs, homes, and friends. Thus, there is a weekly need for many guest stars, who can logically appear and fade out of the series.

The story line can last forever. Kimble could, plausibly, stay on the run the rest of his life, without ever finding the one-armed man or being found by Lt. Gerard. The producers and writers can also weave in and out of the basic "fugitive" concept and allow some episodes to mainly consist of small character studies of the guest stars, like the short plays that made up much of the best TV dramas in the golden age. Kimble can just be the skeleton the scripts are wrapped around.

The plot also allows for legitimate tension, drama, and action. Kimble has to take menial, low-status jobs that do not require much background checking and he cannot stand up for himself out of fear of drawing attention. He is, after all, avoiding an unjust death sentence. Recapture could mean his life, and so narrow escapes and lucky coincidences abound in *The Fugitive,* adding spice to what could be a somewhat slow-moving character piece. Viewers can know that Kimble will not get captured and still not lose interest in watching the fox narrowly escape the hound one more time.

Beyond the format of *The Fugitive,* the acting is first class. David Janssen perfectly captures the feelings of a man on the run, in a portrayal that could only work on the small TV screen where everything is squashed together and viewers get to appreciate the subtle nuances of a character. Janssen portrays Kimble in a subdued and tactful way, with a slew of low-key physical mannerisms that tell much more about the man than loud expositions. He is super reserved in displaying emotions, since vivid emotions only draw attention to him, but he develops a wry, sardonic, pessimistic view of life that is telegraphed by his quick half smiles that look almost like twitches. Kimble knows that most of the surface trappings of people's lives can disappear very quickly, since *everything* can be taken away from you for no just reason, as happened to him.

The overall production quality of *The Fugitive* is to be expected from the show's executive producer, Quinn Martin, the man responsible for such high-grade material as *The Invaders, Streets of San Francisco, The Untouchables, The F.B.I.,* and *Cannon.* You can't miss the trademark Quinn Martin touch of breaking the hour drama into four "acts" (plus an epilogue). An added plus is the deep, resonant voice of William (*Cannon*) Conrad as the serious, pessimistic narrator.

Finally, *The Fugitive* deserves praise for going out in style. Most shows with specific premises never bother to wrap up the concept when the show ceases production. The final two episodes of *The Fugitive* reach a high point of TV series drama, as Kimble, Gerard, and Johnson (the one-armed man) all come together for a climactic resolution of the saga. Hearing that the one-armed man has been captured, Kimbles gives himself up, in hopes he will now be exonerated. The one-armed man escapes, however, and Kimble is in hot water until he manages to talk Gerard into allowing him to go free, to track down the one-armed man. Kimble finally corners his prey on top of an amusement park tower, the one-armed man finally confesses to killing Mrs. Kimble, but, alas, nobody else hears the confession. Kimble and Johnson fight and Gerard, arriving on the scene, must instantly decide who to save. After years of tracking down Kimble in a sincere belief that the doctor was guilty, Gerard now sides with Kimble and shoots the one-armed man, who falls from the tower and dies. With Gerard now behind him, Kimble's conviction is overturned and, in the series' final scene, Dr. Kimble, arm in arm with a pretty new girlfriend, leaves the courthouse a free man and walks off into a sunny summer afternoon. Seen around the world for the first time on the same day, the last episode wraps up with William Conrad intoning "Tuesday, August 29, 1967, the day the running stopped." With that, one of the best TV drama series concludes a classy, entertaining run. ■

**FULL HOUSE (*½) 30 min (44ep at Fall 1989 Color; 1987– ABC) Situation Comedy** *with Bob Saget as Danny Tanner, Candace Cameron as Donna Jo "D. J." Tanner, Jodie Sweetin as Stephanie Tanner, John Stamos as Jesse Cochran, David Coulier as Joey Gladstone, and Lori Loughlin as Rebecca Donaldson*

If you find the idea of a trio of young men floundering at the task of raising three young girls without any maternal assistance to be funny, well, then chances are you will *still* think *Full House* is pretty lame.

Bob Saget (who had a brief stint on CBS's unlamented morning program *The Morning Program*) plays Danny Tanner, a TV sportscaster turned talk show host whose wife dies and leaves him with three daughters, D. J. (ten), Stephanie (five), and Michelle (nine months). Tanner's solution to his dilemma is to have his rock musician brother-in-law Jesse and aspiring stand-up comic pal Joey move in to help take care of the kids. The guys deal with dirty diapers as if they were contaminated moon rocks. The central idea wears thin real fast on *Full House,* and the kids are the usual batch of know-it-alls who populate TV sitcoms.

**FUNNY FACE (**) 30 min (13ep Color; 1971 CBS) Situation Comedy** *with Sandy Duncan as Sandy Stockton, Valorie Armstrong as Alice McRaven, Kathleen Freeman as Kate Harwell, and Henry Beckman as Pat Harwell*

Sandy Duncan is sweet and perky as Sandy Stockton, a student teacher in Los Angeles who earns money on the side by acting in TV commercials. The primary focus in *Funny Face* is on the problems Stockton, a girl from Small Town, USA, has in dealing with the raucous life-style in Tinsel Town.

*Funny Face* shut down production after thirteen episodes so that the star could undergo eye surgery. Once Duncan recovered, the Sandy Stockton character was revived in *The Sandy Duncan Show.*

**FUNNY PEOPLE (*½) 60 min (6ep Color; 1988 NBC) Comedy Magazine** *with Rita Rudner, Scott Blakeman, Blake Clark, and Leeza Gibbons as hosts*

Producer George Schlatter, who gave us both *Laugh-In* and *Real People,* combines elements of those two series in this obscure offering. Along with some "straight" stand-up comedy, *Funny People* presents short feature reports on comedians, oddballs, and anything else that might strike someone as funny. It's an unwieldy format, which only works occasionally, but Schlatter deserves credit for trying something new.

**THE FUNNY SIDE (*½) 60 min (13ep Color; 1971 NBC) Comedy-Variety** *with Gene Kelly as host*

One of those time capsule series that captures the mainstream view of an era (the early 1970s). You know exactly where this one is going by looking at the premise: comedy sketches (and songs) illustrating the funny side of life as faced by couples from every level of society. Five pairs of performers play the respective character types, including John Amos and Teresa Graves (blacks), Warren Berlinger and Pat Finley (blue collars), Dick Clair and Jenna McMahon (sophisticates), Michael Lembeck and Cindy Williams (counterculture teens), and Burt Mustin and Queenie Smith (seniors). Even tackling such timeless topics as taxes and children, this series is guaranteed to make you wince. (And then there's sex and marriage!) But since nearly every performer has a long list of other television work, the shows end up functioning much like a high school or college yearbook: They're a collection of familiar faces in a setting that seems a lifetime away.

**FURY (**½) 30 min (114ep B&W; 1955–1960 NBC) Drama** *with Bobby Diamond as Joey Newton, Peter Graves as Jim Newton, William Fawcett as Pete, Roger Mobley as Packy Lambert, and Gypsy as Fury*

Set in the modern-day West, *Fury* is a kindly series about a poor orphan boy, Joey, who is adopted by bachelor policeman/rancher Jim Newton. Jim raises Joey on his Broken Wheel Ranch and gives the boy a black stallion, named Fury. Boy and horse bond close and foster father Jim gives Joey loads of words of wisdom. This is one of the better father/son western series, and it doesn't go overboard on the schmaltz.

*Fury* was the first series for Peter Graves, later the popular Mr. Phelps on *Mission: Impossible. Fury* is also known as *Brave Stallion.*

**FUTURE COP (*) 60 min (6ep & 90 min pilot & 2 hr sequel Color; 1977 ABC) Police Drama** *with Ernest Borgnine as Joe Cleaver, John Amos as Bill Bundy, Michael Shannon as John Haven, Herbert Nelson as Capt. Skaggs, and Irene Tsu as Dr. Tingley*

There is not much to *Future Cop* other than the silly concept. *McHale's Navy* veteran Ernest Borgnine stars as Los Angeles seasoned police officer Joe Cleaver (no relation to Beaver). Cleaver's new, weird assignment is breaking in officer John Haven, who is a very human-looking android that is supposed to be the "perfect" cop, the cop of the future. Cleaver's regular partner, Bill Bundy, knows nothing about Haven's lineage, so Cleaver goes through all sorts of squirming to keep the secret from Bundy. This concept would work a lot better if it were played for laughs (which it was in another series, the sitcom *Holmes and Yoyo*).

In spite of the tepid reception *Future Cop* received when it first aired, the producers were bold enough to try to revive the show in a two-hour 1978 TV movie called *The Cops and Robin.*

**GALACTICA 1980** **(see *Battlestar Galactica*)**

**THE GALE STORM SHOW (**) (125ep B&W; 1956–1960 CBS & ABC) Situation Comedy** *with Gale Storm as Susanna Pomeroy, ZaSu Pitts as Esmeralda "Nugey" Nugent, Roy Roberts as Capt. Huxley, and Jimmy Fairfax as Cedric*

Long before the *Pacific Princess* set sail on *The Love Boat,* the *S. S. Ocean Queen* was plying the waters of TV-land, bringing out the humor present in the setting of a floating luxury liner. Gale Storm plays Susanna Pomeroy, the social director on the *Ocean Queen,* and Storm brings the same effervescent charm to the role that she did to the title character in *My Little Margie.* Just like Margie, Susanna is forever cooking up schemes that get her involved in innocent misunderstandings. Hollywood film mainstay ZaSu Pitts is a classic as the flustered Nugey (the ship's beautician), Susanna's partner in high jinks. Nothing momentous ever transpires, but, like a cruise voyage, time passes effortlessly on this program.

*The Gale Storm Show* has also been known as *Oh, Susanna.*

**GALLAGHER (*½) 60 min (9ep Color; 1965 & 1967 NBC) Adventure** *with Roger Mobley as Gallagher, Edmond O'Brien as Mr. Crowley, Anne Francis as Adele Jones, and Beverly Garland as Laurie Carlson*

Originally broadcast as a segment of *Walt Disney's Wonderful World of Color, Gallagher* presents the exploits of a young newspaper copyboy in the Old West who dreams of being a real reporter.

**THE GALLANT MEN (**) 60 min (26ep B&W; 1962–1963 ABC) War Drama** *with Robert McQueeney as Conley Wright, William Reynolds as Capt. Jim Benedict, Richard X. Slattery as 1st Sgt. John McKenna, Robert Ridgely as Lt. Frank Kimbro, and Eddie Fontaine as PFC Pete D'Angelo*

Set in Italy during World War II, this series follows the progress of the American Army's thirty-sixth infantry company as seen through the eyes of foreign correspondent Conley Wright. As such it comes off as talky and cerebral, spending too much time with the brass or paying tribute to those "brave, gallant men, who have died so that we might be free" but not offering enough combat action showing the "grunts" at work. Robert Altman directed the pilot episode, then headed to a different field of battle in *Combat.*

In civilian TV life, William Reynolds (company leader Jim Benedict) also appears as the title character in *Pete Kelly's Blues* and as agent Tom Colby on *The F.B.I.,* while Richard X. Slattery (the freewheeling Sgt. McKenna) frequently turns up as an authority figure such as police lieutenant Modeer in *Switch.*

**GAME, SET, AND MATCH (***½) 60 min (13ep Color; 1988 UK Granada) Drama** *with Ian Holm as Bernard Samson, Mel Martin as Fiona Samson, Gottfried John as Erich Stinnes, Michael Degen as Werner Volkmann, Michael Culver as Dicky Cruyer, and Amanda Donohoe as Gloria Kent*

You have to pay strict attention watching this British espionage tale (based on a trilogy of spy novels by Len Deighton: *Berlin Game, Mexico Set,* and *London Match*), but it's worth it. There are layered storylines, continuing character intrigues, and perplexing cases of loyalty and betrayal. Most of all, though, there are excellent performances all around, led by Ian Holm as Bernard Samson, a one-time top British agent forced to a desk job after allegedly botching a mission in Poland five years before. But now there's a security leak in the high-grade spy "cell" he set up back then (the shadowy Brahms Network) and Samson finds himself reactivated and sent to Berlin. There he must deal with Fiona, the head of the underground data processing unit known as the "Yellow Submarine," who also happens to be his wife, and with Berlin-born Werner Volkmann, a boyhood friend Samson originally recruited as one of his operatives.

This is top-notch stuff, filmed on location in England, Germany, and Mexico. The series first aired Stateside on *Mystery.*

**GANGBUSTERS (**) 30 min (26ep B&W; 1952–1953 NBC & Syndication) Police Drama** *with Phillips H. Lord and Chester Morris as narrator*

*Gangbusters* is similar in concept to *Dragnet,* but not nearly as good. Both programs are based on real-life cases from police and FBI files, but *Gangbusters* has no continuing character, just a narrator to explain each week's offering. On *Dragnet,* despite all of Joe Friday's faults, the central continuing character adds some much needed continuity to the show. With no such focus, *Gangbusters* is just another cops and robbers show.

*Gangbusters* is the successor to a long-running (1936–1957) network radio show. The TV version is syndicated under the title *Captured,* with Chester Morris (Boston Blackie in several 1940s films) replacing creator/producer Phillips Lord as narrator. ■

**THE GANGSTER CHRONICLES (***) 60 min (13ep Color; 1981 NBC) Crime Drama** *with Michael Nouri as Charles "Lucky" Luciano, Joe Penny as Benjamin "Bugsy" Siegel, Brian Benben as Michael Lasker, Kathleen Lloyd as Stella Siegel, Madeline Stowe as Ruth Lasker, Chad Redding as Joy Osler, and E. G. Marshall and Danny Dark as narrators*

Television's answer to The Godfather films, *The Gangster Chronicles* is one of the best TV series about gangsters. Like *The Godfather, The Gangster Chronicles* presents the action from the point of view of the mobsters, showing their private lives as well as their business activities. This humanizing portrait is quite a relief from the years of portrayals of hoods as one-dimensional bad guys. While the mobsters in *The Gangster Chronicles* are humanized, they still come across as pretty nasty fellows. That subtlety of characterization is rare on a TV series.

The major surface difference between *The Gangster*

*Chronicles* and *The Godfather* films is that the TV series focuses on two real-life gangsters, Lucky Luciano and Bugsy Siegel. Michael Lasker, the third of the big three hoods here, is described as a composite of several famous criminals. In spite of the dab of reality, the story lines are only loosely based on the documented lives of the gangsters portrayed. The story lines follow Luciano, Siegel, and Lasker from their days as boyhood friends on New York's Lower East Side around 1907, through their ascendancy to the top of the underworld, up to the end of Prohibition in 1932. ■

**GARRISON'S GORILLAS (*½) 60 min (26ep Color; 1967–1968 ABC) War Drama** *with Ron Harper as Lt. Craig Garrison, Cesare Danova as Actor, Rudy Solari as Casino, Christopher Cary as Goniff, and Brendon Boone as Chief*

Inspired by the 1967 film *The Dirty Dozen, Garrison's Gorillas* boldly swipes the hit film's premise in toto and comes up with a pale copy that leaves the viewer searching for the original in the local video store. Lt. Garrison is a ramrod-straight West Pointer who leads a squad engaged in death-defying missions against the Nazis during World War II. Garrison's Gorillas (as the squad is known) consists of convicts removed from jails just to fight the Germans. The squad members are not given real names, just titles, describing their talents. Actor is a slick con man. Casino is a safecracker. Chief is an American Indian who handles switchblades. Goniff is a thief, as those proficient in Yiddish (such as executive producer Selig Seligman) would know.

*Garrison's Gorillas* is quite a letdown from Seligman's previous series, *Combat,* which presented a more engrossing version of the same war.

**THE GARRY MOORE SHOW (**½) 60 min (B&W & Color; 1958–1964 & 1966–1967 CBS) Comedy-Variety** *with Garry Moore and Durward Kirby*

One of the numerous quality variety hours that ran on CBS during the late 1950s and early 1960s, *The Garry Moore Show* is an easygoing low-key program that always presented the best in up and coming comics. Carol Burnett became a star through her stint as a regular from 1959 to 1962. Allen Funt's *Candid Camera* concept was a weekly feature in 1959 and 1960. John Byner and Jackie Vernon starred in the 1966 one-year revival of the show.

**GAVILAN (*) 60 min (10ep Color; 1982–1983 NBC) Adventure** *with Robert Urich as Robert Gavilan, Patrick Macnee as Milo Bentley, and Kate Reid as Marion Jaworski*

With two quality actors, *Gavilan* should be more than just the passable fare it is. A silly, contrived premise drags the show down to being a boring waste of sixty minutes. Robert Urich (*Vega$, Spenser: For Hire*) plays Robert Gavilan, an ex-CIA agent who now has an amorphous consulting job to an oceanographic institute in Malibu, California. Gavilan's roommate in his beach house is an expatriate Latin American (inexplicably played by the ultra-British Patrick Macnee, star of *The Avengers*). Gavilan does some work for the institute, but mostly becomes involved in spy missions. *Gavilan*'s executive producer, Leonard Goldberg, had more success with *Charlie's Angels* and *Fantasy Island.*

**THE GEMINI MAN (*) 60 min (7ep & 2 hr pilot Color; 1976 NBC) Adventure** *with Ben Murphy as Sam Casey, William Sylvester as Leonard Driscoll, and Katherine Crawford as Abby Lawrence*

The Invisible Man strikes again. This time, though, there's a needlessly unwieldy gimmick: certain death following visibility. Government agent Sam Casey has been exposed to a dose of radiation from an underwater explosion that has rendered him invisible. But Abby, his friend at the agency (INTERSECT), comes up with a device (looking suspiciously like a wristwatch) that counteracts the effects of the radiation and makes him visible, but only for short periods of time. If Sam uses this device for more than fifteen minutes in a twenty-four hour period, he'll die.

Even if you keep a stopwatch by your television, all that mumbo-jumbo doesn't add any suspense to the stories—it's really just an excuse to have both an invisible man and a real-life visible title character in the same series. That's understandable, but not as much fun as watching the late 1950s British *Invisible Man* to see a disembodied robed figure peel the last of the wraparound bandages from his face to reveal . . . nothing!

Not that you'd want to even bother with this one, which is strictly routine fantasy adventure. If you're really interested, though, catch the pilot (currently circulating under the title *Code Name: Minus One,* and cut to fit a ninety-minute slot). At least it has future *L. A. Law* senior partner Richard Dysart in the role of agency head Leonard Driscoll.

**THE GENE AUTRY SHOW (**) 30 min (86ep: 71 B&W & 15 Color; 1950–1956 CBS) Western** *with Gene Autry and Pat Buttram as themselves*

Gene Autry, the singing cowboy who captured the hearts of Americans, young and old, through movie serials in the 1930s and 1940s, was one of the first western heroes to make the move to TV, along with the Lone Ranger. His amiable series is filled with the usual good guys–bad guys Pablum that kids sopped up for years in Saturday matinees at the Bijou. Autry plays Autry, a good man who aimlessly roams the West with his faithful pal Pat and his noble steed Champion, helping to bring justice to those in need. Gene frequently gets to sing, and his theme song "Back in the Saddle Again" deserves its status as a classic.

## GENE AUTRY'S MELODY RANCH (*) 30 min (19ep Color; 1966 Syndication) Musical-Variety *with Gene Autry as host*

The singing cowboy star presents country and western talent, set in Gene's spread, the Melody Ranch.

## THE GENERAL ELECTRIC THEATER (***) 30 min (200ep B&W; 1953–1962 CBS) Drama Anthology *with Ronald Reagan as host*

Numerous famous actors and actresses of 1950s Hollywood turn up in this eclectic anthology series. Offerings range from serious drama to light entertainment. Ronald Reagan appears as host in all but the earliest episodes and, like most TV drama anthology hosts of the 1950s, the future president pops up in several episodes, some as co-star with wife (and future first lady) Nancy Davis. Keep a sharp eye peeled for the episode "A Turkey for the President" from November 1958, starring the Reagans (and Ward Bond) as Indians. No kidding.

For a while, these dramas were syndicated under the title *Star Showcase,* with Reagan's narration excised and replaced with that of another old Hollywood actor, Edward Arnold. ■

## GENERAL ELECTRIC TRUE (*½) 30 min (33ep B&W; 1962–1963 CBS) Drama Anthology *with Jack Webb as host/narrator*

*Dragnet* impresario Jack Webb not only hosts this show but narrates it, stars in several episodes, and helps produce and direct some of the episodes. All of the stories come from the files of long-forgotten *True* magazine, and are supposed to be the God's honest truth. Numerous actors and actresses who later became famous appear, but there are not as many big stars as in *General Electric Theater,* the series that *General Electric True* succeeded.

In syndication, this show is simply known as *True.*

## GENTLE BEN (**½) 30 min (56ep Color; 1967–1969 CBS) Adventure *with Dennis Weaver as Tom Wedloe, Clint Howard as Mark Wedloe, Beth Brickell as Ellen Wedloe, Rance Howard as Henry Broomhauer, and Bruno as Ben*

*Gentle Ben* is about the adventures shared by a young boy, Mark Wedloe, and his pet 650-pound black bear, Ben. Considering the size of Mark's pet, it is fortunate that the Wedloe clan does not live in the average TV suburban house, but rather in the Florida Everglades, where father Tom Wedloe is a game warden.

It is not fair to just snidely say that *Gentle Ben* is wholesome, for that word connotes blandness. Wholesome without being bland, *Gentle Ben* is good, quality, family entertainment that youngsters can get a big kick out of and that parents won't die of boredom watching. Star Clint Howard is the brother of TV/movie star and director Ron Howard, and their father Rance appears as a friend of the Wedloe family.

*Gentle Ben* comes from Ivan Tors, who also brought us *Daktari, Flipper,* and *Sea Hunt.*

## THE GENTLE TOUCH (**) 60 min (29ep Color; 1979–1980 UK London Weekend Television) Police Drama *with Jill Gascoine, William Marlowe, and Leslie Schofield*

The home and office adventures of Britain's first female police detective (thus the condescending title), with cases set chiefly in the Soho and Covent Garden areas of London. Competent but nothing outstanding—certainly no threat to *Cagney and Lacey.*

## GEORGE AND MILDRED (**) 30 min (30ep Color; 1976–1980 UK Thames) Situation Comedy *with Brian Murphy as George Roper, Yootha Joyce as Mildred Roper, Norman Eshley as Jeffrey Fourmile, Sheila Fearn as Anne Fourmile, Nicholas Bond-Owen as Tristam Fourmile, Avril Elgar as Ethel, and Reginald Marsh as Humphrey*

A highly successful spin-off from *A Man About the House* (the British model for *Three's Company*), taking the Ropers into a posh new executive neighborhood. There, as in *The Ropers* spin-off in the United States, the two are regarded with initial disdain by some of the established residents. But unlike the Stateside version, it's easy to understand why they consider the Ropers to be social inferiors.

Unlike Stanley and Helen Roper (in the United States), George and Mildred are fairly unsympathetic. Mildred is pushy and somewhat of a social climber. George is (to be blunt) lazy and rather stupid. So they often seem to get exactly what they deserve.

Fortunately this class-conflict comedy is well played, so the episodes are quite funny, if occasionally cruel to their protagonists.

## THE GEORGE BURNS AND GRACIE ALLEN SHOW (****) 30 min (239ep B&W; 1950–1958 CBS) Situation Comedy *with George Burns, Gracie Allen, Harry Von Zell, and Ronnie Burns as themselves, Bea Benaderet as Blanche Morton, and Fred Clark and Larry Keating as Harry Morton*

No, George Burns has not been around since creation (though he did provide some after-the-fact advice while understudying the part of God). But he did come up with one very important element in the creation of the Burns and Allen television series: that he be able to step out of the action, talk to the audience, and then step back in. It's an original contribution he has no doubts about claiming because he specifically remembers stealing the gimmick from Thornton Wilder's play, *Our Town.*

Which is exactly the type of observation he'd make in the monologues, sharing a wry sense of self-awareness with viewers. It's an irresistible style and one key reason *The George Burns and Gracie Allen Show* remains fresh and entertaining even today. Another, of course, is Gracie Allen.

In a sitcom world that embraces empty-headed screwball females, Gracie stands in a class by herself. Instead of being dumb, she is brilliant, but operating on a totally different plane of logic and reality. Such an approach requires clever scripts and flawless delivery, and this series has both. Without ever cracking her character facade, Gracie deftly argues illogical logic, leaving anyone who dares match wits with her near tears. (One running gag on the series has a closet filled with hats left behind by people who have quietly slipped out in defeat rather than face another round with Gracie.) It's no wonder that a successful Gracie Allen type is one of the highly prized catches of any comedy, though only a few have ever come close to the original (among the best: Woody on *Cheers* and Clara on *No, Honestly*).

The strength of George and Gracie's individual witticisms also emphasizes another unique aspect of this series: It's almost all talk. Though there are barebones plots and occasional physical schtick, the bulk of each episode is devoted to conversation. In fact, the specific plot complications are clearly there just to spark the exchanges because, at any time, a few words of explanation will clear everything up. George sometimes alludes to that fact in his monologues (he's the only character who knows that this is just some silly sitcom and none of it is really happening), often trying to decide how he can goose things along with a well-placed phone call or a deliberately misunderstood statement. Sometimes he considers his next move while using the famous George Burns television set, which allows him to watch scenes with the other cast members (especially next-door neighbors Blanche and Harry Morton). They don't know he can hear and see them, so they often have a few laughs at his expense, only to be left gaping in amazement when he later deliberately refers to their private comments.

Over the course of the 239 filmed episodes of the *Burns and Allen Show,* the setting changes from Beverly Hills to a New York high-rise apartment building and then back to Beverly Hills (which is when George's magic television turns up). Son Ronnie first appears as another character, then joins the cast as himself. Harry Morton is played by two different people, but not at the same time (so Blanche is still an honest woman). Announcer Harry Von Zell is probably fired and rehired more often than anybody in employment history. And even though the series setup clearly establishes George and Gracie as the stars of a successful TV comedy, we never break into an episode of *that* Burns and Allen show. Why bother? The one we're all watching is just fine.

In addition to the 239 filmed episodes, there are also two seasons of episodes (from 1950 to 1952) that were done live in a New York theater, but they are not included in the syndication package. (Kinescopes of a few occasionally turn up on home video.) If you look closely at the earliest film episodes, though, you can see remnants of the stage days: The action begins after the curtain rises, with the proscenium arch briefly framing the scene before the camera moves in. And, of course, the closing Burns and Allen routines ("Well, Gracie, which of your relatives shall we talk about tonight?") come straight from the vaudeville stage. ■

**THE GEORGE BURNS SHOW (**½) 30 min (B&W; 1958–1959 CBS) Situation Comedy** *with George Burns, Harry Von Zell, Ronnie Burns, and Judi Meredith as themselves, Bea Benaderet as Blanche Morton, Larry Keating as Harry Morton, and Lisa Davis as Miss Jenkins*

When Gracie Allen decided to retire from show biz, George Burns took his first stab in decades at a solo act. Well, he wasn't exactly alone out there. Sensibly, he stayed with the familiar performers from the *Burns and Allen* setup, from neighbors Blanche and Harry Morton to announcer Harry Von Zell. Even son Ronnie is around, with a new girlfriend, Judi Meredith. The premise is a slight variation from the original, only this time we occasionally get to see the variety acts theatrical producer George Burns has booked. Actually, the overall effect is pretty good, though at times the series takes on a *Waiting for Godot* air because Gracie is still very much on everybody's mind (they talk about her during the stories) and you keep expecting her to show up. She never does. ■

**GEORGE BURNS COMEDY WEEK (***) 30 min (13ep Color; 1985 CBS) Comedy Anthology** *with George Burns as host*

Producers Steve Martin and Carl Gottlieb sneak in some truly offbeat comedy with George Burns as the reassuring front man to introduce each story.

As with any anthology, the settings, characters, and premises change from episode to episode. However, unlike many, this one offers a satisfying variety in its lineup. There's a nice mix of veteran comedy faces (including Don Knotts, Harvey Korman, and Don Rickles), the *Saturday Night Live/SCTV* crowd (including Laraine Newman, Catherine O'Hara, and Eugene Levy), and a host of others (including Martin Mull, Fred Willard, Bronson Pinchot, Sandy Baron, Howard Hesseman, Patrick Duffy, and Tim Matheson).

The stories range from standard silly situations ("The Couch" with Harvey Korman and Valerie Perrine chasing a used couch down the streets of Beverly Hills) to mock adventure ("Home for Dinner" with Eugene Levy on a fishing trip with his neighbors that turns into a rescue mission in a foreign country) to downright surreal ("The Assignment" with Elliott Gould and Telly Savalas in pursuit of a supposedly extinct animal in the jungles of 1940s Africa).

There is even a Christmas tale, "Christmas Carol II: The Sequel," with James Whitmore as Ebenezer Scrooge, who is once again visited by Marley's ghost—this time because the one-time tightwad and champion of humbug has let his newfound generous and jovial nature turn him into a patsy.

Unfortunately, *Comedy Week* didn't survive past this first run of episodes, even though it was probably the best of what was billed at the time as a revival of the anthology format (*Amazing Stories,* the new *Twilight Zone,* and *Alfred Hitchcock Presents* also hit the air back then). Ironically the series did generate a spin-off when "The Couch" begat *Leo and Liz in Beverly Hills.*

**THE GEORGE SANDERS MYSTERY THEATER** (*½) **30 min (13ep B&W; 1957 NBC) Drama Anthology** *with George Sanders as host*

Movie fans know George Sanders best as the suave British actor who won an Oscar for his role as a drama critic in *All About Eve.* TV fans may recall Sanders as Mr. Freeze, one of the colorful villains in *Batman.* Sanders was an odd duck who committed suicide in 1972 and left a note explaining that he was bored by life. In this series, his only lead TV role, Sanders casually hosts a series of mildly interesting "who dun it?" mysteries.

**GEORGE WASHINGTON** (**½) **(8hr miniseries Color; 1984 CBS) Drama** *with Barry Bostwick as George Washington, Jaclyn Smith as Sally Fairfax, Patty Duke Astin as Martha Washington, Lloyd Bridges as Caleb Quinn, Hal Holbrook as John Adams, and Jose Ferrer as Robert Dinwiddie*

History is turned into a backdrop for seething passions in this adaptation of James Thomas Flexner's four-volume biography of America's first president. Barry Bostwick (nerdy Brad Majors in *The Rocky Horror Picture Show* theatrical film) turns in a good performance as the young Washington, portraying the Virginian from the death of his father in 1743 to his retirement as head of the American Army after the Revolutionary War. Much attention is given to George's lust for Sally Fairfax, his best friend's wife.

David Gerber, producer of *Police Story,* produced this miniseries and the 1986 four-hour TV movie sequel, *George Washington: The Forging of a Nation,* which reprises Bostwick and Patty Duke Astin as the first "first couple" after Washington takes office at the end of the Revolutionary War.

**THE GERTRUDE BERG SHOW** (see ***Mrs. G Goes to College***)

**GET CHRISTIE LOVE!** (*) **60 min (22ep & 90 min pilot Color; 1974–1975 ABC) Police Drama** *with Teresa Graves as Christie Love, Charles Cioffi as Lt. Matt Reardon, and Jack Kelly as Capt. Arthur P. Ryan*

No, this is not a show about a woman who desperately needs affection, as its title might imply. Rather, it is a flashy antiestablishment cop show from the 1970s that uses the character's name as cheap wordplay in the title (always a bad sign).

Christie Love is a beautiful, black, undercover policewoman in Los Angeles, who doesn't like working by the silly old stodgy rules established by the police. She goes her own way, showing lots of leg as she does, while her boss (first Lt. Reardon, then Capt. Ryan) fumes.

Teresa Graves is much better than this role. Originally a singer with the Doodletown Pipers, she was briefly a regular on *Laugh-In.* The pilot for this series has Harry Guardino as the frustrated boss, named Lt. Casey Reardon.

**GET SMART** (***) **30 min (138ep: 1 B&W & 137 Color & 2 hr sequel; 1965–1970 NBC & CBS) Situation Comedy** *with Don Adams as Maxwell Smart, Barbara Feldon as Agent 99, Edward Platt as The Chief, Bernie Kopell as Conrad Siegfried, Dave Ketchem as Agent 13, King Moody as Starker, Dick Gautier as Hymie the Robot, and Robert Karvelas as Larrabee*

Hatched and executed by Mel Brooks and Buck Henry in the mid-1960s, *Get Smart* is a genre parody that still wears well. The reason? Though set up as a spy spoof, the series successfully works several comedy fronts at once.

Some of it is pure mechanics. Secret agent Napoleon Solo works for U.N.C.L.E. and fights THRUSH, so Maxwell Smart (secret agent 86) works for CONTROL and fights KAOS. James Bond and Solo are usually armed with miniaturized gadgets disguised as innocent everyday objects like a pen or watch, so Smart comes equipped with a portable telephone hidden in his shoe. Napoleon Solo enters U.N.C.L.E. headquarters through a secret door at the back of a changing room in a New York City tailor shop, so Smart enters a phone booth at the end of a long corridor, dials a number, and drops through the floor to CONTROL.

But the real key to *Get Smart*'s humorous setup is the character of Maxwell Smart himself. He stands in dramatic contrast to the typically suave, erudite spies such as Bond or Solo. Agent 86 is sincere but clumsy, dedicated but easily confused, disciplined but often oblivious to what is really going on around him. Fortunately he also has enough luck (usually in the form of Agent 99) to complete his assignments successfully.

To poke fun at the spy world's already larger-than-life schemes for world domination, *Get Smart* downsizes the whole enterprise into just another routine job. Episode after episode, there is always some madman waiting to destroy the planet or steal some code, so Smart and 99 punch in and go to work. Sometimes in the course of their battles they run into the same foes (such as Conrad Siegfried), so they take the opportunity to catch up on the latest gossip, talk shop, compare pension plans, and even laugh about outwitting each other in the past. They may be enemies, but they do share the same profession. The characters also enjoy sharing the same stage in specific send-ups of other series or theatrical films such as *The Maltese Falcon, Casablanca, The Fugitive, I Spy,* and *The Avengers.*

Rounding out the *Get Smart* story lines are episodes that take spying as a routine job to its logical conclusion, using the world of espionage as backdrop for domestic comedy. This followed years of flirting in the field as Max (certain they were both about to die) proposes to 99, who immediately figures out a way for them to escape certain death. Later they get married, set up housekeeping, and eventually have children (twins). In doing so, they emerge as one of the few adventure couples to have comfortable runs both while flirting and in domestic bliss.

One word of warning: If you can't stand such Don Adams catch phrases as "Sorry about that, Chief!" "Would you believe . . . ?" "I asked you not to tell me that!" "And loving it!" and "Missed it by *that* much!" you'll have to skip this series completely. They turn up *all* the time, though that's part of their charm.

About half a decade too early (baby-boomer television nostalgia had not yet become chic in 1980), Adams returned to the *Get Smart* role for a theatrical feature film, *The Nude Bomb*—though without Ed Platt (who had died), Barbara Feldon, or CONTROL (he worked instead for PITS—Provisional Intelligence Tactical Service). This film was retitled *The Return of Maxwell Smart* for television movie packages. There was another revival in 1989, *Get Smart Again,* a two-hour TV movie. This time the job was done right, with the old cast members out in full force, including 99, Hymie the Robot, and KAOS agents Siegfried and Starker.

Don Adams has also lent his distinctive voice and persona to the title characters of two stand-out cartoon series. In *Tennessee Tuxedo* (from 1963), he plays a well-meaning city zoo penguin who is always trying to understand how things work so he can apply the same principles to improving his life at the city zoo. With his walrus friend Chumley, he usually gets the science part right, but manages to turn the project into an amusing slapstick disaster some other way.

With *Inspector Gadget* (86 episodes from 1982 to 1983), Adams is in a comfortably close approximation of the *Get Smart* setting. Gadget is a half-bionic crime fighter who (with the cry "Go Go Gadget!") can sprout rocket jet feet, elongated legs, or buzz saw arms. However, he's also prone to rash assumptions and bumbling bad timing (just like Max). Fortunately he has Agent 99-type support in Penny, his young genius niece, and Brain, his dog. Appropriately Gadget's chief nemesis is Dr. Claw, the name used by one of Maxwell Smart's first foes.

**GETTING TOGETHER (*½) 30 min (15ep Color; 1971–1972 ABC) Situation Comedy** *with Bobby Sherman as Bobby Conway, Wes Stern as Lionel Poindexter, Susan Neher as Jennifer Conway, Jack Burns as Rudy Colcheck, and Pat Carroll as Rita Simon*

Bobby Sherman, then a newly minted bubble gum rock star ("Julie, Do Ya Love Me"), plays a struggling rock songwriter in *Getting Together.* Sherman's character, Bobby Conway, writes the tunes, while his tone-deaf partner Lionel writes the words. To add domesticity, Conway is the guardian of his twelve-year-old sister Jennifer. Conway, Lionel, and Jennifer live together in poor but humble surroundings, waiting for the songwriting team to hit the big time. This show ought to be at least cutely nostalgic, but it has little to offer, even for aging fans of Mr. Sherman.

The original pilot for *Getting Together,* called *A Knight in Shining Armor,* aired on *The Partridge Family* and relates how the Partridges first introduced Conway to Lionel.

**THE GHOST AND MRS. MUIR (**) 50ep Color; 1968–1970 NBC & ABC) Situation Comedy** *with Hope Lange as Carolyn Muir, Edward Mulhare as Capt. Daniel Gregg, Reta Shaw as Martha Grant, Kellie Flanagan as Candice Muir, Harlen Carraher as Jonathan Muir, and Charles Nelson Reilly as Claymore Gregg*

Daniel Gregg is a nineteenth-century sea captain still haunting his old New England coast home, Gull Cottage, in the twentieth century. He doesn't like visitors, scaring them off every time his still-alive nephew, Claymore, attempts to rent the place. Then a widow, her two children, their housemaid (Martha), and their dog (Scruffy) turn up. Captain Gregg likes them, shows himself to the widow, and he and Mrs. Muir develop a genuine friendship.

The series is inspired by a successful 1947 theatrical feature, but since the film tied up most of the loose ends, this television version is more an alternative scenario rather than a continuation. As in the original, Mrs. Muir is a writer (occasionally helped by Captain Gregg), but she specializes in freelance articles not romantic tales. And while she's interested in romance, she's also content to raise her children and live her life quite independently. In the meantime, she goes through fairly standard warm family comedy complications, peppered with instances of unbridled silliness, especially from Charles Nelson Reilly as Gregg's nephew. No matter what, though, the captain is always there to chat with his good friend.

Though it's never clear how anything really *could* develop between Mrs. Muir and Captain Gregg, one disappointment of this series is the realization that nothing ever will. Even with a relatively low-key approach to the ghost angle, the captain is still just one more magic friend, like George and Marion Kirby in *Topper,* Samantha on *Bewitched,* and Jeannie on *I Dream of Jeannie,* but without the wedding bells.

**GHOST STORY/CIRCLE OF FEAR** (*) **60 min (22ep Color; 1972–1973 NBC) Suspense Anthology** *with Sebastian Cabot as Winston Essex, the host*

Sebastian Cabot's final TV series role is, unfortunately, quite forgettable. He is totally superfluous in the role of Winston Essex, the proprietor of Mansfield House, a spooky hotel where all sorts of ghosts, vampires, and witches hang out. Cabot, as Essex, is simply window dressing to introduce each week's mild episode of supernatural suspense. After thirteen episodes, when Cabot's expendability evidently became clear to the producers, Cabot is dumped and the show is renamed *Circle of Fear* for the final nine episodes. The focus is now just suspense in general, merely pointing out this show's basic problem: The stories are not very good.

**GIBBSVILLE** (**½) **60 min (8ep & 90 min pilot Color; 1976 NBC) Drama** *with John Savage as Jim Malloy, Gig Young as Ray Whitehead, Biff McGuire as Dr. Michael Malloy, Peggy McCay as Mrs. Malloy, and Bert Remsen as Pell*

Though it will never rank as a cult classic, this sadly overlooked series has a lot going for it. Based on a few short stories by John O'Hara, *Gibbsville* is set in the 1940s, in a small Pennsylvania mining town of the same name. Jim Malloy, prodigal son of Dr. Malloy, returns in shame after being booted out of Yale. Young Malloy takes up journalism at the *Gibbsville Courier*, the bottom of the newspaper barrel. Jim is apprenticed to Ray Whitehead, former *Courier* superstar who went on to national acclaim only to return home as a sorry booze hound.

Gig Young, in his final TV series role, is alluring as Whitehead. Young, a former Hollywood leading man and himself no stranger to the bottle, died in a confusing murder/suicide incident only two years after filming *Gibbsville*. The problem with *Gibbsville* is John Savage, who fails to bring much character to the crucial Jim Malloy role.

The 1975 pilot is called *The Turning Point of Jim Malloy*. The series is produced by David Gerber, who had better luck with *Police Story*.

**GIDEON, C.I.D.** (**) **60 min (26ep B&W; 1964 UK ATV) Crime Drama** *with John Gregson as Commander George Gideon, Alexander Davion, and Daphne Anderson.*

A standard British crime drama following the cases of a London police inspector in the C.I.D. division. Also called *Gideon's Way*. A few years later Gregson found himself in a more entertaining setup as straightman to Shirley MacLaine in her 1971 globe-trotting comedy, *Shirley's World*.

**GIDEON OLIVER** (**) **2 hr (5ep Color; 1989 ABC) Adventure** *with Louis Gossett, Jr., as Gideon Oliver*

In the tradition of the Indiana Jones theatrical films, Lou Gossett, Jr., plays a globe-trotting anthropology professor with a nose for mystery and adventure. He does a good job with the character (based on a series of books by Aaron J. Elkins), coming off as believably tough (he was, after all, the no-nonsense drill instructor in the film *An Officer and a Gentleman*) but with the necessary dollop of good humor.

Unfortunately, all this is wasted in violent formula stories that often leave Gideon's friends (for that episode) dead by the closing credits. Even Jessica Fletcher would think twice before visiting.

**GIDGET** (**½) **30 min (32ep Color; 1965–1966 ABC) Situation Comedy** *with Sally Field as Francine "Gidget" Lawrence, Don Porter as Russell Lawrence, Lynette Winter as Larue, Betty Conner as Anne Cooper, and Peter Deuel as John Cooper*

Gidget is a nubile California beach bunny, just feeling her oats as a young woman. She joins a more "mature" set (the surfers) and becomes romantically involved with various bronzed Adonises. Her exploits revolve around boys, beaches, and boring adults. She never ages very much. She never changes. Yet remakes of Gidget keep turning up.

The Gidget saga began with the 1959 beach movie starring Sandra Dee that caught the public's fancy. This movie led to the inevitable sequels, *Gidget Goes Hawaiian, Gidget Goes to Rome,* etc. Next came this mid-1960s TV series, starring Sally Field. In the 1970s and 1980s, feature-length revivals tried to age Gidget slightly, in *Gidget Grows Up, Gidget Gets Married,* and *Gidget's Summer Reunion,* before the 1980s *New Gidget* TV series presented her as something of a grown-up. What with all the previous permutations of Gidget, we can look forward to seeing *Gidget Goes Through Menopause* and *Gidget Goes to a Nursing Home* before too long.

Considering the lightweight nature of the character, it is not surprising to realize that few of the actresses who have played Gidget are known for acting depth. Sandra Dee, Deborah Walley, Cindy Carol, and Monie Ellis are on few lists of the top actresses of our time. Sally Field is the exception. She began her acting career as an eighteen-year-old just out of high school, lucking into the lead of the *Gidget* TV series. She struggled through two other eminently forgettable series (*The Flying Nun* and *The Girl with Something Extra*) and then broke through her silly perky girl typecast to star in several quality movies (such as *Sybil* and *Norma Rae*) and win recognition as a top-level actress.

Sally Field is the best reason to watch *Gidget.* Aside from her, it is an enjoyable but somewhat innocuous mid-1960s sitcom, neither very good nor very bad. This is not to imply that Field turns in Emmy or Oscar performances in *Gidget.* She looks for all the world like an eighteen-year-old in her first big role.

Still, Field adds a lot of life to *Gidget.* Her Gidget is

not just some bimbo on the beach, but rather an intelligent young woman going through all the pitfalls of the teen years while trying to make some sense out of the world. Sure, she gets swept off her feet by older men or dashing surfers and sure, she takes part in silly schoolgirl pranks, but that's what teenage girls do. Field, as Gidget, makes all those traits seem natural, not just a plot device. It is not hard to see the germ of her acting skills through all the fluff.

Aside from Sally Field, Don Porter turns in a solid acting job as Russ Lawrence, Gidget's widower father. Professor Lawrence does his best trying to raise Gidget on his own and he comes up with a few helpful words of advice. Both father and daughter realize, though, that Gidget is growing up and has to fend for herself at times. There is real affection between Gidget and her father and this adds to the natural feeling of the show. All the other characters in *Gidget* are plastic and right out of the standard sitcom mold.

Don't forget to catch the great *Gidget* theme song, written by early 1960s pop tunesmith Howie Greenfield and sung by Johnny Tillotson (of "It Keeps Right on A-Hurtin' " fame).

**GIDGET, THE NEW (*) 30 min (44ep & 2 hr pilot Color 1986–1987 Syndication) Situation Comedy** *with Caryn Richman as Francine "Gidget" Lawrence Griffin, Dean Butler as Jeff "Moondoggie" Griffin, Sydney Penny as Danni Collins, Jill Jacobson as Larue Wilson, Lili Haydn as Gayle Baker, and William Schallert as Russ Lawrence*

The saga of Gidget, once a carefree girl/woman who hung out at California beaches ogling the hunk surfers (like Moondoggie), is pointlessly updated in this series that tries to drag the Gidget character into early middle age. Now married to ex-surf star Moondoggie, Gidget runs her own travel agency and has to deal with her live-in teenaged niece Danni, who is really the "old" Gidget updated for the 1980s. None of this is really worth noting, unless you happen to be planning a Ph.D. dissertation on the evolution of Gidget over the decades. The series pilot, called *Gidget's Summer Reunion,* is a tad more watchable, but not by much.

**GILLIGAN'S ISLAND (*) 30 min (98ep: 36 B&W & 62 Color & 3 sequels: two 2 hr & one 90 min; 1964–1967 CBS) Situation Comedy** *with Bob Denver as Gilligan, Alan Hale, Jr. as Jonas (the "Skipper") Grumby, Jim Backus as Thurston Howell III, Natalie Schafer as Lovey Howell, Tina Louise as Ginger Grant, Russell Johnson as Roy (the "Professor") Hinkley, and Dawn Wells as Mary Ann Summers*

If we are lucky, our civilization will not be judged by our progeny on the basis of *Gilligan's Island* alone, for if it *is* we're going to be written off as simpletons. Through some quirk of popular culture, this silly little show has developed into a staple of rerun syndication. Its distinctive setting and familiar characters have come to symbolize television in the mid-1960s, and it now conjures up warm, cuddly remembrances from the generation of kiddos who were weaned on this Pablum. If we don't watch out, people will start trying to say it really is a comedy classic.

For the few who may have forgotten, *Gilligan's Island* concerns the shipwreck of the tiny charter boat *Minnow.* Ostensibly leaving Hawaii for a three-hour tour, the *Minnow* is caught in a sudden storm and sent far off course to some "uncharted desert isle." There, the two-man crew (the Skipper and first mate Gilligan) and the five passengers (millionaire Thurston Howell III and his wife, a high school science teacher called the Professor, a curvaceous movie star named Ginger, and a pretty country clerk from Kansas named Mary Ann) must cope with primitive island life on the supposedly uninhabited island. Like modern-day Robinson Crusoes, the seven castaways adapt to their new surroundings, while always hoping for rescue someday.

The concept is fine. Placing modern civilized people on a remote uninhabited island is a well-used literary device. Still, Sherwood Schwartz, creator and executive producer of *Gilligan's Island,* takes this flexible format and turns it into mush. The primary problem is the characters. The Skipper is a blustery, glad-handing nincompoop, who probably should have figured out the storm was coming before the shipwreck. Gilligan is a dunderhead who is a pawn in everyone else's games. The Professor is bland and uninteresting. Ginger is a minor league Marilyn Monroe, who thinks she is a lot sexier than she is. Mary Ann is okay, but like the Professor, has few outstanding traits. The Howells are the only saving graces. Veteran Jim Backus (the voice of Mr. Magoo) overplays outrageously as the grown-up preppie Thurston Howell and he and his wife are fairly funny in their attempts to keep up the front of high-class living on the remote island.

The characters interact like children, stuck in grown-up bodies. It's almost slapstick, but it isn't even good slapstick. Aside from the Howells, the cast and crew are nothing but stick figures, designed only to be placed into highly contrived stories.

The weakness of the writing can be demonstrated by noting some questions that regular *Gilligan's Island* viewers have pondered for decades. For example, if the *Minnow* was only out for a three-hour cruise, how can the castaways be so far from civilization? Oh, perhaps the storm blew them quite far, but there is no good answer to this one. If the cruise was to last for just three hours, how come people like the Howells brought along suitcases full of clothes? The only realistic answer is that the writers just didn't care about logic and needed a convenient plot device to play up the Howells' wealth. Most important, if Gilligan's Island is uninhabited, how come so many other people keep turning up? Simple, because the writers ran out of ideas involving just the cast and crew in about five weeks. As a result, this "uncharted desert island" is visited by: a movie producer, an exiled dictator, a famous painter, an underworld mobster, an incompetent pilot, a Hawaiian surfer, a butterfly collector, a mad scientist, a World War II Japanese sailor, a pair of Russian Cosmonauts, a rock-and-roll group, a gorilla, a lion, a robot, doubles for Gilligan, Ginger, and Mr. Howell, and so on (ad nauseum). Needless to say, none of these island interlopers ever take our seven castaways with them when they leave.

*Gilligan's Island* does have some merit. The theme song (co-written by Sherwood Schwartz) is memorable. The show has some nice laughs now and again, and, giving the program every benefit of the doubt, *Gilligan's Island* can be described as a simple series easy to laugh at and with. Still, it is filled with cheap, easy gags, cardboard characters, and a numbing banality that really starts to drag after a few episodes. Adding it up, *Gilligan's Island* stands as a monument to how vapid and empty a sitcom can be.

Even though the series originally lasted only three seasons, the saga of *Gilligan's Island* dragged on for more than another decade. In 1974, seven years after *Gilligan's Island* headed into reruns, five of the original seven cast members supplied the voices to one season's cartoon continuation of the saga of the *Minnow,* titled *The New Adventures of Gilligan.* The absentees were Dawn Wells and Tina Louise (who had the grace never to play Ginger again). In 1978, NBC presented *Rescue from Gilligan's Island,* the first of three TV-movie sequels, with Dawn Wells resuming her role as Mary Ann and Judith Baldwin playing Ginger. A tidal wave provides the locomotion to send the castaways back out to sea, where they are rescued and brought to Hawaii. In an ending only TV writers plotting a new series could plan, the gang later reunite for a reunion cruise on the *Minnow II* and are, you guessed it, again shipwrecked on the *same* island. From 1979, *The Castaways on Gilligan's Island* (with Judith Baldwin again as Ginger) features the troupe leaving the island once more, via a plane the Professor has concocted from a World War II wreck. The plane malfunctions, but the Coast Guard comes to the rescue in the nick of time. Back in civilization, Thurston Howell *buys* Gilligan's Island (from whom?) and turns it into a tropical resort. The seven former castaways become partners in The Castaways hotel on the island as this second sequel ends (again, looking like a series pilot). The third and final TV movie is from 1981 and is the embarrassing *The Harlem Globetrotters on Gilligan's Island* (with Constance Forslund as Ginger). Somehow, the black basketball team winds up staying at The Castaways hotel and battles an evil genius (Martin Landau, from *Mission: Impossible* and *Space: 1999*) who wants to take over the world. In this permutation, the seven ex-castaways are only backdrops for a very silly plot. Fortunately, no new *Gilligan's Island* series ever developed out of these TV movies.

The *Gilligan's Island* story does not quite end there. In 1982, a new animated cartoon series, *Gilligan's Planet,* appeared, with the six loyal originals supplying voices (Dawn Wells now doubling as both Mary Ann *and* Ginger). Here, the *Gilligan's Island* story goes to its ultimate extreme. Somehow still shipwrecked on the island, the Professor builds a rocket ship that takes the seven into outer space, where it (oh no, not again) crash lands, this time on a uncharted *planet.* At last check, the Skipper, Gilligan, the millionaire, his wife, the movie star, the Professor, and Mary Ann are still up there, in the cosmos, trying to get home. Judging by their past record, their chances do not look good.

**GIMME A BREAK (**) 30 min (137ep Color; 1981–1987 NBC) Situation Comedy** *with Nell Carter as Nell Harper, Dolph Sweet as Chief Carl Kanisky, Kari Michaelson as Katie Kanisky, Lauri Hendler as Julie Kanisky Maxwell, Lara Jill Miller as Samantha Kanisky, Howard Morton as Officer Ralph Simpson, Jonathan Silverman as Jonathan Maxwell, Joey Lawrence as Jody Donovan, John Hoyt as Grandpa Stanley Kanisky, and Telma Hopkins as Addy Wilson*

Usually when a series comes up with an episode about some local charity show or awards banquet production you know it's just an excuse for the cast members to take center stage for song and dance and comedy numbers more appropriate to a variety format. (Even *Cagney and Lacey* and *The Paper Chase* pull this stunt!) In most cases, you quietly groan and tolerate the indulgence because you like the characters anyway and you know things will be back to normal next time around. With *Gimme a Break,* though, you almost wish for the opposite: more of Nell Carter performing as Nell Carter and less time devoted to the silly sitcom setting.

Unfortunately such a variety format would not have been able to match *Gimme a Break's* run of more than half a decade, so we take what we can get: Nell as irrepressible housekeeper to a police chief widower (Carl Kanisky) with three cute if troublesome children. Both Nell and the chief start out quite tubby, so there are plenty of fat jokes, along with the semiobligatory housekeeper-to-employer wisecracks, smart-tongued comments from the kids, and family schemes and counterschemes. Naturally there's also plenty of hugs and love to go around, with everyone going through the familiar pains of growing up and growing older. Just as in any real-life family, this growth includes some amusing changes (Nell Carter's tremendous loss of weight practically redefines her character) and some sad ones (in real life Dolph Sweet died about halfway through the series run, so his character of the chief dies as well).

One of the best additions to the cast comes about a third of the way in when former *Bosom Buddies* regular (and one-time member of the singing group Dawn) Telma Hopkins turns up as Nell's best friend, Addy Wilson.

There's excellent chemistry between the two, which carries through to the end of the run. By then the kids have pretty much grown, so for the last batch of episodes Nell and Addy leave California and head for New York City, with Grandpa and an adopted young orphan, Joey, tagging along. There Nell is back at her roots (Carter's major performing breakthrough was in the Broadway musical tribute to Fats Waller, *Ain't Misbehavin'*) and they all have a loose, entertaining time winding down their series.

**THE GIRL FROM U.N.C.L.E. (**) 60 min (29ep Color; 1966–1967 NBC) Spy Adventure** *with Stefanie Powers as April Dancer, Noel Harrison as Mark Slate, and Leo G. Carroll as Alexander Waverly*

Imagine Mr. Roper and Miss America as a daunting spy duo! It almost happened that way. When the pilot for a *Girl from U.N.C.L.E.* spin-off ran as an episode of *The Man from U.N.C.L.E.* ("The Moonglow Affair"), former Miss America (of 1959) Mary Ann Mobley had the role of up-and-coming agent April Dancer while future *Three's Company* landlord Norman Fell played veteran Mark Slate. Their characters played off each other rather well, almost like a father–daughter team.

Apparently that was not quite the chemistry U.N.C.L.E. was looking for because when the new series began six months later, singer Noel Harrison (Rex's son) had the role of Mark (who was transformed into a British U.N.C.L.E. agent transferred from London), while Stefanie Powers was cast as April. It's unlikely either was prepared for what was about to hit them.

*The Girl from U.N.C.L.E.* went into production just as campy comic book television adventures (led by the success of *Batman*) were reaching their peak. So instead of being staged as a lightly tongue-in-cheek spy adventure (like its parent series for the first two seasons), *The Girl from U.N.C.L.E.* comes off as a gimmicky romp, casting aside plot and story line in favor of outrageous props, silly dialogue, and unbelievable Batman-clone foes.

Even worse, April and Mark never have the chance to develop a comfortable rapport like Napoleon Solo and Illya Kuryakin. Instead April spends far too much time as the damsel in distress (in such ridiculous traps as a giant toaster), with Mark riding to the rescue at the last minute.

The best moments in this series come from its ties to the original. For instance, the unflappable Alexander Waverly is there to hand out the assignments. And there are even a couple of crossover appearances with Solo and Kuryakin, most notably "The Mother Muffin Affair" (with Robert Vaughn joining the battle against Mother Muffin, played with aplomb by Boris Karloff) and (on *The Man from U.N.C.L.E.*) "The Galatea Affair" (a parody of Rex Harrison's *My Fair Lady*, with guest Joan Collins).

All to no avail. But on a particularly silly night it is fun to watch an episode or two now, preferably after *Batman*. Or right before *Hart to Hart*, where Stefanie Powers later had considerably more success.

**THE GIRL WITH SOMETHING EXTRA (*½) 30 min (22ep Color; 1973–1974 NBC) Situation Comedy** *with Sally Field as Sally Burton, John Davidson as John Burton, Zohra Lampert as Anne, Jack Sheldon as Jerry Burton, William Windom as Stuart Kline, Stephanie Edwards as Angela, and Teri Garr as Amber*

The last fluffy Sally Field television series before she turned to roles with a harder edge, both on TV (such as *Sybil* in 1976) and in feature films (such as *Norma Rae* in 1979). This one certainly put her good-time spunkiness to the test, casting her as a young bride with one tiny "extra" little secret: She has extra sensory preception. In other words, she can read her husband's mind (or anybody else's). That alone would be enough to send most people over the edge (imagine constantly wading through other people's random internal clutter), but she and John are determined it won't get in the way of their marriage or his career as a lawyer.

So they press on with plenty of silly complications and awkward revelations (Sally discovers what her new mother-in-law thinks of her, or that one of John's clients really is guilty), along with more traditional sitcom plots (John tries to keep Sally's birthday gift a secret), and the semiobligatory early 1970s touches of relevancy and topicality (Sally's friend Anne wants to become a single mom, Sally's parents may separate, John is asked to do a nude centerfold). The gimmick, though, really does get in the way—tapping into someone else's personal thoughts is downright intrusive. If you enjoy Sally Field in her more innocent, perky days, go with *Gidget* over this one. Even *The Flying Nun* might be a better bet—you might be taken aback by a Sister soaring overhead, but at least your private thoughts would still remain your own.

**THE GLEN CAMPBELL GOODTIME HOUR (**½) 60 min (80ep Color; 1968–1972 CBS) Musical-Variety** *with Glen Campbell*

The first thirteen episodes of this series aired under the tongue-twisting name of *The Summer Brothers Smothers Show*, since it was the summer replacement for *The Smothers Brothers Comedy Hour*. Campbell, a fine guitarist and a popular singer of gentle ballads, features several regulars from the Smothers Brothers series such as Pat Paulsen and Leigh French. As time goes on, Campbell relies more on his own brand of regulars, who tend toward the country side (such as Jerry Reed). The material is dated, but good music is always entertaining.

**GLENCANNON (*) 30 min (39ep B&W; 1958–1959 UK) Adventure** *with Thomas Mitchell as Colin Glencannon and Patrick Allen as Bos'n Hughes*

The low-budget seafaring adventures of Colin Glencannon, skipper of the freighter *The Inchcliffe Castle.* Veteran Irish-American character actor Thomas Mitchell puts a light spin on these minor productions, just barely balancing the cheesy location footage. Based on a series of stories written by program creator Guy Gilpatrick.

**GLITTER** (*) **60 min (13ep Color; 1984–1985 ABC) Drama** *with David Birney as Sam Dillon, Morgan Brittany as Kate Simpson, Christopher Mayer as Pete Bozak, Arthur Hill as Charles Hardwick, Tracy Nelson as Angela Timini, Dianne Kay as Jennifer Douglas, and Timothy Patrick Murphy as Chester "Chip" Craddock*

All flash and no substance is the apt description of a series titled *Glitter.* This simplistic drama comes from Aaron Spelling and Douglas Cramer, the masters of cotton candy TV (such as *The Love Boat*). The paper-thin setting of this program is *Glitter* magazine, a *People*-ish rag focusing on celebrities and fads. Sam Dillon and Kate Simpson are the magazine's two leading reporters, who serve the function of introducing and interacting with the various weekly guests, who make or break each episode (just as in *The Love Boat*).

**GLORIA** (**) **30 min (21ep Color; 1982–1983 CBS) Situation Comedy** *with Sally Struthers as Gloria Bunker Stivic, Burgess Meredith as Dr. Willard Adams, Jo de Winter as Dr. Maggie Lawrence, Lou Richards as Clark Uhley, and Christian Jacobs as Joey Stivic*

In this final *All in the Family* spin-off series, Archie's little girl, Gloria, gets the last word on her frequently bumpy marriage to Michael Stivic. She's back in New York with son Joey in tow, ready to begin a new life as a single mother—the reason: The "Meathead" left them both to join a California commune. (Bet that continuity thread would have been reversed if this series had been called *Michael.*) As part of their fresh start, Gloria moves from Queens and lands a job in upstate New York, assisting small-town veterinarian Willard Adams. The series then settles into a relatively low-key effort, focusing on small-town life for Gloria, Joey, her new circle of friends and associates, and, of course, all those cute scene-stealing animals.

Surprisingly, after the welcome home hugs with Archie in the *Gloria* pilot (which first played on *Archie Bunker's Place*) and the quick dispatching of Michael in setting up the new premise, there is virtually no tie-in with Gloria's past in the rest of the series. About the only continuing reference seems to be the name of Joey's pet dog, Archie. That's too bad because the one and only season of *Gloria* coincided with the final season of the parent *Archie Bunker* program, and might have served as an excellent stage for a series of crossover appearances. Instead, Sally Struthers simply went on to join the *9 to 5* working world in its first-run syndication version.

**GLYNIS** (*½) **30 min (13ep & 30 min pilot B&W; 1963 CBS) Situation Comedy** *with Glynis Johns as Glynis Granville, Keith Andes as Keith Granville, and George Matthews as Chick Rogers*

The concept of a fairly normal husband with a wacky wife who gets him involved in numerous adventures had worked before for producer Jess Oppenheimer in *I Love Lucy.* It doesn't work for him in *Glynis,* where the husband is a successful lawyer and the scatterbrained wife is a writer of mystery stories who likes to dabble in real-life sleuthing.

The pilot is known as *Hide and Seek.*

**THE GODFATHER SAGA** (***½) **(9hr miniseries Color; 1977 NBC) Drama** *with Marion Brando and Robert De Niro as Vito Corleone, Al Pacino as Michael Corleone, James Caan as Sonny Corleone, and Robert Duvall as Tom Hagen*

An unlikely triumph, this miniseries combines footage from two Oscar-winning theatrical films (*The Godfather* and *The Godfather II*) into an "underworld epic." Yet, this is not just a cut-and-splice job on the stock copies of the two movies. Instead, Francis Ford Coppola (director of both) was personally involved (working from the Philippines while shooting *Apocalypse Now*), approving a careful and deliberate reworking of the material including the restoration of outtake passages and scenes that had been cut from both films (primarily due to time limitations in theatrical release). In addition, when explicit dialogue had to be trimmed to conform to over-the-air network standards, Coppola insisted that instead of merely cutting out the offending lines, new acceptable passages be recorded by the original actors and dubbed in.

The result is a true rarity: a successful television presentation of a theatrical film that stands on its own as a powerfully effective alternative work of art. Unlike the two separate originals (especially the second, which incorporates flashbacks and flashforwards), all the scenes play out in a single chronological narrative. Even if you've seen both films already, it is definitely worthwhile to catch this version as well.

Officially, the title of this miniseries is *Mario Puzo's The Godfather: The Complete Novel for Television,* but inevitably the shorthand *Godfather Saga* is used to identify it. ■

**GOING MY WAY** (**½) **60 min (39ep B&W; 1962–1963 ABC) Comedy-Drama** *with Gene Kelly as Fr. Chuck O'Malley, Leo G. Carroll as Fr. Fitzgibbon, Dick York as Tom Colwell, and Nydia Westman as Mrs. Featherstone.*

Twenty years after the fact, the producers were obviously not going to get Bing Crosby and Barry Fitzgerald for the television series version of the classic 1944 feature film, but they found some able substitutes in Gene Kelly and Leo G. Carroll. At the time of its original airing, the series was no big deal, just a low-key comic drama doing an acceptable job recreating the spirit of the Crosby/Fitzgerald conflict between the fresh young priest and the set-in-his-ways pastor. Nowadays, though, it comes off as a delightful treat for nostalgic TV fans who instantly recognize Kelly (from *Singing in the Rain*), Carroll (from *The Man from U.N.C.L.E.*), and future *Bewitched* hubby Dick York (who plays the head of a local community center). Though at times the stories may be a bit too slow, gentle, and amiable for contemporary times, there are few other series in which such treatment somehow seems so appropriate.

**THE GOLDBERGS (*½) 30 min (39ep B&W; 1949–1956 CBS & NBC & DuMont & Syndication) Situation Comedy** *with Gertrude Berg as Molly Goldberg, Robert H. Harris and Harold J. Stone and Philip Loeb as Jake Goldberg, Tom Taylor and Larry Robinson as Sammy Goldberg, Eli Mintz as Uncle David, and Arlene McQuade as Rosalie Goldberg*

Don't be fooled by cheap imitations. Although *The Goldbergs* ran for years as a live TV sitcom, if you run into it these days, it will likely be from the show's disappointing final season of thirty-nine filmed episodes, a poor, watered-down version of the original. Unfortunately, it is about all we have left of a comedy classic, one of the first sitcoms in TV history.

Gertrude Berg created the character of Molly Goldberg in the late 1920s and *The Goldbergs* was one of the first big comedy hits on radio. The concept stayed the same for decades. Molly, the archetypal Jewish mother, was a warm, loving soul who spoke with a Yiddish accent and kept up with all the neighborhood gossip. She was the real head of her extended household, which consisted of easygoing husband Jake, children Rosalie and Sammy, and Molly's Uncle David. The shows were filled with simple, enjoyable comedy. Molly's salt-of-the-earth wisdom, spiced with her humorous dialect-filled malapropisms, somehow overcame whatever semicrises arose in each episode. Much of the flavor of the show came from its lower-middle-class Brooklyn setting, where the hustle and bustle of various immigrant groups rubbing shoulders provided endless story lines.

After twenty years of success on the radio, *The Goldbergs* came to TV in 1949, where the show lasted more than five seasons. It was a hit at first, but soon faded as viewers' tastes changed. *The Goldbergs* and other warm, simple, ethnic-based sitcoms of the radio era (*Amos'n'Andy, Lum and Abner, Life with Luigi*) either never caught on with TV viewers or quickly were surpassed by the new TV generation of sitcoms such as *I Love Lucy*.

The original TV version of *The Goldbergs* was faithful to its radio roots, and the few kinescopes that remain from the era of all-live television are enjoyable. By the mid-1950s, the show's popularity was gone. In a last, desperate effort to stay alive, *The Goldbergs* went from live TV to film and, horror of horrors, the setting was changed from Brooklyn, a real town filled with very real people, to Haverville, one of the amorphous, cookie-cutter suburbs that was sprouting in the 1950s both in America and in TV sitcom land. It is this one-year batch of filmed *Goldbergs* that survives today.

Aside from the fact that Molly's supporting cast here is weak (Tom Taylor as Sammy and Robert H. Harris as Jake are letdowns from the originals in those roles), the whole basic premise of the Haverville *Goldbergs* is wrong. What made *The Goldbergs* work was that the family belonged in the original setting, Brooklyn. By placing Molly and family in split-level land, the show loses focus. In Brooklyn, the Goldberg family was one of the gang. In Haverville, they seem weird, eccentric, and lost. After all, who is Molly going to swap gossip with—June Cleaver and Harriet Nelson? Fat chance.

As a historical artifact, the thirty-nine filmed *Goldbergs* (sometimes known as *Molly*) serve a purpose. As entertainment, they strike out. If one of the few surviving Brooklyn episodes turns up, tune in; otherwise avoid *The Goldbergs.* ■

**THE GOLDEN AGE OF TELEVISION (****) 60 min & 90 min (9ep B&W; 1981 Syndication Package) Drama Anthology**

When you hear people reminisce about the golden age of television drama in the 1950s, they may well be referring to a very specific stretch of time (generally regarded as beginning with the 1953 presentation of "Marty" and ending somewhere in 1957 after the first season of *Playhouse 90*). More likely, though, they are thinking of an attitude or a feeling from that era. They remember when ABC, CBS, and NBC were the only major networks and that the anthology format was a key element of their schedules. What was so great about that? In truth, on many nights, nothing. But there was always the potential for something exceptional, especially with writers and performers stretching themselves in the young medium. It hadn't all been done yet. Instead the productions often went out live, with a heady sense of a Broadway opening night. And more people would see that play in one hour than would turn up in a year of stage performances. Who wouldn't get excited?

Still, if you press the point and ask for specific examples of particular stories from the drama anthologies, you'll find not more than a few dozen titles turning up again and again on people's lists, which leads to an obvious question: Why not a series showcasing some of these titles? Let us judge for ourselves if the great golden age was really all that great. With *The Golden Age of Television* you can do so.

First packaged in 1981, this series offers a superb selection of performers and writers, fresh and confident. Because most of these plays were done live in a pre-video tape era, the only available copies are the kinescope recordings made at the time. The recordings involved filming a live presentation from a video screen, so there is a certain graininess to the picture. Nonetheless, once you get used to that, it's very easy to concentrate on what's really important: the dramas. The lineup is quite impressive, including "Marty" with Rod Steiger, "Bang the Drum Slowly" with Paul Newman, "The Comedian" with Mickey Rooney, "The Days of Wine and Roses" with Piper Laurie and Cliff Robertson, "Patterns" with Ed Begley, "No Time for Sergeants" with Andy Griffith, and the ninety-minute "Requiem for a Heavyweight" with Jack Palance. The stories are alternately moving, funny, intense, sad, challenging, and all quite memorable. It's like coming across a cache of great movie performances that had been hidden in the vaults for decades. Indeed many of these dramas were later turned into feature films, often with some of the same cast members.

And that, by the way, is probably the real reason that the golden age of live drama had such a short life span: There was so much more money to be made by writers, directors, and performers working on feature films rather than television. But, for now, it's good to have these dramas as examples of the best from that short but important era in television history.

Note that "The Golden Age" is a very common term and has often appeared as an umbrella title for collections of old series of every sort. On cable, A&E has used the title for reruns of the half-hour filmed Alcoa/Goodyear drama anthologies. There's even a series called *The Golden Years of TV,* but that features a mix of episodes from mostly average 1950s series. So if you tune in expecting "high class" and find an episode of *The Adventures of China Smith* instead, rest assured you have the wrong package. Even on an off-night, the drama anthologies were never that bad. ■

**THE GOLDEN BOWL (**½) 60 min (6ep Color; 1973 UK BBC) Drama** *with Cyril Cusack as Bob Assingham, Barry Morse as Adam Verver, Gayle Hunnicutt as Charlotte Stant, Kathleen Byron as Fanny Assingham, Jill Townsend as Maggie Verver, and Daniel Massey as Prince Amerigo*

Surprisingly entertaining adaptation of a novel by Henry James focusing on the lives of some well-to-do American expatriates. Their story is seen through the eyes of their friend, Bob Assingham, who also serves as narrator. Cyril Cusack does an excellent job in that role, moving the story along, especially when it comes to weaving his way through the sometimes complicated verbiage used by James. And it all starts with a tiny, almost matter-of-fact incident: a remark by a shopkeeper selling a golden bowl to a young woman as a birthday present to her art collector father. By the time it's over, four lives have been changed forever.

**THE GOLDEN GIRLS (***) 30 min (102ep at Fall 1989 Color; 1985– NBC) Situation Comedy** *with Bea Arthur as Dorothy Zbornak, Betty White as Rose Nylund, Rue McClanahan as Blanche Devereaux, and Estelle Getty as Sophia Petrillo*

Before *The Golden Girls,* Susan Harris was mostly known for creating offbeat cult series such as *Fay* and *Soap.* In *The Golden Girls,* Harris finally hits pay dirt, with a program that is mainstream enough to capture and keep a large audience, while intelligent and witty enough to earn critical respect and praise.

As with all Harris series, *The Golden Girls* focuses on people not usually represented in the TV sitcom world, in this case, post-menopausal women. Dorothy, Rose, and Blanche live together in a semblance of harmony in Blanche's home in Miami. All are without a mate from divorce or death. Dorothy is the tart-tongued urban type, now serving as a substitute teacher. Rose is a daffy leftover of the June Cleaver era who is forever (and for no good reason) bubbly and cheerful, in spite of her job as a grief counselor. Blanche is aptly named for Blanche Dubois of *A Streetcar Named Desire* fame. Both Blanches are relics of the antebellum South, hiding a somewhat shady past with veils of practiced gentility.

Into this mixed cauldron comes the fourth element, Sophia, Dorothy's slightly senile mother, on loan from the local nursing home. With no pretenses left at her age, Sophia serves as the source of the zingy putdowns that deflate the egos of the three younger women. Together the four women deal with the trials of life in the so-called golden years. Other than Sophia, none are ready to admit their years of romance and active life are over, and their efforts to keep socially active are both humorous and instructive. They may be prone to calamity in their exploits, but they always maintain dignity amidst the slow decline of their powers.

Watching *The Golden Girls* is like watching an all-star dinner theater troupe, with performers who are perfectly schooled in their craft. This professionalism is to be expected from such a veteran combo. Bea Arthur starred in *Maude,* the premier sitcom about mature women. Rue McClanahan co-starred with Arthur in *Maude,* as Maude's best friend, Vivian. Betty White is the perfect choice to lampoon the peaches and cream innocence of the 1950s image of TV womanhood, since White served years in that role, in various sitcoms and game shows and as TV hostess of the Tournament of Roses parade. White had already been liberated from her goody-two-shoes image by playing Sue Ann Nivens, the venomous manhunter of *The Mary Tyler Moore Show.*

**THE GOLDEN YEARS OF TV (**½) 30 min (77ep B&W; 1985 Syndication) Anthology**

This should not be confused with *The Golden Age of Television* series (which repackages classic dramas from such programs as *Playhouse 90*), though the idea behind it is similar. Rather than attempt to slot the full production run of adventure or comedy programs from the 1950s such as *Captain Gallant, Annie Oakley, Mr. Peepers, Charlie Chan,* or *Sherlock Holmes,* this series take one or two episodes from each of these (as well as from forty-nine other series) to form a sampler anthology of the era. In many cases, the material selected is definitely typical of what you might have seen on TV back then, though that doesn't necessarily mean it is the *best* from the period. Still, sit down with this series in its entirety and you'll see all you'd ever want to of such programs as *China Smith* or *Doctor Fu Manchu* (where even one episode is one too many), along with pleasant visits with the likes of Jack Benny, Ozzie and Harriet, and Leo G. Carroll's *Topper.*

## GOLDIE (see *The Betty Hutton Show*)

## GOMER PYLE, U.S.M.C. (**½) 30 min (150ep: 30 B&W & 120 Color; 1964–1970) Situation Comedy *with Jim Nabors as Pvt. Gomer Pyle, Frank Sutton as Sgt. Vince Carter, Ronnie Schell as Pvt. Gilbert Slater, Barbara Stuart as Bunny Olsen, Forrest Compton as Col. Edward Gray, Allan Melvin as Sgt. Hacker, Roy Stuart as Cpl. Charles Boyle, and William Christopher as Pvt. Lester Hummel*

Gomer Pyle may look harmless. With his wide-eyed innocence and hayseed nasal drawl, he seems an easy mark for any bully, manipulative con man, or overconfident administrator. Yet as Deputy Barney Fife discovered on *The Andy Griffith Show* (where Gomer first appeared, pumping gas at the Mayberry filling station), a pure, unrestrained innocent can be the most powerful, uncontrollable force around. For example, when Barney executed an illegal U-turn moments after handing Gomer a ticket for the same offense, he was stopped dead by Gomer's cry of, "Citizen's arrest! Citizen's arrest!" and eventually spent time in the slammer.

After only one season's worth of episodes on *The Andy Griffith Show,* Jim Nabors shifted his Gomer Pyle character to his spin-off series as Gomer enlisted in the peacetime U.S. Marines. Appropriately, Andy Griffith's Sheriff Taylor character escorted Gomer to the new setting, sending him off into a new world strangely reminiscent of Griffith's own successful run in the 1950s as the country innocent of *No Time for Sergeants* (as a TV play, a stage production, and a feature film). Once again, the armed forces would never know what hit them.

Gomer is enthusiastic and eager to please, much to the puzzlement, frustration, but finally admiration of his immediate superior, Sgt. Carter. He knows Pyle might not be the smartest one around to map out the nation's defense strategy, but he also knows there's not a more loyal, honest, caring, and generous soldier in the outfit. (Then again, maybe he *should* be in charge of the Pentagon.) In the meantime, he learns to live with Pyle's pigheaded adherence to instructions (not letting Carter pass a check point without the proper identification), his literal interpretation of typical drill sergeant sarcasm ("Gol-lee, Sgt. Carter, you're right! This *is* fun!"), and his tendency to babble on enthusiastically about whatever is on his mind. Eventually Carter evolves from Gomer's nemesis to his number one protector (even if Gomer ends up protecting the sergeant more than he'd care to admit).

Though quite a bit more slapstick and situation oriented than *The Andy Griffith Show, Gomer Pyle* still shares the simple, homespun humor of its parent series. (The closest you'll come to Marine swearing are Gomer's pet phrases "Shazam!" and "Surprise! Surprise! Surprise!") Appropriately there are also one or two crossover appearances by *Andy Griffith Show* characters (Andy, Opie, Aunt Bee). And, of course, Jim Nabors is there for the 1986 *Return to Mayberry* reunion movie, still pumping gas with his cousin Goober.

Perhaps the strangest aspect of Gomer Pyle is that it left actor Jim Nabors permanently associated with that country hayseed twang and image, even though in real life he has a rich, deep singing voice. No doubt to counter the character stereotyping, Nabors hosted a musical-variety series in the early 1970s after *Gomer Pyle* ended its run. (Then again, Frank Sutton was one of the regulars on *The Jim Nabors Hour,* so he wasn't trying that hard to distance himself from the very successful Gomer setting.) Nabors also frequently turned up on the *Carol Burnett Show,* where she insisted he was her good luck charm for the opening show of each season. (Burnett, in fact, had appeared several times on *Gomer Pyle,* too.) But no matter how many such appearances he makes, Gomer proudly endures.

## GOOD GUYS (*) 30 min (42ep Color; 1968–1970 CBS) Situation Comedy *with Bob Denver as Rufus Butterworth, Herb Edelman as Bert Gramus, and Joyce Van Patten as Claudia Gramus*

Bob Denver will always be known as Gilligan (or, at least, Maynard G. Krebs). He will never be known as Rufus Butterworth, which is fine for everyone concerned. Rufus and his chum Bert are boyhood pals who go into business together, running Bert's Place, a Los Angeles diner. Rufus is a klutz, whose crazy get-rich-quick schemes are always getting Bert in hot water.

Look for two of Bob Denver's fellow castaways on Gilligan's Island. Alan Hale, Jr. (the Skipper), pops up now and again as Big Tom, Rufus's friend. Jim Backus (Thurston Howell III) plays Henry Arsdale, Bert's father-in-law.

## GOOD HEAVENS (*½) 30 min (13ep Color; 1976 ABC) Situation Comedy *with Carl Reiner as Mr. Angel*

In *Good Heavens,* Carl Reiner plays a kindly angel who finds deserving mortals and grants them one wish, as long as it is not for money. Each week brings a new setting and new cast, but the idea never gels into anything very funny.

Reiner, whose credits include *Your Show of Shows* and *The Dick Van Dyke Show,* produces as well as stars in this program.

**THE GOOD LIFE (*½) 30 min (15ep Color; 1971–1972 NBC) Situation Comedy** *with Larry Hagman as Albert Miller, Donna Mills as Jane Miller, David Wayne as Charles Dutton, Hermione Baddeley as Grace Dutton, and Danny Goldman as Nick Dutton*

On the surface, *The Good Life* is merely another forgettable sitcom, no better and no worse than numerous others. Albert and Jane Miller are a suburban married couple who drop out of the rat race and pass themselves off as a polished butler/maid duo. They are hired to be live-in servants to millionaire industrialist Charles Dutton, and humor is meant to follow from the Millers' efforts to be efficiently servile.

The more interesting aspect of *The Good Life* is the professional relationship between the cast and crew. Larry Hagman, already a star from *I Dream of Jeannie,* went on to become a mega star as J. R. Ewing in *Dallas,* a show produced by Lee Rich, who first produced Hagman here in *The Good Life.* Donna Mills, who plays Hagman's wife in *The Good Life,* also went on to star in a later Lee Rich series, *Knots Landing,* a spin-off from *Dallas,* where she played the devious Abby Cunningham, who had an affair with J. R. Ewing!

**THE GOOD LIFE** **(see also *Good Neighbors*)**

**GOOD MORNING MISS BLISS (**) 30 min (13ep at Summer 1989 & pilot Color; 1988– Disney & NBC) Situation Comedy** *with Hayley Mills as Carrie Bliss, Joan Ryan as Tina Palladrino, Heather Hooper as Nicki, Lark Vooheis as Lisa, Duston Diamond as Screech, Mark-Paul Gosselaar as Zach, Max Battimo as Mikey, and T. K. Carter as Mylo Williams*

Carrie Bliss teaches ninth-grade history and social studies in Indiana's John F. Kennedy Junior High School. She's British, unattached, has a sense of humor, and scores well with the semiobligatory mix of student character types: charming Zach, opinionated Nicki, bubble-headed Lisa Palladrino, misfit Screech, and prankster Mikey. Art teacher Tina is Carrie's best adult friend at the school.

All this is rather broadly played on about the same level as *Welcome Back, Kotter,* though Hayley Mills (as Carrie) is a lot easier to accept as a responsible adult than Gabe Kaplan's Gabe Kotter. The production deal behind this series was a first, with NBC co-producing for an initial run on the Disney cable channel to be followed by its own slotting. However, when Disney canceled the show after only thirteen episodes, NBC revamped the package into *Saved by the Bell* (targeted for a Saturday morning slot).

In the *Good Morning Miss Bliss* pilot (which originally aired on NBC), Carrie is a second grade teacher and married. (Charles Siebert plays her husband.)

**GOOD MORNING WORLD (***) 30 min (26ep Color; 1967–1968 CBS) Situation Comedy** *with Joby Baker as Dave Lewis, Ronnie Schell as Larry Clarke, Billy DeWolfe as Roland B. Hutton, Jr., Julie Parrish as Linda Lewis, and Goldie Hawn as Sandy Kramer*

Produced and developed by *The Dick Van Dyke Show* veterans Carl Reiner, Sheldon Leonard, Bill Persky, and Sam Denoff, this series draws inspiration from its predecessor's hit formula, but uses a slightly different spin in execution. Or, more accurately, a double-play combo, following the home and office lives of a wacky pair of early-morning disc jockeys—Lewis and Clarke—working the morning drive time shift (6 A.M. to 10 A.M.) at a Los Angeles radio station. They do silly voices, drop-in bits, and comic chat in between records and commercials.

Dave Lewis is the married one with a loving wife (a Rob and Laura Petrie relationship), Larry Clarke is the self-styled available bachelor (a younger Buddy, without wife Pickles), and Billy DeWolfe is their overbearing boss, station manager Roland B. Hutton (a combination of Mel Cooley and Alan Brady). Back at home, Goldie Hawn (pre–*Laugh-In,* but using that same daffy voice) plays Sandy, neighbor to Dave and Linda.

The stories are well done, nicely mixing plots involving both domestic and show-biz situations. For instance, in one on the home front, football fan Dave decides to drive 200 miles to a motel with a television in order to see a game blacked out in Los Angeles. Needless to say, by kickoff time he's nowhere near a screen. Back in the performing arena, a story involving a local telethon reveals that Billy DeWolfe's Roland character used to play the vaudeville circuit. Naturally that leads to an on-air piece for him. Finally, in some unintentional foreshadowing of another comedy classic, there's an episode set at a radio awards dinner (the Golden Mikey Awards) that plays an awful lot like one of those Teddy Awards stories on *The Mary Tyler Moore Show.*

Maybe the cast and characters of *Good Morning World* didn't become household names from this series, but they turned in some excellent performances. This series is definitely worth searching out.

**GOOD NEIGHBORS (***) 30 min (28ep & one 60 min special; 1974–1978 UK BBC) Situation Comedy** *with Richard Briers as Tom Good, Felicity Kendal as Barbara Good, Penelope Keith as Margot Ledbetter, and Paul Eddington as Jeremy Ledbetter*

A delightful and well-written character comedy following two next-door neighbor couples, the Goods and the Ledbetters. Both husbands work for the same company (with Jeremy Ledbetter higher up the corporate ladder) until the day Tom decides he's had enough of the rat race. Before it's too late, he wants a shot at the good life, like in the old days when you could grow your own food and make your own clothes. So he and his wife decide to try self-sufficiency for about a year.

The twist is that they're doing it right from their existing suburban house, much to the astonished embarrassment of Margot Ledbetter. As a rule, she is quite concerned about proper appearances, and she knows a goat grazing next door simply isn't done. But Margot and Jeremy come to take a protective interest in their foolish young neighbors, admiring their dedication if not their cause. Tom may walk in with a truly handmade wool-knit suit (unfortunately dyed green), but he's still Tom, a good friend, and a good neighbor. The self-sufficiency gimmick hook aside, the blossoming of their mutual friendship is really what makes this series work.

In U.S. syndication, the title of this series was changed from *The Good Life* (as it plays in Britain) to *Good Neighbors,* perhaps to avoid confusion with the U.S. *Good Life* series with Larry Hagman. Following this series, Penelope Keith took her character type intact to a country estate on *To the Manor Born,* while Paul Eddington worked his way to the top of the political ladder in *Yes, Minister.*

**GOOD TIME HARRY** (*½) **30 min (7ep Color; 1980 NBC) Situation Comedy** *with Ted Bessell as Harry Jenkins, Eugene Roche as Jimmy Hughes, Marcia Strassman as Carol Younger, and Jesse Welles as Billie Howard*

It may be typecasting, but it is rather difficult to swallow the idea of Ted Bessell playing a swinging ladies man, when he is best known to one and all as the eunuch-like boyfriend to Marlo Thomas in *That Girl.* Nonetheless, Bessell tries hard as a newspaper sports reporter in San Francisco, whose work keeps interfering with his social life.

**GOOD TIMES** (**) **30 min (133ep Color; 1974–1979 CBS) Situation Comedy** *with Esther Rolle as Florida Evans, John Amos as James Evans, Jimmie Walker as James Evans, Jr., (J. J.), Ralph Carter as Michael Evans, BernNadette Stanis as Thelma Evans, Ja'net DuBois as Willona Woods, Ben Powers as Keith Anderson, and Janet Jackson as Penny Gordon*

This series seems torn in two directions. On the one hand, there's the tug of tough realism in the basic premise: a struggling black couple in a Chicago high-rise project trying to make a better life for themselves and their three children. Esther Rolle and John Amos anchor that part of the story, standing tall as the strong and loving parental figures, coping even during the seemingly endless lean times. (In that light, the series title carries more than a touch of irony, with the catchy gospel-tinged opening tune an almost defiant declaration of hope.)

One of the family's never-ending challenges is keeping the kids on the right track, especially the smart-mouthed J. J. (played by popular comic Jimmie Walker). The prominence of J. J.'s rubbery-faced mugging to the camera (punctuated by his trademark phrase "Dyn-o-mite!") over the course of the series provides a clue to the forces pulling at *Good Times* from a different direction: that of jive-talking silliness.

Frankly, neither aspect is automatically better than the other—in fact, without heavy doses of humor this setup could very well have turned into a grim ghetto drama. It's just that mixing the two is a very tricky proposition, with J. J. the hustling aspiring artist often just a hair away from J. J the smart-ass caricature. That's one aspect of the scripting that led to the permanent departure of John Amos from the series after three seasons and Esther Rolle's temporary absence for one. During Rolle's absence, the character of next-door neighbor Willona becomes surrogate mother for the series, with young Janet Jackson (Michael's younger sister) joining the cast as her adopted daughter, Penny. Despite the controversy surrounding scripts, though, strong individual stories still turn up anywhere through the series run. However, the best episodes are probably the first and last batches. Often your affection for a particular story may well hinge on your tolerance for J. J.'s antics. (Toward the end of the run, keep an eye out for Gary Coleman doing his prototype smart-aleck kid shortly before landing the lead in *Diff'rent Strokes.*)

*Good Times* started life as a spin-off of a spin-off, taking the Florida Evans character from *Maude* (itself a spin-off from *All in the Family*) and moving her from New York to Chicago.

**GOODBYE MR. CHIPS** (***) **30 min (6ep Color; 1984 UK BBC) Drama** *with Roy Marsden as Charles Edward Chipping (Mr. Chips), Jill Meager as Katherine, Anne Kristen as Mrs. Wickett, Susan Dowdall as Aunt Elizabeth, Eryl Maynard as Amanda Farrell, and Peter Baldwin as Dr. Merivale*

Leisurely rendition of the 1933 James Hilton novel, with the title character played by Roy Marsden (more familiar as inspector Adam Dalgliesh in a series of detective adventures). The story takes him from his arrival at the ivy-covered halls of Brookfield right before the beginning of the twentieth century through to his reflective eighties in retirement. Along the way, he develops from an uncertain new teacher into the quintessential English schoolmaster, loved and respected by his pupils—who give him the nickname Mr. Chips. Best of all, when he's comfortably settled into his late forties bachelor routine, there's suddenly the possibility of romance in the air . . .

When this series aired on *Masterpiece Theatre,* the six half-hour episodes were packaged into three one-hour offerings.

**THE GOODIES** (**) **30 min (26ep Color; 1973–1978 Color) Comedy-Variety** *with Graeme Garden, Tim Brooke-Taylor, and Bill Oddie*

One of those attempts to bring to television the chaotic style of radio's infamous *Goon Show* (a legendary BBC Radio vehicle of the 1950s with Peter Sellers), filling in the specifics that with radio could be left to each listener's imagination. As a result, the episodes are packed with sight gags, nonsequiturs, pratfalls, lots of noise, strange costumes, skits, and more noise. Give them points for sheer energy and definitely tune in if you like that style of humor. For many people, though, the breathless one-upmanship wears thin quickly, so be sure to mix in doses of *Monty Python* (for more cerebral silliness) and *Benny Hill* (for . . . well, you know).

**GOODNIGHT, BEANTOWN** (**) **30 min (18ep Color; 1983–1984 CBS) Situation Comedy** *with Bill Bixby as Matt Cassidy, Mariette Hartley as Jennifer Barnes, Tracey Gold as Susan Barnes, George Coe as Dick Novak, and G. W. Bailey as Albert Addelson*

"Goodnight, Beantown" is the sign-off used by Matt Cassidy, long-time sole anchorman on WYN-TV in Boston. As this series begins, the chauvinistic, egocentric Cassidy suddenly has to deal with the presence of a new co-anchor, and a *female* co-anchor to boot. Jennifer Barnes, the new co-host, is new to the city and winds up living, with her young daughter Susan, in the same apartment building where bachelor Cassidy resides. As a result, the two anchors are at each other's throat all day at work, and then continue to bicker at home.

The addition of the "home" aspect really detracts from this show. *Goodnight, Beantown* can't figure out if it wants to be a smart sitcom in the *Mary Tyler Moore Show* vein or just another cute family sitcom. On top of that, the writing here is dull, and it is somewhat difficult to build up much feeling for either of the two leads.

Bill Bixby is best known from *My Favorite Martian* and *The Incredible Hulk.* Interestingly enough, a few years after *Goodnight, Beantown* ceased production, Mariette Hartley put in a brief stint as a real-life anchor, on CBS's short-lived and unlamented 1987 morning news show, *The Morning Program.*

**GOODTIME GIRLS** (**½) **30 min (13ep Color; 1980 ABC) Situation Comedy** *with Annie Potts as Edith Bedelmeyer, Lorna Patterson as Betty Crandall, Georgia Engel as Loretta Smoot, Francine Tacker as Camille Rittenhouse, and Adrian Zmed as Frankie Millardo*

The crew that produced *Happy Days* and *Laverne and Shirley* gets credit for trying a unique setting in *The Goodtime Girls.* Moving back ten years before *Happy Days,* this program is set in 1942 Washington, D.C. At the time, the capital is filled with bureaucrats working on the war effort (causing a housing shortage) and most of the eligible men are serving Uncle Sam.

Edith, Betty, Loretta, and Camille are four disparate women sharing an apartment. Camille is a snooty reporter, Edith works for the government, Betty is a "Rosie the riveter" defense plant worker, while Loretta, married to an overseas soldier, works in the Pentagon.

The acting here is fresh, the writing is sprightly, and the laughs come easily.

**GOODYEAR TELEVISION PLAYHOUSE** (see ***Turn of Fate; The Golden Age of Television***)

**THE GOVERNOR AND J. J.** (*½) **30 min (39ep Color; 1969–1970 CBS) Situation Comedy** *with Dan Dailey as Gov. William Drinkwater, Julie Sommars as Jennifer Jo "J. J." Drinkwater, Neva Patterson as Maggie McLeod, and James Callahan as George Callison*

Popular Hollywood actor Dan Dailey is perfectly cast as the even-tempered governor of an unnamed midwestern state in this unassuming sitcom. Gov. Drinkwater is a widower, so he uses the talents of his nonconformist twenty-three-year-old daughter J. J. as social director and acting first lady. J. J. is more comfortable in her regular job, assistant zoo curator, but she is quite ready to espouse her opinions on life and politics when in the governor's mansion.

Producer Leonard Stern (*Get Smart*) also cast Dailey as his leading man in *Faraday and Company.*

**GRADY** (*) **30 min (5ep Color; 1975–1976 NBC) Situation Comedy** *with Whitman Mayo as Grady Wilson, Carol Cole as Ellie Marshall, and Joe Morton as Hal Marshall*

The Grady Wilson character originated in *Sanford and Son* as Fred Sanford's slow-witted buddy. *Grady* is a well-intentioned effort to spin off the character into a show of his own, but it just won't work. Grady is not interesting enough to carry an entire program. In his series, Grady is presented as the doting grandfather to the two young children of his daughter and son-in-law Ellie and Hal Marshall. Unlike the Sanfords' neighborhood, the Marshalls live in upscale Santa Monica and, since both parents work, Grady spends his days babysitting.

**GRANDPA GOES TO WASHINGTON** (*) **60 min (11ep Color; 1978–1979 NBC) Comedy-Drama** *with Jack Albertson as Sen. Joe Kelley, Larry Linville as Maj. Gen. Kevin Kelley, and Sue Ane Langdon as Rosie Kelley*

Larry Linville should have stayed in *M*A*S*H.* At least in *M*A*S*H,* Linville's Frank Burns character could bounce his stupidity off the wise-guy barbs of Hawkeye and Trapper. Here, playing Gen. Kevin Kelley, a virtual clone of Maj. Burns, Linville gets to bounce off of Jack Albertson. While Albertson is a consummate acting pro, his character as old coot Joe Kelley, political science professor turned U.S. senator, is almost as annoying as Linville's Gen. Kelley character.

Most of the attempts at humor here are in having senior citizen Senator Kelley really be a rebellious anti-establishment type, the sort you would expect to be a Young Turk. Instead, he is an old Young Turk, whose rambunctious antics constantly embarrass and befuddle his son, Gen. Kelley, a functionary at the Pentagon.

**THE GRAY GHOST (**½) 30 min (39ep B&W; 1957–1958 Syndication) Adventure** *with Tod Andrews as Maj. John Singleton Mosby and Phil Chambers as Lt. St. Clair*

At the end of the 1950s, as the centennial of the Civil War approached, there were several films and TV shows about the War Between the States. *The Gray Ghost* is quite possibly the only TV series about the Civil War that presents the Confederates as the good guys. Maj. Mosby is a dashing Virginian whose lightning raids on Union troops earn him the nickname of the Gray Ghost.

This show is based on the exploits of the real-life Maj. Mosby, as presented in several books about the Southern hero by Virgil Carrington Jones.

**THE GREAT ADVENTURE (**½) 60 min (26ep B&W; 1963–1964 CBS) Drama Anthology** *with Van Heflin and Russell Johnson as narrators*

Long before John Houseman became famous for playing the imperious Prof. Kingsfield in the film and video versions of *Paper Chase,* he had been a fabled producer and director of plays, movies, and several honored TV series. *The Great Adventure* is not Houseman's best work in TV (*Seven Lively Arts,* a Sunday afternoon show from 1957, might classify as such), but it is worth catching nonetheless.

Each episode presents another story from American history, with numerous famous actors and actresses guest starring. Respected Hollywood actor Van Heflin narrates the first thirteen segments, while Russell Johnson narrates the final thirteen episodes. Johnson later became better known as the Professor on that monument of American history, *Gilligan's Island.*

**THE GREAT AMERICAN DREAM MACHINE (***½) 90 & 60 min (Color; 1971–1972 PBS) Comedy** *with Marshall Efron as host*

An extremely ambitious series that broke ground in several areas, *The Great American Dream Machine* is a virtual counterculture news magazine from the middle Nixon years, when little, if any, true social satire could be found on TV. It was produced for PBS, which is a real shocker, since PBS has not exactly been known as a storehouse of humor unless, of course, it comes from England.

The show is rather dated, but much of its content is still funny and fresh, and *The Great American Dream Machine* is one of the direct progenitors of *Saturday Night Live* (check for the appearance of a young Chevy Chase as the pantomime face near the start of many episodes). Andy Rooney (before he became a *60 Minutes* institution), Nicholas von Hoffman (a newspaper columnist), and Studs Terkel (a social historian who had dabbled in TV in its infancy) are regular contributors. The roly-poly presence of host Marshall Efron is delightful.

**GREAT CIRCUSES OF THE WORLD (**) 60 min (7ep Color; 1989 ABC) Variety** *with Mary Hart as host*

Mary Hart, the leggy lady best known for co-anchoring *Entertainment Tonight,* serves as host of a pleasant series showing the highlights of some of the world's best circuses. Big Top stops include Japan, Mexico, West Germany, and even New York City. Producer Joe Cates tried the same format in the mid-1960s, with *Coliseum.*

**THE GREAT GILDERSLEEVE (*) 30 min (39ep B&W; 1955 Syndication) Situation Comedy** *with Willard Waterman as Throckmorton P. "Gildy" Gildersleeve, Stephanie Griffin as Marjorie Forrester, Ronald Keith as Leroy Forrester, and Lillian Randolph as Birdie Lee Coggins*

*The Great Gildersleeve* was a great radio show. It is not a very good TV show. By the time this series was filmed, the bloom was off the Great Gildersleeve rose. Originated by Harold Peary on the *Fibber McGee and Molly* radio show in the 1930s, the blustery figure of Throckmorton P. Gildersleeve, the water commissioner of the town of Summerville, was spun off to his own radio show in 1941. When Peary left the role, Willard Waterman took over the Gildy role on the radio in 1950 and Waterman took the role to TV.

Gildy is a bachelor uncle who raises his orphaned niece and nephew in between his august duties as water commissioner. The humor comes almost exclusively from Gildy's constant bouts of fevered exasperation at the denseness of all those around him. This gambit wears thin fast.

**GREAT MYSTERIES, ORSON WELLES' (*) 30 min (26ep Color; 1973–1974 Syndication) Mystery Anthology** *with Orson Welles as host*

In the 1950s, many fading film stars were tacked on (as hosts) to undistinguished drama anthologies just to add some star title to the show. This is a sad example of the same concept, but from the 1970s. Orson Welles, one of America's film geniuses of the 1940s, had become just another old actor doing commercials ("We shall sell no wine before its time") around the time this bland mystery series roped him into providing short introductions.

**GREAT PERFORMANCES (***) Various (Color; 1974– PBS) Variety**

One of PBS's most successful series, *Great Performances* is actually an umbrella title under which numerous types of programs appear. A great deal of the

*Great Performances* offerings are single-episode productions concerning drama, dance, or music, but there are several memorable series that have appeared under this title. *Brideshead Revisited,* an eleven-part adaptation of Evelyn Waugh's novel, and *Tinker, Tailor, Soldier, Spy,* a six-part version of John LeCarre's spy story, first appeared in the United States as *Great Performance* episodes. See those titles for more details. ■

## THE GREATEST AMERICAN HERO (***½) 60 min

**(42ep & 2 hr pilot & 60 min sequel Color; 1981–1984 ABC & Syndication) Adventure** *with William Katt as Ralph Hinkley/Hanley, Robert Culp as Bill Maxwell, Connie Sellecca as Pam Davidson, Faye Grant as Rhonda Blake, and Michael Pare as Tony Villicana*

This is one of the gems in producer Stephen J. Cannell's production catalogue, a superhero series that manages to strike the perfect balance between stunts and character interaction. It's done with good humor, sly self-awareness, and a sense of romance. If you liked the tone of the first two *Superman* theatrical feature films, you should really enjoy this.

The story begins one night in the California desert, when a pair of strangers have a close encounter with a huge alien spaceship. One is a gung-ho FBI agent, Bill Maxwell (Robert Culp), whose partner (John) was just fatally wounded as part of their latest field operation. The other is an idealistic young school teacher, Ralph Hinkley (William Katt), who is walking the highway alone trying to find help for his stalled school bus. As they watch in amazement, the area is bathed in light, and then Bill's deceased partner appears, with his voice coming out of the car radio. John explains that Ralph and Bill have been chosen by the aliens for a special assignment, and hands Ralph a box with a bright red "supersuit" that will give him (and only him) amazing powers when he wears it. What powers? They're all explained in the instruction book with the package. And why the two of them? Well, apparently, it's their destiny. More than that, the aliens aren't saying (in fact, they don't even show themselves). Then John disappears. So does Bill, who wants no part of an operation that requires some civilian dressed in a crazy-looking costume.

That leaves Ralph high and dry, so he walks back to civilization from this remote desert site. And, on the way, he loses the instruction book. A bad break for him, but a wonderful plotting device because it means that he never knows the full extent of his powers or how to completely control them. This gives the writers plenty of leeway to try out different abilities as they suit (pardon the expression) particular stories. Eventually the main powers that Ralph learns to control are super strength, invulnerability (but only where the suit covers his body), flying (wobbly, and usually with crash landings), invisibility, and "holograph vision" (holding an object, he can lock in on the "vibes" from whoever touched it and in his mind see where they are now).

Of course, that's if and when he decides to use his powers. One of the delightful aspects of the series is Ralph's reaction to all this. He's just an average guy who doesn't quite know what he wants to do. But after overhearing some upbeat "truth, justice, and the American way" rhetoric on the superhero cartoon show his son Kevin is watching, Ralph decides to give this a try. One of his first tasks: flying to the courtroom where he's scheduled to appear as part of a custody fight for his son. Unfortunately for Ralph, he takes three steps, jumps (like the comic books say), and runs smack into a brick wall, knocking himself silly. He wakes up in protective custody, leaving his attorney, Pam Davidson (Connie Sellecca), seriously doubting his sanity (and abilities as a divorced dad). His only solution: reveal his secret to her, which she believes only after he lifts her car.

Meanwhile, Bill has second thoughts on this scenario (especially after Ralph rescues him from a tight spot) and decides that maybe a civilian could work out as a partner. With visions of Ralph and the "red jammies" as the ultimate weapon against the bad guys (especially the "Commies"), Bill sets out his agenda. Unfortunately for him, Ralph is far more interested in assignments such as "save the whales," so Bill has to constantly cajole "the greatest American hero" to his style of action. After a while, though, Ralph starts to feel more comfortable in his superpowered role and finds he really enjoys being a hero, albeit a secret one. He also comes to genuinely like Bill, and begins to trust his instincts for what assignments might be worth taking on (which is probably why the aliens teamed them up in the first place).

Ralph doesn't take any super-duper name and he keeps his exploits carefully hidden. He's just this guy who shows up, saves the day, disappears, and lets Bill Maxwell notch another successful capture on his FBI record. And what about the people he captures? Most of them quickly learn that describing a flying guy in a red suit and cape guarantees them a ticket to the psycho ward.

Oddly, Ralph's son soon disappears from the story line, no doubt spending most of his time with his mom. However, Pam Davidson remains a key part of the action, both romantically and in his life as a superhero. In fact, she frequently finds herself moonlighting from her law offices to help Ralph and Bill on the latest assignments. The chemistry between Ralph, Bill, and Pam is perfect, and manages to keep the adventures on a very human, accessible level, even when they involve plots that leave the world teetering on the eve of destruction. Oh yes, most of the episodes are peppered with bits of music, often sung over flying sequences or battle scenes. Stephen Geyer performs most of these (usually those sequences are trimmed in the syndication package), though Joey Scarbury does the opening theme song, "Believe It or Not" (a hit record in 1981).

Over the course of the series, Bill and Ralph eventually meet the aliens and learn the full story behind the suit. (The success of the theatrical film *E. T.* probably had something to do with the decision to show what Bill describes as the "little green guys.") After a while, Ralph and Pam become engaged and eventually get married. (Lois Lane, eat your heart out.) And, increasingly, references to Ralph's "day job" as a teacher are pretty much phased out (in the early episodes, members of his class often turn up in the stories, with Rhonda and Tony the main student characters).

When the series hit postnetwork syndication, four episodes produced for the final ABC season received their first airing. Currently an unsuccessful mid-1980s sequel pilot for a follow-up series (*The Greatest American Heroine*) also turns up in the syndication package. In this pilot, Ralph inadvertently reveals his identity rescuing a woman in full view of the public, turning him into an instant celebrity. He even receives a medal from the president, who calls him the "greatest American hero" (clever, eh?). Unfortunately, much to Pam's displeasure, Ralph starts to enjoy the limelight so much (making talk show appearances and such) that he loses his special innocence and idealism. The aliens bring Ralph and Pam to the ship and tell him that he's to retire and hand the suit over to someone else of their choosing. Eventually they select Holly Hathaway (Mary Ellen Stuart), an altruistic environmentalist with a seven-year-old foster daughter, Sara (Mya Akerling). After tearful goodbyes, Ralph and Pam drive off into the sunset, while Bill stays around to work with this new partner.

**THE GREATEST SHOW ON EARTH** (**) **60 min (30ep B&W; 1963–1964 ABC) Drama** *with Jack Palance as Johnny Slate and Stu Erwin as Otto King*

Based on a 1952 Cecil B. DeMille film, this series combines the drama behind the scenes in staging the Ringling Brothers Barnum and Bailey Circus with the excitement of the acts that make the circus a world-renowned attraction. Jack Palance is tough, as usual, as the circus boss. Most attention goes to the weekly guest stars, who appear as circus performers. Look for Annette Funicello, Buster Keaton, Joe E. Brown, Fabian Forte, and Edgar Bergen, among others, as guests.

**GREEN ACRES** (***½) **30 min (170ep Color; 1965–1971 CBS) Situation Comedy** *with Eddie Albert as Oliver Wendell Douglas, Eva Gabor as Lisa Douglas, Pat Buttram as Mr. Haney, Tom Lester as Eb Dawson, Hank Patterson as Fred Ziffel, and Frank Cady as Sam Drucker*

This is the best of Paul Henning's rural-based comedies of the mid-1960s, taking the deceptively simple premise of *The Beverly Hillbillies* backward (city folk move to the country) and using it as the springboard for some truly absurdist television. The setting is a broken-down Hooterville farm, near the folks of *Petticoat Junction,* and members of both casts go back and forth in a number of episodes (though general store owner Sam Drucker is the only one to be a regular on both). What sets *Green Acres* apart from its predecessor, however, is its emphasis on broad exaggeration, complicated wordplay, illogical logic, and pop culture in-jokes (often involving the opening credits or onscreen subtitles). And, of course, its two lead characters.

To start, there's the delicious contradiction of the initial premise, spelled out in the program's catchy theme song as lawyer Oliver Douglas sings the praises of country living while his wife, Lisa, talks about all the wonderful things New York has to offer. He wins that battle when they move to Hooterville, but Lisa wins the war because she's the one who has virtually no problem adapting (perhaps it's her Hungarian roots). Maybe she can't cook very well (her coffee could grease an airplane), but she manages to make herself quite at home in the broken down old farm house, putting her wardrobe, assorted knickknacks, and luxury bedroom set in place as if they always belonged there.

Oliver is another matter. With his big-city assumptions and expectations intact, he is a man with a vision of the way things should work and he won't let anything (not even common sense) stand in his way. Like any good lawyer, Oliver can turn a benign situation into a complicated mess with just a few well-placed letters of complaint, virtually destroying the area's mail delivery system, telephone service, and crop rotation plans (to name just a few of his fiascoes) in the process. And, of course, he finds himself constantly at odds with the other characters (even Lisa), insisting that they see the world as he (a well-educated New Yorker) knows it really is. Trouble is, they seem to know something he doesn't. For instance, before heading to Washington for a visit, everyone tells Oliver to be sure and see the Eiffel Tower there, prompting him to point out time and again that the famous landmark is really in Paris, France. But, sure enough, when Lisa opens the curtains and balcony window of their Washington hotel room, there's the Eiffel Tower in plain sight.

Perhaps what everyone else realizes (and Oliver doesn't) is that they really are in a different world, the silly world of a television comedy. That's not a constantly explicit theme (like the monologue asides by George Burns in his various series), but it does mean that there's a totally different logic system at work here. So animals such as Arnold the pig are treated as full-fledged characters, complete with occasional subtitled conversations—such as when Arnold chats with a Hollywood horse he is slated to replace in a popular television comedy. And that's also why the local lodge band might break into the program's theme song, or why part of the opening credits might appear on the back of Oliver's bathrobe, with Lisa commenting, "I wondered where those would turn up." Obviously, Gracie Allen would get along fine here. City slicker Oliver doesn't stand a chance. He's a marked man doomed to fall to the latest money-grabbing scheme of Mr. Haney (who sold him the farm, sight unseen, in the first place) or to the deceptively innocent requests of their young farmhand, Eb Dawson.

But that's fine because Eddie Albert's exasperated rendering of his character is priceless. Besides he has Lisa to bail him out because, after all, he's her husband and they're in this together. Which is probably the final reason this series works so well. Like George Burns and Gracie Allen, Oliver and Lisa make a sexy, loving pair that obviously enjoy being married to each other. Even in the midst of some comic disaster (like the total collapse of the Hooterville telephone switchboard system), they still have time for some affectionate double-entendres and cuddles. It's all a part of that fine country living.

**THE GREEN HORNET (**) 30 min (26ep Color; 1966–1967 ABC) Adventure** *with Van Williams as Britt Reid/The Green Hornet, Bruce Lee as Kato, Wende Wagner as Casey, Lloyd Gough as Mike Axford, and Walter Brooke as D. A. Frank Scanlon*

A true cult series, and not because of any overwhelming interest in masked crime fighters brought to television from 1930s radio. Or in the trumpet music of Al Hirt, who played the solo for the program's opening theme (a variation of "Flight of the Bumblebee"). It's not even the distinctive announcing style of narrator William Dozier (who also served as executive producer). Instead, what keeps this series turning up in the oddest slots is its second banana, Bruce Lee. The future superstar of martial arts feature films (most notably, the 1973 hit *Enter the Dragon*) plays Kato, chauffeur (and fellow crime fighter) to newspaper publisher Britt Reid and his secret alter ego, the Green Hornet. His chops at each episode's crooks may be brief, but they're exciting to watch. And certainly more believable than anyone else's fighting moves, even the Green Hornet's. (His dialogue delivery, on the other hand, easily explains why he never received a spin-off series of his own.)

Otherwise, this mid-1960s *Batman* cash-in (from the same production company) is a well-staged but fairly routine crime adventure series, without the bizarre schemes of the Caped Crusader's "Rogues Gallery" of strangely costumed foes. In fact, it's how *Batman* might have been done if it hadn't gone "camp." The Green Hornet and Kato dutifully chase after relatively normal bad guys, though they do sport a supercharged car worthy of the Batmobile, the Black Beauty (a customized 1966 Chrysler Imperial). They also operate outside official police channels (though Scanlon in the D. A.'s office knows their secret), and so are sometimes regarded as villains themselves. That's what happens when the duo makes its one and only crossover appearance on *Batman* (against Colonel Gumm, a stamp thief)—eventually there's a face-off between the suspicious crime-fighting pairs. Bruce Lee follows the script and restrains himself, so Robin and Kato end up fighting to a draw. But we all know who should have won the contest, hands down. There was never time for a no-holds-barred rematch because *The Green Hornet* lasted only one season.

**GRIFF (*½) 60 min (12ep Color; 1973–1974 ABC) Detective Drama** *with Lorne Greene as Wade "Griff" Griffin, Ben Murphy as Mike Murdoch, Patricia Stich as Gracie Newcombe, and Vic Tayback as Capt. Barney Marcus*

Fresh from his long-running role as Pa Cartwright on *Bonanza,* Lorne Greene shifts gears here, as he portrays Griff, a Los Angeles police captain who quits the force and goes into the private detective business. Griff is aided by a handsome hunk, Mike Murdoch. Vic Tayback, before he was Mel in *Alice,* is the new police captain that Griff must deal with.

*Griff*'s producer, David Victor, also produced *Marcus Welby, M. D.*

**GRINDL (*) 30 min (32ep B&W; 1963–1964 NBC) Situation Comedy** *with Imogene Coca as Grindl and James Millhollin as Anson Foster*

Imogene Coca, a fine comedic talent who co-starred with Sid Caesar in *Your Show of Shows,* is wasted in this slight sitcom about Grindl, a domestic worker who is placed each week in a different temporary job by her boss, Mr. Foster. *Grindl*'s producer, Harry Ackerman, also produced the very similar series *Hazel.*

**GRIZZLY ADAMS, THE LIFE AND TIMES OF (**½) 60 min (37ep & 2 hr sequel Color; 1977–1978 NBC) Adventure** *with Dan Haggerty as James "Grizzly" Adams, Denver Pyle as Mad Jack, Don Shanks as Nakuma, John Bishop as Robbie Cartman, and Bozo as Ben*

When Dr. Richard Kimble of *The Fugitive* was convicted of a crime he did not commit, he escaped and ran around the country to avoid the police. When James Adams is charged with a murder he did not commit, he hightails it to the woods, where he avoids human contact as much as possible, in order to live in peace with nature.

*Grizzly Adams* is a kind-hearted but slow-moving saga of James Adams, who is renamed Grizzly when he befriends and raises a stray grizzly bear named Ben. Adams doesn't wear leather or eat meat and is kind to animals. The show usually involves some sort of animal adventure. It's all lovely and morally uplifting for the kiddies tuning in, but adults will begin to snooze after a bit.

The TV series grew out of a 1976 movie of the same name, where Dan Haggerty originated the character. A 1982 TV movie sequel is titled *The Capture of Grizzly Adams.* ■

**THE GROUCHO SHOW** (see *You Bet Your Life*)

**GROWING PAINS** (**½) 30 min (92ep at Fall 1989 Color; 1985– ABC) Situation Comedy *with Alan Thicke as Jason Seaver, Joanna Kerns as Maggie Seaver, Kirk Cameron as Mike Seaver, Tracey Gold as Carol Seaver, Jeremy Miller as Ben Seaver, Josh Andrew Koenig as Richard "Boner" Stabone, and Bill Kirchenbauer as Graham Lubbock*

It's likely that Alan Thicke will, for some time, be best known as the amiable dad/psychiatrist-working-at-home of *Growing Pains.* Before this series debuted, Thicke, a true Renaissance man of TV, had dabbled in all aspects of the medium. He began as a comedy writer in Canada, came to Hollywood as the writer for variety specials by the likes of Bill Cosby, Kenny Rogers, and Richard Pryor, wrote and produced the zany 1970s talk-show parodies *Fernwood 2-Night* and *America 2Night,* failed spectacularly as host of his own "serious" talk show (*Thicke of the Night*), wrote the theme songs to *Diff'rent Strokes* and *The Facts of Life,* and recorded an album or two of rock music. After failing at becoming a star from all that work, Thicke (who always kept a self-deprecating air about him) at least deserved a steady job that paid well, such as starring in this popular sitcom.

As Jason Seaver, Thicke plays the ultimate TV dad of the mid-1980s, one who engages in a little role reversal with his wife. Jason moves his psychiatric practice into the family home, to allow wife Maggie to return to the work place. Jason must now juggle caring for his patients with supervising his three over-active offspring. Chief attention among the kiddos goes to fifteen-year-old son Mike (described by Maggie as "a hormone with feet"). Playing Mike, Kirk Cameron became the preteen female heartthrob of the moment through his barely pubescent mildly macho swagger.

Keep an eye open for the fleeting appearance by zany comic Bill Kirchenbauer. His vibrant character of Coach Lubbock quickly graduated to his own show, *Just The Ten Of Us.*

**GUESTWARD HO!** (*) 30 min (38ep B&W; 1960–1961 ABC) Situation Comedy *with Joanne Dru as Babs Hooten, Mark Miller as Bill Hooten, J. Carrol Naish as Chief Hawkeye, and Flip Mark as Brook Hooten*

*Guestward Ho!* sounds a lot funnier on paper than it is. The Hootens, Bill and Babs (honest!), decide to leave the tensions of life in Manhattan behind, so they buy a dude ranch called Guestward Ho in New Mexico. Husband, wife, and son Brook move out west and discover that the ranch is a run-down mess, sorely in need of refurbishing. The local character they befriend is Chief Hawkeye, local Indian bigwig who runs the region's general store. The Chief reads the *Wall Street Journal* and sells cheap souvenirs made in Japan.

*Guestward Ho!* could be a modern *F Troop,* but it's not. The writing is very silly and the characters (mostly the Hootens) are much too straight-laced to be interesting. Chief Hawkeye is fun, but a little too fake, even for TV sitcom standards. Ethnically ambiguous J. Carrol Naish, who plays the Chief, played an Italian in the lead role of *Life with Luigi* and Oriental sleuth Charlie Chan in *The Adventures of Charlie Chan.*

**GUN SHY** (*½) 30 min (6ep & 60 min pilot Color; 1983 CBS) Situation Comedy *with Barry Van Dyke as Russell Donovan, Tim Thomerson as Theodore Ogilvie, Geoffrey Lewis as Amos Tucker, and Pat McCormick as Col. Mound*

Based on the Disney studio's two popular late 1970s films, *The Apple Dumpling Gang* and *The Apple Dumpling Gang Rides Again, Gun Shy*, like most TV versions of hit movie comedies, lacks the zing of the cinema original. The story concerns Russell Donovan, a gambling playboy in California in the late 1860s, who somehow "wins" two orphaned children in a poker game and then has to adjust his life-style as he tries to raise them right. The two kids soon join with Theodore and Amos, two klutzy types who long to be famous outlaws, to form the Apple Dumpling Gang, a gang that does *good* deeds.

In the movies, Bill Bixby played Donovan, Don Knotts played Theodore, and Tim Conway played Amos. Those three former TV stars were too busy to agree to reprise the role in the TV series, so lesser lights were brought in. Barry Van Dyke (son of Dick) is adequate as Donovan. Tim Thomerson (memorable in bit parts in *Quark* and *The Associates*) is a lot of fun as Theodore. Geoffrey Lewis is forgettable as Amos.

The one-hour pilot, from 1982, is called *Tales of the Apple Dumpling Gang,* and has a very different cast. John Bennett Perry plays Donovan, while Ed Begley, Jr., and Arte Johnson play Amos and Theodore.

**GUNG HO** (*) 30 min (9ep Color; 1986–1987 ABC) Situation Comedy *with Scott Bakula as Hunt Stevenson, Gedde Watanabe as Kaz Kazuhiro, Sab Shimono as Mr. Saito, Patti Yasutake as Umeki Kazuhiro, and Clint Howard as Googie*

Ron Howard, of *Andy Griffith Show* and *Happy Days* fame, left TV to first star in and then direct movies. One of his more lightweight film offerings was *Gung Ho,* from 1986. The film starred Michael Keaton as a fast-talking American who convinces a Japanese car maker to reopen a closed auto plant in Keaton's depressed middle-America town. The humor came from the clash of cultures as the individualistic American workers had to deal with the corporate mind-set of their new Oriental employers, and vice versa.

This TV version of the film is even less weighty than the airy original. The only significant cast carryovers are Gedde Watanabe as Kaz (the plant manager) and Clint Howard (brother of Ron) as Googie, one of the workers. Even more than the movie, TV's *Gung*

*Ho* all too often takes the easy comedic route of playing up ethnic stereotypes of the Oriental and occidental characters.

**THE GUNS OF WILL SONNETT (*½) 30 min (50ep Color; 1967–1969 ABC) Western** *with Walter Brennan as Will Sonnett and Dack Rambo as Jeff Sonnett*

Another inconclusive western quest. This time, a tough old former cavalry scout (Will Sonnett) sets out to find his wayward son, James, who had left *his* son, Jeff, behind as an infant. While granddad Will was raising young Jeff, James became a notorious gunfighter. Now nearly twenty, Jeff wants to meet his dad, face-to-face, so he and Will wander the West of the 1870s, searching. Along the way they run into plenty of people with opinions about James, but he remains elusive till the end, appearing on camera only a few times (played by Jason Evers). It's a workable premise, produced and co-created by Aaron Spelling (*The Love Boat, Dynasty*), but the individual stories never break from typical western formulas. The series was last dusted off from rerun storage when Dack Rambo landed the Jack Ewing role on *Dallas*.

**GUNSLINGER (*½) 60 min (12ep B&W; 1961 CBS) Western** *with Tony Young as Cord, Preston Foster as Capt. Zachary Wingate, Charles Gray as Pico McGuire, and Dee Pollock as Billy Urchin*

The leading man in *Gunslinger* is some guy known only as Cord, who poses as a hotshot gunslinger, while actually serving as an undercover agent for the U.S. Cavalry. Cord serves under Capt. Wingate in New Mexico, in the immediate post-Civil War era. The only interesting tidbit about this undistinguished western is that one of Cord's cohorts, Pico, is played by English actor Charles Gray, best known as the criminologist/narrator with no apparent neck in the cult film classic *The Rocky Horror Picture Show.*

**GUNSMOKE (****) 30 & 60 min (635ep: two hundred thirty-three 30 min B&W & one hundred seventy-six 60 min B&W & two hundred twenty-six 60 min Color & 2 hr sequel; 1955–1975 CBS) Western** *with James Arness as Matt Dillon, Amanda Blake as Kitty Russell, Milburn Stone as Galen "Doc" Adams, Dennis Weaver as Chester Goode, Ken Curtis as Festus Haggen, Burt Reynolds as Quint Asper, and Buck Taylor as Newly O'Brien*

*Gunsmoke* is *the* TV western. It created the concept of "adult western" that dominated TV in the late 1950s and it stands head and shoulders above most of the copycat shows that followed its lead. *Gunsmoke* lasted long after most of the other oaters had ridden off into the sunset. It rolled up an impressive record of twenty seasons in prime time, a massive output of 635 episodes that no weekly show with continuing characters has yet matched.

The premise of *Gunsmoke* is simple, and it hardly ever changes throughout its long run. Matt Dillon, U.S. Marshal in Dodge City, Kansas, in the late 1800s, is forever serving as the one and almost only bulwark of law and order in a frontier town never far removed from its lawless roots. Dillon is tall, lean, sparse of tongue but gentle of heart. He undergoes some merciless beatings throughout the 635 episodes, and he sometimes bends but he never breaks.

An intriguing part of Dillon's character is his relationship with Kitty Russell, owner and operator of the Longbranch Saloon, Dodge City's social center. If Kitty followed the traditional pattern in Old West folklore, she would be a prostitute, or a former prostitute. In *Gunsmoke,* the question of whether Kitty is or was a prostitute is alluded to only in subtle ways and never answered. For twenty years, she and Marshal Dillon carry on a close, but never formalized, relationship, the physical aspects of which are not made clear. Matt and Kitty may just not be the marrying type. What is more likely is that Kitty's scarlet past (or even present) creates a social obstacle that local lawman Dillon cannot overcome, in spite of his stature in town. A marriage between the lawman and the saloon keeper (a role tantamount to harlotry in "refined" Old West circles) just would never do, even in a small frontier town like Dodge City. Thus, Matt and Kitty must carry on an apparently arms-length relationship, one that gives *Gunsmoke* a lot of its zing. Kitty's social and economic independence set her apart from other women of her era, and she can go back and forth between loving Matt (from afar, perhaps) and then next week joining up with townspeople opposing him on some issue.

In spite of *Gunsmoke*'s lengthy run, there are only a small number of important regulars. Aside from Matt, the only other Dodge City resident to last all 635 episodes is Doc Adams (Kitty bails out before the last season). Doc is the only evidence of an educated man in Dodge City, and even he is willing to admit that his knowledge is limited by his unspectacular medical training. Doc serves the role of learned confidant and companion for Matt. Doc's only real faults are his proclivity for a nip now and then and his frequently acerbic personality. Both "faults" can probably be chalked up to the fact that Doc spent most of his life as the only person within a few hundred miles who could read Latin.

Beyond the central trio of Matt, Kitty, and Doc comes the comedic relief of Matt's deputies, first Chester Goode and then Festus Haggen. Both mean well, and do provide Matt with some much needed backup, but they have odd personalities that are usually good for a laugh. Chester walks with a noticeable limp, takes great pride in his home-brewed coffee, takes himself quite seriously, and is somewhat prissy. Chester, in fact, might be described as a more solemn version of Mayberry's Deputy Barney Fife.

After nine seasons, Chester departs and is replaced by Festus, who is much more in the hillbilly vein. His back country ways come in for a lot of ribbing, but Festus is a good judge of character and it is he who frequently smells out the villain first.

The next level of male support for Matt comes from more traditional clean-cut he-man types. Young Burt Reynolds shows up for three seasons as Quint Asper, a half-breed Indian blacksmith. Soon after Asper leaves the series, gunsmith Newly O'Brien arrives for an extended stay, serving as a bland, strong fellow who was better to look at than Festus. Newly did not add much more to the show than his looks.

As the first true adult TV western, *Gunsmoke* is largely responsible for raising the cowboy format out of the kiddie action-adventure mold that *The Lone Ranger* and *Hopalong Cassidy* brought from the days of movies. *Gunsmoke* presents more realistic stories of more realistic characters, in a setting much closer to the true West than in the simple sagas that came before.

The very nature of Matt Dillon's character symbolizes the growing up of the western. Unlike previous sagebrush heroes, he does not always prevail over the bad guys, he does not always know what to do, and he frequently anguishes over what is right and what is wrong. Matt's somber solitude is a far cry from the hearty piousness of the Lone Ranger.

The credit for *Gunsmoke*'s stature belongs to Norman Macdonnell, the show's producer for the first nine of its twenty seasons. Macdonnell had produced the original radio version of *Gunsmoke* in 1952 (with William Conrad, later of *Cannon,* as Matt), a show still considered one of the best of network radio's heyday.

The original half-hour TV episodes of *Gunsmoke* are frequently syndicated under the title of *Marshal Dillon.* The *Gunsmoke* gang reunite in a tepid 1987 two-hour made-for-TV movie (*Gunsmoke: Return to Dodge*) that is not quite up to the dramatic standards of the twenty-year series.

**HAGEN** (*½) **60 min (9ep Color; 1980 CBS) Crime Drama** *with Chad Everett as Paul Hagen and Arthur Hill as Carl Palmer*

Chad Everett and Arthur Hill head north in California from their previous signature series roles (Everett as a Los Angeles doctor in *Medical Center,* Hill as a Santa Barbara lawyer in *Owen Marshall*). Hill is still an attorney (polished and cagey Carl Palmer), though Everett has gone back to nature to become Paul Hagen, an expert animal tracker from Idaho now stalking the most dangerous game of all, "the two-legged animals who prowl the neon jungle of San Francisco." Naturally, Hagen and Palmer team up as private-eye legman and legal eagle, chasing the usual suspects (drug dealers, syndicate types, errant teens)—in strictly formula dramas.

**HAIL TO THE CHIEF** (*½) **30 min (7ep Color; 1985 ABC) Situation Comedy** *with Patty Duke Astin as Pres. Julia Mansfield, Ted Bessell as Gen. Oliver Mansfield, Herschel Bernardi as Helmut Luger, Quinn Cummings as Lucy Mansfield, Murray Hamilton as Sen. Sam Cotton, Dick Shawn as Premier Dmitri Zolotov and Ivan Zolotov, and Glynn Turman as LaRue Hawkes*

From Paul Junger Witt, Tony Thomas, and Susan Harris, the trio that created *Soap,* comes this potentially funny, but ultimately empty, sitcom about America's first woman president. Patty Duke Astin is a great choice as the first truly *first* lady, Ted Bessell (*That Girl*) is perfect as the first *first* husband, and Herschel Bernardi is cute as a presidential advisor. The problem is that *Hail to the Chief* just doesn't know what to be, a social satire sitcom (like *All in the Family*) or one that just aims for laughs, plain and simple (such as *The Partridge Family,* where a young Susan Harris did some writing). While some of the outlandish plot lines will evoke memories of *Soap, Hail to the Chief* just doesn't have the spark that kept *Soap* a treat to watch.

**THE ½ HOUR COMEDY HOUR** (*½) **30 min (6ep Color; 1983 ABC) Comedy-Variety** *with Arsenio Hall and Thom Sharp as hosts*

One of Dick Clark's instant variety productions of the 1980s, which originally filled a few weeks for ABC in the summer of 1983 (before cable turned into stand-up comedy heaven). The show provides the usual "past-lives" snapshots of repertory performers such as Victoria Jackson and Jan Hooks (later *Saturday Night Live* regulars), John Paragon (later Jambi on *Pee Wee's Playhouse*), and "overnight" star Arsenio Hall (later cohort of Eddie Murphy in the feature film *Coming to America* and host of his own late night talk show).

**HALF-NELSON** (*½) **60 min (7ep & 2 hr pilot Color; 1985 NBC) Comedy-Drama** *with Joe Pesci as Rocky Nelson, Victoria Jackson as Annie O'Hara, Fred Williamson as Chester Long, Dick Butkus as Kurt, Bubba Smith as Beau, and Dean Martin as himself*

Glen A. Larson, the producer of such popular shows as *B. J. and the Bear, Buck Rogers in the 25th Century, The Fall Guy,* and *Battlestar Galactica,* turns offbeat in *Half-Nelson,* one of the few TV series to star a very short man. Rocky Nelson is short, very short, but his height doesn't stop him from being a private eye, and he hopes it doesn't stop him from being an actor. Naturally the best place for a combination aspiring actor and private eye to locate is Los Angeles, which is where Rocky sets up shop. Nobody seems to take Rocky very seriously, due to his short stature, but he still manages to hang out with Dean Martin, who turns up now and again, playing himself, supposedly a friend of the little guy. Too bad Frank Sinatra, Sammy Davis, Jr., and the rest of Martin's "rat pack" didn't accompany Dino; it might have helped perk up this show. Former NFL behemoths Dick Butkus and Bubba Smith (who previously teamed up in the equally forgettable *Blue Thunder*) literally provide Rocky with much needed muscle.

**HALF THE GEORGE KIRBY COMEDY HOUR (**) 30 min (26ep Color; 1972–1973 Syndication) Comedy-Variety** *with George Kirby as host*

In the early 1970s, there was much demand for non-threatening black comedians. George Kirby was one of the best. His rotund frame and impressions of famous blacks were all over TV in that era. This series is his only showcase. Steve Martin, then a virtual unknown as a comedian, is a regular.

**HALLMARK HALL OF FAME (****) 60 min, 90 min, 2 hr & 3 hr (1951– NBC & CBS & ABC & PBS) Drama Anthology** *with Sarah Churchill and Maurice Evans as hostess and host*

One of TV's most distinguished drama showcases, the *Hallmark Hall of Fame* first aired in 1951 and has been around, off and on, ever since, rarely in any regular slot. From 1952 to 1978, the series aired on NBC. Several episodes ran on PBS in the early 1980s, but CBS has been the primary home of the show since leaving NBC. Sarah Churchill (daughter of Winston) served as hostess from 1952 to 1955, while noted Shakespearean actor Maurice Evans served as host from 1955 to 1958. Since then, there has been no regular host.

Among *Hallmark's* more memorable productions are "Amahl and the Night Visitors" (1951), "Hamlet" (1953), "Alice in Wonderland" (1955), "A Doll's House" (1959), "The Fantasticks" (1964), and "The Man Who Came to Dinner" (1972). Some more recent productions include George C. Scott and Trish Van Devere in "Beauty and the Beast" (1976), Henry Fonda and John Houseman in "Gideon's Trumpet" (1980), Anthony Perkins and Derek Jacobi in "Hunchback of Notre Dame" (1982), and John Lithgow and Richard Bradford in "Resting Place" (1986). ■

**HALLS OF IVY (*½) 30 min (39ep B&W; 1954–1955 CBS) Situation Comedy** *with Ronald Colman as Dr. William Todhunter Hall, Benita Hume as Vicky Hall, Mary Wickes as Alice, and Herb Butterfield as Clarence Wellman*

The one and only TV series starring Hollywood matinee idol Ronald Colman is a poor offering that uses a play on the lead character's name in the title. Colman is William Hall, president of Ivy College. Colman's real-life wife Benita Hume plays Mrs. Hall. The theme song is old-fashioned college boolah-boolah, and the tone is quiet, but the somnambulant Ivy College in this show is from an era long gone. Drop out of Ivy College while you can.

**THE HAMPTONS (**) 60 min (5ep Color; 1983 ABC) Drama** *with Michael Goodwin as Peter Chadway, Leigh Taylor-Young as Lee Chadway, Craig Sheffer as Brian Chadway, John Reilly as Jay Mortimer, and Bibi Besch as Adrienne Duncan Mortimer*

Gloria Monty, the power behind *General Hospital,* produces this true example of prime-time soap opera. Set in the fashionable Long Island resort area known as the Hamptons, the series revolves around the battling, bickering, and bedding between the Chadway family and the Mortimer family.

**HANGING IN (**) 30 min (4ep Color; 1979 CBS) Situation Comedy** *with Bill Macy as Louis Harper, Barbara Rhoades as Maggie Gallagher, Dennis Burkley as Sam Dickey, and Nedra Volz as Pinky Nolan*

Far more interesting for what it isn't than what it is, *Hanging In* was originally designed as a revamped version of *Maude.* In that set-up, Beatrice Arthur's character moves to Washington as a newly installed member of Congress (replacing a deceased member). Despite the possibilities of that environment, Arthur had decided she did not want to continue as Maude, so the producers reworked the premise into *Onward and Upward,* with John Amos as a former black football star taking over that vacant political office. Then it became *Mr. Dugan* (after Amos and the producers split over creative differences), with Cleavon Little in the title role. But that *isn't* what finally aired. Instead the entire Washington setting was scrapped after some real-life black members of Congress denounced the show following a sneak preview of the premiere. So it was back to the drawing board one more time for *Hanging In* (a self-reflexive title if there ever was one), starring Bill Macy, who (ironically) had played Maude's husband and would have ended up a key part of the original package anyway.

For this version, though, the setting changes to the very fictional Braddock University, where Macy's character is a former football star (oh?) appointed to the presidency. There he has to fight the educational bureaucracy to get his liberal, humanitarian programs through, just like in the halls of Congress.

Actually what they ought to do someday is package all four versions (from *Maude* to *Hanging In*) as a behind-the-scenes broadcast special or even an instructional video tape. With the supporting cast the same through each reworking, this would be a rare glimpse at just how the Hollywood creative process works, fine-tuning the same basic script and cast around various leads and settings. It might even lead to a series, all about working within the entertainment bureaucracy to get a series on the air.

**HANK** (**) **30 min (26ep Color; 1965–1966 NBC) Situation Comedy** *with Dick Kallman as Hank Dearborn, Linda Foster as Doris Royal, Howard St. John as Dr. Lewis Royal, Lloyd Corrigan as Prof. McKillup, Katie Sweet as Tina Dearborn, and Kelly Jean Peters as Franny*

Hank Dearborn is a resourceful young man who will do anything for a college education. He can't obtain one the normal way (have Dad pay for it), because his parents died in a car crash (the favorite choice of sudden death among TV script writers), leaving Hank with little money and his baby sister, Tina, to care for. Hank gets around his lack of funds by simply dropping in, unregistered, in several classes at Western State University. He adopts numerous easy-to-see-through disguises, but college Registrar Lewis Royal can't seem to catch the campus legend (his daughter Doris can, however, since she is Hank's girlfriend and is in on the scam). To make ends meet, Hank performs all sorts of odd jobs around campus, such as running a laundry service and an ice cream truck.

*Hank* is a blissfully innocent series that does not promise much, but provides easy entertainment. Considering how most teens in TV shows these days are either smart-mouthed brats or rich computer geniuses, *Hank* provides a nostalgic look back to an era when getting a college degree was still something held as a proud accomplishment.

**THE HANK MCCUNE SHOW** **(zero) 30 min (6ep B&W; 1950 NBC) Situation Comedy** *with Hank McCune and Larry Keating*

Perfectly awful blundering situation comedy now dutifully noted by pop culture historians as one of the first series to use that classic TV "pleasure enhancer," the dubbed laugh track. You'll probably never see this show on the air, but if you spot it on some home video offering give it a fast scan. Then try to decide which programs needed this innovation the most, yesterday's slapstick or today's caustic innuendo.

**THE HANNA-BARBERA HAPPINESS HOUR** **(½) 60 min (5ep Color; 1978 NBC) Comedy-Variety** *with the voices of Udana Power as Honey and Wendy McKenzie as Sis*

Joseph Barbera (and his partner William Hanna) gave the world such gems as *The Jetsons, The Flintstones, Huckleberry Hound, Scooby-Doo,* and *Hong Kong Phooey.* This hour variety series is Mr. Barbera's unmitigated flop in the noncartoon format. Something akin to the popular *Muppet Show,* this series has puppets as hosts, in this case two females, Honey and Sis. Unlike the Muppets, Honey and Sis are life-size. Real human celebrities show up to interact with the puppets. There is little, if any, comedy, and marginal, if any, variety.

**HAPPY** (**) **30 min (26ep B&W; 1960–1961 NBC) Situation Comedy** *with Ronnie Burns as Chris Day, Yvonne Lime as Sally Day, Doris Packer as Clara Mason, Lloyd Corrigan as Uncle Charlie Dooley, and twins David and Steven Born as Christopher Hapgood "Happy" Day*

Young marrieds Chris and Sally Day operate the Desert Palm Hotel in Palm Springs, California. They have demanding guests, an officious co-owner (Clara Mason), a well-meaning but interfering uncle (Charlie Dooley), and a sweet young infant son, Christopher, better known as Happy. Though he's far too young to talk, he definitely speaks his mind (thanks to voice-over dubbing), dropping acerbic asides to the audience much the same as Cleo the basset hound on *The People's Choice,* or like George Burns delivering his monologues directly to the audience on *The George Burns and Gracie Allen Show.*

The result is a very familiar mix of light domestic and workplace comedy, with likable young leads and an appropriately proper matron. All of them came from good workouts on other series: Ronnie Burns played George and Gracie's son Ronnie on *Burns and Allen;* Yvonne Lime spent time on *Father Knows Best* as Betty's friend, Dotty, and on *Dobie Gillis* as heartthrob Melissa; Lloyd Corrigan was Unce Dan ("that happy man") on Disney's *Corkey and White Shadow* serial; and Doris Packer played the grand dame Clarice Armitage on *Dobie Gillis* (later reworked to become Mrs. Chatsworth Osborne, Sr.). As for the title character, the main problem with Happy (and the series itself) is that smart-mouthed infants aren't nearly as cute as talking animals, or an old vaudeville hoofer with a cigar.

**HAPPY DAYS** (***) **30 min (255ep & 30 min pilot Color; 1974–1984 ABC) Situation Comedy** *with Ron Howard as Richie Cunningham, Henry Winkler as Arthur "Fonzie" Fonzarelli, Tom Bosley as Howard Cunningham, Marion Ross as Marion Cunningham, Anson Williams as Warren "Potsie" Weber, Donny Most as Ralph Malph, Erin Moran as Joanie Cunningham, and Scott Baio as Charles "Chachi" Arcola*

You don't need to get beyond your ten fingers to count all the TV sitcoms that have amassed 255 episodes or more (eleven seasons, approximately). *Happy Days* is one of the more recent additions to the list, and its popularity spawned an entire stable of other comedies, few of which lasted anywhere near as long.

Originally *Happy Days* is set in the 1950s and is as slow-moving and bland as that decade. The central focus is on the Cunningham household. Mr. Cunningham is a gentle father, easy to push around and funny when he gets mad. Mrs. Cunningham is a somewhat addle-brained housewife who comes from the June Cleaver school of mothering. Young daughter Joanie is a little pixie with a smart mouth. Son Richie is the straight arrow, the "good" boy that parents hold up as an example to other children. His pal, Potsie, is more of a troublemaker. Potsie is always coming up with the crazy scheme that lands the duo in hot water.

That is all the original *Happy Days* is about. It is mid-1950s Milwaukee, recreated for mid-1970s viewers, and, aside from the addition of color and some mildly risqué cracks, *Happy Days* could *really* be from the 1950s.

Then comes Fonzie. Originally a minor character relegated to dark looks and motorcycle repair, Fonzie gets more and more attention as *Happy Days* moves into its second and third year. He makes *Happy Days* unique and brings the show out of its bland mentality by getting away from the middle-class niceties that dominate 1950s sitcoms.

Fonzie is working class, he is a juvenile delinquent, he is bad news, and he is *real* trouble. He threatens all the boys and entices all the girls. He is the leader of the youth pack around Arnold's Drive-In, the youth mecca in *Happy Days's* Milwaukee. With Fonzie as a catalyst, *Happy Days* takes off and becomes a real hit show.

When Fonzie first comes to the forefront, he is the prototypical "hood," whose menace serves as counterpoint to the goodness of Richie and Potsie and their other geeky pal Ralph. What takes *Happy Days* one step further into rarefied territory is that Fonzie develops during the show's middle years. Under Henry Winkler's subtle performing, Fonzie moves beyond the simple leather jacket, switchblade, and motorcycle concept to a more human Fonzie, one who can show his feelings and vulnerability *without* sacrificing the essential toughness of his character. Simply put, Fonzie lets his guard down now and then. In this new permutation, Fonzie becomes a combination of father confessor and guru to Richie's pals. Since Fonzie is the epitome of cool, he is the one who can dispense advice, settle disputes, and serve as role model. This is all a far cry from the standard 1950s sitcom, where only parents could dispense wisdom to children, and working class, noneducated teens were threats not role models.

With the prominence of Fonzie, all the characters loosen up a bit, as the 1950s run out and the show chugs toward 1960. Unfortunately *Happy Days* goes overboard on the Fonz angle and the later part of the series run is more formula and less excitement. Fonz actually moves into the Cunningham home (in an apartment above the garage) and thus virtually becomes one of the family. He loses a lot of his threatening nature and actually starts becoming too *good*! He starts lecturing on the value of a good education and on being tolerant of minorities, and before you know it, the Fonz is just *Father Knows Best* in a leather jacket and sideburns. By the last season, when the Fonz has become Dean of Boys at George S. Patton Vocational High School and has adopted a young orphan named Danny, you know the metamorphosis is complete.

The other characters go through less cataclysmic changes during the series. Richie, Potsie, and Ralph all graduate high school, and go to college at the local branch of the University of Wisconsin. After college, Richie and Ralph join the Army, get shipped to Greenland, and virtually leave the show. Richie gets married in absentia (the Fonz stands in at the ceremony) and has a baby. Joanie grows up, falls in love, and eventually marries Fonzie's cousin Chachi.

*Happy Days* began as an episode of *Love, American Style* in February 1972 called "Love and the Happy Days," with only Ron Howard and Marion Ross playing the same roles as in the series. Harold Gould plays Mr. Cunningham and Susan Neher plays Joanie in the pilot. In 1973, Ron Howard played a character very similar to Richie Cunningham in the George Lucas film *American Graffiti,* and the popularity of that film helped revive the old "Happy Days" pilot concept.

*Happy Days* was, itself, the spawning ground of several spin-off series. First came *Laverne & Shirley,* based on two working-class girlfriends of the Fonz, Laverne DeFazio (Penny Marshall, sister of *Happy Days* producer Garry Marshall) and Shirley Feeney (Cindy Williams, another graduate of *American Graffiti,* but no relation to Anson Williams, who plays Potsie here). After a few appearances in the second year of *Happy Days,* the two girls went out on their own and lasted a highly respectable eight seasons. After brief appearances on *Happy Days* in early 1978, the alien Mork from Ork (Robin Williams, no relation to Cindy or Anson) starred in his own hit, *Mork and Mindy.* For a season or two in the early 1980s, Joanie and Chachi even had their own show, titled, appropriately enough, *Joanie Loves Chachi.* The Fonz finally got top billing in a cartoon series spin-off, *Fonz and the Happy Days Gang* at the same time *Happy Days* was winding down.

The original theme song for *Happy Days* is Bill Haley's rock classic "Rock Around the Clock." By the fourth season, a new specially written tune, "Happy Days," took over and became a hit itself.

One intriguing oddity in *Happy Days* lore is that in the first two seasons the Cunninghams have an older son, Chuck (played by Gavan O'Herlihy and then Randolph Roberts). Chuck quickly goes to college and is never seen again. After a few seasons, he is no longer mentioned by anyone in the show. It's as if Chuck Cunningham never existed. Perhaps he did something very nasty to make the family disown him. At any rate, he didn't even get his own spin-off series, so he must have done *some*thing wrong.

**HARBOR COMMAND (**) 30 min (39ep B&W; 1957–1958 Syndication) Police Drama** *with Wendell Corey as Capt. Ralph Baxter*

A lackluster series about the exploits of the police unit assigned to protect the harbor of a major metropolitan coastal city, *Harbor Command* is the first TV series for nondescript Hollywood leading man Wendell Corey.

**HARBOURMASTER** (**½) **30 min (26ep B&W; 1957–1958 CBS & ABC) Adventure** *with Barry Sullivan as Capt. David Scott, Paul Burke as Jeff Kittridge, and Nina Wilcox as Anna Morrison*

*Harbourmaster* looks good on paper. Barry Sullivan and Paul Burke, the two leads, are TV pros who have appeared in numerous series, always acting with class, if not much sparkle. The setting is unique, in that it is not Los Angeles or New York, or any big city for that matter, but rather the craggy, cold coast of Massachusetts. Finally, the stories do not involve shocking crimes or torrid love affairs, but rather interesting people in a small, tightly knit community.

Capt. Scott is the harbourmaster and pretty much all the law enforcement of tiny Scott Island. Jeff Kittridge is Scott's partner, while Anna Morrison runs the local diner and has eyes for the bachelor Capt. Scott.

Working against the success of this series is its fairly plodding script and the topical restraints that shackled all TV shows in the more restrictive 1950s. With TV's ability to tackle more daring topics these days, the setting of *Harbourmaster* might make a great prime-time soap opera show.

Midway through its original run, *Harbourmaster* changed its name to *Adventures at Scott Island.*

**HARD COPY** (*½) **60 min (8ep & 2 hr pilot Color; 1987 CBS) Crime Drama** *with Michael Murphy as Andy Omart, Wendy Crewson as Blake Calisher, Dean Devlin as David Del Valle, and Charles Cooper as William Boot*

Hard-bitten crime reporter Andy Omart and his associates Blake and David cover the seamy world of big-city crime. All the usual elements are there: secret deals, drug pushers, political pressure to suppress a story, murder, blackmail, and—most of all—the self-righteous commitment to get the facts into print, no matter what the consequences! This series is so intent on being intense that you almost feel guilty about looking for lighter moments (for those, see *Hot Shots,* which hit the CBS schedule in a late-night slot shortly before this program began). Well, at least all this is *fictional* tabloid television, hanging together a bit better than some of those *America's Most Wanted*-type shows. Wendy Crewson was previously on another gritty crime series, *Night Heat.*

**HARD KNOCKS** (**) **30 min (4ep Color; 1987 Showtime) Comedy-Adventure** *with Bill Maher as Gower Rhodes and Tommy Hinkley as Nick Bronco*

Gower and Nick are two mismatched private eyes. Gower is a relic of the 1960s hippie era, while Nick is his aggressive macho partner. Together they attempt to solve mysteries without stepping on each other's toes too often.

**HARD TIME ON PLANET EARTH** (*) **60 min (13ep Color; 1989 CBS) Science Fiction-Adventure** *with Martin Kove as Jesse and Danny Mann as the voice of Control*

A violent warrior from another planet is convicted of a serious infraction of his world's laws and is sentenced to serve his time on the backward planet known as Earth (hence the title). The point is that the alien, who only understands force and violence, is supposed to learn kindness and compassion from the earthlings. Adopting human form, the alien calls himself Jesse (it was the name sewn on the gas station uniform he finds soon after arriving) and heads immediately to Los Angeles, that well-known bastion of kindness and compassion. There, he attempts to do good deeds, in hopes of proving to the gang back home that he has reformed. The problem is that Jesse knows zilch about human nature and habits, and he must try to make sense of what he observes, both in person and from watching TV. The judges back on Jesse's world keep tabs on the convict through an electronic observer, called Control. Looking like a floating eyeball, Control talks to, and helps, Jesse, but nobody else can see or hear it.

Jesse is thick and unlikable, sort of a surly E. T. who has pumped a lot of iron. Control is whiny and obnoxious. The numerous references to old movies and TV shows seem far too trendy, and fail to cover the fact that the individual stories themselves rarely make much sense.

**HARDCASTLE & MCCORMICK** (**) **60 min (67ep & 2 hr pilot Color; 1983–1986 ABC) Adventure** *with Brian Keith as Judge Milton G. Hardcastle, Daniel Hugh-Kelly as Mark "Skid" McCormick, John Hancock as Lt. Michael Delaney, and Joe Santos as Lt. Frank Harper*

No doubt every lawyer, judge, and police officer feels there are guilty parties that escaped punishment due to some loophole in the system. Judge Hardcastle even has a list of all those that "got away" during his thirty years on the bench. Now that he's retired, he has the time to check up on them and see if they're doing anything now that might warrant punishment, with a young hotshot race driver as his muscleman.

You can take such a premise very, very seriously and turn it into a series of Charles Bronson-style revenge tales or a kangaroo court setup like *The Star Chamber* (a 1983 theatrical film with Michael Douglas). Or you can use it as a jumping-off point for some light, quasi-legal adventures featuring high-speed car chases, sparring lead characters, and a sound track of contemporary-style music. With Stephen J. Cannell as executive producer, you know which option this series takes. It runs true to formula, with the color of the judge's flashy Hawaiian shirt about the only major variation from episode to episode. Otherwise, Hardcastle sputters and fumes, McCormick displays his muscle, some bad guys get caught, and another hour runs by. Fun for a while.

**THE HARDY BOYS** (**½) **11 min (32ep B&W; 1957 ABC) Mystery** *with Tim Considine as Joe Hardy, Tommy Kirk as Frank Hardy, Russ Conway as Fenton Hardy,*

*Sarah Selby as Gertrude Hardy, and Carole Ann Campbell as Viola Morton,* **THE HARDY BOYS/NANCY DREW MYSTERIES (**½) 60 min (54ep total Color; 1977–1978 ABC) Mystery Adventure split into THE HARDY BOYS (36ep)** *with Parker Stevenson as Frank Hardy, Shaun Cassidy as Joe Hardy, Edmund Gilbert as Fenton Hardy, Edith Atwater as Gertrude Hardy, Lisa Eilbacher as Callie Shaw, and Jack Kelly as Harry Hammond,* **NANCY DREW (10ep)** *with Pamela Sue Martin as Nancy Drew, William Schallert as Carson Drew, and Jean Rasey and Susan Buckner as George Fayne,* **THE HARDY BOYS AND NANCY DREW MYSTERIES (8ep)** *with above casts combined except Janet Louise Johnson as Nancy Drew (later episodes)*

Brothers Frank and Joe Hardy, sleuthing sons of the famous detective, Fenton Hardy, have been widely read heroes in a popular series of young boys' adventure books since the 1930s. And why not? They live the teenage male dream: Always on summer break or winter vacation, the two travel throughout the country (and sometimes overseas) solving mysteries, with easy access to such status symbols as flashy cars, motorcycles, speedboats, and even small private planes. Over the decades, the Stratemeyer Publishing Company (using the house pen name of Franklin W. Dixon) has churned out more than seventy books featuring the characters, periodically rewriting older titles to give the adventures a more contemporary flair. Along the way, the Hardy Boys have also had several television incarnations.

The first was as young teens in two serialized tales originally presented on the 1950s version of *The Mickey Mouse Club* (and subsequently rerun on the Disney Channel): *The Mystery of the Applegate Treasure* (a twenty-episode search for "gold doubloons and pieces of eight," very loosely based on the first Hardy Boys novel, *The Tower Treasure*) and *The Mystery of Ghost Farm* (a twelve-episode original, involving counterfeiters). The *Applegate Treasure* story is definitely the stronger of the two, though the cliffhangers and adventures in both are relatively tame and definitely "G" rated, even compared to the original books. Brother Joe (Tim Considine) later played brother Mike on *My Three Sons*.

In 1967, there was an unsuccessful pilot, with Tim Matheson (then spelled Matthieson) as Joe, Rick Gates as Frank, and Richard Anderson as their dad. A rock and roll cartoon series followed in 1971, with the boys solving mysteries while on concert tours. At last, in 1977, the Hardy Boys characters returned for full-fledged adventure treatment in 1977. Actually, they shared the spotlight with another star from the Stratemeyer Publishing Company, Nancy Drew, whose history also stretched back to the 1930s. Like the Hardy Boys, she always had time away from school, drove a stylish coupe, carried plenty of spending money, and lived with an understanding dad (attorney Carson Drew, a widower) who had no problem with his daughter's many adventures. Though the character did not have any television vehicles in the 1950s and 1960s, she did appear in four theatrical films in 1938 and 1939.

The 1970s television showcase (*The Hardy Boys/Nancy Drew Mysteries*) was set up to alternate between the two sets of characters. Though none of the stories were based directly on any of the novels, they might as well have been. They were pure pulp adventure in a contemporary setting, perhaps a little shy on sleuthing but strong on teen appeal. In fact, by the end of the second season, Shaun Cassidy (half-brother of David) was a real-life teen idol outside his Joe Hardy role, scoring three consecutive top ten hits on the pop charts ("Da Doo Ron Ron," "That's Rock'n'Roll," and "Hey Deanie"). Cassidy's success seemed to guarantee that the episodes based on the Hardy books would have a lot of teenage girls tuning in. Appropriately, Pamela Sue Martin provided a very attractive Nancy Drew for the guys, though she was always dressed tastefully enough to make the family-hour standards. (Later, a *Playboy* spread and a stint as Fallon on *Dynasty* gave Martin a chance to display other aspects of her performing persona.) Martin split from the series when the producers completely eliminated *Nancy Drew* as a separate segment, so Janet Johnson took the role for the last four Hardy Boys/Nancy Drew team-up adventures.

There's a cute in-joke in one of the final episodes of the series ("Assault on the Tower"), when the brothers discover that their dad fought in World War II alongside a suave English agent known only as "S." With *Avengers* star Patrick Macnee (John Steed) playing the character, it's pretty clear who that man is supposed to be. ■

**HARPER VALLEY (*½) 30 min (30ep Color; 1981–1982 NBC) Situation Comedy** *with Barbara Eden as Stella Johnson, Jenn Thompson as Dee Johnson, Anne Francine as Flora Simpson Reilly, Fannie Flagg as Cassie Bowman, and George Gobel as Mayor Otis Harper, Jr.*

Not many songs are spun off into TV series, especially not thirteen years after the song is on the music charts. Country songwriter Tom T. Hall wrote "Harper Valley PTA" as a humorous protest song in the late 1960s, when country music didn't go in much for protests. Jeannie C. Riley had a big hit with the song in 1968, when the lyrics about a bold woman putting down the stodgy hypocrites of the local PTA rang true during that year of revolt.

In 1978, for no good reason, the song was used as the basis for a Hollywood film, starring Barbara Eden, an actress who had her own struggle with silly hypocrites during *I Dream of Jeannie,* when she was not allowed to show her belly button. The film fared poorly at the box office, but garnered great ratings when it first aired on TV in 1980. This success resulted in the *Harper Valley* TV series, with Eden reprising her film role. The original thirteen episodes, called *Harper Valley PTA,* are produced by Sherwood Schwartz (of *Gilligan's Island* fame) and the comedy level is appropriately simple and 1960s-ish in feel. After Schwartz departs, the final seventeen episodes drop the PTA idea and are marginally more humorous. George Gobel is fun in both versions of the TV series as the tipsy mayor of the town.

**HARRIGAN AND SON** (**½) **30 min (34ep B&W; 1960–1961 ABC) Situation Comedy** *with Pat O'Brien as James Harrigan, Sr., Roger Perry as James Harrigan, Jr., Georgine Darcy as Gypsy, and Helen Kleeb as Miss Claridge*

Take *The Defenders,* turn it into a sitcom and, voila, you have *Harrigan and Son.* Both shows focus on father and son legal teams, with the father trying to impart some real-world wisdom to the mounds of book learning the son brings from law school.

Pat O'Brien, Hollywood's professional Irishman for decades, plays dad in this show, his only TV series role. O'Brien, as always, has a gleam in his eye and a smile is never far from his lips. Roger Perry, as son, unfortunately does not add much to the story, leaving the dapper O'Brien to carry the load himself.

**HARRIS AGAINST THE WORLD** (**) **30 min (13ep Color; 1964–1965 NBC) Situation Comedy** *with Jack Klugman as Alan Harris, Patricia Barry as Kate Harris, Claire Wilcox as Deedee Harris, David Macklin as Billy Harris, and Guy Raymond as Cliff Murdock*

Jack Klugman's first regular TV series role is that of Alan Harris, the superintendent of a big Hollywood movie studio whose life is complicated by his free-spending wife and his two active kids. The Harris clan resides at 90 Bristol Court, an apartment complex that serves as the locale for two other sitcoms, *Tom, Dick, and Mary* and *Karen.*

**HARRIS AND COMPANY** (***) **60 min (4ep Color; 1979 NBC) Drama** *with Bernie Casey as Mike Harris, David Hubbard as David Harris, Renee Brown as Liz Harris, Lia Jackson as Juanita Priscilla "J. P." Harris, and James Luisi as Harry Foreman*

The Harris family is that all-too-rare species, the realistic black TV family. No jive-talking kiddies here, no big-breasted mammies, no slicked-up young bucks, just a widowed father of five who leaves the Detroit assembly line for the sunny promise of L. A. Once in California, Mike Harris opens up a garage business with Harry Foreman, but the focus here is on Harris's home life and the problems he faces raising his children alone. It's not all pathos, though, and there are some nice moments of fun and laughs to brighten up the show.

**HARRY** (**½) **30 min (6ep Color; 1987 ABC) Situation Comedy** *with Alan Arkin as Harry Porschak, Richard Lewis as Richard Breskin, Matt Craven as Bobby Kratz, Holland Taylor as Nurse Ina Duckett, and Barbara Dana as Dr. Sandy Clifton*

After two decades as a well-respected Hollywood actor (*The Heart Is a Lonely Hunter, Catch-22, The In-Laws*), Alan Arkin's first TV starring role is as Harry Porschak, a wheeler-dealer who is head of purchasing for a large urban hospital. Harry's cunning and guile wind up helping to save lives, of course, but his abrasive personality makes him unloved among the hospital administration, especially Nurse Duckett.

Arkin's character takes some getting used to, and the focus on such a blue-collar type amidst TV's favorite professionals (doctors) is highly unusual. Still, the result is always intriguing, if not hilarious. *Harry*'s producers include Arkin himself and Barry Levinson, who produced the hit films *Diner, Tin Men, Good Morning, Vietnam,* and *Rain Man.*

**HARRY-O** (***) **60 min (44ep & 2 pilots: one 90 min & one 2 hr Color; 1974–1976 ABC) Detective Drama** *with David Janssen as Harry Orwell, Henry Darrow as Manny Quinlan, and Anthony Zerbe as K. C. Trench*

David Janssen made a career out of playing laconic loners. His most famous role was Dr. Richard Kimble in *The Fugitive,* where he hardly ever cracked a smile. Before that, he starred in *Richard Diamond, Private Detective,* playing another tight-lipped hero. *Harry-O* is, arguably, Janssen at his best, as he combines the quirky outsider tics that are his trademark with a wry sense of humor to liven things up.

Harry Orwell is an L. A. policeman, shot in the back while breaking up a drugstore burglary. The resulting spinal injury ends his police career and he moves to a small beachfront house near San Diego, where he collects disability. Unwilling to sit on his duff all day, Orwell becomes a part-time private eye, taking only the cases he wants. Orwell is an irascible grouch, who doesn't like to waste time in idle chitchat. As with all such grumpy TV heroes, though, he really has a heart of gold.

Tight-lipped gumshoes are a dime a dozen in the annals of movies and TV. What makes Harry Orwell stand out is Janssen's complete believability in the role and the lengths the producers go to make him unique. It is not enough to have him be close-mouthed and full of wise-guy remarks when he does talk. It is not enough to have him live like a bohemian on the beach, far from the madding crowd. No, to top it off, Orwell doesn't even drive a car. Oh, he owns a car, but it always seems to be broken or something, so he rides the bus, picking it up at the end of the line right by his house. Exhaustive TV history research has yet to find any other private eye who rides the bus on any regular basis.

Since Orwell takes public transportation, do not expect many tire-squealing car chases in *Harry-O.* Instead look for good character development, intriguing stories, and low-key excitement. Those are the pluses. For minuses, *Harry-O* is saddled with the traditional by-the-book cop insider who is supposed to counterbalance the star's rebel qualities. This gimmick wears out very easily in *Harry-O,* as it does in the numerous other cop shows where it is used. At first, Manny Quinlan, of the San Diego police, is the pain in the rear in Orwell's life. About halfway through the show's run, Quinlan is killed off, Orwell moves to Santa Monica (closer to L. A.) and K. C. Trench, of the LAPD, picks up where Quinlan left off.

*Harry-O* goes downhill in the Santa Monica-era episodes. Orwell frequently forsakes the bus, for slightly more conventional motor transportation (an old jalopy) and Orwell loses much of the cranky quirkiness that made him stand out from the other private eyes. Even the gunshot wound in his back seems to clear up in the L. A. smog.

In the earlier, better, San Diego episodes, look for Orwell's next-door neighbors, Farrah Fawcett (later of *Charlie's Angels*) and Loni Anderson (later of *WKRP in Cincinnati*). This dream pair of unmarried women perk Orwell's interest, but no romance develops, another mark of *Harry-O*'s uniqueness.

The early development of the Harry Orwell character can be followed by catching the two made-for-TV movie pilots that predate the regular series. The original 1973 pilot, titled *Harry-O,* is Orwell at his best. This pilot has Orwell's gunshot injury, his putting down stakes in San Diego, and a great guest performance by Martin Sheen as the gunman who wounded Orwell. The second pilot, from 1974, titled *Smile Jenny, You're Dead,* features guest star Jodie Foster.

**HARRY'S GIRLS (*½) 30 min (15ep B&W; 1963–1964 NBC) Situation Comedy** *with Larry Blyden as Harry Burns, Susan Silo as Rusty, Dawn Nickerson as Lois, and Diahn Williams as Terry*

If you accept the series premise that a vaudeville-style dance act with three beautiful women was too old-fashioned for success in the States, but perfect for a European tour, why would anyone expect a series about that act on tour to be very popular here? It wasn't, though the location footage (shot in southern France) wasn't bad. Apparently inspired by the 1957 George Cukor film *Les Girls,* with Larry Blyden taking the Gene Kelly role of the women's talent manager.

**HART TO HART (**) 60 min (112ep Color; 1979–1984 ABC) Adventure** *with Robert Wagner as Jonathan Hart, Stefanie Powers as Jennifer Hart, and Lionel Stander as Max*

We're talking real money here. Jonathan Hart is a self-made millionaire, head of his own conglomerate, and someone who loves adventure. So does his wife, Jennifer, who developed her sleuthing skills as an international journalist. With plenty of time, money, and social connections at their disposal, Mr. and Mrs. H (as they're referred to by their chauffeur, Max) have developed a unique hobby: solving murders.

The Harts are probably the most comfortably situated private eyes since Nick and Nora Charles (and their dog, Asta) in the *Thin Man* theatrical films (the Harts even have a pet dog, Freeway). They're happily married, well respected, popular, and—best of all—they work only when they want to (or when they stumble on a case). The tone of the series reflects that satisfied air, with the Harts almost casually strolling through their jet-set intrigues and international adventures. They're very good at what they do, and they know it.

Oddly, that's the main problem with the series. The central cast is good and the tone is appropriately light, but, given all that talent, you expect a little more sizzle. Instead the plots, villains, and banter are too often cookie-cutter predictable, without the extra zing. The Harts look great and love each other, but they just don't radiate sexual excitement. For example, there's the final-season "origin" episode ("Two Harts Are Better Than One"), which at last explains just what Max means when he says, "When they met, it was murder." The episode does indeed reveal how the two first met, but it seems more like a rush to run through plot points (including a murder) rather than a love story, with Jonathan's proposal (a banner atop a London bridge) coming almost out of nowhere. Granted, this isn't meant to be a deep character study, but you can't help wishing for scripts with just a little more romance.

Still, despite disappointment over what might have been, this series is definitely a safe slice of light entertainment, with three entertaining leads.

**THE HARVEY KORMAN SHOW (*½) 30 min (6ep & 30 min pilot Color; 1978 ABC) Situation Comedy** *with Harvey Korman as Harvey Kavanaugh, Christine Lahti as Maggie Kavanaugh, Milton Selzer as Jake Winkleman, and Barry Van Dyke as Stuart Stafford*

Harvey Korman, the perennial second banana to Carol Burnett, doesn't do much with his first chance to star in his own show. Korman plays Harvey Kavanaugh, an aging bit actor still trying to hit the big time. Korman's affected mannerisms, acceptable in a secondary role, are a bit distracting in the lead actor.

In the 1977 pilot, Korman's character is known as Francis Kavanaugh, and his daughter Maggie is played by Susan Lawrence.

**THE HATHAWAYS (zero) 30 min (26ep B&W; 1961–1962 ABC) Situation Comedy** *with Jack Weston as Walter Hathaway, Peggy Cass as Elinore Hathaway, Harvey Lembeck as Jerry Roper, and the Marquis Chimps (Charlie, Enoch, and Cindy) as themselves*

The stories are standard screwball sitcom fodder: misunderstood situations, balancing a household budget, arguments between friends and neighbors, and jealousy within the family. The key difference with this series is that three members of the Hathaway family are chimps. They share in all the household activities—eating, drinking, playing, getting dressed, and even bringing home a paycheck. (Elinore, their manager, and Jerry, their agent, handle the paperwork.) But they don't talk, not even through the magic of overdubbing, and this may be one reason the series seems so maddeningly dumb. Sure, Lassie and Flipper couldn't talk either, but they weren't dressed in cute bonnets and given plates at the breakfast table. Here we have to watch the cast go through the excruciating humiliation of playing second banana to the scene-stealing chimps without even getting the illusion of humanlike asides (a la Mister Ed, Cleo the basset hound, or even Lancelot Link, Secret Chimp). Around the time this series originally aired, Newton Minow (then the commissioner of the FCC) made his famous speech describing television as a "vast wasteland." He couldn't have asked for better evidence than *The Hathaways.*

**HAVE FAITH** **(*½) 30 min (6ep Color; 1989 ABC) Situation Comedy** *with Joel Higgins as Msgr. Joseph "Mac" MacKenzie, Ron Carey as Fr. Vincent Paglia, Stephen Furst as Fr. Gabriel Podmaninsky, Frank Hamilton as Fr. Edgar Tuttle, and Francesca Roberts as Sally Coleman*

In this lightweight comedy, Joel Higgins (*Silver Spoons*) plays the Monseigneur of St. Catherine's church in Chicago. Higgins is teamed up with three other graduates of popular ensemble series, Ron Carey (from *Barney Miller*), Stephen Furst (from *St. Elsewhere*) and Francesca Roberts (from *Frank's Place*). Monseigneur MacKenzie (known as "Mac") is an easygoing fellow with a fondness for the Chicago Cubs. Father Paglia (played by Carey) is the penny pincher in charge of finances, Father Podmaninsky (played by Furst) is the tubby young priest just out of the seminary, while Father Tuttle is the strict old-timer who must adapt to Mac's relaxed regime. Sally Coleman (played by Roberts) is the no-frills black secretary who tries to keep Mac organized.

In *Have Faith,* most of the jokes are pretty obvious and pretty simple. There are a few attempts at making "serious" points, but mostly the show is one-liners and easy "priest" gags. The cast is better than the material.

**HAVE GUN WILL TRAVEL** **(***½) 30 min (225ep B&W; 1957–1963 CBS) Western** *with Richard Boone as Paladin*

*Have Gun Will Travel* is one of the purest, most imaginative examples of the golden age of TV westerns. It presents the underlying concept in all TV westerns, the battle of good versus evil, in a setting we can easily understand. Its quality comes from its restraint, its style, and its ability to transcend its sparse setting.

Richard Boone plays a college-educated Civil War veteran who sets up business in the swank Hotel Carlton in sophisticated San Francisco. Boone's character is known only as Paladin, a word meaning "paragon of chivalry" or "heroic champion." A paladin is also the name for a knight in the game of chess, and that chess piece serves as Paladin's symbol on his business card. The card simply reads "Have Gun—Will Travel. Wire Paladin, San Francisco." Paladin's business is that of a hired gun who, for pay, will serve as investigator, bodyguard, courier, or enforcer.

Paladin's true nature, however, is more intriguing. On the one hand, he is the typical offbeat private eye, set in a western framework, full of dark cynicism and deep-down warmth. On the other hand, Paladin can also be viewed as an avenging angel, a force for good in a world overflowing in corruption and evil. He is no simple hired gun, for Paladin will turn on his employers, if it turns out that *they* are the guilty ones.

Paladin can do what mortal men cannot: He can confront evil face to face and *shoot it dead.* It is truly the case of having a dirty job that somebody has to do. Still, Paladin is tainted by the power he must exert, and, unlike most good guys in westerns, Paladin wears black (the traditional symbol of evil), even in the God-forsaken blazing wastes of the desert. The inner contradiction is thus made obvious, as Paladin, the force for good, must act like evil at times, in helping good triumph.

Richard Boone turns in an acting gem in this show, presenting Paladin as a tower of strength who is still wracked by inner turmoil when forced to use his deadly strength. Boone, in fact, directed twenty-seven episodes and exerted his influence over many areas of writing and production.

Paladin is the anchor of *Have Gun Will Travel.* Aside from the mysterious gunman, the only continuing character is Paladin's deferential Oriental servant, perversely named "Hey Boy" (Kam Tong). For one season, Hey Boy is spelled by the equally subservient Hey Girl (Lisa Lu). Aside from these aides, Paladin is truly the lone gun. He seems to have no family, few friends, and little, if any, love in his life. He is, you might say, serving a life sentence of helping others who cannot help themselves.

**HAVING BABIES** **(**) 60 min (8ep & three 2 hr pilots Color; 1978–1979 ABC) Medical Drama** *with Susan Sullivan as Dr. Julie Farr, Mitchell Ryan as Dr. Blake Simmons, and Dennis Howard as Dr. Ron Danvers*

This medical series can't seem to decide what it wants to be. In its first incarnation, *Having Babies I,* a 1976 TV movie originally called *Giving Birth,* the focus is on a series of women about to have children, and the personal crises they are going through. *Having Babies II,* from 1977, keeps the focus on expectant couples, but places the character of obstetrician Dr. Julie Farr in the mix as the medical focus of the story of the parents-to-be. *Having Babies III,* from 1978, creates the setting that became a series. Dr. Farr is now the primary focus, and it is how her life and loves are affected by her demanding job and her expectant patients that takes up most of the show. The characters of elder Dr. Simmons and younger Dr. Daniels (later called Dr. Danvers in the series) serve as buffers for Dr. Farr.

The *Having Babies* series picks up where the third pilot left off, but, after three episodes, the title is changed to *Julie Farr, M. D.,* and the emphasis is moved even further away from the pregnancy angle and focused more on Dr. Farr as young female medico.

**HAWAII FIVE-O (***) 60 min (200ep & 2 hr pilot Color; 1968–1980 CBS) Police Drama** *with Jack Lord as Det. Steve McGarrett, James MacArthur as Det. Danny Williams, Kam Fong as Det. Chin Ho Kelly, and Khigh Dhiegh as Wo Fat*

If you mated *Dragnet* and *Hawaiian Eye,* the offspring would be *Hawaii Five-O.* From *Dragnet, Hawaii Five-O* would inherit all the tough-guy, tight-lipped policeman routines, where common peons never fully understand the problems the police must face to rid the streets of the vermin of society. From *Hawaiian Eye, Hawaii Five-O* would inherit the filmed on location lush tropical scenery, featuring lots of swaying palms and curvaceous native women, plus colorful characters from a culture noticeably different from that of the mainland.

*Hawaii Five-O* is the tale of a special police unit (called Five-O) based in Honolulu and nominally affiliated with the Hawaiian State Police. Head of Five-O is the tall, rugged, intense Steve McGarrett, who has the independence to bypass the officials at the Hawaiian State Police and answer only to the governor. No petty bureaucrats need get in the way of McGarrett and his men, so they are free to use whatever methods of persuasion are at hand to bring the evildoers to bay.

It is hard to argue with success, and *Hawaii Five-O* lasted longer than almost every cop show on TV, but there is a huge emptiness in this program and that emptiness is humanity. McGarrett is virtually humorless, has no private or home life to speak of, and his men are driven to follow in his example. The Polynesian flora and fauna are easy on the eyes, and the drama and suspense of the shows are put together well, but you keep wanting McGarrett to play hooky one day and go to the dog track or something. No such luck. All he lives for is cleaning up the island paradise from the unending parade of spies, drug dealers, hoodlums, and punks that pop up each week. McGarrett's fervid trademark expression of "Book 'em, Danno!" is about as emotional as the guy gets.

The only interesting characters on *Hawaii Five-O* are the bad guys, since they are the only ones allowed to express any emotion other than gritty determination. Best known of the Hawaiian crime czars is Wo Fat, a burly, sinister, Oriental reminiscent of Oddjob from the James Bond film *Goldfinger.* Wo Fat is the equal of McGarrett, forever eluding the Five-O cops until an obligatory final episode when truth and justice are made to prevail at last and Wo Fat is sent to the slammer. Another, less renowned, villain from the series is Tony Alika, mob boss, played by the always inventive Ross Martin (of *Wild, Wild West* fame).

Keep on the lookout for the original two-hour pilot episode, containing most of the regular characters (including Wo Fat). The only major change, and the way to recognize the pilot, is that McGarrett's top aide, Det. Danny "Danno" Williams, is played by Tim O'Kelly in the pilot, while James MacArthur filled the role during the regular series run.

Episodes of *Hawaii Five-O* have been rerun under the title *McGarrett.*

**HAWAIIAN EYE (**) 60 min (134ep B&W; 1959–1963 ABC) Detective Drama** *with Robert Conrad as Tom Lopaka, Anthony Eisley as Tracy Steele, Grant Williams as Greg MacKenzie, Connie Stevens as Cricket Blake, Poncie Ponce as Kazuo Kim, and Troy Donahue as Philip Barton*

*Hawaiian Eye* is one of the slew of Warner Bros. action/adventure series that blossomed on ABC in the late 1950s and early 1960s and frequently cross-pollinated with one another. These series were designed around the same format: a few good-looking hunk leads, a pretty female auxiliary and an offbeat character for local color, all set in an exotic setting and revolving around fighting crime.

*Hawaiian Eye* fulfills all the requirements of this Warner Bros. mold. Stars Robert Conrad, Anthony Eisley, and Grant Williams are appropriately handsome as the three private eyes running the Hawaiian Eye agency out of a poolside office in a swank Honolulu hotel. Connie Stevens provides the curves as a local nightclub singer/photographer who provides entertainment, hot tips, and hot photos to the tropical gumshoes. Poncie Ponce runs a taxi business, is the butt of most of the show's "crazy native" jokes, and helps out by enlisting his widespread family in the crime-fighting efforts.

It takes a genealogist to keep track of the inbreeding that occurs among the various Warner Bros. shows that followed this format. In *Hawaiian Eye,* Eisley leaves after three seasons, to be replaced by Troy Donahue, formerly of Warner's *Surfside Six.* Efrem Zimbalist, Jr., makes several guest appearances here, in his role as Stuart Bailey of *77 Sunset Strip,* the first and best of Warner's action/adventure shows.

**HAWAIIAN HEAT (*) 60 min (12ep Color; 1984 ABC) Police Drama** *with Jeff McCracken as Andy Senkowski, Robert Ginty as Mac Riley, Tracy Scoggins as Irene Gorley, and Mako as Maj. Taro Oshiro*

Flashy Hawaiian settings and wisecracking buddies fill this formula cop show about two Chicago cops who ditch the Windy City for jobs as undercover police detectives in Hawaii. Turn the sound down and watch the pretty scenery.

**HAWK** (***) **60 min (17ep Color; 1966 ABC) Police Drama** *with Burt Reynolds as Lt. John Hawk, Wayne Grice as Det. Dan Carter, Leon Janney as Gorten, and John Marley as Sam Crown*

For nothing else, *Hawk* is worth catching simply because it is the first TV series that Burt Reynolds starred in (he previously had supporting roles in *Riverboat* and *Gunsmoke*). Beyond that, *Hawk* is an enjoyable show on its own, one of the original of the "outsider" cop school of shows that proliferated in the late 1960s and early 1970s.

Reynolds plays John Hawk, a full-blooded Iroquois who is a member of an elite troop of undercover detectives with the New York City police force. Hawk works mostly by night and the tone of *Hawk* is dark and somewhat sinister. The series was filmed on location in and around the Gotham area, adding a welcome touch of realism. Reynolds, himself part Indian, plays his role with a lot more solemnity than a viewer weaned on his later *Smokey and the Bandit* films might expect. *Hawk* is produced by the versatile Hubbell Robinson, who also produced *ABC Stage '67, 87th Precinct,* and some *Playhouse 90* episodes.

**HAWKEYE AND THE LAST OF THE MOHICANS** (*½) **30min (39ep B&W; 1956–1957 Canada CBC) Adventure** *with John Hart as Nat "Hawkeye" Cutler and Lon Chaney, Jr., as Chingachgook*

Based somewhat on the famous James Fenimore Cooper book, this Canadian series follows Nat Cutler, known as Hawkeye, a white fur trader and scout, and his blood brother Chingachgook, the "last" of the Mohican tribe, in the frontier of the 1750s. The pair work for the U.S. calvary and battle the hostile Huron tribe of Indians.

John Hart served briefly as the Lone Ranger in the popular 1950s TV series. Lon Chaney, Jr., will forever be known as the original Wolf Man in the 1941 film classic of that name.

**HAWKINS** (**) **90 min (8ep Color; 1973–1974 CBS) Law Drama** *with James Stewart as Billy Jim Hawkins and Strother Martin as R. J. Hawkins*

A reasonably good vehicle for Jimmy Stewart, faithfully incorporating his slow, hesitant drawl and homespun country boy manner so familiar to television viewers from countless rerun showings of his theatrical classics (including *It's a Wonderful Life, You Can't Take It With You,* and *Mr. Smith Goes to Washington*). Here he plays a one-time deputy D. A. turned to private practice in rural West Virginia, but often called out of town to handle murder cases anywhere in the country. His cousin R. J. comes along as legman assistant and together the two of them clear their clients and find the real culprits. Unfortunately, even for a short-flight series, you don't run into many scripts on a par with Frank Capra's classics, so this is best seen as harmless visits with an old celluloid friend.

**HAZEL** (**) **30 min (154ep: 34 B&W & 120 Color; 1961–1966 NBC & CBS) Situation Comedy** *with Shirley Booth as Hazel Burke, Don DeFore as George Baxter, Whitney Blake as Dorothy Baxter, Bobby Buntrock as Harold Baxter, Ray Fulmer as Steve Baxter, Lynn Borden as Barbara Baxter, and Julia Benjamin as Susie Baxter*

George Baxter is a highly successful, highly organized corporate lawyer who is all thumbs when it comes to doing much around the house. His wife Dorothy is a wealthy matron who does not want to be bothered by the mundane demands of running a home and keeping a close eye on their young son Harold. What the Baxters need is a housekeeper/maid to run things for them, and that need is filled by Hazel.

Hazel goes beyond the traditional roles of housekeeper and maid to become the *real* head of the household. She winds up running the Baxters' lives, sorting out their problems, and keeping everyone in line. The humor is supposed to come from Hazel's awkward, unpolished way of solving problems that the Baxters, in their upper-crust formality, just can't seem to deal with.

Hazel's supremacy over the Baxters is wryly amusing, but becomes fairly annoying afer a few episodes. She seems more like a meddlesome busybody, who sticks her nose into other people's business more than is necessary. The Baxters truly are a bunch of twits who need a lot of guidance, but Hazel goes too far. You begin to wish that George or Dorothy would stand up to Hazel and yell "Leave me alone! I'll handle this myself!"

In its last season, *Hazel* revamps its format. The Baxters are shipped to Saudi Arabia, due to George's business. Hazel is left with the Baxter's son Harold, and the two move in with George's younger brother Steve, his wife Barbara, and daughter Susie. Steve Baxter shows a tad more backbone than brother George, but Hazel makes short work of taking over this new Baxter household as well. Perhaps George and Dorothy Baxter were not really transferred to Saudi Arabia. Perhaps they just made up the whole story to get out of town and get rid of Hazel. Hopefully they found a nice quiet town somewhere and began living a more independent life, free of domination from their domestic.

**HE & SHE** (***½) **30 min (26ep Color; 1967–1968 CBS) Situation Comedy** *with Richard Benjamin as Dick Hollister, Paula Prentiss as Paula Hollister, Jack Cassidy as Oscar North, Kenneth Mars as Harry Zarakardos, Hamilton Camp as Andrew Hummel, and Harold Gould as Norman Nugent*

An excellent ensemble comedy with real-life husband and wife Richard Benjamin and Paula Prentiss playing a happily married young career couple in New York City. Dick is a successful cartoonist (his biggest creation "Jetman" even runs as a TV show) while Paula is a wacky but well-meaning social worker. The stories are an excellent mix of mild domestic and work-related complications, ranging from silly squabbles (Dick grows a beard while out of town and Paula wants him to shave it off) to sweetly romantic gestures (for a birthday gift Paula gives Dick their special rock—the one that hit him on the head during their first date).

Naturally, Dick and Paula also get involved with their next-door neighbor. Actually it would be hard for them to avoid Harry, a fireman at the station next door, because he's often literally at their window—passing the time standing on a wooden plank he's put between the two buildings (so he's still within earshot of the alarm bell). Rounding out their home life is the building's janitor, Andrew, a man just slightly off his rocker.

The success of "Jetman" also means that Dick and Paula get to spend time with Oscar North, the vain, self-centered braggart who plays the character on television. Jack Cassidy's portrayal of North is hilarious and so strikingly similar in spirit to Ted Knight's Ted Baxter (on *The Mary Tyler Moore Show* a few years later) that when the time came to introduce Ted's brother, Cassidy was a natural for the role. Though not at all related, the two looked as if they were indeed long-lost kin. (And from the production side, future *Mary Tyler Moore Show* team members Jay Sandrich, Allan Burns, and David Davis all put in time on *He & She*.)

A highly recommended series.

**HE'S THE MAYOR** (**) **30 min (10ep Color; 1986 ABC) Situation Comedy** *with Kevin Hooks as Mayor Carl Burke, Al Fann as Alvin Burke, Mari Gorman as Paula Hendricks, Wesley Thompson as Wardell Halsey, and Pat Corley as Chief Walter Padget*

Kevin Hooks, who played eager young Morris Thorpe in *The White Shadow*, plays Carl Burke, the young, black mayor of a small town who bumps up against a cynical police chief played by Pat Corley. Mayor Burke relies frequently on the advice of his father Alvin, a veteran janitor in City Hall. The actors are good here, but the scripting is mundane.

**HEAD OF THE CLASS** (***) **30 min (68ep at Fall 1989 Color; 1986– ABC) Situation Comedy** *with Howard Hesseman as Charlie Moore, William G. Schilling as Dr. Harold Samuels, Tannis Vallely as Janice Lazarotto, Daniel Schneider as Dennis Blunden, Brian Robbins as Eric Mardian, Dan Frischman as Arvid Engen, Jory Husain as Jawaharlal Shoudhury, Leslie Bega as Maria Borges, Khrystyne Haje as Simone Foster, Tony O'Dell as Alan Pinkard, Kimberly Russell as Sarah Nevins, Jeannetta Arnette as Bernadette Meara, and Robin Givens as Darlene Merriman*

Charlie Moore is one of those relics from the 1960s who is still idealistic enough to believe he can make a difference. He has the tricky task of teaching history to a group of super-whiz honor students (at Millard Fillmore High School in Manhattan) who are experts in practically everything (science, math, music, foreign languages). However, they still need lessons on social interaction and perspectives on life, which Mr. Moore is definitely equipped to supply. They may be I.Q. geniuses, but they are still just high school kids. He, on the other hand, lived through the days of Richard Nixon and Watergate. (Yes, he's a liberal, but the kids like him anyway!)

This is a smooth and comfortable vehicle for Howard Hesseman, easily his best role since Dr. Johnny Fever on *WKRP in Cincinnati.* Just as important, the kids on this series are intelligent and interesting individuals who frankly enjoy Moore's approach and appreciate his concern for them. He's a calming influence, especially in contrast to the school's principal, Dr. Samuels, who sometimes gets too caught up in his own boosterism efforts on behalf of these prize pupils.

*Head of the Class* is a good bread-and-butter series and definitely worth following for a while—you'll need to see more than a few episodes anyway just to get the names of all the students in the class straight (though you already know about Robin Givens from the gossip column treatment of her involvement with boxer Mike Tyson). Along the way, definitely keep an eye out for the "glasnost" episodes, featuring some counterpart genius students from Russia. They go head-to-head with a team of Moore's students in a competitive question and answer contest (reminiscent of the old *College Bowl* TV series). The first match is staged Stateside, but the follow-up takes place in Russia, with the entire episode done on location.

**HEADMASTER** (***) **30 min (13ep Color; 1970–1971 CBS) Comedy-Drama** *with Andy Griffith as Andy Thompson, Jerry Van Dyke as Jerry Brownell, Claudette Nevins as Margaret Thompson, and Parker Fennelly as Mr. Purdy*

After eight years of playing easygoing folksy sheriff Andy Taylor of Mayberry, N. C., Andy Griffith left his own popular show and, two years later, tried something completely different in *Headmaster.* His name is still Andy, and he still plays an easygoing guy, but Griffith's new role as Andy Thompson, a headmaster at Concord Prep School, is far more modern and dramatic than Sheriff Taylor. Trying to hit the same note of drama and levity that *Room 222* did so well, *Headmaster* focuses on the personal problems of the students and Andy Thompson's home life.

Jerry Van Dyke is quite distracting as the school's physical education teacher. His slapstick nature (better suited for the lead role in *My Mother the Car*) grates against the more serious tone the show is attempting. That tone of seriousness, however, does tend to get a bit overbearing at times. All in all, *Headmaster* is a nice try at something different that doesn't quite work.

A special treat in *Headmaster* is the theme song, sung by Linda Ronstadt, a tune that never turned up on any of her albums.

**HEART OF THE CITY** (*) **60 min (13ep 90 min pilot Color; 1986–1987 ABC) Drama** *with Robert Desiderio as Wes Kennedy, Christina Applegate as Robin Kennedy, Jonathan Ward as Kevin Kennedy, and Dick Anthony Williams as Lt. Ed Van Duzer*

Wes Kennedy is a tough-guy cop whose wife was brutally murdered by some wacko, leaving Wes with a giant chip on his shoulder (not to mention severe emotional problems) and two teenaged kids to raise. Kennedy works the night shift and even his co-workers think the guy needs to loosen up. This muddled drama wears its heart on its sleeve far too much, resulting in a morass of haphazard emotions.

**HEART OF THE CITY** (see *By-Line: Steve Wilson*)

**THE HEART OF THE DRAGON** (**½) **60 min (12ep Color; 1984 PBS) Documentary** *with Anthony Quayle as host*

This series profiles modern day China in everything from marriage to farming to trade with the rest of the world, paying particular attention to social attitudes (often in stark contrast with Stateside values) and the side-by-side existence of traditional and modern day practices even in areas such as medicine. ■

**HEARTBEAT** (*) **60 min (17ep & 2 hr pilot Color; 1988 ABC) Medical Drama** *with Kate Mulgrew as Dr. Joanne Springsteen (a.k.a. Dr. Joanne Halloran), Laura Johnson as Dr. Eve Autry (a.k.a. Dr. Eve Calvert), Ben Masters as Dr. Leo Rosetti, Gail Strickland as Nurse Marilyn McGrath, Lynn Whitfied as Dr. Cory Banks, and Julie Ronnie as Nurse Alice Swanson*

The trendy concept here is a health clinic (Women's Medical Arts) run by and for women. The lady medicos spend a lot of time railing against the male-dominated medical profession that surrounds them. While this may be a valid concern, it is played out in a simplistic manner that drags the concept down to vacuous soap opera posing.

A co-production effort from Aaron Spelling (*Charlie's Angels*) and Esther Shapiro (*Dynasty*), *Heartbeat* contains appropriately spicy interactions between some of the women doctors and the few token males in the show. One odd aspect of *HeartBeat* is the original names of the two lead female doctors, Springsteen and Autry. While no mention is made, one would guess that they are no relation to singers Bruce and Gene, respectively. At the start of the second season, the two characters' names have been inexplicably altered to the more mundane Halloran and Calvert.

**HEARTLAND** (*) **30 min (10ep Color; 1989 CBS) Situation Comedy** *with Brian Keith as B. L. McCutcheon, Kathleen Layman as Casey Stafford, Richard Gilliland as Tom Stafford, Jason Kristofer as Johnny Stafford, Devin Ratray as Gus Stafford, and Daisy Keith as Kim Stafford*

Set in Nebraska, *Heartland* presents the artificial and largely annoying Stafford household. Patriarch B. L. McCutcheon (played by *Family Affair*'s Brian Keith) grouses too much about his life and his son-in-law (still considered not good enough for his daughter). Vietnam veteran Tom Stafford, the son-in-law, is too dull as the prime operator of the family's 350-acre farm. Wife Casey is too sweet. Oldest son Johnny wants to be a punk rocker and move to Los Angeles. Younger son Gus is a chubby nerd who is preoccupied with the farm animals. Adopted Asian daughter Kim (played by Brian Keith's real daughter, Daisy) has an annoying high-pitched squeak for a voice. The rural setting is refreshing for the urban-obsessed late 1980s, but who needs a show where one episode's minor bit is Johnny's urgent need to "take a wicked whiz." The title song, by 1960s rocker Dion ("Runaround Sue," "Abraham, Martin and John"), is nice, however.

**HEC RAMSEY** (**) **90 min & 2 hr (10ep Color; 1972–1974 NBC) Mystery Adventure** *with Richard Boone as Hec Ramsey, Harry Morgan as "Doc" Amos Coogan, Richard Lenz as Sheriff Oliver B. Stamp, and Sharon Acker as Norma Muldoon*

The former Paladin moves into the twentieth century, with Richard Boone playing a grizzled old gunfighter who takes a job as deputy sheriff in the town of New Prospect, Oklahoma. Even though he's probably twice the age of his nominal boss, young Sheriff Stamp, Hec Ramsey is actually quite plugged into the latest turn-of-the-century methods of criminology, favoring deductive reasoning, dusting for fingerprints, and good old-fashioned legwork over his legendary six-gun. No surprise there, since this is a Jack Webb production. As with most of the series that originally played in one of those *Mystery Movie* slots, the stories are shamelessly padded and saved only by the character performances. Fortunately, Boone is pretty good and Webb's old mate, the reliable Harry Morgan, is also there for ad hoc medical support.

**HEE HAW** (***) **60 min (517ep at Summer 1989 Color; 1969– CBS & Syndication) Comedy-Variety** *with Roy Clark and Buck Owens as hosts*

Who says variety is dead? Who says you can't have a hit with cornball vaudeville-style humor? And who says viewers will tune out if you let the musical acts go on too long?

Not the fans of *Hee Haw*. This series first turned up in 1969 on CBS as a countrified knockoff of *Rowan and Martin's Laugh-In,* complete with a pair of genial hosts (veteran country singers Roy Clark and Buck Owens), celebrity cameos, a company of players, and a never-ending string of one-liners and drop-in bits. All of this tickled the funny bone of the program's animated donkey, whose "hee-haw" reminded folks of just what they were watching.

When CBS dropped *Hee Haw* from its lineup in 1971 as part of the network's "rural purge" (shifting from the likes of *Green Acres* to more urban-oriented fare like *All in the Family*), *Hee Haw* just rolled into first-run syndication and kept right on going . . . far longer than any of those newfangled "city-slicker" shows. Currently it still plays with its patented mix of cornfield humor, country music (old and new), a long alumni list of supporting players, and an easygoing welcome from Roy Clark. (Buck Owens left the co-host spot in 1986, after a mere seventeen years.) Perhaps the ultimate surprise of the program is that, unlike *Laugh-In, Hee Haw* barely shows its age. The series hasn't really dated because it has been in its own detached universe from the very beginning. And doing just fine, y'all.

**HEE HAW HONEYS (*) 30 min (26ep & 30 min pilot Color; 1978–1979 Syndication) Situation Comedy-Musical-Variety** *with Kathie Lee Johnson as Kathie Honey, Misty Rowe as Misty Honey, Gailard Sartain as Willie Billie Honey, Lulu Roman as Lulu Honey, and Kenny Price as Kenny Honey*

The sitcom part of this show is atrocious. Five regulars from the popular country and western comedy-variety show *Hee Haw* are spun off as members of the Honey family (parents Kenny and Lulu and their three grown children), who run Honey's Club, a Nashville restaurant/lounge. The son cooks, while the two daughters wait tables and try to break into show business as singers. The humor is corny, as expected, but it lacks the level of topicality and looseness that makes *Hee Haw* entertaining.

The variety part of this show is acceptable, in that several famous country singers pop in at Honey's every so often and perform. The problem is that if you want good country music you can catch the same people on *Hee Haw*.

**HELL TOWN (**) 60 min (11ep & 2 hr pilot Color; 1985 NBC) Drama** *with Robert Blake as Father Noah "Hardstep" Rivers, Natalie Core as Mother Maggie, Vonetta McGee as Sister Indigo, Whitman Mayo as One Ball, Jeff Corey as Lawyer Sam, and Tony Longo as Stump*

Imagine popular TV cop Baretta as an ex-con. Well, that's not hard, Baretta always seemed like a two-bit crook anyway. Now imagine Baretta as an ex-con who became a *priest*. What a concept! You now have the format of *Hell Town*, a well-meaning series where always cantankerous actor Robert Blake gets to act like a renegade again.

Blake's ex-con padre character, Father Rivers, known on the street as Hardstep, doesn't take any . . . uh, lip from anyone. In the Hell Town ghetto area of East L.A., Hardstep is always battling for homeless orphans or kindly bag ladies, which is admirable in theory, but is portrayed in a simplistic, preachy way here. Hardstep could take some lessons in subtlety and believability from Karl Malden's crusading priest character in the film *On the Waterfront*.

**HELLO, LARRY (*) 30 min (33ep Color; 1979–1980 NBC) Situation Comedy** *with McLean Stevenson as Larry Alder, Donna Wilkes and Krista Errickson as Diane Alder, Kim Richards as Ruthie Alder, Joanna Gleason as Morgan Winslow, and Meadowlark Lemon as himself*

In *Hello, Larry,* McLean Stevenson (four years out of *M*A*S*H*) plays Larry Alder (originally called Adler), a successful radio talk-show host who moves to Oregon with his two teenaged daughters after splitting from his wife. The primary focus of humor is that Larry has all the glib answers to life's problems while hosting his show (called "Hello, Larry"), but he is a total klutz in real life at home. *Hello, Larry* tries hard, but it just isn't very funny.

The characters from the more popular sitcom *Diff'rent Strokes*, produced by the same company, turn up now and again in an effort to boost interest in *Hello, Larry.*

**HEMINGWAY (**) 6hr miniseries Color; 1988 Syndication) Drama** *with Stacy Keach as Ernest Hemingway, Josephine Chaplin as Hadley Richardson, Rebecca Potok as Gertrude Stein, Marisa Berenson as Pauline Pfeiffer, Lisa Banes as Martha Gellhorn, and Pamela Reed as Mary Welsh*

The life (and loves) of the great American writer Ernest Hemingway is dramatized in a somewhat superficial manner in this miniseries. His numerous wives take up a lot of time, and a great deal of the literary luminaries Hemingway met put in merely cameo appearances. Stacy Keach makes a valiant effort to put some grit into his portrayal of "Papa" Hemingway.

**HENNESEY (***) 30 min (96ep B&W; 1959–1962 CBS) Situation Comedy** *with Jackie Cooper as Charles "Chick" Hennesey, Abby Dalton as Martha Hale, Roscoe Karns as Capt. Walter Shafer, James Komack as Harvey Spencer Blair III, and Arte Johnson as Seaman Shatz*

The multitalented Jackie Cooper (former child star in the *Our Gang* comedies and later a TV producer and director) is very enjoyable as the amiable Chick Hennesey, a medical officer at a naval base in San Diego. Hennesey romances and eventually marries his nurse, Martha Hale. Unlike many military sitcoms (*McHale's Navy, F Troop*), *Hennesey* is more witty and less slapstick. The show even avoids using a laugh track, a true rarity among 1950s sitcoms.

The actors and actresses in *Hennesey* are worth noting. Abby Dalton played Joey Bishop's wife in his early 1960s sitcom, and went on to play the mentally deranged Julia Cumson on *Falcon Crest.* Roscoe Karns was a star of the early TV cop show *Rocky King, Inside Detective.* Arte Johnson became a famous regular on *Laugh-In,* while James Komack is best known as the producer of *Welcome Back, Kotter* and *Chico and the Man.*

## HENRY FONDA PRESENTS THE STAR AND THE STORY (see *The Star and the Story*)

**HERBIE, THE LOVE BUG (*½) 60 min (5ep Color; 1982 CBS) Comedy-Adventure** *with Dean Jones as Jim Douglas, Patricia Harty as Susan MacLane, Richard Paul as Bo Phillips, and Larry Linville as Randy Bigelow*

"Herbie" is a battered Volkswagon "Bug" automobile with the magical ability to act on its own. Dean Jones starred in the original Herbie adventure, Disney's hit 1969 film *The Love Bug,* and in the 1977 film *Herbie Goes to Monte Carlo,* one of the three somewhat less successful movie sequels. In this TV version, Jones's character, racing car driver turned driving school instructor Jim Douglas, woos and weds comely divorcée Susan MacLane. Along with Susan come three children from her first marriage. Susan's old boyfriend Randy Bigelow, played by *M*A*S*H* graduate Larry Linville in his usual energetic Frank Burns manner, tries to thwart the new romance.

The star, of course, is Herbie, the VW Bug. It can do all sorts of tricks on its own, but at least it doesn't talk, like the auto in *My Mother the Car.*

**HERE COME THE BRIDES (**½) 60 min (52ep Color; 1968–1970 ABC) Comedy-Adventure** *with Bobby Sherman as Jeremy Bolt, David Soul as Joshua Bolt, Robert Brown as Jason Bolt, Joan Blondell as Lottie Hatfield, and Mark Lenard as Aaron Stempel*

In newly founded Seattle in the 1870s, the Bolt brothers' logging camp is in danger of foundering because the workers have no female companionship. Instead of shipping in a boatload of prostitutes (which wouldn't be proper for a family show), the Bolt brothers ship in a boatload of single women from Massachusetts (mostly widows from the Civil War) and play matchmaker to the loggers. This way, propriety is preserved and the logging camp keeps running.

The primary interest in this show is watching two of the more popular pinup boys of the 1970s. Bobby Sherman, who had garnered little attention on the musical-variety series *Shindig* in the mid-1960s, became a teen idol during *Here Come the Brides,* with numerous records ("Julie, Do Ya Love Me") topping the music charts. David Soul, who makes his first regular TV series appearance here, also attempted a side career as a singer (to litle avail). Sherman's popularity overshadowed Soul's presence in *Here Come the Brides,* and it was not until Soul co-starred in *Starsky & Hutch* in the late 1970s that he became a heartthrob as well.

**HERE WE GO AGAIN (**) 30 min (13ep Color; 1973 ABC) Situation Comedy** *with Larry Hagman as Richard Evans, Diane Baker as Susan Evans Standish, Nita Talbot as Judy Evans, and Dick Gautier as Jerry Standish*

Here's the character road map on this one: easygoing Richard and super-aggressive Judy get divorced after seventeen years (incompatibility); trusting Susan and roving Jerry get divorced after ten years (philandering); Richard and Susan meet, fall in love, get married, and set up housekeeping at her place (heartwarming); but their respective former mates both live only a short distance from the newlyweds, and are constantly intruding in their new lives (masochistic for all concerned).

Actually, in the 1930s and 1940s there were a number of clever "divorce comedy" theatrical films (such as *The Awful Truth* and *The Gay Divorcee*), but it's a tough act to pull off in a comedy series (especially when the "right" couple is already in place). The cast is pretty good (especially Larry Hagman and Dick Gautier), and there are plenty of zingers. But maybe such complicated interpersonal connections are best done as straight soap opera fodder (which Larry Hagman later handled just fine on *Dallas*), where characters routinely hover near ex-lovers beyond all common sense.

Oddly, Nita Talbot found herself observing another split couple (but with a more believable continuing friendship between them) as the receptionist in the late 1980s comedy *Starting from Scratch.*

**HERE'S BOOMER (*½) 30 min (24ep & 60 min pilot Color; 1980–1982 NBC) Adventure** *with Boomer as himself and Tom Moore as the voice of Boomer*

The canine version of *Route 66, Here's Boomer* presents a mongrel dog roaming the countryside. Each week Boomer meets up with some new humans who need the help a good dog can bring. After performing his good deed, Boomer is off again, in search of more adventure on the road. For an episode or so, Boomer's thoughts are heard through an offscreen narrator. The 1979 pilot, *A Christmas for Boomer,* presents Boomer's attraction for a saucy French poodle named Celeste.

**HERE'S LUCY (*½) 30 min (144ep Color; 1968–1974 CBS) Situation Comedy** *with Lucille Ball as Lucy Carter, Gale Gordon as Harrison Otis Carter, Mary Jane Croft as Mary Jane Lewis, Lucie Arnaz as Kim Carter, and Desi Arnaz, Jr., as Craig Carter*

First, the good news. This is the only Lucille Ball vehicle to have her real-life children, Lucie and Desi, Jr., as regulars in the cast. They play (no surprise) the teenaged children of their mom's latest Lucy character, bringing some generational humor hooks to the Lucy Carter living room. Both do just fine, though only Lucie stays for the entire run of the series. Otherwise, Gale Gordon and Mary Jane Croft are back as regulars (as they had been on *The Lucy Show*), with Vivian Vance turning up in occasional guest shots as well. This time the premise is set in Los Angeles with Lucy playing a widow working for the employment agency run by her brother-in-law, Harrison.

Now, the bad news. Though a hit when it originally aired on CBS, this version of the wacky redhead versus the world premise starts to look shopworn and tired. Giving familiar performers new names and occupations doesn't really help because they're all still doing the same old thing. In fact, it only underscores how irrelevant the characters have become. It doesn't matter what moniker they wear, because everyone is just going through some very, very familiar moves. Lucy and Gale Gordon. Lucy and Vivian Vance (or Mary Jane Croft). Lucy and virtually any piece of machinery in the prop room. They all look terribly cramped and limited. Oddly, even the opening credit sequence reflects this, with the real Lucille Ball nowhere to be seen—instead, a caricature of Lucy (using a 1970s equivalent to Claymation) comes onstage to open the curtain to the episode.

As for plots, very often the episodes seem more like variety show skits strung together. This is particularly true when Lucy and some famous guest star mug through a bit. Sometimes those sequences are quite funny, or appropriately weird, as when Richard Burton and Elizabeth Taylor appear in a story revolving around the million-dollar diamond gift Burton had given Taylor at the time. But no matter what the hook, if they all turned to the camera after their routine for a curtain call ("Ladies and gentleman, Liz and Dick! Let's hear it for them!"), it would have seemed acceptable. They would not have been breaking character because, sadly, there was often nothing there to break.

Probably the worst aspect of this series, however, is that by going out a ratings winner in the 1970s, it no doubt helped convince Lucille Ball that Lucy-doing-Lucy was the only way the public wanted to see her. As a result, for her 1980s *Life with Lucy* comeback, she didn't try anything else. In any case, if you want to see Lucy shine after the *I Love Lucy* days, your best bet is *The Lucy Show*.

**HERITAGE: CIVILIZATION AND THE JEWS** (**½) **60 min (9ep Color; 1984 PBS) Documentary** *with Abba Eban as host*

Noted Israeli diplomat Abba Eban hosts this well-researched but somewhat lifeless overview of 3,000 years of Jewish history. ■

**THE HERO** (***) **30 min (16ep Color; 1966–1967 ABC) Situation Comedy** *with Richard Mulligan as Sam Garret, Mariette Hartley as Ruth Garret, Bobby Horan as Paul Garret, and Victor French as Fred Gilman*

*The Hero,* a sadly overlooked series from the mid-1960s, pokes fun at TV itself, long before doing so became a popular pastime. The show-within-a-show concept has Richard Mulligan (the loud bumbling Burt Campbell of *Soap*) playing Sam Garret, the star of a TV western called *Jed Clayton—U.S. Marshal.* On screen, Garret plays a fearless western lawman, adept on the draw and an expert horseman. In "real" life, Garret is a complete klutz, much to the amusement of his friends and neighbors.

Aside from the always exuberant Mulligan, *The Hero* features early performances of Mariette Hartley and Victor French. Production is handled by Leonard Stern (*Get Smart* and *He and She*) and Jay Sandrich (*The Mary Tyler Moore Show* and *The Bob Newhart Show*). *The Hero* may be somewhat silly, but its wry humor makes it worth tracking down.

**HEY, JEANNIE** (*½) **30 min (32ep B&W; 1956–1957 CBS) Situation Comedy** *with Jeannie Carson as Jeannie MacLennan, Allen Jenkins as Al Murray, and Jane Dulo as Liz Murray*

Another vintage 1950s sitcom premise, with a perky young Scottish immigrant named Jeannie landing in New York City with no place to stay and no one to take care of her—and then finding both in New York cab driver Al Murray, who inexplicably offers to act as her sponsor while giving her a cab tour of the city. Suddenly, Jeannie's living with Al and his sister Liz, and working as a waitress in a donut shop. The rest of the series flows just as believably.

This was set up as a showcase for British comedienne Jeannie Carson, who was pegged at the time as a hot up-and-coming star. That never happened, but the two other members of the cast had their moments. Allen Jenkins later provided the voice for Officer Dibble on *Top Cat,* while Jane Dulo turned up in a host of comedy and drama roles over the next three decades, including Nurse Molly Turner on *McHale's Navy,* 99's mother on *Get Smart,* and Grandma Kanisky on *Gimme a Break.*

**HEY, LANDLORD** (**) **30 min (31ep Color; 1966–1967 NBC) Situation Comedy** *with Will Hutchins as Woody Banner, Sandy Baron as Chuck Hookstratten, Pamela Rodgers as Timothy Morgan, and Michael Constantine as Jack Ellenhorn*

Lee Rich, the producer of *The Waltons* and *Dallas,* puts in an early production job on *Hey, Landlord.* This minor mid-1960s show is about an Ohio rube who inherits a Manhattan apartment building and learns all about life in the big city while living in and managing the place. Woody Banner, the rube/landlord who wants to be a writer, rooms with Chuck Hookstratten, a city boy who wants to be a stand-up comic. Sally Field, in between *Gidget* and *The Flying Nun,* pops in on a few episodes as Woody's sister Bonnie.

**HEY MULLIGAN** **(see *The Mickey Rooney Show*)**

**THE HIGH CHAPARRAL** (**½) **60 min (98ep Color; 1967–1971 NBC) Western** *with Leif Erickson as John Cannon, Cameron Mitchell as Buck Cannon, Mark Slade* *as Billy Blue Cannon, Linda Cristal as Victoria Cannon, and Frank Silvera as Don Sebastian Montoya*

In Arizona in the 1870s, Big John Cannon runs the High Chaparral, the biggest ranch in those parts. When Big John's wife is killed by Injuns, he marries the daughter of his biggest competitor, the Mexican Don Sebastian Montoya. *The High Chaparral* follows the struggles among the two rival, but somewhat united, clans, the perennial struggle with the land and the ongoing struggle with the restless Injuns. If this sounds a little like *Bonanza* without all the family warmth, it's because this show is produced by David Dortort, the producer of *Bonanza.*

**HIGH MOUNTAIN RANGERS** (**) **60 min (13 ep & 2 hr pilot Color; 1988 CBS) Adventure** *with Robert Conrad as Jesse Hawkes, Christian Conrad as Matt Hawkes, Shane Conrad as Cody Hawkins, Tony Acierto as Frank Avila, P. A. Christian as Robin Kelly, Timothy McLachlan as Izzy Flowers, and Roy Conrad as Dr. Fenton*

Robert Conrad makes this a true family affair, with daughter Joan producing, sons Christian and Shane in the supporting cast, and himself as series creator—as well as writer and director of the series pilot. (Note: Roy Conrad is no relation.) The premise is a wonderful excuse to film in some of the most beautiful mountain areas of the United States, the Sierra Nevadas near Lake Tahoe. Conrad plays Jesse, the retired leader of the High Mountain Rangers, who lives with his son, Cody, while elder son Matt continues as the present-day leader of the Rangers. Inevitably, they end up in the rescue business, including such obvious candidates as turned-around campers, explorers, and visitors, along with people heading for the high country to escape something or someone. There are also plenty of references to protecting the ecology. Overall the plots of the series are pretty cut-and-dried, but for anyone who enjoys stomping through the snow, those outdoor settings look really good. However, if you prefer a photogenic urban backdrop, simply follow the Conrad clan to the 1989 follow-up spin-off series, *Jesse Hawkes*—set in San Francisco.

**HIGH PERFORMANCE** (*½) **60 min (4ep Color; 1983 ABC) Adventure** *with Mitchell Ryan as Brennan Flannery, Lisa Hartman as Kate Flannery, Rick Edwards as Shane Adams, Jack Scalia as Blue Stratton, and Jason Bernard as O. T. "Fletch" Fletcher*

This strictly formula high-tech action series is about three instructors at some swank security school who moonlight as real rescue and investigation operatives.

**HIGH RISK** (*) **60 min (5ep Color; 1988 CBS) Adventure Magazine** *with Wayne Rogers*

A glitzy modernized version of *You Asked for It, High Risk* presents short features on folks who accomplish daring feats. Wayne Rogers (formerly Trapper John on *M*A*S*H*) serves as the glib host of this series produced by Alan Landsburg (*That's Incredible*).

**HIGHCLIFFE MANOR** (*½) **30 min (6ep Color; 1979 NBC) Situation Comedy** *with Shelley Fabares as Helen Blacke, Eugenie Ross-Leming as Frances Kiskadden, Stephen McHattie as Rev. Mr. Ian Glenville, Audrey Landers as Wendy, Gerald Gordon as Dr. Felix Morger, Christian Marlowe as Bram Shelley, and Harold Sakata as Cheng*

A combination gothic horror and soap opera send-up, this is one of those setups that plays better as a one-shot skit than a series. In fact, the character lineup sounds like what you might get from a well-lubricated Second City improvisational theater performance—"quick, we're looking for audience suggestions to populate a spooky mansion located on some desolate island." Not surprisingly, one of the program's executive producers (and stars), Eugene Ross-Leming, was a Second City company performer.

In brief, this series follows the eccentric residents of the Blacke Foundation, an island scientific think-tank with dark and deadly secrets. There's Helen Blacke, the put-upon widow seemingly oblivious to everything around her; Frances, the scientist building herself a bionic man dubbed Bram Shelley—an allusion to writers Bram Stoker (Dracula) and Mary Shelley (Frankenstein); Rev. Mr. Glenville, a mysterious South African clergyman who paddled to the island by canoe; Dr. Felix Morger, seeking to seduce the vulnerable Helen; and so on. What is the real secret identity of Bram Shelley? Is Helen really a widow? And why are all those corpses piling up in the basement crypt? Maybe they'll release this series on home video and we can all find the answers. Or maybe we should just ask Count Floyd.

**HIGHWAY PATROL** (**) **30 min (156ep B&W; 1955–1959 Syndicated) Police Drama** *with Broderick Crawford as Chief Dan Matthews and Art Gilmore as the narrator*

This low-budget crime adventure became one of the biggest first-run syndicated hits of the 1950s and turned Broderick Crawford's Dan Matthews character into an American cultural icon. Matthews is a beefy, gravel-voiced law enforcement chief who works with local highway patrol forces on the wide-open roadways of the western United States, nailing smugglers, thieves, and murderers (exactly the types of characters he used to play in films in the 1930s and 1940s). The stories are typical grade-B formula fodder, with plenty of chase scenes, roadblocks, and shoot-outs, but you've got to see it at least once to watch Crawford at the patrol car radio barking his radio tag trademark phrase, "ten-four, ten-four."

**HIGHWAY TO HEAVEN** (**½) 60 min (115ep Color; 1984–1989 NBC) Drama *with Michael Landon as Jonathan Smith and Victor French as Mark Gordon*

Michael Landon, formerly of *Bonanza* (Little Joe) and *Little House* (Charles Ingalls), plays an angel on probation who is sent to Earth to earn his wings by helping people. This "probationary angel" angle was used in the mid-1960s on the Smothers Brothers' ill-fated original sitcom, where it was played for laughs. Here Landon plays the concept straight (with nice touches of levity), as he goes about his noble task of do-gooding.

The aspect of picking out people almost at random and bestowing blessings upon them is reminiscent of *The Millionaire,* though, of course, here the reward is not as materialistic as cold cash, but rather, peace of mind. Landon travels the land in the guise of a common laborer, using his angelic powers only when pressed, which brings to mind the roaming social work of David Janssen in *The Fugitive.*

Landon is aided in his travels by Victor French (another *Little House* alumnus, who played Isaiah Edwards), in the role of an ex-cop who was "saved" by the good deeds of Landon's angel.

Like the *Little House* series before it, *Highway to Heaven* is totally dominated by star–executive producer Landon. Both series come very close to being cloying and sappy, but usually avoid it, resulting in very clean entertainment that leaves you feeling good for a while.

**THE HIGHWAYMAN** (*½) 60 min (9ep & 2 hr pilot Color; 1988 NBC) Fantasy Adventure *with Sam Jones as the Highwayman, Jacko as Jetto, Jane Badler as Ms. Tania Winthrop, and Tim Russ as D. C. Montana*

Sam Jones (lead character in the 1980 theatrical remake of *Flash Gordon*) plays a troubleshooting federal marshal covering Broderick Crawford's old *Highway Patrol* beat, the wide-open stretches of the southwestern United States. Of course, this Highwayman drives something a bit more powerful: a high-tech, eighteen-wheel, supercharged truck. And he has a loud and powerful sidekick named Jetto—played by a muscular Australian wrestling type, Jacko, who screamed his way to prime-time attention at the time in commercials hawking "energized" flashlight batteries. Sort of a cross between the Australian theatrical *Mad Max* films and a stylized wrestling match, this series is done as tongue-in-cheek mayhem by Glen Larson's production company (home of *The Fall Guy* and *Knight Rider*), complete with futuristic plot hooks liable to lead almost anywhere. These include such concepts as subhuman clones, radioactively charged bodies, and even a twister trip back to 1945 (a la Dorothy and Toto). Jane Badler (previously the evil Diana on *V*) is also aboard as their tough dispatcher, while D. C. keeps all the electronic gear in order. This head-banging nonsense first appeared in a 1987 made-for-TV movie series pilot.

**HILL STREET BLUES** (****) 60 min (146ep Color; 1981–1987 NBC) Police Drama *with Daniel J. Travanti as Capt. Frank Furillo, Veronica Hamel as Joyce Davenport, Michael Conrad as Sgt. Phil Esterhaus, Michael Warren as Bobby Hill, Charles Haid as Andy Renko, Bruce Weitz as Det. Mick Belker, Rene Enriquez as Lt. Ray Calletano, Kiel Martin as Det. Johnny "J. D." LaRue, Taurean Blacque as Det. Neal Washington, James Sikking as Lt. Howard Hunter, Joe Spano as Sgt./Lt. Henry Goldblume, Betty Thomas as Lucy Bates, Barbara Babcock as Grace Gardner, Barbara Bosson as Fay Furillo, Ed Marinaro as Joe Coffey, Dennis Franz as Lt. Norman Buntz, and Robert Prosky as Sgt. Stan Jablonski*

Whatever it is that you look for in a TV show, chances are you will find it on *Hill Street Blues.* Action? Plenty of action here. You can be assured of about one act of senseless violence in every episode. There is also almost always a shoot-out or a hostage-taking to boot. Romance? *Hill Street Blues* contains some of the steamiest scenes in TV history, outside of soap operas. Drama? The interplay of the numerous characters features a wide assortment of human emotions in conflict. Humor? No matter how dark the situation, somebody on *Hill Street* is always cracking a joke, or the writers will toss in a wry comment that the characters miss and only the audience gets. On and on the list goes. Good writing, tight direction, great actors, topical plots, innovative production, a hit theme song. What else do you want?

From the overused setting of a police station in a big city, *Hill Street* manages to redefine the entire TV cop show format. The Hill Street station is in a decaying ghetto region of an unnamed northern city (several exterior shots in the opening credits were filmed in Chicago). There is always a lot of background activity, with a jumble of voices competing for viewers' attention. Use of a somewhat jumpy hand-held camera adds to the flavor of realism. Capt. Frank Furillo is the captain of the precinct, and the supervisor of all who work at the station. Below Furillo are Lt. Calletano (one of the highest-ranking Hispanics on the force, but something of a windbag) and Lt. Hunter (the militaristic leader of the local SWAT squad).

On the sergeant's level are Phil Esterhaus, the gentle giant who leads the daily morning roll call (always ending with the warning of "Hey, let's be careful out there!"), and Henry Goldblume, the token bleeding-heart liberal whose job it is to talk crazed maniacs out of whatever crime they had planned. The plain-clothes detectives are J. D. LaRue (a con man at heart), his proud, black and tight-lipped partner Neal Washington, and Mick Belker (a wild man who operates solo and who can't avoid his mother's nagging telephone calls). Among the original batch of uniformed officers are black and white partners Bobby Hill and Andy Renko (both shot in the opening episode) and male and female partners Lucy

Bates and Joe Coffey (who never really resolve their growing attraction for each other).

Capt. Furillo's private life keeps leaking into his professional one, as his ex-wife Fay is forever barging into his office to complain about something or other, and his secret romance with feisty and beautiful public defender Joyce Davenport threatens to burst into the open and pose conflict-of-interest problems for both. Sgt. Esterhaus' private life is also threatening to become public, as he must try to satisfy the increasingly torrid romantic demands of Grace Gardner, a policeman's widow who also makes unannounced visits to the police station, but for more sensual reasons.

It is *Hill Street*'s deft combination of various artistic styles that results in its strength. Like the prime-time soap operas, there are convoluted stories that stretch on and on. Plots intersect, carry over from episode to episode, and may be revived in the future. The personalities take on distinct attributes that can be relied on to carry a few episodes now and again. From the MTM studios' brand of 1970s sitcoms (such as *The Mary Tyler Moore Show*) comes the concern for examining the human side of the main characters. Another MTM style, the topical and whimsical drama (*The White Shadow, Lou Grant*), is then added, combined with the cop show structure, and the result is close to TV perfection. The influence of the MTM studios is to be expected, as *Hill Street* is, itself, a product of the MTM production house.

Considering the length of *Hill Street*'s run, it is amazing how well the quality of the writing holds up throughout. This is partly a result of the many characters the writers have to focus on, but the large cast helps only because the individual characters are so well drawn. Mick Belker goes from being an ankle-biting caricature to a warm and loving father. J. D. LaRue vacillates marvelously from lascivious lecher and money-grubbing welsher to a frightened alcoholic unsure of his professional or personal future. Capt. Furillo, the tower of strength, is shown as both a man of virtue in a field all too often full of venal corruption and a rigid formalist who sometimes can't deal with the realities of human life.

Another sign of the care put into the production of *Hill Street* is how the continuing story lines rarely stagnate, and how new, interesting characters keep arriving to replace departing ones. When Frank and Joyce's secret romance starts becoming old hat, the couple make their relationship public. After another season or so, it's becoming tiring to hear Joyce constantly dance around the issue of getting married, so the couple is married in a simple lunchtime ceremony. Viewers are slowly teased as to whether Lucy and Joe will become lovers, until it is made clear that they have drawn the line and will go no further. Henry Goldblume eventually has to face up to the fact that his temperament and concern for others may be a detriment to being a good policeman, so he considers quitting and becoming a writer.

In the later seasons (by which time many hit shows rest on their laurels), *Hill Street* is revived by new blood. The untimely cancer death of Michael Conrad forces the writers to replace his Phil Esterhaus character with that of Stan Jablonski. The portly Pole is an entirely different sort of man than Phil, much more from the "old school" of policemen. There will be no steamy passion sessions for Jablonski, but his loneliness results in a touching growing friendship with Belker. The chief addition in the later years is Lt. Buntz, an extraordinary character who combines the shiftiness of J. D. LaRue and the trigger-happy sentiments of Lt. Hunter with a genuine concern for others. Buntz comes across at first as a bozo, an uncouth lout in a loud tie, but he develops into the strongest member of the force. He may seem harsh and unrefined, but he knows that the high gloss of education and style often hides a lack of knowledge of reality. In one of the series' most memorable episodes, Buntz is held captive by a crazed gunman, who threatens to shoot him at any moment. Only through Buntz's razor sharp verbal maneuvering and bold bluffing does he survive until help arrives. When finally rescued, Buntz freely admits he was scared out of his mind. Still he stayed in control and overcame his ordeal. After that episode, Buntz can never be seen as a simplistic buffoon.

Like religious disciples, the production crew of *Hill Street Blues* spread over the TV landscape, bringing the feel and style of the series to other series and other formats. The series' primary creative force, Steven Bochco, transplanted the *Hill Street* concept almost verbatim to the world of lawyers in *L. A. Law.* He also helped create *Hooperman,* a more lighthearted look at police work (where Bochco's wife, Barbara Bosson, exchanged her *Hill Street* role as Furillo's nagging wife for that of police precinct captain). Another *Hill Street* producer, Anthony Yerkovitch, went on to create *Miami Vice,* a far more stylized police drama.

*Hill Street Blues* knew to quit while it was ahead. Seven seasons is plenty for any quality show. Viewers are spared having to watch the program slowly sink into the west. *Hill Street* leaves behind a valuable tradition of production excellence and a much emulated style of concern for nuances of character. Like any serialized program, *Hill Street* requires some period of indoctrination for viewers unfamiliar with the cast of characters. Beyond that, it requires an audience's attention. It is a well-made piece of work, and like all such creations, it can only be fully appreciated by focusing on it. Unlike so much of what TV throws at the viewer, *Hill Street* must be savored, not gulped.

**HIRAM HOLIDAY, THE ADVENTURES OF (*) 30 min (26ep B&W; 1956–1957 NBC) Situation Comedy** *with Wally Cox as Hiram Holiday and Ainslie Pryor as Joel Smith*

Meek and mild Hiram Holiday (played by the ever

meek and mild Wally Cox) is sent around the world by his employer, a newspaper, accompanied by Joel Smith, a reporter.

**THE HITCHHIKER** (*) **30 min (65ep at Fall 1989 Color; 1983– HBO & USA) Suspense Anthology** *with Nicholas Campbell and Page Fletcher as The Hitchhiker*

If *this* is the type of original programming that will dominate cable TV, we were better off with our old nineteen-inch black-and-white Motorolas with rabbit ears. *The Hitchhiker,* one of the early efforts at series programming on cable, is essentially a boring suspense anthology with bare female breasts and somewhat graphic violence occasionally tossed in to make it seem "adult" and different from regular over-the-air TV. The program concentrates on spooky, supernatural-type stories. The extremely thin thread of continuity is the superfluous regular presence of the unnamed, broody hitchhiker, who pops up at the start or end of the episode, looks meaningful, and provides heavy-handed comments to the viewers. He does not deserve to be the title character of the show. To be fair, *The Hitchhiker* does have some talented guest actors and some fairly interesting plots, but on the whole, it is a waste. ■

**THE HITCHHIKER'S GUIDE TO THE GALAXY** (**½) **30 min (6ep Color; 1981 UK BBC) Science Fiction Satire** *with Peter Jones as the Voice of the Book, Simon Jones as Arthur Dent, David Dixon as Ford Prefect, David Lerner as Marvin the Paranoid Android, Stephen Moore as the Voice of Marvin, Mark Wing-Davey as Zaphod Beeblebrox, and Saundra Dickinson as Trillian*

Writer Douglas Adams has gotten extraordinary mileage out of this uniquely warped view of life, the universe, and everything that comes with it. Books. Records. A computer game. Cassette books. And a television series.

But it all started on British radio in March 1978. That's when the BBC presented the first of (eventually) twelve half-hour episodes that followed the adventures of the only survivors of Earth's untimely demise.

Our planet, you see, has to be demolished to make way for an interstellar hyperspace bypass. It is only through the timely intervention of an alien visitor (going by the name Ford Prefect) that Earthman Arthur Dent finds himself escaping the carnage. Instead of dying, Arthur is given the unique opportunity to hitchhike his way through time and space and to discover what an absolutely perplexing mess the universe really is.

Such adventures are perfectly suited to radio, where planets, spaceships, and alien worlds could be created with just a few words of narration mixed with selected sound effects. They also come off reasonably well in print (in a series of four novelizations, beginning in 1979).

But television demands visual execution, with specific traits spelled out rather than left to each person's imagination. Sometimes the translation is easy. Arthur Dent is supposed to be dressed only in his bathrobe and slippers throughout the entire story, so that's just the costume Simon Jones wears. On the other hand, Zaphod Beeblebrox is most inconveniently described on radio as having two heads, so Mark Wing-Davey has to carry around the extra appendage on camera.

Still, some radio concepts do surprisingly well on video. For instance, the name *The Hitchhiker's Guide to the Galaxy* actually refers to a book . . . a talking book, that is—a notion tailor-made for radio where the voice of the book could take the form of a voice-over narrator. But it also works for television because the book contains a video screen. So while the book speaks, its video portion fills the home screen with appropriate images.

"The Restaurant at the End of the Universe" segment also works well, as Arthur and his companions explore Milliway's, an eating establishment whose floor show consists of the destruction of the entire known universe. At the restaurant, Peter Davison (from *All Creatures Great and Small, Doctor Who*, and, in off-screen life, the husband of Saundra Dickinson, who plays Trillian), has a cameo as the "Dish of the Day"—a specially bred animal that *wants* to be consumed. (He's not, at least not on camera.)

The weakest aspect of the *Hitchhiker* television series is its special effects such as space flight, which occasionally look pretty cheesy. So does the awkward nuts-and-bolts figure of Marvin, the manic-depressive paranoid android (though in his case, a decrepit cartoonish look is most appropriate). Still, when Arthur Dent and Ford Prefect discover why the Earth was made, who was really running it, and the answer to the ultimate question of life, the universe, and everything . . . their facial expressions are priceless.

In packaging the six-part BBC television version of *The Hitchhiker's Guide to the Galaxy*, one U. S. syndicator stretched the material into seven half-hour segments. In that, there's quite a bit of recap in the last episode.

**HIZZONER** (*) **30 min (7ep Color; 1979 NBC) Situation Comedy** *with David Huddleston as Mayor Michael Cooper, Will Seltzer as James Cooper, Kathy Cronkite as Annie Cooper, Don Galloway as Timmons, and Diana Muldaur as Ginny Linden*

*Hizzoner*'s mild claim to fame is that it is the only TV series about a small-town mayor who breaks into song just about every week. David Huddleston, a portly chap who has a lengthy acting resume with no distinguishing entries, is both star and producer here, as he plays a widowed mayor with two grown kids. One is a feminist lawyer; one is an unreconstructed hippie. Kathy Cronkite, the feminist daughter, is the real-life daughter of CBS newsman Walter Cronkite.

## THE HOGAN FAMILY (see *Valerie*)

**HOGAN'S HEROES (***) 30 min (168ep: 1 B&W & 167 Color; 1965–1971 CBS) Situation Comedy** *with Bob Crane as Col. Robert Hogan, Werner Klemperer as Col. Wilhelm Klink, John Banner as Sgt. Hans Schultz, Richard Dawson as Cpl. Peter Newkirk, Robert Clary as Cpl. Louis LeBeau, Ivan Dixon as Cpl. James Kinchloe, Larry Hovis as Sgt. Andrew Carter, and Kenneth Washington as Sgt. Richard Baker*

In the beginning there was *Stalag 17,* an Oscar-winning movie from 1953 that set the pattern for the plethora of World War II prisoner-of-war sagas that followed. *Stalag 17* combined comedy and drama, with an emphasis on drama, as it presented a ethnic grab bag of Allied soldiers scheming and plotting to outwit their German guards, in order to do what they could to help defeat the Nazis.

*Hogan's Heroes* takes the *Stalag 17* concept several steps into the zone of farce. There is the same POW camp in some bleak region of the Nazi empire, although this camp is Stalag 13, not 17. There is the same ethnic mixture of wisecracking Allied soldiers. There is the same constant effort to outwit the Hun. The difference is that, while Stalag 17 might be considered a reasonable model of an actual German POW camp, Stalag 13 is a wild exaggeration, stretched beyond the limit of believability for purposes of humor. Obviously no real German POW camp was ever like Stalag 13, but, then, nobody ever said *Hogan's Heroes* was supposed to be a documentary. It's a comedy.

In *Hogan's Heroes,* the Allied prisoners actually run the camp, unbeknownst to the dim-witted Germans in nominal command. Col. Robert Hogan and his men have turned the camp into a virtual Allied underground command center in the heart of Germany. So, unlike most POW epics, in *Hogan's Heroes* the central aim of the prisoners is *not* to escape, but rather to stay put, keep the Germans in the dark, and continue to aid the Allied cause from the inside.

The primary appeal of *Hogan's Heroes* is the wonderful collection of character actors who populate the camp. Col. Hogan is full of Yankee ingenuity and charm. He is quick-witted enough to outfox the Nazis, but still Main Street enough to relish poking fun at the German's Old World pomposity and formality. He is a perfect example of the American wisecracking handsome leading man. Hogan can both beat the Germans at their own game and still win the hearts of all the eligible frauleins in the neighborhood.

Backing up Hogan is the stereotypical Frenchman, LeBeau, who is a wiz at cooking and tailoring, and the stereotypical cockney Englishman, Newkirk, whose brash salt-of-the-earth attitude comes in handy when bravado is needed. Technical support comes from two other familiar U.S. caricatures, the nerdy farmboy who can fix anything that moves (Sgt. Carter) and the black electronics expert (Cpl. Kinchloe). This black caricature is actually fairly new for the era of *Hogan's Heroes,* but is also seen in *Mission: Impossible*'s Barney Collier, who arrived one year after Cpl. Kinchloe. This black character type allowed TV to respond to the growing demand for more blacks in nonservile roles, but both Kinchloe and Collier studiously avoided any romantic involvement with white women, to forestall any potential controversy about mixed-race love affairs.

The German side in Stalag 13 is represented by two figures designed especially to avoid making any *real* Nazis look good. Col. Klink is an officious, obsequious milquetoast. Klink is no Nazi, but he is more than willing to butter them up if it aids his own career. This, of course, is exactly the type of person who allowed the Nazi regime to run a country as sophisticated as Germany for more than a decade, but viewers cannot really hate Klink, because, deep down, Klink knows that the Nazis are evil and he is merely trying to hide under some rock until they go away.

Sgt. Schultz is overweight and more interested in having a good time than in the hustle and bustle of war and politics. He is never a threat to anyone, although he sees himself as a brave soldier. His desire to always look the other way and avoid trouble (and possible shipment to the dreaded Russian front) is of immeasurable help to Hogan and his men.

The real Nazis are represented by Gen. Burkhalter (Leon Askin) and Maj. Hockstedder (Howard Caine). These men are presented as pure evil. While they are always a threat, they can usually be defeated by Hogan and company, because they are both too blinded by their Nazi zealotry to outthink the Allied POWs, and they get no real support from the non-Nazi Germans (like Klink and Schultz), who do not have their hearts in the war.

In its early days, *Hogan's Heroes* tries to keep a little bit of the *Stalag 17* combination of comedy and drama. The plots of Hogan and his men are exciting and, although farfetched, realistic enough to maintain a level of believability. As the series wears on, the comedy element overcomes the small drama strain and the program recedes into virtual slapstick. *Hogan's Heroes* goes about two seasons too long and the silly scripts that turn up in the last few seasons indicate that the writers have run out of ideas for exploiting the POW camp setting.

The first episode of *Hogan's Heroes* (the original pilot) is in black and white, while the remainder of the series is in color.

**HOLIDAY LODGE (**) 30 min (13ep B&W; 1961 CBS) Situation Comedy** *with Johnny Wayne as Johnny Miller, Frank Shuster as Frank Boone, and Maureen Arthur as Dorothy Jackson*

Wayne and Shuster, a pair of Canadian comics who made numerous appearances on the *Ed Sullivan Show* in the 1960s, star in this lightweight series set in a resort hotel in New York's Catskills. The duo are the social directors of the hotel, named Holiday Lodge.

**HOLLYWOOD (A CELEBRATION OF THE AMERICAN SILENT FILM) (***) 60 min (13ep Color; 1979 UK Thames) Documentary** *with James Mason as Narrator*

A loving appreciation of silent film, Hollywood style. Each episode takes the time to place the material in historical context, as well as to examine in detail the contributions of the directors, on-screen talent, stunt performers, and special effects artists. Most important, the films themselves are shown in the best available condition, at the proper speed, and with appropriate accompanying music. The result forever destroys the cliché of "silents" as those silly two-reelers with people walking in unnatural jerky motion. Naturally, this fond, well-researched stroll through essential American popular culture comes from Britain, and usually turns up Stateside on PBS stations.

**HOLLYWOOD AND THE STARS (**) 30 min (31ep B&W; 1963–1964 NBC) Documentary** *with Joseph Cotten as host*

David Wolper, one of the premier documentary producers of TV (*Biography, The Making of the President 1960*), who later turned to miniseries (*Roots, The Thorn Birds*), produces this informative look at American movies and their stars.

**HOLLYWOOD BEAT (*) 60 min (9ep & 90 min pilot Color; 1985 ABC) Crime Drama** *with Jack Scalia as Nick McCarren, John Matuszak as George Grinsky, Jay Acovone as Jack Rado, and Edward Winter as Capt. Wes Biddle*

Nick McCarren and Jack Rado are two more scruffy undercover cops who help the "little people" in spite of the big bad meanies who run and ruin everything in this world. The duo have the glittery job of patrolling the seamy underside of Hollywood, with help from George Grinsky, a former NFL linebacker who is openly gay (played by John Matuszak, a real former NFL star).

**THE HOLLYWOOD PALACE (**½) 60 min (B&W & Color; 1964–1970 ABC) Variety**

ABC's 1960s answer to *The Ed Sullivan Show, The Hollywood Palace* showcases a wide-ranging collection of talent, from old-style vaudeville (Ed Wynn), through mid-century pop (Bing Crosby, Judy Garland), to new-fangled rock'n'roll (The Rolling Stones). With no regular host, guest hosts handle the continuity. Nick Vanoff serves as executive producer. ■

**HOLLYWOOD WIVES (*) (6hr miniseries Color; 1985 ABC) Drama** *with Candice Bergen as Elaine Conti, Joanna Cassidy as Marilee Gray, Mary Crosby as Karen Lancaster, Angie Dickinson as Sadie LaSalle, Anthony Hopkins as Neil Gray, Roddy McDowall as Jason Swankle, and Suzanne Somers as Gina Germaine*

A vapid tour of Rodeo Drive, *Hollywood Wives* features numerous famous actresses playing rich, spoiled women. This garden of glitz (adapted from Jackie Collins' novel) is, appropriately, produced by Aaron Spelling and Douglas Cramer, of *The Love Boat* fame.

**HOLMES AND YOYO (**) 30 min (16ep Color; 1976 ABC) Situation Comedy** *with Richard B. Shull as Det. Alexander Holmes, John Schuck as Gregory "Yoyo" Yoyonovich, Bruce Kirby as Capt. Harry Sedford, and Andrea Howard as Maxine Moon*

The "android as cop" concept flopped as drama in *Future Cop,* but it does a bit better in *Holmes and Yoyo.* L.A. police officer Holmes, a thick, old-fashioned cop, is teamed up with Yoyo, an android with a photographic memory that can eat anything and process film to boot. Yoyo is just a test model, so he keeps malfunctioning at comically inappropriate times. Officer Maxine Moon, like most of the characters, doesn't know Yoyo is not one of us, so her romantic moves on Yoyo are doomed to failure.

*Holmes and Yoyo* is pretty silly, but it's fun. John Schuck, a good second banana from *McMillan and Wife,* is appropriately deadpan as the robot. Leonard Stern, the executive producer of *Holmes and Yoyo,* dabbled in robotics in his earlier hit, *Get Smart,* with the minor character of Hymie the Robot.

**HOLOCAUST (***½) (9½hr miniseries Color; 1978 NBC) Drama** *with Fritz Weaver as Josef Weiss, Michael Moriarty as Erik Dorf, Meryl Streep as Inga Helms/Weiss, James Woods as Karl Weiss, Rosemary Harris as Berta Weiss, Joseph Bottoms as Rudi Weiss, Deborah Norton as Marta Dorf, Robert Stephens as Kurt Dorf, Sam Wanamaker as Moses Weiss, and David Warner as Reinhard Heydrich*

At one count a few years ago, it was estimated that there is more in print about the holocaust than any other subject in human history. You would need a lifetime just to read and absorb all the extant written material, much less interpret it.

Out of practical necessity, the only way to focus on the event is to move past the mountains of data to some particulars—approaching such sweeping questions as *how* and *why* did it happen through the more accessible drama-oriented hook of simply *what* happened.

*Holocaust* does an excellent job of putting faces to the potentially numbing facts, mixing wartime romance, life-and-death street battles, and bureaucratic schemes against the everybody-watching-at-home-knows-it's-coming backdrop of "the final solution."

The series focuses on two families, one led by Dr. Josef Weiss (Fritz Weaver), the other by Erik Dorf (Michael Moriarty). At the beginning of the story (1935), both men are pressed for their opinions on the political climate in Germany. Both protest, claiming little interest in such matters. Within a few years, of course, both are part of that political situation, whether they like it or not. And we follow them through to the bitter end—of the war and of their lives.

That's a lot of territory to cover, so of necessity the story jumps around a bit, compressing events and conveniently placing the main characters at key points of the Nazi campaign against the Jews. But the particulars of the plot are not all that important; they're just the framework for carefully crafted individual scenes, images, and characters that carry the dramatic thrust of the series.

Moriarty's Dorf is probably the best, presented as the definitive "professional" Nazi, no doubt to answer the question: What kind of man would do all this?

Well, a good boy. A baker's son. Dorf was in the top ten of his law class. He likes poetry and music. He's a devoted father.

But truth be told, Dorf joins the rising Nazi party only because his status-climbing wife practically forces him to do so. He doesn't even like guns. And he doesn't have any deeply held moral beliefs. He's the nightmare caricature of a soulless lawyer: a master manipulator of words that hide what's really being said.

Moriarty does a superb job of transforming Dorf into an increasingly cold and creepy paper pusher who remains insecure and constantly on edge despite his promotions and status in the party. He buries his doubts in bureaucratic procedures and rationalizations, eventually becoming one of the architects of the many plans to eradicate the Jews. His rise and fall are epitomized in two powerful scenes.

In the first, he must personally execute about a dozen Jews, shooting them at the side of the road. He hesitates, aware that he's about to cross the line from words to deeds. And then Dorf discovers a horrible fact—after the first murder, the rest come easy.

Much later, as Allied forces sweep across Europe, Dorf faces another moment of truth. Arrested and confronted by an American officer with pictures of murdered Jews and sworn testimony of his involvement, Dorf is knocked from his arrogant rationalizations to confront a terrifying future—he will be held accountable at a war crimes trial. At first, he falls back on the line "I was only following orders," but even he chokes on his own words as he attempts to explain away the execution of innocent children.

On the other side, the entire Weiss family feels the effects of the Nazi policies against the Jews, so their fates in *Holocaust* serve as a convenient microcosm of the millions caught in the struggle.

The spector of death hangs over them all. Even worse is a nagging doubt that somehow whatever they're doing is too little, too late. They should have seen this coming and resisted. Or run away sooner. In short, they wonder how *they* could have *let* this happen.

It's especially painful to Josef and his wife, Berta. At the beginning of the story, she blithely plays a classical piano piece over a montage of clips showing the rise of Hitler's power through the next three years. Then, suddenly, the whole family is confronted with the reality of a new Germany. When Josef and Berta at last sit down to discuss the situation, their faces are already worn with confusion, fear, and regret.

Yet there are also images of resistance and attempts to overcome the apparently hopeless situation. At the Jewish ghetto in Warsaw, for instance, Dr. Weiss attempts to save as many lives as he can in what soon becomes an intolerable situation. Eventually when the ghetto explodes into armed rebellion, Josef's brother Moses is one of those leading the attack. Josef's son Rudi does the same behind enemy lines as part of a guerrilla band.

Other forms of resistance don't involve guns, but require just as much courage. When Josef's other son, Karl, is sent away to prison, his wife Inga (from a respectable Christian German family) nonetheless stands by her husband and her new in-laws. She insists that her own family take in Josef's wife and daughter. Later, Inga bribes a prison officer with sex just to get letters to her husband.

Karl, meanwhile, carries on resistance of a different sort. He and other artists secretly sketch the conditions around them, determined to document the atrocities they fear will otherwise be hidden from history.

That, ultimately, is the overpowering image of *Holocaust,* as the characters force themselves to watch the unwatchable and to think the unthinkable, determined never to forget.

At the end those who survive (and not many do) wear a toughened look as they wander through streets suddenly awash with sunlight. They're alive and apparently safe. There's even talk of heading to a new Jewish homeland. But their safety is guarded in their hearts with memories and the vow, "never again."

*Holocaust* is tough, but well worth watching. With exceptional performances throughout, it successfully turns a litany of statistics into an engrossing drama. It is probably best seen now on video tape, with the pacing intact and uninterrupted by commercials. ■

**HOME TO ROOST (**) 30 min (7ep Color; 1989 UK YTV) Situation Comedy** *with John Thaw, Reece Dinsdale, and Elizabeth Bennett as Enid*

A long-divorced, set-in-his-ways father is suddenly stuck with the care and feeding of his grown-up son who's come home to roost. This is a well-cast formula package with all the prerequisite generational conflicts and arguments in place. Stateside, this sitcom set-up was turned into *You Again,* starring Jack Klugman. In an unusual instance of trans-Atlantic character consistency, Elizabeth Bennett (Enid the housekeeper) plays exactly the same role in both the British and U.S. versions.

**HOMETOWN** (**) 60 min (9ep Color; 1985 CBS) **Drama** *with Franc Luz as Ben Abbott, Jane Kaczmarek as Mary Newell Abbott, John Bedford-Lloyd as Peter Kincaid, Margaret Whitton as Barbara Donnelly, Daniel Stern as Joey Nathan, and Andrew Rubin as Christopher Springer*

If *The Big Chill* launched the age of the Yuppie in the movies, then *Hometown* did the same for TV. Bearing a striking resemblance to that earlier hit film, *Hometown* is about a gang of college friends from the 1960s who reunite in the 1980s (originally for the marriage of long-time couple Ben and Mary) and endlessly relive the good old days. A lot of kvetching about current problems goes on as well. *Hometown* trods familiar ground, and presents few, if any, new insights. Daniel Stern, who played an early 1960s kid in the movie *Diner,* is good as the nonmaterialistic Joey, a restaurant cook. He later served as the off-screen narrator of *The Wonder Years.*

**HOMICIDE** (**) 60 min (36ep Color; 1965–1975 Australia Crawford Productions) Crime Drama *with Charles Tingwell as Inspector Lawson, George Mallaby as Det. Peter Barnes, and Don Barker as Det. Harry White*

Straightforward police detective series set in Australia and following members of the Victoria Homicide Squad. Though the program ran for nearly a decade, only a few dozen episodes are currently in U.S. syndication. Good for spotting faces later in such Australian exports as *Prisoner: Cell Block H* and *All the Rivers Run.*

**HONDO** (**) 60 min (15ep Color; 1967 ABC) Western *with Ralph Taeger as Hondo Lane, Kathie Browne as Angie Dow, Buddy Foster as Johnny Dow, and Noah Beery, Jr. as Buffalo Baker*

Hondo Lane is a 1960s hippie dropout, but he is set in the post–Civil War West. Hondo had fought for the Confederates, lived with the Indians, and been sickened by all the unnecessary bloodshed he saw along the way. Now Hondo is a loner, traveling the Arizona Territory with his dog Sam, and his sometimes scout Buffalo Baker, working a bit for the U. S. Cavalry. Hondo is always rubbing the military types the wrong way and protesting innocent widows and orphans.

The origins of *Hondo* lie in a Louis L'Amour book and a good 1953 film with John Wayne as Hondo.

**HONEY WEST** (**½) (30ep B&W; 1965–1966 ABC) **Detective Drama** *with Anne Francis as Honey West, John Ericson as Sam Bolt, and Irene Hervey as Aunt Meg*

Long before Laura Holt found clients so skeptical of a female private detective that she needed to create a male front (*Remington Steele*), Honey West won them over the old-fashioned way—she postured, teased, seduced, and then went in for the kill. Anne Francis is perfect in the part, dispatching the bad guys with her feminine wiles—as well as with sharp karate and judo moves, perfect marksmanship, and latest electronic gadgets, and even her pet ocelot, Bruce. She's aided by associate Sam Bolt, who is obviously smitten with his boss but can't seem to get any private time between cases.

Both characters were first introduced on an episode of *Burke's Law* ("Who Killed the Jackpot?"), though it's too bad the producers decided to go with the half-hour adventure format for the *Honey West* series—in a full hour, they might have been able to develop an Amos Burke–style of sophisticated mysteries with more character interaction. Or at least gotten a bigger budget, especially for some of the technical gear (such as the television spy camera equipment), which really looks like it came from the cardboard prop department. Luckily, Honey's wardrobe is just fine, from her black jumpsuit for field work to furs and other stylish attire for activities in the trenches.

**THE HONEYMOONERS** (****) 30 & 60 min (118ep: one-hundred seven 30 min B&W & eleven 60 min Color & four 60 min Color sequels; 1952–1957 & 1966–1967 CBS) **Situation Comedy** *with Jackie Gleason as Ralph Kramden, Art Carney as Ed Norton, Audrey Meadows and Sheila MacRae as Alice Kramden, and Joyce Randolph and Jane Kean as Trixie Norton*

Simple pleasures are often the best, and the simple joys of *The Honeymooners* represent American TV at its finest. By deliberately setting a modest goal and sticking to basics, *The Honeymooners* overcomes its minimalist surroundings to stand as the closest thing to pure comedy we are ever likely to see on the tube. Styles and mores may fluctuate and waver, but as long as men and women live together, as long as people struggle to earn a living, *The Honeymooners* will be rerun somewhere and somebody will be laughing along.

Ralph Kramden and his wife Alice are no longer exactly honeymooners, having been married for some time (even in the earliest episodes). They have lost all of the innocent glow that newly married couples carry around with them. Instead the Kramdens appear to be locked into a no-win, never-ending treadmill of hardship. He is a chubby bus driver in New York. She is a housewife, nothing more, nothing less. They live in a spartan apartment on Chauncey Street in Brooklyn. Their best friends are their upstairs neighbors, the Nortons. Ed Norton is a sewer worker for the Department of Sanitation and his wife Trixie is a housewife. Both couples live from paycheck to paycheck and rarely have anything left over for luxuries. Ralph keeps hoping (dreaming?) that he will come up with some plan, some scheme, that will catch fire, make them rich, and propel them out of their grimy neighborhood and into the gold-plated life of Easy Street, a life that seems tantalizingly close but always out of reach.

He never does strike it rich, of course. Through the years of *The Honeymooners,* the Kramdens and the Nortons just plod on, making the best of what they have. This ever-present theme of blue-collar reality gives *The Honeymooners* its majesty. By focusing on the most common of Americans, the program glorifies the most common themes that Americans share, and therefore the program appeals to almost everyone.

The abject simplicity of *The Honeymooners* setting is breathtaking, especially to modern eyes. While many episodes of *The Honeymooners* venture out of the Kramden apartment, most of the main action occurs inside those four walls. With regular props that are no more complex than two doors, a table, some chairs, a window, a stove, a sink, a chest of drawers, and an ice box, the four main characters act out their lives.

The stories are simple. Ralph is having trouble at the bus company. Alice's mother is coming to stay for a while. Ralph and Ed want to go bowling, or to their cherished men's club (the Raccoon Lodge). Alice and Trixie try to decide how to inject a little more romance into their marriages. Ralph and Ed try to work out the details of Ralph's latest get-rich-quick scheme. Ralph is to be audited by the IRS. Nothing elaborate. No trendy issues. Just the mundane daily trivia of twentieth-century American life.

Just focusing on the basics of life, in the wrong hands, could be deadly dull. In the hands of Jackie Gleason, however, all this simplicity is given a spark that makes it come alive. Gleason's Ralph Kramden is electric. Ralph is, on the one hand, a loud, pushy, self-centered lout. He erupts into tirades and berates his friends and family. He frequently threatens to send Alice to the moon, courtesy of a well-placed Kramden right hook. Over and over again, Ralph gets himself (and others) in trouble simply as a result of his pigheadedness. He is very easy to dislike.

Having Ralph be so grating is great. Too many central characters on TV (especially in the 1950s) overflowed with the milk of human kindness. Finding an annoying ornery braggart like Ralph on TV is a deliverance from the waves of blandness that otherwise issue forth from the tube.

He is not, however, just a figure of scorn. Ralph Kramden is an American everyman. He may be poor, he may be just a working slob, but, by God, he is king of his castle (better check with Alice about that), master of his little corner of the world. He is also highly vulnerable, likely to feel deep remorse when he sees (finally!) the error of his ways. He *can* be saved. By possessing appealing touches of warmth in addition to a gruff exterior, Ralph emerges as a more intriguing personality. Ralph will freely admit, in his moments of lucidity, that he needs Alice badly, to keep him on an even keel. He may boast about ruling the roost, but he knows he can't make it alone. He knows that, as he often tells his wife during the ending hug, "Baby, you're the greatest!"

The character of Alice is also intriguing for her era. She is as strong-willed a wife as you will find in 1950s sitcoms. She sees right through all of Ralph's blustering bravado, and knows how to cut him down to size when she wants to. She stands up to Ralph and demands that he consider reality when he launches himself on one of his flights of fancy. She has few illusions about how the rest of their lives will go, and she is more interested in some small tenderness than in some grand cockamamie scheme to win millions. Alice's strength and pragmatism set her apart from virtually every other sitcom wife of the decade.

Ed Norton is a whimsical creation, mixing broad humor and gentle pathos. As portrayed by Art Carney, Ed is a fount of hilarious physical flourishes and quirks that ripen over the series' run. Ed's fidgety physical flourishes and his loosey-goosey manner blend perfectly with Ralph's bulldozer wrath and pop-eyed double-takes. Norton may be played mostly for laughs, but his guileless honesty and trusting spirit serve as potent counterpoints to Ralph's chicanery. Ralph and Ed, together, make the greatest buddy pair on TV. They are so compatible in social standing and so divergent in personality that one can always fill in where the other leaves off.

As for Trixie (Ed's wife), there is not much to say. She does little more than serve as a sounding board for Alice and constitute the fourth hand in a game of cards. Trixie has none of the gumption of Alice and none of the ability to see beyond her husband's latest whim. Trixie stands by her man, even if he is standing in a sewer.

Considering the seminal nature of *The Honeymooners* to American TV humor, it's amazing to realize how limited, relatively, its exposure has been. Until recently, *The Honeymooners* has largely only been seen in the form of endless reruns of one season's worth of thirty-nine filmed episodes. This is due to the show's convoluted history.

*The Honeymooners* began in 1951 as a skit on the *Cavalcade of Stars,* a variety show hosted by Jackie Gleason on the old DuMont network. It was only one skit among many that Gleason featured on a regular basis. Gleason was Kramden, Pert Kelton played Alice, Carney soon arrived as Norton, and Joyce Randolph later became Trixie. After Gleason and his company attracted a loyal following, CBS lured them away from low-budget DuMont in the fall of 1952. With Audrey Meadows replacing Pert Kelton in the move to CBS, *The Honeymooners* skit became a regular feature of *The Jackie Gleason Show* on Saturday nights through the early 1950s.

These early CBS *The Honeymooners* were performed live, preserved only on low-quality kinescopes, and ran for varying lengths. Some skits were just a few minutes; some ran for a good chunk of the Gleason hour. There were no reruns. Once the skits aired, they were never seen again.

By the mid-1950s, Gleason wanted a break from the demands of a weekly hour program, so the *Jackie Gleason Show* was shut down. Gleason decided to focus just on *The Honeymooners* skits, so he filmed a series of thirty-nine half-hour episodes in front of a live audience and those thirty-nine episodes ran during the 1955–1956 season as Gleason's sole TV showcase. The filmed series did not fare as well as Gleason's old variety showcase, and, with Gleason fearing that his writers were running out of ideas for *The Honeymooners,* the thirty-minute filmed format was scrapped after just that one year. In the fall of 1956, Gleason resumed his live one-hour *Jackie Gleason Show* series that again contained various-length *Honeymooner* skits, along with his other familiar characters. After one more season of the weekly grind, Gleason temporarily left TV in the spring of 1957, marking the virtual end of production of *The Honeymooners* for almost a decade.

In 1966, Gleason (who had returned to weekly TV four years earlier) briefly reactivated *The Honeymooners* as an occasional segment of his weekly *Jackie Gleason Show* series. Art Carney is back as Ed Norton, but now Sheila MacRae plays Alice and Jane Kean plays Trixie. Almost all of these skits are hour-long revamped versions of the "Honeymooners Win a Trip to Europe" theme that had already been staged (with only lukewarm response) in the 1956–1957 season. For fans of the old black and white *Honeymooners,* these color episodes with music are something of a letdown. They are more like Broadway revues (with original music and dancing) than situation comedy. The acting is not as deft (Sheila MacRae does not compare with Audrey Meadows' cool determination as Alice) and the songs are fairly lame. These episodes are best left ignored. One year after Gleason left weekly TV forever in 1970, eleven of these hour-long segments from the late 1960s were packaged as *The Honeymooners,* airing one winter on CBS and then going into syndication.

The final installments of *The Honeymooners* are a set of four one-hour specials that aired between 1976 and 1978. Audrey Meadows returns to the role of Alice, while Jane Kean remains as Trixie. The first of the four specials (*The Honeymooners Second Honeymoon*) is perhaps the best, with the Kramdens and the Nortons reuniting to celebrate the Kramdens' twenty-fifth wedding anniversary. In the final installment (*Jackie Gleason's Honeymooners Christmas*), we leave the gang in a familiar situation, with Ralph gambling both his and Ed's life savings on lottery tickets that he hopes will finally bring him the untold riches he has lusted after for so long. Needless to say, the riches elude Ralph and he must make do with his life as it is.

Because only the thirty-nine *Honeymooner* episodes from 1955–1956 were filmed, it is those thirty-nine that have cemented the *Honeymooner* legend over the years, being rerun over and over again. It was not until 1985 that the best of the so-called lost episodes (those that aired live on CBS from 1952 to 1955 and in the 1956–1957 season) reappeared, greatly expanding the *Honeymooner* archives. Gleason himself had been holding on to these old kinescopes all that time, and chose to reissue them before his death from cancer in 1987. The lost episodes originally resurfaced on the Showtime cable channel in 1985–1986, in their original irregular length. After that run, the lost episodes were trimmed a bit and repackaged in the form of sixty-eight thirty-minute shows, which have now joined the classic thirty-nine segments to form a healthy 107-episode body of material running in syndication. The lost episodes take some of the mystical allure away from *The Honeymooners,* since there is now more than just that one shining season of work available. Nonetheless, by almost tripling the amount of *Honeymooners* material in view, the lost episodes flesh out the previously sketchy genius of the concept. *The Honeymooners* now can be appreciated in more generous portions, and it is a couch potato's dream come true to feast on such a grand repast. With the addition of the lost *Honeymooner* episodes to the syndication market, a key historical gap in American TV history has been filled. ■

**HONG KONG (**½) 60 min (26ep B&W; 1960–1961 ABC) Adventure** *with Rod Taylor as Glenn Evans, Lloyd Bochner as Neil Campbell, and Jack Kruschen as Tully*

One of the few decent action/adventure shows of the early 1960s that did not come out of the Warner Bros. sausage factory, *Hong Kong* leaves out the silly patter and the excessive gimmicks that ultimately sank *Surfside Six, Hawaiian Eye,* et al., while leaving in the exotic locales (here, Britain's colony on mainland China) and the intrigue. Rugged Australian actor Rod Taylor (star of Hitchcock's *The Birds*) plays an American journalist who is always wrapped in some Oriental excitement. Lost amidst the many similar shows at the time, *Hong Kong* now stands out a bit, thanks to its restraint.

**HOOPERMAN (**½) 30 min (42ep Color; 1987–1989 ABC) Police Drama** *with John Ritter as Det. Harry Hooperman, Barbara Bosson as Capt. Celeste Stern, Clarence Felder as Officer Boris "Bobo" Pritzger, Felton Perry as Insp. Clarence McNeil, Debrah Farentino as Susan Smith, and Alix Elias as Betty Bushkin*

Created by the *L. A. Law* team of Steven Bochco and Terry Louise Fisher, *Hooperman* is a John Ritter showcase and he rises to the occasion, carrying the series through some rough spots with his likable personality. The main problem with the program is that at times is seems like an hour ensemble package squeezed into a half-hour single character setup, with the patented Bochco *Hill Street Blues* approach (several concurrent, occasionally overlapping, plots in one episode) racing to make the wrap-up. Even Hooperman's character comes with a few too many cute hooks: He's a cop, an amateur musician, a dog lover, the inherited owner of his apartment building, and seriously involved with Susan, an aspiring writer in the building. By the end of the first season, she's pregnant and Hooperman's facing fatherhood. Fortunately things loosen up a bit with the second season episodes, and Ritter has more opportunities for well-balanced comic moments.

In a sly character reversal, the no-nonsense captain of Hooperman's precinct is played by Barbara Bosson, who played the nagging ex-wife of precinct captain Frank Furillo on *Hill Street Blues.*

**HOPALONG CASSIDY (**) 30 min (52ep B&W; 1951–1952 Syndication) Western** *with William Boyd as Hopalong Cassidy and Edgar Buchanan as Red Connors*

*Hopalong Cassidy* is where the TV western started. In the late 1940s, when TV stations were desperate to fill their empty hours with anything cheap, they turned to the sixty-six old Hopalong Cassidy "B"-movies produced in the 1930s and 1940s. They were inexpensive and attracted a surprising number of young viewers. When the films became huge hits on local TV stations, NBC placed them in prime time and ABC ordered a TV version of *The Lone Ranger* to compete.

William Boyd, who played Hopalong in all the old films (and had wisely purchased the rights to the films just before they appeared on TV), then produced and starred in a series of fifty-two new western adventures filmed especially for television. In these new episodes, Hopalong is aided by sidekick Red Connors, played by Edgar Buchanan, later renowned as the slow-moving Uncle Joe on *Petticoat Junction.*

The character of Hopalong Cassidy, as played by Boyd in the theatrical and TV versions, is a far cry from the original Hopalong Cassidy character created by author Clarence E. Mulford. In the books, Cassidy was a big drinker who chewed tobacco, swore, and had a limp (hence his nickname). Boyd transformed Cassidy into a morally upright western idol, who always wore black (even in the desert!), spoke perfectly, and was kind, reverent, and obedient. This paragon of virtue style of kiddie western heroes would stay dominant until the adult western (i.e., *Gunsmoke*) appeared in the mid-1950s.

Hopalong's horse is named Topper, not to be confused with the banker of the same name who saw ghosts in a TV series (*Topper*) in the 1950s.

**HOT L BALTIMORE (**) 30 min (13ep Color; 1975 ABC) Situation Comedy** *with James Cromwell as Bill Lewis, Richard Masur as Clifford Ainsley, Conchata Ferrell as April Green, Al Freeman, Jr. as Charles Bingham, and Jeannie Linero as Suzy Marta Rocket*

Set in the once glamorous but now seedy Hotel Baltimore (the "e" in the hotel sign is burned out), *Hot l Baltimore* is Norman Lear's first sitcom failure. At the time the show was produced, Lear could do no wrong as his *All in the Family* was both a critical and popular smash.

*Hot l Baltimore,* based on a play of the same name by Lanford Wilson, focuses on the seedy, run-down characters who inhabit the seedy, run-down hotel. Bill Lewis is the desk clerk, Clifford Ainsley is the manager, April Green is the "nice" prostitute, and Suzy Rocket is the "bad" prostitute. There are numerous other offbeat characters, who all engage in offbeat activities.

What makes *Hot l Baltimore* so intriguing—its weird collection of characters—may also lead to its downfall. It is a bit hard for audiences to work up a warm relationship with this bunch. Usually critics reply that audiences *would* get involved if only the networks would support odd shows like *Hot l Baltimore.* Maybe. Maybe not. It is doubtful this show would have ever caught on. It is just too weird. At best, it should have been designed as a six-part comedy miniseries.

**HOT OFF THE WIRE** **(see *The Jim Backus Show—Hot Off the Wire*)**

**HOT PURSUIT (*½) 60 min (9ep Color; 1984 NBC) Drama** *with Kerrie Keane as Kate Wyler/Cathy Ladd, Eric Pierpoint as Jim Wyler, Dina Merrill as Estelle Modrian, and Mike Preston as Alec Shaw*

It's not sacrilegious to try and update a successful TV idea, but the updates rarely, if ever, measure up to the original. *Hot Pursuit* takes nearly every concept from *The Fugitive* and leaves out the quirky loneliness that made the original so good.

In *Hot Pursuit,* instead of a doctor unjustly accused of killing his wife, we have the trendy idea of a female race car driver, Kate Wyler, unjustly framed for the murder of her wealthy employer. The boss's nasty wife Estelle used a double of Kate (the shadowy Cathy Ladd) to trap the poor girl. Kate's loyal veterinarian hubby Jim arranges for her escape from jail and the loving couple become fugitives, roaming the United States, interacting with people and trying to avoid a . . . (get this!) one-*eyed* man (Alec Shaw), who is tracking them on behalf of evil Estelle. The show never gets around to filming a denouement, so Jim and Kate are probably still out there.

**HOT SHOTS (**½) 90 min (13ep Color; 1986–1987 CBS) Crime Drama** *with Dorothy Parke as Amanda Reed, Booth Savage as Jason West, Clark Johnson as Al Pendleton, Heather Smith as Cleo, and Paul Burke as Nicholas Broderick*

Nothing like the smell of a big story to get a couple of competing reporters to work together, especially when it means prestigious bylines for both. The fact that Amanda and Jason find each other attractive (though both constantly deny it) may also have something to do with it. Obviously yet another of the bickering-but-they're-really-turned-on couplings of the mid-1980s (*Cheers, Remington Steele, Moonlighting*), this Canadian-produced entry features a pair of home-grown talents in the lead roles—with Dorothy Parke a 1984 winner from the syndicated *Star Search* talent show. Paul Burke (as their editor) is the familiar U.S. performing face, from such series as *Twelve O'Clock High* and *Dynasty.*

**HOTEL (**) 60 min (88ep Color; 1983–1988 ABC) Drama** *with James Brolin as Peter McDermott, Connie Sellecca as Christine Francis, Anne Baxter as Victoria Cabot, Shea Farrell as Mark Danning, Nathan Cook as Billy Griffin, Shari Belafonte-Harper as Julie Gillette, and Bette Davis as Laura Trent*

Once you know that *Hotel* is produced by Aaron Spelling and Douglas Cramer, the men who produced *The Love Boat,* you know what this series will be like. The setting is an opulent resort, where people of all walks and shapes come and go. The series focuses on a few guests each week, with a few regulars around to hold it all together. Does this format sound vaguely familiar to you?

Unlike *The Love Boat, Hotel* is not played quite as much for laughs. After all, we are not on a Caribbean cruise liner, but in a swank San Francisco hotel, and a bit more decorum is called for. James Brolin, having grown a dapper beard since his days as Dr. Kiley on *Marcus Welby, M. D.,* plays Peter McDermott, the urbane manager of the St. Gregory Hotel, while Connie Sellecca, fresh from her role as William Katt's girlfriend in *The Greatest American Hero,* plays Brolin's glamorous assistant Christine Francis. Like *The Love Boat,* chief draw of *Hotel* is the parade of famous guest stars who check in and out each week. Bette Davis was to appear regularly as the hotel owner, but due to illness she only appears in the first episode or so. Anne Baxter, Davis's co-star in the 1950 film *All About Eve,* steps in to replace Davis as Victoria Cabot, the sister-in-law of the owner, who watches things while the owner is on a cruise somewhere (on the *Pacific Princess* perhaps?).

Avoid the later episodes, where a romance between Peter and Christine is pumped up to sustain this series, which had already run out of gas. The other pointless aspect of the later episodes is a *Falcon Crest*–like battle over control of the hotel, once Victoria dies and leaves one-half to Peter. The other one-half is controlled by other members of the Cabot clan, who are awfully nasty to Peter before he buys them out.

**HOTEL DE PAREE (*) 30 min (33ep B&W; 1959–1960 CBS) Western** *with Earl Holliman as Sundance, Judi Meredith as Monique Deveraux, Jeanette Nolan as Annette Deveraux, and Strother Martin as Aaron Donager*

One of the many gimmicky westerns that flooded the screen in the late 1950s, *Hotel De Paree* is set in Georgetown, Colorado, in the amorphous 1870s. Sundance is a local who just got out of prison for killing a man. Now he goes into business with some of the dead man's family, running the Hotel De Paree, the grandiose name of the only hotel in the county. Sundance's job is still to act as a tough guy, and he uses silver dollars in his hat brim to temporarily blind troublemakers with reflected light (huh?). With his adversaries thus unnerved, Sundance shoots them or beats them up or bounces them out of the hotel. Life was sure rough in the Old West.

**HOTHOUSE (*½) 60 min (6ep & 2 hr pilot Color; 1988 ABC) Drama** *with Josef Sommer as Sam Garrison, Art Malik as Ved, Michael Learned as Marie, Tony Soper as Matt, Ann-Sara Matthews as Abby, Peter Friedman as David, Michael Jeter as Art, Katherine Borowitz as Issy, Alexis Smith as Lily, and Susan Diol as Claudia*

This short-run medical drama presents the soapy lives and loves of the staff and patients at the Garrison Medical Center, also known as the "Hothouse," where they "treat minds with hearts." Located in New England, the facility is a specialized psychiatric clinic with an emphasis on trust and self-awareness along with the latest techniques (such as the use of video tape at sessions to allow both the staff and sometimes the patients to watch themselves).

Though the Hothouse is not set up as an equivalent to such real-life celebrity dry-out facilities as the Betty Ford Clinic, one story has a stressed-out performer using it for just that (completely disrupting the normal hospital routine in the process), with Marsha Mason playing an actress who suffered a breakdown on the set of her latest picture. Edward Herrmann plays her studio-exec husband, torn between concern for her and for the bottom line of the film.

Naturally the staff members have their own internal dramas: the conflict between the center's founder, Sam Garrison, and his son, Matt, who wants to keep a tighter eye on the budget; the romance between Ved and Marie (played by Art Melik from *Jewel in the Crown* and Michael Learned from *Nurse*); the friendship triangle between Claudia, Lily, and Issy; and much more.

Far too much more. It's a unique setting, but this series is too slow, too sudsy, and ultimately too pretentious.

**HOUSE CALLS (**½) 30 min (57ep Color; 1979–1982 CBS) Situation Comedy** *with Wayne Rogers as Dr. Charley Michaels, Lynn Redgrave as Ann Anderson, David Wayne as Dr. Amos Weatherby, Sharon Gless as Jane Jeffries, Ray Buktenica as Dr. Norman Solomon, Marc L. Taylor as Conrad Peckler, and Deedy Peters as Mrs. Phipps*

Despite the different title and the character names.

this series is *really* the Trapper John spin-off from *M*A*S*H*. At least, this is closer to what *Trapper John, M. D.* might have been as a half-hour comedy with Alan Alda's old bunk mate, Wayne Rogers, in the lead. So even though all the respective legal departments will dutifully point out that this series is based on a completely different source (the 1978 hit feature film starring Walter Matthau and Glenda Jackson), we'll all just nod knowingly, wink, and enjoy Trap (er, Wayne as Charley Michaels) in action.

The setting is Kensington General Hospital in San Francisco, where Charley Michaels operates both as a respected surgeon and a popular ladies' man. He's also a stickler about bending the administrative rules, especially when there's a greater good to result (a habit he probably picked up in the Korean War—whoops). Naturally this causes him untold trouble when he falls for Ann Anderson, an attractive English woman hired as the hospital's new administrative assistant. (She *appreciates* paperwork.) As in the original feature film, the two attempt to develop their relationship while still maintaining their own stubbornly individualistic outlook on life. They both also keep a protective eye on the hospital's chief of surgery, Amos Weatherby, whose absentmindedness occasionally borders on senility. (Art Carney played that role to the hilt in the film.)

Perhaps the most unusual aspect of this series is that even with a few loose words about sex and malpractice insurance, the program seems to belong to another era. On closer examination that's no surprise, though, because the original film script (and series premise) comes from the pen of *Dobie Gillis* creator Max Shulman, who specialized in very clean and direct comedy, with simple lessons about responsibility, respect, and love. So even though this series originally aired in the late 1970s, it's very easy to place the action just down the street from the Gillis grocery store, only a few years after Korea, in the timeless never-never land of California.

The most disappointing aspect of the series is that the relationship between Ann and Charley never gets properly resolved. Due to a dispute with the producers, Lynn Redgrave found herself written out of the program, with Sharon Gless stepping in as her replacement, Jane Jeffries. Though presented as a former love interest to Charley, they don't have much time to rekindle the flames before the series comes to an end.

**HOUSTON KNIGHTS** (*½) **60 min (30ep & 2 hr pilot Color; 1987–1988 CBS) Police Drama** *with Michael Pare as Sgt. Joey La Fiamma, Michael Beck as Sgt. Levon Lundy, Robyn Douglass as Lt. Joanne Beaumont, and John Hancock as Chicken*

Hard-nosed, uptight Chicago cop Joey La Fiamma is transferred to the Houston force after his partner is killed in a mob shoot-out. Joey is teamed with easygoing Texas cop Levon Lundy and sparks fly as their differing attitudes clash. Their boss, Lt. Beaumont, is a woman. Everybody in this series is much too good-looking.

**HOW GREEN WAS MY VALLEY** (**½) **60 min (6ep Color; 1976 UK BBC) Drama** *with Stanley Baker as Hwilym Morgan, Sian Phillips as Beth Morgan, Rhys Powys as Huw Morgan, Mike Gwilyn as Owen Morgan, Norman Comer as Ifor Morgan, Keith Drinkel as Ianto Morgan, and Gareth Thomas as Rev. Mr. Gruffydd*

Particularly authentic television adaptation of the Welsh novel by Richard Llewellyn, with most of the cast (and the script adapter) Welsh as well. The setting is a Welsh mining town, with the focus on a close-knit Welsh family, the Morgans, facing personal and economic hardships at the turn of the century. Nothing flashy, just a good earthy tale of a tough professional life made tolerable by family triumphs.

This is probably one of the most famous modern Welsh tales around. John Ford directed a 1941 Oscar-winning feature film version, and *Monty Python* did its send-up of the setting with the tale of a rebellious son of a theatrical family leaving the stage for the glamorous allure of coal mining.

**HOW THE WEST WAS WON** (**½) **3 hr & 2 hr & 60 min (24ep: three 3 hr & twelve 2 hr & nine 60 min, plus 2½ hr pilot Color; 1977–1979 ABC) Western** *with James Arness as Zeb Macahan, Eva Marie Saint as Kate Macahan, Bruce Boxleitner as Luke Macahan, Kathryn Holcomb as Laura Macahan, William Kirby Cullen as Josh Macahan, Fionnula Flanagan as Molly Culhane, and Vicki Schreck as Jessie Macahan*

This epic effort to revive westerns on TV in the post-*Gunsmoke* era failed to bring that once-popular format back, but it was not for lack of trying. The costly production, the fancy on-location photography, the star-studded cast, and the soap opera aspects of the scripts should have captured an audience. In the original 1976 pilot (*The Macahans*), Zeb Macahan leads some of his family out West in the 1860s. In the series that follows, Zeb returns to Virginia to lead the rest of the family to the West, just as the Civil War breaks out. Eventually, through much travail and action, the Macahans wind up in the far West, in the Grand Teton mountains, raising appaloosa horses.

Due to irregular scheduling when *How the West Was Won* was first produced, the series exists in confusing lengths. Adding up all the three-hour, two-hour and one-hour episodes, the grand total (not counting the pilot) comes to forty-two hours of material. In syndication, the series is usually chopped into single hour segments.

The TV series was produced by John Mantley, who also produced the epic TV western *Gunsmoke* that James Arness had just concluded when the original pilot aired. *How the West Was Won* was also a 1963 epic movie, directed by John Ford and starring John Wayne.

**HOW TO MARRY A MILLIONAIRE** (**½) **30 min (52ep B&W; 1958–1959 Syndication) Situation Comedy** *with Merry Anders as Michele "Mike" Page, Barbara Eden as Loco Jones, Lori Nelson as Greta Lindquist, and Lisa Gaye as Gwen Laurel*

While the concept of three man-hungry females using all their feminine wiles to trap unwary rich men into matrimony may seem quite out of date these days, *How to Marry a Millionaire* is still undeniably funny. Based on a hit 1953 film starring Marilyn Monroe, Betty Grable, and Lauren Bacall, this series changes the lead characters' names from the film's, but keeps the same light and breezy tone. The show is worth watching for nothing else than to see the TV series debut of twenty-three-year-old Barbara Eden (later the genie of *I Dream of Jeannie*) in the Monroe-esque role of nearsighted dumb blonde.

**HULLABALOO** (**) **30 & 60 min (44ep: twenty-eight 30 min & sixteen 60 min Color; 1965–1966 NBC) Musical-Variety**

Network television has a truly abysmal record when it comes to rock'n'roll. A few shows (such as *American Bandstand*) found a niche in offbeat time slots, but prime time and rock just don't seem to mix, since the networks have never believed there is an audience for rock shows. Consequently programmers always hedged their bets when staging rock'n'roll by toning it down or adding some more "wholesome" elements in hopes of attracting a wider range of viewers. *Hullabaloo* demonstrates how that pussyfooting concept results in neither fish nor fowl.

Before *Hullabaloo,* Gary Smith, the show's producer, was best known for producing *The Judy Garland Show.* Smith later teamed up with Dwight Hemion and became one of the tube's premier producers of middle-of-the-road music-variety shows in the 1970s. The Garland show was fine television, but Smith was always a man more at home with Broadway than the big beat. Not surprisingly, *Hullabaloo* looks as if it is the youth auxiliary of *The Ed Sullivan Show,* except that each week's show is hosted by a guest star. The premier episode's host is Jack Jones, a crooner whose biggest hit was the syrupy "Lollipops and Roses." The other performers joining Jones are eclectic, if nothing else: Woody Allen, the New Christy Minstrels, Joey Heatherton, Gerry and the Pacemakers, the Zombies, and a New Jersey high school band.

The opening night lineup is symbolic of the show's concept, mixing hit rock groups with more sedate singers and other variety acts. Visually, the show aims for a dash of hipness by affecting the discotheque look with lots of screaming kids and a troupe of mini-skirted, perpetually gyrating, Hullabaloo Dancers. Best remembered of all the dancers is Lada Edmund, the Hullabaloo Dancer forever locked in a cage suspended somewhere above the stage.

Real rock fans will be bored by guest hosts such as Jerry Lewis and Mickey Rooney. More sedate variety fans won't make heads or tails out of Marianne Faithful or the Moody Blues. All that is left of *Hullabaloo* (aside from aging fantasies about Lada Edmund and her cage) are some nice video clips of famous 1960s rock groups, captured performing at their peak. ■

**HUNTER** (**) **60 min (26ep Color; 1968 Australia) Spy Drama** *with Tony Ward as John Hunter, Glyn Fernande as Eve Halliday, and Nigel Lovell as Blake*

John Hunter is another Bond surrogate, working for some western super-secret organization to save the world from crazed evil geniuses.

**HUNTER** (**) **60 min (13ep & 60 min pilot Color; 1977 CBS) Spy Drama** *with James Franciscus as James Hunter, Linda Evans as Marty Shaw, and Ralph Bellamy as Gen. Harold Baker*

This is the second of three drama series named *Hunter* with the lead character named Hunter. As with the 1968 Australian series of the same name, this *Hunter* is about a guy named Hunter who is a spy for the good guys. In this case, Hunter is played by James Franciscus, the super-straight all-American type from *Mr. Novak.* He has the good luck to be teamed up with super-sexy agent Marty Shaw (played by pre-*Dynasty* Linda Evans). The producing duo of Lee Rich and Philip Capice, who created *Dallas,* are at the helm in *Hunter* as well.

The 1976 pilot episode has Broderick Crawford (*Highway Patrol*) as the boss man to the spies, a role taken over by Ralph Bellamy in the series.

**HUNTER** (**) **60 min (110ep at Fall 1989 Color; 1984– NBC) Police Drama** *with Fred Dryer as Sgt. Rick Hunter, Stepfanie Kramer as Sgt. Dee Dee McCall, James Whitmore, Jr. as Det. Bernie Terwilliger, Michael Cavanaugh and Arthur Rosenberg as Capt. Lester Cain, and Garrett Morris as Arnold "Sporty" James*

Fred Dryer, former pro football star for the Los Angeles Rams, gets to perform some mayhem on the streets of L.A. in *Hunter,* a nasty little program from Stephen J. Cannell (*The A-Team, The Rockford Files*). Dryer plays Rick Hunter, one of the army of tough, no-nonsense TV cops who has to handle the tidal wave of urban violence *his* way. Hunter's attitude ensures a lot of run-ins with his stick-in-the-mud superiors, who insist on following police rules. The most interesting angle here is that Hunter is from a family overrun with mobsters, so he knows the crime business from the inside out and keeps running into relatives who don't appreciate his working on the side of the law. Another slightly different aspect about *Hunter* is that his partner is *female,* a tough little number named Dee Dee McCall, known to her friends as the "brass cupcake."

Dryer does well for a new actor, but *Hunter* goes a little overboard on the violence, and it's hard to get too wrapped up in the characters. A little more *Rockford*-esque humor would help.

**THE HUNTER** (**½) **30 min (26ep B&W; 1952–1954 CBS & Syndication & NBC) Spy Drama** *with Barry Nelson and Keith Larsen as Bart Adams*

One of the few anti-Communist series from the 1950s that have a trace of humor, *The Hunter* is almost an early version of *I Spy* in its mix of adventure and smiles. Unlike the 1960s *I Spy, The Hunter* is about just one U.S. agent, in this case Bart Adams, who poses as a wealthy American playboy while battling the Red menace across Europe. Adams is a master of disguises and whistles the tune "Frere Jacques" to identify himself to compatriots. Barry Nelson, star of the hit sitcom *My Favorite Husband* and the first man to portray James Bond (in a 1954 TV production of *Casino Royale*), plays Bart Adams in all but a few episodes.

**HUSBANDS, WIVES & LOVERS** (*) **60 min (11ep and 60 min pilot Color; 1978 CBS) Situation Comedy** *with Jesse Welles as Helene Willis, Ron Rifkin as Ron Willis, Stephen Pearlman as Murray Zuckerman, Cynthia Harris as Paula Zuckerman, Eddie Barth as Harry Bellini, and Lynne Marie Stewart as Joy Bellini*

*Husbands, Wives & Lovers* is an ambitious, but failed, effort to create an hour-long sitcom about five contemporary couples in southern California. Created and co-written by comedienne Joan Rivers, this series has none of the biting sarcasm that makes Rivers so memorable. The couples range from blue collar to proto-Yuppie, but none of them stand out. The 1977 pilot is known by the shorter name *Husbands and Wives* and has most of the cast from the series, although numerous character names are slightly different.

**I, CLAUDIUS** (***½) **60 min (13ep Color; 1976 UK BBC) Drama** *with Derek Jacobi as Claudius, Brian Blessed as Octavian/Augustus, Sian Phillips as Livia, John Hurt as Caligula, John Paul as Agrippa, Christopher Guard as Marcellus, Frances White as Julia, George Baker as Tiberius, David Robb as Germanicus, Patrick Stewart as Sejanus, Patricia Quinn as Livilla, and James Faulkener as Herod*

A large number of the fancy British drama series imported to the United States are stuffy, drawing room stories of stifling Victorian emotions. *I, Claudius* is none of those things. Set in Rome around the time of Jesus, *I, Claudius* views the reign of the first five Roman emperors through the eyes of Claudius, a member of the royal family with a strong speech impediment that leads nearly everybody to consider him a retarded fool. Claudius spends most of his youth sheltered from the cruelness of imperial politics. When he does learn how heartless those in power can be, he makes it a point to avoid the limelight, hiding behind his supposed mental thickness in order to stay alive while all those around him are being poisoned and exiled. Finally, amidst a military revolt against the depraved and insane Emperor Caligula, Claudius is made emperor, mostly as a joke. Suddenly given the trappings of power, Claudius shows his mental strength and astounds Rome by actually serving as a wise and kind ruler. In time, of course, palace intrigue dooms Claudius, and he makes way for Nero, another incompetent monarch.

The acting in *I, Claudius* is stunning. All of the major characters (and several minor ones) are memorable. Best of the lot are Brian Blessed as the powerful but friendly Octavian (renamed Augustus when he becomes Rome's first emperor), Sian Phillips as his wife Livia (a schemer of the first magnitude), John Hurt (who later starred in the film *Elephant Man*) as the mad emperor Caligula, and Derek Jacobi, who is unforgettable as Claudius. Watch as Claudius's stutter begins to fade as he asserts himself as emperor.

*I, Claudius* is based on a series of novels by Robert Graves that purport to be historically accurate. Whether they are accurate or not is irrelevant for the TV viewer, who will be hard pressed to find another historical drama with the exciting mix of fine acting, writing, steamy kinky sex, intelligence, and intrigue of *I, Claudius*. ■

**I DREAM OF JEANNIE** (***) **30 min (139ep: 30 B&W & 109 Color & 2 hr sequel; 1965–1970 NBC) Situation Comedy** *with Barbara Eden as Jeannie, Larry Hagman as Maj. Anthony Nelson, Bill Daily as Maj. Roger Healey, Hayden Rorke as Dr. Alfred Bellows, Emmaline Henry as Amanda Bellows, and Barton MacLane as Gen. Martin Peterson*

When his test mission has to be aborted in mid-flight, U.S. Air Force astronaut Tony Nelson parachutes to safety on a deserted South Pacific island. There he finds a strange old bottle, opens it, and releases a genie named Jeannie. She immediately offers to grant his every wish, mainly because that's what genies are supposed to do (and he did release her). Magically, the rescue helicopter appears. Tony is shocked, grateful, confused, and soon dead certain he'll be diagnosed as nuts if the medical team at the base hears much talk from him about magical powers and a 2,000-year-old genie. So, even as Jeannie accompanies him home, they begin to work out a routine that limits her magic antics enough to keep him judged sane and still flying. Which isn't easy once skeptical base psychiatrist Dr. Bellows sets his sights on proving otherwise.

Of course, we all know what we'd do if some good-looking magically endowed spirit offered to grant us any wish, but that probably wouldn't play five seasons as light family entertainment. (Co-producer Sidney Sheldon saved the steamier stuff for subsequent ventures such as the TV movie *Rage of Angels*.) Still, this is more fun and believable (as these things go) than, say, *Bewitched*. For one thing, as a military pilot Tony leads an occasionally dangerous life, so he really could use a comrade-in-arms like Jeannie. And, in truth, he really seems to enjoy watching her pull those miraculous stunts that leave the brass (or whoever is making his life miserable) dumbfounded—almost as much as she delights in messing up his love life so that, eventually (no surprise), he'll realize they're destined to be married (after all, she's fallen in love with him).

Larry Hagman and Barbara Eden play their roles perfectly, obviously having fun with the silly premise and the many opportunities for well-timed comic denials, deadpans (following one of Jeannie's stunts), and unexpected pratfalls (Hagman is surprisingly good at those). Perennial sidekick Bill Daily (as Tony's buddy, Roger) fits right into the mix, bringing his patented style of professional competence hidden behind nervous confusion. Because Jeannie lets Roger see her in action, he's able to join their side of a scheme or adventure, sometimes even being the one to concoct a cover story for Tony. It's fun watching Roger attempt a bluff with a straight face, especially when coupled with the image of his similar civilian life role as Howard Borden on *The Bob Newhart Show*.

In the final season of *I Dream of Jeannie*, Jeannie and Tony at last get married and set up housekeeping as husband and wife. We get to see how well things turned out over the long run in a 1985 made-for-TV movie reunion ("I Dream of Jeannie: 15 Years Later"), though Wayne Rogers subs for Larry Hagman (obviously quite busy down in *Dallas*) as Tony. The big news in the revival is that Barbara Eden finally shows her belly button—something she never had the chance to do in the entire original run of the series.

**I HAD THREE WIVES (*½) 60 min (6ep Color; 1985 CBS) Detective Drama** *with Victor Garber as Jackson Beaudine, Maggie Cooper as Mary Parker, Teri Copley as Samantha, Shanna Reed as Liz, and David Faustino as Andrew Beaudine*

The title of this show is cute, a play on words on the 1950s Cold War spy series *I Led Three Lives*. The premise is interesting: an easygoing private eye is assisted by his three ex-wives (an actress, a journalist, and a lawyer). If *I Had Three Wives* only had some good acting and writing, it would be worth watching.

**I LED THREE LIVES (***) 30 min (117ep: 78 B&W & 39 Color; 1953–1956 Syndication) Spy Drama** *with Richard Carlson as Herbert Philbrick, Virginia Stefan as Eva Philbrick, and Patricia Morrow as Constance Philbrick*

If you want to capture a real taste of life in the early 1950s, watch *I Led Three Lives*. All the paranoia, all the Red-baiting, all the "us versus them" philosophy that Sen. Joseph McCarthy exploited and promoted is here in one easy-to-watch thirty-minute saga. If ever there was a show that mixed propaganda with entertainment in order to brainwash an audience, *I Led Three Lives* is it.

The genesis of the show is the real-life Herbert Philbrick, the man who led three lives for the benefit of his country. Posing as a normal sober citizen, Philbrick was an undercover agent for the FBI who infiltrated the American Communist Party and pretended to be one of the Red's undercover operatives, all the while reporting back to J. Edgar Hoover and his boys in Washington. Philbrick came out from undercover to write a best-selling book about his turbulent life, and the book served as the basis for the series.

Richard Carlson is the perfect choice to play Philbrick, for Carlson is the embodiment of the xenophobic science fiction film classics that proliferated during the Red-baiting decade. In films such as *It Came from Outer Space* and *Creature from the Black Lagoon*, Carlson always played the average American who suddenly had to deal with aliens or horrible prehistoric creatures among us that had to be destroyed before they ruined our way of life.

Most of these sci-fi films were loosely sheathed allegories for the fears of the nation struggling to get through the Cold War. Those in high places kept indicating that anyone or anything somewhat out of the ordinary might be a Communist, trying to bring down the U.S. of A.

In *I Led Three Lives*, this usually understated theme is prominently up front. Here everyone who is somewhat out of the ordinary probably *is* a Communist, and will be seen plotting awful, nefarious schemes that almost succeed. Only Philbrick, who pretends to be one of the Reds, can unmask the alien menace that poses as one of us.

This is America the way J. Edgar Hoover saw it (his FBI troops reviewed all the scripts before airing). Why any college professors or labor unions or bohemians were questioning the status quo was simple . . . they were Reds, only trying to weaken the nation and get it primed for revolution.

Aside from the fascinating civics lesson that *I Led Three Lives* provides, it is a whale of a good drama show. The premise is, after all, fraught with tension, the stakes are high, and the writing and production are quite good, as long as you accept the central philosophy of communists everywhere. Carlson is Everyman, USA, and he is so likable and earnest that you root along with him and start believing that your local librarian fighting for that banned book really might be a pinko.

**I LOVE LUCY** (****) **30 min (180ep B&W; 1951–1957 CBS) THE LUCY-DESI COMEDY HOUR** (**½) **60 min (13ep B&W; 1957–1960) Situation Comedy** *with Lucille Ball as Lucy Ricardo, Desi Arnaz as Ricky Ricardo, Vivian Vance as Ethel Mertz, William Frawley as Fred Mertz, Mary Jane Croft as Betty Ramsey, Frank Nelson as Ralph Ramsey, and Richard Keith as Little Ricky Ricardo*

Lucy and Ricky and Fred and Ethel are probably the most recognized neighbors in television history. Everyone has seen them in action, whether at the New York brownstone owned by the Mertzes, in Hollywood for Ricky's big movie screen test, in Europe on tour with Ricky's band, or in Connecticut, learning to adjust to suburban life. Their schemes and situations seem more familiar than the pictures in your own family album: Lucy and Ethel on a candy assembly line; Lucy stomping grapes in Italy; the Ricardos and the Mertzes driving cross country to California; the birth of Little Ricky; Lucy attempting to say and sell Vitameatavegamin; and so on.

If you haven't seen them lately, just check your local listings. This series is virtually guaranteed to be showing in any area of the country almost any day of the week. Sometimes it seems as if there's never been a time without *I Love Lucy* somewhere on the dial. As a result, it's easy to take the series for granted. Fortunately, while the fashions and prices referred to on the show may have changed since the 1950s, most of what made *I Love Lucy* special back then still applies today.

First and foremost, there is an excellent ensemble. While Lucy is clearly the lead character, the strength of Ricky, Fred, and Ethel helps to keep the stories from getting stale. It's not just Lucy versus the world. Sometimes it's the husbands versus the wives, or the Mertzes versus the Ricardos, or even all of them versus some common concern. As a result, they really do come off as lifelong friends and neighbors. Even better, everyone has a chance to win and lose. Lucy may fail to land a walk-on movie part in Italy (after stomping those wine grapes), but she does manage to overcome a sunburn and successfully model a dress in California. In one episode, Ricky and Fred might succeed in dragging Lucy and Ethel to the fights, as a "night out," but in another the girls triumph by derailing the guys' scheme to put them on a strict time schedule at home.

The set pieces are another timeless strength, especially the physical schticks that center around Lucy. Though *I Love Lucy* certainly did not invent the screwball comedy format (it thrived in feature films long before), few series have been as successful in transferring the form to television. Nearly every episode has some broad physical stunt, such as Lucy hanging outside a penthouse window, Lucy and Ethel baking a twelve-foot-long loaf of bread, or Lucy watching in horror as a rubber nose she's wearing as a disguise bursts into flame. These episodes are always well-played and essentially timeless.

There are also plenty of opportunities for light showbiz song and dance. Fred is conveniently an old hoofer from Vaudeville, Ricky is a nightclub performer, and Lucy . . . well, Lucy always wants to get into showbiz so she'll do anything (even honk squeeze-horns like a trained seal). All four turn up in a number of community theater benefit performances, or in special nightclub routines.

Finally ,the producers and writers (who turned out some superb scripts) were clever enough to change various elements of the package to keep the series fresh. One major change was dictated by real life when Lucille Ball became pregnant (Lucy Ricardo followed suit), a perfectly logical development for a young couple in the early 1950s. In fact, that particular plot helped solidify *I Love Lucy* as the number one show in viewers' affections, with the actual birth episode being one of the highest rated television episodes ever. Other developments are less dramatic, such as shifting locales several times (Hollywood, Europe, and Connecticut), working in more celebrity guest stars (usually playing themselves), and promoting Ricky to owner of his own club. In the Connecticut-based stories (which begin in the program's final season of half-hour episodes), Lucy and Ethel do get new neighbors, Ralph and Betty Ramsey, and Little Ricky becomes a more active member of the cast (he plays drums and performs with his dad). For the final half-hour episode (in which the Ricardos dedicate a statue), the real-life Arnaz children (Lucie and Desi, Jr.) have a cameo.

Although it is easy to find *I Love Lucy*, tracking down the last batch of episodes featuring the Ricardos and the Mertzes is much more difficult. There are thirteen of those, but they originally aired over a three-year period as one-hour specials, so they don't fit the *I Love Lucy* rerun rotation. Sometimes they turn up as a short run series (*The Lucy-Desi Comedy Hour*), but not all that often—understandable because, in truth, the stories are often a bit padded. (One contemporary syndication package—*We Love Lucy*—neatly solves that problem by trimming three hour-long episodes to fit a two-hour slot.)

All of the hour-long tales are set in Connecticut (or in some exotic foreign locale), and feature a celebrity guest star. The best one is the first, "Lucy Takes a Cruise to Havana," a flashback on how Lucy met Ricky, with Ann Sothern along in her Susie MacNamera role from *Private Secretary*. Ethel and Fred have just a walk-on cameo in this one, but it's worth looking for because Fred is sporting a full head of hair!

Another episode ("Lucy Makes Room for Danny") is a crossover appearance with the entire Danny Thomas clan, culminating in a frenzied snowball fight between Danny and his family and the Ricardos and the Mertzes. True completists should also watch for Lucy and Ricky on *Make Room for Daddy,* with (no surprise) Lucy and Kathy Williams teaming up against Ricky and Danny. (Lucy also appears solo in an episode of *The Ann Sothern Show,* playing matchmaker to Sothern's Katy O'Connor.)

Oddly, for a series that practically defines the word rerun, there's even one rare half-hour *I Love Lucy* episode that has never been repeated: a 1956 Christmas episode set up as a nostalgic flashback story.

Obviously, *I Love Lucy* has had a tremendous influence on television programming, in everything from the way it was filmed (before a live audience using a special three-camera system), to the countless screwball comedies that followed in its wake, to the growth of Lucy and Desi's own independent production company, Desilu. Production people from *I Love Lucy* went on to success in many, many other programs, including scripts for the very different sitcom world of *All in the Family.* Even in the 1980s, *Kate and Allie* couldn't resist staging an episode to look and play just like *I Love Lucy.*

If you're a big fan of the series, you might seriously consider picking up some of the video cassette packages. After decades of watching worn station copies of the series, you'll probably be jolted by the sight of clean, unedited versions of your favorite stories. Why, you can almost make believe you're back in the 1950s, watching CBS on Monday night at 9:00 P.M. (8:00 P.M. Central). ■

## I MARRIED DORA (½) 30 min (13ep Color; 1987–1988 ABC) Situation Comedy *with Daniel Hugh-Kelly as Peter Farrell, Elizabeth Pena as Dora Calderon, Jason Horst as Will Farrell, Juliette Lewis as Kate Farrell, and Henry Jones as Hughes Whitney Lennox*

The basic premise of *I Married Dora* is so convoluted and calculated that it turns what would otherwise be inoffensive fluff into a truly awful program destined to be a cult classic of bad TV. Peter Farrell is a conservative architect with a wife and two kids (daughter Kate and son Will). So far so good, right? Well, Mrs. Farrell decides one day that married life is for the birds and she leaves husband, daughter, and son to fend for themselves. For a 1980s sitcom, that's not so unusual, but this is where it gets weird. Mom hops a plane, heading for an idyllic locale, but the plane is hijacked and goes down, leaving her a presumed victim of international terrorism.

Peter Farrell responds to these unsettling developments by hiring Dora, a comely young lady from Latin America, to be housekeeper/nanny. However, Dora has problems of her own. It seems she is in the United States illegally and is about to be deported to an unfriendly reception south of the border. To prevent any harm to lovely Dora, Farrell decides to marry her so she can stay in the country. The marriage is supposed to be platonic, you see, but who can tell what might happen. Oh, by the way, the producers felt obliged to add a disclaimer to the première, noting that marrying an illegal alien just to keep her (or him) in the country is a federal offense and should not be done by the kiddies watching at home. What have we come to when a silly sitcom must issue a warning that its basic premise is a federal offense?

The final episode is, to be fair, kind of cute. Peter is about to fly to Bahrain to work for an Arab sheik for two years (leaving the kids in Dora's sole charge), but at the last minute he lets the plane leave without him. He explains to Dora that he did so because the series has been canceled! The camera than pulls back to show the cast and crew, waving good-bye. Nice touch.

## I MARRIED JOAN (**) 30 min (98ep B&W; 1952–1955 NBC) Situation Comedy *with Joan Davis as Joan Stevens, Jim Backus as Judge Bradley Stevens, Hope Emerson as Minerva Parker, and Beverly Wills as Beverly Grossman*

For several years after the megahit of *I Love Lucy,* virtually every housewife on TV was a screwball. Joan Stevens is one of the screwiest of the lot, and *I Married Joan* is one of the most heavy-handed in its treatment of the distaff side of the nation.

As the series opens each week, Judge Bradley Stevens faces another case in domestic court. In his attempt to resolve the dispute, the judge begins to recount a story of the antics of his dippy wife Joan, and the courtroom scene fades into the judge's recollections. Most of the episode is then taken up by another example of Joan's childish shenanigans.

Star Joan Davis, a popular comedienne at the time this series was produced, controlled *I Married Joan* through her production company, but her character turns out to be rather annoying. Whereas Lucy was inventive and crafty in her zaniness, Joan is just a lunkhead, trying far too hard to do right. She usually winds up needing her husband, the judge, to fix things in the end. It's almost embarrassing to watch Joan goof over and over again.

In the beginning, Joan's chief cohort is her neighbor, Minerva Parker. When Parker leaves after the first season, Joan then gets into hot water with her equally trouble-prone younger sister, Beverly Grossman (who is played by Joan Davis's real-life *daughter,* Beverly Wills).

Jim Backus, the actor playing Judge Stevens, was already famous as the voice of Mr. Magoo when *I Married Joan* was filmed, and the familiar corniness of the Magoo character keeps sliding into the judge's actions. Backus went on to play Thurston Howell III in *Gilligan's Island.*

The best thing that can be said about *I Married Joan* is that it has the corniest yet catchiest theme song of all of the early 1950s sitcoms. ■

## I REMEMBER MAMA (see *Mama*)

**I REMEMBER NELSON: RECOLLECTIONS OF A HERO'S LIFE (**½) 60 min (4ep Color; 1982 UK Central) Drama** *with Kenneth Colley as Lord Horatio Nelson, Anna Massey as Lady Fanny Nelson, Geraldine James as Emma Hamilton, John Clements as Sir William Hamilton, and Timothy Pigott-Smith as Captain Hardy*

The trick in this biographical drama is that the story of British naval hero Admiral Horatio Nelson is told through the eyes of four people, a different one in each episode. It starts with his wife, Anna ("Love"), then moves to the husband of his mistress ("Passion"), one of his friends ("Duty"), and—no surprise—a hero-worshiping young sailor ("Battle") witnessing his triumph at the Battle of Trafalgar. Of course, you may come away from this admiring Nelson's accomplishments but not thinking very much of the man, who is portrayed as cold, arrogant, and ruthless. At least that makes the final episode's tragic events easier to take.

**I SPY (*½) 30 min (39ep B&W; 1955–1956 Syndication) Spy Anthology** *with Raymond Massey as Anton*

Raymond Massey, later Dr. Gillespie on *Dr. Kildare,* plays a bloke known as Anton, the Spy Master (really!), who introduces stories about spies throughout modern history. It's unlikely, but do not confuse this *I Spy* with the mid-1960s show of the same title, with Robert Culp and Bill Cosby.

**I SPY (***) 60 min (82ep Color; 1965–1968 NBC) Spy Adventure** *with Robert Culp as Kelly Robinson and Bill Cosby as Alexander Scott*

*I Spy* is a top-notch tongue-in-cheek spy saga from the mid-1960s. Robert Culp plays a world-class tennis pro, with Bill Cosby as his trainer. The catch is that they are really undercover spies for an unnamed U.S. espionage organization. The tennis cover is a wonderful excuse to send the boys off to all the glamorous cities of the world, where they can do good for Uncle Sam.

The primary allure of *I Spy* is seeing Cosby in his formative years. Already a popular stand-up comic and veteran of numerous TV variety show appearances when *I Spy* was produced, Cosby breaks ground here by crossing over in two categories. First, Cosby shows that a good comic can take a semiserious role and be believable. Second, Cosby shows that blacks can be portrayed as intelligent, powerful, lead characters. These discoveries may be old hat now, after Cosby's 1980s sitcom spent most of the decade as America's favorite TV show, but in the days of *I Spy,* comedians did not star in action shows and blacks were unseen outside of variety and comedy shows.

Cosby and Culp are a memorable duo, who show that they can banter with the best of them. Culp, looking very much like the classic dashing hero, is adept at poking holes in the superspy macho myth by pleading ignorance or confusion in many crunch situations. Cosby finds a way to sneak in lots of his comedy routines. Together Culp and Cosby seem like two grown fraternity preppies who can't quite believe they are in the real world, battling real-life foes.

Much of the credit for the intelligent, witty tone of *I Spy* must go to producer Sheldon Leonard, who was the brains behind Danny Thomas's *Make Room for Daddy, The Andy Griffith Show,* and *The Dick Van Dyke Show.* ■

**ICHABOD AND ME (**½) 30 min (36ep B&W; 1961–1962 CBS) Situation Comedy** *with Robert Sterling as Robert Major, George Chandler as Ichabod Adams, Christine White as Abigail Adams, and Jimmy Mathers as Benjie Major*

This easygoing light comedy is set in small-town New England, where New York City reporter Robert Major has taken refuge from the madness of the big city. Buying the town's only newspaper, Major (a widower) and his young son Benjie become involved in the town, especially with Ichabod Adams, the former owner of the paper and all-around busy-body.

The gentle humor of *Ichabod and Me* is typical of producers Joe Connelly and Bob Mosher (*Leave It to Beaver*). The *Beaver* connection is evident in the presence of Jimmy Mathers, brother of Jerry Mathers (a.k.a. Beaver), as Major's son Benjie.

The 1960 pilot is titled *Adams' Apples.*

**I'M A BIG GIRL NOW (**½) 30 min (20ep Color; 1980–1981 ABC) Situation Comedy** *with Diana Canova as Diana Cassidy, Danny Thomas as Dr. Benjamin Douglas, Rori King as Rebecca Cassidy, Sheree North as Edie McKendrick, Walter Douglas as Michael Durrell, Deborah Baltzell as Karen Hawks, and Martin Short as Neal Stryker*

*Soap* fans know that when Corrine Tate (Diana Canova) says good-bye to her mom at the beginning of the fourth season's batch of episodes, she's really just walking across the hall to the set of her own series. It's a performer, not a continuity spin-off (she plays a completely different character, with no plot connections to *Soap*), put together by the same production company, Witt-Thomas-Harris. Which also accounts for the presence of another cast member, veteran Danny Thomas—his son, Tony Thomas, talked him into doing it.

A wise decision. Danny and Diana play off each other pretty well in a premise that sounds a bit like *The Odd Couple* put through a Cuisinart: father and daughter as recent divorcés sharing an apartment together, along with her seven-year-old daughter. Of course, Diana has to constantly remind dad that she's no longer *his* little girl, completely dependent on him. (Hence, the series title.) She has a job, outside interests, and an eye out for available dates. But, surprise, so does he. (After all, what else can he do after losing his wife to his former dental partner?) Of course, Danny is still Danny, so his famous Lebanese temper is there for their arguments, only slightly mellowed. Fortunately, Diana can hold her own. The result is a good mix of rather contemporary home and office comedy along with archetypal warm family scenes, such as their first Christmas together in the apartment, both missing their respective mates.

Rounding out the cast are Diana's neurotic brother, Walter, and several office characters (she works for a Washington think tank), including Martin Short (fresh from *The Associates*) as a minor co-worker. At the end of the series' brief run, there was some tinkering with the work setting (changing the think-tank office into a newspaper, with all the characters becoming writers, editors, or reporters), but it failed to win renewal for a second season. Later in the 1980s, Canova had more success with *Throb,* a comedy done directly for syndication.

**I'M DICKENS, HE'S FENSTER (**½) 30 min (32ep B&W; 1962–1963 ABC) Situation Comedy** *with Marty Ingels as Arch Fenster, John Astin as Harry Dickens, Dave Ketchum as Mel Warshaw, Emmaline Henry as Kate Dickens, and Frank DeVol as Myron Bannister*

This sitcom from the early 1960s is worth a watch or two, if not for the show itself then at least for the great cast. The setting of the show has Dickens and Fenster as handymen/carpenters. They are two solid blue-collar types amidst the morass of middle-class, middle-management males who populated most early 1960s sitcoms. Dickens is married, henpecked, and wacky, while Fenster is a swinging bachelor and even wackier. Together they are always getting into some sort of predicament, to the constant frustration of Mr. Bannister, their vain boss.

Marty Ingels, whose voice became more familiar than his face (thanks to work in commercials and cartoons such as *Great Grape Ape, Cattanooga Cats,* and *Motor Mouse*), is an American version of Marty Feldman, with his pop eyes and loony looks. John Astin later became renowned as the bon vivant Gomez Addams in *The Addams Family,* and here demonstrates his already developed ability to deftly combine zaniness within a normal exterior. Frank DeVol, the multitalented actor-musician who wrote the popular theme songs to *Family Affair* and *My Three Sons* and appeared on *Fernwood 2-Night* as band leader Happy Kyne, is a delight as Mr. Bannister. The self-centered boss is more concerned with getting his toupee to fit right than with running his business. Dave Ketchum, who appears as another of Bannister's carpenters, later teamed up with DeVol in the frothy kiddie summer camp comedy *Camp Runamuck.* Behind the scenes of *I'm Dickens, He's Fenster* is young producer Leonard B. Stern, who later turned out more polished gems such as *Get Smart, He and She,* and *McMillan and Wife.*

**THE IMMORTAL (*½) 60 min (15ep & 90 min pilot Color; 1970–1971 ABC) Adventure** *with Christopher George as Ben Richards, Don Knight as Fletcher, David Brian as Arthur Maitland, and Carol Lynley as Sylvia Cartwright*

*The Immortal,* the only nonvampire show involving lust for human blood, is a weird tale concerning handsome race car driver Ben Richards. Ben's blood contains mysterious elements that make him immune to aging, and therefore virtually immortal. Needless to say, many people not so young and handsome as Richards would like to borrow some of Ben's blood, even if it means enslaving the guy. Richards spends the entire show running away from sick old rich men and their flunkies.

The 1969 pilot, of the same name, is just as muddled as the series. Christopher George, who plays Ben Richards, was better as Sam Troy, the leader of *The Rat Patrol.*

**IN CONCERT (**½) 90 min (52ep Color; 1973–1975 ABC) Musical-Variety**

All the superstars of early 1970s rock music show up in this series of edited concerts. Don Kirshner, music man behind The Monkees, created this series.

**IN SEARCH OF . . . (**½) 30 min (144ep Color; 1976–1982 Syndication) Documentary** *with Leonard Nimoy as host*

All of the standard topics of lurid magazine tabloids, such as UFOs, the Bermuda Triangle, ghosts, and the Loch Ness monster, are given fairly serious treatment here. Leonard Nimoy, America's favorite alien from *Star Trek,* is the super-sober host who keeps *In Search Of . . .* from going off the deep end. Alan Landsburg, who *did* go off the deep end with *That's Incredible!*, is the producer. ■

**IN THE BEGINNING (*) 30 min (9ep Color; 1978 CBS) Situation Comedy** *with McLean Stevenson as Father Daniel M. Cleary, Priscilla Lopez as Sister Agnes, Priscilla Morrill as Sister Lillian, and Jack Dodson as Msgr. Francis X. Barlow*

*In the Beginning* presents McLean Stevenson playing Father Daniel Cleary, a very unlikable old-fashioned Irish priest. Father Cleary is assigned to some storefront mission in inner city Baltimore with a crusading, progressive nun, Sister Agnes. The padre and the sister represent the old versus the new and nothing unexpected occurs. Mort Lachman, of *All in the Family,* produces this tired rehash of the 1970s social commentary sitcom style.

**IN THE HEAT OF THE NIGHT (***) 60 min (28ep at Fall 1989 & 2 hr pilot Color; 1988– NBC) Drama** *with Carroll O'Connor as Chief Bill Gillespie, Howard Rollins as Det. Virgil Tibbs, Anne-Marie Johnson as Althea Tibbs, Alan Autry as Dep. Bubba Skinner, Hugh O'Connor as Dep. Jamison, Jill Carroll as Barbara Giles, Lois Nettleton as Joann St. John, and Geoffrey Throne as Wilson Sweet*

Surprise! Carroll O'Connor in a role at least a little different from Archie Bunker, complete with a mean southern accent. Surprise again! This television series version of the 1967 Oscar-winning feature film actually works! O'Connor and Howard Rollins (best known from his roles in the theatrical films *Ragtime* and *A Soldier's Story*) mesh perfectly in the characters originated by Rod Steiger and Sidney Poitier, playing (respectively) white southern police chief Bill Gillespie and his new chief of detectives, Virgil Tibbs, a black man.

They're working together in the small town of Sparta, Mississippi, an area they both know quite well: Gillespie has lived there all his life; Tibbs was born and raised there before going to Philadelphia (where he learned modern criminology methods). As in the feature film, racial tension is still one of the themes, though the conflict between Tibbs and Gillespie is more often one of newfangled science versus old-fashioned instinct. (Or headstrong young hotshot versus the set-in-his-ways veteran.) However, since both styles and methods seem to lead them to the guilty parties, they develop a healthy professional respect for each other. Followed, of course, by a grudging personal bond.

The series also does a good job with its "gritty" portrayal of the area, which must rank with Cabot Cove (on *Murder, She Wrote*) as one of the most dangerous small towns in the country—there's always a domestic squabble, murder, blackmail scheme, or drug deal simmering somewhere.

For a few episodes filmed in 1989, Joe Don Baker substitutes for Carroll O'Connor (then undergoing surgery), playing a similarly styled law enforcement friend of Chief Gillespie's, acting Chief Tom Dugan.

**THE INCREDIBLE HULK (**½) 60 min (85ep & two 2 hr sequels Color; 1979–1982 CBS) Adventure** *with Bill Bixby as David Bruce Banner, Lou Ferrigno as The Incredible Hulk, and Jack McGee as Jack Colvin*

Surprisingly faithful television translation of the long-running Marvel comic-book character, following the transient life of scientist David Banner and his big green alter ego, The Hulk. For Banner, the nightmare begins with an accidental exposure to a massive dose of radiation, which causes his metabolism to change in response to the state of his emotions. When he becomes angry or excited, he changes into the beast, reverting back to human form only when he has calmed down or is exhausted.

What makes both the comic book and this television series so effective is that Banner has virtually no control over this process, nor can he even remember what he does from one guise to another. He can attempt to stay calm and not change, but sometimes events overwhelm his efforts at self-control. As a result, he is not really a superhero, ready to leap into battle with superior strength and a secret identity. Rather, he is as much a victim as anybody he meets, with a beast inside that can emerge at a moment's notice—and usually does, though only one or twice a story. Fortunately, while terribly strong and potentially violent, the Hulk is more like Rin Tin Tin than Godzilla, instinctively focusing his attacks on deserving bad guys. There's also a hint of Frankenstein's monster in him, responsive to a gentle touch and a soothing spirit (which soon turns him back into Banner).

The series is structured as a wandering anthology, with Banner traveling and working odd jobs like Richard Kimble on *The Fugitive.* Of course, the sensible thing for him to do would be to find some dedicated fellow scientists and stay with them, searching for a solution to his problem, but that wouldn't play for very long. Besides, he doesn't trust himself, so he stays on the road, which also helps him avoid the prying eyes of reporter Jack Colvin (who suspects the Hulk of murder) while trying to figure out a cure on his own. And no doubt to search for a source of good, cheap clothing since his transformations into the Hulk leave whatever he's wearing in tatters.

The stories are good though pretty interchangeable. Surprisingly they rely far less on superpowered stunts than you'd expect, and one two-hour story ("Married") does a surprisingly effective job on that time-bomb premise (Mariette Hartley plays Banner's wife). *The Incredible Hulk* began as a pair of two-hour made-for-TV movies, graduated into a series, and also played briefly (with a completely different cast) as a Saturday morning cartoon. The double-length pilot episodes are usually incorporated into the one-hour syndicated package as four episodes. A 1988 *Return of the Incredible Hulk* two-hour movie revival at last has Banner hooking up with some research center, but then a TV adaptation of another long-running Marvel comic book character (Thor) shows up. And it's bye-bye potential cure. The sequel adventures continue with the 1989 two-hour TV movie, *The Trial of the Incredible Hulk,* directed by Bill Bixby and introducing still another Marvel comic book hero, Daredevil (played by Rex Smith). ■

**INCREDIBLE SUNDAY** **(see *That's Incredible*)**

**THE INNER SANCTUM (**) 30 min (39ep B&W; 1954 Syndication) Suspense Anthology** *with Paul McGrath as Mr. Raymond*

*The Inner Sanctum,* one of network radio's best mystery series, is turned into an undistinguished anthology for TV. Paul McGrath, who narrated the show for a while on radio, serves as the unseen host and narrator, Mr. Raymond. The show's trademark squeaky door is not as spooky as it was on radio.

**THE INNES BOOK OF RECORDS (**½) 30 min (12ep Color; 1981–1982 UK BBC) Musical-Variety** *with Neil Innes*

Neil Innes is the one who created the musical identity for that dead-on 1977 Beatles spoof, The Rutles. He cut his teeth on musical and media parody in the 1960s as part of the Bonzo Dog Band, appearing in the Beatles' made-for-TV special "Magical Mystery Tour" and scoring an international hit in 1968 with the Paul McCartney-produced song "I'm the Urban Spaceman." Though not one of the formal members of Monty Python, he has worked frequently with the troupe on a variety of British projects, and even joined them onstage for their various U.S. concert appearances. In 1976, he collaborated with Eric Idle on the *Rutland Weekend Television* series (where the Rutles first took root), at last getting his own short-lived "solo" showcase in 1981. Through it all, his humor alternates between broad exaggeration (such as walking across stage wearing shoes with heels more than a foot high) and very, very dry and deadpan (some of his musical parodies are so polished and close to the source that they could pass for the originals). For some, an acquired taste. For others, the absolute master of his genre. There's also a record of musical selections from the series, but it has only been released in Britain.

## THE INNOCENT AND THE DAMNED (see *Aspen*)

## THE INSIDERS (*) 60 min (13ep Color; 1985–1986 ABC) Crime Drama *with Nicholas Campbell as Nick Fox, Stoney Jackson as James Mackey, and Gail Strickland as Alice West*

Nick Fox and James Mackey are two more handsome hunks who battle the forces of evil in the bottomless pit of crime in and around Los Angeles. Nick, the blonde white guy, is a freelance magazine writer looking for hot stories. James is his duded-up ex-con black pal.

## INSPECTOR MORSE (***) 60 min (12ep at Fall 1988 Color; 1987– UK Central) Mystery *with John Thaw as Chief Inspector Morse, Kevin Whately as Det. Sergeant Lewis, and Peter Woodthrope as Max*

Chief Inspector Morse is based in the English university town of Oxford, where he enjoys crossword puzzles, Thomas Hardy novels, Mozart, and "real ale" (sometimes to near excess). He's a paunchy middle-age bachelor with a steadfast and stubborn manner, little patience for the idle rich, and a caustic deadpan delivery. Morse is also the man called in for some of the homicide department's toughest cases.

This series has a touch of *Columbo* to it, with Morse (like the American lieutenant, his rank seems to be his first name) doggedly peppering each suspect with question after question as part of his "inspirational methodology." However, unlike the *Columbo* series, we don't know who the guilty party is from the beginning and, frankly, it's obvious Morse usually doesn't either. But that's fine because it's fun to see a detective character who really seems to have to work at it, without the apparent cocksure certainty of other British investigators like Sherlock Holmes or Miss Marple.

Besides, Morse knows his methods work—they just take a while. He believes in deductions, not theories, looking at his growing stockpile of facts, grabbing another pint, and continuing to dig, knowing that eventually the clues will all fall into place. Ironically, sometimes that last flash of inspiration comes from an inadvertent remark or action by his faithful young assistant, Sergeant Lewis, who is often the target of Morse's cutting remarks because of his naivete and inexperience.

This is clearly a character showcase series, with John Thaw's portrayal of Morse refreshingly grumpy, even nasty. (Not surprisingly, Thaw's previous major television role is that of the hard-bitten Inspector Regan on *The Sweeney*, a mid-1970s British cop show.) Most cases in the *Inspector Morse* series last for two episodes. The show first aired in the United States on *Mystery!*, beginning in 1988.

## INTERNATIONAL DETECTIVE (**) 30 min (39ep B&W, 1959–1960 Syndication) Detective Drama *with Art Fleming as Ken Franklin*

Art Fleming, then known as Arthur Fleming and later known as the host of the game show *Jeopardy* in the 1960s, plays Ken Franklin, the chief detective for the William J. Burns Detective Agency. As you might guess from the show's title, Franklin's work takes him to various countries. The series is filmed mostly in England.

## THE INTERNS (*½) 60 min (24ep Color; 1970–1971 CBS) Medical Drama *with Broderick Crawford as Dr. Peter Goldstone, Mike Farrell as Dr. Sam Marsh, Stephen Brooks as Dr. Greg Pettit, Christopher Stone as Dr. Pooch Hardin, Hal Frederick as Dr. Cal Barrin, Sandra Smith as Dr. Lydia Thorpe, Elaine Giftos as Bobbe Marsh, and Skip Homeier as Dr. Hugh Jacoby*

One of those early 1970s efforts swimming in television social relevancy. This one is decked out in good intentions and pseudo hipness, right down to its carefully mixed lineup of dedicated young interns (including one black man, one woman, a young married man, and a couple of bachelors). Naturally they receive expert guidance from their semiobligatory father figure, played by crusty Broderick Crawford. With solid scripts and a sense of perspective, this series would have been a good effort. Unfortunately it has neither. But you may want to tune in for part of one episode just to see a post–Highway Patrol Crawford, a post–*Dan Raven* Skip Homeier, and a pre–*M*A*S*H* Mike Farrell.

## INTERPOL CALLING (**) 30 min (39ep B&W; 1960 Syndication) Police Drama *with Charles Korvin as Paul Duval*

Paul Duval is the chief inspector for Interpol, an international police organization that tracks down miscreants all over the planet.

**THE INVADERS** (***) **60 min (43ep Color; 1967–1968 ABC) Science Fiction** *with Roy Thinnes as David Vincent and Kent Smith as Edgar Scoville*

The primary theme that runs through the best of the 1950s black and white grade B science fiction movies is paranoia. In the original versions of *Invasion of the Body Snatchers* and *Invasion from Mars,* the fear of realizing that the enemy is not just coming but is amongst us and may *be* us perfectly matched the rabid anti-Communist hysteria sweeping the country in the early Eisenhower era. By the late 1960s, the anti-Red phobia had mostly subsided, but *The Invaders* captures that old theme of finding the enemy in our midst better than any other TV series since the anti-Communist classic *I Led Three Lives.*

*The Invaders* deals with aliens from outer space, not from behind the Iron Curtain. David Vincent, a respectable, well-educated architect, spots a huge UFO disgorging aliens one night when he takes the proverbial wrong turn on a country road. These aliens, Vincent learns, have come to Earth in order to take over and colonize the planet, since their home world is dying. The aliens have taken human form, but they usually can be detected by a bent pinky finger. The aliens also have no heartbeat (since they have no heart) and, when they die, their bodies evaporate, leaving no trace.

Vincent leaves architecture aside and devotes his life to uncovering aliens and to alerting a skeptical world to the danger from outer space. Most citizens, naturally, think Vincent is another kook, like those who populate the talk shows claiming close encounters with men from Mars. Vincent never seems to get his hands on any real proof, at least not long enough to show anyone important. The aliens avoid killing him, out of fear that his death might lend credence to his warnings. Still they keep a close eye on Vincent and do their best to thwart his efforts.

The paranoia element in *The Invaders* that best fits the late 1960s is the fact that the aliens have infiltrated various high governmental and big business positions. This leaves Vincent always unsure of who he can trust in trying to unmask the enemy. Coming from the late 1960s when large numbers of Americans began to distrust the leaders of society for the first time, both in the public and private sector, *The Invaders* fits into this mind-set perfectly.

Producer Quinn Martin (famous for other stylized, docudrama-ish series such as *The Untouchables, The F.B.I.,* and *The Fugitive*) brought several trademarks to *The Invaders.* William Conrad, who provided the deep doomsday narration for *The Fugitive* also serves as narrator on *The Invaders.* Each of the hour show's four segments are labeled as separate acts (with an epilogue at the end). The theme music is lively, distinctive, and appropriate. The acting is top-notch and famous guest stars abound.

The problem with *The Invaders* is that the premise sets up a no-win situation. If Vincent convinces the world of the alien invasion, the show ends. Yet there are only so many ways to try to warn people. Later episodes add more elements of *The Fugitive* by focusing on Vincent as a man on the run, who meets up with interesting people on the road. This tends to serve as a distraction from the alien element that is the central reason for the show's existence. Thinnes does seem like a understudy for *The Fugitive*'s David Janssen, in that Thinnes is rugged yet sensitive and fairly tight-lipped.

Halfway through the series' run, some help arrives in the form of Edgar Scoville, a big business tycoon who believes Vincent's story and does his best to help. This winds up hurting the show, because Vincent is best as the lone man warning the world, not some hotshot executive reporting to the boss each week. Besides, with his aloof coolness, Scoville seems too much like the aliens who have infiltrated big business, and you keep waiting for Scoville to show his bent pinky.

Unlike *The Fugitive,* no climactic final episode of *The Invaders* was ever produced. It would be nice to see Vincent triumph and hit the TV talk show circuit, putting all those other UFO authors out of business. ■

**THE INVESTIGATORS** (*) **60 min (13ep B&W; 1961 CBS) Detective Drama** *with James Franciscus as Russ Andrews, James Philbrook as Steve Banks, Al Austin as Bill Davis, and Mary Murphy as Maggie Peters*

*The Investigators* concerns three insurance investigators in and around New York City. Tune in for each episode as they check up on fraudulent insurance claims. Sound terribly exciting? Not really.

James Franciscus is the only high point here, as he makes the transition from the cop of *Naked City* to the goody-two-shoes teacher in *Mr. Novak.*

**THE INVISIBLE MAN** (**) **30 min (26ep B&W; 1958–1959 UK ATV) Science Fiction** *with Jim Turner as Dr. Peter Brady, Lisa Daniely as Diane Brady, Deborah Watling as Sally Brady, and Ernest Clark as Sir Charles*

A young British scientist, Peter Brady, finds himself turned permanently invisible during some experimental work. Though he immediately begins efforts to find a way to reverse the process, he decides not to waste his new talent in the meantime. Ever a solid citizen, Brady offers to help British intelligence with some of its more puzzling or ticklish espionage efforts throughout Europe. In his travels, he usually walks around wearing gloves with his head wrapped in bandages, items quickly discarded when he needs to use his invisibility. Better than you'd expect, and closer in spirit to the original H.G. Wells novel, *The Invisible Man,* than just about any other attempt at the gimmick premise. No doubt this was due to the skills of series producer Ralph Smart and his writing team, several of whom came along for Smart's next espionage series, *Danger Man* (with Patrick McGoohan).

And in the footnotes to history department: Throughout the entire run of this series, the name of the performer playing Peter Brady was never revealed. Nor did it slip out for about twenty-five years afterward. But in the 1980s, British writers Leslie Halliwell and Philip Purser got the scoop and unmasked the Invisible Man as . . . Jim Turner! (Who?) Actually it was more fun not knowing.

**THE INVISIBLE MAN (*½) 60 min (13ep & 90 min pilot Color; 1975–1976 NBC) Adventure** *with David McCallum as Dr. Daniel Westin, Craig Stevens as Walter Carlson, and Melinda Fee as Dr. Kate Westin*

It's a long way from the original H. G. Wells story to this TV show, but the concept of an invisible human is always good for another run-through. David McCallum, in his first (and so far only) American TV series after *The Man from U.N.C.L.E.,* is Dr. Daniel Westin, the noble scientist who discovers the formula for invisibility. Westin ingests the serum and runs off with the formula when the bad bureaucrats in the Army want to use the invention for nasty military purposes. The problem is that Westin never found out how to become *visible* again, so he has a *very* lifelike mask of his face made up in order to operate in everyday society. While avoiding Uncle Sam, Dr. Westin works on sensitive security missions for a shadowy organization. Whenever he needs to vanish, Westin takes off his mask and clothes.

Harve Bennett, of the equally 1970s high-tech *The Six Million Dollar Man* and *The Bionic Woman,* produces this interesting but somewhat plodding series. The 1975 pilot has Jackie Cooper in the role of Walter Carlson, Westin's boss.

**THE IRISH R. M. (**½) 60 min (13ep Color; 1983–1984 UK C4) Drama** *with Peter Bowles as Sinclair Yeates, Doran Godwin as Philippa Yeates, Bryan Murray as "Flurry" Knox, Lise-Ann McLaughlin as Sally, and Beryl Reid as Mrs. Knox*

This light comic drama is set in the Irish countryside, circa 1900, when the area was still under clear and undisputed British rule. Peter Bowles (veteran of such comedies as *To the Manor Born*) takes the title role of Sinclair Yeates, a proper British major who resigns his army commission to become a local British resident magistrate (legal arbiter) in Ireland. He arrives ready to administer the law of the land without a hitch, but soon discovers that the bucolic setting hides a whole world of passionate personal interests tied up in seemingly innocuous matters of dispute—often over animals (horses, foxes, and such).

Though not as delightfully mannered as *Rumpole of the Bailey* or as down-home sincere as *All Creatures Great and Small, The Irish R. M.* does manage to tap some of the potential charm from its setting, especially in the sequences featuring the occasionally gullible Yeates in over his head without knowing it. (He has to be especially alert when dealing with Flurry, the landlord of his country home.) Adapted from an 1899 book *Some Experiences of an Irish R. M.,* co-authored by Martin Ross (pseudonym of Edith Somerville) and Violet Florence Martin.

**IRON HORSE (*½) 60 min (47ep Color; 1966–1968 ABC) Western** *with Dale Robertson as Ben Calhoun, Gary Collins as Dave Tarrant, Bob Random as Barnabas Rogers, and Ellen Burstyn (then known as Ellen McRae) as Julie Parsons*

Ben Calhoun is the proverbial western roving gambler/playboy who wins a decrepit railroad in a high-stakes poker game. He spends the rest of this easy-to-ignore series trying to make the trains run on time. Calhoun is one of the few western TV heroes with a pet raccoon (named Ulysses).

Star Dale Robertson was better, and had more to work with, in *Tales of Wells Fargo.*

**IRONSIDE (**½) 60 min (198ep & 2 hr pilot Color; 1967–1975 NBC) Police Drama** *with Raymond Burr as Robert Ironside, Don Galloway as Ed Brown, Barbara Anderson as Eve Whitfield, Don Mitchell as Mark Sanger, and Elizabeth Baur as Fran Belding*

Raymond Burr was a bit hard to warm up to when he played Perry Mason, the know-it-all lawyer who never seemed to lose a case. He is even harder to like as Robert Ironside, one of the grouchiest, snarliest, good guys you will bump into on TV reruns. Ironside has a good reason to be grouchy. After clawing his way through the ranks to become chief of detectives in the San Francisco police department, he is nearly killed by a would-be assassin's bullet while on a rare vacation. He is left crippled for life, confined to a wheelchair. Rather than collect disability payments, Ironside bullies his way into being appointed as a special consultant to the force who literally lives in police headquarters. Assisted by clean-cut Sgt. Ed Brown and comely Sgt. Eve Whitfield, Ironside carries on his war against crime, roaming the city in a customized van. Black ex-street punk Mark Sanger, now following the straight and narrow, serves as Ironside's "legs."

Ironside was grouchy before he was shot and he is twice as grouchy afterward. He is forever frustrated by his inability to do everything he could do before, and by the inability of the rest of the world to be as smart as he is and figure out the crimes that he is solving. Oh, Ironside means well, and there are times he softens up and tells his trio of helpers that he appreciates them, but mostly *Ironside* is a lot of listening to Raymond Burr grumble about something or other.

*Ironside* has a lot of mid-1960s feel to it. Eve Whitfield represents the emerging new woman, who is liberated enough to work for the police, but is still not taken completely seriously by anyone. Mark Sanger is a young version of Sidney Poitier, in that he is too good to be true, a common problem with the way blacks were portrayed in the 1960s. Sanger is supposed to have been a juvenile delinquent, but he is so polite and well mannered that you would think he went to prep school. As the series progresses, he even manages to squeeze law school into his busy schedule and becomes a lawyer by the time the series ends.

*Ironside* is full of good, solid, police action. The characters are interesting and the premise is novel. After a few seasons, however, the policeman in a wheelchair motif wears thin and the series loses steam about the time Eve Whitfield disappears (when actress Barbara Anderson left the show after a contract dispute). For the last four seasons, policewoman Fran Belding carries on in Eve's place.

Try to catch the well-written two-hour pilot episode, where Ironside is gunned down. After seeing the portly Burr waddling around before he is shot, you will know why the producers chose to have him sit out the rest of the series in a chair.

Finally, it seems much too cute to have Burr's character named Ironside even *before* he is confined to a wheelchair. It is almost as if he was destined to be crippled. Obviously, "ironside" also connotes a tough exterior, but few policemen outside of the Dick Tracy comics wind up with given names that define their personality. Ironside should have been the character's nickname.

**THE ISLANDERS (*½) 60 min (24ep B&W; 1960–1961 ABC) Adventure** *with William Reynolds as Sandy Wade, James Philbrook as Zack Malloy, and Diane Brewster as Wilhelmina "Steamboat Willie" Vandeveer*

A frothy early 1960s exotic adventure show, *The Islanders* concerns a one-plane airline in the Spice Islands of the East Indies. Sandy and Zack are the two pilots, while shapely Steamboat Willie is the wily business manager who looks out mostly for herself. On a rainy Sunday afternoon, *The Islanders* could prove mildly entertaining.

**IT TAKES A THIEF (***) 60 min (65ep & 90 min pilot Color; 1968–1970 ABC) Adventure** *with Robert Wagner as Alexander Mundy, Fred Astaire as Alister Mundy, Malachi Throne as Noah Bain, and Edward Binns as Wallie Powers*

"Let me get this straight—you *want* me to steal?" That's the amazed reaction of professional thief Alexander Mundy to an offer from the SIA, a covert U.S. government spy agency. Ordinarily Mundy might have dismissed it out of hand, but the government pitches it when he's at somewhat of a disadvantage: he's sitting in jail. So Mundy agrees to use his considerable skills and charms on government-sponsored cases—in exchange for limited freedom (he's under house confinement between jobs).

After about a year of this, Mundy's father, Alister, negotiates a much better deal: complete freedom as a free agent, able to come and go as he pleases. Obviously, Alister (himself an experienced international thief) understands exactly how covert government agencies work and how much they're willing to pay their players, even ex-cons.

Of course, this elaborate premise is just an excuse to put Robert Wagner in some lovely European settings for some chic international intrigue, reminiscent of Cary Grant in the classic jewel thief film *To Catch a Thief.* Wagner is perfect for the part, handling it with wit, style, and charm. The setup is even more fun when Fred Astaire makes occasional appearances as Mundy's father. Wagner and Astaire play off each other perfectly in some delightfully complicated capers. One of the best ("The Second Time Around") involves the simultaneous theft of a roomful of solid gold bars by Alexander while Alister takes care of the casino action downstairs.

Twenty years later, as a sign of changing perceptions, perhaps the most surprising thing about *It Takes a Thief* is that Mundy was taken aback by the SIA offer to hire a convicted criminal. Nowadays, he'd not only expect it but he'd probably demand a much better deal, including retention of all book and film rights.

**IT TAKES TWO (**) 30 min (22ep Color; 1982–1983 ABC) Situation Comedy** *with Richard Crenna as Dr. Sam Quinn, Patty Duke Astin as Molly Quinn, Helen Hunt as Lisa Quinn, Anthony Edwards as Andy Quinn, Billie Bird as Anna "Mama," Richard McKenzie as Walter Chaiken, and Della Reese as Judge Caroline Phillips*

The *Soap* production team of Susan Harris, Paul Junger Witt, and Tony Thomas team up in *It Takes Two,* a mild sitcom about the modern problems of a two-earner couple. Sam Quinn is a top Chicago surgeon. Wife Molly, after raising two kids, went to law school and is now an assistant D. A. They work so darn hard that all they have time to do is trade witty bon mots with each other.

Considering the top level of acting here (Richard Crenna and Patty Duke Astin have long resumes in good TV shows), *It Takes Two* should be better than it is. As it is, the scripts are just average and the tone is a bit stilted. Sam and Molly Quinn seem more like mouthpieces for jokes than a real couple.

**IT'S A GREAT LIFE (**) 30 min (78ep B&W; 1954–1956 NBC) Situation Comedy** *with Michael O'Shea as Denny David, William Bishop as Steve Connors, James Dunn as Uncle Earl, Frances Bavier as Amy Morgan, and Barbara Bates as Kathy Morgan*

Two swinging single ex-GIs come to sunny southern California to find fame, fortune, and fun. Since it's the mid-1950s, they wind up living not in a condo but in a boarding house run by a kindly widow who has a wiseguy live-in brother and a cute daughter.

This is the first TV series appearance of Frances Bavier, and she is already playing the spinster type, a role she continued on *The Andy Griffith Show* as Aunt Bee.

**IT'S A LIVING/MAKING A LIVING (***) 30 min (120ep Color; 1980–1982 & 1985–1989 ABC & Syndication) Situation Comedy** *with Marian Mercer as Nancy Beebe, Ann Jillian as Cassie Cranston, Susan Sullivan as Lois Adams, Gail Edwards as Dot Higgins, Barrie Youngfellow as Jan Hoffmeyer, Paul Kreppel as Sonny Mann, Louise Lasser as Maggie McBurney, Crystal Bernard as Amy Tompkins, Richard Kline as Richie Gray, Richard Stahl as Howard Miller, and Sheryl Lee Ralph as Ginger St. James*

Set in the Above the Top restaurant, a swank eatery in Los Angeles, *It's a Living* focuses on the largely female staff of the joint. While sex and sexiness is a prime topic and concern, *It's a Living* rarely degenerates into titillation or smarminess. The waitresses represent a fair cross section of young female America (TV style) and there are numerous cast changes as the series goes on, much as waitresses frequently change in real restaurants.

The two stand-outs in the cast are Marian Mercer as the nasty, yet vulnerable, maitre d', and Ann Jillian, as the bold and brassy blonde. Paul Kreppel is funny but very obvious as Sonny Mann, the self-absorbed lounge piano player. The characterizations are rather broad, as is typical in shows produced by Paul Junger Witt and Tony Thomas (two-thirds of the producers of *Soap*).

After the first fourteen episodes, the title of this series changes to *Making a Living* for fifteen episodes and then reverts to its original in new episodes produced for syndication.

**IT'S A MAN'S WORLD (**) 60 min (19ep B&W; 1962–1963 NBC) Comedy Drama** *with Glenn Corbett as Wes Macauley, Ted Bessell as Tom-Tom DeWitt, Randy Boone as Vern Hodges, and Mike Burns as Howie Macauley*

Some good-lookin' guys sharing a houseboat look at life in Ohio—at least the part that can be seen while docked at the college town of Cordella. There's Tom-Tom and Wes, who attend the nearby college; Wes's kid brother, Howie; and Vern, a free-spirited guitarist. For them, it's truly a man's dream world in the most carefree time of their lives. Of course, in a later decade, this setting (especially in the hands of hack relevant comedy writers) would definitely have evolved into something embarrassingly topical—with hip jargon and significant issues lurking around every river bend. But in the early 1960s, it's a quite disposable yet safe stage for some occasionally silly college high jinks stories. The three faces you want to catch are Corbett (who went right from here to *Route 66* as Linc Case, the substitute for George Maharis's Bud), Bessell (boyfriend of Marlo Thomas on *That Girl*), and Boone (who took his guitar-strumming characterization onto *The Virginian* the very next season).

**IT'S ABOUT TIME (zero) 30 min (26ep Color; 1966–1967 CBS) Situation Comedy** *with Jack Mullaney as Hector, Frank Aletter as Mac, Imogene Coca as Shad, and Joe E. Ross as Gronk*

This may not be the *worst* sitcom in TV history, but any fair observer must concede that it belongs in the bottom ten. Like any contender for the dubious honor of worst show ever, *It's About Time* has an extraordinarily contrived premise. Hector and Mac, two clean-cut American astronauts, run into space turbulence while testing their newfangled rocket and are accidentally sent back in time. Stranded in the Stone Age, they are befriended by a group of prehistoric Neanderthals who live in caves.

So you can see from the start we are not talking cinema-verite documentary here. Still, other TV shows with premises just as stupid have managed to be funny. What sets *It's About Time* apart from other sitcoms is its moronic level of humor. There are possibilities here, with the twentieth-century astronauts trying to cope with the cavemen and vice versa, but only the easiest, most obvious, jokes are trotted out. Worse yet, the two astronauts are not interesting at all. In fact, they both tend to be sour and unlikable.

The Neanderthals are not much better. Joe E. Ross (Sgt. Rupert Ritzik in the Sgt. Bilko series and Officer Gunther Toody in *Car 54, Where Are You?*) plays Gronk, one of the cavemen. The problem is that Ross plays all three of his famous characters, Ritzik, Toody, and Gronk, pretty much the same way and there is nothing very funny about any of them. Ross's patented laugh line of "oooh, oooh, oooh" becomes annoying almost immediately. Imogene Coca, who plays Gronk's wife Shad, gives the show what little life it has, but she is constantly dragged down to the sorry level of humor that permeates the show. Coca played characters just as silly druing her collaboration with Sid Caesar, but at least in *Your Show of Shows* the silly characters were meant to be satirical. In *It's About Time,* the audience laughs *at* the show, not with it.

To be fair, the producers recognized that this show stank and tried to make it better. Halfway through its run, a complete format change occurs. The astronauts fix their ship and return to the twentieth century, with two stowaways, Gronk and Shad. Now tables are turned and it is the two Neanderthals who must adapt to a strange new world. In this permutation, without the ridiculous Stone Age trappings, *It's About Time* rises to the level of a mediocre sitcom, sort of like *I Dream of Jeannie* on one of its bad days. This slight improvement probably keeps *It's About Time* from winning the "worst sitcom ever" award.

The series does have a very catchy theme song, with lyrics written by its producer, Sherwood Schwartz. He seems to have a golden touch with tunes, as Schwartz also penned the words to the theme for his best-known series, *Gilligan's Island*. Too bad that golden touch didn't extend beyond the theme songs in either show.

**IT'S GARRY SHANDLING'S SHOW** **(***) 30 min (54ep at Fall 1989 Color; 1986– Showtime) Situation Comedy** *with Garry Shandling as himself, Molly Cheek as Nancy Bancroft, Michael Tucci as Pete Schumaker, Bernadette Birkett as Jackie Schumaker, and Scott Nemes as Grant Schumaker*

If you can imagine a young Jimmy Carter with a stylish perm haircut, you have an idea of what Garry Shandling looks like. In his first TV series, and just about the first regular comedy series on cable TV to garner any degree of popularity, Shandling manages to update TV sitcoms by bringing them back to their roots.

At the heart of *It's Garry Shandling's Show* is the concept of constantly alluding to the fact that everybody on the program, especially Garry, knows that they are working on a TV show. Characters will therefore refer to earlier scenes they "watched" on the TV monitor. Garry will address the TV audience at home directly or walk off the stage and deal with the technicians taping the program or the studio audience. On top of that, the events on the program are supposed to be actually occurring to Garry and his friends. The result is an exciting mix of standard sitcom fare with offbeat directing that livens up what could otherwise be mundane.

Shandling's opening monologues and asides to the home viewers are strongly reminiscent of the old *Burns & Allen* show, where George Burns would keep up with events offstage by watching them on TV, and then talk directly to the home viewer. What Shandling does is take this fun concept and update it for the 1980s. Shandling is forever playing the good-natured schmuck, a fellow always yearning for romance but racked with enough self-doubt to torpedo any serious relationship. Much like *The Honeymooners,* the plots here tend to take place chiefly on one set, Garry's living room, where his friends and neighbors are always dropping by.

Shandling can get a little whiny at times, but the frequent novel directions the show takes make up for that. One episode is a cute tip of the hat to *The Fugitive,* with Garry's friend Nancy bringing over an old pal named Dr. Richard Kimble (looking nothing like David Janssen). Ever the ardent TV watcher, Garry is convinced this guy must be an escaped murderer, and it turns out the doctor *is* on the run. Garry and Nancy unsuccessfully try to help the man escape the police, but find out at the end that the doctor *is* guilty—in fact, he has only one arm, just like the infamous one-armed man David Janssen looked for so assiduously in *The Fugitive.*

**IT'S NOT EASY** **(*½) 30 min (7ep Color; 1983 ABC) Situation Comedy** *with Ken Howard as Jack Long, Jayne Meadows as Ruth Long, Rachael Jacobs as Carol Long, Evan Cohen as Johnny Long, Bert Convy as Neal Townsend, and Carlene Watkins as Sharon Long Townsend*

Ken Howard (*The White Shadow*) stars in this formula TV sitcom that comes with a highly contrived but catchy concept that tries real hard to be trendy. The result is failure, in spite of a good cast. The story involves Jack Long, who has divorced Sharon Long. Sharon has since remarried, with Neal Townsend as her new hubby. Jack and Sharon have two kids, Carol and Johnny. To solve the problem of who will have custody, Jack and Sharon decide to live across the street from each other. Jack lives with his nagging mother Ruth. Sharon lives with Neal, who is as confused as the audience is by this situation.

**IT'S YOUR MOVE** **(*½) 30 min (18ep Color; 1984–1985 NBC) Situation Comedy** *with Jason Bateman as Matthew Burton, David Garrison as Norman Lamb, Caren Kaye as Eileen Burton, and Tricia Cast as Julie Burton*

Jason Bateman, brother of *Family Ties* star Justine Bateman, plays a smart-aleck kid (Matthew) who bosses his widowed mother (Eileen) and pesters his older sister (Julie) in this mildly annoying series. Matthew's made-to-order situation is disrupted when a struggling writer (Norman), who begins dating Eileen, sees through all of the youngster's stratagems.

**IVAN THE TERRIBLE** **(**) 30 min (5ep Color; 1976 CBS) Situation Comedy** *with Lou Jacobi as Ivan Petrovsky, Maria Karnilova as Olga Petrovsky, Phil Leeds as Vladimir, and Manuel Martinez as Raoul Sanchez*

*Ivan the Terrible* is not terrible, but it's not very good either. The show does deserve praise, however, for its wildly offbeat premise. This show is apparently the one and only series in American TV history (so far) set in Moscow. More particularly, the setting is the very cramped three-and-a-half bedroom Petrovsky apartment that has nine people living in it. The focus of the show is Ivan, the head waiter at Moscow's swankiest hotel, the Metropole. This position of august power does little for Ivan's ranking at home, where he is constantly outvoted, outshouted, and outmaneuvered by his wife Olga, their three children, Olga's mother and first husband, Ivan's daughter-in-law, a Cuban exchange student, and even Ivan's dog Rasputin.

*Ivan the Terrible* takes virtually all the standard American TV family sitcom concepts and transplants them, hardly changed, to a Moscow setting, while at the same time working in every Russian stereotype imaginable (right down to the "catchy" title). Alan King, popular stand-up comedian from the Ed Sullivan days, is the executive producer of *Ivan the Terrible,* which explains a lot of the funny but corny jokes on the show.

**IVANHOE** (**½) **30 min (39ep B&W; 1957–1958 Syndication) Adventure** *with Roger Moore as Ivanhoe, Bruce Seton as King Richard, Robert Brown as Gurth, and John Pike as Bart*

Roger Moore, the one-time James Bond, makes his first TV series appearance in this British-produced program. Moore plays Ivanhoe, a chivalrous knight in medieval England. The character comes from Sir Walter Scott's venerable novel.

**J. J. STARBUCK** (**) **60 min (14ep Color; 1987–1988 NBC) Detective Drama** *with Dale Robertson as J. J. Starbuck and Ben Vereen as E. L. Turner*

At first glance, this is a bit like Columbo played by McCloud, with Dale Robertson (the lead in the 1950s western *Tales of Wells Fargo*) in the title role of the gregarious and ingratiating private eye. The major difference: As an eccentric Texas millionaire, J. J. Starbuck really is doing this just for the hell of it. About halfway through, producer Stephen J. Cannell pumps some extra life into the premise, bringing in Ben Vereen as E. L. Turner, a character from one of his previous series, *Tenspeed and Brownshoe* (which had flashed briefly for ABC in 1980). Not a bad combination, but also short-lived.

**JACK AND MIKE** (*) **60 min (9ep & 90 min pilot Color; 1986–1987 ABC) Drama** *with Shelley Hack as Jackie "Jack" Shea, Tom Mason as Mike Brennan, and Kevin Dunn as Anthony Kubacek*

This pretentious show about Yuppie angst is a must to avoid. Jack and Mike are a couple of young, urban professionals in Chicago (she is a controversial newspaper columnist; he is a restaurant entrepreneur) who are married, but, gee, their jobs are just so danged exciting, they never have time for a snuggle in front of the tube, unless one calls the other and makes an appointment.

Former model Shelley Hack gets to show more acting skill here than she did as replacement for Farrah Fawcett on *Charlie's Angels.* Still, both her character and that of saxophone-playing husband are too trendy for their own good. David Gerber, the executive producer of *Jack and Mike,* should have stuck with cop shows, where he scored with *Police Story.*

**THE JACK BENNY PROGRAM** (***½) **30 min (343ep B&W; 1950–1965 CBS & NBC) Situation Comedy** *with Jack Benny, Don Wilson, Eddie "Rochester" Anderson, and Dennis Day as themselves*

In the early 1950s, Jack Benny made a smooth transition from network radio to network television and, like so many other comedy-variety stars in the 1950s, he thrived in the new medium. But unlike most of them, his shows hold up pretty well today, because most of the time his programs are not really pure variety shows—they are situation comedies about Jack Benny. The situation? Why, putting on a variety show.

Benny had used the one step removed from reality approach on radio during the 1930s and 1940s, giving his entire crew the chance to develop their performing characters as well as variety show talent. So listeners got to know them all as part of Jack Benny's fictionalized daily life, from the booming voice of announcer Don Wilson, to the sharp-tongued raspiness of valet Rochester, to the high-pitched innocence of singer Dennis Day. Jack's real-life wife, Mary Livingston, was also there, along with the man of a thousand voices, Mel Blanc (who did such characters as Benny's frustrated violin teacher and his sputtering old Maxwell automobile). Most important was the character of Jack Benny himself—with a comic persona of stinginess (he kept his money in an underground vault beneath his home), vanity (forever insisting that he was only thirty-nine years old), and musical ineptness (screeching through his violin solos). Yet he was also quite vulnerable, often emerging as the helpless victim in his crazy world.

These characters sounded great on radio and work even better on television. There Benny adds his pained facial expressions when delivering his patented, exasperated catch phrases such as "Well!" or "Wait a minute! Wait a minute!" or "Now cut that out!" He wisely brings along virtually all of his successful radio characters and concepts, so viewers could see their favorites—his legendary vault, his portly announcer, his classic car. Best of all, Benny uses marvelously silly bits to connect everything (even some commercials), turning what could have been just routine variety sketches into a continuing visit to an absurd world.

Perhaps the main contemporary criticism of the series is that Jack Benny should have dispensed with the actual variety program he was hosting. In some episodes the show runs straight, complete with dated musical guests, opening monologue, and typical variety show stunts.

Otherwise *The Jack Benny Show* is a resilient program and one of those seminal series widely admired by generations of viewers, writers, and performers. You can see stylistic touches still being embraced decades later. For the best example of how the idea works in the 1980s, catch an episode of *It's Garry Shandling's Show.* ■

**JACK LONDON'S TALES OF THE KLONDIKE** **(see *Tales of the Kondike*)**

**JACK THE RIPPER** (*½) **60 min (6ep Color; 1973 Syndication) Drama** *with Sebastian Cabot as host, Alan Stratford-Johns as Det. Jack Barlow, and Frank Windsor as Det. Frank Windsor*

Fascination with the story of nineteenth century London murderer Jack the Ripper never ends (nor will it ever be cleared up). Add to the dramatized histories this adequate 1973 fictional investigation, set in the 1880s. In the 1980s, Michael Caine appeared in a multipart TV movie, covering much the same territory. Though it's unlikely anyone will ever succeed in this "Search for Historic Jack," that certainly won't keep many more from mining this territory.

**THE JACKIE GLEASON SHOW (***) 60 min (B&W & Color; 1952–1955, 1956–1957, 1962–1970 CBS) Comedy-Variety** *with Jackie Gleason, Frank Fontaine, and Sammy Spear and His Orchestra*

*The Honeymooners* will always stand as Jackie Gleason's crowning achievement on television, but *The Honeymooners* was almost always presented as part of Gleason's hour-long variety series, *The Jackie Gleason Show,* which aired on network TV off and on between 1952 and 1970. The 1950s episodes of the Gleason variety hour were all performed live and preserved only on fair-quality kinescopes. The 1960s episodes were produced on video tape, and the final four years are in color.

Keep in mind when watching the 1960s version of *The Jackie Gleason Show* that *The Honeymooners* will not show up as a sketch for the first four of the eight seasons. The format is the "American Scene Magazine," a loosely structured variety potpourri, all *very* loosely tied together by topics dealing with the American scene. This variety show consists of Gleason's familiar characters (developed throughout his earlier stage and TV career) plus a few new ones and lots of music, singing, and dancing.

Among the familiar characters are the Poor Soul, Reginald Van Gleason III, and Joe the Bartender. The Poor Soul is Gleason paying homage to Marcel Marceau and Charlie Chaplin. A silent, unassuming type dressed in simple threads, the Poor Soul wants nothing more out of life than to be kind to others and to go his own way. In skits, he keeps running into others who complicate his life, get him in trouble, and take advantage of his naivete. The Poor Soul skits are sometimes sappy, but they tend to be surprisingly touching, and fairly amusing as well.

Reginald Van Gleason III is one of Gleason's earliest creations and quite a switch from Gleason's best-known character, Ralph Kramden, of *The Honeymooners.* "Reggie," a top-hatted, tuxedoed, cane-bearing aristocrat, appears to be everything Kramden is not, such as rich, sophisticated, and debonair. However, Reggie and Ralph share more in common than either would care to admit. Reggie may be wealthy, but he is still a boastful braggart, just like Ralph. Reggie considers himself a smooth operator, but he winds up being a clumsy oaf more times than not, just like Ralph. The chief difference between these two Gleason characters is that Reggie knows when to remain silent (something Ralph does *not*), demonstrating again (as with the Poor Soul) Gleason's love for pantomime. Reggie can say a lot with his swagger, his twitching moustache, and arching eyebrows without ever opening his mouth. Just watching the overdressed Reggie prance into a room, with the band playing his overbombastic theme music, is worth several laughs.

Joe the Bartender is the character who appears most frequently during the "American Scene Magazine" format of the 1960s Gleason show. Taken directly from Gleason's Brooklyn youth, Joe is a straight-talking regular bloke who will bend your ear with topical tales of local doings or national news. Joe talks to the TV camera directly, as if it were a patron named Mr. Dunahy, a regular at Joe's drinking establishment. After a few remarks, Joe usually calls out Crazy Guggenheim (Frank Fontaine), an idiot savant worker at the bar who switches from a ridiculous crazy dialect to a rich, deep baritone when asked to sing (the same trait Jim Nabors demonstrated when he stepped out of his Gomer Pyle voice). Crazy Guggenheim is an acquired taste, best described as a relic of the old days of vaudeville.

A Gleason show would not be a Gleason show without lots and lots of pretty girls to dress up the scenery. *The Jackie Gleason Show* has plenty of girls, from the multitalented June Taylor dancers to the pretty but pointless "Glea-Girls" such as "Christine Clam" (Barbara Heller). Another feature of the show is Gleason's easygoing opening monologue. Usually delivered while the "Great One" sips from a tea cup containing *some*thing strong ("Mmm, How sweet it is!"), the monologue will wrap up with Gleason's trademark line of "and *away* we go!"

At the start of the third season of the 1960s "The American Scene Magazine" format, the Gleason show leaves cold, gray New York for the sun and fun capital of the world, Miami Beach. After the fourth season, the "American Scene Magazine" concept vanishes and *The Honeymooners* once again becomes a recurring skit on Gleason's show (albeit briefly). Reunited with cohort Art Carney for the first time (on a regular basis) in nine years, Gleason and Carney step into their Ralph Kramden and Ed Norton roles, with new spouses. Sheila MacRae is the new Alice and Jane Kean is Ed's wife Trixie. Many of these *Honeymooners* bits run for most, if not all, of various episodes of the hour-long *Jackie Gleason Show,* and there is a large emphasis on musical and dance numbers absent from the more popular 1950s *Honeymooners* skits. These later *Honeymooners* episodes are the weakest. Gleason and Carney seem to be along for the ride, MacRae is simply adequate as Alice, and the musical numbers drag down what was always the prime appeal of the sketch, its gritty realism.

The 1960s *Jackie Gleason Show* is available in the form of 216 hour-long episodes, but is more likely to appear edited down to thirty-minute lengths. In 1979, one hundred of these half-hour highlights were released as *The Best of Jackie Gleason.* A less extensive series of 1960s highlights titled *The Best of Gleason* was released in 1988, comprising twenty-six half-hours and three two-hour specials.

Non-*Honeymooners* highlights of the 1950s Gleason series have been packaged as twenty-six half-hour episodes titled *Gleason: He's the Greatest.* The 1950s-era series features frequent appearances by two other Gleason characters, loud-mouthed braggart Charlie Bratton and clumsy and incompetent Rudy the repairman.

See *The Honeymooners* for a more complete discussion of that skit. ■

**THE JACKSONS (**½) 30 min (12ep Color; 1976–1977 CBS) Musical-Variety** *with Michael, Marlon, Randy, Jackie, Tito, Maureen "Rebbie", LaToya, and Janet Jackson*

Eight of the nine talented Jackson brothers and sisters appear in this variety show (the ninth, brother Jermaine, was already out on his own as a solo act and does not appear). Brother Michael is the de facto leader on *The Jacksons,* which was produced just before Michael went off on his own and became one of the biggest solo music acts of the 1980s. As with most variety shows of the 1970s, the nonmusical material on *The Jacksons* is shoddy, but being able to see Michael Jackson and his famous clan when they were all still fairly young is worth it.

**JAKE AND THE FATMAN (*½) 60 min (35ep at Fall 1989 & 2 hr pilot Color; 1987– CBS) Police Drama** *with William Conrad as Jason Lochinvar "Fatman" McCabe, Joe E. Penny as Jake Styles, and Alan Campbell as Derek Mitchell*

William Conrad has one of the great deep voices of our times (he served as the voice of Matt Dillon on the original radio version of *Gunsmoke* and narrated *Rocky and Bullwinkle* and *The Fugitive*), and he has overcome his large and somewhat dumpy build to star in a successful TV series of his own (*Cannon*). It's sad, therefore, to see him stoop to the level of *Jake and the Fatman.* Oh, Conrad's character on the show (a district attorney inelegantly, but all too correctly, dubbed the "Fatman") is not that much different from that of Frank Cannon. Both characters grumble a lot, do things their way, and manage to get their man in the end.

The problem with the character of the Fatman is that while Cannon was endearingly chunky, the Fatman is . . . well, just fat, and looks like an old wino to boot. It's a miracle the guy can move around at all, not to mention catch a thief. That, of course, is why there is Jake to help the Fatman out. Jake is some young, oily hotshot who works undercover to do the legwork that would result in an immediate massive coronary if the Fatman tried to rise from his torpor to duplicate the task. So since Jake looks like the kind of guy who will proposition your fourteen-year-old sister and the Fatman looks like he just got let out of the detox street mission, there isn't much chance you're going to get real involved with the characters in this show.

The setting of *Jake and the Fatman* shifts from flashy southern California to tropical Hawaii in the show's second season. Commendably enough, the Fatman sheds a few pounds on his way out to the island, and he no longer looks quite so grungy. Maybe the pair should look up Steve McGarrett and see if they can join his Five-O outfit.

**JAMES AT 15/16 (**½) 60 min (21ep & 2 hr pilot Color; 1977–1978 NBC) Drama** *with Lance Kerwin as James Hunter, Linden Chiles as Paul Hunter, Lynn Carlin as Joan Hunter, Kim Richards as Sandy Hunter, Deirdre Berthrong as Kathy Hunter, David Hubbard as Ludwig "Sly" Hazeltine, and Susan Myers as Marlene Mahoney*

Since teens are so often portrayed on TV as either smart-aleck brats or hormone-mad delinquents, it is refreshing to see a touch of honesty in a series about a teenager. In the beginning, James Hunter is fifteen and his life changes abruptly as his father changes jobs and moves the family from Oregon to downtown Boston. Most of the original episodes deal with the problems James has fitting in at a new school, making friends, and all the usual puppy-love crises that fifteen-year-olds have. The exploits of James and his family and friends will ring true to many people and the show deftly mixes drama and light moments.

*James at 15* hits a bump in episode eleven, when it is retitled *James at 16.* Aside from reaching an age milestone in that episode, James has his first sexual encounter, with (lucky him) a Swedish exchange student, Christina Kollberg (played by Kirsten Baker). The producers try real hard to handle the touchy topic with aplomb, but the rites of passage concept comes across as too forced. The awkwardness of the protrayal of James's fumblings reflects the central problem of the program. The series makes a big effort to be realistic and noble, but winds up a tad stilted and too perfectly constructed. *James at 15/16* is certainly worth catching for a while, but it is unlikely that many viewers will become hooked.

*James at 15/16* is one of the few post-1970 productions of Martin Manulis, a man of admirable talent who turned out both great drama (*Playhouse 90*) and great comedy (*Dobie Gillis*) in TV's early days.

**JAMES CLAVELL'S** **(See *Noble House, Shogun*)**

**JANE EYRE (**½) 60 min (5ep Color; 1980 UK BBC) Drama** *with Juliet Waley and Sorcha Cusack as Jane Eyre, Michael Jayston as Edward Rochester, Isabelle Rosin as Adele, and John Phillips as Mr. Brocklehurst*

Charlotte Bronte's oft-filmed novel is turned into an adequate British TV production. Poor Jane Eyre is a poor orphan who grows up to become a governess in a wealthy home (Thornfield Hall) and mistress of her employer. ■

**THE JANE WYMAN SHOW** **(**) 30 min (163ep B&W; 1955–1958 NBC) Drama Anthology** *with Jane Wyman as hostess*

Star of numerous big-budget Hollywood hits in the 1930s (*Stage Struck*), 1940s (*The Lost Weekend, Johnny Belinda*), and 1950s (*Magnificent Obsession*), Jane Wyman was also Ronald Reagan's first wife (from 1940 to 1948). Her best-known TV work, until she became the wily matriarch of *Falcon Crest*, was as host and occasional star in a series of weekly drama shows. The series was originally entitled *The Fireside Theater* and ran for six years before she took over as hostess. Her fancy gowns, breezy introductions, and star demeanor proved so popular that the title changed to *Jane Wyman Presents the Fireside Theater* and then just *Jane Wyman Theater*. It is now distributed as *The Jane Wyman Show*.

**JASON KING** **(*½) 60 min (26ep Color; 1971–1972 UK ATV) Adventure** *with Peter Wyngarde as Jason King*

More pulp fodder in this spin-off continuation of *Department S*, with mystery writer Jason King taking on puzzling (but routine) assignments for the government, probably to adapt later in his "Mark Cain" mystery novels. (It works for Jessica Fletcher.)

**THE JEAN ARTHUR SHOW** **(*½) 30 min (12ep Color; 1966 CBS) Situation Comedy** *with Jean Arthur as Patricia Marshall, Ron Harper as Paul Marshall, Leonard Stone as Mr. Morton, and Richard Conte as Richie Wells.*

Jean Arthur, a popular husky-voiced actress in Hollywood films from the mid-1930s to the mid-1950s, stars in her one and only TV series, in which she plays that rarest of creatures in the 1960s, a female lawyer. In this twist on *The Defenders* and *Harrigan and Son*, the lady lawyer (named Patricia Marshall) is in business with her young son (Paul) who just got out of law school. To complicate things, Patricia, a comely widow, is pursued by Richie Wells, an ex-con with love on his mind.

**JEAN SHEPHERD'S AMERICA** **(***) 30 min (26ep Color; 1971–1972 & 1985 PBS) Documentary** *with Jean Shepherd as host/narrator*

Jean Shepherd's career has been based on telling whimsical tales about growing up in the sooty shadow of the Indiana steel mills, serving as sort of a wise-guy, urban variation of Lake Wobegon's Garrison Keillor. Shepherd spent two decades spinning yarns nightly on New York radio, was a regular contributor of humor pieces to *Playboy*, and brought his boyhood stories to film in a series of PBS TV-movies and the 1983 hit theatrical film *A Christmas Story*.

In *Jean Shepherd's America*, Shepherd leaves his boyhood and Indiana behind and goes on the road, Charles Kuralt style, while keeping his sharp tongue and offbeat view of life in the forefront. Each episode is a Shepherd essay on a place (Alaska), an event (vacation), or an institution (beer). The locals make appearances, but Shepherd is the star, both on-screen and as narrator.

There are no deep meanings here, no great insights into the American psyche, just thirty minutes of an inventive mind stretching the bounds of television. As always with offbeat shows, a fair number of episodes miss the mark a bit and even fall flat, but the ones that work are a treat. Only Shepherd could turn a snowbound layover in a truck stop in Little America, Wyoming, into an enjoyable half-hour of TV.

The second series of thirteen episodes, produced more than a decade after the first, lack some of the punch of the originals, but are a bit smoother in production values.

**JEFFERSON DRUM** **(**) (26ep B&W; 1958–1959 NBC) Western** *with Jeff Richards as Jefferson Drum, Eugene Martin as Joey Drum, Cyril Delavanti as Lucius Coin, and Robert Stevenson as Big Ed*

Jefferson Drum, a crusading newspaper publisher, attempts to protect the law-abiding citizens of Jubilee, a gold-mining town, during the 1850s. However, when the power of the press is not enough, he and his friends Lucius and Big Ed are ready to back it up with gunfire.

This is one of a handful of drama/adventure series produced by Mark Goodson and Bill Todman, who usually devoted their energies to game shows such as *I've Got a Secret* and *Family Feud*. The results are just average for the times.

**THE JEFFERSONS** **(**½) 30 min (253ep Color; 1975–1985 CBS) Situation Comedy** *with Isabel Sanford as Louise Jefferson, Sherman Hemsley as George Jefferson, Marla Gibbs as Florence Johnston, Franklin Cover as Tom Willis, Roxie Roker as Helen Willis, Mike Evans and Damon Evans as Lionel Jefferson, Berlinda Tolbert as Jenny Willis Jefferson, and Zara Cully as Mother Olivia Jefferson*

The Jefferson family first appeared on *All in the Family* in that program's première season, presented as a black equivalent to the Bunkers. There was a liberal young adult like Gloria (Lionel), a reasonable wife like Edith (Louise), and a pigheaded loud-mouthed husband like Archie (George, though he did not turn up on camera for more than two years). After nearly four seasons of regular appearances on *All in the Family*, the next-door-neighbor Jeffersons sold their house (to Mike and Gloria) and "moved on up" from Queens to Manhattan—and into their own series.

Only this one turns out just a little bit different. In contrast to *All in the Family* (or other program spin-offs such as *Maude* and *Good Times*), *The Jeffersons* plays much more like a traditional sitcom almost from the start. As such, it avoids the overly serious, somber (occasionally self-righteous) tone that sometimes infects the others. Oh, the usual ideologically correct trappings are there—interracial marriage, for instance—but the series does not wrap itself in these matters, holding a sign saying "great issues of the day." Instead *The Jeffersons* gets right down to the business of being funny.

The long incubation period on *All in the Family* no doubt helped, allowing the central characters plenty of time to establish their credibility. It also helps that the Jeffersons have plenty of money—George had successfully turned his one dry cleaning establishment into a lucrative chain (a Horatio Alger story he shares shamelessly and often). So when the family arrives at their "deluxe apartment in the sky," they are ready for some fun. For instance, one of the first things George does is to make sure that Louise has a maid, although he comes to regret this as the sharp-tongued Florence Johnston (Marla Gibbs) proves an able match to his own huffing and puffing.

Actually the entire series is quite a contest. Sherman Hemsley's George Jefferson is a great comic lightning rod. Without hesitation, he goes on the verbal offensive against Florence, his family, his next-door neighbors (Helen and Tom Willis, a black woman married to a white man), and anyone else that passes by. In doing so, he gets off some funny lines and also sets himself up for some obvious retorts. It's insult comedy, pure and simple, rounded out with plenty of complicated schemes and situations, and a bit of physical humor (Hemsley even does a Charlie Chaplin impression).

Oddly, *The Jeffersons* (and the character of George Jefferson, in particular) has attracted a fair share of negative criticism over the years (especially from some black groups), even though it presents a successful upper middle-class black man pretty much in control of his own situation. No doubt George Jefferson's character traits (he's scheming and self-serving, loud, officious, and a braggart) have a lot to do with such discomfort with the show.

Yet these traits are also key to why the sitcom works. There is a confident glee to George Jefferson as he embarks on another blatantly self-serving venture (like Ted Baxter on *Mary Tyler Moore*) or gets ready to unleash his anger (like Gale Gordon's characters from *Our Miss Brooks* to *Here's Lucy*). He's earned the right. Besides, he really does love his family and friends—it's just that he doesn't forget to love himself first.

After the decade-long run of *The Jeffersons*, Hemsley successfully transplanted his basic characterization to another series, *Amen*, which also became a hit. After a short-lived *Jeffersons* spin-off (*Checking In*), Marla Gibbs also scored with a follow-up hit, *227*.

**JENNIE: LADY RANDOLPH CHURCHILL (**½) 60 min (7ep Color; 1975 UK Thames) Drama** *with Lee Remick as Lady Randolph Churchill, Ronald Pickup as Randolph Churchill, Cyril Luckham as the Duke of Marlborough, Rachel Kempson as the Duchess of Marlborough, Dan O'Herlihy as Mr. Jerome, Helen Horton as Mrs. Jerome*

Essential viewing for those consistently fascinated by the lives and loves of Sir Winston Churchill and his extended family. This one dramatizes the story of his American-born mother, Lady Randolph Churchill (nee Jennie Jerome), as she takes her adopted country by storm.

**JENNIFER SLEPT HERE (*) 30 min (13 ep Color: 1983–1984 NBC) Situation Comedy** *With Ann Jillian as Jennifer Farrell, John P. Navin, Jr., as Joey Elliot, Georgia Engel as Susan Elliot, Brandon Maggart as George Elliot, and Mya Akerling as Marilyn Elliot*

Ghost shows can be fun—just look at *Topper.* Ghost shows can also be trite—just look at *Jennifer Slept Here.* Jennifer is an ex-Hollywood film star who died at the height of her fame and beauty. Five years later, a boring family from New York (the Elliots) moves into Jennifer's Hollywood mansion. It turns out that Jennifer is still around in the form of a ghost. A friendly, sexy ghost to be sure, but a ghost nonetheless. She only appears to fourteen-year-old Joey, a nice squirt who is slogging his way through puberty. Jennifer, an expert in matters of the heart, provides advice and guidance. Everybody else, who can't see Jennifer, thinks Joey is nuts for talking when there is nobody around (apparently).

This all sounds better than it is. Ann Jillian is a marvelous actress (she lit up *It's a Living*), but she is wasted here as a sultry tart. *Jennifer Slept Here* has an odd undercurrent of lasciviousness that adds an unwanted air to the proceedings. You keep expecting Jennifer to seduce the poor kid.

**JERICHO (**) 60 min (16ep Color; 1966–1967 CBS) War Drama** *With Don Francks as Franklin Sheppard, Marino Mase as Jean-Gaston Andre, and John Leyton as Nicholas Gage*

Norman Felton hit it big as producer of the offbeat spy show *The Man from U.N.C.L.E.* in the mid-1960s. He failed with *Jericho*, an average World War II action show from the same era. Jericho is the code name of an elite squad of Allied commandos working behind Nazi lines. The squad is made up of a Yank (specializing in psychological warfare), a Frenchman (munitions expert), and a Brit (demolition man).

**JERRY LESTER & DAGMAR** (see ***Broadway Open House***)

**JESSE HAWKES** (**) **60 min (5ep & 2 hr pilot Color; 1989– CBS) Crime Drama** *with Robert Conrad as Jesse Hawkes, Christian Conrad as Matt Hawkes, and Shane Conrad as Cody Hawkes*

This urban-based continuation of Robert Conrad's *High Mountain Rangers* series relocates Jesse and his sons Matt and Cody from the Sierra Nevada mountains to San Francisco for some generally adequate big city crime adventures. In the pilot, they come to town in pursuit of some bad guys (drug dealers) and before long find themselves involved in a CIA case (through an old Marine buddy of Jesse's). Though they all gripe about dealing with the urban environment, by the time the pilot wraps up they've pretty much decided to stick around as professional bounty hunters.

As with *High Mountain Rangers*, this series is a true family showcase: Conrad's sons Christian and Shane continue to play the Hawkes brothers while Conrad's daughter Joan is executive producer. Appropriately, one episode (about an elite military outfit) sports an impressive lineup of other performing offspring, including Griffin O'Neal (son of Ryan and brother of Tatum), Chad McQueen (son of Steve), Ethan Wayne (son of John), Ryan Cassidy (son of Jack Cassidy and Shirley Jones; brother of David, Patrick, and Shaun), and Ramon Sheen (son of Martin and brother of Charlie and Emilio Estevez).

**JESSICA NOVAK** (*) **60 min (7ep Color; 1981 CBS) Drama** *with Helen Shaver as Jessica Novak, David Spielberg as Max Kenyon, and Andrew Rubin as Phil Bonelli*

Jessica Novak is the typical local TV reporter (female division). Her boss (in this case Max Kenyon) wants her to do fluff pieces on children, dogs, and flowers. She wants to do crusading journalism. They bicker, but Jessica always scoops the competition. All in all, all these people take themselves far, far too seriously.

Helen Shaver, who was very unlikable in Larry Gelbart's *United States*, is only mildly unlikable in *Jessica Novak*.

**JESSIE** (*) **60 min (7ep Color; 1984 ABC) Police Drama** *with Lindsay Wagner as Dr. Jessie Hayden, Tony LoBianco as Lt. Alex Ascoli, and Celeste Holm as Molly Hayden*

Lindsay Wagner, trying to break out of her stereotyping as the Bionic Woman, plays a police psychologist who probes the troubled psyches of arrested criminal suspects. In order not to scare away the average viewer, the producers toss in numerous gratuitous car crashes and gunfights. The two elements don't mix and *Jessie* is a sloppy mess whose original good intentions can't save the show.

**JESUS OF NAZARETH** (***½) **(8hr miniseries Color; NBC 1977 & 1979) Drama** *with Robert Powell and Immad Cohen as Jesus Christ, Olivia Hussey as the Virgin Mary, Anne Bancroft as Mary Magdalene, James Farentino as Simon Peter, Ian McShane as Judas, Michael York as John the Baptist, Christopher Plummer as Herod Antipas, Laurence Olivier as Nicodemus, Ralph Richardson as Simeon, James Mason as Joseph of Arimathea, Peter Ustinov as Herod, Anthony Quinn as Caiaphas, Rod Steiger as Pilate, Claudia Cardinale as the Adulteress, and Stacy Keach as Barabbas*

If you want a video version of the story of Jesus Christ that's reverential and true to the Bible yet also accessible and dramatically entertaining, this is it.

Theatrical film director Franco Zeffirelli manages to avoid the garish spectacle of past Bible epics and instead brings an authentic and controlled tone of the presentation. The location footage (shot in Tunisia and Italy) and costuming are stunning, conveying the sense of another land and another time. The music (by Maurice Jarre, who scored the feature film *Dr. Zhivago*) is tasteful and appropriate. Most important, the script (co-authored by Zeffirelli, Anthony Burgess, and Suso Cecchi d'Amico) manages to bring new life to the sometimes overly familiar text without resorting to silly modern colloquialisms. Because the gospels are essentially a series of short stories strung together, the overall narrative flows very well.

One important reason for this success goes back to a basic strength of miniseries versus theatrical film: There is time to linger at a scene and play it as more than famous quotes from the Bible. So, for instance, Zeffirelli devotes attention to Jesus as a young boy (played by Immad Cohen) growing up in Nazareth and helping Joseph (Yorgo Voyagis) with his carpentry work. In these early years, Olivia Hussey (who had played Juliet in Zeffirelli's 1968 theatrical film version of *Romeo and Juliet*) is particularly effective as the Virgin Mary.

Once Christ begins his public life, Robert Powell takes over that difficult role, handling it with quiet strength and dignity. As the story unfolds, Zeffirelli does an excellent job balancing the action and characters, making certain to present preaching as well as miracles. In both areas, acting—not bolts of lightning—carries the drama. So when Jesus delivers his parables, you end up listening to *what* he's saying because they come off as helpful conversational tales rather than some grand pronouncements. And miracles, such as the raising of Lazarus or the expelling of a demon, seem to flow from the inner authority of Christ rather than the special effects department.

Zeffirelli also manages to keep in check any star tendencies to overplay such familiar (but relatively minor) characters as Simeon. Essentially glorified walk-ons, they nevertheless come across as smoothly integrated components of the overall story that don't call attention to themselves. It's a welcome contrast to the infamous delivery a dozen years before (by such celebrities as John Wayne playing a centurion) in the theatrical biblical epic, *The Greatest Story Ever Told.*

*Jesus of Nazareth* does not end with the crucifixion and death of Christ, but takes the story through to his resurrection and subsequent limited appearances to his disciples. This method provides a very reassuring and uplifting conclusion for the faithful, with the risen Jesus sitting among his followers and comforting them in his final moments on earth.

This miniseries was originally presented by NBC in 1977 and rerun with additional footage in 1979. ■

**JET JACKSON, FLYING COMMANDO (See *Captain Midnight*)**

**THE JETSONS (**½) 30 min (65ep & two 2 hr sequels Color; 1962–1963 & 1986–1987 ABC & Syndication) Cartoon** *with the voices of George O'Hanlon as George Jetson, Daws Butler as Elroy Jetson and Henry Orbit, Janet Waldo as Judy Jetson, Penny Singleton as Jane Jetson, Mel Blanc as Cosmo G. Spacely, Don Messick as Astro, and Jean VanderPyl as Rosie*

*The Jetsons* premiered in prime time during a rush of such animated fare in the early sixties. It was ABC's first regular color series and an obvious mirror-image companion to the successful *Flintstones.* The premise was simple: Set a typical suburban family sitcom in the twenty-first century. And don't worry about building expensive futuristic sets—at the drop of a pen, there can be scout outings on the moon, a Hazel-type robot as maid, and the most expressive and energetic character on the series, the family's dog, Astro.

After one season, the program ceased production and the existing episodes immediately hit the kiddie cartoon rerun circuit. In 1986, after two decades of rerunning those same twenty-four half-hours, Hanna-Barbera at last began turning out new episodes. These are easily recognized by the inclusion of a new pet for Elroy, Orbitty (an ugly alien thing of no particular importance to the stories).

Though the characters in *The Jetsons* never caught on with the general public in the same across-the-board manner as Fred Flintstone and Barney Rubble, that push-button world of the future has warmed the hearts of several generations of kids. Perhaps because there were so few episodes, they also embraced the series in the same way that older viewers came to love the original thirty-nine half-hour *Honeymooners* stories, memorizing the plots and dialogue of each one verbatim.

In 1988, the Jetsons also starred in two made-for-TV movies, *Rockin' with Judy Jetson* and (appropriately) *The Flintstones Meet the Jetsons*, followed in 1989 by *The Jetsons—The Movie*, a theatrical release. ■

**THE JEWEL IN THE CROWN (****) 60 min (14ep: thirteen 60 min & one 2 hr Color; 1984 UK Granada) Drama** *with Tim Pigott-Smith as Ronald Merrick, Art Malik as Hari Kumar, Susan Wooldridge as Daphne Manners, Geraldine James as Sarah Layton, Wendy Morgan as Susan (Layton) Bingham, Charles Dance as Guy Perron, Rachel Kempson as Lady Manners, Judy Parfitt as Mildred Layton, Eric Porter as Count Dimitri Bronowsky, and Peggy Ashcroft as Barbie Batchelor*

One of the most prestigious television productions ever, adapted from four novels (known collectively as "The Raj Quartet") by Paul Scott. *The Jewel in the Crown* (also the title of the first book) virtually defines the miniseries novelization form, especially as practiced in Britain.

It also provides a unique opportunity to compare an excellent miniseries with an excellent movie on essentially the same subject (a clash of cultures in India), released at the same time (1984), and even including a few of the same performers (most notably Peggy Ashcroft and Art Malik). So warm up for the fourteen-hour *Jewel in the Crown* by watching the three hours of *A Passage to India.* This movie will also provide you with helpful historical background because *A Passage to India* is set in the 1920s, two decades before *The Jewel in the Crown.*

Though the time periods and particular characters are different, the central conflicts are strikingly similar: British rule versus the native desire for an independent India, competition and clashes among both Indian and British social classes, and (the key dramatic charge that hangs over both) the alleged rape of a white English woman by her Indian friend.

The chief difference between the two presentations underscores the strength of the miniseries format at its best: in *The Jewel in the Crown* there is much more screen time, thus allowing for a far greater delineation of the subtleties behind the characters and conflicts. There are greater opportunities for both foreshadowing and for following the consequences of actions among the many characters. Though the key action focuses on about a half-dozen characters, there are many more (both major and minor) who weave in and out of the narrative. The story runs from 1942 (the height of World War II) to 1947 (the eve of independence), starting with a fundamental conflict of race and class.

At a mission sanctuary, the articulate, Indian-born (but prep-school educated in England) Hari Kumar comes face-to-face with Ronald Merrick, the town's British police superintendent. It's hate at first sight. As a Briton with only limited education and a lower-class background, Merrick loathes all that Kumar represents. Merrick sees Kumar as a man who doesn't know his place, a member of the racially inferior rabble parading around like he's a white Englishman. To Merrick the only true relationship between the races should be one of fear (of the British) and disdain (by the British).

These feelings translate to a very personal vendetta against Kumar when both men take an interest in the same young English woman, Daphne Manners. Newly arrived in India after the war left her an orphan, she is a bit shy and innocent, but well-bred (her late uncle was governor of a province) and good-hearted (she helps at a local hospital). Daphne stays with an influential native family friend, Lady Lili Chatterjee (Zohra Segal), and soon entertains invitations from both Merrick and Kumar. Quickly she finds herself drawn to Kumar, much to Merrick's horror. Desperate, he warns her of the dangers of mixing with Kumar's "kind," but when he launches into a vitriolic racial diatribe (almost without realizing it), he completely and irrevocably alienates Daphne.

Ironically, Kumar is also very aware of racial considerations because he faces a very difficult personal adjustment. After spending most of his life (from age two) in Britain, he finds himself unable to adjust (even to speak the language well) in his native country. Most Britons automatically consider him just another brown face, while his Indian friends mock his breeding—and question his being seen with a white woman.

But the attraction is there. And late one evening, in the empty outdoor gazebo of a local temple (the Bibighar Gardens), Kumar and Daphne touch, embrace, and become lovers. Then their nightmare begins. A group of street hoodlums (who were watching from the bushes) accost them both and gang rape Daphne, forcing Kumar to watch, gagged and bound to a pillar. When they leave, the distraught Daphne begs Kumar not to say a word about what happened. She says she'll insist he was not there at all—that he didn't see any of it. She'll report the rape and that will be the end of it.

Merrick, though, has other ideas. As superintendent of police, he knows exactly how he wants to conduct the subsequent investigation. Merrick arrests some young Hindus (including one of Kumar's friends) found drinking nearby and then picks up Kumar as well. He plants some evidence (Daphne's bicycle) and then subjects all the "suspects" to humiliating verbal abuse and physical torture.

Faithful to Daphne's request, Kumar doesn't say a word, suffering in silence. Daphne sticks to her plan, but soon discovers that she has less control over the situation than she expected. The jailing (and suspected torture) of the Indians turns the incident into a local cause, and they soon become political symbols (and prisoners), with no quick release in sight. Daphne, meanwhile, can only look on—powerless, heartbroken, and increasingly detached.

Though the characters of Daphne Manners and Hari Kumar soon virtually disappear (in person) from much of the rest of the story, the moral injustice of the events at Bibighar Gardens remains at the heart of everything else. Author Paul Scott himself called it "the core of a plot and a system that ended with the spectacle of two nations in violent opposition." Thus, ripples from this situation continue to touch many other people, directly or indirectly, while India makes its way to a final, violent separation from British rule.

So World War II rolls on and *The Jewel in the Crown* shifts focus to the Layton family and their friends and associates. In a touching transition, Sarah Layton (a sergeant in the British army) visits with Daphne's aunt, who is staying next door. Later, Sarah describes all the controversy surrounding the rape to a newly arrived retired missionary (Barbie Batchelor, played by Peggy Ashcroft). "You seem to be haunted by it," Barbie observes perceptively. "Someone should be," is the reply.

Ronald Merrick is, but not by any personal feelings of guilt. Rather he finds himself the target of occasional rocks or graffiti—even a bicycle (or the symbol of one) left in a prominent position (alluding to the evidence he planted). But these faceless attacks are surprisingly gentle and seem to be more reminders rather than revenge. They are not yet his moment of reckoning. Instead, Merrick remains very much in control of his immediate environment, in the next five years doing little to discourage harsh judgments against him. He transfers from local police work into the wartime army and there finds plenty of opportunities for advancement, in spite of (or perhaps because of) his crude but effective style. Eventually, though, he does have to face the consequences of all his actions.

And so do the many characters of the series, including the aging Mabel Layton (Barbie's best friend, played by Fabia Drake), the stubborn Moslem Mohammed Ali Kasim (Zia Moyheddin), Ali's son Ahmed (Derrick Branche), historian and soldier Guy Perron (Charles Dance), and the mysterious Count Bronowsky (Eric Porter). Even if their actions have been as deceptively harmless as merely being a part of the ruling class of India, they have to look at things in a way they had never thought about before.

All this challenges their self-confidence, their self-worth, even their faith in life itself, leading to some extremely graphic, violent, and frightening scenes. In one, for instance, a distraught young English mother (feeling alone and helpless at the death of her soldier husband) decides to "free" her young infant boy. She places the child on the ground, with a lace blanket of butterflies, pours a circle of kerosene around him, and lights the fire. In another, there is a bloody clash between Hindus and Moslems at a train, leading Sarah Layton to declare bitterly, "after 300 years of India, we've made this whole damned bloody senseless mess."

It is these moments that make *The Jewel in the Crown* a particularly effective *literary* miniseries. It is quite rich in subtexts. Dialogue, action, and specific visuals consistently allude to larger themes and reoccurring imagery. In fact, *The Jewel in the Crown* demands that you view it with the same care and concentration you bring to reading a novel. You can see this series several times and still find plenty to think about. ■

**JIGSAW** (*) **60 min (8ep Color; 1972–1973 ABC) Police Drama** *with James Wainwright as Lt. Frank Dain*

This forgettable exercise in variations on a common theme is set in the California State Police Department of Missing Persons. Lt. Dain is the top detective, renowned for his uncanny ability to solve the most puzzling mysteries, hence the show's title.

**JIGSAW JOHN** (**) **60 min (15ep & 90 min pilot Color; 1976 NBC) Police Drama** *with Jack Warden as "Jigsaw" John St. John, Alan Feinstein as Sam Donner, Pippa Scott as Maggie Hearn, and James Hong as Frank Chen*

Just another grumpy 1970s antiestablishment cop, "Jigsaw" John St. John got his nickname by piecing together the clues to the many crime mysteries he solves. As is expected, his individualistic methods just exasperate his officious superiors. St. John dates nursery school teacher Maggie Hearn, but he's too busy to marry her.

The 1975 pilot is called *They Only Come Out at Night*, and in the pilot St. John has a wife named Helen (Madeleine Sherwood).

**THE JIM BACKUS SHOW—HOT OFF THE WIRE** (**) **30 min (39ep B&W; 1960–1961 Syndication) Situation Comedy** *with Jim Backus as John Michael "Mike" O'Toole, Nita Talbot as Dora Miles, and Bobs Watson as Sidney*

The familiar Jim Backus, the voice of Mr. Magoo and the actor who portrayed Gilligan's Island refugee Thurston Howell III, stars in this forgettable series about the struggles of Mike O'Toole to keep his news organization one step ahead of its creditors.

**JIM BOWIE, THE ADVENTURES OF** (**) **30 min (76ep B&W; 1956–1958 ABC) Western** *with Scott Forbes as Jim Bowie and Peter Hanson as Rezin Bowie*

This innocuous kiddie western is based on a real-life personality, Jim Bowie, the inventor of the knife that bears his name. Set in the Louisiana–Texas region during the 1830s (a welcome change from the bland 1870s and 1880s), the series loves to drag in other contemporary celebrities as guests, such as Andrew Jackson, John James Audubon, and Davy Crockett. ■

**THE JIM HENSON HOUR** (**½) **60 min (13ep Color; 1989– NBC) Variety** *with Jim Henson as host, and John Hurt as "the storyteller"*

Jim Henson, the creator of the Muppets, brings his most famous creations to this offbeat variety hour. Combining the elements of the 1970s *Muppet Show* (Muppet regulars sing and joke with guest celebrities) and *The Storyteller* (a series of late 1980s Henson specials of high-tech versions of old fairy tales), *The Jim Henson Hour* works hard to attract both youngsters and parents with a grab bag of attractions.

**THE JIMMY STEWART SHOW** (**) **30 min (24ep Color; 1971–1972 NBC) Situation Comedy** *with Jimmy Stewart as Prof. James K. Howard, Julie Adams as Martha Howard, Jonathan Daly as Peter Howard, Ellen Geer as Wendy Howard, and John McGiver as Dr. Luther Quince*

Hollywood film star Jimmy Stewart is wasted in this mundane sitcom. Stewart plays James Howard, a college anthropology professor who learns some new facts about life when he allows his married son to "temporarily" move back home, along with a wife and child. This doubling of the Howard household population results in typical TV sitcom mayhem.

**JOANIE LOVES CHACHI** (*½) **30 min (17ep Color; 1982–1983 ABC) Situation Comedy** *with Scott Baio as Charles "Chachi" Arcola, Erin Moran as Joanie Cunningham, Al Molinaro as Al Delvecchio, Ellen Travolta as Louisa Delvecchio, and Art Metrano as Uncle Rico*

A lot of good things came out of *Happy Days*, but *Joanie Loves Chachi* was not one of them. Joanie Cunningham was the youngest of the Cunningham children on *Happy Days* and as she grew into a pretty teenager she became the focus of more and more episodes. A romantic interest for Joanie turned up when the Fonz's young cousin Chachi moved to Milwaukee and took up with the *Happy Days* gang.

The next logical step was for Joanie and Chachi to get their own show, so, voilà, *Joanie Loves Chachi* was born. The premise is that Chachi's widowed mother Louisa marries Al Delvecchio, co-owner of Arnold's Drive-In, the local teen hangout featured so often in *Happy Days.* The newlyweds and Chachi leave Milwaukee for the big city, Chicago, where Al opens a family restaurant. Taken in by Louisa's Uncle Rico, a shyster talent agent, Al hires one of Rico's worst acts, a going-nowhere rock group, to supply music at the restaurant. To help improve the band, Chachi joins as lead vocalist and he invites girlfriend Joanie to leave her home and family in Wisconsin, move to Chicago to live with his family, and join him in the band as they make their move to stardom.

Sometimes secondary characters on a TV show can go out on their own and star in a spin-off, but Joanie and Chachi are much too cute. This show treats the pair as if they really were teen singing idols, with new songs on most episodes. The music is just fair, the humor is sparse, and the characters are too weak. After a few episodes, the gang calls it quits in the Windy City and moves back to Milwaukee and *Happy Days.*

**JOE AND MABEL** (*½) **30 min (15ep B&W; 1955–1956 CBS) Situation Comedy** *with Larry Blyden as Joe Sparton, Nita Talbot as Mabel Spooner, and Luella Gear as Mrs. Spooner*

Joe is a cab driver. Mabel is a manicurist. They have been going together for some time. Mabel wants to get married, real soon. Joe wants to get married, but not just now. Mabel tries to get Joe to set the date. That's it.

**JOE AND SONS** (*) **30 min (13ep & 30 min pilot Color; 1975–1976 CBS) Situation Comedy** *with Richard Castellano as Joe Vitale, Jerry Stiller as Gus Duzik, Barry Miller as Mark Vitale, and Jimmy Baio as Nick Vitale*

Douglas Cramer has a certain knack for producing glitzy, escapist series that catch the public's fancy (such as *The Love Boat, Vega$,* and *Wonder Woman*). He has less success with the more traditional sitcom format of *Joe and Sons.* Here the setting is as far from the swank world of *The Love Boat* as possible: the working-class confines of Hoboken, N.J.

Joe is a widowed factory worker with two teenaged sons. He wants them to be doctors and lawyers and such. They want to party. The only entertainment here is watching veteran comic Jerry Stiller (without longtime partner Anne Meara) play Joe's factory chum, and keeping an eye on Jimmy Baio (Billy Tate on *Soap*), who plays one of Joe's sons.

In the pilot the setting is Pennsylvania and Mitch Brown plays Jimmy Baio's role.

**JOE AND VALERIE** (**) **30 min (7ep Color; 1978–1979 NBC) Situation Comedy** *with Paul Regina as Joe Pizo, Char Fontane as Valerie Sweetzer, Bill Beyers and Lloyd Alann as Frank Berganski, and Pat Benson and Arlene Golonka as Stella Sweetzer*

It's the late 1970s, disco is king, and *Saturday Night Fever* is the rage. Joe is an apprentice plumber and Valerie is a salesgirl in a department store. They meet on the disco dance floor, where they can rise above their humble Brooklyn surroundings and find true love and a good dance partner.

Joe and Valerie are nice people, but a bit too straight for their own good. Their friends and family are slightly offbeat, but no really interesting people shine from this show, which is produced by Linda Hope (daughter of Bob).

Oh, by the way, Joe and Valerie do get married, during the final three episodes, when some of the cast changes.

**JOE BASH** (***) **30 min (6ep Color; 1986 ABC) Situation Comedy** *with Peter Boyle as Joe Bash, Andrew Rubin as Willie Smith, and DeLane Matthews as Lorna*

There may be more offbeat TV shows than *Joe Bash,* but there probably aren't any that are more unsettling and disturbing. The program is listed as a situation comedy, because it really doesn't fit any other category. Peter Boyle, the balding, burly actor who appeared in several hit films (*The Candidate, Young Frankenstein, Joe*), makes a rare TV appearance here in the lead role. As Joe Bash, he plays a veteran New York City policeman whose mind is more on putting in his time until his upcoming retirement and pension than on catching criminals. Bash is teamed with eager-beaver patrolman Willie Smith and the two have real problems relating to each other.

Despite that fairly normal setup, *Joe Bash* constantly roams in directions highly unusual for a TV comedy. Boyle's characterization of Bash goes way beyond the lovable grouch mold of Ralph Kramden (*The Honeymooners*) and Archie Bunker (*All in the Family*), so much so that Bash is genuinely unlikable at almost any level. The only compassion a viewer can feel is sympathizing with the years of thankless drudgery that made Bash what he is. Bash's quasi-romance with Lorna, a hooker, is staggeringly honest and excruciatingly heartfelt. Bash's almost cruel treatment of the woman will leave viewers raised on standard TV with mouths agape.

*Joe Bash* is nowhere near mass entertainment. It could never work as a long-running series. It may not even be very easy to watch. Still the audacity and boldness of producer Danny Arnold (best known for easygoing quality shows such as *Barney Miller* and *My World . . . and Welcome to It*) must be congratulated. Anyone willing to take such a creative risk on network TV deserves a lot of leeway.

**JOE FORRESTER** (*½) **60 min (22ep & 2 hr pilot Color; 1975–1976 NBC) Police Drama** *with Lloyd Bridges as Joe Forrester, Patricia Crowley as Georgia Cameron, and Eddie Egan as Sgt. Bernie Vincent*

This cop series from *Police Story's* David Gerber looks as if it is all heart, at least on the surface. Joe Forrester, longtime policeman, declines a cushy desk job and a fancy patrol car so he can walk his beloved ghetto streets and rap with all the locals. Nonetheless, when trouble rears its ugly head, Joe is quick on the draw and not squeamish about blasting away suspects who don't cooperate. All the violence is sugar-coated by playing up Joe's humanity. He cares a lot, about many things, and he has a nice girlfriend he snuggles with. Still, there is too much of squealing tires and busted glass. Catch *Blue Knight* instead, for a better treatment of much the same concept.

**JOE'S WORLD** (*) **30 min (11ep Color; 1979–1980 NBC) Situation Comedy** *with Ramon Bieri as Joe Wabash, K. Callan as Katie Wabash, Christopher Knight as Steve Wabash, Misty Rowe as Judy Wilson, Russ Banham as Brad Hopkins, and Frank Coppola as Andy*

Another of those annoying salt-of-the-earth relevant comedies, with Ramon Bieri as a Detroit house painter with five kids (including Christopher Knight, previously Peter Brady on *The Brady Bunch*) and his own small business. Over the short run of this series Joe has to face such issues as employee health (the dangers of paint fumes), military service by his daughter, and even his own mortality (wife Katie makes estate plans for the kids). Even on the job, sexy Judy (played by Misty Rowe, one of the *Hee Haw* Honeys) insists on nursing her baby.

It's a wonder he gets anything done. Bob and Norm would never hire him for work on *This Old House*.

**THE JOEY BISHOP SHOW (**½) 30 min (123ep: 53 B&W & 70 Color; 1961–1965 NBC & CBS) Situation Comedy** *with Joey Bishop as Joey Barnes, Marlo Thomas as Stella Barnes, Madge Blake as Mrs. Barnes, John Griggs as J. P. Willoughby, Abby Dalton as Ellie Barnes, Guy Marks as Freddie, Corbett Monica as Larry, and Joe Besser as Mr. Jillson*

There were two different settings for Joey Bishop's Joey Barnes character (and his trademark phrase, "Well, son-of-a-gun."). The initial twenty-six episodes (the first season) cast him as an available bachelor working as an assistant to a Los Angeles press agent, J. P. Willoughby. For the remainder of the series, he has an entirely different supporting cast and plays the part of a newly married television talk show host, with Abby Dalton as his wife, Ellen. The attraction of either setup pretty much depends on your interest in Joey Bishop's low-key comic persona, which remains unchanged throughout.

Ironically the original one-season format is probably more appealing to present-day viewers, especially with regulars Madge Blake (later Aunt Harriet Cooper on *Batman*) as Joey's mom, Joe Flynn (later Capt. Binghamton on *McHale's Navy*) as Joey's brother-in-law, and Marlo Thomas (in her first continuing character role) as Joey's unmarried sister. Appropriately the pilot for this version aired as an episode of *The Danny Thomas Show*.

But version two (the talk show years) continues the Danny Thomas connection as well (for good reason: the series is from Thomas's production company). Appropriately, in this format, *The Joey Bishop Show* is essentially *Make Room for Daddy—Mark II:* the at-home and onstage life of a real-life entertainer. There's even a convenient character crossover with Danny's TV world in some episodes which originally aired immediately after Thomas ended production of his own series. Not only do Danny and son Rusty (Rusty Hamer) turn up at the Barnes household, Rusty even moves in for a while when he enrolls in a California college.

The life-imitates-art circle continued a few years after *The Joey Bishop Show* ended its original run. That's when ABC tapped Bishop as host for a talk show opposite *Tonight*'s Johnny Carson.

**THE JOHN FORSYTHE SHOW (*½) 30 min (30ep Color; 1965–1966 NBC) Situation Comedy** *with John Forsythe as Maj. John Foster, Elsa Lanchester as Margaret Culver, Ann B. Davis as Miss Wilson, Guy Marks as Ed Robbins, and Peggy Lipton as Joanna.*

On paper this show has a great deal going for it. The star, John Forsythe, is a proven TV commodity (*Bachelor Father, Dynasty*). His second bananas are top-rate, such as Ann B. Davis, TV's most popular girl Friday/maid (*Love That Bob, The Brandy Bunch*); Elsa Lanchester, the wonderful English actress who makes a rare TV appearance here; and Guy Marks, a funny borscht-belt comedian who did well in *The Joey Bishop Show*. In addition, the original format is stretched but workable: Air Force Major inherits a girls boarding school run by stuffy old bats.

Somehow it all doesn't work. The acting is good, but the plots are thin and not many laughs result. Near the end of the series, the entire girls school concept is virtually canned and only Forsythe and Marks (as his Air Force buddy) remain, as spies for Uncle Sam who use the girls school as their base. This weird switch kills whatever fun the program had in its original permutation.

Look for Peggy Lipton, pre–*Mod Squad*, as one of the students at the boarding school.

**JOHNNY MIDNIGHT (*½) 30 min (39ep B&W; 1959–1960 Syndication) Detective Drama** *with Edmond O'Brien as Johnny Midnight, Arthur Batanides as Sgt. Sam Olivera, and Yuki Shimoda as Aki*

Johnny Midnight (what a great name!) is a private eye with a rather unusual past: He used to be an actor. Set in New York City, *Johnny Midnight* does not have much to attract viewers other than the solid presence of character actor Edmond O'Brien in the lead role.

**JOHNNY RINGO (**) 30 min (38ep & 30 min pilot B&W; 1959–1960 CBS) Western** *with Don Durant as Johnny Ringo, Karen Sharpe as Laura Thomas, and Mark Goddard as Cully Charlcey*

One notable feature of *Johnny Ringo* is that it is one of the first series created and produced by Aaron Spelling, who went on to produce *The Mod Squad, The Love Boat*, and *Fantasy Island*, among others.

Johnny Ringo is an ex-gunfighter who goes straight and becomes the sheriff of Velardi, Arizona, in the 1870s. The series is now syndicated, along with episodes of *Black Saddle, Law of the Plainsman*, and *The Westerner* under the title *The Westerners*. The pilot is known as both *The Loner* (not to be confused with a Lloyd Bridges series of the same name) and *Man Alone*.

**JOHNNY STACCATO** **(see *Staccato*)**

**JOKEBOOK** (**½) 30 min (4ep Color; 1982 NBC) **Animated Cartoon**

*Jokebook* is an innovative cartoon series from the Hanna-Barbera studios best known for *The Flintstones, Huckleberry Hound*, and *Scooby-Doo*. The series presents animated shorts of all sorts: domestic, foreign, professional, student, etc. A noble effort.

**THE JONATHAN WINTERS SHOW** (**) 60 min (45ep Color; 1967–1969 CBS) **Comedy-Variety** *with Jonathan Winters, Abby Dalton, and Dick Curtis*

By the time he received his own full-length prime-time comedy-variety series, Jonathan Winters had been performing on television for about a dozen years, usually as a guest on other people's programs (though he did have his own fifteen-minute slot in the mid-1950s, right after the network news). The 1960s Jonathan Winters series is a standard comedy-variety package (music, guests, sketches) set apart by its energetic and inventive host and his cast of characterizations (including his famous Maude Frickert). Unlikely to be picked up these days, but a good candidate for some future "best of" package. ■

**JONNY QUEST** (***) 30 min (26ep Color; 1964–1965 ABC) **Animated Cartoon** *with the voices of Tim Matheson as Jonny Quest, John Stephenson as Dr. Benton Quest, Mike Road as Roger "Race" Bannon, Danny Bravo as Hadji, and Don Messick as Bandit.*

One of the few animated cartoon series to be produced especially for prime time, *Jonny Quest* is a great adventure yarn for youngsters of all ages. Jonny, an eleven-year-old who spells his first name funny, avoids such mundane things as school in order to accompany his scientist father Dr. Benton Quest on worldwide expeditions. Along with the Quests are Race Bannon (personal bodyguard and thickheaded jock), Hadji (a young Indian boy who is Jonny's friend), and Bandit (Jonny's know-it-all dog).

Aside from the fun stories, which are full of close calls, natural disasters, and subterfuge, *Jonny Quest* is memorable for the character of Hadji. Not only is Hadji a foreigner (an Indian) but he's smart and speaks good English! Usually foreigners in cartoons are simpletons who say silly things due to their unfamiliarity with the language. Hadji is an eye-opening lesson in international tolerance for kids used to rooting just for Americans.

*Jonny Quest* is one of the best productions from the prolific Hanna-Barbera studios, home of *The Flintstones, Yogi Bear*, and *Scooby-Doo.*

**THE JOSEPH COTTEN SHOW** (**) 30 min (27ep & 30 min pilot B&W; 1956–1957 NBC) **Drama Anthology** *with Joseph Cotten as host*

Joseph Cotten, acting chum of Orson Welles (*Citizen Kane, The Magnificent Ambersons*), hosts yet one more collection of dramas from the 1950s. The series' hook is that each episode is based on actual legal trials from around the world, hence the show's original title, *On Trial.*

**JOURNEY TO THE UNKNOWN** (*½) 60 min (17ep Color; 1968–1969 ABC) **Suspense Anthology**

This British-produced series attempts to tread where *The Twilight Zone* and *Alfred Hitchcock Presents* have trod before, presenting tales of horror, suspense, and the supernatural. Some episodes are interesting, but not many.

**JUDD, FOR THE DEFENSE** (**) 60 min (50ep Color; 1967–1969 ABC) **Law Drama** *with Carl Betz as Clinton Judd and Stephen Young as Ben Caldwell*

Carl Betz will forever be typecast in most viewers' minds as the super-nice, super-boring Dr. Alex Stone from *The Donna Reed Show.* Betz probably was sick and tired of playing such an innocuous guy, and must have leapt at the chance to play Clinton Judd just one year after *The Donna Reed Show* ceased production.

Clinton Judd is a flamboyant, individualistic Texan defense attorney, in the mold of Melvin Belli and Percy Foreman. Judd likes to defend clients everyone else thinks are guilty, and then win. Judd does not win on these picky legal technicalities that most citizens hate, but rather on good, old-fashioned evidence, by showing that somebody else did it.

Somewhat akin to a flashy Texas version of Perry Mason, Judd wears fancy clothes, ten-gallon hats, and string ties and talks with a faint southern drawl that almost sounds believable. Like Mason, Judd wins virtually every time. Straight-laced but handsome Ben Caldwell is Judd's associate, who is around to do some of the dirty work and to be lectured by his boss.

*Judd, for the Defense* makes an effort to be topical in a 1960s sort of way, so lots of civil rights workers, draft evaders, and hippies turn up in Judd's hands. Considering that at the time real-life Texas courts were handing out ninety-nine-year sentences for marijuana possession, someone with Judd's win record was sorely needed.

The producer of *Judd, for the Defense* is Paul Monash, who also produced *Peyton Place*, a very different series indeed.

**JUDE THE OBSCURE** (**) 60 min (6ep Color; 1971 UK BBC) **Drama** *with Robert Powell as Jude, Alex Marshall as Arabella Donn, Fiona Walker as Sue Bridehead, John Franklyn-Robbins as Richard Phillotson, Daphne Heard as Aunt Drusilla, Gwen Nelson as Mrs. Edith, and Gary Rich as Little Jude*

Reaction to this story upon first publication in 1895 was so violently negative that author Thomas Hardy retreated to his poetry, vowing to give up writing novels. When you watch this adaptation, you'll understand why: This is a very cruel and depressing tale. Perhaps it accurately reflects social and religious snobbery of the

Victorian times, but because it's so bleak and nasty you'll probably find yourself wondering (just as the main characters do): Why go on with life?

Still, if you're ready for some self-flagellation, Robert Powell does an excellent job as Jude, the poor naive young man from a small village who wants to better himself. Though he's warned to be content with his lower-class lot in life, he attempts to win a spot in the British university system, where you need either money or influence to be admitted (he has neither). In preparation for a try at the ministry, he then decides to take on the near-impossible task of learning Greek and Hebrew on his own.

He's not much more realistic on the romantic front, becoming involved first with the voluptuous but exploitative Arabella Donn, and then with his cousin, Sue Bridehead. Eventually they're all caught in a hopelessly complicated marital arrangement guaranteed to generate mind-numbing guilt. And then things *really* turn bad.

Several years later, Powell took the lead role in the far more uplifting miniseries, *Jesus of Nazareth.*

**JUDGE ROY BEAN, THE ADVENTURES OF (**) 30 min (39ep B&W; 1955–1956 Syndication) Western** *with Edgar Buchanan as Judge Roy Bean, Jack Beutel as Jeff Taggert, Jackie Loughery as Letty Bean, and Russell Hayden as Steve*

Rascal Edgar Buchanan as a self-appointed judge in the lawless West of the 1870s. Typical low-budget 1950s western, but it's always fun to see Buchanan connive. This series comes about halfway between his sidekick stint in *Hopalong Cassidy* and his "movin' kinda slow" days on *Petticoat Junction.*

**THE JUDY GARLAND SHOW (***) 60 min (28ep B&W; 1963–1964 CBS) Musical-Variety** *with Judy Garland, Jerry Van Dyke, Ken Murray, and The Mort Lindsay Orchestra.*

*The Judy Garland Show* is a near gem of a show that failed at the time it was produced but shines brightly now in retrospect. Judy Garland, former child movie star, had already been through numerous ups and downs in her performing career before she tried her one and only TV series, about five years before her death. Garland starred in several hit TV specials in the late 1950s and early 1960s and her weekly series should have been just more of the same. Unfortunately the program goes through a lengthy identity crisis that almost ruins it. In the beginning, *The Judy Garland Show* is a production of George Schlatter, a veteran of the old *Colgate Comedy Hour.* He was adept at producing comedy-variety, not musical-variety, and this first version of Garland's show is a hodgepodge of music and laughs. The always shy yet volatile Judy is teamed with Jerry Van Dyke, Dick's overreacting brother. After five shows, Schlatter is canned (he went on to focus on comedy, his strong suit, and to create *Rowan and Martin's Laugh-In*).

Schaltter's replacement, Norman Jewison, who had produced some of Judy's earlier TV specials, was much better suited for the role. The focus of the series now, rightly, centers on Judy and her music. The show settles down at this point, but numerous other production changes go on throughout the year, and a solid format is never established. Ken Murray turns up now and again to show his innocuous home movies of Hollywood stars and various groups of dancers come and go.

In spite of all this hubbub, *The Judy Garland Show* comes up with some fine moments of magic. In a few episodes, Judy just sings, all by herself, for an hour. In others, she sings wonderful duets with Barbra Streisand, Mickey Rooney, old *Wizard of Oz* alumnus Ray Bolger (the Scarecrow), and even her two young daughters, Lorna Luft and Liza Minnelli. These moments are worth reliving, even if you must sit through some Jerry Van Dyke routines and Ken Murray movies. ■

**JUKE BOX (**) 30 min (42ep Color; 1978–1979 Syndication) Musical-Variety** *with Twiggy and Britt Ekland as hostesses*

The tops in pops are presented by (first) famed fashion model Twiggy and (later) sexy actress Britt Ekland.

**JULIA (**½) 30 min (86ep Color; 1968–1971 NBC) Situation Comedy** *with Diahann Carroll as Julia Baker, Lloyd Nolan as Dr. Morton Chegley, Lurene Tuttle as Hannah Yarby, Marc Copage as Corey Baker, Michael Link as Earl J. Waggedorn, and Betty Beaird as Marie Waggedorn*

In 1968, this show was a breakthrough, casting a black woman (Diahann Carroll) as the lead character in a situation comedy. This had not been done since *Beulah* in the early 1950s. *Julia* was quite a step up from that scatterbrained maid setting. Carroll's character was an attractive widow with a young son (Corey), a good job (a nurse at an aerospace company in Los Angeles), and a nice apartment.

*Julia* preceded the rush to relevancy that came on the heels of Norman Lear's success with *All in the Family*, though it certainly had its share of points to make. Julia's husband died in Vietnam, her apartment was in a thoroughly integrated complex, and her son's best friend, Earl, was a young white kid. Perhaps the biggest difference from Lear's material was that this series had a minimum of shouting. So the individual stories emerge as a comfortable mix of mild domestic crises and minor complications at the office.

In reruns in the 1970s and early 1980s, this approach came off as a bit too precious and noble. But with the success of Bill Cosby's wholesome *Cosby Show* in the mid-1980s, the genre seems to have come full cycle: It's okay to have a low-key comedy about a professional adult black woman who doesn't go around yelling or spouting street talk. (Besides, after her stint as

Dominique Deveraux on *Dynasty* we know Diahann Carroll can be wicked if she wants to be!)

Nowadays *Julia* occasionally still seems a bit self-conscious (and dated with its use of the word *negro*) but otherwise it plays well enough as a straightforward home-and-work sitcom. At the office, Lloyd Nolan (the lead in *Martin Kane, Private Eye* in the 1950s) is the typically irascible boss with a heart of gold, while Lurene Tuttle (the mom on *Life with Father* and *Father of the Bride* in the 1950s) is the sarcastic head nurse. On the domestic dating front, Julia doesn't do too badly. Paul Winfield plays boyfriend Paul Cameron for two seasons, followed by Fred Williamson as Steve Bruce for the final run.

**JULIE FARR, M.D.** **(see *Having Babies*)**

**THE JUNE ALLYSON SHOW (**) 30 min (57 ep B&W; 1959–1961 CBS) Drama Anthology** *with June Allyson as hostess*

June Allyson, who played the sweet girl-next-door in many MGM Hollywood musicals in the 1930s and 1940s, hosts and occasionally stars in this series of mildly interesting unrelated dramas. Her husband, actor Dick Powell, produces the series and also appears in an episode or two.

When this show originally aired, it was titled *The DuPont Show Starring June Allyson.*

**JUNGLE JIM (**½) 30 min (26ep B&W; 1955 Syndication) Adventure** *with Johnny Weissmuller as Jungle Jim, Martin Huston as Skipper, and Norman Fredric (a.k.a. Dean Fredricks) as Kassim*

Johnny Weissmuller, U.S. Olympic swimmer in the 1920s, is best known as the star of twelve of the many Hollywood versions of the Tarzan legend. After his Tarzan flicks, he appeared in several films as Jungle Jim, a somewhat refined character who wore more clothes than Tarzan, but still knew his way around the African interior. He carries on the role of jungle scout Jungle Jim in this series, the only TV program Weissmuller ever starred in.

**JUST FRIENDS (*½) 30 min (13ep Color; 1979 CBS) Situation Comedy** *with Stockard Channing as Susan Hughes, Lou Criscuolo as Milt D'Angelo, Mimi Kennedy as Victoria Chasen, and Gerrit Graham as Leonard Scribner*

Stockard Channing was supposed to be the next Mary Tyler Moore, but it never seemed to work out. This series, Channing's first, vaguely resembles *The Mary Tyler Moore Show* in concept, but is updated for the late 1970s. Channing's character, Susan Hughes, is a bona fide divorcée (an idea still too radical for Moore's show just nine years earlier) who leaves cold, snooty old Boston for sunny, swinging Los Angeles. Susan gets a job working at a Beverly Hills Health Spa (how trendy can they get?) and the show deals with the funny cast of characters found in and around the spa and Susan's apartment.

In theory, this show should have clicked the way Mary Tyler Moore's program did. Channing, like Moore, is an appealing actress viewers can relate to, but the stilted concept and the mediocre support cast of *Just Friends* doom the program to oblivion. The show's full title is *Stockard Channing in Just Friends.*

**JUST IN TIME (**½) 30 min (6ep Color; 1988 ABC) Situation Comedy** *with Tim Matheson as Harry Stadlin, Patricia Kalember as Joanna Farrell, Kevin Scannell as Jack Manning, and Alan Blumenfeld as Steven Birnbaum*

Tim Matheson, in his youth the voice of cartoon character Jonny Quest, serves as both star and co-executive producer of this sprightly sitcom. Matheson plays Harry Stadlin, the new, high-pressure editor brought in from Chicago to boost circulation for a weekly west coast magazine, the "West Coast Review." Stadlin's efforts to increase the lighter features puts him at odds with Joanna Farrell, the magazine's no-nonsense hard news political reporter. The two match retorts and begin developing some romantic sparks. This concept is very similar to, and actually much better executed than, Mary Tyler Moore's failed *Mary* sitcom from the mid-1980s.

**JUST LIKE FAMILY (**) 30 min (5ep at Fall 1989 Color; 1989 Disney) Situation Comedy** *with Cindy Williams as Lisa Burke, Mark Hudson as Tom Burke, Gabriel Damon as Coop Stewart, Grace Johnston as Emily Stewart, Patrick B. McCormick as Jake Crawford*

Real-life husband and wife Cindy Williams and Mark Hudson play Lisa and Tom Burke, a New York City couple relocating to Red Rock, Nevada. The reason for the move: Tom has lost his cushy executive job and (after five months of surviving on Fruit Loops) he reluctantly accepts a position out west with Giddyup Clothes (even though New York is where Lisa would rather stay). Unfortunately, the company has a policy that its executives be "family men" (have children)—a point Tom fudges when applying for the job. (When reminded that there's a federal law against such requirements, company V. P. Jake Crawford succinctly summarizes their official position: "We don't care.")

As luck would have it, soon after arriving in Red Rock, Tom and Lisa run into two conning orphans, Coop and Emily, who are eager to exploit the situation. They live with their gambling uncle, "Lucky" Stewart (played by Dan Hedaya), in a dumpy trailer camp, where they are schooled by him in such important tenets of life as "Never split up two pair for three of a kind." In exchange for "big bucks," though, they agree to act as surrogate children, until the Burkes start trying to straighten them out. Disgusted at such a prospect, they head back to Uncle Lucky, but not for long—he's soon arrested in Las Vegas. Rather than turn the kids over to some welfare authorities, Lisa and Tom decide to take them in and raise them, well, just like family. Reluctantly, the kids agree.

Though the stories are just average, Cindy Williams (previously Shirley Feeney in *Laverne and Shirley*) has a nice edge to her character, while Hudson is fine as the straight man. The kids are played as conniving brats, but Williams manages to keep them from completely stealing the show.

This series is based on the 1986 Disney TV movie, *Help Wanted: Kids*, which starred Williams and Hudson, with Chad Allen and Hillary Wolf as their kids.

**JUST OUR LUCK (**½) 30 min (11ep Color; 1983 ABC) Situation Comedy** *with T. K. Carter as Shabu, Richard Gilliland as Keith Barrow, Ellen Maxted as Meagan Huxley, Rod McCary as Nelson Marriott, Richard Schaal as Chuck, and Hamilton Camp as Professor Bob*

On the surface *Just Our Luck* may look like *I Dream of Jeannie*, but it's a lot more imaginative than that old 1960s sitcom staple. In *Just Our Luck*, nebbish TV weatherman-turned-reporter Keith Barrow winds up with a genuine ancient genie (Shabu) by buying an enchanted old bottle. Shabu is a riot with his disdain for his lowly new master and he displays that condescension by using his magic powers to play practical jokes on Barrow. Meanwhile, Barrow's status at KPOX-TV is always in jeopardy from management, which doesn't like him, and from Professor Bob, the weatherman who took Barrow's old job.

It's all a somewhat confusing mix of styles, but *Just Our Luck* has much more sparkle than many sitcoms that lasted far longer. The show's executive producer, Ronald Frazer, also displayed his wit in the hip teen sitcom *Square Pegs*.

**JUST THE TEN OF US (**½) 30 min (24ep at Fall 1989 Color; 1988– ABC) Situation Comedy** *with Bill Kirchenbauer as Graham Lubbock, Deborah Harmon as Elizabeth Lubbock, Heather Langenkamp as Marie Lubbock, Brooke Theiss as Wendy Lubbock, Jamie Luner as Cindy Lubbock, Jo Ann Willette as Constance Lubbock, Matt Shakman as J. R. Lubbock, Heidi Zeigler as Sherry Lubbock, and Frank Bonner as Father Robert Hargis*

The character of Coach Lubbock first popped up in *Growing Pains*, where he was a coach to Kirk Cameron's character in a Long Island high school. As this spin-off series begins, Coach Lubbock is let go from his job and he accepts a new position coaching at an all-boy Catholic school in Eureka, California. Relocating the large Lubbock clan across the continent is no small feat. Once everyone is moved in, the coach's prime concern becomes keeping the boys in the new school away from his numerous young daughters. *Just the Ten of Us* is fairly lightweight, but it has a lot of easy-going blue-collar humor that is refreshing.

Bill Kirchenbauer, who plays Coach Lubbock, is a truly madcap comic, whose rotund, balding physique leads towards playing gauche personalities. Fans of the talk show parody *Fernwood 2-Night* may recall Kirchenbauer as the ultra-uncouth lounge singer Tony Roletti. Frank Bonner, who played the equally uncouth Herb Tarlek on *WKRP in Cincinnati*, interacts well with Kirchenbauer here as the slick Father Hargis.

**THE KALLIKAKS (*) 30 min (5ep Color; 1977 NBC) Situation Comedy** *with David Huddleston as Jasper T. Kallikak, Edie McClurg as Venus Kallikak, Bonnie Ebsen as Bobbi Lou Kallikak, Patrick J. Peterson as J. T., Jr., and Peter Palmer as Oscar Heinz*

This is the story of a man named Jasper, a poor Appalachian coal miner who one day strikes oil. Unfortunately this "Texas tea" is in the form of gasoline—located at a run-down two-pump gas station that he inherits in Nowhere, California. So he loads up the family (wife Venus, daughter Bobbi Lou, and son J. T.) and heads West. There he tries to beat the system and con his way to some bonanza in the land of swimming pools and movie stars—not that any are likely to show up in his part of the state.

Bonnie Ebsen, daughter of Buddy Ebsen (Jed Clampett of *The Beverly Hillbillies*), plays the daughter, while Edie McClurg (the future Mrs. Poole on *Valerie*) is her mom.

**KANE & ABEL (**½) (7hr miniseries Color; 1985 CBS) Drama** *with Peter Strauss as Abel Rosnovski, Sam Neill as William Lowell Kane, David Dukes as David Osborne, Ron Silver as Thaddeus Cohen, Fred Gwynne as Davis LeRoy, Tom Byrd as Richard Kane, Jill Eikenberry as Susan Lester, and Richard Anderson as Alan Lloyd*

In epic miniseries, somebody is always clawing their way to the top. It must be some sort of TV regulation. In *Kane & Abel*, it is Abel who does the clawing. He is a dirt-poor Polish immigrant to the United States at the turn of the century who wants some of the wealth he finds around him. Abel does reach the top and then spends his efforts trying to destroy Kane, a Boston Yankee born to wealth who unintentionally became Abel's lifelong enemy.

Peter Strauss and Sam Neill, both popular miniseries actors (*Rich Man, Poor Man* and *Amerika*, respectively), are very good and very intense in the lead roles. The story comes from the Jeffrey Archer novel of the same name.

**KAREN (*½) 30 min (26ep Color; 1964–1965 NBC) Situation Comedy** *with Debbie Watson as Karen Scott, Richard Denning as Steve Scott, Mary LaRoche as Barbara Scott, and Gina Gillespie as Mimi Scott*

All you need to know about *Karen* is:

(1) The theme song ("Karen") is performed by the Beach Boys and has never appeared on any of their records;

(2) the series is produced by Joe Connelly and Joe Mosher, who hit it big with *Leave It to Beaver* and *The Munsters*, but had a poor track record otherwise;

(3) this show should not be confused with another sitcom called *Karen* from the 1970s starring Karen Valentine, even though both shows are pretty bland;

(4) *Karen* originally aired as part of the sitcom umbrella series *90 Bristol Court.*

(5) Least important—the show is about a perky, pretty lass in southern California who has a tomboy younger sister.

**KAREN (**) 30 min (13ep Color; 1975 ABC) Situation Comedy** *with Karen Valentine as Karen Angelo, Charles Lane as Dale W. Busch, Dena Dietrich as Dena Madison, Aldine King as Cissy Peterson, and Oliver Clark as Jerry Siegel*

The *M*A*S*H* production crew of Gene Reynolds, Larry Gelbart, and Burt Metcalfe go Stateside for this tepid topical sitcom set in Washington. Karen Valentine (the perky English teacher on *Room 222*) stars as a young idealistic staff worker for Open America, a lobbyist organization dedicated to exposing corruption and fighting for citizens' rights. Aldine King plays Cissy, her black roommate, who works for the F.B.I. And Charles Lane, the quintessential irascible codger of 1960s sitcoms (he was Homer Bedloe on *Petticoat Junction*), plays the organization's founder, Dale Busch.

**KAREN'S SONG (**½) 30 min (9ep Color; 1987 Fox) Situation Comedy** *with Patty Duke as Karen Matthews, Lewis Smith as Steven Forman. Lainie Kazan as Claire, Teri Hatcher as Laura, and Granville Van Dusen as Zach*

Nearing her fortieth birthday, Karen Matthews, a divorced literary agent, is amazed to discover that she's quite taken with a young man twelve years her junior, Steven Forman. Why, he was only there to cater a meal! But does she dare take the next step?

Karen decides it's worth the risk, so she begins to pursue the relationship. To her relief, the attraction seems mutual, though that still doesn't remove all the uncertainty and awkwardness. Should she invite Steven to her upcoming birthday? Should she spend a night at his place and wake up far from her own dressing room mirror? And how will she explain all this to people who think Steven's there to date her eighteen-year-old daughter?

This is one of those series (like *The Golden Girls* and *Designing Women*) with women in on the production and writing side (including Linda Marsh and Margie Peters of *Valerie*) as well as in front of the camera. Unfortunately, they didn't really have a chance to get past dealing with the initial hook (a woman dating a much younger man) before the series ended its short run.

**KATE AND ALLIE (***) 30 min (140ep Color; 1984–1989 CBS) Situation Comedy** *with Susan Saint James as Kate McArdle, Jane Curtin as Allie Lowell, Ari Meyers as Emma McArdle, Allison Smith as Jennie Lowell, Frederick Koehler as Chip Lowell, Paul Hecht as Dr. Charles Lowell, John Heard and Harley Venton as Max McArdle, and Sam Freed as Bob Barsky*

While a member of the "first generation" of *Saturday Night Live* performers, Jane Curtin found herself playing the part of a straight-laced homemaker in many parody sketches. She just seemed perfect and comfortable as a nonthreatening middle-class mom.

As Allie Lowell, Curtin gets her chance to take that characterization to a more consistent sitcom world setting, with one major change: Allie is a divorced mother raising a family. So is her lifelong friend, Kate (Susan Saint James). The two decide that one combined household can live more cheaply than two separate ones, so they all move into a spacious Greenwich Village apartment. Two moms, three kids. Allie remains the homemaker, while Kate heads to the office.

Combining households of children is a well-worn sitcom path, previously taken by widows and widowers in such series as *The Brady Bunch.* There's a good reason for that—such a setting allows for a good run of solid domestic comedy including such tried-and-true hooks as balancing a budget, keeping the house in order, and sending the kids (or each other) out on dates. Acknowledging its roots in classic comedy, the producers even staged one episode with Curtin and Saint James playing it like a black-and-white episode of *I Love Lucy.*

Still, there are some nice touches that help *Kate and Allie* stand out. Each episode begins and ends with a relaxed conversation between the two women. At the beginning, they are usually walking outdoors sharing some memory, dream, or wistful reflection—none of which have anything to do with that episode's plot. It's a chance for them just to be friends. At the end, they sit talking in the apartment living room. For this wrap-up conversation, Kate and Allie usually bring a more cutting tone to their thoughts and reactions, saving their sharpest comments for men in general and their former husbands (Max and Charles, respectively) in particular. The two men appear occasionally to receive abuse in person, as well as to complicate the lives of their former wives.

But even after such harsh comments and confrontations, Kate and Allie remain incurable romantics, still daring to dream that one day the *right* man will come along. Only this time they know that even if they remarry, their friendship will remain one of the most important continuing relationships in their lives. And, sure enough, when Allie finds her new Mr. Right (Bob Barsky, a radio sportscaster who proposes over the air), the revised premise (incorporating Allie and Bob's marriage) has

Kate living with the newlyweds in their new apartment. The excuses given are that Bob will be commuting from New York to a TV anchor job in Washington (so Allie needs company), there's plenty of room, and Kate can help with the expenses, but we all know the real reason is so that Kate and Allie can continue to be . . . *Kate and Allie.*

**KATE LOVES A MYSTERY** **(see *Mrs. Columbo*)**

**KATE McSHANE (**) 60 min (10ep & 90 min pilot Color; 1975 CBS) Law Drama** *with Anne Meara as Kate McShane, Charles Haid as Father Ed McShane, and Sean McClory as Pat McShane*

Anne Meara plays a gutsy, single, independent L.A. lawyer with the prerequisite heart of gold. Kate McShane is from a tight-knit Irish-American family, so it's not surprising that she hires her dad, Pat (a former cop), as her chief investigator. And for those sticky questions about morality and the law, there's always her Jesuit-priest brother Ed (played by Charles Haid, Andy Renko on *Hill Street Blues*).

Though her performing background is primarily comedy, Anne Meara (half the husband-and-wife comedy team of Stiller and Meara) does an acceptable job. The series does suffer from bouts of mid-1970s heavy-handed topical relevancy.

**KAY O'BRIEN, SURGEON (*½) 60 min (10ep Color; 1986–1987 CBS & Lifetime) Medical Drama** *with Patricia Kalember as Dr. Kay O'Brien, Lane Smith as Dr. Robert Moffitt, Brian Benben as Dr. Mark Doyle, Tony Soper as Dr. Cliff Margolis, Franc Luz as Sam, Keone Young as Dr. Michael Kwan, and Priscilla Lopez as Rosa Villanueva*

Life is rough for Kay O'Brien (everyone calls her Kayo). She's a twenty-eight-year-old second year surgical resident at Manhattan General Hospital. Aside from the mind-numbing hours of long shifts she works and the constant pressure of saving lives, she struggles with the eternal quandary of the beautiful TV working woman of the 1980s: how to keep her job and her man at the same time.

This show means well and has some nice moments, but Kayo is a bit too cool, and there's no reason to watch this if a good quality medical show (such as *St. Elsewhere*) is on.

**KAZ (**) 60 min (21ep Color; 1978–1979 CBS) Law Drama** *with Ron Leibman as Martin "Kaz" Kazinsky, Patrick O'Neal as Samuel Bennett, Linda Carlson as Katie McKenna, and Gloria LeRoy as Mary Parnell*

Martin Kazinsky, known to all as Kaz, touches all the bases for crime show personalities. First, he had been a cop, to prove he was gritty and a man's man. Next, he was a convict, serving a six-month jail sentence for auto theft, to show he had a touch of the bad-boy rebel in him and that he could relate to the down and out in our society. Finally, he hit the jackpot, he became a lawyer, so he could be set in the flashy, moneyed world of professionals.

With all that background, Kaz is not the typical kind of TV lawyer, and his varied personality is well portrayed by craggy-faced Ron Leibman. The actual stories never quite measure up to all the potential of Kaz's triple-decker background, but the novelty of the premise is good enough to sustain interest through a few episodes. *Kaz* is produced by Lee Rich, of *The Waltons*, *Dallas*, and *The Blue Knight.*

**KEEP IT IN THE FAMILY (**) 30 min (31ep Color; 1980–1981 UK Thames) Situation Comedy** *with Robert Gillespie, Pauline Yates, Glyn Houston, and Stacy Dorning*

The folks live upstairs, their attractive teenage daughters live in the downstairs apartment. This is the routine British version of the premise that became *Too Close for Comfort* in the States.

**KEEP ON TRUCKIN' (**) 60 min (4ep Color; 1975 ABC) Comedy-Variety** *with Fred Travalena as host*

Fourteen up-and-coming comedians appear in this brief collection of comedy bits. The most interesting feature of this show is never seen. *Twilight Zone*'s Rod Serling, not a man known for appearing in comedy shows, was to appear at the start of each episode, to set the scene. Tragically, Serling died after open-heart surgery about three weeks before *Keep on Truckin'* premiered. Serling's introductions were never used and have never publicly aired.

**KENNEDY (*½) (7hr miniseries Color; 1983 NBC) Drama** *with Martin Sheen as John F. Kennedy, Blair Brown as Jacqueline Kennedy, John Shea as Robert Kennedy, E. G. Marshall as Joseph Kennedy, Sr., Geraldine Fitzgerald as Rose Kennedy, and Kevin Conroy as Teddy Kennedy.*

From the 1961 presidential inauguration to the 1963 Dallas assassination, this miniseries glosses over the brief, but memorable, Kennedy years.

**KENTUCKY JONES (**½) 30 min (26ep B&W; 1964–1965 NBC) Drama** *with Dennis Weaver as Kenneth Yarborough "Kentucky" Jones, Ricky Der as Dwight Eisenhower "Ike" Wong, and Harry Morgan as Seldom Jackson*

This is the series that Dennis Weaver left *Gunsmoke* for. A much less violent show, *Kentucky Jones* also lacks a lot of the human drama that made Weaver's previous series a twenty-year institution.

Weaver plays K. Y. Jones (whose initials result in his nickname Kentucky), a veterinarian and owner of the forty-acre Jones Ranch in California. Mrs. Jones died before the series starts, leaving Kentucky a reluctant single foster parent when the young Chinese orphan boy he and his wife had arranged to adopt arrives soon after the funeral.

The program follows Kentucky's efforts to raise little Ike Wong, with help from ranch hand Seldom Jackson (played by TV regular Harry Morgan, later of *Dragnet* and *M*A*S*H*).

**KHAN! (**½) 60 min (7ep Color; 1975 CBS) Detective Drama** *with Khigh Dhiegh as Khan, Irene Yah-Ling Sun as Anna Khan, Evan Kim as Kim Khan, and Vic Tayback as Lt. Gubbins*

TV has had crime shows featuring Greeks, Poles, Jews, and Italians, so why not Chinese? Khan (no first name) is a Chinatown gumshoe in San Francisco, who uses his criminologist daughter and college grad son to crack cases.

Khigh Dhiegh, star of *Khan!*, is best known as the evil Wo Fat in *Hawaii Five-O.* Vic Tayback, who went on to star as Mel in *Alice*, is a San Francisco policeman that Kahn deals with.

**KILROY (**) 60 min (4ep Color; 1965 NBC) Comedy** *with Warren Berlinger as Oscar Kilroy, Celeste Holm as Helen Fuller, Allyn Joslyn as Sam Fuller, and Philip Abbott as Ed Barrett*

Oscar Kilroy is an ex-marine who moves in with the family of his old chum from the service. Soon installed as town dogcatcher, Kilroy becomes a local personality. This series originally was broadcast as part of *Walt Disney's Wonderful World of Color.*

**KING (**½) (6hr miniseries Color; 1978 NBC) Drama** *with Paul Winfield as Martin Luther King, Jr., Cicely Tyson as Coretta Scott King, and Ossie Davis as Martin Luther King, Sr.*

Almost every top black actor and actress of the mid-1970s turns up in this well-produced but somewhat overly reverential docudrama about the life of civil rights leader and Nobel prize winner Martin Luther King, Jr. ■

**KING OF DIAMONDS (*½) 30 min (38ep B&W; 1961–1962 Syndication) Adventure** *with Broderick Crawford as John King and Ray Hamilton as Casey O'Brien*

Broderick Crawford growls his way through standard grade-B investigations, playing the part of a security chief for the diamond industry. He and his assistant, Casey, chase down and recover those precious stones in some surprisingly violent confrontations. Overall, though, it's pretty routine stuff from John Robinson, a co-producer of *Wanted: Dead or Alive.*

**KING OF KENSINGTON (**½) 30 min (111ep Color; 1975–1981 Canada CBC) Situation Comedy** *with Al Waxman as Larry King, Fiona Reid as Kathy King, and Helene Winston as Gladys King*

The Archie Bunker from the Great White North, Larry King (not to be confused with the real-life talk show host) runs King's Variety Store in Kensington, near Toronto, Canada. Larry also is the big cheese in his neighborhood, thus giving the show's title its double meaning. Larry is always shooting off his mouth about something or other. He may not be as essentially lovable as Archie Bunker, but King is usually good for several zingers during each episode.

**KING'S CROSSING (*) 60 min (7ep Color; 1982 ABC) Drama** *with Bradford Dillman as Paul Hollister, Mary Frann as Nan Hollister, Linda Hamilton as Lauren Hollister, Marilyn Jones as Carey Hollister, Daniel Zippi as Billy McCall, and Beatrice Straight as Louisa Beauchamp.*

A close-knit but shattered family moves from Chicago to the small California town they left a decade before, King's Crossing. Can the husband control his drinking? Will daughter Carey survive her first affair? Or will wealthy and powerful Aunt Louisa destroy them all?

Not enough time to tell. This was an unsuccessful soaper from Lorimar Productions (*Dallas, Falcon Crest, Knots Landing*) that ended up as just a brief stopover for performers headed to or from other soapy dramas. Linda Hamilton and Marilyn Jones (playing the teenage daughters) and Daniel Zippi (as daughter Carey's stable-hand lover) came from *The Secrets of Midland Heights.* Beatrice Straight, playing the wealthy aunt, was a veteran of *Beacon Hill*, while Bradford Dillman went on to *Falcon Crest* and Mary Frann fell into small-town intrigues of quite a different sort with *Newhart.* However, no one could match the romantic complications Hamilton would face later as one-half of television's most unusual couple on *Beauty and the Beast.*

**KING'S ROW (**) 60 min (7ep B&W; 1955–1956 ABC) Drama** *with Jack Kelly as Dr. Parris Mitchell, Nan Leslie as Randy Monaghan, Peggy Webber as Elsie Sandor, Robert Horton as Drake McHugh, and Victor Jory as Dr. Alexander Tower*

Based on a popular 1942 film (which contained what is generally considered Ronald Reagan's finest onscreen acting role), the TV version of *King's Row* is set in the small midwestern town of King's Row at the start of the twentieth century. Jack Kelly plays Dr. Mitchell, a hometown boy who returns to set up a psychiatric practice in an era and an area where psychiatry was still considered mostly mumbo-jumbo. It is not the medical angle that is dominant here, however, as the romantic intrigues of small-town life (a la *Peyton Place*) get the most attention.

*King's Row* is an early effort by the Warner Bros. film studio to break into TV. The studio had much better luck with the format of the western (such as *Maverick*, which has two alumni of *King's Row*, co-star Jack Kelly as Bart Maverick and producer Roy Huggins) and the action/adventure hour (such as *77 Sunset Strip*, also produced by Huggins).

**KINGSTON: CONFIDENTIAL (*½) 60 min (13ep & 2 hr pilot Color; 1977 NBC) Drama** *with Raymond Burr as R. B. Kingston, Art Hindle as Tony Marino, Pamela Hensley as Beth Kelly, and Nancy Olson as Jessica Frazier*

The premise of *Kingston: Confidential* makes little sense. Hefty Raymond Burr, a favorite from *Perry Mason* and *Ironside*, plays R. B. Kingston, a top executive for a corporate conglomerate that owns newspapers and TV stations. Kingston was an investigative reporter in his younger (and slimmer) days. Now he can't help dropping his high-level executive tasks to run after some breaking crisis, in order to get the scoop. Why bother having him as an executive? By doing so, his forays into beat reporting seem odd and out of place and they sap the series of what little cohesion it has.

Produced by David Victor, a man more successful with medical dramas such as *Marcus Welby, M.D.* and *Doctor Kildare, Kingston: Confidential* begins with a two-hour 1976 pilot titled *Kingston: The Power Play.*

**KIT CARSON, THE ADVENTURES OF (*½) 30 min (104ep B&W; 1951–1955 Syndication) Western** *with Bill Williams as Christopher "Kit" Carson and Don Diamond as El Toro*

It's easy to see why Bill Williams was chosen to play Kit Carson, legendary Indian scout of the Old West. After all, Williams fits the hero profile from the early days of TV kiddie westerns, in that he is blond, rugged, and clean-cut. He had also starred in several post–World War II action flicks (such as *Thirty Seconds over Tokyo*).

Don Diamond, who plays Kit's Mexican sidekick El Toro (The Bull), makes his TV series debut in *Kit Carson.* He later put in a season as Corporal Reyes, Sgt. Garcia's flunky on *Zorro*, and then hit his stride as Crazy Cat, the wheeler-dealer second banana among the "ferocious" Hekawi Indians on *F Troop.* Interestingly enough, both Williams and Diamond were born in Brooklyn, New York, which is about as far from the Old West as you can get.

*The Adventures of Kit Carson* contains all the staple elements of a kiddie TV western, such as a roaming hero and his buddy, lots of horses, Indians, and gun fights, few women, and simple, simple, simple stories. Don't look for any surprises here.

**KLONDIKE (*) 30 min (18ep B&W; 1960–1961 NBC) Adventure** *with Ralph Taeger as Mike Halliday, James Coburn as Jeff Durain, Mari Blanchard as Kathy O'Hara, and Joi Lansing as Goldie*

It's Alaska, in the 1890s, at the height of the gold rush. Fortunes are to be made, and stolen. Mike Halliday is the good-guy prospector. Kathy O'Hara is the good-gal hotel proprietress amidst the swill of gold-fevered miners. Jeff Durain (played by the deliciously evil James Coburn) is the bad-guy hotel proprietor who does his mining through deceit and flimflammery.

The setup sounds half interesting, but the execution is boring and predictable. When *Klondike* shut down, the two male leads reappeared in *Acapulco*, quite a change of scenery, *Klondike* is directed by Sam Peckinpah, master of violent movies (*The Wild Bunch, Straw Dogs*).

**KNIGHT RIDER (**) 60 or 30 min (90ep 60 min or 91ep 30 min Color: 1982–1987 NBC) Adventure** *with William Daniels as the voice of KITT, David Hasselhoff as Michael Knight, Edward Mulhare as Devon Miles, Patricia McPherson as Bonnie Barstow, and Rebecca Holden as April Curtis*

At the same time William Daniels was earning his Emmy awards as the sharp-tongued chief of surgery in *St. Elsewhere*, he was also toiling on the other side of the critical tracks with the fantasy adventures of a dashing young hero and his faithful car. Daniels plays the car.

More specifically, he provides the voice for the sleek super-car (named KITT) driven by undercover adventurer Michael Knight. Daniels infuses KITT with intelligence, warmth, wit (occasionally laced with sarcasm), and an honest concern for his all-too-human partner. As a result, the two emerge as one of television's great adventure duos even though Daniels never appears onscreen.

KITT (nickname for the fictional Knight Industries Two Thousand car) is a flashy stand-in, a black customized Trans-Am that's toured the country doing promotional appearances for the series. Kids and car buffs love it. Meanwhile, former daytime soap opera hunk David Hasselhoff (from *The Young and the Restless*) draws the females with his portrayal of Michael Knight as a brave, sensitive, and somewhat vulnerable hero.

The stories are harmless cartoon fluff, following in the initial fantasy-tinged premise: A dying millionaire genius named Wilton Knight (Richard Basehart) rescues a fatally injured undercover cop named Michael Long. Knight gives Michael a new face, a new identity (that of Michael Knight), and a new job. Then Wilton Knight dies, leaving Michael's future assignments to associate Devon Miles, who manages Knight's Foundation for Law and Government. Teamed with KITT, Michael thrives in his new role.

In syndication, *Knight Rider* is also offered in a condensed thirty-minute format.

**KNIGHTWATCH (*) 60 min (8ep Color; 1988–1989 ABC) Crime Drama** *with Benjamin Bratt as Tony Maldonado, Don Franklin as Calvin, Joshua Cadman as Condo, Ava Haddad as Casey, Calvin Levels as Burn, Gale Mayron as Baldwin, Paris Vaughn as Leslie, and Tom Bower as Father Jim*

An occasionally violent urban crime series, focusing on the Knights, a fictional independent crime-fighting group, obviously inspired by the real-life Guardian Angels—a nonviolent volunteer group operating in cities such as New York and Chicago. Dressed in distinctive caps (or other identifying garb), the Guardian Angels usually ride the public transportation systems of the city, offering an unofficial but friendly presence to potentially nervous passengers (especially those riding alone at night).

The black-vested fictional Knights have a longer agenda but subscribe to similar precepts (no weapons, but they do use the martial arts for defense). They operate out of the basement of an old church, where they train, socialize, and attempt to reach out to their immediate community. In a sequence similar to the morning roll call on *Hill Street Blues*, Tony, their leader, talks about areas they plan to patrol and things to keep an eye out for, ending the session with everyone joining hands in a circle of spiritual unity. Your reaction to this sequence pretty much indicates if you're going to buy into the whole setup.

Allusions to *Hill Street Blues* are appropriate because the surface structure and feel are very similar, shifting from the dramatic administrative actions of Tony to incidents on patrol to interactions and camaraderie within the group. Still, it's a thin line between a vigilante group and dedicated citizens trying to make a difference, and that lack of official status colors the tone of the stories. The Knights may not institute trouble, but they sure seem to be a lightning rod for it. In just the opening episode, one of the Knights is booted from the organization for crossing the line (during a struggle, he flips a knife-wielding perpetrator over the edge of a roof), which leads to a media circus of charges and countercharges.

*Knightwatch* is wrapped in appropriately hip camera work, colors, and music (by Stanley Clarke and the tune "Fragile" by Sting). Yet, ultimately, it comes across as a typical teen-oriented cop series, most likely to seem as dated in five years as such 1970s offerings as *The Mod Squad* appear today.

**KNOTS LANDING (***½) 60 min (246ep at Fall 1989 Color; 1979– CBS) Drama** *with Ted Shackelford as Gary Ewing, Joan Van Ark as Valene Ewing, Michele Lee as Karen Fairgate MacKenzie, Kevin Dobson as M. Patrick "Mack" MacKenzie, Constance McCashin as Laura Avery, John Pleshette as Richard Avery, Don Murray as Sid Fairgate, James Houghton as Kenny Ward, Kim Lankford as Ginger Ward, Donna Mills as Abby Cunningham Ewing, Lisa Hartman as Ciji Dunne and Cathy Geary, Nicollette Sheridan as Paige Matheson, and William Devane as Gregory Sumner*

In the beginning of this *Dallas* spin-off, Gary Ewing, alcoholic brother of J. R. and Bobby Ewing, decides to start his life anew—away from the oppressive surroundings of the Southfork ranch. So, Gary leaves daughter Lucy with Miss Ellie, makes up with his estranged wife, Val, and moves with her to southern California (into a neighborhood known as Knots Landing), where extramarital affairs and deceitful, back-stabbing people are a dime a dozen. There, Gary joins Alcoholics Anonymous, gets a job working for Sid Fairgate (the owner of a fancy car dealership), and everything seems hunky-dory.

But, as even a casual soap viewer knows, this kind of blissful serenity can't last long, and it doesn't. The big shake-up begins with the arrival of Sid Fairgate's divorced sister Abby, who moves into Knots Landing just before Sid is killed off. Abby is a vixen who only needs to look longingly at a man to wreck a marriage, something she seems to enjoy doing. Sure enough, Gary and Val soon break up and Gary marries Abby. Naturally, they're hardly a permanent match either, but the relationship does last several seasons worth of episodes.

Actually, that's one of the strengths of *Knots Landing* over the long haul. This series is very well paced, getting maximum mileage out of its plot complications and character conflicts, following the full ramifications of a story line rather than jumping willy-nilly from one formula denouement to another (the chief sin of soaps in the *Dynasty* mold). Along the way, the characters have plenty of room to develop beyond the role of plot pawns as they deal with the personal intrigues of their cul-de-sac community. Even more important, when characters seem to have gone as far as they're going to, they are very effectively written out and new ones are brought in. For example, William Devane's Gregory Sumner (a state senator) adds local political power manipulations to the continuity, while Nicollette Sheridan's Paige Matheson (illegitimate daughter of attorney Mack MacKenzie) is part of the "next generation" of *Knots Landing* movers and shakers. (Of all the prime time soaps of the 1980s, this series is most successful at bringing in fresh faces.) The program is also willing to take chances with scripts, such as in an episode that has the performers "improvising" in character as they share their thoughts on the death of neighbor Laura Avery.

As a result, *Knots Landing* emerges as one of the best of the prime-time soap opera dramas, every bit as good as *Dallas* (sometimes even better). In fact, though a number of folks from Southfork drop by now and again (as in a one-shot coupling of the manipulative J. R. and Abby), *Knots Landing* generally carries on quite independently from its parent series. The Ewing fortune may have given Gary the start-up money to play in high-stakes ventures (such as California real estate), but he (and the series) definitely stand up quite well on their own terms.

**KODIAK (*) 30 min (13ep Color; 1974 ABC) Police Drama** *with Clint Walker as Cal "Kodiak" McKay, Abner Biberman as Abraham Lincoln Imhook, and Maggie Blye as Mandy*

Clint Walker, the tall, laconic lead from *Cheyenne*,

plays the tall, laconic Kodiak McKay, an Alaskan state policeman, whose turf consists of 50,000 miles of outback. Not much transpires on *Kodiak*, but the scenery (shot on location in the 49th state) is nice.

**KOJAK** (***½) **60 min (118 ep at Fall 1989 & 3 hr pilot & two 2 hr sequels Color; 1973–1978 CBS) Police Drama** *with Telly Savalas as Lt. Theo Kojak, Dan Frazer as Chief Frank McNeil, Kevin Dobson as Lt. Bobby Crocker, and George Demosthenes Savalas as Det. Stavros*

One of the more memorable and distinctive police characters in TV history, Theo Kojak is the archetypal rebel within the system. Kojak works totally inside the established structure of our culture (he is a policeman on the New York City force) yet in his heart he is a loner, a man who does not mentally accept the trappings of conformity. This apparent contradiction fuels the energy of Theo Kojak and helps make *Kojak* one of TV's better cop shows.

Theo Kojak is one of the top plainclothes detectives in Manhattan's 13th Precinct, now working under Frank McNeil, his former partner. McNeil had played along more with the powers that be and had risen through the ranks to be chief detective. Kojak didn't go in for that kind of subservience and paid the price by being passed over for promotion. Kojak is still on the street, solving crimes, doing things his way, cracking jokes, sucking on lollipops, and stepping on the toes of those higher up.

Part of the allure of *Kojak* is the heavy dose of reality that comes through. The series is peppered with interprecinct bickering, police politics, and the gritty, day-to-day routine legwork that takes up much of a real policeman's workday. Some on-location scenery from around New York during the show's later seasons adds to the reality, but primarily the allure is Telly Savalas, TV's first bald policeman. Savalas portrays Kojak as a tough, no-nonsense guy with deep feelings for the work he does and the people around him. Kojak's tendency to thumb his nose at bigwigs is always appealing to viewers who wish they could do the same, and the frequent interludes of violent action in *Kojak* always appeal to large chunks of the audience. Kojak's obvious ethnicity (Greek) also sets him apart as a unique character, when too many other TV cops (Joe Friday, Steve McGarrett) are WASPs with no distinguishing characteristics. Previously an overlooked heavy, Savalas became a worldwide superstar through his role in *Kojak*.

The original 1973 pilot episode for *Kojak*, titled *The Marcus-Nelson Murders*, is an outstanding TV movie, based on a real-life racial incident from 1963.

The first sequel to *Kojak*, a 1985 TV movie titled *Kojak: The Belarus File*, is disappointing. The bald policeman fits poorly in a script jerry-rigged from John Loftus's spy novel *The Belarus Secret*. In the second *Kojak* sequel, *Kojak: The Price of Justice*, from 1987, Theo Kojak is finally promoted to inspector. Here again the script is poorly adapted from a non-Kojak novel, in this case Dorothy Uhnak's *The Investigation*. In the Fall of 1989, though, *Kojak* began a full-fledged revival as part of the two-hour *ABC Mystery Movie* rotation. ■

**KOLCHAK: THE NIGHT STALKER** (***) **60 min (20ep & 2 90 min pilots Color; 1974–1975 ABC) Adventure** *with Darren McGavin as Carl Kolchak, Simon Oakland as Tony Vincenzo, Jack Grinnage as Ron Updyke, and Ruth McDevitt as Emily Cowles*

Here's the *Kolchak* formula: Chicago reporter Carl Kolchak knows there's something strange going on. Several people are dead, killed by someone or something that appears to have supernatural or extraterrestrial powers. The police deny it. Tony, his boss, doesn't want to believe it (his ulcer is in bad enough shape already). But the pattern fits . . . if you're willing to believe in zombies, werewolves, vampires, alien invaders, and the like.

Kolchak does. Eventually it falls on him to save humanity from its worst nightmares. He researches his subject as best as he can and discovers (or stumbles upon) the "fatal weakness," which he uses in a final one-on-one confrontation.

Triumphant, Kolchak dictates the story into his portable tape recorder. That's as far as it will go, though, because either the authorities have ordered it suppressed or he wasn't able to get any documenting photos to accompany his tale. Once again he's denied his shot at national fame and glory.

It's all pretty hokey, which is probably what makes his series so much fun. With his rumpled white sports coat and ill-fitting straw hat, Darren McGavin's Kolchak looks like he just walked off the set of a 1940s horror film in search of some monster. As in those classics, the creatures stay mostly in the shadows (more frightening that way). They also really kill people (rather viciously), adding a genuine sense of horror to the tales. Kolchak's narration caps it off, with such sardonic observations as comparing an alien visitor that sucks bone marrow from humans to an earthly motorist getting a snack at a truck stop.

If you love the formula, you'll probably want to catch every episode. Otherwise you might prefer the two made-for-TV movies that led to the series, *The Night Stalker* and *The Night Strangler* (set in Las Vegas and Seattle, respectively). Tony's there too, getting booted out of town along with Karl.

What they both need is a better agent. Or at least someone to give them the number for a publication like *The Weekly Tabloid News*, where an artist's rendering will do in place of photo corroboration. By now Carl and Tony would probably be running the place. ■

**THE KOPYKATS** (**½) **60 min (7ep Color; 1972 ABC) Comedy-Variety** *with Rich Little, Frank Gorshin, George Kirby, Marilyn Michaels, Charlie Callas, and Fred Travalena*

The best comic impersonators of the early 1970s team up to parade their talents by appearing as other well-known celebrities. Most of these episodes originally aired under the title *ABC Comedy Hour.*

**KRAFT SUSPENSE THEATER (**) 60 min (53ep Color; 1963–1965 NBC) Suspense Anthology**

Kraft Foods was one of the first major sponsors to get involved in television, and numerous regular series bore the Kraft name from the 1940s into the 1970s. This series is a collection of mildly interesting hour-long suspense dramas featuring several famous Hollywood stars. It is also syndicated as *Suspense Theater.*

**KUNG FU (*½) 60 min (62ep & 2 hr sequel Color; 1972–1975 ABC) Western** *with David Carradine and Radames Pera as Kwai Chang Caine, Keye Luke as Master Po, and Philip Ahn as Master Kan*

A pretentious, heavy-handed effort to take some of the concept of *The Fugitive* and add lots of stylized violence, *Kung Fu* reeks of early 1970s relevance. David Carradine, hippy-ish member of the renowned Carradine acting clan, plays half-Chinese, half-American Kwai Chang Caine, a spaced-out refugee from imperial China in the 1870s. Trained in mystical philosophy and the martial arts by Shaolin monks Master Po and Master Kan, young Caine (played in numerous flashbacks by Radames Pera) kills a member of the Chinese royal family and must flee to America. He is tracked by Chinese agents and other bad guys (while he searches for his long-lost half-brother). In the states, Caine also must deal with the crass, vain, sinful, wild West that does not respect the higher ideals of Eastern philosophy and does not particularly care for Orientals, even half-breed Orientals like Caine.

Caine wanders around, trying to avoid capture and trouble (something like *The Fugitive's* Dr. Richard Kimble). When Caine gets mad or is cornered by his enemies, he lashes out with lethal kung fu attacks that are played in excruciating slow motion. When the bad guys are laid low, Caine will pop off with some words of Oriental wisdom and shuffle along.

*Kung Fu* may seem to have its heart in the right place, espousing peace and tranquility, but the amount of butt-kicking violence Caine both dishes out and receives makes one think that perhaps the show protests too much. The mysticism of *Kung Fu* went out with lava lamps. The flashback scenes with Master Po and Master Kan are unintentionally campy.

Keye Luke (Master Po) starred as Charlie Chan's number one son in numerous Charlie Chan films in the 1930s. The executive producer of *Kung Fu*, Jerry Thorpe, got to perfect his touches of *The Fugitive* with the real thing, David Janssen, as producer of Janssen's mid-1970s series *Harry O.*

The *Kung Fu* sequel, *Kung Fu: The Movie* from 1986, does little to advance the basic story. Caine is still roaming the West, followed by yet another imperial hit man (played by Brandon Lee, son of martial arts patron saint Bruce Lee).

In 1987, an attempt to revive the series, but set in the modern era, resulted in a sixty-minute pilot, *Kung Fu, the Next Generation.* David Doran plays Caine's great-grandson, who is seeking a reconciliation with his own wayward son (played by the ubiquitous Brandon Lee).

**L. A. LAW (***) 60 min (61ep at Fall 1989 & 2 hr pilot Color; 1986– NBC) Law Drama** *with Harry Hamlin as Michael Kuzak, Susan Dey as Grace Van Owen, Jill Eikenberry as Ann Kelsey, Corbin Bernsen as Arnie Becker, Richard Dysart as Leland McKenzie, Michael Tucker as Stuart Markowitz, Michele Greene as Abby Perkins, Alan Rachins as Douglas Brackman, Jr., Jimmy Smits as Victor Sifuentes, Susan Ruttan as Roxanne Melman, Blair Underwood as Jonathan Rollins, and Larry Drake as Benny Stulwicz*

Americans are deeply wedded to the egalitarian precepts that helped found our nation. Consequently our heroes of popular culture tend to be representatives of the teeming middle and lower classes. When the upper class is portrayed in American pop culture, it tends to be either in a derogatory manner or with a sense that the well-off are somehow inherently evil. As a result, American TV has always championed simple folk such as Lucy Ricardo and Ralph Kramden, while the rich and powerful such as Blake Carrington and J. R. Ewing are seen in a fairyland of opulence and chicanery.

*L. A. Law* tries to balance this tendency. By all standards, the Los Angeles lawyers seen in this show are the upper crust of modern society. They are rich and powerful and (mostly) good-looking. The great achievement of the series is to portray this power elite as, at heart, just the same as everybody else. The L. A. lawyers get mad, act out of spite, make wrong choices, and struggle their days away just like their lower-class countrymen. This trend of looking behind the working surface to see the human side of hard-working professionals flowered in the early 1980s with *Hill Street Blues* and *St. Elsewhere. L. A. Law* does for lawyers what those two shows did for policemen and doctors. The connection is obvious, since Steven Bochco produced both *Hill Street Blues* and *L. A. Law.*

Bochco carries over the *Hill Street* format almost intact, with a large central cast, overlapping story lines, and a deft combination of human tragedy and whimsy. The setting is a venerable Los Angeles law firm, run by a paternal senior partner (Leland McKenzie) and a balding, penny-pinching son (Douglas Brackman, Jr.) of one of the firm's founders. One step down the rungs of power are handsome and compassionate young workhorse Michael Kuzak and venal and opportunistic divorce lawyer Arnie Becker. Next comes warm but publicly reserved Ann Kelsey and squirrelly little tax expert Stuart Markowitz. Two of the newer additions to the firm are bright and self-assured Hispanic Victor Sifuentes and idealistic and troubled young associate Abby Perkins. The original central cast is rounded out by Grace Van Owen, a languid and icy deputy district attorney who soon becomes romantically involved with Kuzak, and Roxanne, Arnie's long-suffering secretary.

With such a large and vibrant collection of characters, *L. A. Law* can indulge in the luxury of focusing on various cast members through its run, thereby allowing a wide gamut of story lines that keep the show fresh. One week Kuzak may be facing Van Owen in the courtroom after a heavy night of passion together. The next week Arnie's mother may be asking her son to defend her in a divorce action against his own father. Aside from the well-rounded look at the way a real law firm operates, the program can delve deeply into the juicy personal sides of the characters' lives. Stuart, a most unlikely Romeo, engages in a long but ultimately successful pursuit of Ann. Brackman goes through a messy separation from his wife. Arnie turns out to be an insecure guy who just wants some real affection. Even dour Leland has a fling with a sultry young law student. It is this combination of professional and personal details that brings so much depth to the stories and paints such fascinating human portraits of the characters.

While the lawyers of *L. A. Law* cannot face instant death each week as believably as the cops of *Hill Street*, producer Bochco does his best to translate the professional crises so familiar to viewers of TV cop shows (and medical shows, for that matter) to the more cerebral but just as chancy world of legal intrigue. Numerous shows have tried to dramatize non–life-threatening professions before, but with the exceptions of the oil-drenched prime-time soap operas (*Dallas, Dynasty*), few have succeeded as well as *L. A. Law*.

At times, though, it is quite possible to step back from all the wailing and gnashing of teeth on *L. A. Law* and say, "Geez, what are these people griping about? They've got it pretty good." An overlitigious America may not need a TV series that sympathizes with the lawyer's lot in life, but *L. A. Law* demonstrates with aplomb that even the most outwardly successful among us have their own inner trials that constitute high drama. ■

**LACE (***) (5hr miniseries Color; 1984 ABC)/LACE II (**) (4 hr miniseries Color; 1985 ABC) Drama** *with Phoebe Cates as Lilli, Bess Armstrong and Deborah Raffin as Judy Hale, Brooke Adams as Jennifer "Pagan" Tralone, Arielle Dombasle as Maxine Pascale, Anthony Higgins as Prince Abdullah, Francois Guetary as Pierre Boursal, James Read as Daryl Webster, and Patrick Ryecart as Werner Graff*

A monument of swill, a high-water mark of low-brow titillation, *Lace* (and, to a lesser extent, its sequel *Lace II*) is pure, unadulterated trash. Once you accept this fact you can really get into the preposterous story and the brazen bitchery of all the lead characters.

Judy, Pagan, and Maxine are three high school chums, one of whom becomes pregnant after a school dance. The resulting baby girl is put up for adoption, placed with foster parents, and grows up, never knowing who her mother was. The three young women all grow up and attain a modicum of wealth and power. Maxine marries into money, Pagan weds a renowned scientist, and Judy goes into journalism and starts her own magazine, called *Lace*.

When the abandoned baby girl (Lilli) grows to become a renowned movie sex star, she somehow discovers that one of these three renowned ladies is her mother. Lilli goes bonkers and flies off on a rampage to find out which one it is (in order to kill the "rich bitch"), and the petulant starlet will stop at nothing (libeling the ladies in print, seducing their sons) to get her way. Lilli finally confronts all three suspects and utters the memorable line, "All right, which of you bitches is my mother?"

After Lilli finds the answer, daughter and mother have a tear-jerker climax, which sets up *Lace II*, where Lilli turns her anger to a new quest, finding out which "bastard" was her father: an American astronaut, an Arab prince, or a European conductor. Be thankful you aren't related to Lilli.

The original *Lace* is adapted from Shirley Conran's novel, but *Lace II* is a TV original based on Conran's work.

**LADIES' MAN (*) 30 min (15ep Color; 1980–1981 CBS) Situation Comedy** *with Lawrence Pressman as Alan Thackeray, Louise Sorel as Elaine Holstein, Karen Morrow as Betty Brill, Natasha Ryan as Amy Thackeray, and Herb Edelman as Reggie*

At the office, Alan Thackeray is the only male staffer on a woman's magazine (*Women's Life*), working under a tough, sophisticated boss (Elaine Holstein) and surrounded by beautiful co-workers. Naturally he lands such feature article assignments as "sexual harassment of working women" or "why women pose nude for male magazines," which have to be written with the magazine's primary readership in mind. At home he has to face the trials and tribulations of raising his young daughter, Amy, as a divorced single parent (though he gets advice from his earthy neighbor, Betty). Somewhere in this setup lurks the potential for a clever role reversal comedy, but it doesn't show up here. Instead the series settles for half-baked mocking twists on some legitimate female workplace complaints.

**LADY BLUE (*) 60 min (13ep & 2 hr pilot Color; 1985–1986 ABC) Police Drama** *with Jamie Ross as Det. Katy Mahoney, Danny Aiello as Chief Terry McNichols, and Ron Dean as Sgt. Gina Ginelli*

Shoot first; ask questions later. That's the motto of tempestuous red-haired Katy Mahoney, an undercover lady cop in Chicago with a .357 magnum hidden in her dress. Some nasty old lady cocaine smuggler offed Katy's lover boy, and that really made her angry. Now as a sort of female Dirty Harry, she wages a one-woman war against all the nasty druggies and other vermin. Oh, she carries a badge, but she doesn't let police procedure get in the way of a good chase or an easy shoot-out with some suspect.

**LANCER (**) 60 min (51ep Color; 1968–1970 CBS) Western** *with James Stacy as Johnny Madrid Lancer, Wayne Maunder as Scott Lancer, Andrew Duggan as Murdoch Lancer, and Elizabeth Baur as Teresa O'Brien*

No, this is not a show about a frontier doctor who treats boils. Instead it is another male-only family saga in the *Bonanza* mold. Murdoch Lancer owns a ranch covering most of California's San Joaquin Valley in the 1870s. All the pesky peon farmers around him want to break up the large Lancer holdings, and Murdoch finds it hard to hold them off by himself (with only help from pretty young Teresa O'Brien, daughter of Lancer's dead foreman). Old man Lancer calls in his reinforcements, his two sons by different wives. Scott is a half-Irish Bostonian college man, while Johnny is a half-Mexican bandito. The two half-brothers do not agree on much, other than a yen for Teresa.

**LAND OF THE GIANTS (*) 60 min (51ep Color; 1968–1970 ABC) Science Fiction** *with Gary Conway as Capt. Steve Burton, Don Matheson as Mark Wilson, Stefan Arngrim as Barry Lockridge, Don Marshall as Dan Erikson, Deanna Lund as Valerie Scott, Heather Young as Betty Hamilton, and Kurt Kasznar as Cmdr. Alexander Fitzhugh*

The three-person crew and four passengers on a routine commercial rocket flight from New York to London in 1983 go through some sort of weird warp and wind up crash-landed and stuck on a planet resembling Earth. The problem is that everything in this new world is about twelve times as big as on Earth. The seven wee folk are, for no good reason, hunted by the authorities of the gargantuan world.

*Land of the Giants*, like all Irwin Allen shows (*Time Tunnel, Lost in Space, Voyage to the Bottom of the Sea*), has great special effects, but there is not much in the way of plot or characterization here.

**LANIGAN'S RABBI (**½) 90 min (4ep & 2 hr pilot Color; 1977 NBC) Detective Drama** *with Art Carney as Chief Paul Lanigan, Bruce Solomon as Rabbi David Small, Janis Paige as Kate Lanigan, Janet Margolin as Miriam Small, and Barbara Carney as Bobbie Whittaker*

Good Art Carney vehicle that originally slipped on the air the closing days of the *Mystery Movie* slot (home of *Columbo, McMillan and Wife*, and other similar fare) for a very short run. As with the other entries, the emphasis is on character interaction as well as crime, with the wives of police chief Lanigan and his rabbi friend David joining in. In addition, Carney's real-life daughter, Barbara, turns up as a reporter for the local small-town newspaper. The curly-haired Bruce Solomon (Sergeant Foley from *Mary Hartman, Mary Hartman*) plays the rabbi, though Stuart Margolin had the role for the 1976 made-for-TV movie pilot, sometimes rerun in local movie slots under the title *Friday the Rabbi Slept Late* (the name of the novel by Harry Kemelman the series was based on).

**LARAMIE (**) 60 min (124ep: 64 B&W & 60 Color; 1959–1963 NBC) Western** *with John Smith as Slim Sherman, Robert Fuller as Jess Harper, Hoagy Carmichael as Jonesy, Bobby Crawford, Jr., as Andy Sherman, Dennis Holmes as Mike Williams, and Spring Byington as Daisy Cooper*

Slim Sherman takes control of the family ranch near Laramie, Wyoming, after the death of his father at the start of *Laramie.* During the four-season course of the series, drifter Jess Harper settles down to become Slim's partner and Slim's younger brother Andy drifts away, as does laconic ranch hand Jonesy. All the while, wholesome housekeeper Daisy cleans up after the men.

*Laramie*, a solidly produced series, has little to distinguish it from the countless other westerns of the late 1950s and 1960s, other than the appearance of famed songwriter Hoagy Carmichael ("Georgia on My Mind," "Star Dust") as Jonesy.

**LAREDO (**½) 60 min (56ep Color; 1965–1967 NBC) Western** *with Neville Brand as Ranger Reese Bennett, Peter Brown as Ranger Chad Cooper, William Smith as Ranger Joe Riley, Robert Wolders as Ranger Erik Hunter, and Philip Carey as Captain Edward Parmalee*

A western done with a lighter touch, beginning with Neville Brand being cast against his usual tough bad-guy type (for instance, he was Al Capone on *The Untouchables*), and turning up instead as an old-time gunfighter in the Texas Rangers. Two relative youngsters, Chad and Joe, are his closest comrades (later joined by Erik Hunter) with the banter and ribbing among them a welcome contrast to the usual somber faces in such TV western setups. Their straight-laced commander, Captain Parmalee (a phonetic relative to Captain Parmenter of *F Troop*), finds their attitude an annoyance but tolerates it as long as they get the job done. It's not exactly *Maverick*—more like some of the humorous episodes of *Bonanza*. This series has its roots in an episode of *The Virginian* ("We've Lost a Train"), which played the season before *Laredo* began its original run. Both Philip Carey and Peter Brown later went on to successful stints on various daytime soap operas, while William Smith popped up on the prime-time soaper, *Rich Man, Poor Man.*

**LASSIE** **(***) 30 min (533ep: 369ep B&W & 164ep Color; 1954–1974 CBS & Syndication)** *with Tommy Rettig as Jeff Miller, Jan Clayton as Ellen Miller, George Cleveland as "Gramps" Miller, Donald Keeler as "Porky" Brockway, Jon Provost as Timmy, Cloris Leachman and June Lockhart as Ruth Martin, Jon Shepodd and Hugh Reilly as Paul Martin, Todd Ferrell as Boomer Bates, Andy Clyde as Cully Wilson, Robert Bray as Corey Stuart, Jed Allan as Scott Turner, Jack De Mave as Bob Erickson, Ron Hayes as Garth Holden, Larry Pennell as Keith Holden, Pamelyn Ferdin as Lucky Baker, and Larry Wilcox as Dale Mitchell. And, of course, Lassie.*

The photogenic collie first hit the screens in a 1943 theatrical feature, *Lassie Come Home* (with a cast including young Elizabeth Taylor, Roddy McDowall, and Nigel Bruce), and quickly followed with other films, a radio program, and this extraordinarily long-running television series. During the television years, Lassie goes through many different caretakers. There are cute children with loving families (the Millers with their son, Jeff; then the Martins, adopting the young orphan, Timmy), dedicated forest rangers (Corey, Scott, and Bob), and a kind ranching family, the Holdens (with assistant Dale Mitchell and young neighbor Lucy Baker). All are good-hearted people who instinctively trust the golden collie to lead them through difficult situations. Lassie barks out warnings of oncoming disasters, fetches help for the injured, guides the lost and confused, attacks bad guys if necessary, and sometimes even takes such human tasks as working a water pump into her own paws.

The result is a shamelessly sentimental but effective family adventure no matter what the situation. More than half the stories (those involving Jeff and Timmy) are set on a small farm with the primary hook being the love between Lassie and her young caretaker (a boy and his dog). Of the two, the Timmy episodes are stronger, due primarily to a better supporting cast.

After more than 300 such tales (over the course of a decade), the setup for *Lassie* changes dramatically. Timmy and his adopted parents move to Australia and have to leave the collie behind due to animal quarantine restrictions. So after a brief time with an old friend of the family, Cully Wilson, Lassie ends up living at a forest ranger's station. There she has far more time to wander off on her own and eventually (for three seasons' worth of episodes) she even leaves that base and has no permanent human companions at all. Instead it's Lassie in the forest or on the road, often just sticking with other animals in trouble. (That's when she falls in love with another collie, resulting in a litter of puppies.)

You have to give the writers and producers credit for trying something different and for a while Lassie solo isn't a bad idea. But it soon becomes clear why you need those silly people around to say the obvious ("Look, there's the guy who started the fire!")—if they don't, no one else will! During this period, what passes for plot has to be simplified so much (or explained with flashbacks seen through Lassie's eyes) that the program sometimes lurches very close to self-parody. Luckily for the end of the original twenty-season run of *Lassie* episodes, she's back with a human family, this time living on a California ranch.

Since then, the character of Lassie has continued in a number of ventures. There was a passable two-season (forty-eight episodes in 1973 and 1974) animated series, *Lassie and the Rescue Rangers.* Then there were two full-length films in 1978: *Lassie: A New Beginning*, a muddled two-hour made-for-TV movie that did not lead to a subsequent new live-action series; and the *The Magic of Lassie*, a bland theatrical remake of *Lassie Come Home* with Jimmy Stewart, Mickey Rooney, Pernell Roberts, and Stephanie Zimbalist.

At last, in 1989, a new *Lassie* series began production (with twenty-four new episodes) for first-run syndication in the Fall of 1989. The cast for this includes *E. T.* mom Dee Wallace Stone, her real-life husband, Christopher Stone, and (appropriately) a grown-up Jon Provost (who played owner Timmy in the late 1950s and early 1960s).

In reruns, Lassie's early adventures with Jeff and Timmy sometimes play under the titles *Jeff's Collie* (103 episodes) and *Timmy and Lassie* (232 episodes), all in black and white. Or, they air with the balance of the package (198 episodes: 34 black-and-white plus 164 color) under the original title, *Lassie.*

Through all three versions of the Lassie legend, there have been at least a half dozen collies who have taken the title role, all of them male. ■

**THE LAST CONVERTIBLE** **(**) (6hr miniseries Color; 1979 NBC) Drama** *with Perry King as Russ Currier, Bruce Boxleitner as George Virdon, Edward Albert as Ron Dalrymple, John Shea as Terry Garrigan, Michael Nouri as Jean R. G. R. desBarres, Deborah Raffin as Chris Farris, Kim Darby as Ann Rowan, and Sharon Gless as Kay Haddon*

This adequate adaptation of the Anton Myrer novel traces the lives of five Harvard roommates from the class of 1944 to their 1969 reunion. Russ, George, Ron, Terry, and Jean are the comrades who share their golden college years as well as an affectionate interest in both a Packard convertible and a beautiful young Radcliffe student named Chris. Naturally she's the focus of some tense moments among them all. There are the usual miniseries celebrity cameos (including one by John Houseman), but, frankly, all this pining for lost youth starts to come off as rather trite. The six-hour miniseries has also been packaged into five one-hour segments.

**THE LAST DAYS OF POMPEII** **(***) (7hr miniseries Color: 1984 ABC) Drama** *with Ned Beatty as Diomed, Brian Blessed as Olinthus, Ernest Borgnine as Marcus,*

*Lesley-Anne Down as Chloe, Olivia Hussey as Ione, and Duncan Regehr as Lydon*

This unintentionally funny saga of the sordid lifestyle of volcano-doomed Pompeii in 79 A.D. is a riot. It looks as if the producers took a script from some modern-day New York City drama of corporate intrigue and revamped the story to an ancient Roman setting, without altering the characters much. Ned Beatty plays some petty merchant (a refugee from the Seventh Avenue garment trade?), Duncan Regehr is a pretty-boy gladiator (an ancient version of a health club instructor), Olivia Hussey is the timeless spoiled beauty, and Ernest Borgnine brings a little touch of a Brooklyn-bred football coach to the role of manager of the gladiators. It's nice to know that all these nasty people get boiled in steaming lava at the end.

**THE LAST OF THE BASKETS (**) 30 min (13ep Color; 1979 UK Granada) Situation Comedy** *with Arthur Lowe, Ken Jones, and Patricia Hayes*

Predictable vehicle for the portly British character actor, Authur Lowe (from *A. J. Wentworth, Bless Me, Father*, and *Coronation Street*), who plays a factory boiler tender named the sole male heir to an ancient house. This inheritance also includes the honor of continuing the line of the Earl of Clogborough with all modern-day rights and privileges. In short, all the outstanding debts land in his lap.

**THE LAST OF THE MOHICANS (**½) 30 min (13ep Color; 1972 UK BBC) Drama** *with Kenneth Ives as Hawkeye, Andrew Crawford as Colonel Munro, Patricia Maynard as Cora, Tim Goodman as Heyward, Philip Madoc as Magua, Joanna David as Alice, Richard Warwick as Uncas, and John Abine as Chingachgook*

James Fenimore Cooper's "Leatherstocking" series, focusing on the English Indian scout Natty Bumppo (also known as Hawkeye), is a sturdy (if at times silly) adventure saga, with *The Last of the Mohicans* novel (published in 1826) the most popular entry. It's been done as a theatrical feature film (in 1936), an animated series, a 1977 made-for-TV movie, and as two different full-fledged series.

The first is a Canadian-produced package from the 1950s called *Hawkeye and the Last of the Mohicans* (emphasizing Bumppo's character), while this 1970s BBC production goes with the original novel title. Both do an acceptable job with the tale, focusing mainly on the American colonists and their various Indian allies during the French and Indian War (fought in North America between 1754 and 1763). Most notably, there's Hawkeye and his Mohican companions, Uncas and Chingachgook, who attempt to deal with the home-territory effects of a foreign war waged between two empire builders (Britain and France).

This BBC production was packaged into eight one-hour episodes for *Masterpiece Theatre* in the early 1970s.

**LAST OF THE WILD, LORNE GREENE'S (**½) 30 min (104ep Color; 1974–1979 Syndication) Documentary** *with Lorne Greene as host*

The former patriarch of the Cartwright clan from *Bonanza* hosts and narrates a series of nature documentaries concerning endangered species.

**THE LAST PLACE ON EARTH (**½) 60 min (6ep: five 60 min & one 90 min Color; 1985 UK Central) Drama** *with Martin Shaw as Robert Falcon Scott, Sverre Anker Ousdal as Roald Amundsen, Susan Wooldridge as Kathleen Scott, Michael Maloney as Teddy, Richard Morant as Oates, Stephen Moore as Bill, and Sylvester McCoy as Birdie Bowers.*

A competitive trek to the South Pole in 1911–1912, with crews led by British explorer Robert Scott and Norwegian explorer Roald Amundsen. Unfortunately for Scott, his was to be an ill-fated venture. According to this less than heroic portrayal of the man, many of the problems were of his own making. Moody, vain, and egotistical, he is a leader who alienates some of his best men, losing their trust and dedicated skills just when he needs them the most. Based on the biography by Roland Huntford, *Scott and Amundsen*, this series pays particular attention to the physical details of such an exhausting undertaking, which comes across as incredibly demanding. The polar scenery may look beautiful at first glance, but to Scott's cold and miserable men attempting the trek it quickly becomes desolate and unforgiving. In fact, the middle part of this series—pretty much stuck in the frozen wilderness—is downright depressing. Nonetheless, it's worth sticking around for the harrowing final sprint, as Scott and his men push forward to the bitter end.

**THE LAST PRECINCT (½) 60 min (7ep & 2 hr pilot Color; 1986 NBC) Situation Comedy** *with Adam West as Captain Rich Wright, Jonathan Perpich as Sgt. Price Pascall, Rick Ducommun as Officer William "Raid" Raider, Ernie Hudson as Det. Sgt. Tremaine "Night Train" Lane, and Randi Brooks as Officer Mel Brubaker*

Imagine something like *Airplane II: The Sequel* meets *Police Academy 2: Their First Assignment*, but without the obscenities or grossness of those theatrical films. What's left? As many one-liners, slapstick bits, and dumb lugs as can squeeze into an episode—with the stories set at the outermost ("last") precinct of the Los Angeles area. Super-straight commander Rich Wright (played by former Batman Adam West) looks on helplessly as some of the city's bottom-of-the-line police department oddballs ply their trade under his jurisdiction. Maybe this could have worked as a *Police Squad!* type parody series, but not with the material stretched to fill an hour.

**THE LAST RESORT (**½) 30 min (16ep Color; 1979–1980 CBS) Situation Comedy** *with Larry Breeding as Michael Lerner, Stephanie Faracy as Gail Collins,*

*Robert Costanzo as Murray, Zane Lasky as Duane Kaminsky, Walter Olkewicz as Zach Comstock, Ray Underwood as Jeffrey Barron, Dorothy Konrad as Mrs. Trilling, and John Fujioka as Kevin*

Created by the man behind *Family Ties*, Gary David Goldberg, and apparently drawing from his memories of work as a waiter, this series focuses on the summertime employment of four college students putting in time at a vacation resort in the Catskill Mountains. Action is split mostly among the kitchen, dining room, and dorm settings, where Zach (stocky and clumsy), Duane (shy bookworm), Jeffrey (snooty), and Michael (well-meaning romantic) interact with each other, the guests, and their fellow workers. The workers include Gail, a cute but unskilled pastry chef; Kevin, a Japanese cook who frequently chooses not to understand English; Mrs. Trilling (Zach's constant target for fat jokes); and Murray, the insufferable maitre d'. They are a solid ensemble, with plenty of back-and-forth banter.

The series runs with the sexual innuendo so popular at the time but manages to work it into some well-written (if occasionally off-the-wall) scripts (Zach falls for a nun, Murray reveals a love affair that's been going on for sixteen years, Michael and Gail have a disastrous tryst). It's also the beginning of Gary David Goldberg's development of his own series concepts (still under the MTM banner), after years of scriptwriting and production chores for other MTM series such as *The Bob Newhart Show, The Tony Randall Show*, and *Lou Grant.*

**LATE NIGHT WITH DAVID LETTERMAN (***½) 60 min (Color; 1982– NBC) Comedy-Variety** *with David Letterman as host and Paul Shaffer as leader of "the world's most dangerous band" with performers including Calvert DeForest as Larry "Bud" Melman and Chris Elliott*

Descriptions of David Letterman quickly start to resemble one of his own silly "top ten" lists . . .

• He's this generation's Steve Allen.

• He was once a regular on such variety series as *The Starland Vocal Band Show* (featuring the group that sang that annoying "Afternoon Delight" song) and Mary Tyler Moore's 1978 bomb *Mary* (the same program that gave us the Ed Asner Dancers).

• He's this generation's Ernie Kovacs.

• He started out as a local TV weatherman in Indiana, which probably accounts for the nationwide rise in aspiring talk show hosts applying for such positions.

• He's this generation's Johnny Carson.

• His first network talk show was cleverly placed by NBC in a 10:00 A.M. Monday through Friday slot, leaving the few who tuned in more than once totally confounded. Note: This was before Geraldo Rivera got his own syndicated series.

• He's this generation's Barth Gimble.

• Between the end of his morning series and the start of his late-night slot, he did a cameo for a sitcom on another network, *Open All Night*, asking for directions and then wondering aloud if this appearance was going to help or hurt his career.

• He's the Bryant Gumbel of the nineties.

• He was sharp enough to choose as his bandleader sidekick Canadian Paul Shaffer, whose previous network credentials include *Saturday Night Live* and *A Year at the Top.*

• He's Tom Snyder's worst nightmare: a successful late-night replacement for the *Tomorrow* show.

(So that's eleven, but who really counts these things anyway?)

Obviously any future rerun packagings of David Letterman's show will require a careful culling of material, probably pulling classic bits or at least compressed versions of particular episodes. That's because what's hip and sassy on a night-to-night basis often comes off as obtuse or dated down the line—just ask previous late-night personalities Steve Allen and Johnny Carson, both of whom went with comedy highlight packages for rerun syndication. Still what helps Letterman is that many of his goofy bits such as stupid pet tricks, the "dancing waters" fountain in front of his desk, and the "Late Night Thrill-Cam" are truly timeless—as funny now as they'll ever be. And, like Ernie Kovacs, he is definitely a comedian playing with television, not just a comic who happens to be on television. This results in technical tricks such as the "360-degree episode" (in which the picture slowly rotates over the course of an hour, meaning that halfway through the show everything is completely upside down) as well as a true "child of television" subtext, constantly poking fun at the very fact that a guy like him even *has* a network talk show.

In short, *Late Night with David Letterman* is a familiar television format with a new-generation twist, effectively appealing to cynical baby boomers raised on the medium and its conventions. The series even carries the stamp of approval of late-night king Johnny Carson, who previously slotted Letterman as a guest and guest host dozens of times on *The Tonight Show*—and whose production company distributes Letterman's program.

**LAUGH-IN, ROWAN AND MARTIN'S (**) 60 min or 30 min (140ep at 60 min or 120ep at 30 min Color; 1968–1973 NBC) plus (6ep at 60 min Color; 1979 NBC) Comedy-Variety** *with Dan Rowan, Dick Martin, and casts including Gary Owens, Goldie Hawn, Arte Johnson, Henry Gibson, Ruth Buzzi, Lily Tomlin, Eileen Brennan, Alan Sues, Teresa Graves, Larry Hovis, Richard Dawson, and Robin Williams*

This will be a hard one to explain to the grandchildren. In fact, it's a hard one to explain to ourselves.

In the 1960s (1968, to be exact.) *Rowan and Martin's Laugh-In* was the hottest, freshest, funniest program on the air. We baby boomers used to walk around the day after each broadcast quoting such hip program phrases as "Sock it to me!" "You bet your sweet bippy!" and "Here comes the judge!"

The series topped the ratings charts for about two years, and hung around a total of five. Its alumni list includes the likes of Goldie Hawn, Eileen Brennan, Gary Owens, Arte Johnson, and Lily Tomlin—as well as congenial hosts Dan Rowan and Dick Martin.

So why do syndicated reruns of the program seem so "out of it" (to use a phrase of the era)? What happened?

Well, everything.

In the late 1960s, this was a genuine groundbreaking program with a unique style of presentation: flashy colors, special camera effects, rapid-fire editing. Nowadays, a kid sees all of this in ten minutes on MTV. Adults have seen it a lifetime of commercial messages. So any contemporary audience naturally ends up looking past the technical tricks to what is actually on the screen. And that's where the problems begin.

Each hour-long program was made up of several hundred blackout bits and one-liners. Sometimes these consisted solely of some catch phrase or mild double entendre. There was not even a joke as such. Instead the humor came from juxtaposition, repetition, and sometimes the fact that you usually didn't expect to see or hear such material on television. Today, though, you'll routinely find far more explicit references up and down the dial. And who cares about yesterday's catch phrases?

That frenetic structure also limited the talented cast, which rarely had the chance to develop sustained characters in any sort of extended sketch setting. Everything and everybody was just dropped in, from Lily Tomlin as Ernestine the obnoxious telephone operator, to Henry Gibson as a flower child poet, to Arte Johnson as a furtive German soldier peering from the bushes, to Ruth Buzzi as a lonely woman on a park bench constantly being propositioned by a "dirty old man" (also played by Johnson).

Only Dan Rowan and Dick Martin got much time for lengthy pieces, usually in their monologues. Those were (and are) highly entertaining, but pretty much drawn from their nightclub banter—not exactly groundbreaking television.

Faced with the limitations of dealing with such a dated period piece, the producers preparing the syndication package managed to salvage the situation with some timely editing, tightly trimming back the original one-hour length. These 120 half-hour segments were lifted from about 65 of the original 140 one-hour episodes. This editing gives *Laugh-In* a new identity—less a comedy-variety program and more a celebrity scrapbook. As such, it's fun to see guests such as Johnny Carson, Rock Hudson, James Garner, the Smothers Brothers (and so on) twenty years back. The same holds true of such *Laugh-In* regulars as Lily Tomlin, Goldie Hawn, Ellen Burnstyn, and Richard Dawson. You may also get a chuckle from Tiny Tim (singing "Tip Toe Through the Tulips"), or "news of the future"—with a dateline of the 1980s. If you read the closing credits carefully, you'll even catch the name of *Saturday Night Live* creator Lorne Michaels listed among the writers. Obviously he came from this experience knowing exactly what he *didn't* want to do in a comedy-variety format.

Oddly, given all these limitations, NBC and *Laugh-In* producer George Schlatter still attempted to revive the series (sans Rowan and Martin) in 1979. But, pulled from its original sixties context, the *Laugh-In* style and format came off as decidedly ordinary, just a standard package carrying the familiar name. The only reason to catch those episodes is to see a struggling Robin Williams in the supporting cast, just a year before Mork from Ork touched down.

**LAVERNE AND SHIRLEY (**½) 30 min (178ep Color; 1976–1983 ABC) Situation Comedy** *with Penny Marshall as Laverne De Fazio, Cindy Williams as Shirley Feeney, Phil Foster as Frank De Fazio, David L. Lander as Andrew "Squiggy" Squiggman, Michael McKean as Lenny Kosnowski, and Eddie Mekka as Carmine Ragusa*

In the beginning, there was *Happy Days*, and *Happy Days* begot *Laverne and Shirley*. And lo, *Laverne and Shirley* was a hit, almost as big as *Happy Days*. Almost.

The time is still the late 1950s; the place is still Milwaukee, Wisconsin, just like in *Happy Days*. Taking a cue from the popularity of the Fonz, a lower-class pseudo juvenile delinquent, *Happy Days* producer Garry Marshall (brother of Penny) created two females cohorts of the Fonz, Laverne and Shirley, and tested them on a few episodes of *Happy Days*. When the response was favorable, the two girls got their own show.

Like the Fonz, Laverne and Shirley are not in the college-prep world of Richie Cunningham (the nominal lead character of *Happy Days*). Out of school, the two ladies work as assembly-line bottle cappers at the Shotz Brewery in beer-mad Milwaukee. Their work is, to put it simply, pure mechanical drudge work, with a regular paycheck as its only redeeming value. Laverne, the tall, big-toothed one (with the big "L" on her sweaters) is all tough and nasty on the outside, but she breaks down into quivering insecurity without much coaxing. Shirley, the dark-haired cute one, quivers with insecurity most of the time and her naiveté and trusting nature often get her in tight spots that bring out her somewhat tougher side.

There is more to the pair than quivering, however. When they get mad (as one or both frequently are) or are duped by something or someone (as one or both frequently are), then Laverne and/or Shirley will launch onto some emotional skyrocket of anger that is fun to watch.

The working-class atmosphere, which is fairly unique

on TV sitcoms of the modern era, allows the producers to bring in such colorful sidemen as Lenny and Squiggy, neighbors of Laverne and Shirley and truck drivers for Shotz Brewery. These two wonderfully wacked-out losers are weirdos who do not seem to understand that they are not refined society. Their well-meaning efforts to provide friendly advice to the girls usually result in some good laughs, because everything they touch comes out wrong. Another fine creation is Carmine, Shirley's sometimes boyfriend who is trying to live out the Italian stallion macho myth.

The other notable aspect of the show is the very fact that it features two women. There are scores of male "buddy" movies and series, but only a few female "buddy" shows. Just the same, *Laverne and Shirley* is no classroom exercise. It is lower-class, slapstick-based, "nothing serious" humor. The jokes are broad, the overacting is frequent, and the subtlety is sparse, but there are enough jokes and fun characters to keep an audience entertained.

Like *Happy Days*, *Laverne and Shirley* goes through several big changes in its time. The basic format, the two girls at the beer plant in Milwaukee, lasts into the show's fourth season. In an attempt to revive interest in the waning series, the producers then have the girls laid off from Shotz and moved (with most of their family and friends) to California. Now on true TV turf, the girls wind up with equally menial jobs (wrapping clerks at a department store), but the allure of tinsel town is catching. Laverne and Shirley are trying to break into the movies and Lenny and Squiggy open up a talent agency.

In the last season, a more radical change occurs. Due to contract squabbles with Cindy Williams, the Shirley character is phased out (she is suddenly married to a medic and then shipped overseas with her new man). In the end, it's just Laverne, who now works at the Ajax Aerospace Company (it's California, remember). All these changes are for the worse. What simple, earthy charm the show has results from its realistic midwestern roots. In L.A., it's just more of the same old sitcom fluff.

At the height of the popularity of *Laverne and Shirley*, lead actresses Marshall and Williams lent their voices to a silly animated cartoon version of the show, where the girls are in the army, taking orders from Sgt. Squeely, a talking pig.

## THE LAW AND HARRY MCGRAW (*½) 60 min (14ep & 2 hr pilot Color; 1987–1988 CBS) Detective Drama *with Jerry Orbach as Harry McGraw, Barbara Babcock as Ellie Maginnis, Shea Farrell as Steve Lacey, Juli Donald as E. J. Brunson, and Peter Haskell as Tyler Chase*

A spin-off from *Murder, She Wrote, The Law and Harry McGraw* follows loud, rumpled Boston private eye Harry McGraw in his efforts to track down bad guys and verbally spar with his polar opposite: the refined, classy, criminal lawyer Ellie Maginnis. Ellie is recently widowed and she sets up her office just across the hall from Harry's hovel. The result is sparks between the two as they rub elbows, both professionally and personally.

Barbara Babcock has the coquettish middle-aged classy woman role down pat, after appearing for a few years as sex-obsessed Grace Gardner on *Hill Street Blues*. Jerry Orbach, however, is a bit much as Harry McGraw (a character he first portrayed in a few episodes of *Murder, She Wrote*). His intensity and hang-over eyes look more suited for a Manhattan setting, rather than for the more sophisticated world that TV always paints for Boston.

## THE LAW AND MR. JONES (**½) 30 min (45ep B&W; 1960–1962 ABC) Drama *with James Whitmore as Abraham Lincoln Jones, Janet DeGore as Marsha Spear, and Conlan Carter as C. E. Carruthers*

Good showcase for James Whitmore, who effectively weaves his way through the legal system as Abraham Lincoln Jones, a compassionate, supremely honest attorney. He is aided in this task by his young law clerk, C. E. Carruthers, and faithful secretary, Marsha Spear. And here's a switch—usually Jones doesn't get involved in murder cases. Instead these to-the-point dramas cover such issues as upholding contracts or fair housing requirements. Not exactly headline grabbers but in fact much closer to the real effect of the law on day-to-day life. Through occasionally a bit heavy-handed in making its underlying ideological points (especially in the area of prejudice, a favorite early 1960s cause), Whitmore's charm and eloquence manage to smooth such rough spots.

## THE LAW ENFORCERS (see *The Protectors*)

## THE LAW OF THE PLAINSMAN (***) 30 min (30ep & two 30 min pilots B&W; 1959–1960 NBC) Western *with Michael Ansara as Buck Heart/Sam Buckhart, Dayton Lummis as Andy Morrison, Gina Gillespie as Tess Logan, and Nora Marlowe as Martha Commager*

Lebanese–American Michael Ansara, who played Apache chief Cochise in *Broken Arrow*, plays an Apache commoner, originally known as Buck Heart, in *The Law of the Plainsman*, an interesting western that aims for a more moderate view of the cowboy-Indian struggle of the late 1800s.

Buck Heart helped and became friends with a Harvard-educated cavalry captain after a cavalry-Apache battle. When the captain dies, all his money goes to Buck Heart, who uses the dough to go to Harvard (as Sam Buckhart) and become a convert to the white man's way of life. After graduation, Sam returns to the New Mexico Territory, as deputy to U.S. marshal Andy Morrison, and tries to justly resolve disputes between the warring red and white races.

Both pilots for *Law of the Plainsman* originally aired

in episodes of *The Rifleman.* One is called "The Indian," and the other is called "The Raid." In syndication, *Law of the Plainsman* is grouped with episodes of *Black Saddle, Johnny Ringo,* and *The Westerner* under the title *The Westerners.*

**LAWBREAKER, LEE MARVIN PRESENTS (**) 30 min (32ep B&W & Color; 1963–1964 Syndication)** *with Lee Marvin as host and narrator*

An early 1960s version of television's fascination with real-life crime cases. Former *M Squad* tough cop Lee Marvin is the host and narrator to this mix of dramatizations, interviews, and commentary, frequently filmed at the actual site of the crimes and (if possible) including the people involved with them. After twenty-five years, though, don't expect these films to include an "800" number for you to call with your tips, guesses, or latest clues—these were all pretty much wrapped up a lifetime ago.

**THE LAWLESS YEARS (*½) 60 min (52 ep B&W; 1959–1961 NBC) Crime Drama** *with James Gregory as Barney Ruditsky and Robert Karnes as Max*

Crime in New York City during the Roaring Twenties fills this series, very loosely based on the real-life cases of New York detective Barney Ruditsky. Reminiscent of *The Untouchables* (though in fact this show actually pre-dates that series), with gritty plots and a stone-faced lead in James Gregory who battles the usual vices of the time: speakeasies, flappers, and bathtub gin. Not quite as many later familiar faces as in the Eliot Ness tales, but Burt Reynolds, Vic Morrow, and Jack Weston are among those that do show up. Gregory later returned to the New York City beat with a lighter touch as Inspector Luger on *Barney Miller.*

**LAWMAN (**) 30 min (156ep B&W; 1958–1962 ABC) Western** *with John Russell as Marshal Dan Troop, Peter Brown as Johnny McKay, and Peggy Castle as Lily Merrill*

A cookie-cutter western from the Warner Bros. studios, *Lawman* is set in Laramie, Wyoming in the 1870s, and methodically follows straight-arrow marshal Dan Troop as he cleans up the frontier. For some reason, Troop never seems to bump into the gang from *Laramie*, who should be just down the road.

**THE LAWRENCE WELK SHOW (**½) 60 min (352ep Color; 1971–1982 Syndication) Musical-Variety** *with Lawrence Welk*

Smart-mouthed critics laughed at Lawrence Welk when he came to network TV in 1955. They laughed at him for years thereafter, as Welk became a Saturday night institution on ABC. They laughed at him in 1971, when the network canceled his show for drawing *too many* viewers (too many that were old and rural, that is, and not enough that were young and upscale). They laughed at Welk when he kept his show going without ABC, assembling an ad hoc network of his own to air his weekly syndicated series.

All in all, a lot of people laughed at Lawrence Welk, but the fact is that for twenty-seven years Welk turned out a popular, simple, uncluttered hour of musical entertainment. Only Ed Sullivan and Johnny Carson are in the same league when it comes to television longevity. Welk may well have been easy to ridicule, but he obviously had a great appeal to a lot of viewers.

The 352 *Lawrence Welk Show* episodes still available are the eleven years of syndicated prime-time shows that Welk turned out after his abrupt dismissal by ABC. In these shows, Welk is already slowing down and is content to stay with his standard musical format: melodic, "easy listening" tunes of decades gone by. There are a few nods at the post–World War II era, but little effort is made to attract younger, "hipper" audiences.

Welk's format really never changed for twenty-seven years. He is forever the thickly Germanic-accented bandleader/accordionist who is surrounded by a stable of clean, wholesome performers who sing, dance, and play. There is no fancy talk; there are few elaborate production numbers; there is no deep meaning. There is only music, Welk's kind of music, the kind he calls "Champagne music."

By the time these syndicated episodes were produced, Welk had already parted ways with many of his more popular disciples, such as Alice Lon, the Lennon Sisters, Pete Fountain, and Lynn Anderson. However, such hearty regulars as Myron Floren, Larry Hooper, Dick Dale, and Bob Lido stayed with the maestro till the bitter end.

There is little middle ground on Lawrence Welk. He either is a square anachronism of another world or he is a bastion of stability and taste in a world gone to hell in a handbasket. For most people, Lawrence Welk will always be seen as a happy man with a huge grin, surrounded by an orchestra and a torrent of ubiquitous bubbles, tapping a baton and intoning his timeless musical introduction: "ah-vun and ah-two and ah-tree . . ." He may not have done much, but what he did, he did very well. ■

**THE LAWYERS (**) 60 min (27ep & two 2 hr pilots Color; 1969–1972 NBC) Law Drama** *with Burl Ives as Walter Nichols, Joseph Campanella as Brian Darrell, and James Farentino as Neil Darrell*

Originally one of the elements of the umbrella series *The Bold Ones, The Lawyers* is a competent run-through of the TV lawyer genre. The firm of Nichols, Darrell and Darrell is made up of three types of lawyers. Senior partner Walter Nichols is the sagacious old gentleman, whose experience is useful to his less mature junior partners, who are brothers. The elder brother, Brian, is bookish and precise. Younger Neil is handsome and brash, and roots for the underdog. Together the three serve as counterbalances to each other in a restrained series that does not insult your intelligence.

Roy Huggins, of *Maverick* and *77 Sunset Strip* fame, serves as producer of *The Lawyers* and its two-hour pilots, the 1968 *The Sound of Anger* and the 1969 *The Whole World Is Watching.* Guy Stockwell plays the older Darrell role (then called Brad) in the first pilot.

**THE LAZARUS SYNDROME (**) 60 min (7ep & 90 min pilot Color; 1979 & 1986 ABC & Lifetime) Medical Drama** *with Louis Gossett, Jr., as Dr. MacArthur St. Clair, Ronald Hunter as Joe Hamill, Sheila Frazier as Gloria St. Clair, Peggy Walker as Virginia Hamill, and Peggy McKay as Stacy.*

When patients think of their doctor as some sort of godlike miracle worker, it's called the "Lazarus syndrome" (referring to the biblical story of Jesus raising Lazarus from the dead). Joe Hamill is one patient who pulls a twist on that, because after Doctor MacArthur St. Clair (chief of cardiology at Webster Memorial Hospital) treats him for a heart attack, Hamill leaves his job as a journalist and (in the pilot) becomes an administrator at the hospital. There the idealistic former journalist joins St. Clair in the toughest fight of all: matching wits with the medical bureaucracy. (Talk about expecting miracles.) This is a high-minded series appropriately guilty of its title syndrome, taking battles of conscience very, very seriously. Fortunately, Lou Gossett, Jr., turns in a very strong performance, so it's worth a look—the ninety-minute pilot film usually turns up in some movie slot.

Or else you could wait for the Lifetime cable service (formerly the Health Channel) to rerun it. After all, that's where some of the episodes not aired by ABC at last had their television debut, about half a decade after they were completed. ■

**LEARNING THE ROPES (*½) (24ep at Fall 1989 Color; 1988– Syndication) Situation Comedy** *with Lyle Alzado as Robert Randall, Yannick Bisson as Mark Randall, Nicole Stoffman as Ellen Randall, Cheryl Wilson as Carol Dixon, Barry Stevens as Jerry, Richard Farrell as Mr. Mallory and Grant Cowan as Bertie Baxter*

The perfect programming lead-in to some wrestling slot on the schedule, this is the series that answers the burning question: What are wrestlers like in their off-hours? If the life of Robert Randall (a.k.a. The Masked Maniac) is any indication, they're pretty normal—for sitcom land. He's a former football player (just like Lyle Alzado, a former Oakland Raider in real life), a full-time school teacher, and a temporarily single father of two sharp-tongued teens. He and his wife of nineteen years are separated, parting on amicable terms: He kept the kids and she went to England to get her law degree. Eventually she sets up practice there.

Though Robert's son and daughter know about his wrestling career, no one else at Ridgedale Valley Preparatory School does—especially Carol, a teaching colleague with a crush on him. Not that it would be hard to guess his secret. Sometimes Robert has a few of his ring buddies over for cards and coffee. And what do they watch on television? Why, wrestling, of course—usually matches featuring themselves. In fact, the scene sometimes shifts to the on-screen action in the ring, making it easy to forget just what you were watching in the first place: a sitcom or a wrestling match. Stick around, though, because some regular scheduled TV wrestling program should be on any minute.

**LEAVE IT TO BEAVER (****) 30 min (234ep & 30 min pilot B&W & Colorized 1957–1963 CBS & ABC) Situation Comedy** *with Hugh Beaumont as Ward Cleaver, Barbara Billingsley as June Cleaver, Tony Dow as Wally Cleaver, Jerry Mathers as Theodore "Beaver" Cleaver, Ken Osmond as Eddie Haskell, Frank Bank as Clarence "Lumpy" Rutherford, Richard Deacon as Fred Rutherford, Rusty Stevens as Larry Mondello, Madge Blake as Mrs. Mondello, and Pamela Beaird as Mary Ellen Rogers,* **STILL THE BEAVER/THE NEW LEAVE IT TO BEAVER (**) 30 min (119ep at Fall 1989 Color & 2 hr pilot; 1984– Disney & WTBS) Situation Comedy** *with Barbara Billingsley as June Cleaver, Tony Dow as Wally Cleaver, Jerry Mathers as Theodore "Beaver" Cleaver, Kipp Marcus as Kip Cleaver, John Snee as Oliver Cleaver, Janice Kent as Mary Ellen Rogers Cleaver, Kaleena Kiff as Kelly Cleaver, Troy Davidson as Kevin Cleaver, Ken Osmond as Eddie Haskell, Eric Osmond as Freddie Haskell, Christian Osmond as Bomber Haskell, and Frank Bank as Clarence "Lumpy" Rutherford*

*Leave it to Beaver* is the *American Gothic* of the video era. Grant Wood's famous 1930 painting of a taciturn pitchfork-wielding Iowa farmer and his dour wife was first denounced as being condescending, but it has come to be treasured as the personification of an older America filled with simple yet rugged individualists. Whether such an America really ever existed is somewhat beside the point, for popular culture tells us it did, and we tend to compare the real modern America with such an idealized past.

Likewise, *Leave It to Beaver*, a late 1950s TV sitcom, was originally ridiculed for its pristine view of the American suburban family. As the 1950s generation of children has grown up and warily donned the mantle of adult responsibility in a society quite different from the one portrayed in the old TV series, *Leave it to Beaver* has become a video tintype. It seems to confirm our nostalgic notion that things were simpler and better when we were children.

At first glance, *Leave It to Beaver* appears to merit its original scorn. Both the setting in the cookie-cutter town of Mayfield and the well-scrubbed look of the Cleaver clan conjure up all the derogatory comments usually associated with 1950s family sitcoms. Everybody is well-dressed, everybody is a WASP, everybody is aggressively middle-class, and everybody seems untouched by the typical sort of human miseries that beset most everybody else.

These criticisms miss the point, somewhat. *Leave It to Beaver* was never designed to accurately mirror American life. Instead the show is designed more to show the accepted *ideal* of what a good family should be through the humorous interaction of the two Cleaver boys with their parents and their friends and neighbors.

Ward, the head of the Cleaver family, is an accountant, a popular bland occupation for 1950s TV dads. He tries hard to keep his children in line and to set a good example for them. He dispenses kindly words of advice when a problem arises, but is not averse to yelling at the boys when they are bad. He still recalls enough of his own boyhood to know that only a certain level of obedience is to be expected from Wally and the Beaver.

June Cleaver is a far more hilarious character, albeit filled with a good chunk of realism. In true 1950s style, she is a woman whose world barely extends beyond her front yard. Her life consists of cooking, cleaning, worrying about her boys, and little else. She only feels that all is right with the world when the house sparkles and the Cleaver men are well-fed and decked in semi-formal attire.

What sets *Leave It to Beaver* apart from quality contemporaries such as *Father Knows Best* and *Ozzie and Harriet* is the centering of the program on the Cleaver *children*, rather than on the parents. Wally and the Beaver (and their cronies) are probably the most accurate TV examples of 1950s suburban youth, containing all the pluses and minuses common to that species.

At the beginning of *Leave It to Beaver*, Wally is twelve, just entering the mine field of the teen years. He is good-looking, but somewhat uncoordinated and shy. His primary objective in life is to try to combine his essentially goody-goody upbringing with the teen requirement of appearing "cool," especially to the opposite sex. Wally is torn between the admonishments of his parents and the siren song of selfishness sung by his best friend, Eddie Haskell.

If for nothing else, *Leave It to Beaver* is memorable solely for the presence of Eddie Haskell, the slipperiest, most two-faced schemer to grace the TV screen until the arrival of J. R. Ewing. Eddie will literally bow and scrape before the adults in order to maintain an image of wholesomeness, but when they are out of the room, his true nature will slither out. He is cruel and insulting to all those he considers beneath him (meaning just about everyone), and he constantly goads Wally into activities both know are wrong. Nonetheless, when it comes to the crunch, be assured that Eddie will show himself as a complete coward.

And then, of course, there is the Beaver, little Theodore, known to all by his nickname (the result of his big-toothed grin, perhaps?). Beginning the show at age seven, Beaver is still heavily involved in trying to figure out how the world works. He is essentially very trusting, friendly to all, yet still full of mischief. Beaver may be a nice kid, but he still lets his childish nature get the best of him at times. The Beaver will act badly and know that he has been bad. This trait makes the Beaver a far more believable child than the slew of other TV tykes who tend to get into trouble only through silly misunderstandings.

By painting the children on the series with a more realistic brush and by leaving the adults as slightly more secondary characters, *Leave It to Beaver* connects with real children (no matter how grown up) on a more direct level than its contemporary competition. As a result, it only makes sense that the children who watched the show when it originally aired would come to interweave the TV series with their own fading memories of childhood in the 1950s.

Not much changes on *Leave It to Beaver* during the six seasons of its original run. Wally and the Beaver grow some, of course, and the series ends at the right time, just when Wally is ready to ship out to college and Beaver is reaching the start of his more mature teen years. Production of the show ended in 1963, which is appropriate. It was in that year that John Kennedy was assassinated, a convenient landmark noting the start of a big change in the American social scene. For a long time thereafter, *Leave It to Beaver*, while always popular in reruns, seemed to have little to say to an America rushing pell-mell into a brave new world of personal freedoms and nonnuclear families.

By the time the 1980s and the Reagan years rolled around, the view of *Leave It to Beaver* had softened. Championing warm, close-knit families became fashionable again, even if only in the theoretical world of modern sitcoms such as *The Cosby Show*. In 1983, the original *Leave It to Beaver* cast (minus the recently deceased Hugh Beaumont) reunited for a two-hour made-for-TV movie, *Still the Beaver*. The intervening two decades had taken a bit of a toll on the Cleaver clan. Ward was gone. Widow June still lived in the family home. Wally had married high school sweetheart Mary Ellen Rogers and become a lawyer. The Beaver, however, had not found adult life to be easy. At thirty-three, he was out of work, didn't relate well with his two young sons, and had just been dumped by his wife Kimberly. Now surrounded by his family, however, the Beaver begins to put his life back in order. Wally handles the Beaver's divorce proceedings and secures custody of the two boys for his brother. By the end of the film, the Beaver and his sons move into the old Cleaver home, to live again with Mom (the Beaver can't ever really cut the cord). In retrospect, June always seemed destined to be the perfect doting grandmother.

The popular response to the *Still the Beaver* film

resulted in the resumption of the *Beaver* series, under the *Still the Beaver* title. A few minor cast changes are made from the film (Beaver's oldest son is now named Kip, not Corey), but June, Wally, the Beaver, Eddie Haskell, and Wally's tubby pal Lumpy all return, older, grayer, but essentially the same. After one season (twenty-five episodes) the show's title is changed to *The New Leave It to Beaver*, under which moniker the series happily chugs along.

The revival series is not as memorable as the original, but it really would be asking too much to expect otherwise. June and Wally haven't changed much. Eddie Haskell has become a dishonest construction tycoon (how appropriate!) and has a son with much of his father's personality (Eddie's children are played by actor Ken Osmond's real-life offspring).

And still there is the Beaver. Where once the young Jerry Mathers turned in a surprisingly guileless performance, the elder Mathers seems highly artificial. Where cohort Tony Dow has kept his teenage Wally good looks, Mathers has grown a spare tire and looks more like an older version of his portly childhood pal Larry Mondello than a grown Beaver. The plastic performances by Mathers (plus the average level of writing) drag *The New Leave It to Beaver* down to the level of cute but ultimately forgettable sitcom. Much of the attention in the revival is of the new generation of Cleavers, which only seems right, but the kids look too much like more typical TV children. It's nice to tune the new show in now and again to see how your old friends are doing, but there isn't much reason to stick around.

The original *Leave It to Beaver* series was created, produced, and often written by Joe Connelly and Bob Mosher. It is said they based a number of scripts on exploits of their own young children, which sounds right, considering the believable portrayal of the kids on the show. While Connelly and Mosher had another hit with *The Munsters*, on the whole they never duplicated their success with *Beaver*. They did, however, give Jerry Mathers' brother Jimmy his one and only starring role in a TV series on *Ichabod and Me*.

Fans of the *Leave It to Beaver* series should search out the original 1957 pilot for the show, titled "It's a Small World" (which is included as a special episode of *The New Leave It to Beaver* series). Barbara Billingsley and Jerry Mathers play their familiar roles, but Paul Sullivan plays Wally and Max Showalter (then calling himself Casey Adams) plays Ward. Future *Saturday Night Live* contributor Harry Shearer plays Frankie, an early version of the Eddie Haskell character. ■

**LEAVE IT TO CHARLIE (**) 30 min (7ep Color; 1978 UK Granada) Comedy-Drama** *with David Roper as Charlie Fisher, Peter Sallis, Jean Heywood, Gwen Cherrill, and Sally Kinghorn*

This is *not* a Monty Python sketch. Honest. But the main character in this series is an insurance man operating out of the small British Lancashire town of Bolton. Answering the adventurous call of insurance duty, Charlie Fisher risks life and limb (he's accident prone) on everything from assessing the prospects of individual clients to starring in a local amateur theatrical production. A pleasant, unthreatening, short-run series.

**LEE MARVIN PRESENTS LAWBREAKER** **(see *Lawbreaker*)**

**LEG WORK (**) 60 min (10ep Color; 1987 & 1988–1989 CBS & Lifetime) Detective Drama** *with Margaret Colin as Claire McCarron, Frances McDormand as Willie Pipal, and Patrick James Clarke as Lt. Fred McCarron*

An independent Manhattan private investigator who (according to one network tout) is "not afraid to put her life on the line or her credit over the limit." Well, she does spend a lot on her Porsche, but that's because it's always in the shop. Otherwise, just living in modern-day New York City means she has to follow pulp fiction's oldest motivation for taking good-paying, dangerous cases—she needs the money to balance her checkbook . . . and to cover the costs of her other lush indulgences: oatmeal raisin cookies and electric trains. But that's reason enough to send her into settings and cases with a high-fashion glitz, even if some of the stories make only slightly more plot sense than an average episode of *Miami Vice*. Actually the mini-skirted Claire is pretty good at the investigating game, working with prosecutor Willie Pipal and her brother, Fred, at the NYPD information office. Still you'll have to decide if the series title refers to her mode of operation or her character's appearance (or both).

In setting up the series premise, there's a neat implicit reference back to Margaret Colin's previous series, *Foley Square*, where she played a dedicated assistant at the Manhattan district attorney's office. For this series, it's established that Claire McCarron used to work for the Manhattan D. A. before setting off on her own as a private eye.

**THE LEGEND OF JESSE JAMES (*) 30 min (34ep B&W; 1965–1966 ABC) Western** *with Christopher Jones as Jesse James, Allen Case as Frank James, John Milford as Cole Younger, Tim McIntire as Bob Younger, and Robert Wilke as Marshal Sam Corbett*

Hey, Jesse James wasn't such a bad guy. Okay, so he and his brother Frank killed a lot of people in Missouri in the 1860s, and they robbed a whole lot of trains and banks. But, gee, they *had* to do all that stuff, cause the bad old banks and railroads had been mean and nasty to all the peaceful local folk, like Jesse's mom. So what's the poor boy to do but turn outlaw and rob from the rich to give to the poor (and keep a bunch for yourself to cover expenses, you understand).

*The Legend of Jesse James* goes much too far in

trying to make the old outlaw a proto-hippie hero. All that's missing from this silly revisionist western is Jesse picking up a guitar and singing "Blowing in the Wind" as he prepares for armed robbery.

**LEGMEN** (*) **60 min (7ep Color; 1984 NBC) Detective Drama** *with Bruce Greenwood as Jack Gage, J. T. Terlsky as David Taylor, Don Calfa as Oscar Armismendi, and Claude Akins as Tom Bannon*

The plot of *Legmen* is thinner than air. Jack and David, two college student hunks in Los Angeles, decide to earn extra cash by moonlighting as assistants (or "legmen") to a sleazy private eye outfit, the Tri-Star Bail Bonds Agency. Bright and breezy banter fills up most of the show that is also occupied by screaming tires, busted glass, and busty blondes.

**LEO AND LIZ IN BEVERLY HILLS** (*½) **30 min (6ep Color; 1986 CBS) Situation Comedy** *with Harvey Korman as Leo Green, Valerie Perrine as Liz Green, Deborah Harmon as Diane Fedderson, Julie Payne as Lucille Trumbley, Sue Ball as Mitzi Green, and Michael J. Pollard as Leonard*

Based on characters introduced in "The Couch" episode of *George Burns Comedy Week*, this rather predictable comedy follows a self-made couple (Leo and Liz, played by Harvey Korman and Valerie Perrine) trying to fit into posh Beverly Hills with only New Jersey pedigree. The prominent placement of "in Beverly Hills" in the series title suggests that the success at the time of the hot "snobs versus slobs" theatrical feature film *Down and Out in Beverly Hills* may have helped Leo and Liz win their network shot.

For some arcane reason, the Emmy Lou Harris version of "Mr. Sandman" (a hit in 1981) serves as the opening theme for the series.

**LEWIS & CLARK** (**) **30 min (13ep Color; 1981–1982 NBC) Situation Comedy** *with Gabe Kaplan as Stewart Lewis, Guich Koock as Roscoe Clark, Ilene Graff as Alicia Lewis, Michael McManus as John, and Wendy Holcombe as Wendy*

Leaving the urban madness of New York behind him, Stewart Lewis uproots his family and moves to the rural madness of Luckenbach, Texas (a real Texas crossroads glorified in a 1977 singing duet between Waylon Jennings and Willie Nelson). Lewis buys a down-and-out country/western bar, renames it the Nassau County Cafe (after his Long Island home county), and begins to learn about the "quaint" local populace. Roscoe Clark is the hick Texan who manages the cafe and isn't as dumb as he lets on.

Gabe Kaplan was better in *Welcome Back, Kotter.* Guich Koock was the same in *Carter County.* This format was just as forgettable in *Guestward Ho!*

**THE LIBERACE SHOW** (**) **30 min (117ep B&W; 1953–1955 Syndication) Musical-Variety** *with Liberace and George Liberace*

It is very difficult today to comprehend the public furor Liberace created when he burst onto the national stage in the 1950s. These days, when ostentatious wardrobes, homosexual lifestyles and semiserious celebrities are a dime a dozen, Liberace seems old hat. Not so in the fifties, however. Liberace's aggressive flamboyance, his tongue-in-cheek approach to "serious" music, his long wavy hair, his outlandish costumes, and his distinctive silky voice all were in direct opposition to the straight-laced, serious tone of the early Eisenhower era. Women, especially older women, loved him. Men were either befuddled by his appeal or felt threatened by his somewhat effeminate mannerisms.

Born Wladziu Valentino Liberace, but known to friends as "Lee," Liberace used television to vault into national prominence. His early successes on local Los Angeles TV and on a few short network series led to *The Liberace Show*, his syndicated series from an era when syndicated series were few and far between.

All of the trademarks of early Liberace are present in *The Liberace Show.* Lee is bedecked in his usual fancy outfits. His piano is adorned with a fancy candelabra. The maestro runs through some classical standards in his proficient yet flashy way, and he banters with his musical director/orchestra leader/violinist, his brother George. The bantering between Lee and George is all the more interesting, due to the fact that two years after *The Liberace Show*, Lee and George split up and Lee relegated the character of George to the butt of his mild onstage jokes.

*The Liberace Show* was at one time a staple of syndication, turning up year after year on many stations. Since the advent of color, the series has not been seen much. Liberace also hosted a brief summer TV series in 1969, also called *The Liberace Show.*

**THE LIEUTENANT** (**½) **60 min (29ep B&W; 1963–1964 NBC) Drama** *with Gary Lockwood as Lieutenant William Rice, Robert Vaughn as Captain Ray Rambridge, Stephen Franken as Lieutenant Samwell Panosian, Don Penny as Lieutenant Harris, and Carmen Phillips as Lily*

This idealized peacetime service drama follows the seasoning of William Rice, the new second lieutenant at Camp Pendleton Marine base in California (where portions of this series were filmed). Rice is very easygoing and relaxed, much to the professional distress of his immediate superior, Captain Rambridge, who wants to toughen the young officer. Though the stories are sometimes overly stiff and solemn, this series is definitely worth a look in order to see some favorites at work. To start, both producers for *The Lieutenant* were on to very popular productions: Norman Felton became an executive producer to *The Man from U.N.C.L.E.*, while Gene Roddenberry created *Star Trek.* Robert Vaughn, of course, was Felton's leading man on *U.N.C.L.E.* Stephen Franken previously played the pompous Chatsworth Osborne, Jr., on *Dobie Gillis.* And among the guest performers there's Bill Bixby, Robert Duvall, Eddie Albert, Ricardo Montalban, Dennis Hopper, the real-life Gregory "Pappy" Boyington (whose adventures were the basis for *Black Sheep Squadron*), and future *Star Trek* legends Walter Koenig and Leonard Nimoy.

**THE LIFE AND ADVENTURES OF NICHOLAS NICKLEBY (see *Nicholas Nickleby*)**

**THE LIFE AND LEGEND OF WYATT EARP (see *Wyatt Earp*)**

**THE LIFE AND TIMES OF EDDIE ROBERTS (**) 30 min (60ep Color; 1980 Syndication) Comedy Serial** *with Renny Temple as Eddie Roberts, Udana Power as Dolores Roberts, Allison Balson as Chrissy Roberts, Stephen Parr as Tony Cranpool, and Daryl Roach as Turner Lequatro*

Not many series abbreviate their titles, but this series is better known as *L.A.T.E.R.* Trying to outhip *Mary Hartman, Mary Hartman, L.A.T.E.R.* has a slew of totally oddball characters. Eddie Roberts is a professor of anthropology at a California university, lusting for tenure, who volunteers for an experiment to find a male contraceptive. His wife Dolores aspires to be the first female big league baseball player. His boarder, Turner Lequatro, is a black ex-radical who now sells carpets at Sears. You get the picture.

*L.A.T.E.R.* deserves credit for trying to be different, but it usually tries too hard, frequently forgetting to be funny.

**THE LIFE AND TIMES OF GRIZZLY ADAMS (see *Grizzly Adams*)**

**THE LIFE OF LEONARDO DA VINCI (**½) 60min (5ep Color; 1972 CBS) Drama** *with Phillipe Leroy, Alberto Fiorini, and Arduino Paolini as Leonardo Da Vinci, and Bruno Cirino as Michelangelo*

The incredible life of Leonardo Da Vinci, painter, sculptor, engineer, and all-around Renaissance man in fifteenth-century Italy, is presented in this series produced by RAI, the primary Italian TV network.

**THE LIFE OF RILEY (**) 30 min (226ep B&W: 1949–1950 & 1953–1958 NBC) Situation Comedy** *with Jackie Gleason and William Bendix as Chester A. Riley, Rosemary DeCamp and Marjorie Reynolds as Peg Riley, Lanny Rees and Wesley Morgan as Chester Riley, Jr., Gloria Winters and Lugene Sanders as Barbara "Babs" Riley, and Sid Tomack and Tom D'Andrea as Jim Gillis*

This is really two shows, not one. There are two separate TV versions of *The Life of Riley* (the original 26 episodes with Jackie Gleason and the more popular 200 episodes with William Bendix), and the better-known version is not necessarily the better version.

William Bendix originated the role of Chester A. Riley on radio in the mid-1940s, capturing a huge audience with spiffy catch phrases such as "What a revoltin' development this is!" The stories focused on Riley, a blue-collar worker in a California aircraft plant, and his very nuclear family (wife Peg, daughter Babs, and son Junior). Chester A. Riley's life was never the proverbial "life of Riley," since someone in the family (often Riley himself) was always producing some sort of trouble that got in the way of Riley getting to relax.

When it came time to bring the popular Riley character to TV, Bendix was unavailable. An edict from his major employer, a motion picture studio, decreed that none of its actors could appear on that evil upstart, television. Thus, the first *television* Chester A. Riley was Jackie Gleason, making his first appearance in a TV series.

The Gleason *Rileys* are bargain basement television. No expense was incurred to turn out these episodes, and the lack of support shows. The sets are atrocious, the scripts are weak, and the direction is slow. This sounds like a recipe for disaster, but there is something about the Gleason *Rileys* that is instinctively appealing. In spite of the poor production, the cast almost (just almost) saves the show. Gloria Winters, who later captured many young male hearts in her spunky performance as Penny in *Sky King*, is fun to watch as the Riley's daughter Babs. Rosemary DeCamp, who went on to star as Bob Cummings's sharp-tongued widowed sister in *Love That Bob*, is warm and almost believable as Chester's wife Peg.

That leaves, of course, Jackie Gleason as Riley. Almost any show with Gleason is worth watching, but Gleason's first TV series is must viewing for students of the medium. This is the only time Gleason ever was really *thin* during a series, and his relatively svelte form brings out new aspects of his personality. Gleason's Riley is more down-to-earth, more realistic, and more human than the silly caricature that Bendix portrayed for so long. Gleason does not yet have the powerful explosive temperament that marked his *Honeymooners* role as Ralph Kramden, but the basic elements are there in *Riley.* Bendix's Riley was always a pushover for his snooty wife and bratty kids, but with Gleason you get the feeling that this guy might actually haul off and belt the kids or tell his wife to . . . well, to go to the moon, that is, if she likes cheese.

The Gleason *Rileys* won one of the first Emmy awards (for best filmed TV show, which was not much of a prize since it was about the *only* filmed show on TV at the time), but did not catch on with the viewers who had spent too long listening to Bendix to accept Gleason in the role. After one short season of Gleason as Riley, the series halted production. About three years later, when William Bendix's employers relaxed their "no TV" ban, an entirely new production crew revived the *Riley* format, with Bendix, the radio Riley, as star.

The 200 Bendix episodes of *Riley* are much more familiar, but much more bland than Gleason's. The banality and silliness (and relative popularity) of the Bendix version is a perfect example of everything that was wrong with 1950s Hollywood TV sitcoms. Most of the characters are foolish or unlikable, the laughs are forced, the family lives in some nameless suburb in the Los Angeles area where it never rains or gets cold, and, worst of all, everybody is too nice. Still the Bendix episodes are more professionally produced than the Gleason ones.

The only aspect of *The Life of Riley* (Bendix version) that is at all different from the standard filmed 1950s sitcom is that Riley is still a blue-collar worker, not the standard white-collar office automaton. This small distinction can be easily chalked up to the fact that *Riley* is a holdover from the days of network radio in the 1940s, when blue-collar folk filled the air waves.

**LIFE ON EARTH (***) 60 min (13ep Color; 1979 UK BBC) Science Documentary** *with David Attenborough as host and narrator*

David Attenborough offers a fascinating account of how life emerged and developed on our planet, starting with the earliest known geological periods and continuing to the present. As with any such project, an enthusiastic style and the clear articulation of particular concepts is vital in carrying not only each episode but the vision of the entire series. Attenborough comes through on both counts. ■

**LIFE WITH ELIZABETH (**) 30 min (23ep B&W; 1953–1955 Syndication) Situation Comedy** *with Betty White as Elizabeth White, Del Moore as Alvin White, and Lois Bridge as Chlorine "Chloe" Skinridge*

Don Fedderson, the producer of such solid series as *The Millionaire* and *My Three Sons*, produces this first TV starring role for Betty White, who was later renowned as Sue Ann Nivens of *The Mary Tyler Moore Show* and Rose Nylund of *The Golden Girls*. White and Del Moore play young newlyweds on the west coast who own a 185-pound St. Bernard and a tiny Pekinese. What sets *Life with Elizabeth* apart from traditional sitcoms is its structure: Each episode is a collection of three story vignettes.

**LIFE WITH FATHER (*½) 30 min (26ep B&W; 1953–1955 CBS) Situation Comedy** *with Leon Ames as Clarence Day, Sr., Lurene Tuttle as Vinnie Day, and Ralph Reed and Steven Terrell as Clarence Day, Jr.*

In the 1920s, the real Clarence Day, Jr., wrote some nostalgic articles about his youth in turn-of-the-century America for *Harper's* and *The New Yorker*. The success of the articles led to a hit book titled *Life with Father*, which in turn led to a highly successful (eight years) Broadway play and a 1947 film with William Powell. After these memorable works of art comes this rather mediocre TV version. The story is the same: Victorian dad refuses to acknowledge the fading of his era as he is firm yet fair, with his four red-haired boys. The comedy is warm, not raucous, but the spark of the film version is just not here.

**LIFE WITH LUCY (zero) 30 min (13ep Color; 1986 ABC) Situation Comedy** *with Lucille Ball as Lucy Barker, Gale Gordon as Curtis McGibbon, Ann Dusenberry as Margo Barker McGibbon, Larry Anderson as Ted McGibbon, Jenny Lewis as Becky McGibbon, and Philip Amelio II as Kevin McGibbon*

"Lucille Ball does not make pilots." That was the accepted reasoning at ABC when the network made a deal in 1986 for Lucy's first network series in more than a decade. And, at first glance, it seemed to make sense. After all, millions still watched and enjoyed *I Love Lucy* reruns everyday, and the new sitcoms promised to use some of her old writers. Lucy herself had scored well in the 1960s and 1970s in *The Lucy Show* and *Here's Lucy*, and the new sitcom was bringing back her longtime comedy foil, Gale Gordon. Best of all, with television nostalgia on the rise, Lucy seemed to have a built-in audience on curiosity value alone. What was there to work out?

Unfortunately, plenty. In fact, one of the major problems facing any new Lucille Ball series was the continued popularity of the originals. After more than a quarter of a century of reruns, people were now more familiar with the various bits in those than even the writers, producers, and performers involved in them. As a result, the absolute worst strategy was to trot out the old-style routines without any major reworking—they had, in fact, already begun to fray in the *Here's Lucy* days. Asking Lucy to do the same things again twelve years later was courting disaster. Yet that's just what happened. Even though her character was written as being a grandmother of two, everyone seemed to fixate on predictable physical schtick using the new setting of a hardware store owned jointly by Lucy Barker and Curtis McGibbon. Backfiring foam fire extinguishers? Third aisle, please. Falling merchandise? Right under this ladder, sir. Banana creme pies? We'll get to those in just one moment. Even a relatively straight piece of simple comic mime (Lucy chases a fly while demonstrating a fly swatter for a customer) shows its age, with the fly obviously just a sound effect dubbed from offstage.

The real irony is that at seventy-five, Lucille Ball was in surprisingly good physical shape and gamely performed every stunt. But the problem wasn't in the execution—it was in the concept and scripts. Frankly there was no reason for Ball to come back just to redo old Lucy bits, not when the success of such programs as *The Golden Girls* clearly demonstrated that there was definitely an audience for familiar performers in an over-fifty setting. In fact, Ball herself had already demonstrated a willingness to break from her standard character type the previous season, starring as a bag lady in the successful 1985 made-for-TV movie *Stone Pillow*. It's unfortunate the new comedy series did not reflect the same willingness to experiment.

Despite a contractual commitment for a full slate of episodes, neither side raised a fuss when only eight aired. The total production package contains additional episodes not shown on the network, but it is unlikely they will air any time soon.

**LIFE WITH LUIGI (**) 30 min (21ep B&W; 1952–1953 CBS) Situation Comedy** *with J. Carrol Naish and Vito Scotti as Luigi Basco, Alan Reed and Thomas Gomez as Pasquale, and Jody Gilbert and Muriel Landers as Rosa*

As with other hit ethic-based sitcoms of network radio (*Amos'n' Andy, The Goldbergs*), *Life with Luigi* endured a painfully brief run on TV. In the early 1950s, an era when suburban WASP-ishness was the rage (see *Life of Riley, Ozzie and Harriet*), a sitcom about a badly accented Italian immigrant to Chicago turned viewers off. Luigi, who runs an antique store, was brought to this country by Pasquale, the scheming owner of a spaghetti emporium, in hopes Luigi would marry Pasquale's fat daughter Rosa. Luigi is portrayed as a bumbler, but mostly out of his ignorance of American customs.

*Life with Luigi* is rather simple and very old-fashioned, but it is a quaint relic of another era that deserves more respect than it received when it first aired. Most of the talented original cast (including Alan Reed, later the voice of Fred Flintstone, as Pasquale) is dumped near the end of the series and replaced by lesser lights. ■

**LIFE WITH THE ERWINS** **(see *The Stu Erwin Show*)**

**LIFESTYLES OF THE RICH AND FAMOUS (*) 60 min (156ep Color; 1984–1988 Syndication) Interview-Profile** *with Robin Leach*

There is not much point in criticizing this show. It is so crass, so shallow, so materialistic, and so inane that it defies serious analysis. On the other hand, it's also a classic example of a show that is *so* bad, it's good (in a campy sort of way). In each episode, English-born host Robin Leach guides the viewer through a puff profile of some public celebrity or private moneybag, with lots of views of sumptuous homes, fancy cars, and high living. Leach asks some softball questions seemingly written by publicity agents and that's about it.

Very little real information is conveyed during this show, but of course that is its point. *Lifestyles of the Rich and Famous* is designed to feed off public fantasies of wealth, fame, and power, and it does that all too well. Leach is positively shameless in his fawning over guests and his loud, abrasive voice and personality will grate on any viewer who pays attention.

The only saving grace is that Leach at least has a sense of humor and does not take all this too seriously. He is obviously having a good time (who wouldn't?) and, if you look at the show as a parody of itself, *Lifestyles* can be most amusing. No parody, no *Saturday Night Live* take-off could ever quite capture Leach's relentless gold-digging lust as he describes some opulent European villa. If the Communist paranoia of cheap syndicated spy shows such as *I Led Three Lives* perfectly captures the feeling of the early 1950s, then *Lifestyles of the Rich and Famous* perfectly captures the "go for it" mood of pure greed in the mid-1980. ■

**LILLI PALMER QUALITY THEATER (*) 30 min (36ep B&W: 1956 Syndication) Drama Anthology** *with Lilli Palmer as hostess*

In the 1950s, every Hollywood actor and actress with any kind of marquee value served as host and occasional star for a series of usually syndicated drama anthologies. Most are eminently forgettable. This is no exception.

German-born Lilli Palmer, who was married to Rex Harrison from 1943 to 1958, starred in many English films as well as those from Hollywood.

**LILLIE (**½) 60 min (13ep Color; 1978 UK London Weekend Television) Biographical Drama** *with Francesca Annis as Lillie Langtry, Anton Rodgers as Edward Langtry, Cheryl Campbell as Sarah Bernhardt, Peter Egan as Oscar Wilde, John Castle as Prince Louis of Battenberg, Catherine Feller as Dominique, Ann Firbank as Princess Alexandra, Patrick Hott as Dean Le Breton, Jennie Linden as Patsy, Peggy Ann Wood as Mrs. Le Breton, and Denis Lill as the Prince of Wales*

Lillie Langtry was the first celebrity to endorse a commercial product (Pears Soap), and that fact alone would be enough to warrant a biographical TV-movie. But there's more. The British-born rags-to-riches beauty was also the object of affection by the likes of Oscar Wilde, Texas lawman Judge Roy Bean, and the Prince of Wales. Wilde camped on her doorstep, Bean named a town after her, and Prince Edward risked the ire of Princess Alexandra to pursue her. Add to the mix Lillie's weak-willed, alcoholic husband (Edward) and her own fiercely independent lifestyle and pursuit of career in the late nineteenth century (an era just learning to deal with such decisions by women), and you have more than enough to fill a miniseries. This is an entertaining, boisterous bit of celebrity gazing, with Francesca Annis appropriately bold and beautiful in the title role.

**LIME STREET (**) 60 min (7ep & 90 min pilot Color; 1985 & 1987 ABC & Lifetime) Adventure** *with Robert Wagner as James Greyson Culver, John Standing as Edward Wingate, Samantha Smith as Elizabeth Culver, Maia Brewton as Margaret Ann Culver, and Lew Ayers as Henry Wade Culver*

Robert Wagner always plays dashing, romantic, and

wisecracking heroes, such as Alexander Munday in *It Takes a Thief*, Pete Ryan in *Switch*, and Jonathan Hart in *Hart to Hart*. As J. G. Culver in *Lime Street*, Wagner is no longer so dashing or so wisecracking, although he dabbles in both. Culver has a classic Wagner-esque job as an investigator for a London-based insurance conglomerate (something like Lloyd's of London). Edward Wingate is Culver's British cohort and their exploits take up a good chunk of *Lime Street*. The rest of the show focuses on Culver's mundane home life on a Virginia farm, raising fancy horses and two cute daughters (thirteen-year-old Elizabeth and eight-year-old Margaret Ann) with the help of his crusty old dad (played by Lew Ayers).

Elizabeth Culver is played by Samantha Smith, a Maine girl who became a world celebrity in 1983 when her letter to Soviet leader Yuri Andropov urging peace earned her an audience with the Soviet chief. Her fame led to several acting roles, including this one, her first TV series. It was also her last. She and her father were killed in a plane crash just a month before *Lime Street* first aired.

Two episodes of *Lime Street* that never aired on ABC during its original run first appeared on the Lifetime cable service in 1987.

**THE LINEUP (**½) 30 & 60 min (201ep: One hundred and eighty-three 30 min & eighteen 60 min B&W; 1954–1960 CBS) Police Drama** *with Warner Anderson as Lt. Ben Guthrie, Tom Tully as Matt Grebb, Marshall Reed as Fred Asher, William Leslie as Dan Delaney, and Tod Barton as Charlie Summers*

Even though *The Lineup* has more than 200 episodes, few remember it these days, since it was forever in the shadow of *Dragnet*, the other fact-based West Coast police show that originally aired in the same era.

*Dragnet* is set in sun-cracked, hard-nosed Los Angeles, while *The Lineup* is set in more laid-back San Francisco. Otherwise, the concept is the same. Real cases from the S.F.P.D. serve as the basis for each episode, as police detective Ben Guthrie and his two aides, Matt Grebb and Fred Asher, track down suspects.

For the final season, the series expands to one hour and Grebb and Asher are replaced by Dan Delaney and Charlie Summers.

The five years of thirty-minute episodes are also known as *San Francisco Beat*. In 1958, while the series was still in production, a theatrical film version of *The Lineup* was released, directed by Don Siegel (later the director of Clint Eastwood's *Dirty Harry*).

**LITTLE HOUSE ON THE PRAIRIE (**½) 60 min (208ep Color & 2 hr pilot & three 2 hr sequels; 1974–1983 NBC) Drama** *with Michael Landon as Charles Ingalls, Karen Grassle as Caroline Ingalls, Melissa Gilbert as Laura Ingalls, Melissa Sue Anderson as Mary Ingalls Kendall, Lindsay Greenbush and Sidney Greenbush as Carrie Ingalls, Victor French as Isaiah Edwards, Merlin Olsen as Jonathan Garvey, Matthew Laborteaux as Albert Ingalls, Dean Butler as Almanzo Wilder, Patrick Laborteaux as Andy Garvey, Katherine MacGregor as Harriet Oleson, and Richard Bull as Nels Oleson*

Not so much a western as a prairie soap opera, *Little House* is the brainchild of producer–star–writer–director Michael Landon, who learned the craft of turning out family-oriented frontier sagas from his thirteen years as Little Joe Cartwright on *Bonanza*. *Little House* has all the earmarks of a good prime-time soap opera, in that it has a huge, ever-changing cast of characters, many of whom come and go, marry, suffer from blindness, are cured from blindness, move to the big city, leave the big city, and disappear over the course of the series' run.

Charles Ingalls is the youngish patriarch of a Kansas family in the 1870s, who heads north with his brood to the frontier town of Walnut Grove, Minnesota. Over the years, the Ingalls family, like their TV soul mates from the twentieth century, the Waltons, grow up and cope with the harsh realities of life.

It is hard to say anything really bad about *Little House* because, like all soaps, if you get involved with the characters you can overlook many minor flaws and weaknesses in the show. Landon deserves credit for placing the family saga in a time and place we are used to seeing only in the realm of cowboy and Indian stories. Still, Landon just looks too much like blow-dried Hollywood 1970s to pass for rugged prairie 1870s.

Among the hordes of supporting cast, the two standouts are Victor French as neighboring farmer Isaiah Edwards and his replacement Merlin Olsen as Jonathan Garvey. Both French and Olsen play big hulking he-men types that are not afraid to show their feelings. This, of course, is a very 1970s Hollywood trait and it is not typical for big, hulking he-men types usually seen in films or TV shows about the western frontier. As a result, the three male leads, Landon, French, and Olsen, seem a bit out of place.

The most significant of *Little House*'s constant cast changes when Landon leaves the show after eight seasons. The focus shifts to daughter Laura and her husband Almanzo Wilder, and the show's title changes to *Little House: A New Beginning*. After twenty-two episodes under that name, *Little House* winds up with three two-hour specials from 1983 and 1984 (*Look Back to Yesterday*, *Bless All the Dear Children*, and *The Last Farewell*) that follow the events in Walnut Grove, Minnesota, up to the flaming finale when the whole town burns down.

*Little House on the Prairie* is based on a series of autobiographical books by the real Laura Ingalls Wilder and, much like John Boy in *The Waltons*, the character of Laura Ingalls serves as narrator on *Little House*. ■

**THE LITTLE PEOPLE** **(see *The Brian Keith Show*)**

**LITTLE VIC** (*) **30 min (6ep Color; 1977 Syndication) Drama** *with Joey Green as Gillie Walker, Carole Anne Seflinger as Clara Scott, and Doney Oatman as Julie Sayer.*

Little Vic is a horse. Gillie Walker is a fourteen-year-old black orphan who becomes a jockey and rides Little Vic. Surprise! They win the big race.

**LITTLE WOMEN** (**½) **Drama in two major versions 30 min (9ep Color; 1972 UK BBC)** *with Jo Rowbottom as Meg March, Angela Down as Jo March, Sarah Craze as Beth March, Janina Faye as Amy March, and Stephanie Bidmead as Margaret March* **60 min (4ep & 4 hr pilot Color; 1978 & 1979 NBC)** *with Susan Dey (pilot) and Jessica Harper as Jo March, Meredith Baxter Birney (pilot) and Susan Walden as Meg March, Ann Dusenberry as Amy March, Eve Plumb as Beth March and also as Melissa Jane Driscoll, Dorothy McGuire as Margaret March, William Schallert as Rev. Jonathan March, William Shatner (pilot) and David Ackroyd as Prof. Friedrich Bhaer, and Robert Young as James Lawrence*

The 1972 BBC series is a straightforward adaptation of the Louisa May Alcott books, *Little Women*, and its sequel, *Good Times*, tracing the lives of the March girls from adolescence to young adulthood growing up in New England in the 1860s. In the U.S. production, the 1978 four-hour made-for-TV movie pilot pretty well covers the original novel, with the follow-up short-run series taking off into new territory, switching a few performers in the process. Perhaps the most unusual change involves Eve Plumb's character of Beth, who dies and is replaced by her look-alike cousin, Melissa, also played by Plumb.

The U.S. version comes off more as a soap-opera-style tale of Victorian manners (against the backdrop of the American Civil War), while the British production plays like a properly correct presentation perfectly acceptable for a high school literature class.

**LITTLE WORLD OF DON CAMILLO** (**½) **30 min (13ep Color; 1980 UK BBC) Comedy-Drama** *with Brian Blessed and Mario Adorf*

Sparkling adaptation of the books (actually, collections of short stories) written by Giovanni Guareschi about life after World War II in a small Italian village. The tales focus on the clever byplay between the town's communist mayor, Peppone, and its wily Catholic priest, Don Camillo, as they work out the mutual accommodations necessary for day-to-day life. Along the way, of course, they both attempt to score symbolic points over each other. Blessed (most familiar for his role as Augustus in *I. Claudius*) and Adorf are in fine form facing off in their respective roles.

**THE LITTLEST HOBO** (*½) **30 min (83ep: 57ep B&W & 26ep Color; 1963–1964 & 1980–1981 Syndication) Adventure**

London, a homeless German Shepherd, is the "hobo" of the title, roaming cities and towns with the uncanny ability to find dangerous situations and help out the slow-witted humans. There are no human regulars in this series, which was produced in Canada.

**LIVE! DICK CLARK PRESENTS** (*) **60 min (7ep Color; 1988 CBS) Variety** *with Dick Clark as host*

Highly reminiscent of Clark's lame late 1970s live variety series *Dick Clark's Live Wednesday*, *Live! Dick Clark Presents* features the never-aging Clark as host to an odd collection of guests. Some are regular well-known performers (such as Harry Belafonte), while some are more esoteric (such as a mentalist and an escape artist). A big fuss is made over the fact that the show (as originally aired) is live. Who cares?

**LIVE-IN** (½) **30 min (9ep Color; 1989 CBS) Situation Comedy** *with Lisa Patrick as Lisa Wells, Chris Young as Danny Matthews, Hugh Maguire as Ed Matthews, Kimberly Farr as Sarah Matthews, David Moscow as Peter Matthews, Lightfield Lewis as Gator, and Jenny O'Hara as Muriel Spiegleman*

Cheaply titillating, *Live-In* revolves around the hormonal aspirations of a young teenage boy, resulting in a sophomoric series that should be avoided. Soon after the birth of her third child, Sarah Matthews is heading back to her corporate job in Manhattan. Rather than leave little Melissa at day-care, Sarah and her husband Ed hire (sight unseen) Lisa Patrick from the Australian outback to serve as a live-in babysitter (known as an "au pair" in trendy circles). Lisa turns out to be a blond knockout in skimpy miniskirts and revealing blouses who is not that much older than eldest son Chris. Lisa's beauty soon has Chris in a post-puberty frenzy, but she wants to keep her relationship with him on a strictly platonic basis. Chris (and his Eddie Haskell-ish buddy, known as "Gator") are far too annoying with their youthful macho swaggering, and the rest of the Matthews clan is too bland. You know this show is bad news when the first episode concerns the efforts by Chris and Gator to drill a hole in the bathroom wall, in order to spy Lisa *au naturel* in the shower. The disco-ish bump-and-grind effects the show resorts to as Lisa starts to disrobe are embarrassing to all involved in this mistake.

**THE LIVING PLANET** (***) **60 min (13ep Color; 1984 UK BBC) Science Documentary** *with David Attenborough as host and narrator*

David Attenborough's follow-up to *Life on Earth*, this series focuses on change and adaptation, presenting it rather like environmental dominoes. His point: When the surface of the Earth changes, so do the lives of its colonists—plants, animals, and humans. As with *Life on Earth*, Attenborough avoids scientific jargon as much as possible, preferring to make his points through straightforward narration and some stunning location footage (including visits to the volcanic "furnaces of the Earth," baking deserts and plateaus, and rich jungle rain forests). In each location he shows basic cause, effect, and adaptation. As often happens with such programs, humans come in from some scolding for abusing the planet (though there is also admiration for constructive efforts). Overall, this is a top-notch nature series and an effective environmental treatise as well. ■

**THE LLOYD BRIDGES SHOW (**) 30 min (34ep B&W; 1962–1963 CBS) Drama** *with Lloyd Bridges as Adam Shepherd*

You can't fault *The Lloyd Bridges Show* for not trying a different format. Bridges plays Adam Shepherd, a freelance reporter who becomes so involved with his stories that he literally becomes part of them (as one of the main characters). The result is a collection of unrelated drama anthology segments, each opening with an investigation by Bridges' Shepherd character. It's a novel idea, but one that doesn't really add up to much.

Aaron Spelling (*The Mod Squad, The Love Boat*) is the producer of *The Lloyd Bridges Show.*

**LOBO, THE MISADVENTURES OF SHERIFF (**) 60 min (37ep Color; 1979–1981 NBC) Police Comedy** *with Claude Akins as Sheriff Elroy P. Lobo, Mills Watson as Deputy Perkins, Brian Kerwin as Deputy Birdie Hawkins, Leann Hunley as Sarah Cumberland, and Nicolas Coster as Chief J. C. Carson*

If Jackie Gleason's southern sheriff character from the *Smokey and the Bandit* movies had ever received his own television series, it probably would have played something like this show. Technically a spin-off from *B. J. and the Bear, The Misadventures of Sheriff Lobo* follows the comic adventures of the slightly larcenous sheriff of Orly County, Georgia, who consistently manages to stumble his way into nabbing the bad guys. Of course, that's far behind such interests as watching the pretty women in town (especially Sarah Cumberland, who runs the local hotel) while ignoring his paperwork. Naturally such dedication results in a promotion for Lobo and his two naive deputies: The governor doesn't realize Lobo's district has such a low crime rate because the sheriff doesn't bother reporting anything. As the program title changes to the much more concise *Lobo*, the sheriff, Perkins, and Birdie find themselves reassigned to a special police task force in Atlanta. There they quickly bumble their way to success once again (maybe the governor knew exactly what he was doing), much to the annoyance of Atlanta's chief of detectives, J. C. Carson.

Claude Akins obviously has a fine time playing the title character in these totally disposable and interchangeable adventures. Of course, if you have all three *Smokey and the Bandit* movies in your videotape collection, you'll probably want to catch all thirty-seven episodes of *Lobo.*

**LOCK UP (**) 30 min (78ep B&W; 1959–1961 Syndication) Law Drama** *with Macdonald Carey as Herbert L. Maris, John Doucette as Jim Weston, and Olive Carey as Casey*

*Perry Mason* on a shoestring budget, *Lock Up* concerns attorney Herbert L. Maris, who helps out the innocent in need of intense legal help. Macdonald Carey, who plays Maris, is best known as Dr. Tom Horton from the daytime soap opera *Days of Our Lives.*

**LOGAN'S RUN (*½) 60 min (13ep & 90 min pilot Color; 1977–1978 CBS) Science Fiction** *with Gregory Harrison as Logan, Heather Menzies as Jessica, Donald Moffat as Rem, and Randy Powell as Francis*

Based on the 1976 theatrical film of the same name (with Michael York and Farrah Fawcett), this series presents life on Earth in the year 2319, recycling some of the sets, stock footage, and plot hooks of that standard "utopia of the future with a dark underbelly" setting. The twist in this one: a hedonistic life of pleasure until you're thirty, then termination. That sounds all right for Logan, who works for the City of Domes as an elite policeman (a "sandman") charged with rounding up those marked to die, until he notices *his* thirtieth approaching. Suddenly he becomes very interested in a forbidden concept: life outside the city. He flees, accompanied by a young woman (Jessica) and an android (Rem). But hot on their trail is another young policeman (Francis) who is promised a bonus (he won't be killed come age thirty) if he captures them. The series follows all four as they encounter a wide variety of other colonies of twenty-second century Earth survivors, sort of like hopping from plant to planet without bothering with a spaceship. Unfortunately it's not a very interesting world—much of Earth's civilization may have been wiped out by a long-ago nuclear holocaust, but its dramatic clichés managed to survive intact. A weak series taken from a weak film, though Gregory Harrison (later Gonzo on *Trapper John, M.D.*) shows a little more life in the lead role than York does in the theatrical version. Ironically, Donald Moffat's android character probably shows more personality than anyone else around.

**THE LONE RANGER (***) 30 min (221ep: 182 B&W & 39 Color; 1949–1957 ABC) Western** *with Clayton Moore and John Hart as John Reid/The Lone Ranger and Jay Silverheels as Tonto*

*The Lone Ranger* is a pure Saturday matinee kiddie western. There are no complex characters, no shades of gray, just the good and the bad, the innocent and the guilty.

The Lone Ranger started out as John Reid, a Texas Ranger, who was left for dead after a shoot-out with bad guys. Nursed to health by Tonto, an Indian, Reid goes under cover (a black mask) to seek revenge on the bad guys who shot him, in particular, and all the bad guys in Texas, in general.

What stands out sharply in *The Lone Ranger* is the crystal clear code of morality that infuses each episode. As with kiddie matinee heroes of the past, the Lone Ranger is a force of pure good who combats evil almost totally out of the goodness of his heart. Yes, he started his quest as a mission of revenge against his attackers, but that quickly fades into the background. The Lone Ranger is a modern-day knight in shining armor, motivated by chivalry.

Although motivated only by good, the Lone Ranger adopts the guise of evil. He is always known as the "masked man." In the old West, a masked man was an outlaw, one to be feared. What is more, the Lone Ranger is accompanied by an Indian, which is also unusual. For the average white settler, the Indian was seen as the enemy, or, at best, one to distrust. As a result, most everyday citizens who come across the Lone Ranger distrust him at first after spotting the mask and noting his cohort.

Because of their extraordinary popularity and their immaculate morality, the Lone Ranger and Tonto are hard to take seriously today. You keep wanting them to start acting with campy overtones, like Batman and Robin do in *Batman.* This tendency must be overcome in order to enjoy *The Lone Ranger*, because the show only works on the level it was designed for—pure, wholesome, action-packed homilies for America's youth. Accepted for who they are, the Lone Ranger and Tonto have aged quite well, appearing as beacons of goodness and brotherhood from an era (both the mythic old West and the real 1950s) that was not filled with too much of either.

*The Lone Ranger* is a familiar show to many, but it can be seen today in numerous forms that might be a bit confusing. The well-known opening narration by Fred Foy ("a fiery horse with the speed of light . . ."), accompanied by the strains of the "William Tell Overture," is missing on some episodes. The familiar figure of Clayton Moore as the Lone Ranger is replaced for two seasons by the more mundane wooden solidness of John Hart. There are also two theatrical *Lone Ranger* films from the mid-1950s starring Clayton Moore and Jay Silverheels (*The Lone Ranger* and *The Lone Ranger and the Lost City of Gold*) that were produced while the TV series was at the peak of its popularity.

There is also a disposable 1981 theatrical feature, *The Legend of the Lone Ranger* (with Klinton Spilsbury in the title role).

**THE LONE WOLF (*) 30 min (39ep B&W; 1953–1954 Syndication) Detective Drama** *with Louis Hayward as Michael Lanyard*

Michael Lanyard is a detective who roams the globe solo, fighting the good fight against bad guys of all nationalities. Lanyard's solitary ways earn him the title of "Lone Wolf."

Based on stories by Louis Joseph Vance, *The Lone Wolf* (also known as *Streets of Danger*) was a network radio series in the late 1940s. There was also a series of *Lone Wolf* movies produced in the 1930s and 1940s. ■

**THE LONER (**½) 30 min (26ep B&W; 1965–1966 CBS) Western** *with Lloyd Bridges as William Colton*

One year after the demise of the original *Twilight Zone*, Rod Serling returned to television with *The Loner*. Officially a western, *The Loner* is really more of a philosophical search for identity such as *Route 66, The Fugitive*, and *The Prisoner*. The series concerns William Colton, a Union calvary soldier from the Civil War who had received a medal for bravery. Just one month after the war's end, he resigns his commission. Colton, not your typical military hero, decides to head west, he says, "to get the cannon smoke out of my eyes, the noise out of my ears, maybe some of the pictures out of my head." The program follows Colton's solitary saga as he roams the West, running into various sorts of people and interacting with them.

Such a low-key, introspective format is very unusual for a TV series and it foreshadows the national cultural introspection just around the corner in the late 1960s (keyed off by the Vietnam War).

Serling created *The Loner* and wrote several of the scripts. It is not too farfetched to postulate that the character of Colton is a bit of a surrogate for Serling. Having gained wealth and fame from his days of writing hit TV drama scripts and creating *The Twilight Zone*, Serling was always highly frustrated by the shackles put on his creative powers due to the corporate structure of film and TV production.

Aside from Serling's presence, *The Loner* also benefits from the presence of Lloyd Bridges, already a popular TV star from four years on *Sea Hunt.* Bridges always came off well in *Sea Hunt* as a tight-lipped no-nonsense macho hero and he continues to shine in that same vein as the troubled but strong Colton.

Also behind the scenes in *The Loner* is executive producer William Dozier, a man best known for his campy hi-tech shows (*Batman, Green Hornet*, and *Rod Brown of the Rocket Rangers*). In *The Loner*, Dozier gets to air out his softer, more realistic side that surfaced only rarely in his more popular series.

**LONESOME DOVE (***) (8hr miniseries Color; 1989 CBS) Western** *with Robert Duvall as Augustus "Gus" McCrae, Tommy Lee Jones as Woodrow F. Call, Anjelica Huston as Clara Allen, Ricky Schroder as Newt Dobbs, Diane Lane as Lorena Wood, Robert Urich as Jake Spoon, Danny Glover as Joshua Deets, D. B. Sweeney as Dish Boggett, Chris Cooper as July Johnson, and Frederic Forrest as Blue Duck*

This sprawling miniseries begins in the sleepy, dusty, south Texas town of Lonesome Dove in the 1870s. Gus McCrae, a retired Texas Ranger with a love of good stories and beautiful women, runs a small cattle ranch near the Rio Grande with his taciturn old Ranger comrade Woodrow Call. A third ex-Ranger, Jake Spoon, turns up, on the run from an Arkansas sheriff who is after Spoon for accidentally killing a man. Spoon's ramblings about the wonders of the "Big Sky" country in far-away Montana plant a seed in Call's mind. Almost off-handedly, it is decided that the three ex-Rangers will lead the first cattle drive from Texas to the blustery Montana wilderness, where they plan to set up a profitable ranching operation. The logistics of organizing and leading the cattle drive are cumbersome, and nothing goes quite as planned during the long trek north.

Based on the lengthy novel by Larry McMurtry (who also wrote *The Last Picture Show* and *Terms of Endearment*), *Lonesome Dove* ably mixes lots of Western action (cattle stampedes, Indian attacks, prostitutes with hearts of gold) with great character development (a McMurtry staple). The combination of epic Western scenery and top-quality acting makes for an appealing saga that makes good use of the extended time frame of a long miniseries. Robert Duvall is outstanding as the earthy and philosophical McCrae, while Tommy Lee Jones is appropriately stern as the close mouthed Call.

**THE LONG, HOT SUMMER (***) 60 min (26ep B&W; 1965–1966 ABC) Drama** *with Edmond O'Brien and Dan O'Herlihy as Will Varner, Roy Thinnes as Ben Quick, Nancy Malone as Clara Varner, Paul Geary as Jody Varner, and Lana Wood as Eula Harker*

A valiant effort to bring some steamy, sexy, adult drama to TV years before it could realistically be done, *The Long, Hot Summer* is based on the hit 1958 movie starring Orson Welles, Paul Newman, Joanne Woodward, and Tony Franciosa. The film, in turn, was based on several short stories by William Faulkner, such as "The Hamlet" and "The Barn Burning."

Set in sweltering pre-air-conditioning Frenchman's Bend, Mississippi, *The Long, Hot Summer* pits old, corpulent, corrupt Will Varner (the "boss" of Frenchman's Bend) against young Turk Ben Quick. Returning to town to avenge his dead father, who had been "hounded" to death by Varner and his machine, Quick becomes entangled with Varner's beautiful but unmarried daughter Clara. Quick thus is at odds with Boss Varner on both personal and professional grounds.

The standout in the cast is Edmund O'Brien as Boss Varner. O'Brien had already adeptly played a deep-fried southern redneck boozehound in the film *Seven Days in May* (which earned him an Academy Award nomination), and he carries on with flourish in the TV show. Unfortunately halfway through *The Long, Hot Summer*, O'Brien is replaced by another Irishman, Dan O'Herlihy, who had recently starred in the hit film *Fail Safe*. O'Herlihy, however, no matter how hard he tried, could never be as mean and nasty as O'Brien, and thus the series lost a lot of pizazz.

Roy Thinnes appears as Ben Quick, the Paul Newman role from the movie. While no Newman, Thinnes is good at acting the silent sulking hero who seems capable of all sorts of trouble. Thinnes carried on his sulking ways in his later series *The Invaders*. Lana Wood, as sexy Eula, is Natalie Wood's kid sister.

In spite of the talented cast, *The Long, Hot Summer* is hampered by the fairly strict unwritten rules as to how daring a prime-time show could be in the mid-1960s, and it is too tame for its own good. A truer, more steamy version turns up in a 1985 made-for-TV movie with Jason Robards, Don Johnson, Judith Ivey, and Cybill Shepherd.

**LONG JOHN SILVER, THE ADVENTURES OF (**) 30 min (26ep Color; 1955–1956 Syndication) Adventure** *with Robert Newton as Long John Silver, Kit Taylor as Jim Hawkins, and Connie Gilchrist as Purity Pinker*

The 1950 Disney film classic, *Treasure Island*, made Robert Louis Stevenson's pirate character Long John Silver a children's favorite. In this series, Robert Newton, who played Silver in the Disney film, reprises his role. Set in the 1700s, on the British island of Porto Bello, the program has Silver using his pirate arts in support of the British crown, in battle against the Catholic fleet of Spain.

**LONGSTREET (**½) 60 min (23ep & 90 min pilot Color; 1971–1972 ABC) Detective Drama** *with James Franciscus as Mike Longstreet, Marlyn Mason as Nikki Bell, Peter Mark Richman as Duke Paige, and Ann Doran as Mrs. Kingston*

A gimmick detective series—the hero is blind—created by Sterling Silliphant (the man responsible for *Naked City*, where James Franciscus played Detective Jim Halloran). The 1971 made-for-TV pilot film sets up the premise as New Orleans insurance investigator Mike Longstreet is caught in an explosion that leaves his wife dead and his eyesight gone. But driven by his personal passion he overcomes his new handicap and collars her killers. He subsequently taps some of that same energy to carry on his own professional and personal life, with a little help from his German Shepherd guide dog (Pax), an electronic cane (to help him calculate distances), fellow workers Nikki and Duke, and (in an occasional role) Bruce Lee as Li Tsung, Longstreet's self-defense instructor. This is low-key and generally well-written, with Franciscus bringing to his character a sense of personal dedication similar to his portrayal of principled high school English teacher John Novak on *Mr. Novak*.

**LOOSE CHANGE (**) (6hr miniseries Color; 1978 NBC) Drama** *with Cristina Raines as Kate Evans, Season Hubley as Tanya Berenson, and Laurie Heinemann as Jenny Reston*

This predictable exercise in trivializing the 1960s follows the exploits of three women, a journalist (Kate), an artist (Tanya), and a social activist (Jenny). The miniseries was retitled *The Restless Years* for its second network TV run in 1979.

**LORD MOUNTBATTEN: THE LAST VICEROY (***) 60 min (6ep Color; 1985 UK) Drama** *with Nicol Williamson as Lord Mountbatten, Janet Suzman as Lady Edwina Mountbatten, Ian Richardson as Jawaharlal Nehru, Sam Dastor as Mahatma Gandhi, Vladek Sheybal as Mohammed Ali Jinnah, Nigel Davenport as Ismay, Wendy Hiller as Princess Victoria, and Malcolm Terris as Winston Churchill*

A different viewpoint, for those familiar with the events leading to the birth of modern India from the series *The Jewel in the Crown* or the theatrical film *Gandhi.* This time the story is told more from the perspective of Britain's representative, Lord Mountbatten, who is given the very difficult role of supervising the transition of power in India from colony status to an independent country. Or, as he soon discovers, into two independent countries, India and Pakistan. In any case, when his term as viceroy is finished, that will mark the end of British rule (thus, his status as the "last viceroy"). Nicol Williamson does an outstanding job in the title role, but there's also considerable time devoted to the characters of Indian leaders Gandhi and Nehru, as well as Jinnah, the founder and first governor-general of Pakistan.

**LORD PETER WIMSEY (***) 60 min (31ep at Fall 1989 Color; 1972–1975 & 1987– BBC) Mystery** *with Ian Carmichael and Edward Petherbridge as Lord Peter Wimsey, Glyn Houston and Richard Morant as Bunter, Mark Eden and David Quiller as Chief Inspector Parker, and Harriet Walter as Harriet Vane*

More than a half-dozen stories featuring the character of Lord Peter Wimsey first aired as serials on either *Masterpiece Theatre* or *Mystery*, introducing the aristocratic British detective of the 1920s to U.S. audiences. The tales are faithful adaptations of the mystery novels written by Dorothy L. Sayers, with a strong emphasis on the period-piece setting and tone. Both Ian Carmichael (who originated the TV role) and Edward Petherbridge play the lead character as a crisp and proper English gentleman, steel-eyed, reserved, and respectful of friends and associates (such as his personal aide, Bunter, or Inspector Parker). He prefers a world with everything (and, at times, everyone) in just the right order, which may even be one of the reasons he uses his ample leisure time to solve mysteries: Murder leaves things so messy and out-of-sorts.

Like the books, the stories are sometimes quite diffuse. They read, look, and sound fine as long as all you're doing is admiring the people and the scenery—but should you actually attempt to solve the mystery, you'll find the clue path surprisingly sketchy on close examination. So the key to enjoying the series is to focus on Wimsey and Bunter and prepare to be genuinely surprised at the outcome. Two of the more interesting cases involve people closely connected to Lord Peter: *Clouds of Witness* (Wimsey's brother, accused of murdering their sister's fiancé) and *Strong Poison* (Wimsey falls for a client accused of murder). In these cases, Wimsey cracks his veneer and approaches the investigations on a more personal level. However, the most fascinating case by far is *The Nine Tailors*, which probably has the most memorable conclusion and solution of all the stories dramatized.

The *Lord Peter Wimsey* stories packaged on *Masterpiece Theatre* or *Mystery* include *Clouds of Witness* (5ep), *Unpleasantness at the Bellona Club* (4ep), *Murder Must Advertise* (4ep), *The Nine Tailors* (4ep), *Five Red Herrings* (4ep), *Strong Poison* (3ep: new cast begins), *Have His Carcase* (4ep), and *Gaudy Night* (3ep).

**LORETTA YOUNG SHOW, THE NEW (*½) 30 min (26ep B&W; 1962–1963 CBS) Comedy/Drama** *with Loretta Young as Christine Massey, James Philbrook as Paul Belzer, Celia Kaye as Marnie Massey, Beverly Washburn as Vickie Massey, Dirk Rambo as Dirk Massey, and Dack Rambo as Dack Massey*

This series is called "new" to differentiate it from the long-running *Loretta Young Theater*, a drama anthology hosted by former film queen Loretta Young. This "new" series has Young as a continuing character, a widowed mother of seven kids who earns a living writing articles in magazines such as *Belzer's Woman's Journal.* Loretta's character falls in love and finally marries the publisher of Belzer's, Paul Belzer. Twin brothers Dack and Dirk Rambo play two of Loretta's kids. Dack went on to star in *Sword of Justice* and to play Jack Ewing on *Dallas.*

**THE LORETTA YOUNG THEATER (**½) 30 min (261ep B&W; 1954–1961 NBC) Drama Anthology** *with Loretta Young as hostess*

Amidst the large number of drama anthology series from the 1950s that star fading lights from Hollywood, *The Loretta Young Theater* stands out as one of the more successful. The elegant, glamorous Loretta Young, an Oscar winner in 1947 for *The Farmer's Daughter* and an Oscar nominee in 1949 for *Come to the Stable*, stars in most of the early episodes of this series, but cuts back her appearances as time goes on. The plays are mostly solid, morally uplifting tales that seem somehow corny these days.

The first season was originally titled *Letters to Loretta*, in reflection of the original concept, which was to have each episode open with Young reading a letter from one of her fans. The letter tells of a problem that the fan is having and requests Loretta's advice. The play then dramatizes the problem posed and suggests a wholesome solution. The letter concept is phased out after two seasons. The most memorable aspect of this series, Young's elaborate gowns and her concluding remarks that frequently quote scripture, were chopped out of the syndicated reruns at her request, since the gowns she wore were out-of-date. ■

**LORNE GREEN'S** **(see *Last of the Wild; New Wilderness*)**

**LOST EMPIRES (**½) 60 min (8ep Color; 1986 UK Granada) Drama** *with Colin Firth as Richard Hardcastle, John Castle as Uncle Nick, Laurence Olivier as Harry Burrard, Carment De Sautoy as Julie, Beatie Edney as Nancy, Brian Glover as Tommy, and Jim Carter as Inspector Crabb*

*Lost Empires* is an adaptation of a novel by J. B. Priestly, following life on the British music hall circuit, circa 1913. This was Britain's equivalent to the U.S. vaudeville stage, a mixture of song, pie-in-face slapstick, sexy dancing, and comedy that played in local theaters long before television (or even radio) really caught on. (In fact, the title of this series refers to the Empire chain of theaters, now mostly lost to the wrecking ball.) The main action centers on young Richard Hardcastle, a lad from the North Country who comes to work for his Uncle Nick, a magician in a traveling company. Naturally, with all those empty hours to fill on the road (and backstage), Richard quickly loses whatever innocence he may have had, falling first for Nancy, then Julie. Trouble is, he's not the only one with a romantic heart, and sometimes his competition (such as the fiery Tommy) has quite a nasty temper. A nicely paced drama, ending (as so many British dramas do) with the ominous rumblings of war (this time, World War I).

**LOST IN SPACE (*½) 60 min (83ep: 29 B&W & 54 Color; 1965–1968 CBS) Science Fiction** *with Guy Williams as John Robinson, June Lockhart as Maureen Robinson, Jonathan Harris as Zachary Smith, Mark Goddard as Don West, Marta Kristin as Judy Robinson, Billy Mumy as Will Robinson, Angela Cartwright as Penny Robinson, Bob May as the Robot, and Dick Tufeld as the voice of the Robot*

This is the show CBS chose instead of *Star Trek*, which shows you how little TV executives know about science fiction. *Lost in Space* is a simplistic saga of space, aimed at children, with only its nostalgia value making it worth watching today.

The setting is a futuristic version of the venerable Johann Wyss children's story, *Swiss Family Robinson*. This time, the date is 1997, not the 1800s, and the family's destination is Alpha Centauri, not the tropics. Prof. John Robinson, his biochemist wife Maureen, their three children (precocious Penny and Will and nubile Judy), and dashing young pilot Maj. West plan to rocket to another star system in the Jupiter II spaceship, in hopes of establishing the first human colony on another world. Their plans are knocked askew by Dr. Zachary Smith, an enemy agent who sneaks on board in the last seconds before blast-off. While the crew is already in suspended animation for the long flight, Smith arranges for the Jupiter II to self-destruct shortly after lift-off. Due to Smith's ineptitude that will display itself in virtually every episode, he fails to get off the ship in time and thus joins the Robinsons and Maj. West in their journey. Awakening the others, Smith is able to avoid total destruction of the spaceship, but his sabotage causes enough damage to send the Jupiter II wildly off course. Soon thereafter, the vessel crash lands on the proverbial uncharted planet. The series focuses both on the Robinsons' efforts to repair their craft and salvage their mission and on Smith's spineless attempts to sell the others down the river whenever there is any chance of returning to Earth.

A key weakness of *Lost in Space* is its mediocre writing. As the writers of *Gilligan's Island* discovered, there is only so much you can do with people shipwrecked on a deserted isle. Other characters are forever turning up to menace the series regulars, but there is very little rhyme or reason for all the company, other than as a plot device. The stories are trite tales that almost always end (or start, depending on how you look at it) with a cliff-hanger. *Batman* tried the same trick, but it worked because that series was designed as camp fun. In *Lost in Space*, when the cliff-hanger is for real, it seems hackneyed.

*Lost in Space* is not without its own cute charm, however. The attraction between Maj. West and Judy Robinson adds a little sizzle to the program. Not much is made of this platonic affair, but both young people act as if they are ready to begin producing a new generation of settlers immediately. The relationship between young Will and the huge, intelligent, powerful, walking, talking robot is a nice turn on the old *Lassie* saga of a boy and his dog (something June Lockhart, a veteran mom from the *Lassie* show, should know about). The robot, a virtual clone of Robby the Robot of the 1956 sci-fi film classic *Forbidden Planet*, keeps a watchful eye out for all of the crew, especially Will. Instead of barking, like Lassie, to warn its masters, the robot shouts "Warning! Warning! Danger! Danger!"

The best reason to watch *Lost in Space* is to watch Dr. Smith, the slimiest villain this side of Boris Badenov. Smith is not averse to doing anything that might save his own skin, no matter how much it would hurt the others. Smith is greedy, vain, pompous, incompetent, cowardly, deceitful, and obnoxious. Furthermore, Jonathan Harris's portrayal of Smith is highly affected and very broad. The venomous remarks tossed back and forth between Dr. Smith and the robot are far more pungent than the rest of the bland scripts.

*Lost in Space* bears the marks of its producer, Irwin Allen, who went in for overproduced special-effects-laden series such as *Voyage to the Bottom of the Sea* and *The Time Tunnel*, before moving to disaster movies such as *The Towering Inferno*. Allen obviously felt a kinship with the *Swiss Family Robinson* saga, for after three seasons of *Lost in Space*, Allen produced a short-lived series that mostly stuck to the original shipwrecked-on-a-desert-island concept, called *Swiss Family Robinson*.

There is a one-hour animated "spin-off" episode of *Lost in Space* that originally aired on the *ABC Saturday Superstar Movie*. Produced by veteran cartoonist William Hanna and Joseph Barbera, the cartoon *Lost in Space* is quite different from the TV series, with only the characters of Dr. Smith and the Robot carried over. (Jonathan Harris does the voice of Dr. Smith.) The "Space Family Robinson" angle is dropped and the new commander is named Craig Robinson. ■

**LOTSA LUCK** **(**½) 30 min (24ep Color; 1974–1975 NBC) Situation Comedy** *with Dom DeLuise as Stanley Belmont, Kathleen Freeman as Iris Belmont, Wynn Irwin as Arthur Swann, Beverly Sanders as Olive Swann, and Jack Knight as Bummy Fitzer*

Dom DeLuise, a popular portly comic, stars in his first sitcom, produced by *Dick Van Dyke Show* alumni Bill Persky and Sam Denoff. *Lotsa Luck* should be wonderful, but it is only mildly interesting. DeLuise plays Stanley Belmont, a blue-collar flunkie for New York's bus department. The focus is on Stanley's crowded home life, where his mother Iris bosses him, his sister Olive gets in his way, and his lazy, shiftless brother-in-law Arthur mooches from him.

Like numerous comedy series of the 1970s, *Lotsa Luck* is based on a hit British series, in this case *On The Buses*.

**LOTTERY$** **(*) 60 min (15ep Color; 1983–1984 ABC) Drama** *with Ben Murphy as Patrick Sean Flaherty and Marshall Colt as Eric Rush*

If *Lottery$* sounds like *The Millionaire*, it is totally planned. Like that earlier 1950s series, this show concerns ordinary folk who suddenly win millions in a lottery. Perversely, however, *Lottery$* spends too much time on the efforts of Patrick Sean Flaherty (do you think he's Irish?), local representative of Ireland's Intersweep Lottery, who tracks down the lucky winners, along with handsome IRS hunk Eric Rush, who tags along to get Uncle Sam's cut. There is not enough attention paid to the winners. Each episode contains two or three segments, each focusing on a different winner.

**LOU GRANT** **(***½) 60 min (114ep Color; 1977–1982 CBS) Drama** *with Ed Asner as Lou Grant, Mason Adams as Charlie Hume, Robert Walden as Joe Rossi, Linda Kelsey as Billie Newman (McCovey), Nancy Marchand as Margaret Pynchon, Jack Bannon as Art Donovan, Daryl Anderson as Dennis "Animal" Price, Allen Williams as Adam Wilson, Rebecca Balding as Carla Mardigian, and Lance Guest as Lance Reinecke*

There's surprisingly strong life after the final curtain for Ed Asner's Lou Grant following seven seasons on *The Mary Tyler Moore Show*. In this series, Lou heads west for a job as city editor at the *Los Angeles Tribune*. It's a career change that actually makes sense because on *Mary Tyler Moore* it was established that Lou had started out in newspapers in Detroit. The unexpected twist was the decision by MTM to make Lou Grant's new show the company's first hour-long drama, rather than another situation comedy.

It was a gamble that paid off, as the best elements of the MTM approach to comedy were adapted to the new form: a good supporting cast, a strong central character, and clever, well-paced scripts with believable dialogue. The stories are good and well-told. Asner's Grant had been barking orders for years, so he falls into place almost immediately. Surrounding him are character types that at first seem to come straight out of such theatrical newspaper film hits as *The Front Page* and *All the President's Men*: the irascible, editor-in-chief (Charlie Hume), the pushy young male investigative reporter (Joe Rossi), the sensitive but independent young female reporter (Billie Newman and, for a few episodes at the beginning, Carla Mardigian), the unkempt photo hound (Dennis "Animal" Price), a handsome well-spoken assistant city editor (Art Donovan), and an older woman as owner and publisher (Margaret Pynchon).

In a very short time, however, each of these develops into a well-rounded character, continually growing over the five-year run of the series and providing plenty of background fodder. For instance, there's an intense professional rivalry between Billie and Rossi in covering stories. In the world of corporate politics, Mrs. Pynchon and Charlie Hume often find themselves grinding through boardroom concerns as time-consuming as the pursuit of the latest news. And there's always plenty of office gossip about everyone at the paper, ranging from possible romantic ties (Donovan and Billie? Lou and a policewoman? Rossi and that new black reporter?) to juicy personal secrets (Is one of the editors an alcoholic? A spy for the CIA?)

And, of course, there's a constant interaction with characters from the outside world who share detailed information and insights on a variety of topics (from black-market babies to building a nuclear bomb in your very own basement). The facts are presented effectively without sounding like part of a lecture or a dull laundry list. Instead they are a reasonably natural part of the dialogue that you might expect among reporters and their subjects, reporters and their editors, and even reporters arguing with one another. Of course, everybody is focusing on the finished story for the paper and sometimes this information even gets that far.

But sometimes it doesn't. That is perhaps the best aspect of *Lou Grant*'s treatment of the news business—recognizing the fact that occasionally there's just no front-page story there. Or, at best, there's just a throwaway item on page 53. It doesn't really matter, of course, because we've already learned the important details in the episode. But it is an important admission, in contrast to the usual implication in reporter dramas that a crusading newspaper can wipe out evil with a headline. Instead *Lou Grant* deals with the reality of chipping away, day-by-day, at issues, perceptions, and personalities.

This approach really helps the credibility of the series in tackling its selected issues. Generally the writers wisely stay away from trying to solve everything in one hour and focus instead on one or two particular aspects of a topic. Or they choose more elusive concepts like respect, trust, and accountability, sometimes juxtaposing seemingly unrelated subplots to make their points. And, surprisingly, these issue dramas often include arguments from a number of sides, even questioning presumably ideologically correct stands. For instance, one time Charlie chews out Billie when she begins to make assumptions about what a woman in a story she's covering (about unwed mothers) should do with her life. He pointedly reminds Billie that it's the woman's decision to make, not hers.

Much to the disappointment of some viewers, none of the other main cast members from *Mary Tyler Moore* ever show up on *Lou Grant*, though the character of Mary's journalist aunt, Flo Meredith (Eileen Heckart), does appear in one episode, covering the same political campaign as Billie. (This show often gets pulled for broadcast at election time, so watch for it then.) In the other direction, though, *Lou Grant* has a postproduction legacy of its own. You can bet that if a character in another MTM-produced series (such as *Remington Steele*) is reading a newspaper in Los Angeles, it'll be Lou's paper, the *Trib*.

**LOVE, AMERICAN STYLE (*½) 30 & 60 min (224ep: one hundred twelve 30 min & one hundred twelve 60 min Color; 1969–1974 ABC) Comedy Anthology**

On one hand, *Love, American Style* is a great concept. It is a series of comedy vignettes of varying lengths featuring different guest performers each episode, with short skits in between featuring a troupe of regulars, all tied together by only the slenderest of threads: the theme of love. This format is so free-form, so different from just about everything else on TV, that the show deserves credit just for being unique.

On the other hand, *Love, American Style* is mostly a failure. With such a great concept, the show wastes its potential by usually sticking to silly, overly cute romps that seem pretty dated. This show comes from the late 1960s and early 1970s, at the height of the so-called sexual revolution, and *Love, American Style* is just too proud of itself for trying to be bold and daring. In fact, it's often just loud and trite.

All of the stock characters of the era show up: the libidinous bachelor, forever on the make in the era of free love; the beautiful young lass who spouts words of female liberation, but resorts to all the old coy tricks of flirting and chastity when it comes to the clinch; and the older generation that seems desperate to get in on all of the action.

Everybody in *Love, American Style* tries to act hip, but it's sort of Las Vegas hip, somehow artificial and distant from the real thing. Most of the guest stars were already old hat when the show was produced (George Gobel, the Lennon Sisters, Martha Raye) and few of the youthful band of regulars from the short comedy skits went on to make much of a name for themselves in comedy.

In retrospect, *Love, American Style*'s only claim to fame in TV history is its role as the vehicle for the pilot episode of *Happy Days*, which was aired in 1972 as "Love and the Happy Days." In 1986, *The New Love, American Style* briefly revived the series as a daytime thirty-minute offering.

**LOVE AND MARRIAGE (*½) 30 min (26ep B&W; 1959–1960 NBC) Situation Comedy** *with William Demarest as William Harris, Jeanne Bal as Pat Baker, Murray Hamilton as Steve Baker, and Stubby Kaye as Stubby Wilson*

This musty old artifact provides a look at an aspect of the music business now mostly forgotten, the music publishing racket. In the pre-rock'n'roll era, the music publisher held a central role in a song's popularity, by shopping the song around (called "plugging") to bands and singers. With the advent of rock, the music publisher receded into the background.

It is this change of era that is at the heart of *Love and Marriage.* William Harris runs a Los Angeles music publishing business that is dying due to his stubborn refusal to adapt to the new wave in music, rock'n'roll. His daughter, Pat, becomes his partner, in hopes that her more modern sensibilities will save the family business.

The setting here may be fascinating as a social memento, but the actual series is far too mediocre to be truly memorable. Look for William Demarest, in his pre-Uncle Charley (*My Three Sons*) stage, and veteran song and dance man Stubby Kaye in a rare TV series role.

**THE LOVE BOAT (**) 60 min (255ep & 3 pilots: two 2 hr & one 90 min Color; 1977–1986 ABC) Situation Comedy** *with Gavin MacLeod as Capt. Merrill Stubing, Bernie Kopell as Dr. Adam Bricker, Fred Grandy as Burl "Gopher" Smith, Ted Lange as Isaac Washington, and Lauren Tewes as Julie McCoy*

*The Love Boat* is *Love, American Style* on water. The aquatic version has the same general concept (comedy vignettes featuring weekly guest stars that focus on the overall theme of love), but it anchors the tales in a continuing setting (the cruise liner *Pacific Princess*) with a continuing cast serving as the crew of the boat. Even through the stories on *The Love Boat* are just as fluffy and vapid as the tales on *Love, American Style*, the seagoing series wins the dubious honor of being the better of the two similar shows.

The continuing setting of the cruise liner and the presence of the familiar crew help things by providing a thin veneer of reality within which to set the tales of the heart. It is at least conceivable to have syrupy sweet, simplistic tales of love yearned for, love found, and love lost set aboard a cruise ship. The common view of cruises, after all, is that they are floating parties filled with either couples searching for romance or singles on the lookout for a dream date. Cruises are sold to the public as fantasy excursions, so why shouldn't a show set on a cruise ship be all fantasy?

For the crew of the *Pacific Princess*, this cruise stuff is a business. They do their best to create the setting of romantic fantasy that the passengers want, but they also provide helpful down-to-earth matchmaking advice when the guests need assistance.

At least *The Love Boat* makes no effort to appear trendy and hip, which dated *Love, American Style* almost as soon as it aired. *The Love Boat* is more mature (if that term can be used at all in connection with the show) in its portrayal of love. The focus is more democratic, not just centering on young swingers, but including everyone from young children to retirees, and placing them in settings that are more natural for their age group.

Still one should not get too carried away in praising *The Love Boat*. It is still pure formula TV, there is very little zip to the scripts, the famous guest stars tend to walk through their roles, and there is not much humor in the show. As many episodes were actually filmed on board a cruise ship, it is not surprising that the feel is laid back, but it is a little too much so. The program could use more creative drive. As it is, *The Love Boat* is mostly flashy, mindless programming, a specialty of the show's two producers, Aaron Spelling (*Fantasy Island*) and Douglas Cramer (*Wonder Woman*).

An insight into the refinement of *The Love Boat* concept can be obtained by tracking down the three pilot episodes that aired as specials. *The Love Boat I, The Love Boat II*, and *The Love Boat III* have the familiar *Love Boat* format, but play around with the tone and the crew. Ted Hamilton stars as the Captain in *Love Boat I*, where none of the series regulars appear, although the characters of Gopher and Isaac the bartender exist with other actors. In *Love Boat II*, Quinn Redeker is Captain, but Fred Grandy, Bernie Kopell, and Ted Lange appear in the familiar roles they play in the series. Finally, in *Love Boat III*, Gavin MacLeod comes aboard as Captain and Lauren Tewes takes over as cruise director, and the chemistry is right. The cast from *Love Boat III* is carried over to the series.

**LOVE FOR LYDIA (**½) 60 min (13ep Color; 1977 UK LWT) Drama** *with Mel Martin as Lydia Aspen, Christopher Blake as Edward Richardson, Jeremy Irons as Alex Sanderson, Michael Aldridge as Rollo Aspen, Peter Davison as Tom Holland, Rachel Kempson as Aunt Juliana, and Beatrix Lehmann as Aunt Bertie*

Adaptation of a novel by Herbert E. Bates set in Britain's version of the Roaring Twenties following a luscious young British flapper who inherits a small-town factory. Mel Martin is quite effectively sexy as the young femme fatale courted by (eventually) four suitors (including young hopefuls played by Jeremy Irons and Peter Davison). This is a carefree period ripe for loose morals and lustful living, and Lydia takes every advantage available (and then some). Though at times the simple story is really stretched to fill the length of the series run, there is just an undeniable fascination watching people in the middle-class town become caught up in the jazz-age pursuit of fun, gingerly following Lydia's lead on the road to decadence. Of course, there is retribution and the Great Depression is just around the corner, but until then there are the parties and the conquests. And despite some slow moments, it still comes off better than such U.S. vehicles as *Beacon Hill.*

**LOVE IN A COLD CLIMATE (*½) 60 min (8ep Color; 1980 UK Thames) Drama** *with Michael Aldridge as Lord Alconleigh, Judi Dench as Lady Alconleigh, Lucy Gutteridge as Linda Alconleigh Radlett, John Moffatt as Lord Merlin, Vivian Pickles as the Countess of Montdore, Isabelle Amyes as Fanny Logan, Selena Carey-Jones as Louisa, Anthony Head as Tony, Rosalyn Landor as Polly Montdore, and Michael Williams as Uncle Davey*

Adaptation of the 1949 Nancy Mitford novel about an eccentric English gentry family closely resembling her own. The first hour is exceptionally weak, almost like looking at real-life home movies, though the production soon picks up and settles into its true metier: unadulterated, adolescent soap opera. Naturally the head of the household, Lord Alconleigh, is (to be kind) a bit eccentric, and not very appreciative of the really important concerns of the young women. Linda and her cousin Fanny, for instance, are "lounging adolescents waiting for love," which they try to find at young Louisa's coming-out ball. Alas, all appears lost that day until a kindly neighbor, Lord Merlin, magically transforms Linda's life. Soon she is face to face with a handsome young man, Tony, and the young couple is soon engaged. Unfortunately for them, both their families oppose the union.

It never gets much better than that. A good example of the twaddle that occasionally turns up on *Masterpiece Theatre.* Worth remembering the next time someone says all British television is better than our Stateside offerings.

**LOVE ON A ROOFTOP** (**½) **30 min (30ep Color; 1966–1967 ABC) Situation Comedy** *with Peter Deuel as David Willis, Judy Carne as Julie Willis, Rich Little as Stan Parker, Barbara Bostock as Carol Parker, Herbert Voland as Fred Hammond, and Edith Atwater as Phyllis Hammond*

A warm sitcom with its heart in the right place, *Love on a Rooftop* is stuck halfway between standard early 1960s domestic sitcom fare and the more offbeat sitcoms of the late 1960s and early 1970s.

The central conflict is the disparate backgrounds of young newlyweds David and Julie Willis. David is a struggling architect with a meager income. Julie is the pampered daughter of crass but wealthy used car dealer Fred Hammond. The young couple's first apartment is a cramped, windowless top-story flat, whose only saving grace is its proximity to the apartment building's roof, thus affording David and Julie a "patio" with a wonderful view of the San Francisco bay area. The plots revolve around the lovey-dovey ongoing honeymoon of David and Julie, the constant interruptions by the Parkers (their talkative neighbors), and the butting in of Julie's apparently well-meaning parents.

The new twist is the show's focus on a young childless couple. At the time, virtually all TV sitcom couples lived in the suburbs and had cute kids. The fact that the Willises put their love above money is big news in TV land. One of the old features of the show is the stereotypical blustery father-in-law, who can't stand seeing his precious daughter married to some schmuck like David.

Most of the top cast and crew are well-known to TV aficionados. Peter Deuel (who plays David) is better known as Hannibal Heyes of *Alias Smith and Jones*. Judy Carne (Julie) went right from *Love on a Rooftop* to mega-stardom as the "Sock It to Me" girl on *Laugh-In*. Rich Little makes his first appearance as a TV show regular here (as nosy neighbor Stan Parker), and he went on to greater fame as a comic impersonator on numerous variety shows. Herb Voland, who plays Julie's dad, is always adept at playing irascible, nasty big shots, such as Gen. Clayton in the early years of TV's *M*A*S*H*. *Love on a Rooftop*'s executive producer, Harry Ackerman, produced scores of middle-level sitcoms, such as *Gidget* (which Deuel also appeared in), *Bachelor Father, The Farmer's Daughter, Occasional Wife*, and *The Second Hundred Years*.

**THE LOVE SCHOOL** (**) **90 min (6ep Color; 1975 UK BBC) Historical Drama** *with Ben Kingsley as Dante Gabriel Rossetti, David Burke as William Morris, and David Collings as Ruskin*

The lives of Britain's Pre-Raphaelite painters, a relatively small, intensely romantic group from the late 1800s. Plenty of posturing and soapy romantic sighs, directed especially toward William Morris' wife, Jane, whose face seems to turn up constantly on all their canvases. Ben Kingsley (who played the title character in the 1982 theatrical film, *Gandhi*) plays Rossetti, the most respected (and successful) from the group. Fine for limited viewing, but too precious to remain for the entire series.

**LOVE, SIDNEY** (**) **30 min (37ep & 2 hr pilot Color; 1981–1983 NBC) Situation Comedy** *with Tony Randall as Sidney Shorr, Swoosie Kurtz as Laurie Morgan, and Kaleena Kiff as Patti Morgan*

*Love, Sidney* is a sad example of a supposedly innovative idea turning into a morass of syrupy mush. In the beginning, in *Sidney Shorr: A Girl's Best Friend*, the 1981 TV movie that became the pilot for this series, Sidney Shorr is American TV's first explicitly gay leading character. He is a sad, lonely, forty-year-old New York City commercial artist, who befriends Laurie Morgan, a pretty actress half his age who can't afford housing in the big city. After finding out that Sidney is gay, Laurie talks Sidney into allowing her to share his apartment, on a strictly platonic level. Her presence cheers up old glum Sidney and they become buddies.

Up to this point, the concept is different and interesting. Sidney's homosexuality is central to the working of the relationship, but not emphasized. The September-May nature of Sidney and Laurie's interaction is also unique, an interesting twist on the Felix Unger-Oscar Madison prissy-slob relationship in Tony Randall's other hit show, *The Odd Couple*.

At this point, the pilot film begins to go awry. After Sidney and Laurie become pals, he becomes jealous of her boyfriends and then shocked when she becomes pregnant from a married man who has no intention of marrying her. Sidney talks Laurie out of having an abortion and so little Patti is born.

Suddenly the film jumps five years ahead. Laurie decides to marry, leave Sidney's nest, and move to California. Sidney wants to keep Laurie and Patti in his home. They go to court to fight for custody of Patti and the court rules that Laurie must bring Patti to New York to live with Sidney for summers.

From this muddled premise comes the series *Love, Sidney*, where Laurie (now split up from her husband) decides to return to New York permanently and she and Patti move back in with the overjoyed Sidney. The plots focus on mother-hen Sidney watching over his two chicks. Tony Randall overdoes it as the fastidious type who flutters about at the slightest ruffle. Swoosie Kurtz is all wisecracks as Laurie, and Kaleena Kiff is much, much too much the typical know-it-all overly cute TV kid.

Oh, by the way, Sidney is not gay anymore. To be more precise, Sidney's sexual presence is no longer referred to. At all. He is neutered, and so is the show.

The idea behind *Love, Sidney* was tough to work out. With the dropping of Sidney's homosexuality and the polishing up of the main characters for TV series consumption, *Love, Sidney* becomes neither fish nor fowl. Tony

Randall's presence is the chief reason, if any, to catch this show.

In the pilot, Lorna Patterson (star of the TV version of *Private Benjamin*) plays Laurie.

**LOVE STORY** (*) **60 min (12ep Color; 1973–1974 NBC) Drama Anthology**

The title and the theme song are the same as the 1970 hit film, but this TV *Love Story* has nothing else in common with the Ryan O'Neal-Ali MacGraw movie. Rather, *Love Story* is just a collection of unrelated dramatic and humorous tales of love, produced by George Schaefer, who won numerous Emmy awards for his *Hallmark Hall of Fame* efforts.

**LOVE THAT BOB** (**½) **30 min (173ep B&W; 1955–1959 NBC) Situation Comedy** *with Bob Cummings as Bob Collins, Rosemary DeCamp as Margaret MacDonald, Ann B. Davis as Charmaine "Shultzy" Schultz, and Dwayne Hickman as Chuck MacDonald*

The concept of the playboy seems out of fashion in this liberated age, when equality of the sexes is the party line espoused by mainstream culture. The leering, dapper, man-about-town now is portrayed as a heartless boor, who is psychologically immature for not being able to settle down and who may be spreading noxious diseases to boot.

In these enlightened times, it is nonetheless entertaining and almost downright educational to observe firsthand how a "real playboy" lived in the halcyon days of the 1950s, and *Love That Bob* is as good an example of playboy chic as you can find.

*Love That Bob* (officially titled *The Bob Cummings Show* when it first aired) follows the amorous adventures of Bob Collins, ace fashion photographer and professional bachelor. Collins lives with his widowed sister Margaret and her teenage son Chuck (Dwayne Hickman, in his pre–*Dobie Gillis* days). Shultzy, Collins' loyal female assistant, is plain as dish water, but pines away for Bob just the same. Her chances are slim, since Bob is forever surrounded by curvaceous models, who occupy most of his thoughts.

There is something inherently funny about picturing the Bob Collins character as a swinging playboy, since his theatrical mannerisms and clichéd lines were out of style within a few years after the series ceased production. In fact, Bob Collins is a virtual walking definition of uncool, unhip, and square, at least when viewed through post-1960 eyes. So just accepting Collins as somebody that nubile young lovelies would swoon over takes a large leap of faith. After all, it was just a few years after *Love That Bob* that Bob Cummings, in films such as *Beach Party* (with Frankie Avalon and Annette Funicello), was playing a very similar character who was portrayed as a lecherous square oldster who keeps sniffing around the young beach bunnies, hoping to muscle in on the teen action. When watching *Love That Bob*, keep in mind that at the time the youth revolution was still in the future. The ideal of sexy manliness was not the primitive hunk or the brooding youth, but the swank, sophisticated, middle-aged urbanite, the sort who took Hugh Hefner's *Playboy* philosophy to heart and lived it.

In spite of, or perhaps because of, the dated nature of the program, *Love That Bob* is good for a kick. The scripts are funny, even without the added benefit of dated campiness. The supporting cast is top-notch and they frequently steal the show from Cummings, which is not an easy task considering Cummings' ability to overact. Cummings may not be a great actor, but he can milk a leer, a glance, and a wink for all they are worth. If the playboy is an endangered species, then *Love That Bob* catches the species in late full bloom.

Keep an eye out for the character of Pamela Livingston, played by Nancy Kulp. This is a test run for Kulp's later starring role as Jane Hathaway in *Beverly Hillbillies*, which, like *Love That Bob*, was produced by Paul Henning.

**LOVE THAT JILL** (***) **30 min (13ep B&W; 1958 ABC) Situation Comedy** *with Anne Jeffreys as Jill Johnson, Robert Sterling as Jack Gibson, Betty Lynn as Pearl, and James Lydon as Richard*

Somewhat ahead of its time in its view of the male-female relationship, *Love that Jill* is something of a hidden treasure. Anne Jeffreys and Robert Sterling, married in real life and the actors who played the ghostly Kirbys in *Topper*, are wonderful as the bickering, aggressive heads of competing Manhattan model agencies. They have a repressed attraction for each other, but their competitive business drive will not let them act on that attraction. This even-handed view of the battle of the sexes, and this powerful business position played by Anne Jeffreys (she even has a male secretary), is highly unusual for the 1950s, which might explain the unfortunate brief original run of *Love That Jill.*

**LOVE THY NEIGHBOR** (*) **30 min (12ep Color; 1973 ABC) Situation Comedy** *with Harrison Page as Ferguson Bruce, Janet MacLachlan as Jackie Bruce, Ron Masak as Charlie Wilson, Joyce Bulifant as Peggy Wilson, Milt Kamen as Murray Bronson, and Herbie Faye as Harry Mulligan*

A young black couple (the Bruces) moves into a previously all-white suburban development, becoming next-door neighbors to the Wilsons. Then it turns out Ferguson Bruce is the new efficiency expert at Turner Electronics, where Charlie Wilson works as union shop steward. (Oh-oh, looks like sparks will be flying now!) This early 1970s comedy followed in the wake of *All in the Family.* Push-button predictable, it was even dutifully based on a British hit of the same name (and for good measure there was a seven-episode Australian version as well). Everyone is better seen elsewhere, including Harrison Page on *Sledge Hammer* (as Captain Trunk), Joyce

Bulifant on *Mary Tyler Moore* (as Murray's wife, Marie), and, most appropriately, Janet MacLachlan with the *original* relevant 1970s lead on *Archie Bunker's Place* (as Polly Swanson).

**LOVES ME, LOVES ME NOT** (**½) **30 min (6ep Color; 1977 CBS) Situation Comedy** *with Susan Dey as Jane Benson, Kenneth Gilman as Dick Phillips, Art Metrano as Tom, and Udana Power and Phyllis Glick as Sue*

Susan Harris, Tony Thomas, and Paul Junger Witt preceded their hit sitcom *Soap* with *Loves Me, Loves Me Not*, a more normal comedy about life and love in the mid-1970s. Jane is a beautiful grammar school teacher. Dick is a bumbling newspaper reporter. They meet at the wedding of mutual friends and start going out together.

Susan Dey, already past her Laurie Partridge days, but not yet Yuppie Grace Van Owen in *L. A. Law*, is pretty as ever as Jane.

**LUCAN** (*) **60 min (11ep & 90 min pilot Color; 1977–1978 ABC) Adventure** *with Kevin Brophy as Lucan, John Randolph as Dr. Don Hoagland, and Don Gordon as Lt. Prentiss*

*Lucan* just can't make up its mind what it wants to be. At first it's a Tarzan-type story of a young human boy who was left in the wilds and raised by wolves. The boy is found at age ten and taught the ways of humans by scientists. Ten years later, the grown boy, named Lucan, is searching for his parents while trying to deal with his half-animal, half-human history.

The series then becomes something of an antiestablishment series, with Lucan being tracked by a bounty hunter hired by the scientist who taught the boy, since they do not trust Lucan's ability to live as a human on his own. Finally *Lucan* becomes a cheap *Fugitive* rip-off with Lucan falsely accused of a crime. Appropriately he is even chased by a police lieutenant obsessed with his capture.

**LUCAS TANNER** (**) **60 min (24ep & 90 min pilot Color; 1974–1975 NBC) Drama** *with David Hartman as Lucas Tanner, Rosemary Murphy as Margeret Blumenthal, John Randolph as John Hamilton, Robbie Rist as Glendon Farrell, and Kimberly Beck as Terry Klitsner*

This is David Hartman just before he became host of ABC's *Good Morning, America.* Here he pursues a far nobler profession, that of English instructor Lucas Tanner, a former baseball player and sportswriter who turns to teaching after an auto accident kills his wife and son. Starting fresh, Tanner pulls up stakes and settles in St. Louis to teach at Harry S Truman Memorial High School, where his relaxed and open style sometimes puts him at odds with the already established faculty members but endears him to kids like Glendon and Terry.

Like executive producer David Victor's big hit at the time, *Marcus Welby, M.D.*, *Lucas Tanner* emphasizes personal integrity and communication, while slipping in some contemporary moralizing on the side. Not as heavy-handed as it could have been, but still of interest today chiefly because of Hartman. Appropriately, Hartman's real-life decisions on sports and education read like a page from one of the show's scripts. Though he had been a star athlete in high school, he chose college over a baseball contract after graduation.

**THE LUCIE ARNAZ SHOW** (**) **30 min (6ep Color; 1985 CBC) Situation Comedy** *with Lucie Arnaz as Dr. Jane Lucas, Tony Roberts as Jim Gordon, Karen Jablons-Alexander as Loretta and Todd Waring as Larry Love*

The daughter of Lucille Ball and Desi Arnaz plays a radio psychologist who glibly dispenses wisdom to others, but has lots of difficulties dealing with her own problems. Produced by *Dick Van Dyke Show* and *That Girl* alumnus Sam Denoff, this series was based on the British TV series *Agony.*

**THE LUCY-DESI COMEDY HOUR** **(see *I Love Lucy*)**

**THE LUCY SHOW** (**½) **30 min (156ep: 30 B&W & 126 Color; 1962–1968 CBS) Situation Comedy** *with Lucille Ball as Lucy Carmichael, Vivian Vance as Vivian Bagley, Charles Lane as Mr. Barnsdahl, Mary Jane Croft as Mary Jane Lewis, Dick Martin as Harry Conners, Candy Moore as Chris Carmichael, Jimmy Garrett as Jerry Carmichael, Ralph Hart as Sherman Bagley, and Gale Gordon as Theodore J. Mooney*

Lucy and Viv, on their own. When this show first premiered in 1962, there was considerable doubt that Lucille Ball could score another hit sitcom outside the *I Love Lucy* format. But she wisely brought along her old sidekick, Vivian Vance, and together they pulled off the transition by playing two single moms on tight budgets sharing a home in Connecticut (the final season of *I Love Lucy* episodes had been set in Connecticut, too). Lucy Carmichael is a widow, Vivian Bagley is a divorcée, both have children, and both are looking for a new Mr. Right. At least that's a main theme in the first season (the black and white episodes) as Lucy and Viv vie for their latest dream heartthrobs—in between typical Lucy misunderstandings and slapstick skits (for example, there's a circus elephant standing on a thousand dollar bill Lucy got from the bank by mistake and needs to return so . . .).

In the second season (as the color episodes begin), Gale Gordon joins the cast as acerbic banker Theodore J. Mooney. Gordon had appeared several times on *I Love Lucy* (and had been a regular on Lucy's hit radio series of the late 1940s, *My Favorite Husband*), and he brings his patented sarcasm intact for this latest go-around. The Lucy versus Mr. Mooney relationship carries through the remainder of the series. Whether she's attempting to borrow money, or just involved in her latest disaster as his part-time secretary, Lucy is destined to cause Mooney no end of heartache. The relationship is maintained even when the series shafts locale to San Francisco in its fourth season—Mr. Mooney takes a job at a bank out there, foolishly hiring Mrs. Carmichael again as his secretary.

Viv does not come out West, though she does visit in a handful of episodes. Lucy's new cohort is Mary Jane Lewis, played by Mary Jane Croft (who had played a similar role in the final season of *I Love Lucy*). But the new face really doesn't change things. By then the series formula is etched in carbon paper: Lucy and Mooney, or Lucy and Mary Jane, or Lucy and a guest star—all leading to Lucy versus the world. Over time in subsequent permutations (*Here's Lucy*), this approach would begin to wear thin. But for this series it still works.

Nonetheless, the best episodes of *The Lucy Show* are the initial batch of black and white ones. Though Gale Gordon is not there, Charles Lane does a fine job as a similarly fuming banker. Best of all, there's the sense of the characters as characters, who just may surprise you and grow.

**LYTTON'S DIARY (**) 60 min (13 ep Color; 1985–1986 UK Thames) Drama** *with Peter Bowles, Bernard Lloyd, Trevor Peacock, Bernard Archard, Anna Nygh, and Holly de Jong*

Light drama vehicle co-created by Peter Bowles (from *The Irish R. M.* and *To the Manor Born*), casting him as a respected and articulate Fleet Street gossip columnist.

**M*A*S*H (****) 30 min (255ep & 2½ hr finale Color; 1972–1983 CBS) Situation Comedy** *with Alan Alda as Capt. Hawkeye Pierce, Wayne Rogers as Capt. Trapper John McIntyre, McLean Stevenson as Lt. Col. Henry Blake, Harry Morgan as Col. Sherman Potter, Loretta Swit as Maj. Margaret "Hot Lips" Houlihan, Mike Farrell as Capt. B. J. Hunnicut, Larry Linville as Maj. Frank Burns, Gary Burghoff as Capt. Walter "Radar" O'Reilly, William Christopher as Father Francis Mulcahy, Jamie Farr as Cpl. Maxwell Klinger, and David Ogden Stiers as Maj. Charles Emerson Winchester III*

Ardent *M*A*S*H* fans have a tendency to break the long-running series (eleven seasons) into favorite eras. The most obvious dividing point occurs at the end of the third season, when two major cast members, Trapper John and Henry Blake, depart—replaced by B. J. Hunnicut and Sherman Potter for the balance of the series.

Another split takes place at the end of the fourth season, when series co-creator Larry Gelbart ends his stint as a writer and director of the program. Or there's the overbearing foil division between Frank Burns (first five seasons) and Charles Winchester (thereafter). Some even use Radar O'Reilly's departure (during the eighth season) as a marker, since he was the only cast member who also played the same role in the original 1970 *M*A*S*H* theatrical feature film.

And then there are the truly cynical who bluntly divide *M*A*S*H* into two indisputably different eras: when it was funny, and when it wasn't. No matter what measurement you use, though, it is clear that *M*A*S*H* at the end of its run is a far different series from the program that kicked things off. In a way, though, that's one reason this series has been so successful both in its first run and in reruns: There are really several different series (or at least several different approaches to the same subject matter) running under the title.

The approach of the first three seasons (with Hawkeye, Trapper, and Henry Blake) is the most freewheeling and deliberately raucous (especially the first), mixing the gore of war with the joy of sex, booze, and general anarchy (very much in the spirit of the original film). Not surprisingly, these are the episodes that come off as the most fun and deliberately comic today, with the company's top surgeons, Hawkeye and Trapper, prone to self-indulgent drinking binges and amorous affairs. Their well-meaning but easily manipulated commander, Henry Blake, is perfectly willing to look the other way just as long as they can get the job done in the operating room. In fact, Blake is anything but "regular army" and occasionally enjoys such activities himself. These *M*A*S*H* stories are also frankly nasty to the by-the-books pair of Margaret Houlihan (whose promiscuous behavior has earned her the nickname "Hot Lips") and Frank Burns (nicknamed "Ferret Face" just because it's insulting), with Hawkeye and Trapper constantly needling the pair about their not-very-secret affair.

Yet in between the insanity, there is also something serious going on. War. Which is probably why there's such personal insanity in the first place—it's about the only way to cope. So even as *M*A*S*H* dispenses accessibly silly plots (for instance, during a cold snap a pair of long johns passes from one character to another), it also sneaks in slyly effective dramatic pieces. In one of the best of these shows ("Sometimes You Hear the Bullet"), Hawkeye has to deal with the fact that he couldn't save an old friend from dying on the operating table. Even the deceptively easygoing Henry Blake shines in this one, explaining to Hawkeye the two rules of war he learned in his officer's training exercises: (1) Patients die, (2) Doctors can't change rule 1.

Through the second and third seasons, the series tones down the excesses of Hawkeye and Trapper just a touch, but perfects a delightfully sardonic tone. The paranoid CIA agent Colonel Flagg (Edward Winter) first shows up in this run, as well as army psychiatrist Sidney Freedman (Allan Arbus). There's even an appearance by future C. O. Harry Morgan as a completely different character, a flipped-out spit-and-polish Army general who attempts to court-martial Hawkeye. The program's sense of black humor reaches a peak of sorts with "Iron Guts Kelly," the story of a visiting general who suffers a fatal heart attack while having a sexual liaison with Margaret. In order to save the general's image, his aide arranges for the dead body to be shipped into the nearest battle zone so he could "die in action" (a different sort of "action," that is). This leaves even Henry, Trapper, and Hawkeye gaping in amazement, no doubt wondering why people call *them* crazy.

By the final Henry Blake and Trapper John episode, *M*A*S*H* is at the peak of its form. Frankly, if the series had ended its run then, it would have still earned a well-deserved spot of honor in television history. But even with the departure of two-thirds of the lead cast, the producers felt confident enough to press on. However, the tone of the series certainly begins to change with the replacement characters, especially Sherman Potter, who is actually a creditable commander. The stories are still funny, but the opportunities for pure therapeutic anarchy are far less frequent. *M*A*S*H* is beginning to shift from being a comedy with dramatic overtones to a drama with comic overtones. Appropriately, then, this first B. J./Potter season ends with a black-and-white news documentary episode (inspired by a similar real-life report by newsman Edward R. Murrow during the Korean war) without a laugh track, done cinema verité style.

After another season, Frank Burns, the most cartoonish character on the series, is gone. His replacement is upper-crust Bostonian Charles Winchester, an articulate, competent surgeon. Margaret Houlihan is a more well-rounded character, a married woman (well, only for a season), and is no longer referred to as "Hot Lips." (However, she does have a one-time liaison with Hawkeye behind enemy lines.) Even Corporal Klinger (the man attempting to win a "section eight" discharge) changes strategy by acting "crazy" in a variety of more benign ways (such as dressing as an Arab camel jockey) than wearing women's clothes. And Hawkeye is well on his way to near sainthood, dropping nearly all his vices except for his smart mouth. In short, *M*A*S*H's* transformation from its madcap early days is essentially complete. Still, with the arrival of Winchester as fresh blood, and the increased prominence of Klinger and company chaplain Fr. Mulcahy, the program continues to work surprisingly well.

However, when Radar departs in the next season, the program promotes from within (Klinger becomes the new company clerk), instead of bringing in another performer. This essentially freezes everybody in place for the final three seasons, and it is obvious the writers are really stretching to find something new for these now very well-developed characters to say and do. This results in some terribly weak episodes, such as yet another visit by a USO troupe or Col. Potter bordering on senility when taking a required driver's test. Oddly, one episode makes it clear that this really must be a "parallel world" *M*A*S*H* cast: "A War for All Seasons" begins on New Year's Eve, 1951 and concludes on New Year's Eve, 1952, clearly contradicting the previous continuity that has Colonel Potter arriving in September 1952. Perhaps that explains why the characters also have a tendency to spout 1980s ideology in the midst of the early 1950s—it's just a different world.

Yet even during its weakest period, *M*A*S*H* still comes up with outstanding episodes, though usually in the area of drama, not comedy. In "The Life You Save," for instance, Charles becomes obsessed with learning about death after realizing (from a hole in his hat) that he was inches away from being killed himself. He impulsively heads to the battalion station on the front lines and, in a moving conclusion to the story, he holds a young soldier's hand and talks to him while he slips away, absorbing every moment with almost prayerful intensity. Another episode, "Follies of the Living—Concerns of the Dead," could have played on *The Twilight Zone*, with a fever-ravaged Klinger being the only one who can talk to the spirit of a young boy who has just died.

If they could have compressed those last fifty-seven stories into about a dozen, the overall series would stand even stronger today. Still, even on a bad day, *M*A*S*H* is in a class by itself, as one of the best written, filmed, and performed series ever. Besides, you can easily place the era of an episode simply by scanning the opening cast credits, so there's no problem skipping those you don't like even before the story begins.

Currently the two-and-one-half-hour final episode of *M*A*S*H* ("Goodbye, Farewell and Amen") is not included in the syndication package. However, it has been released on home video. Though this was one of the highest rated television programs in its original broadcast, obviously there are still millions who have never seen it. If you are one of those, you should definitely at least rent the video, though be forewarned that it is *M*A*S*H* at its best and its worst.

The first hour or so is powerfully dramatic. Hawkeye has finally cracked. He sits talking to Sidney Freedman, babbling about everything except the trauma that landed him there. What makes this setup work so well is that going in Freedman knows exactly what is wrong with his patient. In fact, everybody in the story does (they saw the events take place). The only ones in the dark are Hawkeye—and the audience. As a result, the conversations between Hawkeye and Freedman play like a psychological mystery, dropping tantalizing clues to an inevitable resolution.

While those scenes are taking place, the other characters have to face the semiobligatory final episode problems. Most are fairly trivial (Fr. Mulcahy's partial deafness is just plain silly), but Charles Winchester shines in a beautifully rendered relationship with a group of North Korean musicians who are held a while at the 4077th as prisoners of war. Though they can't speak a word to each other, Charles and the musicians develop a deep and affectionate friendship based completely on their mutual love of music.

About forty-five minutes into the episode, Hawkeye comes face-to-face with his personal demon in a gut-wrenching confrontation with Freedman, cursing him even as he breaks into tears. This moment is truly moving.

Unfortunately the rest of the episode pales in comparison. Stick around (after all, you did rent the tape) to follow the story of Charles and the musicians, and to see each character "exit" from the set in the final scene. (The final departing helicopter shot is a nice touch, forming a perfect bookend with the program's standard opening.) However, it's unlikely you'll be able to sit through the mawkish farewell dinner speeches without riding the fast forward button. Again, though, pause at Charles—his comments are probably the most bluntly honest in the group.

Because *M*A*S*H* ended its original run with very strong ratings, it was virtually impossible to resist the temptation to keep things going with a spin-off series, so Harry Morgan, William Christopher, and Jamie Farr agreed to continue their characters in *AfterMASH*. Previously, the character of Trapper John was also spun off into a separate series, *Trapper John, M.D.*, but without Wayne Rogers. ■

**M SQUAD (***) 30 min (117 ep B&W; 1957–1960 NBC) Police Drama** *with Lee Marvin as Lt. Frank Ballinger and Paul Newlan as Capt. Grey*

*M Squad* is for those who like their cop shows straight up, no chaser. There are no frills, no cute little touches, no warm family interludes. Just cops and robbers. Mostly it's just one cop. Lt. Frank Ballinger. Plainclothes. In M Squad. A branch of the Chicago police force. Frank don't say much. When he does, he don't say much.

In spite of the laconic nature of the lead character and the simplicity of the plotting, *M-Squad* delivers the goods. It is simply an entertaining thirty minutes of good guys versus bad guys, which is always a workable plot, if it's done right.

It is difficult to analyze *M Squad* without mentioning *Dragnet*, since on the surface they are so similar. Simply put, *M Squad* is everything *Dragnet* should have been. Both shows are documentary in nature, with the lead actor doing voice-over narration and the action almost exclusively focused on the handling of each week's case. Both shows champion the work of the professional crime fighter and both shows have little sympathy for the crooks.

What sets *M Squad* apart from *Dragnet* is that Frank Ballinger, unlike Joe Friday, does not hate everyone who does not wear a badge. Ballinger shows *some* emotion and can be downright mean to bad guys, but he does not have the condescending air to civilians that makes Joe Friday so ultimately disturbing.

What's more, *M Squad* is set in Chicago, not Los Angeles. The difference in the two towns is that of substance over glitter. While Joe Friday may be tracking down some deranged psychopath endemic to the west coast, Ballinger is more likely to shoot it out with mob gangsters or some neighborhood punks.

Another plus is that Ballinger is in M Squad, a special police branch that only handles the tough cases the regular cops can't crack or won't touch. Thus, the stories are more exciting than the usual *Dragnet* episode. Since Joe Friday is just a regular cop, he is often busy with penny-ante criminals.

The best advantage *M Squad* has over *Dragnet* is in the lead actor. Lee Marvin makes his one and only TV series starring appearance in *M Squad* and his soulful face and deep, menacing voice are much more interesting than Jack Webb's basset-hound looks.

Modern viewers beware: *M Squad* is from the days before the Supreme Court's *Miranda* ruling and other legal protections for criminals' rights. When Frank Ballinger goes after a bad guy, he goes after him with all resources at his disposal. Numerous laws are bent in Ballinger's pursuit of justice. That's just the way things were done back then. Modern TV cops have to play by the rules much more often.

The theme for *M Squad* (in all but the first year) is a jazzy number composed by Count Basie.

**THE MACAHANS** **(see *How the West Was Won*)**

**MACGRUDER AND LOUD (**) 60 min (14ep & 2 hr pilot Color; 1985 ABC) Police Drama** *with John Getz as Det. Malcolm MacGruder, Kathryn Harrold as Det. Jenny Loud MacGruder, Frank McCarthy as Sgt. Myhrum, and Ted Ross as Sgt. Debbin*

MacGruder and Loud are two police officers who are partners in their daily squad car patrols. They are also secretly married to each other. The marriage must remain secret because the force has a rule against married couples teaming up. The hocus-pocus that is involved in keeping the bond secret takes up a lot of time that could best be used elsewhere. Aaron Spelling, of *The Mod Squad* and *Charlie's Angels*, is the producer of this show.

**MACGYVER (**½) 60 min (85ep at Fall 1989 Color; 1985– ABC) Adventure** *with Richard Dean Anderson as MacGyver, Dana Elcar as Pete Thornton, Bruce McGill as Jack Dalton, and Teri Hatcher as Penny Parker*

They ought to hire MacGyver for some "school is cool" campaign, especially to promote the sciences. In each episode, he demonstrates the "practical" applications for basic physics, biology, and chemistry in a way even daydreaming high school kids can appreciate: They're a key part of success in espionage adventures.

MacGyver does it from scratch, without carrying the usual spy bag of electronic tricks. He applies his knowledge to ordinary objects he finds along the way. A telescope? No problem. Just give MacGyver access to a magnifying glass, a watch crystal, and a newspaper and he'll have one made in no time.

He's a pretty good role model overall. Honest, dependable, generous, and athletic. MacGyver loves hockey and used to play semiprofessionally. Oh, and he also works for one of those private think-tanks, the Phoenix Foundation, under the supervision of a former government soldier, Pete Thorton (played by Dana Elcar, special agent Polk in *The Sting*). That's who sends MacGyver out as a one-man Impossible Missions force (or is it a one-man A-Team?). The assignments range from testing top secret security systems to rescuing operatives from sensitive overseas assignments that have gone sour. In between these, friends Jack and Penny manage to con him into some off-hours operations as well. No matter what the challenge, MacGyver is up to it—and in the process he's guaranteed to make you consider paper clips, belts, tin foil, and other everyday objects with new respect.

This series is well-paced adventure done with style and humor. For about the first dozen episodes, the producers borrowed an effective gimmick from such feature films as *Goldfinger* and *Indiana Jones and the Temple of Doom*, beginning with the self-contained conclusion to one adventure, then moving to a completely different one for the rest of the hour.

**MACKENZIE'S RAIDERS (*½) 30 min (39ep B&W; 1958–1959 Syndication) Western** *with Richard Carlson as Col. Ranald S. MacKenzie*

Richard Carlson, a man more familiar with chasing communists on TV (*I Led Three Lives*) or aliens in movies (*It Came from Outer Space*), plays Col. MacKenzie, with the much more mundane task of chasing Mexican border-crossing bandits in Texas in the 1870s. The series is based on the exploits of the real Col. MacKenzie, who conducted covert operations for the U.S. Cavalry.

**THE MACKENZIES OF PARADISE COVE (*) 60 min (6ep & 90 min pilot Color; 1979 ABC) Drama** *with Clu Gulager as Cuda Weber, Shawn Stevens as Kevin Mackenzie, Lory Walsh as Bridget Mackenzie, Moe Keale as "Big" Ben Kalikini, and Sean Tyler Hall as "Little" Ben Kalikini*

The five orphaned Mackenzie children, who lost their parents in a sailing accident, stick together by arranging for salty old Cuda Weber, a fishing boat operator in Hawaii, to unofficially adopt them.

The 1978 pilot is titled *Sticking Together* and has a slightly different cast.

**MAD MOVIES WITH THE L. A. CONNECTION (**½) 30 min (128ep Color; 1985–1987 Syndication) Comedy**

The Los Angeles-based comedy troupe, the L. A. Connection, provides the humorous voices for reedited and redubbed old movie classics. Ernie Kovacs, on some of his 1950s TV specials, and Woody Allen, in the 1966 theatrical film *What's Up, Tiger Lily?*, tried the same basic idea.

**MADAME BOVARY (***) 60 min (4ep Color; 1975 UK BBC) Drama** *with Francesca Annis as Emma Bovary, Tom Conti as Charles Bovary, Kathleen Helme as Madame Bovary, Richard Beale as Rouault, Gabrielle Lloyd as Felicite, David Waller as Father Bournisien, Brian Stirner as Leon Dupuis, Denis Lill as Rodolphe Boulanger, and John Carter as Lhereux*

This adaptation of Gustave Flaubert's novel covers a lot of the same territory as Leo Tolstoy's *Anna Karenina*, but with more gusto over less time. Francesca Annis plays the title role of a young woman bored with the dull routine of her marriage to Charles, a sweet but simple country doctor. So she dreams of the high life, spends a small fortune (in credit) on expensive clothes and knicknacks, and is primed and ready for an adulterous affair (or two). Yet even that ecstasy leaves her limp, as she finds herself drowning in passion and haunted by the consequences of her sins (not to mention her overspending). Eventually she contemplates suicide as an escape from it all. Annis is quite effective as Emma, though she definitely has to share the spotlight with Tom Conti, who does an excellent job in the sympathetic role of Charles, the source of her boredom.

**MADAME'S PLACE (½) 30 min (150 ep Color; 1982–1983 Syndication) Comedy** *with Wayland Flowers as the voice of Madame, Judy Landers as Sara Joy Pitts, Susan Tolsky as Bernadette van Gilder, Johnny Haymer as Walter Pinkerton, and Corey Feldman as Buzzy St. James*

The puppet character of Madame (popularized by Wayland Flowers over many years of variety show appearances) finally gets her own series, as host of a talk show set in her own mansion. Madame is assisted by various humans. Some real-life guest celebrities drop by to chat. Most of the show, however, is Madame's constant barrage of off-color innuendos and loud laughter. Madame is an acquired taste.

**MADIGAN (*) 90 min (6ep Color; 1972–1973 NBC) Police Drama** *with Richard Widmark as Sgt. Dan Madigan*

Better known as a Hollywood movie star, Richard Widmark makes a rare TV appearance as solitary New York City plainclothes detective Dan Madigan, a man with little in his life except work. The *Madigan* series is an outgrowth of a far better 1968 film of the same name, which also starred Widmark. Unlike the TV program, the *Madigan* movie provided detective Madigan with a great support cast, especially Henry Fonda as the overworked police commissioner. Compared to the film, the TV Madigan is too sparse and dry.

**MAGGIE (**) 30 min (8ep Color; 1981–1982 ABC) Situation Comedy** *with Miriam Flynn as Maggie Weston, James Hampton as Len Weston, Billy Jacoby as Mark Weston, Christian Jacobs as Bruce Weston, Judith-Marie Bergan as Buffy Croft, and Doris Roberts as Loretta Davenport.*

This is a fictionalized TV personification of Erma Bombeck's world, lovingly described in dozens of bestselling books (such as *The Grass Is Always Greener Above the Septic Tank*) and a widely distributed syndicated column. It's a place that revolves around discount grocery coupons, clogged drains, minor kiddie disasters, a well-groomed lawn, and other triumphs of day-to-day suburban living. Bombeck herself created and developed the series, with Miriam Flynn standing in for her as Maggie Weston.

The look is perfect—messy but still squeaky clean—and Flynn does a very good job treating minor domestic complications like important international disasters. She swaps gossip with her local hairdresser, Loretta (played by Doris Roberts, already an expert in hair care from her stint at the beauty parlor on *Angie*), shops, keeps an eye on the kids, and enjoys the company of her loving husband. But, ultimately, the series falls short, never quite transforming Bombeck's many cute phrases and concepts into the basis for a coherent character comedy or story line. As in the columns, there are moments, but for television continuity they're not quite enough.

**MAGGIE BRIGGS, SUZANNE PLESHETTE IS (**) 30 min (6ep Color; 1984 CBS) Situation Comedy** *with Suzanne Pleshette as Maggie Briggs, Kenneth McMillan as Walter Holden, Shera Danese as Connie Piscipoli, Stephen Lee as Sherman Milslagle, and John Getz as Geoff Bennett*

As the title makes perfectly clear, Suzanne Pleshette (Bob's sexy and independent wife Emily on *The Bob Newhart Show*) plays Maggie Briggs, a hard-news reporter for the *New York Examiner* who is shifted to the "softer" Modern Living features section. It's a disappointing change with the new assignments obviously a letdown for her character and the overall series setup simply not up to Emily's old standards. Though everyone around seems to be Maggie's exact opposite (fluffy, agreeable, acquiescent), it's not enough. She needs a strong mixer as an opposite number because in a short-run series like this, instant chemistry is essential. Still the program recovers from a weak pilot to turn out five fairly enjoyable episodes, though obviously never leading to anything more.

**THE MAGICAL WORLD OF DISNEY** **(see *Walt Disney*)**

**THE MAGICIAN (**) 60 min (21ep & 90 min pilot Color; 1973–1974 NBC) Adventure** *with Bill Bixby as Anthony Blake, Keene Curtis as Max Pomeroy, Todd Crespi as Dennis Pomeroy, and Joseph Sirola as Dominick*

This is not some spooky cult series. Instead, Bill Bixby plays a troubleshooting stage magician, Anthony Blake, once falsely convicted and imprisoned for a crime. Blake has a special affection for people who feel trapped or helpless, drawing on his expertise at illusion and sleight of hand when coming to their aid. He also reaches into his magic hat to pull out help from newspaper columnist Max Pomeroy, Max's son Dennis, and his own personal pilot, Jerry.

For about half the stories, Blake takes up residence at Hollywood's famous Magic Castle (a real place), allowing him to sneak in a few more magic tricks done either by himself or by guest performers. (Bixby developed his skills as an amateur magician in conjunction with this series.) This is an offbeat Bill Bixby vehicle, caught somewhere between *My Favorite Martian, The Incredible Hulk*, and *The Courtship of Eddie's Father*. Oddly, viewers usually have an easier time accepting the pure fantasy of those series than the authenticity of the real-life tricks shown here, often guessing that everything was unfairly "fixed" in advance of the filming. The series is probably best sampled simply with the original ninety-minute pilot film, with Anthony Blake investigating the mysterious circumstances surrounding a plane crash.

**MAGNUM, P.I. (***½) 60 min (162ep & 2 hr finale Color; 1980–1988 CBS) Detective Drama** *with Tom Selleck as Thomas Magnum, John Hillerman as Jonathan Higgins, Roger E. Mosley as Theodore "T. C." Calvin and Larry Manetti as Orville "Rick" Wright*

Set in Hawaii, this stylish adventure series comes with two strong leads, Tom Selleck and John Hillerman. Selleck plays Thomas Magnum, a former Naval intelligence officer (and Vietnam vet) turned private eye after leaving the service. His number one ongoing assignment is to provide security for the estate of Robin Masters, a wealthy but reclusive pulp fiction writer, in exchange for lodging and use of an expensive red Ferrari. Oddly, Masters never seems to be around, giving his orders by phone and letter to Jonathan Higgins, day-to-day manager of the estate. At least that's what Higgins says. After a while, Magnum starts to wonder if Higgins and Masters might well be one and the same. Okay, Magnum does hear the voice of Masters a few times, only it sounds an awful lot like Orson Welles (that's because it is, probably before the writers decided to play up the Higgins/Masters question).

But that's a point Magnum doesn't clear up until the

finale episode. In the meantime, over the eight-year run of the series, the two characters provide a strong foundation for some solid adventures. Selleck's Magnum is obviously the lead figure (the show *is* named after him), and he narrates each episodes in a light, breezy manner. Magnum likes sports (especially basketball and baseball) and is in great physical shape—during the original run of the series, Tom Selleck often found himself the subject of "gorgeous hunk" articles. Despite his pinup good looks, though, Magnum also comes across as a cuddly teddy bear with a disarming sense of humor (epitomized by his raised eyebrows in the opening credits). The scripts reflect this light, entertaining tone, often casting him as the good-natured slightly put-upon hero, at times reminiscent of James Garner's Jim Rockford (an appropriate passing of the baton because Selleck played detective Lance White in a few episodes of *The Rockford Files* before landing the *Magnum* lead).

Hillerman, too, has his moments to shine, with Higgins the perfect vehicle for his patented caustic but oh-so-proper character type (previously displayed on such series as *The Betty White Show* and *Ellery Queen*). He has a good deal of fun with the role, constantly sparring with Magnum and occasionally with himself (Higgins has several look-alike relatives, with Hillerman playing both roles). Like Magnum, Higgins is also an experienced military man, having served with the British forces in World War II (fighting in the African campaign against General Rommel).

What sets *Magnum* apart from most other light adventure series is that there are also a good number of episodes with more serious tones. Both Higgins and Magnum are complex characters, and over the course of the series we learn quite a bit about their past, especially Magnum's time in the service (he was stationed in Vietnam). That's where he met his top associates, chopper pilot T. C. and legwork friend Rick. It's also where he found love, possibly fathered a child, and made some powerful enemies. As a result, this is definitely worth following in a regular syndicated slot because there are a lot of fine character points you can pick up, especially when you know how things wrap up.

Probably the most famous *Magnum* story is the one that *almost* wrapped up the series, with Thomas hovering near death. Through the entire episode he appears as an unseen spirit, egging on the other characters of the story before walking into the clouds, apparently dead. "Not so fast!" came the public outcry at the time. So in an elaborate follow-up, one final batch of episodes gave the characters a proper send-off, ending with a two-hour movie. Once and for all you learn the relationship between Higgins and Robin Masters. Sort of. The script coyly plays it *both* ways, so this time there's no doubt they can do a sequel.

In the meantime, while viewing the reruns, keep an eye out for some excellent guest shots by Carol Burnett, Frank Sinatra, and series crossovers with *Murder, She Wrote* and *Simon and Simon*.

**MAKE ROOM FOR DADDY (***) 30 min (336ep B&W; 1953–1964 ABC & CBS) Situation Comedy** *with Danny Thomas as Danny Williams, Jean Hagen as Margaret Williams, Marjorie Lord as Kathy Williams, Rusty Hamer as Rusty Williams, Sherry Jackson and Penney Parker as Terry Williams, Angela Cartwright as Linda Williams, and Amanda Randolph as Louisa*

Now here's a situation comedy with a truly admirable and believable father figure. Hardworking. Intelligent. Dedicated to his wife and children. And he yells.

In fact, Danny Williams (alter ego for Danny Thomas) fairly bellows—with the authority and spirited energy of a real ethnic parent (he's Lebanese). Though this is sometimes obviously just a setup for a typical sitcom misunderstanding and reversal, there's no mistaking the "I'm the head of the house" delivery. It's one of the reasons the whole setup of *Make Room for Daddy* rings so true: Danny Thomas seems so natural and comfortable in his role.

In part that's because he virtually plays himself, a talented nightclub comedian and singer with strong family ties. Even the series title refers primarily to a situation in his real life: When Danny returned home from tours in his early days, the kids would have to shift bedrooms in order to "make room for daddy." (Thomas even alludes to his real-life children with the name of his production company, "Marterto"—standing for *Mar*lo, *Ter*ry, and *To*ny.)

His TV family is true to that supportive spirit, but also not above taking advantage of the soft heart beneath Danny's stern words. Still even the clever comments and repartee from his family and friends at least make sense as part of an entertainer's household, where everyone (even Louise the maid) can hardly help but pick up dad's sense of comic timing. They're all very clever, but not overbearing.

That mix of showbiz and domestic settings also allows Danny the opportunity to interchange both at a moment's notice. He's liable to burst into song while rehearsing in the living room, backed by a full—though invisible—orchestra. Or he'll resolve a family conflict on the nightclub stage, often publicly admitting just how much he cares for them all. Though at times such scenes come off as a bit overly sentimental, there's never any doubt that Danny's comments come straight from the heart.

Over the course of the series, there are a number of changes in Danny's TV family. Margaret, his wife of the first three seasons, was written out when Jean Hagen left the program. After a season of courting as a widower, Danny marries widow Kathleen O'Hara, who remains with him through the rest of the run, bringing along her daughter Linda from a previous marriage.

With her stubborn Irish heritage, Kathy serves as an ideal match for Danny's fiery Lebanese spirit.

When Sherry Jackson (daughter Terry) left the series, that character remained. Her absence was explained by having her attend college in Europe. After about a year, she returned—as a new performer assumed the role. Before long, Terry gave Danny the opportunity to experience every dad's dream: his daughter, in love, and radiant in her bridal gown. For about a year, Danny even worked with Terry's new husband, Pat Hannegan (played by Pat Harrington, Jr.), as his musical collaborator.

There were many other characters introduced over the decade-long run of the series, including Sheldon Leonard as Phil Brokaw, Danny's agent; Gale Gordon as Mr. Heckendorn, the landlord of Danny's apartment building; Annette Funicello as Gina, a foreign exchange student; William Demarest as Kathy's father; Sid Melton as Charlie Halper, the owner of Danny's main performing venue (the Copa Club); and—best of all—Hans Conried as Danny's Uncle Tonoose. Usually arriving unannounced, Tonoose would burst through the door with his trademark greeting ("Hello family!"), ready to interfere with any and every aspect of his nephew's life.

*The Danny Thomas Show* (as the program was renamed in its fourth season) eventually became one of the top-rated series of its time, with Thomas himself expanding his interests into producing other programs. Look for spin-off pilot appearances by Andy Griffith (as the smooth-talking sheriff of Mayberry), Joey Bishop (as public relations man Joey Mason, changed to Joey Barnes for his subsequent series), and Bill Dana (as elevator operator Jose Jimenez). There are also strong guest star shots by such performers as Jack Benny (playing himself and the Devil), Bob Hope (as himself), and Lucille Ball and Desi Arnaz (as Lucy and Ricky Ricardo, paying a return visit to the Williams family after their guest appearance on *The Lucy-Desi Comedy Hour*).

Actually, toward the end of the series, some of these guest shots occasionally came off as just elaborate celebrity walk-ons. But they only reflected the changing orientation of the series: At the very begining, there's much more emphasis on domestic interaction, while the later episodes showcase Danny's increasingly comfortable niche as a successful showman.

After a hiatus of several seasons in the mid-1960s, Thomas revived the *Make Room for Daddy* setup in several variety specials, beginning in 1967. This led to a full-fledged new series, *Make Room for Granddaddy*. Meanwhile, syndicated reruns of *The Danny Thomas Show* reverted to the old *Make Room for Daddy* title, though usually picking up the story with his marriage to Kathy. ■

**MAKE ROOM FOR GRANDDADDY (**½) 30 min (24ep Color; 1970–1971 ABC) Situation Comedy** *with Danny Thomas as Danny Williams, Marjorie Lord as Kathy Williams, Rusty Hamer as Rusty Williams, Angela Cartwright as Linda Williams, Roosevelt Grier as Rosey Robbins, and Michael Hughes as Michael*

"We're back!"

Those are the first words of *Make Room for Granddaddy*, as Danny and Kathy come through the front door of their apartment. Okay, they're supposed to be returning from a lengthy trip to Europe, but we know that they're really referring to the revival of the *Make Room for Daddy* format.

In short order, most of the old characters also reappear, including Linda (looking surprisingly good after being *Lost in Space* for three years), Rusty, Charley Halper, Uncle Tonoose, and even daughter Terry—who drops off her six-year-old son, Michael, with the folks while she and her soldier husband are shipped abroad. (Thus, the "granddaddy" hook.)

Unfortunately, in 1970 this show was about a decade too early. Instead of being embraced with loving nostalgia, the patented Thomas formula was viewed with puzzled bemusement as out of step with an era caught in the trappings of hip relevancy. Even with a black man as a new regular—former football star Roosevelt Grier played Danny's accompanist—it all seemed too old hat. Besides, the stories weren't quite as good as the originals. These days the series plays as a more than acceptable update of a special TV family. In fact, the familiar faces and sentimental plots that probably made the program appear so dated back in the 1970s are its chief attraction today.

**MAKIN' IT (*) 30 min (8ep Color; 1979 ABC) Situation Comedy** *with David Naughton as Billy Manucci, Greg Antonacci as Tony Manucci, Denise Miller as Tina Manucci, Ellen Travolta as Dorothy Manucci, Lou Antonio as Joseph Manucci, Ralph Seymour as Al "Kingfish" Sorrentino, and Gary Prendergast as Bernard Fusco*

The late 1970s disco craze came and went fairly quickly, but it left behind some really awful TV shows in its wake. No disco TV series got quite as close to the font of disco culture, the 1977 film *Saturday Night Fever*, as did *Makin' It*. The setting in this series is almost the same as in the film. Billy, the John Travolta–type character, is a young Italian-American male living with his folks in the New York City area (here, it's Passaic, New Jersey). He is torn between his two goals in life, education and dancing. The education is so Billy can become a teacher. The dancing is so Billy can outshine brother Tony at The Inferno disco.

*Makin' It*, just like *Saturday Night Fever*, has a Travolta as a star (John's sister Ellen, who plays Billy's mom), lots of Bee Gees music in the background, and some production help from the Robert Stigwood organization. The difference is that the star of *Makin' It*, David Naughton, is far too clean-cut and wholesome, in comparison to John Travolta's animal brutishness in the film. Furthermore, with disco fever abated these days,

*Makin' It* seems like a relic from a long-gone era. The dance or die philosophy rings even more hollow nowadays than in 1979.

**MAKING A LIVING (see *It's a Living*)**

**THE MAKING OF A CONTINENT (**½) 60 min (6ep Color; 1986–1987 PBS) Documentary**

This series explains geologically, the creation of the North American continent and why the land is shaped the way it is.

**MAKING THE GRADE (**½) 30 min (6ep Color; 1982 CBS) Situation Comedy** *with James Naughton as Harry Barnes, Graham Jarvis as Jack Felspar, Alley Mills as Sara Conover, Steve Peterman as Jeff Kelton, and George Wendt as Gus Bertoia*

Franklin High School in St. Louis is the setting for this well done sitcom produced by Gary David Goldberg, who went from *Making the Grade* directly to the more successful *Family Ties.* Harry Barnes, dean of boys at Franklin, is beset by all the problems of running a modern school, such as rampaging youth gangs. George Wendt, who went from this show directly to *Cheers*, where he played Norm Peterson, makes his first TV series appearance as a regular as the gym teacher.

After *Making the Grade*'s brief production run, producer Goldberg revamped and changed the concept into *The Bronx Zoo*, with an entirely new cast and mostly new character names.

**MALIBU RUN (see *The Aquanauts*)**

**MALICE AFORETHOUGHT (**½) 60 min (4ep Color; 1979 UK BBC) Mystery** *with Hywel Bennett as Dr. Bickleigh, Judy Parfitt as Julia Bickleigh, Cheryl Campbell as Madeleine, Belinda Carroll as Ivy, and Rohan McCullough as Gwynfryd*

Based on the 1931 novel by Francis Iles, this show is not so much a whodunit as it is a case of suspicion and pursuit. A timid doctor is unhappily married to a shrewish and demanding wife. Shortly after he develops an intense crush on another woman, his wife turns up dead. But was it murder or natural causes? More to the point, will the doctor be accused, arrested, and convicted? Even with such a limited range of suspects (one), this production manages the tricky task of maintaining an air of uncertainty until fairly late in the story. In addition, the focus here is on the characters involved in the death, not on some scene-stealing detective figure like Inspector Morse or Sergeant Cribb.

This series first aired in the United States in 1981 on *Mystery.*

**MAMA (**½) 30 min (13ep B&W; 1956–1957 CBS) Comedy-Drama** *with Peggy Wood as Marta "Mama" Hansen, Judson Laire as Lars "Papa" Hansen, Dick Van Patten as Nels Hansen, Rosemary Ricè as Katrin Hansen, and Toni Campbell as Dagmar Hansen*

While this popular series ran for eight years, only the final thirteen weeks were produced on film. All the previous episodes were aired live, and are therefore mostly lost forever. This is a pity, for *Mama* is a monument to simple early television done well.

Set in pre–World War I San Francisco, *Mama* deals with the Hansen family—Mama, Papa, and children Nels, Dagmar, and Katrin. It is the reminiscences of Katrin that frame each episode, as she recalls many scenes from her youth, and that most of all "I remember Mama."

The slow pace and dignified air of *Mama* is wildly divergent from the *I Love Lucy* school of 1950s family series, but it is just this difference that stands out now in retrospect. Dick Van Patten, who plays Nels, later played Tom Bradford, a popular TV dad on *Eight Is Enough.*

A few episodes of the live version of *Mama* have been released on video cassette. ■

**MAMA MALONE (*) 30 min (13ep Color; 1984 CBS) Situation Comedy** *with Lila Kaye as Renate Malone, Randee Heller as Connie Karamakopoulos, Evan Richards as Frankie Karamakopoulos, Don Amendolia as Dino Forresti, and Ralph Manza as Padre Guardino*

Ethnicity runs rampant in *Mama Malone.* Renate Malone, the Mama of the title, is an Italian widow who picked up an Irish last name from her departed policeman husband. Mama's daughter (Connie) married and then divorced a Greek gentleman, winding up with a young son (Frankie) and a very long last name. Meanwhile, Mama hosts a very loose cooking show ("Cooking with Mama Malone") on local cable TV. The series is set in Mama's kitchen in her Brooklyn apartment and her friends and family keep walking on stage to kibitz and offer advice.

You can't get more colorful characters than on *Mama Malone.* Unfortunately they are a bit overdrawn and somewhat unlikable. *Mama Malone* gets credit for an off-beat premise, but it has little else to make it worth catching.

**MAMA'S BOY (*½) 30 min (6ep Color; 1987–1988 NBC) Situation Comedy** *with Bruce Weitz as Jake McCaskey, Nancy Walker as Molly McCaskey, and Dan Hedaya as Mickey*

Bruce Weitz, the grizzly Belker from *Hill Street*, is not given much to work with as the star of this poorly designed series. Weitz, without his *Hill Street* stubble and grungy clothes, plays Jake McCaskey, a big city newspaper sports reporter. Jake is a real *man's* man. He drinks beer, plays poker with the boys, and tells bawdy stories about his latest romantic conquests. However, he is reaching middle age and lives alone. His aging mother (the feisty Nancy Walker) leaves her Florida condo and wants to move in with sonny boy. Jake thinks this arrangement will look sort of . . . well, sissy.

Still he swallows hard, lets mom move in, and has to deal with ribbing from the guys.

The concept is different, the stars are quite talented, but *Mama's Boy* goes nowhere. Is it a "male buddy" show? Is it a warm family show about the ties that bind? After about three weeks, what can you do differently about the fact that Jake is living with mom? The producers obviously struggle with these questions, but no answer develops before the show disappears.

**MAMA'S FAMILY (**½) 30 min (110ep at Fall 1989 Color; 1983–1985 & 1986– NBC & Syndication) Situation Comedy** *with Vicki Lawrence as "Mama" Thelma Harper, Ken Berry as Vinton Harper, Dorothy Lyman as Naomi Oates Harper, Rue McClanahan as Fran Crowley, Betty White as Ellen Jackson, Eric Brown as Vinton "Buzz" Harper, Jr., Karin Argoud as Sonja Harper, Beverly Archer as Iola, and Allan Kayser as Bubba*

"Mama" Thelma Harper is one of those roles a performer dreams of. Instantly recognizable. Brassy. Resilient. Adaptable. And one Vicki Lawrence has played (on and off) for more than a decade.

The character first appeared in a long-running series of sketches on Carol Burnett's comedy-variety show in the 1970s. As just one comic element in the program, Mama was not tied down to any complicated continuity trappings that would have to have been developed in advance for a situation comedy debut. Consequently, Lawrence had plenty of time just to play with the role, growing in it along with Burnett and Harvey Korman (who portrayed, respectively, Mama's daughter, Eunice Higgins, and Eunice's husband, Ed).

This setup seemed to reach a dramatic conclusion in March 1982 with a ninety-minute special, "Eunice." The special traced the family's history in four acts, beginning in the mid-1950s when Eunice and Ed first met, going through their unhappy marriage, and ending with the family's reaction to the death of Mama. Along the way, Eunice had to come to grips with her many failed dreams, especially when she saw the success of her brother Philip (Ken Berry) as a writer. So with Mama gone she decided to take a chance at last, leaving town and her sister Ellen (Betty White), and going to the big city with her brother to try to make it as an actress.

But that ending turned out to be only the beginning. After all, just because the cast and writers had shown one conclusion to the story of Mama and her family, this did not mean that it was the *only* way the show could end. So they put together a brand new half-hour comedy package, *Mama's Family*.

In the beginning, Carol Burnett and Harvey Korman made occasional appearances in character, but clearly the new show was not going to be built around them. Instead, Mama directed her sharp tongue toward other family members, and anyone else that got in her way. (Korman did turn up in another role, that of Alistair Quince, who introduced some episodes as if they were a part of a *Masterpiece Theatre*–type presentation.)

Ken Berry was there as her son, but now named Vinton and considerably less successful. Vinton was a recently divorced locksmith moving back in with Mama, and bringing along his teenage son and daughter (Buzz and Sonja). Mama's next-door neighbor Naomi soon got her hooks into Vint and married into the family household as well.

Betty White was also back, this time as Mama's niece, Ellen. Rue McClanahan rounded out the cast as Ellen's mother (and Mama's sister), Fran. In 1985, McClanahan and White moved on to *The Golden Girls* after *Mama's Family* ended its network run on NBC.

But that still wasn't the end of the story. The series was soon revived with new episodes for first-run syndication without Brown, Karin Argoud, McClanahan, and White (though the last two made occasional guest appearances). Instead, Allan Kayser came aboard as Eunice's dumb son, Bubba, while Beverly Archer played Iola, Mama's best friend and neighbor. No matter. Just as long as there's someone for Mama to spar with.

**A MAN ABOUT THE HOUSE (***) 30 min (39ep Color; 1973–1976 UK Thames) Situation Comedy** *with Richard O'Sullivan as Robin Tripp, Sally Thomsett as Jo, Paula Wilcox as Chrissy Plummer, Brian Murphy as George Roper, Yootha Joyce as Mildred Roper, and Doug Fisher as Larry Simmons*

A real oddity in the cross-pollinating world of U.S. and British adaptations of hit series. Not only did the premise (and even some character names) come across from Britain to the States essentially intact (as *Three's Company*) but the U.S. producers also followed the same blueprint for spin-offs. In both countries, the landlord Ropers landed their own series (*The Ropers* in the United States, *George and Mildred* in Britain) and the main male lead carried his character into a follow-up series (*Three's a Crowd* in the United States, *Robin's Nest* in Britain).

Most surprising, both the U.S. and U.K. versions of each series turn up in Stateside syndication, so there's a chance for side-by-side comparisons. In these, *A Man About the House* holds up quite well.

As in *Three's Company*, two women (Jo and Chrissy) and a cute guy (Robin) share an apartment, though unlike the American version, they don't pretend he's gay in order to justify the cohabitation. The economics (coming up with the monthly rent) is apparently enough to satisfy the British Ropers. As in the States, there are plenty of misunderstandings and physical pratfalls, with O'Sullivan's Robin Tripp quite good as the aspiring cooking student. To add just the right touch of confusion to Stateside viewers, Chrissy in this series is the responsible, level-headed one.

There is no upheaval in roommates, so the trio stays together until Robin goes off to run his own restaurant in *Robin's Nest*.

**MAN AGAINST CRIME (*) 30 min (82ep B&W; 1949–1954 & 1956 CBS & NBC) Detective Drama** *with Ralph Bellamy and Frank Lovejoy as Mike Barnett*

Coming from the earliest days of TV private eyes, *Man Against Crime* follows the exploits of Mike Barnett, a tough guy who doesn't need a gun to chase and capture his prey. The eighty-two filmed episodes featuring Ralph Bellamy from 1951 through 1954 are the only episodes generally available these days, and they are frequently titled *Follow That Man.* The episodes with Frank Lovejoy (where Barnett finally straps on a gun) aired live in 1956 and are rarely seen. ■

**MAN AND THE CHALLENGE (*) 30 min (36ep B&W; 1959–1960 NBC) Adventure** *with George Nader as Dr. Glenn Barton*

Produced in the late 1950s, when the United States was in a post-Sputnik frenzy to catch up with the Russians in the field of science, *Man and the Challenge* is an odd amalgam of action, boring science, and government training film. The loose plot concerns Glenn Barton, a doctor/research scientist/athlete working for the Institute of Human Factors, a government agency dealing with human endurance. Each week Barton gets involved in some bizarre experiment where something always goes wrong, but not before he obliquely gives the viewers a dose of science lecture. *Man and the Challenge*'s producer, Ivan Tors, did a much better job on the more mainstream *Sea Hunt*, and even did this same general concept much better in the syndicated *Science Fiction Theater.*

**THE MAN AND THE CITY (**) 60 min (13ep & 2 hr pilot Color; 1971–1972 ABC) Drama** *with Anthony Quinn as Mayor Thomas Jefferson Alcala, Mike Farrell as Andy Hays, Mala Powers as Marian Crane, and Carmen Zapata as Josefina*

In the early 1970s, the TV screen was littered with main characters who really *cared.* They cared about people, life, animals, children, peace, love . . . you name it. Most of these shows look pretty silly now. *The Man and the City* frequently falls into the same pothole, with its major saving grace the presence of Anthony Quinn. The Academy Award-winning actor (*Viva Zapata, Zorba the Greek*) makes an extremely rare TV series appearance as Thomas Alcala, the mayor of an unnamed city in the U.S. southwest (the series was filmed in Albuquerque, New Mexico). Having served as mayor for sixteen years already, Alcala stays popular by spending a lot of time among his constituents, listening to their problems and trying to help. The mayor can only do so much, and his city still has problems after his long tenure, but he tries hard.

The 1971 pilot film (*The City*), produced by Frank Price (*Ironside, It Takes a Thief*), is better than the series. The pilot is a lot grittier and goes against TV convention more assiduously. The regular series, produced by David Victor (of *Dr. Kildare* and *Marcus Welby, M. D.* fame), is a little more sanitized and pasteurized and lacks some of the allure of the pilot. Still, Quinn is fun to watch. Look for pre–B. J. Hunnicut (*M*A*S*H*) Mike Farrell as the mayor's clean-cut aide.

**THE MAN BEHIND THE BADGE (*½) 30 min (38ep B&W; 1955 Syndication) Police Anthology** *with Charles Bickford as narrator*

This undistinguished series of filmed half-hour plays revolves around the theme of law enforcement. Each week's hero is some policeman, judge, army officer, park ranger, or the like, who holds back the wave of crime.

An earlier live version of this series ran on CBS in 1953 and 1954 with Norman Rose as narrator.

**A MAN CALLED HAWK (**½) 60 min (13ep Color; 1989 ABC) Crime Drama** *with Avery Brooks as Hawk, and Moses Gunn as "Old Man"*

The tight-lipped character of Hawk first appeared in *Spenser: For Hire*, where he was the well-dressed enforcer for the literate Boston detective. Now, the cool, bald, black man with not much to say goes out on his own in a series set in Hawk's home turf, Washington, D.C. It's still not clear what Hawk's full name is, or what he does for a living. He is usually found acting as an agent of justice, seeking out bad guys, and serving as protector of the weak and put-upon (all the while wearing his trademark sunglasses). When he needs advice, Hawk seeks out the "Old Man," a personal guru from his past.

While Hawk was a wonderful counterpart for Spenser, his character is a bit thin to anchor his own series. His pithy, bare-bones comments compare with the Oriental musings in *Ohara* for terse (and occasionally meaningless) dialogue. Still, Avery Brooks brings a lot of poise and dignity to the cardboard title character, and the plots tend to have a nice twist to them.

**A MAN CALLED INTREPID (**) (6hr miniseries Color; 1979 NBC) Adventure** *with David Niven as William Stephenson, Michael York as Evan Michaelian, Barbara Hershey as Madeline, and Paul Harding as Col. Jurgen*

William Stephenson is a World War II spy with the code name "Intrepid" who sets up an espionage network for the Allied powers. A Canadian, he is recruited by none other than Winston Churchill himself.

**A MAN CALLED SHENANDOAH (*½) 30 min (34ep B&W; 1965–1966 ABC) Western** *with Robert Horton as Shenandoah*

Amnesia victims do not, as a rule, fare very well as stars of TV series (look up the checkered history of *Coronet Blue*). After all, how can the audience get involved with a guy if he doesn't even know who he is?

In *A Man Called Shenandoah*, Robert Horton plays a mystery man in the Old West who is found on the prairie with a bullet wound and no memory. The guy calls himself Shenandoah and spends the entire series roaming about, trying to find clues to his identity. Not much turns up.

Horton should have been quite familiar with the western landscape from his numerous journeys west as Flint McCullough on *Wagon Train*.

**A MAN CALLED SLOANE (*) 60 min (12ep & 2 hr pilot Color; 1979–1980 NBC) Spy Drama** *with Robert Conrad as Thomas Remington Sloane III, Ji-Tu Cumbuka as Torque, Dan O'Herlihy as The Director, Karen Purcill as Kelly, and Michele Carey as the voice of Effie*

Substandard *Man from U.N.C.L.E.* clone only a decade too late, with Robert Conrad (sporting a mustache) stuck in the role of Sloane, top agent for UNIT. He and his partner, Torque, travel the world to thwart the evil plans of KARTEL. (Sorry, no acronym explanations for either name.) UNIT's secret New York headquarters is hidden behind a toy shop and stocked with typical secret agent weaponry and electronic gear, including "Effie," a computer with a sexy female voice.

The original two-hour pilot (filmed in 1979 but not aired until 1981, under the title *Death Ray 2000*) had Robert Logan in the lead role and Ji-Tu Cumbuka as one of the villains—same name (Torque), sporting a deadly mechanical steel hand, and destined to die. Imagine, NBC canceled *Black Sheep Squadron* and brought Conrad in for *this* instead. ■

**THE MAN CALLED X (*) 30 min (39ep B&W; 1956 Syndication) Spy Adventure** *with Barry Sullivan as Ken Thurston*

There is nothing new in this formula Cold War saga of American spy Ken Thurston, whose code name is, you guessed it, "X."

**MAN FROM ATLANTIS (**) 60 min (20ep: sixteen 60 min & three 2 hrs & one 90 min Color; 1977–1978 NBC) Science Fiction adventure** *with Patrick Duffy as Mark Harris, Belinda Montgomery as Dr. Elizabeth Merrill, Alan Fudge as C. W. Crawford, and Victor Buono as Mr. Schubert*

This was the first American entertainment TV program ever shown in mainland China, ironically giving Patrick Duffy far more notoriety there for his webfooted lead role than for his subsequent work in *Dallas*. Imagine, somewhere in China there are television viewers complaining that the tube has gone downhill ever since they took off *Man from Atlantis*.

Actually the first three two-hour episodes aren't bad, with a stranger in a strange land innocence. Mark Harris, last surviving Atlantean, washes ashore unconscious, where he's found and nursed back to health by ocean scientist Elizabeth Merrill. He agrees to join her scientific exploration team because, well, they both have much to discover. In the subsequent one-hour episodes, they definitely learn to avoid Victor Buono's Mr. Schubert, a mad scientist interested in slicing, dicing, and otherwise "testing" Mark's gills, strength, and speed. They just don't make love stories like this anymore. ■

**MAN FROM BLACKHAWK (*½) 30 min (37ep B&W; 1959–1960 ABC) Western** *with Robert Rockwell as Sam Logan*

From the era when they were obviously running out of gimmicks for TV westerns, this one follows the adventures of an insurance agent in the West in the late 1800s. The former Mr. Boynton from *Our Miss Brooks*, Robert Rockwell, plays investigator Sam Logan, sent by the Blackhawk Insurance Company to look into cases of fraud. Actually this is more of a standard crime series than a western, but it's still fairly uninspired stuff.

**MAN FROM COCHISE (**) 30 min (156 ep B&W; 1956–1960 Syndication) Police Drama** *with John Bromfield as Sheriff/Marshal Frank Morgan, Stan Jones as Deputy Olson, Robert Brubaker as Deputy Blake, and James Griffith as Deputy Tom Ferguson*

Modern-day Arizona is the setting for this series focusing on lawman Frank Morgan. In the first 78 episodes, Morgan is sheriff of Cochise County, Arizona, and he engages in lots of car chases. In the final 78 episodes, Morgan has been promoted to U.S. marshal and he covers the entire state. The Cochise County episodes orginally aired as *The Sheriff of Cochise*, while the later episodes aired as *U.S. Marshal*. In rerun syndication, all 156 episodes are combined under the title *Man from Cochise*.

**THE MAN FROM INTERPOL (*) 30 min (39ep B&W; 1960 NBC) Police Drama** *with Richard Wyler as Anthony Smith and John Longden as Superintendent Mercer*

In this pedestrian police series with a few touches of spy intrigue, Anthony Smith (even his name is boring) is a policeman for England's Scotland Yard. Smith is assigned to the International Police Force (a.k.a. Interpol).

**THE MAN FROM U.N.C.L.E. (***) 60 min (105ep: 29 B&W & 76 Color & 2 hr sequel; 1964–1968) Spy Adventure** *with Robert Vaughn as Napoleon Solo, David McCallum as Illya Kuryakin, and Leo G. Carroll as Alexander Waverly*

Premiering at the height of the James Bond theatrical film frenzy in 1964, *The Man from U.N.C.L.E.* offered breezy spy adventures on a weekly basis—and for at least half the episodes it mostly hits the mark.

Quite properly, the series should be called the "men" from U.N.C.L.E. because it very quickly evolves into a team effort, with top agent Napoleon Solo joined by fellow operative Illya Kuryakin. They receive their assignments from the venerable Alexander Waverly, U.S. head of the worldwide super-secret United Network Command for Law and Enforcement. Its main headquarters is hidden behind the back wall of a changing room in the innocent-looking Del Floria's Tailor Shop, right in the middle of New York City. But Solo and Kuryakin can reach it from almost anywhere in the world by simply using their communication devices, disguised first as cigarette packs, then as fountain pens. ("Open channel D.")

Inevitably, the men from U.N.C.L.E. find themselves up against the minions of THRUSH, with both sides engaged in back and forth maneuvering that never results in total victory or defeat for either camp (much like Cold War actions between eastern and western powers in the real world). Sometimes Solo and Kuryakin also square off against an assortment of mad scientists, ambitious generals, or international power brokers not directly affiliated with THRUSH.

A weekly dose of new schemes that could threaten the entire world might have quickly become a bit dull and repetitive, but the excellent scripts and entertaining banter between Solo and Kuryakin keep the stories moving. So does the structure. Each episode is broken into four acts (each carrying its own cute subtitle) and within each act transitions between scenes are accompanied by a high-speed visual "whir" of light across the screen.

And there is another very clever gimmick: In each story, some civilian (usually a woman) becomes caught in the action. These everyday operatives range from housewives out shopping who just stumble into the fray to people specifically sought by U.N.C.L.E. because of their specialized knowledge of or connection with a targeted foe. Whatever the case, they bring a sense of innocent wonder to the action, which for most of them will be their adventure of a lifetime.

This method also gives *U.N.C.L.E.* two sets of guest stars to feature: the innocents and the villains. Some superb billings result, including innocent William Shatner versus villains Werner Klemperer and Leonard Nimoy in "The Project Strigas Affair," June Lockhart versus Ricardo Montalban in "The Dove Affair," and Jill Ireland (David McCallum's wife at the time) versus Anne Francis in "The Quadripartite Affair."

Most of the best episodes of *The Man from U.N.C.L.E.* are from the first season. These shows demonstrate an almost perfect balance between parody and genuine danger. Unfortunately, because they are in black and white, these episodes are shown least often in reruns. Stations sometimes run just the first black and white one, "The Vulcan Affair," then jump right to the color episodes that began the second season.

Of course, that's not a bad place to start either, because the series reaches a peak of sorts with its first color adventure, the two-part "Alexander the Greater Affair." With Rip Torn as a would-be Alexander the Great and Dorothy Provine as the guest innocent, this tale comes complete with a genuine cliff-hanger between episodes. In a setting straight out of a 1930s serial, Torn leaves them all to die slowly in a tomb: Solo is tied to a slab beneath a swinging scimitar blade while Illya and Provine are tied together and hung from a thick rope over a pit, with a flickering candle slowly burning through the fibers. Of course, they escape.

The series is spotty in the next two dozen episodes, embarrassingly cute and comic thereafter (reaching a low point of sorts in the "My Friend, the Gorilla Affair"). This decline reflects the unfortunate decision at the time to go "camp" a la *Batman* (phenomenally popular back then), a strategy that pushed the series over the line from humorous to silly. At any time along the way, individual stories manage to recapture some of the original magic, but not often enough.

Nonetheless, *The Man from U.N.C.L.E.* stands as a genuinely entertaining slice of 1960s television adventure. It even works quite well in a one-shot made-for-TV movie revival, "The Fifteen-Years-Later Affair," complete with a cameo appearance by one-time James Bond George Lazenby and a new head of U.N.C.L.E. played by former *Avengers* lead Patrick Macnee.

Three *U.N.C.L.E.* television adventures that were converted into U.S. color theatrical features occasionally turn up in TV movie slots: *One Spy Too Many* ("The Alexander the Greater Affair"), *The Spy with My Face* ("The Double Affair"), and *To Trap a Spy* ("The Vulcan Affair" combined with about twenty minutes of "The Four Steps Affair"). ■

**MAN IN A SUITCASE** **(*½) 60 min (28ep Color; 1967–1968 UK ATV) Detective Drama** *with Richard Bradford as John McGill*

The title of this series conjures up intriguing images of a show about some poor bloke who fell into his valise while abroad and, locked inside, each week tries another ingenious stratagem in order to escape the confines of his suitcase.

Unfortunately, the reality of *Man in a Suitcase* is much more mundane. John McGill is a discredited U.S. spy now roaming Europe as a freelance private eye, who would love to find evidence to clear his name.

**MAN OF THE WORLD** **(**) 60 min (20ep B&W; 1962 UK ATV) Adventure** *with Craig Stevens as Michael Strait*

Craig Stevens shifts from his suave lead role in *Peter Gunn* to that of an international photographer inevitably drawn into the thick of adventure. Perfectly adequate package produced on location by *Secret Agent*'s Ralph Smart.

**THE MAN WHO NEVER WAS** **(***) 30 min (18ep Color; 1966–1967 ABC) Spy Drama** *with Robert Lansing as Peter Murphy/Mark Wainwright, Dana Wynter as*

*Eva Wainwright, Murray Hamilton as Col. Jack Forbes, and Alex Davion as Roger Barry*

The basic plot is unbelievably contrived, the general concept is old hat, but still *The Man Who Never Was* is something of a lost classic of the mid-1960s. Peter Murphy is a U.S. spy operating in East Berlin. Discovered by the nasty Red Huns, Murphy scoots over the line into West Berlin (where's the wall?). Inexplicably, the East Germans follow, in hot pursuit. Murphy then stumbles into a socialite gathering thrown by Mark Wainwright who (can you believe it?) is Murphy's "exact" double. When the East Germans see Wainwright, they think he's Murphy, and they kill him. Nobody else sees the murder, so Murphy escapes alive. He decides to adopt Wainwright's identity as a cover and convinces Wainwright's widow (the one person who *can* tell the difference between the two men) to go along with the scam in order to keep the Wainwright fortune out of the evil clutches of the dead man's half-brother, Roger Barry.

There's a lot going on here, probably too much for the good of the show, but it's exciting. Much of the credit for the sparkle of this series is from rugged lead actor Robert Lansing (Frank Savage from *12 O'Clock High*) and multitalented producer John Newland, a fine actor who also hosted and directed the creepy *One Step Beyond.*

**THE MAN WHO WAS HUNTING HIMSELF (**½) 60 min (3ep Color; 1973 UK BBC) Drama** *with Donald Burton as David Foster, Carol Austin as Caroline Foster, David Savile as Captain Mason, Garfield Morgan as Planner, and Conrad Phillips as Martin*

Simple but effective spy thriller about a British government employee stalked by a look-alike killer. First aired in the United States in 1973 on *Masterpiece Theatre*, demonstrating the program's willingness to occasionally present stories without a tie-in to an existing book (this is an original television drama by N. J. Crisp) or to any famous British ruler.

**MAN WITH A CAMERA (**) 30 min (29ep B&W; 1958–1960 ABC) Crime Drama** *with Charles Bronson as Mike Kovac, Ludwig Stossel as Anton Kovac, and James Flavin as Lt. Donovan*

For the legion of Charles Bronson fans, who followed the tough little guy from his early starring movie roles (*The Great Escape, The Dirty Dozen*) to his mega-violent film opuses (such as *Death Wish* and *Telefon*), *Man with a Camera* will be of historical interest, since this is Bronson's very first TV series role.

Bronson plays ethnic World War II combat photographer Mike Kovac, who is back in civilian life now, eking out a living as a freelance photographer. He will snap shots for anyone in need of a photo, and his work resembles that of a blue-collar private eye. A good chuckle comes from recognizing the actor who plays Mike Kovac's father, Anton. The actor's name (Ludwig Stossel) may not ring a bell, but his voice will sound very familiar, since it was heard for years during the 1960s in commercials for wine (Stossel was "that little old winemaker, me").

**MAN WITHOUT A GUN (*½) 30 min (52ep B&W; 1957–1959 Syndication) Western** *with Rex Reason as Adam MacLean and Mort Mills as Marshal Frank Tallman*

A crusading newspaper editor attempts to use the power of the press, rather than a six-gun, to bring law and order to the Dakota territory of the 1880s. Marshal Tallman is there in case the bad guys can't read. Rex Reason went straight from this pulp potboiler to *The Roaring Twenties.*

**MANHUNT (**½) 30 min (78ep B&W; 1959–1961 Syndication) Police Drama** *with Victor Jory as Lt. Howard Finucane and Patrick McVey as Ben Andrews*

It's a police show, it's set on the West Coast, and it's based on real-life cases from the local police department. Is it *Dragnet*? No, it's *Manhunt*, but any confusion between the two shows is purely intentional.

Two plot gimmicks set *Manhunt* apart from Jack Webb's *Dragnet.* For one thing, *Manhunt* is set in San Diego and *not* Los Angeles. Granted, San Diego is not *that* far from L. A. but, hey, most 1950s TV producers did not want to get *too* bold. Second, the leading male duo are *not* police partners, but rather a police lieutenant and a newspaper reporter (who are friends). In *Dragnet*, a *real* cop would never befriend "slime balls" like journalists.

**MANHUNTER (**½) 60 min (22ep & 90 min pilot Color; 1974–1975 CBS) Detective Drama** *with Ken Howard as Dave Barrett, Robert Hogan as Sheriff Paul Tate, Hilary Thompson as Lizabeth Barrett, Ford Rainey as James Barrett, and Claudia Bryar as Mary Barrett*

Ken Howard is mostly known to TV viewers as the basketball-playing high school coach of *The White Shadow* or as the refined Garrett Boydston of *Dynasty* and *The Colbys.* Before these roles, he played a highly unusual role in *The Manhunter*, a little-known period piece produced by Quinn Martin, the master of quality crime/detective series from the 1950s through the 1970s (*The Untouchables, The Fugitive, The F.B.I.*).

Howard plays Dave Barrett, an Idaho farmer in the early 1930s who leaves the farm after a close friend is killed in a bank holdup. Barrett turns bounty hunter–detective, ranging all over the land in search of criminals. The format is flexible and the setting is innovative, but somehow the mixture does not quite come together. Still it's worth a watch.

The 1974 pilot (also called *Manhunter*) can be recognized by Shirley O'Hara playing the role of Dave's sister Lizabeth.

**MANIMAL** (*) **60 min (8ep Color & 90 min pilot; 1983 NBC) Crime Drama** *with Simon MacCorkindale as Jonathan Chase, Melody Anderson as Brooks McKenzie, and Michael D. Roberts and Glynn Turman as Ty Earle*

This is not a very good show. This is, however, a very imaginative show that deserves some credit for trying.

Since TV is always filled with cop shows, producers go out of their way to make their heroes seem different from all the other crime fighters. In *Manimal*, the hero, Jonathan Chase, is *really* different. He can turn himself into an animal. Not just one type of animal, mind you, but a veritable menagerie of beasts. The premise involves some mumbo-jumbo about how Chase (what a name for a crime fighter!) learned this supernatural trait of transformation from his father, who in turn had picked it up in the jungle somewhere. Chase dabbles as a professor of animal behavior (what else?) and chooses to use his awesome power for good, so he tracks villains down using these powers. Only comely police detective Brooke McKenzie and Chase's black Vietnam buddy Ty Earle are in on the secret.

*Manimal* is really a mix of *Superman* and *The Incredible Hulk*, and the concept is all that is astounding about the show. In execution, *Manimal* never seems to know what to do with the wild and crazy premise it has. Lots of time is spent focusing on Chase's transformation from man to beast, in the tradition of *Dr. Jekyll and Mr. Hyde*. The special effects are nice, but there is not much else to *Manimal*.

*Manimal* is one of the productions of action TV whiz Glen A. Larson, the man behind *Battlestar Galactica* and *The Fall Guy*. Veteran actor William Conrad provides the serious narration for *Manimal*.

**MANNIX** (**) **60 min (194ep Color; 1967–1975 CBS) Detective Drama** *with Mike Connors as Joe Mannix, Gail Fisher as Peggy Fair, Robert Reed as Lt. Adam Tobias, Larry Linville as Lt. George Kramer, and Joseph Campanella as Lou Wickersham*

If you enjoy slick crime shows packed with violent car chases, shoot-outs, and fistfights, catchy music (from Lalo Schifrin of *Mission: Impossible* fame), and at least a vague reason for all the mayhem, this long-running formula series should fit the bill. Mike Connors plays the square-jawed independent investigator who starts out in the first season's episodes as a loner within a large detective firm, Intertect. At this point, the series (created by Richard Levinson and William Link of *Columbo* fame) has a man versus computer subtext as Joe constantly spars with his boss, Lou, over the best way to conduct the latest investigation. Lou wants to rely on the company's extensive computer analysis system and other electronic and scientific support devices. Joe wants to go with his gut, hit the streets, and nail the bad guys. For the remainder of the series, that's just what he does, bringing along a no-frills black-and-white bluntness reminiscent of the 1950s and early 1960s (when Connors starred in the adventure series *Tightrope*), dropping the association with Intertect. Joe Mannix puts out his shingle as a solo operative, with only his secretary Peggy there to back him up.

Connors and Gail Fisher are fine in their respective roles, but the series does go on an awfully long time virtually unchanged. Try to catch a few episodes from the first season (which is where the boxy split screen title graphics come from, alluding to the computer theme), then a handful from just about anywhere else in the run. You'll probably hit a few socially relevant tales (hard to avoid those in the early 1970s) and, if you're lucky, an episode or two in which Peg gets to do more than just answer the phone, act as a hostage, and dodge a few bullets. Joe, of course, is always one step away from a life-or-death final confrontation. About half a decade after *Mannix* ended its run, Connors found himself part of *Today's F.B.I.*

**MANY HAPPY RETURNS** (**½) **30 min (26ep B&W; 1964–1965 CBS) Situation Comedy** *with John McGiver as Walter Burnley, Elinor Donahue as Joan Randall, Mark Goddard as Bob Randall, Jesslyn Fax as Wilma Fritter, Mickey Manners as Joe Foley, Elena Verdugo as Lynn Hall, and Russell Collins as Owen Sharp*

In the 1960s, many large stores used to have an entire staff dedicated to dealing with customer complaints, actually working to resolve them to the buyer's satisfaction. This period-piece comedy follows the trials and tribulations of Walter Burnley, manager of the complaint desk at Krockmeyer's department store. Walter faces the twin task of attempting to convince both his penny-pinching boss (Owen Sharp) and his customers that the solutions he comes up with are fair to all concerned.

This plot device is not quite enough comedy to carry a series. In truth, the chief attraction of this package is watching Walter's service-oriented attitude spill over into every part of his life. As a widower he's an easy mark for fellow employees, neighbors, scout troops, and, most of all, for his grown daughter Joan and her husband Bob. If there's a hint of trouble on their road of wedded bliss, he's there to offer a solution. This is a cute, low-key comedy with an unusual premise and absolutely no chance of running for more than a single season. But John McGiver is quite good at holding things together, while Elinor Donahue (from *Father Knows Best* and *The Andy Griffith Show*) is sweet as the loving daughter and Mark Goddard is ruggedly handsome as her husband. Right after this series, Goddard joined the *Jupiter II* crew as Major Don West for an extended stint on *Lost in Space*.

**THE MANY LOVES OF DOBIE GILLIS** **(see *Dobie Gillis*)**

**MARBLEHEAD MANOR** (**½) **30 min (24ep Color; 1987–1988 Syndication) Situation Comedy** *with Linda Thorson as Hilary Stonehill, Paxton Whitehead as Albert*

*Dudley, Bob Fraser as Randolph Stonehill, Phil Morris as Jerry Stockton, Rodney Scott as Dwayne Stockton, Dyana Ortelli as Lupe, and Michael Richards as Rick*

For the better part of the 1970s and 1980s, if you were on a package theater tour of London your lineup of plays would almost inevitably include *No Sex Please, We're British*, an unadulterated farce serving as a relaxing, undemanding break. Though the production received its share of condescending snickers over the years, a good farce is a work of art, with broadly sketched characters, amazing coincidences, mistaken identities, and split-second timing (including lots of swinging doors). Oddly, there haven't been that many Stateside attempts to pull off such a format in a TV series, probably because you don't need to do more than one season of episodes—and even that's stretching the material. Besides, we've generally favored screwball situation comedies over pure farce.

*Marblehead Manor* is a rare exception, a one-season visit with the wealthy Stonehill family (of Marblehead, Massachusetts) and their fractious estate staff. The setting is ideal: There are doors and rooms galore, allowing for plenty of well-timed (or poorly timed) entrances and exits. There's at least a pretense of maintaining proper decorum (a farce is no fun unless there's something to hide). And, of course, Randolph Stonehill (the "lord and master") has a roving eye and a bad temper guaranteed to set off almost anyone—Albert the butler, for one, but he never lets anyone but the audience see his impatient annoyance with Randolph. (He knows the man is a jerk, but Albert does have a spark of affection for him, probably because the two men grew up together.) Besides, Albert gets on quite well with Stonehill's wife, Hilary (played by Linda Thorson, formerly Tara King on *The Avengers*), who really runs things on the manor. The rest of the staff ranges from dedicated and competent (chauffeur Jerry Stockton, played by Greg Morris's son, Phil) to downright spacy (Rick the gardener, played by former *Fridays* cast member Michael Richards). Of course, the particular plots are essentially irrelevant. Rest assured, though, they are faithful to the genre of look the other way/drop your trousers/who were you talking to dear?

The pilot for this series first aired on CBS in 1984 as *At Your Service*, but only Michael Richards carried his role to the series version.

**MARCO POLO (***) (10 hr miniseries Color; 1982 NBC) Drama** *with Ken Marshall as Marco Polo, Denholm Elliott as Niccolo Polo, Burt Lancaster as Teobaldo, John Gielgud as Doge, Anne Bancroft as Marco's mother, Sada Thompson as Aunt Flora, Leonard Nimoy as Achmet, and Kathryn Dowling as Monica*

The proverbial cast of thousands highlights this epic, one of the few commercial TV historical miniseries that devote at least as much time to the sweep of history as to the heaving of almost bared breasts.

Beginning in thirteenth-century Italy, *Marco Polo* follows the title character to the Middle East, Persia, and on to his famous stay in Kubla Khan's China.

**MARCUS WELBY, M. D. (**½) 60 min (172ep & 2 hr pilot & two 2 hr sequels Color; 1969–1976 ABC) Medical Drama** *with Robert Young as Dr. Marcus Welby, James Brolin as Dr. Steven Kiley, Elena Vardugo as Consuelo Lopez, Sharon Gless as Kathleen Faverty, and Pamela Hensley as Janet Blake Kiley*

Admit it, even if you think this series is a hopelessly sugar-coated and unrealistic view of the modern medical world, don't you find yourself secretly longing for someone with the calm, reassuring manner of Doctor Welby when you're in for treatment? No doubt, that sense of positive identification and wish fulfillment had a lot to do with the success of *Marcus Welby* in its original run. Even today, the growing movement toward holistic health treatment seems like a page right out of Welby's prescription book, which stresses treating the whole patient, not just the illness.

For Marcus Welby (and his young associate, Steven Kiley), that approach means getting intimately involved in the personal lives of the patients who turn up at their Santa Monica, California, office. After all, if they came for help, there's simply no other choice—even if it means dealing with family problems, love relationships, job conflicts, and personal self-worth. Through it all, Robert Young's Welby is warm but firm (appropriately reminiscent of his *Father Knows Best* character of Jim Anderson), determined to help his charges understand that in this world "Doctor Knows Best."

With episodes from the early 1970s, the story lines sometimes fall into the semiobligatory issues of the day (the war in Vietnam, radical students, and drug-popping hippies), with predictable resolutions. Apart from these issues, the series does a good job on each disease of the day, painting a generally positive image of the medical profession. Though Welby and Kiley have the kind of success record mocked in the 1980s by the death-dispensing world of *St. Elsewhere*, it is consistent with their dramatic setting—and the positive approach of producer David Victor in that program (similar to his other efforts such as *Dr. Kildare*, *Lucas Tanner*, and *Owen Marshall*).

Eight years after the series ended its original run, Robert Young came back for a 1984 sequel, *The Return of Marcus Welby, M. D.* (battling attempts to put him out to pasture). This sequel was followed in 1988 with *Marcus Welby, M. D.: A Holiday Affair*, filmed in France and Switzerland, with a strong touch of romance coming to the good doctor in the form of Tessa Menard (played by Alexis Smith).

During the time between the series and the sequels, Robert Young remained a familiar TV dispenser of advice, offering cups of Sanka to high-strung friends apparently suffering from too much caffeine.

**MARGIE** (*) **30 min (26ep B&W; 1961–1962 ABC) Situation Comedy** *with Cynthia Pepper as Margie Clayton, Dave Willock as Harvey Clayton, Wesley Tackitt as Nora Clayton, Penney Parker as Maybelle Jackson, Hollis Irving as Phoebe Clayton, Tommy Ivo as Heywood Botts, and Richard Gering as Johnny Green*

Most TV series set in the 1920s are drama shows that concern themselves, one way or another, with prohibition and gangsters (*The Roaring Twenties, The Untouchables*). *Margie* is one of the few sitcoms set in that era. There are no speakeasies in Margie Clayton's small New England town of Madison, and no squealing roadsters with machine-gun-toting hoodlums. Instead there are the familiar problems of a pretty high school girl with a penchant for trouble. This show proves that you can make a boring family sitcom set in any decade, not just the 1950s.

**MARIAH** (*½) **60 min (7ep Color; 1987 ABC) Police Drama** *with Philip Baker Hall as James Malone, John Getz as Ned Sheffield, Tovah Feldshuh as Dr. Deena Hertz, Chris Wiggins as Father Timothy Quinlan, and Kathleen Layman as Brandis LaSalle*

The dark, ominous cloud of human troubles hangs low and heavy over Mariah State Penitentiary. The prisoners are always grumbling, suicides are attempted daily (it seems), political pressures force superintendent Malone to make tough choices, and socialite/activist Brandis LaSalle wants to unionize the prisoners' families. Yup, things are tough all over. *Mariah* is only for the terminally depressed.

**MARK SABER MYSTERY THEATER** (**) **(57ep B&W; 1951–1954 ABC) Police Drama** *with Tom Conway as Mark Saber and James Burke as Sgt. Tim Maloney*

The character of Mark Saber has a long and highly complicated history on TV, one that stretches over a decade, two networks, and at least six different titles. Essentially it boils down to the fact that there were really *two* series involving a lead character named Mark Saber, and the two have very little in common.

This version of the Mark Saber saga is the original version, with Saber as a suave British homicide detective on the New York City police force. Sort of a modern-day Sherlock Holmes, this Saber has slow-witted Sgt. Maloney as his Dr. Watson.

This series has also been known as *Mystery Theater, Inspector Mark Saber—Homicide Squad, Homicide Squad, and The Vise*. The other Mark Saber series, where Saber is a one-armed Scotland Yard inspector, is known as both *Saber of London* and *Detective's Diary*. ■

**MARKHAM** (*) **30 min (60ep B&W: 1959–1960 CBS) Detective Drama** *with Ray Milland as Ray Markham and Simon Scott as John Riggs*

Though often shot on location in Europe, the globe-trotting adventures of investigator Ray Markham still come off as surprisingly dull and ordinary. Part of the problem is with the character himself, a wealthy but bland New York attorney who decides to become a detective just for a change in professional venue. With this flat beginning, he needs some good supporting roles and stories. Unfortunately, Milland has to carry the series almost completely on his own (there's a legman named John Riggs, but only for a handful of episodes), saddled with weak plots and a limited character type. If you're a Ray Milland fan, you'll probably prefer his comedy series (*The Ray Milland Show*) instead, or even his slightly camp rendition of self-centered space politician Sire Uri on *Battlestar Galactica*.

**MARRIED: THE FIRST YEAR** (*) **60 min (4ep Color; 1979 CBS) Drama** *with Leigh McCloskey as Billy Baker, Cindy Grover as Joanna Huffman Baker, Claudette Nevins as Barbara Huffman, K. Callan as Cathy Baker, and Stanley Grover as Bert Baker*

Lee Rich and Philip Capice, the boys who brought us trauma-ridden nouveau riche Texans in *Dallas*, can't seem to hit the mark here in this tale of the simple woes of a young married couple whose families do not get along. The show is a valiant effort to focus on normal, regular folk, but it all seems too strained to be real.

**MARRIED . . . WITH CHILDREN** (***½) **30 min (55 ep at Fall 1989 Color; 1987– Fox) Situation Comedy** *with Ed O'Neill as Al Bundy, Katey Sagal as Peg Bundy, David Garrison as Steve Rhoades, Amanda Bearse as Marcy Rhoades, Christina Applegate as Kelly Bundy, and David Faustino as Bud Bundy*

This is a very cynical, very mean, but very funny sitcom. And it's a contrasting world apart from the successful upper middle-class Brooklyn setting of its contemporary, *The Cosby Show*, where mom and dad are successful professionals with loving children and unlimited potential.

Peg and Al Bundy feel stuck with their disappointing lives. With their two children. With their irritatingly happy neighbors. At one time, they might have been head-over-heels in love (or at least in lust) with each other, but after sixteen years the magic is definitely gone. He's just a mediocre shoe salesman, and she's a lackluster homemaker.

It's not that they hate each other—actually, very *very* deep down there is still a spark of affection. They both simply make no secret of how unhappy they are with the way things turned out.

Ironically, this means venting their respective spleens at the only people who would notice—themselves, their neighbors, and their children. Maybe it won't change their lives, but at least they each have a laugh and some brief triumph in their titular kingdom. That's probably why they never get divorced. Why take a chance with some new losers when you've got your current routine down cold?

So Peg does a minimal amount of housework. Al, in turn, treats sex with her as a tremendous burden that he graciously endures for a few minutes each month. As a result, Peg spends most of her days "horny" while Al spends most of his free time watching TV or trying to convince his next door neighbor Steve to be more like him.

That would be the triumph of small triumphs in his world. Steve and his wife Marcy are recently married and still lovey-dovey. They are not yet burdened with children. They're both working at a neighborhood bank, still on an upward career cycle. Worst of all, Steve purports to be a liberated man who generally treats Marcy with respect. They represent a world apart from Peg and Al.

But not that far away. After all, if they are really that successful, what are they doing as neighbors to the Bundys? In fact, until they reach the top, Steve and Marcy are not above scoring a few ego points of their own, usually at Peg and Al's expense. Steve makes certain to flaunt any raise he gets in front of Al, while Marcy often lets slip how much great sex she gets at home. (In one deadpan, she wondered aloud to an envious Peg whether "an hour-and-a-half of pleasure" was really worth all the trouble.)

Even the two Bundy children catch the spirit. They bring true sibling rivalry and snitching to sitcomland, while trying to have as much irresponsible fun as possible before they grow up. With parents like Peg and Al, they certainly can't be looking forward to married life.

All in all, *Married . . . with Children* provides one of the most entertainingly unhappy family settings to grace the sitcom world since *Fawlty Towers.* There are no scenes of everyone hugging and making up at the end, just a refreshingly nasty edge that gives even typical sitcom complications and misunderstandings some badly needed spice.

## THE MARTIAN CHRONICLES (***) (6hr miniseries Color; 1980 NBC) Science Fiction *with Rock Hudson as Colonel John Wilder, Gayle Hunnicutt as Ruth Wilder, Fritz Weaver as Fr. Peregrine, Roddy McDowall as Fr. Stone, Nicholas Hammond as Arthur Block, Bernadette Peters as Genevieve Seltzer, Maria Schell as Anna Lustig, Joyce Van Patten as Elma Parkhill, and Darren McGavin as Sam Parkhill*

Ray Bradbury's 1950 book *The Martian Chronicles*, is a tough one for screen adaptation because often it is not as much a novel as it is a series of short stories, sometimes only vaguely connected. As a result, the book constantly shifts moods and characters, going from gentle whimsy to genuine fright. Nonetheless, several threads do carry throughout: the mysterious disappearance of the crews from the first two Earth-to-Mars probes, the threat of nuclear annihilation on Earth, and the elusive search for a real-life native inhabitant of the mysterious red planet. They form the basis for this television presentation.

Rock Hudson stars as Colonel John Wilder, commander of the third expedition to Mars. He is determined to lead a successful landing party and, if possible, to find out what happened to the members of the first two. This time, mysteriously, all goes well. Though the fate of the original crews remains an unanswered question, Wilder sends word back to Earth that Mars is safe for colonization. For many, that's a welcome relief because the situation on the war-prone home world is growing increasingly tense. Mars seems to offer the last safe haven. And, for ornery pioneering spirits, it seems a welcome new expanse of emptiness, allowing them to get as far away as possible from interfering civilization. So the colonists set out for their new world, with the rest of the series alternately focusing on their adventures and the personal puzzlement of Colonel Wilder. He is haunted by secrets that seem just out of sight and more than anything else he wants to meet a Martian. After a while, Wilder begins to wonder if they're really much closer than even he imagines.

The real surprise of *The Martian Chronicles* is that the miniseries manages to convey some rather subtle images and concepts, very much in the spirit of Bradbury's original book. It also keeps the drama moving through several settings and characters, with Darren McGavin being one of the best scene stealers, playing a western cowpoke with unique insights into the truth about Mars. Reflecting the original book, some sequences are awfully tough to figure out. But stick around—eventually it all hangs together. And, yes, by the end you will have seen the Martians. ■

## MARTIN KANE, THE ADVENTURES OF (**) 30 min (39ep B&W; 1957–1958 Syndication) Detective Drama *with William Gargan as Martin Kane*

The character of Martin Kane has a convoluted and confusing history on television. Kane began on TV in 1949, in a live series known as *Martin Kane, Private Eye*, with William Gargan in the title role. In this first variation, Kane was a New York City private eye who collaborated with the police. Gargan was later succeeded in the Kane role by Lloyd Nolan and Lee Tracy and the series title was shortened to *Martin Kane.* In 1953, a one-year filmed series called *The New Adventures of Martin Kane* appeared, set in Europe with Mark Stevens as Kane, now a world-touring investigator. These episodes have been syndicated as *Assignment: Danger.*

Finally, in 1957, came this series, *The Adventures of Martin Kane*, which is also set in Europe, but stars William Gargan (yes, the same man who played the original Kane). This final permutation is also known as *The Return of Martin Kane.*

## THE MARTY FELDMAN COMEDY MACHINE (**) 60 min (14ep Color; 1971–1972 UK ATV) Comedy-Variety *with Marty Feldman*

Feldman was a manic, very physical, British writer and bug-eyed comedian, who reached a mass audience as one of the players in such Mel Brooks genre-parody feature films of the mid-1970s as *Young Frankenstein* and *Silent Movie*. This series was originally produced for a late 1971 to early 1972 British run, with excerpts packaged for U.S. consumption as a 1972 spring to summer series on ABC. *Monty Python's* Terry Gilliam does the animations, and regulars include the likes of Spike Milligan (from *The Goon Show*). Worth a peek just to catch Feldman right before he hit it really big.

**MARY (**½) 60 min (11ep Color; 1978 CBS) Comedy-Variety** *with Mary Tyler Moore, Dick Shawn, Swoosie Kurtz, David Letterman, Judy Kahan, and Michael Keaton*

Mary Tyler Moore, who did so well in sitcoms (*The Dick Van Dyke Show, The Mary Tyler Moore Show*), makes a valiant effort here to revive the comedy-variety format. *Mary* is the first of two late-1980s comedy variety hours starring Moore, both of which have exceedingly brief histories.

The crew of *Mary* is top-notch. Producers Tom Patchett and Jay Tarses did well with *The Bob Newhart Show*. The supporting players include Dick Shawn (who portrayed a bad actor playing Adolph Hitler in Mel Brooks' *The Producers*), David Letterman (who had yet to host his first talk show), and Michael Keaton (later a film star in *Mr. Mom, Beetlejuice* and the 1989 *Batman*). The format is flexible, with lots of comedy sketches, singing, dancing, and so on. The show has all the elements for success, and it probably would have been a hit if it was produced in the late 1960s instead of the late 1970s. For some reason, the comedy-variety format had fallen out of fashion, and *Mary* is a casualty of that change in fashion. A revamped version of this show is titled *The Mary Tyler Moore Hour.*

**MARY (**½) 30 min (13ep Color; 1985–1986) Situation Comedy** *with Mary Tyler Moore as Mary Brenner, James Farentino as Frank DeMarco, Katey Sagal as Jo Tucker, John Astin as Ed LaSalle, Harold Sylvester as Harry Dresden, Derek McGrath as Ronnie Dicker, David Byrd as Vincent Tully, Carlene Watkins as Susan Wilcox, and James Tolkan as Lester Mintz*

No, this is not the continuation of the Mary Richards story from *The Mary Tyler Moore Show*. However, this series does use a clever opening setup to instantly tap the mood and memory of the wrap-up to that series: In the first scene, Mary Brenner walks into her office at a high-fashion magazine and discovers she's out of a job—the publication has folded. So, like Mary Richards when we last saw her (handed her walking papers by WJM), Mary Brenner is looking for work.

Like Lou Grant, Mary finds employment in the world of newspapers, though this is a far cry from the bright and noble world of the *Los Angeles Tribune*. The *Chicago Eagle* is a third-rate daily tabloid, churned out in cramped quarters under the direction of aggressive managing editor Frank DeMarco, a connoisseur of the sensationalistic. Frank is also a handsome ladies' man who instantly takes a liking to Mary, which is probably why he hires her despite some reservations (she may not be pushy enough). She becomes the new "Helpline" columnist, a consumer advocate type handling reader requests for aid in resolving minor business disputes or cutting bureaucratic red tape. Rounding out the office staff is nightlife critic Ed LaSalle, cynical Mike Royko-style "Mainline Chicago" columnist Jo Tucker (an unrepentant chain-smoker with a desk opposite Mary's), sportswriter Ronnie Dicker, crime reporter Harry Dresden, and the nearly blind union-protected copy editor, Vincent Tully.

This is a strong workplace lineup with plenty of comic possibilities, just like the old *Mary Tyler Moore Show*, yet sufficiently different to take the plots into fresh territory. (For instance, unlike Lou Grant, Frank DeMarco has more than a fatherly mentor interest in Mary.) On the other hand, Mary's home setting initially fizzles, with an oddly mismatched engaged couple (Susan and Lester) as the chief characters there. Nonetheless, with some careful nurturing, this package could have developed into another reliable vehicle for Moore. Instead it was dropped by all concerned after only half a season—though it is definitely worth seeking out in the rerun circuit.

One odd footnote to the premise is the name of the paper, which changed from the *Chicago Post* to the *Chicago Eagle* at the very last minute of production. This was the result of a real-life lawsuit by a local Chicago-area small circulation weekly with the *Post* name—much to the annoyance of the production company and the bemusement of most Windy City residents, who found it hard to remember the last time they had seen that paper at their local newsstands.

**MARY HARTMAN, MARY HARTMAN (**½) 30 min (325ep Color; 1976–1977 Syndication)/FOREVER FERNWOOD (**½) 30 min (130ep Color; 1977–1978 Syndication) Serial Comedy** *with Louise Lasser as Mary Hartman, Greg Mullavey as Tom Hartman, Dody Goodman as Martha Shumway, Philip Bruns and Tab Hunter as George Shumway, Debralee Scott as Cathy Shumway, Claudia Lamb as Heather Hartman, Mary Kay Place as Loretta Haggers, Graham Jarvis as Charlie Haggers, Dabney Coleman as Merle Jeeter, Victor Kilian as Raymond Larkin, Martin Mull as Garth Gimble and Barth Gimble, Sparky Marcus as Jimmy Joe Jeeter, Susan Browning as Patty Gimble, Shelley Fabares as Eleanor Major, Judith Kahan as Penny Major, and Fred Willard as Jerry Hubbard*

For years, many people have made fun of soap operas, but until *Mary Hartman, Mary Hartman* nobody had the nerve to try and out-soap the soaps at their own game. Structured on the surface like a typical soap opera, *Mary Hartman, Mary Hartman* pokes merciless fun at not only the soap opera conventions but also a whole range of TV shibboleths all at once. While the series may not work all the time, its frequent boldness and imagination usually outweigh the lapses in the production.

At first glance, *Mary Hartman, Mary Hartman* seems to fit right into the daytime drama mold. Mary is a youngish housewife in the small town of Fernwood, Ohio. Her marriage to Tom Hartman had its ups and downs, centering on Tom's reccurring bouts with impotence, which only provides more grist for Mary to chew over with her mother Martha and neighbor Loretta. Like most of the men in Fernwood, Tom and Charlie Haggers (Loretta's husband) work at the local auto plant. The Hartmans have a young pre-pubescent daughter (Heather), and Mary's sister Cathy, father George, and grandfather Raymond Larkin are always around to kick in their two cents.

From this fairly normal background, executive producer Norman Lear launches on flights of fancy. Mary, it turns out, is not your average housewife. She is addicted to TV, especially commercials (which she believes in fervently). So right up there with Tom's impotence are Mary's problems such as her fear of developing "waxy yellow buildup" on her kitchen floor. Sister Cathy is sexually promiscuous, Grandpa Larkin is the town flasher, and Mary's mother is even more out of touch with reality than Mary is.

The rest of Fernwood is likewise perverse. The town's celebrity, eight-year-old evangelist Jimmy Joe Jeeter, is electrocuted when a television set falls into his bathtub. Jimmy Joe's venal father Merle becomes mayor of Fernwood. Loretta takes up country and western singing. Garth Gimble (husband of Mary's friend Patty) is impaled on an aluminum Christmas tree, only to have his twin brother Barth (also played by actor Martin Mull) turn up some months later.

As with any good soap, *Mary Hartman, Mary Hartman* milks these plot twists for all their worth, since there are five shows a week to fill. The intense sense of zaniness here is the model for the equally wild *Soap*, and it's worth watching *Mary Hartman* just to see what weird event will turn up next. The acting is loose but spirited, and the series actually works on both tracks, as a comedy *and* as a soap.

A dramatic and quality high point occurs at the end of the first season, when Mary fulfills the lifelong dream of all true couch potatoes such as herself: She is interviewed on a TV talk show about *her* life. While on the air, spilling her guts to the nation, Mary has a nervous breakdown that is both funny and touching.

After two seasons, Louise Lasser leaves *Mary Hartman, Mary Hartman* and the show tries to continue. As *Forever Fernwood*, the saga of the small Ohio town goes on, with most of the original cast but without some of the spark. The most inspired moment comes when Tab Hunter suddenly turns up as George Shumway, Mary's father. The explanation for the change in appearance from actor Philip Bruns is that George, another worker at the auto plant, fell into a vat of Rustoleum at work and had extensive plastic surgery. After a few months of milking this joke, Hunter disappears and Bruns reappears as George, with the explanation that he was in a car crash and had yet more plastic surgery. A show with the nerve to spin these plot lines deserves a salute.

The humor in *Mary Hartman* is sometimes too smug, and at times it may veer *too* close to the glacierlike pacing of the soaps it set out to satirize. Still, the series (especially the first season's episodes) can be appreciated for its wit and chutzpah.

Barth Gimble and Jerry Hubbard (Loretta's manager) turn up in *Fernwood 2-Night*, another Norman Lear on-target parody (of TV talk shows this time) set in Fernwood, which mutated into *America 2Night.* ■

**THE MARY TYLER MOORE HOUR (**) 60 min (11ep Color; 1979 CBS) Comedy-Variety/Situation Comedy** *with Mary Tyler Moore as Mary McKinnon, Joyce Van Patten as Iris Chapman, Michael Lombard as Harry Sinclair, Michael Keaton as Kenneth Christy, and Dody Goodman as Ruby Bell*

Mary Tyler Moore's second late-1970s effort in the comedy-variety genre is less satisfying than the first (*Mary*). In this later attempt, Mary borrows from the venerable show within a show concept mined for so long by Jack Benny. The idea is that Mary Tyler Moore plays Mary McKinnon, the star of a mythical TV variety series (*The Mary McKinnon Show*). *The Mary Tyler Moore Hour* thus revolves around the trials and tribulations of the production of *The Mary McKinnon Show*, focusing both on the studio crew who assist the star and the star's home life. It's a workable concept, but hard to pull off.

As always, Moore surrounds herself with great talent. Producer Perry Lafferty was one of the kings of early 1960s TV variety (*The Andy Williams Show, The Danny Kaye Show*). Joyce Van Patten (sister of Dick), who had been a regular on *The Danny Kaye Show*, plays Mary McKinnon's secretary. Veteran trooper Dody Goodman (from the old *Jack Paar Show* and Mary Hartman's crazy mother in *Mary Hartman, Mary Hartman*) plays Mary McKinnon's maid. Up and coming comic Michael Keaton, the only holdover from *Mary*, plays a brash studio page. In a more perfect world, this show (and *Mary*) would have been a hit. As the world is not perfect, both shows are only intriguing curios.

Keep an eye out for a fun reunion of Moore with her old sitcom co-star Dick Van Dyke. The two present a skit showing Rob and Laura Petrie about twelve years after the end of *The Dick Van Dyke Show*, and we learn the surprising news that their son, Ritchie, is now gay.

**THE MARY TYLER MOORE SHOW** (****) **30 min (168ep Color; 1970–1977 CBS) Situation Comedy** *with Mary Tyler Moore as Mary Richards, Edward Asner as Lou Grant, Ted Knight as Ted Baxter, Gavin MacLeod as Murray Slaughter, Valerie Harper as Rhoda Morgenstern, Cloris Leachman as Phyllis Lindstrom, Georgia Engel as Georgette Franklin-Baxter, John Amos as Gordy Howard, and Betty White as Sue Ann Nivens*

Mary Richards is newly arrived in Minneapolis. She's determined to make it on her own, striking off on an independent path after seeing her boyfriend pull out of their wedding plans. In short order she finds an apartment, lands a new job (as an associate news producer for television station WJM), and even gets the chance to kiss off her former fiancé when he shows up expecting her to come running back to him. And this is just the first episode. Her new boss, gruff newshound Lou Grant, pegs her perfectly. Mary has spunk. He *hates* spunk, but he likes her. And so does everybody else.

This series is probably one of the most influential in television history, with its success (and that of the MTM production company) establishing a nurturing environment for a crop of writers, producers, and performers dedicated to its particular style and approach to storytelling (both in comedy and drama). That influence is still evident today, with series ranging from *The Cosby Show* to *Cheers* to *Alf* to *The Tracey Ullman Show* all having alums from MTM.

Yet with all that history to follow, probably the best way to appreciate *The Mary Tyler Moore Show* is to try to catch it at the beginning of its rerun cycle. Then you can see all the elements in place from the start and watch as both the writers and the performers help the characters to grow, reacting to situations like real people might. Along the way, you'll also be treated to clever dialogue, funny situations, superb timing, and an ensemble of performers that evolves into a wonderful surrogate family. In short, you might want to follow this series from beginning to end.

The first season is particularly interesting because the characters are making their first impressions. Mary's friend Rhoda is at her self-deprecating best here as the two of them hit the singles dating scene, with Mary being the one the guys inevitably go after. There's also an innocent excitement about being involved with television (even if WJM has the lowest-rated news program in town), with Rhoda volunteering to help run the election night tote board just to be on camera (her legs, anyway) and to see the station's handsome anchor man, Ted Baxter, in person. (She quickly discovers that's no big deal.)

Baxter, of course, is almost a complete cartoon caricature at this point, the epitome of the self-centered, uninformed, blow-dried news reader. He's falsely sincere, a crybaby, and hilarious to watch. Over the long haul this character could become grating, but at the beginning it's just fine. Another annoying character, Rhoda and Mary's landlord, Phyllis, is also tolerable at this stage, though she never gets the same softening treatment as Ted, even after leaving *The Mary Tyler Moore Show* for a *Phyllis* spin-off series.

In these early episodes, newswriter Murray Slaughter quickly establishes himself as the Morey Amsterdam of the newsroom, firing off insults at Ted in the tradition of Buddy Sorrell attacking Mel Cooley on *The Dick Van Dyke Show*. Lou Grant (always referred to as "Mister Grant" by Mary) also stakes out his territory quickly as a boss whose gruff facade often hides a soft, sympathetic interior. Except when it doesn't. Then he can be sarcastic and angry (especially toward Ted), and sometimes even resentful (when he and his wife split). Of all the characters on the series (aside from Mary), Ed Asner is probably the most fascinating to watch, with Lou Grant a constant source of surprise.

After the first season's establishing shots, the program marches on confidently, developing all the characters in Mary's surrogate home and office families. Even Ted Baxter begins to spruce up his act, as he gets a permanent girlfriend, Georgette. And a new face enters the picture, Betty White's Sue Ann Nivens, host of WJM's *Happy Homemaker Show*. Sue Ann is bright, bitchy, manipulative, and perfectly willing to use sex to further advance her career. She's a particularly good verbal sparring partner to Murray, and has her eyes on Lou as the ultimate catch.

With the departure of Valerie Harper to a *Rhoda* spinoff series (and less frequent appearances by Phyllis), the last three seasons effectively merge the home and office worlds, with the focus shifting almost completely to the family of characters at WJM. (Mary even moves into a new apartment.) This era has such classic episodes as Mary's night in jail for refusing to reveal a news source; Ted Baxter's "Famous Broadcasters School" (total enrollment: one); Ted and Georgette's Sunday morning wedding (performed by John Ritter as a minister decked out in this tennis togs); Lou's competitive jousts with Mary's Aunt Flo; and, of course, the gallows humor surrounding the death of Chuckles the Clown.

Naturally the famous final episode is required viewing, with a good mix of hugs, kisses, and tears, along with a cute comic twist (everyone is fired except the incompetent Ted), and the clever use of the song "It's a Long Way to Tipperary" as a farewell theme. Ed Asner, of course, continues in character for another five seasons on *Lou Grant*, though there's only one other major character crossover (Eileen Heckart as Mary's Aunt Flo).

Since this series, Mary Tyler Moore has tried with limited success for the television character hat trick (on *Mary* and *Annie McGuire*, for example). In the meantime, she has two classic portraits hanging in our collective living rooms: Laura Petrie from *The Dick Van Dyke show* and Mary Richards of *The Mary Tyler Moore Show*. ■

**MASADA** (***) **(8 hr miniseries Color; 1981 ABC) Drama** *with Peter Strauss as Eleazar Ben Yair, Peter O'Toole as Cornelius Flavius Silva, Richard Pierson as Emphraim, David Opatoshu as Shimon, Anthony Quayle as Gallus, Barbara Carrera as Sheva, and David Warner as Falco*

A biblical epic in the grand Hollywood style, *Masada* tells the story of the final Jewish resistance to Roman occupation in the year 73. The last band of Hebrew rebels is cornered by the Roman legions on a mountaintop called Masada. The strategic mountaintop locale balances the Roman might for a while, and a lengthy standoff ensues. Jewish leader Eleazar gets to know and respect Roman leader Flavius, and vice versa, but Roman might overcomes in the end. The Jews at Masada take the ultimate revolt and deprive the Romans of their victory by committing mass suicide just before the legions scale the walls.

Money was no object in this production, filmed in Israel, and movie mogul Cecil B. De Mille would have been proud of the complexity of the battle scenes. The acting is somewhat wooden, with most of the good guys being too good, and most of the bad guys being too bad. Peter O'Toole (a veteran of Hollywood epics such as *Lawrence of Arabia*) is the highlight of *Masada* through his strong and very human portrayal of the military commander with a heart, who reluctantly follows orders. ■

**THE MASK** (*½ ) **60 min (14ep B&W; 1954 ABC) Law Drama** *with Gary Merrill as Walter Guilfoyle, and William Prince as Peter Guilfoyle*

Television's first hour-long crime series with continuing characters, *The Mask* is a forgettable exercise focusing on a two-brother law firm that pursues and "unmasks" various crime figures, while helping the needy along the way.

**MASQUERADE** (**) **60 min (11ep & 90 min pilot Color; 1983–1984 ABC) Spy Drama** *with Rod Taylor as Mr. Lavender, Kirstie Alley as Casey Collins, and Greg Evigan as Danny Doyle*

The list of spy series from the 1980s is relatively short, and *Masquerade* is not one of the more memorable entries on that list. Produced by Glen A. Larson (*Battlestar Gallactica, B. J. and the Bear*) *Masquerade* is sort of the *Love Boat* of spy series, since it focuses on a different guest spy each week. The main continuing character is Mr. Lavender, the head of the NIA, yet another CIA clone. The NIA needs spies (the regular ones are dropping like flies), so Lavender recruits average Americans overseas to perform tasks for Uncle Sam on a freelance basis.

Rod Taylor, who plays Lavender, is best known for his early 1960s action/suspense roles (in Hitchcock's film *The Birds* and TV's *Hong Kong*). Lavender's two young aides are Kirstie Alley (making her first TV series appearance, after playing half-Vulcan Lt. Saavik in 1982's *Star Trek II*, but before taking over from Sam Malone as the proprietor on *Cheers*) and Greg Evigan (who was B. J. in Larson's *B. J. and the Bear*).

**THE MASTER** (*) **60 min (12ep Color; 1984 NBC) Adventure** *with Lee Van Cleef as John Peter McAllister, Timothy Van Patten as Max Keller, and Sho Kosugi as Okasa*

John Peter McAllister served with the U.S. Army in Japan after World War II and stayed there at war's end, learning the skills of the Ninja sect, a warrior society that specializes in the martial arts. After learning that he has a grown daughter he never knew of back in the States, McAllister breaks his Ninja vows and leaves Japan for home, searching for his offspring. Pursued by Ninja hit man Okasa, who aims to kill McAllister for breaking ranks, McAllister roams around the United States looking for his daughter. He teams up with young drifter Max Keller, who is anxious to learn the Ninja ways from this western master of Oriental combat. As in *Kung Fu*, lots of bad guys get stomped, kicked, and gouged here, in displays of Ninja prowess.

Lee Van Cleef, making his first TV series appearance, is best known as the star of several "spaghetti" western films produced in Italy (such as *The Good, the Bad and the Ugly*). Timothy Van Patten, of the large and talented Van Patten acting family, previously played Salami, the streetwise Italian white kid in the inner city basketball series *The White Shadow*.

**MASTER OF THE GAME** (**) **(9hr miniseries Color; 1984 CBS) Drama** *with Dyan Cannon as Kate Blackwell, David Birney as David Blackwell, Leslie Caron as Solange, Harry Hamlin as Tony Blackwell, Ian Charleson as Jamie MacGregor, and Cliff DeYoung as Brad Rogers*

Adapted from Sidney Sheldon's novel, this miniseries is a sumptuous romp through one hundred years of the Blackwell family. The Blackwells become one of the world's most powerful (and bitchy) families, beginning with a rich South African diamond mine in the 1800s.

**MASTERPIECE THEATRE** (****) **60 min (Color; 1971– PBS) Drama Anthology** *with Alistair Cooke as host*

For some, this series defines American public television: high-brow, literary, with an almost obsessive interest in history and literature (especially British). That's understandable. *Masterpiece Theatre* is probably the most widely recognized public television programming package, with parodies of long-time host Alistair Cooke seated in his comfy chair turning up in comedy routines since the early 1970s (done everywhere from Johnny Carson's *Tonight Show* to *SCTV* to *Mama's Family* to the Disney Channel's *Mousterpiece Theater* with George Plimpton). Actually such a focus on Cooke (born and raised in Britain, but a U.S. citizen since the 1930s) is appropriate because he is probably one of the key reasons this anthology initially took hold.

Obviously Cooke is not the first person ever to host a drama anthology. But he is probably the first to treat his material with the respect previously reserved for serious literature, subscribing to the astonishing notion that television entertainment presentations are worth talking about on their own merits. Sure, the stories are based on classic novels or biographies or are historical pieces, but there is no condescending implication that "you should be reading the original books instead of watching TV." (Though that would be nice.) Rather, these television programs are taken as just one more legitimate way of appreciating the material—right beside live theater, theatrical feature films, and books. (In fact, nineteenth-century writers such as Dickens and Thackeray first presented many of their stories as serialized adventures in popular newspapers.)

Because all but a handful of *Masterpiece Theatre* offerings are miniseries (most more than three parts), Cooke has great latitude in his wraparound comments, usually speaking before and after each episode. At the beginning of the miniseries run he sketches the historical and social background of the subject matter. Other times he notes some particularly striking developments in the story. But most often he simply shares thoughts that occurred to him while watching the presentation, sometimes drawing on personal memories (school, World War II, international travel), other times taking an appropriate passage from the book being dramatized or from some other work he just feels inspired to read from. Unlike the typical anthology host (Ronald Reagan on *G. E. Theater*, for instance) Cooke is not only very well read but he's viewed the programs himself, writing his own scripts in advance of marathon taping sessions for his commentaries. The result is an entertainingly informative visit with a fellow TV watcher.

Sadly, this approach is rarely taken elsewhere, not even in England, where nearly all of these miniseries come from. There, as here, programs generally run "cold"—without any scene setting, background, or shared thoughts. Stateside programmers find particularly absurd the prospect of turning over perfectly good commercial time for such activities, though there are a few rarely shown clips in the syndication packages of series such as *M*A*S*H* or *I Love Lucy* that have introductory comments to particular episodes (usually by cast members describing their favorite scenes).

As to what goes on between Alistair Cooke's comments, *Masterpiece Theatre* is reassuringly consistent. The productions really shine in their scrupulous eye for detail in sets, costuming, and overall cinematography—items receiving high marks even if a particular drama is weak. (*The New York Times* once noted in amazed admiration that for the series *Lillie* the costumes were truly authentic, down to the women's underwear, which included corsets, bustles, and petticoats of the period.) Though at times some adaptations are a bit overly somber and serious, most manage to strike a balance between being faithful to the source material and realistic about television pacing. The fact that the stories often contain legitimate elements of high-gloss soap opera, including some revealing costumes, doesn't hurt viewer interest. (There are even flashes of nudity in such series as *Therese Raquin* and *I, Claudius.*)

Inevitably, most of the dramas are the product of British television services (chiefly the BBC, but also others such as London Weekend Television, ITC, and Granada), though material from other countries also turns up (*A Town Like Alice* is an Australian production). In adapting the various books and biographies for television, all of them take a different approach from the usual U.S. treatment of series. Instead of going for an open-ended run with the potential of taking the characters and settings through hundreds of episodes season after season, they turn out self-contained relatively short-run tales. Most have fewer than a dozen segments, but even those that go on longer (such as London Weekend's *Upstairs, Downstairs*, with sixty-eight episodes) produce stories at a much less hectic pace than a U.S. company. In fact, the success of these miniseries on *Masterpiece Theatre* beginning in 1971 led directly to the flowering of the form in the United States, starting with *QBVII* in 1974. Of course, the Stateside product more often favors the likes of writers such as Jackie Collins and Judith Kranz rather than Alex Haley and Herman Wouk.

This is not to suggest that all British television is made with *Masterpiece Theatre* in mind (*Benny Hill* instantly disproves that rash assumption). In fact, the show's producers at Boston's WGBH have to sort through (and discard) hundreds of potential entries before arriving at each season's lineup. But overall the material selected demonstrates that the British producers, directors, writers, and performers behind them happen to be particularly adept at the serialized drama formula. And that approach happens to work very well with the material they tackle, often leading to more complete treatment of the classics than would be possible even in a big-budget theatrical film. They simply have more time to flesh out the author's thesis, to tell the stories more completely, and to develop characters more fully—in short, to let time pass and life change. In addition, they can take detours that on the surface seem to contribute little to the final plot resolution but in fact may be quite illuminating to the overall character interaction.

Best of all, unlike the States (where for too long there was a stigma associated with "doing TV" once you hit the big time in movies or on stage), the lead performers don't treat television work as "slumming." The same holds true for the many strong supporting performers. While it's not exactly a repertory company, one of the pleasures of following the many different miniseries on *Masterpiece Theatre* is the opportunity to see what soon become reliable familiar faces, as well as stars-in-the-making and established veterans. These include performers such as Jeremy Irons (*Love for Lydia*), Anthony Andrews (*Danger UXB*), Ben Kingsley (*Silas Marner*), Glenda Jackson (*Elizabeth R*), Lesley-Anne Down (*Upstairs, Downstairs*), Bob Hoskins (*Flickers*), Tom Conti (*Madame Bovary*), Bryan Brown (*A Town Like Alice*), Kate Nelligan (*Therese Raquin*), Diana Rigg (*Bleak House*), and Peggy Ashcroft (*The Jewel in the Crown*). After a while, you'll also start noticing the *Masterpiece Theatre* performers on other imports, and sometimes on U.S. productions—for instance, *Poldark*'s Robin Ellis turns up on an episode of *Fawlty Towers*, Gareth Thomas (from *By the Sword Divided* and *How Green Was My Valley*) stars in *Blake's 7*, Peter Davison (*Love for Lydia*) is on *All Creatures Great and Small* and *Doctor Who*, Pierce Brosnan (Robert Shaw in *Nancy Astor*) went to the States for *Remington Steele*, Sylvester McCoy (Birdie Bowers on *The Last Place on Earth*) became the seventh lead in *Doctor Who*, and Robert Powell (the title character in *Jude the Obscure*) plays the title role in *Jesus of Nazareth*.

With so many British series to choose from and relatively few weeks to fill (most seasons have about thirty-one new episodes), *Masterpiece Theatre* is remarkably consistent in what it does. If you like this type of television drama, you'll rarely be disappointed. If you're coming in cold to the series, you might want to ease in with programs offering the most accessible material or familiar performers, such as *I, Claudius, Upstairs, Downstairs, Elizabeth R, Poldark*, or *The Flame Trees of Thika*, or consult the more detailed write-ups for each series elsewhere in this volume under their individual titles.

Over the years there have been relatively few clunkers, though *Strangers and Brothers, My Son, My Son*, and *Love in a Cold Climate* would probably not be among the first titles you'd want to search out. Ironically, Alistair Cooke himself, in retrospect, has described *Masterpiece Theatre*'s inaugural series, *The First Churchills*, as one that "fizzled into orbit and limped to Earth." But, obviously, the program survived that takeoff and continues to thrive.

Perhaps the biggest change to *Masterpiece Theatre* going into the 1990s (aside from making provisions for Alistair Cooke's inevitable departure as host sometime in the decade) is its conscious shift to tales with fewer episodes and more contemporary settings and source material. Fortunately, the quality of such offerings as *Christabel* (based on a recent British bestseller) or *A Very Special Coup* (a timely political intrigue) is every bit as good as the stories set in the royal courts of Elizabethan or Edwardian England.

Mobil Oil (corporate underwriter for the series) and WGBH (the U.S. producer) found the *Masterpiece Theatre* packaging so successful that in 1980 they launched a spin-off, *Mystery*, showcasing high-gloss adaptations of assorted literary detectives.

In 1988, selections from *Masterpiece Theatre* were included in a special discount sales/rental project (dubbed "Video Classics") set up by the MacArthur Foundation to stock libraries with vintage PBS programs. The goal: to make the tapes available to anyone with a library card. For a series created as a showcase for books brought to television, this was a particularly appropriate development, bringing the process full circle, back to the library shelves where it all started.

The following list is of series airing in the United States under the *Masterpiece Theatre* umbrella. With only a few exceptions (several two-hour made-for-TV movies and two-episode presentations, each indicated by an asterisk), all the titles listed below (in alphabetical order) are discussed as separate entries. [The date in brackets is when the series began its original run on *Masterpiece Theatre*.]

**All for Love** (Anthology) [3/31/85]
**All Passion Spent** [1/1/89]
**Anna Karenina** [2/5/78]
**The Barchester Chronicles** [10/28/84]
**Bleak House** [12/1/85]
**The Bretts** [10/11/87 & 6/11/89]
**By the Sword Divided** [3/23/86 & 8/28/88]
**Cakes and Ale** [4/4/76]
**The Charmer** [4/30/89)
**Christabel** (2/12/89]
**The Citadel** [11/20/83]
**Clouds of Witness** (see *Lord Peter Wimsey*) [10/7/73]
*__Cold Comfort Farm__ [12/26/71] (2 hr)
**Country Matters** (Anthology) [2/4/79 & 2/2/75]
**Cousin Bette** [11/5/72]
**Crime and Punishment** [9/28/80]
**Danger UXB** [1/4/81]
**David Copperfield** [3/27/88]
*__Day After the Fair__ [3/6/88] (2 ep)
**Dickens of London** [9/28/77]
**Disraeli: Portrait of a Romantic** [6/1/80]
*__Drake's Venture__ [3/27/83] (2 hr)
**The Duchess of Duke Street** [10/22/78 & 12/16/79]
**Edward and Mrs. Simpson** [11/15/81]
**The Edwardians** [7/7/74]
**Elizabeth R** [2/13/72]
**The First Churchills** [1/10/71]
**Five Red Herrings** (see *Lord Peter Wimsey*) [12/19/76]
**The Flame Trees of Thika** [1/3/82]
**Flickers** [5/23/82]
**Fortunes of War** [1/7/88]
*__The Gambler__ [11/14/71] (2 ep)
**The Golden Bowl** [3/25/73]
*__The Good Soldier__ [1/9/83] (2 hr)
**Goodbye Mr. Chips** [1/4/87]
*__Heaven on Earth__ [12/4/88] (90 min)
**How Green Was My Valley** [11/7/76]

**I, Claudius** [11/6/77]
**I Remember Nelson: Recollections of a Hero's Life** [2/21/82]
**The Irish R. M.** [1/29/84 & 5/25/86]
**The Jewel in the Crown** [12/14/84]
**Jude the Obscure** [10/3/71]
***Kean** [9/9/79] (2 hr)
**The Last of the Mohicans** [5/14/72]
**The Last Place on Earth** [10/20/85]
**Lillie** [3/11/79]
**The Little Farm** (see *Country Matters* Anthology) [12/30/73]
**Lord Mountbatten: The Last Viceroy** [1/26/86]
**Lost Empires** [1/25/87]
**Love for Lydia** [9/23/79]
**Love in a Cold Climate** [3/28/82]
***Love Song** [5/10/87] (2 ep)
**Madame Bovary** [10/10/76)
**The Man Who Was Hunting Himself** [11/11/73]
**The Mayor of Casterbridge** [9/3/78]
**The Moonstone** [12/10/72]
**Murder Must Advertise** (see *Lord Peter Wimsey*) [10/6/74]
**My Son, My Son** [4/13/80]
**Nancy Astor** [4/15/84]
**Nine Tailors** (see *Lord Peter Wimsey*) [4/13/75]
***Northanger Abbey** [12/6/87] (1 ep)
**Notorious Woman** [11/16/75]
***On Approval** [3/13/83] (2 hr)
**Our Mutual Friend** [4/9/78]
**Paradise Postponed** [10/19/86]
**Pere Goriot** [6/13/71]
**A Perfect Spy** [10/16/88]
**Pictures** [10/2/83]
**Point Counter Point** [2/18/73]
**Poldark** [5/8/77 & 6/4/78]
**The Possessed** [5/2/71]
**Pride and Prejudice** [10/26/80]
**Private Schulz** [4/3/83]
**Resurrection** [11/28/71]
**Shoulder to Shoulder** [10/5/75]
***Silas Marner** [3/15/87] (2 hr)
**The Six Wives of Henry VIII** [1/1/72]
**Sons and Lovers** [5/15/83]
**Sorrell and Son** [12/13/87]
**The Spoils of Poynton** [4/4/71]
**Star Quality** (Noel Coward Anthology) [3/21/87]
**Strangers and Brothers** [5/5/85]
**Sunset Song** [4/25/76]
***The Tale of Beatrix Potter** [3/25/84] (2 ep)
**Testament of Youth** [11/30/80]
**Therese Raquin** [4/12/81]
**To Serve Them All My Days** [10/10/82]
**Tom Brown's School Days** [1/14/73]
**A Town Like Alice** [10/4/81]
**Unpleasantness at the Bellona Club** (see *Lord Peter Wimsey*) [12/2/73]
**Upstairs, Downstairs** [1/6/74]
**Vanity Fair** [10/1/72]
**A Very British Coup** [1/29/89]
**Vienna, 1900** (Anthology) [3/2/75]
**Winston Churchill: The Wilderness Years** [1/16/83]
***A Wreath of Roses** [1/22/89] (90 min)

**MATLOCK (**½) 60 min (67ep at Fall 1989 & 2 hr pilot Color; 1987– NBC) Mystery** *with Andy Griffith as Ben Matlock, Linda Purl as Charlene Matlock, Kene Holliday as Tyler Hudson, Nancy Stafford as Michele Thomas, and Don Knotts as Les "Ace" Calhoun*

It's always good to see an old friend succeed in a new venture. We first met Andy Griffith in the 1950s as the innocently wise young country boy of *No Time for Sergeants* (the TV drama, the Broadway stage play, and the feature film). In the 1960s, he landed the role that endeared him to several generations: Mayberry's number one citizen, Sheriff Andy Taylor. During the 1970s and early 1980s, he was all over the place, from the White House (in the miniseries *Washington: Behind Closed Doors*) to a backyard rocket pad (in *Salvage 1*) to the oil fields of Texas (the TV movie *Murder in Texas*).

Then in the late 1980s, Griffith settled in as Ben Matlock, an Atlanta lawyer with a disarming southern drawl and mischievous twinkle in his eye. It's a comfortable role in a well-worn format: part *Perry Mason*, part *Columbo*. No surprise there. *Columbo* veteran Dean Hargrove created the series and served as executive producer with Fred Silverman (who also handled the 1980s *Return of Perry Mason*). Like those previous series, *Matlock* focuses first and foremost on its lead character. That's good because the murder mysteries themselves are mostly average, about on a par with the original *Perry Mason*. But that's not why you're here. You want to see your old friend in action. He doesn't disappoint.

Griffith is a delight to watch. He postures, cajoles, and sweet talks his way through each case. Like Columbo, Matlock latches onto innocent little things and casual slips of the tongue. And he seems so nice that no one could resist talking to him. It couldn't hurt. Later, of course, that sly devil nails the opponent in court.

Upholding the Perry Mason tradition, Matlock gets away with anything and everything before the bench simply by reassuring the judge that eventually his line of questioning *will* become relevant (like when the witness on the stand breaks down and confesses). The prosecutors object in vain, watching their cases come apart. Bested again!

Another victory under his belt, Matlock probably heads back to his home outside town. Maybe he'll sit back with a tall glass and talk with his loyal Paul-and-Della-like associates, daughter and law partner Charlene Matlock, junior partner Michele Thomas, and investigator Tyler Hudson. Or maybe he'll chew the fat with old Mayberry buddy Don Knotts, who turns up as his next door neighbor, Les Calhoun.

We'll just smile, glad to have had the chance to see our old friend again.

**MATT HELM (*) 60 min (13ep & 90 min pilot Color; 1975–1976 ABC) Detective Drama** *with Anthony Franciosa as Matt Helm, Laraine Stephens as Claire Kronski, and Gene Evans as Sgt. Hanrahan*

After watching Dean Martin sing, slug, and sip his way through four theatrical films in the 1960s as agent Matt Helm, then seeing Tony Franciosa play the character as a standard swinging television detective, you have to wonder if anyone involved in such "adaptations" has ever bothered with the original books. Obviously an established fictional character name provides a competitive advantage, but once that is snared it seems to mark an end to any interest in the character's history or persona. Though producers will often ponder every fine detail of a *Masterpiece Theatre*–style offering, too often pulp fiction sources are lucky to get the main character's name spelled right on the way to their television, stage, or feature film incarnations.

Anyway, unless you want to see a slightly updated version of Jeff Dillon (from *Name of the Game*) crossed with Valentine Farrow (from *Valentine's Day*), there's no particularly compelling reason to search out this series. In the meantime, if you're interested in some old-fashioned adventure tales of an agent who is grim, tough, and violent, there are these novels by Donald Hamilton featuring a character called Matt Helm.

**MATT HOUSTON (*½) 60 min (66ep Color; 1982–1985 ABC) Detective Drama** *with Lee Horsley as Matt Houston, Pamela Hensley as C. J. Parsons, George Wyner as Murray Chase, John Aprea as Lt. Vince Novelli, and Lincoln Kilpatrick as Lt. Michael Hoyt*

A lighthearted romp heavily into the *Magnum, P. I.* mold of sensitive male hunk detectives, *Matt Houston* is another bit of engaging fluff brought to us by Aaron Spelling and Douglas Cramer (*The Love Boat*). Matt Houston is a rich Texas playboy who lives off his father's oil and cattle empire, but loves to dabble in private detective work. Assisted by his Harvard-educated lawyer/compatriot C. J. Parsons, Houston is always roaring around in fancy cars or piloting his private helicopter to some crime scene to help out. He rarely makes any money from detective work, but who cares?

After the first season, Houston drops all pretense of devoting any time to the family businesses and becomes a full-time private eye. This allows him to surround himself with gorgeous women all the time, not just in between stints with smelly cattle and filthy oil workers.

**MATT LINCOLN (*) 60 min (16ep & 2 hr pilot Color; 1970–1971 ABC) Medical Drama** *with Vince Edwards as Dr. Matt Lincoln, Chelsea Brown as Tag, Felton Perry as Jimmy, June Harding as Ann, and Michael Larrain as Kevin*

Pretentiousness rules as Vince Edwards, the "you've gotta be cruel to be kind" star surgeon of *Ben Casey,* plays Dr. Matt Lincoln, a totally committed psychiatrist in Los Angeles. Not only does the benevolent Dr. Lincoln run an inner-city telephone counseling center for troubled teens but he also operates a walk-in psychiatry clinic for the emotionally disturbed poor. As we know from numerous other TV shows, Los Angeles is filled with mentally imbalanced people, so Dr. Lincoln is kept pretty busy. Still he squeezes in some time to drive fancy sports cars and hang out at his beach pad.

The 1970 two-hour pilot for *Matt Lincoln* is called *Dial Hot Line,* where the good doctor has the much less messianic name of David Leopold.

**MAUDE (**) 30 min (141ep Color; 1972–1978 CBS) Situation Comedy** *with Beatrice Arthur as Maude Findlay, Bill Macy as Walter Finlay, Adrienne Barbeau as Carol Traynor, Conrad Bain as Dr. Arthur Harmon, Rue McClanahan as Vivian Harmon, Esther Rolle as Florida Evans, and Hermione Baddeley as Mrs. Nell Naugatuck*

As if to prove that stubborn, loud-mouthed, pigheadedness is not an exclusively conservative trait, there's Maude. The character was first presented on *All in the Family* as Edith's upper-class cousin from suburban New York (a liberal counterpart to Archie Bunker), and quickly won her own very successful spin-off series following the same formula: topical issues, a sharp tongue, and lots of confrontational comedy.

Frankly, over the long haul this one is a bit more wearying. For one thing, Beatrice Arthur makes Maude a much more overpowering figure than Archie Bunker, with the decibel level of the household much higher among the characters. And, though Maude may occasionally get her comeuppance, it's usually when someone (such as her divorced daughter Carol or her black maid Florida) catches her in a philosophical contradiction or a case of double standards. ("You claim to be a liberal, but then how could you . . . ?") Archie would just shrug his shoulders and say "So what?" but to Maude such things matter. Lucky thing, though, because otherwise there's simply not much standing in her way. Walter, Maude's fourth husband, is a good-hearted but weak man. Their conservative next-door neighbors (Arthur and Vivian) are just paper tigers. Only Carol and Florida (and later Mrs. Naugatuck, Florida's replacement) seem capable of scoring even minor points.

Unlike *All in the Family,* in which it is clear that Archie's ramblings are supposed to be considered wildly out of touch and ideologically incorrect (even if some fans embrace them as absolutely dead-on), Maude's dyed-in-the-wool liberalism is obviously considered acceptable to the writers, just occasionally taken to an extreme. Unfortunately, that noble stance takes some of the zip out of retorts directed toward her. Perhaps William F. Buckley should have been asked to turn out a few scripts. With stronger opponents, the charismatic Maude would stand as an even better character.

*Maude* had a very successful run in the 1970s, though in reruns the series suffers much more than *All in the Family* from its incessant topicality. Ironically, Beatrice Arthur decided to leave the series after five seasons just as the premise was reworked into a much better excuse for Maude's pet political polemics. In the final three episodes, Maude finds herself taking a seat in Congress and, with Walter in tow, moves to Washington to face the ultimate foe: the federal establishment. Now *that* would have been some battle. (The production company later attempted to rework the cast and new setting into a series without Maude. See *Hanging In* for details.)

Ultimately, *Maude* is best taken in limited doses, to be viewed chiefly as a warm-up for more successful vehicles for the main cast members. Esther Rolle won her own spin-off series, *Good Times,* for her character of Florida. Conrad Bain (neighbor Arthur Harmon) stayed rich but turned liberal as Philip Drummond on *Diff'rent Strokes.* And Rue McClanahan (Vivian Harmon) and Beatrice Arthur both hit their best series roles in the late 1980s with *The Golden Girls.*

**MAVERICK (****) 60 min (124ep B&W; 1957–1962 ABC) Western** *with James Garner as Bret Maverick, Jack Kelly as Bart Maverick, Roger Moore as Beau Maverick, and Robert Colbert as Brent Maverick*

Brothers Bret and Bart Maverick are true legends of the West, with the *Maverick* series a bona fide television classic. Created by Roy Huggins (after a season of producing *Cheyenne*), *Maverick* takes a fresh approach to the western genre, somewhere between kiddie shoot-em-ups and grim adult fare, emphasizing clever scripts, good humor, plenty of action, and engaging characters. In short, this type of package could work in a variety of settings (Huggins himself demonstrated this when producing the pilot to the *Maverick*-like *77 Sunset Strip*). However, the Old West backdrop is particularly well-suited to this style, using the traditional clear-cut good guy/bad guy confrontations as a jumping point for some sly twists on expectations.

Like most western heroes, Bret and Bart wander from town to town (usually in separate adventures). But that's where the resemblance ends. These are heroes of a different sort: not gun-toting marshal types or loners out to clean up the West—they're on the road to make a living as professional poker players. (Not gamblers, they would insist, because success at poker requires more skill than luck.) As such, they prefer to avoid gunfights, or anything else that might lead to death or injury. However, they both also suffer from a near fatal affection for underdogs in distress, especially if they happen to be pretty ladies. And so, inevitably, they find themselves helping someone out of a jam. Even here, though, they prefer to use their wits (and a sense of humor) to save the situation, all the while rationalizing their foolishness (or berating themselves) by quoting an aphorism or two from their "old Pappy."

The stories involving both Bret and Bart are the most fun, usually because there's a sense of competition between the two. One of the best of this type is "Maverick and Juliet," in which Bret convinces two feuding families to allow him to settle their longstanding conflict in a one-on-one poker match, only to discover that the player on the other side is brother Bart. "Pappy" is even better as we get to meet their much-quoted dad, as well as their uncle Beauregard (James Garner and Jack Kelly, respectively, in dual roles).

But the solo episodes are quite good, too. Some of Bart's standout stories include "Three Queens Full" (a *Bonanza* parody), "The Golden Fleecing" (a stock market sting), "The Wrecker" (a sea-based adventure adapted from a Robert Louis Stevenson story), and "Hadley's Hunters" (with cameo appearances by the leads from a half dozen other Warner Bros. series such as *Lawman, Cheyenne,* and even *77 Sunset Strip*).

In truth, though, the Bret episodes are generally the best, with producer Huggins doing some of his best work there. (He didn't do all the stories for both leads because there were two crews turning out episodes simultaneously—one of the reasons for having two brothers in the first place.) Among the many standouts are: "Rope of Cards" (a *Twelve Angry Men*–type story with Bret serving on a town jury), "Gun Shy" (a *Gunsmoke* parody), "The Ghost Soldiers" (Bret defends a fort from an Indian attack using just two soldiers), "A Fellow's Brother" (a hilarious tale of illogical western revenge), and "Greenbacks Unlimited" (a complicated money-switching game).

Though *Maverick* originally ran five seasons, James Garner played in only the first three, leaving the series in a contract dispute. (Roy Huggins also ended his involvement at the same time.) Warner Bros. decided to press on without Garner and cast Roger Moore as British-educated cousin Beauregard. It's too bad Garner and the studio never resolved their differences because Moore does a good job and it would have been fun to see Bret, Bart, and Beau together. (Actually, they all appear in a previous episode, "The Rivals," but Moore plays a different character there.)

Instead, Bart and Beau rarely team up ("Bundle from Britain" and "The Maverick Line" are two occasions), though Beau does have a few of his own typically *Maverick* moments. In "The Town That Wasn't There" he moves an entire town from one spot to another, while in "Bolt from the Blue" he finds himself caught in an *Alice in Wonderland*–style legal dispute that seems destined to leave him in the hangman's noose despite (perhaps because of) the best efforts of a young lawyer (played by guest Will Hutchins, better known as law student Tom Brewster on *Sugarfoot*).

At the time, though, Moore's contract with Warners was up, so the studio brought in yet another Maverick, Brent (played by Robert Colbert), who was dressed to look vaguely like Bret. The cheap substitute didn't work, with those stories being just typical grind-'em-out westerns. When the time came for a *Maverick* revival (beginning with the 1978 TV movie *The New Maverick* and the spin-off series, *Young Maverick*), Bret and Bart acknowledged the existence of Beau (he was young Ben Maverick's dad). However, Brent was mercifully left in oblivion.

After that one-season experiment, the studio decided to play *Maverick* out with a handful of new Bart episodes mixed with reruns of Bret and Bret/Bart team-ups. Surprisingly the new batch of Bart stories are fairly good, and easily identified in the rerun cycle because Jack Kelly's name comes first in the opening credits. Nonetheless, after that run, the series ended. Still the strength of the first three seasons and selected episodes thereafter easily qualify *Maverick* as one of the timeless classics of television.

In the 1980s, James Garner (and Roy Huggins) revived the Bret Maverick character (complete with references to and a guest shot by brother Bart) with the series *Bret Maverick.* Garner also brought that patented *Maverick* mix of practical heroics to other roles, both in feature films (such as *Support Your Local Sheriff,* and *The Americanization of Emily*) and in other series (such as *The Rockford Files*).

**MAX HEADROOM (***½) 60 min (12ep Color; 1987 ABC) Science Fiction** *with Matt Frewer as Edison Carter and Max Headroom, Amanda Pays as Theora Jones, Jeffrey Tambor as Murray, Chris Young as Bryce Lynch, George Coe as Ben Chaviot, William Morgan Sheppard as Blank Reg, Concetta Tomei as Dominique, and Charles Rocket as Grossberg*

Aptly subtitled "Twenty Minutes into the Future," *Max Headroom* is a superbly crafted science fiction series with excellent speculative tales, a caustic sense of humor, rich visual images, and an uncanny sense of the deep and often incestuous relationships between big business, television programmers, sponsors, newsrooms, and viewers. The main hook for the stories: investigative TV reporter Edison Carter (responsible for the popular "I Want To Know" segments on Network 23) and his alter ego, the ever-present video entity known as Max Headroom (a computer-generated character who exists only on screen).

Appropriately this elaborate setting was concocted as an after-the-fact explanation for a real-life television phenomenon in Britain. In 1985, the character of Max Headroom first turned up as the host of a pop music video show, with his screen-only image providing nonstop flip comments (complete with distinctive stutter). At first, background on Max was deliberately vague, with some suggestion that he was just a computer-generated creation. But soon the producers revealed the identity of the real-life actor playing the character (Matt Frewer). That was quickly followed by a one-hour origin tale, *Rebus: The Max Headroom Story,* which explained just where Max supposedly came from. This story (available in the United States on home video) is the prototype for the subsequent adventure series, establishing Max as a creature of the media-saturated future (a time far closer than we'd care to admit), emerging onscreen from the memory impulses of reporter Edison Carter. They are transferred there by boy genius Bryce Lynch, who attempts to use what he thinks will be merely a carbon copy of Carter's brain to retrieve some vital information. Instead, much to his surprise, the process results in a totally new entity with a mind and personality all its own. And why the name Max Headroom? Those were the last words Edison Carter read on a garage gate before crashing a motorcycle and landing in a coma: "Max Headroom, 2.3m." (Obviously, Edison recovers.)

In crossing over to America, Max the character once again preceded his history. He turned up as host to a talk show on a Cinemax cable service (Max on Cine*max,* so to speak), as a commercial spokesman, and even as a guest on other talk shows (such as *Late Night with David Letterman*). Unfortunately those forums tended to emphasize the more obnoxious aspects of the character, with Max coming off as a smug, self-absorbed smart aleck. Well, yes, maybe he is, but at least in the context of a science fiction adventure there's some perspective for his observations. In any event, in the spring of 1987, ABC launched a full-fledged *Max Headroom* drama series, beginning with a chillingly effective reworked version of the original *Rebus* episode.

The U.S. staging of the story recasts all but four roles (Max, Edison, Theora Jones, and Blank Reg), with excellent substitutions across the board. Jeffrey Tambor is particularly good as Edison's immediate supervisor in the newsroom (similar to his role as producer in *Studio 5B*), while Chris Young plays Bryce more as a naive innocent than as a creepy amoral brat. Of course, Amanda Pays had to be carried over for the series (as Edison's studio control contact)—anyone who could make sitting at a computer screen for most of an episode come off as exciting was irreplaceable!

There's also a bigger budget for special effects in the U.S. episodes, so the series has a very slick, very polished look, even as it presents a most depressing vision of a future fixated on television. While the junk-strewn industrial world seems to be coming apart at the seams, television remains the dominant force in everybody's life, with audience measurements taken every second and the major network services desperately competing for any advantage. And that's what leads to the desperate cover-up of the opening tale: the secret side effect of Network 23's blipverts (ads that run by so fast you don't have a chance to change the channel). What happens? Well, you've heard the stories about drying a cat in a microwave oven . . .

Ultimately, of course, what makes this series work is that despite all the clever science fiction trappings, Edison Carter is there to hold the episodes together as old-fashioned investigative reporter adventures. Though the plots are sometimes as convoluted as a Raymond Chandler novel, they do ultimately sort themselves out. And, if the downbeat backdrop seems a bit depressing, don't worry—each episode is peppered with just enough appearances by the irrepressible Max to lighten the tone (but not so many that he becomes as annoying as his cola commercials). You have to wonder, though, if ABC had any idea what it was buying into. At the end of the first episode, for instance, Max poses the following question: How do you know when our network president is lying? Answer: His lips move. (Of course, we all know Max is really referring to *Network 23,* and not implying anything about the contemporary commercial networks.)

Definitely ke-ke-ke-keep an eye out for this one. ■

**MAYA (**½) 60 min (18ep Color; 1967–1968 NBC) Adventure** *with Jay North as Terry Bowen, Sajid Khan as Raji, and Marvin Miller as narrator.*

Shot entirely on location in India, *Maya* is a nice, simple adventure show that kids can enjoy. The two lead characters are both fourteen-year-old boys. Terry is an American searching for his hunter father who is presumed dead. Raji is an Indian orphan who ran off with his elephant Maya in order to save the huge beast from a life of forced labor. Terry and Raji team up to roam the subcontinent and become involved in numerous adventures.

Jay North, who plays Terry, is best known as the precocious Dennis (the Menace) Mitchell.

**MAYBERRY R.F.D.** **(see *The Andy Griffith Show*)**

**THE MAYOR OF CASTERBRIDGE (**½) 60 min (7ep Color; 1978 UK BBC) Drama** *with Alan Bates as Michael Henchard, Janet Maw as Elizabeth-Jane, Anne Stallybrass as Susan, Jack Galloway as Donald Farfrae, Joe Ritchie as Buzzford, and Ronald Lacey as Jopp*

More of writer Thomas Hardy's vision of a bizarre (even grotesque) world hidden within the seemingly benign settings of Victorian times. In this case, there's also fateful retribution hovering over the main character, Mayor Michael Henchard, for a transgression from his past. And it's a lulu. Early in his marriage an ale-soaked Henchard auctions off his wife and young daughter to a sailor at a county fair. By the time Henchard comes to his senses, he has absolutely no idea where they are, or even if they're still alive. Distraught and ashamed, he leaves the area and starts rebuilding his life as a successful businessman and eventually as mayor of the town of Casterbridge, which is where fate has some nasty surprises in store for him. A well-paced adaptation of the novel, with Alan Bates particularly strong in the lead role.

**MCCLAIN'S LAW (**) 60 min (16ep Color; 1981–1982 NBC) Police Drama** *with James Arness as Det. Jim McClain, Marshall Colt as Det. Harry Gates, George DiCenzo as Lt. Edward DeNisco, Carl Franklin as Det. Jerry Cross, and Conchata Ferrell as Vangie Cruise*

After almost twenty-five years of playing the lead in TV westerns (*Gunsmoke, How the West Was Won*), James Arness tries out the modern era, this time as Jim McClain, an old cop. McClain had left the San Pedro, California, police force at age thirty-nine due to a leg injury. Thirteen years later, after his fishing buddy is killed and the police can't seem to get very far in cracking the case, McClain gets himself reinstated to the force in order to track down his pal's murderer.

The basic conflict in *McClain's Law* is between the old-fashioned rough-'em-up philosophy of McClain and the modern scientific methods of McClain's young hunk partner Harry Gates. McClain's superior, Lt. DeNisco, isn't too wild about McClain's tactics either, but, hey, he gets results.

James Arness is a bit too grumpy here, but he is always fun to watch.

**MCCLOUD (**½) 2 hr & 90 min & 60 min (45ep: twenty 2 hr & nineteen 90 min & six 60 min & 2 hr pilot Color; 1970–1977 NBC) Police Drama** *with Dennis Weaver as Sam McCloud, J. D. Cannon as Peter Clifford, Terry Carter as Sgt. Joe Broadhurst, and Diana Muldaur as Chris Coughlin*

The image is incongruous enough to win over any big-city dweller: a lawman dressed in cowboy boots, sheepskin jacket, and cowboy hat riding through the streets of New York on horseback, in pursuit of his quarry. That may not be doing things by the book, but it sure looks like a lot more fun.

A sense of amusement is the key to *McCloud*'s success. Dennis Weaver brings off the part with just the right combination of western swagger and out-of-town innocence. As Deputy Marshal Sam McCloud (from Taos, New Mexico), he first turns up in New York City (in the 1970 pilot film) with a subpoenaed witness, but soon finds himself drawn into a complex murder and kidnapping plot. When the saddle dust clears from that one, he's on temporary assignment to Manhattan's 27th Precinct, ostensibly to study big-city law enforcement methods, but in reality to show the folks in the Big Apple just how it's done. Actually the stories themselves are rather standard cop show stuff, even though the program's producers and writers (such as *The Fall Guy*'s Glen A. Larson and *Columbo*'s Dean Hargrove) inevitably attempt a touch of humor in most of them. No matter what the plot, there's always McCloud. Through it all he never sheds his trademark outfit, always follows his own instincts, and consistently leaves his nominal local superior, Police Chief Peter Clifford, shaking his head in frustrated wonder.

That formula carried *McCloud* through seven years, always alternating with several other series under some umbrella title (*Four-in-One* for the sixty-minute episodes, the various NBC *Mystery Movie* slots for the rest). Afterward, the *McCloud* stories began turning up on their own as a rerun package, though the variation in the running times does make it difficult to place the series in a regular rerun slot. You'll probably end up finding *McCloud* on an irregular basis, most often warming some two-hour TV movie slot.

**MCCOY (**) 90 min & 2 hr (4ep: two 90 min & two 2 hr & 90 min pilot Color; 1975–1976 NBC) Adventure** *with Tony Curtis as McCoy, Roscoe Lee Browne as Gideon Gibbs, and Lucille Meredith as Lucy*

Following on the successful heels of the hit theatrical film *The Sting,* Tony Curtis stars as a professional Robin Hood–style con man who makes quite a comfortable living out of bilking bad guys of their ill-gotten gains. Not only does McCoy get back the money taken from his latest client but there's also a little something extra in it for him—plus the satisfaction of delivering a well-deserved "sting" as punishment. Curtis is very good in the lead role, with able support from Roscoe Lee Browne as his confederate (and part-time nightclub comedian). The stories and production are also strong (from *Columbo* associates Dean Hargrove and Roland Kibbee), except . . . the stories are far, far too long. This series should have been an hour-long one, tops. Instead, because it originally aired in one of NBC's *Mystery Movie* slots, the tales were stretched to ninety minutes or even two hours. The ninety-minute pilot is called *The Big Payoff* and often turns up in regular movie slots.

**MCGARRETT** **(see *Hawaii Five-O*)**

**MCHALE'S NAVY (**½) (138ep & 60 min pilot B&W & Colorized; 1962–1966 ABC) Situation Comedy** *with Ernest Borgnine as Lt. Cdr. Quinton McHale, Joe Flynn as Capt. Wallace Binghamton, Tim Conway as Ensign Charles Parker, Bob Hastings as Lt. Elroy Carpenter, Carl Ballantine as Lester Gruber, Billy Sands as Harrison "Tinker" Bell, Yoshio Yoda as Fuji Kobiaji, Edson Stroll as Virgil Edwards, Gavin MacLeod as Happy Haines, and Jay Novello as Major Mario Lugatto*

World War II may be in progress, but that doesn't stop Lt. Commander Quinton McHale and his men from taking the opportunity to enjoy themselves. After all, how many times in their lives will they be paid by the U.S. Navy to live on a beautiful island in the South Seas? They're even apart from the main military contingent because as a top flight P.T. boat crew, they have to be ready to spring into action at a moment's notice. In the meantime, they gamble, drink, eat gourmet food, and hatch money-making schemes. About the only negatives they have to face are life-threatening missions against the Japanese fleet, and the ire of their base commander, Captain Binghamton. Of the two, Binghamton (nicknamed "Old Lead Bottom") is the bigger pain.

Unlike Colonel Hall on *The Phil Silvers Show,* (spiritual ancestor to *McHale's Navy*), Binghamton does not see any reason to indulge the irresponsible behavior of McHale and his men. For starters, Binghamton honestly dislikes and resents McHale. So whenever there's an opportunity to catch him in some punishable act, Captain Binghamton and his number one assistant, the obsequious Lieutenant Elroy Carpenter, are there to try. Fortunately for McHale and his men, the two are so completely incompetent that they're more an irritant than a threat. In fact, what usually gets McHale and his crew into trouble is their own self-indulgence, kind hearts, or misfired schemes, with Binghamton merely serving as a convenient plot device ("We've got to get things back in shape before Old Lead Bottom arrives!"). Fortunately for McHale, with a wartime setting there's always salvation in the standard service comedy bail-out device: heroics against the enemy. Just when it looks as if they're really nailed this time, the *P.T. 73* can sink a few key vessels in the Japanese fleet and all will be fine again.

With such standard war-comedy plots, the chief reason to follow *McHale's Navy* over the long haul is for the interaction between protagonists McHale and Binghamton, assisted by their number one aides (Ensign Parker and Carpenter). When Parker, McHale, Binghamton, and Carpenter go at it, they essentially carry the episodes with their scheming, sputtering, misunderstandings, grimaces, and groans. Of all the characters, though, Tim Conway's bumbling and naive Ensign Parker probably steals the show most often with his deadpan stumbling and well-timed double takes. In fact, for the second theatrical feature film based on the television series (*McHale's Navy Joins the Air Force,* released in 1965), Ernest Borgnine did not even appear, turning over the reins of the *P.T. 73* to Conway. (The previous year's theatrical film, *McHale's Navy,* does feature the entire crew, including Borgnine.)

In what must rank as one of television's sillier sitcom premise shifts, the final season of *McHale's Navy* takes place on the European front, with the entire cast joining the Allied operations in Italy. Oddly these episodes have a perverse charm of their own because the writers and producers have clearly thrown overboard any pretense of reality. In the other direction, the one-hour comedy/drama pilot for *McHale's Navy* first played in the spring of 1962 on *Alcoa Premiere* as "Seven Against the Sea," with Borgnine and Joe Flynn starring.

After *McHale's Navy,* Conway and Flynn worked together on the short-lived 1970 sitcom, *The Tim Conway Show,* and both turn up in various Walt Disney feature film comedies.

**MCKEEVER AND THE COLONEL** **(*) 30 min (26ep B&W; 1962–1963 NBC) Situation Comedy** *with Scott Lane as Cadet Gary McKeever, Allyn Joslyn as Col. Harvey Blackwell, Jackie Coogan as Sgt. Barnes, Elizabeth Fraser as Mrs. Warner, Keith Taylor as Tubby Anderson, and Johnny Eimen as Monk*

Proof positive that longevity on the rerun circuit bears no relation to artistic quality. *McKeever and the Colonel* is silly and mediocre and never was a hit before or after its original run, yet it has been filling the off-hours of numerous TV stations for almost three decades.

McKeever is a rambunctious preteen cadet at Westfield Academy, a boys' military school. The colonel is the exasperated school commander. The usual youthful high jinks ensue, with highly predictable results. Look for Sgt. Barnes, the colonel's aide, who is played by Jackie Coogan, better known as Uncle Fester of *The Addams Family.*

**THE MCLEAN STEVENSON SHOW** **(*½) 30 min (13ep Color; 1976–1977 NBC) Situation Comedy** *with McLean Stevenson as Mac Ferguson, Barbara Stuart as Peggy Ferguson, Madge West as Muriel "Gram," Ayn Ruymen as Janet, and Steve Nevil as Chris Ferguson*

It is difficult to keep track of the many short-lived series McLean Stevenson appeared in after his stint as Henry Blake on *M*A*S*H,* but this show is the first of the bunch. Stevenson plays Mac Ferguson, a harried suburban guy who runs a hardware store in Evanston, Illinois (home of Stevenson's alma mater, Northwestern University). The Ferguson household is full of familiar TV characters. First there is Mac's boring wife Peggy and Peggy's pushy mother Muriel. Next comes Mac and Peggy's two grown children: son Chris, who can't seem to "find" himself and has turned the basement into a bachelor pad, and recently divorced daughter Janet, who moved back in with the folks along with her two sons. This congestion would tend to make one long for the peace and quiet of a Korean War mobile surgical unit.

**MCMILLAN AND WIFE** **(***) 90 min & 2 hr (39ep: twenty-four 90 min & fifteen 2 hr Color; 1971–1976 NBC) Mystery** *with Rock Hudson as Commissioner Stewart McMillan, Susan Saint James as Sally McMillan, John Schuck as Sgt. Charles Enright, and Nancy Walker as Mildred,* **MCMILLAN** **(**) 90 min (6ep Color; 1976–1977 NBC) Mystery** *with Rock Hudson as Commissioner Stewart McMillan, Martha Raye as Agatha, Richard Gilliland as Sgt. Steve DiMaggio, and Gloria Stroock as Maggie*

Stewart McMillan ("Mac") and Sally, his wife, are a happily married sleuthing pair in the proud tradition of such couples as Nick and Nora Charles (of the *Thin Man* books, theatrical films, and TV series of the 1940s and 1950s). The reason for Mac's interest in mysteries is obvious: He's the police commissioner of San Francisco. Sally has an even better excuse: She feels like it. With her intuition and Mac's professional training, it's only a matter of time before they crack the toughest cases.

Not that the specific crimes matter all that much. The real draw here is character interaction, with Sally and Mac mixing talk of mystery and murder with plans for everyday activities like grocery shopping, vacations, and social events. Their best conversations take place in bed, with the lights still on and their minds clicking away. Sally usually asks most of the questions, in what Susan Saint James later laughingly noted as the writers' chance to review the story and clues to that point. These scenes are a lot of fun because they offer a rare view of an affectionate married couple sharing each other's company in an intimate setting without sex.

There are also two excellent supporting characters, one at home, the other at the office. John Schuck's Sergeant Enright is the sweet, occasionally naive, but always well-meaning assistant to the commissioner, who dutifully follows his assigned task as second banana. He reaches premature conclusions, provides unexpected inspiration, but never is the one to knowingly crack the case ahead of the star. Nancy Walker's role as Mildred, housekeeper to the McMillans, offers more opportunities to steal a few scenes. She's brash, outspoken, curious about everything, and a genial and fun-loving home companion for Sally, often effectively prodding her interest in Mac's latest case.

During its original run in the 1970s, this series (along with *Columbo*) virtually defined the *Mystery Movie* slot produced by Universal Studios for NBC: mysteries done with style. As such, it also shares the chief fault of this format, a tendency to pad the two-hour episodes with everything from pointless car chases (more pointless than usual) to more enjoyable self-indulgent character digressions (Mac takes out the garbage). Unfortunately, when these episodes are cut for rerun slots, the "irrelevant" character scenes are sometimes trimmed in favor of including all the "necessary" action and plot details.

After a successful five-year run, Susan Saint James, Nancy Walker, and John Schuck left the program (the latter two for their own separate series, Saint James to do movies), so it was rewritten into a Rock Hudson solo vehicle. Mac becomes a widower (Sally dies in a plane crash), with a new housekeeper (Agatha, Mildred's sister), a new dim-witted assistant (Sgt. DiMaggio), and a Sally substitute (Maggie, Mac's secretary). Far too many key figures are removed from the original mix, so the short-run *McMillan* series doesn't have the same entertaining bounce.

**MCNAUGHTON'S DAUGHTER (*½) 60 min (3ep & 2 hr pilot Color; 1976 NBC) Crime Drama** *with Susan Clark as Laurel McNaughton, James Callahan as Lou Farragut, Ricardo Montalban as Charles Quintero, and John Elerick as Ed Hughes*

Future *Webster* mom Susan Clark and Ricardo Montalban right before he became *Fantasy Island*'s Mr. Roarke play (respectively) a deputy D. A. and D. A. in this short-lived crime drama. The pilot film turns up most often, sometimes under the title "Try to Catch a Saint," referring to their case in that first outing: attempting to prove a highly respected religious leader killed her young lover. Nothing special.

**ME AND MAXX (½) 30 min (9ep Color; 1980 NBC) Situation Comedy** *with Joe Santos as Norman Davis, Melissa Michaelsen as Maxx Davis, Jenny Sullivan as Barbara, and Jim Weston as Mitch Russell*

Cute, precocious kids pop up like weeds throughout TV history, and Maxx Davis is another of that ilk. She is the eleven-year-old daughter of Norman Davis, a swinging single who dumped his wife and baby eleven years ago when the pressure of impending fatherhood clouded his sunny view of life. After a decade of the stag life, Norman's lifestyle is rudely interrupted when his ex-wife decides to walk out on Maxx as well (to taste the good life of unfettered singles) and dumps Maxx back in Norman's lap.

Norman doesn't really like having Maxx around his pad and Maxx is understandably not wild about being shuttled between parents like a medicine ball. She is also not very appreciative of the swift exit her dad performed when she came into the world. *Me and Maxx* follows the painfully mawkish efforts of father and daughter to coexist, perchance to love.

Joe Santos was much better and more likable as Det. Dennis Becker, the police contact on *The Rockford Files. Me and Maxx*'s producer, James Komack, showed better judgment in *Chico and the Man* and *Welcome Back, Kotter.*

**ME AND MRS. C (½) 30 min (11ep & 30 min pilot Color; 1986–1987 NBC) Situation Comedy** *with Peg Murray as Ethel "Mrs. C" Conklin, Misha McK as Gerri Kilgore, Gary Bayer as Ethan Conklin, and Ellen Regan as Kathleen Conklin*

Perhaps around the turn of the century *Me and Mrs. C* may be a cult classic, one of the worst shows of the 1980s. Until then it just gets logged as a real dog. Gerri Kilgore is "me," a twenty-two-year-old black female college grad who is an ex-con. Ethel Conklin is Mrs. C, a sixty-two-year-old white widowed woman. Mrs. C needs some income, so she rents a room in her house to Gerri. Mrs. C's family thinks she's nuts. Mrs. C doesn't care, and she and Gerri sort of hit it off and become buddies. Nobody in this show resembles anybody you ever met. Hopefully, *Me and Mrs. C* will drift into the oblivion it so richly deserves.

The pilot episode is from 1984, and has a totally different cast and the character names are slightly different.

**ME AND MOM (*) 60 min (6ep Color; 1985 ABC) Detective Drama** *with Lisa Eilbacher as Kate Morgan, Holland Taylor as Zena Hunnicutt, James Earl Jones as Lou Garfield, and Henry Darrow as Lt. Rojas*

Kate Morgan is a beautiful young criminologist. Zena Hunnicutt (presumably no relation to *M*A*S*H*'s B. J. Hunnicut) is Kate's effervescent socialite mother. Lou Garfield is a tough black ex-cop. What else would these three characters do other than team up to run a private-eye business? Only in TV-land. James Earl Jones should have known better.

**ME AND THE CHIMP (½) 30 min (13ep Color; 1972 CBS) Situation Comedy** *with Ted Bessell as Mike Reynolds, Anita Gillette as Liz Reynolds, Scott Kolden as Scott Reynolds, Kami Cotler as Kitty Reynolds, and Jackie as Buttons*

This low-water mark in western civilization is an early creation of Garry Marshall, who later redeemed himself with *Happy Days* and *Laverne and Shirley,* both of which are Shakespeare compared to *Me and the Chimp.* Mike Reynolds is a suburban dentist with a beautiful wife, a nice home, and two cute kids. The kids find a chimpanzee in the park and talk dad into adopting it as a household pet. Apparently a refugee from some military experiment involving primates, the monkey does one thing very well: It presses buttons (hence its name, Buttons). This proclivity for pushing buttons gets everyone into trouble over and over again in this show that brings back painful memories of another simian-based series, the dreaded early 1960s program *The Hathaways.*

Ted Bessell, who endured five years playing Marlo Thomas's boyfriend on *That Girl,* grits his teeth and toughs out the silly role as Mike Reynolds. Daughter Kitty is played by Kami Cotler, who went on to far better things as Elizabeth Walton on *The Waltons.*

**MEDIC (**½) 30 min (60ep B&W; 1954–1956 NBC) Medical Drama** *with Richard Boone as Dr. Konrad Styner*

This is serious drama, mid-1950s style, bridging the stylistic gap between an anthology program and a series with continuing characters. Richard Boone appears in every episode as Dr. Konrad Styner, both the narrator and a character in the series. However, the stories focus primarily on the guest stars, with scripts based on actual case histories (just as *Dragnet* drew its script ideas from real-life police files). But *Medic* goes one step further than Jack Webb's classic and uses footage shot at real hospitals, often including real doctors and nurses for some of the roles. The result is a fictional drama series with trappings of a documentary.

In its original airing, *Medic* was a highly praised venture, focusing on doctors as brave men in white, delivering babies, treating the sick, and comforting the elderly. The scripts are well done, drawing on some excellent writers of the era, including Worthington Miner, Gene L. Coon, and James Moser (who created *Ben Casey* half a decade later). However, today it often comes off as too solemn and dated (back then it was a big deal just to mention a few of the diseases), with some of the "realistic" portrayals of the profession a bit naive, even in comparison to *Ben Casey*—and it's a universe away from the underfunded anarchy of St. Eligius on *St. Elsewhere.* This was Richard Boone's first starring role, but you'll probably enjoy him much more dressed in black as Paladin on *Have Gun, Will Travel.* ■

**MEDICAL CENTER (**½) 60 min (170ep & 2 hr pilot Color; 1969–1976 CBS) Medical Drama** *with Chad Everett as Dr. Joe Gannon, James Daly as Dr. Paul Lochner, Jayne Meadows as Nurse Chambers, Chris Huston as Nurse Courtland, and Barbara Baldavin as Nurse Holmby*

Dr. Kildare had his Dr. Gillespie, Dr. Casey his Dr. Zorba, so in *Medical Center* Dr. Gannon has his Dr. Lochner. It seems as if all medical-related series must revolve around the dynamics of a Young Turk versus Old Sage relationship. Doing so allows the primary focus to be on a young, handsome, eligible physician who can appeal to the dramatic, while the background can be filled by experience, caution, and knowledge, the concepts our public mythology reserves for the medical profession.

This same synthesis is at the heart of *Medical Center,* a resilient series that ties *Marcus Welby, M. D.* as the longest-running TV medical show. Set in the University Medical Center in Los Angeles, the program is a straightforward collection of weekly traumas and crises. Dr. Gannon is the youngish professor of surgery, dealing with the day-to-day life and death decisions, while Dr. Lochner is the chief of staff, supervising the administration of the hospital. Other doctors come and go, nurses decorate the scene, but Gannon and Lochner remain the primary focus.

*Medical Center* is done well (as befits its long run) and fills an hour admirably. Its fault is that it rarely strays from the serious, moral tone believed to be required for medical series. There is some grudging nod to modern times by having Dr. Gannon head a student health service, in order to drag in the early 1970s concern with youth rebellion, but it would not be until the 1980s *St. Elsewhere* that TV would finally let its hair down in medical shows and present physicians as something close to human.

The 1969 pilot for *Medical Center* is called both *U.M.C.* and *Operation Heartbeat,* and has Richard Bradford in the Dr. Gannon role filled by Chad Everett in the regular series.

**MEDICAL STORY (**½) 60 min (13ep Color; 1975–1976 NBC) Medical Anthology**

Television traditionally paints doctors in a pure white light, to reaffirm the trust the average person wants to feel for those who literally have a life or death say in their lives. *Medical Story* is a valiant effort to add nuances of color to that bright white light, by presenting unconnected stories about doctors that show them to be plagued by the same human failings we all share. Partly due to the unwieldy anthology format (rather unusual for the mid-1970s) and partly due to this revisionist view of the medical profession, *Medical Story* did not garner much attention in its original run. This is a pity, for it is a fine piece of work by two quality producers, David Gerber and Abby Mann. Gerber had already had some success painting policemen in a more realistic light in *Police Story.* Mann was one of the top writers from the 1950s era of live TV drama (*Studio One* and *Playhouse 90*), who later produced a respected gritty portrait of blue-collar life in America (*Skag*).

**MEET CORLISS ARCHER (*½) 30 min (39ep B&W; 1954–1955 Syndication) Situation Comedy** *with Ann Baker as Corliss Archer, John Eldridge as Harry Archer, Mary Bain as Janet Archer, Bobby Ellis as Dexter Franklin, and Hy Averback as narrator*

This is actually the second TV version of a successful (1943–1955) network radio series that was based on *Kiss and Tell,* a play by F. Hugh Herbert. The original TV *Meet Corliss Archer* aired live in 1951 and 1952. This syndicated version features only one actor from the video original, Bobby Ellis, who plays Corliss's boyfriend Dexter.

Corliss Archer is a rambunctious teenage girl who is going through all the innocent fun and frolic of puberty in the era before sex, drugs, and rock'n'roll. Producer/narrator Hy Averback later handled equally light and frothy material such as *F Troop* and *The Dukes of Hazzard.*

**MEET MCGRAW (**) 30 min (39ep & 60 min pilot B&W; 1957–1958 NBC) Detective Drama** *with Frank Lovejoy as McGraw*

*Meet McGraw* is as basic and simple a detective series as you could ask for. The only continuing character, McGraw, has no first name, not much of a past, and no real friends or lovers. As he puts it, all McGraw does is go around "minding other people's business" . . . for a price, you understand. No frills, no psychodrama. Just bare-knuckles snooping.

The hour-long pilot, from a 1954 episode of *Four Star Playhouse,* establishes that the mysterious McGraw is an ex-con. Not much else is known about the man.

**MEET MR. MCNUTLEY** **(see *The Ray Milland Show*)**

**MEETING OF MINDS (***) 60 min (12ep Color; 1977–1981 PBS) Interview** *with Steve Allen as host*

When the Monty Python comedy troupe wanted to spoof

celebrity quiz shows, they pretended to have Karl Marx match wits with Nikolai Lenin on questions concerning English soccer championships. In *Meeting of Minds,* Steve Allen spices up the staid format of celebrity talk shows (a format he helped define in the original *Tonight* show of the 1950s). Allen pretends to have a few of the greatest minds of history meet to exchange ideas with each other around a living room table. It sounds like an idea as funny as the Python skit, but *Meeting of Minds* works as serious dramatic fare. You might say this format is *My Dinner with Moses,* or, more correctly, *My Dinner with Moses, Ben Franklin, Genghis Khan and Cleopatra.*

The setting is outside of time, in that all of the characters know that they are dead and are aware of a fair amount of world history that occurred since their individual eras. Each character is dressed in a period outfit and, conveniently, speaks English. Allen, the moderator, is a man of the present time, who handles his famous guests the same way he handled up-and-coming politicians on the *Tonight* show, that is, he combines respectful questioning with typically Allen-esque witty remarks.

This program has virtually no production budget. All the action is verbal and takes place around a single round table. All the money apparently went into historical research (one of the few TV shows that can make that claim). The historical figures speak almost exclusively in words taken from their own writings or speeches, modified a bit to sound more conversational. Sure, it is a history lesson with sugar coating, but this show is one of the best produced, most efficiently budgeted history lessons on TV.

The only real problem is that almost every female historical character is played by Allen's wife, Jayne Meadows. She's a fine actress, but it may strike you as odd to have Cleopatra look a lot like Betsy Ross.

**MEL & SUSAN TOGETHER (*) 30 min (13ep Color; 1978 ABC) Musical-Variety** *with Mel Tillis and Susan Anton*

This series demonstrates how low the variety format had sunk on TV by the late 1970s. Mel Tillis, the popular stuttering country and western singer, is teamed up with tall, blond goddess Susan Anton, who at the time the series was produced was known to the public only for doing sexy ads for Muriel cigars. She had never acted in anything of substance and had never released a record. Tillis, well-known in the South and West, certainly was not renowned enough nationally to be identified just by his first name. Anton was not known by anybody, and certainly not by her first name only. There was no obvious (or hidden) connection between Tillis and Anton that warranted teaming them up. So calling the show *Mel and Susan Together* conveyed absolutely no information to viewers.

Tillis sings songs; Anton stands around looking beautiful. That's it. This mistake is a production of the singing Osmond Brothers.

**MELBA (**) 30 min (6ep Color; 1986 CBS) Situation Comedy** *with Melba Moore as Melba Patterson, Gracie Harrison as Susan Slater, Barbara Meek as Rose, Jamilla Perry as Tracy Patterson, and Lou Jacobi as Jack*

Singer Melba Moore's short-lived sitcom vehicle comes with one of those "high-concept" hooks: Melba plays a black woman (named Melba) with a white sister, Gracie. Well, that's to get your attention. It turns out Melba's mom, Rose, worked as a housekeeper at the Slater home when the two women were girls and she ended up raising them both as her adopted "soul sisters." (Wouldn't it have been easier to say Melba has a close friend who happens to be white and get on with it?) Anyway, Melba is now grown, divorced (with a nine-year-old daughter, Tracy), the director of the Manhattan Visitors Center, and living with Rose. Unfortunately, it's standard stuff (the opener: Melba needs a date for an important social function so she attends a singles party), not giving Moore much of a chance to make her mark outside the musical-variety circles.

**THE MEN 60 min (24ep Color; 1972–1973 ABC)** This is the umbrella title for three unrelated series: *Assignment: Vienna, Jigsaw,* and *Delphi Bureau.* See each title for details.

**MEN (**½) 60 min (6ep Color; 1989 ABC) Drama** *with Ted Wass as Dr. Steven Ratajkowski, Ving Rhames as Charlie Hazard, Saul Rubinek as Paul Armas, Tom O'Brien as Danny McDaniel, Kimberley Pistone as Lisa, Candy Ann Brown as Margaret, and Steve Brinder as Harvey*

A small group of thirty-ish men in Baltimore, mostly members of a 1971 championship high school football team, keep in touch through weekly "men only" poker games. In the opener, one of the gang, policeman Thomas McDaniel, is killed trying to nab a thief spotted as the game broke up. McDaniel's hot-headed younger brother Danny, also a cop, takes Thomas's spot in the poker fraternity. The other regulars consist of black lawyer Charlie Hazard (happily married with two daughters), Jewish newspaper columnist Paul Armas (divorced and heartbroken that his wife plans to remarry), and Polish surgeon Steven Ratajkowski (a rakish womanizer who plays the saxophone). *Men* may be somewhat soapy in its plot complications, but the theme of old chums trying to stay friends as their lives diverge is appealing. The production (from Steve Brown, formerly of *Cagney & Lacey*) is intelligent and well crafted.

**MEN AT LAW (*) 60 min (10ep Color; 1971 CBS) Law Drama** *with Robert Foxworth as David Hansen, Sheila Larken as Deborah Sullivan, David Arkin as*

*Gabriel Kay, and Gerald S. O'Loughlin as Devlin McNeil*

Actually just a slapdash revision of the series *Storefront Lawyers, Men at Law* takes the three totally committed, completely involved young lawyers who staffed the inner-city legal aid office of *Storefront Lawyers* and places them in the more realistic world of a large, downtown law firm. No longer able to devote all their time to noble causes, the three legal eagles chafe under the supervision of Devlin McNeil, the senior partner in the firm who tries to keep the youngster's feet on the ground.

While *Storefront Lawyers* was ludicrous in its plastic air of "relevancy," the revised version, *Men at Law,* is merely preachy. The series should have been put out of its misery before the metamorphosis.

**THE MEN FROM SHILOH** **(see *The Virginian*)**

**MEN IN CRISES (**) 30 min (32ep B&W; 1964–1965 Syndication) Documentary** *with Edmond O'Brien as host/narrator*

An early effort by producer Alan Landsburg (*That's Incredible!, In Search Of . . .*), this series traces great decisions by great leaders of the twentieth century.

**MEN INTO SPACE (*½) 30 min (38ep B&W; 1959–1960 CBS) Science Fiction** *with William Lundigan as Col. Edward McCauley, Angie Dickinson and Joyce Taylor as Mary McCauley, and Charles Herbert as Peter McCauley*

One of the least-known examples of network science fiction fare in the 1950s, *Men into Space* represents a noble but ultimately self-defeating purpose. The goal of this show is to take space travel *seriously.* That means no evil geniuses ruling the asteroids, no bug-eyed monsters devouring Cleveland, and no seductive Venusians sapping our national strength. Instead we get square-jawed American hero Col. Ed McCauley, part of the U.S. Space Service in the near future, hopscotching the solar system in search of knowledge. The object is to present stories dealing with problems the scientists of the late 1950s foresaw as the real problems future space explorers would face.

This semidocumentary concept (reminiscent of *Science Fiction Theater*) seems admirable at first blush, but on long range reflection it is boring. Who wants to see thirty minutes of tests on the effects of weightlessness? Bring on the nasty aliens and the death rays!

The somewhat hidden problem with *Men into Space* is the "assistance" supplied by the U.S. Defense Department. Much as the "guidance" of J. Edgar Hoover to *The F.B.I.* dulled the exciting aspects of that crime series, the government's position in approving the scripts for *Men into Space* assured a bland, boring series more suited for the classroom than prime time. The series was produced soon after the start of the US-USSR "space race" and it reeks of government propaganda for funding American efforts in space.

Another problem with *Men into Space* is the lack of a real cast. Col. McCauley is really the only continuing character seen very much. It would help to have him be a Capt. Kirk type, commanding a crew of regulars. Angie Dickinson makes a brief appearance in the early episodes as Mrs. Col. McCauley, dutiful 1950s hausfrau to the busy space man.

**MEN OF ANNAPOLIS (*) 30 min (39ep B&W; 1957 Syndication) Drama Anthology** *with Art Gilmore as narrator*

The Ziv studio, the most prominent TV syndicator in the 1950s, followed up its success at *West Point* with equal time for the naval branch of our armed services. *Men of Annapolis* dramatizes the lives of the midshipmen at the naval academy in Maryland. The Navy helped produce the series, which explains some of its stilted tone.

**MIAMI UNDERCOVER (*) 30 min (38ep B&W; 1961 Syndication) Detective Drama** *with Lee Bowman as Jeff Thompson and Rocky Graziano as Rocky*

Private eye Jeff Thompson is hired by the Miami Hotel Owners Association to pose as a rich dilettante in order to flush out "undesirables" who might give the southern Florida city a nasty reputation among tourists. Former middleweight boxing champ Rocky Graziano serves as sidekick. The more innocent and pre-Latinized Miami in this low-budget show is quite a bit different from the city seen in *Miami Vice.*

**MIAMI VICE (***) 60 min (111ep & 2 hr pilot Color; 1984–1989 NBC) Police Drama** *with Don Johnson as Det. James "Sonny" Crockett, Philip Michael Thomas as Det. Ricardo Tubbs, Edward James Olmos as Lt. Martin Castillo, Saundra Santiago as Det. Gina Navarro Calabrese, Olivia Brown as Det. Trudy Joblin, and Michael Talbott as Det. Stan Switek*

What could possibly be more appropriate to say about a TV show that best symbolizes the 1980s than it is a triumph of style over substance? From an era when selling the sizzle and not the steak was first raised to an art form, *Miami Vice* presents some style amidst the squealing tire formulas of the TV cop show format.

On the surface, *Miami Vice* appears to be simply another rogue cop program. Sonny Crockett is one more member of the long line of TV cops who work underground, by their own rules, fighting the system while *being* part of the system. Crockett, white, somewhat redneck, is teamed up with black, urban, refined ex–New York City cop Ricardo Tubbs. The duo operates under the supervision of the intensely serious Latin lieutenant, Martin Castillo, thereby covering most of the major ethnic bases in southern Florida. Together Crockett and Tubbs roam the Miami area pursuing nefarious criminals, while Lt. Castillo fumes about the pair's unorthodox style.

From this angle, *Miami Vice* is simply an updated, more ethnic version of *Starsky & Hutch,* though with far more modern sensibilities and feel. The series drags TV cops out of the 1970s mind-set of focusing on Mafia mobsters and crazed urban psychos, and ushers the genre into the 1980s by usually concentrating on drugs. Here the druggies are not the garden variety pothead that used to turn up on *Dragnet,* but rather a seemingly endless parade of immensely powerful drug lords whose far-flung operations make them virtually unstoppable. Crockett and Tubbs track down their share of bigwigs (and a lot more medium wigs), but the theme here is that the men behind the drugs have infiltrated our society far too cleverly to be eradicated by just a cop or two. The resulting sense is one of almost hopeless futility, with Crockett, Tubbs, Castillo, and maybe a few more good cops as the only remaining barriers to a tidal wave of drug-inspired corruption.

The music in *Miami Vice* plays a major role in the show's mood, as it literally sets the tone (aligning the scene changes to changes in the music) and takes over numerous segments. Original music by Jan Hammer and well-known rock tunes complement the emphasis on splashy tropical colors, flashy cars, expensive clothes, pretty faces, and shapely bodies generously exposed to the Florida sun. Appealing to a new, younger generation raised on rock music and adept at dealing with the blend of song and story in quickly edited formats (such as music videos), *Miami Vice* found a receptive audience for its trendsetting style. Chances are, however, that this emphasis on current music will quickly date the series in the rerun market.

Despite the highly professional and intriguing blend of sound and image throughout *Miami Vice,* the series has weak scripting. After several episodes featuring extended takes of Crockett riding through the Miami streets in his black Ferrari with this week's rock hit wrapping itself around the action, and episode after episode filled with megalomaniac Latin American drug kingpins threatening to do something nasty to everybody, you begin to wonder if the producers didn't scrimp a bit on the scripts while laying down extra dough for the production aspects. Some *Miami Vice* episodes just won't make much sense to you if you try to follow the story (which, it seems, you aren't really supposed to do). All you are supposed to need to know is that Mr. X is this week's drug czar and Sonny and Tubbs are in pursuit, all the while being tempted by the apparently easy good life of the criminals.

In spite of its script defects, *Miami Vice* is usually beautiful to watch, innovative in approach, and sincere enough to touch the audience (though the ultra-cool posturing by Crockett and Tubbs does get annoying after a while). The frequent appearances of famous celebrities (such as Little Richard, Lee Iacocca, G. Gordon Liddy) as guests often liven up an otherwise routine episode. ■

**MICHAEL NESMITH IN TELEVISION PARTS** **(see *Television Parts, Michael Nesmith in*)**

**MICHAEL SHAYNE (*½) 60 min (32ep & 30 min pilot B&W; 1960–1961 NBC) Detective Drama** *with Richard Denning as Michael Shayne, Jerry Paris as Tim Rourke, Patricia Donahue and Margie Regan as Lucy Hamilton, Herbert Rudley as Will Gentry, and Gary Clarke as Dick Hamilton*

Set in the exotic locale of Miami Beach, Florida, *Michael Shayne* comes from a series of novels by Brett Halliday. The novels inspired a radio series and several films in the 1940s and eventually this TV show, with Halliday (real name: David Dresser) serving as consultant.

Suave, debonair, detective Michael Shayne is aided by Miami policeman Will Gentry and newspaperman Tim Rourke (played by Jerry Paris, who directed and appeared in *The Dick Van Dyke Show,* as neighbor Jerry Helper).

The 1958 pilot appeared as *Man on a Raft* in the series *Decision,* and had a completely different cast (Mark Stevens played Shayne). ■

**MICHELOB PRESENTS SUNDAY NIGHT** **(see *Sunday Night*)**

**MICKEY (*) 30 min (17ep B&W; 1964–1965 ABC) Situation Comedy** *with Mickey Rooney as Mickey Grady, Emmaline Henry as Nora Grady, Sammee Tong as Sammy Ling, Tim Rooney as Timmy Grady, and Brian Nash as Buddy Grady*

Mickey Rooney, a child star in movies, never fared very well in series television. This sitcom is his second effort in the field, and it is fairly unmemorable. Rooney plays Mickey Grady, a midwesterner who inherits a beachfront hotel in California. He moves there with his wife and two kids, only to discover that the hotel is run-down and operated by Sammy Ling, a shady Oriental with a lifetime contract. The series involves Mickey's efforts to keep the hotel in the black.

Sammee Tong, who plays Ling, essentially is still playing the Peter Tong butler character he portrayed in *Bachelor Father.* One of the Grady children, Timmy, is played by Rooney's real-life son Tim, who also was a Mouseketeer on *The Mickey Mouse Club.*

**THE MICKEY ROONEY SHOW (**½) 30 min (39ep B&W; 1954–1955 NBC) Situation Comedy** *with Mickey Rooney as Mickey Mulligan, Claire Carleton as Mrs. Mulligan, Regis Toomey as Mr. Mulligan, Joey Forman as Freddie, and Alan Mowbray as the Drama Instructor*

Mickey Rooney, child star of the movies, only graced the small screen sporadically. His first and least known TV series is *The Mickey Rooney Show* (originally subtitled *Hey Mulligan*). This surely must be one of the last times Rooney played a youngster. Famous for his "Andy Hardy" roles as America's favorite young teen in the

1930s and 1940s, Rooney was already in his mid-thirties when he made *The Mickey Rooney Show,* yet he is still in his stereotypical role, the eager beaver kid on the rise. In this series, he is Mickey Mulligan, a young page at some big TV network, who hopes to use his position on the outskirts of show business as a spring board to acting fame. At nights, Mickey attempts to hone his craft with acting classes; still, few people take Mickey's acting dream seriously.

The program is filled with vaguely familiar character actors and actresses you've seen in numerous other roles. Joey Forman, Regis Toomey, and Alan Mowbray all have lengthy acting resumes, but nothing that stands out in the public's mind.

Mickey Mulligan's drive to be considered a real actor seems to parallel Mickey Rooney's career in the mid-1950s, when this series was produced. No longer the child star, Rooney was in the midst of a career slump that ended very slowly. Only over time was he recognized as having dramatic, as well as comedic, talent, a process culminating in Rooney's early 1980s Emmy award–winning role as "Bill," a retarded older man in several TV movies.

Blake Edwards, later famous for producing *Peter Gunn* and hit films such as *10* and the Pink Panther series, was one of the chief writers on *The Mickey Rooney Show.*

**MIDNIGHT CALLER (**½) 60 min (17ep at Fall 1989 Color; 1988– NBC) Crime Drama** *with Gary Cole as Jack Killian, Wendy Kilbourne as Devon King, Dennis Dun as Billy Po, Richard Bradford as Mel King, and Arthur Taxier as Lt. Carl Zymak*

Jack Killian is an ex-cop in San Francisco who accidentally killed his own partner while they were pursuing a felon. Though cleared by the force, Jack decides he's had enough police work and agrees to a request from a local radio station manager, Devon King, to host an overnight call-in show on her station, KJCM (98.3). As with most such radio programs, the topics discussed are essentially whatever is on Jack's mind peppered with comments from listeners (all generally running under the hook of "crime in the city"). Soon, "Jack Killian, the Nighthawk" has a large and loyal audience, including the semiobligatory collection of borderline nutcases who call to involve Jack in their lives. Naturally this often takes him out of the studio and back on the street, sometimes to help out his contact at the police station (Carl Zymak), but usually to go it alone. In the pilot, for instance, he finds himself the chosen target of a pyschotic young prostitute, eventually facing her in a large, empty loft.

Though at times the story lines seem top heavy with deranged killers, topical preaching (on AIDS, for instance), and manipulative establishment types, *Midnight Caller* definitely has a distinctive feel, especially for inside and nighttime scenes. Most of all, though, Gary Cole's portrayal of Jack makes the series. His scenes at the mike while on the air are the highlight of each episode. Though clearly outspoken and in control, he is not an obnoxious creep (in contrast to the character of Barry Champlain in a theatrical feature film at the time, *Talk Radio*). Instead Jack brings a studied intensity to his voice and face, transforming the potentially static visual of announcer, mike, and engineer into an engrossing private conversation with his listeners and, by extension, with the viewers. It's just Jack, engineer Billy Po, and us.

A longtime veteran of the Chicago theater scene, Cole made his first major television splash playing accused killer Dr. Jeffrey MacDonald in the 1984 TV movie *Fatal Vision,* and almost had Don Johnson's role in *Miami Vice.*

**THE MIDNIGHT SPECIAL (**½) 90 min (360ep Color; 1973–1981 NBC) Musical-Variety** *with Wolfman Jack as announcer and Helen Reddy as host*

In the days after rock'n'roll became an accepted part of American life, but before music videos took over the way rock music appeared on TV, shows like *The Midnight Special* were the primary source of presenting rock acts on TV. In *The Midnight Special,* the top acts of the day are seen in concert, in front of throngs of screaming fans. All the boring between-bands equipment shuffling and between-song tuning is edited out and the show is mostly straight music except for commercials. Each week a music superstar acts as host, but only the well-known voice of veteran rock radio DJ Wolfman Jack (nee Bob Smith) turns up week after week.

After a while, the producers of *The Midnight Special* try to tinker with the "only music" format. Easygoing Australian Helen Reddy appears as weekly host for about a year in the middle of the show's run, and she adds little in the way of excitement. Regular "Rock Tribute" profiles of superstars turn up around the same time. These pieces are nice in a documentary sort of way, but they detract from the impact of the live music.

Worst of all are the weekly comedy segments that pop up near the end of the line for *The Midnight Special.* The comics are mostly unknowns and their attempts to be topically funny mostly fall flat. Their appearance turns the show into some form of "hip" Ed Sullivan show, which fails to appeal to anyone.

The original ninety-minute versions of *The Midnight Special* are rarely seen anymore. Much more likely to turn up is *The Best of the Midnight Special,* a series of fifty-two one-hour shows placed in syndication in 1982 packaging the series' best moments in a form that eliminates most of the useless trappings that detracted from the show's main appeal: live music in concert.

**MIKE HAMMER, MICKEY SPILLANE'S (**) 30 min (78ep B&W; 1957–1959 Syndication) Detective Drama** *with Darren McGavin as Mike Hammer* **MIKE HAM-**

**MER, MICKEY SPILLANE'S/THE NEW (**) 60 min (52ep & two 2 hr pilots & 2 hr sequel Color; 1984–1987 CBS) Detective Drama** *with Stacy Keach as Mike Hammer, Lindsay Bloom as Velda, Don Stroud as Capt. Pat Chambers, Kent Williams as Assistant D. A. Lawrence Barrington, Danny Goldman as Ozzie the Answer, and Donna Denton as The Face*

There are two different series packages built around Mickey Spillane's violent pulp detective hero, Mike Hammer. The first originally played in syndication during the late 1950s with the usual dark and gritty formula crime adventures of the time. However, it is fun to watch for an early version of Darren McGavin's patented put-upon gumshoe bit (later perfected in such series as *The Night Stalker*).

The 1980s rendering is another matter. At times (the first batch of episodes), it seems more of a throwback than the black-and-white version, practically celebrating its pulpy clichés with minimal dialogue, smoky back rooms, plenty of violence, and an almost leering attitude toward any female characters. Stacy Keach's Hammer in particular comes off as an appropriately single-minded, two-fisted character who prefers to let his knuckles and his pistol do his talking for him. This softens just a touch in the first set of stories originally run under the banner *The New Mike Hammer,* at least reducing the number of "busty broads" paraded through each episode.

Keach first appeared as Mike Hammer in two 1983 made-for-TV movie pilots. After a production hiatus (caused by Keach's imprisonment in Great Britain on charges of cocaine possession), a new round of episodes began in 1986 with yet another two-hour TV movie, *The Return of Mickey Spillane's Mike Hammer,* followed by *The New Mike Hammer.* (Or should that be *The New Mickey Spillane's Mike Hammer?* Frankly, is there anybody except Mickey Spillane and his agent who considers Hammer's first name to be "Mickey Spillane's Mike"?) One odd feature through many of the Keach episodes is a mysterious brunette (dubbed "The Face"), who seems quite interested in Hammer's actions but always disappears before he can connect with her—until the final episode.

In 1989, Keach's Hammer began yet another revival with some new made-for-TV movies, starting with *Murder Takes All: Mike Hammer in Las Vegas* (with Lynda Carter).

**THE MILLIONAIRE (**½) 30 min (188ep B&W & 2 hr Color sequel; 1955–1960 CBS) Drama** *with Marvin Miller as Michael Anthony and Paul Frees as the voice of John Beresford Tipton*

What would you do with a million dollars? *The Millionaire* is a collection of dramatized answers to that old question. On the whole, the show is simply a thirty-minute drama anthology with the same theme week after week. Considering the wide variety of people in this world, there are numerous ways of working the theme, and that variety is why the show lasted. Some recipients squander the sum in frivolous pursuits. Some show almost biblical kindness and give it away to others who need it more than they do. Some take it as a godsend, and rebuild their lives in ways only dreamed of before.

What makes *The Millionaire* memorable is the way the stories are set up, and the mysterious benefactor who is the moving force behind the scenes. The program always begins in the palatial estate of the fabulously wealthy John Beresford Tipton. Tipton is not just very rich, he is *very, very, very* rich. The Carringtons of *Dynasty* seem as but nouveau-riche cousins of the Clampetts of Beverly Hills when compared to the awesome breadth of the Tipton holdings. Tipton demonstrates a quality that sets the old money apart from the déclassé newly rich, that is, the abhorrence of being in the public eye. Mr. Tipton, however, takes this tendency a bit to the extreme, and the viewer never sees more than the back of Tipton's head, his shoulders, and his arm.

At the start of each episode of *The Millionaire,* Tipton calls his faithful executive secretary Michael Anthony into the Tipton library or conservatory or other room only found in the board game *Clue.* For reasons never fully revealed, Tipton has decided to give away one million dollars every week to a complete stranger. Rather than make contact with the hoi polloi, Tipton instructs Anthony do his legwork for him. Tipton lectures Anthony on some point of wisdom that is tied in to the recipient's life, gives Anthony the check, and instructs him to hand it to "our next millionaire."

Anthony then tracks down the new millionaire and hands over the check to the dumbfounded recipient. The only string attached, Anthony explains, is that the lucky person must never reveal how he or she obtained the money. If this condition was not met, Tipton would somehow find out about it and Anthony would retrieve the unspent portion of the fortune.

It is never made clear how Tipton finds out about the poor slobs who are to win the Tipton lottery. Anthony has never heard of them before and it seems unlikely that Tipton spends his free time slumming around town in search of deserving recipients. One is left to assume he picks the names out of the phone book. Still, Tipton's introductory remarks each week indicate that he knows all about the recipients already. He even seems to know beforehand how each will react to the windfall.

All these preliminaries take about three to five minutes. The remaining part of the half-hour show is devoted to demonstrating how the new millionaire handles sudden wealth. Many times the opening moments with Tipton and Anthony are the most thought-provoking of the program, as the dramas focusing on the recipients tend to be rather sugary and overly sentimental.

The identity of the actor (or actors) who portrays Tipton is never revealed. Paul Frees (the voice of Boris Badenov in *The Bullwinkle Show* and Walt Disney's

Prof. Ludwig von Drake, among others) provides Tipton's voice. *The Millionaire* was produced by Fred Henry and Don Fedderson, who produced the equally sentimental *Family Affair* and *My Three Sons.* The series is loosely based on the delightful 1932 film *If I Had a Million.*

In 1978, Fedderson attempted a revival of the concept in a two-hour made-for-TV sequel (still called *The Millionaire*). The concept is the same (a mysterious benefactor gives away one million dollars through kindly aide Michael Anthony), but the John Beresford Tipton character is omitted. Robert Quarry plays Anthony, handing out checks from an unnamed source.

**THE MILTON BERLE SHOW (**) 60 min (13ep Color; 1966–1967 ABC) Comedy-Variety** *with Milton Berle as host and Irving Benson as Sidney Sphritzer*

Milton Berle became a national superstar by hosting the first successful TV variety show. Berle's vanguard TV series (originally called *Texaco Star Theater*) ran on NBC from 1948 to 1956 and was produced live, in the days before videotapes. Unfortunately this is not that series.

This *Milton Berle Show* is a failed attempted comeback in the 1960s by the man dubbed "Mr. Television" in the 1940s. The format in this series is much the same as in the old *Texaco Star Theater* days. Berle is still the loud, boisterous host and master of ceremonies, who appears in most of the comedy sketches. There is a group of regulars who help out and provide some variety. There is also a list of well-known celebrity guest stars to draw an audience each week.

This format worked for Uncle Miltie in the 1940s and the only real reason it did not work for him in the 1960s was that the audience had changed. Berle was inventing the wheel as he went along in the old days, and people bought TVs just to find out what the hubbub was all about. Twenty years later, TV variety was old hat and Berle smacked too much of the departed days of vaudeville to catch a crowd in the swinging sixties.

*The Milton Berle Show* does not fail for lack of trying. To appeal to the young folk, Berle features singer Donna Loren, a *Shindig* alumnus, and clean-cut pop singer Bobby Rydell, who had some mild hits ("Wild One," "Volare") in the early 1960s. More current chart toppers, such as Paul Revere and the Raiders, turn up as guests. Berle's humor is also more topical than in the restrictive days of *Texaco Star Theater.*

The nonmusical guest list is also impressive. Lucille Ball, Joey Bishop, and David Janssen turn up, along with kung-fu master Bruce Lee (then starring in *The Green Hornet*) and Adam West (from *Batman,* where Berle had guest starred). In a throwback to the vaudeville days, Berle constantly battles insults with Sidney Sphritzer, a planted heckler in the audience.

Still, with all this top-flight talent, the show flops. It is no worse than other comedy-variety shows of the pre–*Laugh-In* era, but no better. At least *The Milton Berle Show* preserves, in bright, living color, one of the giants of TV comedy. This one is of historical interest only.

Highlights of Berle's old *Texaco Star Theater* shows are available on video cassette and on a half-hour syndicated program from the late 1980s, *Milton Berle: The Second Time Around.* ■

**THE MIND (***) 60 min (9ep Color; 1988 PBS) Documentary** *with George Page as host*

A follow-up to the earlier documentary series, *The Brain, The Mind* examines the process by which the human mind thinks, remembers, and works.

**THE MISADVENTURES OF SHERIFF LOBO** **(see *Lobo*)**

**MISFITS OF SCIENCE (**½) 60 min (14ep & 2 hr pilot Color; 1985–1986 NBC) Adventure** *with Dean Paul Martin as Dr. Billy Hayes, Courteney Cox as Gloria Dinallo, Kevin Peter Hall as Dr. Elvin Lincoln, Mark Thomas Miller as Johnny B., Mickey Jones as Arnold Biefneiter, Jennifer Holmes as Jane Miller, and Max Wright as Dick Stetmeyer*

Live action super heroics come to a contemporary crime lab, with an incredible shrinking giant (seven-foot four-inch Elvin Lincoln drops down to about eight inches), a former rock singer with lightning bolt fingers (Johnny B.), and a one-time delinquent with telekinetic powers (Gloria Dinallo). To the rest of the world they're misfits, but here they represent the ultimate crime-fighting unit. At least, that's how Dick Stetmeyer, head of the Humanidyne Research Company, wants to peddle them. But the man in charge of their day-to-day activities, Dr. Billy Hayes, has developed a genuine fondness for the group and instead sees their potential heroic talents as a means to a different end—they're a way for these "freaky" friends to gain some public self-respect, using their powers to help others. The bottom line remains the same, of course: superheroes to the rescue.

Only it's all done with a sense of humor. Not the exaggerated camp of *Batman,* just stories with a comic touch, featuring plenty of sight gags (beginning with the opening credits, sung by a crooner on Billy's television set as he frantically tries to switch it off). Dean Paul Martin (Dean Martin's son) is great as Billy, bringing just the right attitude toward not only his special group of "misfits" but also to the aspiring applicants that are always turning up seeking to join the team. Trouble is, most of them have totally useless or even bogus "abilities," so Billy has to politely send the likes of a "Human Refrigerator" on their way. But they do provide an amusing break.

Besides Martin, this excellent cast includes Jennifer Holmes (Stephanie's cousin, Leslie, on the first season of *Newhart*) as Gloria's probation officer, Max Wright (who later as Willie Tanner met a misfit of a different sort on *Alf*), Kevin Peter Hall (who went on to play the Sasquatch Harry in the feature film *Harry and the Hendersons*), and Courteney Cox as Gloria (in between her romance with Alex on *Family Ties* and her showbiz breakthrough as "the girl who danced with the Boss" in Bruce Springsteen's 1984 "Dancing in the Dark" video). ■

**MISS MARPLE, AGATHA CHRISTIE'S (***) 60 min (14ep at Fall 1989 Color; 1985– UK BBC) Mystery** *with Joan Hickson as Miss Jane Marple*

Since the 1930s there have been many interpretations of Agatha Christie's spinster heroine, Miss Marple (including two made-for-TV movies starring Helen Hayes and pre–Jessica Fletcher Angela Lansbury in the 1980 theatrical film *The Mirror Crack'd*), but Joan Hickson's is probably the most faithful to the written texts. This is Jane Marple as an elderly, somewhat frail English lady, fond of gardening, tea, and conversation. She doesn't pepper suspects with aggressive interrogation boisterously calling attention to herself but instead engages people in quiet chats, usually spending more time listening than talking. She arrives at her conclusions by comparing different descriptions of the same events, by looking at people's personal habits and traits, and, most of all, by searching for something out of the ordinary. It's in the departures from everyday routines that Marple finds her killers.

This series is a co-production by the BBC with an Australian and a U.S. company. Since 1986, they have turned out a half-dozen multiple-episode *Miss Marple* stories featuring Hickson: *The Body in the Library, A Murder Is Announced, The Moving Finger, Nemesis, A Pocketful of Rye* and (one of the best) *Sleeping Murder.* In the United States they have played most prominently on the A&E cable service and on PBS's *Mystery.* ■

**MISS WINSLOW AND SON (*) 30 min (6ep Color: 1979 CBS) Situation Comedy** *with Darleen Carr as Susan Winslow, Roscoe Lee Browne as Harold Devore Neistadter, Elliot Reid as Warren Winslow, and Sarah Marshall as Evelyn Winslow*

Susan Winslow is a twenty-three-year-old woman with an age-old problem: She has a baby but no husband. Dumped by her live-in boyfriend, Susan decides to raise her baby (son Eddie) on her own, to the consternation of her proper Cincinnati parents (Warren and Evelyn). Susan, a freelance art designer, is assisted in attending young Eddie by her neighbor, supercilious black author Harold Neistadter.

This program is utterly forgettable, except for the fact that Susan Winslow may be the first openly unwed mother in U.S. sitcom history. The series is based on the British show *Miss Jones & Son.*

**MISSION: IMPOSSIBLE (***) 60 min (191ep at Fall 1989 Color; 1966–1973 & 1988– CBS & ABC)** *with Peter Graves as Jim Phelps, Steven Hill as Daniel Briggs, Greg Morris as Barney Collier, Peter Lupus as Willy Armitage, Martin Landau as Rollin Hand, Barbara Bain as Cinnamon Carter, Leonard Nimoy as Paris, Lesley Ann Warren as Dana Lambert, Lynda Day George as Casey, Sam Elliott as Dr. Doug Lane, Barbara Anderson as Mimi Davis, and Bob Johnson as the Voice on the Tape, with (for the revival) Thaao Penghlis as Nicholas Black, Tony Hamilton as Max Harte, Terry Markwell as Casey Randall, Phil Morris as Grant Collier, and Jane Badler as Shannon Reed*

This is the definitive formula adventure series, with a story routine that quickly turned into a familiar ritual (no doubt relished and memorized by people like Oliver North). To open nearly every episode, Jim Phelps (and before him for one season, Dan Briggs) receives a recorded message that outlines a proposed unofficial government mission for his consideration. The playback device then self-destructs, so it's never clear just how Jim would formally turn down an assignment if he so desired. But Jim always accepts the challenge, even though he is warned time and again that should he or any of his Impossible Mission forces be caught or killed, "the secretary will disavow any knowledge of your actions." No wonder the final words from the tape (before it dissolves into a cloud of acid smoke) are "Good luck."

Then, with the show's jazzy, rat-a-tat-tat Lalo Schifrin theme playing in the background, Jim looks over the people he might use for this assignment, though it's hard to see why he bothers. Except for cast changes or occasional guest stars, he chooses the same people each time: Barney, an electronics expert; Willy, a powerful muscleman; Rollin (later, Paris), a master of disguise; and Cinnamon (later, Dana, Casey, or Mimi), the key female agent. Later in the series run (and sometimes in local syndication throughout), this sequence is largely eliminated and the team gets right to the planning session.

At these meetings viewers catch snatches of conversation and see maps, graphs, and the latest electronic espionage gadgets, all window dressing for the latest operation. Yet, despite the complex nature of the schemes (requiring split-second timing and audacious bluffing), over the long haul the missions all begin to blend together. Oddly, the superior skills of the team members sometimes hurt the sense of suspense because it's hard to tell when something really has gone amiss and they're actually showing great initiative by adapting to an unexpected snag. These people are so good at what they do, so cool under fire that even with moments of near-discovery, the results never seem in doubt. Still, maybe that's one reason the IMF team always takes on ruthless foreign tyrants (in tiny obscure countries) or domestic underworld operatives—against anyone else their methods would seem like unfair overkill.

Of course, to some viewers the very premise of the series represents overkill of a different sort: In story after story *Mission: Impossible* celebrates unofficial U.S.

government interference with the internal matters of other countries. For some, this was the height of U.S. presumptuous arrogance (especially toward Third World nations), and that may be why toward the end of its original run the series focused more and more on domestic crime lords. More likely, though, the writers just got tired of making up names for yet another season of countries geographically nondescript but somehow essential to U.S. defense.

Besides, for most home viewers, the politics (and even the specific stories) are not really the attraction. At heart, *Mission: Impossible* is about everyday wish fulfillment. In the course of their assignments, the IMF team members use their skills and the latest technology to break into banks, steal gold, fix roulette wheels, jam computers, impersonate police officers, humiliate overbearing bureaucrats, and convince people they're underwater in a sub, in a different country, or even living in a different era—while all the time actually in some warehouse stage set. Who hasn't dreamed of some similarly complex scheme after a particularly frustrating bout with the bureaucracy, or wished for one of Barney's almost magical electronic devices when walking into a real-life gambling casino? No wonder the stories always involve cardboard cut-out bad guys from the underworld or some obscure country—nearly everything the IMF team does is illegal, too!

Still it's a hardy formula that was easily dusted off in 1988 (fifteen years after its original 171 episode run), with Peter Graves again listening to that same faceless voice (this time, on compact disc) and working with another band of talented specialists. (There's even another link to the previous team, with Greg Morris's real-life son, Phil, playing Barney Collier's son, Grant.) At first, Jim Phelps comes out of a fifteen-year retirement to avenge the death of his protégé, Tom Copperfield (seen only in that episode), but he likes his new team so much he decides to stay on. How could he resist?

The revival stories do attempt to inject more uncertainty into the situations—one agent, Casey Randall, even dies in a mission and is "disavowed" (as promised) by the U.S. government. But, otherwise, things go on much as before. (Why tamper with a proven formula?) And, who knows, when the day comes that Peter Graves is no longer available for the series, maybe a programmer searching for a "new" hook might come up with *Mission Impossible: The Lost Copperfield Years.* Different faces, familiar scripts, same music.

**MRS. COLUMBO (zero) 60 min (13ep Color; 1979 NBC) Mystery** *with Kate Mulgrew as Kate Columbo (a.k.a. Kate Callahan), Lili Haydn as Jenny Columbo (a.k.a. Jenny Callahan), and Henry Jones as Josh Allen*

Whenever he is on a case, Lieutenant Columbo always talks about his wife. He describes her likes and dislikes, her cooking, her shopping, her favorite music and movies. Columbo even talks over some of his cases with her. She is obviously quite a woman, though exactly what type of woman is left to viewers' imaginations. She never appears on camera.

In 1979, the brass at NBC decided to change all that and slotted Columbo's never-seen spouse as the lead character in her own series, *Mrs. Columbo* (Kate Columbo, to be exact).

But the program is coy from the very beginning. Is it a murder mystery series? The opening credits show a dark mysterious room in disarray. From a scuffle? A killing? No, actually, the room is just a mess. The shadows made it look more foreboding than it was. Just open the shades, straighten things up, and everything was fine.

Viewers can't even be sure Kate is *the* Mrs. Columbo. At least, she never comes right out and says she is. Or isn't. Instead it is strongly suggested by the title and the fact that Kate enjoys solving mysteries. But is she doing it to follow in the footsteps of her husband, or just as a break from her routine as a housewife?

Whatever the motivation, Kate has plenty of free time during the day while her off-camera husband is at work and her daughter is at school, so she takes a part-time job at her suburban weekly newspaper. That's where she gets her hot leads that inevitably lead to an unsolved murder.

In truth, the program is a disjointed mess. Even worse, the murder stories themselves are dull and plodding—not at all worthy of the good lieutenant's wife! So, in the program's original run, a daring revamping took place midway through: Kate's last name was changed to Callahan, and the series title was changed to *Kate Loves a Mystery.* Apparently viewers were to assume Kate was always getting confused with that *other* Mrs. Columbo, so she reverted to her maiden name (or some other explanation just as preposterous.)

It doesn't matter because even in that version, the series died a quick death. When the show turns up in reruns, it is usually under the *Kate Loves a Mystery* moniker. And no, *Mr.* Columbo (Peter Falk) never makes an appearance.

**MRS. G GOES TO COLLEGE (**) 30 min (26ep B&W; 1961–1962 CBS) Situation Comedy** *with Gertrude Berg as Sarah Green, Cedric Hardwicke as Prof. Crayton, Mary Wickes as Mrs. Maxfield, Skip Ward as Joe Caldwell, Marion Ross as Susan Green, and Leo Penn as Jerry Green*

Gertrude Berg will forever be best known as Molly Goldberg, the Jewish mother from the Bronx and the central character of *The Goldbergs* on radio and TV from 1929 to 1956. In this minor coda to her lengthy career, Berg plays Sarah Green, an aging widow who might as well be Molly Goldberg after the kids have left home and the family has moved out of the city. Sarah decides that after a life of caring for others she will finally fulfill her own personal goal, obtaining a college degree. The humor comes from Sarah's honest way of speaking and from the incongruity of a middle-aged woman attending classes with teenagers.

Sir Cedric Hardwicke, noted English actor, makes an extremely rare TV appearance as Sarah's English professor. Marion Ross, later Mrs. Cunningham on *Happy Days*, makes an early TV appearance as Sarah's daughter. This program is also known as *The Gertrude Berg Show*.

**THE MISSISSIPPI (**½) 60 min (23ep Color; 1983–1984 CBS) Drama** *with Ralph Waite as Ben Walker, Linda G. Miller as Stella McMullen, and Stan Shaw as Lafayette "Lafe" Tate*

Ben Walker, like many busy professionals, yearns for a simpler life closer to nature. Unlike many, Walker actually lives out his dream, leaving behind his successful criminal law practice and buying a riverboat that runs up and down the Mississippi River. Walker's crew consists of Stella McMullen, a former client who now wishes to become a lawyer herself, and Lafe Tate, a black Vietnam veteran who supplies the muscle. Walker's life is not, however, as peaceful as he hoped. As he keeps meeting new folks along the river and getting wrapped up in their lives, Walker falls back on his legal training to help them out.

The premise here is somewhat corny, but at least it is innovative. The series is actually filmed on location on the big river, a welcome break from the usual Los Angeles/Hollywood backdrops. Finally, Ralph Waite is perfect in the Walker role, which is not all that different from Waite's best-known character, papa John Walton in *The Waltons*.

**MR. ADAMS AND EVE (**½) 30 min (66ep B&W; 1957–1958 CBS) Situation Comedy** *with Howard Duff as Howard Adams, Ida Lupino as Eve Adams Drake, and Alan Reed as J. B. Hafter*

This is one series that is definitely all in the family. The two leads, Howard Duff and Ida Lupino, are Hollywood film stars who were then married to each other in real life. In the series, they play two Hollywood stars who are married to each other. To top it off, the series is produced by Collier Young, who used to be married to Ida Lupino. Not surprisingly, the stories in *Mr. Adams and Eve* are said to often be based on incidents from the lives of Lupino and Duff. You may recognize the voice of studio boss J. B. Hafter, since Alan Reed, who plays Hafter, also did the voice for Fred Flintstone.

**MR. & MRS. NORTH (**) 30 min (57ep & 30 min pilot B&W; 1952–1954 CBS & NBC) Comedy/Mystery** *with Barbara Britton as Pamela North, Richard Denning as Jerry North, and Francis DeSales as Lt. Bill Weigand*

Long a popular radio series (and a Broadway play and Hollywood movie), *Mr. & Mrs. North* concerns Jerry North, a level-headed Manhattan publisher of mystery novels who likes to dabble in amateur sleuthing. His scatterbrained wife Pamela, however, is the one who always seems to crack the case. Lt. Weigand of the local Greenwich Village police force is around to arrest the suspect after the Norths turn one up.

The pilot is from 1949, and stars Joseph Allen and Mary Lou Taylor in the title roles. Richard Denning, who plays Mr. North in the series, went on to star in *Michael Shayne* and played Gov. Grey for many years on *Hawaii Five-O*. ■

**MR. BELVEDERE (*) 30 min (92ep at Fall 1989 Color; 1985– ABC) Situation Comedy** *with Bob Uecker as George Owens, Ilene Graff as Marsha Owens, Christopher Hewett as Lynn Belvedere, Rob Stone as Kevin Owens, Tracy Wells as Heather Owens, and Brice Beckham as Wesley Owens*

Bob Uecker is very funny in commercials for Lite Beer, or in interviews reminiscing about his days as a journeyman baseball player in the 1960s. As the head of a TV sitcom family, Uecker leaves a lot to be desired. Uecker's character, George Owens, is the sportswriter head of a two-income couple who don't have the time to care for their three children. The solution to their problem is Mr. Belvedere. A highly proper British sort used to caring for the titled classes, Mr. Belvedere now finds himself nanny to a set of American kids (something akin to the role of Sebastian Cabot's Mr. French in *Family Affair*). Rising to the challenge, Mr. Belvedere quickly wins over the three kiddies and has dad feeling quite the left-out clod before long. Mr. Belvedere's extremely affected manner is a drag and Uecker overacts with abandon.

The character of Mr. Belvedere was portrayed by Clifton Webb in several films in the 1940s and 1950 that are far better than this sitcom.

**MR. BROADWAY (*½) 60 min (13ep B&W; 1964 CBS) Drama** *with Craig Stevens as Mike Bell, Horace McMahon as Hank McClure, and Lani Miyazaki as Toki*

Doctors, lawyers, policemen, and private eyes have been very well represented in TV series through the years. Public relations executives have not. In fact, Mike Bell may well be the only public relations man who is the focus of a TV show. As you might guess from the show's title, Bell operates in Manhattan, hobnobbing with the stars of stage and screen, doing . . . well, whatever it is public relations folk do.

Craig Stevens, who plays Bell, is familiar from his stint as Peter Gunn, and Stevens plays Bell with the same sang-froid coolness. Having an Oriental housegirl (Toki) is evidence that Bell is the epitome of early 1960s male sophistication. *Mr. Broadway* is produced by David Susskind, best known as an intelligent talk show host (*Open End*), a producer of serious drama (*Play of the Week*), and the producer of a few popular series (such as *Mr. Peepers*).

**MISTER DEEDS GOES TO TOWN (**) 30 min (17ep Color; 1969–1970 ABC) Situation Comedy** *with Monte Markham as Longfellow Deeds, Pat Harrington, Jr., as Tony Lawrence, Herbert Voland as Henry Masterson, and Ivor Barry as George*

For this short-run television version of the 1936 Frank Capra film, Monte Markham takes Gary Cooper's character of Longfellow Deeds, a righteous man determined to give away a twenty-million-dollar inheritance. For this series, though, Longfellow's task is tougher. He inherits his unscrupulous uncle Alonzo's multimillion-dollar corporation, and so he heads to New York from the small town of Mandrake Falls, intent on righting some wrongs and making the business more responsible to the people. Luckily, Longfellow's pal Tony comes along to help protect his sometimes naive friend. Good thing, because current chairman of the board Henry Masterson is waiting there for the kill.

A slightly relevant late 1960s package with good roles for future *One Day at a Time* building super Pat Harrington, Jr., and Herb Voland, the familiar face of General Clayton on *M*A*S*H.*

**MISTER DISTRICT ATTORNEY (*½) (78ep: 49 Color & 29 B&W; 1954–1955 Syndication) Crime Drama** *with David Brian as D. A. Paul Garrett and Jackie Loughery as Edith Miller*

This series was very popular as a radio drama in the 1940s, inspired by the real-life prosecution efforts of New York District Attorney Thomas Dewey (later governor of New York and president of the United States for one edition of the *Chicago Tribune*). The program came to television in 1951 with the same main performers and production supervisor as in the radio version, going out live on ABC, but only for one season. Several years later a syndicated film package was released, with different stars but the same dedication to gritty real-life crime as seen through the eyes of Mr. District Attorney, "Champion of the people! Defender of the truth! And guardian of our fundamental rights to life, liberty, and the pursuit of happiness." (Whew! Superman, move over.) Not surprisingly, this plays today as a typical 1950s formula crime drama. Oddly, though, this syndicated version is the first ever to give "the D. A." a character name.

**MISTER ED (***) 30 min (144ep B&W; 1961–1966 Syndication & CBS) Situation Comedy** *with Alan Young as Wilbur Post, Connie Hines as Carol Post, Larry Keating as Roger Addison, Leon Ames as Gordon Kirkwood, and Allan "Rocky" Lane as the voice of Mr. Ed*

Any sane analysis of a show about a horse that speaks, but only to its owner, must inevitably conclude that the program is all air, has no substance, and is probably bad for your health. Yet, if you spend much time following the exploits of Mr. Ed, a big talking palomino, chances are you will think *Mister Ed* is a pretty funny show.

The setup is ridiculous. Wilbur Post and his wife Carol buy a home in the country that comes equipped with a horse. Now, they say that a horse is a horse. Of course, no one can talk to a horse. Unless, of course, the horse happens to be the famous Mr. Ed. Unfortunately for Wilbur, Mr. Ed only talks to him. Wilbur soon gives up trying to convince others that the horse can talk, and a lot of time is spent making Wilbur look foolish to family and friends when people come in the barn unexpectedly, catching Wilbur (but never Mr. Ed) in mid-sentence.

That's it. On paper, that is the whole show, and it does sound silly, or at best weak. Yes, there are a parade of other minor characters, mostly nosy busybody neighbors who think Wilbur is a loony. Even wife Carol is boring, though considering the odd way Wilbur is always acting, she can be excused for being overly straight-laced. What gives *Mister Ed* its zing is the interplay of man and horse. Wilbur really is sort of nutty, but any good psychoanalyst would probably chalk that up to the strains of living a double life, that is, his "Ed" and "non-Ed" life. Mr. Ed was the best thing that ever came into Wilbur's life. With Ed, Wilbur is free to really be himself and do all the wild things he always held in check. Without Ed, Wilbur is just another faceless suburban automaton.

Mr. Ed plays guru to Wilbur, acting as his friend and confidant. Mr. Ed (it seems so fitting to give him the gentlemanly title of "Mister") is no solemn sage, however. It is never made clear where the horse picked up his knowledge, but Mr. Ed is a bon vivant "man" of the world, who likes to bone up on his French and attempt to dance the tango. In fact, Mr. Ed is fairly ribald, always making risqué asides about fillies and such. It is this delightful insouciance, his devil-may-care attitude, that makes *Mister Ed* so appealing. Everything else is fluff. The scripts are otherwise banal and plodding.

Credit for this ability to turn out real humor in such a foolish setting goes to the producers, Al Simon and Arthur Lubin. Simon had helped produce the *Burns and Allen Show,* a classic example of how nonexistent plots can be packaged with flair. Lubin had a little more hands-on training for *Mister Ed,* serving as producer of the Francis, the Talking Mule series of films in the 1950s. The *Francis* films were exactly the same concept, only it was a mule, not a horse that talked. Those movies, like *Mister Ed,* were roasted by critics but a hit with the public.

Allan "Rocky" Lane (a star of scores of 1930s Hollywood B-movie westerns) provides the voice of Mr. Ed, and he adds such expressive vocal touches that the horse *does* seem alive and full of personality. Even the way Mr. Ed always whinnies "Wwwillburr" conveys something of the benign condescension that the horse seems to feel for his "master." Another behind-the-scenes star is the animal trainer who somehow manages to have an apparently normal palomino act in such a way that looks, at least, as if the horse knows what words are being put in his mouth. Some of Mr. Ed's talents, such as dancing, are presented through trick photography, by running a short clip of film over and over, forward and backward, to look like continued motion. Still the horse himself is a real trouper.

There is a final, truly bizzare postscript to the *Mister Ed* story. In the early 1980s, a few years after the horse that portrayed Mr. Ed had died, an evangelical minister in Tennessee claimed that he had found yet another hidden satanic message in popular culture that was leading America's youth astray. This time it was not in some heavy metal rock group's unintelligible lyrics but in the *Mister Ed* theme song, which, the preacher said, if played backward was supposed to praise the devil. Somewhere a great palomino must have had a good snort over that one.

**MISTER GARLUND** **(*½) 30 min (13ep B&W; 1960–1961 CBS) Adventure** *with Charles Quinlivan as Frank Garlund and Kam Ton as Kam Chang*

Garlund is a thirty-ish financial genius with a mysterious background and a nose for intrigue, high finance, and adventure. His closest confidant is his foster brother, Kam Chang (played by Kam Ton, who previously had the role of Paladin's house boy on *Have Gun, Will Travel*), and together they travel in mildly exotic circles. A typical early 1960s formula action series, which also ran under the title *The Garlund Touch.*

**MR. LUCKY** **(**½) 30 min (34ep B&W; 1959–1960 CBS) Adventure** *with John Vivyan as Mr. Lucky, Ross Martin as Andamo, Tom Brown as Lt. Rovacs, and Pippa Scott as Maggie Shank-Rutherford*

A Blake Edwards television adaptation of the 1943 theatrical feature film starring Cary Grant, with lush Henry Mancini theme music throughout and some engaging performances by John Vivyan and Ross Martin. The setup is simple: Lucky operates a gambling boat (the *Fortuna*) just outside the twelve-mile legal limit, offering willing players a posh setting and an honest game. Nonetheless, there's nothing like gambling to stir up trouble, as Lucky and his assistant, Andamo, frequently discover. Sometimes it's a greedy or disgruntled customer; other times it's a person in distress (usually a damsel) or a reluctant request for help from the local police. As much an adventurer as a professional gambler, Lucky inevitably decides to deal personally with virtually every situation.

About halfway through the series, a crusading young woman convince Lucky to change the *Fortuna*'s bill of fare from gambling to fine dining. At the time of its 1960 airing, this switch in the basic premise was attributed in part to image problems haunting the broadcast industry (scandals involving quiz programs and payola), which did not want to be seen as shamelessly celebrating gambling as a reasonable and sophisticated activity. Perhaps that was true, though in fact Lucky had a change of heart in the theatrical film as well, due to the influence of his girlfriend. Whatever the case, the series finishes its run with more emphasis on adventures outside the ship (not too much drama in overcooked mousse). Definitely worth catching for Ross Martin's pre–*Wild, Wild West* performance as well as Vivyan's lanky heroics. Though he's no Cary Grant, he is a creditable hero.

**MR. MAGOO, THE FAMOUS ADVENTURES OF** **(**½) 30 min (25ep Color; 1964–1965 NBC) Animated Cartoon** *with Jim Backus as the voice of Quincy Magoo*

The familiar cartoon character of Mr. Magoo, a nearsighted old crank who first appeared in 1949, hosts, narrates, and stars in one of the few cartoon series to originally run in prime time. Magoo presents the adventures of famous real and literary characters (Rip Van Winkle, William Tell, Long John Silver, Gunga Din, King Arthur), and portrays the central character, thus ensuring that the familiar tale will have a Magoo warp on it. Jim Backus, who is the voice of Magoo, is (unfortunately) best known as Thurston Howell III of *Gilligan's Island.* ■

**MR. MERLIN** **(*) 30 min (21ep Color; 1981–1982 CBS) Situation Comedy** *with Barnard Hughes as Max Merlin, Clark Brandon as Zachary Rogers, Jonathan Prince as Leo Samuels, and Elaine Joyce as Alexandra*

Only on TV would a proud character of fiction such as Merlin the Magician, late of King Arthur's court, be dragged into the present day and set in a dilapidated garage in San Francisco. Merlin (now called Max Merlin and running the garage as a cover) has been ordered by his superiors to train a new sorcerer, so Merlin must put up with the smart-mouthed young brat (Zachary) chosen to be his student. Zachary is more interested in girls and money than mysteries of the universe. Barnard Hughes, a fine actor, is wasted in this silliness.

**MR. NOVAK** **(***) 60 min (60ep B&W; 1963–1965 NBC) Drama** *with James Franciscus as John Novak, Dean Jagger as Albert Vane, Jeanne Bal as Jean Pagano, and Burgess Meredith as Martin Woodridge*

Television is a medium that loves to copy itself. Any show that becomes a hit can be assured that within a year or two numerous clones will appear, usually of far lower quality. Accepting this procedure, there is no shame in calling a series a clone or a rip-off, but some measure of respect for a series is lost when you realize how much of its central premise is copied.

That being said, *Mr. Novak* is a blatant rip-off of *Dr. Kildare.* It is a *good* rip-off, mind you, but it is a rip-off just the same. *Mr. Novak* has virtually the exact same setup as *Dr. Kildare,* with the only difference being that it is a series about a teacher, not a doctor. The setting is Jefferson High School in Los Angeles, not Blair General Hospital. Otherwise the two are Siamese twins. John Novak is a fresh young English teacher in his first job, just as James Kildare was fresh out of medical school. Novak's mentor is craggy old Principal Vane, who terrorizes the young teacher with his harsh criticisms, yet still admires the young man and takes him under his wing as Dr. Gillespie did for Dr. Kildare. Much of the drama of *Mr. Novak* comes from the line of guest stars parading through the show as students, teachers, and so on (as opposed to the patients and other doctors in *Kildare.*) To top it off, James Franciscus, who plays Mr. Novak, might as well be Richard Chamberlain's long-lost cousin. They both are tall, thin, blond-haired WASPs with devastatingly handsome faces, perfectly designed to appeal to women of all ages.

Since "borrowing" a concept from an earlier hit is not really much of a crime in TV circles, the important question is: Is the rip off any good? In the case of *Mr. Novak,* the answer is yes, due to the quality acting, scripts, and production. The series tends to take itself too seriously at times, but not to the point of being obnoxious.

During the last year of *Mr. Novak,* Principal Vane is booted upstairs to the post of superintendent of schools. Martin Woodridge, another of Jefferson High's English teachers, moves up to the post of principal. Burgess Meredith, who plays Woodridge, is a wonderful actor, but he cannot fill the "craggy old mentor" role like Dean Jagger, and the teacher/principal relationship suffers in these later episodes.

One fun reason to watch *Mr. Novak* is to see numerous later-famous faces parade by in semicontinuing roles. Keep an eye out for Marion Ross (Mrs. Cunningham in *Happy Days*) as Nurse Bromfield, Stephen Franken (Chatsworth Osborne, Jr. in *Dobie Gillis*) as French teacher Jerry Allen, Tony Dow (Wally Cleaver in *Leave It to Beaver*) as a student named George, Marta Kristen (the blond Judy Robinson in *Lost in Space*) as student Gail Andrews, Beau Bridges (son of Lloyd and star of movies such as *Norma Rae*) as student Pat Knowland, Shelley Fabares (daughter of Mary Stone in *The Donna Reed Show*) as student Dani Cooper, and Joey Heatherton (later a famous dancer and singer) as student Holly Metcalfe.

**MR. PEEPERS (***) 30 min (100ep B&W; 1952–1955 NBC) Situation Comedy** *with Wally Cox as Robinson Peepers, Patricia Benoit as Nancy Remington, Tony Randall as Harvey Weskit, Jack Warden as Frank Whip, Ernest Truex as Mr. Remington, and Arthur O'Connell as Mr. Hansen*

*Mr. Peepers* is as good an example of how early TV was different from modern TV as you can find. Other better known sitcoms of the era, such as *I Love Lucy* and *The Honneymooners,* do not seem all that different to viewers today because those shows set the pattern that current sitcoms still follow to a large degree. *Mr. Peepers* is from the line of sitcoms that died around the time film and laugh tracks took over.

A quiet, gentle show, *Mr. Peepers* stars Wally Cox, a popular character actor who was forever playing shy, egghead types with a current of excitement just underneath the surface. Appropriately, one of Cox's best-remembered roles was as the voice of Underdog, a shy, retiring cartoon hero of the 1960s. As Mr. Peepers, Cox is his traditional, timid, mild-mannered self, portraying a high school science teacher.

*Mr. Peepers* is blessed with an outstanding supporting cast, featuring a young Tony Randall as Peeper's pal and colleague, history teacher Harvey Weskit. Whereas Peepers is shy and retiring, Weskit is brash and assertive. Together they make an engaging duo that play off each other well. Jack Warden, later a star of numerous series (*Wackiest Ship in the Army, Crazy Like a Fox*), plays Frank Whip, the loud athletic coach. Arthur O'Connell and Ernest Truex, two other low-key character actors of the 1950s, also lend a helping hand.

The big development to watch for in *Mr. Peepers* is the budding romance that grows between Peepers and equally quiet school nurse Nancy Remington. Near the end of the next-to-last season, Peppers and Remington are married in an episode that captured national attention when it first aired.

What sets *Mr. Peepers* apart from much of the TV sitcoms that came later is the intelligent, restrained tone that permeates the show. Due to the fast-paced shows most modern viewers are used to, *Mr. Peepers* may appear slow and dull at first. Once you get into the characters, this feeling should wear off.

Much of the credit for the good taste of *Mr. Peepers* goes to the show's producer, Fred Coe, a giant of the quality TV drama anthologies of the early 1950s, which also died out with quiet sitcoms. Coe's work still is worth watching, even if you have to endure the grainy kinescope quality.

**MR. PRESIDENT (**) 30 min (25ep Color; 1987–1988 Fox) Situation Comedy** *with George C. Scott as Pres. Samuel A. Tresch, Carlin Glynn as Meg Tresch, Maddie Corman as Cynthia Tresch, Andre Gower as Nick Tresch, Conrad Bain as Charlie Ross, and Madeline Kahn as Lois Gullickson*

Any TV series starring George C. Scott is worth noting, but *Mr. President* has little else in its favor. Making only his second TV series appearance (twenty-three years after *East Side, West Side*), Scott plays newly elected President Sam Tresch, a grumpy, tough man in the mold of many of Scott's film characters. The focus in *Mr. President* is on the social side of the president's life, rather than the political, so the first lady and the presidential children receive lots of attention. As befits a George C. Scott role, the humor is restrained, but, unfortunately, not very pointed or poignant.

About halfway through the series, Meg Tresch drops out of the role of first lady (she can't take the public attention), and Meg's dipsy sister Lois steps in as Pres. Tresch's hostess. Like George C. Scott, Madeline Kahn (who plays Meg) has appeared in several quality films (such as *Paper Moon* and *Young Frankenstein*), but her flighty character in *Mr. President* drags the series down to the region of bland farce.

**MR. ROBERTS (*½) 30 min (30ep Color; 1965–1966 NBC) Comedy/Adventure** *with Roger Smith as Lt. Douglas Roberts, Steve Harmon as Ensign Frank Pulver, Richard X. Slattery as Capt. John Morton, and George Ives as Doc*

Nobody is going to forget the original Thomas Heggen book or 1948 play or 1955 movie (with Henry Fonda, Jack Lemmon, and James Cagney) after watching this bland TV version of *Mr. Roberts*. The story is the same: Lt. Roberts serves on the run-down cargo ship *U.S.S. Reluctant* (nicknamed "The Bucket") far out of harm's way in the South Pacific during World War II. Roberts wants to see some action. His commander, Capt. Morton, likes things just as they are and blocks Roberts' attempted move. Ensign Pulver livens up the crew's dull lives with jokes. The difference is that the TV version has little of the sparkle and wit of the earlier versions.

Roger Smith, who plays Roberts, was better cast as the suave and cool Jeff Spencer on *77 Sunset Strip.* James Komack, who went on to produce *Chico and the Man* and *Welcome Back, Kotter,* turns in one of his earliest production stints on *Mr. Roberts.*

**MR. SMITH (*½) 30 min (12ep Color; 1983 NBC) Situation Comedy** *with Ed. Weinberger as the voice of Mr. Smith, C. J. as Mr. Smith, Leonard Frey as Raymond Holyoke, Tim Dunigan as Tommy Atwood, Laura Jacoby as Ellie Atwood, Terri Garber as Dr. Judy Tyson, and Stuart Margolin as Dr. Kline*

After making a splash in feature film appearances with Bo Derek (her remake of *Tarzan the Ape Man*) and Clint Eastwood (as Clyde in *Every Which Way But Loose* and *Any Which Way You Can*), C. J. the orangutan could not have asked for a television package with more potential. The brainchild of former *Mary Tyler Moore Show* producers Stan Daniels and Ed. Weinberger, this series offered him better scripts than *The Hathaways,* a more distinguished wardrobe than *Lancelot Link, Secret Chimp,* and a far more relevant setting than *Me and the Chimp.* C. J. even got a voice (that of co-producer Weinberger) and, unlike Mr. Ed, talks to everybody around him.

The reason this orangutan is so outgoing is simple: The series premise awards C. J.'s character, Mr. Smith, an I. Q. of 256—genius level. That's the result of a lab accident when Smith (then known as Cha Cha) first finds himself in a Washington research center. Briefly unattended, he mixes a batch of chemicals and enzymes, drinks it, and suddenly he's a walking, talking government consultant. Like any good member of a think tank, his immediate concerns are taking care of his own comfort, happiness, and friends. By the end of this first episode, he's wearing impeccably tailored suits and living in a posh suburban home with two human housemates: Tommy (his old trainer) and Ellie (Tommy's sister). They're soon joined by Smith's old buddy, BoBo (with just a normal orangutan brain), rescued from an Atlantic City show. Smith even has an official government caretaker (and comic foil), the prissy but sharp-tongued Raymond Holyoke, an unhappy man accustomed to attending the needs of presidents and ambassadors.

Unfortunately, the series never takes full advantage of the opportunities of its own political satirical setup, settling instead for moderately amusing plot complications (BoBo is mistaken for Smith and kidnapped; Smith falls for an orangutan he sees on television). Or, worse yet, it just falls back on the standard monkey humor hook in which it is assumed hilarious when primates dress as humans and do human things. (Ironically, some of the scenes were not done by C. J. but by a midget in a monkey suit.) But if the thought of Mr. Smith dressed as a doctor walking into the operating room to perform surgery appeals to you, definitely tune in to the dozen episodes that were turned out. Otherwise, you might want to save such escapist affections for a slightly more accessible smart-tongued creature series from another MTM company alum, Tom Patchett's *Alf.*

**MR. SMITH GOES TO WASHINGTON (*) 30 min (13ep B&W; 1962–1963 ABC) Situation Comedy** *with Fess Parker as Sen. Eugene Smith, Sandra Warner as Pat Smith, and Red Foley as Cooter Smith*

If you like the 1939 Frank Capra film classic of *Mr. Smith Goes to Washington* (starring James Stewart), avoid this series. Rent the film, instead.

For the record, Fess Parker plays Eugene Smith, a naive but honest Joe from the heartland who somehow is appointed to fill a vacancy as U.S. senator from his home state. Once in our nation's capital, he must deal with the nastiness and chicanery of life on the Potomac. The stories in the series are pat and pablum, unlike the film, which (in often corny ways) has a lot to say about Americans and their ideals.

Fess Parker is, of course, better known as Davy Crockett from the Disney episodes of the 1950s (where he also served in Congress). Red Foley, who plays the uncle of the new senator, is a country and western singing star from the 1940s and 1950s.

**MR. SUNSHINE (*) 30 min (11ep Color; 1986 ABC) Situation Comedy** *with Jeffrey Tambor as Prof. Paul Stark, Nan Martin as Grace D'Angelo, Barbara Babcock* *as June Swinford, Leonard Frey as Prof. Leon Walters, and Cecilia Hart as Janice Hall*

The list of the main characters of TV series who are blind is very short. A quick check turns up Mike Longstreet, the insurance investigator on *Longstreet,* and Paul Stark, the college professor on *Mr. Sunshine.* It is commendable that *Mr. Sunshine* presents Stark as just another guy, who happens to be blind, instead of some holy martyr in the Helen Keller mold, but the series never goes anywhere. Stark is brilliant, but a real pain in the neck. Not surprisingly, his wife just divorced him, and now his friends and family try to be nice to him, but it's awfully hard. Viewers will overcome their sympathy for his disability real fast and come to dislike him as well.

*Mr. Sunshine,* which *Happy Days*' Henry Winkler helped produce, contains two alumni of *Hill Street Blues.* Star Jeffrey Tambor played the perverse Alan Wachtel, a lawyer turned judge on *Hill Street,* while Barbara Babcock (who plays Mr. Sunshine's landlady) was the hot Grace Gardner.

**MR. T AND TINA (*) 30 min (5ep Color; 1976 ABC) Situation Comedy** *with Pat Morita as Taro "Mr. T" Takahashi, Susan Blanchard as Tina Kelly, Pat Suzuki as Michi, June Angela as Sachi Takahashi, and Ted Lange as Harvard*

No, there is no big black guy with chains in this show. The Mr. T in question is a small, mild-mannered, widowed Japanese inventor who is transferred by his company from Tokyo to Chicago and brings his extended family along. There the inevitable clash of cultures occurs, especially after Mr. T hires a dizzy Nebraska farm girl (Tina) to be governess to his two children. James Komack, who succeeded with *The Courtship of Eddie's Father* and *Chico and the Man,* bombs in this production effort. The pilot of *Mr. T and Tina* is an episode of *Welcome Back, Kotter* titled "Career Day."

**MR. TERRIFIC (zero) 30 min (13ep Color; 1967 CBS) Situation Comedy** *with Stephen Strimpell as Stanley Beamish/Mr. Terrific, John McGiver as Barton J. Reed, Dick Gautier as Hal Walters, and Ellen Corby as Mrs. Beamish*

Some shows are memorable because they were popular, while other shows, such as *Mr. Terrific,* are memorable because they were not popular. *Mr. Terrific* was one of the more memorable flops in the 1960s.

Having first appeared almost one year to the day from the TV premiere of *Batman, Mr. Terrific* tries to spoof a spoof. *Batman* was funny because its superhero was so straight, so square-jawed, and so noble. *Mr. Terrific* goes the other way, turning its superhero into a nerd who acquired superhero powers accidentally.

Stanley Beamish is the only human being the U.S. government can find to ingest some super-secret power pill and then make use of the drug's power (all others who take the pill just get sick). After popping one of the pills, Beamish acquires great strength, which he exploits to fight crime. The problem is that Beamish is a nebbish, a lowly gas station attendant who is a klutz at everything he does, especially being a superhero.

Wishing to help his government, Beamish begins living a double life, both as simple gas jockey and as the fearsome Mr. Terrific. Needless to say, hardly anybody knows about Beamish's double life, and a lot of the plots revolve around trying to keep his secret identity secret. The other basis for plots is that the power pills only have an effect for an hour or two, so Mr. Terrific frequently reverts to his mild-mannered Stanley Beamish self at highly inopportune times.

This overly contrived plot could be the basis for a few laughs or so, but the production is so heavy-handed and the scripts so inane that the whole premise wears off long before Mr. Terrific's power pills. Both *Mr. Terrific* and its nearly identical contemporary competition *Captain Nice* came and went in a flash, never capturing the camp feel of *Batman.* At least *Captain Nice* had some interesting characters. *Mr. Terrific* is just a footnote, not really worth watching.

Dick Gautier, who plays Stanley's unknowing gas station partner Hal Walters, is much funnier as Hymie, the CONTROL robot in *Get Smart.* Ellen Corby, Beamish's mother in *Mr. Terrific,* is best known as Grandma Walton in *The Waltons.*

**MISTRAL'S DAUGHTER (**½) (8hr miniseries Color; 1984 CBS) Drama** *with Stacy Keach as Julien Mistral, Stefanie Powers as Maggy Lunel, Lee Remick as Kate Browning, Stephanie Dunnam as Teddy Kilkullen, Robert Urich as Jason Darcy, Ian Richardson as Adrien Avigdor, and Philippine Leroy Beaulieu as Fauve Mistral*

The title of this miniseries refers to Fauve, the daughter of genius painter Julien Mistral and his third and final love, Teddy. However, the real focus of the show is not on Fauve but on Mistral's life and his loves along the way. First in Mistral's list of conquests is model Maggy, who dumps Julien for an American businessman. Number two is Kate, a rich American, who he throws over for number three, model Teddy, who is (surprise!) the daughter of Maggy and her American love. *Mistral's Daughter* is based on a Judith Krantz novel.

**MOBILE ONE (*) 60 min (13ep & 90 min pilot Color; 1975 ABC) Adventure** *with Jackie Cooper as Peter Campbell, Julie Gregg as Maggie Spencer, and Mark Wheeler as Doug McKnight*

*Mobile One* is more mindless mid-1970s violence from Jack Webb (*Emergency!*). TV reporter Pete Campbell and his crew use the new (for that time) portable TV cameras that local TV news operations love to overuse. Campbell's code name for communications back to the station is "Mobile One." The entire series consists of Campbell and company rushing around, covering one hyped-up story after another. You see enough of that on your local TV news show—why watch more here?

Jackie Cooper, a wonderful actor (*The People's Choice, Hennesey,* and, as a child, one of the *Our Gang/Little Rascals* kids) and TV director (some episodes of *M*A*S*H* and *The White Shadow*) is utterly wasted here. The pilot of *Mobile One* is, confusingly, called *Mobile Two.*

**THE MOD SQUAD (*) (124ep & 2 hr sequel Color; 1968–1973) Police Drama** *with Michael Cole as Pete Cochran, Clarence Williams III as Linc Hayes, Peggy Lipton as Julie Barnes, and Tige Andrews as Capt. Adam Greer*

In its time (the late 1960s), this series managed to have it both ways: giving hippie-type teens a prime-time network showcase as with-it undercover detectives while reassuring concerned adults that those crazy kids could be brought under control as part of the establishment. The stories fairly ooze with hip dudes and slang, "relevant" plots, and adults and hippies that are either sadly misunderstood or deceptively corrupt. There's also a lot of youthful angst among the Mod Squad members befitting their status as topical outsiders: Linc, the brooding black rebel (the one with the sunglasses); Pete, the reject from a wealthy Beverly Hills family; and Julie, the runaway daughter of a prostitute. Though they've all had troubled pasts, under the guidance of Capt. Greer they have a chance to make a difference and help everybody "get it together."

Ironically these days the series does provide common ground among the generations as viewers of all ages find the smarmy pseudo-hipness awfully hard to take. Frankly, if it wasn't for some old-fashioned violence in the stories, this series might be totally a period piece. Not surprisingly, a 1979 made-for-TV movie sequel, *The Return of the Mod Squad* (with all the original leads against a relic-of-the-1960s gunman) did not lead to a series revival.

**MOLL FLANDERS (***) (4hr miniseries Color; 1975 UK BBC) Drama** *with Julia Foster as Moll Flanders, Karin McCarthy as Meg, Patrick Newell as Thomas, Paul Lavers as Robin, and Ian Ogilvy as Humphrey Oliver*

There is plenty of sex, romance, and intrigue in this intelligent British adaptation of Daniel DeFoe's classic novel. The story follows a seventeenth-century woman who is married five times and spends years as a prostitute and thief.

**MOLLY DODD, THE DAYS AND NIGHTS OF (***½) 30 min (39ep at Fall 1989 Color; 1987– NBC & Lifetime) Comedy Drama** *with Blair Brown as Molly Dodd, Allyn Ann McLerie as Florence Bickford, James Greene as Davey McQuinn, William Converse-Roberts as Fred Dodd, Sandy Faison as Mamie Grolnick, and Maureen Anderman as Nina Shapiro*

Molly Dodd lives in the New York City celebrated by Woody Allen in such films as *Manhattan, Annie Hall,* and *Hannah and Her Sisters.* There are nice brownstone apartments, parks, bookshops, jazz clubs, and restaurants filled with people who are capable of having a reasonably intelligent conversation.

That's quite an appropriate setting because *The Days and Nights of Molly Dodd* frequently plays just like one of those Allen films, mixing comic elements into an admittedly upscale slice-of-life drama. It's leisurely and literate, with a rich texture of detail that unwinds slowly, sometimes leading to a moment of comic absurdity, or wistful fantasy, or personal fulfillment.

At the heart of everything is Molly Dodd, a young divorced woman living in a cheery Manhattan apartment. Though she's by herself, Molly is hardly alone. Everyone from her mom (Florence) to her former husband (Fred) to the apartment building elevator operator/doorman (Davey) is interested in her—in fact, they love her. That's not surprising. Molly is warm, open, and engagingly sexy. Her only major shortcoming is that she's still searching for that undefinable "something."—whatever that may be. (Of course, Molly's mom might have a few maternal suggestions, including a well-paying job, a new husband, and grandchildren.)

Blair Brown does a superb job with the title character, keeping Molly fresh and hopeful yet also occasionally wary and worldly. She has some of Bob Newhart's dry humor and "everyman" nervousness, as well as a delightful sense of discovery (it seems that anything can happen when Molly is around). She can write poetry, teach piano, sell real estate, play in a jazz band, and (most of all) provide a sympathetic ear for the many people she encounters.

Perhaps the most striking element of the series is that it does not play out as the typical "everything gets resolved in thirty minutes" TV structure. Instead, people and events drift in and out of the running continuity, almost like a low-key soap opera. The episodes carry cryptic titles such as "Here Are a Few Variations on a Sexual Theme" or "Here Comes That Cold Wind Off the River."

But make no mistake about it, *Molly Dodd* is definitely a comedy, often using such tried and true sitcom hooks as disastrous dates, the lunacy of city living, sibling rivalry, office promiscuity, and an interfering mother who is sometimes simply baffled by her daughter's lifestyle. It's just all executed in an offhand, gentle manner, almost like family gossip told over afternoon tea. In fact, the episodes even open with a voice-over narration by Molly's mom, who fills in viewers on her daughter's latest interests with that mixture of puzzlement and love only a concerned parent can bring.

Though *The Days and Nights of Molly Dodd* has a very strong female point of view, the series was actually created by a male, veteran MTM writer, director, and producer Jay Tarses (whose credits stretch back through the original *Mary Tyler Moore* and *Bob Newhart* shows). With *Molly Dodd* he set out to do something deliberately different from standard sitcom fare, and definitely hit the mark.

**MONA MCCLUSKEY** (**) **30 min (26ep Color; 1965–1966 NBC) Situation Comedy** *with Juliet Prowse as Mona McCluskey, Denny Miller as Sgt. Mike McCluskey, Bartlett Robinson as Frank Caldwell, Herbert Rudley as Gen. Crone, Robert Strauss as Sgt. Gruzewsky, and Elena Verdugo as Alice Henderson*

Granted, money (usually the lack of it) is often a problem in marriages. What happens here, though, is that the male ego of air force sergeant Mike McCluskey runs right into his new wife's paycheck. It's a substantial difference because she's a successful Hollywood star pulling down $5000 per week, versus his $500 per month salary. (Remember, these are mid-1960s figures! Your local recruiter has more up-to-date information.) So in order to prove he could support her, they agree to live in his small two-room apartment, without her income supplementing his. The series complications come from Mona's constant attempts to slip some cash his way, surreptitiously, of course.

Juliet Prowse is fairly good in this thankless role, but the premise is not only annoyingly sexist from a present day perspective ("How dare that woman make more than me!") but also just plain dumb. Why did TV husbands in the 1960s get so uptight about their wives showing off their assets? Darren didn't want Samantha to wiggle her nose on *Bewitched,* Tony had problems with Jeannie's powers on *I Dream of Jeannie,* and here Mike wants Mona to forget she's rich. C'mon guys, wake up! Why not enjoy these opportunities with the new loves of your lives. If magic or money do end up causing problems, at least the two of you can have a good time until then! And *Mona McCluskey* producer George Burns should have known better; for years, one of his standing jokes was how little money he had compared to Gracie. Here, instead, we get just a few chuckles from the silly situation (after all, Mona is nutty enough to agree to the living arrangement), scenes with her Hollywood associates and relatives, and some mildly sexy dancing during her occasional bouts with light housework. The series only ran one season. Bet the marriage didn't last much longer.

**THE MONEYCHANGERS** (**) **(6½hr miniseries Color; 1976 NBC) Drama** *with Kirk Douglas as Alex Vandervoort, Christopher Plummer as Roscoe Heyward, Timothy Bottoms as Miles Eastin, Anne Baxter as Edwina Dorsey, Susan Flannery as Margot Bracken, Joan Collins as Avril Devereaux, and Ralph Bellamy as Jerome Patterson*

Lust and corruption amidst the high and mighty is always a popular theme for glitzy miniseries, and such is the case in this adaptation of Arthur Hailey's novel about the world of banking. At least you know there will be lots of money involved.

**THE MONKEES** (**½) **30 min (58ep Color; 1966–1968 NBC) Situation Comedy** *with Michael Nesmith as Mike, David Jones as Davy, Micky Dolenz as Micky, and Peter Tork as Peter*

A lot of people laughed at *The Monkees* in the mid-1960s. The show was said to be silly and juvenile. The group was decried for its "bubble-gum" appeal to youngsters and for its heavy use of uncredited studio musicians on its recordings. Time has been a little kinder to both the show and the group.

Today, while nobody is willing to say *The Monkees* is a spectacular TV show, or say that The Monkees were on the cutting edge of rock music, both the show and the group are appreciated as mainstream entertainment that featured some touches of avant-garde art.

The Monkees existed only because of The Beatles. The immense popularity of the British Fab Four as record sellers and the surprising critical and box-office success of their 1964 film *A Hard Day's Night* created the burning desire in Hollywood to exploit that popularity by creating a home-grown TV version of The Beatles. Thus, four mostly unknown young men were picked following a lengthy casting procedure and, voila, the world met The Monkees.

The four-man prefab rock group featured Michael Nesmith (the country-ish "smart" one frequently wearing a wool hat), Davy Jones (the short, romantic Britisher, who had already starred on Broadway in *Oliver*), Micky Dolenz (the crazy one, who, as Mickey Braddock, had been the child star lead of *Circus Boy*) and Peter Tork (the quiet, goofy one who was prone to hippie tendencies). The series focuses on their exploits as the group tries to become famous through concert and TV appearances. Meanwhile, in real life the popularity of *The Monkees* series helped transform the foursome into one of the best-selling rock groups of the mid-1960s.

Well-crafted stories are not the point of *The Monkees.* The point is to string together short bits of action with seemingly unrelated inserts, and then add frequent interludes of the group's latest record that plays over some special effects photography of the four guys, such as slow-motion or speeded-up antics. The style is right out of Richard Lester's *A Hard Day's Night,* with some Ernie Kovacs tossed in. At the time, this was quite radical for prime-time TV and the popularity of *The Monkees* helped pave the way for *Laugh-In,* which took the disconnected style of short bits and anarchic humor and developed it even further.

The problem is that *The Monkees* relies too much on the montage of the short clips of film and the special effects. There is little substance to the humor and it all wears thin quickly. The series never really develops beyond the heady, thrilling experiments of its beginning.

In the second season, the show and the group begin to take themselves a bit too seriously as they try to transcend the essentially juvenile formula created at the start. The ends of many of these episodes feature short serious discussions by the offscreen producer and the four stars that seem a bit sophomoric these days. All in all, the show can be appreciated for breaking the staid bonds of formula TV comedy, but faulted for not doing much with the new freedom.

The only area in which *The Monkees* developed during its run is in the presentation of music. While others can claim credit for developing the "first" music video, *The Monkees* is truly the spot where music video began to adopt a style all its own. At first, the weekly presentation of two of the group's songs were featured along with almost random shots of The Monkees being chased by that week's villain, or romping on the beach, or performing at a concert that was part of that episode's plot. Later shows began to create self-contained, almost thematic images to accompany the music, which is the format music videos came to adopt almost a decade later. Michael Nesmith, in fact, became one of the pioneers of music videos in his post-Monkee days, producing one of the first long-form music video projects, *Elephant Parts,* in the era before MTV.

After two seasons of weekly TV production, the Monkees struggled to break out of the teeny-bopper image for which they were originally designed. The group's one feature film, *Head,* from 1968, is a psychedelic, hallucinogenic pastiche of concepts, ideas, music, and celebrities, with heavy doses of anti–Vietnam War statements. The primary theme of the movie is The Monkees rebelling at the concept of being prepackaged media-hyped stars. The film is notable for teaming up Bob Rafelson, the producer of *The Monkees* TV show, and Jack Nicholson, soon to become a celebrity from his *Easy Rider* appearance. Rafelson directed the film and co-wrote the script (what little of it there was) with Nicholson. The two later went on to team up on the much more disciplined film *Five Easy Pieces.*

The group's final effort is 1969's little-seen TV special, "33⅓ Revolutions per Monkee," where a great lineup of early rock'n'rollers and offbeat rock stars join The Monkees in a wild musical free-for-all produced by British rock TV impresario Jack Good.

Years later, in the 1980s, a nostalgic revival of interest in *The Monkees* reunited three of the four (Nesmith excluded) for some live concerts and new recordings. This new outburst of Monkeemania resulted in a spin-off of a spin-off, the undistinguished TV series *The New Monkees,* which presented four new unknowns seeking rock stardom. ■

**THE MONROES (**½) 60 min (26ep Color; 1966–1967 ABC) Western** *with Michael Anderson, Jr. as Clayt Monroe, Barbara Hershey as Kathy Monroe, Keith Schultz as Jefferson Monroe, Kevin Schultz as Fennimore Monroe, Tammy Locke as Amy Monroe, Ron Soble as Dirty Jim, and Liam Sullivan as Maj. Mapoy*

Albert and Mary Monroe take their family of five children (ages six to eighteen) to the God-forsaken Wyoming wilderness in the 1870s, to stake out land Albert had found ten years before. Albert and Mary then drown in the Snake River, leaving the kids to fend for themselves. Clayt, the eighteen-year-old son, and Kathy, the sixteen-year-old daughter, run the family now and try to get a farm going, with the help of kindly Indian Dirty Jim. Nasty land baron Maj. Mapoy wants to kick the kids off and take the land for himself.

*The Monroes* is fine family entertainment that doesn't try to do too much, a rarity among sweeping dramas. The series was filmed largely in the Grand Teton National Park in Wyoming.

**MONSTERS (**½) 30 min (26ep at Fall 1989 Color; 1988– Syndication) Horror Anthology**

As the syndicated *Tales from the Darkside* finished its final season of new episodes, Paul Rubinstein (one of the executive producers) stepped right into production of another first-run syndication anthology. Though the series title is somewhat restrictive, fortunately there are a lot of different ways a monster can exist. (For instance, in "Feverman" it takes the form of a "fever monster" that inhabits your body.) Otherwise, *Monsters* continues the *Tales from the Darkside* formula of lean but imaginative settings with at least one familiar television face per episode (such as David McCallum as Mr. Boil, the Feverman). *Monsters* is not as strong as its predecessor, but it's still an acceptable package, even though sometimes the monster costumes look really silly. This is particularly true of the bug-eyed monster family appearing in the pre-credits sequence, in which they all sit down to watch their favorite television series, *Monsters.* That part earns a "zero" star rating.

**THE MONTEFUSCOS (**½) 30 min (8ep Color; 1975 NBC) Situation Comedy** *with Joe Sirola as Tony Montefusco, Naomi Stevens as Rose Montefusco, Ron Carey as Frank Montefusco, John Aprea as Joseph Montefusco, Sal Viscuso as Nunzio Montefusco, Linda Dano as Angela Montefusco Cooney, and Bill Cort as Jim Cooney*

An interesting mid-1970s stab at reviving the lost art of the ethnic family sitcom, *The Montefuscos* got the bum's rush when it originally aired and never had the chance to develop into the fun series it could have been. Tony and Rose Montefusco, Italian-American parents of three sons and a daughter, live in suburban Connecticut. Each Sunday, the kids and their spouses and children come over for family dinner, where all issues, both family and national, are discussed but rarely resolved. Bill Persky and Sam Denoff, of the old *Dick Van Dyke Show,* serve as producers.

**MONTY NASH** (*) **30 min (31ep Color; 1971–1972 Syndication) Adventure** *with Henry Guardino as Monty Nash*

Monty Nash, a character created by novelist Richard Jessup, is a free-wheeling U.S. spy handling secret missions directly for the White House. Sounds an awful lot like G. Gordon Liddy and the Watergate burglars, doesn't it?

**MONTY PYTHON'S FLYING CIRCUS** (****) **30 min (45ep Color; 1969–1974 UK BBC) Comedy** *with John Cleese, Graham Chapman, Eric Idle, Michael Palin, Terry Jones, and Terry Gilliam*

This is truly something completely different. *Monty Python's Flying Circus* is a brilliantly funny comedy program perfect for fans of bawdy burlesque houses as well as English history and literature majors. The scripts are incredibly literate and witty, and childish and vulgar. There's esoteric highbrow humor and lowbrow pants-dropping punchlines. Nobody named Monty or Python appears on the series, and the show has nothing to do with flying (except for a few sheep) or a circus.

The Pythons started in 1969 as a British contemporary of *Rowan & Martin's Laugh-In.* Like that Stateside program, they included a good number of technical tricks such as quick cuts, bits of animation, and rapid-fire one-liner drop-ins. However, unlike *Laugh-In,* on *Monty Python* the same people conceived, wrote, and performed the material. And they played nearly every role (sometimes assuming multiple characters in the same sketch), including most female parts (which they did dressed in drag). This almost obsessive involvement with the production from the script to the final credits gave *Monty Python* a much greater sense of cohesive identity, rather like British radio's madcap *Goon Show* (with Peter Sellers) in the 1950s. The approach was also much more faithful to the TV ancestor of both *Laugh-In* and *Monty Python,* Ernie Kovacs, who conceived, wrote, and starred in his own journeys into Kovacsland.

Perhaps the greatest single change *Monty Python* brought to comedy was the conviction that with the right segue you could go successfully from any point to any point at any point. This eliminates the need to have a beginning, middle, and end to every bit. Instead great setups without a punch line could zip through to a punch line that need no setup. The cumulative effect is that of disciplined, organized chaos, juxtaposing some incredibly obscure literary (or cricket) allusion with a bit of cheap slapstick. Or combining it, as in a semaphore code version of *Wuthering Heights.*

To illustrate the transitional flow in just part of one episode: A man waiting in a drawing room watches in horror as everything and everybody else in it collapses around him. Then the entire house explodes, so he and some characters from a previous scene walk from the rubble, pass a bishop (who will be in the next episode), and enter a music hall performance of "Seven Brides for Seven Brothers." Two cut-out characters pass in front of the sheet music to the show talking about piggy bank hunting, which then begins in an open field and ends with the body parts of the smashed piggies turning into a meat chart on a butcher shop wall. Which is where the next segment begins.

Yet, in general, that typically mad structure is not meant to hide bad material beneath stylistic tricks. Rather it reflects a half-dozen writers bursting with off-the-wall concepts that they are determined to see played out on television. One time, in fact, they organized an episode so that it almost looks like a regular story, perhaps to demonstrate just how flexible their approach really is. Michael Palin plays Mr. Pither, a young man on a cross-country bicycle trip. The episode begins with him setting off and ends with him continuing his journey. Of course, along the way there are plenty of sidebar bits including a confrontation in a doctor's waiting room, a scientist who thinks he is either Trotsky or Eartha Kitt, and a giant animated singing monster.

Ah, the animation. Initially described by one British paper as the "funniest and cruelest items" on the program, they're the product of the only American in the troupe, Terry Gilliam. Like the rest of the program, the animated bits can lead anywhere and involve anything. For instance, in one version of the opening credits, a short man with wings flies across the sky with a program title banner before being crushed by a giant bare foot from above.

The Pythons not only show little respect for their own opening and closing credits, they also frequently rearrange their placement, dropping them virtually anywhere in the program. Sometimes, they even follow the "end" of their show with official-looking announcements about "other" BBC offerings. But that's only their most gentle ribbing of the medium. The cast really lets itself loose in skewering pompous commentators, pretentious documentary makers, and empty-headed interviewers. Yet in all of these shows, they rarely mock specific current events, preferring instead to dig at timeless targets (virtually anyone in any position of power), working under the assumption that any projected public image is probably a self-serving illusion. How else to explain an interviewer who insists on pressing ahead with questions directed to a tree and a filing cabinet?

But all the philosophical and technical tricks aside, *Monty Python's Flying Circus* works because it is funny. And many of the longer bits even translated quite well to a live stage setting, as the troupe demonstrated with shows in London, New York, and Los Angeles. Even without any video enhancement, audiences still loved watching such sketches as "Blackmail," "The Lumberjack Song," "The Argument Clinic," and, most popular, "The Dead Parrot" (which inevitably touched off a roar of approval when John Cleese entered a pet shop holding a dead parrot and delivered his entrance line, "I wish to register a complaint!").

Though *Monty Python* ran for a little more than three seasons in Britain, there are only forty-five episodes total (thirteen in each full season). John Cleese does not appear in the final six. *Monty Python's Flying Circus* first became a hit in the United States in the mid-1970s, a few years after it had finished its entire run in Britain. The cast used that newfound notoriety to launch dozens of other projects, both as a group and as individuals. They focused primarily on theatrical film ventures, but also turned out a few other television series, including Eric Idle's *Rutland Weekend Television,* Michael Palin's *Ripping Yarns,* and John Cleese's *Fawlty Towers.*

This series runs the full thirty minutes (sometimes a bit over), so be sure to catch it on a service (a public broadcasting station or a cable channel) with a schedule that allots enough time. ■

**MOONLIGHTING (****) 60 min (65ep & 2 hr pilot Color; 1985–1989 ABC) Detective Drama** *with Cybill Shepherd as Maddie Hayes, Bruce Willis as David Addison, Allyce Beasley as Agnes Dipesto, Curtis Armstrong as Herbert Viola, Jack Blessing as MacGilicuddy, Charles Rocket as Richard Addison, Robert Webber as Alex Hayes, and Eva Marie Saint as Virginia Hayes*

Television's first detective show disguised as a comedy-variety drama anthology series. (Or was it the other way around?) This innovative creation of Glenn Gordon Caron (who worked briefly on *Remington Steele*) uses the chemistry between its two leads as the springboard for almost anything.

It all starts innocently enough, with the initial two-hour pilot film and first batch of episodes playing pretty much as a light detective drama sprinkled with some clever dialogue and an obvious attraction between the two main characters (which neither wants to admit to the other, at first). Maddie Hayes is a glamorous fashion model (the seductive symbol used in the promos for "Blue Moon" shampoo) who returns from a trip abroud to discover most of her accumulated fortune (the liquid assets) stolen by her suddenly ex-financial manager. Distraught over having to start all over again, she starts to unload some of her investment properties (mainly because she can't afford them; most were being used as tax losses), including the City of Angels Detective Agency. David Addison, head of the company (who finds Maddie a knockout at first sight), points out that the agency was supposed to lose money, but if it were run with a different goal (profit), it could be a winner. More important, by the end of their first adventure together, he also talks her into sticking around to be an active partner, renaming the business as an affectionate tie to her past (Blue Moon Investigations). It seems the perfect solution to a midlife crisis: The new job gives her something to do and gives David the chance for the two of them to "get horizontal." Or so he dreams.

It would seem unlikely. He's hip, flippant, fiercely noncommittal in the area of romance, sings old rock and soul songs, and is more likely to hold his own at an office limbo party than among the fashionably elite. She, on the other hand, prefers Sinatra to Sam and Dave, feels perfectly comfortable in the most sophisticated circles, prefers order and decorum to chaos, and, most of all, expects the man of her dreams to fit all her preconceived romantic notions. They couldn't be more dissimilar. They argue all the time. And, of course, they soon discover that they're crazy about each other. But that doesn't truly blossom for a while.

In the meantime, they maintain separate but facing offices, go on cases together, and in between attempt to balance the books and manage the agency's staff. However, with the exception of rhyming receptionist Agnes Dipesto, and junior operatives Herbert Viola (her boyfriend) and MacGilicuddy (his chief rival), most of these support people remain anonymously in the background. (Still, just to have a full working staff on a TV detective show is an amazing innovation—it suggests that *someone* has to do all the dull follow-up paperwork or pursue the dozens of boring cases that probably pay the bills while the stars take on the flashy stuff.) Yet just as David and Maddie are getting comfortable with their routine, Caron and his crew give them plenty of chances to break from it.

To start, the writers follow an unusual structure for the cases. Even if a client comes in and says "here's my problem," it probably isn't. Instead, about halfway through the story, viewers have to begin asking themselves: What's *really* going on? And, sure enough, David and Maddie soon end up backing into the real case—the one they discover when wrapping up what they thought was the old one, talking about their investigations. Or while talking about anything. Which is a perfect justification for what soon becomes the real focus of each episode anyway, their rapid-fire exchanges.

It's a feast of clever dialogue, liable to trip into a Dr. Seuss riff, allusions to pop culture, and, increasingly, jibes at the entertainment industry itself (especially their own television show). This sense of self-awareness quickly expands, playfully alluding to the pop culture success of David and Maddie's other identities (Bruce Willis and Cybill Shepherd), and toying with the fact that the adventures of Blue Moon Investigations take place on a television series. As a result, the characters turn up in pre-credits sequences talking about the series, drop comments about plot twists and chase scenes during the show, and even find themselves pursued by the likes of Rona Barrett as part of one of *her* TV reports.

But after a while such media in-jokes can begin to wear thin as dramatic distractions. Fortunately they are accompanied by some excellent writing and a genuine sense of innovation. Caron and crew effectively used the series setting and cast members almost like the repertory company for some drama or variety anthology series. (In fact, they opened one season just like a classic variety series, with everybody dancing and singing on the set. All that was missing was some announcer listing "this week's guest stars," capped with an enthusiastic "And Awaaay We Go!"). Most times, though, everyone is in a regular detective setting—it's just that there's always the option of a different type of tale. One of the first examples is a black-and-white "film noir" episode ("The Flashback Always Rings Twice") introduced by Orson Welles, coincidentally airing about the time of his death. Others include a remake of *It's a Wonderful Life,* a restaging of William Shakespeare's *The Taming of the Shrew,* and the personal observations of a fetus awaiting birth.

But most often the series excels in clever set pieces incorporated into a "regular" story, using them as the best way to illustrate an emotion or to deal with a situation. Usually this means another round of clever dialogue. But it also includes such specialized bits as a stylized dance number (staged by Vincent Minelli to Billy Joel's "Big Man on Mulberry Street"); a pre-date pep-talk song by Ray Charles (playing his piano in David's living room); a violently erotic music-video-style accompaniment to Janet Jackson's hit song "Nasty"; a *Honeymooners* parody with David as Ralph and Maddie as Alice; and a telephone receiver that turns into a clever "Claymation"-style figure of Maddie (during a period in which Cybill Shepherd was pregnant in real life and couldn't appear much on camera).

Still *Moonlighting* plays well in reruns because the dialogue is clever, there is plenty of action (with the semiobligatory chase scenes usually played for slapstick effect), and, of course, Maddie and David really are in love. In fact, for a while (about the time of Shepherd's pregnancy), Caron and the writers seemed driven to push the love story aspect of the Maddie and David tale as hard as they could, apparently determined not to duplicate the *Remington Steele* situation of stretching out courtship without consummation for five years. There's no such hesitation here, though they quickly discovered that the morning after brings its own unique problems, both to the characters and the scripts. After flirting with marriage and parenthood (in a season of episodes playing more like a soap opera than a detective series), Maddie and David pull back to a safer distance in their private and work lives. As a result, later *Moonlighting* plays more like earlier *Moonlighting,* only with some of the anticipation gone.

In *Moonlighting*'s original network run, the series was constantly behind in production (airing fewer first-run episodes than any other successful program), so there were numerous references to those delays in the scripts, drop-ins, and wraparounds. All of that is irrelevant in syndicated reruns, which is probably why most of the opening bits tacked onto the rerun episodes will never turn up again. ■

**THE MOONSTONE (**½) 60 min (5ep Color; 1972 UK BBC) Mystery** *with John Welsh as Sergeant Cuff, Vivien Heilbron as Rachel, Robin Ellis as Franklin Blake, Martin Jarvis as Godfrey Abelwhite, Basil Dignam as Betteredge, and Anna Cropper as Rosanna Spearman.*

Adaptation of the first full-length English detective novel, written by Wilkie Collins in the mid-1800s soon after Edgar Allen Poe's ground-breaking "Murders in the Rue Morgue" short story virtually defined the genre. This tale is set in 1848, tying in with a current event: the establishment of the British rule in the Punjab province of India, symbolized by the presentation of a huge diamond (the Koh-I-Noor) to Queen Victoria from the Maharajah. For the purposes of this mystery scenario, that "moonstone" is a giant yellow diamond stolen from the statue of an Indian god by an English soldier in the midst of a siege in India. And that's what everyone is out to locate. Fortunately the reliable combination of a missing object, plenty of suspects (including the familiar butler and maid), and a top-notch detective (Sergeant Cliff) keeps this prototype story moving quite well.

**MORK & MINDY (***) 30 min (95ep Color; 1978–1982 ABC) Situation Comedy** *with Robin Williams as Mork, Pam Dawber as Mindy McConnell, Conrad Janis as Frederick McConnell, Elizabeth Kerr as Cora Hudson, and Ralph James as the voice of Orson.*

It's easy to get tired watching Mork & Mindy. The pace set by Robin Williams, who plays Mork, is so frenetic that it's tiring just trying to keep up with all the bits of business he tosses in.

The plot is sort of a 1970s update of *My Favorite Martian*, with a little sex appeal tossed in. Mork, an easygoing alien from the planet Ork (where humor has been mostly bred out of the inhabitants), is dispatched to Earth (in an egg-shaped spaceship) to study the strange behavior of the human race. He lands in Boulder, Colorado, and is found by pretty, young, single Mindy McConnell. At first, Mindy is the only one who knows about Mork's background and he talks her into letting him move into her apartment (he sleeps in the attic loft). Mork is Helen Keller to Mindy's Annie Sullivan, in that Mindy goes about teaching Mork how to exist in a human environment. The naturally goony way the alien acts and his misunderstanding of human traits serve as the jumping points for many of the laughs in *Mork & Mindy.*

Secondary characters include Mindy's father Fred, a classical music lover who runs a record shop, and Cora, Mindy's grandmother. Dad is understandably rattled when his eligible daughter starts living with a goofball who says and does very weird things (putting on his clothes backwards, sitting upside down on sofas). Grandma, a perky old lass, is gung-ho on Mork, finding his bohemian nature close to her own heart. Finally there is the unseen but often heard Orson, Mork's superior back on Ork. Mork concludes each episode with a report back to

Orson, thereby providing a chance to neatly wrap up the moral of each show in a short, funny retort.

The alien on Earth concept is always good for laughs. Mork's silly antics and catch phrases in the Orkan language ("na nu, na nu") appeal to kids real fast. Still it is the lightening fast repartee and sly social commentary of Robin Williams that lifts this sitcom out of the ordinary and makes it appeal to older teens and others who like a lot of sarcasm with their humor. Williams is a walking encyclopedia of pop culture. He is liable to slip in some veiled reference to an old hit movie or an old rock'n'roll song in the midst of an otherwise blitzkrieg attack of dialogue. He will pop in and out of numerous characters, each with a distinct personality, faster than many can calculate.

It is unfortunate that after the first season of *Mork & Mindy* (which was an instant hit when it first aired), all sorts of self-defeating changes begin to occur. Characters come and go, for no good reason. Story lines become either far too serious or too confusing. The whole basic foundation of the show, letting Williams go wild as Mork, begins to fall apart. By the third season the program begins to return to its original form, but something of value has been lost. The new side characters only take up space Williams could better fill. The budding romance and marriage of Mork and Mindy seems inevitable, but it winds up not adding much to the plot possibilities.

The only advantage to the changes in *Mork & Mindy* is the final season appearance of Jonathan Winters as Mearth, the fully grown offspring of Mork & Mindy's marriage. The explanation of Mearth's huge size at birth makes no sense at all, but who cares? The presence of Winters (Williams' comic idol) documents the straight line from the 1950s humor of Winters to the 1970s weirdness of Williams. Watching the two comic giants together is worth the bad middle years of *Mork & Mindy*.

The character of Mork first appeared in a February 1978 episode of *Happy Days*, where Mork tried to kidnap Richie Cunningham. The popular response to the character led to the *Mork & Mindy* series, which is produced by Garry Marshall, producer of *Happy Days*. Mork, Mindy, Mr. McConnell, and Orson all pop up again in one season of animated cartoons (from 1982) also titled *Mork & Mindy* (with the original cast providing voices).

**MORNINGSTAR/EVENINGSTAR (**½) (6ep Color; 1986 CBS) Drama** *with Mason Adams as Gordon Blair, Scatman Crothers as Excell Dennis, Sylvia Sidney as Binnie Baylor, Jeff Corey as Bill McGregor, Kate Reid as Martha Cameron, Elizabeth Wilson as Kathy Kelly, Ketty Lester as Nora Blake, Leaf Phoenix as Doug Roberts, Darrell Larson as Bob Lane, and Sherry Hursey as Debbie Flynn*

A short-run series from *Waltons* creator Earl Hamner, Jr., placing a special emphasis on portraying senior citizens as vigorous and active people. (If you liked the 1985 theatrical feature film *Cocoon*, you should love this one.) The setup is simple: A fire at Morningstar orphanage leaves social worker Bob Lane seeking a temporary home for some of his charges. To solve the problem, he and his old friend Debbie Flynn (who runs the Eveningstar senior citizens' center) agree to merge facilities. The result is the opportunity for affectionate, healthy interaction between the old-timers and the kids.

Not surprisingly, the stories are well done, if occasionally over-sentimental. The most familiar faces among the seniors are Scatman Crothers (who did much the same thing in the 1983 *Twilight Zone* theatrical film), Sylvia Sidney (Mama Carlson in the *WKRP in Cincinnati* pilot), and Mason Adams (Charlie Hume on *Lou Grant* and the voice on dozens of commercials such as those for Smuckers jams).

**MOSES THE LAWGIVER (**) 60 min (6ep Color; 1973–1974 UK ATV Italy) Drama** *with Burt Lancaster as Moses, Anthony Quayle as Aaron, Ingrid Thulin as Miriam, Irene Papas as Zipporah, and Laurent Terzieff as Pharaoh*

Filmed on location in Israel, this miniseries covers the same territory as the classic Cecil B. DeMille film of *The Ten Commandments*, only without the spectacular widescreen effects. The cast is good, with Lancaster quite strong in the title role, but the six-hour pace of the series is quite slow without really adding much to DeMille's nearly four-hour 1956 epic.

**THE MOST DEADLY GAME (**) 60 min (12ep Color; 1970–1971 ABC) Detective Drama** *with George Maharis as Jonathan Croft, Yvette Mimieux as Vanessa Smith, and Ralph Bellamy as Ethan Arcane*

The most deadly game is murder, and renowned criminologist Ethan Arcane and his two good-looking assistants Jonathan Croft and Vanessa Smith spend their time solving the puzzle of various murders.

While essentially just a standard whodunit, *The Most Deadly Game* has its moments of pleasure. Considering that the show's executive producer is Aaron Spelling (*The Mod Squad, The Love Boat*), *The Most Deadly Game* is remarkably free of glitz and titillation.

**MOST WANTED (*½) 60 min (22ep & 90 min pilot Color; 1976–1977 ABC) Police Drama** *with Robert Stack as Capt. Linc Evers, Shelly Novack as Sgt. Charlie Benson, Jo Ann Harris as Officer Kate Manners and Harry Rhodes as Mayor Dan Stoddard*

Robert Stack once again takes on the criminal element, this time as head of a special squad from the Los Angeles Police Department, assigned to pursue those on the mayor's most wanted list. A routine exercise, best limited to just the ninety-minute pilot film (with guest star Tom Selleck), showing Stack and his streetwise team in search of a nun killer. ■

**THE MOTHERS-IN-LAW** (***) **30 min (54ep Color; 1967–1969 NBC) Situation Comedy** *with Eve Arden as Eve Hubbard, Kaye Ballard as Kaye Buell, Roger C. Carmel and Richard Deacon as Roger Buell, Herbert Rudley as Herb Hubbard, Jerry Fogel as Jerry Buell, and Deborah Walley as Susie Hubbard Buell*

There is no plot so basic as intersecting families, neighbors who grow up and old together. That is the heart of *The Mothers-In-Law*, a fine little gem of a late 1960s sitcom.

The Hubbards are normal. Herb is a powerful lawyer; Eve is a former golf pro and civic organizer. The Buells are more offbeat. Roger is a TV script writer (this is Los Angeles, naturally) who works mostly at home. Kaye is a lax housekeeper who would rather run everyone's lives. For fifteen years, the Hubbards and the Buells have lived next door to each other and stayed friends. Now the Buell's son Jerry has married the Hubbard's daughter, Susie, and the young couple, who live above the Hubbard's garage, must struggle to establish their own lives amidst so much family.

What makes this show is the cast. Eve Arden is just as sharp as she was when starring in *Our Miss Brooks.* Singer/comedienne Kaye Ballard, a minor league Martha Raye, parlayed her plain looks, strong voice, and loud manner into a long career highlighted by numerous appearances as a guest on TV variety and talk shows. Roger C. Carmel is beloved by *Star Trek* fans as the maniacal Harry Mudd, interstellar con man. Carmel is replaced in the second season by Richard Deacon, Mel Cooley of *The Dick Van Dyke Show*. The presence of so many TV veterans here can be explained by the presence of executive producer Desi Arnaz (*I Love Lucy*), who also appears in the show irregularly as bullfighter Raphael del Gado.

**THE MOUSE FACTORY** (**½) **30 min (40ep Color; 1971–1973 Syndication) Anthology**

More than a decade before there was a separate Disney Channel, the Walt Disney studios developed this first-run syndication series as yet another way to repackage classic footage. On each episode a different guest celebrity (such as John Astin, Wally Cox, Joe Flynn, or even Annette Funicello) "punches in" for a visit to the Disney studios (also known as the "Mouse Factory"), serving as narrator to a selected topic. These are fairly broad subjects (cars, ghosts, flying), allowing just about anything to be pulled and incorporated into the show. While it's always great to see the original full-length presentations, collections like these are fun to watch as scrapbook reminders of favorite moments. They'd be a lot better, though, if the sources of all the bits and pieces were identified.

**MOVIN' ON** (**) **60 min (44ep & 90 min pilot Color; 1974–1976 NBC) Adventure** *with Claude Akins as Sonny Pruitt, Frank Converse as Will Chandler, Rosey Grier as Benjy, and Art Metrano as Moose*

Truck drivers were "in" for about a year or so in the mid-1970s, and *Movin' On* is a result of that fad. Set up just like a lot of the cop shows of that era, *Movin' On* merely changes the police cruiser for the big rig, while keeping the old-fashioned cop versus refined new cop concept that was so popular then. Claude Akins, one of TV's favorite rednecks (*Sheriff Lobo*), plays grizzled trucker Sonny Pruitt. Pruitt is teamed up with Will Chandler, a philosophical law school graduate turned trucker who is looking to find truth on the interstates. Chandler is played by the more cerebral Frank Converse, who played the bright young cop (Johnny Corso) on *N.Y.P.D.*

The 1974 pilot for *Movin' On* is called *In Tandem.* Popular country and western singer Merle Haggard sings the theme song.

**MULLIGAN'S STEW** (*) **60 min (8ep & 90 min pilot Color; 1977 NBC) Comedy-Drama** *with Lawrence Pressman as Michael Mulligan, Elinor Donahue as Jane Mulligan, Johnny Doran as Mark Mulligan, Julie Anne Haddock as Melinda Mulligan, and K. C. Martel as Jimmy Mulligan*

The play on words in the title with the main character's name is the only innovative aspect of this slow saga of the Mulligan clan. High school gym coach Michael, school nurse Jane, and their three kids all live close together but well in another nameless Southern California suburb. Into this nirvana come four more kids, Mike's nephew and nieces, who move in when Mike's sister and her husband are killed. To be topical, one of the adopted kids is a Vietnamese orphan. The kid has great luck, orphaned twice in five years.

**THE MUNSTERS** (**) **330 min (70ep B&W & 2 hr sequel Color; 1964–1966 CBS) Situation Comedy** *with Fred Gwynne as Herman Munster, Yvonne DeCarlo as Lily Munster, Al Lewis as Grandpa Munster, Butch Patrick as Eddie Munster, and Beverly Owen and Pat Priest as Marilyn Munster*

A simple 1960s sitcom family setup, with this gimmick: Members of the Munster clan look as if they just stepped out from the set of some old monster movie. They're dead ringers (so to speak) for Frankenstein's monster (Herman, the dad), a lady vampire (Lily, his wife), a budding future teen wolf (Eddie, their son), an aging Count Dracula (Grandpa, Herman's dad), and the usual victim in such tales (Marilyn, their attractive, normal-looking niece). They all live in a creepy-looking old mansion in the suburban town of Mockingbird Heights and (here's the deliberate twist for the whole series) they think of themselves as a perfectly normal average American family. And so they act like it—even if "normal" for them means steam pouring out of Herman's ears, bubbling potions cooked by Grandpa in the basement, and a hearse as a family car.

Surprisingly most other people don't give their appearance a second thought either. Eddie's school chums nonchalantly drop by to play. Herman has a regular job at the local funeral home. Lily manages the house and talks to Eddie's teachers when necessary. Even their niece doesn't see any reason to move out of the spacious (if incredibly dusty) old home. As a result, while the episodes frequently make use of their "monster" traits (struck by a car, pedestrian Herman is likely to leave the vehicle damaged), most of the stories consist of typical sitcom complications. For examples, Herman goes on a diet so he can fit into his old army uniform, Herman thinks Lily is pregnant, Grandpa leaves home because he feels nobody needs him, and Herman becomes jealous when Eddie admires a kid's TV show "monster" more than him.

All of this is fine, but ultimately a bit disappointing. Why go to all the trouble of getting a house full of neat-looking characters and them have them play through such routine stories? You'd expect at least a little intentionally outrageous behavior rather than such a comfortably settled way of life. But maybe if you've grown up with bats in your belfry, you learn how to take everything in stride.

Besides the original seventy *Munsters* episodes, there is also an unexceptional theatrical feature (*Munster, Go home*, in color) issued in the program's final year (1966). Fifteen years later, Gwynne, DeCarlo, and Lewis reunited for a 1981 one-shot made-for-TV movie revival (*The Munsters' Revenge*). And, for all its weaknesses, *The Munsters* did give *Car 54, Where Are You?* veterans Gwynne and Lewis a chance to get out of their drab cop uniforms. What's more, the original series improves somewhat with age—and almost looks like a Noel Coward classic when compared to its 1988 revival. ■

**THE MUNSTERS TODAY (zero) 30 min (24ep at Fall 1989 Color; 1988– Syndication) Situation Comedy**
*with John Schuck as Herman Munster, Lee Meriwether as Lily Munster, Howard Morton as Grandpa Munster, Jason Marsden as Eddie Munster, and Hilary Van Dyke as Marilyn Munster.*

First, there's the official explanation for all this: According to the show's opening bit, one of Grandpa's experiments went haywire many years ago and the entire Munster family ended up in suspended animation for some two decades (apparently sleeping through their 1981 reunion movie). Now they're awake and performing again, even happily singing the program's theme song (chanting "we're the Munsters" like they're at a basketball pep rally).

Maybe. But perhaps the truth might be closer to this: On a dare, an enthusiastic little community theater group (long on heart, short on experience and funds for scripts and sets) decided to secretly restage one of their favorite TV series on a local cable access channel (estimated audience: about ten). Unfortunately for them, one of their viewers turned out to be an unscrupulous packager who videotaped their crude productions and sold them into syndication. If only they knew, maybe they'd stop.

Or else there's the most frightening possibility of all: A few familiar comedy faces, some relative newcomers, and hapless guest stars were lured into what seemed to be a harmless project—revive the popular *Munsters* characters for first-run syndication—not realizing they were about to become part of something destined to be nominated as one of the worst television series ever.

What's the true explanation? Watch as much of one episode as you can. Then you decide.

**THE MUPPET SHOW (***) 30 min (120ep & 30 min pilot Color; 1976–1981 Syndication) Comedy-Variety**
*with the voices of Jim Henson as Kermit the Frog, Rowlf, Capt. Link Heartthrob, and Waldorf, Frank Oz as Miss Piggy and Fozzie Bear, Dave Goelz as Gonzo and Dr. Bunsen Honeydew, and Richard Hunt as Statler*

Jim Henson created the term "muppet" (part marionette, part puppet) in the late 1950s when he was just starting to appear on local and network TV variety shows. Throughout the 1960s, Henson's expanding troupe of muppets became familiar characters, due to frequent exposure on shows such as *The Jimmy Dean Show* (where Rowlf was a regular). In 1969, with the premiere of *Sesame Street*, the characters of Ernie, Bert, Grover, the Cookie Monster, and Big Bird (all Henson creations) became household names with America's youth.

Yet even with all this fame, Henson and his band of merry men and women could not land a slot on network TV, not even on Saturday morning. A wonderful pilot ran in prime time on ABC in March 1975, but the network passed on the show. It took Sir Lew Grade's ITV network in Britain to fund the thirty-minute series called *The Muppet Show* that became one of TV's biggest first-run syndication smashes in the 1970s.

In format, *The Muppet Show* somewhat resembles the old *Jack Benny Program*, in that it is a show within a show. The characters are always running around, struggling to put on their weekly program. Part of the fun is watching the hectic preparation and last-minute crises behind the curtain, and part of the fun is watching the "real" skits.

Host of the show is Kermit the Frog, a self-effacing, shy pond refugee, whose kindness is frequently taken advantage of. Never far behind Kermit is Miss Piggy, a wonderful creation, the closest thing to a female Ralph Kramden we have. Miss Piggy is loud, boisterous, obnoxious, pushy, self-centered, and fat, yet lovable.

After Kermit and Miss Piggy came a horde of other equally ingenious characters that fill the muppet menagerie. Rowlf is a shaggy piano-playing dog, Gonzo is the trumpet-playing failure, and Statler and Waldorf are the two old sourpusses in the box seats, closing each show with amusingly horrible puns.

What makes *The Muppet Show* so wonderful is its ability to entertain both children and adults. For the kids, the loud, funny muppets are enough. For the adults, the sophisticated humor and the celebrity guest hosts are ample attraction. After following the Muppet saga of *Pigs in Space*, with the exploits of Capt. Link Heartthrob on the spaceship Swinetrek, the old *Star Treks* just never seems the same.

The production here is top-notch. Aside from the obvious complexities of doing a show with a mixed cast of muppets and humans, *The Muppet Show* always manages to come up with novel ways of presenting musical numbers. Guest singers do not just mime their hits but record new versions, often with muppet accompaniment.

Before *The Muppet Show* ceased production, Henson took his clan to the big screen for *The Muppet Movie*, the first in a series of Hollywood movies featuring the muppets. A mediocre Saturday morning cartoon show, *Muppet Babies*, followed in 1984. ■

**MURDER, SHE WROTE** (***) **60 min (110ep at Fall 1989 Color; 1984– CBS) Mystery** *with Angela Lansbury as Jessica Fletcher, William Windom as Dr. Seth Hazlitt, and Tom Bosley as Sheriff Amos Tupper*

You'd think Jessica Fletcher would be the most unwelcome relative ever to come calling. After all, a visit from aunt (or cousin) Jessica is almost certain to involve death, with kin or their close friends usually ending up accused of murder.

Maybe they're just curious to see what might turn up in Jessica's next murder mystery novel. Unlike most other amateur sleuths, Jessica can actually make use of the cases she helps solve, though no doubt she alters a few key names and settings to avoid possible lawsuits.

Or maybe they just want to ask her when she has time to write, in between promotional trips, visits to out-of-town relatives, and everyday life in Cabot Cove. Inevitably, a murder mystery fills her spare time in each of those settings.

However she does it, there's no mystery behind the attraction of *Murder, She Wrote.* For mystery buffs, it's one of the rare television ventures into the form that actually offers a solvable mystery that plays absolutely fair with the audience. All too many TV "mysteries" simply withhold a guilty party's identity until the end. In those, the explanations (if any) are outlandish at best and (more often) simply an arbitrary assignment of guilt.

*Murder, She Wrote* offers clues, opportunities to see the suspects in action, and a clear moment when you (the viewer) should be ready with your solution. This point comes about forty-five minutes into the show, usually when Jessica says to some other character, "*Thank you* very much!" (for inadvertently pointing out a vital piece of evidence). Then she runs off to a final confrontation with the guilty party.

For those with no interest in the machinations of mysteries, the appeal of *Murder, She Wrote* is still perfectly obvious: Angela Lansbury. Though she has a few regulars supporting her in the Cabot Cove stories (most notably Tom Bosley as Sheriff Amos Tupper and William Windom as Dr. Seth Hazlitt), Lansbury is the driving force in the series. She's in virtually every scene (well, except for the murder itself), confronting each character with a mix of tough talk, sweetly innocent inquiry, and diplomatic suggestions for resolving the situation. In some cases, Lansbury has even played a second role (usually a cousin), thus setting up scenes in which she has to confront herself! Now that's a busy woman.

Fortunately, Lansbury is excellent in the role, taking it beyond being just another Miss Marple type. Jessica Fletcher is very active, very outgoing, and very comfortable in virtually any setting.

With about one hundred stories done over the course of the series, there are bound to be some repetitive patterns. Since every mystery fan has a favorite "here's how you solve the case from the opening credits" theory, here's one to try next time you follow the series a while: Scan the guest star list at the beginning and select the performer that is best known for playing a basically good person—for instance, William Christopher (Fr. Mulcahy on *M*A*S*H*) or Gary Sandy (Andy Travis on *WKRP*). If that character is not the victim or the wrongly accused, you've probably found your killer.

Maybe. With long-time mystery buffs Richard Levinson and William Link behind the series, you know that no rule of thumb can be a completely safe bet.

**MURPHY BROWN** (***½) **30 min (22ep at Fall 1989 Color; 1988– CBS) Situation Comedy** *with Candice Bergen as Murphy Brown, Faith Ford as Corky Sherwood, Joe Regalbuto as Frank Fontana, Charles Kimbrough as Jim Dial, Grant Shaud as Miles Silverberg, Robert Pastorelli as Eldin Bernecky, and Pat Corley as Phil*

Murphy Brown is a hard-hitting TV feature reporter who's knocked heads with world leaders, exposed assorted business bigwigs, and absolutely terrorized her fellow workers as a selfish, testy, and demanding superstar. Then she spent a month at the Betty Ford Center excising her physical demons (coffee, booze, cigarettes) and, much to everyone's surprise, comes back an almost reasonable human being. She'll still kill for a story, but now actually allows her co-workers a moment to scurry to safety. Sometimes she's even friendly to them.

This package hits its stride right from the beginning with good writing and an excellent cast, led by Candice Bergen's Murphy. She's a confident, sharp-tongued professional who loves tracking down a lead almost as much as listening to her favorite 1960s soul music tunes (a perfect excuse to work those into the soundtrack). Murphy is accustomed to getting her way, but (thanks to her new outlook on life) she's also able to accept the less than perfect situations thrust upon her—

like a new producer (Miles) so young he's never heard of the Shirelles; or an interior wall painter (Eldin) who has managed to turn a simple two-day job at her home into what seems to be an excuse to move in; and a former beauty queen turned reporter (Corkey), who shares the *FYI* (*For Your Information*) anchor desk delivering her observations on such hard-hitting topics as liposuction. Add to that daily stress such one-time disasters as a gunman who holds the entire *FYI* crew hostage while on the air or a family of kids dropped at Murphy's office at Christmas time (she hates kids) and you can almost forgive her for casting an envious eye on a shot of bourbon, or at least on a cup of black caffeine-rich coffee.

With its focus on an independent female lead, and a nightly news setup as the centerpiece, *Murphy Brown* bears at least a passing resemblance to the 1970s *Mary Tyler Moore Show.* Appropriately, then, the supporting cast is rounded out by Frank, a witty, balding copy writer who wears a toupee when on camera, and Jim, the good-looking deep-voiced main anchor. (Murray Slaughter and Ted Baxter would be proud to know them.) And, best of all, like *Mary Tyler Moore, Murphy Brown* puts its characters into imaginative situations, and then delivers the scripts to support them. It's a potent combination that's a genuine pleasure to watch.

**MURPHY'S LAW (**) 60 min (13ep Color; 1988–1989 ABC) Detective Drama** *with George Segal as Daedelus Patrick Murphy, Maggie Han as Kimiko "Kimi" Fannuchi, Josh Mostel as Wesley Harden, and Lynne Randall as Harriet Tapplinger*

Geroge Segal ought to know better. A talented comedic actor, he's appeared in several fine films (*Who's Afraid of Virginia Woolf?, A Touch of Glass,* and *California Split*) and made several guest appearances on TV variety shows. Now in his mid-fifties, soon after his first TV series (*Take Five*) died a quick death, he appears in *Murphy's Law* as a horny, recovering alcoholic, perpetually broke, divorced insurance investigator with the unwieldy moniker of Daedelus Patrick Murphy. Living with a gorgeous Eurasian model, Kimi, who can't be more than half his age, Murphy is forever being interrupted at an inopportune moment in his constant advances on Kimi. As for Kimi herself, she is a wisecracker who spends a good chunk of the series walking around wearing only a bed sheet or a towel. The relationship between the two is much too coy and Murphy is thick and annoying.

A lot of time is spent on Murphy's efforts to prove he is dried out enough to be awarded visitation rights to see his young daughter. This adds some nice conflicts to the plots, but winds up seeming too much like an element tossed in by the writers just to make Murphy seem more lovable.

**MUSIC HALL AMERICA (*) 60 min (26ep Color; 1976–1977 Syndication) Musical-Variety**

Guest hosts headline this mid-1970s show of country and western talent taped in Nashville.

**THE MUSIC SCENE (***) 45 min (13ep Color; 1969–1970 ABC) Musical-Variety** *with David Steinberg as host*

One of the very few forty-five-minute musical-variety shows in TV history, *The Music Scene* is hardly ever rerun, due to its odd length. Still this program is the source of some valuable clips of the top rock acts of the late 1960s (the Beatles, Janis Joplin, James Brown, Stevie Wonder, Sly & the Family Stone). Interspersed with the fine music is some passable comedy, featuring a troupe of regulars (including pre–*Laugh-In* Lily Tomlin).

**MUSSOLINI: THE UNTOLD STORY (*½) (7hr miniseries Color; 1985 NBC) Drama** *with George C. Scott as Benito Mussolini, Lee Grant as Rachele Guidi Mussolini, Virginia Madsen as Clara Petacci, and Raul Julia as Count Galeazzo Ciano*

Il Duce looks an awful lot like Gen. George Patton in this overly sentimental family portrait of the Italian fascist leader. George C. Scott is appropriately megalomaniacal as the title character.

**MY COUSIN RACHEL (**) 60 min (4ep Color; 1985 UK BBC) Mystery** *with Geraldine Chaplin as Rachel, Christopher Guard as Philip Ashley, John Shrapnel as Ambrose, John Stratton as Kendall, and Amanda Kirby as Louise*

Adaptation of a novel by Daphne du Maurier filled with plenty of juicy plot hooks. Set in Victorian England, this is the story of an unexplained death, two wills, an aristocratic lady with a mysterious past, obsessive love, and romance between cousins. The main characters, Philip and Rachel, are well-played, with the growing bond between them a theme that caries through the entire story, especially as they puzzle out the reasons behind the death of her husband. Unfortunately, the wrap-up is annoyingly obtuse, and fails to offer completely satisfactory answers to many of the questions left dangling. This series first aired in the United States on *Mystery!* in 1985.

**MY FAVORITE HUSBAND (**) 30 min (78ep B&W; 1953–1955 CBS) Situation Comedy** *with Barry Nelson as George Cooper, Joan Caulfield and Vanessa Brown as Liz Cooper, Alix Talton as Myra Cobb and Myra Shepard, Bob Sweeney as Gillmore Cobb, and Dan Tobin as Oliver Shepard.*

This series is famous for who does *not* star in it. *My Favorite Husband* began life in 1948 as a radio sitcom on CBS, starring Lucille Ball, who was then a minor film actress. Ball played the part of Liz Cooper, screwball wife of up-and-coming bank executive George Cooper.

It was the role of Liz Cooper that made Lucille Ball a nationally known comedienne and it was while playing Liz Cooper that Ball developed much of the scatterbrained but lovable housewife character she took to TV in *I Love Lucy* three years later, when *My Favorite Husband* ended its radio run.

After *I Love Lucy* became the number one show on TV. *My Favorite Husband* was quickly revived as a TV series. Ball was obviously unavailable. Former Hollywood ingenue Joan Caulfield was brought in to fill Lucy's shoes, and therein lies the problem. Caulfield is no Lucille Ball. The video stories of Liz Cooper's antics pretty much parallel the antics of Lucy Ricardo, but Lucy's extra zaniness is missing.

The format of *My Favorite Husband* is also more restrictive than that of *I Love Lucy*. The Coopers live in bland suburbia. Husband George is a banker. A nice banker, mind you, but a banker just the same. Barry Nelson, who is a fine actor, is okay as George, but again, the comparison with *I Love Lucy* is unavoidable. Cuban bandleader Ricky Ricardo and his family's Manhattan apartment are much more interesting.

The cast of *My Favorite Husband* changes several times in the show's run. During the final season, Vanessa Brown, another pert Hollywood ingenue, replaces Caulfield as Liz.

**MY FAVORITE MARTIAN (***) 30 min (107ep: 75 B&W & 32 Color; 1963–1966 CBS) Situation Comedy** *with Ray Walston as Uncle Martin, Bill Bixby as Tim O'Hara, and Pamela Britton as Lorelei Brown.*

*My Favorite Martian* is the *Mork and Mindy* of the 1960s. Both shows feature wayward aliens shipwrecked on Earth who are taken in by friendly humans and must learn to cope with the perplexities of life on Earth. *My Favorite Martian*, being from an older era, is slower, more Victorian, and not as topical, but is still worth your attention.

As the series opens, a Martian anthropologist studying the primitive planet Earth crash lands his spacecraft in the Los Angeles area. He is found and brought home by Tim O'Hara, a young newspaper reporter. Conveniently the Martian appears human and speaks English. O'Hara agrees to let the Martian stay in his apartment while repairs are made to the spacecraft. Nobody is to know the Martian's true identity, so Tim passes him off as his long-lost Uncle Martin. A rather likable sort, if a bit weird, Uncle Martin engages in some mutual flirting with Tim's landlady, Mrs. Brown, who never guesses Martin's home port, even though there is an alien spaceship in the garage.

Much fuss is made over Martin's magical Martian powers, which include extending little antennas from his head, practicing levitation on nearby objects, making himself invisible, and reading minds. This all may have seemed wonderfully tricky in the early 1960s, but it loses a lot of its punch these days to an audience weaned on *Star Wars* special effects.

Much of the charm of *My Favorite Martian* is the interplay of Ray Walston and Bill Bixby, two versatile actors. Bixby, then still quite wet behind the ears, plays O'Hara as the eager student. He gets very emotional and worked up over things, but its adept at covering up Uncle Martin's tracks. O'Hara shows a keen interest in the Martian and it must have taken all of his personal loyalty to sit for years on the biggest story in history, without ever writing an exclusive for his newspaper.

Walston is a marvelous character actor who gets a lot of mileage out of the Martian character. Uncle Martin is obviously "slumming" by living amongst the Earthmen, but, like all good anthropologists, he comes to love his observed subjects for their quaint ways.

Three years is just the right length for this series. After a while, there are only so many ways to try to hide Uncle Martin's background. By the third and final season, Uncle Martin might as well be O'Hara's eccentric old uncle. The budding romance with Mrs. Brown never goes anywhere and, although the series never produced a wrap-up episode, one hopes that Martin finally repaired his ship and headed home to Mars, having learned much more than he ever dreamed about Earth.

Bill Bixby, of course, went on to star in *The Incredible Hulk*. Perhaps someday Bixby and Walton will reunite for a TV special where Uncle Martin comes back to Earth for a visit and is shocked to discover that Tim O'Hara was the Incredible Hulk and never told him.

**MY FRIEND FLICKA (**½) 30 min (39ep Color; 1956–1957 CBS) Adventure** *with Gene Evans as Rob McLaughlin, Anita Louise as Nell McLaughlin, Johnny Washbrook as Ken McLaughlin, Frank Ferguson as Gus Broeberg, and Wahama as Flicka*

*My Friend Flicka* is a truly nice show, one that you want to praise and commend. It is nice. It is commendable. It is a little boring, too.

Based on some stories by Mary O'Hara and two movies from the 1940s starring Roddy McDowall, *My Friend Flicka* is set in the lovely ranch country of Montana, where young Ken McLaughlin is growing up alongside his favorite horse, Flicka (Swedish for "little girl"). Ken's parents (Rob and Nell) and ranch hand Gus make up the regular gang at the Goose Bar Ranch.

As in *Lassie*, the boy and his pet are always getting involved in local escapades and excitement, but, in *My Friend Flicka*, Flicka is neither as wise as Lassie nor are the crises as lively. This show is more a mix of *Lassie* with *Little House on the Prairie*, where boy/animal is but one theme alongside the epic continuation of life on the frontier.

While there is nothing wrong with *My Friend Flicka*, *Fury* does a more exciting job of dealing with the same theme.

The producers of *My Friend Flicka* had the forethought to shoot the series in color. When it first aired on network TV, it ran in black and white (as did most all shows then). Only later, when *My Friend Flicka* ran forever in reruns, did the show appear in color. This helped prolong its life, since much of the kiddie western competition was monochrome.

**MY FRIEND IRMA (**) 30 min (70ep B&W; 1952–1954 CBS) Situation Comedy** *with Marie Wilson as Irma Peterson, Cathy Lewis as Jane Stacy, Gloria Gordon as Mrs. O'Reilly, Mary Shipp as Kay Foster, and Richard Eyer as Bobby Peterson*

Much more successful as a radio show than a TV series, *My Friend Irma* is about beautiful but dumb Irma Peterson, secretary to attorney Irving Clyde. Most of the show focuses on Irma's home life, as she shares an apartment in Mrs. O'Reilly's boarding house with first Jane Stacy (who addresses the home audience) and then Kay Foster.

**MY FRIEND TONY (**) 60 min (16ep Color; 1969 NBC) Detective Drama** *with James Whitmore as John Woodruff and Enzo Cerusico as Tony Novello*

Just as *I Spy* was wrapping up its run, producer Sheldon Leonard unveiled another "buddy" adventure setup: a detective adventure series with James Whitmore as an analytical professor of criminology and Italian-born Enzo Cerusico as his legman. Leonard, in fact, had met Cerusico while in Rome filming *I Spy*, casting him in an episode ("Sophia") and then arranging for him to co-star in *My Friend Tony*. In retrospect, Cerusico may have wondered why Leonard went to all the trouble. Besides giving him a chance for some Stateside location shooting, nothing much happened with the detective series, or with Cerusico's subsequent Hollywood career. In any case, *My Friend Tony* is about as well plotted as an average episode of *I Spy*, but without an equivalent to the comfortable banter between Bill Cosby and Robert Culp (which, in truth, was often what carried the series, covering minor holes in the story lines). There is conflict between the two (Tony Novello is a romantic; John Woodruff is more logical), but it's not enough.

**MY HERO (*) 30 min (33ep B&W; 1952–1953 NBC) Situation Comedy** *with Robert Cummings as Robert S. Beanblossom, Julie Bishop as Julie Marshall, and John Litel as Willis Thackery*

From looking at *My Hero*, you'd never guess that Robert Cummings would become a big TV star (*Love That Bob*). In his first TV series, Cummings plays a bumbling real estate salesman who gets by with a little help from his girlfriend, Julie. *My Hero* is one of the earliest filmed sitcoms and looks archaic. The show has also been titled *The Robert Cummings Show.* ■

**MY LITTLE MARGIE (**½) 30 min (126ep B&W; 1952–1955 CBS & NBC) Situation Comedy** *with Gale Storm as Margie Albright, Charles Farrell as Vernon Albright, Clarence Kolb as George Honeywell, Gertrude Hoffman as Mrs. Odetts, Don Hayden as Freddie Wilson, and Willie Best as Charlie.*

In some ways, *My Little Margie* is as typical a screwball 1950s sitcom as you can find. On the other hand, it has elements that set it apart from most other 1950s sitcom hits. The format almost sounds like it might work today.

At first glance, *My Little Margie* reeks of 1950s inanity. The characters are one-dimensional simpleton stereotypes. Vern Albright, middle-aged widowed father to Margie, is the sort of ineffectual TV dad so popular in the 1950s. He works for an investment firm headed by the always fearsome Mr. Honeywell. You can always count on Vern shamelessly kowtowing to Honeywell for a few cheap laughs in almost every episode. Margie looks like she just walked out of a *Family Circle* feature on prim and proper young ladies of 1952. She is only twenty-one, but has the affected grown-up look that teens sought before the rock'n'roll era. Charlie, the black elevator operator in the Albrights' apartment building, is an embarrassing reminder of how blacks were treated, both in real life and on TV. He has no last name and can best be described as, well . . . shiftless. He makes a few lethargic comments now and then, but is mostly around to be laughed at.

All these factors paint *My Little Margie* as typical 1950s fare, and, at first, that is how the show will appear when you watch it. In fact, that is all *My Little Margie* really is. There is no deep hidden message in the program. Nonetheless, after watching a few episodes, you may notice that some things seem a little different here than in most classic Eisenhower-era comedies.

For one thing, there is no Mrs. Albright. Vern is a widower. Most every hit sitcom of the 1950s revolved around nuclear families. The Ricardos, the Nelsons, the Rileys, and the Andersons, all daddy/mommy/kiddie combinations, are the people you think of when you conjure up 1950s TV comedy. Not until Fred MacMurray and *My Three Sons* at the end of the decade do you find another hit comedy show with a widower. The only 1950s equivalents are *Our Miss Brooks*, which has a lead woman with no family and one season of Danny Thomas's character in between wives in *Make Room for Daddy.* While Margie Albright is nowhere near as independent as Connie Brooks, at least Margie is far more free and lively than most of the women seen in 1950s sitcoms.

The fact that the Albright home is one with a single parent is used as the key for much of the plot complications. In another subtle reversal of standard 1950s fare, it is the middle-aged father who is always searching for romance and it is the young daughter who is doing her best to keep dad out of trouble. Margie wants her father to settle down and leave the wild life behind him. Margie has a steady beau (Freddie Wilson), but they might as well be brother and sister for all the sparks that fly between them. For sizzle, it's all up to the dashing, Errol Flynn-ish Vern.

Unfortunately, *My Little Margie* doesn't do much with the possibilities of its slightly unusual setting. On the whole, the series is forgettable fluff. It's occasionally fun to see how Margie schemes with busybody old lady neighbor Mrs. Odetts to keep Vern from falling for some wily widow, or to relish in the sight of Vern abjectly groveling before the demands of his employer, Mr. Honeywell. Still there is not enough good writing to make *My Little Margie* more than a cute period novelty. ■

**MY LIVING DOLL** (**½) **30 min (26ep B&W; 1964–1965 CBS) Situation Comedy** *with Robert Cummings as Dr. Robert McDonald, Julie Newmar as Rhoda Miller, Jack Mullaney as Dr. Peter Robinson, and Doris Dowling as Irene Adams.*

A "classic" series from the deep, dark days of male chauvinism, *My Living Doll* is the ultimate Bob Cummings series. In all his shows (such as *Love That Bob*), Cummings loved to wrap beautiful women around his fingers. In *My Living Doll*, he gets to indulge that predilection to the maximum.

Cummings plays Dr. Bob McDonald, a government psychiatrist who is given possession of Project AF 709, an extremely lifelike robot that is shaped like a gorgeous woman. Bob's job is to mold the lady robot's mind, to make her the perfect woman, one who would obey all commands from her male superior. Somehow or other, the robot (called Rhoda) moves in with Bob, who explains to outsiders that the lady is a patient who needs special care. Sure, Bob.

*My Living Doll* is just overloaded with sexual innuendo, but coming from the mid-1960s, nothing ever really occurs. What cable TV needs to do is produce an X-rated modern update of *My Living Doll* (with somebody younger than Bob Cummings, at least), so the grown boys of the 1960s can finally fulfill their kiddie fantasies.

**MY MOTHER THE CAR** (*) **30 min (30ep Color; 1965–1966 NBC) Situation Comedy** *with Jerry Van Dyke as Dave Crabtree, Maggie Pierce as Barbara Crabtree, Avery Schreiber as Bernard Mancini, and Ann Sothern as the voice of Mother*

This show regularly turns up as nominee for the worst show in TV history, but it does not truly deserve that honor. *My Mother the Car* may well be the weirdest concept ever and it may be a good example of mindless mid-1960s sitcoms, but the sheer audacity of having a TV program about a man who buys an old car that is the reincarnation of his deceased mother deserves some level of respect.

The premise is, you must admit, not really any sillier than *Mister Ed*, where the horse only talked to his owner. In *My Mother the Car*, the 1928 Porter automobile talks only to her son, Dave Crabtree, through the car radio. The difference between the two shows is that the character of Mr. Ed is very appealing, while the mother in *My Mother the Car* might as well still be living in her human form. All mother does is nag her son Dave and give him motherly advice, which is all that TV moms are supposed to do anyway. So why bother trapping her voice inside an old car? A horse, like Mr. Ed, can learn to dance, can walk around, and can bat his tail. A car can just sit there in the garage or slip out of gear and roll downhill. The result is a dead end for the writers and the upshot is that *My Mother the Car* is a very dull show, once you get over the wild premise.

The best that can be said about Jerry Van Dyke's acting is that it must have been a lifelong struggle for Jerry to compete with his older brother Dick, who really had a deft flair for slapstick comedy. Jerry overacts in every episode. Avery Schreiber, better known for his cab driver routines with comedy partner Jack Burns, is wasted here as the foil, a crazed antique car collector who is forever trying to snare the old Porter for his collection, not knowing that the car is actually part of the Crabtree family.

Several of the men behind the scenes of *My Mother the Car* seemed able to produce better work in other shows. The two writer-creators, Allan Burns and Chris Hayward, went on to produce several quality series (*The Mary Tyler Moore Show*, *Rhoda*, and *Lou Grant*, in Burns' case, and *Barney Miller* in Hayward's case). Producer–director Rod Amateau came from the well-respected *Burns and Allen Show*, and later produced the popular (albeit lame) *Dukes of Hazzard* (and its forgettable spin-off *Enos*). Amateau did, however, produce *Supertrain*, one of the most infamous flops of the 1970s.

Like *It's About Time*, another frequent nominee for worst show of all time, *My Mother the Car* has a great theme song.

**MY PARTNER THE GHOST/RANDALL AND HOPKIRK (DECEASED)** (**) **60 min (26ep Color; 1969–1970 UK ATV) Adventure** *with Mike Pratt as Jeff Randall, Kenneth Cope as Marty Hopkirk, Annette Andre as Jean Hopkirk, and Ivor Dean as Inspector Large*

Private detective Marty Hopkirk comes back from the dead to help solve his own murder case, then stays on Earth to continue working with his old partner, Jeff Randall. Of course, only Jeff (and the viewers) can see Marty, but at least he can do all those ghostly things that make ectoplasms such great investigators—and such frustrating partners, since Jeff can't follow Marty into the rafters or to the other side of solid doors. Created by veteran *Avengers* writer Dennis Spooner, this is an attempt at a similar style of adventure stories done with a light touch. Though it doesn't have the same chemistry as that classic, it's worth a look just for the *Topper*-like chatter between Jeff and Marty. Their police contact is Inspector Large, a familiar face from *The Saint* (where Ivor Dean played police inspector, Claude Teal). The series goes by the title *Randall and Hopkirk (Deceased)* in Britain, and *My Partner the Ghost* in the United States.

**MY SECRET IDENTITY (**1/2) (24ep at Fall 1989 Color: 1988– Syndication) Adventure** *with Jerry O'Connell as Andrew Clements, Derek McGrath as Dr. Jeffcoate (Dr. "J"), Wanda Cannon as Stephanie Clements, and Marsha Moreau as Erin Clements*

Superheroics as a fourteen-year-old kid might see them, especially one with an extensive collection of old comic books. Young Andrew Clements hangs out with Dr. Jeffcoate (a.k.a. Dr. J), a moderately successful basement scientist responsible for giving the boy super speed, invulnerability, and the ability to float in the air. Inadvertently, of course. While the doc was away, Andrew wandered into the basement and accidentally stepped into the path of a gamma ray, which gave him those super powers and a new secret identity, Ultra-Man. So when superheroics are needed (and they usually are), Andrew will grab a couple of aerosol cans to propel himself through the air and fly into action (though with contemporary concerns about damage to the ozone, this odd choice of personal booster rockets is soon replaced by cans of compressed air).

If this explanation of the setup isn't enough, you obviously don't follow superhero comic books and you might as well skip this series. Besides, it's all really just an excuse to give a young boy the chance to be the one to help out the adults, especially Dr. J, a rather sweet and bumbling character. So, for instance, when the Doc nervously prepares for a reunion with his college girlfriend, Andrew is always nearby as super-powered backup. Or when Dr. J's workaholic tendencies start to get out of hand, Andrew takes him to a local comic book shop for a live promotional appearance by TV-actor Gene Barry (playing a video version of comic book hero Captain Noble)—and, naturally, there's a daring rescue before the day is over.

Even with some semiobligatory bad guy confrontations, this approach is a relatively gentle one to superheroics, coming off much like a classic Disney production (in the best sense of the word). It's a kid's show for kids. Andrew Clements (Jerry) previously played the part of chubby chatterbox Vern in the theatrical film *Stand by Me*.

**MY SISTER EILEEN (**) 30 min (26ep & 30 min pilot B&W; 1960–1961 CBS) Situation Comedy** *with Elaine Stritch as Ruth Sherwood, Shirley Boone as Eileen Sherwood, Jack Weston as Chick Adams, Raymond Bailey as Mr. Beaumont, Leon Belasco as Mr. Appopoplous, Stubby Kaye as Marty Scott, and Rose Marie as Bertha.*

An old-fashioned aspiring stars setup, with two women moving from Ohio to New York City in their quest for big-time success. Ruth is a writer and her younger sister Eileen is an aspiring actress in need of a protecting eye. In short order they land an apartment, an agent, some typical sitcom friends, and the chance to make it in New York, New York, which they do. This series follows their complications along the way, ranging from apartment house and dating mix-ups to script and staging deadlines, with generally good performances from a well-rounded cast. Immediately after the one-season run of this series, Rose Marie went directly to another New York-based series with a showbiz orientation, *The Dick Van Dyke Show*. Shortly afterward, Raymond Bailey turned up as banker Milton Drysdale on *The Beverly Hillbillies*.

Previously, *My Sister Eileen* was done twice as a theatrical feature film: in 1942 and a musical version in 1955. The pilot for this series first aired on *Goodyear Theater* as "You Should Meet My Sister" (with Ann Helm as Eileen).

**MY SISTER SAM (**1/2) 30 min (42ep Color; 1986–1989 CBS & USA) Situation Comedy** *with Pam Dawber as Samantha "Sam" Russell, Rebecca Schaeffer as Patti Russell, David Naughton as Jack Kincaid, Joel Brooks as J. D. Lucas, and Jenny O'Hara as Dixie Randazzo*

Pam Dawber, the woman who welcomed Mork from Ork, finds herself in a different setting with another unexpected apartment mate, a sixteen-year-old younger sister. Teenaged Patti reminds her older sister Sam of what a free spirit she had been just a few years before, and begs for the chance to stay with her. How could Sam refuse?

Dawber does a good job as the put-upon Sam, a freelance photographer in San Francisco who has to work a high school teen's schedule, interests, and boyfriends into her own home and office life while trying to decide the best way to handle their situation: as best buddies, a surrogate parent, or a conspiring older sibling. With her loft apartment/office as the main setting, the stories easily intertwine Sam's work, family, and social threads. The complications range from Sam's attempt to orchestrate Patti's high school election campaign (treating it like a typical commercial media contract) to Patti's latest punk rock heartthrob boyfriend to the tricky question of premarital sex (on Sam's part—does she consider bringing a man to the loft with Patti there?). Through all the situations, the scripts and characters are generally believable and consistent.

**MY SON, MY SON (*½) 60 min (7ep Color; 1980 UK BC) Drama** *with Michael Williams as William Essex, Frank Grimes as Dermot O'Riorden, Patrick Ryecart* *as Oliver Essex, Gerald Murphy as Rory O'Riorden, and Ciaran Madden as Maeve O'Riorden*

Adaptation of a 1938 novel by Howard Spring following two friends, William and Dermot, from their time together as teenagers through the lives of their children, especially their respective sons, Oliver and Rory. The two young friends connect when William is fifteen and the wealthy Mr. Riorden brings him into the family household to share a room with Dermot. They get on quite well, and continue as friends after they get married and become dads, eagerly showing off their children to each other. This is a workmanlike adaptation of a rather contrived story, with plenty of arbitrary happenstance, convenient tragedies, and heavy-handed resolutions.

The series was produced by the BBC in association with Time-Life in the United States.

**MY THREE SONS (***) 30 min (380 ep; 184 B&W & 196 Color; 1960–1972 ABC & CBS) Situation Comedy** *with Fred MacMurray as Steve Douglas, Tim Considine as Mike Douglas, Don Grady as Robbie Douglas, Stanley Livingston as Richard "Chip" Douglas, Barry Livingston as Ernie Thompson Douglas, William Frawley as Michael Francis "Bub" O'Casey, and William Demarest as "Uncle" Charley O'Casey.*

*My Three Sons* is one of the longest lasting "square" family sitcoms from the 1950s and early 1960s. The all-male bastion of the Douglas household goes through several important changes in the twelve years of the series' run, but the tone never wavers. All is calm and peaceful in suburbia, at least in the Douglas homestead. Fred MacMurray exudes, revels in, and virtually defines bland TV fatherhood in the role of Steve Douglas. He stands as an edifice, a monument to an age of simplicity, both on TV and in our pristine national image of ourselves.

At first, the three sons are Mike (age eighteen), Robbie (age fourteen), and Chip (age seven). Mrs. Douglas is dead and barely missed, to tell the truth. Steve reigns, but "Bub" rules. Steve's retired father-in-law Bub (William Frawley) serves as the grouchy cook and fraternity mascot in the Douglas household. Frawley must have enjoyed this repast of male companionship after serving as the unforgettable Fred Mertz, the lesser light to Lucy Ricardo and wife Ethel in the female-dominated *I Love Lucy.*

After five years, the ailing Frawley leaves *My Three Sons* (it is said Bub took off for Ireland) and is replaced by William Demarest, who plays the brother of Bub, called Uncle Charley by the kids. Uncle Charley is even more grouchy and grumbling than Bub was (not an easy trick), but naturally he is really just an old softie at heart.

Soon after Uncle Charley's arrival, there is another seismic shift in the world of the Douglas clan. Eldest son Mike marries and moves away, to be replaced by Ernie, a spectacled nerd type, who is played by the younger brother of the actor playing youngest son Chip. Ernie was already a semiregular as Chip's friend, so the addition of Ernie to the household is not very jarring. Rearranged in this manner, *My Three Sons* then cruises for another seven years. During that time, the family moves to North Hollywood, Steve remarries, and Robbie and Chip marry and start having kids of their own. By the end, the Douglas family is so extended, it takes a genealogist to keep it all straight. All these changes detract from the show's appeal; without Fred MacMurray bumbling through another day as de facto head of an all-male family, *My Three Sons* becomes just another boring sitcom. In addition, its attempts at dealing with the "relevant" topics of the long-haired late 1960s are unintentionally funny, due to the show's continued straight-laced tone.

Like most of the solid and sober sitcoms of its era, *My Three Sons* is produced with great restraint and taste, containing an almost Victorian touch that dates it. Credit for this tone goes to producer Don Fedderson, who also produced *The Millionaire* and *Family Affair.* The "Bub" era shows are in black and white and are more entertaining than the Uncle Charley era episodes (which are chiefly in color). Until the mid-1980s, when the Bub episodes began rerunning on the Nickelodeon cable network, they were far rarer than the Uncle Charley color episodes in the syndication market.

**MY TWO DADS (*) 30 min (38ep at Fall 1989 Color; 1987— NBC)** Situation Comedy *with Greg Evigan as Joey Harris, Paul Reiser as Michael Taylor, Staci Keanan as Nicole Bradford, Florence Stanley as Judge Wilbur, and Dick Butkus as Ed Klawicki*

A concept like *My Two Dads* would have been unthinkable back in the 1950s, but its trendy premise is just as boring as many of those from that straight-laced decade. Joey Harris and Michael Taylor were college rivals for the affections of Marcy Bradford, and both had their share of success, since both bedded her around the same time. Then, in a much too cute plot twist, Joey, Michael and Marcy split up and never hear from each other again, despite the fact that Marcy was pregnant from one of the guys (she never knew which). The resulting child, Nicole, grows up fatherless.

When Nicole is twelve, her mother Marcy suddenly dies and leaves all her worldly possessions (including Nicole) to be split up between Joey and Michael (didn't the poor woman have any family or any friends since college?). By now, Joey and Michael are quite different. Michael is a conservative financial type in suit and tie. Joey is a wild and crazy artist. Neither, fortunately, has married or fathered any other children. The two guys now must share the raising of Nicole, to the canned snickers of the laugh track.

The extremely stilted plot and the extremely hack gags that fill *My Two Dads* make it a show to avoid. Paul Reiser, who plays Michael, can be prouder of his work in the film *Diner*, and even Greg Evigan, who plays Joey, is better off boasting about his starring role in *B. J. and the Bear.*

**MY WORLD AND WELCOME TO IT (***) 30 min (26ep Color; 1969–1970 NBC) Situation Comedy** *with William Windom as John Monroe, Joan Hotchkis as Ellen Monroe, Lisa Gerritsen as Lydia Monroe, Harold J. Stone as Hamilton Greeley, and Henry Morgan as Philip Jensen*

Here is a series that was truly before its time, if its time has ever come. Based on the works of humorist James Thurber (the creator of Walter Mitty), *My World and Welcome To It* slides back and forth between live action and animation as the story shifts from real life to the fantasy world of John Monroe. Like Thurber himself, Monroe is a writer who can't seem to come to grips with the real world. Insecure about himself and his place in the world (and in his own family), Monroe only finds solace in retreating to a made-up world where, Walter Mitty-esque, he can do no wrong. In this other reality, Monroe is desired by women, admired by men and is the can-do man of action he always wanted to be.

The most obvious oddity about this series is the heavy use of animation, which is unheard-of in a non-cartoon TV show. Another oddity is the very tone of the show. Monroe's persona is seductively anti-social and anti-family, two tendencies not usually found in prime time TV. Finally, this is truly a show about fantasy, which is quite uncommon. There are numerous TV shows that focus on unreal superheroes or fantasy situations, but *My World and Welcome To It* actually occurs largely *in* the fantasy of the main character.

William Windom is perfect for the role of John Monroe. He is familiar to viewers, from his stints as Cong. Glen Morley in *Farmer's Daughter* and Dr. Seth Hazlitt in *Murder, She Wrote*, and has the bookish, otherworldly feel about him that makes sense in the Monroe character. Veteran cynic Henry Morgan provides more off beat musings as fellow writer Philip Jensen.

The behind the scenes crew is equally top notch. The two producers are Sheldon Leonard, of *Make Room For Daddy* and *Dick Van Dyke Show* fame, and, in one of his earliest productions, Danny Arnold, who went on to produce *Barney Miller*.

Even now, years after *My World and Welcome To It* came and went, it is not clear whether viewers, in any mass numbers, would ever flock to this sort of show, but for those who give it a try, it should prove highly rewarding.

Considering how avant garde the show must have seemed in 1969, it is amazing to realize that this was already the second attempt to turn this concept into a TV series. In 1959, Arthur O'Connell starred in a pilot, called "Christabel", for a series to be called *The Secret Life of John Monroe*, which had the exact same premise and virtually the same characters. The pilot, with animation and all, aired once on *Goodyear Theater* and then disappeared for decades. It has resurfaced as part of a *Golden Age of Television* package of 1950s TV dramas and pilots.

**THE MYSTERIOUS WORLD OF ARTHUR C. CLARKE (*) 30 min (13ep Color: 1980 UK) Documentary** *with Arthur C. Clarke as host*

Science fiction writer Arthur C. Clarke's entry in the *Ripley's Believe It Or Not* style of pop documentaries, usually focusing on odd natural phenomena (a rainstorm of frogs, for instance). Clarke travels the world with his camera crew to talk with the locals, resulting in the predictable mix of anecdotes and speculation. Sunday supplement science, easily downed with your juice and then dismissed. Besides, if the phenomenon is still taking place, you know Geraldo Rivera will be there soon, live.

**MYSTERY! (****) 60 min (Color; 1981– PBS) Drama Anthology** *with Vincent Price and Gene Shalit as host*

In 1973, *Masterpiece Theatre* began its successful presentation of stories adapted from the mystery novels of Dorothy L. Sayers featuring aristocratic sleuth Lord Peter Wimsey. They proved quite popular over the next few years and, in 1980, WGBH and Mobil Oil launched a full-fledged spin-off anthology devoted to similarly styled tales, *Mystery!* Like its predecessor, *Mystery!* serves as an umbrella title for a mixed bag of drama, though concentrating on a particular genre: tales of mystery, suspense, and intrigue, usually involving murder.

As with *Masterpiece Theatre*, each drama is presented with background information before and after. Initially NBC's *Today* show movie critic Gene Shalit was host, but his naturally effusive and jovial manner did not quite work with this package. In 1981, horror and suspense film veteran Vincent Price took the task and proved to be a much more appropriate choice. With either one, though, the commentaries were less personal essays (the case with Alistair Cooke) than basic historical and literary background data most conveniently presented by them. In 1989, Diana Rigg succeeded the retiring Price.

In contrast to its parent package, *Mystery!* concentrates on a relative handful of continuing series that turn up with new episodes from season to season. The most popular of these include adventures featuring Sherlock Holmes, Rumpole of the Bailey, Inspector Morse, and Miss Marple. In most cases, particular tales run three weeks or less, chiefly because it's hard to carry a mystery over a much longer period. So a seven-episode run of *Inspector Morse*, for instance, might actually consist of three different stories. For that same reason, *Mystery!* also includes far more one-time specials (a ninety-minute adaptation of the stage play *Sweeney Todd*, for instance) or occasional minianthologies of unrelated stories under some umbrella title.

Only series that have run four episodes or more are included in this book, with detailed write-ups appearing separately, under the following individual series titles: *Agatha Christie Stories* (Anthology), *Charters and Caldicott, Dalgliesh, Father Brown, Game Set and Match, Inspector Morse, Lord Peter Wimsey, Malice Aforethought, Miss Marple, My Cousin Rachel, Partners in Crime* (Tommy and Tuppence), *The Racing Game, Rebecca, Reilly: Ace of Spies, Rumpole of the Bailey, Sergeant Cribb, Shades of Darkness* (Anthology), *Sherlock Holmes, We the Accused*, and *Woman in White*.

**MYSTERY MOVIE (see *ABC Mystery Movie; NBC Mystery Movie*)**

**NBC MYSTERY MOVIE (1971–1977)**

An umbrella anthology title for more than a dozen unrelated mystery/police/detective series. For details, see each of the following titles: *Amy Prentiss, Banacek, Columbo, Cool Million, Faraday and Company, Hec Ramsey, Lanigan's Rabbi, Madigan, McCloud, McCoy, McMillan and Wife/McMillan, Quincy, M. E., The Snoop Sisters*, and *Tenafly*.

**NBC NOVELS FOR TELEVISION (1979 NBC) Drama**

The umbrella title for four miniseries. See *From Here to Eternity, Studs Lonigan, Wheels*, and *Aspen (The Innocent and the Damned)* for details.

**N.O.P.D. (*) 30 min (39ep B&W; 1956–1957 Syndication) Police Drama** *with Stacy Harris as Detective Beaujac and Lou Sirgo as Detective Conroy*

Filmed on location in New Orleans, *N.O.P.D.* is about two detectives on the New Orleans Police Department. The action is strictly formula 1950s cops and robbers.

**N.Y.P.D. (***) 30 min (49ep Color; 1967–1969 ABC) Police Drama** *with Jack Warden as Lt. Mike Haines, Robert Hooks as Jeff Ward, and Frank Converse as Johnny Corso*

Filmed on location in New York City, *N.Y.P.D.* is Gotham's answer to *Dragnet*, in that it is based on real cases taken from police files. Unlike *Dragnet*, the cops of *N.Y.P.D.* are human, understanding, and believable. Mike Haines is the grumpy old-timer, Jeff Ward is the idealistic black man, and Frank Converse is the young white intellectual. The gritty tone is partly due to the on-location filming, and mostly due to the care of the show's creator, TV drama and talk show celebrity David Susskind.

**NAKED CITY (***) 30 & 60 min (138ep B&W: thirty-nine 30 min & ninety-nine 60 min; 1958–1959 & 1960–1963 ABC) Police Drama** *with John McIntire as Dan Muldoon, James Franciscus as Jim Halloran, Horace McMahon as Mike Parker, and Paul Burke as Adam Flint*

*Naked City* is a sexy title that sounds like racy, exploitation TV, but in reality it is serious, gripping crime drama that lives up to the true and unsexy meaning of the word *naked*. This show focuses on the tough world of big-city crime. Thus, it is a naked view of the city, not dolled up and glamorized. Of course, we are talking TV show here, and that imposes numerous restraints of what can and cannot be shown, especially in the late 1950s when this show was produced.

*Naked City* is the sequel to a great 1948 film of the same name. The movie was filmed almost exclusively on location in New York and it presented a no-nonsense view of brutal inner city crime. The TV series continues the on-location in New York theme, which sets *Naked City* apart from most all of its filmed in Hollywood contemporaries.

The heavy dose of New York settings is the only really constant character in *Naked City*, because the show never stops changing its cast. At first, when the show is in its thirty-minute format, the focus is on detectives Muldoon and Halloran. In the midst of the first season, in a move virtually unprecedented in TV cop shows, a main character (Det. Muldoon) is killed in a car chase sequence. Lt. Mike Parker replaces Muldoon as star.

The program takes a year-long break soon thereafter and when it reappears it is as a one-hour show. Det. Halloran is gone and Det. Adam Flint is in. In that form, *Naked City* completes its run.

In an era when light entertainment like *77 Sunset Strip* was considered different, *Naked City* stands out as a show with real muscle behind the glitter. The writing and production are memorable and the acting is good and gets better as the show develops. The departure of James Franciscus, who plays Halloran, is actually a plus, since, to begin with, Franciscus is too baby-faced to play a hard-nosed cop. He is far better suited for his later role, the sensitive young teacher in *Mr. Novak*. The Billy May and Nelson Riddle theme songs in *Naked City* are cool and jazzy.

Look for a tremendous collection of guest stars in *Naked City*, which could draw on Broadway-based talent that the West Coast shows could not. Dustin Hoffman, Jon Voight, Robert Redford, and Peter Fonda all make early TV appearances in the hour-long format.

**NAKIA (*) 60 min (15ep & 90 min pilot Color; 1974 NBC) Police Drama** *with Robert Forster as Deputy Sheriff Nakia Parker, Arthur Kennedy as Sheriff Sam Jericho, and Gloria DeHaven as Irene James*

*Nakia* is preachy, strident, obvious, and outdated in its fervent condescension. Nakia Parker is a Navajo Indian who has become deputy sheriff of Davis County, New Mexico. Sam Jericho is the kindly old white gentleman who is his nominal boss. Nakia doesn't stoop to ride police squad cars; rather he prefers the more humble pickup truck or, better yet, a horse. Nakia agonizes about blending his Indian heritage with his life in the white man's world.

*Nakia* tries real hard to be significant and deep. All it winds up doing is being superficial, trivializing the real efforts of Indians in the modern age.

**THE NAME OF THE GAME (**) 90 min (76ep & 2 hr pilot Color; 1968–1971 NBC) Crime Drama** *with Gene Barry as Glenn Howard, Tony Franciosa as Jeff Dillon, Robert Stack as Dan Farrell, and Susan Saint James as Peggy Maxwell*

Investigative reporting, TV-movie style, following the exploits of three key characters at Howard Publications: Dan Farrell (senior editor of *Crime Magazine*), Jeff Dillon (top reporter for *People Magazine*), and Glenn Howard (urbane owner of the entire influential empire).

Though carrying the same overall title and setting throughout, this show is actually three different series, with Robert Stack, Tony Franciosa, and Gene Barry alternating as the featured character, doing their respective favorite character types (hard-hitting crime buster a la *The Untouchables*, smooth-talking ladies' man a la *Valentine's Day*, and sophisticated man about town a la *Burke's Law*). They rarely appear with each other (in fact, different production teams handled each character's stories), though Susan Saint James does play gal Friday to all of them.

At the time, a ninety-minute adventure series was quite an innovation, offering feature-film-length episodes every week. Unfortunately, despite some nice location footage and good guest stars, too often the program comes off as just a one-hour story padded to fill the extra length. The series also suffers from bouts of late 1960s relevancy, including encounters with "hippie" bad guys and mind-altering drugs.

These days the extra-length running time makes it hard to fit *The Name of the Game* into a prime rerun slot. What often does turn up, though, is the 1966 made-for-TV movie pilot for the series, "Fame Is the Name of the Game." It's an excellent production well worth catching. Though George Macready has the role of Glenn Howard (with Barry and Stack nowhere to be seen), Franciosa and Saint James are there, along with guest stars Jill St. John, Robert Duvall, and Jack Klugman.

**NANCY (½) 30 min (17ep Color; 1970–1971 NBC) Situation Comedy** *with Renne Jarrett as Nancy Smith, John Fink as Dr. Adam Hudson, Celeste Holm as Abigail Townsend, and Robert F. Simon as Everett Hudson*

*Nancy* can be ignored freely, without any fear you are missing some key moment in American history or a source of TV trivia. Nancy Smith is the incessantly perky daughter of the unseen president of the United States. While vacationing in Iowa, she meets and falls in love with a very straight and very dull veterinarian, Adam Hudson. She moves to the Hawkeye State to be near the bland Dr. Hudson, and is chaperoned by Abigail Townsend, press secretary to her mother, the first lady. Shortly before the blessed demise of this series, Nancy and the pig doctor wed. Perhaps the president will drop by and visit the newlyweds in a few years when the next Iowa caucuses roll around.

**NANCY ASTOR (**) 60 min (8ep Color; 1983 UK BBC) Drama** *with Lisa Harrow as Nancy Astor, Pierce Brosnan as Robert Gould Shaw, James Fox as Waldorf Astor, Dan O'Herlihy as Chillie Langhorne, Sylvia Syms as Nanaire Langhorne, Lise Hilboldt as Phyllis Brand, and Julian Glover as Lord Revelstoke*

Turn-of-the-century biography of Nancy (Langhorne) Astor, a sharp-tongued American southern belle who becomes the first woman to enter England's Parliament in its 600-year history. But first there's a long, sufficiently soapy road to travel as seventeen-year-old Nancy heads north to New York from her family home in Virginia. There she meets and marries Robert Gould Shaw, a rich Boston socialite (played by Pierce Brosnan, in a step away from *Remington Steele*) who is also a renowned playboy. The union is a disaster and ends in divorce, but Nancy quickly recovers and finds a new husband an ocean away, British millionaire-philanthropist Waldorf Astor. When he is elevated to the House of Lords, she sets her sights on election to his vacant seat on the House of Commons—and that's when she really starts to set Britain's business-as-usual politicos and society on its ears.

At times Nancy comes off as a most "unladylike lady," leaving the likes of Winston Churchill sputtering in anger, no doubt convinced he's met the definitive pushy, obnoxious American. But, in truth, after one too many "terribly serious and civilized" British miniseries, it's fun to see an irrepressible Stateside force shake things up out there. Unfortunately, the overall tone of the series is sporadic: flashy yet controlled (perhaps the way they wished she had been). As a result, at times (especially toward the beginning) the fiery Nancy Astor is actually rather dull.

**NANCY DREW** **(see *The Hardy Boys/Nancy Drew Mysteries*)** ■

**NANCY WALKER SHOW (**) 30 min (13ep Color; 1976 ABC) Situation Comedy** *with Nancy Walker as Nancy Kitteridge, William Daniels as Kenneth Kitteridge, Beverly Archer as Lorraine, James Cromwell as Glen, and Ken Olfson as Terry Folson*

Talk about a busy career woman. At one time, Nancy Walker was simultaneously the busybody housekeeper on NBC's *McMillan and Wife*, the pushy Jewish mom on CBS's *Rhoda*, and the sharp-tongued operator of

Rosie's diner in commercials for Bounty paper towels. So appropriately her first "solo" series combines elements from all those characters.

As Nancy Kitteridge, she is head of her own Hollywood talent agency (operated from her apartment), a setup that provides plenty of opportunities for confrontations with strange showbiz types at all hours. She is assisted there by her boarder/secretary, an unemployed gay actor named Terry Folson (whose last name is an anagram of the real performer's own: Olfson).

Naturally Nancy also has a troublesome family including a hypochondriac daughter and son-in-law (Lorraine and her husband, Glen). Worst of all, Nancy's own husband of twenty-nine years is back home for good, having completed a successful career as a merchant marine. She truly loves him, but was accustomed to seeing him only two months out of every year. He was at sea the rest of the time, which was when she had forged her independent career. Now he wants to take full advantage of all the time they'll have together.

Unfortunately, once in place this busy premise doesn't really go anywhere. We don't expect Nancy to ever quit her job. But it is fun to see the caustic Walker and equally determined William Daniels square off for control of their shared household.

**THE NANETTE FABRAY SHOW** **(see *Yes, Yes Nanette*)**

**NANNY AND THE PROFESSOR (*½) 30 min (54ep Color; 1970–1971 ABC) Situation Comedy** *with Juliet Mills as Phoebe Figalilly, Richard Long as Prof. Howard Everett, David Doremus as Hal Everett, Trent Lehman as Butch Everett, and Kim Richards as Prudence Everett*

One part *Bewitched*, one part *The Farmer's Daughter*, *Nanny and the Professor* is a mild, unoffensive sitcom about a talented young English girl named Phoebe who becomes nanny to the three children of Prof. Everett. Phoebe has powers and abilities apparently beyond those of normal humans, such as communicating with animals.

**NAPOLEON AND JOSEPHINE: A LOVE STORY (**½) (6hr miniseries Color; 1987 ABC) Drama** *with Armand Assante as Napoleon Bonaparte, Jacqueline Bisset as Josephine de Beauharnais, Anthony Perkins as Talleyrand, Stephanie Beacham as Therese, Patrick Cassidy as Captain Charles, and Jane Lapotaire as Letizia*

A stylish historical romance following Josephine and Napoleon from the aftermath of the French Revolution to exile and death. Stretching from 1794 to 1814, this David L. Wolper–produced series strikes a generally effective balance between the couple's growing personal passion for each other (peppered with stormy disagreements) and their involvement in the era-shaking events of war and empire building. In short, the perfect miniseries combination: power, beauty, and passion. Naturally the settings and costumes are appropriately authentic, and the cast members seem quite comfortable in their respective roles (Armand Assante had even played Napoleon prior to this in a Broadway play), with the Anthony Perkins version of Talleyrand a surprise (and a lot of fun).

**NASHVILLE 99 (*) 60 min (3ep Color; 1977 CBS) Police Drama** *with Claude Akins as Lt. Stonewall Jackson "Stoney" Huff, Jerry Reed as Det. Trace Mayne, and Lucille Benson as Birdie Huff*

The election of Jimmy Carter to the presidency in 1976 inspired a wave of mediocre country-flavored TV shows, *Nashville 99* being one of the more forgettable examples. Claude Akins plays grizzled Nashville cop Stoney Huff, who wears badge number 99. (Akins is a lot more fun as another southern law man, Sheriff Lobo, in *B. J. and the Bear* and its spin-off show, *Sheriff Lobo*.) Real-life country and western singer Jerry Reed plays Huff's deputy. Together the two archetypal good ol' boys fight crime in Music City.

**NASHVILLE ON THE ROAD (**) 30 min (208ep Color; 1975–1983 Syndication) Musical-Variety** *with Jim Ed Brown and Jim Stafford as hosts*

The stars of country music perform on location throughout North America.

**THE NASHVILLE PALACE (**) 60 min (13ep & 60 min pilot Color; 1981–1982 NBC) Musical-Variety**

This hillbilly version of *The Hollywood Palace* features country-flavored music and comedy from Opryland, USA in Nashville. Weekly guests serve as hosts.

Roy Clark hosts the 1980 pilot.

**NATIONAL GEOGRAPHIC (***) 60 min (96ep Color; 1965– CBS & ABC & PBS & Syndication) Documentary** *with E. G. Marshall and Joseph Campanella as narrator*

Documentary specials produced by and with the National Geographic Society have been playing since the mid-1960s, covering a wide range of historical, cultural, and scientific subjects. Generally, the episodes are sufficiently timeless to fit quite comfortably into a rerun slot as a regular series, or as a home video package. Ninety-six selected episodes have been syndicated in a *Best of* package, while new offerings continue to turn up, primarily on PBS. Ted Turner's WTBS also has its own separate series with the organization, *National Geographic Explorer Magazine*. ■

**NATIONAL LAMPOON'S HOT FLASHES (*) 30 min (5ep per week Color; 1984 Syndication) Situation Comedy** *with Lois Robbins as Kimberly Clark, Mark King as John B. Goode, Kevin Pollak as Barry Gold,*

*Franklyn Ajaye as Walter Conkrite, and Wendy Goldman as Samantha*

Satirizing the banal state of local TV news coverage is not really difficult. Satirizing the local news in a funny manner is more difficult, and is beyond the abilities of this slipshod production. The focus is on the preparation and presentation of an evening news show, with the male and female co-anchors, entertainment and consumers reporter, etc. This series has also been rerun as *National Lampoon Presents the News and Other Unimportant Subjects*.

**NATIONAL VELVET (**) 30 min (58ep B&W; 1960–1962 NBC) Drama** *with Lori Martin as Velvet Brown, Ann Doran as Martha Brown, Arthur Space as Herbert Brown, Carole Wells as Edwina Brown, Joseph Scott as Donald Brown, and James McCallion as Mi Taylor*

First a popular novel by Enid Bagnold and then an Oscar-winning 1944 film starring a young Elizabeth Taylor, *National Velvet* is a story about a girl and a horse, and the big horse race they aim to win.

The TV version moves from the movie setting of England to the more mundane Midwest, a dairy farm to be exact. Young Velvet, age twelve, still hopes to ride her horse (King) to victory.

Despite the equine-oriented theme of the novel and the film, the TV *National Velvet* chooses to focus more on the broad standard story ideas of most 1950s agrarian-based series. In fact, *National Velvet* plays very much as *Lassie*, with a girl and a horse replacing the boy and dog. That being said, *National Velvet* does a good job portraying the weather-beaten American farm family. Velvet herself is fairly artificial, but her father, Herbert, exudes a lot of gritty realism.

Unlike the movies' Elizabeth Taylor, TV's Lori Martin left show business soon after playing Velvet.

**NATURE (***) 60 min (Color; 1982– PBS) Documentary** *with Donald Johanson and George Page as hosts*

The exploration of the earth's wildlife is the topic of this educational yet entertaining series. Subjects range from the effects of drought on Kenyan wildlife to a tour of the Galapagos Islands to a visit to a Costa Rican rain forest. ■

**NAVY LOG (**) 30 min (102ep B&W; 1955–1958 CBS & ABC) Drama Anthology**

Produced in cooperation with the U.S. Navy, this could be dismissed as merely passable fifties flag-waving stuff except that a number of famous performers appear. Look for anyone from Robert Montgomery to Clint Eastwood to Stacy Keach to Leonard Nimoy in these stories of regular navy personnel at home or in battle. All reenactments are based on official navy records, so other than the particular guest stars don't expect any surprises. One episode even brings in Senator John F. Kennedy to introduce a drama based on his war heroics aboard the *PT-109.*

**NEAREST AND DEAREST (**) 30 min (47ep Color; 1968–1972 UK Granada) Situation Comedy** *with Hylda Baker, Jimmy Jewel, and Joe Baldwin*

Adapted in the United States in 1973 as *Thicker Than Water*, this is the original British version of the story of sibling rivalry over a pickle factory fortune. An irresponsible brother and spinster sister face off following the death of their dad, while in the States the ailing owner brings the two children together while he's still alive. Both situations feature plenty of brother and sister bickering.

**NEARLY DEPARTED (*) 30 min (6ep Color; 1989 NBC) Situation Comedy** *with Eric Idle as Grant Pritchard, Caroline McWilliams as Clair Pritchard, Stuart Pankin as Mike Dooley, Wendy Schaal as Liz Dooley, Jay Lambert as Derek Dooley, and Henderson Forsythe as Jack Garrett*

Eric Idle (of *Monty Python* fame) plays the late Grant Pritchard (a prissy British professor), who, along with his equally deceased spouse Clair, still inhabits (haunts, actually) the Pritchards' large home in a Chicago suburb more than six months after the couple was killed in a rockslide. What troubles the snooty spirit is that the ultra-déclassé Dooley family has moved into the Pritchard manse.

Stuart Pankin (formerly of *Not Necessarily the News*) plays Mike, the head of the Dooley clan, who has his own "interloper" problem: his seventy-five-year-old father-in-law, Jack, has settled in the house as well. Jack, it turns out, is the only one able to see or hear the Pritchards—a situation he must handle with care since he fears his family might think him senile if he claims to be conversing with ghosts.

*Nearly Departed* is a poor version of the ghost-in-the-house routine that was done better in *Topper* and the film *Beetlejuice*. There are no special effects to speak of (the Pritchards look as alive as anybody in this series), giving *Nearly Departed* the look of a lame stage offering. It's sad seeing Eric Idle trying hard to pump life into his cardboard character and he should never have been allowed to croon this show's theme song (one of lamest of the 1980s).

**NEEDLES AND PINS (**1/2) 30 min (14ep Color; 1973 NBC) Situation Comedy** *with Norman Fell as Nathan Davidson, Louis Nye as Harry Karp, Deirdre Lenihan as Wendy Nelson, Sandra Deel as Sonia Baker, and Bernie Kopell as Charlie Miller*

The schmaltz is flying fast and furious here in this sitcom set in the ultra-Jewish garment district of New York City. Norman Fell (better known as Stanley Roper, the nosy landlord in *Three's Company*) plays Nathan Davidson, the owner of the Lorelei Fashion House, a manufacturer of women's clothing. Louis Nye (from the old Steve Allen show, by way of *Beverly Hillbillies*, where he played spoiled Sonny Drysdale) is annoying and funny as Davidson's good-for-nothing brother-in-law/partner. Into this Semitic setting comes all-WASP Wendy Nelson, right off a Nebraska farm, who joins Lorelei as a designer.

The cast is fine in *Needles and Pins*, the setting is novel and fertile for yucks, but the show lacks any real charm, and just rolls along during its brief run.

**NERO WOLFE (**) 60 min (14ep Color; 1981 NBC) Detective Drama** *with William Conrad as Nero Wolfe, Lee Horsley as Archie Goodwin, George Wyner as Saul Panzer and Allan Miller as Inspector Cramer*

William Conrad plays mystery writer Rex Stout's ultimate armchair detective: A 285-pound reclusive gourmet and horticulturist who solves crimes from the comforts of his own home, in between tending his greenhouse and sampling his favorite gastronomic treats. It's a simple arrangement: Associates Archie Goodwin and Saul Panzer bring Wolfe the facts and then he solves the mystery.

Overall the series is merely adequate, with the stories lacking the detail and class of the original novels. Conrad is sufficiently crusty and self-indulgent in the title role, but too often the production simply stops with him, the eccentric fat man who loves orchids and murder, at the expense of any further plot and character development.

**NEVER MIND THE QUALITY, FEEL THE WIDTH (**) 30 min (36ep: 26 B&W & 10 Color, 1967–1969 UK Thames) Situation Comedy** *with John Bluthal and Joe Lynch*

Nice ethnic humor at a London (East End) tailor shop operated by Jewish Manny Cohen and Catholic Patrick Kelly.

**THE NEW . . . (see *Andy Griffith, Dick Van Dyke, Gidget, Loretta Young, Odd Couple, Phil Silvers*)**

**THE NEW ADVENTURES OF . . . (see *Beans Baxter, Charlie Chan, Perry Mason*)**

**THE NEW BREED (*) 60 min (36ep B&W; 1961–1962 ABC) Police Drama** *with Leslie Nielsen as Lt. Price Adams, John Beradino as Sgt. Vince Cavelli, John Clarke as Joe Huddleston, and Byron Morrow as Capt. Keith Gregory*

Quinn Martin produced numerous hit series (such as *The Untouchables, The Fugitive, The F.B.I.*), but even his less successful shows (*Dan August, Barnaby Jones, Most Wanted*) showed some spark of originality and imagination. *The New Breed*, one of Martin's least successful efforts, shows neither.

What was "new" about *The New Breed* in the early 1960s seems pretty standard cop show stuff these days. The cops are part of some fancy-schmantzy metropolitan squad of the Los Angeles police and they are all trained in the new scientific way of catching crooks, using electronic gadgets and psychological training. The stories are forgettable, and so is the cast, except for Leslie Nielsen. Making his first regular TV series appearance here (though he had starred in Disney's miniseries *Swamp Fox*), Nielsen sent on to play a lot of boring cop and corporate types. This training served him well in his later hilarious parodies of these sorts of characters in the film *Airplane!* and the police satire series *Police Squad!*

**A NEW KIND OF FAMILY (*½) 30 min (8ep Color; 1979–1980 ABC) Situation Comedy** *with Eileen Brennan as Kit Flanagan, David Hollander as Andy Flanagan, Lauri Hendler as Hillary Flanagan, Rob Lowe as Tony Flanagan, Gwynne Gilford as Abby Stone, Connie Ann Hearn as Jill Stone, Telma Hopkins as Jess Ashton, and Janet Jackson as Jojo Ashton.*

There's nothing really new about *A New Kind of Family*; it's just another run-through of the concept of two different types of people sharing an apartment. The loose, free-thinking side is represented by the Flanagans, headed by recently widowed Kit, who moved to (guess where?) Los Angeles from bad old New York. Kit has two sons and a daughter. The Flanagans, through some pointless plot twist, share the same rented house with the Stones, who are the uptight representatives (divorcée Abby is just starting law school). For the last few episodes, the Stones are replaced by the Ashtons, a black divorcée who runs a catering business and her daughter Jojo. The only interesting point of this program is that it is the first TV series appearance for Rob Lowe, who became a teen heartthrob soon thereafter in movies such as *St. Elmo's Fire* and *About Last Night.*

**THE NEW LAND (**½) 60 min (6ep Color; 1974 ABC) Drama** *with Kurt Russell as Bo Larsen, Scott Thomas as Christian Larsen, Bonnie Bedelia as Anna Larsen, Donald Moffat as Rev. Lars Lundstrom, Todd Lookinland as Tuliff Larsen, and Debbie Lytton as Anneliese Larsen.*

Inspired by two successful Swedish films from Jan Troell, *The Emmigrants* (1971) and *The New Land* (1973), this series follows much the same path into the American wilderness of the nineteenth century. The members of the Larsen family (immigrants from Scandinavia) face the challenge of setting up their new home in the wilds of Minnesota. The stories focus on solid family and moral values, but the real draw of the series is the beautiful location footage shot in Oregon and California.

In the later 1970s and 1980s, Debbie Lytton (the young daughter) moved to life in the soaps as Melissa in *Days of Our Lives.*

**THE NEW MONKEES (*) 30 min (13ep Color; 1987–1988 Syndication) Situation Comedy** *with Marty Ross as Marty, Dino Kovas as Dino, Larry Saltis as Larry,*

*Jared Chandler as Jared, and Gordon Oas-Heim as Manford*

There is no direct connection between this program and the mid-1960s series *The Monkees*, other than the desire to rip off a familiar name for the chance at a few ratings points. The concept is the same, with four young guys, members of a band called The New Monkees, living together and hoping for rock stardom. On the way, naturally, are many pitfalls and silly adventures, all mixed with musical interludes in the form of music videos (a form pioneered by The "Old" Monkees). The four new guys try their hardest to be spiffy, cool, and innovative, but come up short. It's almost laughable to say that this show does not reach the level of quality of *The Monkees*, but *The New Monkees* simply isn't very funny. The music is passable, at best.

**THE NEW PEOPLE** (½) **45 min (17ep Color; 1969–1970 ABC) Drama** *with Tiffany Bolling as Susan Bradley, Zooey Hall as Bob Lee, Jill Jaress as Ginny Loomis, David Moses as Eugene "Bones" Washington, Dennis Olivieri as Stanley Gabriel, and Peter Ratray as George Potter*

This ridiculous series is a prime example of the silly lengths TV went to in the late 1960s to look "hip." The concept is hippie heaven: a planeload of multi-ethnic American college students returning from an exchange program in Southeast Asia crash lands on a deserted island called Buamo. The island used to be a U.S. atomic test site, and is unreachable by established society. The stranded college kids use the buildings set up by the government for the atomic tests as the basis of a new "better" society. Nobody seems to worry about radiation residue on Buamo. Not surprisingly, *The New People* is produced by Aaron Spelling, who also produced *The Mod Squad*, another show designed to be "with it."

**THE NEW SHOW** (**) **60 min (10ep Color; 1984 NBC) Comedy-Variety** *with Buck Henry, Dave Thomas, and Valri Bromfield*

In between his two stints as producer of *NBC's Saturday Night Live*, Lorne Michaels produced this very similar series. The concept is exactly the same, mixing offbeat humor, intentionally extreme bits, and guest rock acts. The difference is that the writing on *The New Show* is highly erratic. There are comic gems, such as guest Steve Martin's hilarious parody of Michael Jackson's video clip of the hit song "Billie Jean," but the talented cast is often wasted in meandering bits that miss the mark.

**THE NEW VOICE** (*½) **30 min (24ep Color; 1981–1982 PBS) Comedy/Drama** *with Lorraine Gauli as Lorraine George, Millie Santiago as Millie, Ken Mochizuki as Ken, Claudio Martinez as Claudio, and Shawn Elliott as Mr. Morfi*

Good intentions abound on *The New Voice*, but the end result is a preachy, stilted series about a group of Boston-area high school students who put out a school newspaper, called the *New Voice*.

**NEW WILDERNESS, LORNE GREENE'S** (**½) **30 min (170ep Color; 1982–1987 Syndication) Documentary** *with Lorne Greene as host*

Much the same as Greene's *Last of the Wild* series, this show focuses on endangered animal species. Greene serves as executive producer as well as host.

**NEW YORK CONFIDENTIAL** (**) **30 min (39ep B&W; 1958–1959 Syndication) Crime Drama** *with Lee Tracy as Lee Cochran*

Based on books by Lee Mortimer and Jack Lait, and a 1955 movie starring Broderick Crawford, this routine crime show revolves around the daring exploits of Gotham newspaper reporter Lee Cochran and his crusade against crime in the nation's largest city.

**NEWHART** (***½) **30 min (160ep at Fall 1989 Color; 1982– CBS) Situation Comedy** *with Bob Newhart as Dick Loudon, Mary Frann as Joanna Loudon, Tom Poston as George Utley, Julia Duffy as Stephanie Vanderkellen, Peter Scolari as Michael Harris, Jennifer Holmes as Leslie Vanderkellen, Steven Kampmann as Kirk Devane, and William Sanderson as Larry, Tony Papenfuss as his brother Darryl, and John Voldstad as his other brother Darryl*

Imagine this: Soon after Chicago psychologist Bob Hartley left his practice to write and teach, he and his wife split. He changed his name, became a full-time writer, remarried, and moved east to run a small Vermont inn.

Obviously, that's taking identification with television characters to an extreme, but it does touch a key point: Whatever the title *Newhart* is essentially another version of *The Bob Newhart Show*, with a different setting and supporting cast but the same central performer.

This time the comedy is a bit more leisurely in pace, befitting the bucolic country setting. Newhart plays Dick Loudon, a writer of "How to" books who moves from New York to Vermont to run the 200-year-old Stratford Inn with his wife, Joanna. This inn location effectively combines home and office, so he doesn't need to waste time commuting. Instead, Newhart gets right to the business at hand, reacting to the characters around him—in this case, the entire population of a set-in-its-ways New England community.

Well, actually, this one takes a while to fine-tune. At first it seems as if Dick doesn't have quite enough craziness immediately surrounding him—even with two jobs (writer and innkeeper) and the likes of characters such as laid-back handyman George Utley (played by Tom Poston, "The Peeper" on *The Bob Newhart Show*) and compulsive liar Kirk Devane (owner of the nearby Minuteman Cafe). So in the second season, Dick becomes host of a low-rated Sunday afternoon local TV interview show.

The cast is also revamped a bit. The hotel's level-headed and responsible maid, Leslie, is replaced with her irresponsible cousin Stephanie, a shallow, self-absorbed, spoiled rich girl. She soon finds her perfect soulmate in Dick's TV producer, the equally self-centered and shallow Michael Harris. The two carry on a lengthy courtship built on their mutual love of looking good, avoiding any real work, and giggling at their social inferiors (everybody else). Occasionally, they visit Stephanie's incredibly wealthy parents to remind themselves of what really matters in life: fashion, status, and everything money can buy.

Ownership of the next-door Minuteman Cafe also changes hands, from Kirk to the most popular supporting characters on the show: Larry, Darryl, and Darryl. Only Larry ever speaks, introducing himself and his two brothers each time they enter the scene. The three scruffy siblings are portrayed as the epitome of country innocence (happily at home playing in the woods) mixed with unexpected real-world savvy and sophistication (deftly analyzing network programming strategies or popping off to New York City to catch a hip play such as *Phantom of the Opera)*. They are also self-acclaimed masters of such "social graces" as spitting into the wind and ducking.

Those cast changes are firmly in place by the third season, as the series hits its stride and Newhart's self-conscious character type really has a chance to shine. Whether as a put-upon substitute kiddie-show host, the reluctant best man to Stephanie and Michael's aborted wedding, or the inadvertent killer of a legendary white deer, Dick Loudon is there to take the fall.

Still he never loses his standing as a respected community leader. After all, who else could people approach with their latest problem or hare-brained scheme? Besides, they probably know he is really a professional shrink in disguise. They all watch enough TV—somewhere in between town favorites like *Barnaby Jones* (George's), *The Mod Squad* (the mayor's), and *Gilligan's Island* (Michael's) someone must have seen those *Bob Newhart Show* reruns.

## THE NEXT STOP BEYOND (see *One Step Beyond*)

## NICHOLAS NICKLEBY, THE LIFE AND ADVENTURES OF (***) (9hr miniseries Color; 1982 Syndication) Drama

*with Roger Rees as Nicholas Nickleby, David Threlfall as Smike, Emily Richard as Kate Nickleby, John Woodvine as Ralph Nickleby, Alun Armstrong as Headmaster Squeers, Lucy Gutteridge as Madeline Bray, Edward Petherbridge as Newman Noggs, Janet Dale as Mrs. Wititterley, and Bob Peck as Sir Hawk*

This was quite an undertaking by London's Royal Shakespeare Company, using some thirty-nine performers (playing 150 parts) to transform a 900-page Dickens novel into a daylong live theatrical event. In 1980 and 1981, it played to sold-out houses in both Britain and the United States, on Broadway commanding a hefty $100 ticket.

The production transfers surprisingly well to video, with a performance taped at London's Old Vic Theater. For one thing, as a television event it usually plays in two- or three-hour segments (or at whatever pace you want on videotape), removing that sense of exhausting endurance that inevitably accompanied seeing it live.

The camera work is also very good, diving into the action with close-ups that allow the performers to show off their onstage versatility (all but Rees have multiple roles) and spirit of ensemble interaction.

Best of all, *The Life and Adventures of Nicholas Nickleby* proves that there's more than one way to bring a classic British novel to television. You don't always need expensive on-location settings and meticulous period-piece re-creations of every room in a Victorian house. Instead a mix of good costumes, basic sets, and (above all) exuberant performances can do the job quite well.

## NICHOLS (**½) 60 min (24ep Color; 1971–1972 NBC) Western

*with James Garner as Sheriff Nichols and Jim Nichols, Margot Kidder as Ruth, Stuart Margolin as Mitch, John Beck as Ketcham, Neva Patterson as Ma Ketcham, and Alice Ghostley as Bertha.*

*Nichols* is reportedly one of James Garner's favorite series, bringing his reluctant hero type to an early twentieth century (1914) western setting. Garner plays Nichols, who returns to his family hometown of Nichols, Arizona, after nearly two decades, only to discover that it's now being run by the Ketcham family.

In short order, Nichols finds himself forced into the job of town sheriff, with one of Ma Ketcham's sons as his less than honest deputy, Mitch. As with *Maverick*, this show is not handled as a traditional western setup. Garner's character does not carry a gun, and prefers a car or a motorcycle to a horse. In fact, he's not quite the paragon of virtue, either, spending much of his time planning con games and get-rich-quick schemes, preferably at the expense of the Ketchams.

After about two dozen stories, the setup is changed to introduce a more standard heroic figure—apparently to earn renewal for a second season. Nichols is shot, but then his twin brother Jim Nichols (also played by Garner) turns up to avenge the killing. The series was canceled anyway, so we're left with one of those continuity gaps that will never be resolved.

Still, *Nichols* is an entertaining venture for Garner, nicely bridging the eras between *Maverick* and *The Rockford Files.* And it's worth catching for the cast alone. Besides Garner there's Margot Kidder (Lois Lane in the theatrical *Superman* films), Stuart Margolin (Jim Rockford's snitch, Angel), John Beck (Pam's boyfriend

Mark Graison on *Dallas*), Neva Patterson (Eleanor Donovan on *V*), and Alice Ghostley (Esmerelda on *Bewitched*).

## NICK AND HILLARY (see *Tattingers's*)

## NIGHT COURT (***½) 30 min (123ep at Fall 1989 Color; 1984– NBC) Situation Comedy *with Harry Anderson as Harry Stone, John Larroquette as Dan Fielding, Richard Moll as Bull Shannon, Markie Post as Christine Sullivan, Charles Robinson as Mac Robinson, Selma Diamond as Selma Hacker, Florence Halop as Florence Kleiner, Marsha Warfield as Roz Russell, Karen Austin as Lana Wagner, Paula Kelly as Liz Williams, and Ellen Foley as Billie Young.*

Harry Anderson's stand-up comedy act combines a bit of street hustle, the carny circuit, and classic vaudeville. The role of free-spirited New York night court judge Harry Stone is tailor-made for him, with *Night Court* itself about as close as you can get to a vaudeville act while still remaining a sitcom. Each episode has Harry presiding over a parade of oddball plaintiffs and defendants, as well as a court staff perfectly suited to his humor-oriented approach to dispensing commonsense justice.

In fact, in the world of *Night Court* the joke reigns supreme. No character gets in the way of any punch line and no punch line is beyond any character. No matter what the situation, if there's a setup, just wait two beats and someone will deliver the necessary retort. (For example, "Don't anybody move!" is sure to be followed by everyone's mad scramble from the premises.) And if there's a chance for a double entendre, someone will run with it.

Fortunately it all hangs together, with excellent writing behind the jokes, as well as performers who know how to deliver them. Besides Anderson, John Larroquette is most effective on the show with his portrayal of prosecutor Dan Fielding as a selfish, manipulative, obsequious weasel with a voracious sexual appetite. Dan ends up as both the target and instigator of some great put-down lines.

There are also caustic comments from the bailiffs standing on the sidelines, with six-foot eight-inch Richard Moll usually delivering a setup line with almost childlike innocence to his associate. In an odd coincidence, the second bailiff role had to be recast and rewritten twice as a new character when two successive performers—Selma Diamond and Florence Halop—passed away. Marsha Warfield took over thereafter. There is also character turnover in two other positions: the court clerk (played by Karen Austin, then Charles Robinson) and the female public defender (played by Gail Strickland in the pilot, then Paula Kelly, Ellen Foley, and, after a never-aired test sequence by Shelley Hack, Markie Post).

The series was created by *Barney Miller* alum Reinhold Weege, who found a New York night court the perfect setting for the type of characters and situations that had worked so well at the 12th precinct. In *Night Court*, though, he puts less emphasis on the revolving door of visitors to the scene, concentrating instead on the silly traits of the central cast.

After all, how could you top a judge devoted to funny faces, magic tricks, and Mel Torme?

## NIGHT GALLERY (***) 60 & 30 min (100ep: twenty-eight 60 min & seventy-two 30 min, plus 2 hr pilot Color; 1970–1973 NBC) Suspense Anthology *with Rod Serling as host*

*Night Gallery* is not *The Twilight Zone* by any stretch of the imagination. Nevertheless, *Night Gallery* is an entertaining collection of spooky, intriguing, and even humorous tales, all introduced by Rod Serling, whose quirky narrating style always recalls his earlier *Twilight Zone* success.

Unlike *The Twilight Zone* (which he produced and wrote for), Serling contributes little to *Night Gallery* other than acting as carnival barker, attracting a crowd to get them "in the tent" to watch the show. Serling, in fact, became upset by his lack of input beyond the filmed introductions and occasional stints as writer or adapter of stories. His anger seems justified, as the numerous bland episodes of *Night Gallery* roll on. There are enough quality episodes to make the series watchable and worthwhile (most of the time), but the show will forever pale in comparison with Serling's masterpiece.

Serling's introductions take place in the stilted setting of an art gallery (hence the title) of macabre, grotesque paintings that tie in, at least superficially, with the upcoming segment. Each hour episode might contain three or even four separate segments, while the half-hour episodes stick to one or two.

The twenty-eight hour episodes were produced first, followed by the seventy-two half-hour episodes. Those seventy-two episodes have been packaged, along with severely edited versions of twenty-five episodes of the unrelated, inferior, and silly series *The Sixth Sense* (see that title), starring Gary Collins, under the title *Rod Sterling's Night Gallery*. The presence of *The Sixth Sense* shows really drags down the *Night Gallery* name, and it is best to avoid the Collins episodes, if possible.

The 1969 two-hour *Night Gallery* pilot is a popular rerun, due to "Darker Than Dark," the second of the pilot's three segments. It is the first TV direction work by twenty-two-year-old novice filmmaker Steven Spielberg. Starring aging film queen Joan Crawford, "Darker Than Dark" is the best segment of the pilot, as Crawford plays a rich old bitch who is blind and literally buys the eyes of a gambler who owes her money. ■

## NIGHT HEAT (**) 60 min (66ep at Fall 1988 Color; 1985– CBS) Crime Drama *with Allan Royal as Tom Kirkwood, Scott Hylands as Det. Kevin O'Brien, Jeff*

*Wincott as Det. Frank Giambone, Susan Hogan as Nicole "Nickie" Rimbaud, and Wendy Crewson as Dorothy Fredericks*

It is appropriate that a show about the low-glamour night-shift world of the police department and the local newspaper is portrayed in a low-budget series with few pretensions. Detectives Kevin O'Brien and Frank Giambone handle the crime calls after dusk, while newspaperman Tom Kirkwood tags along to get a scoop.

**NIGHTINGALES (*) 60 min (11ep & 2 hr pilot Color; 1989 NBC) Drama** *With Suzanne Pleshette as Chris Broderick, Barry Newman as Dr. Garrett Braden, Susan Walters as Bridget Loring, Chelsea Field as Samantha "Sam" Sullivan, Kristy Swanson as Rebecca "Becky" Granger, Roxann Biggs as Yolanda "Yolo" Puentes, Kim Johnston Ulrich as Allyson Yates, Gil Gerard as Paul Petrillo, Taylor Fry as Megan, and Fran Bennett as Nurse Ritt*

Aaron Spelling, the master of high-gloss titillation TV (*Charlie's Angels*), serves up this frothy saga of five comely student nurses struggling through their training in a large hospital in (surprise!) Los Angeles. The young angels of mercy endure romantic and professional traumas, while showing as much skin as the writers can squeeze in.

Suzanne Pleshette (wife Emily in the 1970s *Bob Newhart Show*) provides a modicum of respectability as Chris Broderick, the director of student nursing. She keeps a motherly eye on her pupils, who all live in a dormitory, a renovated old mansion called Nightingale House. Barry Newman (*Petrocelli*) plays Garrett Braden, the hospital chief of staff whose late wife was Chris's best friend. Paul Petrillo is Chris's ex-husband, who shows up at the hospital as a guest lecturer, and decides to stay, complicating his ex-wife's life. Throughout *Nightingales*, there is an air of superficiality that is too premeditated to ignore. The young nurses seem better suited to challenge the Roller Derby queens of *Roller Girls* than to help patients.

In the 1988 pilot, *Hill Street Blues* alumnus Mimi Kuzyk plays the director of nursing (called Liz McCarren), there are a few different girls in the program, and Nightingale House is co-ed.

**9 to 5 (**½) 30 min (85ep Color; 1982–1984 & 1986–1988 ABC & Syndication) Situation Comedy** *with Rita Moreno as Violet Newstead, Rachel Dennison as Doralee Rhodes, Valerie Curtin as Judy Bernly, Leah Ayres as Linda Bowman, Sally Struthers as Marsha McMurray Shrimpton, Peter Bonerz as Franklin Hart, Dorian Lopinto as Charmin Cunningham, Fred Applegate as E. Nelson Felb, Edward Winter as Bud Coleman, and Art Evans as Morgan*

There have been several permutations of this sturdy office comedy setup, originally based on a 1980 hit movie in which three big business secretaries (played by Lily Tomlin, Dolly Parton, and Jane Fonda) get revenge on their slimy boss (played by Dabney Coleman). Fonda, in fact, was a co-producer of the initial television series, even appearing on camera as a security guard at the office building. Otherwise, none of the theatrical cast came over, though Dolly Parton's sister Rachel Dennison landed the video version of her big sister's character. The episodes from this phase are on film.

The series changed producers and switched to videotape for the remainder of its network run, also bringing in a new secretary, Linda, to replace Valerie Curtin's Judy. But ABC canceled the series after thirty-three episodes.

A short time later the project was revived for first-run syndication of new episodes, bringing back both Dennison and Curtin in their original roles along with Sally Struthers as Marsha, a new secretary the veterans take under their wings. They're a good team that supports each other both at the office and in off-hours domestic situations.

Though all the video adaptations are far less angry and vindictive than the original film, this latest version is probably the most well-rounded. It may still be set in a male-dominated business world, but at least the bosses come off as more than just insensitive louts. Sometimes they even use their wiles to help the three secretaries. After all, it's cheaper than paying them what they're worth.

Though Dolly Parton wrote and originally performed the hit title song for the feature film, her recording is not used in the opening credits until the syndicated version.

**1915 (***) 60 min (7ep Color; 1982 Australia ABC) Drama** *with Scott McGregor as Walter Gilchrist, Scott Burgess as Billy McKenzie, Sigrid Thornton as Frances Reilly, and Jackie Woodburne as Diana Benedetto*

World War I, as seen from the perspective of two Australians fighting with the British army, is the focus of this well-produced short series based on a novel by Roger McDonald. Walter Gilchrist is the son of a rich man, while Billy MacKenzie is the offspring of a poor drunk. The series (which actually begins in 1913) follows the two soldiers from their peacetime lives, through their early innocent enlistment and into the disillusionment of the reality of warfare.

**1990 (**½) 60 min (16ep Color; 1977 UK BBC) Drama** *with Edward Woodward, Paul Hardwick, Robert Lang, Yvonne Mitchell, and Tony Doyle*

Absorbing portrait of life in Britain reminiscent of the tyrannical bureaucracy in George Orwell's *1984*, with absolute government control in the name of protecting the common good. In one way, stretching out the tale dilutes the message (especially when compared to Orwell's punchy novel), but in another it becomes even more effective with time to dwell on the depressing vision of the future. Naturally, *Equalizer* fans will enjoy seeing how their man (Edward Woodward) does in that setting.

**90 BRISTOL COURT 90 min (13ep Color; 1964–1965 NBC) Situation Comedy** *with Guy Raymond as Cliff Murdock*

A rather innovative but ultimately unsuccessful effort at packaging three separate shows, *90 Bristol Court* is the umbrella title for three mediocre sitcoms, *Harris Against the World, Karen,* and *Tom, Dick and Mary* (see each title). The only connecting link between the three shows is that they all are set in a swank Southern California apartment complex whose address is 90 Bristol Court. The only common character of the three shows is apartment handyman Cliff Murdock.

**THE NIXON INTERVIEWS (**) 60 min (4ep Color; 1977 Syndication) Interview** *with David Frost and Richard Nixon*

Former President Richard Nixon was paid one million dollars to appear in this series of interviews by British-born talk show host David Frost. The chief topic is Watergate (which Nixon says little new about), but Nixon's entire career is covered. These interviews are for historians only, and those who like to watch Nixon's upper lip sweat.

**NO HIDING PLACE (**) 60 min (9ep B&W; 1959–1966 UK Associated Rediffusion) Crime Drama** *with Raymond Francis as Chief Superintendent Lockhart and Eric Lander as Sergeant Baxter*

Only a handful of these straightforward Scotland Yard detective cases are available for Stateside syndication, though in its original British run the series aired more than 150 episodes. Lockhart is one of those minor gimmick independent heroes. His calling card: He uses snuff.

**NO HOLDS BARRED (*) 70 min (4ep Color; 1980 CBS) Comedy-Variety** *with Kelly Monteith as host*

It is extremely difficult to describe exactly what *No Holds Barred* is, which may explain its very small number of episodes. Kelly Monteith, a passable comic, hosts an eclectic collection of almost straight soft news features, comedy parodies, interviews, and rock music performances. None of the contents relate to anything else on the show and none are memorable.

**NO, HONESTLY (***½) 30 min (13ep Color; 1974 UK London Weekend Television) Situation Comedy** *with John Alderton as Charles "C. D." Danby and Pauline Collins as Clara Danby*

"Years from now, we'll look back on this and laugh." That thought has cheered many young couples through their struggling early days together. It also serves as the premise for *No, Honestly*, a gently affectionate comedy on the rituals of courtship and marriage.

Each episode opens and closes with a wraparound bit between Clara and Charles (C. D.) Danby, married ten years. She is an illogically logical Gracie Allen-type who writes children's books about Ollie the Otter. He is a good-looking comic actor with a quick smile and dry wit. Together they talk a bit about the present, then lead us back to their past—from the first time they met to their first wedding anniversary celebration—all comfortably cushioned by a decade's distance (and subsequent success).

The situations are well-staged, with plenty of good-intentioned misunderstanding, affectionate banter, and cute bits. For instance, when C. D. and Clara give their first dinner party they invite people they don't like in order to pay them back for a party they didn't enjoy in the first place (which turns out to be fine because the event is predictably disastrous anyway). Or during one lean stretch between acting jobs, Charles spends his days ironing shoelaces and talking back to the television set while waiting for a call from his agent. Later, at a dreadful job hunting party, he drops to the floor feigning death while Clara solemnly deadpans: "Please don't look. It was my husband's wish not to be 'seen dead' at this party."

After all the silliness, though, the stories inevitably end with an affectionate embrace because these two really love each other. A real-life husband and wife team, the Danby alter-egos of John Alderton and Pauline Collins also played young marrieds on *Upstairs, Downstairs* (as Thomas the chauffeur and Sara the chambermaid) and took on a variety of courting roles in an anthology of stories by P. G. Wodehouse.

**NO SOAP, RADIO (***) 30 min 5ep Color; 1982 ABC) Situation Comedy** *with Steve Guttenberg as Roger, Hillary Bailey as Karen, Bill Dana as Mr. Plitzky, Fran Ryan as Mrs. Belmont, and Stuart Pankin as Tuttle*

This is the closest any American network dared come to copying the anarchic British comedy series *Monty Python's Flying Circus*. To begin, the title makes no sense. Don't even try to figure it out. Next, the basic setting of the show, the seedy Hotel Pelican in Atlantic City, New Jersey, is largely irrelevant, since much of the action is nonsensical and disjointed.

Using the hotel setting as merely a backdrop, the series goes on wild flights of fancy, with frequent interruptions of the narrative for unrelated comedy bits, and numerous impossible transitions in the story (an elevator might open to a totally different city from the hotel lobby where it began).

Roger is the young manager of the hotel, Karen is the desk clerk, and Tuttle is the house detective. Regular hotel guests and irregular weekly drop-ins also populate the landscape.

For viewers weaned on *Petticoat Junction* or *The Brady Bunch, No Soap, Radio* will be like a bad acid trip. For those with a little more flexibility, *No Soap, Radio* is a breathtaking experiment. It may not always work, but it's exhilarating to go along for the ride.

**NO TIME FOR SERGEANTS** (**) **30 min (34ep B&W; 1964–1965 ABC) Situation Comedy** *with Sammy Jackson as Will Stockdale, Harry Hickox as Sgt. Orville King, Paul Smith as Capt. Paul Martin, Kevin O'Neal as Ben Whitledge, and Laurie Sibbald as Millie Anderson.*

This story had already been around the block a few times before it wound up as a regular TV series. Originally a novel by Mac Hyman, *No Time for Sergeants* caught the public's fancy as a 1955 live TV drama (on *The U.S. Steel Hour*) in which Andy Griffith first garnered wide acclaim, playing the first of his many good ol' boy country roles. The success of the TV play led to a Broadway version by Ira Levin that also starred Griffith. Then came a hit 1958 movie where Griffith, still playing the lead, was first teamed up, albeit briefly, with Don Knotts. Finally comes the TV series. Unfortunately it isn't worth the wait.

The story is about Will Stockdale, a deceptively simple Georgia farm boy drafted into the air force. His innocent goodness and open-hearted honesty just don't compute with the more cynical by-the-book military types, but Will's homespun wisdom frequently outwits the air force brass.

Much like a road company version of a hit Broadway play, the inferior cast of the TV series just can't compete with the originals. *Gomer Pyle, U.S.M.C.* (a spinoff from Andy Griffith's successful TV series) turns the rube in the service trick much better than this pale version of *No Time for Sergeants.*

**NO WARNING** (**) **30 min (13ep B&W; 1958 NBC) Suspense Anthology** *with Westbrook Van Voorhis as host/narrator*

Al Simon, a producer far better known for his work in sitcoms (*The Beverly Hillbillies, Mister Ed, Petticoat Junction*), also dabbled in suspense series. In 1957 he produced a show called *Panic*, and *No Warning* is simply a continuation of the *Panic* format.

Westbrook Van Voorhis, the super-serious "voice of doom" narrator from radio's *March of Time* series, adds his distinctive voice to these mildly interesting tales of personal crises. There is nothing really supernatural here, just sudden traumas.

Aside from the original thirteen episodes of *No Warning*, several episodes of *Panic* have aired under the *No Warning* title.

**NOAH'S ARK** (*½) **30 min (23ep B&W; 1956–1957 NBC) Medical Drama** *with Paul Burke as Dr. Noah McCann, Vic Rodman as Dr. Sam Rinehart, and May Wynn as Liz Clark*

Jack Webb, the man from *Dragnet*, temporarily leaves the crime-fighting world for the more mundane profession of veterinarian. Dr. Noah McCann is the young, intense assistant to Dr. Rinehart, a veterinarian emeritus now confined to a wheelchair. There are hints of the Dr. Zorba/Dr. Casey/Dr. Gillespie/Dr. Kildare old/young medical axis here, but it's hard to get too wrapped up in the traumas of a sick animal. After all, there are no pretty young women suffering from amnesia for the handsome young doctor to fall in love with.

**NOBLE HOUSE, JAMES CLAVELL'S** (**) **(8hr miniseries Color; 1988 NBC) Drama** *with Pierce Brosnan as Ian Dunross, John Rhys-Davies as Quillan Gornt, Deborah Raffin as Casey Tcholok, Linc Bartlett as Ben Masters, Julia Nickson as Orlanda Ramos, Khigh Dhiegh as Four Finger Wu, and John Houseman as Sir Geoffrey Allison*

James Clavell takes the tale of a ruthless taipan to television after the flop of a similar hook as a 1986 theatrical feature film, *Tai Pan.*

This time, Pierce Brosnan has the nasty lead role in the corporate intrigue (set in modern-day Hong Kong), playing the cutthroat head (the *taipan,* Cantonese for "supreme leader") of a powerful international trading firm, Struan and Company a.k.a. the Noble House. In need of fresh cash, he seeks help from an American moneyman, Ben Masters, while his chief competitor, Quillan Gornt, attempts to sabotage the deal.

As with many corporate dramas, the going is a bit slow for far too long, though the lavish location footage certainly helps to illustrate what all that money and power they're fighting for can provide. The final two hours are just fine, though, with the back-stabbing, double-dealing, and passionate affairs coming to a head. And through it all Brosnan gets the chance to play against his affable *Remington Steele* character type.

**NOBODY'S PERFECT** (*½) **30 min (8ep Color; 1980 ABC) Situation Comedy** *with Ron Moody as Det. Roger Hart, Cassie Yates as Det. Jennifer Dempsey, and Michael Durrell as Lt. Vince de Gennaro*

Nobody may be perfect, as the title states, but you could at least expect a little more innovation from this mild sitcom. Roger Hart is a shining light from England's Scotland Yard detective force who is inexplicably loaned to a San Francisco police precinct.

This entire series is premised on two jokes. One is Hart's proclivity for clumsiness, in spite of which he is a good cop. The other in his urbane, refined, continental mannerisms, jarring against the more earthly manner of the unwashed American rabble he must work with in San Francisco.

**NORTH AND SOUTH/NORTH AND SOUTH—BOOK II** (**½) **(24hr miniseries Color; 1985–1986 ABC) Drama** *with David Carradine as Justin LaMotte, Philip Casnoff as Elkanah Bent, Lesley-Anne Down as Madeline Fabray LaMotte, Genie Francis as Brett Main Haz-*

*ard, John Stockwell and Parker Stevenson as Billy Hazard, Patrick Swayze as Orry Main, James Read as George Hazard, Kirstie Alley as Virgilia Hazard Grady, Mary Crosby as Isabel Hazard, Jonathan Frakes as Stanley Hazard, Robert Mitchum as Col. Patrick Flynn, Kate McNeil as Augusta Barclay, Elizabeth Taylor as Madame Conti, Johnny Cash as John Brown, Lloyd Bridges as Jefferson Davis, and Hal Holbrook as Abraham Lincoln*

John Jakes' two best-selling long-winded epic novels (*North and South* and *Love and War*) about the American Civil War are turned into two TV miniseries, *North and South* and *North and South—Book II.* Produced by miniseries whiz David L. Wolper (*Roots, The Thorn Birds*), the story follows two families during the course of the years between 1842 and 1865. The Main family own a plantation in South Carolina and represent the Confederacy, while the Hazards run a factory in Pennsylvania and represent the Union. Pre–*Dirty Dancing* Patrick Swayze plays the main Main boy. As is usual in miniseries, historical events fly by like road signs, great emphasis is given to torrid love affairs, and famous actors and actresses pop up in small guest roles.

**NORTHWEST PASSAGE (**) 30 min (26ep B&W; 1958–1959 NBC) Adventure** *with Buddy Ebsen as Sgt. Hunk Marriner, Keith Larsen as Maj. Robert Rogers, Don Burnett as Ensign Langdon Towne, and Philip Tonge as Gen. Amherst*

Based on a 1940 film (with Spencer Tracy, Robert Young, and Walter Brennan) which came from a book by Kenneth Roberts, this series follows the exploits of American wilderness explorer Robert Rogers during the French and Indian Wars (1754–1759). He and his men (dubbed "Rogers' Rangers") are there in Canada and upstate New York searching for an all-water shipping route across the North American continent (the elusive "northwest passage").

Well, actually, they really seem to be out there to help new settlers fight either the French or the Indians, or both. At least this time Keith Larsen, who previously played the Indian title character on *Brave Eagle*, ends up on the winning side.

**NOT FOR HIRE (*) 30 min (39ep B&W; 1959–1960 Syndication) Crime Drama** *with Ralph Meeker as Sgt. Steve Dekker, Lizabeth Rush as Sonica Zametoo, and Ken Drake as Cpl. Zimmerman*

Sgt. Dekker is not for hire . . . he works solely for the U.S. Army's Criminal Investigation Division, prosecuting military types who break the army's rules. This series has also been known as *Sergeant Steve Dekker*.

**NOT NECESSARILY THE NEWS (***) 30 min (73ep at Fall 1989 Color; 1983–1989 HBO) Comedy** *with Anne Bloom, Danny Breen, Rich Hall, Mitchell Laurance, Audrie Neenan, and Stuart Pankin*

John Moffitt, producer of the late, lamented ABC comedy series *Fridays*, went to cable TV to produce *Not Necessarily the News* when his network series was axed. The freedom allowed by cable helps create a wonderful American version of a British classic.

The British series *Not the Nine O'Clock News* earned a reputation of poking merciless fun at public figures and TV newscasters by lampooning them in a newscast setting. *Not Necessarily the News* does the same for American TV, with the ensemble cast serving as reporters for a hypothetical news program. Frequently actual news footage is used and doctored for comic effect. Rotund Stuart Pankin serves as anchorman. Lanky Rich Hall often turns in the funniest moments.

**NOT THE NINE O'CLOCK NEWS (**½) 30 min (28ep Color; 1979–1982 UK BBC) Comedy** *with Rowan Atkinson, Pamela Stephenson, Mel Smith, and Griff Rhys-Jones*

This is the obvious inspiration for the U.S. series *Not Necessarily the News*. The British original has enough timeless gags mixed in with the topical satire to warrant a look a decade later, though it's best seen in highlight/compilation specials. The top-notch cast went on to many other projects including *Black Adder* (Rowan Atkinson), *Saturday Night Live* (Pamela Stephenson), and *Alas Smith and Jones* (Mel Smith and Griff Rhys-Jones, obviously).

**NOTHING IN COMMON (*½) 30 min (8ep Color; 1987 NBC) Situation Comedy** *with Todd Waring as David Basner, Bill Macy as Max Basner, Wendy Kilbourne as Jacqueline North, Elizabeth Bennett as Victoria Upton-Smythe, and Mona Lyden as Norma Starr*

Garry Marshall's 1986 film *Nothing in Common*, with Tom Hanks and Jackie Gleason, was not all that great to begin with. So when you take the film and quickly turn it into a weekly TV sitcom, it's not surprising that the result is eminently forgettable.

Todd Waring steps into Hanks's role as the young advertising phenom whose life is turned upside down when his good-for-nothing father (just dumped by his wife) decides to freeload off him for a while. Bill Macy, who played the long-suffering husband in *Maude*, tries to fill Gleason's shoes as the father.

**NOTHING IS EASY** **(see *Together We Stand*)**

**NOTORIOUS WOMAN (**½) 60 min (7ep Color; 1975 UK BBC) Drama** *with Rosemary Harris as Aurore Dupin (a.k.a. George Sand), Jeremy Irons as Franz Liszt, Alan Howard as Prosper Merimee, Leon Vitali as Jules, Cathleen Nesbitt as Madame Dupin de Francueil, Peter Woodthorpe as Honore de Balzac, Joyce Redman as Sophie Dupin, and George Chakiris as Frederic Chopin*

A biographical drama on one of the nineteenth century's most "notorious" liberated women, Aurore Dupin, a French woman who wrote under the pen name of George Sand. She's an unusual character, walking around Paris in men's trousers, smoking cigars, and speaking out on issues of social and sexual equality. Sand is an aggressively liberated women, sexually active (her lovers include Frederic Chopin), and comfortably at home in the music, art, and other creative circles of her era. The series spends time in all those settings, as the characters discuss "the great issues" while also putting them to the test (especially the sexual theories) in their own personal high-class soap-operatic lives. Rosemary Harris is quite strong in the lead role, with good-looking males such as George Chakiris (Chopin) and Jeremy Irons (as Franz Liszt) always at her side. In truth, though, the series probably does go on a tad too long.

**NOVA** **(****) 60 min (310ep at Fall 1989 Color; 1974– PBS) Documentary**

In the quest to offer the general public accessible scientific information with the fewest technical distractions, *Nova* wins the contest hands down. The narration is usually off-camera and anonymous, without posturing hosts or grand program themes in the way. Instead there is first-rate research, finely detailed camera work, and a wide variety of topics, such as "When Wonder Drugs Don't work," "The Rise and Fall of DDT," "Linus Pauling: Crusading Scientist," "Visions of Star Wars," and "Why Do Birds Sing?" These shows reflect many different tones including those of a *60 Minutes*–style exposé, a leisurely episode of *Biography*, an anecdotal science lecture, or a quiet moment with the natural beauty and wonder of our universe (like the closing minute of peaceful respite on CBS's *Sunday Morning*).

Besides its annual output of new episodes, *Nova* often reruns some of its older episodes in special packages. In addition, more than twenty are available on videotape. ■

**NUMBER 10** **(**) 60 min (7ep Color; 1983 UK YTV) Drama** *with Ian Richardson as Ramsay MacDonald, Dennis Quilley as Gladstone, Bernard Archard as the Duke of Wellington, John Stride as Lloyd George, Richard Pasco as Disraeli and Jeremy Brett as William Pitt the Younger.*

Exploits of various British prime ministers, mostly set at Number 10 Downing Street. For U.S. viewers, the best-known performer is probably Jeremy Brett from his lead role in *The Adventures of Sherlock Holmes.*

**NUMBER 96** **(zero) 60 min (6ep Color; 1980–1981 NBC) Comedy-Drama** *with Barney Martin as Horace Batterson, John Reilly as Chick Walden, James Murtaugh as Roger Busky, Randee Heller as Marion Quintzel, Greg Mullavey as Max Quintzel, Betsy Palmer as Maureen Galloway, and Ellen Travolta as Rita Sugarman*

Sex, sex, sex. It oozes out of every pore of every person on *Number 96*, a show that confuses sophistication with smut.

This series is based on a controversial Australian TV program of the same name that debuted in 1972 and immediately caused waves with its full frontal nudity and emphasis on homosexuality, drug use, rape, etc. This tamer and sillier American version is set in 96 Pacific Way, a Southern California apartment complex populated, it seems, solely by those obsessed with sex, as long as it is with somebody new or different. The cast is huge, and it is hard (and pointless) to keep up with all the couplings going on. Most all the characters are embarrassing to watch and the humor is at the junior high school level. *Number 96* is an embarrassment to the entire American television system.

**NURSE** **(***) 60 min (25ep & 2 hr pilot Color; 1981–1982 CBS) Medical Drama** *with Michael Learned as Nurse Mary Benjamin, Robert Reed as Dr. Adam Rose, Christopher Marcantel as Chip Benjamin, and Dennis Boutsikaris as Joe Calvo*

Michael Learned, the memorable Mother Walton on *The Waltons*, turns in another sparkling performance in *Nurse* as Mary Benjamin, who returns to her nursing career now that her physician husband has died. She serves as head nurse at Grant Memorial Hospital in New York City, and the series focuses both on her professional life of supervising and advising young nurses and her private life with headstrong college son Chip and interesting lawyer/neighbor Joe Calvo. Robert Reed, who deserves more out of life than being recalled as Mike Brady of *The Brady Bunch*, does well as Dr. Adam Rose, Mary's platonic pal at the hospital. ■

**THE NURSES/THE DOCTORS AND THE NURSES** **(**½) 60 min (98ep B&W; 1962–1965 CBS) Medical Drama** *with Shirl Conway as Liz Thorpe, Zina Bethune as Gail Lucas, Edward Binns as Dr. Anson Kiley, Stephen Brooks as Dr. Ned Lowry, Joseph Campanella as Dr. Ted Steffen, and Michael Tolan as Dr. Alex Tazinski*

Beginning life as a female version of *Dr. Kildare, The Nurses* later broadens its scope to cover more than just two central characters. At the beginning, Alden General Hospital head nurse Liz Thorpe plays the sage Dr. Gillespie role, as supervisor and conscience for young student nurse Gail Lucas. Like Dr. Kildare, Nurse Lucas is wonderful to look at and goes through all sorts of professional and personal traumas. This could be a recipe for sleazy soap antics, but in the capable hands of producer Herb Brodkin (*The Defenders, Studio One*), *The Nurses* stays on the respectable path of solid drama.

In the final thirty episodes, the show's title changes to *The Doctors and the Nurses*, and there is an accompanying widening of scope to include the doctors at Alden General (which, in the early 1960s, means men). Dr.

Steffen is the older and wiser physician, while Dr. Tazinski is young, good-looking, and more volatile.

After the ninety-eight episodes, the series reverted to its original title and became a full-fledged soap opera (without any input by Brodkin and with a totally new cast), which ran for two additional years on daytime TV.

**THE O. HENRY PLAYHOUSE** (*½) **30 min (39ep B&W; 1957 Syndication) Drama Anthology** *with Thomas Mitchell as O. Henry*

Most syndicated drama anthologies of the 1950s revolved around some Hollywood figure who acted as host and occasional star. *The O. Henry Playhouse* is unique in its focus on a single writer, in this case O. Henry, the pen name of William Sidney Porter. Irish–American actor Thomas Mitchell appears as O. Henry and hosts and narrates the series, which is made up of dramatizations of O. Henry stories.

**O. K. CRACKERBY** (*) **30 min (17ep: 1 B&W & 16 Color; 1965–1966 ABC) Situation Comedy** *with Burl Ives as O. K. Crackerby, Hal Buckley as St. John Quincy, Brian Corcoran as O. K. Crackerby, Jr., Brooke Adams as Cynthia Crackerby, and Joel Davison as Hobart Crackerby*

TV critics and Broadway types love to moan about how bad TV is, and how they could do a much better job. Well, *O. K. Crackerby* is a lesson that such may not be the case. The series was created by Cleveland Amory, then chief critic for *TV Guide*, and Abe Burrows, Broadway director and composer (*Guys and Dolls, How to Succeed in Business Without Really Trying*) and frequent TV game show panelist in the 1950s. *O. K. Crackerby* is, however, just as inane, just as silly, and just as forgettable as most of the rest of TV, if not more so.

Burl Ives, folk-type singer of the 1950s ("Bluetail Fly," "Big Rock Candy Mountain"), plays zillionaire O. K. Crackerby, an Oklahoman with everything but social standing. O. K. hires St. John Quincy, an out-of-work Harvard graduate, to polish up his three urchins so they can pass in respectable society. The plot doesn't sound like much, because it isn't. Despite the pedigree of its creators, *O. K. Crackerby* is more reflective of its producer, Rod Amateau, the purveyor of *The Dukes of Hazzard, Enos, Supertrain*, and (gulp!) *My Mother the Car.*

**O.S.S.** (**) **30 min (26ep B&W; 1957–1958 ABC) War Drama** *with Ron Randall as Capt. Frank Hawthorn, Lionel Murton as "The Chief," and Robert Gallico as Sgt. O'Brien*

The baby boom generation may not have heard of it, but the O.S.S. (Office of Strategic Services) was America's World War II precursor to the CIA. *O.S.S.* dramatizes the files of the wartime spy agency, as its agents battle for Uncle Sam behind the axis lines.

**OCCASIONAL WIFE** (***) **30 min (30ep Color; 1966–1967 NBC) Situation Comedy** *with Michael Callan as Peter Christopher, Patricia Harty as Greta Patterson, Jack Collins as Max Brahms, Joan Tompkins as Mrs. Brahms, Stuart Margolin as Bernie, and Vin Scully as narrator*

*Occasional Wife* is a kick because the plot is so contrived, so old-fashioned (and yet so modern) that it's appealing. Simply put, Peter Christopher is a hyper money-grubbing M.B.A. type who finds himself locked out of promotions at his job with Brahm's Baby Food Company for the single reason that he is not married (it's the wrong image for a baby food chain). Undaunted, Peter hires a pretty young lady (Greta Patterson) to pose as his wife when the boss comes over and at company functions. This being a 1960s show, Greta insists on separate lodgings, so Peter sets her up in her own apartment two flights above his own (easily reachable by the fire escape). The whole show deals with Peter's always frantic efforts to drag Greta down to his apartment to pose as his wife, without anyone catching on. The mind reels at the hue and cry that would be raised if a series with this wife for hire plot surfaced today.

Despite, or perhaps because of, the far-fetched plot, *Occasional Wife* is full of slapsticklike laughs and quality acting. Credit for the quality goes to producer Harry Ackerman, who produced a slew of mildly popular sitcoms such as *Bachelor Father, Bewitched,* and *Gidget.*

Michael Callan and Patricia Harty, who play Peter and Greta, met while filming *Occasional Wife* and later got married in real life, but were divorced soon after.

**THE ODD COUPLE** (****) **30 min (114ep Color; 1970–1975 ABC) Situation Comedy** *with Jack Klugman as Oscar Madison, Tony Randall as Felix Unger, Al Molinaro as Murray Greshner, Penny Marshall as Myrna Turner, Elinor Donahue as Miriam Welby, Janis Hansen as Gloria Unger, Monica Evans as Cecily Pigeon, Carol Shelly as Gwendolyn Pigeon, Larry Gelman as Vinnie, and Garry Walberg as Speed*

*The Odd Couple* is one of Neil Simon's best and most successful plays, with an instantly accessible hook: a slob and a neatnik sharing the same quarters. It's also a situation ripe for further development.

With Jack Klugman as sportswriter slob Oscar Madison and Tony Randall as tidy photographer Felix Unger, *The Odd Couple* series has one of television's best comic teams ever. Building on the initial setup of the play (newly divorced Felix moves in with previously divorced buddy Oscar), they flesh out the quirks and conflicts of the characters into a fully believable (if sometimes comically rocky) friendship. They also have a ball with their respective faults.

Klugman's Oscar is a dedicated slob who wolfs down obscene combinations of chips, dip, and cigars in the midst of poker games, sports reports, and side bets. Randall's Felix is a fussy hypochondriac (with neck, back, and sinus conditions), obsessive to a fault, and insecurely secure in the knowledge that everything should be done in just the right way (which he just happens to know). There's no mystery as to why the wives of these two men demanded divorces.

Klugman and Randall are helped by consistently strong scripts, a nice assortment of guest performers, and a solid (if fluid) supporting cast, including poker-playing buddies Vinnie, Speed (Garry Walberg, later Lt. Monahan on Klugman's *Quincy*), and Murray the cop (Al Molinaro, later the diner owner on *Happy Days*). Even the Pigeon sisters (two characters in the original play) breeze through in the first season. Other friends, neighbors, and relatives include Oscar's former wife Blanche (an occasional role played by Klugman's then real-life wife Brett Somers), Felix's former wife Gloria and good friend Miriam, and Oscar's secretary Myrna (played by producer Garry Marshall's sister, Penny).

*The Odd Couple* was Garry Marshall's first big TV comedy series and in the early 1970s it was one of ABC's few comedy jewels, so it received a bit of special attention. For instance, Monty Hall and Howard Cosell (two of ABC's biggest stars at the time) appear several times in guest shots, playing themselves. Even Roone Arledge (president of ABC Sports) turns up. And despite the fact that *The Odd Couple* never cracked the top twenty-five shows for the season, ABC gave the series a solid five-year run.

The final episode neatly wraps everything up with a reconciliation between Felix and Gloria. He moves out and Oscar is once again king of the castle.

**ODD COUPLE, THE NEW** **(**½) 30 min (13ep Color; 1982–1983 ABC) Situation Comedy** *with Ron Glass as Felix Unger, Demond Wilson as Oscar Madison, and John Schuck as Murray Greshner*

*The Odd Couple* without Jack Klugman and Tony Randall? Why not *Barnaby Jones* without Buddy Ebsen? Or *Perry Mason* without Raymond Burr? Or *All in the Family* without Carroll O'Connor? Well, why not?

It happens all the time on stage. Even after a performer has done a superb job with a character, this doesn't stop others from taking a turn at the same role. To a lesser extent, this is also true in theatrical films, where successions of actors have played the likes of Sherlock Holmes, Philip Marlowe, and James Bond.

Besides, with its theatrical roots and resilient character conflicts, Neil Simon's *The Odd Couple* was the ideal choice for such a venture. After all, it had survived countless high school and community theater group productions with its laughs intact. More important, in its first television incarnation in 1970, Jack Klugman and Tony Randall had weathered comparisons to Walter Matthau and Jack Lemmon (leads in the original stage and film versions) rather nicely. Why not pass the frying pan and cigars to yet another Oscar and Felix?

And so it happened, with those juicy roles going to a pair of sitcom vets. Ron Glass (previously the sometimes vain and stuffy Sgt. Harris on *Barney Miller*) became the new Felix Unger and Demond Wilson (previously junkshop co-owner Lamont on *Sanford and Son*) was the new Oscar Madison.

Though both main characters were black, the new series was not set up as an all-black production. That gimmick had been tried (and had failed) in 1970 with another Neil Simon play that was turned into a series, *Barefoot in the Park*. Instead, Oscar and Felix (and some of their friends) happened to be black. Otherwise, it was business as usual, even using some of the same scripts as in the original.

Oddly critics at the time seemed to consider restaging a television script cheating. So even though Glass and Wilson and their crew did a fine job, they were branded from opening night and never caught on. It may be, though, that they were attempting the impossible, competing with the same stories rerunning themselves into the national unconsciousness only a twist of the dial away.

But it's too bad. In a medium always searching for some new twist on an old idea, putting new faces into classic TV scripts and settings has the potential to give the mind-warping satirists of *SCTV* a run for their money. Instead, *The New Odd Couple* had the plug pulled on it while barely halfway through its first act. Meanwhile, Neil Simon took the original *Odd Couple* back to the theater and recast it with two women in the lead roles. So there!

**OFF THE RACK** **(**½) 30 min (8ep Color; 1984–1985 ABC) Situation Comedy** *with Ed Asner as Sam Waltman, Eileen Brennan as Kate Halloran, Claudia Wells as Shannon Halloran, Corey Yothers as Timothy Halloran, Pamela Brull as Brenda Patagorski, and Dennis Haysbert as Cletus Maxwell*

In this confrontational comedy, dedicated chauvinist Sam Waltman is forced to work with the new half-owner of his Los Angeles garment company: his deceased partner's wife. Kate is not thrilled at the prospect either, but when she discovers that this was her husband's only asset, she has no choice. Unfortunately the company is nearly bankrupt. So they both have to make it work.

They argue over everything from his cigar smoke to the best styles to use for their sales presentations. Both Brennan and Asner are old hands at irascible behavior, so they let loose with gusto. It's particularly amusing to see Asner play against his more liberal Lou Grant character type. Over the long haul, all their sputtering could get quite annoying, but as a short-flight series it works.

**OFF TO SEE THE WIZARD** (*½) 60 min (25ep Color; 1967–1968 ABC) Children's Film Anthology

Chuck Jones, the multitalented animator responsible for such characters as Bugs Bunny, Porky Pig, and the Road Runner, produces this collection of unrelated films that appeal to children. Many of the films are edited theatrical movies or TV pilots, but one or two are originals. Animated characters from *The Wizard of Oz* (*not* one of the films included) serve as weekly guest hosts.

**OFFICIAL DETECTIVE** (*) 30 min (39ep B&W; 1957–1958 Syndication) Detective Drama *with Everett Sloane as host/narrator*

From the files of long-forgotten *Official Detective* magazine comes this anthology series of stories about detectives, which is also known as *Crime Reporter*.

**OH, MADELINE** (**) 30 min (18ep Color; 1983–1984 ABC) Situation Comedy *with Madeline Kahn as Madeline Wayne, James Sloyan as Charlie Wayne, Louis Giambalvo as Robert Leone, and Jesse Welles as Doris Leone*

Film star Madeline Kahn (*Paper Moon, Blazing Saddles, Young Frankenstein*) deserves more from her first starring TV role than this muddled show. It concerns a boring housewife of the 1980s, who tries to liven up her dull marriage to a romance novelist by flagging down every passing fad. The series is based on a British series called *Pig in the Middle*, which somehow sounds far more interesting.

*Oh, Madeline* is memorable only because it is the first TV series from Marcy Carsey and Tom Werner, who went on to produce *The Cosby Show*.

**OH, SUSANNA** (see *The Gale Storm Show*)

**OH! THOSE BELLS** (*) 30 min (13ep B&W; 1962 CBS) Situation Comedy *with Herbert Wiere as Herbie Bell, Harry Wiere as Harry Bell, Sylvester Wiere as Sylvie Bell, and Henry Norell as Henry Slocum*

The three German Wiere brothers were renowned slapstick comedians. They try to keep the old burlesque form alive in this TV sitcom about three brothers who run a Hollywood prop shop. *Oh! Those Bells* shows that slapstick died for a reason: It comes across as awfully stupid on TV. Watch an old *Three Stooges* short instead.

**OHARA** (*) 60 min (28ep Color; 1987–1988 ABC) Detective Drama *with Noriyuki "Pat" Morita as Lt. Ohara, Robert Clohessy as Lt. George Shaver, Rachel Ticotin as Teresa Storm, and Madge Sinclair as Gussie Lemmons*

Pat Morita is a familiar face from *Happy Days* (as soda shop owner Arnold) and the *Karate Kid* feature films (as mentor to Ralph Macchio). This series attempts to showcase him as the lead in a cop series, at first alluding to his *Karate Kid* persona by presenting Lt. Ohara as a generally nonviolent, reflective, inner-directed man. In this version he's a solo operative who prefers martial arts to a gun, offering wise sayings and a soothing persona to those around him. For the rest of the series, though, he takes on more traditional cop show trappings, including standard issue firearms and a headstrong partner, Lt. George Shaver (played by Robert Clohessy, who earned his stripes in the last season of *Hill Street Blues* as Officer Flaherty). The two work a while for a special federal task force, then go off on their own as independent private eyes. Clohessy and Morita are a pretty good pair of performers, but even with all that tinkering, they never end up with any decent scripts.

**O'HARA, UNITED STATES TREASURY** (*½) 60 min (22ep & 2 hr pilot Color; 1971–1972 CBS) Crime Drama *with David Janssen as James O'Hara and Stacy Harris as Ben Hazzard*

Probably David Janssen's least satisfying series. In contrast to his much more familiar role as an independent outsider (*Richard Diamond, The Fugitive*), he works here as an agent of the U.S. government, investigating cases for such Treasury Department agencies as Customs or the Internal Revenue Service. And, as a Jack Webb production, there's a bit too much emphasis on the investigative routine rather than on characterization.

If you want post-*Fugitive* Janssen, go for *Harry O* instead.

**OIL** (**½) 60 min (8ep Color; 1987 PBS) Documentary

The history of oil exploration and the story of the men who gained power through oil (J. R. Ewing excluded) are examined in this documentary series.

**THE OLDEST ROOKIE** (*½) 60 min (12ep Color; 1987–1988 CBS) Police Drama *with Paul Sorvino as Ike Porter, D. W. Moffett as Tony Jonas, and Raymond J. Barry as Lt. Marco Zaga*

Paul Sorvino is a rather talented character actor, whose pudgy build and plain looks tend to typecast him as a harmless sidebar to the handsome leading man. Sorvino's earlier attempt at playing the leading man (*Bert D'Angelo/Superstar*, where he was a tough New York cop in San Francisco) fared poorly. In *The Oldest Rookie*, he begins the series in a typical Paul Sorvino role, that of Ike Porter, deputy chief of public affairs for the police force. All he does is appear at boring public relations affairs, pumping up the good image of the police. Right away, however, Porter goes through a midlife crisis, quits his cushy job, and starts all over in order to be a "real" cop. He enters the police academy, struggles through, and becomes, you guessed it, the oldest rookie on the force.

Porter is teamed up with hot-headed, handsome Tony Jonas, forming a homely/hunk tandem loved by TV producers. Despite Sorvino's expressive features, *The*

*Oldest Rookie* is strictly formula TV cop stuff, even down to the tough but fair police superior, who wants the stars to operate by the book. Yawn.

**ON OUR OWN (**½) 30 min (22ep Color; 1977–1978 CBS) Situation Comedy** *with Lynnie Greene as Maria Teresa Bonino, Bess Armstrong as Julia Peters, Gretchen Wyler as Toni McBain, and Dixie Carter as April Baxter*

This cute sitcom carries a lot of the feel of New York City, primarily due to its on-location shooting in Gotham. Maria Bonino is an art director and Julia Peters is a copy writer at the Bedford Advertising Agency run by Toni McBain. Maria and Julia are young, eager, and have a lot to learn.

David Susskind, who handled comedy (*Alice*) as well as drama and talk shows, produced *On Our Own* before stories about independent single working women became yet another clichéd TV sitcom format.

**ON THE BUSES (*½) 30 min (74ep B&W & Color; 1970–1975 UK London Weekend Television) Situation Comedy** *with Reg Varney, Anna Karen, Bob Grant, and Stephen Lewis*

Broad comedy of a London bus conductor (played by Reg Varney) dealing with silly passengers, a dim-witted inspector, and his cartoon caricature family. This was the basis for the U.S. series *Lotsa Luck.*

**ON THE ROCKS (**½) 30 min (22ep Color; 1975–1976 ABC) Situation Comedy** *with Hal Williams as Lester DeMott, Jose Perez as Hector Fuentes, Rick Hurst as Cleaver, Tom Poston as Mr. Sullivan, Mel Stewart as Mr. Gibson, and Bobby Sandler as Nicky Palik*

Based on the British hit series *Porridge* (starring Ronnie Barker), this is not quite the inmates running the asylum, but it certainly allows them plenty of chances to tweak the nose of the bureaucracy. Set at Alamesa State Minimum Security Prison, *On the Rocks* focuses on cellmates Fuentes, DeMott, Cleaver, and Nicky and their petty schemes and plots to pass the time, often at the expense of the chief prison officer, Gibson (played by Mel Stewart, who also fumed as Henry Jefferson on *All in the Family*).

Setting up convicted criminals as the heroes of a comedy show is a bit tricky, but Alamesa is obviously not Attica, so the light approach to the criminal justice system in the series usually works.

After putting in his time, Stewart went on to espionage work, playing the departmental spy boss in *Scarecrow and Mrs. King* and *The Greatest American Hero.* His soft-spoken fellow officer (played by Tom Poston) moved on to work at a New England inn with Bob Newhart. And Hal Williams (Lester DeMott) did a hitch in the army as the drill sergeant for *Private Benjamin* (the film and the series) before settling down as husband to Mary Jenkins (Marla Gibbs) on *227.*

**ON TRIAL** **(see *The Joseph Cotten Show*)**

**ONCE A HERO (*½) 60 min (4ep & 90 min pilot Color; 1987 ABC) Adventure** *with Jeff Lester as Captain Justice, Robert Forster as Gumshoe, Milo O'Shea as Abner, Josh Blake as Woody, and Caitlin Clark as Emma*

Unless sales pick up, comic book hero Captain Justice will be canceled—and he and his world will cease to exist. So he steps across the forbidden zone into the real world (where he loses his superpowers), meets his creator, and then sets out to restore interest in his adventures and faith in his principles of honor and fair play. Another comic character, a Sam Spade type called Gumshoe, follows to keep the Captain from hurting himself. By the end of the first episode, Captain Justice is back in the headlines and kids are once again reading his comic book adventures.

This offbeat premise was actually fairly clever for a one-shot made-for-TV movie. But there wasn't too much left for a weekly series, especially one featuring a superhero without superpowers on Earth.

In its original network run, the series was canceled after only two episodes aired, delaying until rerun packaging a story featuring former Batman Adam West playing the star of the television version of Captain Justice. ■

**ONCE AN EAGLE (**) (9hr miniseries Color; 1976–1977 NBC) Drama** *with Sam Elliott as Sam Damon, Cliff Potts as Courtney Massengale, Glenn Ford as George Caldwell, Darleen Carr as Tommy Caldwell, Amy Irving as Emily Massengale, Andrew Duggan as Gen. McElvey, and Lynda Day George as Marge Chrysler*

The lives and loves of Sam Damon and Courtney Massengale, two American doughboys in World War I, are chronicled through World War II in this miniseries based on Anton Myrer's novel.

**ONE BIG FAMILY (**) 30 min (25ep Color; 1986–1987 Syndication) Situation Comedy** *with Danny Thomas as Jake Hatton, Anthony Starke as Don Hatton, Kim Gillingham as Jan Hatton, Anastasia Fielding as Marianne Hatton, Michael DeLuise as Brian Hatton, Alison McMillan as Kate Hatton, and Gabriel Damon as Roger Hatton*

Forever the TV dad, Danny Thomas handled his own brood in the 1950s and 1960s with *Make Room for Daddy* and dealt with grandchildren in *Make Room for Granddaddy* in the 1970s. In the 1980s, Thomas makes another stab at video parenting in *One Big Family*. Little has changed. Thomas is still playing a nightclub entertainer, but this time he inherits rather than fathers the children in the show. When the five Hatton children are orphaned, Thomas's character (Jake) moves out to Seattle to raise them himself. Don, the oldest of the Hatton children, is a married policeman. Jan is his wife. The four other kids range from ages eight to nineteen.

Jake is very much the usual Danny Thomas–type character. He is gruff, abrupt, sharp-tongued, and ultimately a pushover. The kids are all cute.

**ONE DAY AT A TIME (**½) 30 min (209ep Color; 1975–1984 CBS) Situation Comedy** *with Bonnie Franklin as Ann Romano Royer, Valerie Bertinelli as Barbara Cooper Royer, Mackenzie Phillips as Julie Cooper Horvath, Pat Harrington, Jr., as Dwayne Schneider, Richard Masur as David Kane, Michael Lembeck as Max Horvath, Boyd Gaines as Mark Royer, Shelley Fabares as Francine Webster, Nanette Fabray as Katherine Romano, and Howard Hesseman as Sam Royer*

A splintered-family comedy set in Indianapolis, this series follows newly divorced Ann Romano as she moves into a small apartment with her two teenaged daughters, Barbara and Julie. As with most single-parent series, this setup allows maximum plot mileage as Ann faces the problems of raising kids, dating, making a living, and sometimes even dealing with her former husband, Ed Cooper (Joseph Campanella, in an occasional role). Daughters Julie and Barbara (who use their dad's last name) also run through the gamut of typical teen problems, from sibling rivalry at home and at school (Barbara's the responsible "A" student, while older sister Julie is the trouble-prone average kid), to making friends, dating, choosing a career, and getting married.

Though this is a Norman Lear production following in the success of the topical *All in the Family, Good Times,* and *Maude, One Day at a Time* does not constantly wrap itself in the latest issues. Perhaps the image of a hard-working divorced woman raising a family on her own was considered sufficiently relevant to carry the series. However, the popular topic of sex does come up fairly often, at first chiefly in Ann's life, but later in the personal decisions of both children (Barbara definitely remains a virgin until she finds love with husband Mark). It's also item number one with Dwayne Schneider, superintendent and chief handyman of their apartment building, who struts about like a peacock on the prowl. Eventually both daughters get married, with Julie and her husband leaving town (and the series) for a while (as star Mackenzie Phillips was written out of the continuity in order to deal with a drug problem). Upon their return, Julie has a child of her own, but then abandons both husband and baby daughter (as once again, Phillips was written out, this time for health reasons). Surprisingly this did not lead to a male *One Day at a Time* spin-off series (a young father struggling to make it on his own raising his daughter), and both Julie's husband and child remain with the original series to the end.

By then the setup is far different from the initial premise. Having more than proven herself as an independent advertising copy writer, Ann finds herself increasingly open and ready for another long-term relationship, which she finds in Barbara's father-in-law, Sam Royer (played by Howard Hesseman, in between *WKRP* and *Head of the Class*).

In life outside and after the series, Pat Harrington, Jr., took his handyman/fix-it image to the commercial world as a pitchman for such sponsors as a do-it-yourself auto parts chain. Mackenzie Phillips briefly joined her dad, John Phillips, on tour with a reconstituted revival of his old group, the Mamas and Papas. Valerie Bertinelli specialized in miniseries and made-for-TV movies while maintaining her own rock and roll connection as wife of guitarist Eddie Van Halen.

*One Day at a Time* was created by Whitney Blake, best known on screen as the easygoing Dorothy Baxter ("Mrs. B") on *Hazel.*

**ONE IN A MILLION (*½) 30 min (13ep Color; 1980 ABC) Situation Comedy** *with Shirley Hemphill as Shirley Simmons, Keene Curtis as Roland Cushing, Carl Ballantine as Max Kellerman, Mel Stewart as Raymond Simmons, Ann Weldon as Edna Simmons, Richard Paul as Barton Stone, and Dorothy Fielding as Nancy Boyer*

This loud and brassy put-down comedy is designed to have its main characters constantly trading barbs. Shirley Hemphill (the waitress at Rob's place on *What's Happening!*) plays a sharp-tongued New York cabbie who inherits controlling interest in a major conglomerate (Grayson Enterprises) from its founder, one of her regular fares. She turns down offers to buy out her shares, gleefully assumes her position as chief executive, and declares open war on "pompous stuffed shirts"—especially company vice-president Roland Cushing. The two fight it out through the rest of the series.

Former *McHale's Navy* crewman Carl Ballantine plays the owner of Shirley's favorite deli.

**ONE OF THE BOYS (*½) 30 min (13ep Color; 1982 NBC) Situation Comedy** *with Mickey Rooney as Oliver Nugent, Dana Carvey as Adam Shields, Francine Beers as Mrs. Green, Nathan Lane as Jonathan Burns, and Scatman Crothers as Bernard Solomon*

Mickey Rooney is sixty-six-year-old retiree Oliver Nugent, who moves from a retirement home to his grandson Adam's college apartment. (Sure, why not?) Naturally, gramps is interfering but lovable, and popular with the kids on campus, even Adam's other roommate, Nathan.

The frequently predictable plots have plenty of gushy moments, such as Oliver's first date in years or his quest for a new job to help fill his spare time. And when things get dull, Oliver and a neighboring retired entertainer friend (played by Scatman Crothers) are always ready and willing to put on a show at a moment's notice. Dana Carvey (just a few years away from his *Saturday Night Live* stint) is the fresh young face beside these veteran hoofers.

**ONE OF THE BOYS (**) 30 min (6ep Color; 1989 NBC) Situation Comedy** *with Maria Conchita Alonso as Maria Navarro, Robert Clohessy as Mike Lukowski, Dan Hedaya as Ernie, Amy Aquino as Bernice, Michael DeLuise as Luke Lukowski, Billy Morrissette as Steve Lukowski, and Justin Whalin as Nick Lukowski*

Perky ex-waitress Maria Navarro gets a new job as the office manager for Mike Lukowski, owner of Lukowski Construction. On one hand, the young and fetching Maria just wants to be one of the boys in the otherwise all-male business (she aspires to be a construction worker herself). On the other hand, she has her heart set on winning the affections of Mike, her handsome and unmarried young boss. Mike, busy enough with his construction company to run and three sons to raise on his own, can't help but be attracted by Maria's beauty and vivaciousness. Even though he at first has doubts about romancing an employee, the couple quickly hits it off and are married by the fifth episode.

Maria Conchita Alonso, Robin Williams's co-star in the 1984 theatrical film *Moscow on the Hudson*, is attractive as Maria, though sometimes she carries the "fiery Latin temper" routine too far. Robert Clohessy (Officer Patrick Flaherty in the waning days of *Hill Street Blues*) is appropriately macho and vulnerable as single-parent Mike. Dan Hedaya (a great character actor best known to TV viewers as Nick, the ex-husband of Carla from *Cheers*, who had his own brief series, *The Tortellis*) is blue-collar authentic as Ernie, the no-frills foreman. While the acting here is fine, the simplistic scripts hold the series down.

*One of the Boys* comes from Blake Hunter and Martin Cohan, the creators of *Who's the Boss?*

**ONE STEP BEYOND/THE NEXT STEP BEYOND (***) 30 min (118ep: 94 B&W & 24 Color; 1959–1961 & 1978–1979 ABC & Syndication) Suspense Drama** *with John Newland as host/narrator*

*One Step Beyond* is from the same era as the original *Twilight Zone*, and the two shows are very similar. Both deal largely with suspense stories that have a supernatural flavor, and both are anthologies, with no continuing characters other than a serious onscreen narrator who often works behind the camera as well.

In *One Step Beyond* (originally called *Alcoa Presents: One Step Beyond*), the host is John Newland, the director of the show. Newland is much creepier than Rod Serling of *The Twilight Zone*, which is appropriate because *One Step Beyond* is a much creepier program. Serling appeared as an overly tense chain-smoker who told good stories. Newland comes across as a borderline psychotic who really believes in his weird tales. In a promotional spot for the series, Newland is seen sitting on the roof of a building, and he asks the audience "Did you ever have the urge to jump?" He plugs next week's show and then really does jump! *One Step Beyond* also has a relentlessly eerie music track that makes the most innocent setting seem fraught with danger and foreboding.

This extra air of creepiness carries into the stories seen on *One Step Beyond*. While Serling's shows frequently featured warm tales with nostalgic overtones or thinly disguised commentaries on the modern world wrapped in a protective cloak of science fiction, Newland's series is mainly interested in ESP, ghosts, and people possessed by unknown demons. Alas, the writing and acting in *One Step Beyond* are no match for the high level of quality in *The Twilight Zone*. Furthermore, Newland keeps telling you that these stories are true and his breathless enthusiasm for making you believe quickly wears thin. Nonetheless, the shows are frequently entertaining, if your idea of entertainment is becoming nervous about every creak and dark shadow nearby. *One Step Beyond* is best watched alone on a cold and rainy night.

The original episodes from the 1950s are in black and white. The color episodes are from the less memorable revival in the 1970s.

**THE ONEDIN LINE (**) 60 min (50ep Color; 1974–1978 UK BBC) Drama** *with Peter Gilmore as James Onedin, Brian Rawlinson as Robert Onedin, Mary Webster as Sarah Onedin, Anne Stallybrass as Anne Onedin, Jessica Benton as Elizabeth Frazer, and Jane Seymour as Emma Fogarty*

This nineteenth-century Liverpool sea saga follows the business and bedroom exploits of the Onedin family. They own and operate an ambitious cargo-shipping service spearheaded by Captain James aboard his schooner the *Charlotte Rhodes.*

**OPEN ALL HOURS (***) 30 min (Color; 1978–1984 UK BBC) Situation Comedy** *with Ronnie Barker as Arkwright, David Jason as Granville, and Lynda Brown as Gladys Emmanuel*

The setting for this cute British comedy is the corner grocery of Mr. Arkwright, who must stay open all night to compete with the new supermarket in the area. Arkwright must also contend with an unending parade of weirdos who frequent his shop in the late, late hours and his uncooperative nephew, Granville. Arkwright is mostly interested in seducing Nurse Emmanuel, who stops in frequently.

*Open All Hours* served as the basis for the equally sprightly American sitcom *Open All Night.*

**OPEN ALL NIGHT (***) 30 min (11ep Color; 1981–1982 ABC) Situation Comedy** *with George Dzundza as Gordon Feester, Susan Tyrrell as Gretchen Feester, Sam Whipple as Terry Hofmyster, Bubba Smith as Robin, and Jay Tarses as Officer Steve*

A sadly overlooked sitcom gem from the early 1980s, *Open All Night* exudes the oddball charm always found in the work of the show's producers Jay Tarses and Tom Patchett (*The Bob Newhart Show, Buffalo Bill*).

Set delightfully in the perfect blue-collar setting for the 1980s, a twenty-four-hour urban convenience store (hence the title), *Open All Night* features middle-aged survivor Gordon Feester (whose entire life is neatly summarized in the catchy theme song). Gordon and his wife Gretchen handle the unending hours of running the store, while Gretchen's punk son from a previous relationship, Terry, is an updated Maynard G. Krebs (from *Dobie Gillis*). The word *work* is not in his vocabulary.

The all-night convenience store is a workable locale to present a parade of oddballs who drop in for one strange reason or another. Local policemen, such as Officer Steve (producer Tarses doing double duty), stop by to slurp coffee and doughnuts for free. Ex-NFL star Bubba Smith provides the muscle as Gordon's night manager.

Bare bones concepts such as this can easily flop. This show doesn't. The great characters, lively scripting, and intriguing tone merit attention. Producers Patchett and Tarses also wrote the theme song, which is one of the best of the 1980s.

**OPERATION ENTERTAINMENT (*½) 60 min (31ep Color; 1968–1969 ABC) Variety** *with Jim Lange as host*

Chuck Barris, better known as the producer of maniacal game shows such as *The Dating Game, The Newlywed Game,* and *The Gong Show*, plays it mostly straight in this series of variety shows taped at U.S. military outposts around the world. Each week presents different guests.

**OPERATION JULIE (**) 60 min (3ep Color; 1985 UK) Police Drama** *with Colin Blakely as Det. Inspector Lee*

Based on a real-life drug investigation led by the dedicated Inspector Lee, who holds it together despite a seemingly endless series of everyday mishaps and accidents.

**OPERATION PETTICOAT (*) 30 min (31ep & 2 hr pilot Color; 1977–1979 ABC) Situation Comedy** *with John Astin as Lt. Cmdr. Matthew Sherman, Richard Gilliland as Lt. Nick Holden, Yvonne Wilder as Maj. Edna Howard, Melinda Naud as Lt. Dolores Crandell, Jamie Lee Curtis as Lt. Barbara Duran, Randolph Mantooth as Lt. Mike Bender, Robert Hogan as Lt. Cmdr. Sam Haller, Jo Ann Pflug as Lt. Katherine O'Hara, and Hilary Thompson as Lt. Betty Wheeler*

Mix *McHale's Navy* with *Broadside* and what do you get? A waste of time called *Operation Petticoat*. Based on a pretty good 1959 Blake Edwards film starring Cary Grant and Tony Curtis, the TV series is about an American submarine during World War II. Somehow or other, the sub never is completely painted before it must dash off to sea, leaving it pink on the bottom due to the color of the primer layer of paint. So there is one meaning of the title term *petticoat*. The other sense of petticoat is provided by the presence of five army nurses who somehow get aboard. We all know that sailing lore says that women are bad luck on ships. This series at least proves that TV shows about women on ships are bad news. There are a lot of silly junior high pranks about the nurses and the seamen.

John Astin (Gomez of *The Addams Family*) is wasted as ship commander. Budding film actress Jamie Lee Curtis (daughter of Tony) plays one of the nurses. After the first season (twenty-two episodes), virtually the entire cast is canned and Robert Hogan is brought in as the new commander, with Randolph Mantooth playing his executive officer. If anything, the show gets worse. The second season shows were officially called *The New Operation Petticoat.*

**OPERATION: RUNAWAY** **(see *The Runaways*)**

**OPPENHEIMER (***) 60 min (7ep Color; 1981 UK BBC) Drama** *with Sam Waterston as J. Robert Oppenheimer, Jana Shelden as Kitty Harrison-Oppenheimer, David Suchet as Edward Teller, Garrick Hogan as Frank Oppenheimer, Kate Harper as Jean Tatlock, Manning Redwood as Gen. Leslie Groves, and Dave Hill as James Tuck*

This engrossing chronicle follows the rise and fall of University of California professor J. Robert Oppenheimer, head of the U.S. Manhattan Project during World War II, and "father of the atomic bomb." Sam Waterston is superb as "Oppie" (the professor's lifelong nickname), taking the character from his days at Berkeley in 1938 through development of the bomb and his terrible guilt over its use. Later he faces a different sort of challenge: a fight over his security clearance in the midst of Cold War fever.

Ironically, when U.S. public television launched its *American Playhouse* series of homegrown productions in 1982, this British series was one of its first offerings.

**THE OREGON TRAIL (**½) 60 min (6ep & 2 hr pilot Color; 1977 NBC) Western** *with Rod Taylor as Evan Thorpe, Darleen Carr as Margaret Devlin, Charles Napier as Luther Sprague, and Andrew Stevens as Andrew Thorpe*

Evan Thorpe's wife Jessica has died, leaving him with three kids in Illinois in the 1840s. Evan decides to leave the Midwest and join a wagon train to Oregon. Because of his leadership qualities, Evan is elected captain of the travelers. All the bad stuff you can imagine (Indians, drought, robbers) happens to the group on the way.

The 1976 pilot casts Blair Brown (*The Days and Nights of Molly Dodd*) as the doomed Jessica Thorpe.

**ORSON WELLES' GREAT MYSTERIES** **(see *Great Mysteries, Orson Welles'*)**

**THE OSMOND FAMILY SHOW** (*½) **60 min (10ep Color; 1979 ABC) Musical-Variety** *with Donny Osmond and Marie Osmond*

Donny and Marie Osmond, whose *Donny and Marie* show was a medium-size hit for three years, give the rest of their Utah clan (Alan, Wayne, Jay, Merrill, Jimmy, etc.) equal billing in this inoffensive hour.

**OTHERWORLD** (**) **60 min (8ep Color; 1985 CBS) Science Fiction** *with Sam Groom as Hal Sterling, Gretchen Corbett as June Sterling, Tony O'Dell as Trace Sterling, Jonna Lee as Gina Sterling, Brandon Crane as Smith Sterling, and Jonathan Banks as Kommander Nuveen Kroll*

The Sterlings are a wonderful American family, and everything is going along just fine until some weird creature from an Egyptian tomb transports the whole family to a parallel universe and deposits them on an Earthlike planet. They roam this new world, always finding highly unusual societies (one where families are against the law, one where resort guests are killed so that others may live) where they just don't fit in. All the Sterlings want is to get back home, but the bad guys who run this other world have more nefarious plans for them . . . If the family can be tracked down. The idea of *Otherworld* is intriguing, but it is somewhat scattered. If the series had lasted longer, the concept might have come together.

**OUR FAMILY HONOR** (*½) **60 min (12ep & 2 hr pilot Color; 1985–1986 ABC) Drama** *with Eli Wallach as Vincent Danzig, Kenneth McMillan as Patrick McKay, Daphne Ashbrook as Liz McKay, Tom Mason as Frank McKay, Michael Madsen as Augie Danzig, and Michael Woods as Jerry Cole*

This plodding drama follows two New York families: one led by crime czar Vincent Danzig, the other by lifelong cop Patrick McKay. The two had been childhood friends, so their ongoing present-day power struggle often gets quite personal. To further complicate family matters, Liz McKay and Jerry Cole (from the Danzig family) fall in love, in the best Romeo and Juliet tradition. She's also a cop, while he works at a bank, trying to put his secret family connections behind him.

Unfortunately, this series creaks along so slowly that even the typical soap opera-ish plot hooks aren't enough to sustain it.

**OUR HOUSE** (**½) **60 min (46ep Color; 1986–1988 NBC) Drama** *with Wilford Brimley as Gus Witherspoon, Deidre Hall as Jessie Witherspoon, Shannen Doherty as Kris Witherspoon, Chad Allen as David Witherspoon, Keri Houlihan as Molly Witherspoon, and Gerald S. O'Loughlin as Joe Kaplan*

There's oodles and oodles of family affection in *Our House*, yet the program somehow manages to stay one step ahead of being too syrupy. Gruff but lovable Gus Witherspoon, a feisty, independent widower living alone in his big house, has his life changed by the sudden death of his son. Gus's thirty-five-year-old daughter-in-law, Jessie, moves in with him, bringing along her three lovable kids: Kris (fifteen), David (twelve), and Molly (eight). Grandpa learns to relate to the grandkids and the grandkids learn that Grandpa is a cool dude, in his own way. There are lots of hugs doled out.

Wilford Brimley, a talented character actor who finally won public recognition in the film *Cocoon*, adds some wonderful touches of life to the Grandpa role.

**OUR MAN HIGGINS** (*) **30 min (34ep B&W; 1962–1963 ABC) Situation Comedy** *with Stanley Holloway as Higgins, Audrey Totter as Alice MacRoberts, Frank Maxwell as Duncan MacRoberts, Rickey Kelman as Tommy MacRoberts, K. C. Butts as Dinghy MacRoberts, and Regina Groves as Joanie MacRoberts*

TV history is littered with proud British stage actors who wind up debasing themselves playing silly British caricatures in forgettable U.S. series just to earn a little cash. Stanley Holloway, a British thespian best known as Alfred Doolittle (father of Liza) in *My Fair Lady*, wastes his time playing the archetypal stuffy British butler who is "inherited" by the MacRoberts, the archetypal bozo American suburban family. *Our Man Higgins* performs the impossible: It makes the vaguely similar 1980s sitcom *Mr. Belvedere* look good.

**OUR MISS BROOKS** (***) **30 min (127ep B&W; 1952–1956 CBS) Situation Comedy** *with Eve Arden as Connie Brooks, Gale Gordon as Osgood Conklin, Robert Rockwell as Philip Boynton, Richard Crenna as Walter Denton, Jane Morgan as Margaret Davis, Nana Bryant as Mrs. Nestor, Isabel Randolph as Mrs. Nestor, Gene Barry as Gene Talbot, and William Ching as Clint Albright*

Connie Brooks stands out almost alone amidst all of the leading ladies of 1950s TV because she held a steady, paying job. A working woman was a very rare bird indeed on TV in that decade, since virtually every woman in any major role appeared as homemaker and mother.

This emphasis on domesticity reflected, of course, the large percentage of American women who filled that role in real life. Common wisdom dictated that full-time career jobs were only for old maids or unlucky widows. So it is not surprising to note that Connie Brooks is not married in *Our Miss Brooks*, and, in fact, she spends most of the series trying to elicit a marriage proposal out of mousy, shy biology teacher Philip Boynton. Sure, teaching high school English was a well-accepted job for women in the 1950s, but Connie Brooks is a landmark in TV portrayal of women for her spunky independence and her intelligence.

Most of Connie's video sisters from the 1950s are either screwballs (Lucy Ricardo, Gracie Allen) or demure angels (June Cleaver, Margaret Anderson of *Father Knows Best*). Miss Brooks is a breath of fresh air, since she is such a sarcastic wisecracker. Her stance is simply a 1950s version of the postliberation angst of Rhoda or Molly Dodd, the educated woman who will kvetch about how all the good available men are nerds, while pining away for Mr. Right.

Connie Brooks teaches at mid-America Madison High School, an institution under the harsh command of principal Osgood Conklin. Conklin is portrayed by Gale Gordon, who tapped the vein of blustery, pompous bosses for more than two decades, first on *Our Miss Brooks*, then on *The Lucy Show* and *Here's Lucy*. Miss Brooks is chauffered to school each day by geeky student Walter Denton, whose voice approximates the soothing ring of nails on blackboard. Denton is played by Richard Crenna, in his first major role. Denton may look a little long in the tooth to be a high school student, especially in the later seasons, but never has the high school nerd been so faithfully reproduced on TV. Crenna's Denton will be a big surprise for viewers more familiar with Crenna's very different and more famous characters (hunky Luke McCoy of *The Real McCoys*, crusading James Slattery of *Slattery's People*, and as Sylvester Stallone's co-star in the *Rambo* films).

Also adding to the flavor of *Our Miss Brooks* are elderly Mrs. Davis (Miss Brooks' landlady, who is always trying to get Connie married), and the previously mentioned Mr. Boynton, who beats out Mr. Peepers for the shy, retiring type (male category) in 1950s TV.

After four successful years on network radio and three good years on TV, *Our Miss Brooks* gets a drastic overhaul for its final, less successful, season. Madison High is demolished to make way for a superhighway (another omen of things to come) and Miss Brooks and Mr. Conklin both wind up working at a private elementary school. The new school is run by a woman named Mrs. Nestor (who is soon replaced by her sister-in-law, another Mrs. Nestor). Miss Brooks acquires two new suitors, gym teacher Gene Talbot (the manly Gene Barry) and athletic director Clint Albright. The demure Mr. Boynton even turns up again just before the series shuts down.

Throughout all her travails on radio and TV, Miss Brooks never earns that "Mrs." degree she has been pursuing for so long. It is only after her series has run its course that she accomplishes this goal. In a 1956 Hollywood movie coda to the *Our Miss Brooks* saga, Mr. Boynton finally pops the question. Connie's ecstatic reaction appears to be unintentionally sappy, but perhaps Connie was just playing along, finally giving in to the intense 1950s pressure to conform. Knowing Connie, it's unlikely she stayed Mrs. Boynton very long into the changing times of the 1960s.

**OUR MUTUAL FRIEND (**½) 60 min (7ep Color; 1978 UK) Drama** *with Jane Seymour as Bella Wilfer, Leo McKern as Nicodemus Boffin, Kathleen Harrison as Henrietta Boffin, Andrew Ray as Mortimer Lightwood, Duncan Lamont as Jesse Hexam, Lesley Dunlop as Lizzie Hexam, and John McEnery as John Rokesmith*

This adaptation of the 1864 Charles Dickens novel looks at love and deception and the accumulation of material wealth. Or, in the case of "dustman" Nicodemus Boffin, the accumulation of disposable material—what we might call solid waste (also known as garbage). Ah, but is there gold to be found in such dross? Only Boffin knows for sure, and that's a secret to be played out at its proper time (and with relish, by Leo McKern—at his best, just a step away from the title role in *Rumpole of the Bailey*). And that's just one of the fortunes in this story, which also includes several identity switches, two fortune hunters in search of dowry wealth, and a character (Bella Wilfer, played by Jane Seymour) apparently based on Dickens's mistress at the time. Overall, a good interpretation of one of the author's later works.

**OUR WORLD (****) 60 min (13ep Color; 1986–1987 ABC) Documentary** *with Linda Ellerbee and Ray Gandolf as hosts*

There are two basic types of TV documentary. One is the super-serious collection of archive footage, such as *The 20th Century* or *World War I*, which provides interesting glimpses of the past. The other is the high-gloss milking of a trendy current issue, such as specials on violence or the sexual revolution. There are very few TV documentaries, at least on the commercial networks, that do much to place historical events into perspective, in order to make sense of the past. There are virtually no TV documentaries that use humor. *Our World* is the exception to both rules.

Ostensibly a nostalgia showcase, *Our World* focuses each episode on a season, a month, a week, a day, or any arbitrary division of time during the twentieth century. Hosts Linda Ellerbee and Ray Gandolf lead the look back at the faces and events of that era. What makes *Our World* exceptional is its thoughtful weaving together of important and seemingly unimportant events to highlight the mood or feel of a particular time. Sure, all the old familiar film clips are trotted out, but *Our World* goes beyond that. Some of the actual characters from the era in question are tracked down and interviewed to lend some personal hindsight on the events of the past. Furthermore, topical music is woven through each week's show, not just to add period flavor but to actually make a point about the events being discussed.

Ellerbee and Gandolf add offbeat, opinionated comments that are often laced with humor and sarcasm to the recollections. Not only does this add flavor to the historical recollections but it often puts the events in better focus by drawing conclusions that TV documentaries usually shy away from.

Particularly good episodes deal with the spring of 1954 (the battle for school integration) and Halloween 1938 (Orson Welles's "War of the Worlds" scare).

**OUT** (**½) **60 min (6ep Color; 1978 UK Thames) Drama** *with Tom Bell, Katharine Schofield, John Junkin, Brian Croucher, and Robert Walker*

A bank robber released from prison after eight years is obsessed with only one thought: revenge against whoever betrayed him. Along the way, he once again turns the lives of former friends, associates, and family into a state of upheaval. A chilling thriller.

**OUT OF THE BLUE** (**) **30 min (8ep Color; 1979 ABC) Situation Comedy** *with Jimmy Brogan as Random, Dixie Carter as Marion McLemore, Eileen Heckart as the Boss Angel, Clark Brandon as Chris Richards, Olivia Barash as Laura Richards, Tammy Lauren as Stacey Richards, Jason Keller as Jason Richards, and Shane Keller as Shane Richards*

A young angel named Random moves in as a boarder with five recently orphaned brothers and sisters now living with their Aunt Marion. Though she doesn't know his secret the children soon do, so he attempts to teach them important lessons of life while discreetly helping them with his special powers.

Very sweet. Dixie Carter later became one of the leads on *Designing Women*, while Clark Brandon stuck with magic as an apprentice sorcerer on *Mr. Merlin*. Robin Williams (playing Mork from Ork) guest stars in the opening episode.

**OUT OF THE FIERY FURNACE** (**) **60 min (7ep Color; 1986 PBS) Documentary**

Leaving no stone unturned in its quest for offbeat TV fare, PBS serves up the first (and only?) documentary on the *metallurgical* history of civilization. The saga travels from Stone Age tools to Space Age metals.

**OUT OF THE UNKNOWN** (**) **60 min (20ep B&W; 1965–1966 UK BBC) Science Fiction Anthology**

Earthlings meet various aliens, some friendly and some hostile. Acceptable anthology series not quite as scary as its Stateside contemporary, *The Outer Limits.*

**OUT OF THIS WORLD** (**) **30 min (48ep at Fall 1989 Color; 1987– Syndication) Situation Comedy** *with Donna Pescow as Donna Garland, Maureen Flannigan as Evie Garland, Doug McClure as Mayor Kyle Applegate, Joe Alaskey as Beano Froelich, and Burt Reynolds as the voice of Troy*

Donna Garland's story is familiar to many modern women. Donna met this great guy, was swept off her feet, had a brief sexy fling, and then found herself all alone, pregnant, with her new love gone and hard to find. The difference here is that Donna's roaming beau, Troy, is an alien (from outer space, not overseas). Evie, the baby that results from her extra-terrestrial fling, inherits some of her dad's alien powers.

This series begins when Evie is thirteen and first learns of her true heritage, and it focuses on mom's attempts to keep Evie under control despite the kids' otherworldly talents, all the while keeping the neighbors from knowing an alien half-breed lives next door. There are lots of neighbors to keep track of, because Donna runs a private school for rich, smart kids in California. This same general concept is dealt with slightly differently in *Starman* (a TV show based on a hit film).

Donna Pescow, who plays mom in *Out of This World*, had a quick moment of fame at the end of the 1970s, as John Travolta's girlfriend in the film *Saturday Night Fever*, and then as the star of the brief TV sitcom *Angie*.

**THE OUTCASTS** (*) **60 min (26ep Color; 1968–1969 ABC) Western** *with Don Murray as Earl Corey and Otis Young as Jemal David*

Uh-oh. A series called *The Outcasts*, from the late 1960s, from ABC. An hour drama in the west. Sounds like some cheap relevancy show about hippies set in the old west. Maybe with some heavy moralizing, too. Well, *The Outcasts* isn't quite that bad, but it is pretty stilted. Set in the post–Civil War era, *The Outcasts* teams up a white ex-aristocrat who is an ex-slave owner (Earl Corey) and a black ex-slave (Jemal David) and has them become bounty hunters and partners. They can't stand each other and hiss and spit a lot, but, gee, ain't brotherhood great, they learn to get along and live together. If only we could learn that lesson. Hmm. Actually there is a lot of moralizing going on here, after all.

**THE OUTER LIMITS** (****) **60 min (49ep B&W; 1963–1965 ABC) Science Fiction Anthology** *with Vic Perrin as the Control Voice*

*The Outer Limits* just don't get no respect. Whenever people talk about great TV science fiction, usually only *The Twilight Zone* and *Star Trek* get mentioned. While those two shows are true classics, it is highly unfair to omit *The Outer Limits*, one of the great series of the 1960s.

When *The Outer Limits* does get mentioned, it usually is with the condescending compliment that the show has great monsters. That it does, but it also has great writing, great acting, and arguably the best opening in TV history.

*The Outer Limits* is pure anthology. There is no continuity whatsoever, other than the mysterious disembodied "Control Voice" that narrates each episode. Dispensing with the familiar, reassuring presence of a human host, *The Outer Limits* opens with video static and the Control Voice menacingly informing us that "there is nothing wrong with your television set," other than the fact that "we" are controlling transmission, controlling "all that you see and hear." This is a far more conspiratorial view of television broadcasting than existed at any time before Vice-President Spiro Agnew's attacks on the electronic media in 1969.

As an anthology, *The Outer Limits* must survive on the strength of each story. The joy of the program is that many stories are so imaginative. The opening episode ("The Galaxy Being" starring Cliff Robertson and Jacqueline Scott) concerns the first human-alien contact, via radio broadcasts, climaxing with the unexpected teleportation of the alien to Earth, via radio waves, leading to disastrous results. Another episode ("Demon with a Glass Hand" by Harlan Ellison, starring pre-*I Spy* Robert Culp) presents the intriguing notion that the entire human race has been reduced to electronic impulses on a wire in the glass hand of a robot who thinks he is human. Carroll O'Connor (later of *All in the Family*) and Barry Morse (of *The Fugitive*) turn up in "Controlled Experiment" as lighthearted Martians who study the odd behavior of Earthlings by means of a device that can rerun time like a giant instant replay machine. In "The Sixth Finger," David McCallum (later of *The Man from U.N.C.L.E.*) plays a lower-class slob who becomes a bubble-headed genius when used as a human guinea pig in an experiment that greatly accelerates the process of human evolution. Donald Pleasence is ominous in "The Man with the Power" as a mild-mannered college professor who develops the power to cause his deepest, darkest urges to come to pass through a cloud of powerful energy that can kill.

Most of TV's big suspense/sci-fi anthologies stuck to a half-hour, but *The Outer Limits* relishes the benefits of a sixty-minute format. The additional time is well used to provide extensive background, subplots, and complicated endings. A lot of time and money went in to preparing the special effects (mostly each week's monster/alien) and for once the effort pays off as the effects tend to complement the writing and acting. As it turns out, the reason *The Outer Limits* is so "monster"-oriented is that the producers were under considerable pressure from the network to supply easy-to-promote bogeymen. More concerned with developing well-crafted stories, the producers felt obliged to toss in the weekly bugbear to keep the network brass at bay.

The first thirty-two episodes contain the best of *The Outer Limits* material. Produced by the show's creator Leslie Stevens and his successor in day-to-day control of the series, Joseph Stefano, these take the boldest leaps of imagination and are often chilling in their spookiness. The seventeen episodes of the second season, produced by *Perry Mason* alumnus Ben Brady, try too often to cut corners by going light on the scripts and heavy on the ugly monsters. The grim, moralistic intonations of the Control Voice at the open and close of the first season's programs are reduced in the second season to short, bland messages.

The relatively brief run of *The Outer Limits* and its lack of a familiar host work against the show's ranking in TV history lore. The emphasis on bug-eyed aliens gives the program an unwarranted reputation as simplistic and childish. But, to those willing to pay attention, *The Outer Limits* can prove a short but extremely fertile source of TV brilliance. ■

**THE OUTLAWS** (**) **60 min (50ep B&W; 1960–1962 NBC) Western** *with Barton MacLane as Marshal Frank Caine, Don Collier as Will Forman, Jock Gaynor as Heck Martin, and Bruce Yarnell as Chalk Breeson*

There is nothing so rare as a TV western from the late 1950s/early 1960s with an *original* concept. *The Outlaws* almost fits that description. The first season of the series really is different, in that it focuses mostly on a collection of bad guys. Oh, they do get caught in the end, but the series is written from their perspective, as Marshal Caine and his boys close in on the varmints.

For the second season, *The Outlaws* becomes just another TV western, with the focus back where it always is, on the law-abiding folk trying to fight off the bad guys. Marshal Caine is gone, and his deputy, Will Forman, has replaced him. Marshal Forman and his boys hang out in Stillwater, Oklahoma.

**THE OUTSIDER** (**½) **60 min (26ep & 2 hr pilot Color; 1968–1969 NBC) Detective Drama** *with Darren McGavin as David Ross*

Kolchak fans, look for this one. Though it's not quite as light or fantasy-oriented as *The Night Stalker*, this series does feature Darren McGavin once again as the put-upon loner in a classic "genre" setting. This time it's the world of a typical Philip Marlowe detective novel, with McGavin's David Ross pounding the pavement as an underpaid gumshoe who inevitably finds himself involved in convoluted cases, sometimes with double-dealing clients. In the 1967 TV movie pilot, for instance, Ross watches his investigation into an embezzlement scheme turn into a murder case, with him as the number one suspect. Created and produced by Roy Huggins, the man behind such series as *Maverick, The Fugitive,* and *The Rockford Files.*

**OVERLAND TRAIL** (*½) **60 min (17ep B&W; 1960 NBC) Western** *with William Bendix as Frederick Thomas Kelly and Doug McClure as Frank "Flip" Flippen*

What a match up! William Bendix, who went to his grave best known as Chester A. (*The Life of . . .* ) Riley, is mentor to Doug McClure (making his first TV series appearance), young TV stud of the 1960s, best known as suave detective Jed Sills in *Checkmate* and wild cowboy Trampas in *The Virginian.*

The two are like oil and water—they just don't mix. Bendix is supposed to be a cantankerous old coot who is helping to open a commercial stage coach line from Missouri to California in the post–Civil War era, while McClure is his Indian-raised helper. It is typecasting at its worst, but chances are you will keep waiting for

Bendix, when surrounded by bloodthirsty Injuns, to look at the camera with a stupid grin and say . . . "What a revoltin' development this is!"

## OWEN MARSHALL, COUNSELOR AT LAW (**½)

**60 min (69ep & 2 hr pilot Color; 1971–1974 ABC) Law Drama** *with Arthur Hill as Owen Marshall, Lee Majors as Jess Brandon, Reni Santoni as Danny Paterno, David Soul as Ted Warrick, Christine Matchett as Melissa Marshall, and Joan Darling as Frieda Krause*

You can't say much about *Owen Marshall, Counselor at Law* without mentioning *Marcus Welby, M. D.* Both shows come from the early 1970s. Both shows are produced by David Victor. Both shows concern thoughtful, compassionate, aging white men in professions where they dedicate their lives to helping others. In fact, the two series actually overlap at times, with some characters from one popping up on the other (though Marshall never had to defend the good doctor himself, just Dr. Kiley, his associate).

What is good about *Welby* is good about *Marshall*. They both are well-written, thoughtful series with some fine acting and little, if any, sensationalism. What is bad about *Welby* is also bad about *Marshall*. They both are very soap opera-ish, highly paternalistic, too serious, and overly interested in appearing to be important drama.

Owen Marshall is a defense attorney in Santa Barbara, California, who is a widower with a twelve-year-old daughter (Melissa). One highlight for viewers is to keep an eye on Marshall's young associates. Like Welby, he keeps a stable of handsome young protégés nearby to pique female interest. At first, Marshall is helped by the broad-shouldered Jess Brandon (Lee Majors, the *Six Million Dollar Man*). Then Marshall briefly dabbles in ethnic help (Danny Paterno), before returning to the tried and true WASP charm of Ted Warrick (David Soul, the blond Hutch of *Starsky and Hutch*).

## OZZIE & HARRIET, THE ADVENTURES OF (***)

**(435ep: 409 B&W & 26 Color; 1952–1966 ABC) Situation Comedy** *with Ozzie, Harriet, David, and Ricky Nelson as themselves, Don DeFore as "Thorny" Thornberry, Skip Young as Wally Dipple, June Blair as June Nelson, and Kristin Harmon as Kris Nelson*

It is easy to make fun of *Ozzie & Harriet*, especially now that it seems so old-fashioned. The Nelsons are sort of boring, they live in the 1950s suburban world, and Ozzie never seems to go to work. Once you get beyond the surface corniness, *Ozzie & Harriet* can be appreciated as a very important part of TV history and an amazing documentary of how one American family grew up.

The standard joke about Ozzie Nelson's character on *Ozzie & Harriet* is that he never works, has no apparent source of income, and yet supports a family of four in handsome style. The truth is that the real Ozzie Nelson put in almost a quarter century of very hard work resulting in a program that almost always manages to entertain.

Ozzie Nelson began his career as a law school graduate turned bandleader. He married Harriet Hilliard, the singer in his band, and in 1944, they began a weekly sitcom (on network radio) based solely on their own lives, or at least a fictionalized version of their lives. Ozzie and Harriet played themselves but child actors played their two sons, David and Eric (later known as Ricky). Four and one-half years later, David and Ricky themselves replaced the child actors. In the early 1950s, the series was moved to the new medium of television.

From the 1940s to the 1960s, the Nelsons turned up in America's living room every week, with plots as thin as rice paper. At first, Ozzie and Harriet were a young couple with two kids. By the time the TV series began, Ozzie and Harriet were sliding into middle age and the focus shifted to David and Ricky, who were growing into their teen years. In the late 1950s, Ricky became a rock'n'roll star and the two boys went to college. In the 1960s, David and Ricky married and had children of their own. By the time the series ended, the two Nelson boys were not much younger than Ozzie was when he started the weekly family saga.

So after laughing at the bumbling character of Ozzie Nelson keep in mind that following a successful bandleading career he was the prime force behind a program that ran every week for twenty-two years, and produced more episodes (435) than any other sitcom in American TV history. Ozzie and Harriet held their family together for two decades during the strain of weekly television production while their children grew up.

Ozzie also was an unheralded pioneer of rock videos. When son Ricky became a teen idol in the 1950s, Ozzie shrewdly began plugging Ricky's new songs through inserting musical numbers in each week's episode. Often the songs appear at the end of the show, unconnected to that week's story, in a self-contained performance clip. Some clips, such as for "Travelin' Man," add thematic background film and superimpositions that relate to the song lyrics, a style that did not come into common use until the late 1970s.

Strictly as a TV show, *Ozzie & Harriet* is somewhat dull. Not very much happens in any one episode. If you think of this series as a cross between a soap opera and a sitcom, it plays much better. The real story is the lengthy saga of the growing Nelson family, and each week is merely another installment. Appropriately, when first David married and then Ricky married in real life, their new brides joined the show's cast, playing (what else?) the wives of the two sons. The other secondary characters in the series are shallow and forgettable (Wally Dipple, a friend of the two boys who is frequently bedecked in a college letter sweater, is one of the nerdiest guys in TV history). The Nelsons, however, are as real as you can get. They are an aggravatingly nice family, but they interact the way only a real family can. Their problems may seem trivial, but they mirror the trivial day-to-day problems that most all families face. This sense of down-to-earth normality is what kept audiences coming back week after week.

A 1952 feature film, *Here Come the Nelsons*, in effect serves as the pilot for the long-running TV series. The saga of the Nelson family (after David and Ricky have moved away) continued for one season in the early 1970s on *Ozzie's Girls*, where Ozzie and Harriet take in boarders for the boys' old rooms. ■

**OZZIE'S GIRLS (*½) 30 min (24ep Color; 1973–1974 Syndication) Situation Comedy** *with Ozzie and Harriet Nelson as themselves, Susan Sennett as Susan Hamilton, Brenda Sykes as Brenda (a.k.a. Jennifer) MacKenzie, and David Doyle as Professor McCutcheon*

You can't fault the Nelsons for trying to move with the times. In this case, Ozzie and Harriet find themselves facing some contemporary issues when they decide to rent Ricky and David's old rooms. One look at the setup and you know where this one is headed: The new boarders are two college girls, Brenda (black) and Susan (white), who brings the early 1970s generation gap right into the Nelson living room. Perhaps to add an *All in the Family* feel to the production (or just reflecting the tighter budget of a syndicated show), this series is video taped, not filmed, with Ozzie writing and directing, while son David acts as producer.

This series was sometimes uncomfortable to watch in its original run in 1973, perhaps because it was tough to see one of the symbols of television's innocence forced to deal with even the hint of those very angry times. (Not that it was a diatribe on race, sex, and drugs—this was played just like any other lightly relevant comedy at the time.) For thirtysomethings, it's like looking at an old photo album (or, worse yet, watching a home video tape of yourself) and sheepishly wondering, "Did I really put my folks through all that? And did Ozzie and Harriet really have to do something like that to get back on the air?" Unfortunately, those were judgmental times. Even rock-and-roller Rick Nelson ran into problems when he didn't look and sound exactly the way his audience assumed he should (detailed in his 1972 hit, "Garden Party"). Still, an episode of this series should be kept within easy reach for the next time someone complains about the never-never land of the original Nelsons program. Just to show them the less than successful alternative.

**THE PALLISERS (***) 60 min (26ep Color; 1975–1976 UK BBC) Drama** *with John Gielgud as host, Susan Hampshire as Lady Glencora Palliser, Philip Latham as Plantagenet Palliser, M. P., Ronald Culver as the Duke of Omnium, Barry Justice as Burgo Fitzgerald, Donal McCann as Phineas Finn, Fabia Drake as Countess Midlothian, Jeremy Clyde as Gerald Maule, Penelope Keith as Mrs. Hittaway, Jeremy Irons as Frank Tregear, Anthony Andrews as the Earl of Silverbridge, and Derek Jacobi as Lord Fawn*

This lengthy but engrossing adaptation of six novels by Anthony Trollop traces a quarter century of the lives, loves, and political ambitions of the Pallisers, a wealthy Victorian family. At the time of publication, Trollop used the political fortunes of this fictional family as a means of focusing on the many real life developments of the era, when he had made some unsuccessful runs for Parliament himself. The television series retains that sense of history, but also puts more emphasis on the personal aspects of the conflicts. And, like *Upstairs, Downstairs*, each episode can stand on its own as a self-contained story while also functioning as part of a continuing narrative. It all starts with the rise to power of Plantagenet Palliser and concludes a generation later with his son, the Earl of Silverbridge, making a run for Parliament as a member of the same liberal party. Of course, quite a bit happens in between.

Because this series covers so much territory with so many characters (most around for just a handful of episodes), over the course of the production you'll probably spot a lot of familiar faces from other British series (the above cast list should be regarded as just selective highlights) including Barry Justice's disreputable Burgo, Penelope Keith's delightful Mrs. Hittaway, and Jeremy Irons as the politically daring Frank Tregear, who breaks from the Pallisers' circle and casts his lot with the conservatives.

**PALMERSTOWN U.S.A. (**) 60 min (16ep & 2 hr pilot Color; 1980–1981 CBS) Drama** *with Jonelle Allen as Bessie Freeman, Bill Duke as Luther Freeman, Star-Shemah Bobatoon as Diana Freeman, Jermain Hodge Johnson as Booker T. Freeman, Beeson Carroll as W. D. Hall, Janice St. John as Coralee Hall, Michael J. Fox as Willy-Joe Hall, and Brian Godfrey Wilson as David Hall*

This show appears to be a meeting of giants. The two producers of *Palmerstown U.S.A.* are Alex Haley (author of *Roots*) and Norman Lear (producer of *All in the Family* and *Sanford & Son*). Together they should have created a landmark in TV history.

Not quite. *Palmerstown U.S.A.* is a heartfelt tale of two nine-year-old boys growing up in Palmerstown, Tennessee, in the Depression of the 1930s. David is white and Booker T. is black. Their families don't really like each other, but manage to get along. In spite of the fact that the story is loosely based on Haley's own childhood in Henning, Tennessee, the series lacks any real drive. The black-white friendship theme is great, as far as it goes, but it doesn't go very far. Unlike *The Waltons*, set in the same era and region, viewers will not get wrapped up in the families here.

Unfortunately, the biggest claim to fame of *Palmerstown* (the *U.S.A.* was dropped halfway through the series) is that it is the first series appearance of Michael J. Fox, who plays David's older brother. He went on to superstardom as Alex Keaton on *Family Ties* and in the movies (*Back to the Future*).

**PANIC (**) 30 min (31ep B&W; 1957 NBC) Suspense Anthology** *with Westbrook Van Voorhis as narrator*

*Panic* consists of tales of suspense, with *March of Time* voice Westbrook Van Voorhis as narrator. Some of the *Panic* episodes have been packaged with a very similar series, *No Warning.*

**THE PAPER CHASE (***½) 60 min (56ep & 2 hr finale Color; 1978–1979 & 1983–1986 CBS & Showtime) Drama** *with John Houseman as Professor Charles W. Kingsfield, James Stephens as James T. Hart, Tom Fitzsimmons as Franklin Ford III, James Keane as Willis Bell, Francine Tacker as Elizabeth Logan, Robert Ginty as Thomas Craig Anderson, Betty Harford as Mrs. Nottingham, Michael Tucci as Gerald Golden, Clare Kirkconnell as Rita Harriman, and Lainie Kazan as Rose*

John Houseman's Professor Charles W. Kingsfield is tough, which is clear from his remarks in the opening credits sequence of the program's first season, as he warns his first-year students to be prepared for school work unlike any they've experienced before. His stern promise: No matter what the cost, if they can survive the process, he will clear their minds of a lifetime of "mush" and turn them into lawyers.

He wasn't exaggerating. Little did they know that the standard three-year law school program would stretch far beyond that, with graduation day not coming until eight years later. Of course, in between, there was a little problem: network ratings.

Actually, *The Paper Chase* marks a rare instance in which the key members of a U.S. television series reassemble to continue the story line with new episodes. (This happens far more often in Britain.) In this case, the tale began on CBS in 1978 when the network picked up this prestige series, based on a successful 1973 feature film that won Houseman an Oscar for his role. Unfortunately, the network tossed this drama about first-year law students against two of the era's top-rated comedies, *Happy Days* and *Laverne and Shirley*. To absolutely no one's surprise, *The Paper Chase* barely nicked the ratings of the Fonz and his friends. There was some minor tinkering, leading John Houseman to refuse to appear in one episode, a heavy-handed tale about a visiting Russian gymnast who (oh, go on, guess the plot twist). Afterward *The Paper Chase* was canceled and presumably laid to rest alongside other admired but low-rated drama series.

Shortly thereafter, public television stations began airing the series in reruns, and there was talk about attempting to do additional episodes, but funding problems killed the idea. (However, Houseman did turn up as Kingsfield on an episode of the 1979 comedy *The Associates.*) In the early 1980s, cable's Showtime was looking to produce a few original series to help distinguish itself from the competition, so it worked out a production deal, reviving *The Paper Chase*. As a result, in spring 1983, the series was back, carrying on the story of law student James Hart and his friends (only two from the original series, Franklin Ford and Willis Bell), forever laboring under the demanding presence of Charles Kingsfield. The series of twenty episodes carried the subtitle "The Second Year," and was followed by twelve episodes from "The Third Year," three from "The Graduation Year," and, finally (in 1986), a two-hour TV-movie, *The Paper Chase Graduation*. (Fortunately, with the change in focus from just the first year students, there was an excuse to shelve that cloying Seals and Crofts song, "The First Year," in favor of a light classical music piece.)

Currently the entire series plays through as part of the same rerun package, though usually the *Graduation* movie is run as a special. This series is definitely worth following from beginning to end if only to experience a rare instance of a premise being taken to its inevitable conclusion. These students actually do graduate! In addition, you'll also be able to compare scripts tailored for the one-year commercial network run and those for the subsequent cable packaging.

First, the obvious: The stories for CBS have far more flashy, nonclassroom hooks than any of the subsequent episodes. These include a mob shooting, compulsive gambling, that "Russian detente" episode, and some student protest scenes. But there are also some very clever set pieces that deal with more cerebral themes. For instance, in one story the first-year study group helps a student with a photographic memory learn how to think rather than merely recite facts. They drag him into Kingsfield's empty classroom at night and hammer him with question after question, doing their best booming-voice impressions of the professor. In another, a "scavenger hunt" for the answers to an impossible-to-solve Kingsfield test provides plenty of footage showing the campus libraries left in shambles, but also allows Kingsfield the opportunity to make a point on why there is contract law (the subject he teaches).

James Hart, the top student in Kingsfield's law class, embodies this obsession with learning and thinking. In one telling first-year scene, he and his girlfriend (for that episode) sneak into the law library archives and dig into Kingsfield's personal papers. There he comes across the professor's contract law class notebook from his days as a student and pores over it. Hart finds it thrilling to see that Professor Kingsfield was once just like him, and that he and the professor are part of the same continuing chain of knowledge, learning, and thinking. (Frankly we never see Hart half as excited about a date. No wonder he doesn't have many long-term relationships.)

Of course, none of these intellectual concerns would work for a moment without good stories. Here the episodes produced for Showtime are clearly superior, emphasizing issue drama and character conflicts. Oh, there are still flashy hooks (Kingsfield versus a computer or Kingsfield gets mugged), but at least they make sense within the context of a university environment.

No matter what the trappings, though, *The Paper Chase* is ultimately a showpiece of John Houseman's Professor Kingsfield. He may have created the character for the feature film, but in this series he truly defines it, adding subtle nuances and private moments of interaction. One of the best episodes of this type is the "Second Year" story, "My Dinner with Kingsfield," in which the Professor ends up at Hart's apartment one evening during a blinding snowstorm, awaiting a tow truck. They talk, eat, and play a board game together, with Hart alternately awed and ecstatic. But again Houseman consistently steals the show, as when he looks out at the snow-packed streets and declares, "No school today!"

However, even in an intimate exchange like that, one facet of Houseman's Kingsfield remains absolutely unchanged to the very end (even on graduation day): When with his students, he never breaks from his role as professor. No matter what the situation, there are no cute hugs or soft-as-marshmallow looks (though he occasionally allows himself a private smile of pride when they leave). This is not the time for them to think of him as a friend or colleague. He knows that's for later, after they've had time to act as adults in the real world of applied law. That's when they'll win his friendship and respect the old-fashioned way: by earning it.

**PAPER DOLLS (*) 60 min (13ep & 2 hr pilot Color; 1984 ABC) Drama** *with Lloyd Bridges as Grant Harper, Dack Rambo as Wesley Harper, Morgan Fairchild as Racine, Brenda Vaccaro as Julia Blake, Jennifer Warren as Dinah Caswell, Nicolette Sheridan as Taryn Blake, and Terry Farrell as Laurie Caswell*

The usual high-powered lust and intrigue of corporate America flows through this series, set in New York's high-fashion modeling and cosmetics industry. Completely disposable, but the cast contains enough familiar faces from other shows (ranging from Nicolette Sheridan of *Knots Landing* to Lloyd Bridges of *Sea Hunt*) to make it worth a quick once-over.

Based on a 1982 made-for-TV movie featuring a different cast, led by Joan Collins.

**PAPER MOON (**½) 30 min (13ep Color; 1974–1975 ABC) Situation Comedy** *with Christopher Connelly as Moses "Moze" Pray and Jodie Foster as Addie Pray*

Here we have yet another valiant but failed effort to transform a hit film to the small screen. The Oscar-winning 1973 Peter Bogdanovich film *Paper Moon* (based on Joe David Brown's novel, *Addie Pray*) starred Ryan O'Neal and his real-life daughter Tatum. The pixie-ish story dealt with flim-flam man Moze Pray, who sweet-talked Midwesterners out of their money in the Depression, posing as a Bible salesman. Addie was a young waif who latched onto Moze, convinced that he was her father.

The TV series picks up the film story, with Moze and Addie cruising the dust bowl in his roadster. Moze is played with some charm by Christopher Connelly (Norman Harrington from *Peyton Place*). Addie is portrayed by precocious Jodie Foster (already in her second TV series at age eleven), who soon thereafter became a film star (*Taxi Driver, Bugsy Malone*). The concept does not really work as a continuing series, but the few episodes produced are worth catching.

**PARADISE (**½) 60 min (20ep at Summer 1989 Color; 1988– CBS) Western** *with Lee Horsley as Ethan Allen Cord, Jenny Beck as Claire Carroll, Matthew Newmark as Joseph Carroll, Brian Lando as Benjamin Carroll, Michael Carter as Geroge Carroll, and Sigrid Thornton as Amelia Lawson*

Ethan Allen Cord is a grungy gunfighter in the western mining town of Paradise in the 1890s. His life is radically transformed when his dying sister's four children (ages five through thirteen) turn up at his door. The sister figures Ethan is her best bet to raise the kids when she is gone, since he has led her to believe he's a sedate store owner. Not knowing much about this fathering business, Ethan tries hard to give up the gunplay, settle down and become a simple farmer. While dealing with his new brood, he winds up battling the bad guys in town and avoiding the bounty hunters who know he's still a wanted man.

The basic plot here is needlessly convoluted, but it is an admirable late 1980s attempt to revive the nearly moribund western format. Lee Horsley, who plays Ethan, is best known as the star of *Matt Houston*, a *Magnum, P. I.* rip-off of the early 1980s.

**PARADISE POSTPONED (***) 60 min (11ep: ten 60 min & one 90 min Color; 1986 UK Thames) Drama** *with Michael Hordern as Rev. Simeon Simcox, David Threlfall as Leslie Titmuss, Paul Shelley as Fred Simcox, Peter Egan as Henry Simcox, Colin Blakely as Dr. Salter, Eleanor David as Agnes, and Zoe Wanamaker as Charlotte*

An excellent slice of post–World War II England, conceived by John Mortimer (creator of *Rumpole of the Bailey* and adapter of *Brideshead Revisited*) and set in the fictional small-town area of Rapstone Fanner. The story shifts back and forth in time from the present to the immediate postwar days, tracing the activities of two key characters: liberal activist Rev. Simeon Simcox and self-serving Conservative cabinet minister Leslie

Titmuss. There's an added edge of mystery to the flashbacks, however, because at the beginning of the story everyone is shocked to discover that the recently deceased Rev. Simcox has left the bulk of his considerable estate to the despised Titmuss. Simcox's son Henry contests the will and vows to discover the reason for his father's bequest.

So while following the contemporary actions of Henry (and his brother, Fred) in attempting to solve the mystery, the series also shows them in the past with their father, facing a world that wasn't turning out quite the way they had expected. This is the main thematic hook of the drama: attempting to bring the optimism of the postwar world to fruition, even as promises of social advancement, economic justice, and political responsibility fall increasingly by the wayside. It seems that social Paradise, which once appeared within grasp after the war, is destined to be postponed indefinitely. Underscoring this fact is the rise of characters such as Titmuss, working-class conservatives who pull themselves up to power and then maintain that money itself is a virtue, those left in poverty are a personal disgrace, and governmental help for the poor is economic nonsense.

Of course, in between philosophical debates and antinuclear protests, there's plenty of entertaining action. Henry, Fred, and Titmuss have their own careers to pursue, as well as some special women to court (Agnes and Charlotte). Henry is a cynical writer (described by Mortimer as, frankly, himself showing off), Fred is a quiet country doctor and amateur jazz drummer (Mortimer's nicer side), and Titmuss is a rags-to-riches local boy who rises to power in the ranks of Britain's Conservative party. All of them are well-cast and help sustain the drama from beginning to end. In the end, it's Fred who solves the mystery of his father's will, which he reveals to both Henry and Titmuss in the last episode.

**PARIS (**½) 60 min (12ep Color; 1979–1980 CBS) Police Drama** *with James Earl Jones as Woody Paris, Lee Chamberlain as Barbara Paris, Hank Garrett as Deputy Chief Jerome Bench, and Michael Warren as Willie Miller*

James Earl Jones plays a multifaceted Los Angeles police captain. He solves crimes, loves his wife, and teaches a course in criminology at a local university. Unfortunately the entire setup never quite comes together.

However, *Paris* is definitely worth a look not only because of James Earl Jones (who is riveting as ever), but also because it was created by Steven Bochco, whose very next outing was *Hill Street Blues*. *Paris* regular Michael Warren came over to that new series and other future *Hill Street* cast members appear in *Paris* guest slots as well, including Barbara Babcock, Taurean Blacque, James B. Sikking, and Bruce Weitz.

Meanwhile, going in the other direction, Hank Garrett's deputy chief character has roots stretching back to a squad room of a different sort in *Car 54, Where Are You?*, where he played officer Nicholson.

**PARIS PRECINCT (*½) 30 min (26ep B&W; 1954–1955 Syndication) Police Drama** *with Louis Jourdan as Inspector Beaumont and Claude Dauphin as Inspector Bolbec*

Louis Jourdan, French actor and the epitome of suaveness, makes a rare TV series appearance as a Parisian police detective. This series has also been known as *World Crime Hunt*.

**PARIS 7000 (*) 60 min (10ep Color; 1970 ABC) Adventure** *with George Hamilton as Jack Brennan, Gene Raymond as Robert Stevens, and Jacques Aubuchon as Jules Maurois*

What better locale than Paris for a series starring the eternally suave and dapper George Hamilton? The man with the perpetual tan plays a U.S. State Department employee at the U.S. Embassy in Paris, whose job is to help Americans in trouble. His phone number is Paris 7000. Surprisingly, he doesn't get many calls from tourists who lost their traveler's checks.

**PARK PLACE (**) 30 min (5ep Color; 1981 CBS) Situation Comedy** *with Harold Gould as David Ross, David Clennon as Jeff O'Neil, Don Calfa as Howard "Howie" Beech, Alice Drummond as Frances Heine, Cal Gibson as Ernie Rice, Mary Elaine Monti as Joel "Jo" Keene, and Lionel Smith as Aaron "Mac" MacRae*

The idea is workable: a sitcom about a legal aid clinic in New York City, staffed by a group of lawyers who are fairly down-and-out themselves. A kindly old lawyer with a good sense of humor runs the place. The result, *Park Place*, does not live up to its potential. Harold Gould, the father in *Rhoda*, seems destined to forever be a second banana. All his efforts to star in a series have met with little success.

**THE PARTNERS (*½) 30 min (20ep Color: 1971–1972 NBC) Situation Comedy** *with Don Adams as Lennie Crooke, Rupert Crosse as George Robinson, Dick Van Patten as Sgt. Nelson Higgenbottom, John Doucette as Capt. Aaron Andrews, and Robert Karvelas as Freddie Butler*

Don Adams and Rupert Crosse play a pair of mildly bungling police detectives in this disappointingly tame comedy. Though Adams (who created the series) probably didn't want this to be seen as just "Maxwell Smart joins the police force," he definitely pulled in the reins a bit too much.

Another *Get Smart* alum also turns up, Robert Karvelas (who played Larabee, a CONTROL agent even more incompetent than Smart). This time around he's a chronic confessor, Freddie Butler, who obviously embraces that old mystery cliché "The Butler did it."

**PARTNERS IN CRIME** (**½) **60 min (13ep Color; 1984 NBC) Detective Drama** *with Loni Anderson as Sydney Kovak, Lynda Carter as Carole Stanwyck, Leo Rossi as Lt. Ed Vronsky, Walter Olkewicz as Harmon Shain, and Eileen Heckart as Jeanine Caulfield*

The potential is here for the champion "jiggle" show of all time. Loni Anderson (Jennifer Marlowe of *WKRP in Cincinnati*) and Lynda Carter (*Wonder Woman*) are two of the more well-endowed women on TV and pairing them up smacks of cynical exploitation. The reality is, however, that both Anderson and Carter aspire to roles much more meaningful than showcases for tight tops. *Partners in Crime* turns out to be a fairly satisfying mix of action and humor, without many cheap shots at the stars' figures.

Anderson and Carter play two very different ex-wives of Raymond Caulfield, a murdered San Francisco private eye. He wills his detective business and mansion to the two ex-wives, who become, yes, partners in crime—or, more accurately, partners in solving crime. Carter's character is a prim and proper photographer, while Anderson's is a sometimes pickpocket and jazz bass player. Together there is enough friction and resentment about their common ex-husband to fuel a show, while providing material for some fun. After all the "buddy" detective/cop shows with two men, it's about time there was a female "buddy" series with a light touch.

**PARTNERS IN CRIME, AGATHA CHRISTIE'S** (***) **60 min (11ep Color; 1983 UK London Weekend Television) Mystery** *with James Warwick As Tommy Beresford and Francesca Annis as Tuppence Beresford*

Not to be confused with the U.S. series of the same name, this is a particularly entertaining Agatha Christie adaptation, with a fun-loving affectionate pair of jazz-age husband-and-wife detectives, Tommy and Tuppence. The two first meet shortly after World War I, searching for ways to earn money after years of wartime service. They start out as amateur sleuths, but soon turn the venture into a reasonably successful occupation—oh, and they also fall in love and get married. They're a fun couple to watch because they enjoy teasing each other and posturing, especially when they have to don costumes or other proper attire to visit some posh spots. And they enthusiastically pursue their cases, even if they involve their own physical peril. If you like your mysteries mixed with sexy banter and period-piece settings, this is definitely the Agatha Christie series for you. Most of these stories first aired in the United States on *Mystery!* ■

**THE PARTRIDGE FAMILY** (*½) **30 min (96ep Color; 1970–1974 ABC) Situation Comedy** *with Shirley Jones as Shirley Partridge, David Cassidy as Keith Partridge, Susan Dey as Laurie Partridge, Danny Bonaduce as Danny Partridge, Jeremy Gelbwaks and Brian Forster as Christopher Partridge, Suzanne Crough as Tracy Partridge, David Madden as Reuben Kinkaid, and Ricky Segall as Ricky Stevens*

In the late 1960s, there was a mildly successful rock group called the Cowsills. They are best remembered for the hit version of the song "Hair" (from the controversial play of the same name), and other hits such as "Rain, the Park and Other Things" and "Indian Lake." What made the Cowsills unique was that they were family: a mother and her four kids singing together.

The idea behind the Cowsills seemed so cute and so cuddly that it had to be turned into a TV series. It was, and the series is called *The Partridge Family*. Like the Cowsills, the Partridge clan is mom and her kids (three boys and two girls), who sing together and become an overnight sensation (with the simple but catchy tune "I Think I Love You"). The TV show follows the group as they tour the land in their psychedelic school bus with their grumpy manager Reuben Kinkaid.

Following the lead of the Monkees, another group prefabricated for TV, the Partridge Family became a real-life success on the pop charts and David Cassidy, who played the eldest Partridge son, became a true teen heartthrob. (Appropriately, Cassidy is the real-life stepson of his TV mom, Shirley Jones.)

As a music group, The Partridge Family is just another boring bubble gum group from the early 1970s, who may awaken nostalgic memories for some. On the other hand, as a TV show, *The Partridge Family* has not aged well, even recognizing that it was aimed primarily at kids. The problem is that the kids are too cute. Real-life kids can certainly relate to the idea of average suburban children suddenly becoming rock stars, but they won't believe the very nice behavior of the Partridge kids most of the time. Also, the "hippie" flavor of the late 1960s permeates the show (like in the family's painted bus) and seems odd and quaint now.

A much more satisfying view of the same era and somewhat the same concept can be found in *The Monkees*, which is also total fluff but more fun. *The Partridge Family* is worth watching for a few episodes just to see heartthrob Cassidy at his peak and to see budding beauty Susan Dey, who plays Laurie, the eldest daughter. She went on to play yuppie legal whiz Grace Van Owen in *L. A. Law*.

For true yucks, catch an episode of *Partridge Family: 2200 A. D.*, a 1974 cartoon show based on the hit sitcom, where the Partridge clan tours outer space. Most of the original actors (though not David Cassidy) provide the voices.

**PASSPORT TO DANGER** (*) **30 min (39ep B&W; 1954–1956 Syndication) Adventure** *with Cesar Romero as Steve McQuinn*

Cesar Romero, one of Hollywood's Latin lovers of the 1930s and 1940s, waltzes his way through this routine series. As a diplomatic courier for the U.S. government, he always becomes involved in some international intrigue. The strangest thing is that Romero, so obviously Latin in nature, plays a character named McQuinn.

**THE PATTY DUKE SHOW** (***) **30 min (104ep B&W; 1963–1966 ABC) Situation Comedy** *with Patty Duke as Patty Lane and Cathy Lane, William Schallert as Martin Lane, Jean Byron as Natalie Lane, Paul O'Keefe as Ross Lane, Eddie Applegate as Richard Harrison, David Doyle as Jonathan Harrison, Skip Hinnant as Ted Brownley, and Rita McLaughlin as the double for Patty/Cathy Lane*

Identical teenage cousins. On the one hand, there's Cathy, a warm, soft-spoken, well-bred European teenager. And then there's her cousin Patty, an outgoing all-American girl, who loves rock'n'roll, slumber parties, and malt shops. One day they find themselves living under the same roof, as Cathy's dad (a foreign correspondent) sends her to the United States to finish her high school education while he travels through Europe.

Soon after Cathy arrives at the Brooklyn Heights home of Patty's family, the two girls look closely at each other, fascinated by their mutual resemblance. (They're practically identical twins.) They stand face-to-face, as if they were both staring at a mirror, and work to develop the ability to mimic each other's mannerisms. As a pair of high school teens, they just can't resist the opportunities that these similarities offer them. So, despite the exasperated reaction of Patty's parents (and their friends), the two girls often switch roles—or find themselves unintentionally confused with each other.

It's a cute hook that allows for plenty of standard mistaken identity situations, as well as moments of unintended honesty, especially when other characters think they're talking to Cathy rather than Patty, or vice versa. The two cousins also end up serving as reassuring advisors to each other, like two sides of the same personality. Through it all, Patty Duke does an amazingly disciplined piece of acting, infusing the two characters with such distinctive personalities that you almost forget they're both played by the same person. Before long (if you're not careful) you'll start to wonder why the producers bothered to use an obvious stand-in for some scenes with the two girls together!

Appropriately, in the world of TV reruns, there's also a sense of déjà vu to a few other characters, including the father of Patty's boyfriend (who later played John Bosley, the male detective on *Charlie's Angels*), and Patty's parents (who for years played teachers on *Dobie Gillis*). And, of course, series creator Sidney Sheldon is a familiar name to fans of steamy novels turned into steamy TV movies (such as *Rage of Angels*).

Perhaps the biggest surprise of *The Patty Duke Show* is that the stories are very good, with family complications that would have played well even without the look-alike gimmick. It's a durable domestic suburban comedy providing a taste of mainstream teen life in the mid-1960s, down to the hip lingo. And add ten points to your "with-it" score if you can place the theme song reference to a "Ballet Russe."

**THE PAUL HARTMAN SHOW** **(see *Pride of the Family*)**

**THE PAUL HOGAN SHOW** (**½) **30 min (26ep Color; 1981 Australia Nine Network) Comedy-Variety** *with Paul Hogan, Delvene Delaney, John Cornell, Roger Stephen, Graham Mathrick, and Marion Edward*

Paul Hogan, who became known in the United States for appearing in tourist ads for his native Australia and then as the star of the 1986 film *"Crocodile" Dundee*, was already a big comedy hit in his homeland before we got to know him. This Australian series has some of the flavor of *Monty Python's Flying Circus* and *The Benny Hill Show* in its fast-paced, irreverent humor. The "Oz" accent may be a bit thick at times, and some of the references to people and places may not ring a bell, but the show and the star are funny.

**THE PAUL LYNDE SHOW** (*½) **30 min (26ep Color; 1972–1973 ABC) Situation Comedy** *with Paul Lynde as Paul Simms, Elizabeth Allen as Martha Simms, Jane Actman as Barbara Simms Dickerson, John Calvin as Howie Dickerson, Pamelyn Ferdin as Sally Simms, Jerry Stiller as Barney Dickerson, and Anne Meara as Grace Dickerson*

Paul Lynde was a very funny man who talked with a very affected manner and was very good at quips, put-downs, and acting angry. He was great in secondary roles (the play and film *Bye Bye Birdie*, the TV show *Bewitched*, where he played Samantha's Uncle Arthur, and the TV game show *Hollywood Squares*), but he never succeeded as the star of his own series.

*The Paul Lynde Show* is the first of Lynde's two failures as a headliner (*Temperatures Rising* being the second). Lynde plays Paul Simms, a high-strung (what else?) lawyer. His life is disrupted by the marriage of his daughter to Howie Dickerson, a certifiable genius who is a pain in the neck and can't hold a job. The newlyweds live with the Simms and Howie's annoyance of Paul is the prime source of laughs.

The restrictive concept of this show acts as a straightjacket to Lynde's ability. He has flashes of brilliance, but mostly he seems muted and trapped inside a silly sitcom.

**THE PAUL SAND SHOW/PAUL SAND IN FRIENDS AND LOVERS** (***) **30 min (15ep Color; 1974–1975 CBS) Situation Comedy** *with Paul Sand as Robert Dreyfuss, Steve Landesberg as Fred Myerback, Penny Marshall as Janice Dreyfuss, Michael Pataki as Charlie Dreyfuss, Dick Wesson as Jack Reardon, Craig Richard Nelson as Mason Woodruff, Jan Miner as Marge Dreyfuss, and Jack Gilford as Ben Dreyfuss*

Created by James L. Brooks and Allan Burns, the

team responsible for *The Mary Tyler Moore Show*, this is a sleeper of a short-run series with a particularly good cast and an unusual setting. Paul Sand (who played an IRS auditor on an episode of *Mary Tyler Moore*) is a soft-spoken young bachelor named Robert Dreyfuss, a bass violinist with the Boston Symphony Orchestra. It's sort of a male Mary Richards role, with Robert being even more of an incurable romantic than Mary. His brother Charlie is just the opposite—loud, aggressive, and very married (Penny Marshall plays Charlie's wife, just a year away from her Laverne DeFazio role). At work, Robert gets helpful support and advice from his friend Fred (Steve Landesberg, later Dietrich on *Barney Miller*), especially as they both try to deal with their manager, Jack Reardon (played by veteran writer and performer Dick Wesson, Rollo on *The People's Choice*). Naturally this should be a key part of an all-Boston network, slotted alongside *Cheers, Beacon Hill, Banacek,* and *Spenser: For Hire.*

The series was originally called *Paul Sand in Friends and Lovers*, sometimes just *Friends and Lovers*, and finally *The Paul Sand Show.*

**PEARL (**) (6hr miniseries Color; 1978 ABC) Drama** *with Angie Dickinson as Midge Forrest, Robert Wagner as Capt. Cal Lanford, Dennis Weaver as Col. Jason Forrest, Lesley Ann Warren as Dr. Karel Lang, Gregg Henry as Lt. Doug North, and Joseph Campanella as narrator*

Here's another trek through the lives and loves of American military personnel in Pearl Harbor during the days just before the Japanese attack of December 7, 1941. You'd have thought that *From Here to Eternity* (the book, film, miniseries, and TV series) would have covered all the bases on this topic. Sterling Siliphant, screenwriter of *In the Heat of the Night, The Towering Inferno, Naked City,* and *Route 66*, does a good job as producer here, and there are plenty of top-name actors and actresses, but the story is nothing new.

**THE PEARL BAILEY SHOW (**) 60 min (13ep Color; 1971 ABC) Musical-Variety** *with Pearl Bailey*

Pearl Bailey, an outspoken, fun-loving jazz singer, hosts her one big try at TV stardom. It's an hour variety show with Louis Bellson (her hsuband) and his orchestra providing the music.

**PECK'S BAD GIRL (**) 30 min (39ep B&W; 1959 CBS) Situation Comedy** *with Wendell Corey as Steve Peck, Marsha Hunt as Jennifer Peck, Patty McCormack as Torey Peck, and Ray Ferrell as Roger Peck*

The progenitor of this program was a series of films in the 1920s and 1930s called *Peck's Bad Boy*. The films starred a pair of child stars, first Jackie Coogan (Uncle Fester on *The Addams Family*) and then Jackie Cooper (*The People's Choice, Hennesey*) as mischievous young boys who terrorized parents and family. *Peck's Bad Girl* is a late 1950s attempt to revive the concept, with a young girl instead.

Patty McCormack, the child star of the mid-1950s play and film *The Bad Seed* (where she played a murderer), is twelve-year-old Torey Peck. A tomboy approaching puberty, Torey's antics (none of which involve murder, thank goodness) keep her folks on their toes. This series is one of the earlier productions by Norman Felton, who later made a name for himself with dramas and adventures (*Dr. Kildare, The Man from U.N.C.L.E.*).

**PENMARRIC (**) 60 min (12ep Color; 1979 UK BBC) Drama** *with Angela Scoular as Maud Castallack, Paul Spurrier and John Castle as Mark Penmar, and Shaughan Seymour as Giles Penmar*

The British invented the generational family TV drama, and they can knock off competent versions without much effort. *Penmarric* is an example of this talent, as it follows the Penmar family in the mining region of England from the mid-1800s to the start of World War II. The title is the name of the ancient Penmar estate in the area.

**PENNIES FROM HEAVEN (***½) 90 min (6ep Color; 1978 UK BBC) Musical Drama** *with Bob Hoskins as Arthur Parker, Cheryl Campbell as Eileen, Gemma Craven as Joan Parker, Kenneth Colley as The Accordian Man, Freddie Jones as the Headmaster, Hywel Bennett as Tom, and Dave King as the Inspector*

Steve Martin was so taken with this 1978 British musical drama miniseries that he jumped at the chance to star in the 1981 theatrical feature film version. While that is a superb (if sadly overlooked) production with a substantial budget for some major set pieces, the original BBC presentation is also definitely worth searching out. The story line and premise are essentially the same in either case (series creator Dennis Potter did the scripts for both), following the increasingly sad and frustrating life of song salesman Arthur Parker.

It's the 1930s Depression and Arthur makes his meager living as a sheet music salesman and song plugger. Only he really, really loves the songs and wishes that he could find a place where somehow, somewhere the happy sentiments of his favorite tunes were real. In the meantime, he looks for (and finds) love on the road. But Arthur's already a married man, and soon he discovers once again that, unlike those sweet soaring melodies, the day-to-day world holds plenty of grim surprises.

This story is intense, well written by Dennis Potter, capturing the gritty feel of the era and the pain of an unhappy marriage. But Potter's real innovation is in how the characters do the musical numbers. Taking the traditional movie musical approach of people breaking into song for no good reason, he goes one step further and has the performers sing and dance to the music of the times, but mouthing the original recordings, not singing themselves. If only for a few moments, Arthur's fantasy becomes reality as everything stops when the popular songs he loves so much begin to play.

Potter is one of British television's most creative writers, also turning out such material as the 1986 serial *The Singing Detective* and the adaptation script for *The Mayor of Casterbridge*.

**PEOPLE ARE FUNNY (*½) 30 min (259ep: 246 B&W & 13 Color; 1954–1961 & 1984 NBC) Comedy** *with Art Linkletter and Flip Wilson as host*

Art Linkletter, classic quiz and game show master of ceremonies of the 1950s, hosts the 246 black and white episodes (only 150 of which are presently syndicated) of this funny yet somehow demeaning show. In *People Are Funny*, the contestants are asked to perform crazy antics (water and pie throwing is a common theme) in order to win money and prizes. The brief 1984 revival of the show (in color) features black comic Flip Wilson as host, with all the stunts taking place on the streets of Los Angeles.

**THE PEOPLE'S CHOICE (***) 30 min (104ep B&W; 1955–1958 NBC) Situation Comedy** *with Jackie Cooper as Socrates "Sock" Miller, Pat Breslin as Amanda "Mandy" Peoples Miller, Margaret Irving as Augusta "Gus" Miller, Paul Maxey as Mayor John Peoples, and Mary Jane Croft as the voice of Cleo*

*The People's Choice* is a delightful, mostly forgotten vehicle for former child star Jackie Cooper. Along with *Burns & Allen*, it is one of two 1950s sitcoms that feature one of the main characters talking to the home audience with none of the other characters knowing. In *The People's Choice*, the viewers are addressed by Cleo, a basset hound owned by ornithologist Sock Miller. Elected to the City Council of New City while he attends law school, Sock begins wooing Mandy Peoples, the cute daughter of the mayor, his political opponent.

The focus on young adults with real jobs, a light touch on the scripts, and the whimsical side comments of the talking dog make *The People's Choice* one of the more intelligent sitcoms of its day. Unfortunately the show starts sliding downhill in the third and last season, when Sock and Mandy (secretly married at the end of the second season) publicly announce their wedding and Sock changes jobs. He and Mandy move to a new housing development, where he starts selling homes, the angry father-in-law virtually disappears, and *The People's Choice* starts to look like just another suburban 1950s sitcom with a happy husband and wife.

**PERE GORIOT (*½) 60 min (4ep Color; 1971 UK BBC) Drama** *with Michael Goodliffe as Pere Goriot, Andrew Keir as Vautrin, David Dundas as Eugene de Rastignac, June Ritchie as Delphine, Anna Cropper as Victorine, Angela Browne as Anastasie, and Moira Redmond as Mme. de Beauseant*

Pere Goriot is a man obsessed with keeping up appearances. Once rich, he continues to squander what little wealth he still has on trying to buy a spot in "proper society" for his two ungrateful daughters. The result is round after round of deception, eventually leading to adultery, bankruptcy, and murder. This tale of misplaced family ambitions is adapted from a novel by Honore de Balzac, who approached such subjects with a strong sense of moral certainty and candor. The result, quite frankly, is a story filled with pretty dreadful people driven by ambition, greed, and money. They almost deserve everything that happens to them, which is probably the only way to view and enjoy this series.

In 1976, David Dundas (who plays de Rastignac here) hit the U.S. charts with the offbeat single "Jeans On," reaching the top twenty.

**A PERFECT SPY (***) 60 min (7ep Color; 1988 UK BBC) Spy Drama** *with Peter Egan, Benedict Taylor, and Nicholas and Jonathan Haley as Magnus Pym, Ray McAnally as Rick Pym, Rudiger Weigang as Axel, Alan Howard as Jack Brotherhood, and Jane Booker as Mary Pym*

John LeCarre's somewhat confusing semiautobiographical novel about an English spy is turned into a fascinating short TV series by the simple expedient of rearranging the story to follow chronological order.

Magnus Pym is a perfect spy because he has mastered the art of deception. Learned from his con-man father Rick, deception becomes Magnus' way of life as he grows up and enters the British spy network. The only person with whom Magnus ever establishes an honest relationship is a Czechoslovakian communist counterpart, Axel. The two spies secretly exchange information with each other, which results in both being promoted over and over again, due to the impressive trove of material they have brought in from the "other side." This clandestine double-agent work eventually causes Magnus' downfall.

While ostensibly about spies, *A Perfect Spy* is much more concerned with the emotional development of Magnus and his lust for deception than the usual hokuspokus of espionage work. The elder Pym is a fascinating character, a complete charlatan that neither Magnus nor the viewer can entirely dismiss.

The adaptation of LeCarre's novel was performed by Arthur Hopcraft, who served the same function for another British video version of a LeCarre spy novel, *Tinker, Tailor, Soldier, Spy.*

**PERFECT STRANGERS (**½) 30 min (72ep at Fall 1989 Color; 1986– ABC) Situation Comedy** *with Bronson Pinchot as Balki Bartokomous, Mark Linn-Baker as Larry Appleton, Ernie Sabella as Donald "Twinkie" Twinkacetti, Lise Cutter as Susan Campbell, Belita Moreno as Edwina Twinkacetti and Lydia Markham, Rebeca Arthur as Mary Anne, Melanie Wilson as Jennifer, and Jo Marie Payton-France as Harriette Winslow*

In the late 1970s, the weirdest character in a hit sitcom was Latka Gravas, the funny-talking immigrant on *Taxi*, played by the late, great Andy Kaufman. In the late 1980s, the weirdest character in a hit sitcom was Balki Bartokomous, played by Bronson Pinchot. Both Latka and Balki come from indeterminate eastern European countries, have thick and funny accents, and use their naivete about American culture to make humorous cracks. In *Taxi*, Latka was only a second banana. In *Perfect Strangers*, Balki is co-star, the funny man to straight man Mark Linn-Baker's Larry Appleton character. Balki is the ultra-distant cousin of Appleton, a mostly normal all-American nebbish living in Chicago who suddenly has this weird-talking relation move in. Together the two relatives who have never met before (hence the title) form a funny duo who bounce good lines off each other in a highly professional manner.

Balki's rose-colored view of the United States as a land where everyone can become a millionaire overnight is infectious. Unfortunately the secondary characters and the plots never seem to match the dynamism of the Balki–Larry relationship, but *Perfect Strangers* is worth watching, if for no other reason than to see Balki grin and say "Don' be ridikalus!"

## THE PERRY COMO SHOW (**½) 60 min (B&W and Color; 1955–1963 NBC) Musical-Variety *with Perry Como*

One of the most popular singers of the 1940s and 1950s, Perry Como hosts eight strong years of classic musical variety on TV. The ultra-relaxed Mr. C is always joined by top-name guests. For the final two years, the show is titled *The Kraft Music Hall*, a name used on a number of other series. ■

## PERRY MASON (***½) 60 min (271ep B&W; 1957–1966 CBS) and 2 hr (10ep at Fall 1989 Color; 1985– NBC) Murder Mystery *with Raymond Burr as Perry Mason, William Talman as Hamilton Burger, Barbara Hale as Della Street, William Hopper as Paul Drake, Ray Collins as Lt. Arthur Tragg, and William Katt as Paul Drake, Jr.*

This is formula TV at its best, with virtually every story unfolding in the same well-oiled fashion: Someone comes to Perry Mason for legal advice. Mason begins work on the case, but by the halfway point of the episode there's a much bigger concern: murder. So the scene shifts to the courtroom where Perry stands as the last hope to a client charged with the killing.

In court, he carefully questions each witness while deftly outmaneuvering prosecuting attorney Hamilton Burger. To clinch the case, Perry will reveal some important new piece of evidence (often brought in at the last moment by investigator Paul Drake) that inevitably forces the guilty party to publicly confess. Afterward he ties up the loose ends at the office and answers any remaining questions about the case with Paul and secretary Della Street.

It's a deceptively simple setup that works for several reasons. First, the main cast of regulars is excellent, with Raymond Burr and William Talman particularly effective as courtroom adversaries. In fact, unless you really care about the specific details of each case (trying to solve the murder mysteries before Mason does), you can often safely skip the first part of the show and just come in for the court scenes. They're great theater.

When Burr's Mason takes center stage, it's a virtuoso performance. He mixes genuine concern, reassurance, and curiosity with well-timed anger, sarcasm, and outright brow-beating. It reaches a crescendo as Mason hammers away at the inconsistencies of the final witnesses, peppering them with rhetorical questions they don't even have time to answer. ("Isn't it true you then entered the house? Isn't it true you fired the gun? Isn't it all true?") Sometimes the person on the stand isn't the guilty party, but a confession comes anyway—from someone else sitting in the courtroom.

Maybe that's why Perry gets away with as much as he does in court, and why the prosecution ultimately can't be too annoyed with him. After all, he goes well beyond his duty as defense attorney. Rather than just demonstrating reasonable doubt that his client is the guilty one, Perry also finds out who is guilty. So while Burger may be "zero for whatever" against Mason, he's probably batting a thousand against the guilty parties that Perry uncovers.

From its original nine-year run through two decades of reruns, *Perry Mason* became the definitive lawyer series, in the process setting the standards for the general public's perception of the law, courtroom behavior, and the pursuit of justice. It wasn't until *L. A. Law* in the 1980s that another series even came close to its influence.

By then, Burr had dusted off the character again for a series of occasional two-hour TV movie episodes. These begin with *Perry Mason Returns*, in which Mason resigns from his position as a judge. The reason? To return to court as a defense lawyer on behalf of Della, who faces a murder charge. By the end of the first revival story Perry decides to resume his practice, with Della at his side. They're joined by the son of Paul Drake (played by Barbara Hale's real life son, William Katt), who wants to follow in his late father's footsteps. David Ogden Stiers often appears as prosecuting attorney Michael Reston.

For these new tales there are no substantial changes to the old formula, except that with two hours to fill, viewers get to see a lot more of the investigative legwork. In the first new story we even find out what's on one of those documents Paul Drake typically rushes in with at the last moment.

## PERRY MASON, THE NEW ADVENTURES OF (zero) 60 min (15ep Color; 1973–1974 CBS) Murder Mystery *with Monte Markham as Perry Mason, Harry*

*Guardino as Hamilton Burger, Sharon Acker as Della Street, Albert Stratton as Paul Drake, and Dane Clark as Lt. Arthur Tragg*

There's absolutely nothing wrong with another crew taking a shot at the legend of Perry Mason. After all, Raymond Burr's own portrayal of the title character actually represented a departure from both the original Erle Stanley Gardner novels and a successful radio series from the 1940s (in which Mason came off as far more irresponsible and short tempered).

Still, if you're going to tread on sacred ground, you'd better have your vision of things down cold. Unfortunately, no one here does, especially the production team. They can't seem to decide just what to do with this new version of Mason, other than setting the action in more modern courtrooms (carpeted, cold, and sterile) and avoiding the familiar ritual story formula of the previous series. The result is an unfocused mess with stories so confusing that in the first one ("The Case of the Horoscope Homicide") even Mason looks surprised at the climactic witness stand confession he elicits. Like the audience, he's probably trying to remember how this repentant character fits into the threadbare plot in the first place!

Though the performers struggle mightily, it never gets much better.

**PERSON TO PERSON (**½) (B&W; 1953–1961 CBS) Interview** *with Edward R. Murrow and Charles Collingwood as host*

Edward R. Murrow is frequently invoked as the man who set the standards for TV journalism back in the 1950s. This series, also from that era, is a reminder that celebrity interviews were also part and parcel of the package back then, too. Don't look for any hardball *Nightline* style confrontations here—the conversations are quite deferential, though there's a nice variety of personalities involved (ranging from Groucho and Harpo Marx to Senator John F. Kennedy and wife Jacqueline).

Though the program originally ran for more than half a decade (with Charles Collingwood taking over for Murrow for the last two years), only a relative handful of episodes turn up these days, mostly as part of a syndication package prepared for PBS in the late 1970s. ■

**THE PERSUADERS (**½) 60 min (24ep Color; 1971–1972 ABC) Adventure** *with Roger Moore as Lord Brett Sinclair, Tony Curtis as Danny Wilde, and Laurence Naismith as Judge Fulton*

Roger Moore and Tony Curtis play two wealthy adventurers with roots on opposite sides of the tracks. Moore's Sinclair is strictly old money, a British Lord with impeccable taste. Curtis's Danny Wilde is a self-made millionaire from New York, still somewhat rough around the edges.

A retired judge convinces them to use their idle hours to right wrongs that he happens to know about. Since these cases usually involve travel to some of Europe's most romantic spots, the two playboys agree to work together as a sort of international odd couple. It's a light international romp, complete with the usual exotic locales and appropriate John Barry music. ■

**PETE AND GLADYS (**½) 30 min (72ep B&W; 1960–1962 CBS) Situation Comedy** *with Harry Morgan as Pete Porter, Cara Williams as Gladys Porter, Verna Felton as Hilda Crocker, and Gale Gordon as Paul Porter*

Famed as one of the first spin-off series in TV history, *Pete and Gladys* evolved out of Harry Morgan's Pete Porter character from *December Bride*. In that series, Pete was the next door neighbor who always popped over to complain about his (never seen) wife Gladys and the silly things she did. In *Pete and Gladys*, Pete Porter gets center stage and wife Gladys is finally seen, in the person of Cara Williams. It turns out that Gladys is yet one more daffy, addle-brained, TV sitcom housewife, 1950s style.

The most intriguing aspect today about *Pete and Gladys* is the sarcastic nature of the Porters' relationship. Most of the wacky wives of the 1950s (e.g., Lucy Ricardo of *I Love Lucy*) had husbands who just grinned and beared it. Not Pete Porter. He's quite willing to make cutting little cracks to and about Gladys. It is also great to see Harry Morgan, who is forever playing very bland or very nice guys (Bill Gannon in *Dragnet*, Col. Potter in *M*A*S*H*), playing a fellow with a little more backbone, a little more bite.

**PETE KELLY'S BLUES (**½) 30 min (13ep B&W; 1959 NBC) Crime Drama** *with William Reynolds as Pete Kelly, Connee Boswell as Savannah Brown, Than Wyenn as George Lupo, and Phil Gordon as Fred*

*Pete Kelly's Blues* is one of the few innovative and eclectic series produced by Jack Webb, a man better known for his cold, formula cop shows (such as *Dragnet*).

Set in a Kansas City speakeasy of the 1920s, the show focuses on Pete Kelly, jazz cornet player and leader of the house band. Kelly always gets involved in some sort of criminal investigation, or helps out some poor soul in need of a hand.

Webb, a longtime jazz fan, played Pete Kelly in a 1951 radio version of the show, and also directed and starred in a 1955 film that led directly to the TV series. It's hard to imagine *Dragnet*'s Sgt. Joe Friday tapping his toes and saying "Go, man, go!" to some trumpet player, so maybe it's for the best that Webb stays behind the camera here.

**PETER GUNN (***) 30 min (114ep B&W & 2 hr Color sequel; 1958–1961 NBC & ABC) Detective Drama** *with Craig Stevens as Peter Gunn, Lola Albright as Edie Hart, Herschel Bernardi as Lt. Jacoby, and Hope Emerson and Minerva Urecal as Mother*

Every crime fighter on TV who hits it big must have an angle, a catch, a hook to corral viewers. For Peter Gunn, it is cool jazz. Gunn, an early version of the tough, macho private eye with sensitive feelings, inhabits the dark "film noir" world of Los Angeles previously inhabited by Philip Marlowe. Gunn hangs out at "Mother's," an out-of-the-way jazz nightclub where Edie, his girlfriend, sings. Henry Mancini's low-key bluesy jazz background music permeates the show and adds to the wistful mood generated by Gunn's cynical attitude towards life, his clients and the hope for any real justice in this imperfect world.

For modern viewers, Craig Stevens may seem an odd choice to play Gunn. He is much too clean-cut and middle America for the tawdry world of L.A. crime we see on shows set in the same era, such as *Private Eye*. To fit into the modern view, Stevens would need about two days growth of stubble and a dangling cigarette. However, in the 1950s (when *Peter Gunn* was produced) well-scrubbed WASPy leading men were *de rigueur*. Herschel Bernardi (as Gunn's police contact, Lt. Jacobi) is an interesting choice to represent the law, since Bernardi is far more ethnic than most 1950s TV types, especially policemen. Perhaps the show would seem more current if Bernardi played the private eye and Stevens played the cop. If so, the series would have to relocate to Brooklyn.

As it is, *Peter Gunn* is certainly a show to catch. The characters are fascinatingly quirky (at least by 1950s standards), the mood is catchy, and the plots well-written.

Along with all the low-down seriousness of *Peter Gunn*, there are frequent flashes of levity (Gunn is usually good for a few sly cracks each episode). Still, even with the humorous touches, it is surprising to discover that the show's producer is Blake Edwards, who went on to greater fame producing broadly humorous films such as the Pink Panther series starring Peter Sellers. Edwards and Mancini evidently stayed friends, since the famous Pink Panther theme is another Henry Mancini creation.

After becoming famous as a film director, Edwards tried to revive the *Peter Gunn* concept in the 1967 movie *Gunn* (with Mancini again providing the music). Stevens reprises his title role, but Ed Asner stands in for Bernardi and seems miscast in the role. Far more violent than the TV series, *Gunn* can be freely ignored. In 1989, Edwards and Mancini teamed up once more to revive the Peter Gunn character, this time in a made-for-TV movie sequel (titled *Peter Gunn*) set in 1964. Peter Strauss (*Rich Man, Poor Man*) takes over the role of Gunn, while Barbara Williams plays Edie, Peter Jurasik (Sid the Snitch on *Hill Street Blues*) is Lt. Jacoby, and Pearl Bailey portrays "Mother."

**PETER LOVES MARY (**) 30 min (32ep B&W; 1960–1961 NBC) Situation Comedy** *with Peter Lind Hayes as Peter Lindsey, Mary Healy as Mary Lindsey, Bea Benaderet as Wilma, and Alan Reed as Happy Richman*

The misadventures of a married couple trying to balance their Broadway careers with domestic responsibilities at home in Connecticut. The result is just average, which is disappointing considering that the leads were almost tailor-made for the setup—not only were Peter Lind Hayes and Mary Healy married in real life but they had also performed together on television throughout the 1950s, usually in light talk or comedy-variety series.

But there is one prime reason to catch an episode of the series: to see Alan Reed, the original voice of Fred Flintstone, alongside Bea Benaderet, the original voice of Betty Rubble.

**PETER THE GREAT (**½) (8hr miniseries Color; 1985 NBC) Drama** *with Maximilian Schell, Graham McGrath, Jan Niklas, and Denis DeMarne as Peter, Vanessa Redgrave as Sophia, Laurence Olivier as King William III, Omar Sharif as Prince Feodor Romodanovsky, Trevor Howard as Sir Isaac Newton, Elke Sommer as Charlotte, Mel Ferrer as Frederick, and Helmut Griem as Alexander Menshikov*

Robert K. Massie's Pulitzer Prize–winning biography of the Russian czar who brought his country, kicking and screaming, into Western civilization, is turned into a lengthy and ambitious TV miniseries. Production problems plagued this epic, but the result is commendable. On-location scenery in Russia adds to the believability. The classy cast is impressive, with Vanessa Redgrave being a stand-out as Peter's sister Sophia.

**PETROCELLI (**½) 60 min (48ep & 90 min pilot Color; 1974–1976 NBC) Law Drama** *with Barry Newman as Tony Petrocelli, Susan Howard as Maggie Petrocelli, and Albert Salmi as Pete Ritter*

Typical of the mid-1970s tendency toward gimmicky outsiders, *Petrocelli* features Barry Newman as Tony Petrocelli, a Harvard-educated defense lawyer living and working in the small southwestern town of San Remo, far from the uptight pressures of city life. Tony and his wife even live in a camper trailer and use a real cowboy to handle the investigative legwork on the cases.

There are distinctive touches in the program, most notably the clever use of flashbacks that may or may not accurately reflect what really happened at the time of a murder. This technique harkens back to the roots of the series: the 1970 theatrical film *The Lawyer*, directed by Sidney J. Furie (co-creator of the series) and also featuring Newman.

**PETTICOAT JUNCTION (**) 30 min (212ep: 64 B&W & 148 Color; 1963–1970 CBS) Situation Comedy** *with Bea Benaderet as Kate Bradley, Edgar Buchanan as Uncle Joe Carson, Linda Kaye Henning as Betty Jo Bradley Elliott, Jeannine Riley and Gunilla Hutton and Meredith MacRae as Billie Jo Bradley, Pat Woodell* *and Lori Saunders as Bobbie Jo Bradley, Smiley Burnette as Charlie Pratt, Rufe Davis as Floyd Smoot, Charles Lane as Homer Bedloe, Mike Minor as Steve Elliott, June Lockhart as Dr. Janet Craig, and Frank Cady as Sam Drucker*

The middle entry in producer Paul Henning's hit rural sitcom hat trick of the 1960s. At first, this was planned as a direct spin-off from *The Beverly Hillbillies* original, returning to the hills with Bea Benaderet as Jethro's mother, Pearl (a character that had already appeared in the Clampetts' own series). But instead Benaderet stepped sideways into a different (but similar) role, that of Kate Bradley, owner of the Shady Rest hotel in the backwoods town of Hooterville. In either case, this top-billing status was quite a change for Benaderet after life as a talented second banana (most notably as next-door neighbor Blanche to George Burns and Gracie Allen, and as the voice of Betty Rubble on *The Flintstones*).

This is laid-back rural life. People hang around Kate's hotel, Sam Drucker's general store, and, of course, the train station where the single-engine, steam-driven Hooterville Cannonball (operated by Floyd and Charlie) comes rolling in. Kate's daughters (Billie Jo, Betty Jo, and Bobbie Jo) use the nearby water tower as a perfect spot for skinny dipping (just during the opening credits, hanging their petticoats over the side as the train rolls in, apparently to explain the program's otherwise obtuse title). Uncle Joe spends most of his time sitting on the porch, avoiding work and hatching unsuccessful money-making schemes. The only major complications are from the outside world, when city types show up—like Homer Bedloe, a vice-president at the C. F. & W. Railroad (owner of the Cannonball), who has this strange notion that such a nonprofitable line should be shut down. Otherwise there are minor spats between characters, but nothing very exciting.

Which may be why *Petticoat Junction* seems like such an oddity these days in reruns. Unlike Paul Henning's next entry, *Green Acres*, which used the same town setting for some truly bizzare humor, *Petticoat Junction* does not wear as well today. Life in this program moves way too slowly and respectably, coming off less as a comedy than as a warm family soap opera with a few safe sitcom complications. The main continuing theme seems to be finding husbands for Billie Jo, Betty Jo, and Bobby Jo. In the end, only Betty Jo (played by producer Paul Henning's daughter) lands a mate (pilot Steve Elliott), though that may be partially due to the slight but disconcerting physical changes her sisters experience over the years (as five different performers play the two roles). Otherwise, Uncle Joe's antics and the very minor in-town character conflicts are downright dull. Ironically the funniest episodes of *Petticoat Junction* are those featuring crossover character appearances from Henning's other series: Oliver and Lisa Douglas (Eddie Albert and Eva Gabor) from *Green Acres* and, occasionally, members of the Clampett clan from *The Beverly Hillbillies.*

Still, *Petticoat Junction* might play a little better if all the episodes were in the syndication package. Instead the first two black and white seasons are not available, even though those are the stories that come off freshest in both the characters and the tone. Worse yet, that eliminates nearly half of Bea Benaderet's time on the series, and she's the most important and entertaining member of the Bradley family—the real source of believable homespun wisdom and guidance. For instance, when Kate is asked by a food executive to set up a kitchen to mass produce one of her hometown recipes, she and her sponsor discover that there are some things you just can't get into assembly line cooking, like individual enthusiasm and love. It's a lesson that could have come right out of Aunt Bee's kitchen on *The Andy Griffith Show*. Unfortunately, Bea Benaderet passed away as production began for the program's sixth season (she had also been absent due to illness in previous years), leaving the series without its bedrock character. June Lockhart came in as a new mature figure (playing a doctor), but it wasn't the same.

Though it was a big hit in its time, today *Petticoat Junction* is best taken in small doses. But you do have to watch it at least once because it has a great theme song just like the other two Paul Henning hits.

**PEYTON PLACE (***) 30 min (514ep: 267 B&W & 247 Color & two 2 hr sequels; 1964–1969 ABC) Serial Drama** *with Dorothy Malone as Constance Mackenzie Carson, Mia Farrow as Allison Mackenzie Harrington, Ed Nelson as Dr. Michael Rossi, Warner Anderson as Matthew Swain, Paul Langton as Leslie Harrington, Ryan O'Neal as Rodney Harrington, Barbara Parkins as Betty Anderson Harrington, Christopher Connelly as Norman Harrington, Kasey Rogers as Julie Anderson, and James Douglas as Steven Cord*

Before *Dallas*, before *Dynasty*, before any of the famous prime-time soap operas, there was *Peyton Place*. Designed much more like a traditional daytime soap opera than its later progeny, *Peyton Place* is pure mid-1960s kitsch. It has all the Victorian ultra-repressed sexual tension that the swinging sixties brought into the open.

Sex oozes, drips, secretes, and flows out of every aspect of *Peyton Place*. If it's not illicit sex from the deep dark past, it's extramarital sex in the present, or premarital sex among the rebellious youth. Everybody is somebody's bastard child, and everybody, no matter how pure they seem on the surface, is hiding some awful secret (often so secret, the person involved doesn't even know).

The setting is the small New England town of Peyton Place, setting of Grace Metalious's originally scandalous novel, the 1957 movie with Lana Turner, and the tepid 1961 follow-up film, *Return to Peyton Place*. Amidst the prim and proper Yankee locale, the seething passions of the townsfolk seem all the more shocking.

Today none of the horrible secrets bandied about on *Peyton Place* would even raise an eyebrow among devotees of frank and explicit TV talk shows, so it's almost cute to watch the townsfolk of Peyton Place squirm in order to avoid a hint of revelation.

As with any serial, the tempo in *Peyton Place* can be glacial. On the other hand, change occasionally is shockingly abrupt, as when a major star (such as Mia Farrow) walks from the show after two seasons and her character just vanishes from town without a trace (sort of).

Primary interest for modern viewers, aside from the dated nature of the scandals, is the presence of Mia Farrow and Ryan O'Neal. Farrow, daughter of actress Maureen O'Sullivan, makes her TV debut here. She went on to briefly serve as Mrs. Frank Sinatra before starring in hit films such as *Rosemary's Baby* and *The Great Gatsby*. She then hooked up (romantically) with Woody Allen and appeared in several of his films (*Purple Rose of Cairo, Hannah and Her Sisters*). Ryan O'Neal had already starred in *Empire* before *Peyton Place*, and, like Farrow, he went on to film success (*Love Story, What's Up Doc?,* and *Paper Moon* with his daughter Tatum).

The *Peyton Place* saga continued beyond the 514 episodes of this series. Like the 1957 movie, the TV series spawned a spin-off titled *Return to Peyton Place*, this time an early 1970s daytime soap opera with new actors and actresses filling in for the more famous prime-time cast. In 1977, a TV-movie sequel appeared, *Murder in Peyton Place*, starring old regulars Dorothy Malone and Ed Nelson, among others. The murders (or alleged murders) in question are that of Allison Mackenzie and Rodney Harrington (Farrow and O'Neal's characters). Much less satisfying is the 1985 TV-movie *Peyton Place: The Next Generation*, which also stars Malone, Nelson, and the gang. Everybody is still talking about Allison Mackenzie, now absent almost twenty years. Considering the popularity of the Peyton Place theme, its doubtful we've seen the last of the proper New Englanders who seem to always be in heat.

**THE PHIL SILVERS SHOW (***½) 30 min (138ep B&W; 1955–1959 CBS) Situation Comedy** *with Phil Silvers as Master Sergeant Ernest Bilko, Paul Ford as Col. John Hall, Joe E. Ross as Sgt. Rupert Ritzik, Maurice Gosfield as Pvt. Duane Doberman, Billy Sands as Pvt. Dino Paparelli, Allan Melvin as Cpl. Henshaw, Harvey Lembeck as Cpl. Rocco Barbella, and Herbie Faye as Pvt. Sam Fender*

Fort Baxter, Kansas (and later, Camp Fremont, California) is part of the 1950s peacetime Stateside army, somewhere between World War II and retirement. There's little for the soldiers to do and plenty of time to do it.

It's the perfect setting for the escapades of fast-talking con man Master Sergeant Ernest Bilko. He manages to keep the camp entertained not only with his countless gambling operations but also with dozens of made-to-order schemes designed to deal with any threat to the comfortable routine at the base. Along the way, Bilko organizes wagers on everything from target practice scores to the length of time it'll take him to get rid of a new captain trying to put an end to gambling at the post.

Everyone respects Bilko's unerring instincts, even the camp's nominal commander, Col. Hall. Though Hall spends half his time trying to figure out what must be behind some seemingly innocuous Bilko request, he also knows that the man can be invaluable in a tight bureaucratic spot. As the camp chaplain once noted, "If it's Bilko versus the Pentagon, Washington doesn't stand a chance."

First and foremost, though, Bilko keeps a fatherly eye on the boys in his company (the camp motor pool), especially when they foolishly let someone else con them out of their paychecks. After all, he needs to keep them solvent for his deals. So, naturally, he's quick to hatch a plan to rescue their cash.

Even the colonel benefits from Bilko's intervention. When Hall is thinking of retiring because he's been passed over again for a promotion, Bilko follows him to Washington and deftly arranges for him to play golf with President Eisenhower. Naturally the doors of power then swung open to welcome Hall, who Bilko certainly does not want to see step down. Breaking in a new base commander could take so much time.

So with all that cunning, why isn't Bilko rich and retired? For one thing, he doesn't really need to be. He's a career soldier virtually in charge of his own base. Where else can he sleep till noon, play poker all night, and successfully avoid anything resembling physical labor? He may have been drafted in World War II, but he manages to fulfill every soldier's dream and take control of the army.

That's probably one reason that the premise of *The Phil Silvers Show* wears so well. Rather than coming off as a selfish huckster, the character of Bilko is a champion against the ultimate faceless bureaucracy.

Besides, truth be told, Bilko has not only a soft heart but also a conscience. For instance, when rocker Elvin Pelvin (an Elvis Presley character type) lands in his company, Bilko is determined to surreptitiously tape him singing and sell the recording to the highest bidder. The deal is virtually signed and sealed until Bilko hears the acetate, which contains an original song Elvin wrote and dedicates to his good friends at the platoon. To Bilko, there is no choice. He calls off the deal and smashes the only copy of the disc.

Though *The Phil Silvers Show* was a hard act to follow, many of its alumni went on to other series. Series creator Nat Hiken brought both Joe E. Ross (Sgt. Ritzik) and Beatrice Pons (Mrs. Emma Ritzik) to his New York cop comedy, *Car 54, Where Are You?*—where they once again played husband and wife.

Maurice Gosfield (the tubby Pvt. Doberman) did the voice of Benny the Ball, a Dobermanlike character in the animated *Top Cat* (a sort of "back-alley Bilko"). Billy Sands (Pvt. Paparelli) became Harrison "Tinker" Bell on *McHale's Navy* (a "briny Bilko"). And Allan Melvin (Cpl. Henshaw on Bilko) turned up as Archie Bunker's pal Barney Hefner on *All in the Family*.

Back when *The Phil Silvers Show* first premiered, it was called *You'll Never Get Rich* (a line from the old song "You're in the Army Now"). That title soon dropped by the wayside in favor of *The Phil Silvers Show*, though most people (then and now) usually refer to the series as either "Sgt. Bilko" or just "Bilko."

**PHIL SILVERS SHOW, THE NEW (**) 30 min (30ep Color; 1963–1964 CBS) Situation Comedy** *with Phil Silvers as Harry Grafton, Herbie Faye as Waluska, Stafford Repp as Mr. Brink, Elena Verdugo as Audrey, Sandy Descher as Susan, and Ronnie Dapo as Andy*

Phil Silvers plays fast-talking factory worker (and occasional con man) Harry Grafton. (What a perfect name!) Unfortunately, what had seemed amusing and harmless in the Sgt. Bilko army setting comes off more like petty theft in civilian life. Attention frequently shifts to home escapades, but those lack the satisfying institutional target worthy of Bilko's skills.

**PHILIP MARLOWE (*) 30 min (26ep B&W; 1959–1960 ABC) Detective Drama** *with Philip Carey as Philip Marlowe*

Though sporting a familiar name from novelist Raymond Chandler's pen, this is just a routine crime series setting the character in the present rather than the 1930s, with standard sets, shoot-outs, and solutions. Remember, just because it's in black and white, that doesn't make it authentic. For a better rendition of the character, catch the color 1980s series.

**PHILIP MARLOWE, PRIVATE EYE(***) 60 min (11ep Color; 1983 & 1986 HBO) Detective Drama** *with Powers Boothe as Philip Marlowe and William Kearns as Lt. Violete Magee*

A sparkling homage to the film noir style of the 1940s, this tangy series spruces up Raymond Chandler's familiar Philip Marlowe character. The setting is still Los Angeles in the 1930s, but the sensibilities reek of the 1980s. Powers Boothe excels as the classic sarcastic, suspicious, unsentimental private eye (quite a switch from Boothe's best known previous role, religious cult leader Jim Jones in a 1980 TV-movie). The stories are full of alluring starlets, nasty studio bosses, steamy sex scandals, and lots of sadistic mobsters, all handled with taste, charm, and allure.

The first batch of five episodes are better than the later six, which scrimps on the writing in favor of more titillation. ■

**THE PHOENIX (*) 60 min (5ep & 90 min pilot Color; 1982 ABC) Science Fiction** *with Judson Scott as Bennu of the Golden Light, Richard Lynch as Preminger, and E. G. Marshall as Dr. Ward Frazier*

Bennu is a superpowered ancient astronaut entombed more than one thousand years ago on Earth, but awakened from his golden sarcophagus by archaeologist Ward Frazier. Unfortunately, Bennu is not quite sure why he is on this planet or where his partner Mira might be buried. That's too bad because apparently Mira knows what their mission is.

In the meantime, a government agent named Preminger is intent on using the golden-haired alien for his own nationalist purposes. So while dodging Preminger, Bennu sets out to find Mira, using his special powers to help people in need along the way.

Far too solemn and pretentious for its own good, this series hasn't even attracted a decent cult following.

**PHYL AND MIKHY (*) 30 min (6ep Color; 1980 CBS) Situation Comedy** *with Murphy Cross as Phyllis "Phyl" Wilson, Rick Lohman as Mikhail "Mikhy" Orlov, Larry Haines as Max Wilson, and Michael Pataki as Vladimir Gimenko*

A mirthless time piece of the late detente era of Soviet/American relations, *Phyl and Mikhy* features a handsome Russian track star who defects in order to marry a beautiful American track star. The young couple set up house with her father, who is also her coach. A burly Soviet operative keeps trying to get the Russian to return home.

**PHYLLIS (*½) 30 min (49ep Color; 1975–1977 CBS) Situation Comedy** *with Cloris Leachman as Phyllis Lindstrom, Lisa Gerritsen as Bess Lindstrom, Barbara Colby and Liz Torres as Julie Erskine, Richard Schaal as Leo Heatherton, Jane Rose as Audrey Dexter, Henry Jones as Judge Jonathan Dexter, Judith Lowry as Sally Dexter, and Burt Mustin as Arthur Lanson*

One of the least satisfying spin-offs from *The Mary Tyler Moore Show*, *Phyllis* takes Mary's nosy, self-centered landlady Phyllis, turns her into a widow, and sends her packing to San Francisco to make her way in the world. During the first season, Phyllis works as an assistant to Julie Erskine, a photographer. The second season finds Phyllis as an administrative assistant to some local government agency. In neither role is she very appealing.

The only interesting character here is Sally Dexter ("Mother Dexter"), aged mother of Phyllis's mother-in law's second husband, who is always good for a wisecrack. Mother Dexter marries even older Arthur Lanson near the end of the series.

**THE PHYLLIS DILLER SHOW** **(see *The Pruitts of Southampton*)**

**PICTURES** (**) **60 min (7ep Color; 1983 UK Central) Comedy-Drama** *with Peter McEnery as Bill Trench, Harry Towb as Ziggy, Wendy Morgan as Ruby L. Sears, Anton Rodgers as Forbes Lawson, Annette Badland as Vera, and Malcolm Jamieson as Graham*

For his thematic successor to *Flickers*, writer Roy Clarke kicks the action into the British cinema world of the 1920s. There's a full lineup of familiar character types, including Ruby, the zany would-be actress schooled on fan magazines and looking for her cinema entree; Bill, the talented young script writer looking for a major studio break; Forbes Lawson, a fading John Barrymore-type actor with a weakness for demon rum; Ziggy, a stereotypical deal-making go-go-go producer; Graham, professional gigolo and seducer of Ruby; and Vera, roommate to Ruby and Forbes.

Unfortunately, compared to *Flickers*, the material seems more shopworn and padded this time around. The characters dash, deal, giggle, drink, smooch, and whiz about, but there is just not as strong a center supporting the whole production (though Bill, Ruby, and Forbes gamely try). Good for a few chuckles, especially at the beginning.

**PIG IN THE MIDDLE** (**) **30 min (7ep Color; 1979 UK London Weekend Television) Situation Comedy** *with Dinsdale Landon as Barty, Joanna Van Gyseghem as Susan, and Liza Goddard as Nellie*

Barty and Susan's marriage has lost some of its pizazz as they enter middle age. Enter Nellie, Susan's best friend, and Barty's idea of an exciting new companion.

Obviously, an aptly named comedy.

**PINK LADY** (zero) **60 min (5ep Color; 1980 NBC) Musical-Variety** *with Jeff Altman and Pink Lady (Mie Nemoto and Kei Masuda)*

It's really inconceivable that this show aired at all. Pink Lady is a Japanese rock act, consisting of two nubile young ladies, Mei and Kei. In Japan Pink Lady (don't ask where the name came from) was a popular combo. In the United States, nobody ever heard of them. For no good reason, they are teamed up with young American comic Jeff Altman and an hour-long variety show is constructed around them. The PInk Lady ladies are shown learning English and giggling. They are shown singing (their song "Kiss in the Dark" did hit the American charts) and giggling. They are shown in bikinis and giggling. Jeff Altman provides translation. *Pink Lady* challenges *Mel and Susan Together* as the most pointless variety show on TV since 1970. At least Mel Tillis and Susan Anton spoke English.

**PISTOLS 'N' PETTICOATS** (*) **30 min (26ep Color; 1966–1967 CBS) Situation Comedy** *with Ann Sheridan as Henrietta Hanks, Douglas Fowley as Andrew Hanks, Ruth McDevitt as Grandma Hanks, Carole Wells as Lucy Hanks, and Gary Vinson as Harold Sikes*

This utterly undistinguished western comedy comes from the mid-1960s rush to cash in on the *Beverly Hillbillies*-inspired rural rube craze. The Hanks clan, made up mostly of women and old men, rule Wretched, Colorado, in the 1870s due to their adept gun handling and the bumbling nature of local Sheriff Sikes. The so-called humor is meant to come from the incongruity of ladies outshooting real rootin'-tootin' western bad guys.

This series emanates from producer Joe Connelly, half of the team that created *Leave It to Beaver. Pistols 'n' Petticoats* is a sad way for star Ann Sheridan to conclude a long entertainment career. She was the Warners "Oomph Girl" in the 1930s, starred in several enjoyable movies, and died of cancer before this series was off the air.

**PLANET EARTH** (**½) **60 min (7ep Color; 1986 PBS) Documentary** *with Richard Kiley as narrator*

This scientific survey series examines the origins of the earth's topography (including theories behind the formation of the continents and oceans), the current condition of our home planet, and its prospects for the future. There's plenty of whiz-bang computer graphics, special effects, and dramatic location footage—with the shots from outer space and deep beneath the oceans the most impressive. ■

**PLANET OF THE APES** (*½) **60 min (14ep Color; 1974 CBS) Science Fiction** *with Roddy McDowall as Galen, Ron Harper as Alan Virdon, James Naughton as Pete Burke, and Mark Lenard as Urko*

TV's nearly perfect record of botching up video versions of hit theatrical movies is kept intact by this toothless adaptation of the 1968 film starring Charlton Heston and Roddy McDowall. The plot is close to the original film, in that American astronauts from our era land on some planet run by apes, with humans in the subservient position. It turns out that the ape-led world is Earth, but it is the Earth of the distant future, when apes have taken over. Ron Harper, last seen battling the Hun in the World War II–era *Garrison's Gorillas*, is the astronaut, with young James Naughton along as sidekick. Roddy McDowall reprises his film role as the ape leader who takes a shine to the nearly hairless bipeds and helps them evade the simians obsessed with their capture (it's considered bad form to let humans run around free). Considering that there had already been four film sequels to the original *Planet of the Apes* movie before this program appeared, there is little that the TV series adds to the concept.

**PLAYHOUSE 90** (***½) **90 min (133ep B&W; 1956–1960 CBS) Drama Anthology**

Generally recognized as one of the best examples of the 1950s golden age of live TV drama, this series had a high budget for quality scripts, sets, and performers, along with a regular weekly slot for its first three seasons. It also had most of the problems inherent to a live drama anthology, including the nightmare of logistics involved with each broadcast and the difficulty of sustaining audience interest week after week with completely different casts, characters, and themes.

But, because video tape was coming into more common use during the run of this series, *Playhouse 90* did emerge with many of its episodes past the second season preserved in that format. In fact, a good number even started to go out that way in their initial broadcasts, at last acknowledging the hard reality that a live production was not necessarily going to result in the most effective presentation of the material. There was nothing morally or artistically wrong with shooting scripts in advance, with time to correct muffed lines and minor technical flaws. And it meant that the production cost of an encore presentation was already covered because the play did not have to be restaged—all they had to do was rerun the video tape. (Which is what CBS did during the summer of 1961, rerunning episodes of the series in a weekly slot.)

As with other top-of-the line drama anthologies from the 1950's this is where established talent mixed with rising newcomers first flexing their TV muscles. Before long, many of them were moving on to regular weekly series or to theatrical feature films. The lengthy list of program alums includes Paul Newman, Buster Keaton, Jackie Gleason, Hoagy Carmichael, Fess Parker, and Robert Redford, along with directors and writers such as George Roy Hill, Aaron Spelling, and Rod Serling. Nowadays such names are usually the hook used to package individual episodes from the series either on videotape or in some golden age highlights program, such as *The Golden Age of Television*, which premièred in the early 1980s with "Requiem for a Heavyweight," probably the best-known *Playhouse 90* presentation. Other famous productions include "The Miracle Worker" (the story of Helen Keller, with Patty McCormack), "The Comedian" (by Rod Serling and starring Mickey Rooney), "The Days of Wine and Roses" (with Piper Laurie and Cliff Robertson), "For Whom the Bell Tolls" (from the Ernest Hemingway novel, with Jason Robards, Jr., and Maria Schell), and "Seven Against the Wall" (a precursor to *The Untouchables*, with newsman Eric Sevareid narrating the story of the St. Valentine's Day Massacre).

Now suppose good-quality copies of just about every presentation could be found and packaged into a rerun series—how well would it play? Probably moderately well, but only if there were some Alistair Cooke–style host to set the stage and the tone and background for each episode. After all, even the dramas that were prerecorded for their original broadcasts are still very "stage-bound." Today's viewers, even those weaned on *Masterpiece Theatre*, are accustomed to extensive exterior footage, detailed costumes, and letter-perfect delivery. They would definitely need some explanation as to why these dramas are good for something more than a round of "spot the star." And a number of them simply aren't worth pulling from the shelf because they come off as stiff, overblown, and heavy-handed. (No surprise. In most cases, that's just what the critics said back then, too!) But when these dramas work, they really are very, very good—and worth a return visit. ■

**PLEASE DON'T EAT THE DAISIES (**½) 30 min (58ep: 1 B&W & 57 Color; 1965–1967 NBC) Situation Comedy** *with Patricia Crowley as Joan Nash, Mark Miller as Jim Nash, Kim Tyler as Kyle Nash, Brian Nash as Joel Nash, Joe Fithian as Tracey Nash, Jeff Fithian as Trevor Nash, and Lord Nelson as Ladadog*

Poking gentle fun at the suburban American family is nothing new to the annals of TV sitcoms, but *Please Don't Eat the Daisies* brings a fresh approach to this familiar theme. The Nash family (Mom, Dad, four sons including twins, and their huge sheep dog Ladadog) reside in pleasant Ridgemont, New York. Dad is an English professor and Mom is a freelance writer. Mom hates housework, and for that reason she deserves a place in the TV Sitcom Moms Hall of Fame. Few of Mrs. Nash's TV sisters ever dared to speak ill about the womanly art of keeping house (at least not until the 1970s). Mrs. Nash sleeps late, doesn't pick up after her kids, and hates to cook. Somehow life goes on, albeit to the consternation of the Nashes' more proper neighbors.

*Please Don't Eat the Daisies* is pretty tame stuff, but its light and breezy style is fetching. Blandness was never done quite so well. The running thread of reality can be chalked up to the series origin, which is Jean Kerr's quasi-autobiographical book, on which a play and 1960 film with Doris Day was based. The first (pilot) episode is in black and white, while the rest of the run is in color.

**PLEASE SIR (**½) 30 min (55ep B&W & Color; 1968–1969 UK LWT) Situation Comedy** *with John Alderton, Joan Sanderson, Erik Chitty, and Deryck Guyler*

John Alderton plays a dedicated young teacher given the school's most notorious class. He wins them over with his dedication, charm, and good humor, much like Gabe Kaplan in *Welcome Back, Kotter* or Sidney Poitier in the 1967 theatrical film, *To Sir With Love.*

**PLEASE STAND BY (*½) 30 min (24ep Color; 1978–1979 Syndication) Situation Comedy** *with Richard Schaal as Frank Lambert, Elinor Donahue as Carol Lambert, Darian Mathias as Susan Lambert, Stephen Schwartz as David Lambert, Bryan Scott as Rocky Lambert, and Marcie Barkin as Vicki Janes*

This is a well-meaning but not very funny sitcom about the tribulations of a big-city tycoon who chucks it all, moves the family to New Mexico, and runs a tiny TV station, largely with his family as the staff.

**POINT COUNTER POINT** (**½) **60 min (5ep Color; 1973 UK BBC) Drama** *with Lyndon Brook as Philip Quarles, Tristam Jellinek as Walter Bidlake, Patricia English as Elinor Quarles, John Wentworth as Sidney Quarles, Max Adrian as John Bidlake, Edward Judd as Everard Webley, and Valerie Gearon as Lucy Tantamount*

A satirical story of life, love, and violent death in the 1920s, adapted from the 1928 novel by *Brave New World* author Aldous Huxley. It's social criticism set in Huxley's own times, with the main character (writer Philip Quarters) shown constructing his new novel by using the lives of his friends as a model, in the process considering their various character types and traits. If his friends weren't so self-absorbed, they might even be insulted by Huxley's rendering, which portrays their society as overly sophisticated, sex-obsessed, and self-devouring. In short, ideal fodder for a soapy TV miniseries.

Actually, Philip is not very involved in the main action—he's more absorbed in writing about the lives of others than in living his own, much to the disappointment of his devoted but ignored wife, Elinor. Instead most of the juicy plot threads wind around his wife's brother (Walter Bidlake), their dad (John Bidlake), and an extramarital suitor (Everard Webley) to the neglected Elinor. For starters, Walter is living with one woman, but infatuated with another, the mysterious beauty Lucy Tantamount. John is just going through the motions on his third marriage. And Everard finds himself in a deadly face-off with a political and philosophical rival.

Downbeat, especially about the institution of marriage, but still a well-done, entertaining message tale.

**POLDARK** (***½) **60 min (29ep Color; 1976–1977 UK BBC) Drama** *with Robin Ellis as Ross Poldark, Jill Townsend as Elizabeth, Angharad Rees as Demelza, Clive Francis as Francis, Nicholas Selby as George Warleggen, Frank Middlemass as Charles Poldark, Judy Geeson as Caroline, Ralph Bates as George, Norma Streader as Verity, and Paul Curran as Jud*

Adapted from a series of novels by Winston Graham set in eighteenth-century Cornwall (England), this is a deliciously soapy and romantic adventure with a sharp sense of humor. The story opens with Captain Poldark returning to his home from fighting against the American rebels, only to discover a "for sale" sign on his estate and, worse yet, the news that his sweetheart, Elizabeth, is engaged to his cousin, Francis. While he soon gets his property in order, the romantic connection between Francis and Elizabeth remains a teasing plot thread throughout the entire series, even when both are already married to other people.

On other fronts, Poldark is the consummate independent hero, ready to jump on his horse at a moment's notice and ride to some new challenging situation. Of course, Poldark is not particularly popular with the other landowners, chiefly because he's such an unconventionally fair man. For instance, when he gets his servant girl, Demelza, pregnant, Poldark actually feels duty-bound to marry her (despite the difference in their classes and even much to her surprise). In the local political and social battles, Poldark's chief rival is George Warleggen, an extremely wealthy man with holdings ranging from mines to ships to large tracts of land. This makes him an appropriate target for symbolic moments of class conflict and retribution, as when one of his trading ships runs aground and hordes of hungry people swarm over the wreckage grabbing everything in sight.

And so it goes, through duels, poaching, smuggling, wenching, and lovemaking, all effectively staged for maximum melodramatic effect. If *Indiana Jones* had been conceived by Steven Spielberg and George Lucas as a British television series, it may well have turned out like this, down to its devilishly handsome lead. During the original run of the series in England, the British press described lead Robin Ellis as "the sexiest man on the telly."

**POLICE CALL** (½) **30 min (26ep B&W; 1955 Syndication) Police Anthology**

This anthology of stories, supposedly based on actual police files, is so cheap that the producers didn't even spring for a few bucks to pay for a down-and-out actor to host it.

**POLICE SQUAD!** (****) **30 min (6ep Color; 1982 ABC) Situation Comedy** *with Leslie Nielsen as Det. Frank Drebin, Alan North as Capt. Ed Hocken, William Duell as Johnny the Shoeshine Snitch, Peter Lupus as Officer Norberg, and Ed Williams as Ted Olson*

A perfectly executed television parody by and for a generation raised on its conventions.

In *Police Squad!*, the team of Jerry Zuker, Jim Abrahams, and David Zuker take the same formula they used on their hit theatrical film parody *Airplane!* and apply it to the tried-and-true world of the TV cop. This means a lot of clever wordplay, bad puns, silly names, visual gags going on in the background behind the main characters, and a matter-of-fact awareness of television and movie personalities of the past and present.

What makes the humor so effective is that the performers (led by veteran Leslie Nielsen, also one of the stars of *Airplane!*) play it deadpan (no mugging to the camera with eyes rolling). No matter how silly the line or setting is, they treat it straight—as if *Police Squad!* were just another cop show. In fact, you might want to warm up for the adventures of Nielsen's Det. Frank Drebin and Alan North's Capt. Ed Hocken by catching an episode or two of *M Squad, Dragnet, Cannon, Barnaby Jones,* or even two previous Leslie Nielsen cop vehicles, *The Protectors* and *The New Breed.*

Or just trust your subconscious memory, because the Zuker/Abrahams/Zuker team has dug deep into it, from the opening credits to the closing freeze frame. To start, each episode begins with a brief program identification: "*Police Squad!* In Color." Anyone that grew up with TV in the mid-1960s can't help but recognize that obscure allusion—it was a gimmick phrase used by ABC before every color show in 1965 to emphasize the network's newfound commitment to color broadcasting.

Then the familiar voice-over announcer from *Barnaby Jones, Cannon*, and dozens of other series introduces the cast for the episode, ending with a story title on the screen completely different from the one he says. And there's a twist to the announced guest stars as well: Within seconds of being introduced ("Tonight's guest star, Lorne Greene") each one is killed. And this is the only time in the episode they appear.

The closing also uses a familiar TV technique, that of freezing the action in the last scene to act as a backdrop for the credits. In *Police Squad!*, the performers do it literally, standing stock still trying desperately to hold their open-mouthed expressions through the closing roll.

And in between . . . plenty of opportunities for visual and verbal jokes. For instance, when Frank and Ed visit "little Italy," the Roman Coliseum and the Leaning Tower of Pisa appear in the background. When two bodies are removed from the scene, they are taken out on a stretcher thirty feet long. And when the cops question a grieving widow about her deceased husband, they have the perfect answer to her complaint about being bothered at such a bad time. "We would have come earlier," they explain, "but your husband wasn't dead yet."

*Police Squad*'s send-up of the typical police tipster is also inspired. Whenever Frank runs into a dead end, he goes to Johnny the shoeshiner, slips him a few bills, and gets a letter-perfect answer to his questions. Then after Frank departs Johnny serves another customer with ready cash and questions. These range from a priest who wants to know about life after death to *American Bandstand*'s Dick Clark wondering about "ska" music. Without missing a beat, Johnny answers them all.

And so it goes, through dozens of silly scenes and lots of clever wordplay. Was a man named "Twice" shot once, or was "Once" shot twice? Isn't that an Olympic-size swimming pool upstairs at police headquarters? And isn't that the strongman guy from *Mission: Impossible* playing Officer Norberg?

No doubt due to its short run, the percentage of successful gags per episode of *Police Squad!* is pretty good, somewhere below Monty Python but above Mel Brooks and *Laugh-In*. Over the years, several of the episodes were edited together for feature film-length releases overseas or issued on home video. But in 1988, the producers and Nielsen reunited for an all-new (but very familiar, too) *Police Squad* theatrical film release, *The Naked Gun*, subtitled "from the Files of *Police Squad!*" (opening the door for numerous sequels, especially in light of the movie's tremendous success). One cute cast change for the film: Officer Norberg is transformed from IMF strongman Peter Lupus to Hertz super-spokesman O. J. Simpson. ■

**POLICE STORY (***) 60 min (105ep Color; 1973–1980 NBC) and 2 hr (5 ep Color; 1988 ABC) Police Drama Anthology**

This may be the definitive big-city police department anthology series, created by former Los Angeles cop turned author Joseph Wambaugh (responsible for such best-sellers about the force as *The New Centurions* and *The Blue Knight*). Wambaugh's approach is to emphasize authentic procedures and the genuinely tough (sometimes traumatic) moments police officers have to face in doing their jobs, and he maintains the same tone throughout as a special creative consultant to the series. As a result, the stories generally reflect a somewhat somber tone, dealing with such subjects as burned-out cops, charges of harassment, watching your partner die, and, most often, dealing with your peers as well as with your own conscience—no matter what the situation. While there are car chases, shoot-outs, and drug busts, they come much closer to the gritty feel of *Hill Street Blues* than the never-never land of *Starsky and Hutch* or *S.W.A.T.*

The series consistently turns out strong scripts, attracting a solid lineup of guest stars, with some performers (and even a few characters) returning for several different stories, including Tony Lo Bianco (as Tony Calabrese) and Don Meredith (as Bert Jameson). Three even landed their own series: Angie Dickinson in *Police Woman*, Lloyd Bridges in *Joe Forrester*, and David Cassidy in *Man Undercover*. Ironically, on their own these spin-offs (especially *Police Woman*) tend toward some of the flashier gimmicks specifically avoided by *Police Story*. In their original release, more than a half-dozen stories ran as two-hour presentations, but in reruns these generally play as multi-part one-hour episodes.

When a writers' strike delayed general series production for the 1988–1989 season, a number of producers began dusting off old scripts from past programs, including *Police Story*. The five new two-hour *Police Story* episodes that emerged from this (featuring lead performers such as Ken Olin, Robert Conrad, and Lindsay Wagner) effectively demonstrate that some material in the TV script vaults is definitely worth another look and another staging.

**POLICE SURGEON (½) 30 min (78ep Color; 1972–1974 Syndication) Medical Drama** *with Sam Groom as Dr. Simon Locke, Len Birman as Lt. Dan Palmer, and Larry Mann as Lt. Jack Gordon*

A very cheaply made police/doctor show from Canada, *Police Surgeon* is sort of a spin-off or outgrowth of *Doctor Simon Locke*. In that earlier show, young Dr. Locke took up practice in a small town. In this series, the good doctor heads for the big city, Toronto, where he hooks up with the city's medical arm of the police force. Your local TV station's newscast stories on today's six-car pile-up on the expressway provide more drama than *Police Surgeon.*

**POLICE WOMAN (**½) 60 min (91ep & 60 min pilot Color; 1974–1978 NBC) Police Drama** *with Angie Dickinson as Sgt. Suzanne "Pepper" Anderson, Earl Holliman as Lt. Bill Crowley, Ed Bernard as Det. Joe Styles, and Charles Dierkop as Det. Pete Royster*

Having already pushed forty when *Police Woman* debuted, Angie Dickinson proves here that, for women, sexy good looks are not limited to young nymphets. Dickinson plays L.A. undercover cop Pepper Anderson, a svelte lady who uses her shapely form to successfully pose as prostitutes and other underworld ladies, in order to catch bad guys (and bad girls). *Police Woman* comes from the era when the idea of a police woman serving as a detective was still considered radical, so there is a lot of needless flack from stodgy old men (both on and off the force) who would rather see Pepper between the sheets than on the beat.

In *Police Woman*'s pilot ("The Gamble") which aired on *Police Story* in 1974, Dickinson's character is known as Lisa Beaumont.

**PONY EXPRESS (½) 30 min (39ep B&W; 1959–1960 Syndication) Western** *with Grant Sullivan as Brett Clark, Bill Cord as Tom Clyde, and Don Dorell as Donovan*

Basic western fodder with Brett Clark as a troubleshooter for the Pony Express. Let it ride by undisturbed.

**THE POPCORN KID (**½) 30 min (6ep Color; 1987 CBS) Situation Comedy** *with Bruce Norris as Scott Creasman, Raye Birk as Leonard Brown, Jeffrey Joseph as Willie Dawson, Penelope Ann Miller as Gwen Stottlemeyer, John Christopher Jones as Marlin Bond, and Faith Ford as Lynn Holly Brickhouse*

After school, sixteen-year-old Scott Creasman works the candy counter at an old-fashioned Kansas City movie palace, the Majestic, dreaming of using the position as his entry into the glamorous world of showbiz—or at least to work up enough nerve to ask the girl of his dreams (dumb blond bombshell Lynn Holly) for a date. Meanwhile, another girl, Gwen (a cute dark-haired intellectual), wishes Scott would notice her because she thinks he's dreamy, while Scott's athletic friend, Willie, wants to be recognized for more than just his sports achievements. And then there's Marlin, the theater's spaced-out projectionist who considers leaving the booth while a film is running akin to opening a submarine hatch while still under water. Majestic manager Leonard Brown wishes they'd all come back down to earth and treat this like any other normal, low-paying job.

This is a pleasant, short-run teen ensemble comedy from MTM productions. It comes off as a more restrained and developed television version of the typical theatrical coming-of-age teen flicks of the time (such as *The Breakfast Club*), with more time for individual character growth. And while Scott never does land his dream job in Hollywood, he does get to meet Ed Asner, who shows up to help promote the Majestic's Ed Asner film festival. (Imagine! *Change of Habit, They Call Me Mister Tibbs,* and *Fort Apache: The Bronx* all on one bill!)

**POPI (*) 30 min (13ep & 30 min pilot Color; 1976 CBS) Situation Comedy** *with Hector Elizondo as Abraham "Popi" Rodriguez, Anthony Perez as Abraham Rodriguez, Jr., Dennis Vasquez as Luis Rodriguez, and Edith Diaz as Lupe*

Based on a nice 1969 film starring Alan Arkin and Rita Moreno, *Popi* is an uninteresting saccharine look at life among the lowly in New York's Puerto Rican ghetto. Hector Elizondo, a fine actor wasted in every two-bit Hispanic role on TV in the 1970s and 1980s, plays Popi, widowed father of two sons, who holds down three jobs to feed his boys.

**PORRIDGE (**½) 30 min (30ep Color; 1974–1977 UK BBC) Situation Comedy** *with Ronnie Barker as Fletcher, Richard Beckinsale, Fulton McKay, and Brian Wilde*

*Porridge* is Cockney slang for "prison" (don't ask), which is the setting for this Ronnie Barker vehicle. He plays a manipulative con man working all the angles from his cell, all the while trying to get along with his cellmate (played by Richard Beckinsale). This show was later adapted for Stateside viewing as *On the Rocks*, while the Barker/Beckinsale sparring continues in a 1978 six-episode follow-up outside the prison walls, *Going Straight.*

**THE POSSESSED (**) 60 min (6ep Color; 1970 UK BBC) Drama** *with Keith Bell as Nikolay Stavrogin, Rosalie Crutchley as Mme. Stavrogin, Anne Stallybrass as Pasha, James Caffrey as Shatov, David Collings as Peter Verkhovensky, Joseph O'Connor as Stepan Verkhovensky, and Eve Belton as Marya Lebyadkin*

Adaptation of Feodor Dostoyevsky's most intensely autobiographical novel, reflecting his obsession with the problems of good and evil, God, and human betrayal. In this case, the story focuses on a group of radicals who must deal with a leader they feel has betrayed their ideals. Unfortunately, it all plays a bit too dark and somber, especially stretched over six episodes.

**POWERHOUSE (*) 30 min (16ep Color; 1982–1983 PBS) Drama** *with Sandra Bowie as Brenda Gaines, Domenica Galati as Jennifer, Jessica Prentice as Pepper, and Michael Mack as Kevin*

In this heavy-handed lecture disguised as a drama show, a multiracial group of inner-city kids who hang out at Powerhouse (an afterschool center for children) learn to live together as they join in adventures and exploits.

**THE POWERS OF MATTHEW STAR (*½) 60 min (22ep & 2 hr pilot Color; 1982–1983 NBC) Science Fiction** *with Louis Gossett, Jr., as Dehay/Walt Shephard, Peter Barton as Ehawk/Matthew Star, Amy Steel as Pam Elliott, and James Karen as Major Wymore*

A young alien prince named Ehawk and his guardian Dehay flee to Earth when their planet Quandris is invaded, disguising themselves as an average California high school student and a science teacher.

While on Earth, Matthew must also develop his tremendous mental powers in preparation for an eventual return home. Not surprisingly, school soon falls by the wayside as the pair takes on more exciting work as special agents of the U.S. government.

*Matthew Star* creator Steven DeSouza subsequently became one of the producers for the weekly series version of *V*, which also focuses on alien visitors to Earth.

**THE PRACTICE (**) 30 min (27ep Color; 1976–1977 NBC) Situation Comedy** *with Danny Thomas as Dr. Jules Bedford, Dena Dietrich as Molly Gibbons, Shelley Fabares as Jenny Bedford, David Spielberg as Dr. David Bedford, Didi Conn as Helen, and John Byner as Dr. Roland Caine*

*The Practice* is hardly perfect, but with the talents of Danny Thomas, it can't be all bad. Thomas, ever the irascible grouch with a heart of gold (as he was in *Make Room for Daddy*), plays elderly, cantankerous yet humanitarian Dr. Jules Bedford. The senior Dr. Bedford has maintained his simple practice on Manhattan's West Side for fifty years. His son, Dr. David Bedford, is a crass, materialistic suburbanite with a swank practice on ritzy Park Avenue. Son is always whining after Dad to see the light, join his practice, and rake in the dough. Dad sticks to his morals, helps widows and orphans, and acts grumpy a lot. Shelley Fabares, another refugee from a popular TV sitcom of the black-and-white days (*The Donna Reed Show*), plays bland wife to Dr. David.

**A PRAIRIE HOME COMPANION (***) 90 min (16ep & 3 hr finale & two 2½ hour sequels Color; 1987 Disney) Variety** *with Garrison Keillor as host*

After more than ten years as a cult favorite on public radio, *A Prairie Home Companion* allowed the TV cameras in for its final episodes, before host and creator Garrison Keillor left America for a brief self-imposed exile in Denmark. Few, if any, concessions are made as a result of the video presence, and this series is truly just a radio show staged in front of cameras. Each episode consists of a ninety-minute cut-down of a two-hour program that aired live on radio. There is a lot of amiable low-key folk music, and Keillor's enrapturing "News From Lake Wobegon" monologues, but this is a treat best enjoyed on radio. The final episode lasts three hours. In 1988 and 1989, Keillor staged "reunion" specials. ■

**PRIDE AND PREJUDICE (**½) 60 min (5ep Color; 1980 UK) Drama** *with Elizabeth Garvie as Elizabeth Bennet, David Rintoul as Fitzwilliam Darcy, Sabina Franklyn as Jane Bennet, Tessa Peake-Jones as Mary Bennet, Clair Higgins as Kitty Bennet, and Natalie Ogle as Lydia Bennet*

This adaptation of Jane Austen's novel follows the comedy of manners courtship between middle-class but strong-willed Elizabeth and the wealthy but vain Fitzwilliam Darcy. Along the way, the four other Bennet sisters also share in the humorous highs and lows of love and courtship rituals. By the numbers, but done well. ■

**PRIDE OF THE FAMILY/THE PAUL HARTMAN SHOW (*½) 30 min (40ep B&W; 1953–1955 ABC) Situation Comedy** *with Paul Hartman as Albie Morrison, Fay Wray as Catherine Morrison, Natalie Wood as Ann Morrison, and Bobby Hyatt as Junior*

Take a well-meaning husband bumbling his way through silly home and office situations and you have yet another mid-1950s simple screwball setup. Supporting cast members Fay Wray and Natalie Wood are the only reasons to catch this.

The series was originally called *Pride of the Family*, but has also been repackaged as *The Paul Hartman Show*.

**PRIMUS (**) 30 min (26ep Color; 1971 Syndication) Adventure** *with Robert Brown as Carter Primus, Will Kuluva as Charlie Kingman, and Eva Renzi as Toni Hyden*

From *Sea Hunt* producer Ivan Tors comes the underwater exploits of oceanographer, explorer, and inventor Carter Primus (played by former *Here Come the Brides* logger Robert Brown). Primus and his assistants explore the waters off Nassau. Routine, but great scenery.

**THE PRISONER (***½) 60 min (17ep Color; 1967 UK ATV) Adventure Drama** *with Patrick McGoohan as Number Six, Angelo Muscat as The Butler, and a variety of performers as Number Two, including Leo McKern and Patrick Cargill*

For a moment, forget the cult following this series has attracted since it first aired in Britain in 1967, as well as the seemingly endless speculation on what it all meant. Instead sit back and enjoy *The Prisoner* as a well-made espionage adventure. With only a handful of exceptions (which we'll get to later), it functions perfectly well on just that level.

First, the setup: Patrick McGoohan plays a British secret agent (reminiscent of John Drake, his character in the *Secret Agent/Danger Man* series) who resigns in anger over what he later describes as some unstated "matter of principle." Immediately afterward, in the midst of packing, he is rendered unconscious and spirited off to a mysterious seaside location (called simply "The Village") which looks like an innocent resort town, but is really an inescapable prison. There his captors demand information—specifically, the reason for his resignation.

For his part, McGoohan's character (known as Number Six) has a few questions of his own: Which side is running this place? Who is ultimately in charge? And, most practically, where am I?

But that's the continuing backdrop conflict, resolved in increments over the run of the series. In the meantime, there are also specific confrontations with a succession of foes (each episode has a different person in the role of Number Two, administrative head of the village). These plots range from assassination attempts to recovering secret formulas to ferreting out double agents—solid spy stuff that just happens to take place in the village. Some of the episodes in this style include "The Chimes of Big Ben," "The Schizoid Man," "The General," "Do Not Forsake Me Oh My Darling," "It's Your Funeral," and "The Girl Who Was Death"—all of which could have played virtually unchanged on *Secret Agent*. These are some of the best stories for casual viewers.

If you're interested in a bit more, such as watching the progress of the running battle between Number Six and his captors, it's probably worth following the entire series—there are only seventeen episodes. While doing so, pay special attention to a shift in tone over the run. At first, Number Six concentrates primarily on escape and is consistently surprised and often outmaneuvered by his captors, who subject him to every mind-altering drug, hypnotic technique, and psychological game they can come up with.

About halfway through the run, the tide turns noticeably. Now more familiar with his surroundings as well as the tactics of his foes, Number Six not only manages to thwart virtually every scheme against him rather quickly but he begins to seize the initiative himself. This reaches a dramatic peak in "Hammer into Anvil," with Number Six brazenly executing a one-man plan to undermine the authority of Number Two himself—without any thought of escape involved! It's laying down the ultimate gauntlet, declaring that he doesn't need to escape to make good his promise to dismantle and destroy the Village.

The final two stories ("Once Upon a Time" and "Fall Out") carry the running battle between Number Six and his foes to its dramatic conclusion—sort of. However, if you have no interest in poetic license and obtuse allusions, you might want to skip these. Or be forewarned that even after you see Number Six come face-to-face with Number One and then launch his final attack against the Village . . . you still won't be all that sure of exactly what happened.

That's because of the other important element in *The Prisoner*: symbolism. Though symbolism is always present throughout the series in everything from the character names (all numbers), to the huge plastic bubbles that "patrol" the Village, to its *1984*-like surveillance cameras, those aspects usually remain in the background to an understandable story. But in a few cases (such as "Free for All," "Dance of the Dead," and especially the final two episodes), the stories themselves can only function on a symbolic level.

Thus, it is supposed to be up to you to figure out the show's significance. Which is probably why *The Prisoner* has retained its enthusiastic cult following for so long, still prompting heated discussions among first-time and veteran viewers more than two decades later. Even if you know the "answers" revealed in the final episode, it's still up to you (and your friends) to make them work in whatever theory you subscribe to.

Fortunately, *The Prisoner* is a well-made show that holds up quite nicely to such intense scrutiny. For the truly dedicated, there is also a "lost" episode of the series (available on video tape), which consists of a working "pilot" version of "The Chimes of Big Ben." In addition, in 1988 Patrick McGoohan authorized a short-run "graphic novel" comic book adaptation of the series looking at Number Six and Leo McKern's Number Two back at the Village in contemporary times. ■

**PRISONER: CELLBLOCK H (***) 30 & 60 min (390ep: two hundred sixty 30 min & one hundred thirty 60 min Color; 1979–1981 Australia 0–10 Network) Serial Drama** *with Kerry Armstrong as Lynn Warner, Val Lehman as Bea Smith, Fiona Spence as Vera Bennett, Carol Burns as Freida "Franky" Doyle, Peita Tommano as Karen Travers, Patsy King as Erica Davidson, Mary Ward as Jeannie "Mum" Brooks, and Elspeth Ballantyne as Meg Jackson*

Finally, here is an adult soap opera worthy of the title *adult*. This low-budget gem is set in the Wentworth Detention Center for Women in Australia and deals honestly, openly, and dramatically with all the problems of women's lives behind bars. Not surprisingly, *Prisoner: Cellblock H* is not an American production, and the lack of standard American TV glitter and titillation makes this Australian show unique.

*Prisoner: Cellblock H* pulls no punches with its writing. The prisoners are rough, both in language and in actions. The female guards are just as rough, and not above beating a recalcitrant prisoner just out of spite. Lesbianism is presented frankly as an issue, but it is not a dominant theme. The warden (called the "governor") is harsh but fair. Some men do appear, as doctors, workmen, visiting friends, and lovers, but this show is almost exclusively populated by women.

This program developed a bad reputation for "graphic violence" that was really unwarranted. It is no more violent than any run-of-the-mill prison picture, but here both the perpetrators and victims are women, which takes a bit of getting used to.

The best aspect of *Prisoner: Cellblock H* is its ability to portray most of its characters as complete human beings, not just cardboard representatives of certain character types. Thus, the viewer finds out *why* a mean character acts so rough, and gets to see her soft side as well. Few, if any, of the prisoners are completely innocent, but at least the writers delve into a bit of explanation of what drove the various women to commit their crimes. Some prisoners serve their time and then survive on the outside; others are just too far gone to operate in normal society, while some never had and will never have a home more stable and secure than jail.

This show is a soap opera, and some of the plot developments are far-fetched, but *Prisoner: Cellblock H* is a refreshing change that puts numerous big-budget American soaps to shame.

**PRIVATE BENJAMIN (**½) 30 min (39ep Color; 1981–1983 CBS) Situation Comedy** *with Lorna Patterson as Judy Benjamin, Eileen Brennan as Capt. Lewis, Hal Williams as Sgt. Ted Ross, Wendie Jo Sperber as Pvt. Stacy Kouchalakas, Lisa Raggio as Pvt. Maria Gianelli, and Robert Mandan as Col. Lawrence Fielding*

A perfectly acceptable series version of Goldie Hawn's 1980 theatrical film. Obviously Hawn's title character had to be recast, but Eileen Brennan and Hal Williams continue in their key roles of army officers determined to mold pampered young Judy Benjamin into a decent soldier. For her part, Judy usually manages to get the brass marching her way, even though it's still a far cry from that "new army" she saw advertised on TV.

As with the original film, the comedy often veers more to the style of 1960s service sitcoms like *McHale's Navy* rather than the relevant drama of *M*A*S*H*. But in the hands of good producers, including *I Love Lucy* veterans Madelyn Davis and Bob Carroll, Jr., that's not such a bad turn.

**PRIVATE EYE (**) 60 min (12ep & 2 hr pilot Color; 1987–1988 NBC) Detective Drama** *with Michael Woods as Jack Cleary, Josh Brolin as Johnny Betts, Bill Sadler as Lt. Charlie Fontana, and Lisa Jane Persky as Dottie Dworski*

First there was Miami in the 1980s, with *Miami Vice*. Then there was Chicago and Las Vegas in the 1960s, with *Crime Story*. Next comes *Private Eye*, set in Los Angeles in 1956. All three shows have similar dark, brooding tones, lots of period music, and common producers (Michael Man for *Miami Vice* and *Crime Story*, Anthony Yerkovich for *Miami Vice* and *Private Eye*). Unfortunately, *Private Eye*, while a sumptuous production you can feast your eyes and ears on, comes up short on the character and plot end. There just isn't enough substance to go along with the sparkle.

Jack Cleary is a square-jawed L.A. cop who is railroaded out of the force in the mid-1950s on trumped-up charges. Soon thereafter, his brother Nick (a cool, suave private eye) is murdered and the police just can't seem to do much to find his killer. Jack, who went off the deep end and hit the bottle pretty hard after being canned, dries out enough to find Nick's killer and then takes over his detective business. Along with the business comes Nick's young assistant Johnny Betts, a ducktailed proponent of the raucous new music fad, rock and roll. Jack, much more of a cool jazz man himself, thinks Johnny is a weirdo, but he needs his help. Thus, the central partnership of *Private Eye* is formed.

Jack is forever cruising Sunset Strip in some crazy 1950s big-finned car, with two days growth of stubble and a dangling cigarette, very much carrying on the Philip Marlowe tradition of L.A. private eyes. He doesn't talk much, and when he does, he mumbles a lot. It's hard to work up much interest in Jack, and even women who are attracted to his well-built physique will ultimately decide he is just a drag to be around. Meanwhile, Johnny looks like a reject from the *Blackboard Jungle* movie casting call.

Your best bet with *Private Eye* is to just catch the original two-hour pilot, which is the program at its best. The scenery and stylishness (and music by Joe Jackson) can be appreciated as fine craftsmanship, without having to endure the slow, spiral, downhill fall the show goes through over its thirteen weeks.

**PRIVATE SCHULZ (***) 60 min (6ep Color; 1981 UK BBC) Comedy Drama** *with Michael Elphick as Private Schulz, Ian Richardson as Major Neuheim, Billie Whitelaw as Bertha Freyer, Cyril Shaps as Solly, and David Swift as Professor Bodelschwingh*

No, this is not a spin-off solo series for John Banner's character from *Hogan's Heroes* (their last names are spelled differently and Banner's Schultz is a sergeant, not a mere private). Still, this short-run series does have one thing in common with the popular U.S. sitcom—it attempts to bring a humorous touch to an otherwise serious subject. Like *Hogan's Heroes*, it generally succeeds, largely due to the sharp performance of lead Michael Elphick as petty Nazi con man Schulz. There are numerous set pieces throughout the series (Schulz eavesdropping on his superiors in a brothel, Schulz at the Dutch border trying to kidnap some British officers), but the main scheme is inspired by a real-life German plot from World War II: print counterfeit British £5 bank notes and destroy the country's economy by flooding it with the phoney paper. Which is just what Private Schulz proposes to the German SS. The question is: Will they succeed in spite of themselves?

An entertaining twist on some familiar character types, written by Jack Pulman, who did the adaptation for another set of schemers, the Romans of *I, Claudius*.

**PRIVATE SECRETARY/SUSIE/THE ANN SOTHERN SHOW** (**½) 30 min (103ep B&W; 1953–1957 CBS) **Situation Comedy** *with Ann Sothern as Susie McNamera, Don Porter as Peter Sands, Ann Tyrrell as Vi Praskins, Jesse White as Cagey Calhoun, and Joan Banks as Sylvia*

A tight, well-done office comedy, with excellent rapport between Ann Sothern and Donald Porter. He plays Peter Sands, head of a successful talent agency, while she's cast as Susie McNamera, his private secretary. Susie is outgoing, efficient, humorous, quite attractive, and often the one whose charms help save a situation or nail down a new client.

Of course, at times she goes overboard managing things in her boss's life, but as in any vintage 1950s sitcom such screwball complications are easily resolved. What really helps the series work more than three decades later is that neither Susie nor Peter is played as a dummy. Instead, they're a great team that simply works well together.

Sothern and Porter were coupled again in the subsequent *Ann Sothern Show*, though sometimes this series plays under that title as well. The series was originally called *Private Secretary*, but the current packaging edits in new title graphics with the *Susie* moniker.

**PROBE** (**½) 60 min (6ep & 2 hr pilot Color; 1988 ABC) **Mystery** *with Parker Stevenson as Austin James and Ashley Crow as Mickey Castle*

A light mystery series with former *Hardy Boys* lead Parker Stevenson as a brilliant young scientist who owns his own think-tank consulting firm (Serendip). He also branches out from the laboratory world to offer his expertise in the world of mystery, tackling some truly baffling crimes. It's no big deal to him. Like Sherlock Holmes, Austin has a memory for obscure facts and familiarity with science, so he can see implications to actions and objects that sail by everyone else, especially the police. Austin's secretary, Mickey, has the faithful Dr. Watson role, contributing at her own average intelligence level, though occasionally kicking in the solution with an inadvertent insight.

This is fun in a *MacGyver* sort of way, with Austin's explanations clear enough to satisfy those of us in the normal I. Q. range. And if that four-degree discrepancy in the victim's body temperature still doesn't make sense, don't worry—the series covers itself with well-paced, breezy production.

Novelist and science writer Isaac Asimov is the cocreator of *Probe*, along with a former *Hill Street Blues* story editor, Michael Wagner. Creative consultant William Link (*Columbo, Murder She Wrote*) rounds out the mix.

**PROFESSIONAL FATHER** (*½) 30 min (13ep B&W; 1955 CBS) **Situation Comedy** *with Steve Dunne as Dr. Thomas Wilson, Barbara Billingsley as Helen Wilson, Ted Marc as Thomas "Twig" Wilson, Jr., Beverly Washburn as Kathryn "Kit" Wilson, Phyllis Coates as Nurse Madge Allen, and Joseph Kearns as Fred*

Most all sitcom dads in the 1950s were professional fathers. All they ever did, at least on screen, was hang around the house, fix things, and have heart-to-heart talks with the kiddos. Their real jobs were almost always off-screen and rarely mentioned. This series is not making an up-front admission about the profession of its TV dad; rather it is trying to contrast the know-it-all attitude Dr. Tom Wilson has on the job (as ace child psychologist) to the klutzy manner he has at home with his own children.

While the plot here is thin and unimaginative, the cast is a couch potato's dream. The Wilsons' neighbors are Joseph Kearns (the original Mr. Wilson on *Dennis the Menace*) and Phyllis Coates (the original Lois Lane in *The Adventures of Superman*). Best of all, the wife of the professional father is Barbara Billingsley, who went on to personify the professional mother of the 1950s as June Cleaver in *Leave It to Beaver.*

**THE PROFESSIONALS** (**) 60 min (52ep Color; 1978–1983 UK London Weekend Television) **Adventure** *with Gordon Jackson, Martin Shaw, and Lewis Collins*

An elite squad of international adventurers led by Gordon Jackson (the butler from *Upstairs, Downstairs*) pursues spies and criminals beyond the reach of the law. Produced by *Avengers* veterans Albert Fennell and Brian Clemens after *The New Avengers* revival, this series emphasizes the action far more than the banter, with the level of violence causing a minor flap in Britain at the time of the original broadcasts. But it's a well-made package, relatively tame by some of today's extreme standards. ■

**PROFILES IN COURAGE** (***) 60 min (26ep B&W; 1964–1965 NBC) **Drama/Biography Anthology**

In 1954, when John F. Kennedy, the junior senator from Massachusetts, spent months recuperating from a delicate back operation, he wrote a book entitled *Profiles in Courage*. It presented the stories of several American politicians who had invited (and often received) public scorn for taking unpopular stands, but whose courageous positions were proved correct by history. When published in 1956, the book won the Pulitzer Prize for biography.

On May 16, 1956, *Kraft Television Theater* presented a dramatization of one chapter of Kennedy's book as "A Profile in Courage." It dealt with Sen. Edmund G. Ross, the man who cast the swing vote against the conviction of Pres. Andrew Johnson in the Senate impeachment proceedings of 1868. Sen. Kennedy served as consultant for the Kraft broadcast and appeared on the show to read the introduction.

Within the next four years, Sen. Kennedy became a national figure and was narrowly elected president. While he was in office, Kennedy approved the production of a television drama series based on his hit book. Before production began, Kennedy was assassinated.

The *Profiles in Courage* series is a finely crafted collection of television productions that would make the slain President proud. Produced by Robert Saudek (famous for his quality series *Omnibus*), *Profiles in Courage* serves double duty as both gripping drama and a valuable history course. Many of the characters featured in the stories have largely been forgotten (how many recall Alabama Sen. Oscar W. Underwood's vocal stance against the Ku Klux Klan in the 1920s?), but their bravery can still serve as a lesson to later generations.

Like most good anthology drama series, *Profiles in Courage* provides a great opportunity to catch several stars-to-be in their early days, such as Carroll O'Connor (*All in the Family*), Barbara Feldon (*Get Smart*), Barry Morse (*The Fugitive*), Edward Asner (*Lou Grant*), Michael Constantine (*Room 222*), Walter Matthau (the *Odd Couple* film) and David McCallum (*The Man from U.N.C.L.E.*). ■

**PROJECT U.F.O. (*) 60 min (26ep Color; 1978–1979 NBC) Drama** *with William Jordan as Maj. Jake Gatlin, Edward Winter as Capt. Ben Ryan, Caskey Swaim as Sgt. Harry Fitz, Aldine King as Libby Virdon, and Jack Webb as narrator*

In *Project U.F.O.*, Jack Webb takes the spicy topic of UFOs (Unidentified Flying Objects) and turns it into a maddeningly boring hour show. Unlike *The Invaders*, where a common man deals with real aliens, this series focuses on dull government officials who methodically track down reports of strange objects. It might as well be Sgt. Joe Friday of *Dragnet* tracking down some report of vandalism in the schoolyard. Most of the reports investigated in *Project U.F.O.* are left unexplained, which is no substitute for a little imagination or creativity.

**THE PROTECTORS (**) 60 min (6ep & 2 hr pilot Color; 1969–1970 NBC) Police Drama** *with Leslie Nielsen as Sam Danforth and Hari Rhodes as William Washburn*

Sam Danforth is the white deputy police chief of some California city, who likes the old school of police etiquette. William Washburn is the black district attorney for the area, who believes in the humanistic school of criminology. Danforth and Washburn clash, but respect each other. Viewers will tire of all this civility after a few episodes.

The two-hour 1969 pilot for the series is titled *Deadlock. The Protectors* (also known as *The Law Enforcers*) originally aired as part of the umbrella series *The Bold Ones.*

**THE PROTECTORS (*½) 30 min (52ep Color; 1971–1972 UK ITC) Adventure** *with Robert Vaughn as Harry Rule, Nyree Dawn Porter as Caroline di Contini, and Tony Anholt as Paul Buchet*

More protection for a helpless world, this time from an organization of the world's best private detectives called The Protectors. *U.N.C.L.E.*'s Robert Vaughn represents the United States, Nyree Dawn Porter (Irene on *The Forsyte Saga*) is there for Britain, and Tony Anholt (First Officer Verderschi on *Space: 1999*) plays a Frenchman, in workmanlike but wooden adventures.

Some of the production team's other credits include the marionette adventure series *Fireball XL-5* and *Supercar*. Unfortunately, while these folks are quite adept at working with puppets, they don't show quite the same flair with international intrigues involving living, breathing humans. Not surprisingly, they later had similar problems with the live-action science fiction of *Space: 1999.*

**THE PRUITTS OF SOUTHAMPTON (**) 30 min (30ep Color; 1966–1967 ABC) Situation Comedy** *with Phyllis Diller as Phyllis Pruitt, Reginald Gardiner as Ned Pruitt, Pam Freeman as Stephanie Pruitt, Gypsy Rose Lee as Regina Wentworth, Grady Sutton as Sturgis, John Astin as Rudy Pruitt, Marty Ingels as Norman Krump, Paul Lynde as Harvey, Richard Deacon as Mr. Baldwin, and Billy DeWolfe as Vernon Bradley*

The wild, raucous humor of Phyllis Diller is hard to squeeze into the confines of a TV sitcom, and this is the main reason why *The Pruitts of Southampton* flops. The original premise is strained and artificial. Diller plays wealthy socialite Phyllis Pruitt, of the Southampton, Long Island Pruitts. It turns out the Pruitts owe a fortune to the IRS, but the IRS will avoid prosecution if the Pruitts don't let on (huh?). Phyllis thus must try to carry on her lavish style while actually pinching pennies.

In mid-series, the title changes to *The Phyllis Diller Show* and, perhaps realizing the show is doomed, Diller lets loose and has a ball. The format alters slightly and she begins to take in boarders, which is a fine plot device to bring in a fabulous collection of co-stars, such as John Astin (*The Addams Family*), Richard Deacon (*The Dick Van Dyke Show*), Paul Lynde, Marty Ingels, and Billy DeWolfe.

**THE PSYCHIATRIST (*) 60 min (6ep & 2 hr pilot Color; 1971 NBC) Medical Drama** *with Roy Thinnes as Dr. James Whitman, and Luther Adler as Dr. Bernard Altman*

For Freudians only, this turgid drama takes the *Dr. Kildare* concept of elderly mentor/young medico and places it in the psychiatric field. Roy Thinnes, who was much better battling the clear and present danger of aliens in *The Invaders*, is extremely intense as Dr. Whitman.

Budding film genius Steven Spielberg directs an episode or two of this series.

**PUBLIC DEFENDER (*) 30 min (65ep B&W; 1954–1955 CBS) Law Drama** *with Reed Hadley as Bart Matthews*

Following the *Dragnet* mold, *Public Defender* bases its stories on real-life tales gleaned from the files of a crime-fighting agency, in this case various public defender agencies around the country.

**PUBLIC EYE (*½) 60 min (33ep: 12 B&W & 21 color; 1969–1973 UK Thames) Detective Drama** *with Alfred Burke*

Reasonably true-to-life cases of a likable, but only moderately successful, British gumshoe. With all these sleuths currently gathering dust on the shelves, someone should start a detective channel. All crime, all the time.

**PUBLIC PROSECUTOR (*) 20 min (26ep B&W; 1947–1948 Syndication) Crime Drama** *with John Howard as the prosecuting attorney, Anne Gwynne as his assistant, and Walter Sande as the police lieutenant*

*Public Prosecutor* holds the honor of being the very first filmed series made especially for television. The concept is crude and simple, following the exploits of an unnamed prosecuting attorney as he tries to put guilty criminals behind bars. What makes *Public Prosecutor* so odd is that it is only twenty minutes long. By the early 1950s, when the show was already in reruns, thirty minutes had become the standard length of TV shows, so many stations that aired *Public Prosecutor* filled out the half hour with panel discussions, quiz segments, or commercials. The series has also run as *Crawford Mystery Theater.*

**PULASKI THE TV DETECTIVE (**½) 60 min (8ep Color; 1987 UK BBC) Detective Drama** *with David Andrews as Larry Summers, Caroline Langrishe as Kate Smith, Kate Harper as Paula Wilson, Nigel Pegram as Gerry Marsh, Rolf Saxon as Jerome, and Timothy Carlton as Hilary*

*Pulaski the TV Detective* is a cute little effort that takes the TV detective concept and has some fun with it. David Andrews plays Larry Summers, a boozy expatriate American actor who stars as a priest turned detective (just known as Pulaski) in a U.S. TV show (called *Pulaski*) being filmed in England. Summers is just an actor, but somehow he keeps becoming involved in real mysteries that he tries to solve with the crime-fighting pointers he picks up on the soundstage. Assisting Summer is his wife, Kate, who also portrays Pulaski's assistant Briggsy on the show within the show. Sometimes, all these plot convolutions become a bit much to follow, but everything in *Pulaski the TV Detective* is done with some humor. Andrews' portrayal of Summers as an overly cool womanizer is a bit too forced, but the nice jabs at the image of the perfect TV gumshoe make up for it.

**PUNKY BREWSTER (*½) 30 min (88ep Color; 1984–1987 NBC & Syndication) Situation Comedy** *with Soleil Moon Frye as Penelope "Punky" Brewster, George Gaynes as Henry Warnimont, Cherie Johnson as Cherie Johnson, and Susie Garrett as Betty Johnson*

A Raggedy Ann doll come to life, seven-year-old Punky Brewster has that wide-eyed, adorable kid look designed to melt the heart of even a cruel taskmaster in a Charles Dickens novel. The stories play such emotions to the hilt, beginning with the opening episode, in which young Punky and her little puppy are found in a vacant Chicago apartment and adopted by the building's crusty but kind-hearted bachelor manager, Henry. He keeps a watchful eye on her, while she brings some long-needed sunshine into his otherwise drab world. And should he stray far from her smiley face view of the world, she will be there, voice dripping with innocent hurt, pleading for him to mend his ways. The series is well done, but sort of like the "It's a Small World" happy-song ride at Disneyland: Either you buy into the premise completely, or you suffer a sugar overdose and begin pulling the stuffing from any doll or plush toy at hand.

Eight-year-old Soleil Moon Frye (younger sister of Meeno Peluce, the lead in such series as *Voyagers*) plays the role as if typecast for it, though the idea of a young character named Punky was (according to network PR) actually based on the object of a childhood crush by NBC programming executive Brandon Tartikoff (who even got the grown woman's permission to use her first name). Appropriately, then, Punky's dog is named Brandon.

One odd aspect of this series is that six thirty-minute episodes actually consist of two separate, fifteen-minute stories (complete with their own individual closing credits). This production accommodation took place because in its original run *Punky Brewster* was slotted after the Sunday football games, which sometimes spilled over. Rather than just drop this program (or run it intact, but throw off the rest of the schedule that night), the network would drop in a fifteen-minute package.

There are also eighty-eight cartoon episodes of *Punky Brewster* (which first aired as Saturday morning fare on NBC from 1985 to 1987), which feature more adventure-oriented tales, often set throughout the world.

**PURSUIT OF HAPPINESS (**) 30 min (10ep Color; 1987–1988 ABC) Situation Comedy** *with Paul Provenza as David Hanley, Brian Keith as Roland G. Duncan, Judie Aronson as Sara Duncan, Wesley Thompson as Vernon Morris, and Wendel Meldrum as Margaret Callahan*

Idealistic history professor David Hanley has been on the road searching for America long enough to actually look forward to returning to classwork in Philadelphia. Even better, he's coming back as a new assistant professor working lifelong idol, Prof. Roland Duncan, a gruff but lovable tenured scholar (played by gruff but lovable Brian Keith). Of course, face-to-face Hanley soon discovers both disappointing and inspiring traits in his hero, such as when they collaborate on an article and the professor spends more time reminiscing than writing. But since this is pretty much a by-the-numbers "generations" sitcom, they both ultimately come to respect each other. There are also some silly but effective supporting cast members (including Duncan's dumb but sexy daughter, Sara, and Margaret, a slightly neurotic Egyptian studies scholar), though the most innovative moments come when Hanley turns to two other idols for fantasy-scene advice: U.S. President Thomas Jefferson (played by Kevin Scannell) and basketball legend "Magic" Johnson (the real-life figure in a cameo).

In a rarity for a short-run series, there is even a neat wrap-up moment in the final episode, with David realizing that the love he was searching for is right in his own office, which he shares with Margaret. She really likes him a lot, and in the last scene, he notices.

Paul Provenza went on to host Nickelodeon's *Kid's Court.*

**QB VII** (**½) (6¼hr miniseries Color; 1974 ABC) **Drama** *with Ben Gazzara as Abe Cady, Anthony Hopkins as Dr. Adam Kelno, Leslie Caron as Angela Kelno, Lee Remick as Lady Margaret Alexander Weidman, Juliet Mills as Samantha Cady, Dan O'Herlihy as David Shawcross, Anthony Quayle as Tom Bannister, John Gielgud as Clinton-Meek, Jack Hawkins as Justice Gilroy, and Judy Carne as Natalie*

One of the earliest American TV miniseries, *QB VII* is a quality adaptation of Leon Uris's bestselling novel. Abe Cady, an American writer, publishes an article claiming that a successful Polish doctor, Adam Kelno, performed unethical experiments on concentration camp inmates during World War II. Kelno denies the charges and sues Cady for libel. The case is tried in a British courtroom, where Kelno's entire life is examined and reviewed.

Compared to later miniseries, *QB VII* is a bit slow and filled with talking heads. Still, it is engaging drama with top-flight acting by a well-known cast. Douglas Cramer (*The Love Boat, Vega$*) does a fine job as producer ■

**Q.E.D.** (**½) 60 min (6ep Color; 1982 CBS) **Adventure** *with Sam Waterston as Quentin E. Deverill, George Innes as Phipps, A. C. Weary as Charles Andrews, Sarah Berger as Betsy Stevens, and Julian Glover as Dr. Stephan Kilkiss*

Sam Waterston is a talented actor who usually sticks to plays (*Much Ado About Nothing*), movies (*The Great Gatsby, Capricorn One, Heaven's Gate*), and PBS miniseries (*Oppenheimer*). *Q.E.D.* is his first attempt at a TV series, and it is well crafted with an undercurrent of humor.

The series *Q.E.D.* is something of a mix of *The Wild, Wild West* and the Sherlock Holmes stories. Set around 1912, the show concerns brilliant Harvard professor Quentin E. Deverill, whose initials are Q.E.D. (the same as the Latin phrase *quod erat demonstrandum*, signifying the solution to a problem). Prof. Deverill quits academia in disgust when his inventions are pooh-poohed by his colleagues. He travels to London, where he puts his inventions to practical use as an amateur detective. There aren't many episodes of *Q.E.D.*, and the show is not really a hidden masterpiece, but it is worth watching. ■

**QUANTUM LEAP** (**½) **60 min (7ep at Fall 1989 & 2 hr pilot Color; 1989– NBC) Science Fiction** *with Scott Bakula as Sam Beckett and Dean Stockwell as Al*

An intriguing twist on the always difficult premise of time travel, *Quantum Leap* is far more down to earth than its more ponderous predecessors, such as *Time Tunnel*. The basic concept is superficially confusing (although ultimately irrelevant): Sam Beckett, a 1990s scientist working on a super-secret time travel project in a deserted part of New Mexico, is the first man to break the time barrier, but nothing else goes as planned. Sam turns up in other people's bodies in various earlier eras. Everybody else sees Sam as the person he has replaced, but to the viewer (and Sam), Sam always looks like Sam (except when he looks in the mirror, and sees how he appears to others). Since everyone accepts Sam as the person he has replaced, the time traveler must laboriously adapt to utterly different surroundings whenever he engages in a "quantum leap" and changes eras. Sam can only confide in Al, a cigar-chomping scientific colleague in the time travel project, whose holographic form is seen and heard only by Sam. Al observes the goings on and brings news of the slow progress back in the 1990s to bring Sam home.

After all that elaborate setup, *Quantum Leap* has a lot of fun with the time travel theme. Sam's task is to change history slightly, making the past come out better than it was supposed to. When his good deed is accomplished, Sam leaps to a new setting, always turning up at inopportune moments, with no idea (at first) who he is this time. Dean Stockwell (*Blue Velvet, Married to the Mob*) is a hoot as the lecherous and frequently hungover Al. Scott Bakula is engagingly vulnerable as Sam.

**QUARK** (***) **30 min (9ep Color; 1978 NBC) Situation Comedy** *with Richard Benjamin as Adam Quark, Conrad Janis as Otto Palindrome, Tim Thomerson as Gene/Jean, Richard Kelton as Ficus, Tricia Barnstable as Betty, Cyb Barnstable as Betty, Bobby Porter as Andy the Robot, and Alan Caillou as The Head*

The setting is space, in the year 2222 A. D., with commander Adam Quark and his crew on a vital continuing mission: to clean up the garbage floating in the void, where far too many have boldly come and gone, and left behind a real mess. They are well-suited for their task as interstellar street sweepers, mainly because there's not much else they're qualified for. Quark (played to deadpan perfection by Richard Benjamin) is a well-meaning but bungling dreamer whose assignment to the United Galaxy Sanitation Patrol was probably the only way he was ever going to become a commander . . . of anything. His crew is equally cut-rate: Andy, a cowardly junk heap robot; Gene/Jean, a male/female transmute who switches from aggressive macho to shy and withdrawn at the most inconvenient times; science officer Ficus, a logical, unemotional humanoid plant with an unerring sense of bad timing; and co-pilots Betty I and Betty II (one is a clone of the other, but neither knows which is which). They're on assignment from space station Perma One, home of Otto Palindrome and the disembodied "Head" of the galaxy—both of whom shudder whenever the safety of the universe is inadvertently put in the hands of Quark and his crew.

This space adventure genre parody was created by Buck Henry (one of the pens behind *Get Smart*), and owed its brief 1978 network run to the success of the initial *Star Wars* film—though only one story is a deliberate takeoff of that blockbuster hit. In that, Hans Conried provides the voice of "The Source," a comic version of "The Force." In fact, the overall series is more a parody of television's *Star Trek* and other classic science fiction tales.

Ironically, because *Quark* ran for such a short time, Henry and the other writers never had to venture much beyond these parameters for plots, instead devoting their energies to fine-tuning the particular story and character parodies and sneaking in plenty of wordplay. This includes using such appropriate character names as Quark (a scientific term borrowed from James Joyce's *Finnegans Wake*), Ficus (literally, a plant), and Palindrome (whose first name, Otto, is an example of one), along with some delightfully bad puns (such as the episode "Goodbye, Polumbus," alluding to Richard Benjamin's theatrical film *Goodbye, Columbus*). Of the story parodies, "All the Emperor's Quasi-Norms" (*Flash Gordon*), "Vanessa 38-24-36" (*2001: A Space Odyssey*), "The Old and the Beautiful" (*Star Trek*), and "May the Source Be with You" (*Star Wars*) are probably the best. Even the twin Bettys are an odd allusion, played by Cyb and Tricia Barnstable, who years before played the Doublemint twins in television commercials for Doublemint chewing gum.

*Quark* is a funny, intelligently written, and well-executed comedy definitely worth searching out. Ironically, just a few months after the series ended its original run, Conrad Janis (Palindrome) found himself working in a space parody setup of a different sort, playing Mindy's dad on *Mork and Mindy.*

**QUATERMASS (**) 30 min & 60 min (22ep: eighteen 30 min B&W & four 60 min Color; 1953, 1955, 1958, & 1979 UK BBC & Thames) Science Fiction** *with Reginald Tate, John Robinson, Andre Morell, and John Mills as Professor Quatermass*

Pioneer British TV science fiction effort (beginning half a decade before the *Sputnik* satellite launching), makes the most of a relatively meager budget to present the terrifying consequences of an astronaut returning to Earth infected with a space virus. The main hope for our planet? The brilliant, bluntly outspoken, Professor Quatermass. During the 1950s the BBC produced three *Quatermass* serials (*The Quatermass Experiment, Quatermass II,* and *Quatermass and the Pit*), each six episodes long, with a succession of three different actors in the title role. But the real importance of this serial is that it began to develop the story, filming, and taping techniques incorporated in the next decade on such British adventure series as *Doctor Who.* There were also three feature film adaptations of the material, released in the United States as *Creeping Unknown* (1956), *The Enemy from Space* (1957), and *Five Million Years to Earth* (1968). In 1979, Thames television put out a four-episode *Quatermass* follow-up, with yet another performer taking the lead. But there was one more person using this name, filmmaker John Carpenter, who took Quatermass as a feature-film-writing pseudonym. ■

**THE QUEEN AND I (*½) 30 min (13ep Color; 1969 CBS) Situation Comedy** *with Larry Storch as First Mate Charles Duffy, Billy DeWolfe as First Officer Oliver Nelson, Carl Ballantine as Seaman Becker, Pat Morita as Crewman Barney, Barbara Stuart as Wilma Winslow, and Reginald Owen as Commodore Dodds*

The "queen" in the title is the *Amsterdam Queen*, an aging ocean liner destined for the scrap heap. Aghast at such a prospect, first mate Charles Duffy decides to do all in his power to save the boat, and not coincidentally his own job (which has plenty of off-the-books perks). No doubt meant as a fresh con man setting reminiscent of *The Phil Silvers Show, McHale's Navy,* or *F Troop* (where Storch played the scheming Corporal Agarn), this one doesn't really hold water. It's missing that important angle of put-upon recruits making the best of their military service. Here, Duffy and such confederates as Seaman Becker (Carl Ballantine, previously Lester Gruber on *McHale's Navy*) and Crewman Barney (Pat Morita, later Arnold on *Happy Days*) come off as just plain grubby. Why shouldn't the ship's owner (Commodore Dodds) sell it—except, of course, to annoy obnoxious First Officer Nelson (played by Billy DeWolfe). If you like such scheming, stick with the Bilko, Agarn, and McHale originals.

**THE QUEST (**½) 60 min (15ep & 2 hr pilot Color; 1976 NBC) Western** *with Kurt Russell as Morgan Beaudine and Tim Matheson as Quentin Beaudine*

A late model western (more than a decade after the peak of the genre in the early 1960s) with strong leads and a workable premise. Kurt Russell and Tim Matheson play Morgan and Quentin, two brothers raised in totally different environments: Morgan spent eight years living as a captive of the Cheyenne Indians (he even has an Indian name, "Two Persons"), while Quentin was educated in San Francisco and plans to be a doctor. But the brothers are united in one quest, to find their long-lost sister, Patricia, who had been captured along with Morgan but sent to a different Indian tribe. It's as good an excuse as any to wander the Old West, giving Morgan and Quentin the chance to get involved with both Indians and settlers. Definitely worth catching for the leads, even if it's only the pilot film (of the same name) in some movie slot. Both subsequently focused more on theatrical films, such as *Animal House* and *To Be or Not to Be* (Matheson) and *Big Trouble in Little China* and *Silkwood* (Russell). Matheson also did two subsequent TV series, *Tucker's Witch* and *Just in Time* (which he also produced).

**THE QUEST** (*½) **60 min (8ep Color; 1982 ABC) Adventure** *with Perry King as Dan Underwood, Noah Beery as Art Henley, Ray Vitte as Cody Johnson, Carrie Welby as Karen Austin, Michael Billington as Count Dardinay, and John Rhys Davies as Sir Edward*

To keep its territory from being absorbed by France (because there is no bloodline successor to its aging king), the tiny principality of Glendora brings over four very (*very*) distant relations from the United States and offers each of them a chance at the throne. Only first they have to compete with each other according to some medieval tests of skill and honor.

Not a bad setup for a made-for-TV movie, but stretching it to a series begins to strain credibility, especially when the tests continue with the entourage stomping around Europe. Wouldn't it have been easier and cheaper for Glendora just to strike a deal with France, maybe bribing some official or buying the land outright?

The series ended production without declaring a winner, but the smart money was on Art (Noah Beery a.k.a. Jim Rockford's dad), who would then name the rest as his royal court.

**QUILLER** (**) **60 min (13 ep Color; 1975 UK BBC) Spy Drama** *with Michael Jayston as Quiller, Moray Watson as Angus Kinloch, and Sinead Cusack as Rosalind*

Yet another stubbornly independent government agent, Quiller often locks horns with his boss, Angus Kinloch, but inevitably turns out to be right in his hunches. This mid-1970s series is loosely based on a 1966 theatrical feature film, *The Quiller Memorandum* (written by Harold Pinter and starring George Segal), which had been a departure in its time from the spy films laden with technical gizmos. By 1975, though, that was nothing really special. The main reason to tune in is to see Michael Jayston in the title rule of Quiller, half a decade before he turned up as Peter Guillam in the 1980 international adventure *Tinker, Tailor, Soldier, Spy*.

**QUINCY, M. E.** (**½) **60 min (148ep Color; 1976–1983 NBC) Police Drama** *with Jack Klugman as Quincy, Robert Ito as Sam Fujiyama, Garry Walberg as Lt. Frank Monahan, John S. Ragin as Dr. Robert Astin, Lynette Mettey as Lee Potter, and Anita Gillette as Dr. Emily Hanover*

Single-minded and principled to a fault, Jack Klugman's Quincy loves his work as a medical examiner at the Los Angeles County Coroner's Office. It's Quincy's business to investigate and certify causes of death and whenever he uncovers *anything* suspicious (often pointing to murder) he uses this information as his carte blanche to take on virtually any cause that sets off his sense of outrage. Whether his suspects include a mob leader or a self-serving bureaucrat, Quincy will find a way to make that person squirm. He savors every moment of confrontation, knowing that he and his assistant, Sam, have uncovered forensic medical evidence from the corpse that the suspect couldn't even imagine. And when there's some larger social issue involved (for example, food poisoning from pesticides), Quincy really shines. And shouts.

Unfortunately, Quincy at times is like Oscar Madison with a medical degree, so loud, pushy, and preachy that you wish someone would slip him a hypo with a sedative. Though definitely worth following for a while, *Quincy, M. E.* is best taken in limited doses. Also, don't bother waiting to hear his first name—even at his wedding ceremony with Dr. Emily Hanover, Quincy just calls himself . . . Quincy!

**R.C.M.P.** (*) **30 min (39ep B&W; 1960 Syndication) Adventure** *with Gilles Pelletier as Cpl. Jacques Gagnier, John Perkins as Frank Scott, and Don Francks as Bill Mitchell*

From the great white North come three mounties, members of the Royal Canadian Mounted Police. As promised, they always get their man.

**THE RACING GAME** (*½) **60 min (6ep Color; 1979 UK YTV) Mystery** *with Mike Gwilym as Sid Halley*

In real life, mystery writer Dick Francis was once a horse jockey for the Queen of England. Then he became a prolific author, specializing in horsey whodunit stories, including the adventures of former steeplechase jockey Sid Halley. Sid is one of those accidental detectives, falling into the business when a personal injury results in an artificial hand, forcing him to hang up his professional riding togs. Those gimmicks aside, this is a strictly formula mystery adventure, without particularly complex plots or characters. All the episodes are self-contained stories and first aired in the United States on *Mystery!* in 1980 and 1981.

**RACKET SQUAD (**½) 30 min (98ep B&W; 1950–1953 Syndication & CBS) Police Drama** *with Reed Hadley as Capt. John Braddock*

Predating the TV version of *Dragnet, Racket Squad* is one of the pioneers of TV cop shows. What sets it apart from the numerous crime shows that followed it, aside from the cheap budget and dated atmosphere, is that *Racket Squad* does not deal with armed criminals. San Francisco police Lt. Braddock is only interested in unarmed robbery, the swindle, the con man, the phony sales pitch, and the like. Braddock goes about his business wising up a gullible public that the stranger you meet is more than likely just itching to pick your pocket, either literally or figuratively. The absence of squealing tires and blazing guns is refreshing, as is the 1950s lingo. Do police still call themselves the "racket squad" or the "bunco squad" anymore? ■

**RAFFERTY (*½) 60 min (13ep Color; 1977 CBS) Medical Drama** *with Patrick McGoohan as Sid Rafferty, Millie Slavin as Nurse Vera Wales, and John Getz as Daniel Gentry*

Patrick McGoohan portrays the title character of this quirky medical series as a tight-lipped enigma with little love for or interest in his fellow medicos. Though he might explode at any moment in an argument (usually over some matter of principle), Rafferty usually just takes matters into his own hands as best as he can. The stories are equally puzzling, reflecting an obvious desire to break from the boundaries of the hospital corridors, but not all that certain where to go. For instance, in one episode there's a car chase scene involving just one car, Rafferty's, as he drives like a madman to reach a playing field to keep some kids from eating contaminated food after a sports practice. Well, at least he gets out of the hospital—one of McGoohan's stated goals for the character. He later described this whole experience as "the most miserable job I've ever done in my life," chiefly because he had absolutely no control over the ins and outs of the series, scripts, and his character (in contrast to his major input in *The Prisoner* or *Secret Agent*). Afterward, he kept his distance from U.S. television productions.

**RAGS TO RICHES (**) 60 min (19ep & 2 hr pilot Color; 1987–1988 NBC) Comedy-Drama** *with Joseph Bologna as Nick Foley, Douglas Seale as John Clapper, Kimiko Gelman as Rose, Tisha Campbell as Marva, Bridget Michele as Diane, Bianca DeGarr as Patty, and Heidi Zeigler as Mickey*

"*Bachelor Father* meets MTV" is an apt description of *Rags to Riches*, a frothy series that dabbles with innovation. Nick Foley is a rich playboy business tycoon living in L.A. in 1961. For reasons that are essentially irrelevant, Foley decides to adopt a few young female orphans, ages seven through sixteen. Before you begin to think of some lurid child-molestation horror saga, be assured that Foley intends no harm to the girls; he just feels having some young girls around the house will help his business (huh?).

Naturally the presence of the girls causes disruptions in Foley's life. The young ladies go through all sorts of puppy-love routines and Foley's butler, Clapper, keeps a doting eye on the gaggle of girls.

The MTV aspect of *Rags to Riches* is the girls' inclination to break into choreographed versions of 1960s rock'n'roll songs when the mood strikes them. All in all, its a crazy-quilt premise that ambles aimlessly through its brief run. ■

**RAISING MIRANDA (*½) 30 min (7ep Color; 1988 CBS) Situation Comedy** *with James Naughton as Donald Marshak, Royana Black as Miranda Marshak, Amy Lynne as Marcine, Steve Vinovich as Bob Hoodenpyle, Miriam Flynn as Joan Hoodenpyle, and Michael Manasseri as Jack Miller*

One day, Donald Marshak wakes up and finds that his wife has left him. Gone. Adios. Sayonara. Why? Who knows! Why she left is irrelevant to the proceedings. All that is important is that Mrs. Marshak is gone, leaving poor Donald, a Racine, Wisconsin contractor, to raise their teenaged daughter Miranda all by his lonesome.

The humor in this show is supposed to come from the awkwardness Donald and Miranda feel when everybody they know offers aid and comfort on their loss and from Donald's fumbling efforts to be both father and mother to Miranda. This territory is all pretty familiar for TV sitcoms, and there is nothing new in *Raising Miranda* to make it stand out. The characters of Donald and Miranda are somewhat appealing, but this show's only claim to fame is that it is, without a doubt, the first TV sitcom set in Racine, Wisconsin.

**RAMAR OF THE JUNGLE (*) 30 min (52ep B&W; 1952–1954 Syndication) Adventure** *with Jon Hall as Dr. Thomas "Ramar" Reynolds and Ray Montgomery as Professor Howard Ogden*

These "authentic" backlot jungle adventures follow Dr. Thomas Reynolds (a.k.a. Ramar—the Great White Doctor) as he tends to the medical needs of natives in both Africa and India. In between, of course, there are the obligatory bad guys to dispatch. Though meant as strictly kid stuff, these don't carry the same sense of heroic legend as *The Lone Ranger* (a contemporary show to *Ramar*), instead coming off as very basic, very cheap, and very dated.

**RANDALL AND HOPKIRK (DECEASED)** **(see *My Partner the Ghost*)**

**RANGE RIDER** (**) 30 min (76ep B&W; 1951–1952 Syndication) Western *with Jock Mahoney as the Range Rider and Dick Jones as Dick West*

With his faithful young companion Dick at his side, this daring and resourceful rider of the range (who never reveals his real name) fights for law and order in the early West. Return now to those thrilling days of yesteryear with this contemporary to *The Lone Ranger*. Produced by Gene Autry's company, these episodes actually have pretty good exterior shots (done on Autry's Flying A ranch), with veteran stuntman Jock Mahoney doing his own flying leaps and chases. But, perhaps because he lacks the Lone Ranger's trademark mask and familiar legend, The Range Rider's exploits do not have much staying power. Within a few years of their original *Ranger Rider* stint, both the stars turned up in other western settings: Mahoney in *Yancy Derringer* and Dick Jones in *Buffalo Bill, Jr.* ■

**RANGO** (*) 30 min (17ep Color; 1967 ABC) Situation Comedy *with Tim Conway as Rango, Guy Marks as Pink Cloud, and Norman Alden as Capt. Horton*

*Rango* is but the first of numerous avoidable sitcoms starring Tim Conway that are absolute bombs. Conway is a very funny man (his sidekick work in *McHale's Navy* and *The Carol Burnett Show* proves it), but whenever he steps in front, he falls flat.

Aside from Conway, the talent behind *Rango* makes it look better than it is. The executive producer is Danny Thomas, no stranger to quality TV comedy. The producer is Aaron Spelling, whose work with *Charlie's Angels* and *The Mod Squad* shows that he can at least turn out popular entertainment. Even Frankie Laine, the pop singer who performed the title song to the epic TV western *Rawhide*, turns up to warble the *Rango* theme song.

Still, *Rango* is no good. Trying to redo the *F Troop* theme of bumbling western heroes, *Rango* has Conway play the klutzy son of the commander of the Texas rangers in the 1870s. He is stuck in the rangers' most out-of-the-way locale, where he teams up with an assimilated Indian con man (played by borscht belt comedian Guy Marks). Much commotion ensues, none of it memorable. Catch *F Troop* instead.

**THE RAT PATROL** (**½) 30 min (59ep Color; 1966–1968 ABC) War Drama *with Chris George as Sgt. Sam Troy, Gary Raymond as Sgt. Jack Moffitt, Lawrence Casey as Pvt. Mark Hitchcock, Justin Tarr as Pvt. Tully Pettigrew, and Hans Gudegast as Capt. Hans Dietrich*

Plenty of banter, explosions, and jeep chases across the North African desert drive this well-paced World War II group adventure. The stories are based on the real-life missions of a British outfit known as the Long Range Desert Group, which made life in the desert just a little more difficult for Nazi General Rommel's elite Afrika Korps. On its way to American television, though, the make-up of the crew changed a bit, with the Rat Patrol becoming three-fourths American and one-fourth British (demolition expert Jack Moffitt)—a point that annoyed British viewers in the original run of the series.

After these war exploits, Christopher George (head of the Rat pack) went on to play the eternally young Ben Richards on *The Immortal*, while Hans Gudegast (leader of the German forces) changed his name to Eric Braeden and eventually turned up on the daytime soap *The Young and the Restless*.

**RAWHIDE** (***) 60 min (144ep B&W; 1959–1966 CBS) Western *with Clint Eastwood as Rowdy Yates, Eric Fleming as Gil Favor, Sheb Wooley as Pete Nolan, Paul Brinegar as Wishbone, Steve Raines as Jim Quince, James Murdock as Mushy Mushgrove, and Robert Cabal as Hey Soos Patines*

This is a manly show: for men, about men. Women do turn up now and again as guests, but the focus is on the guys, doing what guys did in the old west, like driving cattle from Texas to Kansas. Its a rough, dirty job, but somebody's got to do it (at least until the railroad reaches Texas).

What better man to star in this manly show about men than Clint "Dirty Harry" Eastwood? An unknown when *Rawhide* was produced, Eastwood is dynamic with the gritty, low-down power of his personality as he plays number two man in the cattle drive. The cattle boss is played by Eric Fleming, another laconic fellow who fits in well with Eastwood.

The rest of the cast includes assorted cooks, assistant scouts, and one Mexican whose character's name is actually spelled Hey Soos (better known as Jesus, with a Spanish lilt). The action in *Rawhide* is solid, the stories are compact, and there is very little philosophical angst about the vagaries of justice that pop up so often on *Gunsmoke*, a contemporary of *Rawhide*. To top it off, *Rawhide* boasts one of TV's best theme songs, co-written by Dimitri Tiomkin (the Russian-born musician who wrote the themes for films such as *High Noon* and *The High and the Mighty*) and sung by macho man Frankie Laine. *Rawhide* has just about everything you'd want in a TV western, with none of the mushy stuff that turns up when you bring in women to get in the way of the horses and cattle.

**THE RAY BOLGER SHOW** (**½) 30 min (59ep B&W; 1953–1955 ABC) Situation Comedy *with Ray Bolger as Raymond Wallace, Allyn Joslyn as Jonathan Wallace, Richard Erdman as Pete Morrisey, Betty Lynn as June, and Marjie Millar as Susan*

TV has never succeeded with the musical comedy format that works so well on Broadway. *The Ray Bolger Show* is one of the more memorable attempts in that genre. Ray Bolger, the scarecrow in *The Wizard of Oz* and the star of many Broadway musicals, such as *Where's Charley* (where he sang "Once in Love with

Amy"), plays Ray Wallace, a star of numerous Broadway musicals. The concept is akin to that of Danny Thomas in *Make Room for Daddy* or Jack Benny in his show, in that Bolger plays a thinly disguised version of himself and has lots of opportunities to show off his main talent. With Thomas and Benny, that talent is joke telling. With Bolger, the talent is dancing, and that's where the problem comes in. TV viewers just don't seem to dig dancing, so Bolger's lively show had to change.

Originally titled *Where's Raymond* (for the main character's tendency to show up at the theater just moments before the opening curtain), the show becomes *The Ray Bolger Show* in the second season, where dancing is downplayed and sitcom is played up. Ray acquires a girlfriend from Iowa (Susan), and much of the unique charm of the show is lost.

**RAY BRADBURY THEATER (**½) 30 min (18ep at Fall 1989 Color; 1985– HBO & USA) Suspense Anthology** *with Ray Bradbury as host*

The author of *The Martian Chronicles, The Illustrated Man*, and numerous other science fiction classics hosts a series dramatizing his own short stories. Bradbury's work is short on bug-eyed monsters and long on appealing spookiness, but his complex tales deserve better production than is provided in this somewhat low-budget effort. ■

**THE RAY MILLAND SHOW (**) 30 min (76ep B&W; 1953–1955 CBS) Situation Comedy** *with Ray Milland as Prof. Ray McNutley/McNulty, Phyllis Avery as Peggy McNutley/McNulty, Minerva Urecal as Dean Josephine Bradley, and Lloyd Corrigan as Dean Dodsworth*

Ray Milland, a suave leading man of 1930s/1940s Hollywood, stars as a married college professor with a large following of admiring females. At first, the series is called *Meet Mr. Nutley*, is produced by Joe Connelly and Bob Mosher (who went on to produce *Leave It to Beaver*), and has Milland as scatterbrained Prof. McNutley at a girls' college. For the second season, the title changes to *The Ray Milland Show*, the McNutleys become the McNultys, Connelly and Mosher are gone, the setting becomes coed Comstock College, and Peggy, the professor's wife, is the wacky one now. The changes are too confusing. The first season is better, but the entire series is fairly forgettable.

**READY STEADY GO (Highlight Specials) (***½) 30 min (7ep B&W; 1985 UK C4) Music-Variety**

While we can only lament the absence of any highlights packages from the likes of *Hullabaloo* and *Shindig*, at least we have a taste of British pop music, 1960s style, with *Ready Steady Go!* This series flourished in Britain through the Associated Rediffusion television service, and in the mid-1980s reappeared through the efforts of Dave Clark, who had acquired rights to the program tapes. (Yes, Dave Clark of the Dave Clark Five rock group.) In Britain, excerpt specials hit the airwaves both as a limited series on the BBC's Channel 4, and on videotape. Stateside, they first circulated on home video, with any Beatles hook receiving the strongest promotional push. For nostalgic baby boomers, this is the ideal way to enjoy not only British acts such as The Beatles, The Who, and The Rolling Stones but also visiting American performers such as the Beach Boys, Otis Redding, Marvin Gaye, and Jerry Lee Lewis. ■

**THE REAL MCCOYS (***) 30 min (224ep B&W; 1957–1963 ABC & CBS) Situation Comedy** *with Walter Brennan as Grandpa Amos McCoy, Richard Crenna as Luke McCoy, Kathy Nolan as Kate McCoy, Lydia Reed as Hassie McCoy, Michael Winkleman as "Little" Luke McCoy, and Tony Martinez as Pepino Garcia*

*The Real McCoys* is where TV's hillbilly craze started. Before Andy of Mayberry locked up his first town drunk, before Jed Clampett loaded up his clan and moved to Beverly Hills, before Kate Bradley opened the Shady Rest Hotel in Petticoat Junction, and before Eddie Albert talked Eva Gabor into moving to Green Acres, Grandpa Amos McCoy and his brood headed west from West "Virginny" to the promised land of California. The success of the McCoys unleashed a decade-long love affair between the networks and the rural settings that had been strenuously avoided beforehand.

Early TV sitcoms (*The Goldbergs, I Love Lucy*) were ultra-urban in tone, in that most characters lived in downtown apartments in big eastern cities. By the mid-1950s, the move was on to bland West Coast suburbia (*Life of Riley, Leave It to Beaver*). The general assumption among TV executives was that the mass of urban and suburban viewers would not sit still for a show featuring rural "rubes." *The Real McCoys* proved them wrong.

The setting of the series is California's San Fernando Valley (a careful mix of rural and urban), where Grandpa Amos McCoy relocates his ranching business and his family. The family does not include Grandpa's children (they had mysteriously died), but consists instead of his three grandchildren: teenaged Hassie, eleven-year-old "Little" Luke, and big Luke (newly married to Kate, who he calls "Sugar Babe") The McCoys may have moved west, but they still have a lot of West Virginia in them, as their corn pone accents attest. The comedy comes from their efforts to adapt to the new environment, while everyone tries to cope with the iron control of stubborn, irascible, old Grandpa.

One aspect of California life that the McCoys were not ready for is the Mexican farmhand. Pepino Garcia, the McCoys' hired help, does not seem to share the puritanical rugged work ethic the McCoys brought west. Pepino would prefer to take a long siesta and play some music rather than hop to it all day, and this difference in opinion constantly riles Grandpa Amos.

These days, Pepino's character may strike some viewers as being a negative stereotype. Nevertheless, it's always entertaining to see how Grandpa and Pepino interact.

Richard Crenna and Kathy Nolan both turn in fine performances as the not-so-country new generation, struggling to find themselves in a new culture. Clearly, however, the main draw here is Walter Brennan. His Grandpa Amos is a pickled mixture of rural aphorisms and wild exasperations, a cantankerous old coot who never gives in and is usually right. His explosions of wrath are always fun to watch, and Grandpa Amos is one of those rare TV characters who is basically annoying, yet somehow still lovable. Brennan's ability to so adeptly catch the flinty feel of country bumpkinism (a talent he had previously shown in films such as *Swamp Water* and *To Have and Have Not*) is all the more remarkable considering that he was born in Swampscott, Massachusetts, a suburb of Boston.

The essential beauty of the humor in *The Real McCoys* is that the program both satirizes the rough, unsophisticated ways of the country folk (which city slickers chuckle at) and demonstrates that simple backwoods wisdom often overcomes big-city book learning (which confirms what rurals have always felt). Two of the people behind the scenes of *The Real McCoys* later transplanted this concept and cashed in. Executive producer Danny Thomas took the simple country wisdom aspect of *The Real McCoys* and created *The Andy Griffith Show*, while writer Paul Henning took the rubes move West concept and created the biggest comedy hit of the 1960s, *The Beverly Hillbillies*. Young Danny Arnold, one of the show's producers, apparently was untouched by the McCoy phenomenon, since he went on to produce such nonrural shows as *My World and Welcome to It* and *Barney Miller.*

Try to avoid the last season of *The Real McCoys*, when Kate McCoy is killed and the plots revolve around efforts to marry "big" Luke to a string of eligible widows.

**REAL PEOPLE (*) 60 min or 30 min (130ep 60 min or 195ep 30 min Color; 1979–1984 NBC) Personality Interviews** *with Fred Willard, Sarah Purcell, John Barbour, Skip Stephenson, Bill Rafferty, Byron Allen, and Mark Russell*

The tout for this interview and personality feature series is that it celebrates real people from all walks of life. Of course, "real" is somewhat of a misnomer. At the very least, most of the featured subjects have an unusual skill, an odd or eccentric hobby, or some other trait that helps them stand apart from the crowd. They're not quite weird enough to carry a whole hour themselves (with the likes of Phil Donahue or Geraldo Rivera or Oprah Winfrey), but they are (and always have been) ripe for an appearance in the sort of fluffy filler features news reporters such as Charles Kuralt ("On the Road") have been doing for years ("And here's a man who plays the national anthem on a saw!"). It's harmless fun—and in the hands of someone like Kuralt, even a touch poetic—giving a local character a moment of national exposure.

*Real People* also has a crew of permanent celebrity hosts to introduce the features, to welcome guests in the studio, and to go out on the road. After all, what's the fun of being a one-night hometown television celebrity without the chance to hob-nob with some established TV star (that way you can knowingly tell your friends what people such as Sarah Purcell and Fred Willard are "really like"). Unfortunately, these celebrity types are given some truly awful scripts and "spontaneous" lines to deliver. The result is an often condescending package that at times seems more a mockery than a true celebration of Anywhere, U.S.A.

*Real People* was created by George Schlatter (of *Rowan and Martin's Laugh-In* fame), and helped usher in a rush of "pop journalism" still going strong. Like *Laugh-In*, each episode of *Real People* is broken into dozens of smaller self-contained segments. Currently, the 130 hour-long episodes are also available as edited-down thirty-minute offerings (195 episodes), which play a bit better than the full-length originals.

**REBECCA (**) 60 min (4ep Color; 1979 UK BBC) Mystery** *with Jeremy Brett as Maxim de Winter, Joanna David as Mrs. de Winter, Julian Holloway as Jack Favell, Vivian Pickles as Beatrice Lacy, and Anna Massey as Mrs. Danvers*

Based on the same 1938 novel by Daphne du Maurier used by Alfred Hitchcock for his 1940 theatrical feature starring Laurence Olivier, Joan Fontaine, and George Sanders. It's one of those psychological mysteries with the hint of something deep and sinister always lurking at the edge, beginning with our first sight of English aristocrat Maxim de Winter (played by future Sherlock Holmes Jeremy Brett) in Monte Carlo. He's an intense, brooding man haunted by the death of his wife, Rebecca, though such thoughts seem to be set aside when he meets a shy and insecure young American woman (played by Joanna David). The two are married and return to his home, Manderley estate, where the new Mrs. de Winter discovers references to Rebecca almost everywhere. Luckily, Mrs. Danvers is there to help her adjust to this new life, even giving her advice on what to wear to a costume ball. But there's still that nagging sensation that something's not quite right. Will this turn out to be a magical romance, or something quite different?

Actually this story works much better in condensed form as a feature film. But if you are already familiar with the plot details, you might enjoy comparing performances, especially to judge how well Brett stacks up against Sir Laurence. The production first aired in the United States on *Mystery!* in 1980.

**THE REBEL** **(**½) 30 min (76ep B&W; 1959–1961 ABC) Western** *with Nick Adams as Johnny Yuma*

Nick Adams, a minor league James Dean in 1950s films, plays Johnny Yuma, an ex-Confederate soldier in the aptly titled *The Rebel*. Yuma still hasn't gotten over Dixie's defeat. He roams the West, trying to find himself and helping those he meets along the way, making this show something like a western version of *Route 66*. Johnny Cash sings the theme song.

**REBOUND** **(see *Counter Point*)**

**THE RED SKELTON SHOW** **(**½) 30 min or 60 min (130ep 30 min Color; or 99ep B&W & 150ep Color at 60 min; 1962–1970 CBS) Comedy-Variety** *with Red Skelton*

Despite a successful career on radio in the 1940s, former circus clown Red Skelton was much more at home in the movies and, of course, on television. His first weekly TV series began in 1951, and he kept going for two solid decades. The program followed essentially the same formula throughout: opening monologue, main guest stars, an extended sketch featuring one of Skelton's many characters, and (when the series expanded from thirty to sixty minutes) music from David Rose and his orchestra (along with some dancers) before wrapping up with "The Silent Spot" (a pantomime sketch) and a sincere "Good night and may God bless."

None of Skelton's programs from the 1950s are currently being syndicated (though some do turn up on home video tape collections), so the half-hour packages circulating for broadcast are actually cut-downs from the color episodes of *The Red Skelton Hour* from the 1960s. As with other comedy-variety series (such as *The Carol Burnett Show*), this procedure is probably the best, showcasing the comedy segments rather than guest star chat. One thing in Skelton's favor no matter what type of package is that he never really tries to be a headlines-style comic. He'd much rather crack a joke about a pair of seagulls (Gertrude and Heathcliff) than zing the current president. So, to carry his show, Skelton relies on his rubbery face, broad characters, funny voices, physical slapstick, and old-fashioned "seltzer bottle" comedy. This environment is perfect for such Skelton alter egos as simple-minded Clem Kadiddlehopper, The Mean Widdle Kid, Sheriff Deadeye, Boxer Cauliflower McPugg, and con man San Fernando Red. Yet Skelton also balances this comedy with his love of low-key pantomime, especially in sketches involving Freddie the Freeloader.

Over the long, long run of the series, none of these characters ever change. Nor are they joined by any regulars in recurring supporting roles—this really is a one-man showcase. As a result, *The Red Skelton Show* is really not geared toward the long haul broadcast rerun grind. Yet it is perfect for some highlight compilations, if only to allow Skelton's characters to strut their stuff at least once. These highlights are definitely worth seeing and saving. ■

**THE REDD FOXX COMEDY HOUR** **(*) 60 min (16ep Color; 1977–1978 ABC) Comedy-Variety** *with Redd Foxx, Slappy White, and LaWanda Page*

Redd Foxx was wonderful as Fred Sanford in *Sanford and Son*, where overacting was needed. However, having left that sitcom for this hour variety show (the type of show Foxx always wanted to star in), Foxx seems miscast in the role of friendly host.

There are some very funny moments here, but on the whole there is not much worth watching. LaWanda Page, Fred Sanford's nemesis in *Sanford and Son* as Aunt Esther, turns up to bedevil Foxx again.

**THE REDD FOXX SHOW** **(*½) 30 min (13ep Color; 1986 ABC) Situation Comedy** *with Redd Foxx as Al Hughes, Rosana DeSoto as Diana Olmos, Pamela Segall as Toni Rutledge, Barry Van Dyke as Sgt. Dwight Stryker, Nathaniel Taylor and Theodore Wilson as Jim-Jam, Beverly Todd as Felicia Clemmons-Hughes, and Sinbad as Byron Lightfoot*

Redd Foxx, best known from the lead role in *Sanford and Son*, plays Al Hughes, another grouchy widower, in *The Redd Foxx Show*. Instead of running an L. A. junk yard like Fred Sanford, Hughes owns a Manhattan coffee shop/newsstand. A social worker pressures Hughes into adopting an orphaned white girl (Toni), causing Hughes to soften up a bit. At least it's nice to reverse the *Diff'rent Strokes*/*Webster* situation and see a white child adopted by a black parent for a change.

Whatever value *The Redd Foxx Show* has is lost about halfway through the run when wholesale cast changes are made. Toni is shipped to boarding school, and Hughes winds up with a new orphan, this time a boy (Byron). Theodore Wilson, late of the brief *Sanford and Son* spin-off series *Sanford Arms*, takes over as Hughes' pal Jim-Jam. Along with this comes the arrival of Hughes' ex-wife Felicia, yet another loud-mouthed black woman for Redd Foxx to trade insults with. This setup is simply a poor reprise of the great Fred Sanford–Aunt Esther battles on *Sanford and Son*.

**REDIGO** **(*½) 30 min (15ep B&W; 1963 NBC) Drama** *with Richard Egan as Jim Redigo, Roger Davis as Mike, Elena Verdugo as Gerry, Mina Martinez as Linda Martinez, and Rudy Solari as Frank Martinez*

The character of Jim Redigo first appeared in *Empire*, where he was the foreman of a large modern western ranch. In *Redigo*, as the title implies, he becomes the prime figure, now running his own (much smaller) spread.

**REGGIE** **(**) 30 min (6ep Color; 1983 ABC) Situation Comedy** *with Richard Mulligan as Reggie Potter, Barbara Barrie as Elizabeth Potter, Chip Zien as C. J.*

*Wilcox, Jean Smart as Joan Reynolds, Dianne Kay as Linda Potter Lockett, Timothy Busfield as Mark Potter, and Timothy Stack as Tom Lockett*

Mid-life crisis, American style. That describes this U. S. version of the British comedy, *The Fall and Rise of Reginald Perrin*. Richard Mulligan (Burt Campbell on *Soap*) plays the nervously uncertain middle-aged executive, Reggie Potter. He works unhappily at the Funtime Ice Cream Company, under C. J. Wilcox, his obnoxious young boss. Actually, Reggie doesn't really do anything dramatic to shake up his life, but he does fantasize about alternative moments to his routine (which we see acted out). For instance, in his dreams Reggie actually does make a pass at Joan, the good-looking secretary at the office. Outside of such temporary diversions, this is a fairly standard home and office family comedy.

**REGINALD PERRIN, THE FALL AND RISE OF (**) 30 min (21ep Color; 1976–1980 UK BBC) Situation Comedy** *with Leonard Rossiter as Reggie Perrin, Pauline Yates as Elizabeth Perrin, John Barron as C. J., and Sue Nicholls as Joan Greengross*

Reggie Perrin is a middle-aged suburban family man stuck in an incredibly boring dead-end executive position. He's really not all that good at it anyway, succeeding only in spite of himself. Here's the "fall": He gets sacked. Or is that the "rise"? After staring at the inviting waves of the seashore, he decides to fake his own suicide and rise again from the depths with a new name and a new lease on life.

Though still only mildly talented, he starts his own business and finds himself quite successful (but, how could you miss selling Whoopee cushions). He's curious about the life he sort of left behind, though, so he watches and interacts with his former family and work associates in disguise, seeing how they have dealt with his departure—or ignored it. Rule of thumb: You really don't want to be there to see how they act when you're just a memory. Later Reggie heeds the old business adage of repeating your winning formula and "dies" a second time, coming back with yet another identity. And another successful business.

A 1983 U. S. adaptation is called simply *Reggie* and doesn't dwell on the death angle quite as much.

**REILLY: ACE OF SPIES (***½) 60 min (12ep: one 90 min & eleven 60 min Color; 1983 UK Thames) Espionage Drama** *with Sam Neill as Sidney Reilly, Leo McKern as Basil Zaharov, Norman Rodway as Cummings, Jeananne Crowley as Margaret Thomas Reilly, and David Suchet as Inspector Tsientsin*

This series is based on a 1967 biographical book detailing the exploits of real-life British agent Sidney Reilly. Ian Fleming's James Bond obviously owes some of his characterization to Reilly. It's easy to see why.

Reilly is a lifelong professional, born in Odessa in 1874 and spending more than two decades in the world of espionage (working for the British). He's cool, suave, physically fit, and equipped with superb instincts for survival. In addition, he has the confident audacity to carry out some truly daring escapades (such as selling German ships to Russia, then sending their blueprints to London). Reilly seems to take personal satisfaction in the knowledge that his activities really do help shape the destiny of his times, though even he is not successful in every venture (the Russian Revolution still takes place despite his efforts to undermine it). His number one nemesis is Russian agent Basil Zaharov, nicely played by Leo McKern.

*Reilly*'s individual episodes are a combination of multipart adventures and self-contained exploits, so there's a good mix of pacing. The ninety-minute opening tale is particularly good (as Reilly attempts to smuggle stolen oil surveys out of Russia), as is the wrap-up episode. But definitely try to catch the entire series run for historical spy drama at its best.

**REMINGTON STEELE (****) 60 min (94ep Color; 1982–1987 NBC) Detective Drama** *with Stephanie Zimbalist as Laura Holt, Pierce Brosnan as Remington Steele, Doris Roberts as Mildred Krebs, James Read as Murphy Michaels, and Janet DeMay as Bernice Foxe*

They meet on opposite sides of a case. She is protecting a valuable collection of gems, while he is out to steal them. By the end of the adventure, they've felt the first spark of romance. They've also become partners. In fact, he takes over as her boss.

That's quite a promotion, but there happens to be a personnel gap at Remington Steele Investigations—namely, a man named Remington Steele. The oversight was intentional because Laura Holt is the real head of the agency. A detective whiz, she had been frustrated at customer reluctance to hire a female investigator, so she created a masculine superior and put "his" name on the door. Suddenly there were plenty of clients willing to hire Mr. Steele, who was always "out of town" or "keeping a low profile" while Laura (and her assistant, Murphy Michaels) did the front-line work. The setup was working fine until he walked in.

Actually he doesn't set out to assume Remington Steele's identity; it just evolves out of a convenient misunderstanding in the first story. But, upon getting to know Laura ( and confirming that there is no "Mr. Steele"), he decides that this identity would be a fine life for a while. And she agrees, "strictly for business reasons." It makes sense to have a real-life figurehead to trot out for clients.

Of course, the real reason they both agree is that they've found themselves instantly attracted to each other and working together is a wonderful excuse to be together. Over the course of the series, Laura and Steele (he rarely uses his first name and she always calls him "Mr. Steele") go through a most unusual and lengthy courtship, testing each other, verbally sparring, and digging into each other's past, all the while developing a deep and genuine affection. It's clear they both realize this just might be the real thing, so they're determined to be very careful. They don't want to get hurt, and at the same time they don't want to lose an opportunity for true love.

The result is a wonderful subtext to the entire series, with the romantic feelings between Laura and Steele adding a special energy to the stories, reminiscent of the sly affection between John Steed and Emma Peel on *The Avengers*. And, like that classic adventure series, *Remington Steele* also showcases some first-class writing and stylish action.

In its first season, the series splits the adventures between standard agency mystery cases (involving Murphy in the action as well) and solo shots with Laura and Steele. At this point, Steele's deliberately vague background sometimes makes his useful participation in the actual investigations appear more as a matter of luck—he might make an offhand remark that cracks the case, but it will be Laura who picks up on it as the key to the solution. However, he does have an encyclopedic knowledge of theatrical feature films, and he's constantly making analogies between them and whatever situation they might be in.

And so are the writers, who effectively work in subtle references to classic and obscure cinema moments throughout the series run. In fact, the first episode sequence in which Steele initially takes his name is a direct allusion to Alfred Hitchcock's *North by Northwest* (a film that hinges on mistaken identity). Another early story quietly drops in the name George Kaplan (also from *North by Northwest*) without calling attention to that fact. Usually, though, there will be some direct cinema reference and, in particularly strong episodes, the tone of the story itself will reflect that connection. One of the best of this type in the first season is "Vintage Steele," a wine-country murder that doubles as a parody of *Falcon Crest* and an affectionate tribute to the offbeat Hitchcock film, *The Trouble with Harry*.

Beginning with the second season, *Remington Steele* wholeheartedly embraces the romantic adventure genre. Both odd-man-out Murphy and agency secretary Bernice Foxe depart. The new receptionist (and occasional investigating assistant) is a brassy former IRS agent, Mildred Krebs (played by Doris Roberts, the ethnic mom on *Angie*). This role not only eliminates any potential competition for Laura's affections but it also fundamentally changes the setup at the agency because Mildred doesn't know Steele isn't really Steele. In her eyes, they're both experienced investigators—in fact, he really is the boss (a point Laura takes pains to correct). At the same time, Laura also moves into a new apartment, revamps her wardrobe, and drops a few hints about impulsive moments in her own past. (She even reveals herself to be a chocoholic in the delightful story "Steele Sweet on You.")

Now a full investigating partner, Steele himself starts to display consistently greater aptitude in the cases, drawing on skills apparently honed in his mysterious past. One of his old associates, Daniel Chalmers, turns up occasionally, confirming that "Harry" (as he calls Steele) can be quite an accomplished con man operator. (In a particularly appropriate bit of casting, Chalmers is played by Efrem Zimbalist, Jr., a former suave Los Angeles detective himself on *77 Sunset Strip* and the real-life father of Stephanie Zimbalist.) After a while, it becomes clear that the reason Steele hasn't shared much of his past with Laura is that in many cases he's not particularly thrilled to remember it or, in the case of his real name, he doesn't know the answer himself. Steele's quest for his own identity becomes yet another subtext to this series.

In the meantime, *Remington Steele* develops into one of television's best detective adventures, with clever cases, sharp dialogue, occasional international locations, and a sense of humor that never gets in the way of the stories themselves. Unlike the competing romantic twosome on *Moonlighting* (developed by first-season *Remington Steele* writer Glenn Gordon Caron), Laura and Steele don't mug to the camera, settle into soap opera-ish tales, or otherwise rob the series of a sense of danger. Each episode of *Remington Steele* contains a full-fledged adventure, with the romantic subplots carefully worked into the overall story.

Still, four seasons is a long haul for courtship and personal mystery, so in the last batch of episodes (the final season consists of only six hours) all the loose ends are tied up. Steele fills in much of his past (even confronting his long-lost father) and then the question of romantic consummation is settled at last in a tasteful (off camera) closing scene.

Though a neat wrap-up to an excellent series, the abbreviated fifth season definitely left Pierce Brosnan unhappy. At the time he was being touted as one of the leading candidates to succeed Roger Moore in the role of James Bond—assuming no other commitments. When NBC announced the cancellation of *Remington Steele* after four seasons, that seemed to clear the way. However, in the wake of viewer protests (too many points were left hanging), and the publicity surrounding the possible Bond role, the network changed its mind at the last minute and exercised its option for one final season. Good-bye Mr. Bond (Timothy Dalton got the role), hello Mr. Steele. The final six episodes were shot so they could also be run as three two-hour movies. In these episodes, Jack Scalia plays Tony Roselli, another man with a mysterious past, who follows Laura and Steele from Mexico to Los Angeles to London to Ireland.

**RENDEZVOUS (**) 30 min (39ep B&W; 1959 Syndication) Drama Anthology** *with Charles Drake as host*

*Rendezvous* is an utterly undistinguished series of unrelated dramas. The host, Charles Drake, was an appropriately undistinguished bit actor in numerous Hollywood films of the 1940s and 1950s.

**THE RENEGADES (*) 60 min (6ep & 2 hr pilot Color; 1983 ABC) Police Drama** *with Patrick Swayze as Bandit, Tracy Scoggins as Tracy, Randy Brooks as Eagle, Paul Mones as J. T., Robert Thaler as Dancer, Brian Tochi as Dragon, Kurtwood Smith as Capt. Joseph Scanlon, and James Luisi as Lt. Frank Marciano*

*The Renegades* is *The Mod Squad* of the 1980s. Six young men and one young woman, all with long police records and gang affiliations, are rounded up by Lt. Marciano and given the chance to clear their records by serving as stool pigeons for the cops. So the young squad, called The Renegades, goes out and rats on their friends and contemporaries, while railing at the establishment of society in general and the police bureau in particular. It has all been done before, and it wasn't that good to begin with.

This is the first TV series appearance of Patrick Swayze, who went on to star in the film *Dirty Dancing.*

**REPORT TO MURPHY (**) 30 min (6ep Color; 1982 CBS) Situation Comedy** *with Michael Keaton as Eddie Murphy, Olivia Cole as Blanche Nesbitt, Donna Ponterotto as Lucy Webb, Donnelly Rhodes as Charlie Dawson, and Margot Rose as JoAnn Baker*

You could win a trivia contest by identifying *Report to Murphy* as the show where Michael Keaton plays Eddie Murphy. Keaton is the young comic who went directly from fair sitcoms (such as this one and *Working Stiffs*) to film stardom in *Night Shift, Mr. Mom,* and the 1989 revival of *Batman*. Unfortunately, the Eddie Murphy he plays has no relation to the young black comic who was starring on NBC's *Saturday Night Live* at the time *Report to Murphy* was produced.

The Eddie Murphy in this show is a very young, very white parole officer who really gets involved with the ex-cons he keeps an eye on. Naturally his unorthodox style rankles the by-the-book types. Other than Keaton's presence (this is his last sitcom before he became a film star), *Report to Murphy* is nothing more than the answer to a trick question.

**THE REPORTER (**½) 60 min (13ep B&W; 1964 CBS) Newspaper Drama** *with Harry Guardino as Danny Taylor, Gary Merrill as Lou Sheldon, George O'Hanlon as Artie Burns, and Remo Pisani as Ike Dawson*

The *Dr. Kildare* idea of eager young professional supervised by crusty old mentor is adapted to the pre-Watergate world of newspaper journalism in *The Reporter*. The setting is the mythical New York *Globe* daily and reporter Danny Taylor is the *Globe*'s hot young reporter. Lou Sheldon is Taylor's grumpy editor. Taylor's favorite cabbie, Artie Burns, is played by George O'Hanlon, who is best know as the voice of George Jetson on *The Jetsons.*

**RESCUE 8 (*) 30 min (73ep B&W; 1958–1960 Syndication) Adventure** *with Jim Davis as Wes Cameron, Lang Jeffries as Skip Johnson, and Nancy Rennick as Patty Johnson*

More than a decade before the rescue anthology format enjoyed a brief and abysmal reign (with shows such as *Emergency!* and *S.W.A.T*), *Rescue 8* pioneered the concept. Set in Los Angeles (naturally), the Rescue 8 boys are associated with the L. A. County Fire Department and they battle unrelated emergencies each week. The fancy effects and special gadgets are very primitive, compared to similar big-budget shows from the 1970s. Jim Davis is better known as patriarch Jock Ewing from the early days of *Dallas.*

**RESTLESS GUN (**) 30 min (77ep & 30 min pilot B&W; 1957–1959 NBC) Western** *with John Payne as Vint Bonner*

Just what the world needs, another undistinguished western about a loner gunfighter who roams the post–Civil War West and gets involved in people's lives each week.

The only things worth noting about *Restless Gun* are that star John Payne served as executive producer, this is the first series for producer David Dotort (who went on to the more successful western *Bonanza*), and in the 1957 pilot episode the main character is called Britt Ponset.

**THE RESTLESS YEARS (see *Loose Change*)**

**RESURRECTION (**) 60 min (4ep Color; 1971 UK BBC) Drama** *with Alan Dobie as Prince Dimitri, Bridget Turner as Maslova, Eithne Dunne as Agrafena, Constance Lorne as Sophia, and Clifford Parrish as the Court President*

Adaptation of the Leo Tolstoy novel about a Russian prince attempting to make amends for seducing a girl of sixteen who subsequently became a prostitute. Later when she is falsely convicted of a crime he takes her case, even attempting to "appeal" through the beautiful wife of a high government official in the hopes of securing a pardon from the Czar. The attempt fails and eventually the prince and the prostitute find themselves in Siberia, as he struggles to find atonement, redemption, and "resurrection." Despite the noble aspirations, there's still an air of cynicism and heavy polemics hanging over the series—perhaps impossible to avoid when dealing with this material.

**THE RETURN OF CAPTAIN NEMO (*) 60 min (3ep Color; 1978 CBS) Adventure** *with Jose Ferrer as Capt. Nemo, Tom Hallick as Cmdr. Tom Franklin, Burr*

*DeBenning as Lt. Jim Porter, Lynda Day George as Kate Melton, and Warren Stevens as Hamilton Miller*

Producer Irwin Allen (*Voyage to the Bottom of the Sea*) should have known better than to yank Jules Verne's classic nineteenth-century Capt. Nemo character into the twentieth century. Capt. Nemo, the vaguely mad scientific genius who invented a highly efficient submarine in the 1800s, is revived through some preposterous suspended animation plot device in order to team up with the U.S. navy. They use his ancient sub (the *Nautilus*) for Uncle Sam. Star Jose Ferrer is far better than this stilted series.

**THE RETURN OF THE SAINT** **(see *The Saint*)**

**RETURN TO EDEN** **(*½) 60 min (6hr miniseries & 22ep Color; 1984 Australia) Drama** *with Rebecca Gilling as Stephanie Harper and Tara Welles, Wendy Hughes as Jilly Stewart, James Reyne as Greg Marsden, James Smilie as Dan Marshall, and Olivia Hamnett as Joanna Randall*

An Australian-made soaper with Rebecca Gilling as the target of a murder plot by tennis pro Greg Marsden and her best friend, Jilly Stewart. But she survives that barely creditable attack and soon embarks on an assortment of serious revenge schemes, even adopting a new name to accompany a plastic surgery job. The story covers two eras, with the six-hour miniseries taking care of the initial duplicity while the subsequent series skips ahead seven years for new schemes. Stick with the miniseries, which at least dispatches the trashy, repetitious story line in only twice the time it should have taken.

**RETURN TO TREASURE ISLAND** **(see *Treasure Island, Return To*)**

**THE RHINEMANN EXCHANGE** **(**) (5hr miniseries Color; 1977 NBC) Drama** *with Stephen Collins as David Spaulding, Lauren Hutton as Leslie Hawkewood, Roddy McDowall as Bobby Ballard, Claude Akins as Walter Kendall, Vince Edwards as Gen. Swanson, and Jose Ferrer as Erich Rhinemann*

Robert Ludlum's novel of World War II intrigue is turned into a passable TV miniseries. David Spaulding is an American agent operating in Argentina who is trying to pry some valuable material out of Hitler's Germany by dealing with anti-Hitler Germans.

**RHODA** **(***) 30 min (110ep Color; 1974–1978 CBS) Situation Comedy** *with Valerie Harper as Rhoda Morgenstern, Julie Kavner as Brenda Morgenstern, David Groh as Joe Gerard, Nancy Walker as Ida Morgenstern, Harold J. Gould as Martin Morgenstern, Lorenzo Music as the voice of Carlton the doorman, Anne Meara as Sally Gallagher, Ron Silver as Gary Levy, and Ray Buktenica as Benny Goodwin*

TV's premier J.A.P. (Jewish-American Princess), Rhoda was first seen as second banana to Mary Richards in *The Mary Tyler Moore Show*. Together, Mary and Rhoda commiserated about the problems of being female, single, over thirty, and too intelligent to fall for the first line that came their way. Spun-off to her own show, Rhoda moves from Minneapolis (Mary's locale) to her native New York, where she rooms with her younger sister Brenda.

Rhoda is to Brenda what Mary had been to Rhoda, big sister and partner in kvetching about life's problems. Right away, however, Rhoda's success with men picks up and she lands that prized possession, a husband, in the eighth episode. Hubby Joe Gerard is a good-looking, solid guy who runs a wrecking company and puts up with Rhoda's eccentricities.

For the next two seasons or so, the focus on *Rhoda* is the married life of Rhoda and Joe, while sister Brenda fills out the role of man-hungry young single woman. Rhoda's parents ( Ida and Martin, played by the versatile Nancy Walker and Harold J. Gould) add color by joining in the complaining and arguing that occupy most episodes.

After two years, apparently realizing that the whole appeal of Rhoda's character (from the *Mary Tyler Moore* days) was her status as an unattached woman seeking love (and/or husband), the producers of *Rhoda* decide to dump Joe and put Rhoda back in circulation. At first, Joe and Rhoda separate, but a divorce eventually follows.

Unfortunately, *Rhoda* never gets back on track after Joe leaves. Rhoda joins Brenda at the singles bars, but soon finds a new friend, Sally Gallagher, an older divorced airline stewardess. Now Rhoda can play the little sister again. Various boyfriends come and go, to no great result. Rhoda's mom returns from a brief absence, temporarily without Martin (it seems their marriage had its problems as well), so now all the women can complain about men. For the final episodes, Rhoda is working at some run-down costume company and looks like a woman who is heading nowhere fast. Brenda, at least, has a new uninspiring boyfriend (Benny Goodwin) who is talking marriage.

It's really too bad that such a lively, interesting character as Rhoda winds up with so little after eight years (four with Mary Richards, four on her own). Rhoda has a lot going for her, but her whining does get tiresome after a while.

*Rhoda* is a pure mid-1970s sitcom, with the MTM (Mary Tyler Moore) production company stamp all over it. While the MTM people would soon branch out to produce some of the best TV of the 1970s and 1980s (*Hill Street Blues, St. Elsewhere*), *Rhoda* was one of the first MTM hits without Moore herself.

**THE RICH LITTLE SHOW** **(*) 60 min (13ep Color; 1976 NBC) Comedy-Variety** *with Rich Little, Charlotte Rae, Julie McWhirter, R. G. Brown, and Mel Bishop*

Nobody told Rich Little, a very talented comic impressionist from Canada, that comedy-variety shows were passé by the mid-1970s. After guesting on numerous variety shows and playing supporting roles on several series, Little finally gets his own show, and it sinks from its dead weight. It has the same problems of all variety shows in the 1970s: too old-fashioned a format, too rigid a structure, and too many similar shows preceding it.

**RICH MAN, POOR MAN (BOOK I & BOOK II) /BEGGARMAN, THIEF (***) (12hr miniseries & 21ep 60 min series & 4hr miniseries Color; 1976–1977 & 1979 ABC & NBC) Drama** *with Peter Strauss as Rudy Jordache, Nick Nolte as Tom Jordache, Susan Blakely as Julie Prescott, Edward Asner as Axel Jordache, Dorothy McGuire as Mary Jordache, Michael Morgan, Gregg Henry, and Tom Nolan as Wesley Jordache, James Carroll Jordan and Andrew Stevens as Billy Abbott, Susan Sullivan as Maggie Porter, William Smith as Arthur Falconetti, Kay Lenz and Lynn Redgrave as Kate Jordache, Jean Simmons as Gretchen Jordache Burke, Glenn Ford as David Donnelly, Tovah Feldshuh as Monika Wolner, and Bo Hopkins as Bunny Dwyer*

Based on Irwin Shaw's mammoth novel, *Rich Man, Poor Man* follows the complicated tale of the Jordache family from simple beginnings at the end of World War II through the turbulent 1960s. In the original twelve-hour miniseries, the "rich" man is Rudy Jordache, a real go-getter who climbs out of poverty, builds a business empire, and becomes a U.S. senator. Brother Tom is the "poor" man, a sensitive tough guy who gets lost in life and comes to a nasty end.

In *Book II* (the twenty-one-episode series), the focus is on Wesley and Billy (sons of the late Tom and his true love Julie, respectively), and on Senator Rudy's political battles. Fancy locales such as Las Vegas and Aspen spice up the tale, but *Book II* is hurt by the more mundane nature of weekly production and the lack of famous guest stars.

The final chapters, the 1979 miniseries *Beggarman, Thief*, continues the Jordache saga into the late 1960s, with parts of the story set at the posh Cannes Film Festival. By now, Senator Rudy is gone (disappeared after a dispute with Arthur Falconetti), and the focus shifts to Gretchen Jordache, a sister of Tom and Rudy not seen in the earlier programs. Gretchen, a filmmaker, tries to patch up what is left of the Jordache clan.

**THE RICHARD BOONE SHOW (**½) 60 min (25ep B&W; 1963–1964 NBC) Drama Anthology** *with Richard Boone, Robert Blake, Harry Morgan, Warren Stevens, and Guy Stockwell*

Richard Boone, best known from *Have Gun, Will Travel*, stars in and hosts this intriguing anthology series that tried a highly unusual format for TV, that of a repertory anthology. Each week there is a different story, but the actors are the same, just playing different roles. It's a wonderful idea, but far, far ahead of its time for the early 1960s. The supporting cast (including Robert Blake, later of *Baretta*, and Harry Morgan, later of *Dragnet* and *M*A*S*H*) is great, the writers (including Rod Serling) are good, and the show is worth catching if you are lucky enough to find it.

**RICHARD DIAMOND, PRIVATE DETECTIVE (**) 30 min (51ep B&W; 1957–1960 CBS & NBC) Detective Drama** *with David Janssen as Richard Diamond, Regis Toomey as Lt. McGough, Barbara Bain as Karen Wells, and Mary Tyler Moore and Roxanne Brooks as Sam*

Richard Diamond is another ex-cop who winds up as a private eye and uses his old contacts on the force to keep up on breaking crime news. At first, Diamond operates out of New York, his old stomping ground, but like all good film noir shamuses of the 1950s, Diamond goes west after a while to set up shop in the rococo world of Los Angeles.

Each private eye on TV has to have a gimmick and Diamond's gimmick (once he arrives in L.A.) is having a phone in his car (quite unusual in the 1950s), so he can check in with his answering service. Apparently he's either too cheap or too hard-up to hire a full-time secretary. The answering service lady, known only as "Sam," is never seen. Well, at least her face is never seen. Instead she appears in silhouette and only her shapely legs are in the light. Sam's sexy voice and beautiful legs make her a highlight of the Los Angeles episodes, but the show's cast credits never identify the actress playing Sam. It turns out that originally Sam is played by a young actress then called Mary Moore (now better known as Mary Tyler Moore), who is making her first major TV appearance. After a few months in the role, Moore is replaced as Sam by Roxanne Brooks, another young woman with nice legs and a sultry voice.

While on the West Coast, Diamond finds himself a steady girlfriend, Karen Wells. Barbara Bain (also in her first major series role), who plays Wells, would go on to fame as Cinnamon Carter, the alluring undercover agent in *Mission: Impossible.*

The major reason to watch *Richard Diamond* is to see leading man David Janssen who, you guessed it, is also making his first important TV appearance in this show. Janssen doesn't smile much in *Richard Diamond*, but then smiling was not his forte, as evidenced by his tight-lipped roles as Dr. Richard Kimble, a.k.a. The Fugitive, and Harry Orwell, a.k.a. Harry-O, another ex-cop making a living as a private eye in L.A.

*Richard Diamond, Private Detective* has also been known as *Call Mr. D.*

**THE RICHARD PRYOR SHOW (***) 60 min (6ep Color; 1977 NBC) Comedy-Variety** *with Richard Pryor, Allegra Allison, Sandra Bernhard, Victor Delapp, and Robin Williams*

Richard Pryor, the innovative and volatile black stand-up comic, had made the round of all the TV talk and variety shows by the late 1970s. He already was making a name in movies (*Silver Streak, Greased Lightning*), conducted sold-out concert tours, and didn't really need a TV series to prove his worth. Nonetheless, he tried. *The Richard Pryor Show* is classic proof that standard network TV simply cannot deal with offbeat tastes.

Pryor tries to be different in his series, with weird, semiserious bits that are almost as disturbing as they are funny. His supporting cast is made up of mostly unknowns who turn in good jobs. Still, after some expected run-ins with network censors (too complicated and pointless to detail), Pryor shut down the series before it could really get started. What is left to see is really just a taste of what could have been.

A footnote of interest is that *The Richard Pryor Show* is the first TV series appearance of Robin Williams, who went on to superstardom in *Mork & Mindy.*

## RICHARD THE LION HEART (*½) 30 min (39ep B&W; 1962–1963 UK) Adventure *with Dermot Walsh as King Richard*

An occasionally creaky British-produced historical adventure that would probably work best as a companion program to any of the *Robin Hood* series currently kicking about. This one follows Richard from his crowning as king, through the Crusades and his imprisonment afterward, to his return to England. Not exactly *Masterpiece Theatre* material, but it does provide a Classic Comics–type survey of the era.

## RICHIE BROCKELMAN, PRIVATE EYE (**) 60 min (5ep & 90 min pilot Color; 1978 NBC) Detective Drama *with Dennis Dugan as Richie Brockelman, Barbara Bosson as Sharon Deterson, and Robert Hogan as Sgt. Ted Coopersmith*

A tough assignment, following in Jim Rockford's shoes. Twenty-three-year-old Richie Brockelman wants to be a detective just like Jim and after helping out on *The Rockford Files* (and in a 1976 TV-movie, *Richie Brockelman: Missing 24 Hours*) he goes to his own series. Richie depends on his deceptively innocent youthful appearance to hide the fact that . . . he's really quite inexperienced at the private eye game. But he's college educated, enthusiastic, and has a glib tongue, which he uses to talk himself out of the inevitable tight spot. Or to reassure his police contact, Ted, and his secretary, Sharon (played by the future Fay Furillo of *Hill Street Blues*).

This series was created by Stephen J. Cannell and Steven Bochco, and though everybody seems to give it their all, it doesn't quite jell like *Rockford.*

In 1988, Dennis Dugan won a memorable spot in television continuity history on *Moonlighting*, playing the proud husband (for a few episodes) in the impulsive Las Vegas marriage of Maddie Hayes.

## THE RIFLEMAN (***) 30 min (168ep B&W; 1958–1963 ABC) Western *with Chuck Connors as Lucas McCain, Johnny Crawford as Mark McCain, Paul Fix as Marshal Micah Torrance, Joan Taylor as Milly Scott, and Patricia Blair as Lou Mallory*

Here is a good show with its heart in the right place, but there is some absent ingredient that prevents it from standing out as a truly great series. *The Rifleman* is the saga of the McCain family, or, to be more precise, the McCain men. Lucas McCain is a recently widowed rancher who rides into North Fork, New Mexico, with his twelve-year-old son, Mark, to start a new life. The McCains want only to till the soil in peace. Lucas is really serious about trying to be a good father to Mark, hoping that the boy will grow up the right way amidst the hardships and temptations of frontier life.

The only problem with this bucolic rural existence is that North Fork seems to be chock-a-block full of bad guys who are forever riding through town with guns blazing, shooting up the good townsfolk and threatening the peace and quiet of the McCain family.

Normally a western town would have a marshal or sheriff to take care of bad guys. North Fork has a marshal (Micah Torrance) and, heck, he tries hard, but old Marshal Torrance needs help. Fortunately for the marshal, Lucas McCain is a crack shot with his Winchester rifle and apparently has plenty of time to take from ranching to help shoot back at the bad buys. As it turns out, this fits in with Lucas's overall game plan anyway, because all these shoot-outs are a great way to train Mark to be a crack shot like the old man. What better way is there to teach the kid the TV western male burden of facing off against half-crazed killers every week or so?

So it goes, episode after episode. Lucas mows down the bad guys and Mark learns a lesson about life. Some shows, Lucas mows down a lot of bad guys and Mark doesn't learn any lesson to speak of. Some shows, Lucas does not shoot anybody and Mark learns a lot of lessons.

This is all fairly exciting, as westerns go. The production is nice, with some subdued lighting and appropriate background music. Lucas and Mark are as close and as warm a father-son duo as you will find in the annals of western TV shows, but that bonding does not make up for the dearth of other interesting people. During the latter half of the run of *The Rifleman*, the producers bring in some females to spice up Lucas's life. First comes Miss Milly Scott, who runs the local general store. She has an eye for Lucas, but she is just as level-headed and ultimately dour as he is. Next comes Lou Mallory, a hotelkeeper with a little more spunk, but by this time the series has just about run its course, and nothing much comes of her interest in Lucas.

Lucas has his shares of burdens, what with raising Mark all by his lonesome, but he is too somber and unbending to be very likeable. Oh, he shows emotions now and again, but only in moody outbursts reminiscent of characters in an Ingmar Bergman film. He just tries too hard to always do the right thing. What would make Lucas more human would be for him to go get drunk some Saturday evening, spend the night in the local bordello while some bad guys are running amok on the other side of town, and *then* try to explain to Mark about how the old man is not perfect and that sometimes you just have to let your guard down a bit. Mark would learn a lot.

Johnny Crawford, the handsome young Mark McCain, was one of the original Mouseketeers before he starred in *The Rifleman*. The first episode of *The Rifleman* is a re-edited version of the series pilot, which was originally known as *The Sharpshooter.*

**RIKER** (*½) **60 min (5ep Color; 1981 CBS) Police Drama** *with Josh Taylor as Frank Riker and Michael Shannon as Bryce Landis*

Another of the army of outcast/outsider crime fighters of the 1970s and 1980s, Frank Riker is a rogue San Francisco cop. His expulsion from the force is but a ploy to allow him to work undercover for the district attorney, ferreting out information a regular cop couldn't discover.

**RIN TIN TIN, THE ADVENTURES OF** (**½) **30 min (164ep B&W; 1954–1959 ABC) Western** *with Lee Aaker as Cpl. Rusty, James Brown as Lt. Ripley "Rip" Masters, Joe Sawyer as Sgt. Biff O'Hara, and Rand Brooks as Cpt. Randy Boone*

*Rin Tin Tin* is really *Lassie* with a little more action. Both shows focus on a boy and his dog, but the shows differ in what kind of life the two lead.

*Lassie* presents its boy and dog leading the kind of life grown-ups think kids should lead, living on a nice quiet farm with gentle, loving parents and helping to extricate local townspeople from various dilemmas.

*Rin Tin Tin*, on the other hand, presents its urchin and canine duo leading the kind of life most kids dream about, or at least used to dream about, that is, living in a western frontier cavalry fort with no parents and lots of exciting battles with Indians and outlaws that cry out for the assistance that a boy and his dog can provide.

Young Rusty and his faithful German Shepherd Rin Tin Tin are the only survivors of an Indian raid and the pair are adopted by the 101st Cavalry in general and Lt. Rip Masters in particular. Living in Fort Apache, Arizona, Rusty is made an honorary corporal right off the bat when he uses his young wiles to save a visiting general from a fiendish Indian plot (Rin Tin Tin is made honorary private). From then on, Rusty, "Rinty," and the guys have a whale of a time each week, doing stuff much more interesting to young kids than homework, cleaning their rooms or trudging to school.

The Rin Tin Tin character has a long history, much of which has nothing to do with Fort Apache. The dog first turned up in the German army in World War I, starred in several silent films of the 1920s, and had his own network radio show in the 1930s.

In the mid-1970s, new color introductions were temporarily added to the old black and white *Rin Tin Tin* episodes. In these new openings, James Brown reprises his roles as Lt. Rip Masters, relaying stories of Rusty and Rinty to a new generation of children visiting Fort Apache. These "new" introductions were soon shelved and the episodes now usually run as originally aired.

Keep an eye out for Chief Culebra of the Kiowa Indians. He is played by Frank DeKova, who later played the much friendlier Chief Wild Eagle of the Hekawi Indians in *F Troop.*

In the 1980s, Rin Tin Tin reappeared in an entirely new setting, *Rin Tin Tin K-9 Cop.* ■

**RIN TIN TIN K-9 COP** (**) **30 min (26ep at Fall 1989 Color; 1987– Canada CBC) Police Drama** *with Jesse Collins as Hank Katts, Sharon Acker as Alice, Andrew Bednarski as Stevie Katts, and Ken Pogue as Capt. Cullen Murdoch*

Rin Tin Tin, the redoubtable German Shepherd last seen aiding the U.S. Cavalry in the West in a 1950s black-and-white kiddie action show, reappears here in color, assisting the Toronto police force. Assigned to young policeman Hank Katts, the all-knowing hound sniffs out criminals and evidences an amazing understanding of the English language.

This story may be simplistic, but at least it is far more believable than *The Littlest Hobo*, another Canadian update of an old U.S. dog series.

**RIPCORD** (**½) **(76ep: 38 B&W & 38 Color; 1961–1963 Syndication) Adventure** *with Larry Pennell as Ted McKeever and Ken Curtis as Jim Buckley*

Ivan Tors turned out some of the best syndicated adventure shows of the 1950s (*Sea Hunt, Science Fiction Theater*). *Ripcord* makes no claim to greatness, but it is a well-produced half hour of visual entertainment. The concept is slightly far-fetched, but who cares? Ted and Jim run Ripcord, Inc., a sky-diving school. One way or another, they become involved in all sorts of crime investigations. There is a lot of exciting footage of the two guys falling through the air, making daring landings in the middle of action, and so on. Teenagers should be thrilled.

**RIPLEY'S BELIEVE IT OR NOT** (**) **60 min (120ep Color; 1982–1986 ABC) Documentary** *with Jack Palance, Holly Palance, and Marie Osmond as hosts*

Television footage devoted to the oddities uncovered by Robert L. Ripley (and his heirs and successors) has been kicking around since the late 1940s. Ripley himself even hosted a program for a few months in 1949 before he died. The episodes currently in circulation are drawn from the 1980s revival of the series featuring movie tough guy Jack Palance as the main host and narrator. He offers a somber, rock-solid voice of credibility for the reports, which cover subjects ranging from unusual objects (old bones, carvings, antiques) to downright silly stunts (a woman who insisted in her will that she be buried in her automobile). The producers even find ways to deal with static objects that are not inherently "good television," finding creative ways to present the oddities, such as adding appropriate mood music, sending the camera into unusual angles, or providing extensive background information (including location footage). Wisely, all of the episodes are also available in cut-down thirty-minute form.

**RIPPING YARNS (***) 30 min (9ep Color; 1977 & 1979 UK BBC) Adventure Comedy Anthology** *with Michael Palin and Terry Jones*

A series of comic adventures written by and starring Monty Python's Michael Palin and Terry Jones, based on their warped reinterpretations of Victorian and Edwardian juvenile fiction. Each episode is a self-contained genre send-up with such titles as "Tomkinson's Schooldays," "Escape from Stalag Luft 112B," "Whinfrey's Last Stand," and "Across the Andes by Frog." Their eye for authentic detail is amazing as ever, and they're obviously taking vicious pleasure in exaggerating the clichés of the originals, with long, significant looks between characters, bald-faced lies, and, most of all, youthful innocence. Be forewarned that the main problem for most U.S. viewers is that the original books (such as *Tom Brown's Schooldays*) are not a part of our misspent youth and without those subliminal, gut-level memories, the humor sometimes seems far too dry and obtuse. We recognize what Palin and Jones are doing but we can't appreciate the humor on their level—it's like looking into somebody else's dreams. Fortunately, there are still plenty of clichés shared by all children's literature, so it's worth seeing at least one or two of these. ■

**RIPTIDE (**) 60 min (56ep & 2 hr pilot Color; 1984–1986 NBC) Detective Drama** *with Perry King as Cody Allen, Joe Penny as Nick Ryder, and Thom Bray as Murray Bozinsky*

A formula action package bringing the early 1960s *Surfside Six* gimmick (handsome detectives on a houseboat) from Miami Beach to the golden shores of Southern California. Ex-marines Cody and Nick are the two good-looking male-hunk heads of the agency, located aboard the cabin cruiser *Riptide* (docked at Slip 7, Pier 56). In between bouts with the sun (and flirting with the women on the boat next door), they tackle the usual assortment of low-rent cases, aided by another service buddy, Murray ("Boz"), an electronics geek who happens to be a genius with computers. Cody and Nick take particular delight in trying to bring Murray out of his shell and to develop his poise with women rather than with his robot helper/toy, The Reboz.

*Riptide* is a Stephen J. Cannell production with the usual assortment of contemporary music, light humor, and semiobligatory action scenes featuring such crash-and-chase hardware as the team's aging pink helicopter (the *Screaming Mimi*), their trusty old motor boat (the *Ebb Tide*), and any automobile foolish enough to come within smashing distance. It's a good, reliable adventure package, harmless fluff done with a grin.

Definitely catch one episode, "If You Can't Beat Them, Join Them," the program's dig at *Moonlighting*. At the time of this story's filming, *Riptide* was slotted opposite David and Maddie and getting clobbered in the ratings. Cody, Nick, and Murray find themselves hired to babysit a sparring male and female TV detective duo, showing them how "real" detectives work. Though it's a stretch to call the Riptide crew more realistic than their charges, in the context of this parody the concept works. The story even contains an obtuse dig at *Moonlighting*'s perennial production delays and self-referential TV humor, with much of this episode consisting of segments (and a few outtakes) recycled from previous adventures.

**RIVERBOAT (**½) 60 min (44ep B&W; 1959–1961 NBC) Adventure** *with Darren McGavin as Grey Holden, Burt Reynolds as Ben Frazer, William D. Gordon as Travis, and Noah Beery as Bill Blake*

The cast is the prime allure of *Riverboat*, an otherwise mediocre adventure show. Set in the 1840s, it concerns the *Enterprise* . . . not the star ship of *Star Trek* fame, but rather a 100-foot Mississippi River boat. Darren McGavin (*Kolchak: the Night Stalker*) is the jovial Capt. Holden, who won the boat in a card game. Burt Reynolds, in his first TV series role, is Ben Frazer, the boat pilot. In the second season, with Reynolds gone, Noah Beery (James Garner's dad in *The Rockford Files)* comes aboard as Bill Blake, Capt. Holden's new partner.

**RIVIERA POLICE (½) 60 min (26ep B&W; 1964 UK Associated Rediffusion) Crime Drama** *with Geoffrey Frederick and Noel Trevarthen*

This is a premise that virtually demands being shot "on location" to do justice to the "complex" plots and characterizations. At least, that's no doubt what the producers said at the time. Only about half the total series run of twenty-six episodes is currently available for Stateside syndication, which gives us that much less to ignore.

**THE ROAD WEST (*) 60 min (26ep Color; 1966–1967 NBC) Western** *with Barry Sullivan as Benjamin Pride, Andrew Prine as Timothy Pride, Brenda Scott as Midge Pride, Kelly Corcoran as Kip Pride, and Glenn Corbett as Chance Reynolds*

The Pride family moves from dull Ohio to duller Kansas and encounters all sorts of troubles.

**ROALD DAHL'S TALES OF THE UNEXPECTED (see *Tales of the Unexpected*)**

**THE ROARING TWENTIES (*½) 60 min (45ep B&W; 1960–1962 ABC) Newspaper Drama** *with Rex Reason as Scott Norris, Donald May as Pat Garrison, and Dorothy Provine as Pinky Pinkham*

This series is typical Warner Bros. action-adventure TV from the early 1960s. If you like *77 Sunset Strip, Hawaiian Eye,* or *Surfside Six,* the three most popular Warner Bros. efforts of that era, you'll probably get a kick out of *The Roaring Twenties*. The formula is the same: two hunks, a babe, an exotic setting, and lots of gunfights.

Scott Norris and Pat Garrison are two newspaper reporters in Prohibition-era New York. Their beat is crime and their hangout is the Charleston Club, a swank speakeasy featuring sassy songstress Pinky Pinkham. Pinky is always good for a hot tip about some big mobster and then is likely to belt out a jazzy tune, backed up by "The Girls," a bevy of six lovelies who provide more easy viewing. Sooner or later, an old Packard will come screaming around a dark street corner and some faceless thug will rat-a-tat-tat machine gun some poor Joe who tried to buck the "Mob." Scott and Pat will get on the case, barely escape being turned into swiss cheese by other thugs, and then get their scoop. Pinky will serenade the two heroes at the end. Another sixty minutes of your life down the drain.

*The Roaring Twenties* is not all that bad. It's not that good either. Reason and May are one-dimensional leads, with no intriguing eccentricities. Dorothy Provine is unintentionally hilarious as Pinky. She's so squeaky clean that it hurts to listen to her. She looks like she belongs in the church choir, not some illegal booze joint. The trappings of the 1920s in the show are simplistic and obvious. The theme song is fairly lively and the opening montage contains film clips of the "roaring" decade that are recycled every time the 1920s is breezed over by a slapdash TV documentary.

*The Roaring Twenties* is strictly minor league. If you like Prohibition-era drama, seek out Desilu's *The Untouchables.*

**ROBBERY UNDER ARMS (*½) (6hr miniseries Color; 1985 Australia) Drama** *with Sam Neill, Steven Vidler, Liz Newman, Ed Devereaux, and Christopher Cummins*

Sam Neill plays a noble renegade in nineteenth-century Australia who takes to the life of a plundering highwayman. It's a drawn-out adaptation (filmed on location) of a rambling novel, which is probably better served by a much shorter theatrical film version done in the 1950s. Catch that instead and you'll also get performances by Peter Finch and David McCallum.

**THE ROBERT GUILLAUME SHOW (**) 30 min (12ep Color; 1989 ABC) Situation Comedy** *with Robert Guillaume as Edward Sawyer, Wendy Phillips as Ann Shear, Hank Rolike as Henry Sawyer, Kelsey Scott as Pamela Sawyer, and Marc Joseph as William Sawyer*

After playing butler-turned-politician Benson DuBois for nine years first on *Soap* and then *Benson*, Robert Guillaume shifts gears here and plays Edward Sawyer, a black divorced marriage counselor who lives with his father and two teenaged children. In need of a new secretary, Edward hires a flaky, divorced white woman (named Ann). The two have divorce and children in common, and soon, their professional relationship turns personal (making it one of the rare interracial love affairs among American sitcoms). Robert Guillaume is always enjoyable to watch, but *The Robert Guillaume Show* is more pleasant than pleasing.

**ROBERT KENNEDY AND HIS TIMES (***) (7hr miniseries Color; 1985 CBS) Drama** *with Brad Davis as Robert F. Kennedy, Veronica Cartwright as Ethel Kennedy, Beatrice Straight as Rose Kennedy, Jack Warden as Joseph P. Kennedy, Sr., Cliff De Young as John F. Kennedy, Ned Beatty as J. Edgar Hoover, and G. D. Spradlin as Lyndon B. Johnson*

The busy life of Robert Kennedy, attorney general, U. S. senator, and presidential candidate, is portrayed without too much schmaltz in this miniseries based on a biography by Kennedy aide Arthur Schlesinger, Jr.

**ROBERT TAYLOR AND THE DETECTIVES (see *The Detectives*)**

**ROBIN HOOD, THE ADVENTURES OF (**½) 30 min (143ep B&W; 1955–1959 CBS) Adventure** *with Richard Greene as Robin Hood, Bernadette O'Farrell and Patricia Driscoll as Maid Marion, Donald Pleasence and Herbert Gregg as Prince John, Archie Duncan and Rufus Cruikshank as Little John, Alexander Gauge as Friar Tuck, and Alan Wheatley as the Sheriff of Nottingham*

Robin Hood is the man who made theft respectable, just as long as you're stealing from the rich in the name of a good cause (giving to the poor, for instance). It also helps to have thoroughly despicable targets who abuse their money, power, and influence. It's all in place here in eleventh-century England as Robin and his "Merry Men of Sherwood Forest" battle the Sheriff of Nottingham, frontline emissary of the evil Prince John. The prince is after the ultimate prize, the throne of England, scheming to seize it permanently in the absence of King Richard, not yet returned from fighting in the Crusades.

This is a well-done staging of the familiar swashbuckling tale, with excellent performances from the central cast, an authentic setting (filmed entirely in England), good guest stars, and reasonably clever plots. Richard Greene's Robin proves an able champion of the people (a role aptly celebrated in the program's title song) and, though it's a long, long wait, Richard the Lion-Hearted does eventually turn up.

Currently only a relative handful of episodes are circulating in Stateside syndication, so the conflict seems to move much more quickly than you'd expect. Other versions of the Robin Hood legend can be found in the 1970s Mel Brooks comedy series *When Things Were Rotten* and a 1980s adventure with a supernatural touch, *Robin of Sherwood.* ■

**ROBIN OF SHERWOOD (**½) 60 min & 2 hr (22ep: eighteen 60 min & four 2 hr Color; 1984–1986 Showtime) Adventure** *with Michael Praed as Robin Hood, Jason Connery as Robert of Huntington/Robin Hood, Judi Trott as Maid Marian, Nickolas Grace as the Sheriff of Nottingham, Philip Davis as King John, Robert Addie as Guy de Gisburne, John Abineri as Herne the Hunter, and Richard O'Brien as Guinar the Sorcerer*

This reworked Robin Hood legend (filmed in Britain) weaves a thread of magic into the story (Robin has roots to some legendary pagan god), and emphasizes the rugged sexiness of our swashbuckling hero. Michael Praed carries the lead role for the first half of the run, replaced (after Robin's apparent death) by Jason Connery as Robert of Huntington, the "new" Robin Hood. Appropriately, Michael Praed subsequently turned up Stateside in an American showcase for "pagan gods" of a different sort, playing Prince Michael on *Dynasty*. ■

**ROBIN'S NEST (**½) 30 min (48ep Color; 1977–1981 UK Thames) Situation Comedy** *with Richard O'Sullivan as Robin Tripp, Tessa Wyatt as Victoria Nicholls, Tony Britton as James Nicholls, Honor Blackman as Marian Nicholls, and David Kelly as Albert Riddle*

The follow-up to *A Man About the House*, this show was the basis for the U.S. series follow-up to *Three's Company, Three's a Crowd*.

Robin Tripp finds the girl of his dreams, Victoria Nicholls, and the two of them move in together above a defunct restaurant. Soon, Robin uses the available space to open his own bistro, called Robin's Nest, with a hard-working one-armed man, Albert, as his kitchen help.

Eventually Robin and Victoria get married, though not before plenty of encounters with her divorced parents, especially her irascible father. Honor Blackman (Catherine Gale in *The Avengers* and Pussy Galore in the James Bond film *Goldfinger*) plays her mom.

**ROCK FOLLIES/ROCK FOLLIES OF '77 (***) 60 min (12ep Color; 1976–1977 UK Thames) Drama** *with Charlotte Cornwell as Anna Wynd, Julie Covington as Devonia "Dee" Rhoades, Rula Lenska as Nancy "Q" Cunard de Longchamps, and Emlyn Price as Derek Huggin*

The British *Rock Follies* is perhaps the only TV drama series that presents a valid, intriguing look at rock music, along with some very good original music. The story concerns a three-woman rock band, called "The Little Ladies," and follows their tiring, difficult, and drawn-out efforts to become successful rock stars. They try to maintain some dignity, integrity, and originality, while constantly undergoing stylistic changes foisted on them by their manager. A selection of original songs (all co-written by Andrew Mackay of the group Roxy Music) are performed within the story line of the show, something like early music videos.

The first six episodes outshine the later six (called *Rock Follies of '77*), but all twelve are worth watching. The cult success of this series led the American networks to try to copy the format. All that resulted were some really awful, glitzy, jiggly shows (*3 Girls 3, Sugar Time!*) that missed the whole point of the women trying to prove their value while the marketplace wanted them to be Kewpie dolls.

**ROCK'N'ROLL: THE FIRST 25 YEARS (**½) 60 min (6ep Color; 1982 Syndication) Music Documentary** *with Robert W. Morgan as narrator*

This stab at presenting a course in the history of rock'n'roll contains some nice old clips of various rock stars, circa 1951–1980, but the organization is a bit scattered. Various music celebrities such as Tina Turner, Alice Cooper, William "Smokey" Robinson, and Pat Boone (?!) serve as guest hosts for episodes dealing with their specialty.

**THE ROCKFORD FILES (***½) 60 min (123ep & 90 min pilot Color; 1974–1980 NBC) Detective Drama** *with James Garner as Jim Rockford, Noah Beery, Jr. as Joseph "Rocky" Rockford, Joe Santos as Detective Dennis Becker, Gretchen Corbett as Beth Davenport, and Stuart Margolin as Angel Martin*

Roy Huggins and James Garner (the creator and star from *Maverick*) and Stephen J. Cannell (fresh from stints on *Columbo* and *Toma*) team up for a wonderfully offbeat detective series. Garner is once again at his affable, put-upon best, playing an ex-con turned detective. He charges $200 a day, plus expenses—a nice wage, but the work is sporadic. And dangerous. (Rockford is one detective always nursing an injury; there are no illogical ironman heroics here.) Rockford lives and works out of a house trailer in a beachside community, not only to cut costs but because he likes the location. So does his dad, "Rocky," who is always stopping by hoping to get his son interested in a little fishing. Or a better career.

Because Rockford had been falsely imprisoned, he has a weakness for people in dire straits, often reopening cases the police have already considered closed, much to the occasional frustration of his contact at the station house, Dennis Becker. But just as often he seems to find himself forced into situations he really wants no part of. That's when "Jimbo" is at his best, using his wits and his contacts (especially fellow ex-con Angel Martin) to improvise some sort of solution.

The writing on *The Rockford Files* is particularly sharp, with a nice mix of straight-ahead action scenes and humorous set pieces. In "The Big Cheese," for instance, everybody (including Rockford) thinks he's about to receive in the mail a vitally important package of evidence from a deceased reporter friend who was hot on the trail of some underworld figures. Instead, after dodging mob heavies and hit men also interested in retrieving the package, Jim opens it to discover . . . a block of his favorite cheese. Rockford's expression of surprise mixed with disgust ("They're *never* going to believe this!") is priceless, vintage Garner—and typical of the series.

Also keep an eye out for a number of effective guest shots. Future *Magnum* star Tom Selleck plays Lance White, a handsome detective who frustrates Rockford with his abilities to wrap up a case with a minimum of footwork and a lot of undeserved luck. Kathryn Harrold's Megan Dougherty is a blind therapist who turns to Rockford for protection from one of her patients and discovers there's a spark between the two of them. Dennis Dugan appears several times as Richie Brockelman, eventually leading to a short-lived spin-off series. Even old *Maverick* cohort Jack Kelly turns up a few times in various roles, usually as a villain.

Best of all is "Trouble in Paradise Cove" with guest star Mariette Hartley. This show originally aired shortly after Hartley and Garner had appeared in a series of breezy commercials plugging Polaroid cameras and film, one of the classic perfect chemistry ad pairings. Fortunately, that sense of fun effectively carries over into the episode, with the two alternately sparring and flirting with each other. (Hmm. Perhaps we've found the real inspiration for the teasing twosomes of *Moonlighting, Remington Steele,* and *Cheers*?)

The original 1974 ninety-minute *Rockford Files* TV movie pilot has been reedited into two episodes for the syndicated package. (There's a lot of recapping.) In these episodes, Robert Donley plays Jim's dad. Sometimes episodes of the *Richie Brockelman* spinoff series also turn up in the *Rockford Files* rotation as well.

**ROCKY AND HIS FRIENDS** **(see *The Bullwinkle Show*)**

**ROCKY JONES, SPACE RANGER (*½) 30 min (39ep B&W; 1954 NBC & Syndication) Science Fiction** *with Richard Crane as Rocky Jones, Sally Mansfield as Vena Ray, and Scott Beckett and Bill Lechner as Winky*

For devotees of camp only, *Rocky Jones, Space Ranger* is from the deep, dark past of kiddie TV. Somewhat more sophisticated than *Captain Video* (which is not saying much), *Rocky Jones* follows the harrowing exploits of square-jawed Rocky Jones. He is the leader of the Space Rangers, whose mission is to, you guessed it, protect the universe from evil geniuses. ■

**ROGER DOESN'T LIVE HERE ANYMORE (**½) 30 min (6ep Color; 1981 UK BBC) Situation Comedy** *with Jonathan Pryce as Roger Flower, Diane Fletcher as Emma Flower, Alice Berry as Arabella Flower, Benjamin Taylor as Charles Flower, and Kate Fahy as Rose*

Something akin to the "dramadies" that were the rage on American TV in the late 1980s, this intriguing British series combines humor and pathos in telling the tale of recently divorced Roger Flower. Roger, the typical struggling artist, takes up with Rose, his dipsy girlfriend who only likes married men. Roger also must contend with his son and daughter, who have turned against him thanks to his ex-wife's bad mouthing.

**THE ROGUES (**½) 60 min (30ep B&W; 1964–1965 NBC) Adventure** *with Gig Young as Tony Fleming, David Niven as Alec Fleming, Charles Boyer as Marcel St. Clair, Robert Coote as Timmy St. Clair, and Gladys Cooper as Margaret St.Clair*

Once upon a time, there was a family of rogues. Actually, two families—the Flemings and the St. Clairs—whose ancestors had been among Europe's top jewel thieves, reaching back to the time of Marie Antoinette in 1789. They quite proudly carry on the family tradition in modern times, embracing the motto "Honor Before Honesty" as they plan and execute classy thefts and appropriately staged con games.

Nowadays, as in its original single-season run, the immediate attraction of this series is its all-star cast. But, be forewarned, David Niven and Charles Boyer don't appear nearly as often as Gig Young, who plays "American cousin" Tony. Even though Young does a good job, it's usually the European clan (especially Niven and Boyer) that viewers want to see. But no matter what the lineup, it's definitely worth catching at least a few episodes. Of course, the best stories are those few involving the entire family on the same job. Then it's like *Mission: Impossible, The Sting,* and *It Takes a Thief* all rolled into one, with great character interaction. And at the end there's tea and a victory celebration in Aunt Margaret's home across from (where else?) Buckingham Palace. ■

**ROLL OUT! (**½) 30 min (13ep & 30 min pilot Color; 1973–1974 CBS) Situation Comedy** *with Stu Gilliam as Cpl. Carter "Sweet" Williams, Hilly Hicks as Pvt. Jed Brooks, Mel Stewart as Sgt. B. J. Bryant, Val Bisoglio as Capt. Rocco Calvelli, Ed Begley, Jr., as Lt. Robert W. Chapman, Garrett Morris as "Wheels" Dawson, and Darrow Igus as "Jersey" Hampton*

One of the more intriguing of the rash of 1970s black-oriented sitcoms, *Roll Out!* is set in Europe in the final year of World War II. The series revolves around the mostly black 5050th Army transport company, the so-called "Red Ball Express," that transports supplies to American units at the front.

Aside from the somewhat innovative format, the cast and crew are memorable. The show's producer, Larry Gelbart, garnered more fame from his other military sitcom, *M*A*S*H*. Ed Begley, Jr., one of the few whites in the outfit, went on to star as Dr.Victor Erlich in *St. Elsewhere*. Garrett Morris and Darrow Igus became the resident blacks in two late-night comedy-variety shows, *Saturday Night Live* and *Fridays*, respectively.

**THE ROLLER GIRLS (zero) 30 min (4ep Color; 1978 NBC) Situation Comedy** *with Terry Kiser as Don Mitchell, Rhonda Bates as Mongo Sue Lampert, Candy Ann Brown as J. B. Johnson, Joanna Cassidy as Selma "Books" Cassidy, Marcy Hanson as Honey Bee Novak, Marilyn Tokuda as Shana "Pipeline" Akira, and James Murtaugh as Howie Devine*

Roller derby, arguably the first all-TV sport, is a limited ground for humor. The sport is inherently obscure because nobody really understands the rules, few actually watch the sport anymore, and most fans seem to only want to see fights among the players. There is not much of a basis for story hooks.

The one thing people do know about roller derby is that it is one of the few places you can see comely young women knock each other around, an aspect that some find somewhat alluring. As you may guess, this is the hidden ingredient of *The Roller Girls*, an unfunny "comedy" about a troupe of minor league roller derby queens, the Pittsburgh Pitts. The series is a really cheap method of showing curvaceous young ladies in form-fitting outfits doing a lot of locker room talking. In short, it is titillation TV at its most crass.

That in itself would not be fatal (after all, *Three's Company* contained a lot of those elements), but *The Roller Girls* just is not very funny. The girls, who are supposed to be lively and sharp, just seem like bimbos. The social and ethnic mix of the team (one tall, one black, one Eskimo, one blond airhead, one intellectual, etc.) is too blatant. Team owner Don Mitchell is a cheapskate, of course, but is fairly amusing. The only character with some originality is team announcer Howie Devine, an ex–opera commentator now hitting rock bottom and no longer able to keep up his aristocratic airs.

The sole cast member to go on to anything resembling quality TV acting is Joanna Cassidy, who plays a bookworm with her real last name (Selma "Books" Cassidy). She was far more appealing as Jo Jo White, the very understanding sometimes ex-girlfriend to Dabney Coleman's Bill Bittinger in *Buffalo Bill*. *Roller Girls* comes from James Komack, who hit the mark with *The Courtship of Eddie's Father* and *Welcome Back, Kotter*.

**THE ROOKIES (*½) 60 min (90ep & 90 min pilot Color; 1972–1976 ABC) Police Drama** *with Georg Stanford Brown as Terry Webster, Michael Ontkean as Willie Gillis, Sam Melville as Mike Danko, Kate Jackson as Jill Danko, Gerald S. O'Loughlin as Lt. Eddie Ryker, and Bruce Fairbairn as Chris Owens*

*The Rookies* is another of the huge stable of shows produced by Aaron Spelling and Leonard Goldberg. Like the duo's earlier hit, *The Mod Squad*, the focus is on youth, in this case three shiny new cops who view the world differently than their crusty old superior. Where a "traditional" cop would shoot first, ask questions later, these three young police officers prefer, if possible, to solve disputes amicably.

Like most Spelling-Goldberg productions, *The Rookies* is heavy on the sizzle and light on the meat. You can still find some of the heavy-handed moralizing of *The Mod Squad*, a trait the production duo dumped for later megahits such as *Charlie's Angels* and *Fantasy Island*. Kate Jackson, making her TV series debut here, went on to star as one of the "angels" of *Charlie's Angels*, while intense black actor Georg Stanford Brown starred as Tom Harvey in the two *Roots* miniseries and became a noted TV director, working on *Hill Street Blues* and *Cagney & Lacey*.

In the 1972 pilot, Darren McGavin plays the Gerald O'Loughlin role of superior officer.

**ROOM FOR ONE MORE (*½) 30 min (26ep B&W; 1962 ABC) Situation Comedy** *with Andrew Duggan as George Rose, Peggy McCay as Anna Rose, Ronnie Dapo as Flip Rose, Carol Nicholson as Laurie Rose, Anna Carri as Mary Rose, and Timmy Rooney as Jeff Rose*

Try as you might, you'll be hard pressed to find a more warm-hearted TV couple than George and Anna Rose. They already have two wonderful children of their own (ten-year-old Laurie and nine-year-old Flip), but that's not enough. To do their little part to ease the sorrows in this harsh, cruel world, they adopt two orphans, sixteen-year-old Mary and fourteen-year-old Jeff. Everybody gets along just fine, thank you, and, in fact, the Roses would be pleased as punch to adopt still more (hence the title). The philosophy is admirable, but the exposition in the series is dull and slightly banal.

The series is based on the autobiography of Anna Perrott Rose and a 1952 film (first called *Room for One More*, then *The Easy Way*) with Cary Grant and Betsy Drake.

**ROOM 222 (***) 30 min (113ep Color; 1969–1974 ABC) Situation Comedy** *with Lloyd Haynes as Pete Dixon, Denise Nicholas as Liz McIntyre, Michael Constantine as Seymour Kaufman, and Karen Valentine as Alice Johnson*

Most series from the late 1960s and early 1970s that tried to be relevant came out as stilted, preachy, morality plays. Many that featured blacks in lead roles often tried so hard to overcome negative stereotypes that the black characters appeared as lifeless icons, with no trace of humanity other than rage and suffering. *Room 222* avoids both pitfalls, resulting in one of the more pleasant sitcoms from an era of social upheaval in the United States.

The primary setting is Room 222 of Walt Whitman High School, homeroom of Pete Dixon, a black teacher of history in an integrated high school in Los Angeles. Seymour Kaufman is the always put-upon principal who gets through crises with a live and let live philosophy and some Yiddish sarcasm. Liz McIntyre is the black guidance counselor and romantic interest for Dixon. Alice Johnson is the young English teacher just out of graduate school, whose bubbly enthusiasm for teaching is tested by the reality of the bureaucratic educational system.

The primary quality of *Room 222* is the believability of its characters. All of the big issues of the day (civil rights, youth rebellion, sexual revolution, drug abuse, and antiwar sentiment) are dealt with at one time or another, but always within a realistic setting of the high school and with realistic responses from the primary characters. The two main black characters, Dixon and McIntyre, are two of the more normal blacks to appear on TV during the late 1960s. Neither character is a WASP in soul clothing (as was Diahann Carroll in *Julia*), nor are they laughable buffoons such as Jimmie Walker's J. J. in *Good Times*, or stilted paragons of streetwise virtue such as Linc Hayes of *The Mod Squad*. Dixon and McIntyre can be serious about black issues, but they can laugh about race as well. They have faults and problems just like everybody, and being black is not the only reason they exist on the show.

*Room 222* conveys the message that education is very important to young people and that some educators do their best to bring change within an often cumbersome system. Fortunately these valuable lessons are presented within a humorous, entertaining comedy that rarely seems preachy. Pulling off such a delicate feat requires deft management, and *Room 222* has deft management galore behind the scenes. The creator of the series, James L. Brooks, was later responsible for some of the best sitcoms of the 1970s (such as *The Mary Tyler Moore Show, Rhoda, Taxi,* and *The Associates*) before he moved on to hit movies such as *Terms of Endearment* and *Broadcast News*. The primary producer of *Room 222* is Gene Reynolds, who went on to *M*A*S*H*.

The only serious criticisms worthy of note in regard to *Room 222* are that the actors and actresses portraying the students tend to be more stilted than the adult cast members, and the series probably lasted a tad too long. By the final seasons, the premise seems played out and the stories are not as fresh. Otherwise, for quality TV comedy, *Room 222* should be assigned viewing.

**ROOMIES (½) 30 min (8ep Color; 1987 NBC) Situation Comedy** *with Burt Young as Nick Chase, Corey Haim as Matthew Wiggins, and Jane Daly as Ms. Adler*

Nick Chase is a forty-two-year-old marine drill sergeant who retires from the corps and enrolls in college. Matthew Wiggins is a fourteen-year-old child prodigy who enrolls in college years before his contemporaries. This being a TV sitcom, Nick and Matthew are assigned to the same dormitory room, thus becoming "roomies."

There is supposed to be humor in the contrasting personalities of the two freshmen, but *Roomies* is so strained and so divorced from reality that it comes across as merely embarrassing.

**ROOTS (***½) (12hr miniseries Color; 1977 ABC)/ ROOTS: THE NEXT GENERATIONS (***) (14hr miniseries Color; 1979 ABC) Drama** *with LeVar Burton and John Amos as Kunta Kinte (a.k.a. Toby), Cicely Tyson as Binta, O. J. Simpson as Kadi Touray, Edward Asner as Capt. Thomas Davies, Louis Gossett, Jr., as Fiddler, Lorne Greene as John Reynolds, Chuck Connors as Tom Moore, Leslie Uggams as Kizzy, Ben Vereen and Avon Long as Chicken George Moore, Georg Stanford Brown as Tom Harvey, Henry Fonda as Col. Warner, Richard Thomas as Jim Warner, Stan Shaw as Will Palmer, Irene Cara as Bertha Palmer Haley, Christoff St. John, Damon Evans and James Earl Jones as Alex Haley, Al Freeman, Jr., as Malcolm X, and Marlon Brando as George Lincoln Rockwell*

The miniseries that made miniseries a hit, *Roots* quickly established itself in TV mythology by attracting a record number of viewers when it was originally broadcast over eight consecutive nights in 1977. At the time, *Roots* seemed like a radical departure from TV orthodoxy not only in format but also in content and concept. Viewed in hindsight, it certainly deserves recognition for blazing the trail for miniseries, but its content and concept seem much more in line with the stream of miniseries that have followed.

*Roots* is just a big-budget historical miniseries. Like most other shows of this type, it transforms the more impersonal trends of history into specific human terms, using celebrity guests and some judicious sex and violence to attract a mass audience. The range of *Roots* begins in West Africa around 1750 and runs through the end of the American Civil War a little more than a century later. In the sequel, *Roots: The Next Generations*, the story resumes around 1880 and continues to the 1970s. The two programs follow several generations of one black family from the wilderness of West Africa, through slavery in the American South, then on to the hardships of "freedom" in the late 1800s, the slow rise to respectability in the 1900s, and the eventual rediscovery by one black man of his family's heritage. The *Roots* saga is based on autobiographical novels (*Roots* and *Search*) by that man, author Alex Haley.

In the beginning, Haley's great-great-great-great grandfather, Kunta Kinte, is seen going through initiation rituals as a young man in an idyllic, pastoral community in West Africa. Kinte's Eden is disrupted by the arrival of white slave catchers, who capture Kinte while he is away from the village one day and spirit him off to America, where he is sold as a slave. Never giving in to the efforts of his owners to break his independent spirit, Kinte (renamed Toby) loses a foot in an effort to escape. His daughter, Kizzy, is raped by her owner and bears a son later known as Chicken George (due to his adept handling of fighting chickens). George's ability with the battling birds takes him to England, where he enjoys a modicum of freedom. Returning to the States just before the Civil War, George finds it hard to readjust to the old slave ways. With emancipation following the war, George's family (like most former slaves) is hard-pressed to make any headway due to economic and educational deprivation, not to mention the lingering desire by local whites to keep the blacks in as close a position to slavery as possible. George's son, Tom, takes his family to Tennessee, where they hope to make a better future for themselves as the original *Roots* episodes end.

By the start of the sequel, Tom has become a blacksmith and the leader of the local black community. His daughter Cynthia marries Will Palmer, who manages to acquire ownership of a lumberyard. Their daughter Bertha goes to college, where she meets and soon marries Simon Haley, who serves in World War I and becomes a teacher of agriculture in a black college. Their son, Alex, spends twenty years in the Coast Guard before becoming a noted writer. It is Alex's curiosity and eventual mania for tracing his heritage that brings him back to West Africa, where a local oral historian completes the circle by telling Alex the tale of Kunta Kinte, who left the local village one day, never to return.

The endless parade of top-quality actors and actresses is a large part of the reason *Roots* holds up so well over so many hours. While quality performances can be expected from old pros such as Lorne Greene, Ed Asner, Marlon Brando, Cicely Tyson, and James Earl Jones, it is the great work of then unknowns LeVar Burton, Georg Stanford Brown, and Louis Gossett, Jr., that raises *Roots* above the standard miniseries fare. Much credit must also go to executive producer David Wolper, who had previously been known mostly for documentary work (*Biography, The Making of the President 1960*).

The original *Roots* episodes are superior to the sequel, largely because they deal with far more dramatic incidents. The sequel, while no less sweeping, lacks the epic sense of worlds in flux that marks the original hundred-plus years of the story. Ultimately, Haley's personal search for his family heritage is interesting, but cannot compare to the struggle of his ancestors to survive slavery.

As with all "fact-based" miniseries, historians can easily poke holes in numerous aspects of the plot of *Roots*, but that really is meaningless. *Roots* is not, and should not be, a history lesson. Rather it is an epic on the scale of old Hollywood, adapting to a black setting a common American theme: the struggle, ever upward, of a family of people through hardships.

In 1988, two of the stars of the original *Roots* series, LeVar Burton and Louis Gossett, Jr., reprised their roles as Kunta Kinte and Fiddler, respectively, and teamed up with *Roots* producer David Wolper in a *Roots* TV-movie spin-off titled *Roots: The Gift*. Set around Christmas 1775, in Virginia, the sequel diverges from the Alex Haley novel to tell a fictional story of the involvement of the young Kunta Kinte and his reluctant mentor Fiddler with an early version of the underground railroad. ■

**THE ROPERS** **(*½) 30 min (26ep Color; 1979–1980 ABC) Situation Comedy** *with Norman Fell as Stanley Roper, Audra Lindley as Helen Roper, Jeffrey Tambor as Jeffrey P. Brookes III, Patricia McCormack as Anne Brookes, Evan Cohen as David Brookes, Dena Dietrich as Ethel Armbrewster, and Rod Colbin as Hubert Armbrewster*

The best aspect of *The Ropers* is that it freed *Three's Company* of its two most annoying characters. Even though the couple was somewhat effective as plot foils to Jack, Janet, and Chrissy—always good for some surly deadpan laughs—their bored-with-life-and-marriage routine had begun to wear thin, especially their odd attitudes toward sex with each other. Stanley passionately avoids being passionate, recoiling in horror at the thought of sex with his wife. She, in turn, remains faithful but constantly frustrated with him, always looking for any excuse for the two to hop into bed. Perhaps this was supposed to represent the perversions of an uptight generation, or maybe serve as an American equivalent to the British concept of dutiful sex in marriage.

In any case, it made the Ropers the least likable characters on *Three's Company*. So why spin them off? For one thing, that's exactly what happened in Britain, where the *George and Mildred [Roper]* spin-off from *A Man About the House* was a huge success.

Besides, the performers are good and there is always the chance of playing up Stanley as a much put-upon everyman. One way to do this is with comic foils even more unlikable than the Ropers. So when Helen and Stanley sell their apartment building in Santa Monica and buy a condominium in the ritzy Chevoit Hills area, the comedy hook becomes how they struggle to fit in their new, somewhat snobbish, area.

The supporting cast is good, including Jeffrey Tambor (judge Alan Wachtel on *Hill Street Blues*) and Patricia McCormack (with roles back to child-star days on *Mama* and *Peck's Bad Girl*) as the next-door neighbors, and Dena Dietrich (from the "It's not nice to fool Mother Nature" margarine commercials) as Helen Roper's sister, but it still doesn't quite work. Ironically, part of the problem is that the series and characters are probably too faithful to their British roots, where mannered comedy between the classes (pushy, clannish, judgmental, and dumb) plays much better than here.

So the series had a short network run. Currently it usually sneaks into the *Three's Company* episode rotation under the title *Three's Company's Friends, The Ropers.*

**ROSEANNE** (***) **30 min (24ep at Fall 1989 Color; 1988– ABC) Situation Comedy** *with Roseanne Barr as Roseanne Conner, John Goodman as Dan Conner, Lecy Goranson as Becky Conner, Sara Gilbert as Darlene Conner, Michael Fishman as D. J. Conner, Natalie West as Crystal, and Laurie Metcalf as Jackie Harris*

This television setting seems instantly familiar. Roseanne and Dan Conner are chubby middle-class parents with three kids, a comfortable but not extravagant house, and salt-of-the-earth interests like tinkering with cars, bowling, and hanging out with friends. Roseanne puts in an eight-hour day at a plastics factory assembly line (beside her sister, Jackie, and their good friend, Crystal), plus at least that long back home as a self-proclaimed (tongue-in-cheek) "Domestic Goddess" taking care of her family's needs. (John is in construction, which runs hot and cold, so they really need both paychecks to make ends meet.) Even with the exhausting schedule (enough to send a self-absorbed Yuppie running to analysis), the couple is very happy, and it shows in their warm give-and-take. For instance, once while dining out (at a buffet bar special) they discover a friend is getting divorced, so their conversation humorously (but genuinely) turns to the state of marriage in general and their feelings for each other in particular. It's a touching, affectionate scene. And those warm feelings also apply to their children. Though the two may talk of a glorious life without the kids, with Roseanne tossing off seemingly caustic quips and threats ("They've left for school, quick—change all the locks!"), the pair clearly love their family.

If this description begins to sound vaguely like a blue-collar *Cosby Show*, it shouldn't be a surprise. The series comes from the same production company, only this time it's all built around stand-up comic Roseanne Barr (with the setting, quips, and her fictional character strikingly similar to her stage routines). The stories are low-key, containing more plot than a typical *Cosby Show* episode, but still ultimately carried more by the characterizations. And, best of all, the adults (not the kids) steal the show. Besides Roseanne and Dan as the ultimate teddy bear couple, the characters of Jackie and Crystal (both unattached and very interested in finding the right match) provide a good number of plot hooks. Or at least the latest neighborhood and family gossip.

If you enjoy warm contemporary slice-of-life stories, but find even *Cosby* a bit too upscale (and *thirtysomething* a self-indulgent never-never land), this series is definitely the one for you.

**ROSETTI & RYAN** (**) **60 min (6ep & 2 hr pilot Color; 1977 NBC) Law Drama** *with Tony Roberts as Joseph Rosetti, Squire Fridell as Frank Ryan, and Jane Elliott as Jessica Hornesby*

An innocuous but strictly formula lawyer show, *Rosetti & Ryan* teams up aristocratic and suave lawyer Joseph Rosetti with ex-cop streetwise lawyer Frank Ryan. Together they smart-mouth their way through cases, as do many glib male duos of the 1970s and 1980s (*Starsky & Hutch, Simon & Simon*). Tony Roberts, who plays Rosetti, is best known as Woody Allen's "pal" in several of Allen's films (going back to *Play It Again, Sam* and *Annie Hall*).

The 1977 pilot is called *Men Who Loved Women*.

**THE ROUGH RIDERS** (*) **30 min (39ep B&W; 1958–1959 ABC) Western** *with Kent Taylor as Capt. Jim Flagg, Jan Merlin as Lt. Colin Kirby, and Peter Whitney as Sgt. Buck Sinclair*

Totally forgettable, *The Rough Riders* features two ex-Union soldiers (Flagg and Sinclair) and one ex-Confederate (Kirby) who team up to head west in the days just after the Civil War. The trio runs into trouble quite often.

**THE ROUNDERS** (**½) **30 min (17ep Color; 1966–1967 ABC) Situation Comedy** *with Ron Hayes as Ben Jones, Chill Wills as Jim Ed Love, Patrick Wayne as Howdy Lewis, Bobbi Jordan as Ada, and Janis Hansen as Sally*

Never much of a hit either when it was produced or since, *The Rounders* is fun, no more, no less. Ben Jones and Howdy Lewis are two virile red-blooded modern cowboys deeply in debt to the slithery Jim Ed Love. Thus Jones and Lewis must toil for Love and put up with his orneriness.

Patrick Wayne, who plays Howdy, is the son of western film legend John Wayne. Chill Wills, character actor supreme (who appeared with the elder Wayne in *The Alamo*), reprises his wonderfully larcenous role as Jim Ed Love from the 1965 film *The Rounders* that led to the series.

**THE ROUSTERS** (**½) **60 min (12ep Color; 1983–1984 NBC) Adventure** *with Chad Everett as Wyatt Earp III, Jim Varney as Evan Earp, Maxine Stuart as Amanda Earp, Timothy Gibbs as Michael Earp, Hoyt Axton as "Cactus" Jack Slade, and Mimi Rogers as Ellen Slade*

*The Rousters* has a lot of wacky charm. It is another lighthearted hour show from Stephen J. Cannell, the man behind *The Rockford Files, The A-Team*, and *The Greatest American Hero*. Chad Everett (*Medical Center*) plays the proud but simple great-grandson of legendary western lawman Wyatt Earp. This modern-day Earp works at a more mundane job as bouncer and assistant in a carnival. Earp's efforts at leading a somewhat normal life are always under attack from his weird relatives. Brother Evan thinks (incorrectly) of himself as a master mechanic. Mother Amanda makes a fool of herself as an amateur bounty hunter. Meanwhile, Earp's boss, Cactus Jack Slade, frequently is entangled in some shenanigans of his own making.

**ROUTE 66 (***) 60 min (116ep B&W; 1960–1964 CBS) Drama** *with Martin Milner as Tod Stiles, George Maharis as Buz Murdock, and Glenn Corbett as Linc Case*

Route 66 does not exist anymore. For decades it was the main road west in pre-interstate highway America. It winds from Chicago to L. A. for more than two thousand miles. Unlike the modern interstates, which do their best to avoid any contact with the towns near the road, the old U.S. highway system brought you face-to-face with the various forms of life found in this country.

Because it was such a major passageway west, Route 66 connoted freedom and escape for the generations that grew up in the middle of this century. In the 1930s, the Okie dust-bowl refugees took Route 66 to the pastures of plenty in California. In the 1950s, the Jack Kerouac types traveled this highway as they searched for themselves, on the road to setting up the West Coast counterculture.

Joining that long line of travelers are the main characters from *Route 66*. Tod Stiles is a poor young rich boy now on his own after the death of his father caused the collapse of the family fortune. Buz Murdock is a product of the slums of New York. The two team up and head out to look for America. It never is quite clear why the two of them are driving aimlessly around the country, but they are forever becoming involved in other people's lives. Sometimes they help out; other times it is the locals who teach a lesson to the two young men.

In many ways, this concept is the same one that worked in *The Fugitive*, only here Tod and Buz do not *have* to run away—they want to. This gives the scriptwriters a tremendous freedom to place Tod and Buz in any kind of town, with any kind of people, and this freedom gives the series life. The writing is almost always on target and the acting is first-rate. Watch for the guest stars, as some famous actors (Robert Redford, Rod Steiger) turn up. Nelson Riddle's theme song is catchy, and was a minor hit on the pop charts of the early sixties.

In the final season, George Maharis leaves the show and is replaced by Glenn Corbett as Linc Case, possibly the first Vietnam veteran portrayed in a TV series.

The show gives a little too much exposure to Tod's fancy Corvette (the original sponsor was Chevrolet), and the duo are frequently hundreds of miles from the road for which the show is named, but this is an hour's drive worth taking.

**ROWAN AND MARTIN'S LAUGH-IN** **(see *Laugh-In*)**

**ROXIE (*) 30 min (6ep Color; 1987 CBS) Situation Comedy** *with Andrea Martin as Roxie Brinkerhoff, Teresa Ganzel as Marcie McKinley, Mitchell Laurance as Michael Brinkerhoff, and Ernie Sabella as Vito Carteri*

Andrea Martin, a graduate of the SCTV comedy troupe, is wasted in this pointless sitcom about a low-rent UHF TV station in New York City. She plays Roxie Brinkerhoff, the program director who must try to keep the station on the air, despite the loonies who make up the crew. Only two episodes of *Roxie* aired in the show's original run before it was yanked.

The Roxie character first appeared in a few episodes of *Kate and Allie*, where Jane Curtin's Allie Lowell character met Roxie at a local cable TV station. Martin, in her *SCTV* days, had played a funnier character, Edith Prickley, who, as station manager to the fictitious SCTV network, also helped operate a low-budget television outfit.

**THE ROY ROGERS SHOW (**½) 30 min (100ep B&W; 1951–1957 NBC) Western** *with Roy Rogers, Dale Evans, and Pat Brady as themselves*

Boy, whoever said "you can't go home again" was right, and watching old reruns of *The Roy Rogers Show* proves it. Back in the 1950s, to millions of preteen viewers, *The Roy Rogers Show* was the epitome of action and western excitement. Young boys liked Roy's exploits on his horse Trigger and young girls liked the example set by Roy's wife Dale, who helped out in all of Roy's adventures. Everybody got a laugh out of the comical bumblings of sidekick Pat Brady and his jeep Nellybelle, and there was a great theme song (*Happy Trails to You*) to boot.

Well, on sober reflection now, grown-up eyes see *The Roy Rogers Show* as a slow-moving mishmash of styles that the actors merely walk through. The setting makes little sense and certain aspects of the series seem jarring.

The first thing you'll notice is that the setting is not the Old West. It is the *new* West, the modern West (it did always seems strange that Pat drove around in a jeep, a contraption not noticed in other westerns). So there are no roving bands of bad guys or marauding Injuns. Well, there are still bad guys in *The Roy Rogers Show*, but they are just sort of generic ones, western versions of the central casting bad guys that turn up on *The Adventures of Superman*. Nonetheless, there are an awful lot of them hanging around Roy's ranch, the Double R Bar.

Roy's ranch brings up another issue. He plays a rancher who also runs a diner in Mineral City, all in the "modern" West, yet he is always running off to battle crime and stuff. Where does he get the time for these extracurricular activities? Don't they have sheriffs in Mineral City?

Also, why does everybody in this show use their real names? Did you know that Roy Rogers is not his real name, that it is Leonard Slye, and that he is not a real cowboy, that he grew up in Cincinnati, Ohio, and that he got famous just for singing corny little songs in movies in the 1940s? Do you recall that Roy and Dale got real "born again" religious in the 1970s and backed Richard Nixon all the way to the end, and that Roy had Trigger stuffed when the horse died? Well, did you?

Okay, so Roy is no rough, tough cowpoke. So maybe the stories are simple and slapped together. It's still a fun show that captures the imagination of youngsters without blowing up half the galaxy. Besides, the theme song still brings tears to your eyes. ■

**ROYAL PLAYHOUSE (**) 30 min (51ep B&W; 1949–1950 NBC) Drama Anthology**

These unrelated dramas originally aired as part of the venerable *Fireside Theater* series.

**THE RUGGLES (*½) 30 min (13ep B&W; 1949–1952 ABC) Situation Comedy** *with Charlie Ruggles as himself, Erin O'Brien-Moore as Margaret Ruggles, Margaret Kerry as Sharon Ruggles, Tommy Bernard as Chuck Ruggles, Judy Nugent as Donna Ruggles, and Jimmy Hawkins as Donald Ruggles*

From the prehistoric days of TV sitcoms comes *The Ruggles*, which features Hollywood standby Charlie Ruggles (*Ruggles of Red Gap, Bringing Up Baby*) playing himself. Ruggles is portrayed as a refined and debonair elderly gentleman who is beset with a wife and children who make his life difficult. There were far more than thirteen episodes produced, but only thirteen remain generally available today. ■

**RUMPOLE OF THE BAILEY (***½) 60 min (30ep & 2 hr special Color; 1978–1988 UK Thames) Law Drama** *with Leo McKern as Horace Rumpole, Peggy Thorpe-Bates and Marion Mathie as Hilda Rumpole, Peter Bowles as Guthrie Featherstone, Moray Watson as George, Julian Curry as Claude Erskine-Brown, Bill Fraser as Judge Bullingham, Patricia Hodge as Phyllida Trent Erskine-Brown, Peter Blythe as Samuel Ballard, and Samantha Bond as Liz Probert*

The "Old Bailey" is (or at least used to be) the Grand Central Station of English courts. Located in an old part of London, the Bailey serves as the primary criminal court for the English capital. As a result, the traffic of cases, criminals, lawyers, and judges through the Bailey is often quite congested. Cases heard there are not expected to be lengthy, important, or filled with an inordinate attention to every legal detail.

Horace Rumpole is a portly, aging criminal defense lawyer (a barrister, in British terms) whose low-class clients bring him to the Bailey rather frequently. While everyone (judges included) tends to assume that all the defendants in the Old Bailey dock must be guilty, Rumpole often believes in their innocence. Even if he doesn't, he battles to give them the best legal defense possible. The other lawyers with whom Rumpole shares offices are far more refined than the unpretentious Rumpole, and they are far more interested in social status and career advancement than in seeing justice done.

The *Rumpole* stories wonderfully weave in and out between drama and humor, as the gruff legal curmudgeon goes about putting on his best performance before the Old Bailey judges and as he causes feathers to ruffle among his colleagues. Sometimes the actual nuances of the legal matter at hand get lost, but this is more than made up for by the fabulous characterizations that fill the series.

Leo McKern (who played Clang, the Indian high priest in the Beatles' film *Help!*, and was both the second and final Number 2 in *The Prisoner*) is a treasure as Rumpole. His semibombastic oratory has a Churchillian flavor, and his weary battling against the ways of the world is heartening. Rumpole is no saint, for he has more than a small weakness for the cheap wines served at the local legal watering hole, Pomeroy's wine bar. His longtime marriage to Hilda is friendly but distant, as she never fails to remind her husband that he has not lived up to the legend of her father, the judge. He usually refers to her only by the hushed name of "She-who-must-be-obeyed!"

The creator and writer of the *Rumpole* stories is John Mortimer, a former English lawyer who adapted Evelyn Waugh's *Brideshead Revisited* for TV. The five sets of six-episode series of *Rumpole* (and the two-hour TV movie *Rumpole's Return* that precedes the third set) were produced in a staggered fashion over several years. Mortimer (and McKern) kept insisting that each set was the last, but British popular response kept making sequels hard to avoid.

**RUN, BUDDY, RUN (**) 30 min (16ep Color; 1966–1967 CBS) Situation Comedy** *with Jack Sheldon as Buddy Overstreet, Bruce Gordon as Devere, and Jim Connell as Junior*

While sitting in a steamy Turkish bath, average citizen Buddy Overstreet (an L. A. accountant) accidentally overhears some syndicate types discussing a proposed "hit" using such code terms as "chicken little" and "the man in Chicago." Though this language means absolutely nothing to him, when the hoods realize he's been listening they assume Buddy knows too much and take chase. Buddy eludes them for the moment, but then their leader, Mr. Devere, puts out the word to his entire organization: find and kill Buddy Overstreet. And so Buddy becomes an inadvertent fugitive, running for his life from a deadly (but generally inept) gang somewhat obsessed with his capture.

Obviously, this show is a parody of such "man on the run" programs as *The Fugitive* and *Run for Your Life*.

What's truly amazing is that it is a series. This type of setup should be a variety skit, or at best a one-shot presentation on something like *Bob Hope Presents the Chrysler Theater.* The producers (including veterans David Susskind and Leonard Stern) displayed amazing audacity to expect this show to play week after week. Actually it didn't—lasting only sixteen episodes—but surprisingly about a half-dozen stories along the way are fairly good. The main reason is one inspired bit of casting: Bruce Gordon, the man who played mobster Frank Nitti on *The Untouchables* for four seasons, got the role of top hood Devere. He plays it perfectly, no doubt relishing every opportunity to needle his own past image. And the writers give him plenty of opportunities because it seems no matter what job Buddy gets, somehow it connects to Devere. For instance, if Buddy is working at a hotel, you can bet Devere will be checking in any moment. While this series is no *Get Smart*, everyone involved does their best with the one-joke premise and it's worth catching a few episodes. A few years after his running days were over as Buddy, Jack Sheldon turned up as a friend to Sally Field in *The Girl with Something Extra.*

**RUN FOR YOUR LIFE (**) 60 min (85ep & 60 min pilot Color; 1965–1968 NBC) Adventure** *with Ben Gazzara as Paul Bryan*

Essentially an inferior imitation of *The Fugitive, Run for Your Life* takes the same concept of a man on the run and twists it. Richard Kimble was a fugitive because he wanted to escape recapture by the police on a groundless murder charge. Paul Bryan is running because his doctor told him he has an incurable disease, some form of leukemia. Bryan, an apparently hale and hearty thirty-five-year-old lawyer, leaves his business behind, takes his amassed fortune, and travels the globe, trying to live as much as possible in the time he has left.

Since Bryan is not running from anything in particular (other than time), his travels are just jaunts, extended vacations. Sure, Bryan will die soon, but won't we all? Bryan looks perfectly healthy. In fact, if it were not for the opening each week (explaining the premise), a viewer might think he was just some unattached jet-set playboy. Ben Gazzara tries real hard to put some pathos in the Paul Bryan role, but without the cat and mouse chase represented by the police lieutenant chasing Kimble in *The Fugitive* (or any believable substitute), *Run for Your Life* never builds any dramatic tension. The series winds up as a well-produced disappointment.

Roy Huggins (*Maverick* and *Cheyenne*) produced *Run for Your Life* and its original 1965 pilot, titled *Rapture at Two-Forty*.

**THE RUNAWAYS/OPERATION: RUNAWAY (*) 60 min (17ep Color 1978 & 1979 NBC) Drama** *with Robert Reed as David McKay, Alan Feinstein as Steve Arizzio, Karen Machon as Karen Wingate, Michael Biehn as Mark Johnson, and James Callahan as Sergeant Hal Grady*

This show played first as a five-hour short-run series, *Operation: Runaway*, with Robert Reed as a former vice-squad officer turned psychologist specializing in tracking down runaway kids. It resumed a year later as *The Runaways*, with Alan Feinstein taking over the lead role, but still pursuing the same ends. Predictably pat and preachy. Go with milk carton notices instead.

**RYAN'S FOUR (*½) 60 min (4ep Color; 1983 ABC) Medical Drama** *with Tom Skerritt as Dr. Thomas Ryan, Lisa Eilbacher as Dr. Ingrid Sorenson, Timothy Daly as Dr. Edward Gillian, Albert Hall as Dr. Terry Wilson, and Dirk Blocker as Dr. Norman Rostov*

David Victor, the man behind *Dr. Kildare* and *Marcus Welby, M. D.*, and Henry Winkler, who played the Fonz on *Happy Days,* team up to produce this overly somber series about four young interns in some gargantuan L. A. hospital. Dr. Thomas Ryan is the tough but fair director of interns. Expect to hear a lot of complaining by the interns.

**SA 7 (see *Special Agent 7*)**

**SCTV NETWORK (****) 30 min (156ep Color; 1977–1984 Syndication & NBC & Cinemax) Comedy-Variety** *with casts including John Candy, Joe Flaherty, Eugene Levy, Andrea Martin, Rick Moranis, Catherine O'Hara, Martin Short, Robin Duke, Tony Rosato, Harold Ramis, and Dave Thomas*

You know you've come across something completely different when the distinctive whistle from *The Andy Griffith Show* begins a plug for "the next Merv Griffin show." The footage is in black and white and the setting is Mayberry, but Floyd the barber, Deputy Barney Fife, Otis Campbell, and Aunt Bee (played by various *SCTV* cast members) are talking to Merv. Only it's Merv (actually Rick Moranis) dressed in a sheriff's uniform doing an impression of Andy. In short order, this series of "preview clips" neatly summarizes the plot of the Merv/Andy show episode, including an appearance by Dave Thomas playing impressionist Fred Travalena doing Jim Nabors as Gomer Pyle. (Whew!)

This bit takes less than three minutes, but by the end you've had an exhilarating trip through some brilliantly skewed memories. And that's just the beginning. In rapid order *SCTV* juxtaposes promotional clips, full-blown parodies, commercial send-ups, behind-the-scenes station intrigues, original characters, and devastating impersonations. This is where a scene from *Ben-Hur* turns into a *Three Stooges* routine (with John Candy as Curly), or where the laid-back Perry Como performs lying in bed on stage, or where the familiar *Hill Street Blues* opening credits garage door rises to reveal cops dressed in drag running through the streets as part of *The Benny Hill Street Blues Show,* or where Dick Cavett finds the ultimate interview subject: himself. And everything, it seems, can be seen "Thursdays at Nine on SCTV."

The sheer density of the material is amazing. You have to watch this series alertly, several times, much like *Monty Python's Flying Circus*. And, like *Python*, it is very much a writer's show, with most of the cast members scripting the routines and frequently playing many different roles (sometimes several in the same sketch). They delight in broad comedy (such as John Candy's thieving Johnny LaRue) as well as in allusions to high-brow esoterica (Ensign Chekov from *Star Trek* performing in an Anton Chekov play). Most of all, this program constantly cuts and jumbles, deftly applying the *Python* lesson of dropping in sketches of any length anywhere they can squeeze a laugh (even for only a few seconds).

Appropriately this program's production history is nearly as convoluted as some of its episodes. Though it currently plays in reedited thirty-minute segments (with standard opening graphics), *SCTV* originally aired in thirty-minute blocks (seventy-eight episodes over three seasons in first-run syndication), ninety-minute blocks (three seasons on NBC late night), and in forty-five minute blocks (the final season on Cinemax). The series started in 1977 as *Second City Television*; a very, very low-budget package produced by the Canadian branch (in Toronto) of Chicago's famed Second City troupe (the home company of such alums as Bill Murray and Dan Aykroyd). After three nonconsecutive seasons in syndication, the group landed its NBC slot, changing the program title to *SCTV* and filling each episode with a combination of new material, musical guest stars, and occasional golden oldie bits. During this entire run, there was quite a bit of cross-pollination with NBC's *Saturday Night Live* (Don Novello came over as producer for a while on *SCTV*, while Robin Duke, Tony Rosato, and Martin Short all served stints in the *Saturday Night* cast).

Over the program's long run, some of the characters and bits to keep an eye out for include the beer-guzzling McKenzie Brothers (Rick Moranis and Dave Thomas as Bob and Doug); the polka-playing Schmenge Brothers (John Candy and Eugene Levy as Yosh and Stan); the ultimate in self-aggrandizing showbiz types: Sammy Maudlin (Joe Flaherty), Lola Heatherton (Catherine O'Hara), and Bobby Bittman (Eugene Levy); and the conniving SCTV management team of Edith Prickley (Andrea Martin) and Guy Caballero (Joe Flaherty), the man who sits in a wheelchair for effect.

Best of all are the brilliant impressions, as familiar stars (interpreted by the *SCTV* cast) do just what you always wanted them to do. These stars range from Martin Short as Jerry Lewis slobbering his way through serious drama, to Rick Moranis (as Woody Allen), Dave Thomas (as Bob Hope), and Joe Flaherty (as Bing Crosby) restaging Allen's *Play It Again, Sam* as *Play It Again, Bob.* That last sketch alone deserves a spot in the comedy hall of fame, as Woody Allen attempts to script Hope a sure-fire Oscar-winning comedy. ■

**S.W.A.T. (**) 60 min (36ep & 2 hr pilot Color; 1975–1976 ABC) Police Drama** *with Steve Forrest as Dan "Hondo" Harrelson, Rod Perry as David "Deacon" Kay, Robert Urich as Jim Street, Mark Shera as Dominic Luca, and James Coleman as T. J. McCabe*

If you want to remember what was bad about the 1970s, watch *S.W.A.T.* It was a time when people were sick of urban crime and when the impending collapse of the nation's Vietnam effort left great chunks of the nation frustrated about our apparent inability to have our way with small, supposedly backward peoples. *S.W.A.T.* is designed as an antidote to all those ills. For viewers tired of urban crime, here is a fool-proof way to solve it: treat the city as if it were a combat zone. When the put-upon local police cannot deal with a problem, call in the *S*pecial *W*eapons *A*nd *T*actics squad, a troupe of mostly faceless officers in military garb, with fancy, powerful weapons. When summoned, they come swarming out of the S.W.A.T. van, which roams the trouble spots responding at a moment's notice. *S.W.A.T.* is the forerunner of the *Rambo* movies. Here you can see an American quasi-military operation where everything goes *right* this time and "we" always win.

To be fair, *S.W.A.T.* is a very well-produced series. With all the pyrotechnics, it has to be. The problem is the relentless violence. The program is cold and inhuman in its presentation. The S.W.A.T. squad members do evidence some personalities when off duty, but the focus is mostly on explosive urban combat.

*S.W.A.T.* is produced by the giants of 1970s ABC action/adventure, Aaron Spelling and Leonard Goldberg, who were better handling frothier fare, such as *Charlie's Angels* and *Fantasy Island.* The *S.W.A.T.* pilot originally ran as an episode of *The Rookies,* another Spelling/Goldberg cop show. Robert Urich (*Vega$, Spenser: For Hire*), who plays one of the S.W.A.T. goons, makes his first action series appearance here after debuting in the failed sitcom *Bob & Carol & Ted & Alice*.

**SABLE (**) 60 min (7ep Color; 1987–1988 ABC) Adventure** *with Lewis Van Bergen as Nicholas Flemming/Jon Sable, Rene Russo as Eden Kendall, Ken Page as Joe "Cheesecake" Tyson, and Holly Fulger as Myke Blackmon*

By day, Nicholas Flemming is a successful author of children's books living in Chicago. But come nightfall (or at any other appropriate opportunity) he dons a subdued black jumpsuit and hood, spreads greasepaint on his face, and leaps into action as Jon Sable, freelance avenger and righter of wrongs. The only one who knows his double identity is his personal modem to the world of data bases, Cheesecake Tyson, a blind computer hacker. Otherwise, Eden (Flemming's girlfriend and literary agent) and Myke (his illustrator on the books) don't suspect their friend's darker side.

Despite the traditional trappings (costume, girlfriend, double identity), this stylized super hero adventure series definitely reflects the more somber and cynical orientation of many late 1980s comic books. (It is, in fact, based on a contemporary comic book, *John Sable, Freelance*.) So the backdrop world is a cruel one, populated by heartless thieves, manipulative business people, and deranged killers. And, in the fine tradition of such heroes as Billy Jack or Kwai Chang Caine (on *Kung Fu*), while Sable talks passionately against violence (he just hates it) the screen is frequently filled with flailing bodies—sent flying, of course, in response to someone else's violent measures. But Sable does win points for avoiding the usual flashy superhero garb (except for the greasepaint, his "costume" is barely a costume), while still looking dramatically different from most ordinary men. In an unusual final episode, the character of Sable is killed and buried, though Flemming survives.

It's a long way from lighthearted *Batman* camp, but then again so are the comics these days—even *Batman*. Consult your local comic book specialty shop (remember when they used to sell them at drugstores?) for issues of the *Sable* comic along with such titles as *Batman: The Dark Knight Returns* to see how they tone things *down* for television.

**THE SAGA OF ANDY BURNETT** **(see *Andy Burnett*)**

**THE SAINT (***) 60 min (114ep: 71 B&W & 43 Color; 1963–1968 UK ATV) Adventure** *with Roger Moore as Simon Templar and Ivor Dean as Inspector Claude Teal* **RETURN OF THE SAINT (**) 60 min (22ep Color; 1978 UK ATV) Adventure** *with Ian Ogilvy as Simon Templar*

Simon Templar, also known as "The Saint," is a handsome, sophisticated, international adventurer with a weakness for people in distress—especially beautiful women. The character first appeared in a series of books and short stories by Leslie Charteris in the 1930s, but never clicked in feature films, with three different actors taking a crack at the role from 1938 to 1942 (Louis Hayward, George Sanders, and Hugh Sinclair). Then came the 1960s television series with Roger Moore, who instantly seized the character as his own. His easy nonchalance and smooth, articulate manner made it clear that this man was in charge of his own destiny. He begins each episode as the narrator, wryly observing some facet of life in the world of international intrigue, ending the pre-credits teaser with the one and only appearance of a halo above his head, followed by the program's catchy musical signature theme and a stick-figure Saint for the title graphics.

For the black and white episodes, the stories themselves are a cut above average (though sometimes just barely), often carried over the rough spots by Moore's charming manner. However, the scripts are considerably better for the color episodes, providing Templar with a better caliber of foe, more sophisticated plots, and a greater sense of playful humor. By this time, he's also generally trusted by the police, especially his contact at Scotland yard, Claude Teal, and he is frequently asked to help on their latest puzzler (in an unofficial way, of course). Even after the most harrowing of escapes, Moore manages to appear essentially unruffled, the epitome of a dashing fantasy figure. Had he never landed the role of James Bond, succeeding Sean Connery in 1973, Roger Moore would have still been guaranteed a spot in the pop culture Hall of Fame for his work on *The Saint*.

In 1978, following the relative success of *The New Avengers* revival, the ATV production company fashioned a return vehicle for the Saint character dubbed appropriately *The Return of the Saint*. They recast with a dashing new lead (Ian Ogilvy), came up with a reworked signature theme song, and even figured out a way to get that famous stick figure into the opening credits action (ending with a tossed halo and a sexy embrace). The stories themselves, though, are strictly average late-1970s formula adventures.

Yet another update revival began in the late 1980s, first in a 1987 series pilot for CBS (starring Andrew Clarke). Though the revival was rejected, in 1988, D. L. Taffner Ltd. took the challenge to develop a series of two-hour movies (with London Weekend Television) with an eye toward an eventual series. They cast British actor Simon Dutton as the next Simon Templar. ■

**ST. ELSEWHERE (****) 60 min (137ep Color; 1982–1986 NBC) Medical Drama** *with William Daniels as Dr. Mark Craig, Norman Lloyd as Dr. Daniel Auschlander, Ed Flanders as Dr. Donald Westphall, Ed Begley, Jr., as Dr.Victor Ehrlich, Howie Mandel as Dr.Wayne Fiscus, Mark Harmon as Dr. Robert Caldwell, David Morse as Dr. Jack Morrison, Stephen Furst as Dr. Elliot Axelrod, Christina Pickles as Nurse Helen Rosenthal, Denzel Washington as Dr. Phillip Chandler, Eric Laneuville as Luther Hawkins, Byron Stewart as Warren Coolidge, Cynthia Sikes as Dr. Annie Cavanero, Ellen Bry as Nurse Shirley Daniels, Sagan Lewis as Dr. Jackie Wade, Jennifer Savidge as Nurse Lucy Papandrao. Terence Knox as Dr. Peter White, Alfre Woodard as Dr. Roxanne Turner, Bruce Greenwood as Dr. Seth Griffin, France Nuyen as Dr. Paulette Kiem, Cindy Pickett as Dr. Carol Novino, Bonnie Bartlett as Ellen Craig, and Ronny Cox as Dr. John Gideon*

*St. Elsewhere* is a show on the edge. The premise itself is a marked departure from a typical scrubbed and shiny medical drama, focusing instead on the action at a battered old teaching hospital (St. Eligius) located in a decaying Boston neighborhood. The city's other institutions dump their unwanted patients there, dubbing the place "St. Elsewhere."

Off camera, the most amazing thing that happened to this series in its original run was that it kept getting renewed. Not that it didn't deserve being picked up. However, no one could figure out why and how *St. Elsewhere* managed to hang on for six seasons with marginal ratings at best. Among the many theories: NBC president Grant Tinker's son was one of the producers; various NBC executives personally enjoyed it; and the detailed ratings data at the time demonstrated that the audience composition, while not up to the numbers of a prime-time top-ten hit, happened to consist of the right *type* of viewers (those most advertisers really wanted to reach).

Whatever the reason, the producers usually paced each season as if it were their last. Fortunately this meant turning out the best scripts possible, consistently taking chances with the characters, settings, and subject matter. There's a true sense of discovery in the series that leaves viewers wondering where in the world the show will dare venture next. For instance, after being shot, Wayne Fiscus (played by stand-up comic Howie Mandel) journeys to heaven and comes face-to-face with God. Or at the end of one season the hospital building stands inches away from total demolition by a wrecking ball crew. On a lighter note, one episode takes place upstate from Boston, staged just like the play *Our Town*.

As with *Hill Street Blues*, there are continuing plot threads carried over a number of episodes. However, *St. Elsewhere* is particularly adept at turning out strong, self-contained stories as well. For instance, one toward the end of the series run is structured to follow the cycle of life, beginning with a difficult birth in the first act and ending with an old man dying in an orderly's arms to close the piece. A few episodes later, the show does a light parody of disaster film settings like *The Towering Inferno*. That ability to go back and forth between the tender and the audacious is probably why *St. Elsewhere* fans tend to be particularly dedicated to the series.

They also enjoy picking up wry pop culture allusions in the dialogue. Unlike a program such as *Moonlighting*, which often accompanies such references with a wink toward the camera, *St. Elsewhere* plays them straight. If you get them and chuckle, fine. If not, the story goes on and no one is the wiser. Such comments range from simply working in a popular song title ("Use more polythene, Pam" for "Polythene Pam" by The Beatles) to elaborate references to other series. In *St. Elsewhere*'s final episode, for instance, they slip in a restaging of the final chase scene from *The Fugitive*, with a one-armed man climbing a water tower (off camera).

The final five minutes of the final episode shows the program at its mind-stretching best. After neatly tying up a number of plot threads, the camera pulls back to show the hospital building standing there, with snow falling all around. Suddenly, the picture shakes, and we discover that the building is actually one of those miniatures inside a "snow globe." Instead of the hospital, the scene has changed to a working-class neighborhood living room where a young autistic boy sits, staring into the globe. Elsewhere in the room, two of the characters that we know as surgeons are talking to each other, though neither one is a doctor here. One takes the globe from the boy, muttering about how the child can just sit there all day looking into that glass. As they leave the room, he places the globe on top of the family TV set, which is where the final shot lingers.

Well, perhaps sometimes we do spend too much of our lives staring into that glass screen in our living rooms. Still, as long as there are series like *St. Elsewhere*, there are very good reasons to do so.

**SAINTS AND SINNERS (*½) 60 min (18ep & 60 min pilot B&W; 1962–1963 NBC) Newspaper Drama** *with Nick Adams as Nick Alexander, John Larkin as Mark Grainger, Barbara Rush as Lizzie Hogan, and Richard Erdman as Klugie*

The second (after *The Rebel*) and last TV series starring Nick Adams, *Saints and Sinners* is an uninspiring look at newspaper reporting. The show focuses on Nick Alexander, reporter/columnist for a large New York City newspaper. The pilot episode, which aired in 1962 on *The Dick Powell Show* as *Savage Sunday*, had Russell Thorson co-starring as Adams's colleague, Albert King.

**SALLY (**½) 30 min (25 B&W; 1957–1958 NBC) Situation Comedy** *with Joan Caulfield as Sally Truesdale, Marion Lorne as Myrtle Banford, Gale Gordon as Bascomb Bleacher, Johnny Desmond as Jim Kendall, and Arte Johnson as Bascomb Bleacher, Jr.*

This short-run 1950s sitcom comes in two phases. The bulk of the series follows the comic adventures of wealthy Myrtle Banford and her pretty young traveling companion, Sally Truesdale, as they journey throughout the world (well, mostly through the studio backlots). After completing their travel, Myrtle returns to her business, the Banford and Bascomb Department Store, for phase two of the series in which Sally begins work as a salesgirl for the store.

Overall this series is about average for the times, but the program's cast makes it well worth a trip to the storage shelves just to see an episode or two with the blustery Gale Gordon (Lucille Ball's eternal sitcom nemesis), the spacy Marion Lorne (strong support on *Garry Moore, Mr. Peepers,* and *Bewitched*), future *Laugh-In* star Arte Johnson, and Joan Caulfield (*My Favorite Husband*) as the typical 1950s screwball comedy heroine.

**SALTY** **(**½) 30 min (24ep Color; 1974–1975 Syndication) Adventure** *with Julius Harris as Clancy Ames, Mark Slade as Taylor Reed, and Johnny Doran as Tim Reed*

*Salty* has no grandiose ideas about being great art, but it's a fine little family viewing series. Taylor and Tim Reed are orphaned brothers cared for by Clancy Ames, a retired lawyer who runs a marina in the Bahamas. The title character is Tim's pet sea lion.

**SALVAGE-1** **(**) 60 min (18ep Color; 1979 ABC) Fantasy Adventure** *with Andy Griffith as Harry Broderick, Joel Higgins as Skip Carmichael, Trish Stewart as Melanie Slozar, J. Jay Saunders as Mack, and Richard Jaeckel as Jack Klinger*

The initial hook is silly but irresistible.

Professional scrap and salvage man Harry Broderick looks at the moon and realizes that it's littered with abandoned space exploration hardware. Or, as it's known in his business, perfectly good junk ripe for the picking.

So with a little help from Skip (a former astronaut) and Melanie (a fuel and explosives expert), Harry and his assistant Mack build and launch a rocket ship—just a half step ahead of a puzzled local FBI agent, Jack Klinger. Skip and Melanie fly the ship (dubbed the *Vulture*) to the moon, collect the scrap, and return safely.

Sure, why not? Isn't that what private industry and initiative are all about? For an encore, the Salvage-1 team takes on other equally reasonable tasks such as pumping oil from dried-out wells, moving an iceberg from the North Pole to provide water for a drought-stricken island, and ridding a haunted house of its ghosts.

Led by Andy Griffith, the cast just manages to make all this seem credible, though the outlandish comic book science does strain a bit over the long haul. The three best stories (the original voyage to the moon, a subsequent space mission to retrieve a golden satellite, and the iceberg project) sometimes turn up in two-hour TV-movie slots, so you can safely skip the rest of the series.

**SAM** **(½) 30 min (5ep & 30 min pilot Color; 1978 CBS) Police Drama** *with Mark Harmon as Mike Breen, Len Wayland as Tom Clagett, and Sam as Sam*

Sam is a yellow Labrador retriever who barks, points, runs, and sniffs on behalf of Jack Webb's favorite organization, the Los Angeles Police Department. Sam must contend with rabid anticanine prejudice on the force and overcome nasty stereotypes about dogs being unreliable in the crunch. Fortunately for Sam, good-looking cop Mike Breen sticks up for Sam's rights and is assigned to be Sam's partner on the beat. Webb, the producer of Sam, was truly scratching the bottom of his creative barrel with this lame excuse for a crime show.

Mark Harmon (son of Tom), just off the gridiron as star quarterback for UCLA, makes his first series appearance as Mike Breen. Harmon would go on to play Lothario Dr. Robert Caldwell in *St. Elsewhere*.

**SAM BENEDICT** **(**½) 60 min (28ep B&W; 1962–1963 NBC) Law Drama** *with Edmond O'Brien as Sam Benedict, Richard Rust as Hank Tabor, and Joan Tompkins as Trudy Wagner*

Based on the exploits of real-life criminal attorney Jake Erlich, *Sam Benedict* is a nifty series set in San Francisco that deftly mixes standard courtroom antics with a light touch of levity (something sorely lacking in most TV lawyer shows). The always intriguing Edmond O'Brien plays Sam with a lot of verve.

The original pilot for the series, called *333 Montgomery* (which aired in 1960 on *Alcoa Theater*), was produced by Gene Roddenberry (who later created *Star Trek*) and starred DeForest Kelley (Dr. McCoy on *Star Trek*) as the main character, then known as Jake Brittin. By the time Edmond O'Brien replaced Kelley in the actual *Sam Benedict* series, Roddenberry was out and *Mr. Novak* producer E. Jack Neuman was in.

**SAMMY AND COMPANY** **(*) 90 min (55ep Color; 1975–1977 Syndication) Talk-Variety** *with Sammy Davis, Jr., and William B. Williams*

That hip dude himself, Sammy Davis, Jr., tries to emulate Johnny Carson and host a talk/variety show set in Las Vegas, Sammy's home away from home. Lots of fab guests, such as Wayne Newton and Sandy Duncan, rap with the man.

Highlights of this series are packaged as twelve half-hours, under the misleading title of *The Best of Sammy Davis, Jr.*

**SAN FRANCISCO BEAT** **(see *The Lineup*)**

**SAN FRANCISCO INTERNATIONAL AIRPORT** **(*) 60 min (6ep & 2 hr pilot Color; 1970–1971 NBC) Drama** *with Lloyd Bridges as Jim Conrad, Clu Gulager as Bob Hatten, Barbara Werle as June, and Barbara Sigel as Suzie Conrad.*

Okay, so at least this is not another show about cops in Los Angeles. The setting is, well, unique. How many TV series are named after large public transportation terminals? If you can think of more than one, you're a pro. As you can imagine, this series is set in San Francisco's large airport, and it dramatizes the traumas and heartaches that occur each day in running the place (something akin to the then current film hit, *Airport*). Lloyd Bridges, dried off from his run in *Sea Hunt*, is the airport boss. In the pilot, *Bonanza* alumnus Pernell Roberts plays Bridges' role.

It's a good thing *San Francisco International Airport* never caught on, for if it had, we could have been subjected to copy-cat series such as *The Holland Tunnel, The Port Authority Bus Station*, and *The Washington Beltway*.

**THE SAN PEDRO BEACH BUMS** **(zero) 60 min (10ep & 90 min pilot Color; 1977 ABC) Situation Comedy** *with Christopher Murney as Buddy Binder,*

*Stuart Pankin as Anthony "Stuf" Danelli, John Mark Robinson as Edward "Dancer" McClory, Darryl McCullough as Moose Maslosky, and Chris De Rose as Boychick*

Sweeping in its banality, shocking in its lack of subtlety, *The San Pedro Beach Bums* is the low-water mark of producers Aaron Spelling and Douglas Cramer, the pair who claim credit for the likes of *Aloha Paradise, B.A.D. Cats, Glitter,* and *The Love Boat*.

The bums in question are five carefree young men who live on a broken-down tuna boat in the harbor of San Pedro, California. An hour-long sitcom is hard to sustain even when the writing is good. It is excruciating when the writing is insipid. Unlike most shows in this book with a "zero" rating, *The San Pedro Beach Bums* is not even bad enough to be fascinating. It's just bad. The pilot is titled *The San Pedro Bums*, but it, too, takes place near the beach.

**SANCHEZ OF BEL AIR (**) 30 min (13ep Color; 1986–1987 USA) Situation Comedy** *with Reni Santoni as Ricardo Sanchez, Marcia Del Mar as Rita Sanchez, Richard Coca as Miguel Sanchez, and Bobby Sherman as Frankie Rondell*

Something akin to a Hispanic variation of *The Jeffersons, Sanchez of Bel Air* concerns clothing manufacturer Ricardo Sanchez, whose business success allows him to move on up with his family from the barrio of East Los Angeles to a fancy neighborhood in Bel Air. Sanchez is, at least, not as abrasive a figure as George Jefferson, though he does get exasperated at his children's antics. Former teen singing idol Bobby Sherman (*Shindig, Here Come the Brides*) plays the Sanchez's neighbor, Frankie Rondell, an ex–rock'n'roller.

**THE SANDY DUNCAN SHOW (**) 30 min (26ep Color; 1972 CBS) Situation Comedy** *with Sandy Duncan as Sandy Stockton, Tom Bosley as Bert Quinn, Marian Mercer as Kay Fox, and M. Emmet Walsh as Alex Lembeck*

In the 1971 sitcom *Funny Face*, Sandy Duncan had first played a character named Sandy Stockton, who was a UCLA college student with a part-time job in an advertising agency. The Sandy Stockton character reappears here in *The Sandy Duncan Show* (still at UCLA and still working at the ad agency part-time), but otherwise the two shows have different casts and different producers. Both programs are mildly amusing, if you don't mind Sandy Duncan's laboriously effervescent personality. The actor playing Sandy's employer in this show, Tom Bosley, went on to star as Mr. Cunningham in *Happy Days*.

**SANFORD (*½) 30 min (23ep Color; 1980–1981 NBC) Situation Comedy** *with Redd Foxx as Fred Sanford, Dennis Burkley as Cal Pettie, Nathaniel Taylor as Rollo Larson, and Marguerite Ray as Evelyn "Eve" Lewis*

The original *Sanford and Son* brew has been watered down substantially in this tepid continuation of the saga of irascible L. A. junk dealer Fred Sanford. As you may guess from the title, Fred's son Lamont is gone (working on the Alaska pipeline, we are told), so Fred must vent his spleen on both his new business partner, hefty white redneck Cal Pettie, and his neighbor, Rollo. The most surprising development is Fred's acquisition of a comely and wealthy widow girlfriend (Eve Lewis) Other than chalking it up to the old bromide "love is blind," there is no believable reason to think Eve would fall for a curmudgeon such as Fred.

While Lamont's absence doesn't help, the most important element missing from *Sanford* is the feeling of freshness. Fred has yelled and complained a bit too much over the years and the lack of any solid opposing force leaves *Sanford* a sorry wrap-up to a memorable series.

**SANFORD AND SON (***½) 30 min (136ep Color; 1972–1977 NBC) Situation Comedy** *with Redd Foxx as Fred Sanford, Demond Wilson as Lamont Sanford, Whitman Mayo as Grady Wilson, LaWanda Page as Esther Anderson, Nathaniel Taylor as Rollo Larson, Don Bexley as Bubba Hoover, and Gregory Sierra as Julio Fuentes*

Among the short list of popular TV sitcom characters who are basically unlikable, Fred Sanford must be ranked near the top. An aging, selfish, conceited liar, Fred Sanford runs a marginally profitable junk business in Los Angeles with his reluctant partner, unmarried son Lamont. Fred is quite willing to cruise out the rest of his years with help from Lamont, while the son is fearful of wasting his best years on a nowhere business that may not survive the old man. With Fred's wife Elizabeth long dead, Fred and Lamont are all that's left of the family and the father/son team bump against each other not only during work but after-hours as well when they share the family home (next to the junk yard).

Redd Foxx is clearly the motor that drives *Sanford and Son*. It's true that the idea originated in England (in the show titled *Steptoe and Son*). What's more, a lot of the show's impetus came from producer Bud Yorkin (and, to a far lesser degree, Yorkin's erstwhile partner Norman Lear, of *All in the Family* fame). Still, it is Foxx's ability to milk the most out of his lines and to turn the character of Fred Sanford into a national curmudgeon that lifts *Sanford and Son* into the realms of great shows. Demond Wilson is fine in the basically straight-man role of son Lamont, and the supporting cast fills the spaces nicely, but all revolves around Fred.

Much fuss was made at the time *Sanford and Son* appeared about the mostly all-black cast of the show. As time has gone by, and black-oriented shows (especially sitcoms) have become almost commonplace, the quality of *Sanford and Son* is evident. Even without the uniqueness of its racial tone, *Sanford and Son* survives as a very funny show about a very common human condition, the love/hate bonds between an aging man and his grown son. The ethnic element is but an extra attraction to the primary theme. Whereas many of the topical 1970s sitcoms now seem dated and strident, the more down-to-earth and timeless *Sanford and Son* can still be enjoyed.

**SANFORD ARMS** (½) **30 min (4ep Color; 1977 NBC) Situation Comedy** *with Theodore Wilson as Phil Wheeler, LaWanda Page as Esther Anderson, Whitman Mayo as Grady Wilson, Bebe Drake-Hooks as Jeannie, Norma Miller as Dolly Wilson, and Don Bexley as Bubba Hoover*

Imagine *I Love Lucy* with just the Mertzes, or *The Dick Van Dyke Show* with just Jerry and Millie Helper. Sounds boring? Wait until you see *Sanford Arms*!

Fred Sanford and son Lamont, the double leads of *Sanford and Son*, are gone, off to Arizona (if you believe the scripts) for no good reason. The real reason is, of course, the unavailability of stars Redd Foxx and Demond Wilson. Management of the Sanford home and junk business and the rooming house next door owned by Fred's sister-in-law Esther is turned over to an upstanding ex-army man (Phil Wheeler), who tries to keep things going by turning the rooming house into a hotel. Esther shows up to collect the monthly payments that Wheeler owes Fred. Other second bananas from the original hit show (Fred's pals Grady and Bubba) also stick around.

The concept of *Sanford Arms* is ludicrous. Without Fred or Lamont, there is simply no point in continuing the story of the Sanford locale. Fortunately there are only a handful of episodes. They are only for serious professionals researching the *complete* Sanford history.

**SAPPHIRE AND STEEL** (**½) **60 min (39ep color; 1979–1982 UK ATV) Science Fiction** *with Joanna Lumley as Sapphire, David McCallum as Steel, and David Collings as Silver*

Sapphire and Steel are in the same business as Doctor Who, Doug and Tony (from *The Time Tunnel*), and Phineas Bogg and Jeffrey (from *Voyagers*)—making sure that time and the universe (or at least the Earth) remain more or less intact. In this series, the time-traveling heroes are a pair of superpowered "angels" who have assumed human form as Sapphire and Steel (bearing an unmistakable resemblance to Purdey from the *New Avengers* and Illya from *The Man from U.N.C.L.E.*). They wander through time keeping the forces of evil, chaos, and destruction in check. Steel is cold, analytical, ruthless, amoral, and exceptionally strong. Sapphire is much more lovingly emotional, can see through and reverse time, read the history of an object just by holding it, and (her toughest task) can even keep Steel in line. Occasionally they also get help from Silver, an electronics genius who constructs the gadget that saves the day. Frankly this is a pretty weird series, though at least the familiar leads help to get past the obtuse premise. Nonetheless, if you can't fathom programs like *Doctor Who* or *Blake's 7*, about the only thing you'll get out of this one is recognition of how "normal" those seem to be.

**SARA** (*) **60 min (13ep Color; 1976 CBS) Western** *with Brenda Vaccaro as Sara Yarnell, Bert Kramer as Emmet Ferguson, Albert Stratton as Martin Pope, and Mariclare Costello as Julia Bailey*

Imagine a stilted western version of *Harper Valley, PTA* and you have *Sara*. The lead character is Sara Yarnell, a strong and proud woman about a hundred years ahead of her time in the area of women's liberation. The time is the 1870s and the place is a nowheresville western town none-too-subtly named Independence, Colorado. Sara comes west from stuffy old Philadelphia and becomes the town's only teacher. Her independent spirit riles the old fogies of the town, while exciting the few who were closet reformers. The kids love Sara to pieces.

The only reason to watch *Sara* is to see the first TV series performance of noted play and film actress Brenda Vaccaro (*Cactus Flower, Midnight Cowboy, Once Is Not Enough*), who tries hard.

**SARA** (**½) **30 min (13ep Color; 1985 NBC) Situation Comedy** *with Geena Davis as Sara McKenna, Bronson Pinchot as Dennis Kemper, Alfre Woodard as Rozalyn Dupree, Bill Maher as Marty Lang, Mark Hudson as Stuart Webber, and Ronnie Claire Edwards as Helen Newcomb*

A short-run showcase for Geena Davis after her supporting stint on *Buffalo Bill*, where she played the far too trusting Wendy Killian. Here, too, she's good-hearted and vulnerable, this time as a young San Francisco attorney sharing a storefront law office with several other lawyers including Dennis, who is gay; Marty, the sleazy manipulator; and Roz, a principled black woman (and Sara's best friend). Rounding out the setup are Helen, the office secretary (and loving den mother to the pack), and Stuart, Sara's neighbor (recently divorced and trying to raise his son as a single parent).

This package has all the right ingredients, but the final mix is just okay. Everyone turns in fine performances, the scripts are adequate, and there are moments—such as when the very tall Sara dates a significantly shorter man—but ultimately not enough of them. Definitely catch a few episodes, but then plan to see the main performers in other more successful productions: Bronson Pinchot on *Perfect Strangers*, Alfre Woodard on *St. Elsewhere*, and Geena Davis in a host of excellent feature films (including *The Fly, Beetlejuice,* and *The Accidental Tourist*).

**SARGE** (**) **60 min (13ep & 2 hr pilot Color; 1971–1972 NBC) Drama** *with George Kennedy as Father Samuel "Sarge" Cavanaugh, Sallie Shockley as Valerie, Har-*

*old Sakata as Kenji Takichi, and Roman Bieri as Barney Verick*

Here's a contrived plot that smacks of the 1970s infatuation with rogue cops: A police homicide detective's wife is killed in an assassination attempt meant for the cop, so the distraught policeman leaves the force and becomes a priest. Wait! There's more! The cop turned priest graduates from the seminary and is assigned to a church in the *same* neighborhood he used to patrol as a policeman (*what* a coincidence!). As a priest with a background in police work, our hero can fight crime two ways, both as detective and as spiritual advisor.

*Sarge* is not quite so trite as this summary implies, but there really is not much happening on the show other than the stilted concept. George Kennedy (a film star in *Cool Hand Luke* and several disaster films such as *Airport, Airport '77, Airport '79,* etc.) is appropriately tough and gritty as the priest everyone calls "Sarge." The pilot is called *Sarge: The Badge or the Cross,* where Kennedy's character is known as Sarge Swanson.

In syndication, the thirteen episodes of *Sarge* are often run as part of *The Bold Ones*, an umbrella program originally made of four separate series segments.

**SATURDAY NIGHT LIVE (***½) 90 min (Color; 1975– NBC) with syndicated packages of (102ep 30 min or 102ep 60 min Color; 1975–1980 NBC) Comedy-Variety** *with casts including Dan Aykroyd, John Belushi, Chevy Chase, Jane Curtin, Bill Murray, Laraine Newman, Gilda Radner, Garrett Morris, Eddie Murphy, Joe Piscopo, Don Novello, Billy Crystal, Martin Short, Harry Shearer, Jim Belushi, Rich Hall, Jon Lovitz, Nora Dunn, Victoria Jackson, Phil Hartman, Jan Hooks, Kevin Nealon, Dana Carvey, and Dennis Miller*

It started as a groundbreaker, became an institution, and in the process launched at least a half-dozen major careers. Above all, *Saturday Night Live* marked the ascent of a new generation of producers, writers, performers, and viewers, all steeped in a lifetime of television, rock music, and overall love of pop culture.

Yet there was also something almost nostalgic about the series when it began in 1975. For one thing, it was a comedy-variety series, a format that had reached its peak in the 1960s. More important, though, each program went out live, just like *Your Show of Shows* or *Playhouse 90* in the golden age of television. Whatever happened each week, it was television history in the making.

There's nothing like a live performance to pump up a cast and a studio audience. However, the effect on viewers at home is more problematic. Given the choice, some may have actually preferred to see some prudent editing, cutting out flubbed lines and unsuccessful bits. Ironically, that's the way most people these days get to see the performances from the first generation of *Saturday Night Live* (seasons one through five).

When the series first hit syndication, the ninety-minute programs (which actually contained about sixty-six minutes of material sans commercials) were packaged as one-hour cut-downs. This usually involved trimming performances by the musical guests, filler patter ("Next week's host will be . . ."), audience shots, and some filmed bits or flat skits. Even after all this, each episode was still clearly identifiable by its host, graphics, the context of its opening routines, and the overall feel of the show.

This format changed in the subsequent half-hour packages, which opened with a standard *Best of Saturday Night Live* graphic montage. This change made sense because even though the packages were derived from specific episodes (the first time Steve Martin hosted, Eric Idle's second appearance), they were much more a collection of program highlights, picking and choosing from among the available skits in any episode. As a result, any routine might end up opening or closing the program. Sometimes the program host barely turned up.

This way is probably the best for these seasons to play as reruns, showcasing the best moments rather than the entire originals that came live from New York at the time. Contemporary viewers just enjoy the chance to see entertaining bits by some of their favorite performers.

The first five seasons of *Saturday Night Live* have also turned up on video, both in compilation form (on "Best of" packages for John Belushi, Dan Aykroyd, Gilda Radner, and Chevy Chase) and as complete programs.

The twelve episodes from the disastrous *Saturday Night '80* are unlikely ever to see the light of day again. This season followed the departure of producer Lorne Michaels as well as all of the writers and performers from the first five years. It was every producer's (and viewer's) worst nightmare come true, filled with far too many excruciatingly bad moments to be believed. The only bits worth rescuing are those featuring Eddie Murphy and Joe Piscopo. The rest of the cast never really gels, though Charles Rocket (very unsuccessful as the "Weekend Update" news anchor) later redeemed himself in such series as *Moonlighting* and *Max Headroom,* and stand up comic Gilbert Gottfried also recovered nicely. The next two seasons, though, are fine as Murphy and Piscopo reel off one great skit after another, with a solid cast behind them.

Then for one year veterans Billy Crystal and Martin Short led another excellent cast in one of the program's most consistent seasons since the Lorne Michaels days. Michaels himself returned as producer in 1985. After a weak initial season, he seemed to find his rhythm again, deftly showcasing another new generation of performers. As a result, *Saturday Night Live* was once again "back," warmly embraced both by nostalgic critics and fresh young viewers. Appropriately, it seemed that if any troupe could begin to match the legendary innovation of those first golden seasons, this was the one, with such characters as the Church Lady and the best "Weekend Update" anchor (Dennis Miller) since Chevy Chase.

This may also be the cast that accumulates enough episodes for a separate rerun syndication package (with such frequent cast turnovers after the fifth season, there haven't been enough episodes with a consistent lineup to stand on their own). Or, perhaps highlights from different seasons might be combined to run as something like *Saturday Night Live: The Next Generations*.

Whatever the case, this series has compiled a most enviable record, going strong from 1975 into the 1990s. Still live. Still from New York. And still an amazing network institution. ■

## SATURDAY NIGHT LIVE WITH HOWARD COSELL

**(½) 60 min (19ep Color; 1975–1976 ABC) Variety** *with Howard Cosell as host*

Few remember it now, but this show is the *original Saturday Night Live*. In the fall of 1975, an important live variety show premiered on NBC. It featured the "Not Ready For Prime-Time Players," including Chevy Chase and John Belushi, and became a monster hit. However, it was not originally called *Saturday Night Live*, but rather *NBC's Saturday Night*, to differentiate it from the prime-time series premiering the same fall on ABC, starring Howard Cosell.

NBC's live show became a TV classic, but Cosell's program barely made it through the 1975 football season. Cosell, renowned as an opinionated sportscaster, never was cut out to be an amiable master of ceremonies. The incongruity of his vain attempt to play a latter-day Ed Sullivan only increases when viewing the series now.

Guests on the opener range from the overhyped British rock group The Bay City Rollers to Frank Sinatra, Shamu the killer whale, and a live satellite hookup of boxers Muhammad Ali and Joe Frazier from the Orient, where they were preparing for a match dubbed the "Thrilla in Manila."

This series is still available in syndication, but if nobody wanted to see it in 1975, who would bother watching it now? It is for historians only, and maybe for inveterate Cosell haters.

An interesting sidelight is that Bill Murray, who was not in the original crew of *NBC's Saturday Night*, made his network series debut on *Saturday Night Live with Howard Cosell*, as a semiregular in the comedy troupe. Murray did not join the NBC series until around 1977, when that show's title was officially changed to what everyone already called it, *Saturday Night Live*.

## SCARECROW AND MRS. KING

**(**½) 60 min (88ep Color; 1983–1987) Adventure** *with Kate Jackson as Amanda King, Bruce Boxleitner as Lee "Scarecrow" Stetson, Beverly Garland as Dotty West, Mel Stewart as Billy Melrose, Paul Stout as Philip King, Greg Morton as Jamie King, and Martha Smith as Francine Desmond*

Their first meeting is strictly a matter of chance. While on a hot espionage assignment, U.S. agent Lee Stetson (code name: Scarecrow) has to get rid of a small package, so as he dashes down the platform at a suburban Washington train station, he plucks Amanda King from the crowd, gives her the box, and disappears. Understandably, Amanda finds this intriguing. More important, as a super-straight, terribly responsible suburban housewife (divorced), she wants to make sure that the package is properly disposed of . . . and perhaps get another look at that good-looking hunk (just to make sure he's all right). By the end of the first story, she's begun to back her way into a second career, that of a part-time espionage agent.

Perhaps the most amazing aspect of this series is how long it manages to maintain an essentially static setup. Amanda is attracted to Lee, he cares about her, but the two keep an arm's length distance through virtually the entire run. (Okay, they kiss occasionally.) Meanwhile, even as Amanda goes through training as an agent, she never loses her slightly wide-eyed and innocent demeanor, constantly making analogies to domestic situations and explaining her hunches and plans with an eye for everyday homemaking oddities. (But she's usually right, which is why she gets promoted.) Amanda's two children and her mom (Dotty) never seem to tumble onto what's going on in her secret life. For the longest time they don't even formally meet Lee (he's always sneaking in the back door when he sees her at home).

The cases are routine stuff, often torn from the pre-*Glasnost* book of spy clichés. Fortunately the agency characters provide good plot support, with Billy Melrose (Lee and Amanda's immediate superior) properly fatherly and concerned, and Francine Desmond (Lee's old flame) a mild threat to Amanda's affections for Lee. The best strategy for this series is to catch both the first and the last half-dozen stories so you see Lee and Amanda's first hesitant cases together (the series at its most charming) as well as their top-secret marriage.

## THE SCARECROW OF ROMNEY MARSH

**(***) 60 min (3ep Color; 1964 NBC) Adventure** *with Patrick McGoohan as Dr. Syn, Geoffrey Keen as General Pugh, George Cole as Mipps, and Sean Scully as John Banks*

A masked adventure tale set on the southern coast of England in the eighteenth century, following the exploits of the mysterious Scarecrow of Romney Marsh, head of a brazenly successful smuggling operation. His fiendish yell echoes from the marsh to the coast and he rides in the night like a demon ghost, meting out his own brand of justice with cold-blooded ruthlessness and efficiency. At least that's what it looks like to everyone, including the local authorities determined to capture him. But in truth, he's really more like Robin Hood, robbing from the rich to help the poor pay the King's taxes and still have money left over for their own needs. As to ruthlessness? It's really more myth than fact, because in his other identity the Scarecrow is really the town's dedicated vicar, Dr. Syn (Patrick McGoohan), who never takes a life or steals for profit. McGoohan does a convincing job in his double-identity role, nicely understated as Syn, fiendishly manic as the Scarecrow.

Each of these episodes features well-paced self-contained tales, with increasingly dangerous missions—including an unmasked assault directly into the local general's garrison. They originally aired in February 1964 on *Walt Disney's Wonderful World of Color*, slotted opposite the first three appearances of the Beatles on *The Ed Sullivan Show* (thus losing almost the entire teen audience). Unfortunately this series usually turns up severely edited to fit into a typical made-for-TV movie slot. Hold out for the full-length presentation, though you might want to tune in to catch the title song. It's a great heroic ballad. ■

**THE SCARLET LETTER (**½) 60 min (4ep Color; 1979 PBS) Drama** *with Meg Foster as Hester Prynne, Kevin Conway as Roger Chillingsworth, and John Heard as Rev. Arthur Dimsdale*

Nathaniel Hawthorne's classic American novel (from 1850) of forbidden love in colonial Massachusetts is given a respectful turn in this four-part adaptation. Hester, a married woman, and the Rev. Dimsdale have a secret affair. Hester is convicted of adultery and is sentenced to wear an "A" on her clothes. The padre won't admit his part, and Hester won't squeal. Her husband is anxious to discover the identity of the guilty party.

**SCENE OF THE CRIME (*) 60 min (5ep Color; 1985 NBC) Suspense Anthology** *with Orson Welles as narrator*

Sad to say, this is Orson Welles's final TV series work before his death. *Scene of the Crime* is not at all worthy of the great man's name, but, after all, Welles did work on some real dogs in his later years. This short series is a "whodunit" murder mystery. Each episode contains a murder, a handful of suspects, and huffy/puffy Orson lending his stentorian tones to the bland occurrences. ■

**SCHAEFER CENTURY THEATER (*) 30 min (14ep B&W; 1952 Syndication) Drama Anthology**

An undistinguished member of the fraternity of 1950s syndicated filmed drama anthologies. Unlike most shows of this ilk, there is no host.

**SCIENCE FICTION THEATER (**½) 30 min (78ep: 39 B&W & 39 Color; 1955–1957 Syndication) Science Fiction Anthology** *with Truman Bradley as host/narrator*

This workmanlike anthology series straddles the middle ground between out-and-out fantasy and pure science. Truman Bradley, well-known radio voice of the 1940s, is the no-nonsense host. He adds dignity to what are essentially thirty-minute fantasy dramas concerning the outer fringes of scientific knowledge.

Each week some aspect of modern (mid-1950s) science (space flight, ESP, cryogenics) is the basis for an action story that takes then-known facts and goes one step beyond into the realm of what might be. The show may be science fiction, but it is serious stuff. There are no bug-eyed monsters from outer space here, only dedicated scientists pushing the barriers of human knowledge.

Because *Science Fiction Theater* tries to be serious about its fantasies, the stories are a bit limited. One almost wishes a bug-eyed monster would turn up now and again. Science teachers from the 1950s must have thought this show was a load of rubbish, but today's grown-ups who were teens and preteens back then may find the program a cute dose of nostalgia.

*Science Fiction Theater* was one of the first shows produced by Ivan Tors, who later used his adept touch at combining science and nature in an entertaining package in *Sea Hunt, Flipper,* and *Daktari*.

**SCOTT ISLAND, ADVENTURES AT** **(see *Harbourmaster*)**

**SCREEN DIRECTOR'S PLAYHOUSE (**) 30 min (39ep B&W; 1955–1956 NBC) Drama Anthology**

Some famous Hollywood film directors (such as John Ford and Alfred Hitchcock) take turns serving as director of the week in this anthology series with no host.

**SCRUPLES (*½) (6hr miniseries Color; 1980 CBS) Drama** *with Lindsay Wagner as Billy Winthrop Ikehorn, Efrem Zimbalist, Jr., as Ellis Ikehorn, Barry Bostwick as Michael "Spider" Elliott, Marie-France Pisier as Valentine O'Neil, Connie Stevens as Maggie MacGregor, and Gavin MacLeod as Curt Avery*

Judith Krantz's glitzy novel becomes a trashy miniseries. Lindsay Wagner, ex–*Bionic Woman*, plays Billy Winthrop, a poor little fat girl who goes to France, slims down, and becomes a model. She marries rich and old businessman Ellis Ikehorn, who promptly dies, leaving everything to wife Billy. She then opens a trendy Beverly Hills boutique called "Scruples" that caters to the kinky whims of bored rich people. The high gloss of the series may tempt you, but you'll feel somewhat tarnished if you stick around for the whole thing.

**THE SEA HAWK, ADVENTURES OF (**) 30 min (26ep B&W; 1958–1959 Syndication) Adventure** *with John Howard as John Hawk*

Filmed in the Caribbean, *Adventures of the Sea Hawk* focuses on John Hawk, a mechanical whiz who commands the schooner *Sea Hawk*. The boat operates as a floating electronics lab, and the series tosses in lots of 1950s-style atomic age jargon to seem up-to-date.

**SEA HUNT (***) 30 min (177ep 155ep B&W & 22ep Color; 1957–1961 & 1987–1988 Syndication) Adventure** *with Lloyd Bridges and Ron Ely as Mike Nelson and Kimberly Sissons as Jennifer Nelson*

Television has seen an endless parade of offbeat private investigators and cops. Some are bald and suck lollipops, some wear rumpled trench coats, some live on houseboats and keep pet alligators, some are blind, some are crippled, some only ride the bus, and some even talk to their shoe. Only one TV private investigator spends most of his waking day underwater, and that man is Mike Nelson.

Nelson is an ex–navy frogman who turned his diving skills into a profitable business by hiring himself out to investigate various mysteries of the deep. There might be some nasty contraband hidden underwater or a downed boat or plane or some fiendish foreign spy snooping around America's secret naval exercises. All these tasks and more call for the expertise of Mike Nelson and his boat, the *Argonaut*.

It's a great, if somewhat limited, premise, and large chunks of the action actually occur underwater. Nelson provides narration, as if the viewer was at the Nelson home watching thrilling home movies. Considering the difficulties that must have been encountered in production, the result is fabulous, if for nothing else than to get a lesson in underwater ecology.

The original Mike Nelson, Lloyd Bridges, is the ultimate example of 1950s manliness. Tough without bragging and brave without pointless machismo, Bridges' Nelson goes about his business, aware of the risks and knowing his limitations. Women do not play a big role in Nelson's life, other than as clients who need his help. In fact, Nelson leads a solitary, nomadic life, roaming the world in the course of his work. Keep a sharp eye out for Bridges' real-life sons Jeff and Beau, both of whom later became well-known actors. The two boys play various minor roles in several episodes.

In the late 1980s, the Mike Nelson *Sea Hunt* saga resumed, with ex-Tarzan Ron Ely picking up the Nelson role. This new Nelson, a widower, is assisted by his shapely and serious daughter Jennifer. The new color episodes demonstrate the progress of thirty years of TV production experience, but Ely is too much of a 1980s nice guy. Viewers will miss the tough-as-nails curtness of Lloyd Bridges. The underwater scenes do look a lot better in color, though.

**SEARCH (**) 60 min (23ep & 2 hr pilot Color; 1972–1973 NBC) Adventure** *with Hugh O'Brian as Hugh Lockwood, Tony Franciosa as Nick Bianco, Doug McClure as Christopher R. Grover, Burgess Meredith as B. G. Cameron, and Angel Tompkins as Gloria Harding*

TV stalwarts Hugh O'Brian (*Wyatt Earp*), Tony Franciosa (*Name of the Game*), and Doug McClure (*The Virginian*) take turns as lead agent for Probe, a super-sophisticated detective agency that spans the globe. The fancy gadgets seem old-fashioned now. Leslie Stevens, the producer, did better with the very similar *Name of the Game* and the very dissimilar *The Outer Limits*. The 1972 pilot, originally called *Probe*, just features Hugh O'Brian.

**SEARCH FOR THE NILE (***) 60 min (6ep Color; 1972 NBC) Drama** *with Kenneth Haigh as Sir Richard Burton, John Quentin as John Hanning Speke, Ian McCulloch as Capt. James Grant, Norman Rossington as Samuel Baker, Michael Gough as Dr. David Livingstone, Catherine Schell as Florence Baker, and James Mason as the narrator*

James Mason narrates this docudrama-style re-creation of efforts back in the nineteenth century to discover the source of the Nile River by members of England's Royal Geographic Society. The program was produced by the BBC and filmed on location in Africa, attempting as much as possible to use authentic backdrops in the story. Overall, it's a solid (if occasionally esoteric) tale.

**THE SEASPRAY, ADVENTURES OF (**) 30 min (32ep Color; 1967–1968 Syndication) Adventure** *with Walter Brown as John Wells, Susanne Haworth as Sue Wells, Gary Gray as Mike Wells, and Rodney Pearlman as Noah Wells*

Filmed entirely in Australia, *Adventures of the Seaspray* has an entire family floating aimlessly around on a schooner, this one called the *Seaspray*. The concept is that John Wells is a freelance writer searching for ideas for stories. Nice work, if you can get it.

**SEAWAY (*) 60 min (30ep: 28 B&W & 2 Color; 1965–1966 Syndication) Adventure** *with Stephen Young as Nick King and Austin Willis as Admiral Fox*

The stereotypical knock against Canada is that it is pretty but boring, and *Seaway* does nothing to change this view. Set on the normally placid St. Lawrence (connecting the ocean to the Great Lakes), *Seaway* concocts dramas relating to the waterway. Security man Nick King and his boss, Adm. Fox, nip the problems in the bud so ships can sail free to the Atlantic. Yawn.

**SECOND CHANCE (*) 30 min (9ep Color; 1987–1988 Fox) Situation Comedy** *with Kiel Martin as Charles Russell (a.k.a. Charles Time), Matthew Perry as Charles "Chazz" Russell, Joseph Maher as St. Peter, Randee Heller as Helen Russell, William Gallo as Francis "Booch" Lottabucci, and Demian Slade as Eugene Blooberman*

It's a big drop for Kiel Martin from the juicy role of libidinous, shifty police detective J. D. LaRue on *Hill Street Blues* to the purgatory-bound dead man Charles

Russell in this sorry vehicle. It seems the late Mr. Russell (who died in the year 2011) isn't quite good enough for heaven, yet not bad enough for hell. So St. Peter gives Russell's spirit a second chance and sends him back to Earth to earn brownie points. He must keep the fifteen-year-old younger version of himself (called "Chazz") on the straight and narrow. Both versions of Russell, the elder dead one (who adopts the name Charles Time) and the younger smart-aleck one, are unlikable. The dead spirit idea is cute at first, but becomes tiring very fast. When *Second Chance* expired, the series was, itself, given a second chance under the title *Boys Will Be Boys* (with the whole dead spirit angle dropped). That series is even worse than *Second Chance*.

## SECOND CITY TV (see *SCTV*)

## THE SECOND HUNDRED YEARS (**) 30 min (26ep Color; 1967–1968 ABC) Situation Comedy *with Monte Markham as Luke Carpenter and Ken Carpenter, Arthur O'Connell as Edwin Carpenter, and Frank Maxwell as Col. Garroway*

Mild and innocuous, *The Second Hundred Years* boasts an innovative premise that goes nowhere after an episode or two. Luke Carpenter, a young gold prospector, is buried alive in an Alaskan avalanche in 1900. In 1967, Luke's body is found and thawed, reviving the 100-year-old man who has the body and mind of a thirty-three-year-old. Luke's reappearance comes as quite a shock to his sixty-seven-year-old son Edwin, who is now a mild-mannered suburbanite in the Los Angeles area. Luke comes to live with son Edwin and Edwin's thirty-three-year-old son Ken, who is the spitting image of Luke. The difference is that Luke is a brash adventurer, while grandson Ken is a conservative corporate type. Much of the humor comes from Luke's confusion concerning the modern wonders of mid-1960s L. A. and the opposite twins concept of Monte Markham playing both Luke and Ken as contrasting types.

## SECRET AGENT/DANGER MAN (***) 30 min & 60 min (84ep: thirty-nine 30 min & forty-five 60 min B&W; 1960–1961 & 1964–1966 UK ATV) Spy Drama *with Patrick McGoohan as John Drake*

There are two versions of the adventures of Patrick McGoohan's crisp but principled international agent, John Drake. The first was produced during the early 1960s in a half-hour format, with Drake as a stylish operative who travels throughout Europe as a special investigator for NATO. These shows move at a fairly rapid clip, with good stories and sharp performances from McGoohan. This version turned up in the States under its British *Danger Man* title.

A few years later, in the wake of the tremendous success of the theatrical James Bond films, McGoohan dusted off the Drake character and the shows went back into production, this time as one-hour adventures. (Ironically, McGoohan had been offered the role of Bond in *Dr. No* and turned it down.) In England, the new series of episodes retained the *Danger Man* title, but for airing in America (just so there would be no confusing the audience) they were retitled *Secret Agent*, adding a catchy theme song by Johnny Rivers over the opening and closing credits.

With the expanded format, these episodes allow for more complex stories and dramatic action. They also clearly establish John Drake as an agent with a conscience and sense of decency, often not at all happy with the violent consequences of his latest adventure. Some of these themes would surface again in McGoohan's next series, *The Prisoner*.

Overall, this is a well-done adventure series, with a nice mix of more traditional espionage plots and occasional offbeat tales. Three that you might want to keep an eye out for: "Colony Three" (Drake infiltrates a Russian village constructed to look exactly like an English town, discovering two types of people there: those training to be Soviet spies disguised as British citizens, and those workers who can never leave), "The Not-So-Jolly Roger" (Drake works as a DJ at a "private" radio station off the British coast line), and "The Paper Chase" (directed by Patrick McGoohan, with Drake attempting to retrieve valuable papers for a friend in an adventure that takes on almost surrealistic properties at times).

There are two color episodes made at the end of the hour-long series run. These shows were edited into an instant theatrical release *Kiroshi* issued in 1966. ■

## THE SECRET ARMY (**) 60 min (39ep Color; 1979 UK BBC) Drama *with Bernard Hepton as Albert Foiret, Jan Francis as Lisa Colbert, Christopher Neame as John Curtis, and Clifford Rose as Maj. Ludwig Kessler*

The so-called secret army is a legion of Belgian civilians who help captured Allied bombers to escape the Nazis and return to their units during World War II. The code name for the Belgian underground is Lifeline.

## THE SECRET EMPIRE (**½) 20 min (10ep Color; 1979 NBC) Adventure *with Geoffrey Scott as Marshal Jim Donner, Tiger Williams as Billy, Carlene Watkins as Millie Thomas, Mark Lenard as Emperor Thorval, and Diane Markoff and Stepfanie Kramer as Princess Tara*

Barely noticed at the time it was produced, *The Secret Empire* is a very impressive effort at creating a science fiction western, something barely tried on TV (unless you count *The Wild, Wild West*).

Set in Wyoming in the 1880s, *The Secret Empire* has Jim Donner, the local marshal, bump into a society of aliens living underground in a region called Chimera. The Chimera lord is Emperor Thorval, who steals gold from the surface world in order to power a device that keeps his subjects at bay. Marshal Donner tries to fight the nasty Emperor, but must keep his efforts secret from his neighbors, for fear they will think he's nuts.

Originally broadcast as part of the *Cliffhangers* series, *The Secret Empire* adopts the "to be continued" approach of the old movie serials (and TV's *Batman*). Unfortunately no resolution was filmed, so the aliens never are defeated. One nice touch is that the surface scenes are shot in black and white, while the Chimera underground scenes are in color.

**SECRET FILE, U.S.A.** **(*½) 30 min (26ep B&W; 1954–1955 Syndication) Adventure** *with Robert Alda as Major Bill Morgan, Lois Hensen as Colonel Custer, and Kay Callard as Jane Morgan*

Alan Alda's dad plays a "can-do" espionage agent, fighting the "Silent (Cold) War" against the forces identified as threatening the safety and security of the United States. Standard formula adventures, often saddled with heavy-handed righteousness. Filmed mostly in Holland.

**THE SECRET OF MYSTERY LAKE** **(**) 30 min (12ep B&W; 1957 ABC) Drama** *with George Fenneman as Bill Richards and Gloria Marshall as Lanie Thorne*

Groucho Marx's straight man from *You Bet Your Life*, George Fenneman, turns up in the unlikely role of a naturalist who teaches a young girl the wonders of nature in and about a Tennessee lake. This series was originally shown on the 1950s version of *The Mickey Mouse Club*.

**THE SECRETS OF MIDLAND HEIGHTS** **(*) 60 min (13ep Color; 1980–1981 CBS) Drama** *with Bibi Besch as Dorothy Wheeler, Martha Scott as Margaret Millington, Jordan Christopher as Guy Millington, Robert Hogan as Nathan Welsh, Mark Pinter as Calvin Richardson, Lorenzo Lamas as Burt Carroll, and Linda Hamilton as Lisa Rogers*

There is nothing so pointless as a failed soap opera. The effort it takes to explain all the plot complications often takes longer than the entire run of the show. Such is the case of *The Secrets of Midland Heights*, one of several *Dallas* imitators from the early 1980s (albeit one produced by *Dallas* producer Lee Rich himself). The chief angle here is that Midland Heights is a small college community, so there are lots of hot coeds and football stars to play musical beds, while the adults do their part to wreck every marriage in town.

Among the survivors of this show are Lorenzo Lamas (son of Fernando), who went on to play handsome playboy (what else?) Lance Cumson in *Falcon Crest*, and Linda Hamilton (making her first regular TV series appearance here as the girlfriend to Lorenzo's character), who went on to team up with a very different brand of hunk in *Beauty and the Beast*.

**SEE IT NOW** **(****) 30 & 60 min (177 ep B&W; 1951–1958 CBS) Public Affairs** *with Edward R. Murrow as host*

The most revered series in TV news history, *See It Now* was the brainchild of its two producers, Fred W. Friendly and Edward R. Murrow. In the 1940s, Friendly and Murrow combined the then-novel emphasis of on-the-spot news broadcasting with tough, no-nonsense journalism to create a documentary format that utilized actual recordings of famous news events and public figures. The format was first used in a series of records (called "I Can Hear It Now") and a radio series called *Hear It Now*. When Murrow and Friendly brought the idea to video, as *See It Now*, they made TV news a major force in American public life for the first time.

*See It Now* is best remembered for its unflinching exposés on Sen. Joseph McCarthy at the height of his Red-baiting congressional investigations. The series also made waves through an exposé of the Air Force's unfair treatment of a lieutenant whose father was suspected of radical leanings. One episode features atomic scientist J. Robert Oppenheimer, then labeled a security risk, expounding his beliefs on America's nuclear policy. *See It Now* contains one of the first shows to focus on the links between lung cancer and smoking (in spite of the fact that Murrow was a very visible chain-smoker). These shows virtually created broadcast journalism in an era when local and network news were usually limited to reading headlines and showing newsreel footage.

Aside from its pivotal role in the development of TV news, *See It Now* also presents numerous equally memorable shows of a somewhat lighter nature, such as a montage of American troops in Korea and portraits of painter Grandma Moses and comedian Danny Kaye.

Most of what was good about broadcast journalism in the 1940s and 1950s came from the work of Ed Murrow, and *See It Now* is the place to see Murrow at his best. The style and spirit of the program carried over to subsequent TV news shows such as *60 Minutes*, whose two primary behind-the-scenes forces, executive producer Don Hewitt and field producer Joe Wershba, first came to prominence working on *See It Now*. ■

**SEMI-TOUGH** **(**) 30 min (4ep & 30 min pilot Color; 1980 ABC) Situation Comedy** *with Bruce McGill as Billy Clyde Pucket, David Hasselhoff as Marvin "Shake" Tiller, Markie Post as Barbara Jane Bookman, Hugh Gillin as "Big" Ed Bookman, and Ed Peck as Coach Harry Cooper*

*Semi-Tough* keeps TV's record intact for having botched all sports-based sitcoms. Based on the 1977 movie with Burt Reynolds, Kris Kristofferson, and Jill Clayburgh (which was, in turn, based on the Dan Jenkins novel), the series centers on Billy Clyde Pucket and Shake Tiller, two stars of the New York Bulls, an abysmally poor pro football team. Their roommate is childhood chum Barbara Jane Bookman, but there is no hanky-panky here, as everything is quite platonic amongst the trio. Because the more ribald humor of the book/

movie (the best part of the two original formats) is off-limits for commercial network TV, there is not much left for the focus of the video version of *Semi-Tough*. The humor is obvious and sophomoric.

The program does, at least, provide the first TV series slot for David Hasselhoff, who later was a minor heartthrob as Michael Knight in *Knight Rider*. Bruce McGill is best known as "D-Day" from the *Animal House* movie (and *Delta House* TV version). The *Semi-Tough* pilot has an almost totally different cast.

**THE SENATOR (**½) 60 min (8ep & 2 hr pilot Color; 1970–1971 NBC) Drama** *with Hal Holbrook as Sen. Hayes Stowe, Michael Tolan as Jordan Boyle, Sharon Acker as Erin Stowe, and Cindy Eilbacher as Norma Stowe*

The innocent idealism of the late 1960s oozes freely out of *The Senator*, but it still contains some modern entertainment value, due to its good writing and fine cast. Sen. Hayes Stowe is a U.S. senator from California who is always shocked to find out that right and justice are not the sole reasons behind most governmental decisions. He does his best to correct that slight oversight, and is forever bumping against the nasty special-interest lobbyists and corrupt figures from which simple-minded political dramas thrive.

Chief draw for *The Senator* is Hal Holbrook (originally famous for playing Mark Twain in a one-man show) in a rare TV series appearance. *The Senator* originally was one element of the umbrella series *The Bold Ones*.

The pilot film is called *A Clear and Present Danger*, and it features E. G. Marshall playing Hayes Stowe's father, himself a U.S. senator.

**SENTIMENTAL AGENT (*½) 60 min (13ep B&W; 1966 UK ATV) Adventure** *with Carlos Thompson as Carlos Borella*

It's written in the bylaws of international adventure (under *Casablanca*) that, among lead characters, so-called tough exteriors hide soft, sentimental hearts. This show's characters are not the exceptions. Carlos Borella runs a successful import-export business, but inevitably he and his aides (played by Clemence Bettany and John Turner) find themselves involved in chasing down international criminals, obviously for the greater good of society and the elimination of evil. Unfortunately they rarely encounter anything other than run-of-the-mill scripts and adventures—something else that seems to be in the bylaws (under "Budgets, Low").

**SERGEANT CRIBB (**½) 60 min (14ep Color; 1979–1981 UK Granada) Mystery** *with Alan Dobie as Sgt. Cribb and William Simons as Constable Thackery*

A Victorian London detective-sergeant, usually caught up investigating murderous complications among the nineteenth-century leisure set. There are some truly bizzare cases such as a corpse in a crocodile cage ("Mad Hatter's Holiday"), the poisoning of an eccentric elephant enthusiast ("The Last Trumpet"), and murder at a six-day walking marathon ("Wobble to Death"). These stories reflect excellent research into the era for the original novels (by Peter Lovesey), and also provide Sergeant Cribb with a wide variety of unusual settings for his investigations. A solid effort, though placing less emphasis than usual for such series on the driving force of the main character, who comes off as almost low-key in comparison to the likes of Inspector Morse or Adam Dalgliesh.

The *Cribb* episodes generally consist of one-part self-contained stories, most of which first aired in the United States on *Mystery*! between 1980 and 1983.

**SERGEANT PRESTON OF THE YUKON (**½) 30 min (72ep B&W & Color; 1955–1958 CBS) Adventure** *with Richard Simmons as Sgt. Preston*

Enough of those look-alike westerns filmed on some back lot in Hollywood. Enough of the endless parade of savage Injuns and scruffy desperados. Here, finally, is a show set somewhere else. Not in Texas, not on the plains, not in California, but in the Yukon. Yes, Canada's Yukon Territory, home of a gold rush just as crazed as the one in California. The time is the 1890s, and the gold rush to Canada's desolate western frontier is in full swing.

Many of the kiddie western heroes dressed well. The Lone Ranger's outfit was always nicely pressed and Wild Bill Hickok usually looked rather dapper. Still, can any western hero compare sartorially with Sgt. Preston? The guy has the ritzy red Royal Canadian Mounted Police uniform with the puffed-out trousers and the enormous brimmed hat. Don't forget the mustache! Preston had a pencil-thin one like Boston Blackie. Nowadays only oily used-car dealers look like that, but in the good old days, upright, ramrod heroes such as Sgt. Preston *had* to sport a pencil-thin mustache.

So what does this snappy dresser do up there in the frozen north? Oh, the usual, tracking down thieves and murderers who are trying to disrupt the mad dash for cash in the Yukon. While the Sergeant has no sweetie on ice or any boon companion to down some brews with, he does have all the friendship a real man needs. A horse and a dog. Rex the horse and Yukon King the dog. Both will drive themselves to within an inch of foaming exhaustion for their beloved master.

Aside from randy thoughts modern viewers might have concerning the true proclivities of this manly man in the swank outfit, the stories of Sgt. Preston (who is never even called by his first name) are thirty minutes of pure adventure. The show is well done and civil, when many of its contemporaries were neither.

*Sergeant Preston* was created by George W. Trendle and Fran Striker, who were also responsible for *The Lone Ranger* and *The Green Hornet*. It first appeared on network radio from 1947 until 1955.

**SERPICO** (*½) **60 min (15ep Color; 1976–1977 NBC) Police Drama** *with David Birney as Frank Serpico and Tom Atkins as Tom Sullivan*

The TV series *Serpico* is three levels removed from reality, but it demonstrates how fast fact can become hack fiction. In the early 1970s, there really was a New York City police officer named Frank Serpico. He worked undercover to expose organized crime, corruption in big business, and corruption in the police department. As you might expect, Officer Serpico had many enemies, including several police brethren. In 1971, he was shot in the face by a drug dealer and retired from the force, becoming something of a local celebrity. Author Peter Maas wrote a popular biography of Serpico, which was turned into a hit 1974 movie, starring Al Pacino. Two years later, this TV series appeared, starring David Birney. It took just half a decade for Serpico to hit the hat trick of pop culture: a book, a movie, and a TV series.

Each version, of course, got farther and farther away from the reality of Serpico's life, while emphasizing the more dramatic aspects. By the time the TV series came around, most of the rough and tumble flavor of Serpico's world had been neutralized for mass consumption. The TV series pushes the angle of corruption in high places that was popular in the Watergate era.

Birney, a good actor, does a workmanlike job as the unconventional cop with a tough assignment. Tom Sullivan is Serpico's police department contact while Serpico is undercover. Unfortunately there are no good scripts to go along with this juicy format. Stick to the film version of the Serpico story.

**SEVEN BRIDES FOR SEVEN BROTHERS** (**) **60 min (21ep & 90 min pilot Color; 1982–1983 CBS) Drama** *with Richard Dean Anderson as Adam McFadden, Terri Treas as Hannah McFadden, Drake Hogestyn as Brian McFadden, Peter Horton as Crane McFadden, Roger Wilson as Daniel McFadden, Tim Topper as Evan McFadden, Bryan Utman as Ford McFadden, and River Phoenix as Guthrie McFadden*

Give this show an "A" for effort, but a "C" for entertainment. Based on a hit 1954 film musical, *Seven Brides for Seven Brothers* tries to bring the format of the musical to TV, where musicals (what few there have been) have always met a short and cruel fate.

Whereas the 1950s film was set in the old west, the video version is set in modern-day California, on a rural ranch where the first of the seven orphaned McFadden brothers has taken a wife. Poor Hannah must deal with her husband's six rude and rowdy younger brothers. Original music is provided by veteran pop tunesmith Jimmy Webb. Dance numbers are interspersed throughout the show.

Unfortunately this series does nothing to dispel the notion that musicals do not succeed on TV because the cramped nature of the small screen cuts against the wide-open spectacle that makes Broadway musicals so thrilling. The thin plots (a tradition among musicals) do not help. The youngest of the McFadden brothers, Guthrie, is played by River Phoenix, four years away from becoming one of the child stars of the theatrical film *Stand by Me*.

**SEVENTH AVENUE** (**½) **(6hr miniseries Color; 1977 NBC) Drama** *with Steven Keats as Jay Blackman, Dori Brenner as Rhoda Gold, Anne Archer as Myrna Gold, Herschel Bernardi as Joe Vitelli, Alan King as Harry Lee, and Jane Seymour as Eva Meyers*

The rags-to-riches (through rags) story of Jay Blackman fills the heart of *Seventh Avenue*, a TV adaptation of Norman Bogner's novel. Blackman makes a fortune by stepping all over people as he claws his way to the top of New York's garment district fashion business in the 1930s and 1940s.

**79 PARK AVENUE** (*½) **(6hr miniseries Color; 1977 NBC) Drama** *with Lesley Ann Warren as Marja Fludjicki, Marc Singer as Ross Savitch, David Dukes as Mike Koshko, Morgan Fairchild as Myrna Savitch, Barbara Barrie as Kaati Fludjicki, and Raymond Burr as Armand Perfido*

Based on a Harold Robbins novel, this sudsy miniseries mixes love and murder at the Park Avenue "front" location of one of New York City's most renowned madames, Marja Fludjicki. Will she survive the pressure to get at the syndicate types also operating from her building, including the wealthy son of a syndicate boss, Ross Savitch? Or will she rekindle the affection for her old high school sweetheart, who also happens to be a prominent district attorney out to get the crime czars? Just as soapy and trashy as it sounds, this one turns up in one-hour, ninety-minute, and two-hour rerun packages.

**77 SUNSET STRIP** (**½) **60 min (204ep & 90 min pilot B&W; 1958–1964 ABC) Detective Drama** *with Efrem Zimbalist, Jr., as Stuart Bailey, Roger Smith as Jeff Spencer, Edd Byrnes as Gerald Lloyd "Kookie" Kookson III, Louis Quinn as Roscoe, Jacqueline Beer as Suzanne Fabray, Richard Long as Rex Randolph, Byron Keith as Lt. Gilmore, and Joan Staley as Hannah*

The finger-snapping theme song to this series is one of the classics of nostalgic TV sing-alongs. Some people even recall the words to the verses in between the click-clicks, though memories fade when it comes to actual plots. That's chiefly because *77 Sunset Strip* hasn't appeared much in syndication over the past two decades, which is a shame. Though the series is clearly pure formula, it does have a good combination of character types, led by Efrem Zimbalist, Jr., as suave Stu Bailey, head of the detective agency located on Hollywood's swank Sunset Strip. His associates include Jeff Spencer (the standard handsome lead), Roscoe (a transplanted New Yorker with a heart for the horses), Suzanne (their French switchboard operator), and Kookie (the parking lot attendant from next door eventually promoted to a junior partner at the agency). Besides Zimbalist, Kookie (played by Edd Byrnes) is probably the name most associated with this series, which turned Byrnes into a teen heartthrob at the time, even hitting the top-ten record charts with the self-referential "Kookie, Kookie, Lend Me Your Comb" (done with Connie Stevens). Oddly, Byrnes played the villain in the pilot film for the series ("Girl on the Run"), which also featured only Zimbalist from the cast eventually selected for the series.

At the time of its original run, the success of *77 Sunset Strip* set off a mad rush to action-adventures series with distinctive (yet somehow interchangeable) locales and handsome heroes, such as *Surfside Six, Bourbon Street Beat,* and *Hawaiian Eye*. A stock company of sorts traveled from series to series (each produced by Warner Bros.), turning up as bad guys, victims, and clients. Even lead performers hopped around, such as Rex Randolph, who briefly became a *Sunset Strip* partner when his *Bourbon Street Beat* was canceled. There are also crossovers in character (between *77 Sunset Strip* and *Hawaiian Eye*, for instance). But despite all the imitators, the *77 Sunset Strip* original generally came off as the best in the genre.

For most of the stories, everyone plays the standard detective game, solving the usual assortment of robbery, blackmail, and murder cases. There are, however, a few more unusual episodes such as "Reserved for Mr. Bailey" (Bailey as the only person in an abandoned small town wired for remote-control murder) or "The Silent Caper" (a mystery without a word of dialogue). But as the series wound down in its original run, the format was changed for the final twenty stories, produced by Jack Webb. Zimbalist is the only series regular hanging around for these shows (joined by a new secretary/assistant, Hannah), leaving Sunset Strip far behind in search of adventure throughout the world. After dozens of cases, it seemed like time for a change. Later, of course, Zimbalist would go into public service with *The F.B.I.* (as agent Lewis Erskine).

In the 1980s, Zimbalist appeared several times (as con man Daniel Chalmers) with his daughter, Stephanie (as Laura Holt), on her suave detective series, *Remington Steele*. And, for a moment of cosmic continuity, watch for the *77 Sunset Strip* episode "Scream Softly Dear," with a guest female character played by Elinor Donahue (from *Father Knows Best*) named Laura Holt.

## 77TH BENGAL LANCERS, TALES OF THE (*½) 30 min (26ep B&W; 1956–1957 NBC) Adventure *with Phil Carey as Lt. Michael Rhodes, Warren Stevens as Lt. William Storm, and Patrick Whyte as Col. Standish*

The white man's burden is carried on with a very stiff upper lip in this relic from the colonial days of the British Empire. The 77th Bengal Lancers are British cavalry troops defending the crown against pesky little natives in nineteenth-century India. Lt. Rhodes and Lt. Storm are the two main hunks who wear the well-pressed military outfits.

## SHA NA NA (**½) 30 min (97ep Color; 1977–1981 Syndication) Musical-Variety *with Sha Na Na, Avery Schreiber, Pam Myers, and Kenneth Mars*

The 1970s musical group Sha Na Na, who rely on camped-up versions of 1950s rock chestnuts, serve as hosts to this loose but enjoyable thirty-minute variety series. The humor is broad and often banal. The guests range from pointless (Ethel Merman) to splendid (Chuck Berry). At least nobody takes the entertainment too seriously.

## SHADES OF DARKNESS (**) 60 min (9ep Color; 1983 & 1986 UK Granada) Suspense Anthology

Low-key series of supernatural tales adapted from a variety of short stories (most from the 1930s or earlier), first airing in the United States on *Mystery!* in 1984. As usual, you'll spot some familiar faces from other offerings on *Mystery!* and *Masterpiece Theatre* (for instance, Gareth Thomas from *Upstairs, Downstairs* is in "Bewitched") though the plots themselves are awfully tame and predictable.

## SHADOW CHASERS (*) 60 min (9ep & 2 hr pilot Color; 1985–1986 ABC) Comedy-Adventure *with Dennis Dugan as Edgar "Benny" Benedek, Trevor Eve as Prof. Jonathan MacKenzie, and Nina Foch as Dr. Julianne Moorhouse*

Benny Benedek is a reporter for the *National Register*, a sleazy tabloid that features articles about UFOs, ghosts, and black magic. Prof. MacKenzie is an anthropologist who supposedly is trying to conduct "serious" research in parapsychology. Through a tortuous collection of plot devices, Benny and the professor team up to check out reports of supernatural happenings that are passed on by the reclusive Dr. Moorhouse. One would guess that *Shadow Chasers* is meant to cash in on the popularity of the 1984 ghost/comedy film *Ghostbusters*, but it does not even come close to the wild humor of the movie.

## SHAFT (*½) 90 min (7ep Color; 1973–1974 CBS) Detective Drama *with Richard Roundtree as John Shaft and Ed Barth as Lt. Al Rossi*

Anyone familiar with the original films *Shaft* (1971), *Shaft's Big Score!* (1972), and *Shaft in Africa* (1973) knows that heaping doses of steamy sex and heavy violence gave the films the appeal that won them huge audiences. As can be expected, this TV version of the tales of suave black private eye John Shaft has none of the sex and little of the violence. So, what's left? Just another distinctive character playing a TV private eye. Yes, Richard Roundtree continues his film role as Shaft, and the guy has an undeniable appeal with his cool, tough manner. Still, there isn't enough here (in the way of scripts or backing characters) to make up for the loss. At least the TV show still maintains the funky Isaac Hayes theme song from the films.

**SHAKA ZULU (***) (10hr miniseries Color; 1986 Syndication) Drama** *with Henry Cele as Shaka, Edward Fox as Lt. Francis Farewell, Robert Powell as Dr. Henry Fynn, Trevor Howard as Lord Charles Somerset, Christopher Lee as Lord Bathurst, Dudu Mkhize as Nandi, and William C. Faure as the narrator*

The setting is Southeast Africa in the first part of the nineteenth century. In just six years (1816–1822), the powerful warrior king Shaka Zulu has managed to build an impressive empire there, uniting the many tribes of the region under his iron rule and constantly expanding his borders. Eventually, that brings him face to face with British colonial power, which is also looking for new territory. So, at the request of Lord Charles Somerset, governor of the Cape Town colony, British representatives venture into the stronghold of Shaka Zulu. Much to their surprise, they discover not only a powerful warrior army, but also a web of political and personal intrigue worthy of any soapy royal miniseries back home.

Series director William C. Faure plays the narrator, who dutifully notes everything the group sees, along with stories they hear about Shaka Zulu's rise to power. This is an effective framing device that takes us back to the future king's formative childhood days when he and his mother, Nandi, had to flee from their home to escape being killed. We see the development of his personal charisma as a leader (motivated by a passionate desire for revenge), culminating in his elevation to the prophesied all-powerful ruler of the land.

There is an epic sweep to the story, along with a touch of the supernatural, that make this quite an effective package. Be forewarned, though, that the series does contain some fairly explicit scenes involving violence and nudity. ■

**THE SHAKESPEARE PLAYS (***) 2–4 hr (37ep Color; 1978–1984 UK BBC) Drama Anthology**

Television has been rifling the pages of Shakespeare since the long-gone days of experimental broadcasts. Early drama anthologies in particular enjoy adapting the Bard (after five centuries there were no troublesome author's fees to contend with), though they usually stuck to the more famous titles (*Hamlet, Juliet Caesar, A Midsummer Night's Dream, Romeo and Juliet*). Even more important, the plays were inevitably trimmed to fit the demands of television timing, sometimes compressing more than three hours of stage action into sixty minutes (or less, with commercials). Despite all the available drama showcases of the 1950s and 1960s, it was not until 1978 that a serious, systematic effort was launched to produce a television series encompassing the *complete* canon of Shakespeare's plays, staged in their entirety. The brave company tackling the task? Why, the BBC, of course. Thirty-seven plays and seven years later, the project was complete.

For the most part, the watchwords in these productions are "stage it for the ages." You will not find characters in contemporary dress (like the Orson Welles version of *Julius Caesar* with the Mercury Theater in 1937) or offbeat interpretations of famous passages. However, you will see an excellent selection of contemporary performers and directors, including many familiar faces from the *Masterpiece Theatre* world, along with a few stars from pop circles, including rock singer Roger Daltrey from the Who (playing the twin Dromios in *The Comedy of Errors*) and *Monty Python*'s John Cleese (playing Petruchio in *The Taming of the Shrew*). They attempt to walk that careful line between being too respectful toward the original text and coaxing fresh energy from the works at any cost. Though the series probably errs on the side of playing it safe far too often, for the most part it still comes off as a generally faithful rendering of Shakespeare at his most famous and his most obscure.

Of course, when it comes to Shakespeare, you'll never have trouble finding a circle of critics and scholars ready to tell you precisely what was right and wrong about every production ever mounted. Amazingly, PBS (which ran the series in the United States) resisted the temptation to stage such postproduction comment sessions throughout the entire original seven-year run of the series, letting the works speak for themselves. There was some background information, but no Siskel and Ebert (or Harry and Wally) types ready to blast the slightest acting or directing flaws after the final credit roll.

For subsequent reruns, though, commentary shows were allowed. In addition, to make the whole project slightly more accessible, the plays were also packaged into multipart thirty-minute episodes complete with background information and summaries of "the story so far." Probably only a dedicated Shakespeare fan or literature teacher would attempt to sit through every one of these productions, but it is definitely worthwhile to catch at least one comedy and one tragedy, especially if you've never seen any of the plays in an unedited theatrical staging. (With this in mind, *Measure for Measure, The Taming of the Shrew, As You Like It,* and *Henry V* are definitely worth a look.) If nothing else, you'll end up with a greater appreciation for such offerings as *Moonlighting*'s "Atomic Shakespeare" (which is a *Taming of the Shrew* parody). ■

**SHANE (*½) 60 min (17ep B&W; 1966 ABC) Western** *with David Carradine as Shane, Jill Ireland as Marion Starett, Tom Tully as Tom Starett, Christopher Shea as Joey Starett, and Bert Freed as Rufe Ryker*

Herb Brodkin (*The Defenders, Studio One*) tries his

hand at producing a western with a touch of class (that's the intent, anyway). Based on the hit 1953 film of the same name, *Shane* is about a mysterious drifting gunfighter who appears in Wyoming in the late 1800s and winds up working on the ranch of recently widowed Marion Starett. Young son Joey takes a real shine to Shane, but the brooding loner ex-gunfighter knows it's only a matter of time before he moves on. Meanwhile, Shane helps the Staretts fight off the mean and nasty cattle barons who don't like the new homesteaders getting in their way.

David Carradine (pre–*Kung-Fu*) is a bit young for the role of Shane. Christopher Shea, who plays the idolizing Joey Starett, was the original voice for Linus in the first set of *Peanuts* TV specials in the 1960s.

**SHANNON (*) 30 min (36ep B&W; 1961–1962 Syndication) Crime Drama** *with George Nader as Joe Shannon and Regis Toomey as Bill Cochran*

In this dated early 1960s series, Joe Shannon is an investigator for a transportation insurance company. He drives a fancy new car with all sorts of silly "modern" gadgets that look funny today.

**SHANNON (*) 60 min (10ep Color; 1981–1982 & 1984 CBS & USA) Police Drama** *with Kevin Dobson as Det. Jack Shannon, William Lucking as Det. Norm White, Charlie Fields as Johnny Shannon, and Michael Durrell as Lt. Rudy Moraga*

Det. Jack Shannon, not to be confused with Joe Shannon of a similarly titled 1950s series, is a New York City cop whose wife dies, leaving him with Johnny, their ten-year-old son. Detective Shannon then uproots and moves to San Francisco, near his in-laws, where he becomes an investigator for the S.F.P.D.

Three episodes of *Shannon* that did not air during its original run were first broadcast over the USA cable network in 1984.

**SHAPING UP (zero) 30 min (5ep Color; 1984 ABC) Situation Comedy** *with Leslie Nielsen as Buddy Fox, Michael Fontaine as Ben Zachary, Jennifer Tilly as Shannon Winters, and Shawn Weatherly as Melissa McDonald*

*Shaping Up* is an unintentionally perfect self-parody, a snapshot of a fad that came and went and left just this one sitcom.

The fad was the mid-1980s craze for health clubs, which the public media linked to kinky, sexy activity (sort of a disco with more revealing clothes). *Shaping Up* is a brainless comedy set in Buddy Fox's Health Spa in (where else?) California. Buddy is the owner, still fit and trim after his hair has turned gray. Ben is his beefy manager, and Shannon and Melissa are the shapely aerobics instructors.

Leslie Nielsen is totally wasted here as Buddy Fox. This setting cries out for the broad satire of Nielsen's previous show, *Police Squad*, which lampooned TV crime shows. *Shaping Up* is best seen as a historical curio, all too revealing of the sad state of popular culture.

**SHE'S THE SHERIFF (*) 30 min (50ep at Summer 1989 Color; 1987– Syndication) Situation Comedy** *with Suzanne Somers as Sheriff Hildy Granger, George Wyner as Deputy Sheriff Max Rubin, Pat Carroll as Gussie Holt, Nicky Rose as Allison Granger, Taliesin Jaffe as Kenny Granger, Lou Richards as Deputy Dennis Putnam, Guich Koock as Deputy Hugh Mulcahy, and Leonard Lightfoot as Deputy Alvin Wiggins*

This silly TV show features Suzanne Somers (the ultimate TV dumb blonde in *Three's Company*) playing a woman who takes over her dead husband's job as sheriff of Lakes County, Nevada (near Lake Tahoe). The new Sheriff Granger comes with two kids and inherits four deputies who doubt her abilities. The humor here is quite thin. Guich Koock, one of the deputies, previously served in a similar capacity on the police force of *Carter Country*. George Wyner, another of the deputies here, played a more respectable law enforcement type, Assistant D.A. Irwin Bernstein, on *Hill Street Blues*.

**SHEENA: QUEEN OF THE JUNGLE (**) 30 min (26ep B&W; 1955–1956 Syndication) Adventure** *with Irish McCalla as Sheena, Christian Drake as Bob, and Neal as Chim*

Not all the bold heroes of the great 1950s syndicated series were men. Sheena, the White Goddess of the Jungle, is a figure fondly recalled by many. A female Tarzan, Sheena is a beautiful young white woman who was orphaned in Africa and raised by a tribe of local black nobles. Now on her own, she swings from trees in her skimpy leopard-skin outfit, plays around with her pet chimp Chim, and is forever saving her clumsy male friend Bob, a trader who looks like he'd last about ten minutes in the jungle alone. Unfortunately for Bob, Sheena is averse to being tied down to one man, so she swings freely, keeping up the hopes of the young adolescent males in the audience.

Don't expect much in the way of real drama or action here—it's all standard stuff. Still, Sheena is fun to watch, either as an early women's lib role model or as a pinup who fights.

**SHELL GAME (**½) 60 min (6ep Color; 1987 CBS) Adventure** *with Margot Kidder as Jennie Jerome, James Read as John Reid, Marg Heigenberger as Natalie Thayer, Rod McCary as William Bauer, and Chip Zien as Bert Luna*

Is this how Mike Wallace does it? John Reid was once a professional con artist with his wife, Jennie, until they got divorced and went their separate ways. Now he's putting some of those same skills to work as a local Santa Ana television producer of *Solutions*, a combination news/consumer help program. Then Jennie reappears, still running scams but also willing to help her former partner. In short order, she's semireformed and a part of his production team, though still more willing than he is to connect with the right con scheme if one comes along. Of course, working together the two might also find themselves back together on a personal level, much to the distress of John's new fiancée, Natalie. This light adventure tale has a good cast, obviously attempting to duplicate the teasing male/female relationships of *Moonlighting* and *Remington Steele* (where Read put in his time for one season as investigator Murphy Michaels), but with such a short run nothing really has time to develop. Gene Barry also turns up as the conniving dad to Margot Kidder's Jennie Jerome.

## THE SHERIFF OF COCHISE (see *Man from Cochise*)

**SHERLOCK HOLMES (*½) 30 min (39ep B&W; 1954–1955 Syndication)** *with Ronald Howard as Sherlock Holmes, Howard Marion-Crawford as Doctor John Watson, and Archie Duncan as Inspector Lestrade,*
**SHERLOCK HOLMES, THE ADVENTURES OF & THE RETURN OF (***½) 60 min (27ep at Fall 1989 Color; 1984– UK Granada)** *with Jeremy Brett as Sherlock Holmes and David Burke and Edward Hardwicke as Doctor John Watson*

Since the creation of Sherlock Holmes in the 1880s, Sir Arthur Conan Doyle's literary sleuth has been a big pop culture hit in virtually every medium: the original short stories of the *Strand* magazine, in book form, on stage, in feature films, and on the radio. Not surprisingly, Holmes has also been a fixture on television. There have been numerous one-shot TV movies and episodes of drama anthologies, along with several series packages.

At first, individual stations created a de facto Sherlock Holmes series with the fourteen theatrical films from the 1930s and 1940s, usually placing them in a ninety-minute slot (sometimes alternating with *Charlie Chan*). Though the first two (*The Hound of the Baskervilles* and *The Adventures of Sherlock Holmes*) are reasonably faithful to the original texts, the balance of them moved Holmes and Watson into contemporary times. In many of these (produced during the height of World War II), the pair is usually involved in thinly disguised patriotic adventures, with Nazis to fight, spies to expose, and a war to win. Nonetheless, they are still fascinating to watch because of the performances by Basil Rathbone and Nigel Bruce, who soon came to represent the definitive Holmes and Watson for several generations of fans.

The 1950s syndication version (filmed in France) is properly set in the 1890s, though the stories are typical grind-them-out grade-B crime dramas. Even worse, Holmes comes off as an empty-headed eccentric who often treats Watson with no more respect than he gives police Inspector Lestrade. You suspect the only reason Holmes is able to come to his brilliant deductions before anyone else is that he saw a copy of the script and they didn't. Despite its flaws, this version still turns up surprisingly often, probably because the 1980s version is already sold to another station in the same market. That's a poor substitute, though, because *The Adventures of Sherlock Holmes* with Jeremy Brett may well be the definitive rendering of the Doyle stories.

Produced in Britain by John Hawkesworth (*Upstairs, Downstairs*) for Granada television, the 1980s version is a Sherlock Holmes staging that gets all the period details correct, from the cobblestone street scenes to the lush Victorian interiors. In addition, the scripts stick fairly close to the original text, though the adapters aren't afraid to include an extra flourish if it seems appropriate. After all, most of the tales are based on short stories that offer plenty of opportunities to fill in specific visual details.

Of primary importance is the chemistry of the lead characters. Fortunately, Jeremy Brett is one of the best Sherlock Holmes since Basil Rathbone. Brett plays the detective as a man on the edge, capable of instant action and daring courage, but also as one who sometimes needs to just sit and think before reaching his conclusions. Those are truly fascinating moments because you can almost feel the wheels turning inside his head, even though he doesn't move from his chair. Brett is a Holmes of great wit, intelligence, tact, and decorum, who also cannot resist an occasional touch of theatrics when revealing his solution to a mystery. (The breakfast scene in "The Naval Treaty" is a delightful example.)

Brett is also a Holmes who fully respects his friend, Doctor Watson, treating him as a comrade, not a buffoon. (Perhaps Brett's stint playing Watson onstage a few years before this series gave him a greater appreciation for the character.) Rising to the occasion, both David Burke (for the first thirteen stories) and Edward Hardwicke (all the episodes thereafter) portray the character with strength, independence, and intelligence. Of course, Watson is no Sherlock Holmes, but he is someone who can play the deductive game well. In fact, during the period following the "death" of Holmes at Reichenbach Falls fighting Professor Moriarty, Watson continues to work with the police on a number of cases.

Ironically the one minor problem with the series is that it is so faithful to Doyle's original works. Frankly in a number of cases there's not very much happening in the stories, which sometimes were more literary mind puzzles than detective adventures. So be forewarned that in a few instances you're best advised to just enjoy Holmes and Watson at work—the case doesn't really matter.

In 1988, Jeremy Brett and Edward Hardwicke took their respective characters to the London stage for a two-person play, *The Secret of Sherlock Holmes*. ■

**SHINDIG** (***½) **30 & 60 min (B&W; 1964–1966 ABC) Musical-Variety** *with Jimmy O'Neill as host*

The premier rock music prime-time TV show of the 1960s, *Shindig* captures rock'n'roll at one of its high points. It was after the British Invasion launched by the Beatles but before the narcissistic excesses of acid rock dulled the excitement of the genre. Developed by British TV rock pioneer Jack Good (*Oh, Boy!*), *Shindig* (unlike its contemporary competition, *Hullabaloo*) mostly sticks to teen-oriented rock acts. In the show's final months, efforts to broaden the show's appeal (by dragging in such nonrock acts as Zsa Zsa Gabor and Mickey Rooney) diluted its focus.

While all the big names of mid-1960s rock (the Beatles, the Rolling Stones, the Beach Boys) occasionally turn up, the Righteous Brothers, Bobby Sherman, and Glen Campbell appear frequently. The house band, the Shindogs, at various times included James Burton, Leon Russell, Delaney Bramlett, and Glen Hardin. *Shindig*, unavailable in syndication at present, is a gold mine of pre-MTV clips of the best of rock.

**SHIRLEY** (**) **60 min (12ep Color; 1979–1980 NBC) Comedy Drama** *with Shirley Jones as Shirley Miller, Rosanna Arquette as Debra Miller, Tracey Gold as Michelle Miller, Bret Shryer as Hemm Miller, Peter Barton as Bill Miller, Ann Doran as Charlotte McHenry, and Patrick Wayne as Lew Armitage*

Shirley Jones plays a widowed mother attempting to raise several children, just as she did in *The Partridge Family*, only this time there's no million-dollar record contract on the horizon. Instead she heads west from New York City to a new life in Lake Tahoe, California, moving into the house she and her late husband had planned to live in together. The series then follows the adjustments she and her family have to make in their new town, on a tight budget, meeting plenty of new people.

This is a clean and wholesome package generally well done, just ultimately dull. (*Our House* covers the same type of territory somewhat more effectively.) Maybe Shirley and the kids should have tried to book an extended gig at some Tahoe hotel. Fortunately at least the program's character scrapbook does contain some good performances and otherwise familiar faces including Rosanna Arquette (later in the 1985 film *Desperately Seeking Susan*), Tracey Gold (Carol Seaver on *Growing Pains*), Peter Barton (the lead in *The Powers of Matthew Star*), and Patrick Wayne (John Wayne's son) as Shirley's local love interest.

**THE SHIRLEY MACLAINE SHOW** (see *Shirley's World*)

**SHIRLEY TEMPLE'S STORYBOOK** (***) **60 min (40ep B&W; 1958–1961 NBC & ABC) Children's Anthology** *with Shirley Temple as hostess.*

Shirley Temple, the 1930s child film star, serves as hostess for a wonderful series of adaptations of famous children's stories and fairy tales. Assisting her are a noted selection of guest stars. Look for Charlton Heston in "Beauty and the Beast," Agnes Moorehead in "Rapunzel," Elsa Lanchester in "Mother Goose," Jonathan Winters in "Babes in Toyland," and E. G. Marshall in "Rip Van Winkle."

The series has also been known as *Shirley Temple Theater* and *The Shirley Temple Show*.

**SHIRLEY'S WORLD** (*½) **30 min (17ep Color; 1971–1972 ABC) Situation Comedy** *with Shirley MacLaine as Shirley Logan and John Gregson as Dennis Croft*

The first foray into TV series work by film star Shirley MacLaine (*Irma La Douce, The Turning Point, Being There*) is not much. Shirley plays Shirley Logan, a peppy, perky, London-based reporter for a magazine called *World Illustrated*. The job takes her all over the world, where she becomes involved in all sorts of shenanigans, none of which are worth mentioning. This program is also called *The Shirley MacLaine Show*.

**SHIVAREE** (**) **30 min (26ep B&W; 1965–1966 Syndication) Musical-Variety** *with Gene Weed as host*

From the mid-1960s, the high-water mark of rock music on network TV, the era of *Shindig* and *Hullabaloo*, comes *Shivaree*, a lesser-known showcase for rock talent hosted by West Coast radio personality Gene Weed. *Shivaree* is an interesting curio from the post–British Invasion years.

**THE SHOCK OF THE NEW** (**) **60 min (8ep Color; 1981 PBS) Documentary** *with Robert Hughes as host*

The only shock here is that anyone would put together a well-researched documentary series and then give it such an confusing name. Robert Hughes, art critic for *Time* magazine, presents an overview of modern art. It is the bold new art styles that are the shock referred to in the title. ■

**SHOESTRING** (***) **60 min (26ep Color; 1979–1980 UK BBC) Detective Drama** *with Trevor Eve as Eddie Shoestring, Erica Bayliss as Doran Godwin, Michael Medwin as Don Satchley, William Russell as David Carn, and Liz Crowther as Sonia*

Eddie Shoestring works the radio airwaves of West England. His local station, "Radio West," invites listeners to phone in their tips and potential cases to an answering machine set up at the office. A lot of what he's asked to look into is pretty routine, but there's always a few messages that lead to spicier crimes, especially murder. After Eddie takes a crack at the cases (with Radio West footing the bill), he shares the details in a weekly radio program, changing key names and details to avoid potential lawsuits (much to the relief of station lawyer David Carn).

It's a neat variation in the world of private eyes, tapping the appeal of radio as a way to have very private conversations in public. In addition, Shoestring's listeners sometimes serve as a formidable investigative team themselves, tracking down facts for cases still in progress.

What makes this series really work is the credibility of Shoestring himself. A complex character, he can be blunt and determined, yet also occasionally withdrawn, sometimes retreating to the total privacy of an old boat to think. As a former professional computer whiz, Shoestring has a sharp mind and an eye for detail. Literally quick on the draw, he also does sketches of people while talking to them, capturing in an instant his impressions on any handy piece of paper.

Yet, at one point in his life, things were not quite as clear and he entered an institution for emotional therapy treatments. Shoestring knows what it's like to be scared, confused, and overwhelmed, so the rapport he had with his clients and listeners comes off as quite genuine. He may not have started out as a professional broadcaster (Sonia the station receptionist was the one to suggest he do such a show), but he quickly grows in his niche as the "Private Ear" of the airwaves.

Shoestring is also a warm and funny guy. He's an excellent vocal mimic, keeps in touch with the staff and fellow patients from the institution, and literally charms the pants off his landlady, Erica Bayliss. She, in turn, also helps him on some cases, both as an apartment confidante and also in her role as a local bailiff.

All in all, it's an excellent showcase for Trevor Eve, and certainly much better than his first U.S. series a few years later, *Shadow Chasers*.

**SHOGUN (***) (12hr miniseries Color; 1980 NBC) Drama** *with Richard Chamberlain as John Blackthorne, Toshiro Mifune as Lord Toranaga, Yoko Shimada as Lady Toda Buntaro-Mariko, Nobuo Kaneko as Lord Ishido, John Rhys-Davies as Vasco Rodriguez, Michael Hordern as Friar Domingo, Damien Thomas as Father Alvito, Yuki Meguro as Omi, and Orson Welles as the narrator*

This epic dramatization of the James Clavell novel (filmed on location) plays in two versions: the full-length twelve-hour package and a TV movie cut-down (running about two and one-half hours). The movie functions primarily as a teaser for the series, covering the main plot points and battle scenes, though losing a number of subplots completely. (It's the *Classic Comics* version.) However, if you can handle some initial confusion over the very different cultural assumptions at work in seventeenth-century Japan (along with a good deal of dialogue in Japanese), you'll want to go with the complete presentation. It's a fascinating tale of manners, morals, and personal courage.

At the center of the action is John Blackthorne, a shipwrecked English navigator who washes ashore in feudal Japan. There he finds himself caught in storms of a more dangerous sort: the bitter, bloody battle between two competing Japanese warlords (Toranaga and Ishido), the quest for Western influence by Jesuit missionaries and traders from Portugal (colonizing and trading enemy of England at the time), and a passionate affair with a married noblewoman, Mariko. But Blackthorne proves a most adaptable visitor, quickly gaining respect in his newfound country under the protective wing of Toranaga. The Englishman even takes a new "native" moniker (Anjin-san), while striving for the rarefied honor (and power) of becoming the first Western-born Shogun (supreme samurai warrior).

Richard Chamberlain and Toshiro Mifune give standout performances in what often plays as a symbolic war of style and inches, with how you execute your moves as important as the actions themselves. The same holds true even in the steamy scenes with Yoko Shimada, especially as Blackthorne/Anjin-san becomes increasingly assimilated into the Japanese way of life. Of course, if you prefer grand-scale battle footage, there's plenty.

Definitely best enjoyed at your own pace on home video (which also has some nudity and more graphic violence excised from the initial network broadcast). Watch it with a well-informed Jesuit friend and you'll also be treated to a blow-by-blow rebuttal to the drama's portrait of the missionaries in the story. ■

**SHOTGUN SLADE (**½) 30 min (78ep B&W; 1959–1961 Syndication) Western** *with Scott Brady as Shotgun Slade and Monica Lewis as Monica*

The world doesn't really need another western from the late 1950s, but *Shotgun Slade* is actually quite different from the other oater brethren of its day. For one thing, hero Shotgun Slade is really a private detective roaming the old west of the 1860s, as sort of a nineteenth-century Peter Gunn. The analogy to Gunn is heightened by the effusive use of jazzy music (by Gerald Fried) in the background. Look for some very unusual guest stars, such as Ernie Kovacs, Johnny Cash, and assorted minor sports figures from the era.

**SHOULDER TO SHOULDER (**½) 60 min (6ep Color; 1974 UK BBC) Drama** *with Sian Phillips as Emmeline Pankhurst, Michael Gough as Richard Pankhurst, Louise Plank as Adela Pankhurst, Patricia Quinn as Christabel Pankhurst, Angela Down as Sylvia Pankhurst, and Georgia Brown as Annie Kenney*

Set at the turn of the twentieth century, this is a fascinating history of the militant English suffragette movement spearheaded by the Pankhurst family. For them it all begins with the marriage of Richard and Emmeline, both dedicated to the advancement of the rights of women (Richard, in fact, had drafted the first unsuccessful women's suffrage bill in 1870). When Richard dies suddenly in 1898, his widow decides to turn the cause into a crusade, involving her daughters and anyone else they could muster. Unfortunately for them, all their polite lobbying and rallies win them minor attention and ridicule, but mostly indifference. So they turn to a different strategy: becoming a nuisance. And that's when their cause really starts to get attention.

There are some amazing confrontations presented in this series, ranging from force-feeding imprisoned hunger strikers to fire bombs in mailboxes. Definitely worth viewing, both as a relatively accurate docudrama and for the strong performances by all the Pankhurst performers. Ironically, of course, what finally does win the vote for British women has almost nothing to do with such headline-grabbing activities—it's their participation in World War I service jobs.

**SHOWCASE 39 (**) 30 min (39ep B&W; 1956–1957 ABC) Drama Anthology**

This obscure series of filmed thirty-minute dramas originally aired as the final season's episodes of *Ford Theater*, a long-running prestigious series that ran for eight years as an hour-long drama show.

**SIDEKICKS (**) 30 min (22ep & 60 min pilot Color; 1986–1987 ABC) Police Drama** *with Gil Gerard as Sgt. Jake Rizzo, Ernie Reyes, Jr., as Ernie Lee, Frank Bonner as Det. R. T. Mooney, Nancy Stafford as Patricia Blake, Keye Luke as Sabasan, and Vinny Argiro as Capt. Blanks*

The Force is apparently very much alive and functioning on earth, at least as tapped by young Ernie Lee and his grandfather, known as Sabasan. Together they've targeted Jake Rizzo, a bachelor cop, as Ernie's new guardian. That's because grandfather is dying and doesn't want Ernie to land in a foster home, especially after he's passed his secrets of mystical power on to him, dubbing his grandson "The Last Electric Knight." So after a little forceful spiritual persuasion, Rizzo finds himself looking after Ernie, much to the pleasure of social worker Patricia Blake, Grandfather Sabasan, and the boy himself. After a while, even Rizzo has to admit he's found a good partner in life and on the job: Ernie is a bonafide juvenile black belt in karate. He's a perfect back-up to Rizzo and his grown-up partner, R. T. Mooney.

In real life at the time, Ernie Reyes, Jr., actually was a young martial arts expert, whose fast moves ended up as the highlight of each episode. The pilot for this series originally aired as a one-hour drama on the *Walt Disney* anthology series under the title "The Last Electric Knight," with the subsequent series playing as a light police adventure (serious, but not somber).

**SIERRA (*) 60 min (13ep & 90 min pilot Color; 1974 NBC) Adventure** *with James G. Richardson as Tim Cassidy, Ernest Thompson as Matt Harper, Susan Foster as Julie Beck, and Michael Warren as P. J. Lewis*

Take *Emergency!*, tone it down, and set it amidst the flora and fauna of a western national park and you have *Sierra*, another of the plotless Jack Webb–inspired action shows of the 1970s. Like Webb's more successful series *Emergency!, Sierra* only nods at character development, preferring instead to focus on the surroundings and on the unrelated string of action rescues performed by the stars. In the case of *Sierra*, the stars are National Park Service rangers, whose job is to put up with ignorant, selfish, unthinking tourists and to protect them when outside danger looms (the same idea behind Webb's top show, *Dragnet*). The true star of *Sierra* is the scenery of Yosemite National Park, where much of the outdoor footage of this series is shot.

Michael Warren, a former UCLA all-America basketball star who plays token black ranger P. J. Lewis, makes his first TV series appearance in *Sierra*. He later starred as officer Bobby Hill in *Hill Street Blues*. The pilot film is called *The Rangers* and has a slightly different cast.

**THE SILENT FORCE (*) 30 min (15ep Color; 1970–1971 ABC) Police Drama** *with Ed Nelson as Ward Fuller, Percy Rodriguez as Jason Hart, and Lynda Day (George) as Amelia Cole*

The Silent Force is a super-secret U.S. government spy force that operates undercover to penetrate and disrupt the workings of "the Mob," alias organized crime, alias the Mafia. *The Silent Force* is a bland, forgettable series that seems to have been designed by computer, since it has all the elements of hit shows such as *Mission: Impossible* and a bit of *The Mod Squad* without their good writing and slick production.

**THE SILENT SERVICE (*½) 30 min (78ep B&W; 1957–1958) Drama Anthology** *with Rear Admiral Thomas M. Dykers, USN (ret.) as host and narrator*

As a producer, writer, host, and narrator to this series, Admiral Thomas Dykers certainly managed to keep control of his particular vision of military service. The result is a strikingly authentic almost documentary-style drama about various real-life missions of the U.S. Navy's submarine fleet, chiefly in the South Pacific during World War II. You can't fault this portion of the series: It effectively combines actual footage from the era with newly filmed segments (shot with the full cooperation of the navy, using the U.S.S. *Sawfish*). The problem is in the personal drama—or, rather, the lack of it.

Most of the character interaction consists of stiff commands, terse responses, and very concerned looks, though the performers do try their best with the given material. At least Dykers was sharp enough to recognize this show as a docudrama, casting real Hollywood performers as the officers and crew rather than relying on real naval personnel. (We're not talking big-name box office guns at the time, but there are familiar faces such as Craig Stevens, Jim Davis, DeForest Kelley, and Dennis McCarthy.) Acceptable military hype, but only in limited doses.

**SILENTS PLEASE** (**) **30 min (40ep B&W; 1960–1961 ABC) Documentary** *with Ernie Kovacs as host*

Designed as a showcase for some of the classic films of the "silent" era (1900 to 1930), *Silents Please* takes old movies such as *Don Juan* (John Barrymore and Mary Astor, from 1926), *The Black Pirate* (Douglas Fairbanks, Sr., from 1926), and *The Hunchback of Notre Dame* (Lon Chaney, from 1923) and chops them up to fit into thirty-minute time slots. The goal, presenting old film masters to a modern audience, is admirable. The method, chopping the films up, is objectionable, considering that many of the films originally ran about ninety minutes. In the later episodes, eccentric TV comedy genius Ernie Kovacs serves as host. This show is highly obscure and was seen by few, even when it originally aired.

**SILVER SPOONS** (**½) **30 min (116ep Color; 1982–1987 NBC & Syndication) Situation Comedy** *with Ricky Schroder as Ricky Stratton, Joel Higgins as Edward Stratton III, Erin Gray as Kate Summers, John Houseman as Edward Stratton II, Jason Bateman as Derek Taylor, and Franklyn Seales as Dexter Stuffins*

From the early 1980s, when the Reagan revolution was in full swing, *Silver Spoons* led the way in presenting the *new* generation gap. In a reverse of standard 1960s dogma, the parents are cooled-out ex-hippy liberals and the kids are the conservative, business-oriented types. Ricky Stratton is a highly mature twelve-year-old who comes to live with his divorced dad (Edward III) after being raised by mom and attending military school. Thirty-five-year-old dad is rich from a successful toy company he runs and is more of a kid than Ricky. He spends most of his time at home playing with video games and toy trains. The occasionally seen grandfather (Edward II) is like Ricky—very dignified and more interested in material things. Ricky's pal, Derek, is played by Jason Bateman, younger brother of Justine Bateman (who played the older sister alongside Michael J. Fox's conservative Alex Keaton in the similar and contemporary *Family Ties*). Jason Bateman went on to star as the oldest Hogan child, David, in *Valerie* (also known as *Valerie's Family* and *The Hogan Family*).

There is a lot of overly cute son-acting-as-grown-up and father-acting-as-kid here, but versatile child actor Ricky Schroder pulls off his tough assignment fairly well. John Houseman, as granddad, is always riveting when he shows up. At least by the end of the show, dad has matured a bit and finally marries Kate, his secretary, who has been maneuvering to be asked for years.

**SIMON & SIMON** (**½) **60 min (154ep Color; 1981 CBS) Detective Drama** *with Jameson Parker as Andrew Jackson "A. J." Simon, Gerald McRaney as Rick Simon, Mary Carver as Cecilia Simon, Ed Barth as Myron Fowler, Tim Reid as Det. Marcel "Downtown" Brown, and Joan McMurtrey as Lt. Abigail "Abby" Marsh*

Light and breezy to the max, *Simon & Simon* rolls on and on, without any visible means of support. The plots are wafer thin, the characters skin deep, the action just marginal, yet somehow *Simon & Simon* manages to string together entertaining shows that are watchable almost in spite of themselves.

The Simon duo of the title are brother detectives in San Diego. A. J. is the clean-cut, conservative type, while older brother Rick is scruffy and laid back. Together they run (or try to run) a detective bureau. If you can imagine *The Rockford Files* with Jim Rockford split into two people (one neat and one messy), you've sort of got a handle on *Simon & Simon*.

During four of the series' middle years, look for Tim Reid (Venus on *WKRP in Cincinnati* and Frank on *Frank's Place*), who plays the Simon's police contact, Downtown Brown. He adds some welcome spice to the surroundings.

**SING ALONG WITH MITCH** (**) **60 min (41ep & 60 min pilot Color; 1961–1964 NBC) Musical-Variety** *with Mitch Miller as host*

This show was an anachronism when it originally aired, and it is a genuine period piece now. You must see it to believe it. If you are not old enough to remember watching it (or deliberately avoiding it), and even if you are that old, *Sing Along with Mitch* will appear as something out of a time machine, from turn-of-the-century small-town America.

Mitch Miller, a short, goateed, record producer for Columbia Records in the 1940s and 1950s, was an outspoken critic of the rock'n'roll craze sweeping the nation in the late 1950s. An advocate of more sedate, melodic tunes of days gone by, Miller assembled a choral group in 1958, recorded a number of standard favorites, and released a record album. The buyer could sing along with the songs, since the words were printed on the album jacket. The idea caught on, and several sing-along LPs followed. In May 1960, on *Ford Startime*, Miller tried the sing-along concept as a special. It worked. It was simple, with no production numbers, no fancy guest stars, no inane chatter between songs, just music. The music was sung by Mitch's Sing-Along Gang, a collection of about twenty men and women of various vocal ranges. To help the folks at home join in, the words to the songs appeared on screen as the song was sung. All Mitch did was stand in front of the group and wave his baton.

The success of the special resulted in *Sing Along with Mitch* becoming a regular series. For more than three seasons, Mitch leads his Sing-Along Gang, his Sing-Along Kids, and several regular featured soloists, such as Leslie Uggams, Diana Trask, and Sandy Stewart.

The series ceased production soon after the Beatles arrived in the United States, launching a second wave of rock'n'roll hysteria in the land. Miller's loyal followers could not stop the tides of change much longer, and *Sing Along with Mitch* soon receded into the past, like some faded, tinted memory from the family photo album.

There were more than forty-one episodes produced, but only that number are available in syndication. ■

**THE SINGING DETECTIVE (****) 70 min (6ep Color; 1986–1987 UK BBC) Drama** *with Michael Gambon and Lyndon Davies as Philip E. Marlow, Patrick Malahide as Mark Binney/Mark Finney/Raymond Binney, Joanne Whalley as Nurse Mills, Alison Steadman as Beth Marlow/Lili, Bill Paterson as Dr. Gibbon, and Janet Suzman as Nicola Marlow*

This offbeat hallucinatory British series is definitely not for everyone. However, for those with a strong stomach and a craving for imaginative concepts, *The Singing Detective* can prove one of the more fascinating forays into the well-traveled field of detective drama.

Philip Marlow, a grumpy British writer of hack detective stories, is hospitalized with some noxious skin disease that is shown in excruciating detail. To keep his mind alert during his lengthy bed rest, Marlow's mind slips in and out of various tales, some of which are various plots from his old detective novel *The Singing Detective*, some of which are memories of his youth in World War II Britain, and some of which are fantasies about his fellow patients and the hospital staff. Marlow also has a set of fantasies revolving around his wife (Nicola) and her presumed affair with a sleazy film producer who wants to cheat Marlow out of the royalties to a film adaptation of *The Singing Detective*. Got it?

As the series progresses, the various tales imagined by Marlow begin to overlap, with several actors popping up in different roles in a few of Marlow's imaginary dramas. The effect is like going through psychoanalysis with Marlow or like being inside Marlow's mind during a lengthy fever dream. By the end, it's not quite clear what is "real" and what is merely a creation of Marlow's mind.

The production is phenomenal and the writing is deft, which is no surprise, considering that the writer is Dennis Potter, who wrote the 1978 BBC-TV series *Pennies from Heaven* (later turned into an adequate 1981 film starring Steve Martin). Potter's *Pennies from Heaven* also featured lengthy imaginary segments, where the characters would break out in song with the sound provided by actual 1930s records. In *The Singing Detective*, this device is used again, though more sparingly.

The heavy emphasis on Marlow's skin disease will turn off many viewers, but his skin (like his mental state) does begin to clear up by the end. If you stick around, you will be rewarded with truly innovative TV drama.

**SINS (**) (7hr miniseries Color; 1986 CBS) Drama** *with Joan Collins as Helene Junot, Jean-Pierre Aumont as Count Deville, Marisa Berenson as Luba Tcherina, Steven Berkoff as Karl Von Eiderfeld, Joseph Bologna as Steve Bryant, James Farentino as David Westfield, and Timothy Dalton as Edmund Junot*

Joan Collins, who plays "superbitch" Alexis on *Dynasty*, really unleashes her venomous cattiness in *Sins*, a miniseries she and her husband Peter Holm helped produce. In this story based on the Judith Gould novel, Collins plays Helene Junot, a French woman who, as the press releases always say, claws her way to the top. In this case, the top is the head of a fashion magazine publishing conglomerate. Once ensconced in power, Junot makes it her mission to ruin the life of the man who destroyed her family's life during the Nazi occupation of France in World War II.

The primary challenge of watching *Sins* is to see if you can catch all eighty-seven of Collins's costume changes. The southern European scenery is pleasant to look at as well. ■

**SIR FRANCIS DRAKE, THE ADVENTURES OF (**½) 30 min (26ep B&W; 1962 UK ATV) Adventure** *with Terence Morgan as Sir Francis Drake, Jean Kent as Queen Elizabeth I, Roger Delgado as Ambassador Mendoza, Richard Warner as Walsingham, and Michael Crawford as John Drake*

These are fictional adventures of sixteenth-century English explorer and fighter Sir Francis Drake, done with a sharp eye for accurate historical detail in the sets, costumes, and, in particular, Drake's fighting ship, the *Golden Hind*. The stories feature his exploits as an explorer, pirate, spy, and strategist to Queen Elizabeth I (he was a key player in the defeat of the mighty Spanish Armada), with most involving overseas adventures in the American colonies.

A good swashbuckling series, with a solid supporting cast including Roger Delgado (familiar to *Doctor Who* fans as the original Master) and young Michael Crawford (known in the late 1980s for his role in the stage production *Phantom of the Opera*, but then just beginning his successful career as a British stage and feature film performer specializing in light musical comedy).

**SIR LANCELOT, THE ADVENTURES OF (**) 30 min (30ep B&W; 1956 UK ITC) Adventure** *with William Russell as Sir Lancelot du Lac, Jane Hylton as Queen Guinevere, Cyril Smith as Merlin the Magician, Ronald Leigh-Hunt and Bruce Seaton as King Arthur, and Robert Scroggins as Squire Brian*

Yet another British-produced period piece adventure series shipped Stateside in the 1950s, presenting the twelfth-century adventures of Sir Lancelot, one of the knights of the Round Table. There's the usual attempts at historical detail, though a few more anachronisms than usual are slipped in. Actually in this case it would have been more fun to toss history and legend completely out the window and see characters like Merlin and Arthur played in more spectacularly magical ways. (Mickey Mouse as the Sorcerer's Apprentice in the film *Fantasia* might have been a good model.) Instead this show is a merely adequate rendering of a well-worn legend. ■

**SIROTA'S COURT (**½) 30 min (8ep Color; 1976–1977 NBC) Situation Comedy** *with Michael Constantine as Judge Matthew J. Sirota, Cynthia Harris as Maureen O'Connor, Kathleen Miller as Gail Goodman, Fred Willard as Bud Nugent, and Owen Bush as Bailiff John Belson*

Blazing the trail that *Night Court* would follow more successfully a decade later, *Sirota's Court* is a well-crafted series about the lowest rung on the judicial ladder, the urban night court. It is in night court where the dregs of cases and defendants turn up. Legal niceties are frequently overlooked in the spirit of getting things wrapped up as soon as possible, which suits the presiding judge, Matthew Sirota, just fine. Playing Judge Sirota is Michael Constantine, who exhibited the same world-weary supervision as the principal in *Room 222*. The sparring matches between ultra-liberal public defender Gail Goodman and ultra-egotist assistant D. A. Bud Nugent are well written.

**THE SIX MILLION DOLLAR MAN (**½) 60min (128ep & two 2hr sequels Color; 1973–1978 ABC) Science Fiction Adventure** *with Lee Majors as Col. Steve Austin, Richard Anderson as Oscar Goldman, and Alan Oppenheimer and Martin Brooks as Dr. Rudy Wells*

*The Six Million Dollar Man* is one of only a handful of comic-book-style TV series that really remains faithful to the inspiring medium at its simple, heroic best. It plays like a good old-fashioned adventure comic come to life. No "Pow!" or "Zap!" or other condescending camp, just an admittedly simple story structure played absolutely straight.

In this world the improbable is accepted as real. It is inhabited by Bigfoot and visited by alien invaders. Here government forces represented by the OSI (Office of Scientific Information) work tirelessly for the defense of truth, justice, motherhood, and apple pie.

In the opening episode, government scientists rescue American astronaut Steve Austin from certain death following the test site crash of his space vehicle. On the operating table, they not only keep him alive but they "make him better" with new atomic-powered artificial limbs (both legs, his right arm, and his left eye). It's the American dream at its most cocky and confident. All you need is the scientific know-how (and six million dollars, to cover costs) to turn anyone into a virtual superman.

Best of all, Lee Majors as Steve Austin looks super-heroic. He doesn't wear some silly costume or use some ridiculous super-duper name. Dressed in ordinary working clothes, Austin just gets the job done, making it look like fun without making it look funny.

*The Six Million Dollar Man* is often shown along with episodes of its sister series, *The Bionic Woman*, with occasional crossover appearances by Austin and super cohort Jaime Sommers (Lindsay Wagner). Fans had to wait more than a decade, though, to see if this "perfect couple" would ever tie the knot. After two TV movie reunions (*The Return of the Six Million Dollar Man and the Bionic Woman* in 1987 and *The Bionic Showdown* in 1989), Steve Austin at last pops the question.

Some episodes in the syndication package originally appeared as ninety-minute made-for-TV movies, which preceded the series and introduced the character of Steve Austin.

**THE SIX O'CLOCK FOLLIES (**) 30 min (6ep Color; 1980 NBC) Situation Comedy** *with A. C. Weary as Sam Page, Larry Fishburne as Robby Robinson, Joby Baker as Col. Harvey Marvin, and Aarika Wells as Candi LeRoy*

This extremely obscure series deserves at least an honorable mention in the annals of TV history. *The Six O'Clock Follies* is the first TV series set during the Vietnam War. Like *M*A*S*H*, it is also one of the few antiwar comedies in TV history. Unfortunately, *The Six O'Clock Follies* was not a very good show.

Set in 1967 Saigon, *The Six O'Clock Follies* focuses on the men and women who produce and star in the nightly six o'clock TV news broadcast by the U.S. Army to the American soldiers stationed in Vietnam. Sam Page and Robby Robinson are two ex-Chicago reporters now anchoring the news for the army, while Candi LeRoy is the weather girl and Col. Marvin is the commanding officer. The newscast is irreverently labeled the "six o'clock follies" because of the crazy antics of the crew and their attempt to deal with both the terror of the war and the pressure by the army to only air pro-army news. The term "six o'clock follies" had originally been coined during the real-life Vietnam War as the derogatory term that U.S. reporters used to describe the always optimistic daily news briefings given by the army.

*The Six O'Clock Follies* tries to combine the loose comedy feel of *The Mary Tyler Moore Show* newsroom with the seriousness of the *M*A*S*H* surgery unit, but neither aspect works.

**SIX SCENES FROM A MARRIAGE (**) 60 min (6ep Color; 1972 Sweden) Drama** *with Liv Ullmann as Marianne, Erland Josephson as Johan, Bibi Andersson as Katarina, Gunnel Lindblom as Eva, Jan Malmsjo as*

*Peter, Anita Wall as Mrs. Palm, and Barbro Hiort AF Ornas as Mrs. Jacobi*

Director Ingmar Bergman's excruciatingly detailed portrait of an apparently happy marriage gone sour first played in Sweden as a six-part television series. It was subsequently reedited by him for release as a theatrical feature film in 1973, *Scenes from a Marriage*. There are lots of close-ups and introspective discussions here as Liv Ullmann's Marianne tries to deal with her husband Johan's involvement with a younger woman. Does it mean the eventual end of their marriage? What will their friends think? (Don't worry, you'll find out.)

Though the original Bergman series occasionally turns up on Stateside public television stations, if you're in the mood to savor this one you'll probably have to settle for renting the feature film version (running a mere two hours and fifty minutes). Of course, you can always wait for some programmer to rerun the television package, perhaps coupled with a retrospective showing of the American-made *United States* series.

**THE SIX WIVES OF HENRY VIII (***½) 60 min (6ep Color; 1970 UK BBC) Drama** *with Keith Michell as King Henry VIII, Annette Crosbie as Catherine of Aragon, Dorothy Tutin as Anne Boleyn, Anne Stallybrass as Jane Seymour, Elvi Hale as Anne of Cleves, Angela Pleasance as Catherine Howard, Rosalie Crutchley as Catherine Parr, Patrick Troughton as Norfolk, and Sheila Burrell as Lady Rochford*

For anybody who wants to become completely caught up in the world of British royalty and courtly intrigues, this is required viewing. One way or another, this era (and the production) is one that all other miniseries and movies can only hope to match. For starters, historical events and characters just don't get much juicier, beginning with the larger-than-life figure of King Henry VIII.

Keith Michell handles his portrayal of Henry very well, beginning at age eighteen and working his way through all six wives. (The change in his physical appearance over the years is akin to watching Orson Welles balloon from the svelte star of *Citizen Kane* in 1941 to a well-fed wine spokesman of the 1980s.) His King Henry has a commanding presence and an appropriately stubborn, overindulgent, and short-tempered demeanor, though these traits are not why each of his wives stands a very good chance of being either divorced or beheaded. In fact, Henry needs a healthy male heir. And when his first wife, Catherine of Aragon, doesn't produce one, he starts looking elsewhere. After all, it's his royal duty. Besides (especially in the early days), he's handsome, a skilled athlete, well educated, and a great lover (if he does say so himself). And he's the king. So if he wants a new wife, who would dare oppose him?

Those who would and those who don't make up the courtly cast of dealers, double-dealers, conspirators, and loyalists who find themselves caught up in one of the most fascinating times in English history. This era includes England's official split with the Catholic Church and the formation of a brand new religion (which just happens to have the King of England as its head). There are moments of individual heroism, arbitrary executions, self-serving deals, and the constant battle for the dubious (if not downright dangerous) honor of sharing Henry's bed chamber as his queen.

Each episode is devoted to one of the wives and every one is definitely worth watching. Pay attention, take notes, and you should be ready to move on to other royal tales. *Elizabeth R* is the logical follow-up miniseries to look for, then perhaps such theatrical films as *Anne of the Thousand Days* or *A Man for All Seasons*. But be careful. These royal soaps have the potential to become quite addictive. Before long, you may even start to care about third cousins to Winston Churchill.

**THE SIXTH SENSE (*) 60 min (25ep Color; 1972 ABC) Suspense Drama** *with Gary Collins as Dr. Michael Rhodes and Catherine Ferrar as Nancy Murphy*

Stilted and dull, *The Sixth Sense* is a waste of time for those who like good suspense television. Gary Collins plays parapsychologist Dr. Michael Rhodes, who studies the murky world of extrasensory perception (ESP) and goes around questioning people who have had psychic experiences. It all seems more like an episode of Collins's later soapy talk show series *Hour Magazine*, with Collins interviewing just another crackpot who claims to have flown to Venus.

*The Sixth Sense* is now most often seen severely reedited (into thirty-minute stories) and packaged as part of Rod Serling's *Night Gallery*, which is a far better show. However, adding Collins's drivel (edited to the point of incomprehension) to Serling's show really detracts from the appeal of *Night Gallery*.

**60 MINUTES (***½) 60 min (Color; 1968– CBS) Public Affairs** *with Mike Wallace, Harry Reasoner, Morley Safer, Dan Rather, Ed Bradley, Diane Sawyer, Steve Croft, Meredith Vieira, and Andy Rooney*

While not the first of the modern network news magazines (PBS's *PBL* deserves that honor), *60 Minutes* popularized the form. Each week the chief correspondents (first two, then three, four, five, and six) present stories on a wide variety of topics (politics, the arts, investigations, etc.). A brief studio segment (a liberal–conservative debate in the early years, a humorous Andy Rooney commentary in later years) wraps up the show. Throughout, a stopwatch ticks away the sixty minutes of air time.

While *60 Minutes* did much to prove that serious, informative programming can capture an audience, it also popularized the journalist as inquisitor concept, which lesser lights misused, causing a growing distrust of TV reporters. Still, with more than two decades of material, *60 Minutes* is a storehouse of insights into its era. ■

**SKAG (***) 60 min (5ep Color & 3 hr pilot; 1980 & 1982 NBC & The Entertainment Channel) Drama** *with Karl Malden as Peter "Skag" Skagska, Piper Laurie as Jo Skagska, Craig Wasson as David Skagska, Peter Gallagher as John Skagska, Kathryn Holcomb as Patricia Skagska, Leslie Ackerman as Barbara Skagska, George Voskovec as Petar Skagska, and Powers Boothe as Whalen*

One of the most dramatic working-class series in TV history, *Skag* focuses on the hardships of Pete Skagska ("Skag" to his pals), a fifty-six-year-old foreman at a troubled steel mill in Pittsburgh who suffers a stroke in the pilot episode. The series follows Skag as he tries to recover, return to work, and resume his role as foreman. All the while, Skag must battle young Whalen at the mill, who wants to replace him as foreman, and must also deal with his turbulent family.

Skag's second wife Jo is Jewish (an oddity amidst the Orthodox Catholic Skagskas), and she is twelve years younger than him. Eldest son David works with dad at the mill, but is having second thoughts about following in the old man's footsteps. Younger son John is in medical school and rejects the working-class nature of his family for the more materialistic world of the professional. Oldest daughter Pat lives in her own private world and youngest daughter Barbara is promiscuous and overweight. Meanwhile, Skag's partially paralyzed father Petar lives with the family and drains yet more of Skag's emotions.

With all these travails, the Skagska household will never be confused with the Cleavers from *Leave It to Beaver* or the Cunninghams from *Happy Days.* The people in *Skag* are very real and their problems are similar to those faced by millions. The writing and acting in the series meet the challenge of the setting and provide top-class drama.

Despite such great quality, *Skag* was an object failure when it was produced. The most likely reason is that *Skag* is too intense. In spite of the high-quality scripts and acting, *Skag* may well hit too close to home for the audience. Working-class series, as a rule, have a very poor track record on TV, as most viewers seem to need a good dose of escapism or at least distance in their shows. With such pros as Karl Malden and Piper Laurie in the cast, and both Abby Mann (a writer from TV's golden age of dramas and the producer of *Medical Story*) and Lee Rich (producer of *Dallas, Knots Landing,* and *The Waltons*) as executive producers, viewers may well have warmed up to *Skag.* They were never given the chance. The few episodes that exist are worth looking for.

The final two episodes of *Skag* never played on NBC during the original run of the series. They first aired two years later on cable's Entertainment Channel. ■

**SKY KING (*½) 30 min (72ep B&W; 1951–1954 NBC & ABC) Western** *with Kirby Grant as Sky King, Gloria Winters as Penny King, and Ron Hagerthy as Clipper King*

Most kiddie westerns (such as *The Lone Ranger* and *Wild Bill Hickok*) took place in the safe, amorphous late 1800s, when men were men, Indians were Injuns, and criminals were bad guys. Very few westerns dared take on the twentieth century, not to mention the present, figuring that placing the setting in the current era would tend to defeat the prime allure of the western; a sense of frontier justice and classic heroes.

*Sky King* takes the bold step of placing its action firmly in the present, and, horror of horrors, there are few, if any, horses to be seen. Not to leave the kids without anything to marvel at, the focus moves from equine excitement to aerial adventures. The show's hero, Sky King, does his traveling by means of a twin engine Cessna airplane called *The Songbird.* Sky pops up all over the modern West, to help those in need and to right wrongs that modern law enforcement officials have overlooked. Sky is a former World War II fighter pilot turned Arizona rancher (his Flying Crown ranch is huge, thus necessitating the plane), but helping others takes up much of his time. He has no wife or children of his own, but is ably assisted by his niece Penny and his nephew Clipper, two youngsters who also have a lot of free time.

While some young male TV watchers pined away for the slowly developing Annette Funicello of *The Mickey Mouse Club* during the 1950s, others with more discriminating tastes were loyal to Penny King. Penny has already developed an attractive figure and is a girl with evident spunk, as she helps Uncle Sky in numerous exploits. Penny also gets to wear tight-fitting blue jeans and Western shirts long before the girls back east caught on to that style. It is doubtful whether many young female viewers of the 1950s became too excited over young Clipper King. Clipper tends toward the nerdy and is only marginally helpful to Sky in the clinch.

The two gimmicks of *Sky King*, the modern setting and the airplane, are different and result in some unique plot developments, but the stories and the acting are mostly mediocre. Unless you grew up with this program, it won't seem like much. ■

**THE "SLAP" MAXWELL STORY (***) 30 min (22ep Color; 1987–1988 ABC) Situation Comedy** *with Dabney Coleman as "Slap" Maxwell, Susan Anspach as Annie Maxwell, Brian Smiar as Nelson Kruger, Megan Gallagher as Judy Ralston, and Bill Cobbs as the Dutchman*

After turning out one of the more critically acclaimed sitcoms of the early 1980s (*Buffalo Bill*), producers Bernie Brillstein and Jay Tarses and star Dabney Coleman reunite in *The "Slap" Maxwell Story.* Once again, critics seem to prefer this show more than the viewing public. Coleman's "Slap" Maxwell is very similar to abrasive, self-centered TV talk show host "Buffalo" Bill Bittinger. This time, however, Coleman plays a sports reporter for a low-class newspaper (*The Ledger*) somewhere in the Southwest. Time and fame have moved on, leaving Slap a forgotten local hero who now gets by on memories of past glories (which probably never were). The modern trends of TV sports and investigative reporting have made Slap's writing style seem old-fashioned and florid. He still churns out his material on an old manual typewriter. Slap is left to pump up his stories with libelous, defamatory allegations that make him a liability his paper would love to unload. Hence, Nelson Kruger, the managing editor, is always on the verge of firing him.

Slap and his wife Annie have split up and Slap barges in on her at inopportune times (such as when she has a date over for dinner) to make extremely selfish and embarrassing demands for reconciliation. Slap's on-again, off-again relationship with beautiful young secretary Judy is marked by his fluctuations between demands for affection and refusals of any commitment. Slap is mean, snide, and tends toward running off at the mouth (and typewriter). Sounds like a great guy, huh?

Slap Maxwell's numerous personality defects undoubtedly are the reason many viewers have difficulty warming up to him. While this is understandable, *The "Slap" Maxwell Story* is, like other Brillstein–Tarses efforts (including the sadly overlooked *Open All Night*), a marvelous collection of character studies that head in unusual and intriguing directions rarely traversed by standard TV fare.

Slap's undiluted boorishness seems to have gotten to the network overseers near the end of the show's one and only season. In a foolish effort to soften his image, a few late episodes send Slap back to his hometown, where he rekindles a romance with Kitty, an old flame (Shirley Jones). To dilute Slap is to make him meaningless. Give us full-tilt Slap or no Slap at all.

**SLATTERY'S PEOPLE (**) 60 min (36ep B&W; 1964–1965 CBS) Drama** *with Richard Crenna as James Slattery, Paul Geary as Johnny Ramos, Maxine Stuart as B. J. Clawson, and Edward Asner as Frank Radcliff*

A venture into the halls of government from *Medic* and *Ben Casey* creator James Moser, with Richard Crenna (fresh from six years as Luke on *The Real McCoys*) taking on the tough role of James Slattery, minority leader in a fictional state legislature. Within the limits of television drama (i.e., skipping the details of all-night filibusters or some private backroom deals), the series uses the forum of legislative debate to tackle a host of topical and philosophical issues. In some cases, Slattery and his staff manage to change things through a new law, whereas at other times they have to be content with a few rhetorical victories. (Otherwise, this would be *Mr. Smith Goes to Washington* every episode.) Appropriately, Ed Asner is on hand playing a veteran political reporter covering the legislature—no doubt gaining the valuable experience that will serve him later as a TV news producer on *Mary Tyler Moore* and a big-city newspaper editor on *Lou Grant.*

With the growing, dedicated audience for public legislative discussions of every sort on the C-Span cable services, *Slattery's People* may well be due for another round on the syndication market. Its chief problems are in the dialogue (occasionally downright preachy, and sometimes more articulate that you'll ever hear in real life) and in topicality (a brave stand from twenty years ago may be the ideologically incorrect position today).

Still, considering that the actions of both local and national lawmakers have a much more direct, continuing effect on our lives than some flashy police car chase, we might be due for a completely new, similarly styled drama anyway. Or maybe C-Span can use highlights from its coverage of the halls of Congress as the basis for a "pulse-pounding" fictional series. But would *anyone* believe it?

**SLEDGE HAMMER! (**½) 30 min (41ep Color; 1986–1988 ABC) Situation Comedy** *with David Rasche as Sledge Hammer, Ann-Marie Martin as Dori Doreau, and Harrison Page as Capt. Trunk*

This attempt to revive the *Get Smart* style of humor comes complete with silly catch phrases, physical slapstick, an exasperated but impossibly tolerant boss, and a main character often oblivious to what's really going on but blessed with enough luck to complete his assignments anyway.

Stand-up comic David Rasche (pronounced "Rah-She") does a good job developing his character (an L. A. police detective) into an effective exaggeration of the Dirty Harry type of gung-ho supercop popularized by Clint Eastwood. The main problem is that such a super-macho guy is already a caricature, so it's hard to take him too much further without turning him into a total freak.

As it is, Hammer emerges as single-minded to a fault, mouthing knee-jerk conservative clichés against wimps and pinkos while intentionally (or accidentally) knocking about suspects and bystanders in his quest against the bad guys. Yet that dedication also saves him from himself. Though he'll go to any length to squash the scum of the earth, he also really believes in truth, justice, and the American way. Hammer is nobody's willing patsy.

Luckily his partner Dori Doreau is there to help pull him clear when he does become somebody's unwitting (or inadvertent) pawn. Despite his macho image, Hammer honestly respects her abilities as a cop, probably because she also excels in hand-to-hand combat and if provoked might just punch out a "no-good yogurt-eatin' creep" on her own. (Not bad for "only a girl.") Naturally Doreau has a soft spot in her heart for Sledge. When it comes to romance, though, Hammer saves his most tender words for the true love of his life, his .44 magnum. He polishes it, talks to it, and even takes it to bed.

As with *Get Smart*, the series excels when its stock comedy hooks are mixed with other parody elements, such as episodes sending up Crocodile Dundee, Max Headroom, and the feature film *Witness.*

However, the most audacious episode comes at the close of what was expected to be the series' only season. Hammer, Doreau, and Capt. Trunk have to disarm a small nuclear bomb set to destroy Los Angeles. Confident as always, Hammer delivers his trademark line ("Trust me, I know what I'm doing"), then twists the cap to open the device. It detonates and levels the city. Then the series got renewed.

How did the writers get out of that bind? To open the new season, they repeated the scenes leading to the fatal explosion. Then an announcer came on to explain that the new season of *Sledge Hammer* would take place five years before the explosion.

You have to admire their nerve in pulling off such a continuity cop-out. ■

**SMALL & FRYE (½) 30 min (6ep; 1983 CBS) Situation Comedy** *with Darren McGavin as Nick Small, Jack Blessing as Chip Frye, Debbie Zipp as Phoebe Small, and Bill Daily as Dr. Henry Hanratty*

*Small & Frye* is a witless exercise from the Disney studios involving two private eyes. Chip Frye is young, hip, modern, and handsome and can shrink to six inches when he wants to (and sometimes when he doesn't want to) due to some cockamamie laboratory accident. His partner is Nick Small (see, he is *not* the small one), a gumshoe left over from the film noir days of the 1940s when Sam Spade and Philip Marlowe were the private eye rage. Small can't adapt to the high-tech 1980s. Aside from the size reduction gag, *Small & Frye* has nothing to offer, and it wastes the fine acting talent of Darren McGavin, who has demonstrated the ability to mix action and humor on *Riverboat* and *Kolchak: The Night Stalker.*

**SMALL WONDER (*) 30 min (92ep Color; 1985–1989 Syndication) Situation Comedy** *with Tiffany Brissette as Victoria Ann "Vicki" Smith, Dick Christie as Ted Lawson, Marla Pennington as Joan Lawson, and Jerry Supiran as Jamie Lawson*

It's bad enough that most little kids on TV are syrupy sweet tykes. In *Small Wonder*, computer engineer Ted Lawson actually constructs a little girl robot (looking about ten years old) he tries to pass off as a real kid. The robot, Vicki, is maddeningly precocious. The "real" people are maddeningly banal. Only the members of the Lawson family know Vicki's lineage, and much time is wasted trying to keep others in the dark.

**SMILEY'S PEOPLE (***½) 60 min (6ep Color; 1982 BBC) Spy Drama** *with Alec Guinness as George Smiley, Curt Jurgens as General Vladimir, Eileen Atkins as Madame Ostrakova, Sian Phillips as Ann Smiley, Anthony Bate as Oliver Lacon, Bernard Hepton as Toby Esterhase, Michael Byrne as Peter Guillam, and Patrick Stewart as Karla*

This sequel to *Tinker, Tailor, Soldier, Spy,* which is also based on a John Le Carre spy novel, once again presents Alec Guinness as George Smiley, the master spy forever called out of his well-earned retirement to clean up messes made by his successors. At first, the problem seems minor. Smiley is to tidy up the details of the murder of General Vladimir, an aged Russian emigre with loose ties to the British intelligence agency (known as the "Circus"). After investigating the situation, Smiley is led to believe that the General's death is no minor matter, but rather part of an extremely complicated saga leading back to the infamous Karla, Smiley's long-time nemesis who now heads the Russian spy agency.

Having long ago resigned himself to never being able to defeat Karla, Smiley jumps to the challenge and turns his low-level investigation into a continent-wide sting operation that reaches an initial high-point in Switzerland. There, Smiley and several of his favorite former colleagues kidnap a minor Soviet official who easily breaks under Smiley's cunning interrogation and then serves as a direct contact with Karla. The climactic meeting of Karla and Smiley is wonderfully subtle and low-key (with Patrick Stewart, still a few years away from taking command of the *Enterprise* in *Star Trek: The Next Generation,* playing Karla).

Guinness is spectacular as Smiley, just as he was in *Tinker, Tailor, Soldier, Spy.* The story line may be virtually impossible to keep straight at times, but it is definitely worth the effort to follow to its end.

**THE SMITH FAMILY (**) 30 min (39ep Color; 1971–1972 ABC) Drama** *with Henry Fonda as Sgt. Chad Smith, Janet Blair as Betty Smith, Darleen Carr as Cindy Smith, Ron Howard as Bob Smith, and Michael-James Wixted as Brian Smith.*

*The Smith Family* concerns the home and work life of Sgt. Chad Smith, an L.A. plainclothes policeman with twenty-five years on the force. His family is the typical TV collection of wife, teenaged daughter and son, and younger son.

There are only two good reasons for watching *The Smith Family*: to see a rare (and final) TV series appearance by famed Hollywood film legend Henry Fonda, and to see Ron Howard in the brief interregnum between playing Opie Taylor in *The Andy Griffith Show* and playing Richie Cunningham in *Happy Days.*

**THE SMOTHERS BROTHERS COMEDY HOUR (***) 60 min (Color; 1967–1969 CBS) Comedy-Variety** *with Tom Smothers, Dick Smothers, Pat Paulsen, Leigh French, Mason Williams, and Bob Einstein as Officer Judy*

This fabled hour virtually defined cutting-edge TV humor in the late 1960s. "Slow-witted" Tom and his amiable brother Dick serve as hosts to a talented collection of comics and musicians. Poker-faced Pat Paulsen offers wacked-out editorials. Leigh French offers some tips that appear to be laced with some form of illegal weed. Officer Judy is the target for lampoons on the establishment. Many top rock and folk acts turn up for guest musical appearances. This series broke new ground for TV comics who wanted to go beyond stale patter and mother-in-law jokes. The air of topicality is now faded, but still refreshing.

All the hubbub about censorship that dogged this series during its original run will seem quaint now, considering the tame content of the program. In spite of the series' popularity, constant bickering between the network and the Smothers caused CBS to abruptly cancel the show in 1969. The Smothers also hosted a summer 1970 ABC series (*The Smothers Brothers Summer Show*) that featured pre–*All in the Family* Sally Struthers. A thirteen-week NBC show followed in winter 1975 (also called *The Smothers Brothers Comedy Hour*) featuring Steve Martin (a writer for the 1960s series) and Don Novello (a.k.a. Father Guido Sarducci). Afterward the Smothers dropped off TV for more than a decade.

**THE SMOTHERS BROTHERS COMEDY HOUR (**½) 60 min (18ep & 1 hr pilot Color; 1988–1989 CBS) Comedy-Variety** *with Tom Smothers, Dick Smothers, Pat Paulsen, and Jim Stafford*

Almost twenty years after the squabbling Smothers Brothers were booted off CBS, they returned to the network for a reunion special. Its popularity resulted in this series that closely resembles the old 1960s version, only a bit grayer and tamer. Tom and Dick still argue, Pat Paulsen still runs for president, and great musical acts still appear. The only thing really new is Tom's "Yo-Yo Man" character, where he demonstrates his proficiency on the yo-yo.

The first few episodes of this series were produced during a writer's strike, so the comedy material may appear pretty thin at times.

**THE SMOTHERS BROTHERS SHOW (**) 30 min (26ep B&W; 1965–1966 CBS) Situation Comedy** *with Tom Smothers as Tom Smothers, Dick Smothers as Dick Smothers, Roland Winters as Leonard J. Costello, and Harriet MacGibbon as Harriet Costello*

The Smothers Brothers' variety show of the late 1960s is a landmark in TV history, but the Smothers' first TV series was this frothy thirty-minute sitcom about an apprentice angel. Dick Smothers, the serious one with the mustache, plays an up-and-coming corporate type working for Leonard Costello at Pandora Publications. Dick's busy but boring life is disrupted when his brother Tom (the funny one) moves in. The problem is that Tom has been dead for two years, drowned at sea in some accident. It turns out that Tom is merely an apprentice angel and must do good deeds on earth before earning his wings above. Tom, being the same bumbler as he was in life, always seems to get messed up while trying to help others. Dick usually must come to the rescue, taking time away from his job.

This series is much too trite and stilted to work for long. The angel concept wears out fast. The Smothers are, as always, fun to watch going through their paces with their sibling bickering, but the writing is weak and doesn't match the level of comedy viewers have come to expect from the duo. This series is most notable simply as a historical footnote.

**THE SNOOP SISTERS (**½) 90 min (4ep & 2 hr pilot color; 1973–1974 NBC) Mystery** *with Helen Hayes as Ernestine Snoop, Mildred Natwick as Gwendolyn Snoop, Bert Convy as Lt. Steve Ostrowski, and Lou Antonio as Barney*

Two elderly mystery writers (Helen Hayes as spinster Ernestine and Mildred Natwick as widow Gwendolyn) find a second career in real-life sleuthing, much to the frustration of their nephew on the police force. He's probably just annoyed because they're usually right, starting with their work on the mysterious death of a faded starlet in the program's 1972 pilot film (rerun these days in TV movie slots as *Female Instinct*). With a lifetime of mystery writing under their belts, they know how to play the "let's suppose" game, trying out various theories between themselves before sending Barney, their chauffeur (played by Art Carney in the pilot), out on another legwork assignment.

This series is good for a limited run, probably helped by not having to stretch the premise for very many stories. Instead the two leads have the chance to make their mark and then move on, leaving the long-haul investigative work to *Murder, She Wrote*'s Jessica Fletcher and Agatha Christie's *Miss Marple.* Of course, in the latter case, there's Hayes again, at least in two made-for-TV movies: *A Caribbean Mystery* (1983) and *Murder with Mirrors* (1985).

**SOAP (****) 30 min (94ep Color; 1977–1981 ABC) Situation Comedy** *with Katherine Helmond as Jessica Tate, Cathryn Damon as Mary Dallas Campbell, Robert Guillaume as Benson DuBois, Richard Mulligan as Burt Campbell, Robert Mandan as Chester Tate, Billy Crystal as Jodie Dallas, Ted Wass as Danny Dallas, Jay Johnson as Chuck and Bob Campbell, Arthur Peterson as The Major, Diana Canova as Corrine Tate, Jimmy Baio as Billy Tate, Jennifer Salt as Eunice Tate, Sal Viscuso as Father Timothy Flotsky, Rebecca Balding as Carol David, Dinah Manoff as Elaine Lefkowitz, Donnelly Rhodes as Dutch, John Byner as Detective Donahue, Lynne Moody as Polly Dawson, Roscoe Lee Browne as Saunders, Gregory Sierra as Carlos "El Puerco" Valdez, and Robert Urich as Peter Campbell.*

This is the story of two married sisters, Jessica Tate and Mary Campbell, and their respective families. It is also the first big hit series from writer/producer Susan Harris, setting the winning formula she would continue to use on subsequent ventures such as *Benson, The Golden Girls,* and *Empty Nest*: clearly defined characters in a mix of funny pieces, clever plots, and reflective personal moments.

In *Soap*, Harris takes the concept of a sex-laden serial drama and plays it as a fast-paced comedy, taped before a live studio audience. In dramatic contrast to the very slowly paced *Mary Hartman, Mary Hartman*, a soap opera send-up staged much closer in tone to the real thing, both the characters and plots of *Soap* fall into place very quickly, allowing plenty of room for playful manipulation.

On the Campbell side, Mary's new husband, Burt, is suffering from temporary impotency. Unknown to her, the reason is that he feels guilty about inadvertently causing the death of her first husband, a mob hit man. The rubber-faced Richard Mulligan plays Burt as a hilarious bundle of nerves, with a sense of inadvertent slapstick worthy of Dick Van Dyke. Mary's son, Jodie (Billy Crystal), is gay, while her other son, Danny (Ted Wass), who also works for the mob, decides he wants out of the business, and the "Godfather" (Richard Libertini) agrees, but only after Danny kills the man who killed his father. (Oops!) Burt has two sons from his previous marriage: Chuck (played by ventriloquist Jay Johnson), who walks around with a wooden dummy named Bob; and Peter (Robert Urich), a local tennis instructor, who happens to be carrying on simultaneous affairs with Mary's sister, Jessica (Katherine Helmond), and Jessica's daughter, Corrine (Diana Canova).

Which brings us to the Tate household and its initial family complications. Corrine is in love with a Catholic priest, Father Flotsky (a character name used by comedian Lenny Bruce in one of his stage routines), but since she can't have him she's turned to Peter. Jessica, too, has sought out Peter because her husband, Chester (Robert Mandan), never seems to be around (he's busy philandering). Their other daughter, Eunice, is involved with a married senator (played by Edward Winter), sneaking sexual encounters in such places as an airplane restroom. Jessica's son Billy dreams of passing through puberty, while the "Major," Mary and Jessica's senile dad (who lives at the Tate home), still thinks World War II is in progress. The only sane one in the bunch is Benson, butler to the Tates, who can't stand Chester, but stays around because this family really needs his services. (Later, though, Benson finds a situation even more desperate: the household and administrative offices of Jessica's cousin, Governor James Gatling, so Robert Guillaume departs for a *Benson* spin-off series.)

*Soap* spins these situations (and many, many more) into a wonderful web of complications, with each season's episodes ending with a dramatic cliffhanger. The first involves a murder mystery and trial (with future *WKRP in Cincinnati* stars Gordon Jump and Howard Hesseman playing, respectively, the investigating officer and the prosecuting attorney), culminating in Jessica's conviction—even though she is not guilty. At the end of the second season, the main hook involves Burt's abduction by aliens, while the third has Jessica lapsing into a coma. In the program's original airing on ABC, there were summary specials before each new season (highlighting the previous action), but these are not included in the current syndicated packages. For the most part, there is no loss, except for the third special, which features Jessica standing at the Pearly Gates talking to a heavenly administrator played by Beatrice Arthur. This sequence doesn't turn up in any other episode.

But there are plenty of others that do, and over the course of the regular episode run, they provide some amusing as well as touching moments. One cute piece has Jessica, Mary, Corrine, and Eunice all sitting around the kitchen stuffing themselves with a cake they're not even supposed to touch, all the while talking about how much they enjoy sex. Another has Burt and Danny having a father–stepson talk while shaving, faces covered with lather. And throughout every episode there are dozens of clever lines, some almost throwaways. In one instance, Chuck is horrified to discover that Jodie has hidden his dummy, Bob, in the family refrigerator. After retrieving his wooden buddy, Chuck starts to leave the room, but we can still hear Bob tell him "that little light inside really does go off when you close the door."

Some of *Soap*'s most moving moments are when the characters speak from the heart, in between the gags and set pieces. In one such scene, Jodie delivers a passionate defense of his desire to be a gay single parent. Another has Burt face-to-face with an alien double, demanding the right to live his own life. And in the very first season, guest performer Harold Gould plays Barney, a man about to undergo bypass surgery, who explains to a depressed and suicidal Jodie (lying in a hospital bed next to him) why life is worth living. By the end of that monologue, Jodie (who has already swallowed enough pills to kill himself) looks up with a weak smile and a tear in his eye, convinced he's just made the wrong decision. Now he wants to live.

*Soap* is definitely worth following in its entirety. Because of its serialized structure, stations inevitably run the episodes in the correct order. Oddly, there is one frustrating side effect: When the series is used as a seasonal filler, running less than five months in a slot, the story just stops in the middle. As a result, you'll probably end up seeing the first two seasons far more often than the last two.

Of course, the actual final episode does have its share of unresolved cliffhangers—most notably, the fate of Jessica in front of a firing squad. The best you can hope for in resolving this is to watch for a subsequent episode of *Benson* featuring a "ghostly guest appearance" by Helmond. (Jessica also makes a few crossover appearances in *Benson* while she's still very much alive.)

*Soap* has an exceptionally rich cast that went on to roles in a wide variety of other projects, including Katherine Helmond in *Who's the Boss?*, Richard Mulligan in the Susan Harris–produced *Empty Nest,* Billy Crystal on *Saturday Night Live*, Diana Canova on *I'm a Big Girl Now* and *Throb,* Ted Wass as a substitute Inspector Clouseau in *Curse of the Pink Panther*, and Robert Urich in many other series, beginning with *Vega$.*

**SOLDIERS OF FORTUNE (*½) 30 min (52ep B&W; 1955–1956 Syndication) Adventure** *with John Russell as Tim Kelly and Chick Chandler as Toubo Smith*

Tim Kelly and Toubo Smith (where did he get that first name?) are soldiers of fortune. They will fight anyone, anywhere, for any reason, as long as the price is right. Since the plots are paper thin, at least the exotic foreign scenery is nice.

**SOLID GOLD/SOLID GOLD IN CONCERT (**½) 60 min (416ep at Fall 1988 Color; 1980– Syndication) Musical-Variety** *with Dionne Warwick, Marilyn McCoo, Andy Gibb, Rex Smith, and Rick Dees as hosts*

Veteran variety producer Bob Banner (who worked with Perry Como, Dinah Shore, and Garry Moore) updates the old *Your Hit Parade* concept of presenting the top hit records every week. For the 1980s, the songs are accompanied by scantily clad lovelies (the Solid Gold Dancers), while the artists performing the hits are sometimes seen in person, lip syncing to their records. Sometimes music videos of the songs are seen instead. Hosts for *Solid Gold* come and go at a dizzying pace, but Dionne Warwick and Marilyn McCoo hang around the longest. At the start of the eighth season, the show's title is altered to *Solid Gold in Concert* to emphasize the "live" aspect of the performances in an era dominated by filmed music videos.

**SOMETHING IS OUT THERE (*½) 60 min (8ep & 4 hr pilot Color; 1988–1989 NBC) Science Fiction/ Crime Drama** *with Joe Cortese as Jack Breslin and Maryam d'Abo as Ta'ra*

When it began life as a four-hour miniseries, *Something Is Out There* had some promise. The basic idea was exciting, with a "deese, dem, dose" kind of a cop (Jack Breslin) teaming up with a beautiful alien (Ta'ra). Together they attempted to track down a disgusting creature (called a xenomorph) from Ta'ra's world that had escaped to Earth and was chopping up people and adapting to human form at will. He helped her deal with the realities of Earth society, while she helped him figure out how to catch the xenomorph. Meanwhile, the good-looking couple exchanged titillating romantic banter, sort of like an extraterrestrial version of the *Moonlighting* duo.

All this promise began to slowly fade away when *Something Is Out There* began life as a regular series. Now Jack and Ta'ra don't seem as interested in the xenomorph. They prefer to spend their time working on more terrestrial criminals, such as bogus psychics and kidnappers of poor little girls. Ta'ra uses some magic powers now and again, but she might as well be from Bel Air as Betelgeuse.

**THE SONNY & CHER COMEDY HOUR (**½) 60 min (94ep Color; 1971–1974 & 1976–1977 CBS) Musical-Variety** *with Sonny Bono and Cher Bono*

One of the last really successful variety shows on network TV before the format fell out of fashion,. *The Sonny & Cher Comedy Hour* rolls along through the interplay between the married hosts. Sonny plays the somewhat dense but excitable husband, while Cher is the deadpan, put-down wife. Having performed together for years as a singing duo ("I Got You Babe"), Sonny and Cher have the patter down perfectly.

The series has a nice mixture of rock music and comedy bits. The cast of supporting regulars keeps fluctuating, but celebrities-to-be such as Teri Garr and Steve Martin are around for a while.

After three seasons, Sonny and Cher split in real life and shut down their show, each going off to host less successful series. After a year-and-a-half separation, the couple reunite (at least professionally) on what was originally called *The Sonny & Cher Show*. The idea is the same as before, but the zing is gone. The coolness between the couple leaks through, and it's not as much fun watching them bicker.

**SONNY SPOON (**½) 60 min (15ep Color; 1988 NBC) Detective Drama** *with Mario Van Peebles as Sonny Spoon, Terry Donahoe as Carolyn Gilder, Joe Shea as Lucius DeLuce, and Melvin Van Peebles as Mel Spoon*

Popular TV producer Stephen J. Cannell (*The A-Team, The Rockford Files, The Greatest American Hero*) suffered a rare setback in 1980 with the failure of his *Tenspeed and Brownshoe* series, in which Ben Vereen played a smart-talking black detective who used elaborate disguises to crack cases. *Sonny Spoon* is really just another effort by Cannell to succeed with this format. The affable black detective with a knack for costumes is played by Mario Van Peebles, who is so likable that it is hard not to enjoy *Sonny Spoon.* Even so, the series has plots as thin as some of Cannell's weaker shows. At the start of the second season, Van Peebles' real-life father, movie director Melvin (*Watermelon Man*), joins the program as (who else?) Sonny's father.

**SONS AND LOVERS (**) (7ep Color; 1981 UK BBC) Drama** *with Eileen Atkins as Gertrude Morel, Karl Johnson as Paul Morel, Tom Bell as Walter Morel, Geoffrey Burridge as William Morel, Amanda Parfitt as Annie Morel, Leonie Mellinger as Miriam, Lynn Dearth as Clara Dawes, and Jack Shepherd as Baxter Dawes*

This series, based on the 1913 autobiographical D. H. Lawrence novel, is definitely not a love letter to motherhood. In fact, this show was apparently a therapeutic outpouring of the author's deeply held feelings and resentments about his mother's dominating influence in his life. It does mean, though, that we're left with a suffocating, fiery-tongued mom, Gertrude Morel, as the main force in a generally downbeat story. Set in the coal-mining area of Nottinghamshire, this tale is the epitome of working-class social discontent as Gertrude rails at her crude, drunken husband, Walter. But she does keep a watchful and loving eye on her son, Paul. Unfortunately this soon develops into an obsessive intrusion, as she reacts defensively to any outside interests on his part (such as a possible engagement, affair, or even really serious dating). Eileen Atkins turns in a stand-out performance in a difficult role, though the series still gets rather shrill, heavy-handed, and tedious over the long haul.

**SORRELL AND SON (**) 60 min (6ep Color; 1985 UK Yorkshire) Drama** *with Richard Pasco as Stephen Sorrell, Peter Chelsom as Kit Sorrell, Stephanie Beacham, John Shrapnel as Thomas Roland, Sarah Neville as Molly Pentreath, and Michael Troughton as Maurice Pentreath*

Straightforward adaptation of the pulpy 1925 novel by Warwick Deeping, following the dreams of a World War I veteran who is a penniless single parent. Though a former officer and a gentleman, he takes a job as a hotel porter to earn enough to put his son, Kit, through school in pursuit of a medical career. Kit comes through on the scholastic side, but after a while he starts to wonder about his love life. A standard, slightly melodramatic offering.

**SORRY! (**) 30 min (18ep Color; 1982–1983 UK BBC) Situation Comedy** *with Ronnie Corbett as Timothy Lumsden, Barbara Lott as Phyllis Lumsden, William Moore as Mr. Lumsden, Ray Holder as Frank, and Chris Breeze as Chris*

Ronnie Corbett (the short one from *The Two Ronnies*) plays Timothy Lumsden, a forty-year-old bachelor who works at the town library, rides a tiny moped, and lives at home under the watchful eye of his possessive and dominating mother. (Oh, his dad's there, too, but mother clearly rules the roost.) The two of them have never advanced much beyond a mom and kid relationship, even lapsing into singsong baby talk in their normal conversations ("tinklies" for using the washroom, or "pubbies" for going to the pub).

The setup is good for Corbett, playing on his helpless little guy image, while giving him plenty of opportunities for deadpan quips and sight gags. Timothy is nervous and apologetic (the "Sorry!" of the title), with his idea of a big night out consisting of a few beers and conversation at the nearby pub. There his drinking buddy Frank is always trying to set him up, with predictably disastrous results (of course, Tim is extremely uncertain around women). Usually, though, Tim just goes on about his latest mother problem, quickly downing his last drink as the pub phone rings with her checking up on him. Despite his complaints, though, it's clear that Tim is as hesitant to leave the protective cocoon of his upstairs bedroom as his mother is to let him go. It would be sweet if it weren't so sad.

Nonetheless, for a premise that might have played as just one sketch on *The Two Ronnies*, the cast and writers make the most of it. Toward the end there is even a dash to freedom. But will Tim actually escape? Will he find the girl of his dreams? Will he have the nerve to leave his mom behind? (Do you even have to ask?)

**SOUNDSTAGE (***½) 60 min (160ep Color; 1973–1983 PBS) Musical-Variety**

Taped live at the studios of WTTW-TV in Chicago, *Soundstage* presents the cream of rock, folk, and country music from the mid-1970s to the early 1980s. The highlight of the series is a lengthy tribute to Columbia Records executive John Hammond, with many of his finds (including Bob Dylan) showing up to play.

**SPACE (**½) (13hr miniseries Color; 1985 CBS) Drama** *with James Garner as Norman Grant, Susan Anspach as Elinor Grant, Beau Bridges as Randy Claggett, Blair Brown as Penny Pope, Bruce Dern as Stanley Mott, Melinda Dillon as Rachel Mott, David Dukes as Leopold Strabismus, Martin Balsam as Senator Michael Glancey, Ralph Bellamy as Paul Stidham, Harry Hamlin as John Pope, and Michael York as Dieter Kolff*

A fictionalized history of the U.S. space program, based on James A. Michener's lengthy novel, with a high-budget star-studded cast. The story begins at the closing days of World War II, with the scramble to bring Germany's best scientists to American shores—a key job handled by Stanley Mott, who convinces an impressive number, led by Leopold Strabismus. Meanwhile, in the halls of Congress newly elected senator Norman Grant, a war hero, decides to use plans for a long-term commitment to a national space program as a means to help build his own legislative power base. And on the front lines of flight there are test pilots (later astronauts) Randy Claggett and John Pope.

Everyone turns in stand-out performances, though James Garner is pushed a bit with a character that starts out the story in his twenties (during World War II). Yet even as fictional alternative history (so we don't know exactly what's going to happen next), at times this series is a bit dull. The problem may simply be that (as the astronauts in the feature film *The Right Stuff* observed) when Americans hear the word *space* what they really expect is . . . Buck Rogers! Authentic history is fine, but we seem to lap up highly improbable space theatrics. Whatever the reason, about four hours were dropped from this miniseries for its first network rerun airing in 1987. Current repackaging can go either way. If you are transfixed by launching countdowns and care about debates over space funding, you'll probably want to seek out the full-length presentation. Otherwise the shorter version is just fine.

**SPACE: 1999** **(*½) 60 min (48ep Color; 1975–1977 Syndication) Science Fiction** *with Martin Landau as Commander John Koenig, Barbara Bain as Dr. Helena Russell, Barry Morse as Prof. Victor Bergman, Catherine Schell as Maya, and Tony Anholt as Tony Verdeschi*

It is tempting to try to put a fresh spin on this series. Perhaps all the negative criticism that greeted the program in 1975 (and still haunts it today) was just carping from dedicated *Star Trek* fans unhappy with any TV space odyssey except their cherished favorite. Perhaps this series is really just as clever and imaginative in its own unique way as anything that has ever hit television. After all, it brings some big-budget state-of-the-art special effects to television science fiction. Shouldn't this count for something? Perhaps the time has come, at least, to see *Space: 1999* with a new sense of respect and wonder.

There's just one problem. Sit down and watch and you'll see that all the basic shortcomings of this series are still there. Yes, the effects are very nice. Unfortunately other aspects of the series were not given the same loving care. The characters rarely interact well (if at all) and the real-life husband and wife leads (Barbara Bain and Martin Landau) are surprisingly cool in their scenes with each other. Of course, maybe they just couldn't figure out what they were supposed to be doing since the stories are frequently just arbitrary incomprehensible nonsense parading as grand statements and mythical symbols. Or maybe they made the mistake of opening a Science 101 textbook and discovering that the premise for the entire series was quite . . . unlikely.

At the end of this century, Earth has found the perfect spot to dump its nuclear waste, the dark side of the moon. Unfortunately this setup is an accident waiting to happen, as the 311 men and women of Moonbase Alpha discover when some magnetic interference detonates the material. The explosion essentially turns the moon into a giant spaceship, careening out of Earth's orbit and into deep space, with the Alpha crew along for the ride.

When first unveiled, this premise caused even casual viewers to raise their eyebrows, while science writers such as Isaac Asimov could barely contain their professional astonishment, pointing out the blatant absurdity of the setup. For example, assuming the moon was knocked out of orbit, it would probably come crashing toward Earth; but even if it did head to deep space, several lifetimes would pass before it could hope to encounter an unknown inhabited planet.

Why such a truly ridiculous initial premise? Maybe the production team was just trying too hard not to be *Star Trek* and wanted to do away with even the surface similarity of a starship cruising the galaxy. If so, it was a bold effort, but one so silly that it cast the series in a bad light from the start. Still, if the program's stories had made more sense and the characters had acted more human, the so-called scientific impossibilities could have been easily dismissed as esoteric nit-picking. In fact, if the crew had been placed on some asteroid and the explosion had taken place there instead, or if some mumbo-jumbo had been created about tearing a hole in the space-time continuum sending the crew into another galaxy, the writers could have probably gotten away with it. Some critics and science fiction writers might have complained, but at least the situation would not have looked so blatantly wrong to the general public.

To their credit, the production team at *Space: 1999* paid attention to some of the complaints (especially about character interaction and pompous story lines) and attempted to fine-tune those aspects for the second batch of episodes, introducing a new character (an alien named Maya), making the stories more action-oriented, and having Landau and Bain act as if they at least liked each other. But once you've decided not to buy into a science fiction premise, it's awfully hard to take any of it seriously. As a result, this series regularly earns a spot at the top of nearly everyone's list of the worst science fiction series ever. ■

**SPECIAL AGENT 7** **(*) 30 min (26ep B&W; 1958–1959 Syndication) Crime Drama** *with Lloyd Nolan as Philip Conroy*

This boring crime show is one of many that boasts of having its stories based on official files. In this case, the files are those of the Internal Revenue Service, and the main character is a special agent for the U.S. Department of the Treasury. This program is also known as *SA 7*.

**SPENCER** **(*½) 30 min (6ep Color; 1984–1985 NBC) Situation Comedy** *with Chad Lowe as Spencer Winger, Mimi Kennedy as Doris Winger, Ronny Cox as George Winger, Amy Locane as Andrea Winger, Dean Cameron as Herbie Bailey, Grant Heslov as Wayne, and Richard Sanders as Benjamin Beanley*

This teen comedy is built around sixteen-year-old Chad Lowe, younger brother of brat-pack film star Rob Lowe. As is typical for this type of vehicle, the adults are essentially window dressing for the shenanigans of an average contemporary kid. Spencer's escapades range from liberating the white mice in a school laboratory, to keeping a brotherly eye on his younger sister Amy on a date, to making plans for losing his virginity by going out with a "fast" girl.

Before the series was barely in gear, Lowe departed. Some of the characters continued in a revamped premise, *Under One Roof.*

**SPENCER'S PILOTS (*) 60 min (11ep & 60 min pilot Color; 1976 CBS) Adventure** *with Christopher Stone as Cass Garrett, Todd Susman as Stan Lewis, Gene Evans as Spencer Parish, Margaret Impert as Linda Dann, and Britt Leach as Mickey "Wig" Wiggins*

Cass Garrett and Stan Lewis are two hot-shot pilots flying for Spencer Parish's character organization, Spencer Aviation. Cass and Stan will fly anything, anywhere. Oddly enough, nobody asks them to fly packages of white powder from Columbia to the United States.

**SPENSER: FOR HIRE (**½) 60 min (57ep & 2 hr pilot Color; 1985–1988 ABC) Detective Drama** *with Robert Urich as Spenser, Avery Brooks as Hawk, Richard Jaeckel as Lt. Martin Quirk, Barbara Stock as Susan Silverman, and Carolyn McCormick as Rita Fiori*

A literary (not to mention literate) modern private eye is a rare TV commodity. Perhaps this is why *Spenser: For Hire* seems so much out of the TV shamus mainstream. The cause of the nonconformity can be easily traced to Spenser's genesis, a series of wonderful novels by Robert Parker. Spenser himself (no first names, please) is an ex-cop, ex-boxer who can quote Wordsworth and Melville, believes in monogamy, and likes to cook. Here is a true Renaissance man of the 1980s!

*Spenser: For Hire* deserves credit simply for setting itself outside of the Los Angeles area. Shot mostly in Boston, *Spenser: For Hire* has a lot of the charm of this city. The gritty, ethnic realities of the big town fit in nicely with the private eye format. Robert Urich, who served his time in mediocre to passable programs such as *S.W.A.T.*, *Vega$*, and *Gavilan*, finally gets to shine here, as he can combine his rugged good looks with his flair for the humorous. Spenser and his bald, black, ally Hawk form a tough pair that can operate at almost any level of Boston society when the need arises.

The scripts in *Spenser: For Hire* are almost always polished and usually avoid the easy clichés of the genre (such as weekly car cashes). The chief problem is that the producers never seem to figure out what to do about a girlfriend for Spenser. Different romantic interests come and go, with no real chemistry developing.

Spenser's sidekick graduated to his own series, titled *A Man Called Hawk.*

**SPIDER-MAN, THE AMAZING (*½) 60 min (13ep & 90 min pilot Color; 1978–1979 CBS) Adventure** *with Nicholas Hammond as Peter Parker/Spider-Man, Robert F. Simon as J. Jonah Jameson, Michael Pataki as Captain Barbera, and Chip Fields as Rita Conway*

This bland rendition of the Marvel Comics character virtually ignores the aspects that originally set him apart in 1961 from the other long-underwear superhero types in comic books. There, Peter Parker, a young science student turned superhero, found his powers as much a burden as a blessing. Though possessing super strength, a radar sense, and the ability to climb walls (all acquired from a bite on his hand by a radioactive spider), Parker often felt that he was letting down himself and his loved ones. The fact that his Spider-Man identity did not automatically translate into riches and public respect didn't help.

By the time the series pilot hit the air in 1977, Spider-Man was a hot licensing commodity, and even his comic-book stories put a more upbeat, action-oriented spin to his image as a very human, often misunderstood, hero. On television, the transformation is even more complete: The guilt and uncertainty are acknowledged and then essentially ignored in favor of some very traditional formula adventure tales that just happen to involve a costumed, wall-climbing hero. These are so interchangeable that some stations edit several stories together into "feature-length" *Spider-Man* films. (However, two stories—"The Deadly Dust" and "The Chinese Web"—are suitable for such treatment, running as two-part presentations.)

*Spider-Man* has also appeared in several animation packages, including a mediocre batch in the late 1960s (fifty-two episodes, first aired in syndication 1967–1969), a better collection for NBC's Saturday morning cartoon lineup (thirty-nine episodes of *Spider-Man and His Amazing Friends*, first aired on NBC 1981–1985), and another syndication package (twenty-six episodes in 1983) much closer in spirit and execution to the comics. ■

**SPIES (**) 60 min (6ep Color; 1987 CBS) Spy Adventure** *with George Hamilton as Ian Stone, Gary Kroeger as Ben Smythe, and Barry Corbin as Thomas Brady*

This show borders on an SCTV or *Saturday Night Live* parody premise: George Hamilton is the good-looking womanizing spy more concerned with his suntan than his latest mission. Will Gary Kroeger be able to keep him on the case long enough to prevent their boss from firing them both? (Silly question.) Actually, for an episode or two this plays rather well, with Hamilton doing a delightful job of self-parody vanity and former *Saturday Night Live* cast member Kroeger the ultimate in superstraight faithful sidekicks yearning to bust loose like his idol. Even their superior has a silly moniker, referred to as the "C of B" (chairman of the board). Unfortunately, they still have to fill the hours with some sort of plot (unlike a five-minute comedy-variety skit), and this series falls short after the première episode.

**SPIKE JONES SHOW (**) 30 min (B&W; 1954 & 1957 & 1960–1961 NBC & CBS) Comedy-Variety** *with Spike Jones*

Anarchist musician and bandleader Spike Jones had

several brief runs in network variety slots during the 1950s and early 1960s. A number of these appearances turn up on home video. ■

**THE SPOILS OF POYNTON** (**½) **60 min (4ep Color; 1971 UK BBC) Drama** *with Pauline Jameson as Mrs. Gereth, Ian Ogilvy as Owen Gereth, Gemma Jones as Fleda Vetch, and Diane Fletcher as Mona Brigstock*

Based on a Henry James novel with a wonderful plot hook sure to appeal to every stubborn individualist. A mother learns that her deceased husband has willed their house (called Poynton) to their son, Owen, but fears that the son and his bride-to-be will not truly appreciate the many wonderful accumulated possessions inside. So she packs them up and moves these personal treasures to another house (effectively saying to him, "Okay, take the house! I've got everything else!"). Thus, the stage is set for Owen's pursuit of "the spoils of Poynton," which leads him into an unexpected complication, the quietly unassuming woman (Fleda) his mother has hired to take care of the materials at the new place. She is sensitive and cultured and before either of them realizes it, love is on the horizon. And so is a breach-of-promise suit from Owen's fiancée if he isn't careful—though there's an unusual twist resolving the conflict. A good adaptation, translating quite well to the intimacy of television the vaunted Henry James affections for complicated prose and small (some would say microscopic) movements in the action.

**SQUARE PEGS** (***) **30 min (20ep Color; 1982–1983 CBS) Situation Comedy** *with Sarah Jessica Parker as Patty Greene, Amy Linker as Lauren Hutchinson, Tracy Nelson as Jennifer DeNuccio, Merritt Butrick as Johnny "Slash" Ulacewitz, John Femia as Marshall Blechtman, Jami Gertz as Muffy Tepperman, Jon Caliri as Vinnie Pasetta, Steven Peterman as Rob Donovan, and Basil Hoffman as Principal Dingleman*

As Dobie Gillis discovered in the black and white days of the early 1960s, at times high school can be a traumatic social experience, especially when you're a square peg trying to fit into society's round holes. In that spirit, veteran *Saturday Night Live* writer Anne Beatts offers her version of high school hell (early 1980s style), as freshmen Patty and Lauren try to make it with the "in" crowd at Weemawee High. It's a formidable task. Patty is skinny and awkward and wears glasses, while Lauren is short and still has braces. They've never been hip and can only look enviously at the people in the circles they aspire to: Vinnie, the school's good-looking hunk; Jennifer, his rich, attractive, and stuck-up "valley girl" steady; LaDonna, a snobbish black beauty; and Muffy, the self-centered cheerleader booster in love with her own voice. The best Patty and Lauren can do is the likes of Marshall, the incessant class clown, and Johnny Slash, a slightly spaced-out new wave music freak.

Of course, the real irony is that Marshall and Johnny are better friends than all the people in the circles Lauren and Patty dream of joining. In fact, they don't do badly in the world of status symbols, either—especially Johnny who actually knows some of the hip musicians the kids like, and who dresses "cooler" than anyone else on campus . . . they just won't know that for another few years! Best of all, they welcome the girls into their circle and after a while Patty and Lauren start to feel comfortable there themselves.

What hurts *Square Pegs* is when it loses confidence in its own characters. Far too soon after presenting Jennifer, Muffy, LaDonna, and Vinnie as the enemies, they are quickly given occasional sensitive sides. Maybe this would be fine in a second or third season, but not right away. It dilutes any minor victories by the Square Pegs circles over these people, who are self-centered snobs and deserve to be skewered, even as they serve as perfect plot foils.

At times, though, this series is absolutely dead-on, capturing the important crises of high school life, ranging from Patty's clumsy moves without her glasses to Jennifer's withering dismissal of her perceived social inferiors. There are also moments when Johnny Slash seems to be the 1980s embodiment of Maynard G. Krebbs, with an innocent view of the world that makes everything possible. In one story, for instance, the non-athletic Johnny becomes the baseball team's champion home run hitter simply because the bat and ball just feel right in his hands. Everything is fine until the team has an away game—then he looks for the familiar sights (such as the roof of the house across the field) and finds them gone. His career ends because he simply can't handle leaving the home field behind. Illogical, but it makes sense in a Maynard kind of way.

Though this series misses at being the definitive *Dobie Gillis* of the 1980s, it is still worth catching for moments from its own era. Also, look for guest shots by *Saturday Night Live* associates Bill Murray and Don Novello (as Fr. Guido Sarducci), and in the first episode the new wave group The Waitresses performing the title song in person at a school dance.

**STACCATO** (***) **30 min (27ep B&W; 1959–1960 NBC) Detective Drama** *with John Cassavetes as Johnny Staccato and Eduardo Ciannelli as Waldo*

It may be a direct steal of *Peter Gunn,* but *Staccato* is a fine piece of TV work that has not received the attention it deserves. Like *Peter Gunn, Staccato* features a loner private eye, with lots of jazzy music in the background. Unlike Peter Gunn (who was much too clean-cut and WASPy for his loner image), Johnny Staccato really looks like a guy on the outside, someone who would hang out in jazz dives and pick up information from the lowlifes of society. Staccato is, himself, a jazz pianist who branches into detective work, making him one of the few musician/detectives in TV history.

What makes this series fun is the somber, bluesy feel that permeates the series. The show's music is arranged by Elmer Bernstein and performed by Pete Candoli's jazz outfit. Another big plus is the leading man, John Cassavetes, a handsome man with an intriguing, foreign air. A popular actor from the live TV dramas of the 1950s, Cassavetes went on to star in films such as *The Dirty Dozen* and *Rosemary's Baby*. He then became a director, scoring (critically, if not at the box office) with *Faces, Husbands, A Woman Under the Influence,* and *Gloria. Staccato* marks Cassavetes' only TV series. Catch it if you can.

**STAGE 7 (**) 30 min (39ep B&W; 1955 CBS) Drama Anthology**

More filmed thirty-minute drama vignettes from the 1950s. Don Rickles appears in his first dramatic TV role in one episode, "A Note of Fear."

**STAGECOACH WEST (*½) 60 min (38ep B&W; 1960–1961 ABC) Western** *with Wayne Rogers as Luke Perry, Robert Bray as Simon Kane, and Richard Eyer as David Kane*

No, it's not *Wagon Train.* No, it's not *Overland Trail*, but it's about the same idea, taking a load of people west in the days before the railroads spanned the continent. In this case, the method of transportation is the stagecoach, which is slightly more civilized than the wagon train. Despite this step up in comfort, there are lots of marauding bad guys and hostile Indians to contend with.

Since this idea has been ridden to death in other shows, the only interest in *Stagecoach West* is to see the first TV series role for Wayne Rogers (later Trapper John in TV's *M*A*S*H*).

**THE STAR AND THE STORY (**) 30 min (26ep B&W; 1954–1955 Syndication) Drama Anthology** *with Henry Fonda as host*

While Hollywood legend Henry Fonda serves as overall host of this series of plays, the focus is on each week's guest star, who picked the story he or she would star in. The series is also known as *Henry Fonda Presents the Star and the Story.*

**STAR OF THE FAMILY (*½) 30 min (8ep Color; 1982 ABC) Situation Comedy** *with Brian Dennehy as Leslie "Buddy" Krebs, Kathy Maisnik as Jennie Lee Krebs, Michael Dudikoff as Douglas Krebs, and Judy Piolo as Judy "Moose" Wells*

This show just doesn't know what it wants to be. On the one hand, it is the story of Jennie Lee Krebs, a pretty sixteen-year-old who seems on the verge of hitting it big as a singer of country/pop tunes. Her grumpy widowed dad, Buddy, is overprotective of his little girl and afraid of letting her into the big world. On the other hand, the show is a more typical sitcom about a surly boss of the local fire house (Buddy Krebs) and the wacko guys he has working for him. The first concept is interesting and different, while the second is far too familiar and mundane.

On the plus side, *Star of the Family* has Brian Dennehy, a fine hulking character actor who later went on to film success in *Cocoon.* On the minus side is the flip-flopping between concepts. The series was created by Rick Mitz, author of *The Great TV Sitcom Book,* which goes to show that TV historians should probably stick to chronicling past shows and leave the creative writing to others. As a TV historian, Mitz should have known that anyone named Krebs (as in Maynard G. Krebs of *Dobie Gillis* fame) who dabbles in music should play the bongos.

**STAR PERFORMANCE (***) 30 min (153ep B&W; 1952–1956 CBS) Drama Anthology** *with David Niven, Charles Boyer, Dick Powell, and Ida Lupino*

In this program of half-hour filmed dramas, David Niven, Charles Boyer, Dick Powell, and Ida Lupino, four leading lights of Hollywood in the 1940s, became some of the first serious film actors to appear regularly on the upstart medium of television. The four stars rotate their appearances and Niven, Boyer, and Powell also direct some episodes. Powell's recurring character of nightclub owner Willie Dante appears in eight episodes that were later packaged as *The Best in Mystery* and eventually led to a separate series, *Dante* (starring Howard Duff).

*Star Performance* originally aired under the title *Four Star Playhouse*, though it does contain some episodes that were not a part of that series. ■

**STAR QUALITY (**) 60 min (5ep Color; 1987 UK) Drama Anthology**

"Star Quality" is the name of the Noel Coward short story used as an umbrella title for this anthology of five adaptations (first packaged and presented in the U.S. on *Masterpiece Theatre*). They provide a taste of the legendary British artist, actor, and composer's sometimes cynical view of the world, especially as seen from the British stage circuit or as a part of proper society (two areas in which he was personally well-versed). It begins in the 1940s with the appropriately nightmarish experiences of a young dramatist (played by Peter Chelsom) caught in the cross-fire between the production's big-name star (played by Susannah York) and its veteran director (played by Ian Richardson). Though the overall series is spotty at times, it's definitely worth seeing at least one of these for historical research purposes alone. Coward 101, so to speak.

**STAR SEARCH (*½) 60 min (130ep at Fall 1988 Color; 1983– Syndication) Variety** *with Ed McMahon as host*

Ed McMahon, Johnny Carson's long-time second banana, steps out on his own as a latter-day Ted Mack (of *Ted Mack's Amateur Hour*). As host of this talent competition among amateur performers, McMahon provides a familiar face among the unknowns. Each week, competitors in various variety categories seek to prove worthy of a return trip, heading toward the yearly finals. Bob Banner, of *Solid Gold*, serves as producer. *Star Search* served as the launching point for the careers of the country-rock group Sawyer Brown and pubescent singer Tiffany.

**STAR TREK (****) (79ep & 75 min pilot Color; 1966–1969 NBC) Science Fiction** *with William Shatner as Capt. James T. Kirk, Leonard Nimoy as Mr. Spock, DeForest Kelley as Dr. Leonard "Bones" McCoy, James Doohan as Lt. Montgomery "Scotty" Scott, Nichelle Nicholas as Lt. Uhura, George Takei as Mr. Sulu, Majel Barrett as Nurse Christine Chapel, Walter Koenig as Ensign Pavel Chekov, and Grace Lee Whitney as Yeoman Janice Rand*

It has become rather difficult to view the original *Star Trek* series as anything other than a venerable classic. The series is so familiar and so available to even the most casual fan that a lot of what the original seventy-nine episodes were, and were not, gets lost in the nostalgia.

*Star Trek* was and still is a finely crafted show that accomplishes two important tasks. First, it takes science fiction seriously (but not too seriously), thus providing a measure of badly needed respectability to TV science fiction (something akin to what *Gunsmoke* and the adult westerns did for TV westerns). Second, *Star Trek* goes out of its way to dramatize interesting social issues, within the framework of its setting, resulting in a show that can be enjoyed on several levels.

Set about three hundred years in the future, *Star Trek* focuses on the starship U.S.S. *Enterprise*, a combination scientific and military craft exploring and protecting a region of our galaxy run by the United Federation of Planets. The five-year mission of the *Enterprise* is to "explore strange new worlds, seek out new life and new civilizations" and to "boldly go where no man has gone before." Its mission is also to protect frontier areas of the galaxy from the Klingons and the Romulans, the violent enemies of the Federation.

In the tradition of World War II action films, the crew of the *Enterprise* is a racially mixed outfit, thereby emphasizing a belief in equality. Captain Kirk is an American from the Midwest, with all the unpretentiousness and bold ingenuity typical of that region. His two chief subordinates are two extremes. Science officer Spock is half-Earthling and half-Vulcan, although his Vulcan heritage is dominant. Vulcans are all logic and no emotion, so Spock represents the pure science aspect of mankind. Opposing Spock is the ship's doctor, "Bones" McCoy, a traditionalist from the Old South, who puts his stock in emotions, not logic. Whenever Kirk is faced with a crucial choice, Spock and McCoy can be counted on to personify and to argue out loud the debate going on inside Kirk's brain.

The rest of the crew fits classic stereotypes. Chief engineer Scotty is the traditional hard-drinking Scotsman. Chief navigator Sulu is the Oriental technocrat with an inscrutable smile. Assistant navigator Chekov is the impulsive and erratic Russian (who was only added after the first season to provide representation from America's chief space rival). Communications officer Uhura is the 1960s TV black stereotype. She is highly proficient in her trade (to ensure she is not viewed as inferior by anyone), but she shies away from personal revelations and romantic escapades in order to sidestep any potential race mixing that might rile parts of the home audience. With this central crew, the U.S.S. *Enterprise* sails through the galaxy, running into different worlds, different cultures, and different crises each week.

There had been quality science fiction series before *Star Trek* (*The Twilight Zone,* for example), but the best of these earlier shows were, at heart, more mystery and suspense oriented. When it came to blatant science fiction settings, such as outer space and alien races, earlier TV efforts tended toward the juvenile, such as *Lost in Space* (the series CBS chose over *Star Trek*). *Star Trek* demands that space flight and extraterrestrials be taken seriously.

Like *Wagon Train,* the classic TV western, *Star Trek* places a small band of regulars in the wilderness, where they must deal with unknown peoples and places each week, while a parade of guest stars serves to spice up the adventures. The fiction aspect of science fiction does not overwhelm the program's basic concern with familiar emotions and conflicts. Still, the fiction angle is not ignored, and *Star Trek* has great episodes dealing with time travel, beings of pure thought, humanoid robots, and other sci-fi staples. Gene Roddenberry, creator and executive producer of *Star Trek*, emphasized this core concept from the beginning, since he sold the series to NBC by touting it as "*Wagon Train* to the stars."

*Star Trek*'s other major accomplishment, dramatizing social issues, is a direct continuation of a trend begun by Rod Sterling. Just as many of Sterling's *Twilight Zone* tales were really modern social commentaries made "safe" by wrapping them in science fiction, many *Star Trek* episodes are able to deal with current earthbound problems by placing the action far in space. Several *Star Trek* episodes contain morals dealing with racial discrimination, political totalitarianism, religious zealotry, and flawed attempts at creating nirvanas.

It is a credit to Gene Roddenberry that this message aspect of *Star Trek* still packs a punch. Not all of the moralizing has aged well, however. For example, the episode where the *Enterprise* picks up a band of space hippies led by a Timothy Leary-like pied piper with sinister motives seems really hokey now, no matter what your views are concerning hippies.

The aspect of *Star Trek* that seems truly dated is the technical one. The only special effect that seems remotely fancy is the matter transporter. Spoiled as we are by multi-million-dollar special effects film epics (such as *Star Wars*), the original TV series now appears positively cheap by comparison. The papier-mâché boulders on alien planets and the array of pointlessly flashing lights on the ship's equipment panels seem almost quaint (to be fair, the producers did a lot with their tight budget). *Star Trek* is still miles ahead of *Captain Video,* but when the *Enterprise* bridge starts looking less impressive than your own home computer, you know that some of the magic of *Star Trek* is gone.

Nonetheless, the ability to avoid appearing old-fashioned more than two decades after its production is the true mark of quality in *Star Trek.* The adventures are still exciting, the stories are still intriguing, and the show still has a message to viewers. You cannot ask for much more from a TV series.

The popularity of *Star Trek*, which really only mushroomed after the series ceased production and reruns captured a wider audience, spawned several spin-offs. In 1973, twenty-two animated half-hour *Star Trek* cartoons aired on NBC's Saturday morning schedule. The actors and actresses who portrayed Kirk, Spock, McCoy, Uhura, Scotty, Sulu, Chekov, and Nurse Chapel supplied the voices of their animated counterparts. In 1979, the original crew reassembled to star in *Star Trek—The Motion Picture,* the first of a series of films that followed the crew long beyond their five-year mission, and into middle-age paunchiness. The second *Star Trek* movie, *Star Trek II: The Wrath of Khan*, is a direct continuation of the "Space Seed" episode (starring Ricardo Montalban) from the original TV series. In 1987, Gene Roddenberry reinvented the wheel and created *Star Trek: The Next Generation*, a TV sequel with an entirely new cast set several decades beyond the era of the old *Enterprise.*

The original *Star Trek* pilot (from 1964), titled "The Cage," is a very intelligent and exciting story. It features Jeffrey Hunter as Capt. Christopher Pike, who commands the *Enterprise* in place of Capt. Kirk. Leonard Nimoy's Mr. Spock is the only major character from the pilot retained when the series began production. Highlights of the unaired pilot turn up in a two-part *Star Trek* TV episode called "The Menagerie." In 1988, the original uncut pilot was finally reassembled and released. ■

**STAR TREK: THE NEXT GENERATION (***) 60 min (46ep at Fall 1989 & 2 hr pilot Color; 1987– Syndication) Science Fiction** *with Patrick Stewart as Capt. Jean-Luc Picard, Jonathan Frakes as Cmdr. William Riker, LeVar Burton as Lt. Geordi La Forge, Michael Dorn as Lt. Worf, Marina Sirtis as Deanna Troi, Brent Spiner as Lt. Cmdr. Data, Wil Wheaton as Ensign Wesley Crusher, Gates McFadden as Dr. Beverly Crusher, Denise Crosby as Lt. Tasha Yar, Diana Muldaur as Dr. Katherine Pulaski, and Whoopi Goldberg as Guinan*

Revivals of hit TV series have abysmal track records, both on the artistic and popular levels. *Star Trek: The Next Generation* is delightful proof that this trend can be overcome. Eighteen years after the original *Star Trek* TV series closed up shop, *Star Trek*'s creator, Gene Roddenberry, took the basic *Wagon Train* to the stars concept, shuffled it around, and presented it with all new trappings.

The two key decisions that help make the revived *Star Trek* work are bringing Roddenberry back as executive producer and not trying to recast the original characters. Roddenberry's insistence on maintaining the original *Star Trek*'s concern for well-written scripts that have a lesson to teach ensures that the newer series does not just try to cash in on a famous name. Fortunately the show avoids overdosing on pointless special effects (a fault the first *Star Trek* movie fell victim to). By setting *Star Trek: The Next Generation* about eighty years after the era of the original *Star Trek*, Roddenberry ensures that it can be populated with entirely new characters who do not have to battle Trekkies' recollections of Capt. Kirk, Mr. Spock, Bones, and so forth (DeForest Kelley, the original Dr. McCoy, does make a cameo appearance as 137-year-old Admiral McCoy in the revived show's pilot, just to add a touch of continuity).

Of course, the new characters are not entirely new. Roddenberry ingeniously shuffles a lot of the personality traits of the original *Star Trek* crew among the cast. *Star Trek: The Next Generation* still has a half-human who can directly tap into other people's minds, a highly logical top officer, and a funny-looking alien, but it's not Mr. Spock. Rather, it's three characters: Counselor Deanna Troi (a half-Betazoid who can sense emotions), Lt. Cmdr. Data (a very logical android who is anxious to learn the confusing ways of humans), and Lt. Worf (a Klingon). There is also a tough decision-making commander who seems married to the ship and a suave good-looking all-American officer who is not above flirting with the comely alien lassies, but it's not Capt. Kirk. Rather it's two characters: Capt. Picard (a Frenchman older than Kirk who is far more cool and severe) and Cmdr. Riker (Picard's top aide, a somewhat flippant fellow working hard to get his own command soon).

The other main crew members are a less obvious mix of new and old. Lt. LaForge is a black, blind navigator, who can "see" in great detail, thanks to some high-tech wraparound super-duper "glasses." Wesley Crusher is the young son of the ship's first medical officer. It turns out that Wesley has highly advanced powers of intelligence, so Capt. Picard overcomes his natural distrust of children and makes Wesley an ensign. When Wesley's mother is shipped out at the start of the second season, Ensign Crusher sticks around.

The setting is still the *Enterprise*, but a brand new one, named after Kirk's old ship but almost twice as big.

Since Kirk's day, peace has been made with the Klingons (hence Worf's presence) and numerous technical advancements have been made. Still, the mission of the new *Enterprise* (no longer limited to just five years) has not changed; it is to seek out new worlds and new civilizations and do a little police work in the outer galaxy as well.

The advances in twentieth-century technology since the late 1960s really make the original series look like a cheap old war horse, at least technically. The newer show is far sleeker. Its stories hold their own and even occasionally outpace its predecessor. The two-hour pilot about a maniacal super-alien named Q (John deLancie) who toys with Picard and his crew is fair warning that the revival can create highly inventive plots. The "holodeck" on the replacement *Enterprise*, which by means of holograms can recreate any time or place desired so well that it seems real, opens up a flexible escape valve to allow stories to roam far and wide. In the second season, a new bar/rec lounge called "Ten Forward" is added to the ship. Black comedienne Whoopi Goldberg joins the cast as a semiregular named Guinan, a mysterious woman who lends an ear and some choice morsels of wisdom to the crew members who come in for a brew or just to relax.

*Star Trek: The Next Generation* can never have the impact of the old series; because it follows a great tradition, it does not break tradition itself. Still, the newer series is perhaps the best example of revamping and resurrecting a TV classic in the history of the medium. It's a pleasure to see the classy *Star Trek* heritage carried on so nobly.

**THE STARLOST (**) 60 min (16ep Color; 1973–1974 Syndication) Science Fiction** *with Keir Dullea as Devon, Gay Rowan as Rachel, and Robin Ward as Garth*

This science fiction series was created by noted sci-fi author Harlan Ellison, and the plot is appropriately complex. The Earth, you see, was doomed around the year 2300, so a bunch of earthlings were rocketed into space in a highly complex spacecraft that actually resembles Earth. Over time, the residents lost sight of the fact that they were on a spaceship. The huge craft goes off course, and drifts for about 500 years. With that as background, *The Starlost* focuses on the love triangle of Rachel, Devon, and Garth, three inhabitants of the drifting "world." Garth intends to marry Rachel, but then she runs into Devon, who has other ideas. The trio, not the best combination for an action squad, find out the truth about the big ship they are on and team up to find out more information about where they are going.

Keir Dullea (who plays Devon) previously starred in the sci-fi film classic *2001: A Space Odyssey*. Walter Koenig, Ensign Chekov in the original *Star Trek*, turns up occasionally as the alien Oro.

**STARMAN (**½) 60 min (22ep Color; 1986–1987 ABC) Science Fiction** *with Robert Hayes as Paul Forrester, C. B. Barnes as Scott Hayden, and Michael Cavanaugh as George Fox*

This TV series sequel to the 1984 theatrical film of the same name continues the low-key story of love across outer space. Robert Hayes takes the Jeff Bridges role of a being from another planet assuming human form. It's fourteen years later and this time he's here specifically to get in touch with two very special humans: his son, Scott, and his wife, Jenny, both of whom he left behind at his last visit. Using for his earthly guise the body of a freelance photographer Paul Forrester, killed in a wilderness plane crash, the Starman quickly locates Scott in an orphanage. Then he and his son hit the road in search of Jenny, who had left the area years before.

As in the original film, the Starman comes off as a positive force touching a handful of individuals, encouraging people he meets along the way to follow their dreams. However, since no alien visitor story would be complete without a human villain (preferably some military type interested in conducting research), Scott and Paul also have to keep moving to avoid government agent George Fox. Fortunately most of the stories emphasize the character interaction with the people they meet rather than the chase angle, with Fox there mostly to satisfy the perceived programming need for a continuing conflict and as a convenient plot device. For instance, at the end of the run, when Paul does find Jenny (played by Erin Gray from *Silver Spoons*), it turns into a brief reunion. To save him (and Scott, who she doesn't even have a chance to see), Jenny deliberately leads the army away from them, postponing a final reunion for another day—or another season, which never came.

Though the love story probably would have been resolved more cleanly and effectively with just a theatrical sequel (or a single two-hour TV-movie), the series does offer the opportunity for a well-done, generally upbeat, quiet little tale—a positive alien visitor that isn't a supersweet *E.T.* clone.

**STARSKY AND HUTCH (***) 60 min (92ep & 90 min pilot Color; 1975–1979 ABC) Police Drama** *with Paul Michael Glaser as Det. Dave Starsky, David Soul as Det. Ken "Hutch" Hutchinson, Bernie Hamilton as Capt. Harold Dobey, and Antonio Fargas as Huggy Bear*

All of the major elements of the standard antiestablishment cop format of the 1970s are present in *Starsky and Hutch*, yet the show is often able to overcome its stock setting to provide solid, exciting entertainment. Like all rogue cop sagas from the 1970s, *Starsky and Hutch* focuses on policemen who can't work within the system. Dave Starsky and his partner Hutch are undercover officers for the L.A.P.D. They wear casual clothes, drive fancy cars, and do things their way, which usually goes against the book. This causes ruffles in the fur of stock element number two, the by-the-book boss, Capt. Dobey. Oh, the captain will rant and rave at his two bad boys and tell them to act better, but, gee, the duo keeps capturing the bad guys, so how can Capt. Dobey really get mad at Starsky and Hutch? There are lots and lots of squealing tire shots (during the innumerable car chases), lots of violence, and a colorful streetwise informant (in this case Huggy Bear).

Since *Starsky and Hutch* is from the Aaron Spelling and Leonard Goldberg TV factory (*Charlie's Angels, S.W.A.T.*), the highly formula approach here is no surprise. Nonetheless, *Starsky and Hutch* is done well. The lead pair are a great combo. Dark-haired Starsky is the more ethnic, volatile, and earthy one, while blond Hutch is the more WASPy, suave, intelligent one. They banter back and forth in between shooting crooks, muggers, and rapists, and develop a great repartee. All the sexy, exploitative themes of the era (easy sex, drug use, and random urban violence) are milked over and over, but at least Starsky and Hutch themselves seem above it all.

In the 1975 pilot, Capt. Dobey is played by Richard Ward.

**STARTING FROM SCRATCH (**½) (22ep Color; 1988–1989 Syndication) Sitcom** *with Bill Daily as Dr. James Shepherd, Connie Stevens as Helen DeAngelo (Shepherd), Nita Talbot as Rose, Heidi Helmer as Katie, Jason Marin as Robbie, and Carmine Caridi as Frank DeAngelo*

A well-deserved promotion for perpetual sidekick Bill Daily (*I Dream of Jeannie, The Bob Newhart Show*), who gets the lead in this sitcom as small-town veterinarian James Shepherd. The home and office settings are just a doorway apart, so after sessions with his animal patients and their odd owners it's on to the domestic front. Waiting there for James is Helen, his fun-loving former wife (played with perfect comic verve by Connie Stevens). She's back in town with her new husband, Frank, in tow, living in a nearby condominium—and she doesn't hesitate to drop by or call anytime. After all, she still loves the kids, likes James, and (surprise) they feel the same about her. They even like Frank, though sometimes they wonder if his "business" just might involve organized crime. He says they've seen too many *Godfather*-type movies, but then "takes the Fifth." He also "takes a powder" about halfway through as he and Helen split and the series shifts comedy gears to play even more on the obvious continuing attraction between Helen and James. Maybe they *should* get back together.

*Starting from Scratch* was created by British sitcom vet Brian Cooke (who did *Man About the House*, the U.K. version of *Three's Company*) and reflects a similar emphasis on basic misunderstandings rather than on put-downs or insults. (There are some insults, but they are mostly directed toward the pet owners.) It's familiar territory, but with Connie Stevens in excellent form and Daily's patented nervous reactions honed to perfection, this show is a well-executed treat.

**STATE TROOPER (**) 30 min (104ep B&W; 1957–1959 Syndication) Police Drama** *with Rod Cameron as Rod Blake*

*State Trooper* is about Rod Cameron, the chief investigator for the Nevada State police. He tracks down bad guys from the fancy locales of Las Vegas to the barren wastes of the Mojave Desert.

**STEAMBATH (*½) 30 min (6ep Color; 1984–1985 Showtime) Comedy with** *Jose Perez as Morty, Janis Ward as Meredith, Robert Picardo as Rod Tandy, Rita Taggart as Blanche, and Al Ruscio as Davinci*

Bruce Jay Friedman's irreverent off-Broadway play *Steambath* supposed an afterlife set in a New York steambath, with God portrayed as a diminutive Puerto Rican washroom attendant. It was first staged for TV in May 1973 on PBS with Bill Bixby and Valerie Perrine. This effort to turn the concept into a series doesn't really work, because the idea seems stretched beyond need to keep the show going. God, in the guise of the attendant, is called Morty in this TV version.

**STEPTOE AND SON (**½) 30 min (40ep B&W & Color; 1964–1973 UK BBC) Situation Comedy** *with Wilfrid Brambell as Albert Steptoe and Harry H. Corbett as Harold Steptoe*

If you ever vaguely wondered about the prominent role (and casting credit) given to Wilfrid Brambell in the Beatles' first film, *A Hard Day's Night,* this series is the reason. In 1964 in Britain, *Steptoe and Son* was a big hit and consequently Brambell's presence in the movie was considered a coup. Not surprisingly, his character of Paul's grandfather bore a striking similarity to the senior Steptoe: a stubborn, conniving, old codger.

*Steptoe and Son* is also familiar for another reason: It was the basis for the U.S. hit *Sanford and Son.* Again the similarities are striking and deliberate, with American producers Norman Lear and Bud Yorkin bringing the setting (a junkyard), relationship (a sparring father and son), and even some of the scripts to their version. But the original is definitely worth digging up, just to see how two other old pros (Brambell and Harry H. Corbett) handle the concept.

*Steptoe and Son* originally played a few years in the mid-1960s, then returned again at the turn of the decade, accounting for the relatively small number of episodes for such a long-running series.

**STEVE ALLEN'S LAUGH BACK (***½) 90 min (23ep Color; 1976 Syndication) Comedy-Variety** *with Steve Allen, Jayne Meadows, Louis Nye, Bill Dana, Don Knotts, and Pat Harrington, Jr.*

Steve Allen was one of the great TV comics of the early days of the medium. Because most of his best work was done live on variety shows long gone and almost forgotten, it is difficult for modern viewers to appreciate his achievements. This series seeks to remedy the problem by packaging the best of Allen's TV work, interspersed with reminiscences with his famous cohorts.

Allen was the original host of the *Tonight* show (1953–1957), then hosted a prime-time hour series from the mid-1950s through the mid-1960s. His supporting cast was always top-notch, and the great success many have had on their own is tribute to his ability to pick talent. In fact, most people forget that it was through Allen's shows that America first got to know Tom Poston (George Utley on *Newhart*), Don Knotts (Barney Fife on *The Andy Griffith Show*), Louis Nye (Sonny Drysdale on *The Beverly Hillbillies*), Bill Dana (a.k.a. Jose Jimenez), and Pat Harrington, Jr. (Dwayne Schneider on *One Day at a Time*).

*Steve Allen's Laugh Back* is a great way to enjoy some of the best of 1950s TV comedy. Some of Allen's early work may seem dated now, but all of it has the excitement of live TV and the wit and originality that are Allen's trademark. ■

## STEVE CANYON (*) 30 min (39ep B&W; 1958–1959 NBC) Adventure

*with Dean Fredericks as Lt. Col. Steve B. Canyon, Jerry Paris as Maj. Willie Williston, and Ted DeCorsia as Police Chief Hagedorn.*

Steve Canyon, the fearless comic strip character created by Milton Caniff in 1948, is featured in this little-known series. Canyon begins as a hotshot test pilot for the U.S. Air Force, then is promoted to commanding officer at Big Thunder Air Force Base.

Jerry Paris, better known as neighbor Jerry Helper in *The Dick Van Dyke Show*, plays Canyon's buddy, Maj. Williston.

## STEVE DONOVAN, WESTERN MARSHAL (½) 30 min (39ep B&W; 1955–1956 Syndication) Western

*with Douglas Kennedy as Marshal Steve Donovan and Eddy Waller as Deputy Rusty Lee*

The setting, Wyoming in the 1870s, is the standard for this type of show, one more 1950s oater from the era of TV western overflow. Lead actor Douglas Kennedy was a forgettable character actor in Hollywood films in the late 1940s and early 1950s. He is forgettable here as well.

## STILL THE BEAVER (see *Leave It to Beaver*)

## STINGRAY (**½) 60 min (23ep & 2 hr pilot; 1986–1987 NBC) Drama

*with Nick Mancuso as Stingray*

Touted as a combination of *The Lone Ranger* and *Knight Rider*, *Stingray* features a mysterious character who turns up out of nowhere to help people in need, without charge. His identifying trademark: the jet-black 1965 Corvette Stingray he drives. His only requirement: the promise that if and when he returns to ask them for a favor, they will grant it, no questions asked. This show is a good pulp adventure, reminiscent of an atmospheric 1940s radio adventure series such as *The Shadow*, with plenty of tension and suspense. An unexpected treat from Stephen J. Cannell, who manages to turn what could have been just another car-smasher into a distinctive genre piece.

## STIR CRAZY (*½) 60 min (9ep Color; 1985–1986 CBS) Adventure

*with Joe Guzaldo as Skip Harrington, Larry Riley as Harry Fletcher, Polly Holliday and Jeannie Wilson as Capt. Betty, and F vce Applegate and Marc Silver as Crawford*

There's not much comparison between *Stir Crazy*—the TV show and *Stir Crazy*—the movie. The original 1980 film, with Richard Pryor and Gene Wilder (directed by Sidney Poitier), has a lot of loony charm, with Pryor and Wilder overacting in a tale about a black and white duo who wind up in jail. The TV version has two nobodys in the black and white leads, and radically transforms the concept into a parody of *The Fugitive*. The two leads are convicted of a murder they did not commit, break out of jail, and search for the Tattooed Man (named Crawford) who really was guilty, while being followed by Captain Betty, who was in love with the murdered man. If you forget the movie, the TV show is marginally watchable.

## STOCKARD CHANNING IN JUST FRIENDS (see *Just Friends*)

## THE STOCKARD CHANNING SHOW (*½) 30 min (13ep Color; 1980 CBS) Situation Comedy

*with Stockard Channing as Susan Goodenow, Ron Silver as Brad Gabriel, Sydney Goldsmith as Earline Cunningham, Max Showalter as Gus Clyde, and Jack Somack as Mr. Kramer*

Susan is a recently divorced woman who lands a job at a local Los Angeles television station, working as an assistant for its consumer advocate series, *The Big Rip-Off*. Sometimes this position involves undercover research work, but mostly it consists of dealing with her egotistical boss, Brad Gabriel, the host of the show. Susan also gets the chance to take her work home because her friend and neighbor, Earline, is the station receptionist—and the one who helped her land the job in the first place. An average, by-the-book comedy package, not to be confused with the series *Stockard Channing in Just Friends*.

## STONE (**½) 60 min (7ep & 2 hr pilot Color; 1980 ABC) Police Drama

*with Dennis Weaver as Det. Sgt. Dan Stone, Pat Hingle as Chief Gene Paulton, Nancy McKeon as Jill Stone, Beth Brickell as Diane Stone, and Robby Weaver as Officer Buck Rogers*

Producers Stephen J. Cannell and Donald Bellisario have some fun with the image of a cop moonlighting as a bestselling writer (a la Joseph Wambaugh) in this Dennis Weaver vehicle. Stone clearly enjoys the limelight, yet he also hasn't lost his nose for detective work, willingly going from celebrity parties and prestige events to the latest murder call at a moment's notice. Also along for the ride are Nancy McKeon (right before joining *The Facts of Life*) and Robby Weaver, Dennis Weaver's real-life son.

**STONEY BURKE (**) 60 min (32ep B&W; 1962–1963 ABC) Western** *with Jack Lord as Stoney Burke, Bruce Dern as E. J. Stocker, Warren Oates as Wes Painter, Robert Dowdell as Cody Bristol, and Bill Hart as Red*

Contemporary western setting with future *Hawaii Five-O* maven Jack Lord as a champion rodeo rider making the rounds from contest to contest in quest of the ultimate prize, the Golden Buckle. This is as reasonable an excuse as any to have some characters (Stoney and the other rodeo performers) travel through the American southwest, getting involved in other people's lives, though it lacks the obvious dramatic punch of a man on the run setup like *The Fugitive.* An unassuming package, giving you a chance to see Bruce Dern and Jack Lord in cowboy gear. Series producer Leslie Stevens went on from this to create *The Outer Limits.*

**STOP SUSAN WILLIAMS (*½) 20 min (10ep Color; 1979 NBC) Serial Drama** *with Susan Anton as Susan Williams, Ray Walston as Bob Richards, Michael Swan as Jack Schoengarth, and Albert Paulsen as Anthony Korf*

Tall, blond, statuesque, Susan Anton looks like a star. Maybe that's why networks kept treating her like one. While still a virtual unknown to the public, she appeared in several late 1970s series that all went nowhere. In *Stop Susan Williams* (originally one of the three twenty-minute segments of *Cliffhangers*), Anton plays tall, blond, statuesque Susan Williams, a newspaper photographer whose reporter brother was killed while uncovering a nefarious plot by Anthony Korf to blow up the world, or part of it. Susan continued her brother's work, so Korf wants to . . . yes, stop Susan Williams. Each week Susan faces almost certain death, but somehow escapes. Ray Walston (*My Favorite Martian*) is good as her shady boss.

**STOREFRONT LAWYERS (*) 60 min (23ep Color; 1970–1971 CBS) Law Drama** *with Robert Foxworth as David Hansen, Sheila Larken as Deborah Sullivan, and David Arkin as Gabriel Kaye*

An absurdly pompous series, *Storefront Lawyers* presents the sugar-coated story of three young lawyers who form Neighborhood Legal Services in Los Angeles. The trio defend the poor who can't afford legal counsel, a highly admirable concept. The problem with the show is that it plays like a liberal fairy tale, with all the poor people good and all the rich people bad. What's worse, the legal triumvirate are often seen skipping down the main street together, locked arm in arm, like Dorothy, the Cowardly Lion, and the Tin Man. The actors look stupid doing this, and it makes their characters seem foolish.

*Storefront Lawyers* metamorphosed into *Men at Law* to fill out its original production order, but the slightly revised series was almost as bad as the original. See that title for more details.

**STORIES OF THE CENTURY (**½) 30 min (39ep & 60 min pilot B&W; 1954–1955 Syndication) Western** *with Jim Davis as Matt Clark, Mary Castle as Frankie Adams, and Kristine Miller as Jonesy Jones*

Matt Clark is a detective for a huge railroad that runs the newly built transcontinental tracks in the 1890s. In a highly unusual move for a 1950s western, Clark's partner in detective work is a woman, first Frankie Adams, then Jonesy Jones. In the 1954 pilot, called *The Last Stagecoach West*, the leading character is called Bill Cameron, rather than Matt Clark.

**THE STORY OF . . . (*) 30 min (27ep B&W; 1962–1963 Syndication) Docudrama Anthology** *with John Willis as host*

Ace documentary/drama producer David Wolper (*The Making of the President, Roots*) helped create this odd show that dramatizes events in the lives of interesting people. Focusing more on noncelebrities than Wolper's somewhat similar series, *Biography, The Story of . . .* features some of the people actually involved in the events portraying themselves.

**THE STORY OF ENGLISH (**) 60 min (9ep Color; 1986 PBS) Documentary** *with Robert MacNeil as host*

The origins, growth, and mutations of the English language are depicted in this overly slow-moving series hosted by PBS news star Robert MacNeil. ■

**STRAIGHTAWAY (*) 30 min (26ep B&W; 1961–1962 ABC) Adventure** *with Brian Kelly as Scott Ross and John Ashley as Clipper Hamilton*

You can't get much more bland WASPy character names than Scott Ross and Clipper Hamilton, and this series is as bland as the names of the of the characters. Scott and Clipper run the Straightaway Garage, where the duo design, build, and repair racing cars. They become involved in various exploits with the fast car set. Tennis, anyone?

**THE STRANGE REPORT (**) 60 min (16ep Color; 1968 UK ATV) Detective Drama** *with Anthony Quayle as Adam Strange, Kaz Garas as Hamlyn Gynt, and Anneke Wills as Evelyn McLean*

Once again, the police are stumped and have to turn (discreetly, of course) to independent investigators to solve the latest international crimes. Professional criminologist Adam Strange welcomes the chance to step in and show off, combining an appreciation for the latest high-tech resources with his own keen knowledge of criminal behavior. Assistant Hamlyn Gynt and neighbor Evelyn McLean act as his Doctor Watson stand-ins, easily getting caught in the action once the game is afoot. This is an average British-produced crime series distinguished chiefly by Anthony Quayle's presence in the lead role. Though produced in 1968, it turned up on NBC several years later (1971), about the time Quayle was serving as narrator to the CBS presentation of *The Six Wives of Henry VIII.*

**STRANGERS (**) 60 min (13ep Color; 1980–1982 UK Granada) Crime Drama** *with Don Henderson as George Bulman, and Dennis Blanch, Frances Tomelty, John Ronane, Mark McManus, Fiona Mollison, and David Hargreaves*

Scotland Yard sends two agents from its London Murder Squad to battle violent crime in northwestern England. A pretty rough series. One character, Chief Inspector Bulman, continues in the self-titled *Bulman* spin-off series.

**STRANGERS AND BROTHERS (*½) 60 min (7ep Color; 1984 UK BBC) Drama** *with Shaughan Seymour as Lewis Eliot, Sheila Ruskin as Sheila Knight, Nigel Havers as Roy, Elizabeth Spriggs as Lady Muriel, and Alan MacNaughtan as Winslow*

Based on several autobiographical novels by C. P. Snow about life in Britain's ruling class, this story follows young Lewis Eliot as he attempts to rise from his working-class background to a spot in society as a barrister. Along the way, he courts Sheila, a selfish woman he foolishly loves, and develops a demanding friendship with Roy, a brilliant but impetuous scholar at Cambridge. There are lots of dark anguished moments with both, and the result is a slow-moving, at times even preachy, disappointing series.

**THE STRAUSS FAMILY (**½) 60 min (13ep: twelve 60 min & one 90 min Color; 1973 UK ATV) Drama** *with Eric Woolfe as Johann Strauss, Sr., Stuart Wilson as Johann Strauss, Jr., Anne Stallybrass as Anna Strauss, Lynn Farleigh as Adele, Tony Anholt as Eduard, Barbara Ferris as Emilie Trampusch, and Derek Jacobi as Josef Lanner*

The lives, loves, and music of the top waltz composers of the nineteenth century, Johann Strauss, Sr., and Johann Strauss, Jr., The London Symphony Orchestra provides the lush accompaniment to this well-staged biographical drama, covering some seventy-five years of father and son creativity. In 1973, ABC ran seven episodes of this series as a high-brow spring filler. While watching it today (with 1999 just around the corner) you might want to consider nominees for similar treatment looking back at twentieth-century composers. (The Beatles? Rodgers and Hammerstein? Zager and Evans? You decide.)

**THE STREET (*) 30 min (40ep Color; 1988 Syndication) Police Drama** *with Bruce MacVittie as Bud Peluso, Stanley Tucci as Arthur Scolari, Ron J. Ryan as Jack Runyon, and Michael Beach as Shepard Scott*

Four young policemen working the graveyard shift of the Newark, New Jersey police force is the setting of *The Street*, a pointlessly self-conscious cop show that takes itself awfully seriously. Sure, working the Newark night shift is no fun, but jeez guys, lighten up, huh? *The Street* always heads for cheap titillation whenever it can get away with it. The characters use raunchy street language and racial epithets fly fast and furious.

**STREET HAWK (*) 60 min (13ep & 90 min pilot Color; 1985 ABC) Adventure** *with Rex Smith as Jesse Mach, Joe Regalbuto as Norman Tuttle, Richard Venture as Capt. Leo Altobelli, and Jeannie Wilson as Rachel Adams*

Vapid and overly flashy, *Street Hawk* is a cheap effort to cash in on the temporary popularity of pretty-boy singer Rex Smith ("You Take My Breath Away"). Smith plays the none-too-subtly named Jesse Mach, a motorcycle cop recruited to ride Street Hawk, the fastest motorcycle in the world, as part of Uncle Sam's war on crime. Equipped with all sorts of fancy gadgets, Street Hawk allows Jesse to roam the land, looking for good places to let his long locks flow in the wind. The action is mild; the acting and scripts are highly mediocre. ■

**STREETS OF DANGER** **(see *The Lone Wolf*)**

**STREETS OF SAN FRANCISCO (**½) 60 min (119ep Color; 1972–1977 ABC) Police Drama** *with Karl Malden as Mike Stone, Michael Douglas as Steve Keller, and Richard Hatch as Dan Robbins*

Quinn Martin, the man behind some of the best crime drama series in TV history (*The Untouchables, The Fugitive,* and *The F.B.I.*), mellowed out a bit in his later years, but still produced solid, exciting series (*Barnaby Jones* and *Cannon*). *Streets of San Francisco* is from this later (good, not perfect) era of Martin's career.

The stories in *Streets of San Francisco* are just usual crime sagas set amidst one of the nation's most picturesque and interesting cities. The production is classy, but with no special touches to make it memorable. The prime appeal is the match of well-seasoned veteran Karl Malden, in the days before he began shilling for travelers checks, and Michael Douglas, then an acting novice who was still described as the son of Kirk. Later he became a leading man in the movies (*Fatal Attraction*) in his own right.

Malden's blue-collar character (Mike Stone), a twenty-three-year veteran on the force, is teamed with Douglas's (Steve Keller), a college-educated type who is versed in new methods of crime fighting. Each of them bristles a bit at the other's style, but they get along well and learn from each other. The team of old mentor Malden and Young Turk Douglas is notches above most of the similar male duos in medical and cop series throughout TV history. If the scripts were a little better, or if the show was trying to do something a little out of the ordinary, *Streets of San Francisco* might be more than what it is: good-quality entertainment for when you have nothing better to do.

Douglas leaves the series before the final season. His character is said to have quit the force to enter the teaching profession. The final season matches Malden with nondescript pretty boy Richard Hatch and is not worth more than a glance.

**STRIKE FORCE (*) 60 min (19ep Color; 1981–1982 ABC) Police Drama** *with Robert Stack as Capt. Frank Murphy, Dorian Harewood as Det. Paul Strobber, Richard Romanus as Lt. Charlie Gunzer, and Trisha Noble as Det. Rosie Johnson*

Yet more bland crime action from the fecund production duo of Aaron Spelling and Douglas Cramer (*B.A.D. Cats, Glitter, The Love Boat, The San Pedro Beach Bums*), *Strike Force* is about one more elite crime-fighting unit that only handles the tough assignments that regular cops won't touch. The Strike Force operates out of Los Angeles, the world's capital for paramilitary TV crime-fighting organizations. Robert Stack, who was far more interesting and believable as the ultra-noble Eliot Ness in *The Untouchables*, plays the commandant of the unit. ■

**STRUCK BY LIGHTNING (**½) 30 min (6ep Color; 1979 CBS) Situation Comedy** *with Jeffrey Kramer as Ted Stein, Jack Elam as Frank, Millie Slavin as Nora, and Bill Erwin as Glenn*

Delightfully offbeat and wildly unusual, *Struck by Lightning* deserves more attention than its short run would tend to indicate. Set in the run-down Victorian Lodge in rural Maine, the series introduces Boston professor Ted Stein as the man who inherits the place and intends to sell it. He changes his mind when he meets the lodge caretaker, Frank, a repulsively ugly fellow who has quite a tale to tell. Frank is none other than the original monster created more than two hundred years ago by Dr. Frankenstein. Guess who Prof. Ted's great-great-grandfather was? That's right, the mad genius Dr. Frankenstein himself. So Ted decides to keep the place, Frank included, in order to fix it up and make a profit. Ted also hopes to find the formula for his ancestor's ancient elixir, since Frank needs a dose every fifty years in order to keep going.

This story sounds real weird, and it is, but *Struck by Lightning* takes great big leaps of creative farce and that boldness makes up for much of the roughness. Watching veteran movie and TV bad guy Jack Elam play Frankenstein's monster as a grumpy, old, ugly klutz is a delight.

**STRYKER OF SCOTLAND YARD (*) 30 min (13ep B&W; 1956–1957 Syndication) Police Drama** *with Clifford Evans as Inspector Robert Stryker*

From the police files of Scotland Yard come these tales of crime and punishment, featuring the Yard's Inspector Stryker.

**THE STU ERWIN SHOW (½) 30 min (130ep B&W; 1950–1955 ABC) Situation Comedy** *with Stu Erwin as himself, June Collyer as June Erwin, Sheila James as Jackie Erwin, Ann Todd and Merry Anders as Joyce Erwin, Willie Best as Willie, and Martin Milner as Jimmy Clark*

One of the definitive dumb-dad screwball comedies of the 1950s, this series was churned out by the Hal Roach Studios as a showpiece for Stu Erwin (who had played similar roles in feature films and on radio for years). The simple setup casts Stu Erwin as the earnest but blundering principal of suburban Hamilton High School, where he finds his well-meaning plans inevitably going awry. It's the same on the home front, where mom (played by Erwin's real-life wife) is there to pick up the pieces and set things right. Other familiar faces in the cast include Sheila James (Zelda Gilroy on *Dobie Gillis*) as daughter Jackie, Martin Milner (from *Route 66* and *Adam-12*) as daughter Joyce's boyfriend, and Willie Best (the wide-eyed elevator operator on *My Little Margie*) as the family handyman.

This show is perfectly acceptable in small doses (say, on some video cassette package or as part of an umbrella retrospective anthology), but it is awfully hard to take over the long haul. The series has carried many titles over the years (both in its first-run airing and in syndicated reruns), including *The Trouble with Father, Life with the Erwins,* and *The New Stu Erwin Show.* ■

**STUDIO 5B (*½) 60 min (9ep Color; 1989 ABC) Drama** *with Kerrie Keane as Carla Montgomery, Wendy Crewson as Gail Browning, George Grizzard as Douglas Hayward, Kim Myers as Samantha Hurley, Jeffrey Tambor as Lionel, Justin Deas as Jake Gallagher, Kenneth David Gilman as David Chase, and Kate Zentall as Rosemary*

*Studio 5B* is a real network TV prime-time series about a fictional network TV morning show called *Studio 5B.* The real series is about the lives and loves of the people (both in front of and behind the cameras) who put on the fictional five-day-a-week program at an hour when most people are barely awake.

Carla Montgomery is the dragon lady co-anchor, who will step over anyone, glamorously, to maintain her prestige. Her male co-host, Douglas Hayward, is an aging veteran of the TV news wars, who fears he is being put out to pasture. Running things behind the scenes are Lionel, the harried and curt executive producer; David, the producer going through a messy divorce; and Gail, the pretty assistant producer whose on-camera aspirations make her a target for Carla's venom.

One of the messages here is don't expect to juggle a career in TV with a successful marriage. David's wife left him because he spent too much time at work. Gail calls off her wedding at the last moment, partly because of her devotion to finishing her big story on child molesting and partly because her old flame, world-traveling reporter Jake Gallagher, has returned to whisper sweet nothings in her ear.

*Studio 5B* would like to be the *L.A. Law* of the TV journalism set, but its characters are too strident and the writing is too clichéd to reach that goal.

**STUDIO '57 (*) 30 min (38ep B&W; 1954–1956 DuMont & Syndication) Drama Anthology**

The title of this series of undistinguished filmed dramas refers not to the year of original broadcast but to the number of products produced by the show's original sponsor (Heinz).

**STUDIO ONE (***) 60 min (B&W; 1948–1958 CBS) Drama Anthology**

*Studio One* was there to help kick off the 1950s live drama anthology era. Actually beginning back in 1948, this series offered more than 450 episodes in its ten-year television run (following a brief stint on radio), many under the guidance of production guru Worthington "Tony" Miner. The stories range from adaptations of the classics to effective melodramas to powerful originals such as "Twelve Angry Men." As with the other live drama showcases of the era, if the presentations were saved, it was usually as grainy kinescope film recordings. So don't expect to see these turn up on the air, except in highlight form or as part of some anthology sampler (like *The Golden Age of Television*). However, a small number of *Studio One* offerings are available on home video packages, including "Jane Eyre" (with Kevin McCarthy and Frances Starr), and "The Defender" (used as the basis for the subsequent *Defenders* series, with Steve McQueen, William Shatner, Martin Balsam, and Ralph Bellamy).

Oddly, one of the program's famous "You can be sure if it's Westinghouse" commercials may be easier to find than most of the dramas, with such material frequently turning up on home video packages of spots and commercials from the 1950s. ■

**STUDS LONIGAN (**½) (6hr miniseries Color; 1979 NBC) Drama** *with Harry Hamlin as Studs Lonigan, Colleen Dewhurst as Mary Lonigan, Charles Durning as Paddy Lonigan, Jessica Harper as Loretta Lonigan, Brad Dourif as Danny O'Neill, Devon Ericson as Fran Lonigan, and Lisa Pelikan as Lucy Scanlon*

James T. Farrell's novel of an Irish-American boy coming of age in the hustling, bustling, melting pot of Chicago from 1916 to 1931 is given a fine treatment by producers Lee Rich and Philip Capice, two gentlemen better known for *Eight Is Enough* and *Dallas.* The great cast really helps bring the novel alive, and the script by TV drama veteran Reginald Rose (*Playhouse 90, Studio One*) is classy. The only oddity is leading man Harry Hamlin, here appearing in his first major TV role. Later famous as *L. A. Law*'s serious hunk Michael Kuzak, Hamlin is far too dark and non-Gaelic looking to play a son of Ireland.

**SUGAR TIME! (*) 30 min (13ep Color; 1977–1978 ABC) Situation Comedy** *with Barbi Benton as Maxx Douglas, Marianne Black as Maggie Barton, Didi Carr as Diane Zukerman, and Wynn Irwin as Al Marks*

*Sugar Time!*, starring Barbi Benton (one-time playmate of Hugh Hefner) and two other glitzy beautiful young ladies, is the stilted story of a three-woman rock act, called Sugar. They are trying to hit the big time by starting at the bottom, playing and working at Al Marks's Tryout Room. There is an awful lot of what is usually called "T & A" on display here, an awful lot of leering jokes, and just an awful lot that is awful.

Diminutive pop songwriter/performer Paul Williams ("We've Only Just Begun") wrote some of the original songs used in this fiasco. James Komack (*Chico and the Man, Welcome Back, Kotter*) is the producer.

**SUGARFOOT (**) 60 min (69ep B&W; 1957–1961 ABC) Western** *with Will Hutchins as Tom "Sugarfoot" Brewster*

Amidst the hordes of rough and tough macho men who rode tall across the screen in the unending stream of TV westerns in the late 1950s, Tom Brewster (the "Sugarfoot") is a man apart. A law student searching the West for some practical life experiences during the 1860s, Brewster is a novice to the ways of the cowpoke. He is labeled a "sugarfoot," which is even more "green" than a tenderfoot (usually the lowest rank among cowboys). Brewster, an amiable, kind-hearted fellow, gets involved with different people each week, learning to shoot bad guys and to do other things western heroes are supposed to do. The plots are simple, but they can be fun.

**SUNDAY NIGHT, MICHELOB PRESENTS (***) 60 min (26ep at Fall 1989 Color; 1988– Syndication) Musical Variety** *with David Sanborn and Jools Holland as hosts*

With just a minimum of between-numbers patter, this low-key musical showcase gives an eclectic assortment of guest acts the chance to do what they do best: hang loose and play. The emphasis is on jazz and rock, with individual performers of every type teaming up on numbers (for instance, one show features a duet between folk singer Leonard Cohen and jazz sax player Sonny Rollins). Veteran musicians Jools Holland (rock) and David Sanborn (jazz) keep the program moving, but with a clear appreciation and respect for their guests.

Lorne Michaels (creator of *Saturday Night Live*) serves as executive producer of the series, which uses a set reminiscent of his Saturday night hit. Actually, it's not hard to picture this as the open-ended TV stage the musical guests on *Saturday Night Live* would love to perform on after the regular show is over.

The official title of this series is *Michelob Presents Sunday Night* (renamed *Night Music* for the Fall 1989)—reminiscent of the 1950s when the sponsor's name would be up-front, especially on variety shows (*Texaco Star Theater, Kraft Music Hall*).

**SUNSET SONG (**) 60 min (6ep Color; 1971 UK BBC) Drama** *with Vivien Heilbron as Chris Guthrie, Andrew Keir as John Guthrie, Edith Macarthur as Jean Guthrie, Paul Young as Will Guthrie, and Jean Faulds as Aunt Janet*

The story of Chris Guthrie, a young woman coming of age in turn-of-the-century rural Scotland, adapted from a novel by Lewis Grassic Gibbons. The plot focuses on young Chris's dreams, which are frequently shattered by the demands of her family, in particular by her authoritarian father, John. For instance, when he suffers a stroke, he just keeps calling on her to give more and more to the household (and this is after she's already had to leave college to take over the domestic chores). Nicely shot on location, it effectively walks the thin line between melodrama and faithful rendering.

**SUNSHINE (**) 30 min (13ep & 2½ hr pilot & 2 hr sequel Color; 1975 NBC) Comedy Drama** *with Cliff DeYoung as Sam Hayden, Elizabeth Cheshire as Jill Hayden, Meg Foster as Nora, Billy Mumy as Weaver, and Corey Fischer as Givits*

Two very sentimental made-for-TV movies serve as bookends for this series: Sunshine (first airing on CBS in 1973) and Sunshine Christmas (first airing on NBC in 1977). In the initial film, young Kate (played by Cristina Raines) is dying of cancer, but gets considerable moral support from her husband, Sam, and her loving daughter, Jill.

The series follows Sam and Jill a few years later, coping with life as a single-parent family. They're loose and happy together, with Sam pursuing his career as a musician—part of a trio with Givits and Weaver (played by Billy Mumy, from *Lost in Space*)—and supplementing his income with odd jobs. Meanwhile, Jill wouldn't mind seeing Sam remarry, perhaps to his next-door girlfriend, Nora, who seems an obvious candidate for a new lifelong commitment. This low-key combination had a very short run in its original airing on NBC. Nonetheless, it did leave a strong impression and a made-for-TV movie sequel followed two years later. The sequel was probably the best of all the presentations, with Sam taking Jill home to Texas to celebrate Christmas with his family. Not only is she charmed by the setting but Sam finds himself considering remarriage when he sees an old childhood sweetheart.

The two made-for-TV movies turn up most often. It should come as absolutely no surprise to discover that John Denver did the music, with his "Sunshine on My Shoulder" serving as the series theme song. However, Billy Mumy gained further musical notoriety of a different sort in the late 1970s as half of the duo of Barnes and Barnes, who turned out the cult hit record, "Fish Heads."

**THE SUPER (*½)30 min (13ep Color; 1972 ABC) Situation Comedy** *with Richard Castellano as Joe Girelli, Ardell Sheridan as Francesca Girelli, Margaret Castellano as Joanne Girelli, Bruce Kirby, Jr. as Anthony Girelli, and Phil Mishkin as Frankie Girelli*

The 1970s was the era of ethnic-oriented sitcoms, where each ethnic group got to insult all the other groups. *The Super* is a smorgasbord of ethnics, focusing on the Italian Girelli clan. Papa Joe is the large superintendent of a New York City lower middle-class apartment building populated by Jews, Poles, Irish, blacks, Puerto Ricans, and so forth. Lots of complaining goes on, as Joe bitches about the tenants, and the tenants bitch about Joe.

*The Super* is one of the first stabs at behind-the-scenes TV work by Rob Reiner (son of Carl), who was starring as "Meathead" in the ethnic-oriented *All in the Family* when this series was produced. Reiner and series co-star Phil Mishkin serve as the program's writers.

**SUPERBOY (**½) 30 min (24ep at Fall 1989 Color; 1988– Syndication) Adventure** *with John Haymes Newton as Clark Kent/Superboy, Stacy Haiduk as Lana Lang, and Jim Calvert as T. J. White*

In their 1978 *Superman* theatrical film, producers Alexander and Ilya Salkind took a few liberties with the legend of the man of steel. Not that they were the first. Since the character's initial appearance in *Action Comics* number one some four decades earlier, writers in every medium (comic books, cartoons, theatrical serials, television series, comic strips) have added their own adjustments to the particular details. For instance, by the time young Clark Kent leaves Smallville, his foster parents are sometimes both alive, both dead, or his mom is a widow. And he either begins his costumed exploits as Superman, Superboy, or even Superbaby. Ultimately such fine points really don't matter, just as long as the basics are in place: the adventures of a super-powered person (sent to earth as a child from a dying planet) who hides his great abilities behind the guise of mildmannered Clark Kent.

One of the aspects that the Salkinds' *Superman* film dispensed with, though, was Clark's career as Superboy, having him begin his public superhero life as a young adult in Metropolis. Though this idea contradicted more than thirty-three years of comic book adventures, it was actually more in line with the 1939 two-page origin of the character. Still, "the adventures of Superman when he was a boy" is fertile ground difficult to resist exploring, especially when there's little chance that Christopher Reeve will put aside his theatrical career for a new *Superman* television series. And so a decade after the first theatrical *Superman* film premièred, the Salkinds reversed themselves and Superboy took flight.

At least they preserved one of the most important aspects of the first two *Superman* films for the new series: an emphasis on character interaction. Even with excellent special effects (done at Disney's new studio facilities in Florida), the real focus on *Superboy* is on the life of Clark Kent as a college-age hero. A journalism major, he writes for the school newspaper, hangs out with his photographer friend, T. J. (son of the editor of the Metropolis *Daily Planet*), and keeps a loving eye on his good friend from Smallville, Lana Lang. As Superboy, Clark also matches wits for the first time with the self-centered, amoral president of the senior class, Lex Luthor (Scott Wells) and his assistant, Leo (Michael Manno).

Oddly, this confrontation means that even though the very existence of *Superboy* contradicts the *Superman* films, this series is clearly being played as a "prequel" vaguely coexisting with these same films (where both villains played major roles). Actually such an inconsistency is not too surprising because it calls to mind the weakest aspect of the Salkinds' Superman films: the stories. Unfortunately that same flaw turns up in *Superboy*, and it hurts the characters, especially the boy of steel. To compensate at times it looks as if John Haymes Newton is consciously attempting to duplicate the mannerisms used by Christopher Reeve as Superman. That's fine, but the show often misses opportunities for that self-knowing humor that makes Reeve's portrayal so accessible. Sure, as a young teen Clark still needs to grow, but it's not much fun seeing Superboy rather easily duped. Or ignoring plot holes you can fly a planet through.

Newton's second season replacement, Gerald Christopher, faces similar problems. As a result, this series falls short of its potential. Though there are some genuinely exciting scenes, affectionate moments between Clark and Lana, and good camaraderie between Clark and T. J., *Superboy* doesn't soar often enough, even in comparison to the films.

**SUPERCARRIER (*½) 60 min (8ep & 90 min pilot Color; 1988 ABC) Military Drama** *with Robert Hooks as Capt. Jim Coleman, Dale Dye as Capt. Henry "Hank" Madigan, Ken Olandt as Lt. Jack "Sierra" DiPalma, John David Bland as Lt. Doyle "Anzac" Sampson, Cec Verrell as Lt. Cmdr. Ruth "Beebee" Rutowski, and Richard Jaeckel as Sam Rivers*

In this military action series, there are many hotshot navy pilots with flashy nicknames, lots of curvaceous women who do everything from flying planes to changing bed pans, and more than enough shots of the gargantuan supercarrier U.S.S. *Georgetown.* This top-heavy production avoids all the nastiness and ugliness of real war, since it is set in peacetime. Thus, the series can spend more time on the romantic and career conflicts between the stars.

**SUPERMAN, THE ADVENTURES OF (***) 30 min (104ep: 52 B&W & 52 Color; 1953–1957 Syndication) Adventure** *with George Reeves as Clark Kent/Superman, Phyllis Coates and Noel Neill as Lois Lane, Jack Larson as Jimmy Olsen, and John Hamilton as Perry White*

Superman cannot die. Neither the futile gunshots of the world's villains nor the passage of a half century have destroyed a figure close to the heart of generations of admirers. Superman has appeared in many guises and has been portrayed by many mortals, but since 1938, Superman has served as a shining beacon in a cold, cruel world. He is always righting wrongs, always there to lend a helping hand, and never succumbs to the petty tribulations that wear down weak earthlings over time.

Superman has been presented in virtually every form of media known to our age. In 1938, Superman was created by Jerry Siegel and Joe Shuster as a comic book hero. One year later, Superman moved to the newspapers as a daily comic strip. In 1940, there was a radio series (with Bud Collyer supplying the voice of the man of steel). In 1941, the first animated Superman cartoon appeared in theaters, followed in 1948 by the first of a pair of cheap motion picture serials. In the 1950s came the popular TV series *The Adventures of Superman,* starring George Reeves. In the 1960s, a new series of animated television cartoons appeared (again with Bud Collyer as the voice of Superman). In the 1970s and 1980s, multimillion-dollar Hollywood movies, starring Christopher Reeve, demonstrated Superman's arrival in the big leagues of pop culture.

Throughout all these permutations, the basic story that first was told in the June 1938 issue of *Action Comics* remained virtually inviolate. Long ago and far away, the planet Krypton was doomed. As their planet crumbles around them, Jor-El and his wife Lara just have time to pack their young son Kal-El in a small test rocket and launch him toward earth. When baby Kal-El crash lands in Smallville, U.S.A., he is found by John and Martha Kent, two American gothics who name him Clark and raise the boy. It is soon apparent that Kal-El/Clark has powers and abilities far beyond those of mortal men. The boy learns to fly, develops X-ray eyes, and discovers that he cannot be injured by any known device.

As a young man, Clark leaves his rural paradise and heads for the urban corruption of Metropolis. Armed with his Superman suit, made by his Earth mother from his swaddling blanket that accompanied him from Krypton, Kent plans to use his great powers for the benefit of humanity. Keeping his superpowers secret, Clark obtains a job as a reporter for the *Daily Planet*, a great metropolitan newspaper, to be on hand for breaking news stories. At the paper he works with ace reporter Lois Lane and young novice Jimmy Olsen, under the supervision of editor Perry White. When needed, Clark dons his Superman suit and flies to the scene of the crime to battle for truth, justice, and the American way.

As with the Superman legend itself, the 1950s TV series *The Adventures of Superman* has become a cultural icon. The original twenty-six episodes, all in black and white and produced by Robert Maxwell and Bernard Luber, hold up remarkably well. Criticizing the cheap budget is pointless, because the entire series was produced on a shoestring. Superman's flying is a cute novelty that quickly loses its charm, since the same clip of the airborne man of steel is used over and over again. The other special effects are minimal. Superman is always breaking through brick walls, bending steel bars, and deflecting bullets. These actions are only impressive in a low-budget, 1950s sort of way. What is more impressive about these early episodes is that the producers were actually trying to make a believable story about a superhero. As compared to the later episodes, the action is more exciting (some of the bad guys are actually killed), the stories are better written, and the actors are more human.

By the time the later two-thirds of the *Superman* episodes were produced (a majority of which are in color), the program was a hit. Since the budget was still meager and the production schedule was still frantic, there was not much need to fine-tune the show—it was already popular. Consequently the series went from being a drama about an unreal cartoon character to being an unreal cartoonish comic strip come to life.

The major difference between the original and the later episodes is the character of Lois Lane, Kent's main rival as top reporter at the *Planet.* In the first twenty-six episodes, Lane is portrayed by Phyllis Coates as strong-willed, almost a 1950s women's libber in her determination to keep her position as best reporter in town. It is galling for her to be scooped over and over by the mousy man in the glasses who has the inside pipeline to news about Superman. Noel Neill, the replacement Lois, is far more prissy and likely to play the damsel in distress than Coates.

Other characters suffer as well in the later episodes. Perry White changes from hard-nosed newspaper executive to blowhard dunderhead boss, who bellows "Great Caesar's ghost!" at the drop of a hat. Jimmy Olsen, the "cub" reporter, is even more helpless and liable to gulp his big Adam's apple at the slightest danger. Clark has become more self-assured. Since the audience is now familiar with his Superman antics, Clark almost plays to the home crowd by making obvious hints and cute references to his alter ego that only a fool (or a character from the series) could miss.

Even the villains suffer in the later episodes. The bad guys are literally the same crew out of central casting used over and over again as different characters. They never seem to figure out that Superman can't be shot and they lean heavily on the "dem, deese, and dose" brand of gangster portrayal. Nobody is killed onscreen anymore and, as a rule, these new gangsters are not very frightening.

In spite of this litany of criticisms, a good case can be made for dismissing almost all of them. The first series of episodes was aimed at a family audience, as the writing and characterizations reflect. Once the program was a hit, it was directed at its primary target audience: kids. These later *Superman* episodes were simpler and populated by cardboard characters that children could understand. It can be argued that this switch to a more cartoonish format made the show as successful as it was and helped keep *Superman* in reruns for decades after production ended. Still, from more adult eyes, the early episodes show that quality can be produced on a small budget with some imagination and a world-famous central character. ■

**SUPERTRAIN (zero) 60 min (13ep Color; 1979 NBC) Adventure Anthology** *with Edward Andrews as Harry Flood, Patrick Collins as Dave Noonan, Robert Alda as Dan Lewis, and Harrison Page as George Boone*

When you talk about gigantic TV flops of the 1970s, *Supertrain* should be the first show that comes to mind. This overhyped, overproduced series met the fate it so richly deserved—quick cancelation—in spite of a few frantic efforts to rework the program in order to save some of the huge production investment.

The concept is *The Love Boat* on rails. The setting is Supertrain, a fancy atomic-powered train that travels coast to coast in thirty-six hours at speeds up to 200 mph. Supertrain comes equipped with disco, sauna, gym, and swimming pool, Each week the series focuses on the lives of some of the passengers (the guest stars). Some stories are dramatic, some romantic, some humorous. The stories are held together by the continuing characters who work on the train, such as conductor Harry Flood, physician Dan Lewis, social director Dave Noonan, and chief porter George Boone.

Sounds just like *The Love Boat,* right? If *The Love Boat* was a hit, why not *Supertrain*? Part of the reason is that *The Love Boat* acknowledged it was total fluff and never took itself too seriously. *Supertrain* tries to be too many things. It wants the light romance of *The Love Boat*, but it also wants the adventure of *Wagon Train* and the glitz of *Dynasty.* Unfortunately it was unable to perform any of these formats even passably.

So *Supertrain* stinks. So what? Lots of shows flop. What's special about *Supertrain* is the program's enormous production budget and the promotional hype that originally accompanied the series. The elaborate sets for the railroad cars and the detailed miniatures used for the train cost millions. Viewers were supposed to really get into the idea of this atomic-powered locomotive behemoth, as if it was one of the stars. Well, the expensive miniatures looked just like . . . expensive miniatures. When the series first aired, NBC promoted the show unceasingly (with that kind of production budget, they had to), as if *Supertrain* would revolutionize TV. Thus, critics were more than glad to trash the show when it turned out to be a bomb.

Frantic efforts are made about halfway through the series' run to save the show. Producers are changed, the cast is slimmed down, and the show's focus is narrowed to mystery and suspense, but it is too little too late. *Supertrain* soon chugs out of sight, but it lives in the memories of those who savor the many ways a TV network can throw millions of dollars down the drain.

**SURVIVAL (**) 30 min (38ep Color; 1964 Syndication) Documentary** *with James Whitmore as narrator*

James Whitmore, an actor best known for playing Harry Truman and Will Rogers onstage, serves as narrator of this competent series showcasing film footage of famous disasters and the stories of people who survived.

**THE SURVIVORS (**½) 60 min (15ep Color; 1969–1970 ABC) Drama** *with Lana Turner as Tracy Carlyle Hastings, Kevin McCarthy as Philip Hastings, Jan-Michael Vincent as Jeffrey Hastings, Ralph Bellamy as Baylor Carlyle, and George Hamilton as Duncan Carlyle*

More than a decade before hour-long soapy dramas about the ultra-rich dominated TV, *The Survivors* blazed the trail for stories of the angst of the well-to-do. Based on a Harold Robbins novel (and created by Robbins), the series concerns the Hastings and the Carlyles, rich banking families with lives that intertwine. As with the best prime-time soaps, the cast is full of former film stars (Lana Turner, Ralph Bellamy, George Hamilton) and even an up-and-coming young hunk (Jan-Michael Vincent). Sexual hanky-panky, renegade South American dictators, and lusting after power and money are common themes. America may not have been ready for this show in the idealistic late 1960s, but it seems quite tame now.

**SUSIE (see *Private Secretary*)**

**SUSPENSE (*) 30 min (23ep B&W; 1964 CBS) Suspense Anthology** *with Sebastian Cabot as host*

The *Suspense* title has a long, distinguished history at CBS. Beginning as one of the premier network radio drama anthologies, the show ran from 1942 to 1962. From 1949 to 1954, a live TV version of *Suspense* presented many fine actors in tales of tension. The 1964 revival of *Suspense* (the only video version still available), however, is a mild postscript to the famous series. Hosted by rotund British actor Sebastian Cabot (*Checkmate, Family Affair*), this *Suspense* contains mild stories that shock nobody.

**SUSPICION (**½) 60 min (21ep B&W; 1957–1958 NBC) Suspense Anthology**

In its original airing, this series alternated between live and filmed presentations for forty episodes, with Alfred Hitchcock's production company responsible for ten of the films. Hitchcock himself directed only one, "Four O'Clock," with E. G. Marshall as a man who suspects his wife of infidelity and decides to kill her by setting a bomb in the cellar—timed to go off at four o'clock when he is far away. But then some robbers break in, tie him up, and leave him in the cellar, where he struggles to escape from his own trap, with the clock ticking away.

The other episodes from Hitchcock's company also feature clever hooks and strong performances (from the likes of Sebastian Cabot, David Wayne, and Joseph Cotten), making *Suspicion* worth a look at least half the time.

**SUZANNE PLESHETTE IS MAGGIE BRIGGS (see *Maggie Briggs*)**

**SWAMP FOX (**½) 60 min (6ep B&W; 1959–1960 ABC) Adventure** *with Leslie Nielsen as Francis "Swamp Fox" Marion, Myron Healey as Maj. Peter Horry, and Dick Foran as Gabriel Marion*

Walt Disney's presentation in the late 1950s of self-contained continuing series within the framework of the long-running Disney show pioneered the concept of dramatic miniseries on American TV. The first such attempt was the famous Davy Crockett episodes of 1954 and 1955. Not so famous but equally entertaining are the Swamp Fox stories, which are based on a figure from early American history like the Crockett tales. Francis Marion was a Colonial rebel general in the Revolutionary War who fought the British on the less-renowned Southern front. His guerrilla tactics of using the dense natural terrain for cover earned him the nickname Swamp Fox, and his story makes for great TV.

Leslie Nielsen, a fine actor who only gained real fame much later in broad farces such as the film *Airplane!* and the TV series *Police Squad,* deserved greater national fame for playing Marion. He may not have worn Crockett's fabled coon skin cap, but his lively air and jaunty personality are still fresh.

**THE SWEENEY** (**½) **60 min (52ep & 90 min pilot Color; 1974–1978 UK Thames) Crime Drama** *with John Thaw as Inspector Jack Regan, Dennis Waterman as Sgt. George Carter, and Garfield Morgan as Inspector Haskins*

John Thaw (later the dour and acerbic Inspector Morse) stars as the tough, deadpan leader of an elite team of Scotland Yard police detectives ("the Flying Squad" —Cockney rhyming slang for the murderous "Sweeney Todd") assigned to some of the department's toughest cases. Translation: this group means business, dispatching the violent lowlifes of the street with their own brand of rough-and-tumble force. Thaw's Jack Regan in particular frequently takes the pursuit of each villain as his own personal vendetta (as in the pilot film, *Regan,* when he hunts down the killer of a young cop). This series is done well but it is violent, and even shows the police getting drunk, swearing (with some fairly raw language for 1974 television), and taking bribes. If you like your cops down and dirty, this series is for you.

**SWEEPSTAKES** (*) **60 min (10ep Color; 1979 NBC) Drama Anthology** *with Edd Byrnes as Gregg Harris*

Each week three finalists sweat blood as they move closer to winning the big jackpot: the million-dollar prize that will be awarded by Gregg Harris on KBEX-TV in Hollywood. Each week we see how the anticipation, tension, and then either disappointment or jubilation affects the finalists.

*Sweepstakes* is really just an update of the 1950s hit series, *The Millionaire,* but it has none of that show's kindness and seriousness. Instead it is more a modern variation of *The Love Boat.* The major concern is squeezing in guest stars and packing an hour with short vignettes of little, if any, poignancy. It is appropriate that Edd Byrnes, the actor made famous for playing the vapid pretty boy "Kookie" on *77 Sunset Strip*, shows up as the only continuing character here, the master of ceremonies for the weekly lottery drawing.

**SWEET SURRENDER** (**) **30 min (6ep Color; 1987 NBC) Situation Comedy** *with Dana Delany as Georgia Holden, Mark Blum as Ken Holden, Edan Gross as Bart Holden, Christopher Rich as Vaughn Parker, David Doyle as Frank Macklin, and Marjorie Lord as Joyce Holden*

In a break from 1980s orthodoxy, Georgia Holden is a woman with a business career who leaves the workplace to become a full-time mom when she and hubby Ken have their second baby. As the title implies, Georgia's "surrender" to the demands of motherhood has both its good and bad points.

One plus of this series is watching old pros David Doyle and Marjorie Lord. Doyle, who played Charlie's male flunkie in *Charlie's Angels*, plays Georgia's father, while Lord, who earned her TV mom stripes as Danny Thomas's second wife on *Make Room for Daddy*, plays Ken's mother. The two grandparents pepper Georgia with plenty of advice about child raising, much to her chagrin. Dana Delany (who plays Georgia) went on to the role of head nurse Coleen McMurphy in *China Beach.*

**SWISS FAMILY ROBINSON** (*) **60 min (22ep & 2 hr pilot Color; 1975–1976 ABC) Adventure** *with Martin Milner as Karl Robinson, Pat Delaney as Lotte Robinson, Willie Aames as Fred Robinson, Eric Olson as Ernie Robinson, Cameron Mitchell as Jeremiah Worth, and Helen Hunt as Helga Wagner*

Irwin Allen is a producer known for a big, clunky series and films that have lots of hardware, lots of disasters, and minimal character development (*Voyage to the Bottom of the Sea, Lost in Space, The Poseidon Adventure, The Towering Inferno*). His version of *Swiss Family Robinson*, the classic Johann Wyss tale of a nice family marooned in the tropics in the middle 1800s, is appropriately overblown and full of earthquakes, typhoons, and volcanoes. The main problem is that the Robinson clan is far too 1970s to be believable as nineteenth-century seafarers. Daddy Robinson is played by *Route 66/Adam 12* graduate Martin Milner, and one of the Robinson children is named Ernie, a name more appropriate to *My Three Sons* than Victorian Europe.

The most interesting aspect of this show is the extent to which the old Wyss fable served as the model for Allen's previous series, *Lost in Space,* where the marooned family was also known as the Robinsons.

**THE SWISS FAMILY ROBINSON** (**) **30 min (26ep Color; 1975 Canada CTV) Adventure** *with Chris Wiggins as Johann Robinson, Diana Leblanc as Elizabeth Robinson, Heather Graham as Marie Robinson, Micky O'Neill as Franz Robinson, and Michael Duhig as Ernest Robinson*

Far more faithful to the Johann Wyss original than Irwin Allen's version produced around the same time, this Canadian stab at the castaway family story is well-crafted and entertaining, if somewhat slow-moving. The Jamaican scenery is beautiful.

**SWITCH** (***) **60 min (68ep & 90 min pilot Color; 1975–1978 CBS) Detective Drama** *with Robert Wagner as Pete Ryan, Eddie Albert as Frank McBride, Charlie Callas as Malcolm Argos, and Sharon Gless as Maggie*

Frank McBride is a hard-nosed retired bunco squad cop who is amazed to discover that the perfect partner for a private detective agency is someone from the other side: a charming but reformed ex-con artist, Pete Ryan. At least, Pete promises he's reformed, and will only draw on his considerable expertise as needed to solve their cases. (And maybe occasionally to help some old friends, but "Mac" will understand.) Any conflicts of style aside, Pete and Mac really are an ideal team, having seen operations from both sides (running con games and busting them). At first they specialize in cases that require a touch of *The Sting*, or as the title suggests, a last-minute "switch," usually involving the derailment of somebody else's con job with one of their own. Later they apply these same skills to more routine cases, helped by another con man gone straight, Malcolm (a master of disguise), and their faithful office gal Friday, Maggie.

The con games aside, the reason this series works is that producer Glen A. Larson has managed to capture one of the most elusive elements of the hit film *The Sting*, not the convoluted plot twists but the sense of rapport between the two main characters. Wagner and Albert have great give-and-take, sparring over matters of style as well as substance. Yet all the time they are also developing a genuine sense of respect and friendship, with both of them learning from each other. By the end of the series, Pete could probably land a job with any police squad, while Mac can definitely pull an elaborate con with the best of them.

This series is good for *Cagney and Lacey* fans to appreciate Sharon Gless's versatility. In *Switch* she is a typically cute but harmless secretary.

The *Switch* syndication package usually incorporates the 1975 ninety-minute made-for-TV movie pilot into the run, playing it as two episodes.

**SWORD OF FREEDOM** (*½) **30 min (39ep B&W; 1957 UK ATV) Adventure** *with Edmund Purdom as Marco Del Monte, Martin Benson as Duke De Medici, Adrienne Corri as Angelica, and Kenneth Hyde as Machiavelli*

Marco del Monte, sworn enemy of the oppressive Medici family, leads a series of swashbuckling battles against them in fifteenth-century Renaissance Italy. An adequate costume drama from producer Sidney Cole, also responsible for the somewhat similar *Robin Hood* series and, a few years later, *Danger Man*.

**SWORD OF JUSTICE** (**) **60 min (13ep Color; 1978–1979 NBC) Adventure** *with Dack Rambo as Jack Cole, Bert Rosario as Hector Ramirez, and Alex Courtney as Arthur Woods.*

One of the lesser-known efforts of producer Glen A. Larson (*Battlestar Galactica, Magnum, P. I., The Six Million Dollar Man*), *Sword of Justice* is a breezy tale of playboy heir Jack Cole, who is framed on trumped-up embezzlement charges after his rich father's death. After serving a few years in the slammer, Cole comes out bitter, more educated in such practical trades as pickpocketing, and determined to avenge himself on evildoers beyond the reach of the law. Like Bruce Wayne as Batman, Cole poses as social dilettante by day and acts as undercover crime fighter by night. His aide is prison buddy Hector Ramirez.

**SZYSZNYK** (**½) **30 min (15ep Color; 1977–1978 CBS) Situation Comedy** *with Ned Beatty as Nick Szysznyk, Olivia Cole as Mr. Harrison, Susan Lanier as Sandi Chandler, and Leonard Barr as Leonard Kriegler*

Without a doubt the most difficult-to-spell TV series in history, *Szysznyk* (pronounced "Siznick") deserves more notice than that odd-ball honor. The first (and so far only) TV series stint for talented film character actor Ned Beatty (*Deliverance, Nashville, Network*), this show concerns an ex-marine sergeant (Beatty) who takes on the seemingly innocent job of playground supervisor for an inner city community center in Washington, D. C. It turns out that the rigid governmental bureaucracy that runs the center and the wild nature of the kids who frequent the joint are far tougher than expected. Beatty is warm, believable, and funny, and the series shows promise at first, before lack of direction dissipates the show's appeal.

**T AND T** (**½) **30 min (40ep & 2 hr special at Summer 1989 Color; 1988– Syndication) Detective Drama** *with Mr. T as T. S. Turner, Alex Amini as Amanda Taler, Jackie Richardson as Aunt Martha Robinson, David Nerman as Dick Decker, Ken James as Det. Ted Jones, and Sean Roberge as Joe Casper*

Give Mr. T credit—he knows how to play on his own image. With *The A-Team,* he gave his potentially fearsome muscleman character a soft-as-marshmallow inside when it came to kids (or any helpless victim). With this series, he plants his impressive frame in a pinstriped suit and signs on as a former boxer turned legman/investigator to a beautiful attorney. Well, he does keep his Mohawk haircut (albeit trimmed a bit). And since he does have to hit the streets fairly often in his investigations, his famous studded leather outfit is usually only a few scenes away. Then there are the workouts at the gym, with his muscles on display in fine form. Still, you have to admire the man's taste in outfits—he looks sharp in every guise.

The stories are fast-paced half-hour adventures dispatched quickly, cleanly, and with a good mix of formula confrontations. They also include a light touch of professional friendship between T. S. Turner and Amy Taler to play off the action. Obviously fans of *Masterpiece Theatre* are not going to search out this one, but if you like Mr. T, you won't be disappointed.

**T.H.E. CAT** (**) **30 min (26ep Color; 1966–1967 NBC) Adventure** *with Robert Loggia as Thomas Hewitt Edward Cat, R. G. Armstrong as Capt. William McAllister, and Robert Carricart as Pepe*

*T.H.E. Cat* dilutes a decent premise with a few too many "cute" hooks relating to the show's cat theme. Thomas Cat's initials are T.H.E. Cat. He is a former circus acrobat and cat burglar who now uses his skill legally as a bodyguard. He is so adept at his talents that he never uses any weapons. Headquartered in San

Francisco, Cat hangs out at the Casa del Gato (House of the Cat, of course) run by his loyal pal Pepe.

Aside from all the feline trappings, *T.H.E. Cat* is a fair example of mid-1960s TV sleuth work. Robert Loggia, who plays Cat, is always fun to watch.

**T. J. HOOKER (**) 60 min (93ep & 90 min pilot Color; 1982–1986 ABC & CBS) Police Drama** *with William Shatner as Sgt. T. J. Hooker, Adrian Zmed as Vince Romano, Heather Locklear as Stacy Sheridan, and James Darren as Jim Corrigan*

Back on Earth after an extended journey on the U.S.S. *Enterprise* as *Star Trek*'s Captain Kirk, familiar actor William Shatner still anguishes over the burden of command as T. J. Hooker, a veteran police detective who volunteers to return to plainclothes beat work in order to train new cops. Shatner still huffs and puffs through some chases, but most of the physical work is done by the svelte young male and female cops assigned to him. Another aging pretty boy, James Darren, joins halfway through the series.

*T. J. Hooker* is one of the more subdued, rational series produced by Aaron Spelling and Leonard Goldberg (*Charlie's Angels, Fantasy Island, S.W.A.T.*).

**TV 101 (**) 60 min 13ep Color; 1988–1989 CBS) Drama** *with Sam Robards as Kevin Keegan, Brynn Thayer as Emilie Walker, Leon Russom as Edward Steadman, Andrew White as Vance Checker, Mary B. Ward as Penny, Teri Polo as Amanda, Andrew Cassese as Sherman Fischer, Alex Desert as Holden Hines, Matthew LeBlanc as Chuck, Stacey Dash as Monique, and Stewart Goddard as Marty Voight*

The classic Hollywood line "Hey, kids, let's put on a show!" gets a 1980s twist in *TV 101.* The show isn't a cheery musical, but rather a video edition of the school newspaper at Roosevelt High School. Kevin Keegan returns to his alma mater as a young teacher and is put in charge of the school paper he once edited. He does away with all those old-fashioned written words and turns the paper into a video magazine, thanks to some snappy video equipment he picked up. The teens expecting a boring old writing class are all psyched at the thought of producing their own TV shows, just like their favorite anchor people.

Keegan is a familiar modern TV figure: an old-time radical now working within the system. Mr. Steadman, the principal, is the stick-in-the-mud authority figure who does his best to stifle free speech (or video) at Roosevelt High. The kids in Keegan's class are a cross section of 1980s teen stereotypes (one black girl, one jock, one druggie, one valley girl, one handicapped, one nerd, etc.).

*TV 101* carries a jaunty air of humor that makes it easier to accept the somewhat stilted and artificial tone to the goings-on at Roosevelt High. Keegan sometimes gets a little carried away with his tirades on freedom of expression, but it looks as if having him for a high school teacher might be fun.

**TV'S BLOOPERS AND PRACTICAL JOKES (½) 60 min (39ep Color; 1984–1986 NBC) Comedy** *with Dick Clark and Ed McMahon as hosts*

At the bottom of the TV programming barrel lies the "blooper" format, a collection of outtakes and miscues strung together for no other reason than to see people mess up. *TV's Blooper's and Practical Jokes* takes this cheap source of yucks and adds a *Candid Camera*–style collection of filmed practical jokes involving celebrities and two of the fluffiest hosts in TV land (Dick Clark and Ed McMahon).

Some of the clips are funny and it's nice to see some vintage bits involving unknowns who became celebrities, but there is really no reason to have this sort of stuff on every week.

**THE TAB HUNTER SHOW (*) 30 min (32ep B&W; 1960–1961 NBC) Situation Comedy** *with Tab Hunter as Paul Morgan, Richard Erdman as Peter Fairfield III, Jerome Cowan as John Larsen, and Reta Shaw as Thelma*

Lightweight escapist male fantasies from the starched and pressed late 1950s fill *The Tab Hunter Show.*This is appropriate, since Tab Hunter was one of the prefabricated sexless male hunks of the 1950s. In his only TV starring role to date, Hunter plays Paul Morgan, a dashing Malibu Beach playboy. Morgan makes a living drawing a mildly spicy cartoon strip "Bachelor at Large" that is loosely based on his own romantic exploits. Bob Cummings, Annette Funicello, and Frankie Avalon would fit right in with Tab in his Malibu pad.

**TABITHA (*) 30 min (12ep & two 30 min pilots Color; 1977–1978 ABC) Situation Comedy** *with Lisa Hartman as Tabitha Stephens, Robert Urich as Paul Thurston, Mel Stewart as Marvin Decker, David Ankrum as Adam Stephens, and Karen Morrow as Aunt Minerva*

First appearing on the old mid-1960s *Bewitched* series, the character of Tabitha Stephens was the baby girl/witch of Samantha and Darren Stephens. With the series long gone, *Tabitha* is a cheap effort to steal some of the good reputation of *Bewitched* for a mediocre spin-off.

The *Bewitched* connection is loose. None of the major characters continue here. Tabitha, not much of a personality in the old show, is now a grown lady, beautiful and working at a Los Angeles TV station as assistant to airhead newscaster Paul Thurston. She is, of course, a witch, and so she uses some of the tricks her mom made famous, but we've seen all that before in the original *Bewitched.* Tabitha's brother, Adam, also works at the station and helps her out. Lisa Hartman, who plays Tabitha, makes her first TV series appearance here. She later went on to cut some rock records and star as Ciji Dunne and Cathy Geary on *Knots Landing.*

The *Tabitha* series and the 1977 pilot on which it is

based are completely different from the original 1976 *Tabitha* pilot, in which Liberty (a.k.a. Louise) Williams plays the young witch as an assistant in a big San Francisco magazine publishing house.

**TAGGART** (**½) **60 min (12ep Color; 1983 & 1985–1986 Scottish TV) Mystery** *with Mark McManus as Inspector Taggart*

Mark McManus plays the tough-talking Chief Inspector Taggart in a good police mystery saga set in Glasgow. For support (of sorts) he has a university-honed, sharp-tongued assistant (played by Neil Duncan) and his somewhat pedantic wife at home.

The series runs for four three-episode stories, with the first one (in 1983) playing under the title *Killer.* A prime candidate for the U.S. *Mystery!* anthology.

**TAKE A GOOD LOOK** (**½) **30 min (20ep B&W; 1959–1961 ABC) Panel Game & Variety** *with Ernie Kovacs as host*

In the tradition of setting up *You Bet Your Life* as a quiz show just to give Groucho Marx a chance for humorous ad-libs, *Take a Good Look* provides a chance to see Ernie Kovacs show off his peculiar brand of comedy. The premise is that celebrity panelists have to guess the identity of each contestant brought out by Kovacs, taking "a good look" first at the faces (possibly familiar from coverage of a then-recent news event) and then at some clues hidden in various films and skits. Of course, those routines are really why you want to tune in, as Kovacs manages to sneak in some entertaining comedy bits, including some of his own famous characters (such as Percy Dovetonsils). This obtuse material is of only marginal help to such panelists as Hans Conried, Cesar Romero, Edie Adams, and Carl Reiner, but so what? Have you ever cared *which* couple wins the big money on Groucho's show? ■

**TAKE FIVE** (**) **30 min (3ep Color; 1987 CBS) Situation Comedy** *with George Segal as Andy Kooper, Derek McGrath as Al, Bruce Jarchow as Monty, Jim Haynie as Lenny Goodman, Todd Field as Kevin Davis, and Melanie Chartoff as Laraine McDermott*

A tailor-made series for Dixieland band fanatic George Segal, who regularly devoted as much air time as possible to such performances when he visited programs such as the *Tonight* show. On this comedy, Segal's character (public relations man Andy Kooper) regularly relaxes playing music with his pals Lenny, Al, and Monty as the Lenny Goodman Quartet. And Andy has plenty of reasons for some therapeutic tunes: His wife of twenty-one years has divorced him, her dad (his boss) has fired him, one of the band members (Monty) is now dating her, and at Andy's new office his young boss (Kevin) is incompetent while the best and brightest talent there (Laraine) hates him for landing the job she wanted.

The description almost takes more time than the show originally spent on the air (two episodes). It's too bad because Segal is acceptably funny and it's always fun to see Melanie Chartoff perform. Who knows, this may turn up in some obscure cable slot along with previously unused episodes, perhaps disguised as some Dixieland jazz band special.

**TALES FROM THE DARKSIDE** (***) **30 min (92ep Color; 1984–1988 Syndicated) Anthology**

Aspiring to *The Twilight Zone* or *Alfred Hitchcock Presents* status, this anthology series does better than most in that elusive quest. There's good variety in the stories: Sometimes the good guys win; other times the devil himself is triumphant. The approach from episode to episode also varies between obvious tales with a twist (including some wonderfully awful puns and bloody kicker scenes) and uplifting mood pieces, media in-jokes, and outright comedy. There's even room for some old-fashioned Rod Serling–style morality plays. By mixing all these styles, the series avoids the problem of typecasting itself, therefore making it easier for each story to stand on its own. So when a young boy faces "Monsters in My Room," or a frustrated parent tries to deal with a troublesome teddy bear ("Ursa Minor"), there are several ways the stories can turn, rather than automatically following a path to a certain type of twist ending.

As first-run syndicated fare, *Tales from the Darkside* also makes excellent use of a relatively limited budget in both casting and effects. No doubt one of the executive producers, George Romero (famous for his low-budget *Night of the Living Dead* films), had plenty of suggestions to this end. Shot in Canada, the series usually includes at least one familiar U.S. TV performer in each episode, including up-and-coming stars such as Lisa Bonet and veterans such as Bill Macy or Abe Vigoda. Frequently the director is also the writer (or at least the one doing the teleplay), so the stories often reflect a consistent vision in approaching the material.

As with any similar anthology, there are routine tales and standouts that help set it apart. Among the best hooks for this series are tales of a mystic agent who demonstrates that all bestsellers are the result of magic ("Printer's Devil"), a boarding house with a unique disposal system ("A New Lease on Life"), and a radio that tunes in real-life soap operas. "Distant Signals" offers the ultimate TV watcher's fantasy when a man with a briefcase filled with gold attempts to convince the star and writer–producer of a detective series canceled twenty years earlier (*The Max Paradise Show*) to resume production (in black and white) for a few more episodes—just to finish off the plot lines left hanging all those years. Darren McGavin has fun with this one as Van Conway, who plays detective Max Paradise, searching for "a limping man seen leaving the scene of the crime."

Besides Romero, the executive producers for this

series included Jerry Golod (who also worked on *Adderly*) and Richard P. Rubinstein (co-creator of *Monsters,* a similarly styled series that began shortly after *Tales from the Darkside* ended production). ■

**TALES OF THE GOLD MONKEY (***) 60 min (22ep Color; 1982–1983 ABC) Adventure** *with Stephen Collins as Jake Cutter, Caitlin O'Heaney as Sarah Stickney White, Roddy McDowall as Bon Chance Louie, Jeff MacKay as Corky, Marta DuBois as Princess Kogi, and John Calvin as Rev. Willie Tenboom*

If you enjoy old-fashioned cliffhanger adventure films, or their contemporary descendants (features such as *Raiders of the Lost Ark*), this is the perfect way to get your Saturday matinee fix. The series is set in 1938 on the South Pacific island of Boragora, hovering at the front edge of World War II. It comes complete with all the necessary character types: a rugged hero (Jake Cutter), his reliable sidekicks (Corky the mechanic and Jack, a one-eyed dog), a light romantic interest (Sarah White), an evil princess (Kogi), an offbeat tavern owner (Bon Chance Louie), and a German spy (Tenboom). They play their parts to perfection in stories that have just the right mix of serious adventure and a sense of playful humor—as they search for diamonds, idols, secret plans, and whatever else might turn up in their tropical paradise. Producer Donald P. Bellisario also borrows a technique from his biggest hit, *Magnum, P. I.,* and has Jake usually narrate the tales (just like Thomas Magnum).

**TALES OF THE KLONDIKE, JACK LONDON'S (**½) 60 min (7ep Color; 1983 Canada CBC) Drama Anthology** *with Orson Welles as narrator*

These Gold Rush adventures are adapted from Jack London's stories of struggles against nature and society, very effectively filmed on location in Canada. David Cobham—who had previously adapted London's *To Build a Fire* for a BBC TV film in 1970—directs three segments and consults on the rest. Guest stars include Eva Gabor, Robert Carradine, and Canadians Scott Hyland (later Detective O'Brien on *Night Heat*) and John Candy (*SCTV*). ■

**TALES OF THE TEXAS RANGERS (**) 30 min (52ep B&W; 1955–1958 CBS & ABC) Western** *with Willard Parker as Ranger Jace Pearson and Harry Lauter as Ranger Clay Morgan*

This plays more like a western anthology than a continuing series, because from episode to episode the two main characters turn up in a variety of settings, eras, and events. Some are as long ago as the 1830s, while others are set in contemporary times. No matter what the case, the stories are straightforward adventure tales, emphasizing the investigative methods of the Texas Rangers. A cut above standard kiddie western fodder.

**TALES OF THE UNEXPECTED (**) 60 min (8ep Color; 1977 NBC) Suspense Anthology** *with William Conrad as narrator*

With *Tales of the Unexpected,* Quinn Martin, a TV producer best known for crime-related dramas (*The Untouchables, The F.B.I.*), takes a stab at a *Twilight Zone*–type series of unrelated suspense stories. William Conrad (who had worked with Martin before as star of *Cannon*) provides the deep-voiced narration.

This series is also known as *Twist in the Tail.*

**TALES OF THE UNEXPECTED (**½) 30 min (90ep Color; 1979–1984 UK Anglia) Suspense Anthology** *with Roald Dahl and John Houseman as host*

More than half of these tales with a twist are based on the stories of Roald Dahl, with such titles as "Lamb to the Slaughter" and "The Man from the South" already familiar from prior treatment on *Alfred Hitchcock Presents.* But a good story is always worth retelling, and it's fun to compare the different approaches to the same material. To that end, the series also features a good mix of British and U.S. stars, including such performers as Brian Blessed, Julie Harris, Gary Burghoff, Telly Savalas, and Joan Collins. No doubt to avoid comparisons with Hitchcock, the hosts play the introductions rather straight, so we don't get an extra dose of sardonic humor from them. Instead there's just the distinctive carousel theme music over the closing credits.

**TALES OF THE VIKINGS** **(see *The Vikings*)**

**TALES OF TOMORROW (**½) 30 min (84ep B&W; 1951–1953 ABC) Science Fiction Anthology**

This adult-oriented collection of science fiction and fantasy stories includes an excellent mix of famous and obscure tales (including adaptations of *Frankenstein, Twenty-Thousand Leagues Under the Sea,* and *The Picture of Dorian Gray*). The guest casts are equally eclectic (ranging from Boris Karloff in "Past Tense" to Eva Gabor in "The Invaders"), with many performers turning up in a variety of characters (Leslie Nielsen, for instance, appears in several titles including "Twenty Thousand Leagues Under the Sea," "Appointment to Mars," and "Another Chance"). Though obviously working on a tight budget, this series has an authentic "pulp magazine" feel to it. ■

**THE TALL MAN (*½) 30 min (75ep B&W; 1960–1962 NBC) Western** *with Clu Gulager as William "Billy the Kid" Bonney and Barry Sullivan as Sheriff Pat Garrett*

There have been numerous versions of the life of Billy the Kid, the famed western outlaw of the 1870s, and this is a fairly loose attempt to play with the legend. According to history, Billy the Kid was captured by Sheriff Pat Garrett, Billy escaped (killing two deputies), and was tracked down and killed by Garrett. In *The Tall*

*Man,* the series ponders the question of what if history had been different and Billy had made a feeble effort to go straight after his first capture by Garrett. The Sheriff (whose great record in capturing criminals earned him the nickname "the Tall Man") is portrayed in this series as something of a big brother to Billy, trying to keep him out of trouble. As always, Billy the Kid is wild and we all know its just a matter of time before the two face each other at gunpoint.

Playing Billy is Clu Gulager, in his first TV series role. Gulager went on to play Sheriff Ryker on *The Virginian.*

**TALL TALES AND LEGENDS (***) 60 min (9ep at Fall 1988 Color; 1985– Showtime) Anthology** *with Shelley Duvall*

After creating and hosting the stupendous *Faerie Tale Theater,* talented actress Shelley Duvall takes the same idea to more modern folk tales (such as Annie Oakley, as portrayed by Jamie Lee Curtis). Much like that earlier series, *Tall Tales and Legends* contains great gobs of humor, top-of-the-line acting, and cheap but innovative sets. ■

**TALLAHASSEE 7000 (*½) 30 min (39ep B&W; 1959–1960 Syndication) Crime Drama** *with Walter Matthau as Lex Rogers*

Filmed on the usual minuscule TV syndication budget (on location in Florida), these grind-em-out formula adventures are worth a glance for Walter Matthau's lead role. The program title is yet another phone number to add to your TV rolodex, this one for the Miami Beach police—presumably to be used if you can't reach anyone at *Surfside 6.*

**TAMMY (*½) 30 min (26ep Color; 1965–1966 ABC) Situation Comedy** *with Debbie Watson as Tammy Tarleton, Denver Pyle as Mordecai Tarleton, Frank McGrath as Lucius Tarleton, Donald Woods as John Brent, and Dorothy Green as Lavinia Tate*

From a series of novels by Ricketts Summer and three films starring Debbie Reynolds and Sandra Dee, the character of Tammy was already popular with viewers before this TV adaptation arrived. For TV, Tammy (a winsome and love-minded lass in all her appearances) is portrayed as a Louisiana bayou orphan, raised by her grandfather Mordecai and Uncle Lucius. Now grown, she obtains a job as secretary to the fabulously wealthy John Brent. This position earns her an enemy in Lavinia Tate, who wanted the job for her daughter.

*Tammy* the series and Tammy the character are relentlessly chipper and bright. The plots are wafer thin, the personalities are cardboard, and the laughs are obvious. *Tammy* is not really bad enough to be interesting, but young girls may take a liking to the program. Four episodes were strung together in 1967 and released as a film, *Tammy and the Millionaire.*

**THE TAMMY GRIMES SHOW (*) 30 min (10ep Color; 1966 ABC) Situation Comedy** *with Tammy Grimes as Tammy Ward, Hiram Sherman as Simon Ward, Dick Sargent as Terrence Ward, and Maudie Prickett as Mrs. Ratchett*

Renowned as a musical comedy star from the Broadway stage (*The Unsinkable Molly Brown*), Tammy Grimes makes a rare and unsuccessful foray into TV in this series. She plays Tammy Ward, a madcap young heiress who is too young to control the fortune left to her. She must struggle with Uncle Simon, who controls the family funds, and her twin brother Terrence, who is a "square" and tries to thwart Tammy's plans to act recklessly. It's not worth watching.

**TANNER '88 (***) 30 min (11 ep & 60 min pilot Color; 1988 HBO) Political Satire** *with Michael Murphy as Jack Tanner, Cynthia Nixon as Alexandra "Alex" Tanner, and Pamela Reed as T. J. Cavanaugh*

Robert Altman put in some time as a TV director/producer in the 1950s and 1960s (*Bus Stop, Combat, the Gallant Men*) before becoming a popular but eccentric film director (*M*A*S*H, Nashville*). Garry Trudeau came to fame as the creator of the "Doonesbury" comic strip. Together in *Tanner '88,* this talented duo team up to parody the process of nominating presidential candidates.

Altman and Trudeau ably prick at many of the foibles of politicians, politics, and the media through this "mockumentary" of the 1988 Democratic presidential race. Shot on location in the big primary states (New Hampshire, California), and winding up at the 1988 Democratic National Convention in Atlanta, *Tanner '88* follows the fictional campaign of Jack Tanner. The make-believe candidate hustles for votes and bumps into real politicos (Bruce Babbitt, Kitty Dukakis). Michael Murphy (who appeared as a slimy political advisor in Altman's *Nashville*) is very presidential as Jack Tanner. As with many of Altman's recent projects, *Tanner '88* fluctuates between greatness and self-indulgence, but is almost always worth watching.

**TARGET (*½) 30 min (38ep B&W; 1957–1958 Syndication) Drama Anthology** *with Adolphe Menjou as host*

Dapper, conservative Adolphe Menjou (*The Front Page*) acts as host to a passable collection of tales of personal drama.

**TARGET (*½) 60 min (22ep Color; 1977–1978 UK BBC) Police Drama** *with Patrick Mower as Steve Hackett and Vivien Heilbroh as Louise Colbert*

Steve Hackett is the deputy chief of a special police unit handling crimes in the Hampshire area of England.

**TARGET: THE CORRUPTORS (*½) 60 min (35ep B&W; 1961–1962 ABC) Newspaper Drama** *with Stephen McNally as Paul Marino and Robert Harland as Jack Flood*

Reporter as detective is the theme here as investigative newspaper reporter Paul Marino (and his undercover buddy Jack Flood) expose criminals in high and low places.

**TARZAN** (**½) **60 min (57ep Color; 1966–1968 NBC) Adventure** *with Ron Ely as Tarzan and Manuel Padilla, Jr. as Jai*

A rather civilized version of the King of the Jungle. There is no "Me Tarzan, You Jane" dialogue here. This series follows the story of Lord Greystoke farther along the Edgar Rice Burroughs time line. Though raised in the jungle as a child, Tarzan has been back to civilization for formal schooling and now returns to the vines by his own choice, equipped to deal with both worlds as it becomes necessary. Tarzan just happens to prefer the jungle and feels a sense of duty to protect it from poachers and other interlopers.

At times, this show is more like the jungle doctor series, *Daktari,* than the traditional swinging jungle adventures of the more familiar Tarzan movies. There are cute animal scenes, jeeps rushing about, and civilized discussions between Tarzan and his latest jungle visitors. He has a young native ward, Jai,and together they enjoy spending time with the creatures of the wild, especially Tarzan's old chimp friend, Cheetah. (Oddly, Jane is nowhere to be found in this series.) There are also plenty of action scenes, with many stunts done by star Ron Ely himself. (For the famous yell, though, they did go back to the original source and used a recording of Johnny Weissmuller in the role.) This Tarzan may be safe to bring home to a formal dinner, but he's still the man responsible for protecting the jungle from its greatest enemy, man. And he gladly takes on that task because he respects (even prefers) life in the wild over any of the alternatives he's seen.

**TATE** (*) **30 min (13ep B&W; 1960 NBC) Western** *with David McLean as Tate and Patricia Breslin as Jessica Jackson.*

On the outer fringes of gimmick-oriented series from the western glut of the late 1950s is *Tate,* the tale of the one-armed gunfighter. Tate (no first name) had an arm crippled in the Civil War, and now with his bad arm sheathed in leather, Tate roams the West. He uses his good arm to shoot people.

**TATTINGER'S/NICK AND HILLARY** (***) **60 min & 30 min (13ep: nine 60 min & four 30 min Color; 1988–1989 NBC) Drama & Comedy** *with Stephen Collins as Nick Tattinger, Blythe Danner as Hillary Tattinger, Jerry Stiller as Sid Wilbur, Mary Beth Hurt as Sheila Brady, Roderick Cook as Louis Chatham, Yusef Bulos as Chef Alphonse, Simon Jones as Norman Asher, Patrice Colihan as Nina Tattinger, Chay Lentin and Jessica Prunel as Winnifred "Rocco" Tattinger, and Chris Elliott as Spin*

Halfway through the second episode, this series makes its first affectionate continuity connection to *St. Elsewhere* (a real estate salesman turns out to be the cousin of Doctor Elliot Axelrod). It's an understandable nod by *Tattinger's* creators to the tremendous reputation of their previous series association. Fortunately this tale of a struggling but high-class New York restaurant also displays other similarities just as quickly: a strong cast, excellent scripts, respect for the characters, a feel for authentic dialogue, and an affection for occasionally outrageous plot twists. For instance, you can bet that moments after they nailed down the premise, somebody came up with the idea of having a customer die while waiting for service.

Despite the elegant setting, *Tattinger's* also resembles *St. Elsewhere* in another important way: It's about a once proud institution teetering on the brink. In this case, a brief period of mismanagement has put Tattinger's restaurant deeply in the red, a situation that Nick Tattinger must deal with upon resuming ownership and control. (He had given up the business to live in Europe after being shot and severely wounded by a drug dealer, but once back in New York he finds his old love impossible to resist.) So even if he does a perfect job managing, the business will barely stay solvent.

Though the idea of drama at a restaurant (other than Mel's Diner) may sound rather limited, the writers and performers prove equal to the task, actually setting a great deal of the action outside the hardwood walls of Tattinger's. Stephen Collins is particularly good as the undeniably heroic Nick Tattinger. Not so much a father figure as a concerned older brother, he goes to bat in a variety of settings (from a cab barn to city hall) not only for his family, friends, and employees but for total strangers. In another guise (long underwear, superpowers) he could easily pass for a mythic defender of the downtrodden. Instead he has to content himself with small victories in everyday life.

Fortunately he has his share. Though his two daughters (Nina and Winnifred) live with his ex-wife, Hillary (smartly played by Blythe Danner), he's quite involved in their lives—and Hillary's, for that matter (she's co-owner of the business). Their relationship is delightfully adult and affectionate, with the chance of reconciliation always a tantalizing possibility. He also has a reservoir of good will throughout the city, which he taps for everyone, sometimes even for himself.

With a kitchen, bar, and dining area to staff, there's plenty of performing room for the program's large cast, including standout spots by Jerry Stiller as assistant manager Sid, Rob Morrow as Jersey-born bartender Marco, and Mary Beth Hurt as the talented but independent chef Sheila, attempting to enjoy New York City as much as she loved the Colorado Rockies. The restaurant setting also allows for a host of cameo walk-ons (including real-life Broadway producers and writers, New York restauranteurs, basketball players, and performers such as Arlene Francis, Susan Saint James, Jane Curtin, and pianist Bobby Short). Of course, a real *St. Elsewhere*–style casting coup would be a dinner party (in character) with Clifford Huxtable, J. C. Wiatt, Molly Dodd, Rob and Laura Petrie, Danny Williams, and Kate and Allie, with Woody Allen on clarinet. Well, like the natives always say, "It could only happen in New York."

Despite all its good points, *Tattinger's* ran into ratings problems almost immediately upon release. After only nine hour-long episodes aired, the producers reworked the premise into a snazzier half-hour format (which also failed to score well). In *Nick and Hillary*, Hillary revamps the stately old restaurant into a trendy New York night spot while Nick is away in Brazil (unsuccessfully pursuing their thieving accountant). Nick and Hillary *really* have to make the place work upon his return because it is essentially the only asset they have.

Overall, the half-hour package is an effective switch, allowing the series to emphasize the comic elements a bit more. Most of the key characters carry over, with *Late Night with David Letterman* veteran Chris Elliott joining the group as Spin, a far-out maitre d'. Reflecting the producers' incessant interest in pop culture in-jokes, Spin's assistant is a mysteriously silent Charles Addams-ish woman named Marty (played by Anna Levine)—thus making the duo Spin and Marty (which also happen to be the names of the lead characters in a *Mickey Mouse Club* adventure serial from the 1950s).

**TAXI** (***½) **30 min (114ep Color; 1978–1983 ABC & NBC) Situation Comedy** *with Judd Hirsch as Alex Reiger/Rieger, Danny DeVito as Louie De Palma, Tony Danza as Tony Banta, Marilu Henner as Elaine Nardo, Andy Kaufman as Latka Gravas, Carol Kane as Simka Gravas, Jeff Conaway as Bobby Wheeler, Randall Carver as John Burns, and Christopher Lloyd as Reverend Jim Ignatowski*

The premise is simple: the day-to-day lives of the cabbies at New York City's Sunshine Cab Company. Most of them are part-time and would rather be doing something else, but until their individual dreams come farther along, they make the best of their time on the street and in the garage, building friendships in both settings.

And that's it. Of course, what makes this series something special is the on-screen and off-screen talent executing the setup. The actors come with impressive credentials and for the most part the product is superb. Series creators James L. Brooks, Stan Daniels, David Davis, and Ed. Weinberger (all former *Mary Tyler Moore Show* producers) carefully nurture a wide range of scripts, ranging from broad silliness to warm, quiet humor. The performers run the gamut in the same way: the spaced-out Reverend Jim, the other-worldly Latka Gravas, the hot and hungry Tony Banta, the aspiring actor Bobby Wheeler, the quietly committed Elaine Nardo, and the stoic Alex Reiger (also spelled Rieger in some episodes). They handle their characters quite well, and occasionally cross-type, with disheveled Jim sometimes the wisest of the bunch or rock-solid Alex flipping out.

And then there's Louie. This vehicle helped put Danny DeVito's patented "selfish son-of-a-bitch" character on the map. As the dispatcher, he goes about his job totally self-absorbed. He's demanding, manipulative, unscrupulous—and a joy to watch. Louie is absolutely true to himself, so even in a soft, vulnerable moment (as when he's courting Zena Sherman, played by DeVito's real-life wife, Rhea Perlman), he will stop at nothing to get his way. Sure, he should get his comeuppance (often he does), but you can't help but enjoy the unbridled energy of the character. When Louie's on-camera, *Taxi* really sizzles.

DeVito, of course, went on to play similar types in such theatrical feature films as *Romancing the Stone, The Jewel of the Nile,* and *Ruthless People.* The extracurricular credits for the other *Taxi* cast members include Christopher Lloyd in *Back to the Future* and *Who Framed Roger Rabbit?,* Tony Danza as the lead in *Who's the Boss?*, Andy Kaufman in a wide variety of oddball performance specials (this is the man who took his audience out for cookies and milk after a show), and Judd Hirsch in *Ordinary People* and *Dear John.* And the basic behind-the-scenes creative team went on to another working-class setting, the bar life of *Cheers,* bringing along Rhea Perlman as Carla.

**TEACHERS ONLY** (**) **30 min (21ep Color; 1982–1983 NBC) Situation Comedy** *with Lynn Redgrave as Diana Swanson, Norman Fell as Ben Cooper, Adam Arkin as Michael Dreyfuss, Van Nessa Clarke as Gwen Edwards, Teresa Ganzel as Samantha "Sam" Keating, and Tim Reid as Michael Horne*

Lynn Redgrave, part of the noted English Redgrave family of actors (daughter of Sir Michael, sister of Vanessa), is mostly wasted in this mild effort of presenting high school from the teachers' point of view. Most of the action occurs in the teacher's lounge, hence the title. The teachers spend a lot of time bitching about the students and the administration. Norman Fell, the sour Stanley Roper of *Three's Company,* is the sour principal.

The first seven episodes of *Teachers Only* have Redgrave's character as an English teacher in an inner-city Los Angeles high school (Millard Fillmore High). Afterward, the series is radically altered. The setting is moved to Wilson High in Brooklyn, Redgrave's character becomes a guidance counselor, and Normal Fell still plays the principal.

**THE TED KNIGHT SHOW** (*) **30 min (6ep Color; 1978 CBS) Situation Comedy** *with Ted Knight as Roger Dennis, Normann Burton as Burt Dennis, Thomas Leopold as Winston Dennis, and Iris Adrian as Dottie*

After seven years of playing airhead TV newscaster Ted Baxter on *The Mary Tyler Moore Show,* Ted Knight moved on to his own series. Unfortunately it's quite a drop from the famed Moore half hour to this drivel, produced by Lowell Ganz and Mark Rothman (*Busting Loose*). Knight plays Roger Dennis, a character not unlike Ted Baxter, in that both are overtly suave but actually overhyper bumblers. Dennis runs a swank Manhattan escort service financed by his brother Burt. Most of the activity features Dennis surrounding himself with a bevy of beauties and acting befuddled around Burt. The laughs are cheap and the pretty girls are forgettable. Knight was better in *Too Close for Comfort* (which for a while was also called *The Ted Knight Show*). This series is an outgrowth from Ganz and Rothman's *Busting Loose,* where one of the characters worked for the escort service run by Roger Dennis.

**TELEPHONE TIME (*) 30 min (78ep B&W; 1956–1958 CBS & ABC) Drama Anthology** *with John Nesbitt and Dr. Frank Baxter as hosts*

This 1950s anthology series at first dramatizes the stories of author/host John Nesbitt, but later moves on to the works of other writers.

**TELEVISION (***½) 60 min (13ep Color; 1985 UK Granada) and (8ep Color; 1988 US PBS) Documentary**

There are two versions of this exhaustive combination of background history, critical comments, interviews, rare archives footage, and ruminations on what it all means. The original aired in 1985 in Britain, with a shorter Stateside adaptation following a few years later, incorporating new material specifically geared toward American viewers (including narration by Edwin Newman).

The problem faced by both is simple: How do you begin to get a handle on a force that touches nearly every aspect of Western culture yet is still less than a century old? It would have been like trying to evaluate the importance of movable type to fifteenth-century civilization while the ink was still drying on the first run of books. Yet, television has been so quickly and thoroughly incorporated into everyday life that attempting to describe a world without instant global communication begins to sound like science fiction. But you have to start somewhere, and this series marks an excellent beginning.

The truly essential segments fall under the heading "The Race to Invent Television" (with the only episode shown virtually unchanged in both versions of the series), following technical developments from the world of dedicated independent inventors to the corporate and government-sponsored breakthroughs that become the standards used in the national television networks. Some of the old footage and photos demonstrate just how thorough the research for this project was, offering looks at experimental pre–World War II broadcasts throughout the world. This footage is an important reminder that for the longest time content was irrelevant as scientists worked on making the concept of pictures through the air a reality.

Once the technical miracle was in place, people on both sides of the Atlantic have had to decide what to do with it. In attempting to follow those twists and turns, *Television* runs into the inevitable problem of any survey history, the necessity of reducing the subject matter into highlight clips and bits. Lacking a one- or two-year-long weekly series (which could provide time for much more depth on particular subjects ranging from *Playhouse 90* to *Moonlighting* to Edward R. Murrow), it does a respectable job of covering such broad topics as comedy, drama, news, and commercials. If the conclusions don't seem to break any new ground, can we really say we expected them to? This is Television 101, with further studies to follow.

Ironically viewers in both Britain and the United States would probably end up getting a better feel for their respective television systems simply by watching the versions of this series produced for the *other* country. Stateside viewers in particular would not only get to see clips from series never aired here but they would have a chance to see some of our favorite programs through another collective set of eyes. Sounds like a great pledge week double-feature.

**TELEVISION PARTS, MICHAEL NESMITH IN (***) 30 min (8ep Color; 1985 NBC) Comedy-Variety** *with Michael Nesmith, John Hobbs, and Donna Ruppert*

Michael Nesmith will forever be best known as one of *The Monkees* (the one with, yes, the wool hat). However, he went on from that prefabricated series to turn out some fine country-rock albums in the 1970s and to pioneer the music video format (his music/comedy production *Elephant Parts* won the first Grammy Award for videos in 1982). *Television Parts,* his effort to bring an avant-garde view of TV comedy to a larger audience, is a wonderful experiment that, like most experiments, succeeds in some aspects and fails in others. Teamed up with producer Ken Kragen (from various Kenny Rogers and Pat Paulsen TV specials), Nesmith combines standard music videos with weird short comedy bits (some, such as "Five Second Theater," are quite short). The comedy goes from spectacular (Lois Bromfield's "Sorority Girls from Hell"), through innovative (early TV appearances from Whoopi Goldberg and Garry Shandling), all the way to boring and silly. All in all, *Television Parts* is an acquired taste that will provide rich rewards for those willing to try something different. Highlights of the series were issued on two video cassettes issued by Nesmith's Pacific Arts video label.

**TEMPERATURE'S RISING (*½) 30 min (46ep Color; 1972–1974 ABC) Situation Comedy** *with James Whitmore as Dr. Vincent Campanelli, Paul Lynde as Dr. Paul Mercy, Cleavon Little as Dr. Jerry Noland, Joan Van Ark as Nurse Annie Carlisle, Nancy Fox as Nurse Ellen Turner, John Dehner as Dr. Charles Claver, Sudie Bond as Martha Mercy, and Alice Ghostley as Edwina Moffitt*

In version one of this series (the first twenty-four episodes), James Whitmore plays the voice of reason (chief of surgery Vincent Campanelli) at a Washington hospital, attempting to keep his easily distracted staff concentrating on their jobs. Cleavon Little is his number one nemesis, a fast-talking intern (Jerry Noland) with an affection for gambling—especially taking side bets from the staff and patients. For version two (dubbed *The New Temperature's Rising*), Whitmore is replaced by Paul Lynde as a cheapskate administrator (Paul Mercy) running the hospital under the watchful eye of its owner, his mother (Martha Mercy). For the last few episodes, mom disappears and Paul's sister, Edwina, helps him take care of the place. Only Cleavon Little's character sticks around from beginning to end.

But it's hard to imagine why many viewers would remain that long. This is a noisy but hollow package with dull plots and tired jokes. It's the kind of comedy mocked in the P. A. announcements of the original *M*A*S*H* theatrical film: "Watch as the madcap crew of doctors and patients . . . cut and stitch their way . . . to your heart . . . and your funnybone."

**TEMPLE HOUSTON** **(*½) 60 min (26ep & 60 min pilot B&W; 1963–1964 NBC) Western** *with Jeffrey Hunter as Temple Houston and Jack Elam as George Taggart*

Loosely (very loosely) based on the exploits of the son of Texas general Sam Houston, *Temple Houston* has the lawyer/gunfighter son roaming the Southwest in the 1880s. He is equally willing to defend a case as he is to engage in a shootout.

The pilot for *Temple Houston,* called *The Man from Galveston*, is quite different from the series. The star is the same, Jeffrey Hunter, but his character is named Timothy Higgins, and is no relation to Sam Houston. Hunter went directly from *Temple Houston* to star in the original failed pilot for *Star Trek* ("The Cage"), where he played Capt. Christopher Pike.

**TEN WHO DARED** **(**½) 60 min (10ep Color; 1977 Syndication) Documentary** *with Anthony Quinn as host*

The lives of ten famous explorers from history (including Christopher Columbus, Francisco Pizzaro, and Roald Amundsen) are dramatized, one per week, in this British-produced series.

**TENAFLY** **(**½) 90 min (6ep Color; 1973–1974 NBC) Detective Drama** *with James McEachin as Harry Tenafly, Lillian Lehman as Ruth Tenafly, Paul Jackson as Herb Tenafly, and David Huddleston as Lt. Sam Church*

Here's a twist. Harry Tenafly is a happily married Los Angeles detective who goes home to his wife at night, enjoys spending time with his son, and even mows his own very suburban lawn. What's more, these things are included in the stories, just a notch behind the latest murder mystery. A most unusual approach to a crime series from the *Columbo* creative team of Richard Levinson and William Link, who capped the package by also deciding to go against the "bad-ass black dude" cliché of the era and make this champion of middle-class values a sane and sensible black man. It's a low-key package that eschews the era's topical polemics and therefore plays nicely, if quietly, in a rerun package.

**TENDER IS THE NIGHT** **(**½) 60 min (5ep Color; 1985 Showtime) Drama** *with Mary Steenburgen as Nicole and Peter Strauss as Dick Diver*

F. Scott Fitzgerald's story about a mentally unstable woman who falls in love with her psychiatrist is ably adapted here for TV. Miniseries star Peter Strauss (*Rich Man, Poor Man*) and film star Mary Steenburgen (*Cross Creek*) play the two leads.

**TENKO** **(***½) 60 min (30ep & 2 hr sequel Color; 1981 & 1982 & 1984 UK BBC) Drama** *with Ann Bell as Marion Jefferson, Stephanie Beacham as Rose Millar, Renee Asherson as Sylvia Ashburton, Burt Kwouk as Capt. Yamauchi, Claire Oberman as Kate Norris, Joanne Hole as Sally Markham, Jeananne Crowley as Nellie Keene, Maya Woolfe as Gerda, Elizabeth Chambers as Mrs. Van Meyer, Stephanie Cole as Beatrice Mason, Emily Bolton as Christina Campbell, and Louise Jameson as Blanche Simmons*

Whoever survives a war gets to write the history. And if you're on the winning side, your version will probably become accepted as fact. This fascinating and effective World War II drama gives us a chance to see those rules of life in action, presenting the story of a women's prisoner of war camp in the Pacific from before the beginning until after the end. Unlike most such tales, we get to follow both the motivation and the ultimate consequences of some life-or-death decisions, judging for ourselves whether they were justified.

The thirty episodes of *Tenko* break into three runs of ten, first aired by the BBC in 1981, 1982, and 1984. Though they're all part of a continuing story, each section has its special emphasis. In the first, we see a traditional prisoner of war drama setup, beginning with the characters interacting in Singapore. All their lifelong prejudices and assumptions are intact, with the lines between various social circles very clearly drawn. However, the war soon catches up to them, and they find themselves dealing with a new set of rules, as the men, women, and children are split and sent into separate prison camps run by the Japanese. There everyone must prove themselves daily, coping with marches, chores, and uncertainty. Still, at first there's an undercurrent of discovery on both sides (the captors and the prisoners). Everyone seems to feel that the larger events of the war (totally outside their control) will settle down soon. In the meantime, they have to make the best of this situation.

The second batch of ten episodes begins more than a year later. Guarded optimism has been replaced by the need to survive, and hope of rescue has been replaced with the fear of dying in captivity. For everyone the camp has become a totally insulated, self-referential world where the most trivial actions take on exaggerated significance. At the same time, behavior that the outside world would normally judge abhorrent (suicide, for instance) becomes a real option in captivity. Keep a close eye on the actions of both the prisoners and the Japanese captors (especially camp commander Yamauchi), because they will be referred to constantly in the last ten episodes. (In fact, if you have the spare tape, try to keep the first twenty parts handy for a second viewing.)

The last ten episodes begin at the prison camp, but shift with surprising speed into postcaptivity life. This shift is done very effectively, with the prospect of freedom coming as a jolt to the characters on both sides. But soon the prisoners discover that there's an outside world demanding an accounting and waiting to render judgment. The problem is that they find explaining their experiences to anyone else virtually impossible. And when they do speak, actions that seemed clear and justified as a part of camp life suddenly take on new, sometimes sinister, hues.

Though the last batch of episodes seem a bit rambling if you haven't seen any of the camp segments, in the context of the entire series they are essential. If you have the time, *Tenko* is definitely worth following from beginning to end. And if you're a curious completist, keep an eye out for a two-hour TV-movie from 1985, *Tenko Reunion*, set in Singapore in 1950—though be forewarned that it's played more as a period-piece murder mystery.

**TENSPEED AND BROWN SHOE (**½) 60 min (13ep & 2 hr pilot Color; 1980 ABC) Detective Drama** *with Ben Vereen as E. L. "Tenspeed" Turner and Jeff Goldblum as Lionel "Brown Shoe" Whitney*

The two-hour pilot is a Stephen J. Cannell production at its very best, with fast-paced action (lots of great car chases), a sense of humor, and leads that click. Ben Vereen and Jeff Goldblum are perfect foils to each other as the unlikely detective pair of "Tenspeed" Turner (the hustling but charming con man) and "Brown Shoe" Whitney (the well-to-do young stockbroker with fantasies of living in a Humphrey Bogart Sam Spade movie). Just standing there, the deadpan Goldblum and the expressive Vereen look like they come from different worlds. But together they ace their way through their initial case, and it's all gravy from there. Brown Shoe may not be sure just what hit him, but he's really more than happy to go along with his newfound partner.

Though subsequent stories sometimes get a bit silly (with titles such as "The Treasure of Sierra Madre Street" or "It's Easier to Pass an Elephant Through the Eye of a Needle Than a Bad Check in Bel Air"), they're certainly no worse than the mid-1960s tongue-in-cheek style of such programs as *The Man from U.N.C.L.E.* or *I Spy,* with plenty of banter in between the adventure. With such a small number of episodes, it's worth hanging around for the entire cycle.

Oddly, this series was very popular at the beginning of its original run, then quickly faded. Maybe it was ahead of its time. Or perhaps Cannell should have made the pair an unlikely male and female detective team named Maddie and David. In any case, the series obviously has a special place in his heart because more than seven years later he took the opportunity to bring back Ben Vereen's character of Tenspeed Turner for a brief stint in the *J. J. Starbuck* series.

**TESTAMENT OF YOUTH (***) 60 min (5ep Color; 1979 UK BBC) Drama** *with Cheryl Campbell as Vera Brittain, Rosalie Crutchley as Miss Penrose, Michael Troughton as Victor Richardson, Hazel Douglas as Aunt Florence, Rupert Frazer as Mr. Brittain, Joanna McCallum as Winifred, June Tobin as Mrs. Leighton, Jane Wenham as Mrs. Brittain, and Peter Woodward as Roland Leighton*

This excellent autobiographical account of a young nurse's experiences in World War I effectively mines two major themes: the growing sense of identity and self-assertiveness among women, and the devastating effects of that first World War. In both areas, there is almost a feeling of sudden shock, as the characters suddenly discover aspects of the world they hadn't really stopped to consider before.

Vera Brittain's involvement with the war effort comes soon after the heady early days of the action—when even upper middle-class people (such as her fiancé and her brother) volunteered, convinced that this war was going to be brief and easily won. But letters from the front describe a very different world, with soldiers mired in battles that seem to have only one outcome: casualties. She becomes a nurse, first on the homefront, then on the continent, also discovering that the war is a greater nightmare than she imagined.

*Testament of Youth* is actually only the first of several autobiographical books written by Vera Brittain, but the events of the subsequent titles are not included in this series. However, the story does spill over from the war into the growing suffragette movement and other actions of conscience, all effectively told from Vera's point of view. Thoroughly absorbing.

**TESTIMONY OF TWO MEN (**) (6hr miniseries Color; 1977 Syndication) Drama** *with David Birney as Jonathan Ferrier, David Huffman as Harald Ferrier, Linda Purl as Mavis Ferrier, William Shatner as Adrian Ferrier, and Tom Bosley as Dr. Louis Hedler*

Taylor Caldwell's novel of the Ferrier brothers, Jonathan and Harald, is presented as a standard soapy miniseries. Spanning the years from the Civil War to the turn of the century, the story follows Jonathan as he becomes a famous doctor and Harald as he becomes a wastrel playboy.

**TEXACO STAR THEATER** (***) **60 & 30 min (B&W; 1948–1953 & 1954–1955 NBC) Comedy-Variety** *with Milton Berle, Donald O'Connor, and Jimmy Durante as hosts*

An umbrella title for three different TV series, *Texaco Star Theater* was the original title of Milton Berle's seminal live TV variety show, the one that truly can be said to have launched television as a popular medium. The format is variety, and Berle is the host who gets involved with most of the skits. The comedy is very broad, almost slapstick, but the lack of sophistication is compensated for by the historical impact of the show. After Texaco ceased sponsoring Berle's show, Uncle Miltie went on for three more years (1953–1956) under different show titles (*The Buick Berle Show* and *The Milton Berle Show*).

In 1954, the *Texaco Star Theater* title was revived for one season as the overall name for a half-hour show that alternated each week between the comic antics of Jimmy Durante and the music and comedy of Donald O'Connor. These episodes are also known as *The Jimmy Durante Show* and *The Donald O'Connor Show*, respectively.

Some kinescope recordings of the Berle shows remain and have been packaged for syndication and videotape sale. ■

**THE TEXAN** (**) **30 min (8ep B&W; 1958–1960 CBS) Western** *with Rory Calhoun as Bill Longley*

Rugged, handsome, with a background as tough as many of the characters he played, Rory Calhoun appeared in several minor action and western films of the 1950s. In *The Texan*, a competent late 1950s western (which he co-produced), he plays roaming Texan gunfighter Bill Longley. Drifting about the lone star state in the 1870s, Longley always gets involved with someone's problems and usually engages in a shoot-out. ■

**TEXAS JOHN SLAUGHTER** (**½) **60 min (15ep B&W; 1958–1961 ABC) Western** *with Tom Tryon as John Slaughter, Betty Lynn as Viola Slaughter, Brian Corcoran as Willie Slaughter, and Harry Carey, Jr. as Ben Jenkins*

Loosely based on the real-life exploits of John Slaughter, a Civil War era jack-of-all-trades, this series is set in Texas in the 1880s. Slaughter is a local Texas Ranger turned sheriff. Originally aired over three seasons of *Walt Disney Presents, Texas John Slaughter* is a good chance to catch handsome Tom Tryon before he starred in the hit 1963 film *The Cardinal.* Tryon later turned to writing novels, such as *The Other* (which was turned into a 1972 film he produced). ■

**THE TEXAS WHEELERS** (***) **30 min (13ep Color; 1974–1975 ABC) Situation Comedy** *with Jack Elam as Zack Wheeler, Gary Busey as Truckie Wheeler, Mark Hamill as Doobie Wheeler, Karen Oberdiear as Boo Wheeler, Tony Becker as T. J. Wheeler, and Lisa Eilbacher as Sally*

A celebration of pigheaded independence, from the opening theme song by John Prine ("Illegal Smile," an ode to getting high on marijuana) to the chosen lifestyles of Zack (head of the Wheeler clan) and his self-sufficient children. Of course, the kids almost have to be independent because their dad's favorite pastimes are getting drunk and avoiding work. They don't have a mom so they are left scrambling for cash on their own. Sometimes they even find themselves casting envious eyes on their old man's willingness to abandon responsibility. In fact, sixteen-year-old Doobie can hardly wait to leave school and hit the moonshine himself.

This venture is a very unusual one from MTM productions, probably better described as a comedy-drama than as a sitcom. It has a fascinating cast, including veteran film bad guy Jack Elam, Gary Busey (a few years away from *The Buddy Holly Story*), and a pre–*Star Wars* Mark Hamill. This family may not be the most wholesome one you'll ever meet, but it may turn out to be one of the most intriguing. Definitely worth digging up.

**THAT GIRL** (**) **30 min (136ep Color; 1966–1971 ABC) Situation Comedy** *with Marlo Thomas as Ann Marie, Ted Bessell as Don Hollinger, Lew Parker as Lou Marie, Rosemary DeCamp as Helen Marie, Dabney Coleman as Dr. Leon Bessemer, Arlene Golonka as Margie Myer, Morty Gunty as Sandy Stone, Ruth Buzzi as Margie "Pete" Peterson, Bernie Kopell as Jerry Myer (a.k.a. Jerry Bauman), and George Carlin as George Lester*

Time has tarnished the glitter that once adorned *That Girl.* In the late 1960s, *That Girl* was trumpeted as a progressive harbinger of the brave new world of TV sitcoms where women would be presented in a more independent, respectful light, rather than as suburban matriarchs. The program was also championed as a trendsetter in TV's appeal to the new, younger, hipper, postwar generation—the one that would change the nation's tastes.

In the cold, cruel light of reflection, *That Girl* looks like another silly mid-1960s sitcom that is innocuous enough not to offend but bland enough to be boring after a few episodes. The faint banner of relevancy present in the program has yellowed so that only historians can tell that it is anything other than middle-of-the-road pap.

Marlo Thomas (daughter of Danny) plays bright, perky Ann Marie, a young woman who has just left the family nest and is on her own, hoping to turn into a star actress. Meanwhile, she makes a living in Manhattan by taking various menial jobs. Right off the bat, she hooks up with clean-cut young publishing executive Don Hollinger, and the pair become steady daters. The sanitized, pristine romance of Ann and Don is much closer to the *Father Knows Best* era than the more earthy affairs of the later *Mary Tyler Moore/Rhoda* era. Don Hollinger, in fact, could well be the nerdiest, geekiest leading man in 1960s TV. His button-down personality and tame demeanor rival the square antics of Darrin Stephens, husband on *Bewitched.* Hollinger leaves viewers befuddled as to why a lively, exciting girl like Ann would tie herself down with such a dolt. It is intriguing to note that it is not even until the start of the fourth and final season that Don finally gets around to proposing to Ann. They never do get married.

What saves *That Girl* from utter banality is the sprightly action, lively production, and excellent supporting cast. Sam Denoff and Bill Persky, writers on the old *Dick Van Dyke show,* are the producers. Seasoned troupers such as Arlene Golonka and Morty Gunty are in the cast, along with up-and-coming talent such as Ruth Buzzi (pre–*Laugh-In*), Bernie Kopell (pre–*Love Boat*), Cloris Leachman (pre-*Phyllis*), Dabney Coleman (in his first TV series role, pre–*Mary Hartman, Buffalo Bill,* and *"Slap" Maxwell*) and George Carlin (pre-long hair). Star Marlo Thomas is a bit strident here, even before meeting future husband Phil Donahue. Taken in small doses, *That Girl* can fill thirty minutes without much discomfort.

**THAT WAS THE WEEK THAT WAS (***) 30 min (plus 60 min pilot Color; 1964–1965 NBC) Comedy** *with Elliot Reid and David Frost as hosts, and Nancy Ames, Henry Morgan, Phyllis Newman, Buck Henry, Alan Alda, and Burr Tillstrom's Puppets*

A landmark in American TV comedy, *That Was the Week That Was* came from an equally irreverent British TV series of the same name. Produced live by noted Broadway producer Leland Hayward, the American version (nicknamed *TW3*) pioneered the concept of political satire on network television some years before the Smothers Brothers and *Laugh-In.* A lot of the show's bite will mean nothing to modern viewers, unless they were alive during the LBJ (Lyndon B. Johnson) era or immersed themselves beforehand in the catch phrases and topical issues of the mid-1960s. Not until *Saturday Night Live* a decade later would network TV be so topical. Prime time has never topped this show for punch and poignancy.

Beware of cheap imitations. There are two inferior *That Was the Year That Was* specials (from 1972 and 1976) and a one-hour *That Was the Week That Was* rivival pilot from 1985 (with alumnus David Frost as host) that do not measure up to the original. For TV trivia buffs, the original one-hour *TW3* pilot (which aired just before President Kennedy's assassination in 1963) is quite a rarity, and has Henry Fonda as host.

**THAT'S HOLLYWOOD (**½) 30 min (74ep & two 30 min pilots Color; 1977–1982 Syndication) Documentary** *with Tom Bosley as host*

Jack Haley, Jr., who directed the hit 1974 film *That's Entertainment,* brings the same concept of a noncontroversial, surface eye view of Hollywood history to TV in this series. *Happy Days* dad Tom Bosley is narrator of the best of the films of the 20th Century-Fox studios.

Tony Franciosa narrates one of the two 1976 pilots.

**THAT'S INCREDIBLE (½) 60 min (106ep Color) (1980–1984 ABC)/INCREDIBLE SUNDAY (½) 60 min (16ep Color; 1988–1989 ABC) Human Interest** *with John Davidson, Cathy Lee Crosby, Fran Tarkenton, and Cristina Ferrare as hosts*

Chewing gum for the eyes. *National Enquirer* of the air. Tabloid TV. All three critical clichés aptly describe this flimsy series. It panders to everyone's desire to watch people risk their lives or good health in order to perform some unusual or outlandish stunt, in hopes of garnering a moment of celebrity status. The vacuous, pretty hosts introduce short segments concerning daredevils, self-styled wizards, and iron men. Several people were hurt trying to perform the stunts, and several performers were later unmasked as frauds. The content is so vapid that it is not worth getting upset about the show's popularity, but this is truly TV at its lowest common denominator.

*That's Incredible* comes from Alan Landsburg, who also produced *In Search Of . . . , Life's Most Embarrassing Moments, People Do the Craziest Things,* and *Those Amazing Animals* (detect a trend there?). In 1988, the format was briefly revived as *Incredible Sunday,* with former co-host John Davidson teamed up with newcomer Cristina Ferrare.

*That's Incredible* has also been syndicated in 165 thirty-minute cut-downs of the original hour episodes.

**THAT'S LIFE (**½) 60 min (26ep Color; 1968–1969 ABC) Musical-Comedy** *with Robert Morse as Robert Dickson and E. J. Peaker as Gloria Quigley Dickson*

A rare attempt to turn the musical-variety format into a continuing light comedy series focusing primarily on two characters, lovebirds Robert and Gloria. Over the course of the series they go through courtship, marriage, setting up their new home, dealing with the in-laws, having a child, and so forth, with these broadstroke plots punctuated with symbolic musical numbers, celebrity drop-in quips, full-fledged monologues, and assorted sketches. It's all best appreciated today as a nostalgic look at courting rituals of the late 1960s, complete with some of the era's showbiz celebrities.

**THAT'S MY BOY (*½) 30 min (B&W; 1954–1955 CBS) Situation Comedy** *with Eddie Mayehoff as Jack Jackson, Gil Stratton, Jr., as Jack Jackson, Jr., and Rochelle Hudson as Alice Jackson*

This show takes the premise from a fitfully amusing

1951 Jerry Lewis film (also starring Eddie Mayehoff) and stretches it into a series as a former college athlete, "Jarrin" Jack Jackson, attempts to relive his glory days by pushing his bookish son (a freshman in college) to take an interest in more physical activities. A painful setup, with either the dad or the son guaranteed to look foolish—usually, it's the dad.

**THAT'S MY LINE** **(*) 60 min (10ep Color; 1980–1981 CBS) Human Interest** *with Bob Barker as host*

Only tangentially related to the classic live TV game show *What's My Line, That's My Line* is closer to the silly trend of "reality" shows of the early 1980s (*Real People, That's Incredible*). Mark Goodson and Bill Todman, producers of *What's My Line,* rip off the public's goodwill associated with the old show to hype this pointless series focusing on odd people with oddball occupations. Champion TV huckster Bob Barker (*Truth or Consequences, Price Is Right*) serves as host.

**THAT'S MY MAMA** **(*½) 30 min (37ep Color; 1974–1975 ABC) Situation Comedy** *with Clifton Davis as Clifton Curtis, Theresa Merritt as Eloise "Mama" Curtis, Ed Bernard and Theodore Wilson as Earl Chambers, Lynne Moody and Joan Pringle as Tracy Curtis Taylor, and Ted Lange as Junior*

One of the gang of ethnic-drenched sitcoms of the mid-1970s, *That's My Mama* tries to have it both ways. It tries to be progressive by presenting modern, educated, middle-class blacks in nondemeaning roles, such as lead character Clifton Curtis, a twenty-five-year-old bachelor who takes over his late father's barber shop business. Meanwhile, the show relies on slight variations of old standby black figures, such as the domineering big mama (the title character, who tries to run son Clifton's life) and the jive hipster (Junior).

*That's My Mama,* like most of the other ethnic sitcoms of its time, seems a bit loud and forced now. The show's producers, Allan Blye and Chris Bearde, also worked on *The Smothers Brothers Comedy Hour, The Sonny and Cher Comedy Hour,* and Bill Cosby's failed variety series *Cos.* Ted Lange, who plays the jive Junior, later played the far more circumspect bartender Isaac Washington on *The Love Boat.*

**THEN CAME BRONSON** **(*½) 60 min (26ep & 2 hr pilot Color; 1969–1970 NBC) Drama** *with Michael Parks as Jim Bronson*

*Then Came Bronson* was as close as TV got to transforming the film *Easy Rider* into a series. The only continuing character is Jim Bronson, who is directly out of the broody loner school of TV wanderers that previously turned up on *The Rebel* and *The Fugitive.* A promising, bright, young newspaper reporter, Bronson quits his job after his best pal commits suicide. He hops on his dead friend's motorcycle and takes off, in search of America and "The Meaning of Life". He sees a lot of the former and never discovers the latter. He does, however, come across an unending stream of people that he befriends, learns from, teaches, and leaves behind. The scripts are mediocre and dated and Michael Parks's acting is overly dour.

**THERESE RAQUIN** **(**½) 60 min (3ep Color; 1981 UK BBC) Drama** *with Kate Nelligan as Therese Raquin, Brian Cox as Laurent, Kenneth Cranham as Camille Raquin, Mona Washbourne as Madame Raquin, Richard Pearson as Michaud, Jenny Galloway as Suzanne Michaud, Timothy Bateson as Crivet, and Philip Bowen as Oliver Michaud*

They start out as three fairly likable people: Therese, her husband, and her husband's best friend, Laurent. Then Therese discovers that Laurent stirs passionate feelings within her that she's never quite felt before in her marriage. An adulterous affair quickly follows, then a murder scheme. The characters turn nasty, and the script focuses relentlessly on the consequences of their actions, both in personal guilt and in their own private passions. It's all based on an 1867 novel by Emile Zola (which generated considerable shock when first published), with the adaptation capturing both the seductive allure of the initial affair (complete with flashes of nudity and fervid bedroom writhings) and the final sense of justified retribution.

**THICKER THAN WATER** **(**½) 30 min (13ep Color; 1973 ABC) Situation Comedy** *with Julie Harris as Nellie Paine, Richard Long as Ernie Paine, Malcolm Atterbury as Jonas Paine, Jessica Myerson as Lily Paine, and Lou Fant as Walter Paine*

Many of the interesting sitcoms of the 1970s are U.S. versions of British comedies, and *Thicker Than Water* is part of this crowd. Based on the British series *Nearest and Dearest,* the Stateside show has elderly, crotchety, pickle tycoon Jonas Paine drag his two squabbling grown siblings back together, with greed as their motive. Jonas says that if middle-aged spinster Nellie and mid-thirties swinging bachelor Ernie can run the business together successfully for five years, they can become the owners. The two kids grumble and hiss and claw at each other, but the allure of the family fortune is too much to resist.

The concept is different enough and flexible enough to be appealing. The cast is worth watching. Star Julie Harris, mostly seen on Broadway, in films, and in quality TV drama anthologies, makes her first TV series appearance here. Richard Long has the playboy role perfected, having played similar roles in *Bourbon Street Beat* and *77 Sunset Strip.* Series producer Bob Banner has a lengthy resume of producing several hit variety shows (starring Garry Moore, Perry Como, and Dinah Shore).

**THE THIN MAN** **(**½) 30 min (72ep B&W; 1957–1959 NBC) Detective Drama** *with Peter Lawford as Nick Charles, Phyllis Kirk as Nora Charles, Nita Talbot as*

*Beatrice Dane (a.k.a. Blondie Collins), and Jack Albertson as Lt. Harry Evans*

Out of a Dashiell Hammett detective novel came six delightful "Thin Man" films from 1934 to 1947, starring William Powell and Myrna Loy. This heartfelt attempt to bring the popular concept to TV deserves a higher grade for effort than for execution.

As in the films, *The Thin Man* concerns the wealthy Manhattan socialite couple of Nick and Nora Charles. He is a former private eye who officially retired when he married Nora. She is a blithe spirit who always seems to get involved in some mystery that husband Nick can't resist investigating. Accompanying them is their small fox terrier Asta, who provides keen canine assistance in the sniffing department.

The concern here is not on complicated plots or moody atmospherics but in light, devil-may-care banter between the happily married couple who work together well. Unfortunately the TV series rarely reaches the airy heights of the films. Hollywood bon vivant Peter Lawford, in the second of his two TV series, is perfect as Nick. This same concept was later updated in series such as *McMillan and Wife* and *Hart to Hart.*

As with the *Pink Panther* series of films, the title character of the *Thin Man* films and TV series was not one of the lead actors but rather a minor figure in the original movie.

**THE THIRD MAN (**) 30 min (77ep B&W; 1960–1962 Syndication) Drama** *with Michael Rennie as Harry Lime and Jonathan Harris as Bradford Webster*

Graham Greene's tart novel about mysterious double-dealer Harry Lime was turned into a popular 1949 film starring Orson Welles aas the rarely seen Lime. In this joint U.K.-U.S. TV production, Lime is far more visible as a versatile private detective-type who travels the world, solving mysteries and undoing bad guys. Michael Rennie, making his one and only TV starring role here as Lime, is best known as the kind alien in *The Day the Earth Stood Still,* a 1951 sci-fi film classic. Jonathan Harris makes his first TV series appearance as Lime's assistant. He later went on to greater TV fame as the blustery Dr. Zachary Smith in *Lost in Space.*

**13 QUEENS BLVD. (*½) 30 min (8ep Color; 1979 ABC) Situation Comedy** *with Eileen Brennan as Felicia Winters, Jerry Van Dyke as Steven Winters, Marcia Rodd as Elaine Downing, Helen Page Camp as Mildred Capestro, and Susan Elliot as Annie Capestro*

Describing any sitcom starring Jerry Van Dyke as "adult" is clearly a contradiction in terms, yet that's what *13 Queens Blvd.* tries to be. The younger Van Dyke brother and talented actress Eileen Brennan play a long-married couple who reside in an apartment complex in the Queens borough of New York City. Their friends and neighbors always come by to discuss their innumerable problems. The humor is not very funny. The intended pathos is not very deep. Jerry Van Dyke is very out of his element (he seemed more at home in *My Mother the Car*). Producer Bud Yorkin (*Sanford and Son*) has done better.

**THIRTYSOMETHING (***) 60 min (37ep at Fall 1989 Color; 1987– ABC) Drama** *with Ken Olin as Michael Steadman, Mel Harris as Hope Steadman, Timothy Busfield as Elliot Weston, Patricia Wettig as Nancy Weston, Polly Draper as Ellyn, Melanie Mayron as Melissa Steadman, and Peter Horton as Gary Shepherd*

What happens when the generation that embraced such pat phrases as "Don't trust anyone over thirty" finds itself collectively past the "big three-o"? For starters, its members probably watch *thirtysomething.* Or live it. Probably both.

This series is a logical favorite of baby boomers, celebrating their continued fixation with themselves and their fascination with television as a reflection of their own lives. It's the suburban kids of *Leave It to Beaver* or *Father Knows Best* as they probably really would grow up, carefully nurtured by their parents, sent to college during the 1960s and 1970s, and landing in the adult world not quite ready to embrace that moniker. After all, mom and dad are the adults, aren't they? We're not our parents already, are we?

But they are, and this series does a good job focusing on one circle of those "thirtysomething" adults and how they cope with the day-to-day details of life with their families and with each other. Michael and Elliot are partners in their own ad agency, their wives are best friends, and they have several single friends (Gary, a professor at a nearby college; Michael's cousin, Melissa; and Hope's longtime pal, Ellyn). One important consideration for all of them is the state of marriage and parenting: Hope and Michael seem to be the perfect couple, looked at enviously by the other characters. Elliot and Nancy find they just can't seem to cope as well (in fact, they end up filing for divorce) while Ellyn, Gary, and Melissa wonder if maybe they really are missing something living the single life. Of course, Michael and Hope have insecurities of their own, but manage to pull through those rough spots (as when one of Michael's old flames turns up), apparently determined to make their marriage work.

No matter what their concerns, the characters of *thirtysomething* talk about them, constantly. In a way, this just reflects their background (well-educated people raised in an era almost obsessed with the concept of discussing everything to death), though at times these scenes definitely come off as self-indulgent and whiny. Contrary to the program's reputation, these characters are not free-spending set-in-life yuppies, but rather comfortable middle-class professionals, probably about as well off as the Nelsons on *Ozzie and Harriet,* the Andersons on *Father Knows Best,* or the Petries on *The Dick Van Dyke Show.* The difference with *thirtysomething* is that we get to see the scenes when mom and dad worry about paying for needed house repairs or grumble about getting up in the middle of the night to change the baby's diapers, along with discussions about their own expectations and self-images. While they do seem to spend an inordinate amount of time agonizing over relatively simple decisions, that's really more in comparison to the usual whiz-bang world of television comedy than to real life. Unfair as it may seem, most people spend more time fretting about mundane things in their personal routine than on the larger issues of society.

Oddly the series is at its best when simply focusing on such trivial scenes, with the characters coming across as quite effectively genuine—in a way, playing a lot like a married version of *The Days and Nights of Molly Dodd.* (Whether you'd ever like any of these people in real life is another question entirely.) When *thirtysomething* attempts to open up the action the results are mixed: a flashback story to the 1940s with Hope and Michael playing different characters works; a brief black and white restaging of *The Dick Van Dyke Show* doesn't.

Nonetheless, even if you can't stand baby boomers this show is definitely worth catching at least once (if only to confirm your longstanding opinions). Of course, if you are a thirtysomething, it's essential viewing as the ultimate home movie. Or as a peep through the neighbors' curtains.

**THIS IS ALICE (*) 30 min (39ep B&W; 1958–1959 Syndication) Situation Comedy** *with Patty Ann Gerrity as Alice Holliday, Tom Farrell as Mr. Holliday, Phyllis Coates as Mrs. Holliday, and Leigh Snowden as Betty Lou*

Something of a female version of *Dennis the Menace, This Is Alice* is all about a rambunctious nine-year-old girl living in Atlanta, a very unusual setting for a 1950s sitcom. As with many children from 1950s sitcoms, Alice is too cute for her own good.

**THIS IS YOUR LIFE (**½) 30 min (B&W & Color; 1952–1961 & 1971–1972 & 1983–1985 NBC & Syndication) Interview** *with Ralph Edwards and Joseph Campanella as hosts*

Ralph Edwards created a gold mine in 1948 when he began *This Is Your Life* on network radio. After a few years, the series moved to TV and began a lengthy, mostly live, run on NBC throughout the 1950s. Since then, it has popped up again and again in several revivals. The format has remained constant: the host (Edwards, almost exclusively) surprises studio guests (often a celebrity) by bringing them up onstage and reviewing their life. Long-separated or forgotten figures from the guest's past appear, usually resulting in tearful reunions. As long as there are new celebrities, the format can survive.

The only versions currently available consist of 52 episodes from the early 1970s, with Edwards as host, and 130 episodes from the mid-1980s, with Edwards producing but with Joseph Campanella as host. A few hour-long *This Is Your Life* specials, with Edwards once again as host, were produced in 1987. ■

**THIS MAN DAWSON (**) 30 min (39ep B&W; 1959–1960 Syndication) Police Drama** *with Keith Andes as Col. Frank Dawson*

This mild series concerns a former Marine Corps officer who becomes police chief in a big city. William Conrad, the corpulent actor who starred in *Cannon,* serves as producer.

**THIS OLD HOUSE (**½) 30 min (260ep at Fall 1989 Color; 1979– PBS) How-To Documentary** *with Bob Vila as host and Norm Abram as the master carpenter*

From its earliest days, television has been telling us how to do it. Cooking. Fishing. Household hints. Home repair.

For one thing, it's relatively easy to present. Just get people that look as if they know what they're doing, point the camera, and you're in business. There's even a built-in basic plot of sorts, complete with conflict and resolution: Will the cake rise? Will the fish bite? Will the stains disappear? (But of course!)

In 1979, Bob Vila expanded beyond those horizons to ask: Will we be able to completely redo "this old house" over in the next thirteen weeks? To no one's surprise (the show *was* on tape), he did it. But who could have predicted the results? In short order, Bob Vila became the Sir Kenneth Clark of the home renovation set. Only instead of inviting familiarity with the great art masters of Europe, he talked of shims, plumbing, dry wall, insulation, and joint compound.

Like Sir Kenneth, Bob makes it all seem accessible, even fun. He walks into a sorry-looking space, paces, and measures and gestures, goes off to confer with his associate, carpenter Norm Abram, then with the owners, and suddenly work begins. The homeowners put in as much sweat equity (work done themselves) as possible, hiring the necessary professionals to do more demanding jobs. Bob and Norm supply the expertise, along with on-the-spot guidance to get the owners started on something like nailing down a floor. (Did you ever notice, though, that Bob always seems to turn up just in time to hammer in that *last* nail?)

Because these are real houses with real owners who are investing real money in the project, it's easy to get caught up in the changes. As a result, people who don't even own a screwdriver tune in, though it's unlikely they'll ever attempt such a project themselves.

Over the years the series has increasingly emphasized the grunt work done by the owners between episodes, just in case some viewers were getting the impression that thirty minutes a week for three months is all you need to completely redo *your* old house. However, the program's biggest change came in the Fall of 1989 when the producers replaced Bob Vila with Steven Thomas (apparently due to Bob's many home repair commercials, which they began to see as a credibility conflict). ■

**THE THORN BIRDS (***) (10hr miniseries Color; 1983 ABC) Drama** *with Richard Chamberlain as Father Ralph deBricassart, Sydney Penny and Rachel Ward as Maggie Cleary, Barbara Stanwyck as Mary Carson, Jean Simmons as Fiona "Fee" Cleary, Christopher Plummer as Archbishop Contini-Verchese, Ken Howard as Rainer Hartheim, Richard Kiley as Paddy Cleary, and Bryan Brown as Luke O'Neill*

One of the best of the sweeping generational sagas filmed as elongated miniseries in the late 1970s and early 1980s, *The Thorn Birds* comes from Colleen McCullough's bestselling novel about life on the Australian outback from the 1920s to the 1960s. The *Dallas/Falcon Crest*—type power scheming is provided by matriarch Mary Carson (played by Barbara Stanwyck, who played a very similar role in *The Big Valley*). The *Dynasty*-esque forbidden romance comes from the scandalous affair between beautiful young Maggie Cleary and ambitious (and oh, so handsome) priest Ralph deBricassart (played by the king of 1970s/1980s miniseries, Richard Chamberlain, of *Dr. Kildare* fame). Henry Mancini provides the music and the entire epic is produced by miniseries whiz David L. Wolper (*Roots*).

**THE THORNS (½) 30 min (8ep Color; 1988 ABC) Situation Comedy** *with Tony Roberts as Sloan Thorn, Kelly Bishop as Ginger Thorn, Marilyn Cooper as Rose Thorn, Lori Petty as Cricket, Mary Louise Wilson as Toinette, Adam Biesk as Chad Thorn, Lisa Rieffel as Joey Thorn, and Jesse Tendler as Edmund Thorn*

These are really annoying people. The kids are totally self-absorbed, pushy, and spoiled—just like their parents. In fact, nearly everyone in the well-to-do Thorn family obviously deserves whatever bad can happen to them. The problem is that you don't feel like sticking around their posh New York City townhouse to see them get it. Besides, they probably don't even realize how petty and obnoxious they seem. Rose Thorn, the mother of the family, tries to knock some sense into her children's heads, but in this short-flight series she doesn't have nearly enough time.

The Thorns are probably what a lot of Manhattan types that populate Woody Allen's comedies would seem like if he didn't give them such clever lines, or soften their excesses with his own mocking humor. (After all, Tony Roberts's self-centered characters seem just fine in films like *Play It Again, Sam* or *Hannah and Her Sisters.*) Unfortunately even though veteran comedy director Mike Nichols is the producer here, a believable sense of humanity never takes hold. Maybe it would have taken place farther along (always a problem in judging quickly canceled comedies), but from what we see here this family has a long, long way to go before it could spend time with the Huxtables, or even Kate and Allie.

**THOSE AMAZING ANIMALS (*½) 60 min (26ep Color; 1980–1981 ABC) Human Interest** *with Burgess Meredith, Priscilla Presley, and Jim Stafford*

If you take *That's Incredible* and head down the evolutionary chain just a bit, you'll wind up with *Those Amazing Animals,* a pretentious, annoying collection of reports about animals who do amazing things. Produced by *That's Incredible's* Alan Landsburg, *Those Amazing Animals* does have some redeeming features, such as reports by famed naturalist explorer Jacques-Yves Cousteau. Still, the circus atmosphere carried over from *That's Incredible* and the inane banter of the three mismatched hosts drag the series down.

**THREE FOR THE ROAD (*) 60 min (11ep & 90 min pilot Color; 1975 CBS) Drama** *with Alex Rocco as Pete Karras, Vincent Van Patten as John Karras, and Leif Garrett as Endicott "Endy" Karras*

Overly moralistic, boring, and simplistic, *Three for the Road* tells the tale of widower Pete Karras. A freelance photographer, he roams the country taking photos, accompanied by his two teenage sons and his mobile home (called the Zebec). Younger son Endy is played by Leif Garrett, who went on to have a brief fling as a teen heartthrob rock singer in the late 1970s.

**3 GIRLS 3 (**) 60 min (3ep Color; 1977 NBC) Musical-Variety** *with Debbie Allen, Ellen Foley, and Mimi Kennedy*

The spark of a quality show lurks within *3 Girls 3,* but it never really ignites. The concept is innovative: Three unknown actresses play three unknown female stars of a musical-variety show. The program features the trio not only performing but also preparing for their show (like Jack Benny's old show within a show idea). Before you know it, however, the series ends and it's not clear whether the idea could work over time.

Of the three unknowns, Debbie Allen (sister of Phylicia Rashad, of *The Cosby Show*) went on to greater success as dance teacher Lydia Grant in the TV version of *Fame.* Ellen Foley recorded some hit songs with the beefy rock singer Meatloaf and put in one year as Billie Young, the legal-aid lawyer on *Night Court.* Mimi Kennedy sparred with Peter Cook on *The Two of Us* and later played the mom on *Spencer* (with Chad Lowe).

**THE THREE MUSKETEERS (**) 30 min (26ep B&W; 1956 Syndication) Adventure** *with Jeff Stone as D'Artagnan, Paul Campbell as Aramis, Peter Trent as Porthos, and Sebastian Cabot as Count de Brisemont*

This show is a mild run-through of the venerable Alexandre Dumas tale of three noble Frenchmen in the

1620s who protect the king. Produced in Britain, this is the first U.S. TV series appearance for stout Sebastian Cabot (*Family Affair*).

**THREE OF A KIND (**½) 30 min (6ep Color; 1981 UK BBC) Comedy-Variety** *with Tracey Ullman, Lenny Henry, and David Copperfield*

For your developing talent shelf, this is an early 1980s variety vehicle split three ways and including some excellent bits from Tracey Ullman.

**THREE'S A CROWD (**½) 30 min (22ep Color; 1984–1985 ABC) Situation Comedy** *with John Ritter as Jack Tripper, Mary Cadorette as Vicky Bradford, Robert Mandan as James Bradford, Jessica Walter as Claudia Bradford, and Alan Campbell as E. Z. Taylor*

In the last episode of *Three's Company,* Jack Tripper finds the girl of his dreams, airline stewardess Vicky Bradford, and proposes marriage. She turns him down, even though she loves him. It seems her parents' marriage ended in a rocky divorce and she's not quite ready to take a chance yet. But in the meantime she suggests an alternative: cohabitation. Jack reluctantly agrees, and the two move into the apartment above his bistro, much to the consternation of Vicki's wealthy dad, James Bradford (played to the hilt by Robert Mandan, the philandering stuffed shirt Chester Tate on *Soap*). To keep on eye on things, he buys the building, becoming their landlord and part-owner of the restaurant. While Bradford looks for every opportunity to split the couple, Jack dreams of a reconciliation between Bradford and his wife, Claudia, so Vicki would be more prone to marriage.

The series follows the basic sitcom formula used so successfully by *Three's Company*: misunderstood situations, physical humor, and plenty of sexual references. Only this time there's no doubt about what's going on behind those bedroom doors.

John Ritter continues his comfortable role as the affable Jack Tripper, hopelessly devoted to his new paramour. He and Mary Cadorette make a believable cuddling couple. Mandan and Jessica Walter are also a perfect match as Vicky's parents, who take fiendish delight in scoring points at each other's expense long after their divorce. It's easy to understand why Vicky views marriage with such suspicion. And, representing the ultimate in the laid-back California work ethic, Alan Campbell as E. Z. Taylor assists Jack at the bistro.

*Three's a Crowd* is based on *Robin's Nest,* the British spin-off from *Man About the House* (which was the model for *Three's Company*). In syndication, *Three's a Crowd* sometimes plays under the title *Three's Company, Too.*

**THREE'S COMPANY (***) 30 min (174ep Color; 1977–1984 ABC) Situation Comedy** *with John Ritter as Jack Tripper, Joyce DeWitt as Janet Wood, Suzanne Somers as Chrissy Snow, Jenilee Harrison as Cindy Snow, Priscilla Barnes as Terri Alden, Audra Lindley as Helen Roper, Norman Fell as Stanley Roper, Don Knotts as Ralph Furley, and Richard Kline as Larry Dallas*

The morning after the good-bye party for their departing roommate, Janet and Chrissy discover one of the revelers, Jack Tripper, asleep in their bathtub. After he mentions that he needs a place to stay, sealing the request with a superb breakfast (he's studying to be a chef), the two young women invite him to take the place of their old (female) roommate. Sharing the rent, strictly platonic with separate bedrooms. But to get around the objections of their landlord, Stanley Roper, they tell him Jack is gay.

He isn't. Nonetheless, Jack, Janet, and Chrissy (later replaced by Cindy, then Terri) remain true to their agreement. While they may good naturedly flirt with each other, they never get involved, except as good friends. They're more like brother and sisters. Still, they have to deal constantly with the raised eyebrows and snickers of people who learn that two beautiful women and a cute guy are sharing the same apartment. Try explaining that arrangement to your date. "And nothing happens?" is the inevitable, skeptical reaction.

It's that snickering level of humor that probably led to the initial critical reaction to the series in the late 1970s, when it was snidely dismissed within some circles as part of the trend to "jiggle TV." Nonetheless, *Three's Company* was an instant hit and the series remained a consistent ratings winner for ABC throughout its seven-year network run. And it has continued to be a strong program in rerun syndication.

For good reason. Despite the contemporary trappings of opposite-sex cohabitation, this show is primarily a timeless situation comedy cut straight from the *I Love Lucy* world of mild misunderstandings. (Lucy thinks Ricky is planning to murder her) and good old-fashioned physical schtick (Lucy stomps grapes in a wine-making vat). So in that same spirit, *Three's Company* presents such misunderstandings as Janet and Jack suspecting the worst when Chrissy is asked to accompany her new boss on an overnight business trip (not knowing the boss is a woman); while eavesdropping, Mr. Roper mistakenly becomes convinced Chrissy is pregnant; or Chrissy's minister father arrives for a visit not knowing that Jack now lives there.

On the physical schtick side, the routines inevitably focus on Jack. John Ritter does an excellent job handling everything from a simple pratfall to battling an ironing board to carrying on a dinner date while handcuffed to Chrissy at the next table. Through it all, even when caught in some complicated *Lucy*-like deception and sprawling body twist, he manages to pull it off with a likable boy-next-door charm. Even with two beautiful female co-stars, he's really the center of attention whenever he's on camera.

As to the constant talk about sex? That's certainly

different from *Lucy,* though given the context it does make sense. After all, *Three's Company* focuses on attractive young singles living in Southern California, with the pursuit of the opposite sex as topic one in their lives. Besides it soon becomes clear that while the women (and men) might occasionally walk around in exercise tights, bathrobes, and swimsuits, talking about sex is as far as anyone will go on screen. At heart, this is really a pretty wholesome crew, which just happens to believe in premarital sex (though not with each other). Ironically many of the cheap laughs about sex come from Stanley Roper, who doesn't believe in much postmarital sex—much to the frustration of his wife, Helen. He's also the one who provides most of the sneering double entendres about Jack's purported homosexuality.

Over time, some of the leering does get toned down. The Ropers move away (to their own series), leaving the landlord role to the more comically swaggering Don Knotts as the bug-eyed Ralph Furley. Jack gets more adult trappings, with most of the "Jack-is-gay" jokes virtually eliminated (though that's still the excuse for allowing the cohabitation) while Jack's friend, Larry, assumes most of the blatant unbridled male libido lines. At the same time, Jack advances up the cooking ladder, going from a student to a working chef (at Angelino's restaurant) to manager of his own bistro. And each new blonde roommate is more and more responsible, moving from Chrissy (a scatterbrained typist) to Cindy (a clumsy student) to Terri (a nurse). Janet is the sweet, dependable one from the beginning.

The final episode of *Three's Company* leads directly into the follow-up series, *Three's a Crowd.* Sometimes that title and short-lived *Ropers* spin-off are run under the parent show's banner and theme song, using the titles *Three's Company, Too* and *Three's Company's Friends, The Ropers* (kicking the episode total up to 222). *Three's Company* was based on the British hit series *Man About the House,* which also plays in U.S. syndication.

**THRILLER** (**½) **60 min (67ep B&W; 1960–1962 NBC) Suspense Anthology** *with Boris Karloff as host*

Never quite considered in a league with TV's great suspense anthologies *Thriller* deserves a bit more respect. Its hour tales of suspense and horror are heavy on the gothic pathos, which is fitting for the show's host, Boris Karloff, the monster of the old *Frankenstein* movies. The writing is not up to *The Twilight Zone*'s efforts, the tone is not as creepy as the intense *One Step Beyond,* and the hour length tends to drag out stories better fit for thirty minutes. Still, some top actors appear throughout and Karloff is quite spooky by himself. Oddly enough, *Thriller* (also known as *Boris Karloff Presents Thriller*) is produced by Hubbell Robinson, a man more at home with mainstream variety shows (starring the likes of Dean Martin, Mitch Miller, and Jack Paar).

**THROB** (**½) **30 min (48ep Color; 1986–1988 Syndication) Situation Comedy** *with Diana Canova as Sandy Beatty, Jonathan Prince as Zachary Armstrong, Maryedith Burrell as Meredith, Jane Leeves as Blue, Richard Cummings, Jr., as Phil Gaines, and Paul W. Walter and Sean de Veritch as Jeremy Beatty*

There's nothing like seeing the latest aspiring rockers to feel the passing of generations, even if you are only in your thirties. That's one of the hooks for this contemporary music comedy, with former *Soap* star Diana Canova playing Sandy Beatty, a thirty-three-year-old divorcée (with a teenage son) who works at Throb Records, an independent outfit located in a Manhattan loft. She feels young-going-on-adult, probably because she's the most level-headed person at the office—and that's counting her boss, the short, young, enthusiastic Zach. Co-worker Blue even wears the latest-style outfits that make her look more like she's with the band than one of the office employees.

*Throb* is a reaction comedy, with Canova constantly put in situations at home or at the office requiring a response. Whether she's auditioning prospective apartment mates (gaping in amazement at people even stranger than her record company contacts), or gently suggesting to Zach that the two of them can only be good friends, Canova consistently comes through with the appropriate expressions of puzzlement, frustration, and genuine amusement. For half the series, her character of Sandy brings the office relationships home when she and co-worker Blue move in together (splitting the rent on a spacious old apartment). Ironically, Sandy is set up as relatively conservative for her job; in real life Canova apparently has the heart of a rocker, performing the program's opening theme song with the Nylons.

The series also features a good number of guest appearances (mostly cameo) by a wide variety of recording artists, usually visiting the Throb offices and traveling the same circles. These include shots by James Brown, Timothy B. Schmidt, the Tokens, Peggy March, and Donny Osmond. In addition, Deniece Williams ("Let's Hear It for the Boy") and Nicolette Larson ("Lotta Love") take minor character roles, while Kip Lennon (brother to the Lennon sisters) plays Skye Night, Throb's very punky number one act.

**TIGHTROPE** (**½) **30 min (37ep B&W; 1959–1960 CBS) Police Drama** *with Mike Connors as Nick Stone*

Not just another police saga of the 1950s, *Tightrope* has a great premise and a great star. Mike Connors, later the lead in *Mannix* and making his TV series debut here, plays an undercover police agent who infiltrates organized crime and thus walks a tightrope all the time, in fear of blowing his cover. Each episode has Connors on a new case, adopting a new false name, as he poses as a criminal. The character's real name, Nick Stone, is hardly, if ever, used. The thirty-minute format (then *the* length for cop shows) limits the character and plot development possible with the concept. The late 1980s update of the format, *Wiseguy,* works better as an hour series, carrying one undercover identity setting over multiple episodes.

**TILL DEATH US DO PART** (**½) **30 min (50ep Color & B&W; 1966–1968 & 1972–1974 and 7ep sequel Color 1985 UK BBC) Situation Comedy** *with Warren Mitchell as Alf Garnett, Dandy Nichols as Else Garnett, Una Stubbs, and Anthony Booth*

This show is the original model and inspiration for *All in the Family,* though sometimes even the closing credits on that series mistakenly identify the adaptation source as *Till Death Do Us Part* (reversing the "Us Do"). In any case, this comedy did its groundbreaking in Britain half a decade before the Bunkers, playing with a somewhat nastier caricatured edge but containing the same basic relationships: a loud-mouthed working-class bigot dad (Alf Garnett), his long-suffering "silly old moo" of a wife, their daughter, and her "scouse git" of a husband. Alf and his son-in-law are particularly vocal toward each other, looking at the world through diametrically opposed blinders (a died-in-the-wool Conservative versus a know-it-all Marxist), railing on about race and religion and the government. Though Alf is clearly supposed to be the wrongheaded one of the series, like Archie Bunker he ends up winning the sympathy of many viewers, maybe because he seems so put upon by the changing state of the world.

*Till Death Us Do Part* played until 1968, was withdrawn by its producer, Johnny Speight, over what he identified as censorship problems with the BBC, then returned in the early 1970s in the wake of *All in the Family*'s success. In 1985, Warren Mitchell and Dandy Nichols reunited for a seven-episode sequel, *In Sickness and in Health,* but the death of Nichols precluded any further stories together. Neither series has been syndicated in the States so we've never had the chance to compare them side-by-side with *All in the Family.* Today, of course, U.S. viewers would probably perceive the Garnetts as Bunker knock-offs, with their particular controversial issues too far removed to be relevant to us. Nonetheless, a very important show, still fondly remembered in Britain today, and a key item for broadcast museum setups, if only to help convey how ideas have been interpreted on both sides of the Atlantic.

**THE TIM CONWAY COMEDY HOUR** (*½) **60 min (13ep Color; 1970 CBS) Comedy-Variety** *with Tim Conway, McLean Stevenson, Sally Struthers, and Art Metrano*

Tim Conway makes no headway here in his doomed efforts to leave behind the world of second bananas (*McHale's Navy, Carol Burnett Show*) and become a star of his own show. This grab-bag hour of comedy-variety is just one of his many flops as a headliner. Appropriately, Conway picks as *his* second banana pre-*M*A*S*H* McLean Stevenson, who would go on (after *M*A*S*H*) to star in five bombs. Sally Struthers (pre–*All in the Family*) also appears.

**THE TIM CONWAY SHOW** (½) **30 min (13ep Color; 1970 CBS) Situation Comedy** *with Tim Conway as Timothy "Spud" Barrett, Joe Flynn as Herbert T. Kenworth, and Anne Seymour as K. J. Crawford*

A truly horrific show, *The Tim Conway Show* is another of Tim Conway's failures as the star of his own series. Here he is teamed up again with his *McHale's Navy* cohort, Joe Flynn (who played Capt. Binghamton in that older hit program). The pair play the bumbling personnel of a rinky-dink charter airline. It's impossible to resist saying that this show never gets off the ground.

**TIME EXPRESS** (*) **60 min (4ep Color; 1979 CBS) Drama** *with Vincent Price as Jason Winters, Coral Browne as Margaret Winters, James Reynolds as Richard Jefferson "R. J." Walker, and William Phipps as E. Patrick Callahan*

A dab of *The Twilight Zone,* a dollop of *Fantasy Island,* and a touch of *The Millionaire* are combined to make a mish-mash of a show. *Time Express* postulates a mysterious train that can take people back in time to key moments of their past, so that maybe, just maybe, errors can be undone.

Vincent Price is wasted in this, a rare TV series acting role for the horror movie veteran. He and his real-life wife Coral Browne play the hosts to each week's guest stars who are chosen to relive and hopefully rectify their past.

**THE TIME TUNNEL** (**½) **60 min (30ep Color; 1966–1967 ABC) Science Fiction** *with James Darren as Tony Newman, Robert Colbert as Doug Phillips, Lee Meriwether as Dr. Ann MacGregor, Whit Bissel as Gen. Heywood Kirk, and John Zaremba as Dr. Raymond Swain*

*The Time Tunnel* is an inventive series that could have been much better. Set in 1968 (which was the not-too-distant future when the series was produced), *The Time Tunnel* involves a super-secret U.S. government experimental time travel project at a military base deep underground in the Arizona desert. When a penny-pinching bureaucrat threatens to shut down the massively expensive project, brash young scientist Dr. Tony Newman decides to play human guinea pig and sends himself back into the uncharted mists of time. Newman's colleague, the slightly more levelheaded Dr. Doug Phillips, soon follows in hot pursuit, in hopes of bringing Newman back to present-day Arizona. The remaining crew at mission control can now and again see the duo and occasionally make voice contact, but generally headquarters is powerless to help the pair. Most efforts to bring Newman and Phillips home simply result in sending them to yet another unplanned stop along the time-space continuum.

It is best not to spend too much time contemplating the script inconsistencies while watching *The Time Tunnel,* because a lot of what happens makes no sense. Whenever they are about to be sent to a new destination, Newman and Phillips have the amazing ability to instantaneously change back into the clothes they were wearing when first sent through time. The duo is forever turning up at key points in history, such as the sinking of the *Titanic,* the battle of Gettysburg, or the assassination of President Lincoln. They never seem to show up in boring towns on the outskirts of civilization or calm tropical isles or, for that matter, in the middle of the ocean. No matter where Newman and Phillips turn up, people are never very happy to see them.

After watching a few episodes, you will realize that our heroes cannot change the past. So all their thrashing around, trying to convince people that they know what will occur, starts becoming tedious.

*The Time Tunnel* is at its best when it does something different, such as when the drifting duo turn up in Pearl Harbor in (when else?) December 1941. Naturally they try to no avail to thwart the imminent Japanese attack. The more imaginative aspect of the story, which works rather well, focuses on Dr. Newman's efforts to befriend his own father, who will die in the upcoming battle. Another interesting episode has Newman and Phillips making a grueling jaunt from one million B.C. to one million A.D., all in one hour.

The two main faults with this show are the writing, which could have been much better, and the restrictions imposed by a limited budget. The time tunnel apparatus itself looks nifty, with an 800-story complex and millions of flashing lights. The images of Newman and Phillips traveling in time are pure 1960s psychedelia. Still, the producers were faced with the awesome task of outfitting a Roman coliseum one week, an erupting volcano the next, and a lunar rocket base the third. There is no way an eclectic concept such as *The Time Tunnel* could be done right within the financial limits of weekly TV production. Consequently the show occasionally stoops to using file color footage from Hollywood historical epics to pad its scenes of the past.

*The Time Tunnel* was produced by Irwin Allen, the man responsible for other flashy hi-tech science fiction series such as *Lost in Space* and *Voyage to the Bottom of the Sea.*

## TIMES SQUARE PLAYHOUSE (see *The Unexpected*)

## TINKER, TAILOR, SOLDIER, SPY

**(***½) 60 min (7ep Color; 1979 UK BBC) Spy Drama** *with Alec Guinness as George Smiley, Ian Richardson as Bill Haydon, Bernard Hepton as Toby Esterhase, Terence Rigby as Roy Bland, Michael Aldridge as Percy Alleline, Sian Phillips as Ann Smiley, Michael Jayston as Peter Guillam, and Alexander Knox as Control*

Alec Guinness is superb as weathered British spy George Smiley in this complicated espionage tale adapted from the book by John Le Carre. Briefly, Smiley is called out of a forced retirement from the British intelligence agency (nicknamed "the Circus") in order to ferret out a double agent that Smiley's old boss (Control) suspected of feeding information to the Soviets. Control suspected most of his top assistants and gave them code names such as "Tinker," "Tailor," "Soldier," and "Poor Man" during his investigation. Before Control could narrow the field, he was forced out of office (along with Smiley). The British cabinet minister overseeing the Circus brings Smiley back to continue Control's investigation when evidence turns up to corroborate the "mole" suspicions.

Guinness perfectly captures Smiley's world-weary mood as he slowly, methodically narrows the suspects one by one. The polar opposite of the flashy spy image of James Bond, George Smiley is a rumpled, dour old man who is taken seriously by few and ignored by his free-spirited wife. His precise, calculating mind, however, allows him to uncover clues that others would ignore. After numerous plot detours, the story comes together and Smiley is almost as shocked as his aides when the double agent's identity is revealed.

*Tinker, Tailor, Soldier, Spy* is blessed with a highly talented pool of actors, and a thick, detailed production that rewards careful viewers. Producer Jonathan Powell and Alec Guinness teamed up again in 1982 for a sequel, *Smiley's People,* based on another Le Carre novel.

## TO ROME WITH LOVE

**(**) (48ep Color; 1969–1971 CBS) Situation Comedy** *with John Forsythe as Michael Endicott, Joyce Menges as Alison Endicott, Susan Neher as Penny Endicott, Melanie Fullerton as Mary Jan Endicott, Kay Medford as Aunt Harriet Endicott, Vito Scotti as Gino Mancini, Peggy Mondo as Mama Vitale, and Walter Brennan as Grandpa Andy Pruitt*

Former *Bachelor Father* John Forsythe once again plays a sole parent, this time as a widower with three daughters relocating to Rome shortly after the death of his wife. He's there as a college professor at the American Overseas School, living in a bustling boardinghouse run by Mama Vitale. This comedy is simple, with much of the humor coming from the naive American assumptions about life in the Endicotts' new home and the expectations of the Endicott daughters as typical (if squeaky clean) teens. For the first half of the series, Michael's sister (Aunt Harriet) comes along to help keep an eye on the girls, but she's replaced by *Real McCoys* veteran Walter Brennan as crotchety Grandpa Pruitt (Michael's father-in-law) for the remainder of the run. He has no illusions about his new temporary home—it had better be just like back in Iowa, or else!

This is a bland, harmless series oddly reminiscent of such 1960s Walt Disney Fred MacMurray theatrical fare as *Bon Voyage!* (an American dad overseas) or *Follow Me Boys.* It also has a direct connection to the cuddly *Family Affair* (from the same producer, Don Fedderson) with the casts of both series crossing over for one-episode guest spots.

**TO SERVE THEM ALL MY DAYS (***) 60 min (13ep Color; 1980 UK BBC) Drama** *with John Duttine as David Powlett-Jones, Frank Middlemass as Algy Herries, Alan MacNaughtan as Howarth, Patricia Lawrence as Ellie Herries, John Welsh as Cordwainer, Susan Jameson as Christine, Kim Braden as Julia, and Belinda Lang as Beth*

David Powlett-Jones, a Welsh miner's shell-shocked son, returns from World War I and (obviously still a bit confused about reality) decides to seek refuge as a teacher. Much to his surprise, his application for a position at an exclusive upper-class boy's school is accepted and so the would-be Mr. Chips begins what will be a long association there. The series has a good mix of stories, ranging from light romance (David falls for Beth, a pretty nurse) to typical teacher/student conflicts (fighting for control of the class sessions), to the demands and priorities of the postwar world (David locks horns with a local alderman over a war memorial). Eventually, David becomes headmaster and, as if to bookend his experiences, has to face the distressing prospect of another generation of young men going off to die in a world war. A compelling adaptation of the 1972 novel by R. F. Delderfield.

**TO THE MANOR BORN (***) 30 min (20ep Color; 1979–1981 UK BBC) Situation Comedy** *with Penelope Keith as Audrey Forbes-Hamilton, Peter Bowles as Richard DeVere, Angela Thorne as Marjorie Frobisher, John Rudling as Brabinger, and Daphne Heard as Mrs. Puovivitch*

A charming comedy of courtship and class, with Penelope Keith taking on her oh-so-proper character type (similar to Margot on *Good Neighbors*) to the English countryside as Audrey Forbes-Hamilton. She's strictly old money, which is why she's so distressed to discover that her recently deceased husband has left her bankrupt, forcing the sale of their manor house and estate grounds. What's worse, the buyer is a new-money capitalist, Richard DeVere, a Czechoslovakian millionaire bachelor who runs a multinational grocery business. (Canned peas and things—how very common!) And as a final indignity DeVere and his mother actually move in and attempt to run the place, while Audrey can only afford to live just across the way in what should be a servants' coach house. Armed with a pair of binoculars (and aided by her only domestic, Brabinger, and her good friend, Marjorie), she keeps a critical eye on DeVere and his handling of Grantleigh manor!

Audrey soon discovers that DeVere is not a bad sort at all. In fact, if she still had her money and position, she might well consider him a likely candidate for a second marriage. DeVere is surprised to find himself respecting, even liking, Audrey—despite her obvious resentment at his ownership of her family home. Naturally, Richard's mother instantly sees an obvious development for the two of them: They should get married. And they should. Audrey and Richard are two strong, self-confident characters who complement each other's strengths and weaknesses perfectly. In his heart, Richard knows this, but he also realizes that marriage will never happen as long as Audrey feels it wouldn't look right—she would appear to be marrying DeVere just to win back her lost property. Instead he concentrates on fitting in with the community and trying to win Audrey's grudging approval, step-by-step.

The bulk of the series concentrates on the mild complications of English country life and society. Some of the plot hooks include Audrey's battle to keep the town train station from being shut down and sold (the potential buyer? DeVere's company, of course!); Audrey's attempt to fake an overseas holiday by spending two weeks under a sunlamp in her home; and DeVere's delicate efforts to have Audrey agree to organize the manor's annual gala.

It's well worth sticking around for the entire run of episodes, even though the final two set up a slight cheat on the premise in the name of love and matrimony. But you really wouldn't want it to turn out any other way.

**TODAY'S FBI (**) 60 min (13ep Color; 1981–1982 ABC) Police Drama** *with Mike Connors as Ben Slater, Joseph Cali as Nick Frazier, Richard Hill as Al Gordean, Charles Brown and Harold Sylvester as Dwayne Thompson, and Carol Potter as Maggie Clinton*

There is no direct connection between this show and the long-running series *The F.B.I.* that preceded it by about a decade, but *Today's FBI* is really just an update of Quinn Martin's old program starring Efrem Zimbalist, Jr. In place of Zimbalist is Mike Connors, a TV familiar from his days as a lone wolf private eye on *Mannix.* Connors plays Ben Slater, a twenty-year FBI man who now supervises a quartet of up-and-coming law enforcement talent. Like *The F.B.I., Today's FBI* is based on the files of the real FBI and, laboring under the bureau's heavy-handed supervision, it paints an incredibly rosy and pristine picture of the agency. Slater's four charges are spotless and a little levity would go a long way here, but hardly ever shows up.

**TOGETHER WE STAND/NOTHING IS EASY (*) 30 min (13ep Color; 1986–1987 CBS) Situation Comedy** *with Elliott Gould as David Randall, Dee Wallace Stone as Lori Randall, Katie O'Neill as Amy Randall, Scott*

*Grimes as Jack Randall, Ke Huy Quan as Sam, Natasha Bobo as Sally, and Julia Migenes as Marion*

Elliott Gould has starred in some wonderful movies, such as *M*A*S*H, The Long Goodbye,* and *Harry and Walter Go to New York.* Unfortunately, Gould's efforts on TV (this dud and the short-lived *E/R*) are nowhere near the usual level of his film work. This sappy, syrupy mess has him playing David Randall, a rumpled suburban dad who has a wife (Lori) and son (Jack). The Randalls adopted daughter Amy some time ago, and they now adopt another child, an Asian boy named Sam who turns out to be a teenager, not the toddler they expected. For good measure, the Randalls also adopt a six-year-old black girl named Sally. So now we have all the major races living together under one roof. Oh, there are some little spats, but everybody loves everybody. Yawn, what a snoozer.

About halfway through the program's run, the format changes drastically. The title becomes *Nothing Is Easy* Gould's character is killed off (a car accident, the death of choice among TV script writers), and Lori must raise the brood on her own. She receives some help from Marion, her wisecracking next-door neighbor. Losing Gould only makes the series worse, if that is possible.

**TOM BROWN'S SCHOOLDAYS (**½) 60 min (5ep Color; 1973 UK BBC) Drama** *with Anthony Murphy as Tom Brown, Iain Cuthbertson as Dr. Thomas Arnold, Simon Turner as Ned, Gerald Flood as Sir Richard Flashman, John Paul as Squire Brown, and Valerie Holliman as Rosy*

This adaptation of the novel by Thomas Hughes is part biography (of headmaster Dr. Thomas Arnold), part autobiography, and part stinging social criticism. The setting is an English boarding school for the rich and nearly rich (and others who can work their way in), complete with limited curriculum, physical abuse, and even student servants (nicknamed "fags," though not with any intended gay double meaning) for the school's prefects (senior students with the authority to discipline). Much to the admiration of Hughes, Dr. Arnold reforms and transforms this system, rounding out the courses in Latin and Greek with such "radical" additions as math, history, English, and geography, sharply limiting the physical punishment of the students, and (above all else) working to turn out well-rounded and intelligent future leaders not only of Britain but of the world.

Of course, this system is not quite in place during Tom Brown's school days, so he faces some tough, occasionally cruel, adventures. It's a setting in which the older boys bully, mock, and abuse the younger kids, even blaming the youngsters for their own teen mischief. But with its roots in nineteenth-century social criticism, the story does mete out justice and retribution by the end.

**TOM, DICK AND MARY (*½) 30 min (13ep Color; 1964–1965 NBC) Situation Comedy** *with Don Galloway as Dr. Tom Gentry, Joyce Bulifant as Mary Gentry, Stephen Franken as Dr. Dick Moran, and Guy Raymond as Cliff Murdock*

The Gentrys, Tom and Mary, a white bread boring young couple, can't quite afford the rent of their apartment on Tom's meager salary as an intern. Tom's friend Dick, another intern who is not married and lives the traditional swinging singles life, moves in and shares the expenses. Sparks fly as the trio gets in each other's way. *Tom, Dick and Mary* originally ran as part of the *90 Bristol Court* trio of sitcoms. Don Galloway (who plays Tom) later played Raymond Burr's top aid in *Ironside,* while Stephen Franken (who plays Dick) was the insufferably rich Chatsworth Osborne, Jr. on *Dobie Gillis.* Joyce Bulifant (who plays Mary) was the wife of Gavin MacLeod's Murray Slaughter character on *The Mary Tyler Moore Show.*

**THE TOM EWELL SHOW (*½) 30 min (32ep B&W; 1960–1961 CBS) Situation Comedy** *with Tom Ewell as Tom Potter, Marilyn Erskine as Fran Potter, and Mabel Albertson as Irene Brady*

A minor league film star with two hits to his name (*Adam's Rib* from 1949 and *The Seven Year Itch* from 1955), Tom Ewell plays Tom Potter, a middle-of-the-road, middle-America, middle-class kind of guy. He sells insurance in the workaday world and then comes home to a house full of women. Along with wife Fran, there are three daughters (ages fifteen, eleven, and seven) plus a mother-in-law.

**TOMA (**½) 60 min (24ep & 90 min pilot Color; 1973–1974 ABC) Police Drama** *with Tony Musante as Det. David Toma, Simon Oakland as Inspector Spooner, Susan Strasberg as Patty Toma, Sean Manning as Jimmy Toma, and Michelle Livingston as Donna Toma*

One of the better and more humane of the horde of 1970s loner cop/private eye shows, *Toma* is loosely based on the real-life exploits of Newark, New Jersey, undercover cop David Toma. A master of disguise, Toma infiltrates the underworld and has a great record of catching his prey. He likes to avoid gunplay (a true rarity in this genre) and he is also seen interacting with his wife and kids (another rarity). However, Toma does have the familiar by-the-book superior who is always frustrated by his lone wolf tactics.

Produced by Roy Huggins (*Maverick, The Outsider, Cheyenne*), *Toma* was completely revamped after its only season. The entire cast and crew were dumped, the format was altered, and the title became *Baretta*. Under that name, as a virtually new series (starring Robert Blake), it became a hit.

**TOMAHAWK** (*) **30 min (26ep B&W; 1957 Syndication) Western** *with Jacques Godin as Pierre Radisson and Rene Caron as Medard*

Produced in Canada, *Tomahawk* is set in the Great Lakes frontier of the 1700s, where scouts Pierre Radisson and Medard assist newly arrived settlers.

**TOMBSTONE TERRITORY** (**) **30 min (91ep B&W; 1957–1960 ABC & Syndication) Western** *with Pat Conway as Sheriff Clay Hollister and Richard Eastham as Harris Calibourne*

Tombstone, a town in the Arizona Territory of the 1880s, is called "the town too tough to die." The two main reasons it doesn't die are Sheriff Hollister, who fights the forces of crime, and Harris Calibourne, editor of the local newspaper (the Tombstone *Epitaph*), who fights the forces of ignorance.

*Tombstone Territory* was one of the first TV series to continue to produce new episodes for syndication after cancelation by a network.

**THE TONIGHT SHOW STARRING JOHNNY CARSON**
**(See *Carson Comedy Classics*)**

**THE TONY RANDALL SHOW** (***) **30 min (44ep Color; 1976–1978 ABC & CBS) Situation Comedy** *with Tony Randall as Judge Walter Franklin, Barney Martin as Jack Terwilliger, Allyn Ann McLerie as Janet Reubner, Rachel Roberts as Mrs. Bonnie McClellan, Brad Savage as Oliver Wendell Franklin, Devon Scott and Penny Peyser as Roberta "Bobby" Franklin, and Diana Muldaur as Judge Eleanor Hooper*

This show portrays the home and office life of Philadelphia Judge Walter Franklin, played with sharp-tongued vigor by Tony Randall in a setup concocted by *Bob Newhart Show* producers Tom Patchett and Jay Tarses. They give Randall a variety of settings that allow him the chance to react (much like their favorite shrink), and he responds with gusto in court, at home, and (in later episodes) as a part-time teacher for some night school law classes. Naturally, Judge Franklin has the least success in his home turf, where the competition is fierce from his slightly addled housekeeper (Mrs. McClellan), his precocious son (Oliver), and his ambitious daughter in law school (Bobby). Then again, sometimes he doesn't do all that well with his work circles, once losing a contest for a State Supreme Court position to a dead man.

This is an untypical comedy for Randall, giving him a character with a harder edge than usual (more like his real-life interview persona when visiting the *Tonight Show* rather than *The Odd Couple*'s Felix Unger), but he manages to pull it off. This well-written, well-executed gem got lost in its original network run but it is a special treat to discover on the rerun circuit.

**TOO CLOSE FOR COMFORT/THE TED KNIGHT SHOW** (**½) **30 min (142ep Color; 1980–1986 ABC & Syndication) Situation Comedy** *with Ted Knight as Henry Rush, Nancy Dussault as Muriel Rush, Deborah Van Valkenburgh as Jackie Rush, Lydia Cornell as Sara Rush, JM J. Bullock as Monroe Ficus, Audrey Meadows as Iris Martin, and Pat Carroll as Hope Stinson*

Here is a series that begins with little more than a well-known star and some curvaceous females and winds up becoming a fairly successful program. The star of the show is Ted Knight, who made his name playing pompous, nervous TV anchorman Tex Baxter on *The Mary Tyler Moore Show*. In this program, Knight plays Henry Rush, a somewhat less pompous but equally nervous individual.

Rush is a professional cartoonist, the creator of the "Cosmic Cow" comic strip for children. He is very staid and conservative, and he displays all the traditional parental concern over the lives of his two grown and gorgeous daughters. He figures he can keep a better eye on the girls by having them move into the ground floor apartment of his double-decker San Francisco home, but this closeness only provides more reason to worry, as Henry can see the boyfriends come and go.

Much of the series is carried on Knight's shoulders. He fumes and sputters at the girls, they try to assure him all is well, and wife Muriel tells him to cool out. Over time, the one-note theme of nervous dad recedes and the other characters come to the forefront. A whole slew of talented supporting players pop up, and somehow the series just keeps going, with hardly any plot at all. The program is really not that funny, but the crew blend together well.

For the final thirteen episodes, the format changes drastically, as does the show's title. As *The Ted Knight Show,* Henry and wife Muriel leave the San Francisco double-decker home and Henry leaves "Cosmic Cow." The couple move to Marin County, outside of San Francisco, and Henry buys an interest in a small newspaper. The two girls are gone (finally on their own), and the focus is now on Henry, Muriel, and their small son born late in their marriage. The untimely cancer-related death of star Ted Knight in 1986 abruptly ended the series.

*Too Close for Comfort* is based on a British sitcom, *Keep It in the Family.*

**TOP CAT** (***) **30 min (30ep & 2 hr sequel Color; 1961–1962 ABC) Animated Cartoon** *with the voices of Arnold Stang as Top Cat, Maurice Gosfield as Benny the Ball, Marvin Kaplan as Choo Choo, and Allen Jenkins as Officer Dibble*

In the early 1960s, animated cartoons made a brief foray into prime-time television. *Top Cat* is one of those shows that seems like a classic now, but only lasted a brief time when it first aired.

Loosely based on the Phil Silvers/Sgt. Bilko theme (Maurice Gosfield worked on both shows, always playing a dumb fatso), *Top Cat* concerns the exploits of a pack of alley cats in New York City. Their leader is street-smart Top Cat. T. C., as his close friends get to call him, is forever trying to swindle somebody out of something he and his boys want, be it food, provisions, or privilege. Top Cat is also bedeviled by the denseness of his henchmen, always feeling he is the only sophisticated cat around.

Although larcenous in spirit, Top Cat (like Sgt. Bilko) has the prerequisite heart of gold. He is always going out of his way to help someone truly in need if the situation arises.

The *Top Cat* theme song is great and the actors are far better than in most cartoons. Credit must be given to producers William Hanna and Joseph Barbera, masters of TV animation, who usually rely on easy, simplistic characters (*The Flintstones, Scooby-Doo, Huckleberry Hound*) to fill their cartoons.

In 1988, Hanna-Barbera reunited most of the original voices of *Top Cat* and produced a two-hour animated sequel, called *Top Cat and the Beverly Hills Cats,* in which Benny the Ball inherits a fortune and moves to the swank world of Beverly Hills, along with T. C. and the guys.

**TOPPER (***) 30 min (78ep B&W; 1953–1955 CBS) Situation Comedy** *with Leo G. Carroll as Cosmo Topper, Anne Jeffreys as Marion Kerby, Robert Sterling as George Kerby, Lee Patrick as Henrietta Topper, Kathleen Freeman as Katie, and Buck as Neil*

Like a breath of fresh air amidst the stale, stuffy sitcoms of the 1950s, *Topper* is a wonderful little gem that mostly maintains its luster in spite of the passing decades. Aside from a fabulous premise and a top cast, *Topper* is one of the more modern-thinking series of the 1950s.

Like the decade itself, most 1950s sitcoms are very staid and conservative. They champion hard work, normality, and sensibility. *Topper* subverts that philosophy, by championing freedom, liveliness, fun, and an equality of the sexes largely unheard of at that time.

Based on Thorne Smith's novel and a delightful 1937 film starring Cary Grant, Constance Bennett, and Roland Young, *Topper* concerns a fun-loving young couple, George and Marion Kerby. While skiing in Switzerland, they are killed in an avalanche along with the Saint Bernard dog (Neil) who was trying to rescue them. The ghosts of the Kerbys (and Neil) take up residence in the Kerbys' old home, now owned by middle-aged bank vice-president Cosmo Topper and his prim and proper wife Henrietta. The catch is that only Cosmo can see and hear the ghosts of George, Marion, and Neil, and everybody else thinks he is crazy when they walk in on conversations he is having with the unseen specters. Through film special effects, the Kerbys and Neil appear transparent when they materialize before Topper and there are others present. When only Topper is around, the ghosts appear solid.

The basic premise is fun enough, but the way the characters interact lifts *Topper* out of sitcom mediocrity. The amiable Kerbys act as social counselor to Cosmo, urging him to loosen up and enjoy life a little more. They begin to bring out his almost buried side, in which he lets his hair down and acts a little wild. This behavior comes as a rude shock to wife Henrietta, who would prefer the old fuddy-duddy Cosmo, who dutifully follows her social-climbing whirl of proper behavior and idle society chitchat.

While Cosmo at first seems really boring, the slow but steady influence of the Kerbys turns him into a lovable chap. Meanwhile, wife Henrietta becomes the foil, representing the forces of constricting decorum. The Kerbys themselves are, hands down, the fun couple of 1950s TV sitcoms. This may be largely due to the fact that actors Anne Jeffreys and Robert Sterling, who play the Kerbys, were newlyweds in real life when the series began, and their infectious camaraderie, good-natured one-upsmanship, and undeniable fiery passion for each other come across clearly to the viewer. Furthermore the Kerbys are a far more modern couple than the usual male-dominated 1950s pair, in that they are equal partners, with both taking turns calling the shots.

Along with all these qualities comes the sprightly English charm of lead actor Leo G. Carroll, later the suave Mr. Waverly on *The Man From U.N.C.L.E. Topper* does have a particularly annoying laugh track (as did many sitcoms of its era) and the stories occasionally become a tad plodding, but its basic charm still shines through. Several aborted efforts have been made to create a new version of *Topper* (*Topper Returns,* a thirty-minute 1973 pilot with Roddy McDowall, Stefanie Powers, and John Fink, and *Topper,* a two-hour 1979 TV movie with Jack Warden, Kate Jackson, and Andrew Stevens), but they all fade before the 1950s TV original. ■

**THE TORTELLIS (**) 30 min (13ep Color; 1987 NBC) Situation Comedy** *with Dan Hedaya as Nick Tortelli, Jean Kasem as Loretta Tortelli, Timothy Williams as Anthony Tortelli, Mandy Ingber as Annie Tortelli, Carlene Watkins as Carlotte Cooper, and Aaron Moffatt as Mark Cooper*

On the surface, Nick Tortelli seems an unlikely choice for a spin-off series. An occasional character on *Cheers,* the slightly hunched, inarticulate Nick earned a well-deserved reputation as a truly slimy human being. He's the one who proposed marriage to Carla with the heartfelt romantic observation that since he had "knocked her up" and she knew his address, they'd probably have to get hitched. Yet that never stopped him from constantly breaking her heart with his wandering eye, eventually leading to their divorce. The running gag with Nick, though, is that somehow he is able to attract women like flies, leaving even super-hunk Sam Malone shaking his head in wonder because Nick turns around and treats his women like flies, too.

To set up the new series, Nick marries again on *Cheers,* choosing an empty-headed blonde named Loretta, who dreams of a singing career in Vegas—which is where they find themselves for this series. But first, there's a real premise puzzler.

After going to all the trouble of establishing a self-serving lowlife like Nick as having nearly magical powers of persuasion, especially over women, in the opening moments of the first episode the producers decide to give him a conscience. This is the result of a symbolic dream (a great scene, with Rhea Perlman appearing as Carla) in which he faces the consequences of his sins while riding the bus to Las Vegas. So he promises to mend his ways and, amazingly, attempts to stick to his word throughout the series.

A noble gesture, but perhaps one that could have waited for later in the run because it helps turn *The Tortellis* into a surprisingly routine venture, with Nick and Loretta coming off as an almost typical struggling sitcom couple. They end up as part of an extended television family, sharing the home of Loretta's sister, Charlotte (and her young son, Mark) along with Nick's son, Anthony, and his new bride, Annie, who turn up on the doorstep. But can this really be Nick Tortelli in action? While waiting for Loretta's career to blossom (she's just awful enough to make it there), Nick takes an honest job, operating a television repair shop in the garage—with Anthony helping. How the slimy have fallen! And even though Nick's hormones eventually get the better of him later in the series as he tries to cheat on Loretta, the damage has already been done. The Nick Tortelli myth has been shattered.

In one episode, George Wendt and John Ratzenberger show up as Norm and Cliff from *Cheers,* but otherwise there aren't too many reasons to come visiting *The Tortellis.* Afterward, Annie and Anthony turn up again on *Cheers,* still married.

**A TOUCH OF GRACE** (**½) **30 min (Color; 1973 ABC) Situation Comedy** *with Shirley Booth as Grace Simpson, J. Patrick O'Malley as Herbert Morrison, Marian Mercer as Myra Bradley, and Warren Berlinger as Walter Bradley*

A rare and kindly look at older folks makes *A Touch of Grace* a heartfelt show that stands out from the sitcom pack. Shirley Booth, destined to always be known as the star of *Hazel,* plays Grace Simpson. A sixty-five-year-old widow still full of life, Grace moves in with her stodgy daughter and son-in-law. She begins courting Herbert Morrison, the widowed gravedigger who tends her late husband's grave. The daughter and son-in-law are shocked, feeling Grace is lowering herself to associate with such a commoner. Undeterred, Grace presses on, and the older couple becomes engaged in the series finale.

Since *A Touch of Grace* seems so out of the ordinary for American sitcoms, it is not surprising to learn that it is based on a British series, *For the Love of Ada.*

**TOUGH COOKIES** (*) **30 min (6ep Color; CBS 1986) Situation Comedy** *with Robby Benson as Detective Cliff Brady, Lainie Kazan as Rita, Matt Craven as Richie Messina, Adam Arkin as Danny Polchek, Elizabeth Pena as Officer Connie Rivera, and Alan North as Father McCaskey*

Uneasy combination of street drama and comedy, with Robby Benson playing a Chicago police detective returning to his old neighborhood, an area full of "tough cookies." But he knows the territory, the players, the problems, and some offbeat solutions. For instance, in the opening episode he challenges an old high school basketball rival now collecting protection money from the local merchants to a game of one-on-one, winner take all. (Or maybe that was just an excuse to drop an allusion to Benson's 1977 film, *One-On-One.*) With only a handful of episodes produced, this one never finds its rhythm.

**TOUR OF DUTY** (**½) **60 min (36ep at Fall 1989 Color; 1987– CBS) War Drama** *with Terence Knox as Sgt. Zeke Anderson, Stephen Caffrey as Lt. Myron Goldman, Ramon Franco as Alberto Ruiz, Stan Foster as Marvin Johnson, Joshua Maurer as Pvt. Roger Horn, Dan Gauthier as Lt. Johnny McKay, Kim Delaney as Alex Devlin, and Betsy Brantley as Dr. Jennifer Seymour*

TV's first regular drama series about the Vietnam War, *Tour of Duty* begins in 1967 and focuses on the men of Bravo Company, an infantry unit of grunts battling it out in the jungles of Southeast Asia. As it seems all American war dramas must, this program presents an ethnic grab-bag of soldiers. Marvin Johnson is an urban black. Alberto Ruiz is a Puerto Rican from the Bronx. Danny Percell is a farm boy from Iowa. Myron Goldman is a Jewish graduate of officer's candidate school. Roger Horn is a war protester who was drafted. Zeke Anderson is neutral, just an all-American beefy guy. Lt. Goldman is (nominally) in control, but Goldman's battlefield virginity and by-the-book mentality lead him to rely on Sgt. Anderson, who is the real leader of the fighting men.

*Tour of Duty* begins in the mold of *Combat,* a 1960s series about the infantrymen of World War II. Both ignore the overall picture for the microcosm of one fighting unit. *Tour of Duty* cannot bring out the harshness and horror of the Vietnam War as well as movie works such as *Platoon* or *Full Metal Jacket,* but it does as good a job as one can expect from a regular TV series.

The second season brings a positive change as *Tour of Duty* tones down the *Combat*-like grimness a bit and adds some new directions. Some stories take place in cities such as Saigon (instead of the jungle setting favored in the first season), and some women are added to the cast, providing some love interests for a few of the regulars. *Tour of Duty* and its contemporary competition, *China Beach,* serve as an effective male/female variation on the same theme. ■

**A TOWN LIKE ALICE** (**½) **60 min (6ep Color; 1980 Australia The Seven Network) Drama** *with Bryan Brown as Joe Harman, Helen Morse as Jean Paget, Gordon Jackson as Noel Strachan, Dorothy Alison as Mrs. Frith, Melissa Crawford as Robyn, Maggie Dence as Mrs. O'Connor, John Lee as Lester, Cicily Poison as Eileen, Mary Volska as Sally, and Yuki Shimoda as Sgt. Mifune*

A love story carried from a death march in Malaya during World War II to the postwar streets of London and eventually to the tiny Australian town of Alice Springs. Joe and Jean first meet under the worst of conditions, both prisoners of war during the Japanese invasion of Malaya. Though they feel some initial attraction, they don't have much time to act on it. She's a ragged sunburnt figure bullied by her captors, while he is tortured, whipped, and crucified. When their individual prisoner groups go their separate ways, they both can only guess whether the other survives.

But they do, though neither knows it at first. The rest of the story traces their sometimes frustrating efforts to locate each other, with an even more difficult challenge ultimately awaiting them: Will they be able to fit into their respective postwar worlds? The heightened emotions of a wartime encounter are one thing; the challenge of fitting into a town like Alice Springs is another.

This lump-in-the-throat romance is faithful to its source (a popular novel by Nevil Shute) and is carried by three very strong performances: Bryan Brown and Helen Morse (as the dedicated couple) and Gordon Jackson (best known as Mr. Hudson on *Upstairs, Downstairs*) as Jean's British boss and the narrator of the story. ■

**THE TRACEY ULLMAN SHOW** (***½) **30 min (58ep at Fall 1989 Color; 1987– Fox) Comedy-Variety** *with Tracey Ullman, Julie Kavner, Dan Castellaneta, Joseph Malone, and Sam McMurray*

British comedienne Tracey Ullman gets right down to the business of comedy without any distracting opening numbers or lengthy monologues. It's all comedy all the time, like the half-hour syndicated rerun version of the *Carol Burnett Show* (only these are brand new routines). Even in between, there are only brief bits of transition, usually in the form of unusual animation skits drawn by Matt Groening, (the "Life in Hell" newspaper comic strip) featuring the Simpson family (given their own cartoon spinoff series in 1989, *The Simpsons*).

The sketches in *The Tracey Ullman Show* are generally self-contained and easily identified—they all carry titles and individual writing and directing credits, no doubt with half an eye toward future "best of" repackaging. When repackaging is done, it'll be a tough choice because the quality of the material is quite high, effectively showcasing Ullman's amazing versatility as a comic, mimic, singer, dancer, and overall performer.

With such a strong lead, the show demonstrates a refreshing emphasis on female characters, just like Carol Burnett's show. However, unlike that previous series, the Tracey Ullman writers spend very little time doing parodies of specific movies or television series. Instead they just lampoon show business types in general and then move on to unusual character pieces more reminiscent of an improvisational theatrical company such as Second City.

As with any good variety series, they do latch on to a handful of continuing bits and characters, including a pair of busy yuppie parents determined to spend quality time with their child; Kaye, a long-suffering working woman who is constantly put upon by her bosses (but still has time to look after her mum); and Francesca, a precocious child raised by two gay men while her mom wanders the globe.

Also unlike Carol Burnett's program, Tracey Ullman's skits frequently reflect a genuine affection for rock and roll. Sometimes the main portion of a bit will incorporate heartfelt renditions of rock chestnuts such as "Stand By Me," more raucous numbers like "Paint It Black," or relative obscurities like "Radio Radio."

Ullman closes each show with a mini-monologue, which usually consists of one or two quick jokes followed by a screaming admonishment to the audience to "Just go home!"

**TRACKDOWN** (**) **30 min (71ep B&W; 1957–1959 CBS) Western** *with Robert Culp as Hoby Gilman*

This average western about a Texas Ranger roaming the west of the 1870s, battling bad guys, is memorable for only two reasons. First, it is the only western based on actual cases from the files of the Texas Rangers (big deal). Second, it is the TV series debut of Robert Culp (later of *I Spy*), who plays lead ranger Hoby Gilman. In fact, in a few *I Spy* episodes, Culp's Kelly Robinson character is called "Hoby" by his cohort, played by Bill Cosby, in a cute reference to this series.

**TRAINING DOGS THE WOODHOUSE WAY** (**½) **30 min (10ep Color; 1980 UK BBC) Instructional** *with Barbara Woodhouse as the instructor*

If you always wondered how James Bond managed to tame that tiger in *Octopussy* with just one well-spoken word ("Sit!"), then you have to see this series. Of course, it is best to leave the wild animals to 007 and concentrate instead on the domestic stars of this Barbara Woodhouse showcase: the most affectionate dogs you've ever seen. No doubt they're overjoyed to be working with someone who knows what she's doing—someone who operates under the precept that "there is no such thing as a bad dog . . . it is simply an inexperienced owner." True enough, the owners look far more nervous than the canines, so Woodhouse is constantly at their sides, correcting their handling techniques like a patient school marm.

**TRAPPER JOHN, M. D. (**) 60 min (154ep Color; 1979–1986 CBS) Medical Drama** *with Pernell Roberts as Dr. John "Trapper John" McIntyre, Gregory Harrison as Dr. George Alonzo "Gonzo" Gates, Christopher Norris as Gloria "Ripples" Brancusi, Charles Siebert as Dr. Stanley Riverside II, Madge Sinclair as Ernestine Shoop, and Tim Busfield as Dr. John "J. T." McIntyre*

Only loosely related to the Trapper John character of *M*A*S*H, Trapper John, M. D.* turns out to be a very mediocre medical series with visions of grandeur.

The character of Trapper John McIntyre, anarchist surgeon deluxe from the Korean War days, had been played on *M*A*S*H* by Wayne Rogers. This series takes that character, drags him into the 1980s, and presumes that he would have mellowed considerably and become chief of surgery at a large San Francisco hospital. Playing the older Trapper John is the bearded and balding Pernell Roberts, a rebel in real life who walked off the hit show *Bonanza* in the mid-1960s (he played son Adam Cartwright). The cute hook in *Trapper John, M. D.* is that the formerly fearless Trapper John must now confront young surgeon Gonzo Gates, himself a M*A*S*H surgical veteran (from Vietnam), who is full of the fire Trapper John once nurtured.

After a few seasons of this "father/son" interaction, the focus shifts more to Gonzo and his maturing process. Near the show's end, Trapper's son, J. T., turns up as a young resident. Doctors and nurses come and go, but *Trapper John, M. D.* stays an acceptable hospital saga, one that wishes mightily it was *St. Elsewhere,* but never reaches that dream. The final season is a waste, as Gonzo suffers a stroke and is written out of the series. This last batch of episodes is a case clearly calling for mercy killing.

**TRAUMA CENTER (*) 60 min (10ep & 2 hr pilot Color; 1983 ABC) Medical Drama** *with James Naughton as Dr. Michael "Cutter" Royce, Dorian Harewood as Dr. Nate "Skate" Baylor, Wendie Malick as Dr. Brigitte Blaine, Lou Ferrigno as John Six, and Jack Bannon as Buck Williams*

An unending parade of accident victims are dragged, flown, and wheeled into an emergency treatment unit of some big Los Angeles hospital. *Incredible Hulk* star Lou Ferrigno lumbers about as one of the paramedics.

**THE TRAVELS OF JAIMIE MCPHEETERS (**) 60 min (26ep B&W; 1963–1964 ABC) Western** *with Dan O'Herlihy as Sardius "Doc" McPheeters, Kurt Russell as Jaimie McPheeters, James Westerfield as John Murrel, Sandy Kenyon as Shep Baggott, Michael Witney as Buck Coulter, Hedley Mattingly as Henry T. Coe, and Charles Bronson as Linc Murdock*

A wagon train is heading west in the late 1840s, and the McPheeters are on board. Irish-brogued Doc McPheeters and his twelve-year-old son Jaimie are but a small part of the horde heading to the promised land (California). This series is filled with all the exploits you would imagine in a wagon train concept. Kurt Russell (as Jaimie) makes his first regular TV series appearance here, although he had been in numerous specials before. He later played Elvis Presley in the 1979 TV movie *Elvis* and starred in films such as *Silkwood, Used Cars* and *Overboard.* Dan O'Herlihy, a fine Irish actor (in such features as the 1952 theatrical film version of *The Adventures of Robinson Crusoe*) plays Jaimie's father a bit too broadly, and looks out of place on the prairie with his stovepipe hat. Michael Witney is too pretty as the original wagonmaster, Buck Coulter. After only a few episodes, Coulter is killed (trampled while saving Jaimie's life). The new wagonmaster, Linc Murdock, is more authentically rugged and is played by Charles Bronson, in his last TV series appearance before becoming a movie star. Look for the four harmonizing religious Kissel sons, played by the Osmond Brothers (who sing the show's theme song), making their first TV series appearance.

This series is based on a 1958 novel of the same name by Robert Lewis Taylor.

**TREASURE ISLAND, RETURN TO (**½) 60 min (8ep & 2 hr première Color; 1986 Disney) Adventure** *with Brian Blessed as Long John Silver, Christopher Guard as Jim Hawkins, Morgan Sheppard as Boakes, and Kenneth Colley as Ben Gunn*

Set ten years after the original Robert Lewis Stevenson book (and the 1950 Disney theatrical film), this sequel follows Long John Silver on his quest back to Treasure Island to retrieve the loot he and Jim Hawkins left behind on their last visit. Brian Blessed is a worthy successor to Robert Newton (from the feature film) as the scheming Silver. ■

**TRIAL AND ERROR (*½) 30 min (6ep Color; 1988 CBS) Situation Comedy** *with Eddie Velez as John Hernandez, Paul Rodriguez as Tony Rivera, John de Lancie as Bob Adams, Debbie Shapiro as Rhonda, and Stephen Elliott as Edmund Kittle*

This short-run comedy barely set up its odd couple living situation before grinding to a halt. Too bad because there's potential here with two familiar Hispanic performers, Eddie Velez (an *A-Team* member from that program's final season) and Paul Rodriguez (from the comedy *a.k.a. Pablo*), as lifelong friends from East Los Angeles sharing living quarters as adults, but with completely different daytime jobs. John is a recent law school graduate working at a prestigious lily-white law firm, while Tony peddles T-shirts near downtown L. A. Naturally their separate circles are always on a collision course. Sort of *L. A. Law* meets *Perfect Strangers,* but without time to develop the mix.

**THE TRIALS OF O'BRIEN (**½) 60 min (22ep B&W; 1965–1966 CBS) Law Drama** *with Peter Falk as Daniel J. O'Brien, Joanna Barnes as Katie O'Brien, David Burns as The Great McGonigle, Elaine Stritch as Miss G, Ilka Chase as Margaret, and Dolph Sweet as Lt. Garrison*

It is tempting to regard this series as merely a character warm-up for Peter Falk's *Columbo,* but that shortchanges the premise. This is also a very unusual television law drama, with Falk's Daniel J. O'Brien a wonderfully earthy but charmingly flamboyant attorney who lives just beyond his considerable means (with money always going to cover his expensive apartment, his alimony payments, and his weakness for gambling). He'll take any and all cases (a fee is a fee) because, of course, when it comes to the courtroom he's beyond reproach. This series has consistently good writing and a strong assortment of guest stars (including Gene Hackman, Faye Dunaway, Angela Lansbury, Alan Alda, and Roger Moore). It is well worth searching out, if only to see Falk sharply dressed for court, and to keep an eye out for even a brief appearance by a rumpled raincoat.

**THE TRIPODS (***) 30 min (26ep Color; 1984–1985 UK BBC & Australia 7 Network) Science Fiction** *with John Shackley as Will Parker, Jim Baker as Henry, and Ceri Seel as Beanpole*

Suppose the invading alien forces in the H.G. Wells tale *War of the Worlds* had won? What would life on earth be like under the entrenched rule of visitors from another planet? This entertaining science fiction adventure (set primarily in Britain and France in 2089) offers one vision of such a future.

Though not directly connected to the classic *War of the Worlds* tale (this one is based on a trilogy of books written by John Christopher), the series evokes visions of those desperate battles because the alien "Tripod" machines are just as menacing and apparently unbeatable. But, since they've been triumphant and in control for about 100 years, the Tripods rarely need to use their might. Instead, through their human agents, they've kept the general populace in check by kicking available technology back to 18th century levels. Even more important, they've instituted a "capping ceremony" on each child's sixteenth birthday, implanting a mind-controlling device that supposedly offers peace of mind and great understanding, but actually quashes any rebellious urges and destroys the will to resist.

After seeing that happen to one of his friends, young (and independent) Will Parker decides to take the biggest risk of his life. So, on the eve of his ritual capping, he and his younger cousin Henry (also uncapped) run away from home. Their goal: the White Mountains (Switzerland) where, legend has it, they might find the last stronghold of resistance to the Tripods. After a harrowing journey across the English channel, they meet a young French boy (nicknamed Beanpole) who joins them on their quest.

Though the series contains the close calls and demonstrations of alien firepower you'd expect in such a science fiction adventure, it also stands apart with its own unique tone. As in the very best literary "quest" adventures, *The Tripods* dares to linger in particular settings, offering a taste of the deceptively peaceful, almost medieval world of the 21st century. It manages to convey a true sense of discovery among the three boys as they grow from runaway waifs to front-line freedom fighters.

The series is quite involving, but be forewarned: This adaptation only gets through two-thirds of the trilogy (a third batch of thirteen episodes was never produced). So, if you want to see how it turns out, you'll have to read all about it in the novels themselves: *The White Mountains, The City of Gold and Lead,* and *The Pool of Fire.* ■

**THE TROUBLE WITH FATHER (see *The Stu Erwin Show*)**

**TROUBLESHOOTERS (**) 30 min (26ep B&W; 1959–1960 NBC) Adventure** *with Keenan Wynn as Kodiak and Bob Mathias as Frank Dugan*

Kodiak (a man, not a bear) is chief troubleshooter for a big construction company. He is sent to handle emergencies (fires, accidents, strikes, earthquakes) that occur on the job, so work can go back to normal. Kodiak has a new trainee, Frank Dugan, and the two operate in tandem. Bob Mathias, who plays Dugan, was an Olympic decathlon champion in 1948 and 1952.

**TRUE (see *General Electric True*)**

**TRYING TIMES (**½) 30 min (6ep at Summer 1989 Color; 1987 & 1989– PBS) Comedy Anthology**

Though individual public television stations import a good number of British comedies, when it comes to homegrown product they've often been accused of coming up short on humorous offerings. (Intentional humor, that is—*The McLaughlin Group* is beyond the scope of this book.) This anthology represents a positive move in the direction of laughter, with a variety of writers, directors, and performers invited to participate in some offbeat setups.

They all follow the same basic framing structure, with a main character narrating a flashback tale meant to explain what caused this latest trying time. The series kicks off with "A Family Tree" (directed by Jonathan Demme), featuring Rosanna Arquette as a young woman meeting her future in-laws for the first time at a special family dinner. Just so there's no doubt about the disastrous consequences, she begins her tale at the charred remains of their suburban home.

The stars and hooks in some of the other episodes include Teri Garr (in "Drive, She Said") as a New York apartment dweller determined to learn to drive in order to get over an unhappy relationship; Steven Wright (in "Get a Job") as a perpetual student forced to consider employment at age thirty when his parents stop supporting him; and Spalding Gray (in "Bedtime Story") as a man suffering from insomnia, caused by the ticking of his girlfriend's biological clock.

Clearly such material is not going to give the gang at *Night Court* anything to worry about—this is not a gag-a-minute program. Instead it's a view of the world that would be quite at home in a Woody Allen film or on *thirtysomething.* In fact, the overall look of the series is reminiscent of Allen's *Annie Hall,* with the various characters standing in front of a neutral background to deliver their observations in between bits of action. Nonetheless, there's nothing wrong with that. After all, why bother to turn out just another network sitcom? (Plenty of those come and go each season.) Perhaps it would be nice to break once in a while from this particular slice of the known universe (mostly the Manhattan/California axis), but for the moment let's just consider this show a small but important first step on the road to more chuckling on PBS.

**TUCKER'S WITCH (**) 60 min (12ep Color; 1982–1983 CBS) Detective Drama** *with Tim Matheson as Rick Tucker, Catherine Hicks as Amanda Tucker, Barbara Barrie as Ellen Hobbes, and Bill Morey as Lt. Sean Fisk*

There is nothing inherently bad about the idea of a husband and wife detective team in which the wife is a working witch. The problem is that *Tucker's Witch* takes this idea and does little with it. As a result, it is nothing more than a gimmick series that runs out of steam fast. There is some humor here, since wife Amanda's powers are quite fallible, but the series never quite gels.

**TUGBOAT ANNIE, THE ADVENTURES OF (**½) 30 min (39ep B&W; 1957–1958 Syndication) Situation Comedy** *with Minerva Urecal as "Tugboat" Annie Brennan and Walter Sande as Capt. Horatio Bullwinkle*

Amidst a decade filled with happy homemakers, daffy redheads, prim and proper young ladies, and an occasional independent spinster or two, Tugboat Annie is virtually the only woman in 1950s TV who gets her hands dirty. Built like a Mack truck, with a voice like a foghorn, Tugboat Annie pilots the tug *Narcissus* in a Pacific Northwest harbor. Annie is forever trading insults and epithets with Capt. Bullwinkle (who is not a moose). The emphasis is on humor here, but there are enough adventures tossed in to fill any dead spots.

The Tugboat Annie character originated many moons ago in a series of *Saturday Evening Post* articles by Norman Reilly Raine. She captured the public's eye in a 1933 film starring Marie Dressler and Wallace Beery.

**TURN OF FATE (**) 30 min (38ep B&W; 1957–1958 NBC) Drama Anthology**

This show is an odd, short-run remnant of the long-running *Goodyear TV Playhouse* and its alternating companion in the later years, *The Alcoa Hour,* two respected drama anthology series from the 1950s. For most of their respective runs they specialized in live offerings, but beginning in the fall of 1957, they presented thirty-eight filmed dramas under the umbrella title *Turn of Fate,* with Hollywood film stars Robert Ryan, Jane Powell, Jack Lemmon, David Niven, and Charles Boyer taking turns (in a variety of roles) as the lead performer. That entire package is still available for syndication, though today it comes off as just an average collection of suspense melodramas.

**TURNABOUT (*) 30 min (7ep Color; 1979 NBC) Situation Comedy** *with John Schuck as Sam Alston, Sharon Gless as Penny Alston, Richard Stahl as Jack Overmeyer, and Bobbi Jordan as Judy Overmeyer*

Sam Alston is a gruff macho sportswriter. His wife Penny is an executive for a women's cosmetics company. Forever arguing over who has a tougher life, the pair bump into some gypsy potion that magically "turns them about," placing *her* mind into *his* body, and vice versa. To top it off, they can't undo the switch. So "he" must try to act normal in her body, and "she" must do likewise.

There is an awful lot of overly obvious humor here. The idea is sort of cute, but not for more than an episode or two. Sharon Gless went on to star as Chris Cagney in *Cagney & Lacey.*

**TURN-ON (zero) 30 min (2ep Color; 1969 NBC) Comedy-Variety**

One of the most famous flop series of the late 1960s, *Turn-On* is a half-hour *Laugh-In* clone from executive producer George Schlatter. Only one episode aired before the program was canceled, though there was another finished and ready for broadcast. Supposedly as many as four others were in various stages of completion, with the Monkees even slotted to appear in one.

What went wrong? Essentially, this is *Laugh-In* done at double speed but without the reassuring presence of Dan Rowan and Dick Martin as supervising hosts. Instead, a company of players and the guest star (Tim Conway on the only episode broadcast) play second fiddle to a computer supposedly churning out the material. Unfortunately, it plays like pure formula comedy generated by an oily old adding machine. Even a dollop of "controversial" phrases (on such subjects as the birth control pill) can't save it. Still, if you have the chance to see this (especially the unaired episodes) take it. *Turn-On* is a genuine historical curiosity (Tim

Conway still enjoys referring to it on the talk show circuit) showing off "pseudo-hip" late 1960s television at its most embarrassing.

**12 O'CLOCK HIGH (***) 60 min (78ep: 61 B&W & 17 Color; 1964–1967 ABC) War Drama** *with Robert Lansing as Gen. Frank Savage, John Larkin as Gen. Wiley Crowe, Paul Burke as Capt./Maj./Col. Joe Gallagher, Andrew Duggan as Gen. Ed Britt, and Chris Robinson as Sgt. Sandy Komansky*

A gritty and heartfelt view of an American fighter bomber squadron involved in the European theater of World War II, *12 O'Clock High* stands out as one of the better war series on TV. Produced by Quinn Martin (*The Fugitive, The F.B.I.*), *12 O'Clock High* even takes the unheard-of step of killing off its main character after the first season. Gen. Savage is shot down and rapidly rising officer Joe Gallagher takes over.

The early black-and-white episodes with Robert Lansing (and his brooding eyebrows) are the best and pack an emotional punch. As the series ages, especially during the final color season, it begins to lose its fine flavor for detail.

The series is based on a 1949 Oscar-winning film with Gregory Peck.

**THE 20TH CENTURY (***½) 30 min (222ep B&W; 1957–1966 CBS) Documentary** *with Walter Cronkite as narrator*

Part of the great CBS tradition of entertaining yet informative documentary series, *The 20th Century* focuses each week on some event or movement of this century. The show provides a great overview of each topic, using archival photographs, newsreels, and interviews. Walter Cronkite (not yet a deified news icon) is at his fervid best providing the emphatic narration. The only problem is that World War II receives an inordinate amount of attention due to the excess of available stock film.

After nine seasons, *The 20th Century* was revamped and became *The 21st Century.*

**THE 20TH CENTURY-FOX HOUR (*½) 60 min (45ep B&W; 1955–1957 CBS) Drama Anthology**

One of the earliest efforts by a major film studio to produce a weekly TV series, this collection of filmed dramas consists mostly of adaptations of famous 20th Century-Fox movies, cut down to an hour and featuring different actors.

**THE 21ST CENTURY (**½) 30 min (55ep Color; 1967–1970 CBS) Documentary** *with Walter Cronkite as narrator*

After exhausting the first two-thirds of this century in *The 20th Century,* CBS News tried to keep the concept going with a look to the future. In this series, scientific and social advances that may bear fruit in the next century are discussed and explained. The lack of exciting film footage and the unavoidable theoretical nature of many of the topics covered drag this admirable series down and leave the viewer somewhat deadened. The passage of time since the program was produced also renders a lot of it outdated. ■

**21 BEACON STREET (*½) (34ep B&W; 1959–1960 NBC) Detective Drama** *with Dennis Morgan as Dennis Chase, Joanna Barnes as Lola, Brian Kelly as Brian, and James Maloney as Jim*

Grind-em-out cases with a brilliant private investigator (Dennis Chase), his sexy secretary (Lola), a dedicated law student (Brian), and a master of disguise and dialects (Jim). No one cares about these anymore. Besides, the kids on Jump Street are a lot more fun.

**21 JUMP STREET (**½) 60 min (54ep at Fall 1989 & 2 hr pilot Color; 1987– Fox) Police Drama** *with Jeff Yagher and Johnny Depp as Tom Hanson, Peter DeLuise as Doug Penhall, Holly Robinson as Judy Hoffs, Dustin Nguyen as Harry Truman "H. T." Ioki, Frederic Forrest as Capt. Richard Jenko, Steven Williams as Capt. Adam Fuller, and Richard Grieco as Dennis Booker*

*The Mod Squad* for the "just say NO" generation, *21 Jump Street* follows the trendy exploits of four baby-face undercover cops who mingle with high school students in Los Angeles. Handsome hunk Tom Hanson, muscle man Doug Penhall, sultry black Judy Hoffs, and lighthearted Oriental H. T. Ioki battle drug dealers and teen gangs, while helping their younger contemporaries deal with AIDS, teen suicides, and prejudice. The quartet operates out of an abandoned church at 21 Jump Street and report, at first, to free-spirited police superior Capt. Richard Jenko. Giving in to TV cop show conformity, *21 Jump Street* soon kills Jenko off, to replace him with a more typical by-the-book superior (Capt. Fuller), who can rail at the young cops' nonconformist behavior.

Produced by TV cop show pro Stephen J. Cannell (*The A-Team, Rockford Files*), *21 Jump Street* brings a little fresh air to the crime-fighting mold, by focusing on policemen that teens can really relate to. Unlike *The Mod Squad* of the 1960s/1970s, this show mostly avoids moralistic heavy-handedness and has enough flashy images and car chases to entertain fans of TV crime action. The little public service messages the cast take turns giving at the end of most episodes are admirable, but slightly hokey.

**26 MEN (*½) 30 min (87ep B&W; 1957–1959 Syndication) Western** *with Tris Coffin as Capt. Tom Rynning and Kelo Henderson as Clint Travis*

A bargain basement version of *Tales of Texas Rangers, 26 Men* moves slightly west, to the Arizona Territory at the turn of the century. The local legislature established the Arizona Rangers, but limited its size to twenty-six men. Based on the files of the Arizona Rangers, this series has the usual assortment of gunfights, Indian attacks, and bank robbers.

**20/20** **(**½) 60 min (Color; 1978– ABC) Public Affairs** *with Hugh Downs and Barbara Walters as hosts*

This show is ABC's version of *60 Minutes,* though it has a somewhat lighter tone than the CBS program. Principal host Hugh Downs (a *Today* show alumnus) tends toward more kindly conversations than Mike Wallace–style grillings. Co-host Barbara Walters (another *Today* graduate) specializes in celebrity interviews. Geraldo Rivera, who spent seven years (1978–1985) as a regular contributor to *20/20,* adds his usual excess of flash to his investigative reports. While not really a memorable series, *20/20* is a fine show, with many interesting and informative pieces.

The very first episode of the series is a unique rarity. It is the one and only appearance by the original hosts, *Esquire* editor Harold Hayes and Australian art critic Robert Hughes. The pair, both TV novices, were dumped immediately and replaced by the more familiar Downs.

**THE TWILIGHT ZONE** **(****) 30 & 60 min (248ep: 136 B&W 30 min, 18 B&W 60 min, and 94 Color 30 min, plus 60 min B&W pilot; 1959–1964 & 1985–1987 & 1988–1989 CBS & Syndication) Science Fiction Anthology** *with Rod Serling as host, and Charles Aidman and Robin Ward as narrators*

*The Twilight Zone* may well be television at its best. When it comes to great dramas, the written novel rules supreme. For lively musicals, TV can't compete with the Broadway stage. Great sweeping epics always look better on the huge silver screen. Yet for small, intimate, simple stories of human conflict, thirty-minute black and white productions with restricted budgets such as the original *Twilight Zone* possess a simple beauty that is unrivaled.

Rod Serling, creator of *The Twilight Zone,* may not have agreed that these short playlets were the highest video art form possible. He earned his reputation in the mid-1950s, writing some of the most powerful dramas of TV's so-called golden age. Two such plays ("Patterns" and "Requiem for a Heavyweight") both won Emmy awards and were later turned into Hollywood films. By the late 1950s, however, the live drama anthologies that featured Serling's scripts were dying and being replaced by filmed series from Hollywood that strove to agitate nobody and mollify everybody.

*The Twilight Zone* is Serling's valiant effort to combine the best aspects of the old drama anthologies with the trend toward filmed series with continuing characters. He takes the wide scope of topics possible in an anthology format and wraps the tales in the guise of science fiction and suspense so that the moral is more subtle.

Serling's contribution to *The Twilight Zone* is not, of course, only as a writer, though he did write or adapt over half the original episodes. He also serves as an on-screen host and narrator whom regular viewers can rely on for a modicum of stability. His chiseled looks and staccato delivery have become hallmarks, but they serve their purpose in focusing the viewer's attention and setting the appropriate tone.

The original *Twilight Zone* episodes are so powerful because Serling takes full advantage of the limitations of the program's format. A thirty-minute show does not allow much time when you must create a new universe each week. Serling thus focuses his attention on innovative situations, ones that are too farfetched or cumbersome to last for any extended period of time. They are, however, just right to serve as the basis for a quick morality lesson or a fast sleight-of-hand with reality.

For example, in "The Hitch-Hiker," Inger Stevens (*The Farmer's Daughter*) plays a woman driving from New York to California who inexplicably keeps seeing the same ominous hitchhiker beckoning to her along the way, even though it is made clear that the man couldn't possibly be traveling so fast by normal means. After building up the suspense for most of the episode, Stevens's character learns that she is dead as a result of a car crash at the site where she first saw the stranger. She realizes that the stranger is Death, who is beckoning her to accept her fate and cross into eternity with him.

In "The After Hours," Anne Francis (*Honey West*) plays a woman who stumbles into a bizarre and nearly empty ninth floor of a large department store. After purchasing a thimble from a mean saleslady, Francis's character returns to the ground floor and attempts to complain of her treatment, but is shocked to learn that the store has no ninth floor. The nasty saleslady turns out to be a mannequin, and (double surprise!) Francis's character turns out to be a mannequin as well, one who overstayed her allotted time of living amongst the humans and now must return to the stationary existence meant for her.

The often fuzzy line between reality and illusion serves as one of the most common themes of *The Twilight Zone.* Is a business executive really who he thinks he is, or is he just an actor portraying a businessman and having a breakdown? Is a man slated to go to the electric chair really a convicted murderer, or is everyone around him merely an element of the convict's mind, created as part of his recurring dream?

In numerous episodes, wicked twists of fate crush the main character at the story's end. A bookworm is the sole survivor of a nuclear war, and he comes to joyously accept his status, since he now has time to read all the books he wants, with no interruptions. Unfortunately he then breaks his glasses, leaving him virtually blind for the rest of his life. In another, a government decoding expert can't seem to decipher a book entitled

*To Serve Man* that is brought by super-developed aliens who promise to share their immense knowledge with humanity. As the expert boards a shuttle rocket to the aliens' home planet, he learns that *To Serve Man* is a cookbook, and he is that day's main course.

*The Twilight Zone* reaches its peak in some episodes that are just plain spooky. In one, Billy Mumy (*Lost in Space*) is a young child who becomes preoccupied with talking to his dead grandmother on a toy telephone the old woman gave him before her death. The boy's parents finally must plead with the grandmother's spirit to let the boy go, so he can live his own life. "The Invaders" (one of the most innovative episodes) contains virtually no dialogue and features only one person, Agnes Moorehead (*Bewitched*). As a simple farm woman, Moorehead suddenly is thrust into a life-and-death battle with strange tiny aliens who land in her cottage. After thirty minutes of tense struggle, during which the viewer roots for the old lady, she kills the invaders. Only then do we learn that the "aliens" are really American astronauts who landed on a world of giants. It is Moorehead's character who is the alien.

These stories are simple, the morals are sometimes simplistic, the special effects are minimal at best, but *The Twilight Zone* almost always engages the viewer's mind by positing an intriguing premise or taking you where you did not expect to go. This is done through deft writing, good production, and fine acting. It sounds so simple, yet so many others have tried to accomplish much more and failed. By accomplishing its limited goals and maintaining its creative dignity, *The Twilight Zone* must be considered a complete success.

As with any artistic endeavor, *The Twilight Zone* has its ups and downs. The first season contains a very high percentage of memorable episodes. Six installments in the second season are videotaped, rather than filmed, and most of them look pretty cheap. By the third season, some of the scripts start becoming a little trite. The series was actually canceled after three years, but popular demand brought it back for a truncated fourth. The eighteen episodes from the fourth season are all an hour in length, and very few benefit from the extra time. The additional half-hour seems to be taken up with superfluous exposition that cries out for editing. The fifth and final season of the original program reverts to the thirty-minute format, and contains some of the best and some of the worst stories.

After 154 installments, the old black and white *Twilight Zone* fades to black. It would take almost two decades to revive the concept. By the mid-1980s, Rod Serling had been dead almost ten years. His masterpiece, however, had grown in stature with the passage of time. In 1983, the film *Twilight Zone—The Movie* showed how the concept could work with more modern high-tech trappings. The film strung together four stories (three remakes of old *Twilight Zone* stories and a fourth inspired by a Serling tale) and used the talents of four top modern directors (Steven Spielberg, John Landis, Joe Dante, and George Miller). The movie's moderate success led to an actual revival of the TV series in 1985 (in color).

Wisely avoiding the pitfalls of replacing Serling directly, the 1980s episodes make do with a succinct off-screen narrator. These newer stories do not reach the level of the originals, but they are distinguished additions to the *Twilight Zone* collection.

The new edition of the series began as an hour program, but consisted of two to three stories per episode. Soon after the start of the second season, the new *Twilight Zone* reverted to a thirty-minute show, with just one story each. Some of the already produced hour-long installments were chopped up to fit the shorter format. These mid-1980s *Twilight Zones* are now only distributed in the half-hour length.

After only one and one-half seasons' worth of episodes were produced, the new *Twilight Zone* went back into hibernation. It was revived once again in 1988 as a syndicated half-hour program combining thirty new episodes with some of the chopped-up hour shows and some of the remaining thirty-minute episodes from the mid-1980s. The program thus came full circle, returning to the original structure of a simple, low-budget series that didn't try to do too much. The lesson here is that there is always room for a good short story, told well, with few pretensions of grandeur.

One of the most obscure *Twilight Zone* entries is the 1958 hour-long black and white pilot, "The Time Element," which originally aired on *Desilu Playhouse.* In it, William Bendix (*Life of Riley*) plays a man who goes back in time to Pearl Harbor, two days before the Japanese attack, and has little luck warning the locals of the impending disaster. ■

**TWO FACES WEST (*½) 30 min (39ep B&W; 1960–1961 Syndication) Western** *with Charles Bateman as Ben January and Rick January, and Joyce Meadows as Julie Greer*

In *Two Faces West,* star Charles Bateman plays two roles, those of twin brothers Ben and Rick January. Clean-living Ben is the only doctor in the town of Gunnison, while Rick is more of a fun-loving gunfighter.

**240-ROBERT (*) 60 min (15ep Color; 1979–1981 ABC) Adventure** *with John Bennett Perry as Theodore Roosevelt "Trap" Applegate III, Mark Harmon as Dwayne "Thib" Thibideaux, Joanna Cassidy as Morgan Wainwright, Stephan Burns as Brett Cueva, and Pamela Hensley as Sandy Harper*

From the end of the 1970s comes this forgettable remnant of the wave of TV rescue anthology shows (such as *Emergency!* and *S.W.A.T.*) that emphasized unrelated action over character development. The focus in *240-Robert* is on an Emergency Service Detail of the Los Angeles County Sheriff's office; "240-Robert" is the code name of the three-person unit. The final few episodes bring in an almost totally new cast, but keep the setting the same. Hunk-in-training Mark Harmon appears in the early episodes. *240-Robert* is produced by Rick Rosner, who had a hit with the somewhat similar *CHiPs.*

**TWO MARRIAGES** (**) 60 min (13ep Color; 1983–1984 ABC) Drama *with Tom Mason as Jim Daley, Karen Carlson as Ann Daley, Michael Murphy as Dr. Art Armstrong, Janet Eilber as Nancy Armstrong, and Kirk Cameron as Eric Armstrong*

Marriage in the confused social landscape of the 1980s is the topic of *Two Marriages,* a production of Philip Capice of *Dallas* and *Eight Is Enough* fame. The two families featured are the modern Daleys (both work and both have kids from previous marriages/relationships) and the more traditional Armstrongs (he's a surgeon and she's an unhappy homemaker). Set in Iowa, *Two Marriages* is fairly interesting as a middle America character study, but the characters are not all that compelling.

One highlight of *Two Marriages* is catching the TV series debut of teen heartthrob-to-be Kirk Cameron (who plays the Armstrongs' son), before he became popular on *Growing Pains.*

**THE TWO OF US** (**½) (19ep Color; 1981–1982 CBS) Situation Comedy *with Peter Cook as Robert Brentwood, Mimi Kennedy as Nan Gallagher, Oliver Clark as Cubby Royce, Dana Hill as Gabrielle "Gabby" Gallagher, and Tim Thomerson as Reggie Cavanaugh*

The setting for this series is the New York City apartment of local television celebrity Nan Gallagher (co-host of the light chat show *Mid-Morning Manhattan*). She's a divorced single mother with a smart-tongued daughter and no sense of housekeeping order. Enter the stern voice of reason in the form of Robert Brentwood, a very British gentleman's gentleman with a firm voice, expert culinary and organizational skills, and a healthy disdain for less than proper order in anything. Normally he'd never touch a household like Nan's, but he is in need of a job—and she really, really needs him. So Brentwood accepts the position.

This show is the U.S. version of a successful 1975 British comedy, *Two's Company* (which had Elaine Stritch and Donald Sinden as an American writer in Britain and an acerbic British butler, respectively). What gives the Stateside setting a truly authentic touch is the presence of Peter Cook in the role of Brentwood. As one of the top names in British comedy (best known for his years of work with Dudley Moore), he makes the character instantly creditable with his sarcastic tongue, patented deadpan wit, and withering gaze. The rest of the cast seems to rise to his challenge and they turn in good performances, but overall the series still comes off as too soft too often. If only Cook had been hired to write some episodes as well! The show would still have warmth and affection but would also have some lengthy devastating invective. And this would not just come from Brentwood; Nan's running battle with her egotistical co-host, Reggie Cavanaugh, begs for a spirited series of put-downs.

Instead, *The Two of Us* is an average comedy lifted by better than average casting. It's definitely worth following, at least for a few episodes.

**THE TWO RONNIES** (**½) (48ep Color; 1977–1979 UK BBC) Comedy-Variety *with Ronnie Corbett and Ronnie Barker*

Though both Ronnie Corbett (the smaller one with glasses) and Ronnie Barker (the bigger one with glasses) have had several sitcom vehicles in Britain (especially Barker), this sturdy British comedy-variety package has been their most successful Stateside showcase. It's a durable setup in which the delivery is usually more important than the material. Each episode is essentially the same: They both participate in a brief mock newscast (strictly gags, nothing topical), promising "a packed program tonight." Then it's off to a bar or party sketch, a solo monologue from Corbett sitting in a huge chair, an elaborate musical parody production number, some closing news stories, and "It's goodnight from him . . . and goodnight from him." Standard stuff, but absolutely reliable. If you want to catch the Ronnies in one of their comedies, your best bets are Corbett's *Sorry* and Barker's *Open All Hours* and *Porridge.* ■

**227** (**½) 30 min (91ep at Fall 1989 Color; 1985– NBC) Situation Comedy *with Marla Gibbs as Mary Jenkins, Hal Williams as Lester Jenkins, Alaina Reed Hall as Rose Lee Holloway, Helen Martin as Pearl Shay, Regina King as Brenda Jenkins, and Jackée Harry as Sandra Clark*

Marla Gibbs takes the personality type that won her fame as Florence, the maid on *The Jeffersons,* and refines it into Mary Jenkins, a happily married woman living in a Washington, D.C. apartment house (number 227). Mary has a responsible husband (played by former *Private Benjamin* drill sergeant, Hal Williams), a budding teenage daughter, and plenty of friends—including Rose (owner of the building), Pearl (a nosy old-time resident), and Sandra (a sharp-tongued looker thoroughly enjoying her search for the perfect man). Together they build a nice sense of resident camaraderie, swapping quips along with salient plot and character points on the front stoop of the building, especially regarding Sandra's latest escapades.

**TWO'S COMPANY** (**½) 30 min (29ep Color; 1975–1976 UK London Weekend Television) Situation Comedy *with Elaine Stritch as Dorothy McNab and Donald Sinden as Robert Hiller*

Dorothy McNab is a successful Stateside mystery writer living in and working from a London townhouse.

She fits the English caricature of a pushy, abrasive, and ill-mannered American right down to her love of "cheroots" (cigars). Robert Hiller is a gentleman's gentleman, the epitome of supreme self-confidence in managing a household, and a proud champion of England's unmatched good taste and decorum. He is also McNab's butler. Though it presents quite a challenge, Robert likes the situation because it pays well, he has his own private quarters, and he usually manages to keep his employer in line.

Though this clash of character types (symbolized by an animated American eagle and British lion singing the title song) is nothing new, it works pretty well as a showcase for two veteran performers. American-born Elaine Stritch had several decades of comedy on stage, in films, and on television (including *My Sister Eileen* in the 1960s) before taking this role (shortly after relocating to Britain in the early 1970s). Before this series, British born Donald Sinden turned up primarily in theatrical films ranging from the *Doctor in the House* feature in 1954 to *The Day of the Jackal* in 1973, usually playing rather nondescript parts.

In 1981, Peter Cook and Mimi Kennedy starred in a Stateside version of this setup, *The Two of Us.*

**THE TYCOON (*) 30 min (26ep B&W; 1964–1965 ABC) Situation Comedy** *with Walter Brennan as Walter Andrews, Van Williams as Pat Burns, Jerome Cowan as Herbert Wilson, Janet Lake as Betty Franklin, and Pat McNulty as Martha Keane*

Danny Thomas produces and Walter Brennan stars in this disappointing comedy about an elderly slightly eccentric millionaire (Walter Andrews) who runs the Thunder Corporation, a West Coast-based conglomerate. We never really know what Thunder does, but we do get to hear a lot of guff from Andrews, who is sort of a refined and rich version of Grandpa McCoy (of *The Real McCoys*), Brennan's most famous role. Andrews is quick to tell everyone how everything should be done. Since he is the boss, everybody must kowtow and say "yes, sir."

**U.F.O. (**) 60 min (26ep Color; 1970 UK ATV) Science Fiction** *with Ed Bishop as Ed Straker, George Sewell as Colonel Alec Freeman, Gabrille Drake as Lt. Gay Ellis, Michael Billington as Colonel Paul Foster, and Peter Gordeno as Captain Peter Karlin*

The aliens are here. Today. Only the dedicated forces of SHADO (Supreme Headquarters Alien Defense Organization) stand between us and a rather grisly fate. Operating from two main locations—a bunker hidden beneath the Harlington-Straker film studios in London, and a secret moon base—SHADO fights the aliens in the air, at sea, and on land, using supercharged vehicles such as the *Skydiver* and SHADO-mobile.

If the movement of those seem vaguely familiar, there's a good reason: This was the first live-action TV series for "supermarionation" creator Gerry Anderson, best known for such kiddie super-charged vehicle adventures as *Supercar, Stingray,* and *Fireball XL-5.* This venture definitely benefited from the technical action skills honed in those other series. Unfortunately the characters seem a bit stiff and humorless—we expect a bit more from living, breathing human beings.

On the other hand, consider the reason the aliens are supposedly here—they can't reproduce, so the only way for them to survive is by cannibalizing humans for body parts. Perhaps that's the ultimate in-joke, an oblique reference to the interchangeable limbs from those puppet casts of the previous Anderson series. ■

**U. S. BORDER PATROL (*) 30 min (39ep B&W; 1958–1959 Syndication) Police Drama** *with Richard Webb as Don Jagger*

With the records of all of the important crime-fighting agencies already rifled by other TV producers in search of story lines, the gang here falls back on the files of the U.S. Border Patrol. Sounds pretty boring. It is. Richard Webb formerly starred in *Captain Midnight.*

**U. S. MARSHAL (see *Man from Cochise*)**

**THE UGLIEST GIRL IN TOWN (½) 30 min (20ep Color; 1968–1969 ABC) Situation Comedy** *with Peter Kastner as Timothy "Timmie" Blair, Patricia Brake as Julie Renfield, and Garry Marshall as Gene Blair*

It's a pity that this show is so obscure, for it probably deserves at least an honorable mention in the worst shows of all time list. Tim Blair is an L. A. talent scout who falls for a British actress in town to shoot a movie. When Julie, the starlet, flies home to London, Tim can't afford to chase her and instead pines away. Soon thereafter, Tim's photographer brother Gene uses Tim, dressed in drag, as an emergency stand-in for a fashion shoot about the "mod look" (this is the late 1960s when long hair and the unisex look were in vogue). Gene's photos catch the eye of some London fashion mogul and Tim (now labeled Timmie) is flown to London to be the new Twiggy. Tim, a.k.a. Timmie, is happy, because now he can pursue Julie, albeit while trying to maintain his second identity as a female fashion star.

This plot sounds extremely complicated and it is. The sitcom itself is not very funny, and the sight gags and expected laugh lines about Tim/Timmie and his/her secret are all pretty obvious. *Bosom Buddies* pulled off an American sitcom in drag, but *The Ugliest Girl in Town* fails. Rather than being racy and bawdy, it's just ridiculous and inane.

**UNDER ONE ROOF** (**) **30 min (7ep Color; 1985 NBC) Situation Comedy** *with Mimi Kennedy as Doris Winger, Ross Harris as Spencer Winger, Harold Gould as Ben Sprague, Frances Sternhagen as Millie Sprague, and Dean Cameron as Herbie Bailey*

The revamped version of *Spencer,* following the departure of Chad Lowe from that title role. This time, there is more emphasis on the adults as the series changes to three generations under one roof: Spencer (now played by Ross Harris, the son on *United States*), his mom, Doris (now a single mother, abandoned by her husband for some nineteen-year-old), and Doris's parents, Ben and Frances. All this gives adult characters such as those played by Mimi Kennedy and Harold Gould a few minutes at center stage in between the teen plots. That's a bit of an improvement over *Spencer,* but not much.

**THE UNDERSEA WORLD OF JACQUES COUSTEAU** (***) **60 min (36ep Color; 1967–1976 Syndication) Documentary** *with Jacques Cousteau and Rod Serling as narrator*

Though originally aired as a series of specials, these delightful nature explorations (led by French undersea explorer Jacques Cousteau) often turn up today in a regular rerun slot. The scenery is spectacular, the water life (such as dolphins, penguins, and whales) irresistible, and the rhythm of the narration perfectly suited to the image of a worldly wise "old salt" sharing his favorite sea stories. In some of the episodes, former *Twilight Zone* host Rod Serling also acts as narrator. ■

**THE UNEXPECTED** (*) **30 min (39ep B&W; 1952–1953 Syndication) Suspense Anthology** *with Herbert Marshall as host*

Versatile English character actor Herbert Marshall hosts this tepid collection of tales of suspense. These films are also known as *Times Square Playhouse.*

**UNICORN TALES** (**) **30 min (8ep Color; 1977 Syndication) Children's Anthology**

Several classic children's fairy tales are adapted for modern children in this anthology. These pale before Shelley Duvall's *Faerie Tale Theater.*

**UNION PACIFIC** (**) **30 min (39ep B&W; 1958 Syndication) Western** *with Jeff Morrow as Bart McClelland, Judd Pratt as Bill Kinkaid, and Susan Cummings as Georgia*

The final link-up of the transcontinental Union Pacific railroad is the basic setting for this forgotten western.

**UNITED STATES** (**½) **30 min (13ep Color; 1980 & 1983 NBC & A&E) Situation Comedy** *with Beau Bridges as Richard Chapin, Helen Shaver as Libby Chapin, Rossie Harris as Dylan Chapin, and Justin Dana as Nicky Chapin*

Richard and Libby Chapin are a successful young married couple with two children and a nice suburban home. It's a familiar sitcom setting, but in *United States* they do a most un-television-like thing: They talk. To, with, and at each other. And they don't use typical sitcom babble. Instead the two of them intelligently discuss sex, death, personal doubts, feelings of guilt, and painful memories, sometimes revealing secrets they had kept hidden from each other since before they were married. (Though it's hard to imagine that they would have anything left unsaid by this time in their marriage.)

And that's it. There is no laugh track, no catchy theme music, no screwball neighbors, no elaborate pratfalls. In fact, sometimes the two main characters don't even leave their bedroom.

*United States* represents quite a departure for producer Larry Gelbart. Even in his adaptation of the film *M*A*S*H* as a TV series, he stuck a bit closer to conventional television sitcom structure, at least in the beginning. This time he aimed for something completely different from the very start. For its original network run in 1980, the immediate results were a ratings disaster. Viewers tuned out in massive numbers, adamant in their dislike.

But those who stayed were just as strong in their support. As a result, *United States* has a passionately divided reputation: Viewers have alternately described the series as either one of the most daring breakthroughs in television comedy, or the ultimate in pretentious, self-indulgent clap-trap. There's only one thing on which everyone seems to agree: This is not a typical situation comedy, though in truth is it certainly not at either critical extreme.

Perhaps the best way to approach the series is to think of it as eavesdropping on conversations between the couple next door. Once you get to know them, you can't help but get caught up in the mundane details of their lives—that's what gossip is all about. Since Beau Bridges and Helen Shaver make an attractive couple, on this level alone *United States* will probably work for about one or two episodes.

If you like the theatrical film *My Dinner with Andre* (consisting of engaging dinner conversation between two old friends), you'll probably stick around a while longer. And, of course, if you love Woody Allen's "serious" films such as *Interiors* or *September,* or almost anything by Ingmar Bergman, you'll stay for the whole series—though you might find that *United States* is a bit too fast-paced and entertaining in comparison. (Only eight episodes aired in its original NBC release, with the balance shown a few years later on the A&E cable service.)

Whatever your judgment, *United States* emerges as a true television rarity. For better or worse, people certainly never forget having seen it.

**UNIVERSE, WALTER CRONKITE'S** (**½) **30 min (25ep Color; 1980–1982 CBS) Science Magazine** *with Walter Cronkite as host*

This show was an appropriate bookend to Walter Cronkite's stint as chief anchor (and symbol of authority) for CBS News. Twenty-five years before, he had served as host for a popular documentary series, *The 20th Century.* Now he had the opportunity once again to display his personal fascination (even delight) with the wonders of science.

Set up in a news magazine format (similar to *60 Minutes*), *Universe* presents several reports during each episode, drawing on some of the network's top correspondents. Cronkite holds it all together both as host and correspondent himself.

**UNSOLVED MYSTERIES (*) 60 min (37ep at Summer 1989 Color; 1987– NBC) Mystery/Public Interest** *with William Conrad and Robert Stack as host*

The sleazy "reality" format of the late 1970s enjoyed a renaissance in the late 1980s, through shows such as *Unsolved Mysteries.* The idea is to string together short segments of weird events and suspicious mysteries, reenact the high points, and toss in some super-serious narration by Robert Stack (ex–*The Untouchables*). The extra catch is that it includes viewer participation by trying to solve the mysteries through the help of the folks at home (who are given a phone number to call). Once you've seen one town that's been visited by UFOs, you've seen them all.

*Unsolved Mysteries* began as a series of irregularly scheduled specials in 1987 (with William Conrad as host), before graduating to a weekly time slot in 1988 (with Stack stepping in).

**UNSUB (*½) 60 min (8ep Color; 1989 NBC) Crime Drama** *with David Soul as Wes "Westy" Grayson, M. Emmet Walsh as Ned Platt, Joe Maruzzo as Tony D'Agostino, Jennifer Hetrick as Ann Madigan, Andrea Mann as Norma, Kent McCord as Alan McWarters, and Richard Kind as Jimmy Bello*

Wes Grayson is the no-nonsense head of the Department of Justice's Behavioral Sciences Unit, a crime-fighting team that uses only the latest in technical miracles. They solve nasty crimes committed by perpetrators the police label *unsubs* (for *unknown subjects*). Assisting Grayson is an eclectic bunch of crime-fighters. Ned Platt is a grizzled ex-cop, who still knows his stuff, but carries a foam cushion for his hemorrhoids. Ann Madigan is the cool, beautiful researcher. Tony D'Agostino is a psychic who "feels" vibes from the criminal by walking around the scene of the crime. The crimes on *UNSUB* tend to be brutal and disturbing. Grayson and his gang are very, very gung-ho. The technical jargon gets a bit thick at times.

David Soul, who plays Grayson, was more appealing as the comely Hutch in *Starsky and Hutch.* Stephen J. Cannell, who produces *UNSUB,* was more interesting in *The Rockford Files* and *Wiseguy.*

**UNTAMED WORLD (**) 30 min (156ep Color; 1968–1975 NBC & Syndication) Documentary** *with Phil Carey as narrator*

Natural history, concerning both rare endangered animal species and isolated human tribes, is the topic of this long-running documentary series.

**THE UNTOUCHABLES (***) 60 min (118ep & 2 hr pilot B&W; 1959–1963 ABC) Crime Drama** *with Robert Stack as Eliot Ness, Bruce Gordon as Frank Nitti, Nick Georgiade as Agent Enrico Rossi, Paul Picerni as Agent Lee Hobson, Steve London as Agent Rossman, Abel Fernandez as Agent William Youngfellow, Jerry Paris as Agent Martin Flaherty, and Walter Winchell as the narrator*

It never seemed real. From the beginning, *The Untouchables* stood apart from other series as a virtual checklist of every G-man versus the mob cliché and caricature. Though originally touted as a docudrama-type presentation based on the real-life 1930s cases of government agent Eliot Ness, *The Untouchables* really comes off more like a peek into another world—specifically the tabloid newspaper world of screaming headlines and scandals. All the familiar elements are there, only they're run at a much faster pace, punctuated by the breathless Walter Winchell news-as-it's-happening narrative style. Even the exaggerated violence seems somehow appropriate as part of a very different, very frightening, way of life.

But it works, partially because it's hard not to get caught up in these tales of good guys, bad guys, and innocent pawns. Even if they start as caricatures, the characters and settings quickly lure us into their particular dramatic conflict, taking it further than we might expect at first. In addition, the series attracted a good number of famous and later-to-be-famous performers for the guest shot roles, including Robert Duvall, Lee Marvin, Barbara Stanwyck, and Telly Savalas. And Robert Stack's Eliot Ness stands as a rock-hard symbol of law and order and hope, backed by his small band of incorruptible "untouchables."

The series shines at its two plot extremes. At one end are the stories of various big-name crime bosses and lieutenants as they square off against Ness or, just as likely, each other. These shows are like watching a championship fight, with the top contestants from both sides trading blows and looking for a killer punch (literally). Some of the contenders here include performances by Peter Falk, Lloyd Nolan, Neville Brand, and—as the number one lieutenant behind Al Capone—Bruce Gordon as Frank Nitti.

However, some of the best stories take place farther down the hierarchy, when crime is brought to a very personal level. These are played out against a strong backdrop of moral consequence that frightens the innocent and shows penny-ante hustlers the real costs of trying to move into the big time. "Snowball" is typical of this type, with Robert Redford playing an ambitious young operator manufacturing his own "hooch," but with impurities that result in a terrible side effect: blindness.

Ness and his men dispatch them all, though at times it seems like an impossible assignment. For every underling they lock up, dozens more stand ready to take over. Even on the verge of some small victory, a gun-toting mob agent might turn up, fire, and change Ness's assurances of government protection into just a hollow promise.

Still, there were enough successes on *The Untouchables* to turn Eliot Ness into law enforcement's equivalent of Perry Mason. This was reportedly much to the dismay of the F.B.I's J. Edgar Hoover, whose department had to constantly answer fan mail explaining that Eliot Ness was an agent of the Treasury Department, not of the F.B.I.

More than two decades after *The Untouchables* ended its original television run, director Brian De Palma brought the characters back for an original 1987 theatrical feature film. The film concentrated chiefly on Eliot Ness's pursuit of Al Capone, also the subject of the original 1959 *Untouchables* pilot (a two-part presentation that first aired on *Desilu Playhouse*). In 1962, this pilot story was edited into a theatrical film, *The Scarface Mob*. ■

**UP AND COMING (**) 30 min (15ep Color; 1980 PBS) Comedy/Drama** *with Yule Caise as Marcus Wilson, Cindy Herron as Valerie Wilson, L. Wolfe Perry, Jr., as Kevin Wilson, Robert DoQui as Frank Wilson, and Gamy L. Taylor as Joyce Wilson*

Set in modern-day San Francisco, *Up and Coming* tries to present a lighthearted drama about a middle-class black family's trials and tribulations after moving into an integrated neighborhood. The effort is commendable, but the story is thin and stilted.

**UPSTAIRS, DOWNSTAIRS (****) 60 min (68ep: 63 Color & 5 B&W; 1970–1975 UK London Weekend Television) Drama** *with Gordon Jackson as Angus Hudson, Angela Baddeley as Kate Bridges, Jean Marsh as Rose, Simon Williams as James Bellamy, David Langton as Lord Richard Bellamy, Rachel Gurney as Lady Marjorie, Jacqueline Tong as Daisy, Christopher Beeny as Edward, Pauline Collins as Sarah, John Alderton as Thomas, Gareth Hunt as Frederick, Meg Wynn Owen as Hazel, Jenny Tomasin as Ruby, and Lesley-Anne Down as Georgina*

This is a television original that gives soap opera stories a good name. The premise is simple but sturdy: early twentieth-century life at a somewhat upper-class British household, following the activities of both the "upstairs" Bellamy family and their "downstairs" domestic help. Both are treated with loving care and concern, avoiding the clichés of the wise domestic versus the idiot boss (*Hazel*) or the exciting upper class and their nearly irrelevant servants (John Galsworthy's *Forsyte Saga*).

Such even-handedness reflects the divergent backgrounds of the creative team behind the series. The program was conceived by performers Jean Marsh and Eileen Atkins (both with personal roots in the "downstairs" world), then nurtured and supervised by writer-producer John Hawkesworth (definitely from the "upstairs" circles). They and their associates brought to the project a fine eye for detail (including a blueprint of all five levels of the Bellamy home at 165 Eaton Place), a feeling for the times (focusing both on major historical developments and on such "minor" items as the appropriate slang of the era), and, most important, the desire to explore many facets of the characters (their flaws and prejudices as well as their brave hearts).

There is a very strong cast to carry this series, both upstairs and downstairs. Some are there for the duration, others for just a short time, but they all help to convey the authentic feeling of watching some close friends grow with the times. On the domestics' side, chief butler Hudson is the obvious and respected leader, a confident, consummate professional with little doubt on what should be done and who should be doing it (he even keeps a self-scribed guidebook on how to be a gentleman's gentleman). But he is flexible enough to realize when exceptions should be made. Mrs. Bridges, head of the kitchen, is his gregarious comrade, a little more direct about her interest in gossip than Hudson would prefer, but otherwise they're a perfect team.

Series co-creator Jean Marsh gave herself the role of Rose, the steady, reliable maid who's there from the beginning to the final scene of the last episode. Some of the other domestics include the chubby, promiscuous Sarah; faithful housemaid Daisy and her husband Edward; two ambitious footmen, Thomas and Frederick; and the fragile and dependent Ruby.

Upstairs, Lord Richard and Lady Marjorie Bellamy are surprisingly loyal and committed employers who respect the expertise of their staff (especially Hudson). They provide a solid foundation for the household and their extended family, including the children (already young adults), Elizabeth and James. Eventually, a family cousin, Georgina, also moves to Eaton Place, where she blossoms from an uncertain young debutante to a confident young woman ready for marriage (to a suitor played by Anthony Andrews).

Perhaps the best conceptual decision in this series was the careful makeup of the Bellamy family's social and financial status. They are well-off, but not royalty-rich, living in a comfortable London townhouse, not on some thousand-acre country estate. Their household staff is not an extravagant one and occasionally the Bellamys even face relatively rough financial times over some unexpected major expenses (such as estate taxes). In fact, their assets (such as Eaton Place) come primarily from Lady Marjorie, as inherited wealth. Yet because

Richard Bellamy is an active public official (a member of Parliament), their need to maintain a "proper" and fully staffed household makes sense: They have to be ready to entertain royalty if need be (as when King Edward VII comes for dinner), putting forth all the proper social graces and accoutrements. This public life also means there is a legitimate reason to be concerned about potentially scandalous behavior by family members or servants—it can threaten Richard's career. A philandering king or prince may be able to get away with virtually anything, but not a middle-level government official. He has to have a sense of responsibility.

The importance of being responsible is one of the strongest themes throughout the series. The relationship between the Bellamys and the domestics is strong: They all feel a commitment to each other, to their home, and to their country and the world. They're all part of a team—divided into different classes, of course, but a team nonetheless. Led by Mr. Hudson, the staff does a top-of-the-line job maintaining order because they're supposed to. They make the beds, prepare the meals, listen deferentially to their employers, and deftly handle potentially embarrassing situations (such as a birth taking place during the king's visit). The Bellamys, for their part, attempt to use their time and talents in the pursuit of a rich, full life that also gives something back to society. Why? Because this is what a good citizen is supposed to do. In fact, one reason son James is such a fascinating character is that he has a difficult time living up to his potential. He wants to be a responsible adult, but he just can't seem to find his niche. As a result, he emerges as strangely sympathetic even as he's making all the wrong moves.

That's quite a rich foundation for any series, especially when combined with the ever-changing backdrop of real-life historical events. Thus, we get to see the characters go from turn-of-the-century optimism through the challenges of World War I, the unsettling social changes of peacetime and the jazz age, and finally into the puzzling aftermath of the 1929 stock market crash. In doing so, they bring an intimate accessibility to grand events (even the sinking of the *Titanic*), making it more like paging through a family album than a history book. So, it's not just millions of people who lost money in the stock market—it's two in particular, James and Rose. And how they each handle the situation probably tells us more about society as a whole than any litany of statistics from the era.

In its original U.S. run on *Masterpiece Theatre* during the 1970s, *Upstairs, Downstairs* was the offering that lured millions of viewers to public television for the first time. It even inspired an unsuccessful commercial network attempt to duplicate its success in an American setting (*Beacon Hill*). Surprisingly, the original *Upstairs, Downstairs* package for *Masterpiece Theatre* (and a subsequent repackaging in the late 1980s) omitted thirteen episodes from the series—five that were in black and white due to a television labor dispute at the time in England, and eight that were deemed objectionable by mid-1970s standards (dealing with such subjects as suicide, homosexuality, and adultery). But with the success of other "lost episode" packages, they have started turning up here at last.

For most of the cast, *Upstairs, Downstairs* will probably remain their signature series. (For instance, when Angela Baddeley passed away, the British papers mourned the passing of "Mrs. Bridges.") But they've all turned up in many subsequent productions, including adventure series (Gareth Hunt as Mike Gambit in *The New Avengers,* Gordon Jackson leading *The Professionals*), comedies (real-life husband and wife Pauline Collins and John Alderton in *No, Honestly,* and also in their *Upstairs, Downstairs* characters as *Thomas and Sarah*), prestigious miniseries (Anthony Andrews in *Brideshead Revisited*), and feature films (Lesley Anne-Down in *The Pink Panther Strikes Again*). ■

**V and V: THE FINAL BATTLE (***) (4 hr & 6 hr Color; 1983 & 1984 NBC) plus V as a series (**) 60 min (19ep Color; 1984–1985 NBC) Science Fiction** *with Marc Singer as Mike Donovan, Faye Grant as Juliet Parrish, Jane Badler as Diana, Michael Ironside as Ham Tyler, Blair Tefkin as Robin Maxwell, Jenny Beck and Jennifer Cooke as Elizabeth Maxwell, Robert Englund as William, Richard Herd as Supreme Commander John, June Chadwick as Lydia, and Howard K. Smith as the newscaster*

The original *V* miniseries offers a frighteningly effective portrait of just how quickly we can be fooled into handing over control of our lives to a clever oppressor. In this case, alien visitors from another planet land on the Earth and quickly convince the general populace that their interests are peaceful. It all seems harmless enough—they even look like humans (though with dark glasses and slightly metallic voices). And all they claim to need are some chemicals we earthlings can easily supply. In exchange, they offer to help us modernize communications and industry, and even supply many of their people as workers. This clever lure of something for virtually nothing, along with the very real human dream of meeting benign visitors from another planet, results in the alien landing parties being welcomed with open arms, cheering crowds, and a brass band (playing the theme from *Star Wars*). They're even referred to as the "visitors," an innocuous sobriquet that reinforces their image as temporary residents of the planet. Within a surprisingly short time, most people think nothing of seeing a huge alien "mother ship" hovering over dozens of important regions of the world.

But not everybody is convinced. Among the skeptical

is television reporter Mike Donovan, who manages to sneak aboard the main orbiting alien ship with a portable camera. There he gets on tape some peculiar alien habits (they eat white mice, whole) and learns that they are really lizardlike creatures wearing sophisticated masks and costumes to appear humanoid. Most important, contrary to their claims, the visitors are following a calculated plan to take over, control, and sack the planet Earth.

Donovan is discovered but manages to escape from the ship and return to his station with the story of the century—one certain to shake the world from its complacent acceptance of the Visitors. As he prepares for a special news broadcast, he discovers it's already too late. By blithely handing the visitors control of so many things (including maintenance of the country's communications lines), humans have surrendered without firing a shot. Not only does the tape never get on the air but what goes over instead is staged footage of some "street riots and sabotage" (supposedly led by "dissident scientists and educators")—leading to a government "request" that the Visitors move in with their weapons and help restore order. But once they're in position, they don't give up control. And so the real war begins.

It's no coincidence that the bulk of the original *V* miniseries and the follow-up (*V: The Final Battle*) plays like a World War II saga. That's exactly what it is, a contemporary restaging of some sturdy wartime themes, pulling them from the history books and giving them new punch. So when the Visitors hunt down scientists, intellectuals, and other dissidents, it's an obvious parallel to Nazi Germany. So, too, are the ambitious human politicians who work with the enemy, as well as the cruel soldiers that carry out the policies of subjugation. Yet, as in the best war tales, there are also brave individuals who risk their own lives to resist in dozens of major and minor ways. (The program title graphic—a single letter "V"—represents one such act: spray painting that "V" symbol over the Visitors' propaganda posters.) Even a few of the aliens, appalled at their own race's plans, help protect the humans. (One of the first to do so is the soft-spoken William, played by Robert Englund, later Freddy Krueger in the *Nightmare on Elm Street/Freddy's Nightmares* stories.) The key to the entire series is an active underground movement that wages a seemingly hopeless battle against the overwhelming might of the Visitors. Donovan joins this group after fleeing from his station's control room.

Of course, this story is primarily science fiction, so there are also plenty of special effects and unusual twists, including space flight footage, a mind-control torture chamber, and the dramatic birth of an alien-human child. And behind it all is the appropriately cold and ruthless commander of the Visitor forces, Diana—played with gleeful evil by Jane Badler (previously Melinda on the daytime soap *One Life to Live*). She's a classic tough foe, cut from the same ruthless mold of baddies as Ming the Merciless.

It's a long fight, but by the end of *V: The Final Battle,* the symbolic restaging of World War II is pretty much wrapped up. Only this is not quite the end of the story. A subsequent series picks up the battle in a Cold War–style setting, with both sides jockeying for position while searching for a final, decisive victory. Unfortunately, the framework is not as clear-cut as the original miniseries setup, so the stories have a shopworn sameness to them. Also, even though the per-episode budget was substantial, the series could not afford the same concentration of special effects as the original.

Nonetheless, taken together, *V* and *V: The Final Battle* represent a rare instance of television science fiction working particularly well and handling a difficult theme, especially when compared to *Amerika,* which took twice as long to say half as much.

**VACATION PLAYHOUSE (*½) 30 min (59ep B&W & Color; 1963–1967 CBS) Anthology**

These shows are a collection of failed pilot episodes from TV series that never were produced. Stars such as Orson Bean, Eve Arden, Barbara Rush, Ginger Rogers, and Jimmy Durante headline an episode each, in doomed efforts to launch their own programs.

**VALENTINE'S DAY (**) 30 min (34ep B&W; 1964–1965 ABC) Situation Comedy** *with Tony Franciosa as Valentine Farrow, Jack Soo as Rocky Sin, and Janet Waldo as Libby Freeman*

Tony Franciosa plays publishing house editor Valentine Farrow, an amorous big-city playboy. He's a likable enough guy, though the series tries a little too hard to be a sophisticated comedy, especially within the limits of television standards at the time. (It's really not much racier than *Love That Bob* from the 1950s.)

Many of the best moments come from Jack Soo, who plays Valentine's chief cook and bottle washer, a dedicated gambler with a deadpan wit. It's a perfect prototype for his Sgt. Nick Yemana character on *Barney Miller* a decade later. Meanwhile, Franciosa went on to bigger and better publishing assignments on *The Name of the Game.*

**VALERIE/VALERIE'S FAMILY/THE HOGAN FAMILY (**) 30 min (75ep at Fall 1989 Color; 1986– NBC) Situation Comedy** *with Valerie Harper as Valerie Hogan, Jason Bateman as David Hogan, Danny Ponce as Willie Hogan, Jeremy Licht as Mark Hogan, Josh Taylor as Michael Hogan, Christine Ebersole as Barbara Goodwin, Edie McClurg as Patty Poole, Sandy Duncan as Sandy Hogan, Willard Scott as Peter Poole, and Tom Hodges as Rich*

Sitcoms of the 1980s are full of single parents (the decade's largest growth industry). Valerie Hogan is married to jet pilot Michael, but she might as well be a single parent. Michael's frequent foreign travels leave Valerie alone most of the time, with three kids to raise while working at her own job. Ah, a time-pressed dual-income couple trying to be good parents. How 1980s can you get?

Valerie Harper, the star of the 1970s sitcom hit *Rhoda,* is appropriately harried as Valerie Hogan, though her kvetching doesn't seem as cute as it did in *Rhoda.* After one full season as Mrs. Hogan, Harper abruptly walked off the series (in a contract dispute) and the producers scrambled to keep the show going, resulting in several confusing cast and title changes.

At the start of the second full season, it is announced that Valerie Hogan is dead (the result of a car crash), and the title changes to *Valerie's Family.* The new lead is perky Sandy Duncan, who portrays Sandy Hogan, divorced sister of Michael Hogan. She moves into the Hogan home as replacement mom, and the stories begin to focus more on the Hogan offspring. Willie and Mark, the twins, are around in order to be cute. David, the oldest, is available for proto-macho swaggering as he heads for college, where he can pursue girls full-time. Jason Bateman (brother of Justine on *Family Ties*), who plays David, is angling for the teen swoon-of-the-month award.

By the third full season, the title changes once more, to simply *The Hogan Family* (Valerie is rarely mentioned). The infrequently seen paterfamilias, Michael, now turns up more often and begins dating. With all these changes, it is difficult to keep up with this program. Other than serving as a showcase for ogling at Jason Bateman, this series provides routine stories and amiable, if not memorable, characters.

**VAN DER VALK (**½) 60 min (13ep Color; 1972–1973 UK Thames) Detective Drama** *with Barry Foster as Van der Valk, Susan Travers, and Sydney Tafler*

A Dutch police detective dealing with corporate and governmental crime along with the usual accompaniment: bullets, beautiful women, and (momentarily) baffling mysteries.

**VAN DYKE AND COMPANY (**½) 60 min (11ep & two 60 min pilots Color; 1976 NBC) Comedy-Variety** *with Dick Van Dyke, Andy Kaufman, and the L. A. Mime Company*

Comedy-variety shows were dead on arrival through the late 1970s, but *Van Dyke and Company* is one of the better of the failed lot. Dick Van Dyke, best known as a sitcom star, has always been equally adept in pantomime and sketch comedy, and he features both here. He tries real hard, has help from a talented band of unknowns (including Andy Kaufman, later Latka on *Taxi,* making his TV series debut), and deserved a longer run than twelve episodes.

The two pilot episodes originally ran as comedy specials in 1975.

**THE VAN DYKE SHOW (*) (6ep Color; 1988 CBS) Situation Comedy** *with Dick Van Dyke as Dick Burgess, Barry Van Dyke as Matt Burgess, Kari Lizer as Chris Burgess, Maura Tierney as Gillian, Billy O'Sullivan as Noah Burgess, Paul Scherrer as Eric Olander, and Whitman Mayo as Doc*

Sometimes the right role, setting, and scripts are there for a quiet follow-up for a respected television legend. Raymond Burr landed *Ironside* after *Perry Mason,* Andy Griffith found *Matlock,* and Buddy Ebsen went from *The Beverly Hillbillies* to *Barnaby Jones.* None of these shows will ever overshadow the respective performers' original claim to fame, but they're fine for an encore bow.

Unfortunately for Dick Van Dyke, this series doesn't make it. Unlike those other programs, the setup for this one is far too underdeveloped and sketchy. Dick plays a performer who after a lifetime on the road decides to spend some time with his son, Matt (and his family), living in the small town of Arley, Pennsylvania. Once there, Dick hangs out either at the house or at the struggling-to-survive small theater (the Arley Playhouse) he co-owns with Matt. Where this plot is supposed to go is not clear. Dick tells a few old showbiz stories to the other characters (in a relaxed, conversational style), participates in some slapstick bits (attempting to seat people at an oversold performance), has a few minor complications with his son, and that's about it. This plot line seems more like an outline for a low-key bit from a comedy-variety show, not for the makings of a series.

There are a few moments. When Dick first shows up, he walks onto the stage in the middle of a performance without realizing it, and has to improvise accordingly. And since Van Dyke's real-life son plays Matt, there is definitely the sense of authentic father and son rapport (the voices of the two men are hauntingly similar). But it's just not enough. Maybe if they had started with a few episodes focusing just on Matt and his family, then had dad turn up later (perhaps as a reoccurring guest star), we might have cared more about the overall situation. As it is, everyone seems like a prop in a once loved but now discarded vaudeville bit.

Besides the half-dozen episodes shown in the original run, there is also an unaired pilot.

For a better example of Dick Van Dyke's work after the original *Dick Van Dyke Show,* try *The New Dick Van Dyke Show* instead.

**VANITY FAIR (**½) Drama in two major versions: 60 min (5ep Color: 1972 UK)** *with Susan Hampshire as Becky Sharpe, Marilyn Taylerson as Amelia Sedley, Michael Rothwell as Sir Pitt Crawley, John Moffatt as Joseph Sedley, Roy Marsden as George Osborne, and Bryan Marshall as Dobbin* **30 min (21ep Color; 1987 UK BBC)** *with Eve Matheson as Becky Sharpe, Rebecca Saire as Amelia Sedley, Freddie Jones as Sir Pitt Crawley, James Saxon as Joseph Sedley,*

*Benedict Taylor as George Osborne, and Simon Dormandy as Dobbin*

William Thackeray's novel about nineteenth-century London femme fatale Becky Sharp charming and clawing her way up the ladder of society is perfect grist for this pair of melodramatic television adaptations. She's very good at playing the game and assumes everybody else is doing the very same thing. (In most cases they are, which is probably why Thackeray gave it the subtitle "A Novel Without a Hero.") Even under the shadows of war, Becky takes advantage of the opportunities for a score, skillfully teasing everyone from battlefield generals to her easily manipulated soldier husband, Pitt Crawley. And in between Becky's schemes there are other conflicts and heartbreaks, chiefly those in the life of another young woman, Amelia Sedley—far too passive and vacillating to fill a hero or heroine's shoes. This story is best done as a fast-paced soapy melodrama, which the 1987 version does quite well.

**VEGA$ (**½) 60 min (66ep & 90 min pilot Color; 1978–1981 ABC) Crime Drama** *with Robert Urich as Dan Tanna, Phyllis Davis as Bea Travis, Bart Braverman as Bobby "Binzer" Borso, Judy Landers as Angie Turner, Greg Morris as Lieutenant Dave Nelson, Naomi Stevens as Sergeant Bella Archer, and Tony Curtis as Philip "Slick" Roth*

In *Vega$,* Aaron Spelling and Douglas Cramer, two producers adept at turning out hit shows with high glitz (*The Love Boat, Hotel*), succeed at combining a highly exploitable setting with stories with a modicum of substance. Private eye Dan Tanna (one of the great TV names) hangs around Las Vegas, a town where there is always a crying need for someone to snoop on somebody else. Tanna is wonderfully rebellious in his blue jeans, naughty boy smile, flashy sports car (Thunderbird convertible), and show girl sweeties. His chief client is Phil Roth, zillionaire owner of several hotels and casinos. Tanna's chief gopher is Binzer, an ex-hood who tries hard but never seems to get anything done. As a nod to the new era of sexual equality, Tanna's aide-de-camp is the beautiful and brainy Beatrice.

The stories are filled with the usual stuff: car chases, gun battles, alluring ladies, nasty villains, and thick policemen. Still, the sprightly acting by Robert Urich and the quality second string of performers make *Vega$* an amiable hour of diversion. ■

**A VERY BRITISH COUP (***) 60 min (1ep & 2 hr finale Color; 1988 UK Channel 4) Drama** *with Ray McAnally as Harry Perkins, Geoffrey Beevers as Wainwright, Alan MacNaughtan as Percy Browne, and Jim Carter as Foreign Secretary Newsome*

The setting is the near future in England (complete with references to "the King," not Queen Elizabeth), as Harry Perkins rides a landslide election victory to become the new prime minister of Britain. Harry is a dramatic contrast to the immediate past: a third generation steelworker, a dedicated socialist, a self-styled man of the people . . . and an anathema to vested interests of both sides of the Atlantic. As a result, Prime Minister Perkins soon finds himself the target of a frighteningly effective attempted "coup," hatched by perfectly "respectable" business and government leaders who have little use for his left-wing politics and his willingness to stand up for what he believes.

This well-paced tale of political conspiracy and justified paranoia is based on a novel by Chris Mullin which drew inspiration from real life rumors about attempts to destabilize British Prime Minister Harold Wilson's government in the 1970s (a subject dealt with in Peter Wright's book *Spycatcher*). *A Very British Coup* first played in the U.S. on *Masterpiece Theatre* as part of that program's deliberate effort in the late 1980s to expand its scope to more contemporary settings.

**VICTORY AT SEA (***) 30 min (26ep B&W; 1952–1953 NBC) Documentary** *with Leonard Graves as narrator*

*Victory at Sea* was the first major made-for-TV documentary series. In twenty-six episodes, the history of the U.S. Navy's operations during World War II is detailed in a classy production that is still used as an example of how to put together a good TV documentary.

The producers culled through film from both Allied and Axis sources in order to present an inside look at how the naval battles occurred. An intelligent, informative script ties it all together. An original music score by Robert Russell Bennett, conducting the NBC Symphony Orchestra, adds drama and tension to an already exciting story.

The only possible criticism of *Victory at Sea* is that it is obvious that the producers received enormous assistance from the U.S. Navy in assembling the show. While this assistance undoubtedly aided the production, it also gives the series a bit of an in-house feel that cries out for a touch of journalistic distance. In the years just after World War II, when faith in government ran high, this close interaction of government and press was common, but it is somewhat unusual today. ■

**VIENNA, 1900: GAMES WITH LOVE AND DEATH (**½) 60 min (6ep Color; 1981 UK BBC) Drama Anthology**

These adaptations of stories written by Vienna-born doctor turned author Arthur Schnitzler, focus on turn-of-the-century lives, loves, and death. All were frequent topics in his tales, in particular the special magic that occurs in the attraction between a man and a woman, even if sometimes the results are destined to disappoint. The stories include "Spring Sonata," a tale of death and penance with Lynn Redgrave and Jacqueline Pearce; "Mother and Son," with Dorothy Tutin and Christopher Guard as the title characters; and "A Confirmed

Bachelor," with Robert Stephens as a doctor destined to lose his status after treating the ailing daughter of one of his clients, played by Sheila Brennan. These stories were first slotted in the United States on *Masterpiece Theatre* during the mid-1970s.

**VIETNAM: A TELEVISION HISTORY (****) 60 min (13ep Color; 1983 PBS) Documentary** *with Stanley Karnow as narrator and chief correspondent*

If you're under the impression that the Vietnam War consisted only of drugs, Doors music, and Marlon Brando, this is an essential primer on the subject. It is a sweeping history that manages to set U.S. involvement in Vietnam within a larger context, attempting to analyze and clarify just what was going on long before this country sent one soldier to fight, and then what happened as our troops topped half a million.

Correspondent-narrator Stanley Karnow (a journalist who covered Asian affairs for two decades) doesn't come with a political ax to grind, but he also does not hesitate to point out squandered opportunities, faulty assumptions, and—based on the history of the region—the almost inevitable dead-end nature of both French and U.S. involvement.

The series proceeds chronologically, carrying the historical narrative with a deft combination of archives footage and new discussions with participants from all sides. The sheer volume of film and video tape available to draw from worldwide (including many interviews and news reports from the time) underscores again why this war was so aptly called "the first television war." The series might use clips from the past to describe a particular event or battle from the point of view of a front-line soldier, political and military leaders from both the United States and Hanoi, and the Vietnamese people who were there. Then contemporary interviews (sometimes with the same people) reflect on the very same events in hindsight.

When this documentary first aired, this even-handed treatment of "the enemy" outraged many supporters of the war. Yet whether for or against U.S. involvement in Southeast Asia, it's hard to escape the sense of betrayal that seems to have left its mark on everyone touched by the war—from U.S. presidents to village peasants.

On balance, *Vietnam: A Television History* is not so much a "pro" or "anti" war piece as it is a treatise on appreciating the global, political, and personal consequences of such a massive military venture half a world away.

Reflecting the true international nature of interest in the subject, *Vietnam* was produced by WGBH in Boston, in cooperation with British and French broadcasters (Central Independent Television and Antenne-2). ■

**THE VIETNAM WAR WITH WALTER CRONKITE (**½) 60 min (14ep Color; 1986 Syndication) Documentary** *with Walter Cronkite as narrator*

White House legend has it that U.S. President Lyndon Johnson knew he had lost the public relations battle over the Vietnam War in 1968 when CBS news anchor Walter Cronkite ("one of the most trusted names in journalism") began publicly questioning the venture. Not that Cronkite was leading marches in the streets or anything like that—he and his news team just brought an informed but increasingly skeptical view of the events into mainstream America. However, with television coverage of the conflict the chief source of most people's information, that was quite a potent force. This series draws on the extensive CBS news footage from the war, with Cronkite serving (appropriately) as anchor/narrator to the story. Though not quite as detailed or politically hard-hitting as *Vietnam: A Television History*, this is still a good, basic *Reader's Digest*–type overview of the way it was back then. ■

**A VIEW OF THE WHITE HOUSE BY H. R. HALDEMAN (*) 60 min (6ep Color; 1981 Syndication) Documentary** *with H. R. "Bob" Haldeman as narrator*

Bob Haldeman was the stern chief of staff for President Richard Nixon from 1969 to 1973. He captured a lot of the comings and goings at the White House during those years on home movies. This oddball series presents the highlights of those movies, with Haldeman as narrator giving his view of his years at the right hand of power.

**VIKINGS, TALES OF THE (*) 30 min (39ep B&W; 1960–1961 Syndication) Adventure** *with Jerome Courtland as Leif Ericson, Walter Barnes as Finn, and Buddy Baer as Also*

These nondescript formula adventures of Leif Ericson and his Viking raiders (circa 1000 A.D.) feature plenty of grim-faced confrontations soaked with sea spray—and not much else. By the 1980s, Walter Barnes managed to work his way Stateside for the *Walking Tall* series. *Vikings* producer George Cahan was also responsible for *Union Pacific, Cowboy in Africa,* and *It's About Time.*

**THE VIRGINIAN/THE MEN FROM SHILOH (***) 90 min (248ep Color & 30 min B&W pilot; 1962–1971 NBC) Western** *with Lee J. Cobb as Judge Henry Garth, James Drury as the Virginian, Doug McClure as Trampas, Charles Bickford as John Grainger, John McIntire as Clay Grainger, Stewart Granger as Col. Alan MacKenzie, Gary Clarke as Steve Hill, Pippa Scott as Molly Wood, David Hartman as David Sutton, and Lee Majors as Roy Tate*

Truly an epic, *The Virginian* is more of a western movie anthology than a series. The first weekly ninety-minute TV western, *The Virginian* is set in the Wyoming emptiness of the 1880s. The action revolves around the Shiloh Ranch near Medicine Bow and the people who live, work, and die there. Over the run of the series, the

Shiloh Ranch is owned by four different men: Judge Garth, John Grainger, Clay Grainger, and the British Col. MacKenzie.

Unlike most of the other long-running adult westerns of its era (*Gunsmoke, Bonanza*), the central characters in *The Virginian* do not become friendly household buddies over time, but rather remain distant, aloof and mysterious. Only two characters last all 248 episodes (Trampas and the Virginian), and they never reveal their full names. The title character never reveals any part of his name, just going by the laconic handle "the Virginian." Instead of focusing on the leads, *The Virginian* emphasizes guest stars and characters who come and go with intermittent regularity over the years, anthology-style (something akin to *Wagon Train*). In fact, John McIntire, who plays Clay Grainger, the owner of Shiloh for one season, had played the wagonmaster in *Wagon Train* for four years.

Because *The Virginian* is so long, lasting for so many episodes and featuring so many guests, the quality fluctuates from episode to episode. It can always be relied on, however, for solid western entertainment, without a lot of the gimmicks that cluttered up many of the other adult westerns of its time.

The final twenty-three episodes are titled *The Men from Shiloh,* but other than bringing in the fourth and final boss of Shiloh Ranch (Col. MacKenzie), the new title does not indicate any significant alteration in theme or plot. The original 1958 thirty-minute pilot now is part of one of the *Golden Age of Television* packages and has a somewhat different feel from the series. James Drury is still the Virginian, but he plays the stranger as more of a die-hard Confederate partisan. Robert Burton plays the judge who owns the ranch.

*The Virginian* evolved from a 1902 western novel by Owen Wister, a classic 1929 film starring Gary Cooper (source of the classic line "Smile when you say that!"), and a so-so 1946 film remake with Joel McCrea.

**THE VISE (*) 30 min (91ep B&W; 1954–1957 ABC) Crime Anthology** *with Ron Randell as host*

These British-made grade-B crime tales feature people caught in webs of their own making. For U.S. viewers, episodes with guest stars already familiar from other series or feature films (such as Christopher Lee, Honor Blackman, and Patrick McGoohan) are of the most interest. Otherwise the anthology is only routine. After sixty-five episodes, the format changes and the series title ends up serving as the umbrella for a run of *Mark Saber* crime adventures, with Donald Gray as the former Scotland Yard inspector turned private investigator.

**VIVA VALDEZ (*) 30 min (13ep Color; 1976 ABC) Situation Comedy** *with Rodolfo Hoyos as Luis Valdez, Carmen Zapata as Sophia Valdez, James Victor as Victor Valdez, and Nelson D. Cuevas as Ernesto Valdez*

Ho-hum. This is another typical, derivative mid-1970s "relevant" comedy, this time focusing on a Mexican-American family living in East Los Angeles.

**VOYAGE TO THE BOTTOM OF THE SEA (**) 60 min (110 ep: 32 B&W & 78 Color; 1964–1968 ABC) Science Fiction** *with Richard Basehart as Adm. Nelson, David Hedison as Capt. Lee Crane, Robert Dowdell as Chip Morton, Terry Becker as Chief Sharkey, and Del Monroe as Kowalsky*

The next time you're arguing about whether or not *Star Trek* is really all that great, consider for a moment Irwin Allen's *Voyage to the Bottom of the Sea* (based on the 1961 feature film).

After all, they have a lot in common. Both series were set up to explore strange new worlds—it's just that the *Seaview* and its crew stayed on the home planet and wandered through liquid space about two hundred years earlier. But it was still where no one had gone before.

And along the way the ship's commander, Admiral Nelson, encounters the usual: dozens of alien life forms, would-be invaders, and megalomaniacs (many coveting the visiting vessel as the key element to some grand scheme), and occasional rewrites of classic literature (how could a submarine series not redo the stories of Moby Dick or Jonah and the Whale?).

No doubt Nelson and *Star Trek*'s Captain Kirk would exchange knowing glances at some of their common problems and situations. Like that deck that just won't stay horizontal (seems that somebody is always attacking the ship and sending the crew flying off-camera). Or that supposed superpowered nuclear engine that's either running dangerously close to overload ("We're gonna blow!") or sitting drained and idle. And how about that annoying habit of some crew members letting various alien forces take over their minds willy-nilly!

The main difference between the two: Kirk and his crew seem to have such a good time, even in the worst situations. In contrast, *Voyage to the Bottom of the Sea* is so grim! At the beginning (the black and white episodes) it's Cold War–style intrigues. Then it's one scaly creature after another. And, throughout, the all-male crew looks pretty cramped and glum.

After a while, it's hard for viewers to avoid that feeling as well. *Star Trek* may have its flaws, but at least it soars. *Voyage* just sort of sinks to the bottom and stays there.

**VOYAGERS! (**) 60 min (21ep Color; 1982–1983 NBC) Adventure** *with Jon-Erik Hexum as Phineas Bogg and Meeno Peluce as Jeffrey Jones*

This is time travel, done with a tip of the hat to *Doctor Who,* the 1981 theatrical film *Time Bandits,* and even the classic Jules Verne literary tale *Around the World in Eighty Days*—the character name Phineas Bogg is a playful allusion to Verne's hero, Phileas Fogg. Appropriately, Bogg is often in a fog, which is why he's lucky to have as his accidental traveling companion eleven-year-old Jeffrey Jones. The young boy is a history buff, and Bogg is weak on such facts—odd, actually, because Bogg is a member of a race of time travelers ("Voyagers") dedicated to keeping history on course.

Apparently this is a big problem. It seems that occasionally people become displaced in time and find themselves a half-step away from a totally different destiny—Franklin Roosevelt as a Hollywood film director instead of president, for instance. Such moments are when a Voyager like Bogg pops up to set things right. Or sort of right until young Jeffrey helps him figure out just what is supposed to happen.

Unfortunately it quickly becomes clear that all the specific historical names, dates, and places are apparently there just to give the series some aura of "painless" education slipped in with the entertainment. Consequently, the action is limited to past events on Earth—in contrast to the far-flung reaches of future time and space explored on *Doctor Who.* But as a result both the action and the education are pretty much reduced to the wooden simplicity of a *Classic Comics* story.

Still, the chance to set history right is an attractive hook. Given enough time, Jeffrey might have even helped himself out (in another series) with a trip back to the old western town of Copper Creek (setting for *Best of the West*). There he could have convinced marshal Sam Best to let son Dan (also played by Meeno Peluce) head back to a comfortable home in the East. ■

**W.E.B. (*) 60 min (6ep Color; 1978 NBC) Drama** *with Pamela Bellwood as Ellen Cunningham, Alex Cord as Jack Kiley, Richard Basehart as Gus Dunlap, and Andrew Prine as Dan Costello*

Even if you love the back-biting, cut-throat world of corporate intrigue that is the reality of TV network programming, you still will find *W.E.B.* fairly distasteful. In the series, Ellen Cunningham is the brash and bold twenty-nine-year-old female programming whiz kid at the Trans Atlantic Broadcasting network. She is always battling the "boys only" attitude among the network brass. The plots are designed to be quite soapy, but the characters are so concerned with their work that they hardly have time for sexual affairs. *W.E.B.* is therefore reduced to something of a business school exposé, with a feminist twist.

*W.E.B.*'s producer, Lin Bolen, should have been familiar with the plot line. She was NBC's daytime programming boss (one of the first women in such a position) and, reportedly, was the model for Faye Dunaway's workaholic character in the theatrical film *Network* (which does a much better job in skewering TV).

One nagging unanswered question about *W.E.B.* is why is the title made up of initials. The title does not seem to refer to a TV station's call letters (i.e., WCBS), which do not use periods anyway. Likewise, even though "web" is a slang phrase for a TV network, the word is not an abbreviation and does not use periods either.

**WKRP IN CINCINNATI (****) 30 min (90ep Color; 1978–1982 CBS) Situation Comedy** *with Gary Sandy as Andy Travis, Gordon Jump as Arthur Carlson, Loni Anderson as Jennifer Marlowe, Tim Reid as Gordon "Venus Flytrap" Sims, Frank Bonner as Herb Tarlek, Richard Sanders as Les Nessman, Jan Smithers as Bailey Quarters, Carol Bruce as Mama Carlson, and Howard Hesseman as Johnny "Dr. Johnny Fever" Caravella*

If you're the type that constantly switches stations on your car radio when a song comes along that you can't stand, consider how the disc jockeys must feel if they're stuck playing records they hate. They must dream of smashing every offending disc, preferably on the air. *WKRP in Cincinnati* kicks off with just such a therapeutic scene.

On his first day as program director, Andy Travis tells morning disc jockey John Caravella that the low-rated station's format is changing from "beautiful music" to rock and roll. Caravella, a one-time West Coast legend cooling his heels in Cincinnati after being booted off the air in L. A. for saying "booger," rises to the occasion. He takes fiendish glee in dragging the needle across the bland song in progress, turns on the mike, and starts talking, taking on the persona of an old-fashioned medicine show revival preacher (spontaneously dubbing himself "Dr. Johnny Fever"). He rolls one of the rock records Andy left with him, punctuating this inaugural moment with one final word: "booger."

This abrupt change in format sends shock waves through the tiny station: Specifically it brings station manager Arthur Carlson's mother down to the office. "Mama" Carlson is the owner of WKRP, and a sharp business woman. She is also against the change in format (even with Andy's promise of profits within two years) until her son, normally a pushover, rises to defend Andy's change. She's so impressed to see some backbone in him that she agrees to give rock a chance. Though Arthur Carlson personally can't fathom the music himself, he's genuinely excited at the prospect of working on a project that has a chance of success. He's not even deterred when the meeting with Mama comes to an abrupt end with the appearance of a tall black "dude" in a flashy outfit (new nighttime DJ Venus Flytrap, brought in by Andy to fill the evening slot).

Of course, the task won't be easy. Les Nessman, the station's news manager, is in a world of his own, determined to be a first-class newscaster just like CBS legend Edward R. Murrow, but sometimes not at all sure how to go about it. He's an expert at hog news (proudly displaying the Silver Sow award for farm reporting at his desk) and he knows all about the international communist conspiracy, but when it comes to unfamiliar pop culture names (Chi Chi Rodriguez from the world of sports, for instance) Les's mispronunciations give butchering a whole new meaning. Nonetheless, he is genuinely outgoing if somewhat naive, warmly greeting Venus Flytrap with the observation that he's noticed that there are a "a lot of Negroes in sports." Because the station can't afford to give him his own office, Les has outlined with masking tape on the floor where his walls will be, and insists that people knock at a nonexistent door before approaching his desk.

Station sales manager Herb Tarlek is a study in misplaced self-confidence. He has a loud and badly mismatched wardrobe, along with a tendency to approach everything like a high-pressure sales pitch, even flirting with station receptionist Jennifer Marlowe. The main thing Herb has going for himself is that the people in the departments he deals with are as annoying as he is.

And then there's Arthur Carlson himself. Nicknamed the "Big Guy" (Herb was once the "Little Guy"), he's a kindhearted human being but a terrible business manager. (One of Jennifer's top jobs is to steer any real business-related matters away from him—at his request.) Frankly if Andy Travis really wanted to turn WKRP around instantly, Les, Herb, and the Big Guy would be gone. Instead he works with the staff he has.

In addition to Johnny and Venus, Andy encourages Bailey Quarters, a previously underused staff member, to assert herself in promotion, programming, and news. He also discovers that receptionist Jennifer may look like the stereotypical dumb blonde, but she's really the staff member most in control of herself and her environment. She's well-informed, self-confident, and the strictly platonic off-hours companion to a host of wealthy and influential people from all over the world.

Over its four-year run, WKRP slowly brings itself up in the radio ratings, reaching the top ten by the end of the final season. The series itself, though, hits its stride almost immediately, quickly developing into one of television's best ensemble comedies. There is a good mix of radio plot hooks along with stories that emphasize the interaction among the characters.

In the early days, the broadcast plots play on the fact that WKRP is a tiny concern with virtually no audience, so the station will try anything to get attention: Johnny does a remote broadcast from a low-rent stereo store, the station sponsors a concert by a punk rock group called Scum of the Earth (played by the real-life group Detective), and (best of all) Carlson and Herb come up with the ultimate Thanksgiving giveaway, tossing live turkeys from a helicopter over a parking lot (not realizing that turkeys can't fly). Later, though, it is clear that WKRP has become one of the hip, admired stations of the area. Venus, for instance, acts as the emcee for a concert by The Who. And Johnny becomes such a celebrity he even lands his own television disco dance show, leading to an odd Jekyll–Hyde transformation in his character.

In true ensemble fashion, the characters become a mutually supportive family, allowing a truly wide range of plots outside simple radio adventures. These include Carlson's bid for elected office, a late-in-life birth by his wife, and a *Sting*–type plot to keep nude photos of Jennifer from being published. There are also some completely off-the-beaten-track episodes, including a perfect parody of a *Real People* program, *Real Families,* which pokes a prying camera eye into the personal life of Herb and his family.

Be sure to catch the final episode, in which Mama Carlson has a chance to reevaluate her decision about WKRP's move to rock. Her confrontation with Johnny Fever on the issue is a wonderful contest of wills, clearly demonstrating that the laid-back doctor can be a hardball fighter when necessary.

Former *WKRP* cast members constantly turn up in guest shots on other series (often playing very similar character types), with Howard Hesseman and Tim Reid landing the two most impressive vehicles: *Head of the Class* and *Frank's Place.*

**WACKIEST SHIP IN THE ARMY (**) 60 min (29ep Color; 1965–1966 NBC) War Adventure** *with Jack Warden as Maj. Simon Butcher, Gary Collins as Lt. Richard "Rip" Riddle, Mike Kellin as CPO Willie Miller, Rudy Solari as Sherman Nagurski, and Fred Smoot as Seymour Trivers*

Based on a mild 1960 film with Jack Lemmon and Ricky Nelson about the real-life exploits of the *Echo,* a boat used by the United States in World War II, *The Wackiest Ship in the Army* is a fair combination of action and laughs. In the TV series, the ship in question is the *Kiwi,* an old wooden schooner given to the United States by New Zealand after the Japanese attack on Pearl Harbor. The Americans use it as a spy boat, since its wooden shell does not register on radar. The crew pose as Swedish neutrals whenever the Japanese come too close. Command of the boat flip-flops between navy man Lt. Riddle and army man Maj. Butcher, depending on whether the *Kiwi* is at sea or docked on land. Gary Collins, later the host of the *Hour Magazine* interview series, makes his TV series debut here.

**THE WACKY WORLD OF JONATHAN WINTERS (**) (52ep Color; 1972–1974 Syndication) Comedy-Variety** *with Jonathan Winters and Marian Mercer, Mary Gregory, Ronny Graham, and the Soul Sisters*

With his manic energy and gift for improvisation, Jonathan Winters has been a widely admired comic performer for years. Robin Williams confessed to being absolutely thrilled to have Winters on *Mork and Mindy* (first as a guest, then as his son). This syndicated variety series was specifically designed to showcase

Winters as his legendary strength, improvisation. A good idea, though it would have been even better two decades earlier. Though the program is spotty (and some of the musical guests could be dispensed with), you do get a fine sampling of the many characterizations in the Winters repertoire.

**WAGON TRAIN** **(***) 60 & 90 min (253 ep: two hundred twenty-one 60 min & thirty-two 90 min B&W & Color; 1957–1965 NBC & ABC) Western** *with Ward Bond as Maj. Seth Adams, Robert Horton as Flint McCullough, John McIntire as Christopher Hale, Terry Wilson as Bill Hawks, Frank McGrath as Charlie Wooster, Scott Miller as Duke Shannon, and Robert Fuller as Cooper Smith*

*Wagon Train* loads up from St. Joseph, Missouri (the edge of civilization in the days after the Civil War) every season and begins the long trek across the arid wastes, heading for the promised land of TV mythology: California. The continuing characters (the wagonmaster, trail scout, cook, etc.) are simply the skeletons for the real stars of the series, the weekly guests who portray some of the members of the wagon train as it heads west.

With the focus so much on the guest stars who come and go, *Wagon Train* is inordinately flexible in concept, more of a made-for-TV western movie than a regular TV series. It deals with all aspects of western life, while constantly infusing new personalities who can be killed off at will. The program's success helped pave the way for other anthology westerns (such as *The Virginian*) and even nonwestern series that relied heavily on guests (such as *Star Trek,* which was originally touted as "*Wagon Train* to the stars"). John McIntire, who plays the wagonmaster here in the final four seasons, later made the easy transition to *The Virginian,* where he played a similar supervisory character for one season.

The original Ward Bond black and white episodes (later syndicated as *Major Adams—Trailmaster*) are arguably the best. At this point, the show had not yet begun to scrounge around for script ideas to fill each week's quota. The move to ninety minutes in the next to last season was a mistake, requiring too much padding, although the switch to color is helpful. The final season, back to an hour, is uneventful.

The inspiration for *Wagon Train* can be found in a John Ford 1950 film, *Wagonmaster,* which stars Ward Bond, the original *Wagon Train* wagonmaster.

**WAIT 'TILL YOUR FATHER GETS HOME** **(*) 30 min (48ep Color; 1972–1974 Syndication) Animated Cartoon** *with the voices of Tom Bosley as Harry Boyle, Joan Gerber as Irma Boyle, Kristina Holland as Alice Boyle, David Hayward as Chet Boyle, Jackie Haley as Jamie Boyle, and Jack Burns as Ralph*

The yucks are all too obvious on this adult-oriented cartoon series produced by William Hanna and Joseph Barbera (*The Flintstones, Scooby-Doo*). The show is an attempt to create a cartoon version of *All in the Family,* but little of that show's flavor (other than polemical yelling) comes across.

**A WALK THROUGH THE 20TH CENTURY WITH BILL MOYERS** **(***) 60 min (18ep & 90 min pilot Color; 1982 & 1984 CBS Cable & PBS) Documentary** *with Bill Moyers as host*

This show is a far more serious and complex look at this century than CBS's flash *20th Century* (with Walter Cronkite). More than just reviewing old film clips, Bill Moyers digs into the meanings and causes of some of the major events of the times. The comparison of Franklin Roosevelt and Adolph Hitler, two bold leaders who took over a depression-ridden major power in 1933, is a highlight. ■

**WALKING TALL** **(*) 60 min (13ep Color; 1981 NBC) Police Drama** *with Bo Svenson as Sheriff Buford Pusser, Rad Daly as Michael Pusser, Walter Barnes as Carl Pusser, and Heather McAdams as Dwana Pusser*

A vigilante's dream, *Walking Tall* is about a local sheriff who bends the law all out of shape in order to capture the no-goodnicks who are polluting the pristine world of McNeal County, Tennessee. Sheriff Pusser, who packs a four-foot-long club (labeled his "pacifier"), womps a mess of bad guys while seeking revenge for the death of his wife, who was killed in an attempt on *his* life. Lots of violence fills this simple-minded saga. The sheriff is played by Bo Svenson, who starred in two film sequels to the original 1973 *Walking Tall* movie (which featured Joe Don Baker as Sheriff Pusser). There really was a Sheriff Buford Pusser who battled criminals, but he died in a car crash after the 1973 film hit it big.

**WALT DISNEY** **(***) 60 min (Color & B&W; 1954– ABC, CBS, & NBC) Anthology** *with Walt Disney and Michael Eisner as host*

With the Disney cable channel pumping out programming twenty-four hours a day, it's easy to forget that the studio's initial television outlet aired just one hour each week. Even this was a breakthrough at the time (1954) because it marked the first major cooperative effort between an established Hollywood studio and television. The deal was a success for both parties, with the ABC network getting one of its first top-ten hits and Disney demonstrating a program formula that would still be going strong some thirty-five years later. It's a simple mix: theatrical films run as multipart presentations, excerpts from classic Disney animation features and shorts, various "event" tours of the California Disneyland amusement park (and later, Disney World in Florida and other parks overseas), some nature documentaries, and a mixed bag of new adventure serials, made-for-TV movies, and animation specials. The same approach formed the basis for Disney's 1983 pioneer effort into cable as well (though obviously expanded to fill the entire day).

Yet even with its own cable service (and extensive video cassette catalog), Disney has continued to slot material on "free TV," both on a network level (ABC, CBS, or NBC) and in local rerun syndication (offering packages of the hour-long *Walt Disney* series). The reason is simple: Besides producing some of this century's most beautiful animation and family-oriented features, the Walt Disney company has consistently shown absolute genius in promoting itself and its products. So Disney has not stopped servicing the vast audience that doesn't subscribe to its cable channel or may not even have access to cable. After all, those viewers still represent millions of potential customers for the many, many Disney-related products, from record albums to juice glasses.

Yet, even though Disney programming is brimming with implicit and explicit self-promotion (of the company's films, amusement parks, and cartoon character likenesses), the series has been consistently embraced by adults as perfect entertainment for the kids. Of course, some of these same adults might then turn around and decry many Saturday morning cartoon offerings as "one long commercial," forgetting that *Walt Disney* segments on the making of the Disney feature film *20,000 Leagues Under the Sea* or a visit to "Disneyland After Dark" easily fit that definition as well. Even the original title for the weekly series, *Disneyland,* just happened to be the name of the California amusement park. The secret, of course, is the air of class and the quality of Disney projects. Sure you know it's a plug, but you also know that you'll probably enjoy the movie or the amusement park when you go.

A more valid criticism of the *Walt Disney* series is that after the flush of its first decade the episode mix in the 1970s and early 1980s skewed increasingly away from original productions to one main element: slicing Disney theatrical films into multiepisode presentations. And (with exceptions such as *Dumbo*) these presentations were very, very rarely any of the classic full-length animated features (such as *Lady and the Tramp*). Those were only run in excerpt form essentially as teasers for a theatrical re-release or issuing on video cassette. What turned up instead, most often, were the second-string live action films such as *The Computer Wore Tennis Shoes, The Misadventures of Merlin Jones,* or *The Million-Dollar Duck,* which filled the time between the more popular items such as *The Shaggy Dog* or *The Absent-Minded Professor* or *Herbie the Love Bug.* In the 1980s, more new productions did begin to turn up, but very often they were just made-for-TV movie-type offerings sliced into multi-episode presentations looking suspiciously like series pilots.

What has consistently saved the series are its classic episodes, especially those incorporating animated bits (often excerpts from Disney's cartoon shorts as well as from feature-length presentations). There are dozens of these, including "Donald in Mathmagic Land" (narrated by Professor Ludwig Von Drake, a character created especially for the TV series), "From All of Us to All of You" (a Christmas special), "The Legend of Sleepy Hollow," and a variety of humorous instructional or pseudo-history shows featuring Goofy. In addition, during the first decade there were some well-done original miniseries with such characters as Gallagher the newsboy, Texas John Slaughter, and, of course, Davy Crockett.

Perhaps the most important element of the first dozen years of *Disney* presentations was the presence of Walt Disney himself as host. His low-key, friendly uncle style of delivery made whatever followed seem like something very special—a treasure that he had pulled from the vaults and was about to share with the home audience. (These original intros are in the rerun packages on the Disney channel.) It's probably no coincidence that much of the edge disappeared from the weekly Disney series when Walt died in 1966, just as the overall company itself foundered in the aftermath of his death.

Fortunately for the program's late 1980s permutation, the Disney corporation's revitalizing chairman Michael Eisner has brought some of the enthusiasm back to the weekly anthology. For one thing, he has taken on Walt's old role as host, bringing his own older brother style of introduction to the role. He's also slotted a few more originals to the series rotation, including new versions of *Davy Crockett* and *The Absent-Minded Professor.* After all, with a cable service just down the dial, there's no question that these will find a ready home in the world of reruns. And as long as there are kids (of all ages) with their hands at the remote control, there will always be plenty of viewers.

Over the decades the Disney anthology slot has gone through a number of title changes. All of these refer to the same series: *Disneyland, Walt Disney Presents, Walt Disney Presents the Wonderful World of Color, The Wonderful World of Disney, Disney's Wonderful World, Walt Disney, The Disney Sunday Movie,* and *The Magical World of Disney.*

For details on the original miniseries that have aired under the *Disney* anthology umbrella, consult the individual write-ups for: *The Absent-Minded Professor, Andy Burnett, Daniel Boone, Davy Crockett, Elfego Baca, Gallagher, Kilroy, The Scarecrow of Romney Marsh, The Swamp Fox, Texas John Slaughter, Wild Jack McCall,* and *Zorro.* ■

**WALTER CRONKITE'S UNIVERSE** **(see *Universe*)**

**THE WALTONS (***½) 60 min (221ep & 2 hr pilot & three 2 hr sequels Color; 1972–1981 CBS) Drama** *with Ralph Waite as John Walton, Michael Learned as Olivia Walton, Will Geer as Zeb "Grandpa" Walton, Ellen Corby as Esther "Grandma" Walton, Richard Thomas and Robert Wightman as John "John-Boy" Walton, Jr., Judy Norton-Taylor as Mary Ellen Walton,*

*David W. Harper as James Robert "Jim-Bob" Walton, Kami Colter as Elizabeth Walton, Jon Walmsley as Jason Walton, Joe Conley as Ike Godsey, John Ritter as Rev. Matthew Fordwick, and Earl Hamner, Jr., as narrator*

In the eleven years between the December 1971 made-for-TV movie/pilot for *The Waltons* (titled *The Homecoming*) and the November 1982 final sequel made-for-TV movie (titled *A Day for Thanks on Walton's Mountain*), the saga of the Walton clan moves from heart-of-the-depression Christmas 1933 to post–World War II Thanksgiving 1947. In the time span covered by the series, much changes in America and much changes on rural Walton's mountain in Jefferson County, Virginia. The beauty of *The Waltons* is that it is able to deal with the inevitable cast alterations that come to a long-running show and to bring its characters along in time, to show growth and change within the plots, thus helping to forestall the unavoidable decline in freshness that strikes successful series in their later days.

*The Waltons* stands for values that once ruled TV: family, truth, honor, kindness, and responsibility. Those values disappeared from the screen and were even treated as humorous as American society changed through the 1960s and 1970s. The power of *The Waltons,* especially when it originally aired, is that it demonstrated the unchanging significance of these values. By placing the action in depression America and focusing on a poor country family, *The Waltons* put some grit back in goodness. This is not to deny that *The Waltons* gets too sentimental at times, or caught up in its own seriousness, but it does an admirable job of portraying a family drama set in an era and an area frequently overlooked or ignored by the modern media.

The best years are the first five, when the original cast is present: Father John and Mother Olivia Walton, their seven kids and John's aging parents. The show centers on the reminiscences of eldest son John-Boy, who as a child dreams of being a writer and so keeps a detailed journal of the family's tales. Richard Thomas is just right as the overly sensitive yet intelligent John-Boy, the aptly named man-child itching to get out and see the world. Ralph Waite and Michael Learned are superb as kind parents who will never be confused with Ward and June Cleaver, since John and Olivia Walton have serious problems to constantly deal with that dwarf the anxieties of a typical TV sitcom home. Grandpa and Grandma Walton are surly old coots who don't mind speaking their minds and are still active in family affairs.

In the sixth season, John-Boy leaves for New York, to be a writer (Richard Thomas wanted to move on to other things). *The Waltons* thus begins a convoluted series of cast changes caused both by the cast growing up (and, in the case of the older actors, dying) and by the story line slowly moving out of the depression and into World War II. Michael Learned virtually leaves the show during the seventh season, and the show's unity never recovers. The series remains interesting, but the focus is too diffuse and the new characters not as well-developed. The syrupy, soapy side of *The Waltons* begins to take over and the final two years and the three sequels are avoidable.

Not to be missed, however, is the original 1971 Christmastime pilot, *The Homecoming,* which packs an emotional wallop missing in most Christmas specials. Father John is missing after a Christmas Eve bus crash in a snowstorm and the family contemplates the emotional and economic ruin that awaits them if he is dead. His eventual return home, uninjured, to a heartfelt reunion, is sure to start the tear ducts flowing. In this pilot, the Walton children and Grandma Walton are played by the series regulars, but Father, Mother, and Grandpa Walton are played by Andrew Duggan, Patricia Neal, and Edgar Bergen, respectively.

*The Waltons* is the brainchild of co-executive producer Earl Hamner, Jr., who based the story (and the character of John-Boy) on his own history growing up in Schuyler, Virginia. Hamner, in fact, serves as narrator of the series, in the role of the grown John-Boy. The series was also the first TV hit of Lorimar Productions and producer Lee Rich, both of whom went on to become successful with other family-oriented shows (such as *Eight Is Enough*) and more glitzy-style dramas (such as *Dallas*). ■

**WANTED DEAD OR ALIVE (**½) 30 min (94ep & 30 min pilot B&W; 1958–1961 CBS) Western** *with Steve McQueen as Josh Randall*

Steve McQueen stars in these tales of a tight-lipped wandering bounty hunter in the 1870s. Though this is a well-paced loner adventure, McQueen is obviously the main reason to follow this series. The stories are inevitably resolved in some shoot-out with Randall easily besting his foes by wielding his special sawed-off rifle/pistol combination.

If some innovative programmer wants to search the film shelves for a Saturday afternoon rerun double-feature, the pilot episode for this series ("The Bounty Hunter") is part of the *Trackdown* syndication package. Going the other direction, *Wanted: Dead or Alive* was also the title of a terrible 1987 theatrical-release action film, with Rutger Hauer playing Nick Randall, grandson of Josh. Oddly, interest in that connection is dropped almost as soon as the thread is dangled, making the whole exercise rather pointless. ■

**WAR: A COMMENTARY BY GWYNNE DYER (**½) 60 min (8ep Color; 1985 PBS) Documentary** *with Gwynne Dyer as host*

Gwynne Dyer, a Canadian journalist, reviews the history of war and examines battle tactics.

**WAR AND PEACE (***) 60 min (19ep Color; 1973 UK BBC) Drama** *with Morag Hood as Natasha Rostov, Alan Dobie as Prince Andre Bolkonsky, Anthony Jacobs* *as Nikolai Bolkonsky, Angela Down as Maria Bolkonsky, Colin Baker as Anatole Kuragin, David Swift as Napoleon Bonaparte, and Sebastian Cabot as narrator*

Leo Tolstoy's *War and Peace* (the *original* sweeping historical saga), set in Czarist Russia during the Napoleonic Wars of the early 1800s, is adapted for television by the British with admirable attention to detail.

**WAR AND REMEMBRANCE** (***) **29½hr miniseries Color; 1988–1989 ABC) Drama** *with Robert Mitchum as Capt./Rear Adm. Victor "Pug" Henry, Polly Bergen as Rhoda Henry, Hart Bochner as Byron Henry, Michael Woods as Warren Henry, Leslie Hope as Madeline Henry, Jane Seymour as Natalie Jastrow Henry, John Gielgud as Aaron Jastrow, Peter Graves as Palmer "Fred" Kirby, Mike Connors as Col. Harrison "Hack" Peters, Robert Morley as Alistair Tudsbury, Victoria Tennant as Pamela Tudsbury, Barry Bostwick as Lt. Carter "Lady" Aster, Hunt Schlesinger as Louis Henry, Ralph Bellamy as Pres. Franklin D. Roosevelt, Steven Berkoff as Adolf Hitler, E. G. Marshall as Gen. Dwight D. Eisenhower, and William T. Woodson as narrator*

This gargantuan "mini" series picks up where the eighteen-hour miniseries *Winds of War* left off, just after the attack on Pearl Harbor dragged the United States into World War II. As with the previous series, *War and Remembrance* is based on a huge Herman Wouk novel and follows the exploits of the Henry family, both on the field of combat and in the bedrooms. Navy Capt. "Pug" Henry takes command of a cruiser and rekindles his romance with Pamela Tudsbury, daughter of a British war correspondent. Pug's estranged wife Rhoda continues her efforts to sleep with every senior American military officer. Warren and Byron, the Henrys' two sons, are fighting in the Pacific (against the Japanese, not each other). Byron's Jewish wife Natalie is still trying to get out of Nazi-occupied Europe with her Uncle Aaron. And so on and so on.

A good number of the cast from *Winds of War* reprise their roles in this sequel, though Jane Seymour is far more believable than Ali MacGraw as Natalie Jastrow. The spare-no-expense budget is impressive. It's doubtful whether the actual Battle of the Midway cost the parties much more than this recreation of the event. The scenes of the Nazi concentration camps and the German massacre of civilians are chilling, perhaps the most graphic in network TV history.

The first eighteen hours of *War and Remembrance* carry the story from December 1941 through the autumn of 1943 (that's close to one hour for each month). The second installment of *War and Remembrance* spans 11½ hours and takes the regulars through the attempted assassination of Hitler, the D-Day invasion, the battle of Iwo Jima, the explosion of the first atomic bomb, and on to the end of the war in 1945. Dan Curtis, who produced *Winds of War,* also returns for this sequel. ■

**WAR OF THE WORLDS** (**½) **60 min (24ep at Fall 1989 Color; 1988– Syndication) Science Fiction** *with Jared Martin as Dr. Harrison Blackwood, Lynda Mason Green as Suzanne McCullough, Philip Akin as Norton Drake, and Richard Chaves as Lt. Col. Paul Ironhorse*

Presented as a follow-up to the 1953 feature film *War of the Worlds* (starring Gene Barry as Dr. Clayton Forrester), this television treatment continues the tradition of staging this classic H. G. Wells alien invasion story as a contemporary event. Wells himself had done this in 1897, setting his brand new novel in the English countryside of the 1890s. Forty-one years later (on Halloween eve, 1938), Orson Welles made headlines (and pop culture history) with his strikingly effective radio adaptation of the story, updated to the jittery, invasion-conscious United States—only a year away from entering World War II.

The 1950s theatrical film moved the story to California, where some excellent writing and Oscar-winning special effects made this seem more like a frightening documentary rather than just a science fiction thriller. And this is just how the series treats those events: as if they really happened one weekend in 1953. Apparently the U.S. government (and presumably those of other nations as well) chose to believe that when the alien invasion was thwarted by the humblest of creatures (common bacteria), the threat was over. They gathered the thousands of seemingly lifeless alien carcasses, put them in barrels, and stored them alongside other hazardous wastes, including radioactive materials and chemicals. The result: Over three decades the microorganisms died and the aliens were ready to stir. To compound the human error, everyone was so determined to put the terrifying invasion out of mind that when Dr. Forrester wanted to conduct further tests, he was stymied and eventually dismissed as paranoid and out of touch with reality. Fortunately he had an admiring protégé, Dr. Harrison Blackwood, who had witnessed the original invasion when he was only three. He kept Forrester's notes and eventually followed in his footsteps as an astrophysicist. Lucky for us, because the barrels are opening and the aliens are back.

As in the 1953 film, the actual alien bodies are kept mostly in silhouette or shadow, except for powerful "hands" containing three suction-tipped fingers. But to bring them into the light (and to save money on alien costumes and voice effects), the series borrows a page from *Invasion of the Body Snatchers* (crossed with *Alien*). The aliens can seize a human and take over a body, with the cells of the two merging into something totally under the control of the invaders. Worse yet, they can move from one host body to another, each time leaving a puddle of steaming dead flesh behind. In fact, after a while they have to do this because possessed humans eventually develop conspicuous, revealing sores. But there is good news: If you kill the host body, you've killed the alien as well. And since the humans are essentially dead once possessed, there's no reason not to open fire. In the meantime, both sides engage in a double-edged race against time: the aliens (in pursuit of more host bodies and the remaining barrels) versus the humans (in search of the barrels and any possessed humans, so that they can destroy both).

Rather than turn this show into another *Invaders,* with a desperate man no one believes, *War of the Worlds* gets the U.S. government into the story early. By the end of the first adventure, Blackwood and his scientific crew (microbiologist Suzanne McCullough and computer expert Norton Drake) are teamed with a military commando, Paul Ironhorse, and put on government salary. At least this explains how they can afford all that equipment and travel. They are given a clear and simple "impossible mission": destroy the alien menace. (And, by the way, we also learn that the government had something to do with that 1930s Orson Welles broadcast, which was apparently used as a cover-up for a real alien invasion threat.)

*War of the Worlds* is cleverly set up for a credible series run. It starts small, with a handful of revived aliens at a military storage facility, and grows from there. Both the aliens and those fighting them are allowed the chance to score minor victories, and the series is given the latitude to expand into a full-scale war (as in *V*) or to keep the conflicts down to guerrilla size. Best of all, by taking its time, the series makes any final triumph over the aliens more believable because the good guys have had time to work out a successful strategy—other than hoping for another bacteria miracle.

**WASHINGTON: BEHIND CLOSED DOORS (***) (12hr miniseries Color; 1977 ABC) Drama** *with Jason Robards as Pres. Richard Monckton, Cliff Robertson as William Martin, Lois Nettleton as Linda Martin, Stefanie Powers as Sally Whalen, Robert Vaughn as Frank Flaherty, Andy Griffith as Esker Anderson, and John Houseman as Myron Dunn*

The best opening for this miniseries would be a revised version of the old *Dragnet* line, something like: "The story you are about to see is true. The names have been changed to protect the innocent (and the guilty)." Loosely based on the kiss-and-tell novel *The Company* by ex-Nixon aide John Ehrlichman, *Washington: Behind Closed Doors* is arguably the best dramatization of the Watergate saga. The only catch is that all of the characters' names have been changed, to make it a work of "fiction." It won't take long to figure out that Richard Monckton is Richard Nixon, Esker Anderson is Lyndon Johnson, Frank Flaherty is H. R. "Bob" Haldeman, and so on. Jason Robards is inspired as Monckton/Nixon, displaying all the paranoia and strategic cunning that the role requires.

**WASHINGTOON (**) 30 min (13ep Color; 1984–1985 Showtime) Comedy** *with Thomas Calloway as Rep. Bob Forehead, Hilary Thompson as Ginger Forehead, Christine Applegate as Sally Forehead, Jason Naylor as Bob Forehead, Jr., Barry Corbin as Huge "Bunky" Muntner, Beverly Archer as Laura Esterjack, Jack Colvin as Bill Knock, and Jack Riley as Tom Mimmelman*

Based on a weekly comic strip by Mark Alan Stamaty (translated to television by Tom Patchett, producer of *The Bob Newhart Show* and *Alf*) this satirical jab at Washington features Thomas Calloway as Bob Forehead, a television announcer who enters political life and wins a seat in the U.S. House of Representatives. Bob is photogenic (that's no surprise) but hopelessly naive, with little grasp of the ramifications of his new job. He is easily manipulated by everyone around him: Laura, his Congressional secretary; Hilary, his smart and supportive wife; Tom, his staff advisor ("charismatician"), and Hugh "Bunky" Muntner, the House Minority Whip. For instance, Bunky gets Forehead to withdraw a bill calling for a 50% pay-cut for Congress by convincing him that voters would interpret such a drop in salary as Congress refusing to pay its fair share of taxes (which would be lower on that lower income). Forehead honestly thinks he "understands" and is grateful to Bunky for his advice.

Though Forehead's dumb naiveté is key to the series, it also makes him awfully hard to identify with—he really is more a political cartoon caricature than a real character. Fortunately, most of the others (especially Jack Riley's caustic Tom and Beverly Archer's always-in-control Laura) are pretty good. Nonetheless, while an excellent idea with strong individual moments, the overall package never gels into anything more than just average.

**WATER WORLD (**) 30 min (52ep Color; 1972–1974 Syndication) Documentary** *with Lloyd Bridges and James Franciscus as narrator*

As the title implies, *Water World* is about the sea, and the life found in it. The first twenty-six episodes are narrated by *Sea Hunt* veteran Lloyd Bridges, while James Franciscus, who played the teacher in *Mr. Novak,* narrates the second season.

**WATERFRONT (**) 30 min (78ep B&W; 1954–1956 Syndication) Adventure** *with Preston Foster as Capt. John Herrick, Lois Moran as May Herrick, Harry Lauter as Jim Herrick, and Willie Best as Willie Slocum*

Out of the early days of syndicated adventure series, *Waterfront* is a straightforward saga of the home and work exploits of Capt. John Herrick, the pilot of a tugboat in the harbor of San Pedro, California. Considering the early production date of this show, the on-location sea scenery and large cast is impressive.

**WAY OUT (***) 30 min (B&W; 1961 CBS) Suspense Anthology** *with Roald Dahl as host*

One of the missing gems of early TV anthologies, *Way Out* came and went in a flash, and has hardly been seen since, but it deserves to be resurrected. Much more sinister than *The Twilight Zone,* much more sophisticated than *One Step Beyond, Way Out* presents nasty little stories about nasty little people, with a very wicked touch that TV (especially in the late 1950s/early 1960s) usually shies away from. Hosted by Roald Dahl (writer of macabre short stories) and produced by David Susskind (*East Side/West Side, Alice,* and numerous TV drama classics from the golden age of TV dramas), *Way Out* suffers from a cheap budget, but the writing is wonderful. If it ever pops up, catch it, but only if you like being spooked.

**WE GOT IT MADE (*) 30 min (48ep Color; 1983–1984 & 1987–1988 NBC & Syndication) Situation Comedy** *with Teri Copley as Mickey McKenzie, Tom Villard as Jay Bostwick, Matt McCoy and John Hillner as David Tucker, Ron Karabatsos as Max Papavasilios, Sr., and Lance Wilson-White as Max Papavasilios, Jr.*

The titillating elements of *Three's Company* are turned inside out in *We Got It Made,* and the result is far less satisfying. Instead of one male moving in with two eligible females in a platonic arrangement, *We Got It Made* has one shapely female moving in with two horny males. The female, Mickey McKenzie, is a Brigitte Bardot–type (and that may be demeaning to Bardot) who is a live-in maid to the two sloppy guys (conservative lawyer David and grungy Jay).

As salacious as this sounds, keep in mind that *We Got It Made* is a TV sitcom. Be assured that despite innumerable provocative setups and risque dialogue, David and Jay will only lust after Mickey in their hearts.

Three years after the first twenty-four episodes were produced *We Got It Made* resumed production (there certainly was no public demand for its revival) with a slightly revamped cast, but with its silly format intact. The only thing that could help this program would be to move it to the Playboy Channel, so Jay and David could live out their fantasies about Mickey that go unsatisfied for so long. Fat chance, guys.

**WE, THE ACCUSED (***) 60 min (5ep Color; 1980 UK) Mystery** *with Ian Holm as Paul Presset, Angela Down as Myra, and Elizabeth Spriggs as Eleanor Presset*

Paul Presset is a meek and gentle schoolmaster who barely makes enough money to put food on the table, according to his nagging wife, Eleanor. What really hurts is that he knows she's right. The reason they have any comforts at all is because Eleanor has her own private income. And the reason he still has any life and energy left inside with a dead-end job and an unhappy marriage is that he has a girlfriend. And a dream.

At first, it's only a vague notion to break free, but as Paul talks with his lover, Myra, he begins to build the willingness to turn dreams into reality. All he needs is a little courage . . . to make a grab for both his wife's money and a new life with Myra. And all it involves is murder.

This intense tale is based on a novel by Ernest Raymond, with Ian Holm and Angela Down totally absorbing as the desperate lovers. They want so much to build a life together, but soon after Paul takes what he thinks will be the ultimate liberating action of murder, they find themselves on a frightening fast track. They have to keep one step ahead of their friends, neighbors, and the police, while seeing their dream of an idyllic life together put to the ultimate test.

In its original British presentation, this series played in four seventy-five minute episodes. For its first Stateside airing on *Mystery!* in 1983, it ran in five parts.

**WE'LL GET BY (*½) 30 min (13ep & 30 min pilot Color; 1975 CBS) Situation Comedy** *with Paul Sorvino as George Platt, Mitzi Hoag as Liz Platt, Jerry Houser as Michael "Muff" Platt, Willie Aames as Kenny Platt, and Devon Scott as Andrea Platt*

With one of the children in this domestic sitcom called "Muff," you know that we're talking about an early yuppie show. With ex-*M*A*S*H* man Alan Alda as executive producer, you know that this show will feature all sorts of deep feelings and sensitive interactions. Otherwise, *We'll Get By* is an innocuous 1970s sitcom about a suburban New Jersey family that stars Paul Sorvino, a talented actor who rarely gets starring roles.

**WE'VE GOT EACH OTHER (**) 30 min (13ep Color; 1977–1978 CBS) Situation Comedy** *with Oliver Clark as Stuart Hibbard, Beverly Archer as Judy Hibbard, Tom Poston as Damon Jerome, Joan Van Ark as Dee Dee Baldwin, and Martin Kove as Ken Redford*

Many of the best sitcoms of the 1970s (*The Mary Tyler Moore Show, The Bob Newhart Show*) came from the MTM studio, but *We've Got Each Other* is one of MTM's lesser lights from that decade. It is still better, however, than the run-of-the-mill comedy fodder. Produced by Tom Patchett and Jay Tarses (*The Bob Newhart Show, Buffalo Bill*), *We've Got Each Other* dates itself by revolving around the then-trendy concept of sexual role reversals. Hubby Stuart Hibbard works at home (as a copy writer for a mail order catalog) and takes care of the kids. Wife Judy makes the daily commute to downtown (Los Angeles), where she is an assistant to absent-minded photographer Damon Jerome (yet another wonderfully wacko character played by Tom Poston). Everybody is very nice, but there is no real driving force in the show.

**THE WEB (*) 30 min (13ep B&W; 1957 NBC) Drama Anthology**

After four years (1950–1954) as a live series from New York on CBS, *The Web* left the air, only to return in 1957 as a series of filmed dramas. It is these thirteen filmed dramas that survive. The concept is the same as in the live episodes: presenting stories of people caught in events they can't seem to overcome, largely as a result of their own actions (hence the spiderlike title).

**WEBSTER (*½) 30 min (151ep Color; 1983–1989 ABC & Syndication) Situation Comedy** *with Emmanuel Lewis as Webster Long, Alex Karras as George Papadapolis, Susan Clark as Katherine Calder-Young Papadapolis, Henry Polic II as Jerry Silver, Ben Vereen as Phillip Long, and Corin Nemec as Nicky Papadapolis*

The weirdest miniformat fad in TV sitcom history must be that of benevolent white people adopting cute, black, boy orphans who never seem to grow up. The originator was *Diff'rent Strokes* (Conrad Bain adopts Gary Coleman), and *Webster* continues this paternalistic mold with Alex Karras adopting Emmanuel Lewis.

Karras, an ex-NFL defensive tackle who pioneered the jock as a sensitive guy school of celebrities (later followed by Rosy Grier), plays a sensitive ex-pro football type turned sportswriter. He meets, woos, and weds a socialite/consumer activist on a cruise, then brings her home to Chicago where the newlyweds find a seven-year-old black orphan named Webster on their doorstep. Karras's character (George) had promised a black ex-teammate that he would care for his son if anything were to happen to the parents. They were subsequently killed in a car crash, so Webster was sent to live with George. He and his new wife (Katherine) were not expecting a family so soon, and certainly not one of this particular hue, but being sweet folk, they take in the urchin and raise him as their own.

Webster is unsufferably cute, and *Webster* wears its heart on its sleeve far too often. Even avoiding the nasty sociological implications of presenting blacks as cute orphans who need kind whites to raise them, *Webster* is still too sweet for anyone with the slightest taste for reality. As the episodes progress, the producers have the kindness to bring in some black kin for Webster (such as Uncle Phillip), but they begin doing serious shows about child abuse and retarded children that would seem preachy even if aired in the Sunday morning religious schedule. The clash of the fluffy setting and these weighty topics results in a morass of heavy-handed moralizing that just seems awkward.

*Webster* gets by for so long by appealing to the simplest, least offensive, side of the TV audience. While there is no real crime in this, and *Webster* is certainly fit for family viewing, it never really achieves anything of lasting merit.

**WELCOME BACK, KOTTER (**½) 30 min (95ep Color; 1975–1979 ABC) Situation Comedy** *with Gabriel Kaplan as Gabe Kotter, Marcia Strassman as Julie Kotter, John Travolta as Vinnie Barbarino, Robert Hegyes as Juan Epstein, Lawrence-Hilton Jacobs as Freddie "Boom Boom" Washington, Ron Palillo as Arnold Horshack, John Sylvester White as Michael Woodman, Debralee Scott as Rosalie "Hotzie" Totzie, Stephen Shortridge as Beau DeLabarre, and James Komack as the voice of Principal John Lazarus*

The *Dobie Gillis* of the 1970s, *Welcome Back, Kotter* deftly combines touches of reality with slapstick humor, winding up as a funny 1970s ensemble comedy. The reality comes from the dead-end setting of James Buchanan High School in a lower-class section of Brooklyn. Many of the students are just passing through on the way to a tough life of scraping for a living. Only a few break out of that mold, and few of those lucky few ever return. An exception is Gabe Kotter (played by Gabe Kaplan), who ten years after barely graduating from Buchanan High as one of the trouble students returns as a teacher to try and help a new generation of troublemakers. Kotter is assigned to teach the remedial class, the lowest of the low, but he can relate to these kids (called the "Sweathogs") because he was where they are, and not that long ago.

It all sounds pretty grim, but *Welcome Back, Kotter* is nowhere near a mood of despair. Instead it is a sprightly schoolroom stand-up routine, with ex-stand-up comic Gabe Kaplan acting as a Groucho Marx-type straight man to the punch lines tossed in by the Sweathogs. Head Sweathog Vinnie Barbarino is the classic Italian Stallion macho type, with a bevy of adoring young females and an army of respectful young males around him. Juan Epstein is an intriguing combination of Jewish and Puerto Rican cultures, resulting in a fast-talking con man with brains. Boom Boom Washington is the streetwise cool black dude, while Horshack is the class nerd. Numerous other Sweathogs come and go, but the central core serve as primary accomplices for Kaplan's wry humor.

*Welcome Back, Kotter* begins to slide downhill as the youthful cast begins to age. The Sweathogs begin to look a little long in the tooth to be roaming the high school halls by the end, and John Travolta virtually leaves the show to pursue his film career (*Saturday Night Fever*). An attempt to replicate the Barbarino charm in a southern mold, with Cajun heartthrob Beau DeLabarre (what's he doing in Brooklyn?), goes nowhere.

Producer James Komack previously mixed lively humor with touches of realism in other sitcoms (*The Courtship of Eddie's Father, Chico and the Man*). The theme song ("Welcome Back") by John Sebastian (ex–Lovin' Spoonful) is catchy and was a pop hit at the time.

**WELLS FARGO, TALES OF (**½) 30 & 60 min (201ep: one hundred sixty-seven 30 min B&W & thirty-four 60 min Color, plus 30 min pilot; 1957–1962 NBC) Western** *with Dale Robertson as Jim Hardie, Jack Ging as Beau McCloud, William Demarest as Jeb Gaine, and Virginia Christine as Ovie*

There is nobody in this show named Wells Fargo. That's the name of a company, the premier transporter of valuables throughout the Old West. Jim Hardie is chief agent for Wells Fargo, who roams the West as company troubleshooter. He helps the shipments get through despite the efforts of bad guys to abscond with the goodies carried by the company.

The first four seasons (the thirty-minute episodes) just focus on Hardie, with no other continuing characters, and are fine examples of the anthology within a series school of westerns (see *Wagon Train*). For the last season, the show needlessly expands to an hour and Hardie suddenly settles down to run a ranch, which violates the show's basic premise. New side characters are added, to little avail. Ignore the hour shows.

**WENDY & ME (***) 30 min (34ep B&W 1964–1965 ABC) Situation Comedy** *with George Burns as George Burns, Connie Stevens as Wendy Conway, Ron Harper as Jeff Conway, James Callahan as Danny Adams, and J. Patrick O'Malley as Mr. Bundy*

*Wendy & Me* follows the proven formula of the *Burns and Allen* series, down to the character played by George Burns. (He plays George Burns.) The program is derivative and predictable, but so well-executed that even fans of the original can find it an acceptable successor.

George Burns appears as a veteran entertainer who owns a small Hollywood apartment building. (He bought it to practice his singing without having to worry about being evicted.) There he takes particular delight in observing (and interacting with) his tenants, especially first-year marrieds Wendy and Jeff Conway. Jeff is a pilot and Wendy used to be a flight attendant.

Wendy is also the ideal subject for George's attention because she can take the most innocent situation and turn it into an amusing complication, just like Gracie Allen. For instance, when Wendy sees a couple affectionately making up after an argument she concludes that to save her marriage she and Jeff must have an argument and reconcile also.

Jeff accepts and enjoys Wendy's flights of fancy and illogical logic (even at his own expense) because he loves her. He also has a sense of humor, so he relishes watching the rest of the world encounter his determined wife, especially his best friend (and co-pilot) Danny Adams. As a dedicated bachelor living just across the hall, Danny is the perfect foil for Wendy. He's always in pursuit of some beautiful woman and Wendy is always there to complicate his courting with some well-intentioned misunderstanding.

George Burns likes that, too. As in *Burns and Allen,* he (and only he) knows that this is just a television comedy show that depends on silly misunderstandings to help fill a half hour. He takes care of the rest with monologue asides to the audience, his own impish teasing of the characters (especially building superintendent, Mr. Bundy), and lead-ins to the commercial breaks, punctuated by the order, "Do it!" And if the action is still lagging, he'll just step in and stir things up himself.

It's a tried-and-true formula that still plays well after more than two decades. Burns, of course, went on to make a whole new career out of being old. Age catches up with everyone, though, even swinging playboys like Danny Adams. Look for James Callahan playing grandfather Walter Powell on the 1980s comedy *Charles in Charge.*

**WEREWOLF (**½) 30 min (29ep & 2 hr pilot Color; 1987–1988 Fox) Adventure** *with John J. York as Eric Cord, Lance LeGault as Alamo Joe Rogan, and Chuck Connors as Janos Skorzeny*

No, the teen werewolf of this series is not warm and friendly like the cuddly fur ball of the 1985 theatrical film *Teen Wolf.* But unlike many monster movies of the past, Eric does have a way to end it: All he has to do is use the proverbial silver bullet to destroy the first in the bloodline of werewolves that infected him. So between bloody bouts with the moon, Eric searches, also trying to help people he meets along the way (in the best tradition of *The Fugitive* and *The Incredible Hulk*). Unfortunately, as a werewolf, he does have this churlish tendency to kill people (usually bad guys), making him a ripe target for bounty hunter Alamo Joe and an awfully difficult lead character to root for. Instead you end up waiting for Eric's final deadly confrontation with that scarred old sailor who holds the key to ending his curse, Janos Skorzeny (played to great effect by Chuck Connors). It's a tricky (somewhat brutal) premise, but for the short run of this series it works. And, yes, before the end of the series Eric does have that final face-to-face, only it doesn't turn out quite the way he expected.

**WEST POINT (*½) 30 min (39ep B&W; 1956–1957 CBS) Military Anthology** *with Donald May as Cadet Charles C. Thompson*

True life tales from the files of America's military academy, West Point, are dramatized in this modest series. At first, actor Donald May (later Adam Drake in the daytime soap *Edge of Night*) serves as host, while in character as a cadet. He is phased out (and not replaced) by the halfway point of this series, which is also known as *The West Point Story.*

**THE WESTERNER (**) 30 min (13ep & 30 min pilot & 60 min sequel B&W; 1960 NBC) Western** *with Brian Keith as Dave Blassingame and John Dehner as Burgundy Smith*

Sam Peckinpah, director of such violent Hollywood films as *Straw Dogs, Bring Me the Head of Alfredo Garcia,* and *The Killer Elite,* started as a writer and director of TV westerns. *The Westerner* is the only TV series that Peckinpah produced, and it contains some of the stylized violence that later made him famous. Familiar TV nice guy Brian Keith (*Family Affair*) plays laconic loner Dave Blassingame, who wanders through the Old West with his faithful mutt Brown, helping good people and fighting bad people. The 1959 pilot is called "Trouble at Tres Curces."

"The Losers," a 1963 installment of *The Dick Powell Theater,* serves as something of a sequel to *The Westerner,* attempting to revive the main characters, but with different actors. Lee Marvin plays Blassingame, while Keenan Wynn is his pal Burgundy Smith. Aaron Spelling, who had already worked on westerns in Zane Grey Theater, serves as producer of this failed pilot/sequel.

*The Westerner* is syndicated, along with episodes of *Johnny Ringo, Black Saddle,* and other 1950s westerns, under the title *The Westerners.*

**WESTINGHOUSE PLAYHOUSE** **(see *Yes, Yes Nanette*)**

**WESTSIDE MEDICAL (*) 60 min (4ep Color; 1977 ABC) Medical Drama** *with James Sloyan as Dr. Sam Lanagan, Linda Carlson as Dr. Janet Cottrell, and Ernest Thompson as Dr. Philip Parker*

Three ultra-dedicated young medicos open their own clinic in (can you guess?) Los Angeles, so they can devote every minute of everyday to curing people and acting extremely intense.

**WHAT A COUNTRY! (**) 30 min (26ep Color; 1986–1987 Syndication) Situation Comedy** *with Yakov Smirnoff as Nikolai Rostapovich, Garrett M. Brown as Taylor Brown, Gail Strickland as Joan Courtney, Vijay Amritraj as Ali Nadeem, George Murdock as Laslo Gabov, Ada Maris as Maria Conchita Lopez, and Don Knotts as F. Jerry "Bud" McPherson*

Soviet comedian/defector Yakov Smirnoff stars in this tailor-made sitcom about a group of resident aliens studying to become American citizens. Smirnoff plays a talkative Russian cabdriver, who joins with his Hungarian, Pakistani, Mexican, Chinese, and African classmates in trying to make sense of the United States.

The humor is fairly obvious, but it is performed well, with a fair modicum of laughs. Look for *Andy Griffith Show* star Don Knotts, who is brought in at the halfway point of the series as the antsy principal.

**WHAT REALLY HAPPENED TO THE CLASS OF '65? (**) 60 min (14ep & 2 hr pilot Color; 1977–1978 NBC) Drama Anthology** *with Tony Bill as Sam Ashley*

Fictional version of a nonfiction book, written by Michael Medved (later co-host of *Sneak Previews*) and David Wallechinsky. The two had looked up some fellow classmates from their old Los Angeles high school and wrote a best-selling book about what these people had done since 1965. The TV show keeps the title, the year, and the city (why move from television's favorite locale?) for a purely fictional drama anthology narrated by the character of Sam Ashley, a graduate from the class of 1965 teaching at his old high school. Each story begins with a brief flashback to the high school days, then follows the particular student through life after graduation. Not a bad premise, but it suffers from bouts with late 1970s formula relevancy.

**WHAT'S HAPPENING!!/NOW!! (**½) 30 min (131ep Color; 1976–1979 & 1985–1987 ABC & Syndication) Situation Comedy** *with Ernest Thomas as Roger "Raj" Thomas, Fred Berry as Freddie "Rerun" Stubbs, Shirley Hemphill as Shirley Wilson, Haywood Nelson as Dwayne Clemens, Mabel King as Mabel "Mama" Thomas, Danielle Spencer as Dee Thomas, Martin Lawrence as Maurice Warfield, and Ken Sagoes as Darryl*

Loosely based on the 1975 theatrical sleeper hit *Cooley High,* this TV version shifts the action from Chicago in 1964 to contemporary Los Angeles. Nonetheless, it retains a spirit of good fun, with the adventures of three black teens (Rerun, Raj, and Dwayne) wisely played first and foremost for laughs, not heavy-handed relevancy (a strategy successfully used by executive producer Bud Yorkin in the *Sanford and Son* days.) The result is a raucous and entertaining comedy with occasionally topical situations carried by some strong character types: Raj, the aspiring writer; Rerun, the well-meaning overweight clown (and surely one of the "lost" members of the rap group The Fat Boys); Dwayne, the shy one; Shirley, the sharp-tongued waitress at the local diner/hangout (Rob's); Dee, Raj's conniving little sister; and Mabel Thomas, Dee and Raj's hard-working mom.

The series originally played for several seasons on ABC, then did well enough on the rerun circuit with its sixty-five network episodes to warrant a revival more than half a decade later. Rechristened *What's Happening Now!* the series continues with most of the original cast intact, showing the teens as young adults with new (but somehow familiar) problems. Raj is married, Rerun and Dwayne share an apartment, and Shirley is still at Rob's (running the place with Raj). Not surprisingly, the package still works pretty well.

**WHAT'S IT ALL ABOUT, WORLD? (*) 60 min (13ep Color; 1969 ABC) Comedy-Variety** *with Dean Jones as host*

Here is a lame stab at imitating the *Laugh-In/Smothers Brothers* style of satirical topical comedy, while removing all the controversy. The result: inoffensive sophomoric skits. Dean Jones, refugee from Disney films (*The Love Bug*), is way over his head here. The series ends up being called *The Dean Jones Variety Hour,* which at least is a better title than the original moniker, a hippie-esque howler.

**WHEELS (*½) (10hr miniseries Color; 1978 NBC) Drama** *with Rock Hudson as Adam Trenton, Lee Remick as Erica Trenton, Blair Brown as Barbara Lipton, Ralph Bellamy as Lowell Baxter, Anthony Franciosa as Smokey Stevenson, Howard McGillin as Greg Trenton, and John Beck as Peter Flodenhale*

Arthur Hailey's lengthy tome about the automobile industry in Detroit in the late 1960s is turned into a turgid miniseries. There is a heavy emphasis on romantic and corporate intrigue, with the usual bevy of big-name stars. Roy Huggins, of *Maverick* and *Toma* fame, produces.

**WHEN HAVOC STRUCK (**) 30 min (12ep Color; 1978 Syndication) Documentary** *with Glenn Ford as host/narrator*

Somewhat tabloid in its macabre infatuation with disaster, *When Havoc Struck* is a somber and overdramatic look at big disasters of our time. Lots of old film footage is dragged out and actor Glenn Ford is propped up to try (unsuccessfully) to add some class as host/narrator.

**WHEN TELEVISION WAS LIVE (**½) 30 min (7ep Color; 1975 PBS) Variety** *with Peter Lind Hayes and Mary Healy*

The long-running careers of comedian/actors Peter Lind Hayes and real-life wife and partner Mary Healy are relived by the couple themselves in this succinct series. Their careers are brought to life via modern reminiscences and replays of old black-and-white kinescopes of their performances from the early days of TV.

**WHEN THE WHISTLE BLOWS (½) 60 min (13ep Color; 1980 ABC) Situation Comedy** *with Doug Barr as Buzz Dillard, Philip Brown as Randy Hartford, Susan Buckner as Lucy Davis, Tim Rossovich as Martin "Hunk" Kincaid, Dolph Sweet as Norm Jenkins, and Sue Ane Langdon as Darlene Ridgeway*

This show is supposed to be a lighthearted look at the blue-collar world of a work crew for a big L. A. construction company. It is really a patently farcical attempt by producer Leonard Goldberg (*Charlie's Angels, Fantasy Island*) to do a fun show about real people. Everybody in *When The Whistle Blows* is a walking caricature and the plots are silly rather than funny. Goldberg should stick to total fantasy.

**WHEN THINGS WERE ROTTEN (**½) 30 min (13ep Color; 1975 ABC) Situation Comedy** *With Dick Gautier as Robin Hood, Dick Van Patten as Friar Tuck, Bernie Kopell as Alan-a-Dale, Henry Polic II as The Sheriff of Nottingham, Misty Rowe as Maid Marian, Richard Dimitri as twin brothers Renaldo and Bertram, David Sabin as Little John, Ron Rifkin as Prince John, and Jane A. Johnson as Princess Isabelle*

A Mel Brooks comedy production is a precarious combination of elements, playing like a Daffy Duck cartoon crossed with an old vaudeville routine peppered with one-liners, backstage showbiz references, and a touch of vulgarity. This combination is not surprising since it reflects the many facets of Mel Brooks: borscht-belt comic, variety sketch writer, and on-camera comedy performer.

The great strength of Mel Brooks is that he inevitably attempts to shoehorn all these elements into his comedy productions. However, the great weakness of Mel Brooks is that he inevitably attempts to shoehorn all these elements into his comedy productions. It just depends on how well they all fit.

In 1974, Brooks struck box office gold with the western parody film *Blazing Saddles.* This film led to a series of other theatrical genre parodies (of varying success), from *Young Frankenstein* to *Spaceballs.* It also won him an immediate network TV slot for a Robin Hood parody, *When Things Were Rotten.*

This series is typical Brooks from the period, missing only the vulgarity ("fart" jokes and such) from *Blazing Saddles* (this was, after all, on prime-time network television). How well it works depends on your tolerance for obvious physical schtick, anachronisms, bad puns, and creakingly familiar jokes ("Waiter, what's that fly doing in my soup?" "The backstroke?").

A decade later the chief attraction of the series is probably the opportunity to take a peek at familiar performing faces hamming it up, including Sid Caesar as an amorous French Diplomat, Dudley Moore as a rich oil sheik, and Ron Glass as a black knight (literally). Among the regulars, Dick Van Patten's Friar Tuck and Henry Polic II's Sheriff of Nottingham are the most fun, while Prince John and the evil Bertram don't wear quite as well. ■

**WHERE'S HUDDLES (**) 30 min (17ep Color; 1970 CBS) Cartoon Situation Comedy** *with the voices of Cliff Norton as Ed Huddles, Mel Blanc as Bubba McCoy, Dick Enberg as the Sports Announcer, Marie Wilson as Penny McCoy, Jean Vander Pyl as Marge Huddles, Herb Jeffries as Freight Train, Alan Reed as Coach Mad Dog Maloney, and Paul Lynde as Claude Pertwee*

This Hanna-Barbera adult cartoon series brings a familiar lineup of voices to a straightforward home and office comedy setting. In this case, next-door neighbors Ed Huddles and Bubba McCoy both work at the same "office," the football field, where they play professionally for the Rhinos (Huddles at quarterback, McCoy at center). Yet it's all very familiar, with voices straight out of *The Flintstones,* where Alan Reed did Fred, Mel Blanc did Barney, and Jean Vander Pyl did Wilma. And, of course, the Rhino team members all run like Fred and Barney—just watch their feet spin over the ground. Unfortunately, also like *The Flintstones,* the stories are only routine, with typical sitcom complications packaged in animated form.

**WHERE'S RAYMOND** **(see *The Ray Bolger Show*)**

**WHIPLASH (**) 30 min (34ep B&W; 1960–1961 UK ATV) Adventure** *with Peter Graves as Chris Cobb and Anthony Wickert as Dan*

Filmed on location in Australia, and hero Chris Cobb has the bullwhips and boomerangs to prove it. Though the role is a world away from the sophisticated electronic hardware of star Peter Graves's most famous role (that of Jim Phelps on *Mission: Impossible*), it's appropriate in this setting: Australia during the 1850s. In other words, this is a western adventure that happens to be set on another continent, with Graves playing the American owner of a down-under stage coach line, facing the usual assortment of Old West bad guys. *Whiplash* is better than average for its type and times, though don't look for many distinctive Australian accents—the producers went out of their way to make this show sound like a regular Hollywood production.

**THE WHIRLYBIRDS (**) 30 min (111ep B&W; 1956–1959 Syndication) Adventure** *with Ken Tobey as Chuck Martin, Craig Hill as Pete "P. T." Moore, and Nancy Hale as Helen Carter*

Like westerns, adventure shows have to have a gimmick to catch the public's eye. The gimmick in *The Whirlybirds* is helicopters. The two stalwart heroes, Chuck and P. T., run a helicopter charter service in California and get involved in all sorts of daring exploits with their flying machines. The action is plentiful, the stunt work is exciting (don't try this on your own, kids), and the dialogue is minimal.

**WHISPERING SMITH (**) 30 min (25ep B&W; 1961 NBC) Western** *with Audie Murphy as Tom "Whispering" Smith, Guy Mitchell as George Romack, and Sam Buffington as John Richards*

Based on ancient cases from the Denver Police Department, *Whispering Smith* tells the story of Tom Smith, the first detective to use modern and scientific methods to fight crime in the savage West. In spite of the modern methods, Smith still manages to beat up his share of bad guys the old-fashioned way, with guns and fists.

Star Audie Murphy was a well-publicized World War II Medal of Honor winner and the star of several 1950s films (*To Hell and Back*). Co-star Guy Mitchell was also a singer, scoring big with "Singing the Blues" in 1956.

**THE WHISTLER (*) 30 min (39ep B&W; 1954–1955 Syndication) Suspense Anthology** *with Bill Forman as The Whistler*

The opening lines "I am the Whistler, and I know many things, for I walk by night" and the memorable melancholy theme song (mostly whistling, of course) of *The Whistler* captured the minds of a generation, but it wasn't through this version of the show. The original radio version, which debuted in 1942, was a classic of the audio age. This video version is a serious attempt to bring the show to the new medium, but it just doesn't work.

The Whistler is sort of a mysterious avenger who helps people in despair and trouble. The TV series relegates the Whistler to more of a narrator's role, commenting on unrelated tales of suspense that don't match the radio version's ability to create terror by imagination.

**THE WHITE SHADOW (***) 60 min (54ep Color; 1978–1981 CBS) Drama** *with Ken Howard as Ken Reeves, Ed Bernard as Jim Willis, Joan Pringle as Sybil Buchanan, Byron Stewart as Warren Coolidge, Timothy Van Patten as Mario "Salami" Pettrino, Kevin Hooks as Morris Thorpe, Thomas Carter as James Hayward, Ken Michelman as Abner Goldstein, Ira Angustain as Ricky Gomez, and John Mengatti as Nick Vitaglia*

Often, the most exciting basketball contests to watch are the high school games. The plays don't whiz by too fast to follow, the centers aren't always tall enough to dunk every shot, and each drive to score doesn't automatically end with a "swish." Best of all, the kids are still fresh enough to be playing for the fun of it, so a rags-to-riches story is especially satisfying.

And that's what we have here as a talented but not very successful ghetto high school team suspiciously eyes its new white coach, Ken Reeves. He's a former pro (with the Chicago Bulls) forced to retire because of a knee problem, coming to Carver High School at the invitation of his old college roommate, Jim Willis, the principal. Reeves is a straight-talking guy who wants to build a winning team, but who also wants to help the kids grow on a personal basis. After some initial resistance (especially when he institutes some tough practice sessions emphasizing team work) the players begin to develop respect and trust in their coach. Over the next two playing seasons, he builds their self-confidence, sharpens their court skills, and turns them from a group of disorganized show-offs into a tough, balanced, and successful team. They improve in their first year under him and go all the way to the California state finals in their second.

But there's more going on than just basketball. Along the way, the series presents one of the most believable television portraits of teen life, conveying a real sense of youthful discovery and excitement. For instance, when the team has to take a trip in a small commuter plane (for many, their first time flying), their reactions from the moment they enter the airport until they land ring absolutely true. Or when the coach visits some of his players at their homes, they greet him with a mixture of warmth and nervousness, obviously aware that they don't live in the area's most luxurious houses, but still proud to share this part of their lives with him.

The players also have to face some of the other problems of living in a tough area of Los Angeles, such as drugs, gambling, and street violence. They're all basically good kids, so it's usually a matter of pulling them away from the edges of disaster (hanging out at a pool hall) rather than having to rescue them from any truly deep problem (such as selling drugs). This isn't *21 Jump Street.* In fact, one of the team's major brushes with drugs comes through a doctor who normally deals with professionals and just automatically uses a strong painkiller to treat Salami's knee injury. The most dramatic instance of violence takes place on the eve of the big game, when Curtis Jackson is caught in the cross fire of a holdup.

One of the more unusual aspects of *The White Shadow* is its realistic sense of anticlimax in the coach's third year. After basking in the success of his first two seasons during a hometown reunion visit with his dad (played by James Whitmore), he faces the task of starting all over because most of his key players have graduated. Just as he gamely begins, the series winds to its conclusion. Maybe he'll succeed again, or maybe that victory banner will be the only one to hang in Carver High for years to come.

*The White Shadow* was an MTM production created by Bruce Paltrow, who also shared writing chores with (among others) John Falsey, Joshua Brand, and Mark Tinker. All of them worked together again on *St. Elsewhere,* and they used that series for a few final continuity points on *The White Shadow.* Timothy Van Patten turns up in one story line playing a kid gone bad (though he is never specifically identified as Salami). Byron Stewart regularly appears in his Warren Coolidge character, often wearing a Carver T-shirt. Though Coolidge was the one with the best shot at the pros, an injury put an end to his dreams and he ended up instead as an orderly at St. Eligius.

**WHIZ KIDS (**) 60 min (19ep Color; 1983–1984 CBS) Adventure** *with Matthew Laborteaux as Richie Adler, Andrea Elson as Alice Tyler, Todd Porter as Hamilton Parker, Jeffrey Jacquet as Jeremy Saldino, Madelyn Cain as Irene Adler, Dan O'Herlihy as Carson Marsh, and Max Gail as Lew Farley*

Like the 1983 hit film *War Games,* this series is based on the proposition that a sharp high school kid inherently knows and understands more about computer systems than almost any adult. Richie Alder is one such whiz who easily taps into everything from police files to school records along with several of his friends (Alice, Ham, and Jeremy). Fortunately he gets an adult on his side, crusading newspaper reporter Lew Farley (played by Max Gail, Wojo from *Barney Miller*), who helps the kids learn how to work with the system rather than against it. Soon they have a relatively good working relationship with the police (through Farley's brother-in-law on the force) and eventually help from the mysterious Carson Marsh, head of the Athena Intelligence Office. In one episode, A.J. Simon (from *Simon and Simon*) even shows up in a character cross-over.

The stories are standard teen crime adventures (kidnappings, bank robbers, spies, and such), following paths well-worn by the likes of the Hardy Boys, only with more technical gloss—like Richie's glitzy talking computer, Ralf. Soon after this series ended its brief run, Andrea Elson (who plays Richie's friend Alice) found a new out-of-this-world way to make trouble. She became best friends with that furry alien mischief maker, Alf.

**WHO'S THE BOSS? (**) 30 min (120ep at Fall 1989 Color; 1984– ABC) Situation Comedy** *with Tony Danza as Tony Micelli, Judith Light as Angela Bower, Alyssa Milano as Samantha Micelli, Danny Pintauro as Jonathan Bower, and Katherine Helmond as Mona Robinson*

Very little goes a long way on *Who's the Boss?,* a light romp through the sexual role reversals TV found so enticing in the 1980s. Tony Danza, who played the boxer/cabby in *Taxi,* plays equally macho Tony Micelli, a widower with a ten-year-old daughter. Tony decides to leave the madness of New York City for the relative quiet of the suburbs, and he hires himself out as a live-in housekeeper to beautiful divorced business executive Angela Bower. She is too busy at the office to care for her rambunctious seven-year-old son Jonathan. Angela's mother Mona (*Soap's* Katherine Helmond), supervises and chaperones the goings-on.

Angela and Tony are from two different sides of the track, but they learn to respect each other. Tony likes the nice surroundings. Angela likes having a man around young Jonathan. Angela goes through a series of boyfriends, but never hooks up with one. Tony handles his multifaceted role was aplomb, and *Who's the Boss* chugs along, with a minimum of crudeness, for a healthy run.

**WHO'S WATCHING THE KIDS (*½) 30 min (13ep & 60 min pilot Color; 1978 NBC) Situation Comedy** *with Caren Kaye as Stacy Turner, Lynda Goodfriend as Angie Vitola, Scott Baio as Frankie "the Fox" Vitola, Tammy Lauren as Melissa Turner, Marcia Lewis as Mitzi Logan, Larry Breeding as Larry Parnell, and Jim Belushi as Bert Gunkel*

Just as a show, *Who's Watching the Kids* is pretty poor. It's about two gorgeous Las Vegas showgirls who try to raise younger live-in siblings while appearing in some sleazy Vegas dive (the Club Sand Pile). The two younger kids are brash and bratty. All in all, it is the pure late 1970s titillating sitcom format, where the laughs are cheap and the situations are forced.

What makes this show interesting at all is its history and its actors. Produced by Garry Marshall (*Happy Days*), the series borrowed heavily from another failed Marshall sitcom about Las Vegas showgirls, called *Blanskey's Beauties.* Caren Kaye, Lynda Goodfriend, and Scott Baio all appeared in that earlier show, in very similar roles. The pilot for *Who's Watching the Kids* was named *Legs,* and contains most of the cast that made it to this series, but with many characters having slightly different names. The *Legs* version focused more on the showgirls than the kids. Finally, two of the stars of *Who's Watching the Kids* (Goodfriend and Baio) had somewhat better luck in Marshall's big hit show, *Happy Days.* In that series, Goodfriend played Lori Beth, the woman who marries Richie Cunningham and has his baby. Baio became a minor star as Chachi, the young version of the Fonz.

Jim Belushi (brother of John) makes his TV series debut on *Who's Watching the Kids* in a small role.

**WHODUNNIT? (½) 30 min (6ep Color; 1979 NBC) Quiz** *with Ed McMahon as host, and F. Lee Bailey and Melvin Belli as panelists*

More an odd throwback to the neolithic age of TV than a trendsetting breakthrough, *Whodunnit?* offers brief murder dramas that stop just before the murderer is revealed. A panel of contestants then match wits with a celebrity panel (usually including famed lawyers F. Lee Bailey and Melvin Belli, two gluttons for publicity) to try and guess the culprit. *Tonight* show second banana Ed McMahon performs the figurehead function of host. This is pure bottom-of-the-barrel TV that is totally disposable.

**WICHITA TOWN (*½) 30 min (24ep B&W; 1959–1960 NBC) Western** *with Joel McCrea as Marshal Mike Dunbar and Jody McCrea as Deputy Ben Matheson*

A TV western vehicle for a man who truly loved playing a cowboy. After several decades of success in feature film westerns, Joel McCrea rode on the stampede of TV oaters that filled the airwaves in the late 1950s, bringing along his son, Jody. They play sheriff and marshal in some standard western tales, set in Wichita Town, Kansas, during the 1870s. Unfortunately, except for the lead characters, this is nothing special.

**WIDE COUNTRY (**) 60 min (28ep & 60 min pilot B&W; 1962–1963 NBC) Western** *with Earl Holliman as Mitch Guthrie and Andrew Prine as Andy Guthrie*

One of the few of the late 1950s/early 1960s glut of westerns to be set in the modern era, *Wide Country* is about rodeo champ Mitch Guthrie and his younger brother Andy. Mitch is trying to talk Andy out of following in his footsteps. The pilot is entitled *Second Chance.*

**WILD BILL HICKOCK (**) 30 min (113ep: 74 B&W & 39 Color; 1951–1956 Syndication) Western** *with Guy Madison as James Butler "Wild Bill" Hickok and Andy Devine as Jingles B. Jones*

Kiddie-oriented westerns were all over the tube in the early 1950s, after the success of *The Lone Ranger,* but few, if any, equaled the polish and spirit of the tales of the masked man and his Indian companion. *Wild Bill Hickok* is just another competitor of *The Lone Ranger,* with little to differentiate it from the pack, other than the raspy, nails-on-a-blackboard voice of rotund sidekick Andy Devine.

Hickok, a U.S. marshal in the amorphous Old West of the late 1800s, is forever battling evil amidst the prairie and sagebrush. One of the main problems with this show is that Guy Madison, who plays Hickok, is too good-looking. He looks like he should be hanging out at some posh Beverly Hills party, at poolside with a starlet, not rounding up flea-bitten varmints with a 300-pound buffoon who sounds like he gargles with razor blades. Anyone Hickok is protecting should worry that the marshal might give up the chase if it looks as if he might get his outfit dirty.

This program is only for those who have fond memories of watching the series when it originally aired. Otherwise, look for *The Long Ranger.*

**WILD JACK MCCALL (**½) 60 min (3ep at Fall 1989 Color; 1989– NBC) Adventure** *with John Schneider as Jack McCall and Carol Huston as Constance*

An Alaskan wilderness guide is named the trustee of a multimillion-dollar publishing company. Sounds like a great opportunity to (surprise) show those highfalutin city folks a thing or two about life, priorities, and running a business. Former *Dukes of Hazzard* star John Schneider takes the title role in this miniseries first airing as a segment on *The Magical World of Disney.*

**WILD KINGDOM (***) 30 min (529ep at Fall 1989 Color; 1963– NBC & Syndication) Documentary** *with Marlin Perkins, Jim Fowler, Tom Allen, Stan Brock, and Peter Eros as hosts*

The entire animal kingdom, it seems, appears on *Wild Kingdom* at one time or another. Unflappable Marlin Perkins, who began as director of Chicago's Lincoln Park Zoo, serves as host for more than twenty years, with help from other naturalists. The scope of the series is exhaustive. Each episode examines another aspect of animal life. Frequently, Perkins reports on-location in some wilderness.

If *Wild Kingdom* is sometimes pedantic and professorial, so be it. It does its job well, educates and entertains at the same time, and never stoops to cheap thrills to capture an audience. However, Perkins can seem pretty funny (unintentionally) with his convoluted tie-ins of the topic at hand to the sponsor (the Mutual of Omaha insurance company).

After Perkins's retirement in 1985 (he died the next year), his long-time assistant Jim Fowler takes the helm, with Peter Eros as the new number two.

**THE WILD, WILD WEST (***) 60 min (104ep: 28 B&W & 76 Color plus two 2 hr sequels; 1965–1969 CBS) Western Adventure** *with Robert Conrad as James T. West and Ross Martin as Artemus Gordon*

The trouble with many contemporary spy adventures is that there's no way to avoid having the latest technological hardware look dated years later in reruns. *The Wild, Wild West* deftly avoids this problem by setting the action in the 1870s, so that even something as simple as a crude tracking device or a miniature explosives detonator always looks positively state-of-the-art for that time. Of course, with this anachronistic door opened, the writers sometimes play fast and loose with what they sneak along, including supposed interdimensional travel, "magic" elixirs, and mechanical men, all under the guise of top-secret nineteenth-century technology.

But that's part of the fun of this series. Besides, even with a few pseudo-modern devices, this is a world of espionage that calls for plenty of hard work on the part of agents Jim West and Artemus Gordon. Their cases are real and dangerous (if occasionally outlandish for their low-tech times), allowing plenty of opportunities for good old-fashioned heroics. The series has some excellent special effects, amusing set pieces (including the duo's private luxury train car and Arte's trunk of disguises), and a particularly strong assortment of colorful foes, including evil magician Count Manzeppi (Victor Buono), the scheming matchmaker Emma Valentine (Agnes Moorehead), and, of course, Dr. Miguelito Loveless. Standing just a few feet tall, Loveless (played by Michael Dunn, a dwarf in real life) consistently poses the greatest threat of all. This man doesn't just exceed nineteenth-century science, he sometimes gives the twentieth century a run as well.

*The Wild, Wild West* is consistently entertaining, with Ross Martin and Robert Conrad playing their characters perfectly. Unlike *Batman* or *The Man from U.N.C.L.E.*, the series never loses control of its balance between humor and adventure, though the initial black-and-white episodes are less fantasy-oriented than the rest of the run.

There are a pair of two-hour revivals of the series, "The Wild, Wild West Revisited" (1979) and "More Wild, Wild West" (1980), with government intelligence officer Robert Malone (Harry Morgan) calling them out of retirement. In the first, West and Gordon face the son of Doctor Loveless (played by Paul Williams, since Michael Dunn had died), while in the follow-up they battle Professor Albert Paradine II (Jonathan Winters). Both stories suffer from the inevitable padding that accompanies movie-length versions of hour-long adventure stories, but it's still great fun. ■

**WILD, WILD WORLD OF ANIMALS (**½) 30 min (25ep Color; 1973–1978 Syndication) Documentary** *with William Conrad as narrator*

Time-Life Films and the BBC combine to produce this fine series on wild and endangered animals. The familiar voice of William Conrad (star of *Cannon* narrator of *The Fugitive* and *Bullwinkle*) is heard throughout.

**WILDSIDE (**) 60 min (6ep Color; 1985 ABC) Western** *with William Smith as Brodie Hollister, Howard E. Rollins, Jr., as Bannister Sparks, J. Eddie Peck as Sutton Hollister, John Di Aquino as Varges De La Cosa, Jason Hervey as Zeke, Terry Funk as Prometheus Jones, Meg Ryan as Cally Oaks, and Sandy McPeak as Governor J. Wendell Summerhayes*

Wildside, California, in the 1800s, has its own elite squad of law enforcers, sort of a nineteenth-century impossible missions force dedicated to preserving the peace in their part of the world. There are a couple of fast guns (Brodie and his son, Sutton), an explosives expert (Bannister), a master of knives (Varges), and a Hoss-size guy (Prometheus) who's a whiz with a rope. Usually they get their assignments from Governor Summerhayes; other times they find plenty of trouble on their own (ranging from a coal mine disguised as a gold mine to a squad of renegade British soldiers). This is light western adventure attempting to follow a track similar to *The Wild, Wild West,* but only moderately successful. ■

**WILLIAM TELL (**½) 30 min (39ep B&W; 1957–1958 UK ITC) Adventure** *with Conrad Phillips as William Tell, Jennifer Jayne as Hedda Tell, Richard Rogers as Walter Tell, and Willoughby Goddard as Gessler*

Filmed in the Swiss Alps, this series follows the adventures of fourteenth-century freedom fighter William Tell. He's the catalyst for the Swiss people groaning under rule by the tyrannical Austrian Empire and its local representative, Gessler. His despotic arrogance leads to the famous order for Tell to shoot an apple from his son's head, and other abuses. So under Tell's leadership, the drive for Swiss independent takes hold. Another better than average adventure produced by future *Secret Agent* creator Ralph Smart, with a surprisingly energetic story line and the usual collection of familiar British supporting players (Michael Caine, for instance, shows up several times).

For another version of the legend of William Tell, see *Crossbow.*

**WINDOW ON MAIN STREET (**½) 30 min (36ep B&W; 1961–1962 CBS) Situation Comedy** *with Robert Young as Cameron Garrett Brooks, Constance Moore as Chris Logan, Ford Rainey as Lloyd Ramsey, Brad Berwick as Arny Logan, and James Davidson as Wally Evans*

This way station in the TV career of Robert Young came between his two giant hits, *Father Knows Best* and *Marcus Welby, M. D.,* and definitely is worth catching. Young, as he always does, plays a kindly, thoughtful fellow. As widowed novelist Cameron Brooks, he is not as lecturing as Dr. Welby, nor is he as concerned with being the perfect person as Jim Anderson in *Father Knows Best.*

Brooks has returned to his hometown of Millsburg to write about the people close to his heart. He takes a room in the big hotel in town, revives old friendships, and meets new folk.

The pace in *Window on Main Street* is slow. Millsburg could easily be renamed Anytown, USA. Nothing of great importance happens. Still the stories have the warm, friendly flavor of small-town life. This show is easygoing to the extreme, but that may be nice, compared to the frantic nature of most modern shows.

**THE WINDS OF WAR (***) (18hr miniseries Color; 1983 ABC) Drama** *with Robert Mitchum as Victor "Pug" Henry, Ali MacGraw as Natalie Jastrow, Jan-Michael Vincent as Byron Henry, Ben Murphy as Warren Henry, Lisa Eilbacher as Madeline Henry, John Houseman as Aaron Jastrow, Polly Bergen as Rhoda Henry, Peter Graves as Palmer "Fred" Kirby, Victoria Tennant as Pamela Tudsbury, Michael Logan as Alistair Tudsbury, Ralph Bellamy as Pres. Franklin D. Roosevelt, Gunter Meisner as Adolf Hitler, and William Woodson as narrator*

At a total running time of eighteen hours, this miniseries lasts longer than a large number of regular series. Based on Herman Wouk's mammoth novel, *The Winds of War* follows the tried and true formula of historical miniseries, in that it places fictional characters amidst all the real-life occurrences during a crucial historical moment. This formula allows the history lesson part of the show to be sugar-coated with easy-to-understand personalities and exploitable love affairs.

Robert Mitchum, usually a stranger to TV, is admirably gruff as no-nonsense U.S. naval officer Pug Henry. He is stationed in Germany from the outbreak of World War II in 1939 until the U.S. entrance in the war in 1941. Henry, his wife, and his children encounter all the big names of the times: Hitler, Roosevelt, Churchill, Stalin, Mussolini, and so forth. Meanwhile, Pug finds time for an extramarital affair and son Byron marries a Jewish girl who was raised in America and is trying to escape from Italy.

*Winds of War* is very well-produced, using an obviously huge budget. The cast is top-heavy with stars, even for a big miniseries. It's worth eighteen hours of your time, if only to watch Bob Mitchum be so cool that he sometimes hardly moves.

*The Winds of War* spawned an even more mammoth sequel, *War and Remembrance,* in 1988 and 1989.

**WINSTON CHURCHILL—THE VALIANT YEARS (***) 30 min (26ep & 60 min pilot B&W; 1960–1961 ABC) Documentary** *with Gary Merrill as narrator and Richard Burton as the reader of Winston Churchill's memoirs*

Winston Churchill's view of the years just before and during World War II is ably presented in this documentary based on Churchill's own memoirs. Everything about this show is well-done. The writing is clear and informative, the music (by Richard Rodgers) is stirring, and the narration (by Gary Merrill and Richard Burton) is memorable. Aside from some TV plays, movies, and miniseries, and a famous guest spot on *Here's Lucy,* this is Richard Burton's only TV series work in America.

**WINSTON CHURCHILL—THE WILDERNESS YEARS (**½) 60 min (8ep Color; 1981 UK Southern) Drama** *with Robert Hardy as Winston Churchill, Sian Phillips as Clementine, Peter Barkworth as Stanley Baldwin, Eric Porter as Neville Chamberlain, Edward Woodward as Samuel Hoare, Sam Wanamaker as Bernard Baruch, and Tim Pigott-Smith as Brenden Bracken*

No, this is not a look at Churchill's youth riding on horseback through some wide-open wilderness. (That's another series.) Instead, this story covers the decade (1929–1939) that Churchill was on the outs among the power elite. It's a fascinating pause in an otherwise meteoric, ambitious career: a member of Parliament before he was twenty-seven, an officer in the government by age thirty-one, and a cabinet minister by the age of thirty-seven. But then a change in control of Britain's government leaves Chancellor of the Exchequer Winston Churchill facing political unemployment. Even worse, he finds himself at odds with forces within his own Conservative party. But he doesn't stop speaking his mind on a variety of issues, such as his opposition to granting India dominion status. Even as he's marked for political death (one of several such wakes in his career), the winds of war are in the air, setting the stage for his dramatic comeback. This is a well-done, admiring portrayal of Churchill (with Robert Hardy from *All Creatures Great and Small* in the lead), with a good supporting cast (including Tim Pigott-Smith from *The Jewel in the Crown* and Edward Woodward from *The Equalizer*) and a strong sense of the times.

**WIRE SERVICE (*) 30 min (39ep B&W; 1956–1957 ABC) Crime Drama** *with Dane Clark as Dan Miller, George Brent as Dean Evans, and Mercedes McCambridge as Katherine Wells*

Three performers alternate in the lead slot for this international adventure series, covering the world for Trans Globe News. Actually it was probably more like covering the grade-B backlot, since the performers were saddled with some pretty weak plots, settings, and dialogue. As with most low-budget series, the only reason to even glance at this show is for some of the guest star appearances, though in this case there are only a few interesting faces (such as Michael Landon, Lee Van Cleef, and Peter Baldwin). The thirteen episodes featuring Dane Clark (one of the leads on *Bold Venture* just a year later) carry a separate title, *Deadline for Action.*

**WISEGUY (***) 60 min (43ep at Fall 1989 & 2 hr pilot Color; 1987– CBS) Crime Drama** *with Ken Wahl as Vinnie Terranova, Jonathan Banks as Frank McPike, Gerald Anthony as Father Peter Terranova, and Jim Byrnes as Lifeguard*

When producer Stephen J. Cannell gets it right (*The Rockford Files, The Greatest American Hero*), he somehow manages to combine action, adventure, drama, character, whimsy, and poignancy into a form that a mass audience can relate to and critics can applaud. With *Wiseguy,* Cannell heads off on a somewhat more serious direction, and the extra grit wears well.

Vinnie Terranova works with a secret undercover crime-fighting unit (the Organized Crime Bureau) of the federal government whose modus operandi is infiltrating top mobsters. The goal is to catch the big fish in the act, not just the small fry usually caught in federal dragnets. For Vinnie's cover to appear real, he serves eighteen months in the Newark State Penitentiary. Out from the pen, Vinnie's goal is to worm his way into the operations of crime mobs, to become a "wiseguy," one of the underlings who performs tasks for the big shots. The problem is that for the cover to really work nobody (well, almost nobody) is to know that Vinnie is really honest. All of Vinnie's family except for his brother the priest (Pete) turn cold shoulder on him, assuming the worst. Otherwise, only Frank McPike, Vinnie's boss at the OCB, and their communications link (a fellow known as Lifeguard) know what Vinnie is up to. This intense secrecy gives Vinnie a real loner's anguish in performing his tasks, and this anguish is riveting.

The first mobster Vinnie becomes involved with is the best. Ray Sharkey plays Sonny Steelgrave in a fascinating portrait of an Atlantic City gangster, with a complexity unseen outside of the best crime films. Vinnie becomes Sonny's number one aide, and the two men really develop close feelings for each other. Vinnie goes through mental flip-flops trying to rationalize his efforts to undo the one man who shows him the most consideration on a day-to-day basis. The epic two-hour finale, when Sonny and Vinnie lock horns both physically and mentally, is a tour de force that *Wiseguy* will be hard-pressed to top.

After Steelgrave, Vinnie goes to work for crazy Mel Profitt (played by Kevin Spacey), a smuggler of guns and drugs who is working on returning a sympathetic Latin–American dictator to power. It turns out that Profitt's plan is tangled up with a CIA operation and, after Profitt's scheme falls apart through killings, suicides, a congressional investigation, and an apparent assassination, Vinnie is even more troubled than before about the thin line between government and crime. It's no wonder that Vinnie considers leaving the OCB as the second season starts.

*Wiseguy*'s second season opens with the violent death of Vinnie's brother Pete at the hands of a gang of neo-Nazis who are causing trouble in Vinnie's old neighborhood. Soon thereafter, a wonderful five-episode segment features famed comic Jerry Lewis in a rare dramatic role. Lewis plays New York garment honcho Eli Sternberg, who gets ensnared in the mob's clutches when he turns to them for an emergency loan to keep his business afloat. During the Lewis episodes, Vinnie temporarily recedes to the background, due to a real-life broken foot suffered by star Ken Wahl. Vinnie's replacement from OCB is John Raglin, ably played by Anthony Denison (who played top crime figure Ray Luca in *Crime Story*).

The next major storyline brings in several rock musicians (Glenn Frey, Deborah Harry, Mick Fleetwood) and *Rocky Horror Picture Show* graduate Tim Curry, as Vinnie is installed by the OCB as the head of Dead Dog Records in order to uncover music industry criminals.

Ken Wahl may have the looks of a pretty-boy hunk, but he adds some spice to the beef in his portrayal of Vinnie. *Wiseguy* is memorable for its deft combination of glitz and substance. The writing is top-notch and the acting (especially by the guests) is far above average. The life expectancy for a mob infiltrator may not be very long, but *Wiseguy* makes the most of its premise.

**THE WIZARD** **(**½) 60 min (22ep Color; 1986–1987 CBS) Adventure** *with David Rappaport as Simon McKay, Doug Barr as Alex Jagger, Fran Ryan as Tillie Russell, and Cheryl McFadden as Darcy Stafford*

David Rappaport, at three feet eleven inches, must be the shortest star of a TV show ever, not counting Lassie. The miniature British actor first popped up in the offbeat film *Time Bandits,* and soon thereafter he had his own TV show. Rappaport plays Simon McKay, a wondrous chap who designs toys that can perform magical feats. Naturally the government has McKay cook up some toys for them and assigns Alex Jagger to watch over McKay, fearing he might fall into nefarious hands. Meanwhile, McKay just wants to help people in need. A truly unusual series, *The Wizard* has some undeniable charm. It may grow to be a cult classic.

**WIZARDS AND WARRIORS** **(**½) 60 min (8ep Color; 1983 CBS) Fantasy Adventure** *with Jeff Conaway as Prince Erik Greystone, Julia Duffy as Princess Ariel, Walter Olkewicz as Marko, Duncan Regehr as Prince Dirk Blackpool, Clive Revill as Wizard Vector, and Randi Brooks as Witch Bethel*

This sword and sorcery adventure fantasy (set in the time of King Arthur) is an entertaining crib sheet for fans of role-playing games such as "Dungeons and Dragons." Besides displaying a good selection of special effects, settings, and strategies for future reference, the series also injects a lighter tone to the proceedings, shaking off the intensely serious approach that sometimes develops among ardent game players. Having performers with a good sense of comedy helps, including Jeff Conaway (Bobby on *Taxi*), Walter Olkewicz (Zach on *The Last Resort*), Julia Payne (Aggie on *The Duck Factory*), and Julia Duffy (Stephanie on *Newhart*). As a result, even people who don't know what a "Dungeonmaster" is (and never intend to find out) can get a chuckle or two from this.

**THE WOLFMAN JACK SHOW** **(*½) 30 min (26ep Color; 1976–1977 Canada CBC) Musical-Variety** *with Wolfman Jack as host*

The legendary rock'n'roll radio disc jockey Wolfman Jack (born Bob Smith) hosts a series featuring big-name rock and comedy acts and some tame interviews.

**THE WOMAN IN WHITE** **(**) 60 min (5ep Color; 1982 UK BBC) Mystery** *with Deirdra Morris as Anne Catherick, Jenny Seagrove as Laura, Diana Quick as Marian, John Shrapnel as Sir Percival, Daniel Gerroll as Walter Hartright, and Ian Richardson as Fairlie*

Adaptation of a Victorian novel by Wilkie Collins, a book considered in some circles to be the prototype for many modern mysteries (especially those lacking a Sherlock Holmes–style central detective character). There are blackhearted villains, shadowy figures, deep dark family secrets, and, of course, a woman in distress. Actually, there are a few, including Marian (married to the greedy Sir Percival) and Anne (whose chance encounter with Walter, a drawing instructor, in a suburban London park sets the whole story into motion). At times this show is more like a soapy romantic tale than a mystery, but the presentation holds up fairly well.

This production first aired in the United States on cable's Entertainment Channel, then on PBS's *Mystery!* anthology.

**A WOMAN OF SUBSTANCE** **(**½) (6hr miniseries Color; 1984 Syndication) Drama** *with Jenny Seagrove as Emma Harte (through age 49), Deborah Kerr as Emma Harte (at 50), Barry Bostwick as Paul McGill, Diane Baker as Laura Spencer, Liam Neeson as Shane O'Neill, John Mills as Henry Rossiter, Nicola Pagett as Adele Fairley, and Barry Morse as Murgatroyd*

Turn-of-the century Yorkshire servant girl Emma Harte is a woman determined to make her mark in the business world. She travels to the United States and eventually becomes one of the most powerful women in the world (owning a chain of successful American department stores). Good rags to incredible riches story, based on a successful novel by Barbara Taylor Bradford.

Jenny Seagrove, Deborah Kerr, Liam Neeson, and John Mills also appear in a four-hour TV movie sequel to this miniseries, *Hold That Dream*, released in 1986. ■

**WOMEN IN PRISON** **(*½) 30 min (13ep Color; 1987–1988 Fox) Situation Comedy** *with Julia Campbell as Vicki Springer, Peggy Cass as Eve Shipley, C. C. H. Pounder as Dawn Murphy, Wendie Jo Sperber as Pam, Antoinette Byron as Bonnie Harper, and Blake Clark as Clint Rafferty*

Ron Leavitt and Michael G. Moye, the same folks who gave us the refreshingly revisionist view of modern domestic bliss in *Married . . . with Children*, present another unusual view of American life in *Women in Prison.* Set in Bass Women's Prison in Wisconsin, this series takes the grim harshness of Australia's *Prisoner: Cell Block H* and adds some black humor. The result is different, but a bit too tart. The original focus is on basically innocent Vicki Springer, a shoplifter who finds herself rooming with a tough group of cons once she is sentenced to jail. Peggy Cass (oh, it has been a long time since *The Hathaways!*) is a riot as the aging bank robber who rules over the female felons. Wendy Jo Sperber, the lovable chubby one from *Bosom Buddies*, plays Pam, the brainy con sentenced for computer crimes. Also in the joint are Dawn, the "baad black bitch," and Bonnie, the lesbian English hooker.

With a little more self-discipline, *Women in Prison* could have been a real comic gem, poking fun at the highly stereotypical women in jail sexploitation films. As it turns out, the program is merely an oddball offering that will catch your eye, but probably make you squirm.

**WONDER WOMAN** **(**) 60 min (61ep & 90 min pilot Color; 1975–1979 ABC & CBS) Fantasy Adventure** *with Lynda Carter as Diana Prince/Wonder Woman and Lyle Waggoner as Steve Trevor*

One of several comic books come to life from the mid-1970s, this series presents the adventures of Princess Diana of Paradise Island in two distinct setups. For the first run of about fourteen stories, the setting is World War II, with the Amazon princess leaving her secret island home to join the Allied war effort against the Nazis, hiding her identity by working as a U.S. War Department secretary, Diana Prince. In the rest of the series, she battles evil of the present-day world, using the same cover identity but with the IADC (Inter-Agency Defense Command), a covert government organization. (This change coincided with a switch in networks in 1977, going from ABC to CBS.)

Though both versions of the series embrace a simple pulp-magazine view of the world, the initial wartime episodes are played more blatantly as campy live-action period-piece comic books. There are plenty of Nazi villain caricatures, life or death Allied battles, and other superpowered characters—including the evil Faustia (played by Lynda Day George) and Diana's sister Drusilla, a.k.a. Wonder Girl (played by Debra Winger).

For the contemporary adventures, there is a greater emphasis on independent evildoers, including mad scientists, ambitious warlords, alien invaders, and underworld hoods, along with occasional oddball foes such as a pied-piper-type rock singer (played by Martin Mull) who can charm young fans into doing anything he wants. Oddly, these seem more dated than the 1940s stories, probably because they don't carry the automatic aura of wartime nostalgia.

Lyle Waggoner plays Diana's love interest, Steve Trevor, in both settings, though the stories are more than three decades apart. Surprisingly, they even bothered to attempt an explanation of this fact: As a resident of Paradise Island, Diana doesn't age the same way as we do. Trevor, on the other hand, is really the son of the wartime Major Trevor, but happens to be a dead ringer for his dad.

Lynda Carter manages to carry her part as the superpowered heroine fairly well. Her scanty costume with the tiara and golden lasso (accurately based on the original comic book designs by creator Charles Moulton) really does look rather silly, but it was probably one of the chief reasons this series lasted as long as it did.

Originally the *Wonder Woman* series played under several different titles including *The New, Original Wonder Woman* (on ABC) and *The New Adventures of Wonder Woman* (on CBS). There was also a ninety-minute 1974 made-for-TV movie featuring Cathy Lee Crosby in the title role, but she was dressed in regular clothes.

**THE WONDER YEARS (***½) 30 min (22ep at Fall 1989 Color; 1988– ABC) Situation Comedy** *with Fred Savage as Kevin Arnold, Daniel Stern as the voice of Kevin Arnold, Dan Lauria as Jack Arnold, Alley Mills as Norma Arnold, Jason Hervey as Wayne Arnold, Olivia d'Abo as Karen Arnold, Josh Saviano as Paul Pfeiffer, and Danica McKellar as Gwendolyn "Winnie" Cooper*

The children who tend to appear in TV sitcoms usually bear little, if any, resemblance to any real kid that ever lived. However, Kevin Arnold is very similar to a large number of kids, both past and present, and that is why *The Wonder Years* hits home to viewers.

Told as the reminiscences of the off-screen grown-up Kevin Arnold (a la John-Boy's narration of *The Waltons*), *The Wonder Years* relives his junior high years in the late 1960s. All of the trappings of the hippie era (rock music, love beads, flower power) are included to set the mood, but these accoutrements serve only as background filler to what is essentially a very observant portrayal of the early teen years of any middle-class kid since World War II.

The Arnolds live in suburbia, and the mature Kevin does not apologize for that. In the series opener, he poignantly states that while the suburban family may be surrounded by material objects galore, and may be nestled in a dull conformity, they experience joys and sorrows, pain and pleasure, just as any other family. This concept is at the heart of *The Wonder Years* and it is what gives it life and a feeling of honesty. The series takes growing up in the suburbs seriously, but not too seriously.

Kevin Arnold is navigating through the murky waters of puberty, laboring under the yoke of oppression placed upon him by his older brother Wayne and trying to break free of his mother's enveloping control. His father (Jack) is a mysterious figure who inhabits another world (the world of work) that is alien to Kevin. Older sister Karen is a proto-hippy, caught in the excitement and romance of the social protest movement. Her flirtation with the counterculture causes severe grumbling by her parents, who are as mainstream suburban as you can get. The parents, however, are never seen as cardboard authority figures, but rather as products of the 1950s who suddenly found themselves grown up, with a family to raise.

Kevin is neither one of the cool kids, nor one of the nerds, and he is torn between these poles. He longs for the popularity of the cool guys, and questions whether hanging around with his best friend Paul (a decidedly nerdy type) is ruining his social standing. Kevin's major personal dilemma is how to deal with Winnie, the girl-next-door who is blossoming into a beauty. Kevin is angling for a junior high romance with Winnie, but doesn't quite know how to handle it. He fears that if he doesn't act quickly, Winnie will be lost to the older guys, a force Kevin has no ammunition to repel.

Warm-hearted recollections of youth always strike a receptive chord among those whose youth is disappearing from view, but *The Wonder Years* manages to be nostalgic, right on point, genuine and funny at the same time (no small feat). The program does not just rely on old rock songs and worn-out catch phrases to dredge up memories for the old folks. Instead, within the framework of whimsical stories, *The Wonder Years* appeals to all age groups by dealing with some very basic issues that all young people must face: What does friendship mean? What is the value of family? How can the early pangs of love (and lust) be dealt with on a day-to-day basis? How do you come to terms with the world outside your home? These are not issues usually dealt with on sitcoms, and to its credit *The Wonder Years* deals with them in a lighthearted way. It illuminates the hidden memories of everyone who was ever twelve years old.

**THE WONDERFUL WORLD OF DISNEY** **(see *Walt Disney*)**

**THE WORD (**) (8hr miniseries Color; 1978 CBS) Drama** *with David Janssen as Steve Randall, James Whitmore as George Wheeler, and Florinda Bolkan as Angela Monti*

Based on Irving Wallace's fictional account of the discovery of a lost Gospel, this features David Janssen as a New York PR man out to check the authenticity of the newly unearthed ancient manuscript. Both the series and the original novel were obviously inspired by the real-life discovery (shortly after World War II) of the so-called "Dead Sea Scrolls"—the oldest existing copies of portions of the Bible, dating back to the first century, A.D. Ultimately those real-life literary treasures ended up confirming that people had very conscientiously and accurately passed on the biblical texts over the centuries. This miniseries takes the opposite tack, suggesting a major scriptural omission that could shake the foundation of the Christian world . . . and produce the blockbuster publishing coup of all time.

It's an intriguing premise, with an excellent central cast (Janssen, James Whitmore, and Florinda Bolkan), an all-star supporting cast (ranging from Eddie Albert to John Huston), and location footage in Amsterdam and Rome. Unfortunately both the story and the overall production get lost in a muddle of intrigues and meandering plot lines, with the wrap-up far less satisfying than it should have been.

**WORKING STIFFS** (**) **30 min (6ep Color; 1979 & 1987 CBS & A&E) Situation Comedy** *with Jim Belushi as Ernie O'Rourke, Michael Keaton as Mike O'Rourke, Val Bisoglio as Al Steckler, and Allan Arbus as Mitch Hannigan*

A series with a tremendous cast and a painfully short run, *Working Stiffs* has lots of potential that is mostly wasted by silly scripts.

The stars are two of the more talented male comedians of the 1980s, Jim Belushi and Michael Keaton. Belushi started his career under the shadow of his superstar brother John. Jim appeared in a few tepid sitcoms while John captured headlines in *Saturday Night Live* and several movies. Only after John died in 1982 did Jim attract much attention, briefly joining *Saturday Night Live* as a regular in 1983 and then moving to movies such as *About Last Night* (from 1986). Keaton had already served in the comedy troupe of Mary Tyler Moore's two failed variety shows of the late 1970s and later went on to star in comedy movie hits such as *Night Shift* (from 1982), *Mr. Mom* (from 1983), and *Batman* (from 1989).

In *Working Stiffs,* Belushi and Keaton play Ernie and Mike O'Rourke, two young Chicago blue-collar workers (hence the title) who are laid off any job they can land. As a last resort, they wheedle jobs as janitors out of their uncle Harry (Michael Conrad of *Hill Street Blues*), who owns an office building. As it turns out, Uncle Harry is never around, and Ernie and Mike are under the supervision of the building manager, Al Steckler, who would fire the bumbling pair in a flash if they were not related to the building's owner.

When not loafing around on the job Ernie and Mike hang out at the Playland Cafe near their apartment. The Playland is owned by Mitch Hannigan, played by Allan Arbus, best known for his role as psychiatrist Sidney Freedman on *M*A*S*H.*

*Working Stiffs* has a more than adequate cast, a premise capable of producing humor, and a nice blue-collar Chicago setting. Yet the show is constantly disappointing. The scripts are mostly unfunny and silly. The production is very obvious and sophomoric. The characters of Ernie and Mike are almost unlikable, as their incompetence combines with macho braggadocio. There just is not enough humor in *Working Stiffs* to help the audience get around the surface stupidity of the two main characters.

The show's two producers, Arthur Silver and Bob Brunner, came to *Working Stiffs* after flopping with two other late 1970s sitcoms with some potential, the *Animal House*–inspired *Brothers and Sisters* and the TV version of the film hit *Bad News Bears.*

Almost a decade after CBS abruptly canceled *Working Stiffs* (after only four episodes had aired), the remaining two episodes finally appeared when the series was rerun on The Arts and Entertainment cable network. ■

**THE WORLD OF GIANTS** (**) **30 min (13ep B&W; 1959–1960 Syndication) Adventure** *with Marshall Thompson as Mel Hunter and Arthur Franz as Bill Winters*

The art of reasonably priced special effects was simply not well enough developed by the end of the 1950s to allow an imaginative show such as *The World of Giants* to look believable. Marshall Thompson (later the head veterinarian on *Daktari*) plays Mel Hunter, an American espionage agent who is shrunk to miniature size (six inches tall), in order to better carry on the battle against America's foes. Arthur Franz plays Bill Winters, Hunter's normal-size comrade.

The idea of a miniature spy is great (*The Avengers,* for one, tried it in an episode), but the technical wizardry it requires is clearly beyond the simple efforts of the producers of *The World of Giants.* Nice try, though.

**WORLD WAR I** (***½) **30 min (26ep B&W; 1964–1965 CBS) Documentary** *with Robert Ryan as narrator*

Prime-time television on the big three networks used to have time for shows such as *World War I.* Maybe there was less competition from independent channels, cable, and VCRs. Maybe one network (CBS) was so far ahead of the others that it could afford to "waste" a half hour on a documentary. Maybe commercial prime-time TV was not seen simply as a revenue tool. For whatever reason, CBS News filled thirty minutes of prime time for one season with an excellently produced primer on World War I, the first "world" war, the first major conflict covered by motion picture cameras.

Produced by Burton Benjamin, a veteran of such CBS News classics as *20th Century* and *You Are There, World War I* takes a chapter-by-chapter look at the war that ushered out the era of monarchy and gentlemanly society and ushered in the era of mass destruction. Each episode focuses on another aspect of the war, beginning with "The Summer of Sarajevo" and moving on to "America the Neutral," "The Trenches," "They Sank the Lusitania," and "Britain Under Arms."

A tremendous amount of previously overlooked footage, both from Allied and Central Power sources, is presented, along with a very erudite and informative script, read by the familiar voice of actor Robert Ryan. As with any documentary, the show is a slave to its film sources, and *World War I* is hurt by the lack of footage of many crucial aspects of the war. Nonetheless, *World War I* presents a nearly perfect overview of its topic. It is well worth the time for anyone seeking information about and an understanding of one of the major events of this century.

Original music is from noted composer and conductor Morton Gould. ■

**WORLD WAR II** (**½) **90 min (14ep Color; 1981 Syndication) Documentary** *with Walter Cronkite as narrator*

Drawing on combat footage taken by both sides in World War II, this documentary series arranges the story into thematic packages such as "Air War in Europe," "Battleground Italy," and "The Seeds of War". Each one is broken into four episodes, focusing in great detail on particular events (for instance, "Air War in Europe" includes "Target: Ploesti," "Raid on Schweinfurt," "Counterblast: Hamburg," and "Guided Missile"). Though at times this plays more like a real-life Hollywood movie of the war rather than any sort of really deep analysis of the events, the series functions well enough as broadstroke basic history. Former CBS news anchor Walter Cronkite adds the proper air of authority as narrator. ■

**WORLD WAR II: G. I. DIARY** (**½) **30 min (25ep Color; 1978–1979 Syndication) Documentary** *with Lloyd Bridges as narrator*

The "Big War," as seen from the point of view of the grunts risking life and limb in the trenches, on the beaches, and in the air, is the subject of this Time-Life documentary series. It's nice for a change to leave the big picture behind and see how the war was fought on a personal basis. Well-known macho man Lloyd Bridges (*Sea Hunt*) provides the no-frills narration. ■

**WORZEL GUMMIDGE** (**½) **30 min (52ep Color: 1978–1981 UK Southern Television) Fantasy Adventure** *with Jon Pertwee as Worzel Gummidge, Una Stubbs as Aunt Sally, and Geoffrey Bayldon as the Crowman*

Worzel Gummidge is a scarecrow come to life, with former *Doctor Who* lead Jon Pertwee in the title role. Like his scarecrow cousin from Frank Baum's *Wizard of Oz,* Gummidge is also from a series of children's books (written by Barbara Eupahn Todd), where he made his mark as a scruffy but fun-loving man of straw with a romantic heart. (Aunt Sally is the love of his life.) Apparently Pertwee jumped at the chance to do one of his childhood favorites soon after his stint as a Time Lord ended, and his enthusiasm shows in this series. It's also a particularly good showcase for his comedy skills, honed over decades on the British stage and radio circuit (where he earned a reputation as a versatile "man of a thousand voices"). Though the authentic character accents are sometimes a bit thick for Stateside ears, it's worth the effort to listen closely and get used to their distinctive rhythms.

**WRANGLER** (*) **30 min (7ep B&W; 1960 NBC) Western** *with Jason Evers as Pitcairn (the "Wrangler")*

Pitcairn (a name better suited for a remote island than a western hero) is a weird guy who roams the Old West helping good people, killing bad people, and spouting off supposedly deep thoughts.

**WYATT EARP, THE LIFE AND LEGEND OF** (***) **30 min (226ep B&W; 1955–1961 ABC) Western** *with Hugh O'Brian as Wyatt Earp, Morgan Woodward as Shotgun Gibbs, Douglas Fowley and Myron Healey as Doc Holliday, Mason Alan Dinehart III as Bat Masterson, Trevor Bardette as Old Man Clanton, Dirk London as Morgan Earp, and John Anderson as Virgil Earp*

Much overlooked when discussions of the great adult westerns take place, *Wyatt Earp* is perhaps the most realistic western of the 1950s. Loosely based on the career of the real-life Wyatt Earp (a combination lawman/saloonkeeper who died of old age in Los Angeles in 1929), the series more or less follows a specific time frame throughout its run, following the main character from town to town as he changes jobs. What's more, the program reflects the reality of the frontier West, as some of the biggest gangsters actually run their local towns, through crooked henchmen who serve as lawmen.

In the beginning, Earp becomes marshal of Ellsworth, Kansas. He quickly moves to Dodge City, Kansas (where *Gunsmoke*'s Matt Dillon also served as marshal, though the two never meet on screen). For the last two seasons, Earp is marshal of Tombstone, Arizona, where the final five episodes detail Earp's greatest duel, the legendary shoot-out at the O. K. Corral with the Clanton gang.

Hugh O'Brian is rugged and handsome as Earp, but he brings enough humanness and wry charm to make him bearable and believable. Many sidekicks come and go over the six seasons, and none ever rise to the memorable level of a Festus or a Chester from *Gunsmoke.* O'Brian has to shoulder the star role largely alone. The half-hour format and the lack of a quality second banana tend to diminish the reputation of *Wyatt Earp.* However, for quality serious western action, without some of the philosophical angst that crept into *Gunsmoke* over the years, *Wyatt Earp* withstands the passage of time quite well. It helped set the pattern for the adult western craze of the late 1950s, and it still stands as one of the best examples of the genre.

**YANCY DERRINGER** (**) **30 min (34ep B&W; 1958–1959 CBS) Western** *with Jock Mahoney as Yancy Derringer, X. Brands as Pahoo-Ka-Ta-Wah, Kevin Hagen as John Colton, and Frances Bergen as Madame Francine*

Though a cut above the typical westerns being churned out at the same time (the late 1950s), this is still pretty gimmick-laiden. Jock Mahoney plays a former Confederate officer who works New Orleans as both a professional gambler and as a special agent for the city (hired by administrator John Colton). Oh, and he also has a tiny gun in his hat and an Indian cohort at his side. Still, Mahoney (a lifelong stuntman) does make a credible cowboy hero lead. Yancy may be suave and debonair, but at least he looks like he could survive in the West.

After this series ended. Mahoney took a swing at Tarzan in a few theatrical films during the 1960s. In real life, Frances Bergen is the wife of Edgar and the mother of Candice. ■

**THE YEAGERS (**) 60 min (4ep & 2 hr pilot Color; 1980 ABC) Drama** *with Andy Griffith as Carroll Yeager, James Whitmore, Jr., as Willie Yeager, David Ackroyd as John David Yeager, Kevin Brophy as Tony Yeager, Molly Cheek as Carrie Yeager, and Deborah Shelton as Joanna Yeager*

TV veteran Andy Griffith plays another warm-hearted patriarch in *The Yeagers.* As Carroll Yeager, Griffith is the head of a family-run logging and mining company in Washington state. Yeager is a widower with three sons, a daughter, and some extended family.

In the pilot, called *Trouble in High Timber Country,* Carroll Yeager is played by Eddie Albert, who last was in the sticks in *Green Acres.*

**A YEAR AT THE TOP (*) 30 min (4ep & 60 min pilot Color; 1977 CBS) Situation Comedy** *with Paul Shaffer as Paul Durbin, Greg Evigan as Greg, Gabriel Dell as Frederick J. Hanover, Nedra Volz as Belle Durbin, and Mickey Rooney as Mickey Durbin*

No, this is not a fake flashback from *Late Night with David Letterman,* placing Dave's bandleader, Paul Shaffer, in some truly embarrassing situation. Shaffer really did put in his time in this extremely short-lived sitcom. He played one of two young songwriters tempted by the devil's son to exchange their souls for fame and fortune.

But they resist, in part due to the wise counsel of Paul's uncle, played by Mickey Rooney, and his Aunt Belle. So the junior devil (who also doubles as their Hollywood agent, Frederick J. Hanover) teases them with tastes of what it would be like during their "year at the top." All the while, he constantly works to get their names on the dotted line, but they never sign.

Appropriately all those visions of success turned out to be just empty promises, even in real life. *A Year at the Top* was dumped onto the air during the summer viewing doldrums of August, while the companion real-life *Greg and Paul* album release appeared to be issued directly into the cut-out bins.

Eventually the boys received their divine rewards for resisting temptation. After a stint on *B. J. and the Bear,* Greg Evigan (he was B. J.) found himself co-star of a 1980s hit series, *My Two Dads.* Shaffer, of course, hit it big as part of Letterman's series. But before then, Shaffer also worked as a writer and occasional performer on *Saturday Night Live.* There his stock of characters included a devastating dead-on impression of Don Kirshner, who had been the musical supervisor of *A Year at the Top.*

**A YEAR IN THE LIFE (***) 60 min (6hr miniseries & 22ep Color; 1986 & 1987–1988 NBC) Drama** *with Eva Maria Saint as Ruth Gardner, Richard Kiley as Joe Gardner, Wendy Phillips as Anne Gardner Maxwell, Morgan Stevens as Jack Gardner, David Oliver as Sam Gardner, Sarah Jessica Parker as Kay Ericson Gardner, Trey Ames as David Sisk, Jayne Atkinson as Lindley Gardner Eisenberg, and Adam Arkin as Jim Eisenberg*

The original *A Year in the Life* miniseries follows twelve months in the lives of the Seattle-based Gardner family, with one dramatic high point being the death of matriarch Ruth. The regular series picks up where the miniseries left off, with widower Joe leading the family. Daughter Anne moves back home after the breakup of her second marriage. Second daughter Lindley works for the old man's plastics business, and has a lawyer husband and new baby. Oldest son Jack wants no part of the family business and fights with Dad a lot. Conservative youngest son Sam also works for Dad and marries liberal Kay.

For what is essentially another prime-time soap, *A Year in the Life* manages to deal with some weighty topics in a mature manner. There is too much soul-searching among the Gardner clan, but it is easy to get caught up with the family's struggles.

**THE YELLOW ROSE (**½) 60 min (22ep Color; 1983–1984 NBC) Drama** *with Sam Elliott as Chance McKenzie, Cybill Shepherd as Colleen Champion, David Soul as Roy Champion, Edward Albert as Quisto Champion, Chuck Connors as Jeb Hollister, Susan Anspach as Grace MacKenzie, Noah Beery as Luther Dillard, Ken Curtis as Hoyt Coryell, and Jane Russell as Rose Hollister*

Combining some of the best of the adult western format with the *Dallas*-inspired craze for steamy soap operas, *The Yellow Rose* has a lot of promise. The cast is full of well-known faces, the setting is a sprawling Texas ranch (like *Dallas*'s Southfork), there is all sorts of passion bubbling around, and illegitimate children abound. Still the show only lasts 22 episodes, which is a bit of a pity.

The Yellow Rose is a 200,000-acre ranch in west Texas that was owned by Wade Champion. Well, he's dead and now his two sons, Roy and Quisto, are battling each other for control. They are also battling Wade's very nubile twenty-nine-year-old widow Colleen who wants to inherit the spread, and previous owner Jeb Hollister who wants the ranch back. The plot complications are deliciously complex. Jane Russell makes a rare TV appearance in the later episodes.

The only impact *The Yellow Rose* had on TV when it originally aired is that it revived the dormant career of Cybill Shepherd, and paved the way for her success soon thereafter on *Moonlighting.*

**YES, HONESTLY (**½) 30 min (26ep Color; 1975 UK London Weekend Television) Situation Comedy** *with Donal Donnelly and Liza Goddard*

*No, Honestly* producer Humphrey Barclay supervises

this thematic "sequel" to that previous hit. There's no storyline continuity from the original, just a similar setup following a young couple from first love through courtship to marriage.

This time the premise uniting the male and female leads starts with a stronger initial conflict: Donal Donnelly plays a composer who dislikes working with women, but has to seriously reconsider his position when he stumbles across a manuscript he'd like to produce and discovers it was written by a female (played by Liza Goddard).

**YES MINISTER (***) 30 min (16ep Color; 1980–1986 UK BBC) Situation Comedy** *with Paul Eddington as James Hacker, Nigel Hawthorne as Sir Humphrey Appleby, Diana Hoddinott as Annie Hacker, and Derek Fowlds as Bernard Wooley*

This portrayal of behind-the-scenes government machinations is just frivolous enough to pass for the real thing. Paul Eddington does an excellent job as the reform-minded new Parliament member who often says what's between the lines even as he manipulates his way through the entrenched bureaucracy to get the job done. For example, he astutely describes Britain's defense policy as set up to "make the British people believe Britain is defended. Not the Russians. They know it's not." Eventually, he finds himself elected prime minister, with a series title change to *Yes Prime Minister* for the final eight episodes.

**YES, YES NANETTE (**) 30 min (26ep B&W; 1961 NBC) Situation Comedy** *with Nanette Fabray as Nan McGovern, Wendell Corey as Dan McGovern, Bobby Diamond as Buddy McGovern, Jacklyn O'Donnell as Nancy McGovern, and Doris Kemper as Mrs. Harper*

Nanette Fabray starred in numerous Broadway musicals in the 1940s (*High Button Shoes*) and was Sid Caesar's female TV lead in the mid-1950s after Imogene Coca left. She plays a character (Nan McGovern) very close to her real-life self in *Yes, Yes Nanette* (also known as *The Nanette Fabray Show* and *Westinghouse Playhouse*). Nan is a Broadway star who marries a Hollywood writer (Dan McGovern) and moves out West after a whirlwind romance. Suddenly she has to deal with his two bratty kids from his first marriage, the dull housekeeper, and the whole Hollywood lifestyle. Ms. Fabray went through similar experiences when she married Hollywood writer/director Ranald MacDougall, who created this TV show. Dapper Hollywood leading man Wendell Corey plays the Dan McGovern role.

**YESTERYEAR (*½) 45 min (7ep Color; 1982 HBO) Documentary** *with Dick Cavett as host*

Dick Cavett, affable former talk show host, serves as front man for this mild collection of old film clips that skim the surface of some year of recent history. *Our World* showed how to do a quality retrospective series, and *Yesteryear* doesn't match up.

**YOU AGAIN? (*) 30 min (28ep Color; 1986–1987 NBC) Situation Comedy** *with Jack Klugman as Henry Willows, John Stamos as Matt Willows, and Elizabeth Bennett as Enid Tompkins*

Jack Klugman (*Quincy, M. E., The Odd Couple*) has done much better than playing Henry Willows, a grouchy old father, in this annoying sitcom. Ten years after his messy divorce, Willows must suddenly come to terms with his seventeen-year-old son Matt (who Willows has barely seen in a decade), because Matt has returned to the old homestead to live with his old man. They bicker most of the time, which becomes very tiring very fast.

*You Again?* is based on a British sitcom, *Home to Roost,* and Elizabeth Bennett appears in both the U.K. and U.S. versions, playing the same housekeeper role. Her character also has a nasty disposition.

**YOU ARE THERE (**½) 30 min (B&W & Color; 1953–1957 & 1971–1972 CBS) Documentary/Drama** *with Walter Cronkite as host/narrator*

Back in the old days, before being a TV news reporter became something of a religious calling, network news departments could relax a little and try offbeat ideas to stretch the bounds of how to present useful information to viewers. In 1947, CBS Radio came up with *CBS Was There,* a history lesson disguised as a mock news report. The concept centered on re-creating a historical event, as if it were being covered as it was happening by CBS News, using modern electronic reporting equipment. For radio, it makes a lot of sense, if you let your mind accept microphones covering the trial of Socrates, or whatever.

When the series came to TV in the 1950s as *You Are There,* the transition was a bit rocky. Walter Cronkite, then an up-and-coming star at CBS News, is the host. He dresses in modern clothes, sets the stage in serious, stentorian style, and then switches over to some real-life CBS reporter in the field, with the admonishment that "all things are as they were, except *you are there!*" Then magically we are in seventeenth-century Salem for the witch trials, ancient Greece for the fall of Troy, or Civil War Pennsylvania for Lincoln's Gettysburg address. The actors portraying the historical characters are dressed in period costume, though they all speak English. It is the CBS News reporters who look weird. There are familiar CBS reporters such as Winston Burdett, Clete Roberts, Lou Cioffi, and Bill Leonard dressed in standard 1950s dark suits, sticking modern microphones in the faces of Tituba, the slave woman, Helen of Troy, or President Lincoln. Somehow the incongruity is disconcerting. The reporters try to get into the spirit, but always seem a little out of place.

After each episode the reporters throw it back to

Walter Cronkite in the CBS anchor booth. Cronkite then delivers a short wrap-up, ending with the statement that the day featured in that episode was "a day like all days, filled with those events that alter and illuminate our times, and *you were there!*"

After three-and-a-half years on CBS in the 1950s, *You Are There* was put away, only to be revived briefly in the 1970s as a Saturday morning show in color aimed at children. Walter Cronkite is still host, CBS News reporters still turn up in ancient locales, and history comes alive again, if in a somewhat forced manner.

In spite of the odd premise and clunky execution, *You Are There* is a wonderful show that tries to make history exciting in a way that many viewers can understand and appreciate.

In 1989, PBS revived the *You Are There* concept in a series of attractive specials titled *Timeline* (modeled after ABC's *Nightline*), with ex-ABC newsman Steve Bell as anchor. In *Timeline,* unlike *You Are There,* both the anchor and the on-the-scene correspondents wear period costumes.

**YOU ASKED FOR IT (**) 30 min (B&W & Color; 1950–1959, 1971–1972 & 1981–1983 DuMont & ABC & Syndication) Human Interest** *with Art Baker, Jack Smith, and Rich Little as hosts*

The title explains the premise. Viewers send in requests to see something (be it a natural wonder, a demonstration of some science feat or magic trick, or a bit of rare film footage). The genial host reads the request and introduces the segment, and then the request is fulfilled, since "you asked for it." The 1950s episodes (in living black and white) are almost campy now in their stylized innocence (and the omnipresence of pictures of products sold by the sponsor, Skippy Peanut Butter). The 1958–1959 shows, with Jack Smith as host, are the most likely to turn up. Smith also hosted the failed early 1970s revival of the series and replaced comic Rich Little for the last half of the early 1980s re-revival (titled *The New You Asked for It*).

The newer, color episodes suffer from the attempt to modernize an essentially corny concept. Titillating segments are added, filled with the sort of cheap thrills that popped up on *That's Incredible!* ■

**YOU BET YOUR LIFE/THE GROUCHO SHOW/THE BEST OF GROUCHO (**½) (130ep B&W; 1950–1961 NBC) Interview/Quiz Program** *with Groucho Marx as host and George Fenneman as the announcer*

"Folks, won't you come in and meet—Groucho Marx." With those words from announcer George Fenneman, yet another pair of contestants comes face-to-face with the sharp-tongued, cigar-chomping Marx. That's also the way many fans have really gotten to know Groucho. Dick Cavett alluded to this in his opening remarks at Groucho's 1971 stage show at Carnegie Hall, describing "that familiar soft voice that I knew first from the quiz show and then from the movies."

Fortunately this introduction is a good one, with Groucho doing what he does best: having fun at other people's expense. And it's still fun today because even as insult comedy it's really rather gentle (especially compared to the decibel levels of many sitcoms). Groucho finds his opening (usually relating to the profession, name, or demeanor of the contestants) and takes off from there. It's a routine he perfected first on a 1940s radio version of the program, which was specifically set up to give him the opportunity for ad-lib comedy. More than half the show is devoted to conversations with the contestants (though during these they could win money for saying "the secret word"). While those exchanges were not rehearsed, they were cut down from longer filming sessions, eliminating bits that didn't quite work (or were too risqué). And after chatting with each couple Groucho plays it absolutely straight for the quiz portion of the show, giving them all a fair shot at winning some money. (Not an easy task—just try to answer *half* the questions yourself.)

In its original decade-long network run, the series ran under the titles *You Bet Your Life, The Groucho Show,* and (in summer reruns) *The Best of Groucho*—with the last one the title used for the package of selected episodes that plays today. And if some of the camera work looks a little strange by contemporary standards, remember that it wasn't always so—they've cropped and blown up some of the film footage to eliminate shots of sponsor logos from the backdrop. ■

**YOU CAN'T TAKE IT WITH YOU (*½) (13ep Color; 1987–1988 Syndication) Situation Comedy** *with Harry Morgan as Grandpa Martin Vanderhof, Teddy Wilson as Mr. Pinner (nee DePinna), Lois Nettleton as Penny Sycamore, Richard Sanders as Paul Sycamore, Lisa Aliff as Alice Sycamore, and Heather Blodgett as Essie Sycamore*

Since its Broadway première in the 1930s, *You Can't Take It with You* has been one of those George S. Kaufman and Moss Hart stage productions that's almost always playing somewhere, whether on a high school stage or in a full-blown professional revival.

Performers are drawn to such juicy comic roles as that of Grandpa Vanderhof, a stubborn individual who one day just quit his job in order to devote his time and energy to the important things of life (home, family) because he realized "you can't take it with you." Naturally he encouraged the rest of his family to do the same, and within limits they did.

Audiences love the strong sense of absurd comic timing in the play as well as the allure of its central premise. Who hasn't dreamed of chucking it all?

The best part of this short-lived TV series version is that it gives Harry Morgan a chance to play Grandpa (done by Lionel Barrymore in the 1938 film and Jason Robards in a 1980s television production). He obviously relishes the part, dispensing his homespun wisdom both to his family and directly to the audience. Richard Sanders and Teddy Wilson are also good as the eccentric inventors turning out silly new products in the family basement. (Harry Morgan, in fact, played Wilson's character in a 1979 television production of the original play.)

Unfortunately, Kaufman and Hart are a hard act to follow. Even updating the original setting in the 1980s doesn't help much. Though allowing contemporary references and jokes, it still usually leaves the cast trapped in standard sitcomland bits that they just can't take very far.

**YOU'LL NEVER GET RICH** **(see *The Phil Silvers Show*)**

**YOUNG DAN'L BOONE** **(½) 60 min (8ep Color; 1977 CBS) Adventure** *with Rick Moses as Daniel Boone, Devon Ericson as Rebecca Bryan, Ji-Tu Cumbuka as Hawk, John Joseph Thomas as Peter Dawes, and Eloy Phil Casados as Tsiskwa*

There is nothing wrong with the mid-1960s Fess Parker version of *Daniel Boone,* and no reason for the creation of this sappy rip-off of the Boone name. Here, Boone is a comely twenty-five-year-old frontier stud with a pretty girlfriend. Dan'l, of course, has to appear relevant and egalitarian, so he spends lots of time with a Cherokee Indian, a runaway slave, and a twelve-year-old English boy. Rather than battling the frontier wilderness, this Dan'l seems more interested in winning the affirmative action award for 1755.

**YOUNG DR. KILDARE** **(*) 30 min (24ep Color; 1972–1973 Syndication) Medical Drama** *with Mark Jenkins as Dr. James Kildare and Gary Merrill as Dr. Leonard Gillespie*

Look for the Richard Chamberlain–Raymond Massey *Dr. Kildare* original and avoid this cheaply produced effort to update the timeless saga of the wizard in white. Kildare is still young and bold, Gillespie is still stern and demanding, and Blair General Hospital is still massive, but otherwise *Young Dr. Kildare* seems more like *General Hospital* than *Dr. Kildare.* As usual. Gary Merrill (he of the humongous eyebrows) is wasted in another mediocre role far below his fine acting talents.

**THE YOUNG LAWYERS** **(*) 60 min (24ep & 90 min pilot Color; 1970–1971 ABC) Law Drama** *with Lee J. Cobb as David Barrett, Zalman King as Aaron Silverman, Judy Pace as Pat Walters, and Philip Clark as Chris Blake*

It's unfortunate that Lee J. Cobb, an excellent actor who originated the role of Willie Lohman in *Death of a Salesman,* only appeared in two TV series during his life. It is even more unfortunate that the last one of those two was *The Young Lawyers* (the other was *The Virginian*).

Coming from the height of the silly mini-era of TV relevancy programs, *The Young Lawyers* has Cobb play a gruff Boston lawyer who heads up a neighborhood free legal-aid clinic, with the help of some young law students. The proto-lawyers are ethnically/sexually diverse (also following the dictates of the era): one Jewish idealist, one smart, streetwise black female, and one middle-class WASP. As usual with these relevancy shows, the stilted setting and simplistic stories render the whole affair ridiculous. The best that can be said for *The Young Lawyers* is that it is marginally better than the nearly identical series that premièred at the same time, *Storefront Lawyer.*

In the 1969 pilot, there are a great number of differences in character names and cast members from the series. Zalman King and Judy Pace play similar roles to their series characters, but Jason Evers is the elder legal mentor instead of Lee J. Cobb.

**YOUNG MAVERICK** **(**½) 60 min (8ep & 2 hr pilot Color; 1979–1980 CBS) Western** *with Charles Frank as Ben Maverick, Susan Blanchard as Nell McGarrahan, and John Dehner as Marshal Edge Troy*

This moderately effective short-run revival of the Maverick legend, takes up the tale with cousin Beau's son, Ben. Young Maverick is a firm believer in the family traditions of gambling as a profession, flight in preference to fight, and taking advantage of any honorable situation you can. Though Ben is the only member of the Maverick clan regularly appearing in the series, there is an attempt to duplicate the old kinfolk competition (between brothers Bret and Bart) with another sharp western operator, Nell McGarrahan, inevitably turning up in Ben's territory. (And in a way she is kin since Charles Frank and Susan Blanchard were married in real life at the time.) There is also an annoying marshal (originally a sheriff in the pilot) who pursues them both, convinced that they're con artists and determined to catch them in the act. (Well, they are, but without a bounty on their heads, why does he waste his time chasing them?)

With such a short run, the series never really has a chance to establish its rhythm. That's unfortunate because the 1978 two-hour made-for-TV movie (*The New Maverick*) that introduces the character of Ben Maverick has the old style down perfectly. Of course, it also has Jack Kelly and James Garner (as Bart and Bret) playing substantial roles. It's too bad they couldn't have been convinced to join on some guest shot rotation, with Ben carrying most episodes but the two of them around for credibility and authenticity. Then there might have been a quicker sale of the *Young Maverick* series following the successful reception of the TV-movie reunion. Of course, by 1980 Garner was already winding down his *Rockford Files* series and apparently thinking about his own full-fledged solo revival of his Bret Maverick character—which turned up late the very next year in the *Bret Maverick* series.

**THE YOUNG PIONEERS (*½) 60 min (3ep & two 2 hr pilots Color; 1978 ABC) Drama** *with Linda Purl as Molly Beaton, Roger Kern as David Beaton, Robert Hays as Dan Gray, Robert Donner as Mr. Peters, and Mare Winningham as Nettie Peters*

When the pilots for a series run longer than the series itself, you know something is wrong. The two 1976 pilots for *The Young Pioneers* (called *The Young Pioneers* and *The Young Pioneer's Christmas*) establish the setting of the inhospitable Dakota frontier in the 1870s. Teenage newlyweds Molly and David Beaton have settled there in hopes of putting down roots in new soil. The series briefly continues the same tale, with mostly the same cast, but with new producers (Earl Hamner and Lee Rich of *The Waltons*). When last seen, the Beatons were still out there, living on love and the kindness of neighbors.

**THE YOUNG REBELS (zero) 60 min (15ep Color; 1970–1971 ABC) Adventure** *with Rick Ely as Jeremy Larkin, Louis Gossett, Jr., as Isak Poole, Alex Henteloff as Henry Abington, and Hilary Thompson as Elizabeth Coates*

If you were trying to concoct a parody of the insipid "relevancy" trend in late 1960s/early 1970s TV, you would be hard-pressed to come up with anything funnier than *The Young Rebels.* The catch is, of course, that *The Young Rebels* is not meant to be funny.

The goal of this show is to find some cheap way to appeal to the then-current antiestablishment mood of young people, while not really offending anybody, anywhere. The solution? Set a band of ethnically and sexually mixed counterculture types in the era of the American Revolutionary War. They can be out-and-out revolutionaries, but patriotic at the same time!

The four members of the Chester, Pennsylvania–based Yankee Doodle society (an underground guerrilla group aiding the colonial cause against the British establishment) are handsome hunk Jeremy Larkin, noble black ex-slave Isak Poole, liberated lassie Elizabeth Coates, and portly, nerdy yet brainy Henry Abington. Together they bedevil the British, congratulate each other for being so neat, and all in all act very silly and pretentious. If this description sounds something like *The Mod Squad* in tri-cornered hats, you are not far off base, since the producer of *The Young Rebels* is none other than Aaron Spelling, producer of (among other silly shows) *The Mod Squad.*

*The Young Rebels* has one redeeming quality. It is the TV series debut of Louis Gossett, Jr., who went on to star as Fiddler in *Roots* and as the tough drill instructor in the theatrical film *An Officer and a Gentleman.*

**YOUR HIT PARADE (*½) 30 min (5ep Color; 1974 CBS) Musical-Variety** *with Kelly Garrett, Chuck Woolery, and Sheralee*

From 1935 to 1959, first on radio and then on TV, *Your Hit Parade* was one of America's most popular music programs. Each week a stable of regular performers would sing the country's most popular songs. When the show came to live TV in 1950, it became more of a challenge to come up with a novel way of presenting the same song every week, if a song stayed at the top of the charts for ten, eleven, or twelve weeks in a row.

By the late 1950s, with rock'n'roll supplanting the gentler pop tunes of Doris Day and Perry Como, *Your Hit Parade* became an anachronism, and it soon left the air. This brief 1974 revival is a misguided effort to breathe life into a dead horse. Producer Chuck Barris (creator of such low-level gems as *The Dating Game* and *The Gong Show*) tries to mix some of the gentle standards of the post-World War II era with the more raucous rock songs of the 1960s and 1970s. The result is a discordant clash of musical styles that nobody will enjoy.

**YOUR SHOW OF SHOWS (***½) 30 min (65ep B&W; 1950–1954 NBC) Comedy-Variety** *with Sid Caesar, Imogene Coca, Carl Reiner, and Howard Morris*

The parallels with *Saturday Night Live* are impossible to miss. In its original run during the 1950s, *Your Show of Shows* played Saturdays on NBC as a ninety-minute live comedy-variety program. There was a resident company of players, guest hosts (Burgess Meredith was the first), musical guests, and character comedy sketches. Appropriately, like *Saturday Night,* the series is currently available in half-hour highlight form, drawing the best from four seasons of black and white kinescopes, under the banner *The Best from Your Show of Shows.* (Actually this package also includes a few sketches taken from a subsequent series, *Caesar's Hour,* featuring Morris, Reiner, and Caesar with Nanette Fabray and Janet Blair.) To help bridge the generations, series star Sid Caesar provides introductory comments for the package.

The comments are sometimes necessary just to help ease new viewers in because despite the similarities to its 1970s cousin there are also many differences. Most are simply a product of the times. For instance, the main domestic sketch couple (Coca and Caesar as the unhappily married Doris and Charles Hickenlooper) can't help but reflect early 1950s assumptions about men ane women (this was the era of "woman driver" jokes). Once reminded of that, viewers can suspend disagreement with the subject matter involved in the Hickenloopers' latest argument and appreciate the bickering couple as potential next-door neighbors to Ralph and Alice Kramden.

A much more telling departure between decades is in overall tone. From the beginning, *Saturday Night Live* set out to be topical, even nasty, determined to convey a point of view on relevant issues somewhere in the show. *Your Show of Shows,* in contrast, is much more inclined to performance parodies without some underlying sardonic twist, specializing in send-ups of current box office hits, foreign films, television shows, and musical numbers (including operas), as well as domestic scenes. These are well written and executed, revealing the cast's eclectic tastes and versatility, but also require some familiarity with the originals to truly appreciate the twists involved in such sketches as "From Here to Obscurity" (*From Here to Eternity*), "A Place at the Bottom of the Lake" (*A Place in the Sun*), and "La Bicycletta" (*The Bicycle Thief*). But if those films aren't available on another cable channel or at the local video store, the energy of the four main performers (a fairly small repertory group) often compensates for never having seen a moment of any original. For instance, when Howard Morris desperately clings to Sid Caesar's pants leg as part of a parody of *This Is Your Life,* it's a timeless, self-contained moment of madness.

After the series ended, all of the principals went on to other film and television projects. Howard Morris became a familiar guest character performer on everything from *The Dick Van Dyke Show* to the 1986 *Andy Griffith Show* revival, *Return to Mayberry.* Carl Reiner became a very successful producer, writer, and director, beginning with the autobiographical *Dick Van Dyke Show.* Series writers Mel Brooks and Neil Simon eventually emerged as the biggest personal successes, with both of their names virtually synonymous with a particular style of writing and production. Ironically headliners Sid Caesar and Imogene Coca had the most difficult time finding suitable new vehicles for themselves. At one time, Coca even found herself in one of the worst series ever, *It's About Time.* In fact, neither of them ever matched their glory days on *Your Show of Shows.*

In addition to the half-hour syndication format, highlights from the series have also been packaged as a theatrical feature film (*Ten from Your Show of Shows*) and as a series of ninety-minute specials. ■

**YOUR SHOW TIME** **(*½) 30 min (26ep B&W; 1949 NBC) Drama Anthology** *with Arthur Shields as host*

The very first filmed TV drama anthology and the winner of the very first Emmy award, *Your Show Time* dramatizes the classics of literature, with Irish actor Arthur Shields introducing each episode from the confines of a well-stocked book shop. The series is archaic, but a historical novelty.

## Z

**ZANE GREY THEATER** **(**½) 30 min (145ep B&W; 1956–1961 CBS) Western Anthology** *with Dick Powell as host*

Officially titled *Dick Powell's Zane Grey Theater,* this series of western dramas originally centers exclusively on stories written by Zane Grey. Over time, as the master's repertoire runs dry, western stories from other sources are used. Handsome, debonair movie star Dick Powell serves as amiable host and occasional star.

An interesting footnote to this show is that *Zane Grey Theater* is the first TV production work by Aaron Spelling, who would go on to fill TV with gems such as *The Mod Squad, The Love Boat,* and *Fantasy Island.*

*Zane Grey Theater* contains the pilots of several other 1950s westerns, including *The Rifleman* ("The Sharpshooter") and *The Westerner* ("Trouble at Tres Cruces").

**ZERO ONE** **(*) 30 min (39ep B&W; 1962 UK BBC) Adventure** *with Nigel Patrick as Alan Garrett, Katya Douglas as Maya, and Bill Smith as Jim Delaney*

London-based investigator Alan Garrett troubleshoots for Airline Security International. Routine.

**THE ZOO GANG** **(***) 60 min (6ep Color; 1974 UK ITV) Crime Drama** *with Brian Keith as Steven Halliday ("The Fox"), Lilli Palmer as Monouche Roget ("The Leopard"), John Mills as Tom Devon ("The Elephant"), and Barry Morse as Alec Marlowe ("The Tiger")*

Twenty-eight years after the end of World War II, four surviving members of an underground resistance group who fought the Germans in Nazi-occupied France reunite to resume their underground careers. Now, however, they battle crime, not Nazis. The code names of the four principals are all animals, and are the basis for the show's title.

Based on a bestselling novel by Paul Gallico, *The Zoo Gang* has great stars, great action, great scenery (it was shot in Europe), and original theme music by Paul McCartney. Catch this series if you can.

**ZORRO** **(**½) 30 min & 60 min (82ep: seventy-eight 30 min B&W & four 60 min Color; 1957–1959 & 1960–1961 ABC) Adventure** *with Guy Williams as Don Diego de la Vega/Zorro, Gene Sheldon as Bernardo, Henry Calvin as Sergeant Garcia, Britt Lomond as Captain Monastario, and George J. Lewis as Don Alejandro de la Vega*

A great theme song kicks off this old-fashioned Saturday-matinee adventure series about the West's most famous masked swordsman. Set in 1820s Spanish California, *Zorro* presents the exploits of young Don Diego, newly returned to the estate of his father, Don Alejandro, after several years of university study. Much to his dad's disappointment, Diego seems to have turned into a rather timid fop of no apparent use in fighting the forces (such as the corrupt Captain Monastario) ravaging the territory. But it's all just an act, for Don Diego is really that new champion of the oppressed, the mysterious Zorro. Only the mute family servant, Bernardo, knows the truth.

It's a good version of a caped crusader legend that's been kicking around on film since the 1920s, beginning with Douglas Fairbanks, Sr. (in the silent *Mark of Zorro*), and including a twelve-episode Republic cliffhanger serial (*Zorro's Fighting Legion*) that still turns up in obscure TV slots. This one, with Guy Williams in the dual-identity lead, was put together by Walt Disney in the 1950s on the heels of the studio's TV success with a *Davy Crockett* miniseries.

The result is a curious hybrid. Many of the stories play as multiple-part tales, with some new character or concern dealt with over the course of several consecutive episodes, but there are no cliffhangers to cement the connections between each one. With no clear indication that particular conflicts will carry over, some of the stories sputter through the intermediate episodes.

But even then there's always comic relief (usually provided by the corpulent Sergeant Garcia), along with plenty of swashbuckling action for the kids. Also look for guest star shots by other familiar kiddie-adventure performers such as Jonathan Harris (Dr. Smith on *Lost in Space*), Neil Hamilton (Commissioner Gordon on *Batman*), and Disney's number one Mouseketeer, Annette Funicello.

One three-part Zorro adventure was edited into a TV movie, *The Sign of Zorro,* while four one-hour segments aired on the *Walt Disney* anthology series in color. The studio also tried to get some additional mileage out of the characters with a flippant follow-up in the 1980s, the played-for-laughs *Zorro and Son.* ■

**ZORRO AND SON (**½) 30 min (5ep Color; 1983 CBS) Situation Comedy** *with Henry Darrow as Don Diego de la Vega/Zorro, Paul Regina as Don Carlos de la Vega/Zorro, Jr., Gregory Sierra as Commandante Paco Pico, Bill Dana as Bernardo, and John Moschitta as Cpl. Cassette*

The people at the Walt Disney studios are not exactly known for poking fun at the squeaky-clean history of previous Disney films and TV shows, but *Zorro and Son* is a rare exception. The original Disney-produced *Zorro* series from the late 1950s was super-straight in its presentation of Spanish nobleman Don Diego, who comes to Spanish California in the early 1800s and adopts the disguise of Zorro (Spanish for "fox") in order to fight injustice and crime.

This early 1980s send-up of the Zorro legend presents the old fox about twenty-five years after we last saw him. Age has begun to take its toll on the Latin legend, and he can no longer perform the agile physical tasks required of a masked crusader. At the urging of faithful servant Bernardo, Don Diego sends to Spain for his son, Don Carlos, to inject some young blood into the Zorro business. Unlike the old man, Don Carlos is more interested in wooing the señoritas and partying late into the night. Nonetheless, Zorro, Jr. teams up with dad and continues to battle the bad guys, although young Zorro favors more mechanical weapons to the elder Zorro's simple and trusty sword.

*Zorro and Son* is filled with some very broad and very funny humor, which sometimes gets downright silly. Still it's a hoot to see Zorro in this light. Look for John Moschitta, the fast-talking man from the old Federal Express commercials, as the off-the-wall Corporal Cassette, sort of a human recording machine.

*Zorro and Son* was probably inspired by the even more irreverent update of the Zorro legend, the 1981 film comedy *Zorro, the Gay Blade,* with George Hamilton playing a far more fay Zorro.

# VIDEO COLLECTIONS

Why would anyone venture outside their living room for a peek at some old TV series? Aren't nearly a dozen channels (even more in cable households) enough? Ardent TV fans know the answer.

We've yet to find the channel that doesn't do something annoying to our favorite series. Some services are far less guilty than others, but even the best occasionally slip. Among the sins:

- Wholesale chopping, cutting snatches of dialogue or even entire scenes from the program
- Dropping in commercials haphazardly, instead of at the breaks that were designed to accommodate them
- Speeding a program's running time, noticeably altering speech and movement
- Running announcer voice-overs (or even split-screen inserts of some announcer's face) over a program's closing credits
- Clipping the opening and closing credits, sometimes dropping them completely
- Running substandard copies of programs, with such flaws as faded color, scratches, and poor sound
- Never playing the episodes of a series in order, even once.
- Rerunning a handful of series to death, while ignoring hundreds of others unseen for years

So, increasingly, it's not just whether something is available, but when and in what condition. Until someone comes up with the ultimate in viewer-oriented channels (which we'd subscribe to tomorrow, no questions asked), it's definitely worth exploring other avenues, if only to see our favorites when we want to, at our own pace. This section includes tips on two main sources, institutional collections and retail outlets. There's also a section of special notes and helpful hints along with a list of some of the material you just might find out there (approximately 2,000 episodes from nearly 300 different series).

Happy hunting.

## Institutional Collections

Surprise! Your local library (especially the main branch) probably has a decent video department, usually an outgrowth of its long-established audio-video section (previously specializing just in 16mm films and film strips). Though the emphasis in the "entertainment" titles is probably on feature films, television series occasionally turn up, especially historical miniseries, science and history programs, and adaptations of literary works. So if your tastes run to the likes of *Upstairs Downstairs, Nova,* and *I. Claudius*, you owe yourself a visit. Be sure to scan the title lists carefully—you might be pleasantly surprised to see a few classic commercial series there as well, ranging from *Roots* to *The Prisoner* to *The Honeymooners*.

Sometime in the future there will no doubt be many institutions (probably privately funded) specializing in collections of audio and video discs and tapes. At the moment, though, we know of only two currently open to the general public, the Museum of Broadcasting in New York City, and the Museum of Broadcast Communications in Chicago. Though totally separate institutions, they are both dedicated to the ongoing task of collecting and preserving television and radio broadcasts, ranging from popular entertainment to news coverage. Both ask modest admission donations and offer continuing memberships. They have general screening rooms for special exhibitions along with individual cubicles for private viewing. Best of all, they have knowledgeable staff members who know just what treasures are waiting for you in their back stacks of tapes.

The Museum of Broadcasting in New York has the far larger collection (more than 30,000 radio and television programs). Established at the behest of CBS chairman William Paley in 1976, it has become a special selected repository for all three national commercial networks (ABC, CBS, NBC), plus PBS, various cable services, independents, production companies, and even international producers. The extent of the collection is simply staggering—and heartening to a true television connoisseur. If you're in New York City this visit is a must.

Be forewarned, though, that there is great demand for the individual viewing carrels. Be sure to call ahead for information on how and when you can reserve time. But even if those are booked, there's always something playing in the large auditorium screening room.

The Museum of Broadcast Communications in Chicago opened its doors in June 1987 with a collection of more than 3,000 radio and television programs. The emphasis here is on material with Chicago roots, but considering the range of the city's broadcast alumni (from Second City performers to behind-the-scenes news producers), this covers a lot of territory. The collection also has selected episodes of key network series (you couldn't have a TV museum without *The Honeymooners*). The museum's president and founder, Bruce DuMont, has family roots going back to the old DuMont television network, which was started by his uncle.

Both institutions frequently sponsor special events, often with guest speakers and tie-in exhibits. For the latest on these, along with general information about each location, contact them directly at:

The Museum of Broadcasting
1 E. 53rd St.
New York, New York 10022
212/752-4690

The Museum of Broadcast Communciations
River City
800 South Wells St.
Chicago, Illinois 60607
312/987-1500

Remember, of course, that neither place has (nor aspires to have) every episode of every series ever aired. There's a limit to available storage facilities at any one location. Inevitably, as the number of such institutions increases, each will establish a basic core collection and then specialize.

In addition to the broadcast museums in New York and Chicago, there are also collections in other locations (such as the Library of Congress in Washington), but access is more limited, with an emphasis on formal research (usually toward some publication) rather than on casual, off-the-street nostalgic viewing.

## Retail Outlets

Chances are that your local video store does not have a wall devoted to TV series. But look carefully. Often television-related items are scattered into the appropriate feature film categories (Suspense, Comedy, Adventure, Documentary, and the like), placed near some theatrical release with a similar hook, such as episodes of the *Monty Python* series alongside the group's films. Scan the shelves and you'll soon find other appropriately spotted titles such as the pilot films for *Moonlighting* and *L. A. Law*, episodes of suspense series such as *Alfred Hitchcock Presents, The Outer Limits*, and *Kolchak: The Night Stalker*, westerns such as *Bonanza* and the *Lone Ranger*, and comedy offerings such as *Fawlty Towers* and *The Honeymooners.*

Nonetheless, even after digging through the stacks, you'll probably come up with a list significantly shorter than the one that ends this section, especially among the rentals. The reason is simple: The usual assumption with most dealers is that patrons are there for feature films, not television series. As a result, it simply makes economic sense to order a few extra copies of the latest blockbuster theatrical release, rather than too many TV series titles.

Fortunately there are inroads being made. For instance, people are discovering that titles with TV production roots often make good family rental fare. This is obviously part of the motivation behind stocking such series as *Faerie Tale Theater, National Geographic*, and the many releases from such kidvid veterans as Walt Disney and Hanna-Barbera. Beyond that, television-based comedy and adventure programs rarely match the levels of explicit violence, language, and sex of theatrical films.

Still at this point the pitch for television series on video is usually on purchase rather than rental, especially with multiple episodes of the same overall title. For a true fan of a series, that makes sense anyway, especially if it involves relatively obscure, rarely aired titles or fresh copies of a familiar old favorite. Though some material is available only by mail order, most major companies (such as MCA/Universal) don't sell directly to consumers, so you'll have to plan on going through your local video dealers. If they normally sell (as well as rent), there shouldn't be a problem in ordering most in-print titles.

# SPECIAL NOTES AND HELPFUL HINTS

## Mail order: The CBS Video Library

The most prominently promoted mail-order packages are the series touted by the CBS Video Library (part of the CBS Video Club). At this point, it's the only place you can get episodes of *I Love Lucy, The Twilight Zone*, the classic thirty-nine *Honeymooners*, and *The Beverly Hillbillies*, along with special double-feature couplings of *Star Trek* and *Bonanza.* The service also offers three television documentary war series (on World War I, World War II, and Vietnam). All nine are listed in the Video Index, though please note that the volume designations are primarily for sorting purposes and are not necessarily the order in which you'll receive the tapes by subscribing to a title.

For detailed ordering information write to:

The CBS Video Library
1400 North Fruitridge Avenue
Terre Haute, Indiana 47811

Or call the 800 number you see in the ads. We've found the staff there generally very helpful in explaining what is available, and the purchase requirements. At the time of this writing, there are no announced plans for these packages to turn up in general release.

## Mail Order: Catalogs

Mail-order video catalogs also turn up from a variety of companies. Usually these listings cluster television material in one or two main sections. Sometimes you can find out-of-print or public domain titles here.

## Public Domain Television

There are a number of video titles that turn up on a variety of different labels. The reason is that the material involved (chiefly from the 1950s) has been treated by various packagers as falling into the public domain—available for anyone's use.

How did this happen? Back in the early days of television, when many of the variety and drama offerings went out live, the broadcasts were usually considered to be rather disposable (aired once and forgotten). No one could have imagined a market for videotape copies of old shows, and so sometimes they didn't worry much about securing and preserving their claims to the material. Even as recently as the late 1970s, the video market was still not taken all that seriously as a major sales outlet for theatrical feature films—forget about television series! Thus, when companies began to collect and issue this material in the late 1970s and early 1980s (tapping the stockpiles of ardent private collectors), a lot of it went pretty much unchallenged, even if it occasionally did stretch to the breaking point the definition of just what might fall into the public domain.

Today everyone involved is far more aware of the potential and importance of the old shows. Some packagers are even going back and striking new prints from old films (if the negatives can be found), and providing fresh wraparound background footage (which can be newly copyrighted). This treatment greatly increases your chances of spotting such old series in your local store because, recently, there has been a tendency by many dealers to simply avoid public domain–type titles completely (with so many different packages floating around, it was hard to stock and sell them at much of a profit). With versions put out by more mainstream companies (where the dealers they do most of their business anyway), it is easier to justify handling them.

Still, for smaller companies (even those listed in the store's master catalog book) you may be told by your local dealer that it would be cheaper and more convenient to order by mail directly from the company itself. If you're interested in the material, you should definitely do so (those companies are accustomed to direct consumer purchase), but remember one thing: Old public domain material must be approached with care and lowered expectations. It's very tough to get state-of-the-art reproduction from thirty-year-old offerings, especially live performances. Even tapping a television network's own archives might result in just a relatively grainy kinescope recording (a film of a live broadcast shot at the time from a special monitor). As a result, even some official releases will turn out to be a copy of a copy of a copy.

Nonetheless, they are definitely fun in a faded snapshot sort of way, offering glimpses of performers in the first heady days of television (especially on live variety or drama series). Picture quality aside, the old shows are often fresh, funny, and sometimes quite moving. What more could a dedicated television viewer ask for?

Again, though, remember several key points about public domain video: It appears on a wide variety of labels (in packages ranging from unadorned boxes to slip cases with more elaborate artwork); you may end up ordering it yourself, directly from the companies; and the material involved may disappear from the shelves at any time, especially if someone successfully claims ownership (but that's usually for the purpose of launching an authorized new release, so it won't be gone for long).

In our Video Index, we have omitted one particular type of public domain packaging configuration: the potentially endless list of crazy-quilt anthologies containing episodes from two, three, or even four completely different series all on one tape, often under some umbrella theme like "Great Adventures." Instead we have listed only those packages specifically devoted to one series. Along the way, no doubt we've missed a few.

## Limited Use

There are a number of series (usually cultural, historical, or documentary) that are available on videotape, but not for the home retail market. Instead their use is limited, often to classrooms, cultural institutions, and the like. Fortunately, this use often includes public libraries, so even though you can't buy or rent these at your local video store, you can check them out from your local library. We have included a number of such Limited Use titles in the video list, with a cross-reference back to this note. Of course, there is no guarantee that your particular library will have chosen to acquire these. Fortunately the odds are more in your favor on another group of titles: those in the MacArthur Library Video Classics collection.

## The MacArthur Library of Video Classics Project

In 1988, the John D. and Catherine T. MacArthur Foundation launched its Library Video Classics project. In brief, this project set up a special discount deal for libraries, allowing them to purchase episodes from twenty different PBS series at a significant savings (as much as 90 percent), thus stretching their video library dollar. Though most libraries probably will not have every episode from each of these series, they probably will have a few dozen. Each appears in the Video Index, with a list of available episodes. In all but three cases (*The Jewel in the Crown, Vietnam: A Television History, The Story of English*) this project includes material not otherwise available to the public on video.

# GUIDE TO THE HOME VIDEO GUIDE

The Home Video Guide covers the series titles discussed in this book that have been released on video. The format used is as follows.

## EXAMPLES

**SERIES TITLE**
*Package Title*: Individual Episode Titles: 58 vvv
Episode Title 1:57 www/xxx
V.1: 2ep 1:00 yyy
V.2: 2ep 1:00 yyy (LV)
1ep :30 zzz

**SERIES TITLE** (all zzz and 1:00)
Alphabetical Title List or
V.1: Listed by Volume Number

## EXPLANATION

### Series Title

Only series discussed in this book are included in the Home Video Guide, arranged alphabetically.

### Package Title

This is given if it is different from the series title. (For instance, *The Best of Barney* under **The Andy Griffith Show.**) Each package with or without a title, is considered a separate item and begins a new line.

When packages consist of just one episode title, they are listed in either alphabetical order or by volume number (if that's how the company designates them).

### Individual Episode Titles

These are listed, if known, even if the titles never appear on the screen. If there are no titles, the number of episodes is simply indicated (1ep, 2ep).

### Running Times

These are expressed in an hour and minute format (1:57 rather than 117 minutes). Anything less than an hour is simply written in minutes (:32).

Times have been dutifully taken from the packages themselves or from catalog references (:58 rather than 1:00 if the source said so), but in all cases they should be regarded as simple guides (plus or minus as much as ten minutes per hour). The point is to differentiate between, for instance, a thirty-minute and one-hour program, not between episodes running fifty-seven and fifty-eight minutes.

At this point in video-collecting history it's too soon to zero in on many specific cases in which the videotape definitely includes an edited (shorter) version of a story rather than the full-length presentation. One blatant instance we noticed (and confirmed) was the *Doctor Who* release of "The Brain of Morbius," which had been trimmed by one-third (running about 1:00 rather than 1:30) for home release. No doubt there are others, so take careful note.

### Label Abbreviation

This is the name of the company (or companies) releasing the video. The latest addresses can be found in the major reference catalogs (such as VideoLog) used by stores, unless, of course, the company is no longer around. Though every effort has been made to keep this list current at press time, there is no guarantee that every item will still be available.

### Volume Numbers

If there are multiple volumes so designated from the same company, they are listed as Volume 1 (V.1), Volume 2 (V.2), and so on. If different companies have released different sets (each beginning with Volume 1), they are listed separately. Sometimes the roman numeral format (I, II, III) is also used. Occasionally there may be volume numbers used in video catalogs or on a label order form even though the packages themselves do not have any volume number listed.

## Videodisc Designation

If the package has been released on a laser format videodisc as well as on tape, the symbol (LV) appears at the end of the package line. However, if the videodisc coupling is unique (combining material from several tapes, for instance) the symbol (LVo) is used (Laser Disc Only).

There is another type of videodisc (using a completely different, nonlaser format) that was widely available for a few years in the early to mid-1980s, the RCA VideoDisc (also known as the CED format). Though certainly "out of print" (RCA doesn't even make the machines anymore), several of these discs have been included because they contain unique material. These are indicated by (VD) and (VDo).

## Label, Running Time, and Videodisc Designation

If any of these items are the same for all packages under a title, this information is listed after the title as "all"—for instance: (all zzz and 1:00).

## Foreign Releases

With the exception of a few Japanese videodiscs, all the items listed here are domestic (U.S.) releases. Unlike audio products, there has not yet been much international traffic with video, chiefly because of incompatible television systems. (Viewers in Britain and the United States, for instance, get only visual gibberish when they attempt to play back something recorded for the other country's equipment.) Therefore, this list does not include material licensed for foreign video release (such as *Star Trek: The Next Generation*), even if those packages are not yet available in the United States.

Though all the Home Video Guide information has been carefully checked, it is subject to change, errors of omission, and simple misprints (theirs or ours). There is no guarantee that everything is still in print at the time of publication, or that promised catalog items listed won't be held back.

Prices are not listed because they are constantly changing. Remember, material that is out of print may still turn up on an individual store's shelves, in a cut-out bin, or in a second-hand resale shop.

Good luck!

# KEY TO VIDEO LABEL ABBREVIATIONS

acd = Academy Home Video
ach = Active Home Video
amv = Amvest
avp = Ambrose Video Publishing
bel = Bell (Japanese Import)
blh = Blackhawk Films
buv = Buena Vista Home Video
cbf = CBS/Fox Home Video
ccp = Curtain Call Productions
cgr = Congress Video Group
cnt = Corinth Video
con = Concord Video
crw = Crown Video
cvl = CBS Video Library
dct = Discount Video
emb = Embassy Home Entertainment
ent = Enter-Tel, Inc.
fhl = Fox Hills Video
fri = Fries Home Video
got = Goodtimes Video
hbo = HBO/Cannon Video
hls = Hollywood Select Video
hnb = Hanna-Barbera Home Video
ihf = International Historic Films
img = Image Entertainment
iud = Independent United Distributors
ive = International Video Entertainment
j2c = J2Communications
key = Key Video
klr = Karl/Lorimar Home Video
kov = King of Video
lon = London Films
lor = Lorimar Home Video
ltv = Lightning Video (Vestron)
mca = MCA Home Video
mgm = MGM/UA Home Video
mhe = Media Home Entertainment
mon = Monterey Home Video
mpi = MPI Home Video
nsm = Nostalgia Merchant
nwl = New World Video
par = Paramount Home Video
pav = Pacific Arts Video
pio = Pioneer Artists
pla = Playhouse Video (CBS/Fox)
pme = Public Media Video
pre = Premier Promotions
prs = Prism
pyr = Pyramid Film and Video
rca = RCA/Columbia Pictures Home Video
rcd = RCA CED VideoDiscs
reg = Regency Home Video
rhi = Rhino Video
rko = RKO Pictures Home Video

| | | |
|---|---|---|
| rpb | = | Republic Pictures Home Video |
| s&s | = | Simon & Schuster Video |
| she | = | Sheik Video |
| shk | = | Shokus Video |
| son | = | Sony Video |
| tch | = | Touchstone Home Video |
| tem | = | Thorn/EMI |
| tha | = | Thames Video |
| the | = | Today Home Entertainment |
| tml | = | Time Life Video |
| tsa | = | Trans-Atlantic Video |
| twe | = | Trans World Entertainment |
| unc | = | Unicorn Video |
| une | = | United Entertainment, Inc. |
| usa | = | U.S.A. Home Video |
| vcl | = | Video Classics |
| vda | = | VidAmerica |
| vdc | = | Video Connection |
| vdm | = | Video Dimensions |
| ves | = | Vestron Video |
| vhl | = | Video Home Library |
| vir | = | Virgin Vision |
| vls | = | Video Late Show |
| vtn | = | Video Tape Network |
| vys | = | Video Yesteryear |
| war | = | Warner Home Video |
| wds | = | Walt Disney Home Video |
| wlk | = | Welk Home Entertainment |
| wnt | = | WNET Thirteen |
| wov | = | Worldvision Home Video |

# THE HOME VIDEO GUIDE

# A

## ABBOTT AND COSTELLO

V.1: 2ep :50 fhl
V.2: Paperhangers/Lou's Insomnia :50 nsm/fhl
V.3: Lou Adopts Bingo/Hillary's Birthday Party :50 nsm/fhl

## ALDRICH FAMILY

1ep :27 vys

## ALFRED HITCHCOCK PRESENTS (mca)

*The Best of V.1*: Banquo's Chair/Lamb to the Slaughter/Case of Mr. Pelham 1:18
*The Best of V.1* (Laser Version): Banquo's Chair/Lamb to the Slaughter/Case of Mr. Pelham/Back for Christmas 1:46 (LVo)

## ALL CREATURES GREAT AND SMALL

Movie-length ep 1:34 pla

## ALL THE RIVERS RUN

2 vols 4:34 hbo

## AMERICA, ALISTAIR COOKE'S *(Not for Home Retail Market: See notes on MacArthur Library Video Project)*

(all :52)
Ep 1: The New Found Land
Ep 2: Home Away from Home
Ep 3: Making a Revolution
Ep 4: Inventing a Nation
Ep 5: Gone West
Ep 6: A Fireball in the Night
Ep 7: Domesticating a Wilderness
Ep 8: Money on the Land
Ep 9: The Huddled Masses
Ep 10: The Promise Fulfilled and The Promise Broken
Ep 11: The Arsenal
Ep 12: The First Impact
Ep 13: The More Abundant Life

## AMERICAN PLAYHOUSE

Strange Interludes (2 vols) 3:10 fri
True West 1:40 acd
*Four additional titles are available through the MacArthur Library Video Project (See notes)*
The Cafeteria 1:00
Go Tell It on the Mountain 1:33
Private Contentment 1:30
Working 1:30

## THE AMERICAN SHORT STORY COLLECTION (all mon)

Barn Burning :40
+Bernice Bobs Her Hair :48
+Displaced Person (D.P.) :58
The Golden Honeymoon :52
The Greatest Man in the World :51
I'm a Fool :38
Jilting of Granny Weatherall :57
The Jolly Corner :43
Man That Corrupted Hadleyburg :49
Noon Wine 1:21
+Paul's Case :42
Rappacini's Daughter :59
The Sky Is Grey :46
+Soldier's Home :42
*Four of the above titles (indicated by +), as well as two additional, are available through the MacArthur Library Video Project (See notes)*
Almos' a Man :39
The Music School :30
*Two others are also available only for Limited Use (See notes)*
The Blue Hotel :45
Parker Adderson, Philosopher :45

## AMOS AND ANDY (all hls and 1:00 except where noted)

*Anatomy of a Controversy* w. Kingfish Sells a Lot 1:00 mpi
V.1: Getting Momma Married (Pts. 1 & 2)
V.2: Andy Buys a House/The Happy Stevens
V.3: Arabia/Andy Plays Santa Claus
V.4: The Winslow Woman/The Broken Clock
V.5: Leroy Lends a Hand/Call Lehigh 4-9900
V.6: The Birthday Card/Relatives
V.7: Quo Vadis/Kingfish's Last Friend
V.8: Andy Falls in Love with an Actress/Sapphire Disappears
V.9: The Gun/The Turkey Dinner

V.10: Cousin Effie's Will/Superfine Brush
V.11: The Antique Shop/Hospitalization
V.12: The Rare Coin/The Young Girl's Mother
V.13: Kingfish Sells a Lot/Amos Helps Out
V.14: The Diner/Ballet Tickets
V.15: Andy Gets a Telegram/Engagement Ring
V.16: The Adoption/Leroy's Suits
V.17: Ready Made Family/The Convention
V.18: Kingfish Gets Drafted/Traffic Violations
V.19: Kingfish's Secretary/The Society Party
V.20: Vacation/New Neighbors
V.21: Seeing Is Believing/Eyeglasses
V.22: The Boarder/Viva La France

**ANDY GRIFFITH SHOW** (all pre and 2:00 except where noted)

V.1: *The Best of Barney V.1:* Barney's First Car/Up in Barney's Room/Barney's Sidecar/The Lucky Letter
V.2: *The Best of Ernest T. Bass:* Mountain Wedding/Ernest T. Bass Joins the Army/My Fair Ernest T. Bass/The Education of Ernest T. Bass
V.3: *The Best of Floyd:* The Bookie Barber/Floyd, The Gay Deceiver/Convicts at Large/The Case of the Punch in the Nose
V.4: *The Best of Otis:* Aunt Bee the Warden/Deputy Otis/Hot Rod Otis/The Rehabilitation of Otis
V.5: *The Best of Gomer:* Gomer the House Guest/Citizen's Arrest/Andy Saves Gomer/Gomer Pyle, U.S.M.C.
V.6: *The Vintage Years V.1:* Alcohol & Old Lace/The Pickle Story/Man in a Hurry/The Loaded Goat
V.7: *The Best of Barney V.2:* The Return of Barney Fife/The Legend of Barney Fife/A Visit to Barney Fife/Barney Hosts a Summit Meeting
V.8: *The Best of Andy V.1:* A Feud Is a Feud/The Beauty Contest/Andy & the New Mayor/Andy's English Valet
V.9: *The Best of Opie V.1*: Opie's Charity/Opie's Hobo Friend/Mr. McBeevee/Opie the Bird Man
V.10: *The Vintage Years V.2*: The Manhunt/A Plaque for Mayberry/Dogs, Dogs, Dogs/Man in the Middle
V.11: *Bungling Barney Strikes Again*: The Bank Job/Barney for Governor/The Big House/A Black Day for Mayberry
V.12: *Mayberry Classics V.1*: The New Housekeeper/The Inspector/Three's a Crowd/Family Visit
V.13: *The Best of the Darlings*: The Darlings Are Coming/Broscoe Declares for Aunt Bee/Divorce Mountain Style/The Darling Baby
V. 14: *The Mayberry Capers*: Andy & The Gentleman Crook/Crime-free Mayberry/Guest of Honor/The Shoplifters
V.15: *Mayberry Melodies*: Mayberry On Record/Barney & the Choir/The Mayberry Band/Rafe Hollister Sings
V.16: *The Love Life of Barney Fife*: Barney on the Rebound/The Farmer Takes a Wife/Fun Girls/Barney & Thelma Lou, Pfftt
V.17: *America's Favorite Aunt*: Aunt Bee's Brief Encounter/Wedding Bells for Aunt Bee/Aunt Bee's Romance/The Pageant
V.18: *Romance Mayberry Style*: Andy the Marriage Counselor/The Manicurist/The Rivals/A Date for Gomer

**Andy Griffith Show**

Double Feature Series (all pre and 1:00)
V.1: Barney's Sidecar/The Darlings Are Coming
V.2: My Fair Ernest T. Bass/Barney's First Car
V.3: The Pickle Story/Convicts at Large
V.4: Man in a Hurry/Andy's English Valet
V.5: Citizen's Arrest/Fun Girls
V.6: Mountain Wedding/Sheriff Barney
V.7: Barney and the Cave Rescue/The Rehabilitation of Otis
V.8: Goober and the Art of Love/Gomer the House Guest
V.9: Dogs, Dogs, Dogs/The Sermon for Today
V.10: The Education of Ernest T. Bass/Opie the Bird Man
V.11: Barney's Uniform/Ernest T. Bass Joins the Army
V.12: The Haunted House/Christmas Story
V.13: The Return of Barney Fife/The Legend of Barney Fife
V.14: A Visit to Barney Fife/Dinner at Eight
V.15: Barney Comes to Mayberry/Barney Hosts a Summit Meeting
V.16: The Shoplifter/The Haunted House
V.17: Malcolm at the Cross Roads/A Man's Best Friend
V.18: The Big House/The Loaded Goat
V.19: TV Or Not TV/Andy Saves Barney's Morale
V.20: Aunt Bee the Warden/A Black Day for Mayberry
V.21: The Case of the Punch in the Nose/The Manhunt
V.22: Barney Gets His Man/The Luck of Newton Monroe
V.23: If I Had a Quarter Million/Jail Break
V.24: Goodbye Sheriff Taylor/The Great Filling Station Robbery
V.25: Cousin Virgil/The Bookie Barber
V.26: The Bank Job/The Cow Thief
V.27: A Date for Gomer/Andy's Vacation
V.28: Barney & the Choir/Divorce Mountain Style
V.29: Barney's Blood Hound/Lawman Barney
V.30: Aunt Bee the Crusader/The Jinx

**ANNIE OAKLEY**

2ep 1:00 dct
1ep :30 con

**THE ASCENT OF MAN** *(Not for Home Retail Market: See notes on MacArthur Library Video Project)*
(all :52)

Ep 1: Lower Than the Angels
Ep 2: The Harvest of the Seasons
Ep 3: The Grain in the Stone
Ep 4: The Hidden Structure
Ep 5: The Music of the Spheres

Ep 6: The Starry Messenger
Ep 7: The Majestic Clockwork
Ep 8: The Drive for Power
Ep 9: The Ladder of Creation
Ep 10: World Within World
Ep 11: Knowledge or Certainty
Ep 12: Generation upon Generation
Ep 13: The Long Childhood

**THE AVENGERS** (all hls and :53 except where noted)
The Bird Who Knew Too Much
The Correct Way to Kill
The Curious Case of the Countless Clues
Cybernauts
Dead Man's Treasure
Death at Bargain Prices vdm
Death of a Great Dane
Dial a Deadly Number
EPIC
Escape in Time
False Witness
The £50,000 Breakfast
Forget-Me-Knot
A Funny Thing Happened on the Way to the Station
Game
Get-a-Way
The Girl from Auntie
The Gravediggers
Have Guns—Will Haggle
Hidden Tiger
The House That Jack Built
The Morning After
My Wildest Dreams
Positive Negative Man
The Quick, Quick Slow Death
A Sense of History
Silent Dust
Small Game for Big Hunters vdm
Super Secret Cypher Snatch
A Surfeit of $H_2O$
Take-Over
A Touch of Brimstone vdm
Two's a Crowd vdm

# B

**B.A.D. CATS**
Movie-length ep 1:14 klr

**BATMAN**
Theatrical film (1966) 1:44 pla

**BATTLESTAR GALACTICA/GALACTICA 1980** (all mca and :47 except where noted)
Baltar's Escape
Battlestar Galactica 2:05 (LV)
Conquest of the Earth 1:39
Fire in Space
The Long Patrol
The Lost Warrior
The Magnificent Warriors
The Man with Nine Lives
Mission Galactica: The Cylon Attack 1:36
Murder on the Rising Star
The Young Lords

**BEAUTY AND THE BEAST**
Once Upon a Time in the City of New York/A Happy Life 1:40 rpb

**BENNY HILL** (all tem)
*Best of V.1*: 2:00
*Best of V.2*: 1:45
*Best of V.3*: 1:50
*Best of V.4*: 1:35
*Best of V.5*: 1:37
*Best of V.6*: 2:00

**BETWEEN THE WARS** *(See notes on Limited Use) Not For Home Retail Market* (16ep at :24 each)

**BEULAH**
Marriage on the Rocks/Imagination :51 vys
Beulah's Misunderstanding/Beulah the Dance Teacher/Beulah Helps the Hendersons/(5 black exploitation cartoons) 2:00 shk
2 Vols (2ep on each, 1:00) dct
1ep :30 con

**THE BEVERLY HILLBILLIES**
Collector's Edition *(Mail order only from CBS Video Library: See notes for ordering information)* (all cvl and 1:30)
V.1: *The Hillbillies Move to Californy*: The Clampetts Strike Oil/Getting Settled/Meanwhile, Back at the Cabin
V.2–V.10 (3ep each)

**THE BIG VALLEY**
The Explosion 1:28 vda
Legend of a General 1:30 vda

**BILL MOYERS' JOURNAL** *(See notes on Limited Use) Not for Home Retail Market* (40ep at 1:00 each)

**BING CROSBY SHOW**
2ep 1:00 dct

**THE BIONIC WOMAN**
Movie-length ep 1:36 mca

**BLACK BEAUTY** (1970s) (all son and :50)
V.1: The Fugitive/Pet Pony
V.2: A Member of the Family
V.3: A Ribbon for Beauty/A Mission of Mercy
V.4: Lost
V.5: Out of the Night/Good Neighbors
V.6: The Quarry/The Challenge

**BLIND AMBITION** *(See notes on Limited Use) Not For Home Retail Market* (4ep at 1:35 each)

**THE BLUE AND GREY**
Miniseries 4:05 rca

**THE BLUE KNIGHT**
Movie-length ep 1:12 usa

**THE BOAT (DAS BOOT)**
Theatrical film version 2:30 rcd (VDo)

**BOB HOPE** (1950s)
Chevy Show I-III (2ep on each, 2:00) shk

**BONANZA** (all rpb and 1:40)
*Best of V.1*: A Rose for Lotta (pilot)/The Underdog
*Best of V.2*: The Dark Gate/The Honor of Cochise
*Best of V.3*: Hoss & the Leprechauns/The Truckee Strip
*Best of V.4*: To Own the World/The Boss

**BONANZA**
Collector's Edition (*Mail order only from CBS Video Library; See notes for ordering information*) (all cvl and 2:00)
V.1: A Rose for Lotta (pilot)/To Own the World
V.2–V.4: (2ep each)

**THE BRAIN** (*Not for Home Retail Market: See notes on MacArthur Library Video Project*) (all 1:00)
Ep 1: The Enlightened Machine
Ep 2: Vision and Movement
Ep 3: Rhythms and Drives
Ep 4: Stress and Emotion
Ep 5: Learning and Memory
Ep 6: The Two Brains
Ep 7: Madness
Ep 8: States of Mind

**BRAVE EAGLE**
2ep 1:00 dct

**BRIDESHEAD REVISITED** (all vir and 1:38)
Book 1: Nostalgia for a Vanished Past
Book 2: Home & Abroad/Shadows Close In
Book 3: Sebastian Against the World/Julia Blossoms
Book 4: Julia's Marriage/The Unseen Hook
Book 5: Brideshead Deserted/Orphans of the Storm
Book 6: A Twitch Upon the Thread/Brideshead Revisited

**BUCK ROGERS IN THE 25TH CENTURY**
(all mca and :47 except where noted)
A Blast for Buck
Buck Rogers in the 25th Century 1:28
The Guardians
Happy Birthday Buck
Return of the Fighting 69th
Space Rockers
Space Vampire
Unchained Woman
Vegas in Space

**BULLWINKLE & ROCKY & THEIR FRIENDS**
V.1: 1:35 rcd (VDo)

## C

**CAESAR'S HOUR**
3 vols (1ep on each, :45–:59) vys

**CALL TO GLORY**
Pilot 1:36 par (LV)

**CANDID CAMERA** (all ves)
*Best of I* :56
*Best of II* :57
*Candid Candid Camera* (adult-oriented takes) :55
*More Candid Candid Camera* :55
*Candid Candid Camera V.3*: :55
*Candid Candid Camera V.4*: 1:00
*Candid Candid Camera V.5*: :58
*Candid Candid Camera V.6*: 1:00

**CAPTAIN GALLANT**
Boy Who Found Christmas/Gift 1:00 dct
2ep 1:00 dct
1ep :30 con

**CAPTAIN MIDNIGHT/JET JACKSON** (all 1:00)
V.1: Deadly Diamonds/The Frozen Man rhi
V.2: Mission to Mexico/Million Dollar Diamond rhi
Secret Room/Secret Weapon dct
Curse of the Pharoahs/Counterfeit Millions dct

**CAROL BURNETT SHOW** (j2c)
*My Personal Best V.I*: 1:00
*My Personal Best V.II*: 1:00

**CELANESE THEATER** (all vys and 1:00)
On Borrowed Time
Winterset
Yellowjack

**CHIEFS**
2 vols 3:20 total nwl

**CHINA SMITH**
Karpriel Ciper/Yellow Jade Lion 1:00 dct

**CHISHOLMS**
Miniseries 5:00 usa

**CIMARRON STRIP** (reg)
Battleground 1:15
Without Honor 1:15

**CISCO KID**
Pancho Hostage/Quarter Horse 1:00 dct
1ep :30 con

**CIVILISATION** *(Not for Home Retail Market: See notes on MacArthur Library Video Project)* (all:50)
Ep 1: The Frozen World

Ep 2: The Great Thaw
Ep 3: Romance and Reality
Ep 4: Man—the Measure of All Things
Ep 5: The Hero as Artist
Ep 6: Protest and Communication
Ep 7: Grandeur and Obedience
Ep 8: The Light of Experience
Ep 9: The Pursuit of Happiness
Ep 10: The Smile of Reason
Ep 11: The Worship of Nature
Ep 12: The Fallacies of Hope
Ep 13: Heroic Materialism

**CLIMAX** (all 1:00)
Adventures of Huckleberry Finn dct
Casino Royale amv
Dr. Jekyll & Mr. Hyde dct
The Fifth Wheel dct
Lou Gehrig Story vys/dct
A Promise to Murder dct
Wild Stallion vdm/dct

**COLUMBO** (mca)
Murder by the Book 1:19
Prescription: Murder 1:39

**CONNECTIONS** *(See notes on Limited Use) Not for Home Retail Market* (10ep at :52 each)

**THE CONSTITUTION: THAT DELICATE BALANCE** *(Not for Home Retail Market: See notes on MacArthur Library Video Project)* (13ep at 1:00 each)

**COSMOS** *(See Notes on Limited Use) Not for Home Retail Market* (13ep at 1:00 each)

**CREATIVITY WITH BILL MOYERS** *(See notes on Limited Use) Not for Home Retail Market* (12ep at :58 each)

**CRIME STORY**
Pilot 1:36 nwl (LV)
*The Chicago Years* (2ep) 1:35

## D

**THE DAIN CURSE**
Miniseries cut-down 1:58 emb

**DAS BOOT (BOAT)**
Theatrical film version 2:30 rcd (VDo)

**DATE WITH THE ANGELS**
The Three in the Driveway/The Surprise/The Train/ Double Trouble 1:55 shk

**DAVY CROCKETT** (wds)
And the River Pirates (LV)
King of the Wild Frontier 1:28

**DEAN MARTIN SHOW**
1ep :50 vdm

**DEATH VALLEY DAYS**
V.1: No Gun Behind His Badge & 1ep :55 rhi
V.2: Three Minutes to Eternity & 1ep :55 rhi
V.3: Deadly Decision & 1ep :55 rhi
V.4: Battle of San Francisco Bay & 1ep :55 rhi
V.5: Ten Day Millionaire & 1ep :55 rhi
V.6: A Gun Is Not a Gentleman & 1ep :55 rhi
V.2: Kid from Hell's Kitchen/Three Minutes to Eternity/ Deadly Decision 1:15 ive
V.3: Red Shawl/Thar She Blows/Alias James Stewart 1:15 ive/vls
V.4: Ten Day Millionaire/Battle of San Francisco Bay/ A Gun Is Not a Gentleman 1:15 ive
V.1: 2ep 1:00 usa
V.2: 2ep 1:15 usa

**DECOY** (dct and 1:00)
V.1: High Swing/Across the World
V.2: First Arrest/Gentle Gunman

**THE DEVLIN CONNECTION**
2ep at :50 each twe

**DOCTOR FU MANCHU**
Golden God/Master Plan 1:00 dct

**DOCTOR WHO** (all pla)
Brain of Morbius :59
Day of the Daleks 1:30
The Deadly Assassin 1:30
The Five Doctors 1:30
Pyramids of Mars 1:31
Revenge of the Cybermen 1:32
Robots of Death 1:31

**DON KIRSHNER'S ROCK CONCERT**
V.1: 1:17 rcd (VDo)

**DRAGNET** (1950s)
Theatrical film (1954) 1:28 mca
V.1: The Big Shoplift/The Big Bank Robbery/The Big Hit and Run/The Big Secret 1:45 shk
V.2: Big Girls/Big Betty/The Big Trunk/Big Boys 1:40 shk
V.3: The Big Bar/The Big Bird/The Big Bounce/The Big Assault 1:40 shk
V.4: The Big 17/The Big Producer/The Big House Call/The Big Juvenile Gang 2:00 shk
V.1: The Big Girl/The Big Boys 1:00 hls
V.2: The Big Bird/The Big Trunk 1:00 hls
V.3: Big Shoplift/Big Hit and Run 1:00 hls
V.4: Big Betty/Big Counterfeit 1:00 hls
1ep :30 con

**DUCKTALES, DISNEY'S** (all wds)
*Daredevil Ducks*: The Money Vanishes/Home Sweet Homer :44
*Fearless Fortune Hunter*: Earth-Quack/Masters of the Djinni :44

*Fearless Fortune Hunter/Masked Marauders* (combined Laser Disc Version) 1:28 (LVo)
*High Flying Hero*: Hero for Hire/Launchpad's Civil War :44
*Masked Marauders*: Send in the Clones/The Time Teasers :44

### DUPONT SHOW OF THE MONTH
Treasure Island 1:28 vys

## E

### EAST OF EDEN
Miniseries 4:00 usa

### ED SULLIVAN SHOW (as *Toast of the Town*)
2ep includes tribute to *I Love Lucy* 2:00 shk
MGM tribute 1:00 vdm/dct
1ep 1:00 dct

### ED WYNN SHOW (variety)
3ep circa 1949 2:00 shk
1ep Three Stooges :30 con

### EDISON TWINS
Various :45 each rca

### EDWARD AND MRS. SIMPSON
2 vols 4:20 tem

### ELFEGO BACA, THE NINE LIVES OF
Theatrical film adaptation 1:19 wds

### ELLIS ISLAND
2 vols 5:27 usa

### THE EQUALIZER
Memories of Manon 1:36 mca

### ERNIE KOVACS
*Television's Original Genius* 1:26 ves
*Best of V.1*: 1:00 dct
*Best of V.2*: 1:00 dct
*Best of V.3*: 1:00 dct
*Best of V.4*: 1:00 dct

### ERROL FLYNN THEATER
Strange Auction/Sealed Room 1:00 dct

## F

### FAERIE TALE THEATER (all cbf and 1:00)
Aladdin and His Wonderful Lamp
Beauty and the Beast (LV)
The Boy Who Left Home to Find Out About the Shivers (LV)
Cinderella (LV)
The Dancing Princesses (LV)
The Emperor's New Clothes (LV)
The Frog Princess (LV)
Goldilocks & the Three Bears (LV)
Hansel and Gretel (LV)
Jack and the Beanstalk (LV)
The Little Mermaid (LV)
Little Red Riding Hood (LV)
The Nightingale (LV)
Pinocchio (LV)
The Pied Piper of Hamelin (LV)
The Princess and the Pea (LV)
The Princess Who Had Never Laughed (LV)
Puss 'n Boots (LV)
Rapunzel (LV)
Rip Van Winkle
Rumpelstiltskin (LV)
Sleeping Beauty (LV)
The Snow Queen (LV)
Snow White and the Seven Dwarfs (LV)
The Tale of the Frog Prince (LV)
Three Little Pigs (LV)
Thumbelina (LV)
(See also *Tall Tales and Legends*)

### FANTASY ISLAND
*Return to Fantasy Island* (2nd pilot) 1:40 prs

### THE FAR PAVILIONS
6hr miniseries cut-down 1:48 tem

### FAWLTY TOWERS (all cbf)
The Builders/The Wedding Party/The Psychiatrist 1:38
Communications Problems/The Anniversary/Basil The Rat 1:38
Gourmet Night/Waldorf Salad/The Kipper and the Corpse 1:38
The Hotel Inspectors/The Germans/A Touch of Class 1:38

### FIRESIDE THEATER (as RETURN ENGAGEMENT)
Sergeant Sullivan Speaking :24 blh

### FLASH GORDON
V.1: Akim the Terrible/Lure of Light 1:00 dct
V.2: Plant of Death/Struggle to the End 1:00 dct
V.3: Saboteurs from Space/Deadline at Noon 1:00 dct
1ep :30 con
1ep :30 she

### THE FLINTSTONES
Birth of Pebbles/The Time Machine 1:30 hnb
Flintstone Flyer/Hot Lips Hannigan/The Swimming Pool/No Help Wanted (1st 4ep) 1:30 hnb
*Hanna-Barbera Personal Favorites* 4ep 1:30 hnb
2ep :50 wov

### FLIPPER
*Flipper's Odyssey* (1966) 1:17 prs
*Flipper and the Elephant* (1968) cgr

**FOUR STAR THEATER**
1ep :30 w. Charles Boyer con

**FREE TO CHOOSE** *(See Notes on Limited Use) Not for Home Retail Market* (10ep at 1:00 each)

**THE FUGITIVE**
The Judgment (final ep) 1:43 wov/got/rcd (VD)

# G

**GALACTICA 1980** (See *Battlestar Galactica*)

**GANGBUSTERS**
Double Mike Malloy/Gun 1:00 dct

**GANGSTER CHRONICLES**
Miniseries cut-down 2:01 mca

**GENERAL ELECTRIC THEATER**
The Martyr :30 dct
Outpost at Home/American Tour/Return of Gentleman Jim 1:29 vys
Road to Edinburg/Committed 1:00 dct

**GEORGE BURNS AND GRACIE ALLEN SHOW**
V.1: 2ep 1:00 rca (LV)
Christmas Carol :30 vys
2 vols (2ep each, 1:00) dct
2 vols (1ep each, :30) con
2 vols (4ep each, 2:00) shk

**GEORGE BURNS SHOW**
1ep :30 vys

**GODFATHER SAGA**
*The Complete Epic 1902–1959* 6:08 par

**THE GOLDBERGS**
V.1: The Sinner/David's Cousin :54 vcl
1ep :27 vys
2ep 1:00 vtn
2ep 1:00 dct

**THE GOLDEN AGE OF TELEVISION**
Dramas originally appearing on *Goodyear Playhouse* (GOOD), *Kraft Theater* (KRAFT), *Magnavox Theater* (MAGNA), *Philco Playhouse* (PHIL), *Playwrights '56* (PLAY), *Prudential Family Playhouse* (PRUD), and *U.S. Steel Hour* (USS)
Bang the Drum Slowly (USS) :52 vys/dct
The Battler (PLAY) 1:00 dct
Dodsworth (PRUD) vyr
Ernie Barger Is 50 (PHIL) 1:00 vys
Gene Austin Story (GOOD) :51 vys
Kelly (KRAFT) 1:00 vys
Marty (GOOD) :51 mgu
Marty & Wind from the South (GOOD/PHIL) 1:58 mgu
No Time for Sergeants (USS) :50 vys
No Time for Sergeants/Patterns (USS/KRAFT) 1:59 mgu
Three Musketeers (MAGNA) :53 vys
A Wind from the South (USS) :50 vys
(See also *DuPont Show, General Electric Theater, Hallmark Hall of Fame, Playhouse 90*, and *Studio One*)

**GREAT PERFORMANCES** *(Not for Home Retail Market: See notes on MacArthur Library Video Project)*
(all 1:00 except where noted)
Choreography by Balanchine, Part One
Dance Theater of Harlem
The Five Forty-eight (Cheever)
Life on the MIssissippi :54
O Youth and Beauty (Cheever)
The Sorrows of Gin (Cheever)
To Be Young, Gifted and Black 1:30

**GRIZZLY ADAMS, LIFE AND TIMES OF**
At Beaver Dam 1:00 une
The Blood Brothers 1:00 une

# H

**HALLMARK HALL OF FAME** (sometimes packaged as *George Schaefer's Showcase Theater* except *)
Barefoot in Athens 1:16 ent
*A Doll's House 1:29 mgu
Elizabeth the Queen 1:16 ent
Give Us Barabbas 1:16 ent
Holy Terror 1:16 ent
Invincible Mr. Disraeli 1:16 ent
Lamp at Midnight 1:16 ent
*Macbeth 1:43 vys
A Punt Pass & A Prayer 1:16 ent
Soldier in Love 1:16 ent
Tempest 1:16 ent
Victoria Regina 1:16 ent

**THE HARDY BOYS** (all mca and :47)
Acapulco Spies
The Flickering Torch Mystery
The Mystery of King Tut's Tomb
Mystery of the African Safari
The Mystery of the Flying Courier
The Mystery of Witches Hollow
The Secret of Jade Kwan Yin
Wipe-Out

**THE HEART OF THE DRAGON** *(Not for Home Retail Market: See notes on MacArthur Library Video Project)* (all :57)
Ep 1: Remembering
Ep 2: Caring
Ep 3: Eating
Ep 4: Believing

Ep 5: Correcting
Ep 6: Working
Ep 7: Living
Ep 8: Marrying
Ep 9: Understanding
Ep 10: Mediating
Ep 11: Creating
Ep 12: Trading

## HERITAGE: CIVILIZATION AND THE JEWS *(Not for Home Retail Market: See Notes on MacArthur Library Video Project)* (all 1:00)

Ep 1: A People Is Born
Ep 2: Power of the Word
Ep 3: The Shaping of Traditions
Ep 4: The Crucible of Europe
Ep 5: The Search for Deliverance
Ep 6: Roads from the Ghetto
Ep 7: The Golden Land
Ep 8: Out of the Ashes
Ep 9: Into the Future

## THE HITCHHIKER (all lor and 1:30 and LV)

V.1: WGOD Talk Radio/Hired Help/The Curse
V.2: Night Shift/Dead Man's Curve/Last Scene
V.3: Ghostwriter/True Believer/And If We Dream
V.4: Video Date/Face to Face/Man's Best Friend

## THE HOLLYWOOD PALACE

Last Show: 53 vdm/dct
Victor Borge 1:00 dct

## HOLOCAUST

3 vols 7:55 wov/rcd (VD)

## THE HONEYMOONERS: The Hidden (Lost) Episodes (all mpi)

*The Best of the Lost Episodes* (selected clips) :30
*Hidden Episodes V.1*: Letter to The Boss/Suspense/Dinner Guest 1:00
*Hidden Episodes V.2*: Songs & Witty Sayings/Norton Moves In :53
*Hidden Episodes V.3*: Christmas Party/Forgot to Register :55
*Hidden Episodes V.4*: New Year's Eve Party/Two-Family Car :55
*Hidden Episodes V.5*: The Next Champ/Expectant Father :55
*Hidden Episodes V.6*: Move Uptown/Lucky Number :55
*Hidden Episodes V.7*: Little Man Who Wasn't There/Goodnight Sweet Prince :55
*Hidden Episodes V.8*: My Fair Landlord/Income Tax :55
*Hidden Episodes V.9*: Ralph's Sweet Tooth/Cold Pickles :55
*Hidden Episodes V.10*: Cupid/Manager of a Baseball Team :55
*Hidden Episodes V.11*: Vacation at Fred's Landing/Teamwork: Beats the Clock 1:03
*Hidden Episodes V.12*: Great Jewel Robbery/Guest Speaker :52
*Hidden Episodes V.13*: Love Letter/Champagne & Caviar :51
*Hidden Episodes V.14*: Hair Raising Tail/Finger Man :50
*Hidden Episodes V.15*: Hot Dog Stand/Alice Plays Cupid :48
*Hidden Episodes V.16*: Cottage for Sale/Jelly Beans :50
*Hidden Episodes V.17*: Principal of the Thing/Alice's Aunt Ethel :49
*Hidden Episodes V.18*: The Hypnotist/Glow Worm Cleaning :49
*Hidden Episodes V.19*: Two Men on a Horse/The Check-Up :49
*Hidden Episodes V.20*: A Promotion/Hot Tips :49
*Hidden Episodes V.21*: Boys & Girls Together/Anniversary Gift :49
*Hidden Episodes V.22*: This Is Your Life/Halloween Party :49
*Holiday Classics* (2 vols): Christmas Party/Forget to Register/New Year's Eve/Two-Family Car 1:50
*My Man Norton* (Norton skits) :55
*Valentine's Special* :30

## THE HONEYMOONERS: The "Classic Thirty-Nine" *(Mail order only from CBS Video Library: See notes for ordering information)* (all cvl and 1:30)

V.1: TV or Not TV/Funny Money/The Golfer
V.2: Women's Work Is Never Done/A Matter of Life and Death/The Sleepwalker
V.3: Better Living Thru TV/Pal O Mine/Brother Ralph
V.4: Hello Mom/The Deciding Vote/Something Fishy
V.5: Twas the Night Before Christmas/Man from Space/A Matter of Record
V.6: Oh My Aching Back/The Babysitter/The $99,000 Answer
V.7: Ralph Kramden, Inc./Young At Heart/A Dog's Life
V.8: Here Comes the Bride/Mamo Loves Mambo/Please Leave the Premises
V.9: Pardon My Glove/Young Man with a Horn/Head of the House
V.10: The Worry Wart/Trapped/The Loudspeaker
V.11: On Stage/Opportunity Knocks, But/Unconventional Behavior
V.12: The Safety Award/Mind Your Own Business/Alice and the Blonde
V.13: Bensonhurst Bomber/Dial J for Janitor/A Man's Pride

## HULLABALOO

V.1: 1:00 dct
V.2: 1:00 dct

# I

**I. CLAUDIUS** *(Not for Home Retail Market: See notes on MacArthur Library Video Project) (all 1:00)*

Ep 1: A Touch of Murder
Ep 2: Family Affairs
Ep 3: Waiting in the Wings
Ep 4: What Shall We Do About the Children?
Ep 5: Poison Is Queen
Ep 6: Some Justice
Ep 7: Queen of Heaven
Ep 8: Reign of Terror
Ep 9: Zeus, by Jove!
Ep 10: Hail Who?
Ep 11: Fool's Luck
Ep 12: A God in Colchester
Ep 13: Old King Log

**I LOVE LUCY** *(Mail order only from CBS Video Library: See notes for ordering information)* (all cvl and 1:30)

V.1: *Lucy's Trouble Managing Money*: Job Switching/Million Dollar Idea/The Freezer
V.2: *Lucy Wants to Be a Star*: Lucy Does a TV Commercial/Lucy Gets into Pictures/Lucy's Italian Movie
V.3: *Lucy and the Stars*: L. A. at Last/Lucy and Harpo Marx/Lucy and Bob Hope
V.4: *The Ricardos Are Having a Baby*: Lucy is Enceinte/Lucy Hires an English Tutor/Lucy Goes to the Hospital
V.5: *The Mertzes*: Little Ricky Learns to Play the Drum/Ethel's Birthday/The Ricardos Are Interviewed
V.6: *Europe Here We Come*: Ricky's European Booking/The Passports/Bon Voyage
V.7: *Lucy the Clown*: The Handcuffs/Lucy's Show Biz Swan Song/The Ballet
V.8: *Getting into Ricky's Act*: The Audition Show/The French Revue/The Saxophone
V.9: *Crossing the Country*: First Stop/Tennessee Bound/Ethel's Hometown
V.10: *In Europe*: Lucy Meets the Queen/Paris at Last/Lucy Goes to Monte Carlo
V.11: *Lucy in the Country*: Lucy Wants to move to the Country/Lucy Raises Chickens/Lucy Does the Tango
V.12: *Lucy Causing Trouble*: Lucy and the Graumans/Lucy and John Wayne/The Great Train Robbery
V.13: *Lucy and Ricky Perform Together*: Lucy Gets Ricky on the Radio/The Benefit/The Indian Show
V.14: *Neighbors Fights*: The Court Room/Breaking the Lease/Never Do Business with Friends
V.15: *Wrong Conclusions*: Drafted/Lucy Thinks Ricky Is Trying to Murder Her/The Kleptomaniac
V.16: *In Los Angeles*: Lucy in Palm Springs/Ricky Needs an Agent/The Fashion Show
V.17: *Lucy's Hillbilly Episodes*: The Girls Want to Go to a Nightclub/Tennessee Ernie Ford Visits/Tennessee Ernie Ford Hangs On
V.18: *Lucy Interfering in Ricky's Act*: Don Juan and the Starlets/Ricky's Screen Test/Ricky's Contract
V.19: *Lucy Goes Cuban*: Cuban Pals/Lucy's Mother-in-Law/The Ricardos Visit Cuba
V.20: *New Furniture*: Redecorating/Lucy Wants New Furniture/Lucy Gets Chummy with the Neighbors
V.21: *Lucy Wants Attention*: The Inferiority Complex/Pregnant Women Are Unpredictable/Lucy Cries Wolf
V.22: *Battle of the Sexes*: Pioneer Women/Vacation from Marriage/The Camping Trip
V.23: *Happy Anniversary*: The Anniversary Present/Sentimental Anniversary/Hollywood Anniversary
V.24: *Lucy the Author*: Lucy Writes a Play/The Operetta/Lucy Writes a Novel
V.25: *Lucy Stalks the Stars*: The Tour/Lucy Meets Charles Boyer/Lucy Meets Orson Welles
V.26: *Lucy the Dancer*: Bull Fight Dance/The Dancing Star/Lucy and the Dummy
V.27: *Lucy's Car Trouble*: Getting Ready/Lucy Learns to Drive/Ricky Sells the Car
V.28: *The Mertzes Get into the Act*: Little Ricky's School Pageant/Lucy Goes to a Rodeo/Mertz and Kurtz
V.29: *Lucy Gets Jealous*: Ricky's Old Girl Friend/The Charm School/Country Club Dance
V.30: *Lucy's Publicity Stunts*: The Publicity Agent/The Hedda Hopper Story/Don Juan Is Shelved

**I MARRIED JOAN**

Joan Sees Stars/Joan the Matchmaker/Joan Throws a Wedding/Money in the Shotgun 1:45 shk
Joan's Testimonial Luncheon/The St. Bernards :50 vys

**I SPY** (vhl)

V.1: Affair in T'sen Cha/Carry Me Back to Old Tsing Tao 2:00
V.2: So Long Parick Henry/Danny Was a Million Laughs 2:00

**IN SEARCH OF . . .** (all pyr and :24 except where noted)

Amelia Earhart
Anastasia
Ancient Aviators
Astrology
Atlantis
The Bermuda Triangle
Bigfoot
Butch Cassidy
A Call from Space
The Coming Ice Age
The Dead Sea Scrolls
Deadly Ants
Dracula
Earthquakes
The Easter Island Massacre
Firewalkers
The Garden of Eden

Ghosts
Haunted Castles
Hurricanes
Hypnosis
Immortality
Inca Treasure
Killer Bees
Learning ESP
Life After Death
The Loch Ness Monster
The Lost Dutchman Mine
The Magic of Stonehenge
The Man Who Would Not Die
Martians
Mayan Mysteries
Michael Rockefeller
The Mummy's Curse
Nazi Plunder
The Ogopogo Monster
Other Voices
Psychic Detectives
Pyramid Secrets
Reincarnation
The Secrets of Life
Shark Worshippers
Sherlock Holmes/Jack the Ripper/Tower of London 1:15 usa
Strange Visitors
Swamp Monsters
Troy
UFOs
Voodoo
Witch Doctors

## THE INCREDIBLE HULK

The Incredible Hulk 1:34 mca
The Incredible Hulk Returns (1988) 1:33 nwl (LV)

## THE INVADERS (all got and :55)

Beach Head
The Believers
The Condemned
The Experiment
The Ivy Curtain
Labyrinth
Moonshot
The Mutation
Quantity Unknown
The Saucer
The Spores
Wall of Crystal

# J

## THE JACK BENNY PROGRAM

Christmas Show/Railroad Station 1:00 mca
Humphrey Bogart/Jayne Mansfield :52 mpi
Ernie Kovacs :30 vys
Honeymooners Parody :25 vys
Jam Session/Baby Face :58 vys
Visits Walt Disney 1:00 dct
I :30 con
II :30 con
I 3ep 1:50 shk
II 4ep 1:55 shk
III 4ep 2:00 shk
IV: 4ep 1:55 shk

## JACKIE GLEASON SHOW

*The Great Gleason Special* 1:30 mpi
*The Jackie Gleason American Scene* :53 got
as *Cavalcade of Stars* :55 vys

## JANE EYRE

2 vols 3:59 cbf

## JESUS OF NAZARETH

Miniseries 6:11 cbf/rcd (VD)

## THE JETSONS

The Jetsons Meet the Flintstones (1988) 1:34 wov

## THE JEWEL IN THE CROWN (all s&s)

Ep 1–2: Crossing the River/The Bibighar Gardens 2:36
Ep 3–5: Questions of Loyalty/Incidents at a Wedding/The Regimental Silver 2:29
Ep 6–8: Ordeal by Fire/Daughters of the Regiment/Day of the Scorpion 2:28
Ep 9–11: Takers of Silence/An Evening at the Maharanee's/Traveling Companions 2:30
Ep 12–14: The Moghul Rule/Pandora's Box/The Division of the Spoils 2:29

## JIM BOWIE

Squatter/Gambler 1:00 dct

## JIMMY DURANTE SHOW (TEXACO STAR THEATER)

1ep :30 con

## JONATHAN WINTERS SHOW (1950s)

2ep :30 vys

## JUDY GARLAND SHOW

*The Best of* 1:25 rca
*Christmas Show* :55 kov
*Judy Garland in Concert V.1* (2/9/64): 1:00 rko
*Judy Garland in Concert V.2* (3/8/64): :50 rko
*Judy's Favorites* 1:43 img (LVo)

# K

## KING

Miniseries 4:32 tem

## KOJAK

The Belarius File (1985) 1:35 mca

**KOLCHAK: THE NIGHT STALKER**
The Nightstalker (pilot) 1:14 cbf
The Ripper/The Vampire 1:38 mca

# L

**L. A. LAW**
Pilot 1:37 cbf

**LASSIE** (combined episodes) (mgu)
*Lassie's Great Adventure* (1963) 1:44
*Lassie in the Miracle* 1:30

**LAWRENCE WELK SHOW** (wlk)
13 vols (2ep on each, 1:32–1:38)
*On Tour* (1982) 2 vols, 1:30 each

**THE LAZARUS SYNDROME**
Pilot 1:30 usa

**LEAVE IT TO BEAVER** as **STILL THE BEAVER** (1980s) (all wds and 1:00)
V.1: Growing Pains/Thanksgiving Day
V.2: Supply & Demand/Pet Peeves
V.3: Girl Talk/The Gladiators

**LIFE ON EARTH**
Cut-down adaptation from the series 3:53 war

**LIFE ON EARTH** *(Not for Home Retail Market: See notes on MacArthur Library Video Project)* (all :58)
Ep 1: The Infinite Variety
Ep 2: Building Bodies
Ep 3: The First Forests
Ep 4: The Swarming Hordes
Ep 5: The Conquest of the Waters
Ep 6: The Invasion of the Land
Ep 7: Victors of the Dry Land
Ep 8: Lords of the Air
Ep 9: The Rise of the Mammals
Ep 10: Theme and Variations
Ep 11: The Hunters and the Hunted
Ep 12: A Life in the Trees
Ep 13: The Compulsive Communicators

**LIFE WITH LUIGI**
2ep 1:00 dct

**LIFESTYLES OF THE RICH AND FAMOUS**
(all got and :45)
*Celebrity Homes (The Most Fantastic in the World)*
*Money Makers (The Inside Story)*
*Playthings of the Rich and Famous*
*The World's Most Exotic Vacation Resorts*

**LITTLE HOUSE ON THE PRAIRIE**
V.1: pilot 1:38 war/rcd (VD)
V.2: The Craftsman/The Collection 1:37 war
V.3: Remember Me 1:37 war
V.4: The Lord Is My Shepherd 1:34 war

**THE LIVING PLANET** *(Not for Home Retail Market: See notes on MacArthur Library Video Project)* (all :55)
Ep 1: The Building of the Earth
Ep 2: The Frozen World
Ep 3: The Northern Forests
Ep 4: Jungle
Ep 5: Seas of Grass
Ep 6: The Baking Deserts
Ep 7: The Community of the Skies
Ep 8: Sweet Fresh Water
Ep 9: The Margins of the Land
Ep 10: Worlds Apart
Ep 11: Oceans
Ep 12: New Worlds

**THE LONE RANGER**
V.1: The Fugitive + 1ep :55 rhi
V.2: Message to Fort Apache + 1ep :55 rhi
V.3: Six Gun Sanctuary + 1ep :55 rhi
*Count the Clues*: 3ep 1:12 mgu
*Justice of the West*: 3ep 1:11 mgu
Movie (1956) 1:27 mgu

**LONE WOLF**
2ep 1:00 dct

**LORETTA YOUNG SHOW**
1ep :30 con

**LOST IN SPACE**
Pilot :52 vys/vdm
The Space Trader :44 vys

# M

**M*A*S*H**
Goodbye, Farewell and Amen 2:00 cbf (LV) (VD)

**MAKE ROOM FOR DADDY** (w. Jean Hagen)
V.1: Second Honeymoon/Margaret's Career/The Lost Dollar/Rusty's Report Card 2:00 shk
V.2: Danny Has a Baby/Terry Grows Up/Margaret's Aunt/Terry's Boy Friend 2:00 shk
V.3: Margaret's Job/Thanksgiving Day/Danny in Wonderland/The First Allowance 2:00 shk
V.4: Valentine's Day/Danny's Nose Lift/Trip to Wisconsin/Danny Plays the Palladium 2:00 shk
1ep :30 con

**MAMA**
Madame Zodiac :30 vys
Mama's Bad Day :29 vys
Mama's Nursery School/Mama's Bad Day 1:00 dct
Queen of the Bee :29 vys

**MAN AGAINST CRIME**
V.1: 2ep 1:00 vys
V.2: 2ep 1:00 vys

**A MAN CALLED SLOANE**
Death Ray 2000 pilot 1:40 wov

**MAN FROM ATLANTIS**
Pilot 1:36 war

**THE MAN FROM U.N.C.L.E.**
Return of the Man from U.N.C.L.E. 1:36 twe

**MARK SABER MYSTERY**
Case of the Chamber of Death/The Locked Room :53 vys

**THE MARTIAN CHRONICLES** (all fri/usa/img and LV)
V.1: The Expeditions 1:40
V.2: The Settlers 1:37
V.3: The Martians 1:37

**MARY HARTMAN, MARY HARTMAN** (emb and 1:10 and LV)
*Best of V.1*: Ep 1/Ep 43/Ep 325
*Best of V.2*: Ep 2–4

**MARY TYLER MOORE SHOW**
Love Is All Around/The Final Show/Chuckles Bites the Dust/Put on a Happy Face 1:42 rcd (VDo)

**MASADA**
Miniseries cut-down 2:11 mca

**MAX HEADROOM**
*The Original Story* (UK pilot) 1:00 klr (LV)

**MEDIC** (all hls and 1:00)
V.1: My Brother Joe/Flash of Darkness
V.2: A Time to Be/Dr. Impossible
V.3: Breath of Life/Break Through the Bars
V.4: Till the Song Is Done, Till The Dance Is Gone/Death Is a Red Balloon
V.5: Long Tomorrow/The Storm

**MIAMI VICE** (mca and 1:39 and LV)
Pilot
The Prodigal Son

**MICHAEL SHAYNE**
Murder and the Wanton Bride 1:00 dct

**THE MICKEY ROONEY SHOW** as **HEY MULLIGAN**
1 ep :30 con

**MILTON BERLE SHOW** (1950s)
Elvis Presley 1:00 vys
Charlton Heston 1:00 vys
V.1: Buick Berle 2ep 2:00 shk
V.2: Buick Berle 2ep 1:55 shk
V.3: Buick Berle 2ep 1:55 shk
1 ep con
(1960s series) w. Roy Rogers 1:00 vys/dct

**THE MISFITS OF SCIENCE**
Pilot 1:36 mca

**MISS MARPLE, AGATHA CHRISTIE'S** (all cbf)
The Body in the Library 2:31
A Murder Is Announced 2:35
A Pocketful of Rye 1:41

**MR. AND MRS. NORTH**
Anniversary/Busy Signal 1:00 dct
Nosed Out/Trained for Murder 1:00 dct
Scarlett & Violett/Reunion 1:00 dct
2ep 1:00 dct
1ep :30 con

**MISTER MAGOO, FAMOUS ADVENTURES OF**
as Friar Truck 1:23 par/rcd (VD)
as Dr. Watson/Dr. Frankenstein/Count of Monte Cristo/Dick Tracy 1:36 par
in Snow White/Don Quixote/A Midsummer Night's Dream 1:53 par/rcd (VD)

**THE MONKEES** (all rca and :50)
Dance Monkees Dance/Hitting the High Seas
Here Comes the Monkees/I Was a Teenage Monster
Monkees a la Carte/The Prince & the Pauper
Monkees Get Out More Dirt/Art for Monkee's Sake
Monkees vs Machine/Don't Look a Gift Horse in the Mouth (LV)
The Monstrous Monkees Mash/The Devil & Peter Tork

**MONTY PYTHON'S FLYING CIRCUS** (all par) (titles generally refer to opening or very familiar sketches)
V.1: Ep w. Architect's Sketch & Naughty Chemist/Ep w. Dinsdale & Silly Walks 1:00
V.2: Ep w. Money Program & Rat Cuisine & Argument Clinic/Ep w. Spanish Inquisition 1:00
V.3: Ep w. Attila the Hun Show & Killer Sheep/Ep w. Summarize Proust & Travel Agent :58
V.4: Ep w. How to Recognize Parts of the Body & Bruce Sketch/Ep w. Mr. & Mrs. Brian Norris's Ford Popular 1:00
V.5: Ep w. Spam/Ep w. The War Against Pornography & Gumby Surgery 1:00
V.6: Ep w. Peckinpah's Sald Days & Cheese Shop/Ep w. How Not To Be Seen 1:00
V.7: Ep w. Prawn Salad & Blackmail/Ep w. The Nude Man & The Cheap Laughs 1:00
V.8: Ep w. Welsh Coal Miners & Lifeboat/Ep w. E. Henry Thripshaw's Disease & Is There? & Queen Will Be Watching 1:00
V.9: Ep w. Njorl's Saga & Whicker's World/Ep w. School Prizes & Silly Party 1:00
V.10: Ep w. Pantomime Horse & Army Recruitment/Ep. w. Scottish Poetry & Deja Vu 1:00
V.11: Ep w. Blood Bank & Dirty Vicar/Ep w. Meet the Gits 1:00
V.12: Ep w. A Book at Bedtime & Spot the Looney/Ep w. Dennis Moore 1:00

**MONTY PYTHON** (Laser Disc Packages)
(all par and 1:30 and LVo)
V.1: Ep w. Architect's Sketch & Naughty Chemist/Ep w. Dinsdale & Silly Walks/Ep w. Money Program & Rat Cuisine & Argument Clinic

V.2: Ep w. Spanish Inquisition/Ep w. Attila the Hun Show & Killer Sheep/Ep w. Summarize Proust & Travel Agent
V.3: Ep w. How To Recognize Parts of the Body & Bruce Sketch/Ep w. Spam/Ep w. Mr. & Mrs. Brian Norris's Ford Popular
V.4: Ep w. How Not to Be Seen/Ep w. Peckinpah's Salad Days & Cheese Shop/Ep w. The War Against Pornography & Gumby Surgery

**MOONLIGHTING**
Pilot 1:33 war

**MOST WANTED**
Movie-length ep 1:18 wov

**THE MUNSTERS**
The Munsters' Revenge (1981) 1:36 mca

**THE MUPPET SHOW** (all pla)
*Muppet Revue* :56
*Muppets Moments* :55
*Muppets Treasures* :55

**MY HERO**
Horsin Around/Surprise Party/Oil Land/The Photographer 1:40 shk
1ep :30 con

**MY LITTLE MARGIE**
2ep 1:00 dct/ihf

# N

**NANCY DREW** (all mca and :47)
A Haunting We Will Go
The Mystery of Pirate's Cove
The Mystery of The Diamond Triangle
The Mystery of the Fallen Angels
The Mystery of The Ghostwriter's Cruise
The Mystery of the Solid Gold Kicker
Nancy Drew's Love Match
The Secret of the Whispering Walls

**NATIONAL GEOGRAPHIC** (all ves and 1:00 and LV except where noted)
African Wildlife
Among the Wild Chimpanzees
Atocha: Quest for Treasure
Australia's Improbable Animals
Ballad of the Irish Horse
Born of Fire
Creatures of the Mangrove
The Creatures of the Namib Desert
Egypt: Quest for Eternity
Explorers: A Century of Discovery 1:30
Gorilla
The Great Whales
The Grizzlies
Himalayan River Run
Iceland River Challenge
The Incredible Human Machine
The Invisible World
Jerusalem: Within These Walls
Land of the Tiger
Lions of the African Night
Living Treasures of Japan
Man-Eaters of India
Miniature Miracle: The Computer Chip
Polar Bear Alert
Rain Forest
Realm of the Alligator
The Rhino War
Rocky Mountain Beaver Pond
Save the Panda
The Secret Leopard
Secrets of the Titanic
The Sharks
The Superliners: Twilight of an Era
Tropical Kingdom of Belize
White Wolf
Yukon Passage

**NATURE** (all lor and 1:00
V.1: On Dogs
V.2: Leopards
V.3: Yellowstone in Winter

**NIGHT GALLERY**
Pilot: The Cemetery/Darker Than Dark/The Monster Who Wanted to Be a Fisherman 1:35 mca

**NOVA** (all ves and 1:00)
Animal Olympics (LV)
The Bermuda Triangle (LV)
Children & Sex Roles
Einstein: The Private Thoughts of a Public Genius (LV)
Fat Chance in a Thin World (LV)
Hitler's Secret Weapon (LV)
Migration of Gray Whales
Nazi Missile
Science of Murder (LV)
The Secret of the Sexes (LV)
The Shape of Things (LV)
+Signs of the Apes, Songs of the Whales (LV)
Sistine Chapel (LV)
UFO's: Are We Alone (LV)
Visions of the Deep (LV)
+Whale Watch (LV)
*Two of the above titles (indicated by +), as well as eight additional, are available through the MacArthur Library Video Project (See notes)* (all :57)
Acid Rain: New Bad News
Alcoholism: Life Under the Influence
Animal Imposters
City of Coral

Down on the Farm
The Miracle of Life
Nuclear Strategy for Beginners
To Live Until You Die

## NURSE

Pilot 1:40 usa

# O

## ONCE A HERO

Pilot 1:30 nwl

## THE OUTER LIMITS (all mgu and :52 except where noted)

The Architects of Fear
Demon with a Glass Hand
The Forms of Things Unknown
Galaxy Being (pilot) :53
Hundred Days of the Dragon
The Inheritors 1:38
Invisible Enemy
Keeper of the Purple Twilight
Man Who Was Never Born
Man with the Power
Nightmare
The Sixth Finger
Soldier
Specimen: Unknown
The Zanti Misfits
Fun and Games
O.B.I.T.
The Invisibles

## OZZIE AND HARRIET, ADVENTURES OF

(Clustered by label)
Group I: (all hls and 1:00)
*Early Years*
V.1: Separate Rooms/Orchids & Violets
V.2: Pills/Father & Son Tournament
V.3: An Evening with Hamlet/Halloween
*High School Years*
V.4: Hair Style for Harriet/Jet Pilot
V.5: Ricky the Drummer/Fourteen Mile Hike
V.6: A Cruise for Harriet/Ricky's Dinner Guests
*College Years*
V.7: David Goofs Off/Little House Guest
V.8: David Hires a Secretary/The Girl Who Loses Things
V.9: The Fraternity Rents a Room/Making Wally Study 1:00
*Golden Years*
V.10: An Old Friend of June's/Kris Plays Cupid
V.11: Rick's Raise/Breakfast for Harriet
V.12: Trip Trap/Flying Down to Lunch
Group II: (all shk and 2:00)
V.1: 4ep
V.2: 4ep
V.3: Party/A Matter of Inches/Road Race/Little Handprints in the Sidewalk
V.4: David's Birthday/Ball of Tin Foil/David Becomes a Football Coach/An Hour for Oz
V.5: Orchids & Violets/David Picks Up the Tab/Little Visitor/Flying Down to Lunch
V.6: David Wants a Raise/Girl in the Emporium/Rick & Maid of Honor/The Desk Photo
V.7: Father & Son Tournament/The Bridge Group/The Law Clerk/Kris Plays Cupid
V.8: The Editor/Ozzie's Daughters/David the Sleuth/Dave's Other Office
V.9: The Pills/Halloween Party/Ozzie's Night Out/Ozzie the Treasurer
Group III: (all dct and 1:00 except where noted)
V.1: Pancake Mix/New Chairs dct/vdm
V.2: Pajama Game/Ball of Tin Foil
V.3: Tutti-Frutti Ice Cream/Road Race
V.4: Circus/Blue Moose
V.5: Big Dog/Desk Photo
V.6: Girl at the Emporium :30
V.7: Ricky's Horse/Ozzie the Babysitter
Group IV: (various)
Day in Bed/Art Studies 1:00 ihf
Ricky's Horse/Ozzie the Babysitter :55 vys
Wally the Author/The Sheik of Araby :57 vys
1ep :30 con

# P

## PARTNERS IN CRIME, AGATHA CHRISTIE'S (all pav and :51)

*The Affair of the Pink Pearl*
*The Ambassador's Boots*
*The Case of the Missing Lady*
*The Clergyman's Daughter*
*The Crackler*
*Finessing the King*
*The House of Lurking Death*
*The Man in the Mist*
*The Secert Adversary (LV)*
*Sunningdale Mystery*
*The Unbreakable Alibi*

## PERRY COMO SHOW

1ep 1:00 vdm

## PERSON TO PERSON

1ep Groucho & Harpo :30 vys

## PERSUADERS

Five Miles to Midnight 1:00 son
London Conspiracy (combined eps) 1:42 cbf/son
Mission: Monte Carlo (combined eps) 1:36/cbf/son
Overture 1:00 son

Sporting Chance (combined ep) 1:42 cbf/son
The Switch (combined ep) 1:42 cbf/son

**PHILIP MARLOWE** (1980s) (pla and :54)
Finger Man
The Pencil

**PLANET EARTH** *(Not for Home Retail Market: See notes on MacArthur Library Video Project)* (all 1:00)
Ep 1: The Living Machine
Ep 2: The Blue Planet
Ep 3: The Climate Puzzle
Ep 4: Tales from Other Worlds
Ep 5: Gifts from the Earth
Ep 6: The Solar Sea
Ep 7: Fate of the Earth

**PLAYHOUSE 90**
Bomber's Moon 1:25 vys
The Comedian 1:23 mgu/vys
The Days of Wine and Roses 1:29 mgu

**POLICE SQUAD** (par and 1:15 and LV)
*Help Wanted!*: A Substantial Gift/Ring of Fear/Rendezvous at Big Gulch
*More!*: Revenge and Remorse/The Butler Did It/Testimony of Evil

**PRAIRIE HOME COMPANION**
The Last Show (June 13, 1987) 1:54 wds

**PRIDE AND PREJUDICE**
Miniseries 3:46 cbf

**THE PRISONER** (all mpi/img and :52 and LV except where noted)
V.1: Arrival
V.2: The Chimes of Big Ben
V.3: A, B & C
V.4: Free for All
V.5: Schizoid Man
V.6: The General
V.7: Many Happy Returns
V.8: Dance of the Dead
V.9: Do Not Forsake Me, Oh My Darling
V.10: It's Your Funeral
V.11: Checkmate
V.12: Living in Harmony
V.13: Change of Mind
V.14: Hammer into Anvil
V.15: The Girl Who Was Death
V.16: Once Upon a Time
V.17: Fallout
*The Alternate "Chimes of Big Ben" (The Lost Episode)* mpi 1:00

**THE PROFESSIONALS**
Operation Susie/The Heroes 1:39 twe

**PROFILES IN COURAGE** *(See Notes on Limited Use)*
*Not For Home Retail Market* (26ep at :50 each)

# Q

**QB VII**
3 vols 5:13 rca

**Q.E.D.** as **MASTERMIND** (all pla and :48)
The Great Motor Race
The Infernal Device
Target London

**QUATERMASS**
Quatermass II 1:25 ent
Quatermass Conclusion 1:45 tha

# R

**RACKET SQUAD**
Sting of Fate/Case of the Miracle Mud :52 dct

**RAGS TO RICHES**
Pilot 1:36 nwl

**RANGE RIDER** (all dct and 1:00)
V.1: Hideout/Greed Rides the Range
V.2: Silver Blade/Fatal Bullet
V.3: Romeo Goes West/Old Times Trail
V.4: Marshal from Madero/Outlaw's Double

**RAY BRADBURY THEATER**
V.1: Marionettes, Inc./The Playground :58 buv
V.2: The Crowd :28 buv
Banshee/Screaming Woman/Town Where No One Got Off 1:26 hbo

**READY STEADY GO**
V.1: :58 tem/pio (LV)
V.2: :56 tem/pio
V.3: :57 tem (LV)
*The Beatles Live* :20 son (LV)

**RED SKELTON** (1950s)
2ep 1:00 dct
4ep 2:00 shk

**RIN TIN TIN**
*Courage of Rin Tin Tin* (combined eps) 1:30 mon
*Hero of the West* 1:15 (combined eps) colorized mon

**RIPPING YARNS** (all cbf and 1:30)
*Ripping Yarns*: Tomkinson's Schooldays/Escape from Stalag Luft 112B/Golden Gordon
*More Ripping Yarns*: Testing of Eric Olthwaite/Winfrey's Last Stand/Curse of the Claw
*Even More Ripping Yarns*: Roger of Raj/Murder at Moorstones Manor/Across the Andes by Frog

**ROBIN HOOD** (1950s) (all dct and 1:00 except where noted)
Coming of Robin/Money Lender
Thorkill Ghost/Quickness of Hand

Year and a Day/Secret Mission
Youthful Menace/Prisoner
1ep :30 con
1ep :30 vdc

**ROBIN HOOD** (1980s) (all pla)
V.1: Herne's Son 1:41
V.2: And the Sorcerer 1:55
V.3: The Swords of Wayland 1:45
V.4: The Time of the Wolf 1:45

**ROCKY JONES, SPACE RANGER**
Blast Off 3ep 1:15 vdm
The Cold Sun 3ep 1:15 vdm
Crash of Moons 3ep dct
Forbidden Moon 3ep 1:15 vdm
Inferno in Space 3ep dct
Pirates of Prah 3ep 1:15 vdm
Renegade Satellite 1:09 vdm
Trial of Rocky Jones 3ep 1:15 vdm

**THE ROGUES** (rko and :52)
The Day They Gave the Diamonds Away
The Personal Touch

**ROOTS**
Vols. 1–6, 1:30 each war

**ROY ROGERS**
V.1: Minister's Son/Unwilling Outlaw 1:00 dct
V.3: Ride in the Death Wagon/Shoot to Kill 1:00 dct
V.4: Hidden Treasure/Boys' Day in Paradise Valley 1:00 dct
I: Old Man's Gold/Pat Brady Outlaw/Boys' Day in Paradise Valley/Hidden Treasure 1:40 shk
II: Unwilling Outlaw/The Minister's Son/M Stands for Murder/Train Robbery/Money for Charity 2:05 shk
III: Disappearance of Jim Barton/Bad Day at Eagle Rock/Kid with the Map/Bad Neighbors 1:50 shk
IV: Cattle Rustlers/Land Outlaws/Ginger Horse/Attack on the Don Jose Ranch 1:40 shk
1ep :30 con

**THE RUGGLES**
Charlie's Promotion/Charlie's Lucky Day/The Punishment/Perfect Strangers 1:45 shk

## S

**SCTV**
*The Last Polka* (Shmenge Brothers) :54 ves

**THE SAINT** (all ive and 1:40 except where noted)
The Fiction Makers 1:42 cbf
Vendetta for a Saint 1:38 cbf
V.1: Simon & Delilah/A Double in Diamonds
V.2: Counterfeit Countess/Escape Route
V.3: Scales of Justice/Russian Prisoner
V.4: Queen's Ransom/The House on Dragon's Rock
V.5: The Angel's Eye/The Better Mousetrap
V.6: Gadic Collection/The Convenient Monster
V.7: The Reluctant Revolution/The Helpful Pirate

**SATURDAY NIGHT LIVE** (all war except where noted)
on *Best of Chevy Chase* 1:00 lor (LV)
on *Best of Dan Aykroyd* :57
on *The Best of Eddie Murphy* 1:00 par
on *Best of Gilda Radner* 1:00
on *Best of John Belushi* 1:00
Buck Henry 1978 & 1979 2ep 2:00
Carrie Fisher 1:07
Charles Grodin 1977 1:07
Elliott Gould 1976 1:07
Eric Idle 1976 1:04
Eric Idle 1979 :59
Gary Busey 1979 1:09
George Carlin 1:00
Lily Tomlin 1975 1:07
Madeline Kahn 1976 1:08
Michael Palin 1979 1:07
Peter Cook & Dudley Moore 1975 1:07
Ray Charles 1977 1:02
Richard Benjamin 1979 1:04
Richard Pryor 1975 1:06
Robert Klein 1979 1:48
Rodney Dangerfield 1980 1:08
Sissy Spacek 1977 1:08
Steve Martin 1978 1:06
Steve Martin 1978 vol 2 1:50
V.1: George Carlin & Steve Martin 1:52
V.II: Richard Pryor/Steve Martin 1:55

**SCARECROW OF ROMNEY MARSH**
as *Dr. Syn Alias the Scarecrow* 2:09 wds

**SCENE OF THE CRIME**
Scene of the Crime/A Vote for Murder/The Medium Is the Murder (1:14) mca

**SECRET AGENT** (all mpi and :52 except where noted)
V.1: Battle of the Cameras
V.2: Fair Exchange
V.3: Room in the Basement
V.4: Fish on a Hook
V.5: Yesterday's Enemies
V.6: The Professionals
V.7: Man on the Beach
V.8: Dangerous Game
Koroshi 1:40

**SECRET AGENT** as **DANGER MAN** (all mpi and :30)
V.1: Bury the Dead
V.2: Under the Lake
V.3: Affair of State
V.4: View from the Villa

**SEE IT NOW**
3ep + Nixon Checkers Speech 2:00 shk
Automation 1:22 vys

**SHAKA ZULU**
2 vols 5:00 prs

**THE SHAKESPEARE PLAYS**
Midsummer Night's Dream 2:00 key/tml
*The above, as well as six additional titles, are available through the MacArthur Library Video Project (See notes)*
Hamlet 3:36
Julius Caesar 2:40
King Lear 3:05
Macbeth 2:27
The Merchant of Venice 2:37
Othello 3:23
*Additional titles available, but (see notes on Limited Use) not for Home Retail Market:*
All's Well That Ends Well 2:21
As You Like It 2:37
Henry IV, Part 1 2:27
Henry IV, Part 2 2:31
Henry V 2:43
Henry VI, Part 1 2:00
Henry VI, Part 2 2:00
Henry VI, Part 3 2:00
Henry VIII 2:45
Measure for Measure 2:37
Richard II 2:37
Romeo and Juliet 2:47
Taming of the Shrew 2:07
The Tempest 2:30
Timon of Athens 2:00
Twelfth Night 2:04
Winter's Tale 2:04

**SHERLOCK HOLMES** (Brett) (all s&s and :52)
The Blue Carbuncle
The Dancing Men
The Naval Treaty
A Scandal in Bohemia
The Solitary Cyclist
The Speckled Band

**SHERLOCK HOLMES** (Howard) (all dct and 1:00 except where noted)
V.1: Red Headed League/Deadly Prophecy dct/ccp
V.2: Jolly Hangman/Vanished Detective dct/ccp
V.3: Belligerent Ghost/Baker St. Bachelors dct/ccp
V.4: Haunted Gainsborough/Exhumed Client dct/ccp
V.5: Case of Singing Violin/Shoeless Engineer
V.6: Mother Hubbard Case/Case of the Unlikely Gambler
V.7: Case of Diamond Tooth/Careless Suffragette
V.8: Case of Imposter Mystery/Greystone Inscription
V.9: Case of the Thistle Killer/Split Ticket
V.10: Case of Blindman's Bluff/Baker St. Nursemaid
V.12: Case of Cunningham Heritage/Lady Beryl
V.13: Case of Shy Ballerina/French Interpreter
V.14: Case of Pennsylvania Gun/Reluctant Carpenter
V.15: Case of Winthrop Legend/Laughing Mummy
V.16: Case of Neurotic Detective/Impromptu Performance
V.17: Case of Royal Murder/Perfect Husband
1ep :30 con

**SHOCK OF THE NEW** *(See notes on Limited Use) Not for Home Retail Market* (8ep at :52 each)

**SHOGUN**
*The Complete Television Miniseries* 4 vols 9:10 par
Cut-down 1:59 par (LV)

**SING ALONG WITH MITCH**
Holiday Sing Along with Mitch mgu

**SINS**
2 vols 5:36 nwl

**SIR LANCELOT**
Shepherd's War :30 vdc

**60 MINUTES**
*Best of V.1*: 1:02 (LV) cbf
*Best of V.2*: 1:00 cbf

**SKAG**
Pilot 2:25 iud

**SKY KING**
2ep 1:00 dct

**SLEDGE HAMMER!**
*Hammered: The Best of Sledge:* All Shook Up/Witless/Wild About Hammer/Under the Gun 1:44 nwl (LV)

**SPACE 1999**
as *Destination Moonbase Alpha* 1:33 cbf
War Games (as Alien Attack)/Journey Through the Black Sun 1:49 usa
V.1: Alien Attack (combined Breakaway/War Games) 1:00 bel (LV)
V.2: Journey Through the Black Sun 1:00 bel (LV)

**SPIDER-MAN, THE AMAZING** (all pla)
Night of the Clones/Escort to Danger 1:33
Deadly Dust 1:33
2ep 1:33

**SPIKE JONES** (all par)
*Best of V.1*: (8 skits) :51
*Best of V.2*: (13 skits) :53 (LV)
*Best of V.3*: (11 skits) :54 (LV)

**STAR PERFORMANCE** as **FOUR STAR PLAYHOUSE** (all dct and 1:00)
High Stakes/Stacked Deck
The Squeeze/Detective's Holiday
To Die at Midnight/Full Circle

**STAR TREK** (all par and :51 except where noted)
Ep 1: The Cage 1:13
Ep 2: Where No Man Has Gone Before
Ep 3: Corbomite Maneuver

Ep 4: Mudd's Women
Ep 5: The Enemy Within
Ep 6: Man Trap
Ep 7: Naked Time
Ep 8: Charlie X
Ep 9: Balance of Terror
Ep 10: What Are Little Girls Made Of?
Ep 11: Dagger of the Mind
Ep 12: Miri
Ep 13: The Conscience of the King
Ep 14: The Galileo Seven
Ep 15: Court Martial
Ep 16: The Menagerie 1:42
Ep 17: Shore Leave
Ep 18: The Squire of Gothos
Ep 19: Arena
Ep 20: The Alternative Factor
Ep 21: Tomorrow Is Yesterday
Ep 22: Return of the Archons
Ep 23: A Taste of Armageddon
Ep 24: Space Seed
Ep 25: This Side of Paradise
Ep 26: The Devil in the Dark
Ep 27: Errand of Mercy
Ep 28: The City on the Edge of Forever
Ep 29: Operation Annihilate
Ep 30: Catspaw
Ep 31: Metamorphosis
Ep 32: Friday's Child
Ep 33: Who Mourns for Adonais?
Ep 34: Amok Time
Ep 35: The Doomsday Machine
Ep 36: Wolf in the Fold
Ep 37: The Changeling
Ep 38: The Apple
Ep 39: Mirror, Mirror
Ep 40: The Deadly Years
Ep 41: I, Mudd
Ep 42: The Trouble with Tribbles
Ep 43: Bread and Circuses
Ep 44: Journey to Babel
Ep 45: A Private Little War
Ep 46: The Gamesters of Triskelion
Ep 47: Obsession
Ep 48: The Immunity Syndrome
Ep 49: A Piece of the Action
Ep 50: By Any Other Name
Ep 51: Return to Tomorrow
Ep 52: Patterns of Force
Ep 53: The Ultimate Computer
Ep 54: The Omega Glory
Ep 55: Assignment: Earth
Ep 56: Spectre of the Gun
Ep 57: Elaan of Troyius
Ep 58: The Paradise Syndrome
Ep 59: The Enterprise Incident
Ep 60: And the Small Children Shall Lead
Ep 61: Spock's Brain
Ep 62: Is There No Truth in Beauty?
Ep 63: The Empath
Ep 64: The Tholian Web
Ep 65: For the World Is Hollow and I Have Touched the Sky
Ep 66: Day of the Dove
Ep 67: Plato's Stepchildren
Ep 68: Wink of an Eye
Ep 69: That Which Survives
Ep 70: Let That Be Your Last Battlefield
Ep 71: Whom Gods Destroy
Ep 72: Mark of Gideon
Ep 73: The Lights of Zetar
Ep 74: The Cloud Minders
Ep 75: The Way to Eden
Ep 76: Requiem for Methuselah
Ep 77: The Savage Curtain
Ep 78: All Our Yesterdays
Ep 79: Turnabout Intruder

**STAR TREK**: Collector's Edition *(Mail order only from CBS Video Library: See notes for ordering information)* (all cvl and 1:42)

V.1: Ep 16
V.2: Ep 7/Ep 9
V.3: Ep 2/Ep 4
V.4: Ep 24/Ep 22
V.5: Ep 21/Ep 28
V.6: Ep 14/Ep 15
V.7: Ep 38/Ep 44
V.8: Ep 41/Ep 42
V.9: Ep 31/Ep 29
V.10: Ep 34/Ep 25
V.11: Ep 3/Ep 6
V.12: Ep 8/Ep 5
V.13: Ep 18/Ep 52
V.14: Ep 10/Ep 12
V.15: Ep 11/Ep 13
V.16: Ep 19/Ep 20
V.17: Ep 23/Ep 26
V.18: Ep 37/Ep 33
V.19: Ep 49/Ep 50
V.20: Ep 45/Ep 48
V.21: Ep 62/Ep 64
V.22: Ep 30/Ep 17
V.23: Ep 59/Ep 63
V.24: Ep 77/Ep 78
V.25: Ep 57/Ep 56
V.26: Ep 61/Ep 65
V.27: Ep 39/Ep 54
V.28: Ep 43/Ep 35
V.29: Ep 27/Ep 46
V.30: Ep 36/Ep 47

**STAR TREK**: On Laser (all par and 1:42 and LVo exept where noted)

V.1: Ep 6/Ep 8

V.2: Ep 2/Ep 7
V.3: Ep 5/Ep 4
V.4: Ep 10/Ep 12
V.5: Ep 11/Ep 3
V.6: Ep 13/Ep 9
V.7: Ep 17/Ep 14
V.8: Ep 18/Ep 19
V.9: Ep 21/Ep 15
V.10: Ep 22/Ep 24
V.11: Ep 23/Ep 25
V.12: Ep 26/Ep 27
V.13: Ep 20/Ep 28
V.14: Ep 29/Ep 34
V.15: Ep 33/Ep 37
V.16: Ep 38/Ep 39
V.17: Ep 30/Ep 35
V.18: Ep 31/Ep 41
V.19: Ep 32/Ep 44
V.20: Ep 40/Ep 47
V.21: Ep 36/Ep 42
V.22: Ep 46/Ep 49
V.23: Ep 48/Ep 45
V.24: Ep 51/Ep 52
V.25: Ep 50/Ep 54
V.26: Ep 01 1:13
V.27: Ep 53/Ep 43
V.28: Ep 55/Ep 61
V.29: Ep 59/Ep 58
V.30: Ep 60/Ep 62
V.31: Ep 56/Ep 66
V.32: Ep 64/Ep 65
V.33: Ep 67/Ep 68
V.34: Ep 63/Ep 57
V.35: Ep 71/Ep 70
V.36: Ep 72/Ep 69
V.37: Ep 73/Ep 76
V.38: Ep 75/Ep 74
V.39: Ep 77/Ep 78
V.40: Ep 79 :51

**STEVE ALLEN SHOW**
Steve Allen's Golden Age of Comedy :50 mhe

**THE STORY OF ENGLISH** (all pme)
V.1: Ep 1–2 An English Speaking World/Mother Tongue 1:55
V.2: Ep 3–4 A Muse of Fire/The Guid Scots Tongue 1:56
V.3: Ep 5–6 Black on White/"Pioneers O! Pioneers!" 1:56
V.4: Ep 7–8 The Muvver Tongue/The Loaded Weapon 1:55
V.5: Ep 9 Next Year's Words: A Look into the Future :58

**STREET HAWK**
1ep 1:00 mca

**STRIKE FORCE**
Movie-length ep 1:30 ach/stc

**STU ERWIN SHOW as TROUBLE WITH FATHER**
Yvette/What Paper Do You Read :50 shk
1ep :30 con

**STUDIO ONE** (all vys and 1:00 except where noted)
Abraham Lincoln
Black Rain
Bundle of Guilt
A Candle for St. Jude :56
Coriolanus
Collector's Item
Colonel Judas
A Connecticut Yankee in King Arthur's Court :51
The Deep Dark
The Defender 1:44 dct
The Devil in Velvet :59
Hold Back the Night
Human Barrier
Innocence of Pastor Muller
Last Cruise dct
Little Men, Big World
Mark of Cain
Miracle in the Rain :59
Nativity
No Tears for Hilda :59
Of Human Bondage
Pagoda
Passenger to Bali
Plan for Escape
Pontius Pilate :59
Remarkable Incident at Carson Corners :43
The Scarlet Letter :52
The Spectre of Alexander Wolff
The Square Peg :59
Stan the Killer
Ten Thousand Horses Singing
Wuthering Heights :51

**STUDIO ONE SUMMER THEATER** (all vys and 1:00)
The Human Barrier
Jane Eyre
The Man They Acquitted

**SUPERMAN, THE ADVENTURES OF** (all war)
Superman and the Mole Men :59
V.1: Superman on Earth/All That Glitters/Cartoon: Superman 1:03
V.2: Crime Wave/The Perils of Superman/Cartoon: Mechanical Monsters 1:02
V.3: Panic in the Sky/The Big Freeze/Cartoon: Magnetic Telescope 1:00
V.4: The Face & The Voice/Jimmy the Kid/Cartoon: Showdown 1:00

# T

**TAKE A GOOD LOOK**
1ep :30 vys/con

**TALES FROM THE DARKSIDE** (all ive and 1:10)
V.1: Word Processor of the Gods/Djinn, No Chaser/Slippage
V.2: The Odds/All a Clone by the Telephone/Anniversary Dinner
V.3: Mookie & Pookie/It All Comes Out in the Wash/Levitation
V.4: The New Man/Snip, Snip/Pain Killer
V.5: Inside the Closet/The False Prophet/Grandma's Last Wish
V.6: Bigalow's Last Smoke/The Tear Collection/The Madness Room
V.7: In the Cards/A Case of the Stubborns/Trick or Treat

**TALES OF THE KLONDIKE** (all ach and 1:00)
In a Far Country
Race for Number One
The Scorn of Women
The Unexpected

**TALES OF TOMORROW** (nsm and 2:00)
V.1: Frankenstein/Dune Roller/Appointment on Mars/Crystal Egg
V.2: Past Tense/A Child Is Crying/Ice From Space/The Window

**TALL TALES AND LEGENDS** (pla and :52)
Annie Oakley
Casey at the Bat
See also *Faerie Tale Theater*

**TEXACO STAR THEATER** (all 1:00)
1ep (5/29/51) vys/dct
*Best of Milton Berle V.1*: tsa
*Best of Milton Berle V.2*: tsa
See *Jimmy Durante Show*

**THE TEXAN**
2ep 1:00 dct

**TEXAS JOHN SLAUGHTER**
Geronimo's Revenge 1:17 wds
Stampede at Bitter Creek 1:17 wds

**THIS IS YOUR LIFE**
Bebe Daniels and Joe Lewis :50 vys
Laurel & Hardy :30 vys
Laurel & Hardy and Mack Sennett 1:00 dct

**THIS OLD HOUSE**
1ep (Highlights) 1:00 crw

**TONIGHT SHOW** (Carson)
Highlights 1:00 shk

**TOP CAT**
*T.C.'s Back in Town* (4ep) 2:00 hnb
Top Cat and the Beverly Hills Cats (1988) 1:32 hnb
*Loves and Fortunes*: The Missing Heir/Top Cat Falls in Love :50 wov
*25th Anniversary*: A Visit from Mother + 1ep :50 wov
V.1: 2ep :50 wov
V.2: 2ep :50 wov

**TOPPER**
4ep 2:00 usa

**TOUR OF DUTY**
Movie-length ep 1:33 nwl (LV)

**A TOWN LIKE ALICE**
Miniseries 5:10 nwl

**TREASURE ISLAND, RETURN TO** (all wds)
V.1: 2ep 1:41
V.2: 2ep 1:48
V.3: 2ep 1:47
V.4: 2ep 1:47
V.5: 2ep 1:47

**THE TRIPODS**
2:30 son

**THE 21ST CENTURY** *(See notes on Limited Use) Not for Home Retail Market* (6ep at :26 each)

**THE TWILIGHT ZONE** *(Mail order only from CBS Video Library; see notes for ordering information)* (all cvl and 2:00)
V.1: The Invaders/One for the Angels/Eye of the Beholder/The Lonely
V.2: Time Enough At Last/After Hours/Changing of the Guard/Monsters Are Due on Maple Street
V.3: The Living Doll/To Serve Man/Judgment Night/In Praise of Pip
V.4: Walking Distance/Nightmare at 20,000 Feet/Midnight Sun/Purple Testament
V.5: 100 Yards Over the Rim/Deaths Head Revisited/People Are Alike All Over/Five Characters in Search of an Exit
V.6: A Stop at Willoughby/The Last Flight/Night Call/The Last Rites of Jeff Myrtlebank
V.7: Night of the Meek/Mirror Image/The Grave/The Masks
V.8: The Odyssey of Flight 33/Hitch-Hiker/Steel/Two
V.9: The Dummy/Nothing in the Dark/Shadow Play/The Sixteen-Millimeter Shrine
V.10: Little Girl Lost/The Game of Pool/A Short Drink from a Certain Fountain/It's a Good Life
V.11: The Obsolete Man/Long Distance Call/What You Need/A World of His Own
V.12: Escape Clause/Jesse-Belle (1:00)/The Long Morrow
V.13: Mr. Denton on Doomsday/The Shelter/The Lateness of the Hour/The Trouble with Templeton
V.14: Person or Persons Unknown/Miniature (1:00)/King Nine Will Not Return
V.15: The Silence/Kick the Can/A World of Difference/And When the Sky Was Opened
V.16: Where Is Everybody?/Perchance to Dream/The Jungle/Nick of Time

V.17: Will the Real Martian Please Stand Up?/The Execution/The Incredible World of Horace Ford (1:00)
V.18: A Quality of Mercy/The Last Night of a Jockey/Long Live Walter Jameson/The Howling Man
V.19: On Thursday We Leave for Home (1:00)/Nervous Man in a Four Dollar Room/A Passage for Trumpet
V.20: Mr. Dingle, The Strong/Of Late I Think of Cliffordville (1:00)/The Four of Us Are Dying

**THE TWO RONNIES**
*The Best of* :45 cbf

# U

**U.F.O.** (all the)
V.1: Exposed/A Question of Priorities 1:00
V.2–4: 1:00 each

**THE UNDERSEA WORLD OF JACQUES COUSTEAU** (all pav and 1:00 and LV)
The Dragons of Galapagos
The Flight of Penguins
The Forgotten Mermaids
Octopus-Octopus
The Singing Whale
The Smile of the Walrus
A Sound of Dolphins
Whales

**THE UNTOUCHABLES**
*The Scarface Mob* (pilot) 1:38 par

**UPSTAIRS DOWNSTAIRS** (all tem and :50)
The Best of 1: On Trial
The Best of 2: I Dies From Love
The Best of 3: Why Is Her Door Locked?
The Best of 4: For Love of Love
The Best of 5: Guest of Honor
The Best of 6: A Special Mischief
The Best of 7: A Change of Scene
The Best of 8: Desirous of Change
The Best of 9: The Bolter
The Best of 10: A Perfect Stranger
The Best of 11: The Glorious Dead
The Best of 12: Facing Fearful Odds
The Best of 13: Wanted, a Good Home
The Best of 14: An Old Flame

# V

**VARIOUS HIGHLIGHT COMPILATIONS**
*Golden TV Memories of the 50's* Vols 1–3: :55 each mpi
*TeeVee Treasures* Vols 1–3: 2:00 each rhi
*Those Crazy Ol' Commercials* :30 got
*TV Turkeys* (*The World's Worst Television Shows*) 1:00 rhi

**VEGA$**
Pilot 1:17 prs

**VICTORY AT SEA** (all emb)
*Highlights* 1:38
V.1: Ep 1–4 2:30
V.2: Ep 5–8 2:30
V.3: Ep 9–12 2:30
V.4: Ep 13–16 2:30
V.5: Ep 17–21 2:30
V.6: EP 22–26 2:30

**VICTORY AT SEA** (Laser Version) (all emb and LVo)
V.1: I–III 1:30
V.2: IV–VI 1:30
V.3: VII–IX 1:30
V.4: X–XII 1:30
V.5: XIII–XV 1:30
V.6: XVI–XVIII 1:30
V.7: XIX–XXI 1:30
V.8: XXII–XXIV 1:30
V.9: XXV–XXVI 1:00

**VIETNAM: A TELEVISION HISTORY** (all son and 2:00 except where noted)
V.1: Ep 1–2: The Roots of War/The First Vietnam War, 1946–1954
V.2: Ep 3–4: American's Mandarin, 1954–1963/LBJ Goes to War, 1964–1965
V.3: Ep 5–6: America Takes Charge, 1965–1967/With America's Enemy, 1954–1967
V.4: Ep 7–8: Tet, 1968/Vietnamizing the War, 1969–1973
V.5: Ep 9–10: No Neutral Ground: Cambodia & Laos/"Peace Is at Hand"
V.6: Ep 11–12: Home Front U.S.A./The End of the Tunnel, 1973–1975
V.7: Ep 13: Legacies 1:00

**THE VIETNAM WAR** *(narrated by Walter Cronkite) (Mail order from CBS Video Library: See notes for ordering information)* (all cvl and 1:00)
V.1: The Tet Offensive
V.2: Courage Under Fire
V.3: Fire from the Sky
V.4: The World of Charlie Company
V.5: Dateline: Saigon
V.6: America Takes Charge
V.7: America Pulls Back
V.8: The Seed of Conflict
V.9: The Elusive Enemy
V.10: The End of the Road
V.11: The Wall Within
V.12: Morley Safer's Vietnam

V.13: A Nation Divided
V.14: Legacy

**VOYAGERS!**
*Voyager from the Unknown*
(combined eps) (1:31) mca

# W

**A WALK THROUGH THE 20TH CENTURY WITH BILL MOYERS** *(Not for Home Retail Market: See notes on MacArthur Library Video Project)*
(all 1:00 except where noted)
America on the Road
The Arming of the Earth
The Democrat and the Dictator
The Image Makers
Marshall, Texas; Marshall, Texas 1:30
Post-War Hopes, Cold War Fears
The Second American Revolution (Pts 1 & 2) 2:00
The 30-Second President
The Twenties
World War II: The Propaganda Battle
*Additional titles available, but (see notes on Limited Use) not for Home Retail Market:*
Change Change
Come to the Fairs
The Helping Hand
I. I. Rabi: Man of the Century
Out of the Depths—The Miner's Story
Presidents and Politics with Richard Stout
Reel World of News
T. R. and his Times

**WALT DISNEY WONDERFUL WORLD OF COLOR**
(all wds and 1:35 except where noted)
*Series I*
V.1: Mathmagic Land ('61)/Illusion of Life ('81)
V.2: Ranger of Brownstone ('68)/It's Tough to Be a Bird ('69)
V.3: Ducking Disaster with Donald Duck ('76)/Goofing Around with Donald Duck ('76)
V.4: Plausible Impossible ('56)/Ranger's Guide to Nature ('66)
V.5: Yellowstone Cubs ('63)/Flash, the Teenage Otter ('61)
V.6: Bluegrass Special ('77)/Runway on the Rogue River ('74)
V.7: Dad Can I Borrow the Car ('72)/Hunter & the Rock Star ('80)
V.8: Fire on Kelly Mountain ('73)/Adventure in Satan's Canyon ('74)
V.9: Call It Courage ('73)/Legend of the Boy & The Eagle ('68)
V.10: Three on the Run ('78)/Race for Survival ('78)
*Series II*
V.1: Music for Everyone/Fly with Von Drake ('66) 1:37
V.2: Pacifically Peeking with Moby Dick/Man on Wheels ('68) 1:37
V.3: Run Appaloosa Run/The 101 Problems of Hercules ('66) 1:38
V.4: Nature's Better Built Homes/John The Amiable Ocelot ('69) 1:37
V:5: Ida the Offbeat Eagle/The Wahoo Bobcat ('64) 1:37

**THE WALTONS**
*A Decade of* (Highlights) 1:58 klr
The Homecoming 1:38 pla
The Thanksgiving Story 1:36 klr

**WANTED: DEAD OR ALIVE** (vda and :22 and Colorized)
The Medicine Man
Reunion for Revenge

**WAR AND REMEMBRANCE** (all mpi)
Day I: December 15–26, 1941
Day II: Jan–April 1942
Day III: May–June 1942
Day IV: July–Nov 1942
Day V: Nov–Dec 1942
Day VI: Dec 1942–April 1943
Day VII: Feb–July 1943

**WESTINGHOUSE STUDIO ONE & SUMMER**
(See *Studio One*)

**WHEN THINGS WERE ROTTEN**
The Ultimate Weapon/Those Wedding Bell Blues/The French Disconnection 1:18 par (LV)

**THE WILD WILD WEST**
More Wild Wild West (1980) 1:34 pla
Wild Wild West Revisited (1979) 1:35 pla

**WILDSIDE** (all tch and :55)
Buffalo Who?
The Crime of the Century
Delinquency of a Miner
Don't Keep the Home Fires Burning
Until the Fat Lady Sings
Well Known Secret

**A WOMAN OF SUBSTANCE** (all ltv and 1:40)
V.1: A Nest of Vipers
V.2: Fighting for the Dream
V.3: The Secret Is Revealed

**WORKING STIFFS** (par and 1:15)
V.1: The Preview Presentation/Looking for Mr. Goodwrench/Bomb Show (LV)
V.2: Pal Joey/The Bosses/My Boys Are Having a Baby

**WORLD WAR I** (Narrated by Robert Ryan) *(Mail order only from CBS Video Library: See notes for ordering information)* (all cvl and 1:00)
V.1: *Seeds of War*
V.2: *The War Begins*

V.3: *On the Western Front*
V.4: *The Spreading War*
V.5: *America Enters the War*
V.6: *Germany and the Eastern Front*
V.7: *The Loss of Innocence*
V.8: *Other Campaigns*
V.9: *A Change in the War*
V.10: *The War Ends*
V.11: *A Precarious Peace*

**WORLD WAR II** (Narrated by Walter Cronkite) *(Mail order only from CBS Video Library: See notes for ordering information)* (all cvl and 1:00)
V.1: *Europe: The Allies Close In*
V.2: *The Pacific: War Begins*
V.3: *Battleground Italy*
V.4: *Invasion: The Allies Attack*
V.5: *War Against Japan*
V.6: *The Seeds of War*
V.7: *The Pacific Campaign*
V.8: *The Eastern Front*
V.9: *Air War Over Europe*
V.10: *The German High Command*
V.11: *The Scandinavian and Soviet Fronts*
V.12: *The Pacific Perimeter*
V.13: *Europe: Wars Within a War*
V.14: *The Home Front and Victory*

**WORLD WAR II: G. I. DIARY** *(See notes on Limited Use) Not for Home Retail Market* (25ep at :30 each)

**YANCY DERRINGER**
Fair Freebooter/Wayward Warrior 1:00 dct

**YOU ASKED FOR IT**
*Fifth Anniversary Show* (highlights) 1:00 vdm

**YOU BET YOUR LIFE**
I: 4ep 1:50 shk
II: 1:00 pilot & 1ep & *Tell It to Groucho* 2:00 shk
4ep 2:00 shk
2ep 1:00 dct
2ep 1:00 dct/ihf
2 vols (1ep each :30) con

**YOUR SHOW OF SHOWS** (all unc except where noted)
*Ten from Your Show of Shows* 1:32 mhe (LV)
V.1: (7 skits) 1:05
V.2: (8 skits) 1:05
V.3: (8 skits) 1:00
V.4: (7 skits) 1:00
V.5: (7 skits) 1:01
V.6: (7 skits) 1:05
V.7: (7 skits) 1:00
V.8: (8 skits) 1:06
w. Marsha Hunt :25 vys
w. Melvyn Douglas :25 vys

## Z

**ZORRO** (all wds)
V.1: The Secret of El Zorro
V.2: And the Mountain Man 1:15
V.3: And the Mysery of Don Cabrillo 1:15
V.4: Invitation to Death 1:36
V.5: The Gay Charmer (Caballero) 1:38
V.6: The Man from Spain 1:36
The Sign of Zorro 1:29

# INDEX

This index is a guide to the performers appearing in the cast lists (*set in italics*) at the beginning of each series write-up. All names appearing in these lists are in this index.

If a performer appears in more than one italicized cast listing on the same page, that is noted in parentheses after the page number: 19(2)

This index also includes names that appear in the main text discussion for each series. However, only names related to the series under discussion are listed, including performers not in the main cast lists (generally occasional characters or guest stars) along with various production people for the program (producers, directors, writers). These citations are set off by a "t" (19t) after the page number.

If a performer in the series cast list is also mentioned in the discussion text for that series, that will be noted by a "(+t)".

Summary of page citation style of this index:

19 = appears in one series cast list on that page
19t = appears in the discussion text of one series on that page
19(+t) = appears in one series cast list on that page and in the subsequent discussion text of that same series
19,19t = appears in one series cast list on that page and in the discussion text of another series on that same page
19(2) = appears in two series cast lists on that page
19t(2) = appears in the discussion text of two series on that page
19–21t = appears on more than one page of the discussion text of one series which covers several pages

Morrill, Priscilla, 39, 69, 139, 245
Morris, Anita, 50, 140

# ACKNOWLEDGMENTS

We would like to thank the following individuals and organizations for their help in this project:

## BUSINESSES AND INSTITUTIONS

Museum of Broadcasting (New York City)
Special thanks to Ron Simon
Museum of Broadcast Communications (Chicago)
Special thanks to Mike Mertz and Joan Dry
Library of Congress (Washington): Motion Picture Broadcasting and Recorded Sound Division
Special thanks to Gerald Gibson and Kathy Loughney
Georgia Public Television (Atlanta)
Special thanks to Marcia Killingsworth
WTTW (Channel 11 in Chicago)
Special thanks to Rick Kotrba and Shirley Waywood
WPWR (Channel 50 in Chicago)
Special thanks to Neal Sabin and Eileen Muldoon
WGN (Channel 9 in Chicago)
Special thanks to Steve King and Johnnie Putman
Columbia Pictures Television
Special thanks to Susan McLaughlin
MCA/Universal Studios
Special thanks to Tony Sauber
Crew Neck Productions
Special thanks to John Scheinfeld
WGBH (Channel 2 in Boston)
USA Cable Network
A&E Cable Network

For help and advice in the Home Video Guide, very special thanks to:
Brad Burnside at Video Adventure in Evanston, Illinois
Larry Charet at Larry's Comics in Chicago
Robert Griesbaum at Laser Audio/Video in Park Ridge, Illinois
Ted Okuda at Metro Golden Memories in Chicago

## Very Special Thanks To

First and foremost (in alphabetical order) Barbara Brown and Grace Dumelle, for serving as front-line critics of our respective texts. They never hesitated to send material back for rewrite, but were kind enough not to do it *that* often.

Mike Tiefenbacher, for his painstaking critique of the final manuscript, with the type of close reading every author dreams of.

Bill King and Leslie King, for their critical readings and helpful advice, especially on the British-based series.

Our team of genre experts, including Bart Andrews, Mike Class, Cynthia Farenga, John Ferguson, Bernadette Freeman, Jonathan Lehrer, J. Fred MacDonald, Don Wilkie, and Dean Yannias, for keeping us on our toes in everything from Shakespeare to alien life forms.

Jeff Fuerst, Joe Federici, Mark Lewisohn, Ed Mann, Holly Mann, T. Stephen May, Susan Novak, Amy Peck, and Danette Sills, for welcome feedback on the early working manuscript.

Margo Dumelle, Skip Groff, Tom Schultheiss, and Kathy Willhoite for key reference materials.

Peter Sills and Mark Guncheon, for guidance in the world of computer compatibility and data bases.

Richard Stillman, for the primer in computer purchasing in Boston.

Jackie Falk and Theresa Scott, for coming through on requested tapings.

Steve Bulwan, for spotting that red Rolls.

Vince Waldron, for first-hand precinct information.

Kathy O'Malley, for quick confirmation on an L.A. institution.

Robert Feder for last-minute cancellation updates.

John O'Leary, for essential on-site research in Washington, penetrating follow-up analysis, overall direction, and the best collection of technical equipment we've ever borrowed.

Gareth Esersky, for support in the key early days of the proposal.

PJ Dempsey, for shepherding this book into the system and keeping it on track.

Paul Aron, for bringing it home.

And, as usual, Harry would like to thank Wally and Wally would like to thank Harry.

# ABOUT THE AUTHORS

HARRY CASTLEMAN was born in Salem, Massachusetts in 1953, which is starting to seem like an awfully long time ago. After spending too much of his youth watching TV, he headed to the Chicago area and attended Northwestern University. He worked as a news and music producer at a few small radio stations and, soon after graduating college, joined the radio-TV department of the Democratic National Committee in Washington, D.C. He served as a radio producer for the 1976 Jimmy Carter presidential campaign and for several campaigns of Florida governor Reubin Askew. Along with college chum Walter Podrazik, Harry has coauthored seven other books, dealing with The Beatles and the history of television. In a vain attempt to appear a little more respectable, he went to law school (at Boston University) and now is an attorney in Boston, Massachusetts. Harry is married, still watches too much TV, and vigorously denies the claim that he is almost middle-aged.

WALTER J. PODRAZIK grew up in Chicago as part of the first true television generation, complete with Mickey Mouse Club Mousketeer ears, Howdy Doody drinking glass, and Winky Dink magic TV screen. He continued his interest in popular culture right through college, earning a degree from the Radio-Television Department of the School of Speech at Northwestern University. Since then, Wally has lent his consulting expertise to a number of media projects, most notably as part of the media facilities and arrangements setup for every Democratic National Convention and midterm Party Conference since 1976. In dealing with the needs of more than thirteen thousand press people at these, he's seen first-hand how things have changed in the way the whole world watches an international news event.

At the same time, Wally has also written eight other books (seven with Harry Castleman) and is frequently tapped as an informed, articulate, and entertaining pop culture resource person for events ranging from radio talk shows to college symposiums to fan conventions. Currently, he has in the works new volumes on the Beatles and on TV ratings. For now, though, Wally has found the number one attraction of the 1989–1990 season to be his new status as a married man.